DICTIONARY

OF

BRITISH SIGN LANGUAGE/

DICTIONARY

OF

BRITISH SIGN LANGUAGE/ ENGLISH

Edited by David Brien
With an introduction by Mary Brennan

Compiled for the British Deaf Association by
the Deaf Studies Research Unit, University of Durham

faber and faber
LONDON · BOSTON

Production team

1992

First published in 1992 by Faber and Faber Limited
3 Queen Square
London WC1N 3AU

Reprinted 1993

Design and layout:
Ernst Thoutenhoofd
Roy Benzie (Benzie Graphics)

Partly produced on Apple Macintosh
Printed in England by Clays Ltd., St. Ives plc

© Deaf Studies Research Unit, University of Durham, 1992
The visual world of BSL: An introduction © Mary Brennan, 1992

A CIP record for this book is available from the British Library

ISBN 0–571–14346–6

Editor
David Brien

Editorial team
Mary Brennan
Clark Denmark
Frances Elton
Liz Scott Gibson
Graham Turner

Advisory consultants
Martin Colville
Dorothy Miles
Ernst Thoutenhoofd

Models:

Lorna Allsop, Wendy Daunt, Clark Denmark, Frances Elton, Christine Jenkins, Peter Llewellyn-Jones, Helen Todhunter.

Photographers:

Derek Hudspeth, Michelle Johnson, Jane Sutton and Roger Weeks.

Preparation of text:
Mireille Langenbach, Muriel Raine and Mandy Wilson.

Proof-reader:
Nan Anthony.

Photograph facing title page: Allan Brindle Hayhurst MBE
General Secretary of the British Deaf Association from 1966 to 1981
Cover photograph model: Frances Elton

Contents

Acknowledgements

A project of this size has drawn on the expertise of, and received support from, a very large number of people. It is, we regret, not possible to acknowledge the contribution made by each person individually. We are most grateful to the Deaf people, sign language interpreters, linguists, and experts in related fields who have contributed to the work. We wish to pay tribute to the Deaf informants and colleagues of Allan Hayhurst who contributed to his work on the Dictionary: in particular the special contribution made by Irene Hall and Kitty Laidlow. We also acknowledge the contribution made by Mrs. Charlotte Hayhurst to the work of her husband and the British Deaf Association.

We would wish particularly to acknowledge our gratitude to the following individuals and/or organisations:
Her Royal Highness, The Princess of Wales, Patron of the British Deaf Association for the interest she has taken in the project and for providing the Foreword to the dictionary.
The British Deaf Association for supporting the project through to publication: in particular Mr. John Young OBE, Chair of the BDA and the members of the Executive Council; Mr. Hayhurst's successor, Mr. Arthur Verney, and the present Chief Executive, Ms. Elizabeth Wincott, and the staff of the Association.
British Petroleum Company plc for providing grants which enabled initial revision of entries and the publication of the dictionary: in particular Mrs. Tessa Murray of British Petroleum's Community Affairs Department.

The Department of Health and Social Security for providing initial financial support to the project.
Professor Richard Brown and members of the Department of Sociology and Social Policy at the University of Durham for encouraging and contributing to the development of the Deaf Studies Research Unit.
Mr. Roy Benzie and the staff of Benzie Graphics for preparing the text and images for publication and contributing to the design and layout of the dictionary.
Faber and Faber for undertaking to publish the dictionary: in particular Mr. Roger Osborne and Mr. Ron Costley.
Collins ELT, in particular Richard Thomas (Collins Publishing Editor) and Professor John Sinclair (Editor in Chief), for permission to use (and adapt as required) entries from the Collins COBUILD English Language Dictionary (1987) and the Collins COBUILD Essential English Dictionary (1988).
Apple Northeast and Bob Sheehan (University of Durham) who have provided invaluable assistance in matters computational.

As editor, I would wish to thank my colleagues on the editorial team, our consultants and production staff for their dedication and commitment to completing the dictionary: and our partners, families and friends who have supported us throughout the project.

David Brien
Durham 1992

As Patron of the British Deaf Association, I am delighted to welcome the publication of this unique bilingual Dictionary of British Sign Language/English. British Sign Language (BSL) is the fourth most commonly used of Britain's indigenous languages after English, Welsh and Scottish Gaelic and is estimated to be the first or preferred language of over 50,000 people in this country. As a consequence of my involvement with Deaf people I have become aware of the richness of BSL as a distinct and independent language. I know this Dictionary will be seen as a welcome and important bridge-building enterprise.

May 1992

Diana.

1

HOW TO USE THE DICTIONARY

History of the Dictionary

In his history of the Deaf community in Britain, Peter Jackson [1] describes the 1970s and 1980s as a period of considerable change for Deaf people. During this period, signed languages achieved linguistic recognition as natural languages; languages independent of spoken languages. This recognition has led Deaf [2] people in many countries to redefine their situation, identifying themselves as members of a linguistic minority group rather than disabled persons. In Britain, the British Deaf Association (the national representative organisation of Deaf people) has been at the forefront of a campaign to obtain formal government recognition for British Sign Language (BSL), the signed language of the British Deaf community.

The British Deaf Association (BDA) has not confined its efforts to simply campaigning on this issue. In recent years, it has committed a significant proportion of its resources to sponsoring sign language research and training programmes. [3] Its most long-standing commitment has been to the publication of a BSL dictionary which, at last, is achieved with the publication of this volume.

Deaf people's recognition that their preferred means of communication might properly be described as a language considerably predates formal linguistic recognition. At the first British Deaf and Dumb Association [4] Congress (Leeds 1890) the first resolution to be passed read as follows: "That the Congress of the British Deaf and Dumb Association indignantly protests against the imputation....... that the finger and signed language is barbarous. We consider such a mode of exchanging our ideas most natural and indispensable."

Sign lexicography

In 1960, the American linguist William C. Stokoe published the first paper in which the basis for the linguistic analysis and recognition of signed languages was outlined. [5] Five years later, together with his colleagues Dorothy Casterline and Carl Croneberg, he published the first sign language dictionary based on linguistic principles. [6] Entries were presented through a notation system developed for the recording of signs, which described the signs in relation to the location, configuration and movement of the hands. It provided a means to view signs as linguistic phenomena rather than as a characteristic of Deaf people which served only to confirm the severity of their disability. The extent to which this *Dictionary of BSL/ English* has drawn upon the principles of organisation first developed by Stokoe and his colleagues will be readily apparent to those familiar with the 'Dictionary of American Sign Language', which represented a landmark in the study of signed languages and marked the start of sign lexicography.

In claiming such importance for the dictionary designed by Stokoe et al., it is necessary to explain why, in the twenty-five years that followed, the majority of dictionaries published were organised according to very different principles. The notated entries and limited number of illustrations did not make it readily accessible to non-linguists. However, this does not explain why the principles that informed the organisation of entries were not considered appropriate by the compilers of other sign language dictionaries. In order to do this, it

is necessary to locate sign lexicography within the general debate that was taking place during this period on the role of signed languages in the education of deaf children. Although the last twenty-five years may indeed have been the 'best of quarter centuries' [7] for Deaf people, there was (and still is) considerable resistance to implementing social and educational policies based on the linguistic recognition of signed languages such as BSL and American Sign Language (ASL), and their use by Deaf people. This was reflected in the dictionaries produced during this period.

Dictionaries are often defined as being about the words of a language; the volume edited by Stokoe et al. was about the words (i.e. the signs) of ASL. The majority of dictionaries published since 1965 have not been about the signs as used in signed languages but about signs used as supplements to the words of a spoken language, ordered according to the principles of the spoken language. There was usually no reference in such publications to the meanings of the signs—it was implied that these were the same as the single English word 'translation' that usually accompanied each sign. The introduction during this period of the Total Communication approach in the education of deaf children—based not on the use of signed languages, but the use of signs as a support to a spoken language—did not encourage the development of dictionaries of natural sign languages. It has only been in the last five or six years that we have seen the publication of sign language dictionaries organised on similar principles to those advocated by Stokoe and his colleagues over twenty-five years ago. [8]

The BDA's dictionary project

When Allan Hayhurst (former General Secretary of the BDA) commenced work on the BDA's dictionary project, the work of William Stokoe was not known to him. The BDA (then as now) was engaged in seeking to bring about change in the education of deaf children. At that time, education policy was still dominated by the philosophy and practice of oralism. The main aim of the dictionary was to provide hearing parents and teachers with a reference book which would facilitate their communication with deaf children. An English word list was drawn up and signs corresponding to those words were identified. In certain cases, where it was thought a sign did not exist that corresponded to a particular English word, a sign was created or borrowed from Gestuno [9], the then recently published collection of 'international signs'. Photographs were used to illustrate the signs with the addition of artwork to indicate the movements involved. A written description of how to produce each sign accompanied the photograph, along with the English words most commonly associated with the sign. The signs were arranged according to subject headings, e.g. family, school, travel, etcetera.

As the project neared completion, Hayhurst became acquainted with the work of Stokoe and other sign linguists. Sign language research projects had recently been established in Britain at Moray House College of Education and at the University of Bristol. The recognition by linguists that signed languages were natural languages led

1. Jackson (1990).
2. See p. 2 of *The visual world of BSL: An introduction* in this volume for discussion of the distinction between the terms Deaf and deaf.
3. The BDA has sponsored, for example, the following projects at the Deaf Studies Research Unit (DSRU) at the University of Durham: the Dictionary of BSL/English, a sociological study of the Deaf community in Britain (Jackson 1986) and the British Sign Language Tutor Training Course. It has also contributed financially and through the

secondment of staff to the Master of Arts and Advanced Diploma Courses in Sign Language Studies.
4. The word 'Dumb' was dropped from the title in 1970.
5. Stokoe (1960).
6. Stokoe, Casterline and Croneberg (1965).
7. Hacking (1990).
8. See for example Johnston (1989) and Suwanarat et al. (1986).
9. World Federation of the Deaf (1975).

Hayhurst to question the value of publishing the dictionary in its then existing form—a format which he felt would advance the use of signs in combination with spoken English (Sign Supported English) rather than the signed language of the British Deaf community (BSL). He was engaged in consultations as to how the work could be revised when he died. In recognition of his enormous contribution to the dictionary, this work in its final form is dedicated to him and the Deaf community in Britain that he served.

Contribution of the University of Durham
In accordance with Allan Hayhurst's wishes it was eventually agreed that the task of reorganising the contents of the dictionary should be undertaken. The editor of this volume was invited to coordinate the work. In the early years, a number of those who later became consultants to the project, or members of the editorial team, contributed to the work on a part-time, voluntary basis. In later years, the development of a number of sign language projects at the Deaf Studies Research Unit (DSRU) at the University of Durham brought together the group that formed the editorial team.

The reorganisation of the contents was guided by the following objectives:
1 that the signs contained in the dictionary should be BSL signs, i.e. signs identified by Deaf informants as signs they themselves, or other Deaf people, used when communicating in BSL;
2 that the entries should be organised on linguistic principles, appropriate to a sign language;
3 that a guide to the meaning(s) of the signs (and thereby a guide to appropriate usage) be provided;
4 that the dictionary should be of use to both Deaf users of BSL and people wishing to learn the language.

A generous grant from the British Petroleum Company enabled a series of meetings to take place at which Deaf informants, recognised as fluent users of BSL, and drawn from different parts of the country, reviewed all the signs that had been collected by Hayhurst and his colleagues. The aim was to establish the BSL signs, and not the English words, as the starting point of the dictionary. The English words that had been assigned to each sign were removed and the Deaf informants asked to identify those which were BSL signs. Signs which they rejected according to this criterion were replaced with signs which, in their view, were BSL signs. After this had been done, they were asked to identify English words they would associate with each sign. This provided the basic database which the editorial team have drawn upon to produce the dictionary.

Content of the Dictionary
As you will see, the dictionary is in four main sections:
1 *How to use the Dictionary*
2 *The visual world of BSL: An introduction*
3 *BSL* section
4 *English (Guide to meaning)* section.

The *How to use the Dictionary* section which follows provides a detailed explanation of how the *BSL* and *English (Guide to meaning)* sections are organised. In order to emphasise the status of BSL as an independent language, it was agreed that the BSL signs, categorised according to visual-gestural characteristics, should be presented on the left hand pages of the *BSL* section without reference to English. Each photograph of a sign is accompanied by the notation of the sign, demonstrating how signs can be recorded without recourse to English. This policy has also been followed in the *Introduction* where signs have been notated so that the user (should he or she be familiar with the system) does not need to identify the signs by English glosses.

The right hand pages of the *BSL* section provide a description in English of how to produce each sign, with a list of some of the English glosses associated with each sign. The descriptions may be seen as 'translations' of the notations. They are organised in relation to the main parameters of the signs, i.e. handshape and orientation; location, hand arrangement and contact; movement; and, where appropriate, non-manual features. In this way, non-linguists are introduced to the component parts of a sign, and gain an appreciation of the complex structure of signs.

The signs contained in the *BSL* section represent only a very small selection of the signs that constitute the established vocabulary of the language. The fact that the signs were originally chosen in relation to subject headings, and not formational characteristics, has resulted in certain handshape sections containing a very limited number of examples. It was not possible in the main body of the dictionary to add substantially to the collection of signs compiled by Allan Hayhurst. The glosses and reference numbers allow the user to move between the *BSL* section and the *English (Guide to meaning)* section of the dictionary. It should be noted that the editorial team do not claim that the English words (glosses), or the meanings that are given in relation to each sign, are necessarily the only glosses and meanings appropriate to the sign. It was not possible to research the usage of each sign in natural settings. For this reason, the entries have not been described as 'definitions' but rather 'guides to the meaning' of the signs.

The *English (Guide to meaning)* section seeks to serve two functions and meet the needs of two very different potential users of the dictionary. Insofar as the entries provide a guide to the meaning of the signs, it provides information to those seeking a sign relating to a particular meaning, and therefore will be of particular value to people learning BSL. If the dictionary is used in the opposite direction, i.e. from the BSL signs to the English words, it is hoped that it will prove of value to Deaf people studying English as a second language—in particular those attending English classes taught through BSL. In this way, we hope the dictionary will assist both Deaf and hearing people to advance their knowledge of a second language.

The task of writing entries for the *English (Guide to meaning)* section had been started when, prior to publication, information on the first of the Collins COBUILD dictionaries became available. In writing the entries, we had attempted to use a style of English and form of presentation which would make the entries accessible to Deaf people for whom English is a second language. The COBUILD dictionaries had been compiled especially for learners of English as a second language. Their use of complete sentences in definitions written in clear, concise English distinguished them from the other dictionaries we had consulted. We were most fortunate to be granted permission to use entries from the COBUILD dictionaries to provide the basis for the entries in the *English (Guide to meaning)* section of this volume. As with the glosses, we have not sought to be prescriptive with regard to these entries. They represent a descriptive guide to the meanings of the signs based on usage within the Deaf community, as observed by the members of the editorial team fluent in BSL and English, our Deaf informants and consultants.

As stated earlier, in a volume of this size only a small sample of the vocabulary of BSL can be included. The vocabulary of BSL, however, does not consist only of those established signs that can be listed in a dictionary. Of equal importance are the lexical resources used by fluent users of BSL to create new vocabulary. It was therefore considered essential to include information not only on examples of the established lexicon of BSL, but also on the productive lexicon—the meaningful parts of the language which are used to create new vocabulary. The *Introduction* provides the reader with a general introduction to BSL, with particular reference to the nature of the BSL words and the community of people who use the language. Further information on aspects of the productive lexicon may be found in the introductions to the handshape sections.

Completion of the project

The dictionary has taken considerably longer to complete than either the editorial team or the BDA would have wished. The reasons why it has taken so long relate to a combination of issues of which resources, the complexity of the task and technical production difficulties have been the most significant. Without the major financial support of the British Petroleum Company, the Department of Health and Social Security and the BDA itself, the dictionary could not have been completed.

Once the University of Durham had agreed to pursue the project, a combination of new and existing projects undertaken within the DSRU brought together a group of people who, in addition to their other responsibilities, were able to contribute to the development of the dictionary. The demands of these projects (in particular the British Sign Language Tutor Training Course) were at times difficult to accommodate with work on the dictionary. Without such projects, however, it would not have been possible to retain staff essential to the work of the dictionary. In accepting responsibility for the development of the British Sign Language Tutor Training Course, the University of Durham recognised the potential importance of such a programme to the Deaf community: in addition it was realised that the Tutor Training and dictionary projects would clearly complement each other in making a practical contribution to linguistic bridge-building between English and BSL users in the United Kingdom.

The existence of trained Deaf tutors as a consequence of the Tutor Training Course has contributed significantly to changing prevailing views of BSL as a 'simple' language. However, it still appears to be believed that competence in sign language and the training of sign language tutors and interpreters can be achieved in a far shorter period of time than that required in relation to other languages. We trust that the dictionary will encourage a re-examination of such views.

The users of a dictionary are, in the end, the final arbiters of its value. We hope you will find it a useful resource. We would greatly appreciate receiving comments on any aspect of the contents of this volume so that we can, subject to the availability of resources, improve future editions and companion volumes in digital or more traditional formats. Despite our efforts, mistakes will inevitably have been made. We would welcome receiving corrections or additions to entries.

Locating information in the Dictionary

Over the next few pages (xiii to xxxiv), we have tried to set out as clearly as possible *what* information you will find in this Dictionary, *where* you will find it and *how* to make sense of the way in which we have presented it.

Dictionary-makers often say that the one question they have to keep in mind throughout their work is, "How will the readers know where to look for the information they want?" This is especially important to us for three reasons: firstly, in a bilingual Dictionary the organisation of information is twice as complex as it is when only one language is involved; secondly, BSL has no everyday written form, a fact which complicates the process of finding the material readers are looking for; and thirdly, there is no tradition of signed language/spoken language dictionaries which would enable users to be familiar with the kind of format and system we have used in this Dictionary.

This section of the Dictionary tells you how to find your way around within this book.

Moving around in the Dictionary

A key point to remember is that moving from section to section in the Dictionary is the only way to find all the information presented about each sign. Do not expect to use items of information as if they were independent of each other. As you become familiar with the organisation of information you will find yourself becoming more and more able to focus confidently on those details of particular interest to you.

After the *Introduction*, the Dictionary is split into two sections. One of these has the main job of telling you about the production of signs; the other tells you about meanings. It is important that you get used to using the glosses and the entry numbers to move between the two. The glosses enable you to move from BSL to English; the numbers enable you to move from English to BSL.

What the pages look like

On the next page, you will find a sample layout diagram. This shows you at a glance the general format of each page in the *British Sign Language (BSL)* section of the Dictionary. A sample layout from the *English (Guide to meaning)* section then shows you the kind of information we have included about the meanings of the signs and words, and the ways in which they are used in grammatical utterances.

On the following pages, we have described in greater detail what the various symbols and descriptions mean. We have also included an explanation of how to use the many types of information in conjunction with each other, linking up several parts of an entry to get the most detailed picture of the language. On the final *Questions and answers* pages, we tell you how to get from the BSL signs to related English words and how to move from one part of the display to another along a variety of pathways. We have also explained here how to use the Dictionary to work from English to BSL, searching for a potential BSL equivalent for a word or phrase of English.

A basic outline to using the Dictionary

If you start with a BSL sign—

1   Check the right handshape (if the signer is right-handed; left if the signer is left-handed) of the BSL sign.
2   In the *BSL* section of this book, find the chapter with signs using this handshape.
3   You can search in this chapter for the BSL sign or work out exactly where it will be. To find out how to do this, read on in this *How to use the Dictionary* section.
4   If you want to know about the meaning of the BSL sign or about English words which can be used to translate the BSL sign, you must firstly look at the reference number above the photograph.
5   Look at the English words and phrases listed in the glosses column beside this number.
6   Find the appropriate English entries in the *English (Guide to meaning)* section. The words and phrases are listed in alphabetical order.
7   Check the definitions and examples by finding those with the same reference number to see which of them fit the BSL sign you are interested in.

If you start with an English word—

1   Find the English word in the *English (Guide to meaning)* section of the book. The English words in this section are listed in alphabetical order.
2   Look through the definitions until you find one which seems to give the right sense of your English word.
3   If you want to know about the BSL sign or signs which can be used to translate the English word, you must firstly look at the reference number next to the definition.
4   Find the same reference number beside the column of glosses in the *BSL* section of the book.
5   Check any notes marked as relevant to the gloss you are interested in.
6   Find the same number above one of the BSL sign photographs; this entry fits the sense of the English word you are interested in.

Points to remember

— there are two different languages in this book: you can move from one to the other in either direction
— the different items of information are meant to build up into one big picture for each entry: use all the details and your picture will be more complete

---

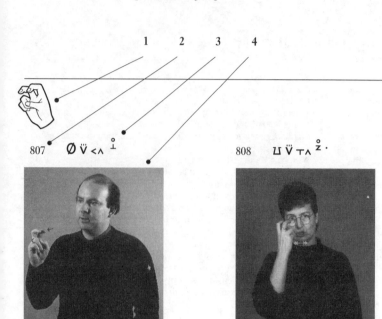

1 *Handshape illustration*
The handshape illustration on the left-hand page shows the handshape used as the dominant (i.e. right) hand for the signs on these pages: see page xvii–xix for more details. Some signs show minor variations; these are discussed in the introduction to each of the handshape sections.

2 *Entry number*
Each sign entry is given a number for reference. This number helps you to find more information about this sign on the facing page and also in the *English (Guide to meaning)* section in the second half of this volume: see page xvi for further information.

3 *Notation*
Sign entries are notated using the BSL notation system developed by linguists in the UK. This is a scientific recording system which gives detailed information on paper about the production of the signs of a visual-gestural language (see pages xvii–xvii for more details about the system of artwork). It is used here to work alongside the *Photographs* and *Production guide* in giving a complete explanation of how to produce each sign.

4 *Photographs*
Sign entries consist of one or more images, which must be 'read' from left to right or top to bottom. These have artwork added to show the movements made as the sign is produced (see pages xxviii–xxix for further information). To get maximum benefit from the range of information presented in the *BSL* section, we recommended that readers al-ways use both images and text (plus *Notation*, for those who are famil-iar with that system) together to find out how the sign is produced.

5 *Handshape symbol*
Each handshape has its own symbol in the notation system (see pages xvii–xix). The symbol shown here relates exactly to the *Handshape il-lustration*. Note especially that neither the symbols nor the handshapes to which they relate are, in fact, representations of letters of the English alphabet, i.e. **A** is not related to 'a'.

6 *Handshape description*
To help you make the handshapes accurately, we give a short descrip-tion of the typical appearance of the dominant handshape (i.e. the right hand) in all the *Photographs* on this page. This description matches up with the *Notation* symbol beside it, and the *Handshape il-lustration* on the opposite page.

7 *Column headings*
The information text is displayed in four columns. The first three col-umns tell you step-by-step how to produce the manual elements of the sign. The fourth column offers a number of English *Glosses* that corre-spond, in various contexts, to the sign entry.

8 *Notes*
Text entries may include additional notes (see page xxxi), which are of two kinds. The symbols *, † and ¶ are used when the information that follows is supplementary—e.g. if a sign is a 'Regional sign', as in entry

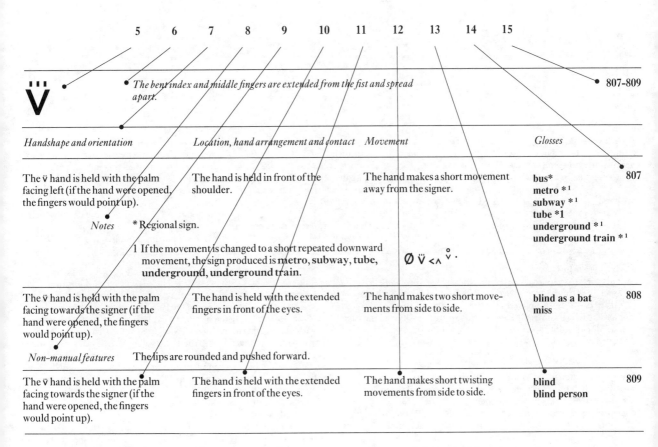

Handshape and orientation	Location, hand arrangement and contact	Movement	Glosses
The v̈ hand is held with the palm facing left (if the hand were opened, the fingers would point up).	The hand is held in front of the shoulder.	The hand makes a short movement away from the signer.	**bus*** 807 **metro** * 1 **subway** * 1 **tube** *1 **underground** * 1 **underground train** * 1
Notes * Regional sign.			
	1 If the movement is changed to a short repeated downward movement, the sign produced is **metro, subway, tube, underground, underground train**.	Ø v̈ <ʌ v̈	
The v̈ hand is held with the palm facing towards the signer (if the hand were opened, the fingers would point up).	The hand is held with the extended fingers in front of the eyes.	The hand makes two short movements from side to side.	**blind as a bat** 808 **miss**
Non-manual features The lips are rounded and pushed forward.			
The v̈ hand is held with the palm facing towards the signer (if the hand were opened, the fingers would point up).	The hand is held with the extended fingers in front of the eyes.	The hand makes short twisting movements from side to side.	**blind** 809 **blind person**

807 above— or explains how a sign *may* be modified. The symbols [1], [2], [3] and [4] are used to explain that a sign *can only* be produced following the instructions in the *Notes*.

9   Non-manual features
If non-manual features are specified, remember that these are integral parts of the sign. The non-manual features are produced at the same time as the manual aspects of the sign. As it has not always been possible to capture the features in the *Photographs*, you should always check here for a description of the non-manual features. See pages xxiv–xxvii for more details of these features.

10   Production guide one
The information in the first column tells you (using *Notation* symbols) which handshapes are used at the start of the sign and how they are orientated in space. Note that the production specification is always given from the signer's own point of view. See page xxx for further information.

11   Production guide two
The second column of texts explains where the hands are held and how they are positioned relative to each other. Follow the information in this and the first column and your hands will be in position to begin the sign (see page xxx).

12   Production guide three
In the third column, you will find a description of the movement made

by the hands in the production of the sign, including any changes in the shape of the hands (see page xxx).

13   Glosses
The glosses column contains a number of entries that can be thought of as possible parellels to the sign given opposite. Two types of additional information are indicated in this column. Firstly, we have used the symbols *, † and ¶ to give supplementary information or to show that the sign with this gloss *may* be modified in certain ways as indicated in the *Notes*. Secondly, we have used the symbols [1], [2], [3] and [4] when the sign with this gloss *can only* be produced following the instructions in the *Notes* (see page xxxi for details).

14   Entry number repeated
Numbers (corresponding to the *Entry numbers* on the facing page) are located at the side of the text. Each number provides a direct link between a section of descriptive text here, the *Photographs* (plus *Notation*) opposite and an entry or entries in the *English (Guide to meaning)* section. See pages xxxii–xxxiv for further information.

15   Page entry contents
In the top corner of the page, you will find numbers showing the range of entries contained on these two pages, to help you locate quickly the information you need (see pages xxxii–xxxiv for more details).

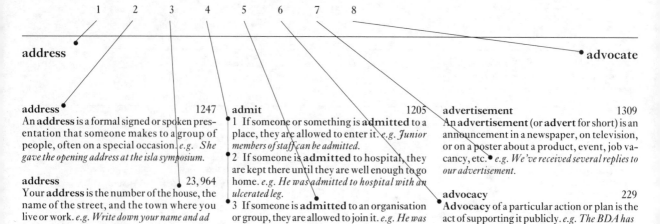

1 2 3 4 5 6 7 8

address   **advocate**

address 1247
An **address** is a formal signed or spoken presentation that someone makes to a group of people, often on a special occasion. *e.g. She gave the opening address at the isla symposium.*

address 23,964
Your **address** is the number of the house, the name of the street, and the town where you live or work. *e.g. Write down your name and ad*

admit 1205
1 If someone or something is **admitted** to a place, they are allowed to enter it. *e.g. Junior members of staff can be admitted.*
2 If someone is **admitted** to hospital, they are kept there until they are well enough to go home. *e.g. He was admitted to hospital with an ulcerated leg.*
3 If someone is **admitted** to an organisation or group, they are allowed to join it. *e.g. He was*

advertisement 1309
An **advertisement** (or **advert** for short) is an announcement in a newspaper, on television, or on a poster about a product, event, job vacancy, etc. *e.g. We've received several replies to our advertisement.*

advocacy 229
Advocacy of a particular action or plan is the act of supporting it publicly. *e.g. The BDA has*

1   *First word*
In the top left-hand corner of every page in the *English (Guide to meaning)* section of this Dictionary, you will find a word printed in black letters **like this**. It is the first item that has an entry on this page. When you want to look through the book quickly, you can easily find the page you want by keeping an eye on this corner of the page (see also *Last word*, below).

2   *Headword*
The glosses listed in the column on the right-hand side of each right-hand page in the *BSL* section are used in this section of the Dictionary as headwords. The headword (printed in bold letters, **like this**) introduces the explanation of the meaning. The headword (and all information laid out in the text below it) actually relates to each one of the signs whose *Reference numbers* appear beside it. If a headword has two or more distinct meanings, each relating to a different sign or signs, then the headword is repeated as a new entry and the relevant sign *Reference numbers* are listed beside it. For example, **address** appears twice as the headword on this page. The first entry is linked to signs 1335 and 872 and its meaning relates to 'a formal presentation'. The second entry is linked to sign 1886 and its meaning relates to 'the place where you live or work'.

3   *Reference number*
The reference numbers used here direct the reader to the appropriate corresponding entry or entries in the *BSL* section of the book. For instance, if the number 1335 appears beside the explanation, then sign entry 1335 will show a BSL sign (photograph, notation, description and relevant notes) whose meaning relates to this explanation. Likewise, if you know the entry number and gloss of a particular BSL sign and you turn from the *BSL* section to the *English (Guide to meaning)* section, remember that only those explanations linked to the relevant reference number will match the BSL sign you have in mind.

4   *Senses and uses*
If there are two or more meanings associated with the sign or signs (see *Reference number*) listed in relation to the given headword, then these are entered as separate numbered paragraphs.

5   *Headword repeated*
In the explanation of the meaning, the *Headword* (or a form of the *Headword* adapted to be as clear as possible in the context of the explanation) is printed in bold letters, **like this**.

6   *Explanation of meaning*
The *Headword* is always explained in full sentences. This means that you can see how it is used in context. Remember, the explanation deals primarily with the meaning of the BSL sign or signs identified by the *Reference numbers* listed beside the explanation, and only secondarily with the meaning of the English word used as the *Headword*. The signs are listed here according to their glosses so that they can be arranged under *Headwords* in alphabetical order (easier to look up) and especially so that the correspondence between the BSL signs and the English words—not necessarily a one-to-one relationship—can be made clear. One BSL sign can often be translated by any of several different words of English: one English word can often be translated by any of several different signs of BSL.

   If we have chosen accurate English glosses—that is, words and phrases which can comfortably be used when translating the sign into English—to use as *Headwords*, then it is logical that the explanation of the meaning of the BSL sign will also be appropriate for this sense of the English word. Even if the English word has many other meanings, these will not be recorded in this Dictionary unless corresponding BSL signs are listed in the *BSL* section of the book: that is why this is only secondarily a guide to the meaning of the English words.

7   *Example sentence*
The example sentences in this Dictionary appear in italics (*like this*) after each *Explanation of meaning*. The examples have been chosen to show typical patterns and structures and, wherever possible, are taken from real language contexts. Although the examples are presented in English, they have been chosen with great care to be applicable both to the English word and to the BSL sign or signs on which the explanation focuses (i.e. the sign or signs whose *Reference numbers* appear above the *Explanation of meaning*).

   Our aim is that the example sentence should represent both a structure of English and a potential sentence of BSL, if the written sentence were translated accurately. We claim that a BSL translation of the sentence *could* use the particular sign referred to, and could be idiomatic and grammatical if this were done.

8   *Last word*
In the top right-hand corner of every page in the *English (Guide to meaning)* section of this Dictionary, you will find a word printed in black letters **like this**. It is the last item that has an entry on this page (see also *First word*, above).

Notation key

The entries in the *BSL* section of this book are listed following a new ordering system. The next few pages (xvii–xxiii) explain how this system works. You do *not* have to know the system in order to use the book.

Most other Dictionaries showing sign languages list the signs in the order of the English words used as translations. As BSL is an independent language, different to English, we do not think this is an appropriate way to organise the signs. We believe it is best to put them in their own order. We decided to organise the *BSL* section of the book by the visual system described below.

When sign language research started, people found that signs had several parts: each hand was held in a *shape* (sometimes called a *dez* by researchers), put in a *place* (sometimes called a *tab*) and made a *movement* (called a *sig*). Each of these parts can be shown using symbols. In time, researchers worked out a *notation system*: that is, a set of symbols which could be used to write down any sign on paper.

It is difficult to imagine how sign language research could have been done without a notation system. This system is an important way of putting clear information about signs onto paper. When we use these symbols, we do not have to try to write about BSL signs using only English words (that is, write an English word such as 'boy', when we really mean the BSL sign which can be translated as 'boy'). In this Dictionary, BSL notation is used for writing BSL signs and English spelling is used for writing English words. BSL and English can clearly be seen as two independent and distinct languages.

On the next few pages, we have laid out all of the symbols used in the notation system. On page xxiii, we explain how to use the information given in notations to work out where any particular sign will be in the Dictionary. In the *BSL* section of the book, each right-hand page has descriptions in English of the information that is given by the notations on the left-hand page.

The first group of symbols are used to show the *shape* of the hand. There are 57 handshapes in the list and you can see that (although the list happens to start with **A**) it does not just use the 26 letters of the English alphabet in 'a,b,c...' order. So, what is the order? Well, the 57 handshapes are grouped in 22 'families'. Some families (like **R**) have just one member. Others (like the **G** family) have as many as eight members. In each family, the handshape with the simple symbol (the one with no extra marks) comes first; second is the one with a 'dot' above it; third is the one with a 'hat'; and so on. If the handshape does not exist in the system—like **R** with a 'hat'—the symbol is not used.

We have also put the 22 families in order based on visual features. We tried to find an order that is easy to remember and makes visual sense. The photographs below show the 22 'family handshapes' in order. You can see that they start with a closed handshape—**A**—and gradually go through closed—open—half-closed—open—closed stages, finishing with **E**. In the *BSL* section of the book, each top left-hand corner of the left-hand page has a picture of the main handshape of all the signs on the page: and each top left-hand corner of the right-hand page shows the notation symbol that matches the handshape.

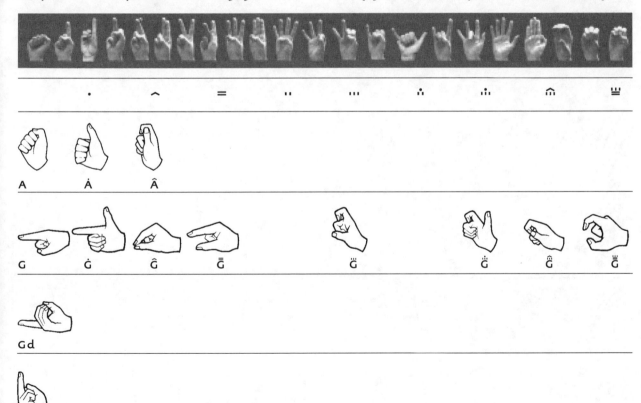

No accent	•	⌃	=	••	•••	⁞•	⁞⁞	⌢	⸺

I   Ï

Y

Y̧   Y̤

ȣ   ȣ̂   ȣ̈

5   5̿   5̈   5̈   5̤

B   Ḃ   B̂   B̄   B̈   B̊

C   Ċ

O

E   Ė

The second group of symbols are used to show the *place* (*tab*) where the sign is made. Again, we have tried to list these symbols in a logical order. The order begins with the 'neutral space' in front of the signer's body, and then moves generally from the top of the head downwards. The list ends with the symbols relating to the arms and legs.

Location

Ø	neutral space in front of the body	[]	chest	>[	left side of the body
∩̄	top of the head	>[]	left side of thechest	]<	right side of the body
∩	upper face	[]<	right side of the chest	⌊⌋	lower trunk
○	whole face	⌈⌉	front of the shoulders	>⌊⌋	left side of the lower trunk
⊔̄	eye	⌈̌⌉̌	on the shoulders	⌊⌋<	right side of the lower trun k
⊔	nose	⌈̌⌉	on the left shoulder	∖	upper arm
3	cheek	⌈⌉̌	on the right shoulder	⁄̇	elbow
⊃	ear	>⌈⌉<	both sides of the upper trunk	⁄	lower arm
◡	mouth and lips	>⌈⌉	left of the upper trunk	ɑ	inside of the wrist
∪	lower face or chin	⌈⌉<	right of the upper trunk	ɒ	back of the wrist
∪̲	under the chin	[	left side of the chest	Ħ	hip
π	throat or neck	]	right side of the chest	!	upper leg

The next group of symbols (called *ori* symbols) give *orientation* information, telling you about the way the handshape is held. First they tell you about the direction the palm is facing: it may be facing up or down, and so on. Then they tell you in which direction the fingers are pointing. To check this, you must imagine the hand opened flat: the direction the fingers point now is what is recorded in the notation. Remember that all notations are written from the signer's own point of view, not from the point of view of another person: when the symbol says 'right', for instance, it means 'to the signer's right'.

Palm orientation

ɑ	up	⊤	towards the signer	<	left
ɒ	down	⊥	away from the signer	>	right

Finger orientation

∧	up	⊤	towards the signer	<	left
∨	down	⊥	away from the signer	>	right

This set of symbols tell you about the arrangement of the hands: side by side, one above the other, and so on. These symbols (sometimes called *ha* symbols) do not have one fixed place in the notation as a whole, so you have to look out for them carefully.

Hand arrangement

Ā	the right hand is held higher than the left hand	×	contacting each other	ꟿ	interlinking
A̲	the left hand is held higher than the right hand	⸱	nearer the body (the hand notated immediately to the left of this symbol is held nearer to the body than the other hand)	⊙	one inside the other
ı	side by side			⊤	crossed over

The next group of symbols tell you what *movement* the hands make. Remember that these symbols (called *sig* symbols) tell you what is happening from the signer's own point of view. Notice that any movement can be repeated: if this happens, the notation has a small dot beside the movement symbols (a small dot *above* the movement symbols means that the movement is sharp).

Movement

ø	no movement	⊙	enter	□	open
∧	up	⊤	cross	♯	close
∨	down	⁌	change places	o	short movement
∿	up and down	℮	move in a circle	·	sharp movement
⊤	towards the signer	×	touch	o·	short and sharp movement
⊥	away from the signer	ω	twist at the wrist	[ ]	handshape after closing or opening
ⲁ	towards and away from the signer	ɑ	palm facing up	∾	alternating movements
<	left	ᴖ	palm facing down	·	repeated movement (this symbol is always placed beside the symbols(s) indicating the movement to be repeated)
>	right	ɲ	bend at the wrist		
z	from side to side	ɱ	bend at the palm knuckles		
÷	away from each other	ɱ	flex at the knuckles		
ϰ	towards each other	ℛ	wiggle		
ⲭ	join together	ᴟ	the thumb rubs across the fingers		

Sometimes we need more precisely to make clear which particular part of the hand is involved in a sign (for instance, which finger touches another part of the body). The last set of symbols tell you how we show these parts of the hand.

Parts of the hand

---

a	thumb	ı	between thumb and index finger
e	index finger	2	between index and middle finger
i	middle finger	3	between middle and ring finger
o	ring finger	4	between ring and little finger
u	little finger		

Notating whole signs

When the notation symbols are used to record whole signs, there are strict rules about the order of symbols on the page. There are three major types of sign, written in three different ways. They are called 'single dez signs', 'manual tab signs' and 'double dez signs'.

Remember, 'tab' is the place where the sign is made; 'dez' is the shape of the hand; 'ori' is the direction of the palm and fingers; 'sig' is the movement of the hands; and 'ha' is the arrangement of the hands.

In each part of the *BSL* section of this book, the 'single dez signs' (where only one hand is involved) are listed first. The way we write these signs is *tab-dez-ori-ori-sig* (for example, notation 1 below). The elements of this notation can be listed as follows:

tab = chin: ∪
dez = the right handshape is an A
ori (palm) = the palm faces towards the signer: ⊤
ori (finger) = imagine that the hand were opened flat; the fingers would point up: ∧
sig = the hand taps the chin; the movement is repeated: × ·

The second group of signs is always the 'manual tab signs', where two hands are involved but only one of them moves. These are written *tab-ori-ori-(ha)-dez-ori-ori-sig*. In this case, though, remember that the tab is the non-dominant handshape (for example, notation 2 below).

The third group of signs is the 'double dez signs', where both hands move. These are written *tab-dez-ori-ori-(ha)-dez-ori-ori-sig* (for example, notation 3 below).

Notes

The rules about which order symbols appear in are strict. Remember especially that in two-handed signs, the non-dominant hand (this means the left hand for right-handed signers) is always shown first. Secondly, remember that palm ori is always written before finger ori.

When sig symbols are in a vertical column, the movements all happen at the same time. When sig symbols are in horizontal rows, the movements happen one after another (starting with the left-most symbol).

Hand arrangement

Hand arrangement symbols normally come in the middle of the notation. However, certain symbols may also appear above or below the first dez symbol, and others may appear immediately before the sig column.

Contacting movement

There are three types of contacting movement. Firstly, if contact is maintained between the moving hand and some other part of the body, the 'touch' symbol is placed at the bottom of the vertical sig column (see notation 4 below). Secondly, if one part of the hand is held in contact with another part of the body while the rest of the hand moves, then the contact symbol is placed at the top of the vertical sig column (see notation 5 below). Thirdly, if the moving hand brushes another part of the body, the contact symbol is placed in the middle of the vertical sig column, and the movement symbols above and below the contact symbol are the same (see notation 6 below).

Circular movement

There are three types of circular movement. The first kind, 'horizontal circles', are like somebody carrying a round tray of glasses: if we actually drew the circle, it would be parallel with the floor. The second type are 'vertical-parallel circles', like somebody holding a car steering-wheel: if we actually drew this circle, it would be parallel with the signer's body. The last type are 'vertical-right-angles circles', like somebody marching with a big bass drum: if we actually drew the circle, it would be at right angles to the signer's body.

The notation of any circular movement needs three symbols in a column. The top one is always ℮. The other two symbols show the direction of the circular movement. We write about these movements as 'clockwise' and 'anti-clockwise'. The sig columns for the various kinds of circle are listed in the table below.

There are four points to remember here when comparing notations against *Production guide* information. Firstly, the circles are described from the signer's own point of view—with one exception. If the circle is a 'vertical-right-angles' circle (like somebody marching with a big drum), to judge whether it is 'clockwise' or 'anti-clockwise' you must imagine that you are looking from the signer's right-hand side. Secondly, when the hands are moving in different directions in a circle, the labels 'clockwise' and 'anti-clockwise' refer to the direction of the right hand movement (the left hand moves in the opposite direction). Thirdly, when both hands move in the same direction, the same sig symbols are written as would be used for a one-handed sign. Finally, if the hands move in the same direction at different times, the alternating symbol ∾ is placed after the last column of sig symbols.

1. ∪ A ⊤∧ ×· (sign entry 30 in the Dictionary)

2. B̄>⊥ | B̊⊥ <° (sign entry 1658 in the Dictionary)

3. Ø F>⊥ | F>⊥ ∧∨ (sign entry 885 in the Dictionary)

4. [] ୪⊤< ×· (sign entry 964 in the Dictionary)

5. — Ba>× G<⊥ ×n z (sign entry 403 in the Dictionary)

6. A>⊥ ? B⊤< ×∨ (sign entry 1294 in the Dictionary)

	hands	clockwise	anti-clockwise
Horizontal plane	1	℮ >	℮ <
	2	℮ ÷	℮ ✕
Vertical-parallel plane	1	℮ >∨	℮ <∨
	2	℮ ÷∨	℮ ✕∨
Vertical-right-angles plane	1	℮ ⊥∨	℮ ⊤∨
	2	℮ ⊥∨	℮ ⊤∨

Searching the ordering system

The notation symbols listed on pages xvii–xxi have been laid out following the order in which they appear in the Dictionary. That is, the basic rule in this Dictionary is that A handshapes come before G handshapes, and so on. This also means that, within one handshape section, signs produced in 'neutral space' (∅ location) come before those produced above the head (⌢ location), and so on.

If you want to find the exact place of a particular sign in the order of entries, you must ask a series of questions. This series of questions is laid out below. Before you start, you will need to decide whether the sign you are looking for is a 'single dez sign' (only one hand involved), a 'manual tab sign' (two hands are used but only one moves) or a 'double dez sign' (two hands, both move).

Now let's take an example. The first question is *What is the (right) handshape?* If we have a single dez sign with a V̈ handshape, we can look in the list of handshape symbols and see that V̈ comes between V̂ and V̈. The V family of handshapes come between H and K. Next we are told to ask *What is the location?* If the sign is made in the area of the eyes, the location symbol is ⊔. In the table on page xx, which lists the location symbols, we can see that this comes between ○ and ⊔. So the sign we want will appear in this part of the V̈ (single dez) section of the Dictionary. As we continue down the list of questions, we get a more and more precise picture, telling us exactly where to find the sign.

Single dez	Manual tab	Double dez
What is the handshape?	What is the right handshape?	What is the right handshape?
	What is the left handshape?	What is the left handshape?
What is the location?		What is the location?
	What is the left palm orientation?	What is the left palm orientation?
	What is the left finger orientation?	What is the left finger orientation?
What is the palm orientation?	What is the right palm orientation?	What is the right palm orientation?
What is the finger orientation?	What is the right finger orientation?	What is the right finger orientation?
	What is the hand arrangement?	What is the hand arrangement?
	What is the left secondary location?	What is the left secondary location?
What is the secondary location?	What is the right secondary location?	What is the right secondary location?
What is the movement?	What is the movement?	What is the movement?

When we get to the movement information, we again need to ask a series of questions.

1 Is there movement? (Signs with no movement come before those with movement)
2 How many columns of movement symbols are in the notation? (Signs with one column come before those with two columns, and so on)
3 How many symbols are in the first column? (Signs with one symbol come before those with two symbols, and so on)
4 What is the top symbol in the column? (The list of movement symbols on page xviii tells you, for example, that < comes before >)
5 Does looking at the first column give a precise answer? (If not, we look at the second column. Signs containing only the symbol [ ], showing a change of handshape, in the second column come first; signs containing only a 'repeated movement' symbol in the second column come second; after these, the movement symbols on page xviii will decide on the order of signs)
6 Does the second column give a precise answer? (If not, we look at the third column, repeating the process outlined above; and so on)

Points to remember

Bear in mind that a number of hand arrangement symbols may be used in one notation. The first symbol from the list on page xxi to appear in the notation (reading left to right) should decide the order of entries. Only if it does not should the second symbol be considered.

'Compound signs'—that is, those signs whose notation has ⫽ in the middle—appear in the order of entries just as if they were simple signs. Only if the first part of the compound does not decide the exact order of entries should the second part be considered.

Within the double dez signs section of any handshape, signs which have a secondary location (that is, signs which behave like manual tab signs but must be held or moved in a particular location) are placed at the end of the handshape section. These signs are distinguished by brackets ( ) separating the secondary location symbol from the rest of the notation.

Within the double dez signs section of any handshape, signs which use two distinct locations (one tab symbol for each handshape) are placed immediately before the 'secondary location' signs described above.

1

2

3

4

5

6

7

8

9

10

11

12

13

14

15

16

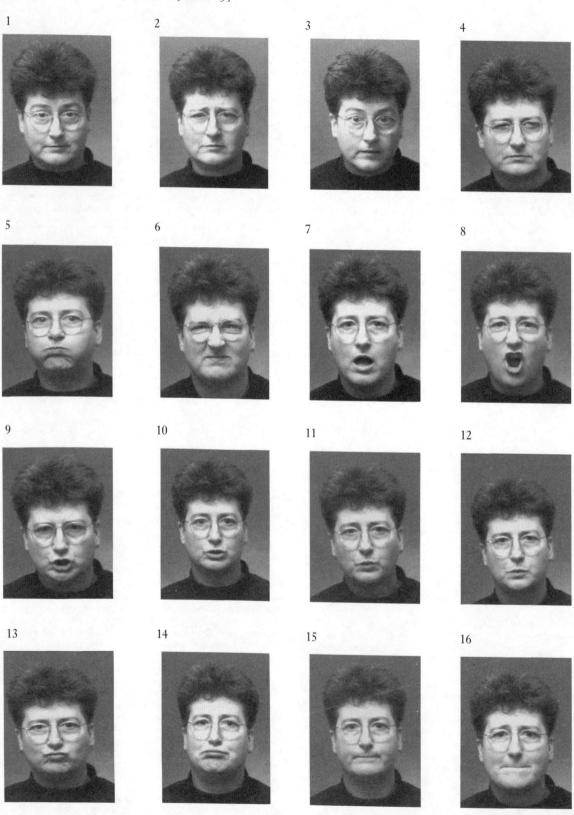

Non-manual features key

When you are producing signs of BSL, your hands are not the only part of your body that is important. In this Dictionary, it has been our aim to give clear information, where possible, about the non-manual features which are an integral part of sign production, vital to the vocabulary and grammar of BSL.

Facial expressions are perhaps the most obvious kind of non-manual feature, but movements of the head, shoulders and trunk are also included under this heading. Indeed, there are signs (e.g. entry 892 in this Dictionary) in which body movements of this kind are the only movements which native signers consider essential to fluent sign production.

The illustrations (numbers 1—30) in this section constitute a key, showing exactly what is meant by each of the descriptive phrases we have used in the *Non-manual features* part of the *Production guide* (see page xiii) in this Dictionary. The English phrases listed below are sometimes slightly modified in the Dictionary: we have tried to give the clearest possible description for each sign.

Some of the non-manual features are not illustrated here. This happens when we either could not give a better picture than the ones used in the Dictionary entries themselves, or when we felt the instructions were intuitively clear—for instance, "The head shakes". Non-manual features 31—44 overleaf give the additional descriptive phrases, with examples of entries where they are used. This list therefore gives a complete index of the non-manual features which appear in this Dictionary.

There are a few signs where we have chosen not to specify a particular non-manual feature, although the signs always require some such features. Two 'umbrella' phrases therefore make occasional appearances as the non-manual specification of Dictionary entries. Here are the two phrases, and a list of the features that are potentially appropriate, and are therefore likely to be seen used, in these contexts:

Appropriate negative non-manual features—one or more of the illustrations numbered 2, 4, 5, 6, 12, 16, 17, 19, 22, 25, 28, 30;

Non-manual features appropriate for questions—one or more of the illustrations numbered 1, 2, 3, 4, 7, 11, 26, 27, 28, 29.

The most effective way to begin to learn how to use these non-manual features like a native signer is simply to get involved in natural sign language conversations. Learning to use parts of the body other than the hands, and to understand the many functions of non-manual features in signed interactions, are vital to all students of BSL. Further information about the role of non-manual features within the language as a whole can be found in the *Introduction* to this book.

Non-manual feature	*Example*
1 The eyebrows are raised	Entry number 510 in the BSL section
2 The eyebrows are furrowed	Entry number 469 in the BSL section
3 The eyes are opened wide	Entry number 725 in the BSL section
4 The eyes are narrowed	Entry number 1072 in the BSL section
5 The cheeks are puffed out	Entry number 1053 in the BSL section
6 The nose is wrinkled	Entry number 590 in the BSL section
7 The mouth is open	Entry number 467 in the BSL section
8 The mouth is open wide with the lips pushed forward and rounded	Entry number 39 in the BSL section
9 The mouth is open with the lips pushed forward	Entry number 111 in the BSL section
10 The lips are pushed forward and rounded	Entry number 161 in the BSL section
11 The lips are rounded	Entry number 460 in the BSL section
12 The lips are tightly rounded	Entry number 41 in the BSL section
13 The mouth is closed with the lips pushed forward	Entry number 48 in the BSL section
14 The lips vibrate	Entry number 1037 in the BSL section
15 The lips are pressed together	Entry number 1643 in the BSL section
16 The lips are closed and drawn back	Entry number 181 in the BSL section

17 18 19 20

21 22 23 24

25 26 27 28

29 30

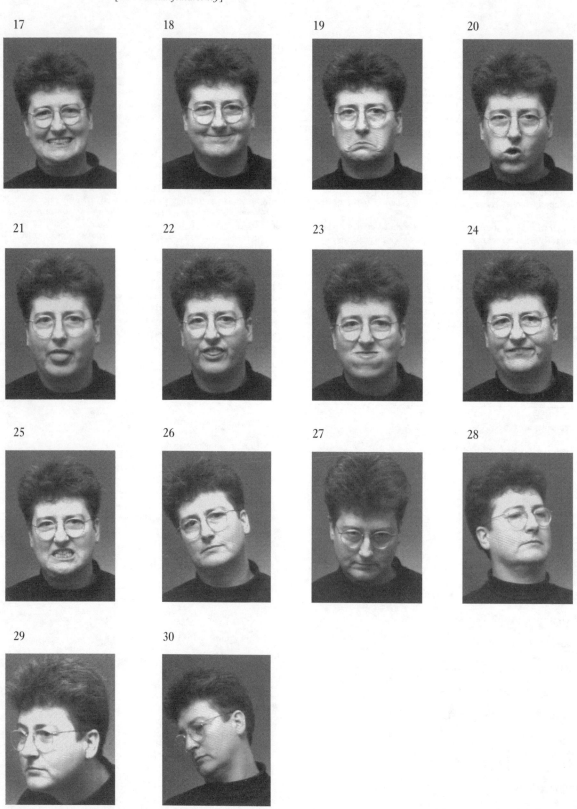

Non-manual feature		Example
17	The lips are stretched	Entry number 188 in the BSL section
18	The corners of the mouth are turned up	Entry number 140 in the BSL section
19	The corners of the mouth are turned down	Entry number 1568 in the BSL section
20	The tongue tip is pushed into the cheek	Entry number 272 in the BSL section
21	The mouth is open with the tongue resting on the lower lip	Entry number 1564 in the BSL section
22	The tongue protrudes	Entry number 1600 in the BSL section
23	The tongue tip is held between the lower lip and the bottom teeth	Entry number 176 in the BSL section
24	The top teeth are held on the lower lip	Entry number 969.2 in the BSL section
25	The teeth are clenched	Entry number 506 in the BSL section
26	The head is tilted to the side	Entry number 34 in the BSL section
27	The head is tilted forward	Entry number 1205 in the BSL section
28	The head is tilted back	Entry number 1161 in the BSL section
29	The head is pushed forward	Entry number 604 in the BSL section
30	The head is twisted to the side	Entry number 1397.1 in the BSL section
31	The head moves from side to side	Entry number 82 in the BSL section
32	The head nods	Entry number 467 in the BSL section
33	The head shakes	Entry number 1731 in the BSL section
34	The eyegaze is directed down and forwards	Entry number 1461 in the BSL section
35	The eyegaze is directed up and forwards	Entry number 126 in the BSL section
36	The eyegaze is directed in line with the movement of the hand	Entry number 1696 in the BSL section
37	The eyes open	Entry number 633 in the BSL section
38	The eyes close	Entry number 508 in the BSL section
39	The eyes are closed	Entry number 633 in the BSL section
40	The mouth closes	Entry number 478 in the BSL section
41	The lower jaw moves from side to side and up and down	Entry number 46 in the BSL section
42	The shoulders are hunched	Entry number 725 in the BSL section
43	The shoulders move forward	Entry number 85 in the BSL section
44	The shoulders move back	Entry number 1632 in the BSL section
45	The body moves forward	Entry number 1397 in the BSL section
46	The body moves back	Entry number 1143 in the BSL section

Artwork key

Each sign entry in the *BSL* section of this Dictionary includes one or more photographs presented with additional artwork. The main feature of this artwork is an arrow system which we have developed to show the complex movements involved in the signs. The type of arrowhead used gives you information about the main direction of the movement.

Combinations of symbols can occur at any time, according to the movements required by the sign. You may find artwork on more than one part of the body; we do this either to make the movements even clearer, or to show that different parts of the body are actually moving in different ways. The *Photographs* alone cannot tell you how to produce the sign, even with the help of artwork: to be sure that you have all the information you need, you must consider them together with the *Production guide* and *Notes*.

Artwork: direction and path

Artwork: type of movement

Direction symbols

These symbols may be used in conjunction with symbols from any other category. The arrowhead indicates the predominant direction of the movement.

> Movement *towards* or *away from* the signer.

▶ Movement to the *left* or *right* or *up* or *down*.

≫ Repeated movement *towards* or *away from* the signer.

▶▶ Repeated movement to the *left* or *right* or *up* or *down*.

≪ ≫ Repeated movement *towards and away from* the signer.

◀◀ ▶▶ Repeated movement from *side to side* or *up and down*.

Path symbols

 Hand or part of a hand moving in a line. When this symbol appears in a curved arrow around the wrist, it indicates a *twisting* movement of the wrist. It may also be used to show the wrist *bending* or a finger either *bending* or *flexing*: only by considering the *Photographs* in conjunction with the accompanying text will you know exactly what movement is indicated.

 Slow movement.

 Fast movement.

 Firm movement.

 Circular movement (see *Notating whole signs* on pages xvi and xvii for explanation of 'horizontal', 'vertical-parallel' and 'vertical-right-angles' circles). Each circle shows the movement of one hand, unless two hands move along the same path—in this case, one circle shows the movements of both hands. Arrowheads show whether the movement is single or repeated. The position of the arrowheads on the circles shows whether the hands move in parallel or in alternating movements.

Circles indicating movement shape have direction symbols which are *in line* with their path. A second, distinct, use of the circle also occurs (see *Interacting movement symbols* on this page).

Internal movement symbols

 'Tapping' movement in which the hand touches another part of the body several times quickly.

 'Crumbling' movement in which the pad of the thumb rubs across the pads of the fingers.

 'Wiggling' movement of the fingers.

Part of the hand closing or part of the hand opening.

 Closed hand opening or open hand closing.

 Closing movement in which the hand becomes a fist.

1 **2** Movements occurring in sequence (this symbol supplements other information only where needed).

Interacting movement symbols

 Stationary hand—no movement.

 The hands maintain contact throughout the movement.

If direction and path symbols are *attached to* the circle, then the hands are held together and move together accordingly.

If symbols are *placed inside* the circle, then the hands do not move together, but still maintain contact throughout. The last two examples on the facing page show these two uses of the 'interacting movement' circle. A second, distinct, use of the circle also occurs (see *Path symbols* on this page).

Artwork: examples

The hand moves in an arc to the left.

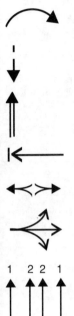

The hand moves slowly downwards.

The hand moves sharply upwards.

The hand moves firmly towards the signer.

The hands move apart while the extended fingers close.

The hand moves away from the signer while opening from a fist.

1 2 2 1

The hands make two parallel upwards movements; the second pair of movements are made nearer to each other than the first pair.

The hand moves in a clockwise horizontal circle.

The hands move (at the same time) in circles parallel to the signer's body; the left hand moves anticlockwise, the right hand moves clockwise.

The hands move downwards together, maintaining contact throughout.

The right hand moves up and down several times, maintaining contact with the stationary left hand throughout.

Photography

Traditionally, dictionaries of spoken languages present their entire contents in written form. British Sign Language, like all other known signed languages, has no comparable system of writing, and therefore presents a special problem to the dictionary-maker. Our solution is to use annotated photographic images to present the words of BSL.

Why photographs? After all, many sign language dictionaries have chosen to produce line drawings of signs. We believe that no line drawing matches a photograph's ability to capture every visible aspect of the sign production. Human beings have developed incredible skills in the recognition of faces and facial expressions, recognition of voice patterns and qualities, and the ability to perceive and differentiate fine details of the shapes and movements made by the hands. All of these skills are put to use in natural communication. Showing signs in such a way that the reader obtains a partial view of the relevant information—and a line drawing would be partial in comparison with what we see in a photograph—cannot do justice to the visual facts which make sign languages rich and efficient linguistic systems. Using photographs allows us to present a relatively full and more complete picture of sign language production.

Of course, photographs need models, and this means that individuals (some of whom are well-known within the British Deaf community) are recognisable in our photographs. Decisions about the signs produced, however, were never the responsibility of these individuals alone: many informants were involved in the process of reaching conclusions about the signs you see on these pages.

Photographs, of course, can only show a single moment in the sign's production. Wherever possible, we have shown the beginning of the sign in the photograph and used the artwork to indicate the movement that follows. Many of the sign entries have two or more photographs: these should be 'read' in top-to-bottom or left-to-right order. We have used multiple photographs in order to show movements as clearly as possible: the last photograph sometimes shows nothing more than the changed position of the hands at the end of the sign. Some signs have evolved over time through the merging of two otherwise independent signs: many of these 'compounds' (see *Introduction*) are still most effectively presented in two parts. Nevertheless, in natural signed communication, no interruption of the fluid movement of the sign should occur in the transition from one photograph to the next.

Finally, it should be noted always that the photographic illustrations represent a kind of neutral form of each sign, isolated from any actual communicative event. When you see the signs in use in natural conversation—even in the context of the example sentences we give in the *English (Guide to meaning)* section of this Dictionary—they may well be modified to suit the context in which they are used.

Production guide

The guide to the production of each sign is presented in four parts (identified on page xv as *Production guide one*, *two*, *three* and *Non-manual features*). The production guide is written as if the manual parts of the signs were constructed in three stages. In real, live signing, this is not the case. For the purposes of a person learning or looking analytically at BSL, though, we feel that it is helpful to put the sign together one step at a time. It is also important to remember that the production guide describes the signs from the signer's own point of view.

The production guide tries to maintain a balance between detail and readability. However, sometimes the photographs on the left-hand pages of the *BSL* section present features of the sign much more clearly than the written English does. It is our aim that the text and the photographs should always be considered together if the reader wishes to get the best possible view of the sign presented.

The information we give about production is not by any means intended to represent the only or the 'best' or 'proper' way to produce the sign. It simply describes one way of producing the sign, which Deaf members of the project team consider to be widely known and used. Some common alternative productions are given in the *Notes* section of the guide. Readers should therefore be aware that the form the sign takes in everyday discourse may vary slightly or significantly from the production presented here.

*Handshape and orientation (*Production guide one*)*

This part of the text tells you which handshapes are used at the beginning of the sign and which way the palms and fingers are directed. The handshapes are shown by using the appropriate notation symbols. To check the handshapes, you will need to look at the top left-hand corner of the left-hand page (where the dominant handshape is illustrated) and at the handshape table on pages xvii–xix.

If you are using these guidelines to practise making the sign, you can now move on to part two of the *Production guide*. However, when you arrange your hands in the given location, be careful not to change the handshape you are making, or twist your hands away from the specified orientation.

*Location, hand arrangement and contact (*Production guide two*)*

This part of the text tells you where the hands are placed and how they are arranged in relation to each other. Taken in combination with the photographs on the left-hand page, the descriptions should give a clear picture of the production. A number of phrases may need practice before becoming familiar. 'Side by side', for instance, means that the hands are held no more than an inch or so either side of an imaginary midline (one may be higher than the other). 'At an angle' means that the palm or fingers are held at approximately 45°—facing neither up nor to the left, for instance, but somewhere midway between the two. It should also be recalled that to say 'the hand is held touching...' in this section is not a description of movement, but of a fleeting still-point before the sign's movement begins.

*Movement (*Production guide three*)*

This part of the text describes the movement of the hands. Whenever there are two or more steps involved in the movement, the description presents these as if they happened one by one without overlapping. In reality, of course, the steps tend to occur in a flowing series of movements with no clear break between one stage and the next.

If the handshape changes during the movement, this is either shown in the words of the description (for instance, 'the index finger flexes') or by using the handshape symbol of the notation within the text. If you are in doubt about the handshape indicated, check the illustrations in the table on pages xvii–xix.

Non-manual features

This part of the text gives you information about the way in which parts of the body other than the hands are used in the sign. Although these are not always used as an integral part of signs, there are many signs which have elements of facial expression, head movement and body posture built into the fabric of the sign. Such elements are recorded in this section of the *Production guide*.

For a number of the signs where we have specified non-manual features in the production guide, we were unable to achieve clear illustrations of these features in the photographs on the left-hand page. As a rule of thumb, if in doubt, trust the text! At times, you may wish to check the table of non-manual feature illustrations on pages xxiv–xxvii for clarification of the exact facial expressions and head movements referred to in the *Production guide* text.

In real, live signing, you will find that people use non-manual features even where these are not indicated in this book. Much of this is due to natural variation from person to person in the exact form a sign takes. People who know BSL well will also recognise that non-manual features may be used to mark grammatical information (for example, eyebrows raised in certain types of question constructions—see *Introduction*) as well as being an element in the kind of lexical information recorded in a Dictionary.

Notes and glosses

The *Notes* in this Dictionary are of particular importance, since they not only give additional information of interest to users and students of BSL, but also record and draw the reader's attention to signs which are not included elsewhere in the book. The signs referred to include both slight variations on the sign described in the *Production guide*, and other signs which differ only in particular fine-detailed features of the production.

Two sets of symbols are used to show two types of *Note*. The symbols *, † and ¶ are used when the information that follows is supplementary, or explains how a sign *may* be modified. The symbols $^1, ^2, ^3$ and ^{4} are used to indicate that a sign *can only* be produced following the instructions in the *Note*. These symbols show which kind of *Note* is intended when used in this section, and also appear in the *Glosses* column to show which glosses are affected—optionally or obligatorily—by the *Note*.

The changes described in the *Notes* may be changes in the non-manual features. For clarification of the facial expressions, head and body movements referred to, readers should check the illustrations on pages xxiv–xxvii. Changes in handshape are recorded in the *Notes* using notation symbols. To check the handshape intended, look at the illustrations listed on pages xvii–xix.

The symbols *, † and ¶ are used:

i. to indicate regional signs, that is, signs which are recognised by members of the British Deaf Community as having a particular regional association. Signs that are not marked in this way can be assumed to have nationwide usage and to be understood throughout the language community. Many regional signs are in fact used in a number of different areas, rather than simply in one well-defined locality. We mark them as 'Regional' simply to indicate that they may not be recognised or understood in all parts of the community.

ii. to indicate those verbs which are considered to be 'Directional Verbs'. This means that the direction of the movement will alter completely in accordance with the meaning of the sign in context. For instance, the sign glossed as **gave** in the sequence 'I gave you the spanner' moves in the opposite direction to the sign glossed as **gave** in 'you gave me the spanner'. Learners are thus warned to be alert to the significance of movement changes of this sort.

iii. to indicate optional variations on the production specified in the main part of the *Production guide*. These variations are not regionally marked (unless such information is given), but are common alternative productions of the sign. They do not include entirely different signs which happen to have the same meaning.

Two or more optional *Notes* may be combined under one symbol when the information given relates to all glosses listed in that sign entry.

The symbols $^1, ^2, ^3$ and ^{4} are used when a sign slightly but significantly different to that described in the production guide can be produced by making small changes to features specified in the text. Those features which must be changed are explained in the *Note*. All elements of the production that are not described as being different remain the same as in the main *Production guide* text. The glosses relating to the sign described in the *Note* are listed: they also appear marked by the numbers $^1, ^2, ^3$ or ^{4} as appropriate, in the *Glosses* column. The meanings of signs described in such *Notes* (and the corresponding English words) can be found in the *English (Guide to meaning)* section as usual.

Glosses are typically used in two different but related ways in the sign language literature. They have been used both to record signs on paper and as translations into English of the meanings of the signs.

Their use as a way of recording signs on paper arises from the fact that BSL is a visual-gestural language without a conventional written form. It is, however, a very inexact way of recording signs as it is not possible (without further information) to identify which specific sign is being referred to. For instance, the gloss **walk** could be used in relation to a number of different signs. As the production of each sign entry in the Dictionary is illustrated by a photograph and explained by notation and written description, it has not been necessary to use glosses in this way in the *BSL* section.

In the Dictionary, the English words that appear in the *Glosses* column are words which correspond to one or more of the meanings of the BSL signs. The glosses are arranged in English alphabetical order within each entry of the *BSL* section: full phrase glosses may begin with just the key word, followed by the full gloss within brackets. All of the glosses in the *BSL* section are listed in English alphabetical order in the *English (Guide to meaning)* section of the Dictionary. In the *BSL* section, glosses which correspond to the sign as shown in the photograph and description are entered first, in alphabetical order.

e.g. Sign 805: **go upstairs,*** **stairs,*** **walk upstairs***

Glosses which carry a superscript number (^{1}) are entered next.

escalator,^{1} **go up by escalator**^{1}

Notice that the addition of symbols *, †, ¶ to glosses does not affect the order of entry. These symbols indicate information which does not involve an obligatory change in the production of the sign. The superscript number (^{1}) indicates that a change in the production, creating a different sign (as described in the appropriate *Note*), is required to produce the meaning or meanings associated with these glosses. Glosses not listed in bold type refer to compound signs made by combining this sign with another sign entered elsewhere in the Dictionary.

In the *Introduction* to this Dictionary, a distinction is made between the established or frozen lexicon and the productive lexicon of the language. The signs associated with the glosses in the glosses column may be considered examples of the established lexicon: however, some glosses have been selected to indicate the productive potential of elements of the signs. You can find further examples of this in the *Introduction* and the introductions to each of the handshape sections.

We do not claim that the glosses entered in relation to each sign are the only appropriate glosses. The glosses chosen represent, in the view of our informants, a range of common meanings associated with each sign. The list of these meanings can be found, arranged in alphabetical order, in the *English (Guide to meaning)* section of the Dictionary.

The inclusion of the glosses enables this book to operate as a bilingual Dictionary. If the glosses had not been included, the Dictionary would, in effect, have been a monolingual Dictionary of BSL in which information on the production and meaning of entries happened to be presented in English. It would be possible to reproduce this information in a signed format (for example, on video) and therefore provide a monolingual BSL Dictionary.

Even so, this Dictionary is not a conventional bilingual Dictionary. In many bilingual Dictionaries, we would simply find a list of words and phrases from one language with corresponding words and phrases of another language. What makes this Dictionary unusual is that we have attempted to give a guide to the meaning of the signs as well as giving equivalents in the other language. The guide also gives some of the meanings of the English words; that is, it gives the meanings insofar as the English words are equivalent to the BSL signs as defined. For instance, one of the glosses used in this Dictionary is **back**. The sign associated with it (entry 1587) relates to the part of the body called the 'back'. However, there is no sign in this Dictionary relating, for example, to the 'back' of a room, although English happens to use the same word for both meanings. This meaning is therefore not listed under **back** in the *English (Guide to meaning)* section of the Dictionary.

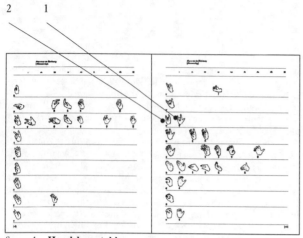

figure 1. **Handshape table**

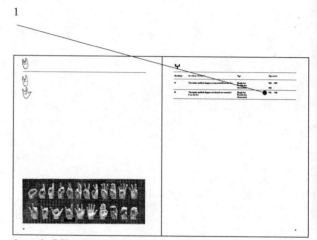

figure 2. **BSL section: introduction to a handshape family**

Questions and answers

On the next three pages, we give some examples of the ways in which you may wish to use this Dictionary. If you follow the instructions listed here—using figures 1 to 4 above to give you a 'bird's eye view' of where information is placed on the relevant pages—when you are actually using the book, you should find the information you need.

Query
I'm a fluent user of BSL and I know some English. I'm writing a letter and I keep having to use one particular English word. I want to know if there are any other English words that have the same meaning. What do I do?

1 In the *English (Guide to meaning)* section of the book, find the English word in the alphabetical listing [figure 4, arrow 1]. Let's suppose it is 'check'.
2 Read the explanations [figure 4, arrow 3] of the meanings of 'check', and see which of them match the meaning you have in mind.
3 See which reference numbers [figure 4, arrow 2] are listed alongside the matching explanations. Suppose you find the numbers 961 and 962.
4 Look for 961 in the column of entry numbers on the right-hand side of the right-hand pages in the *BSL* section of the Dictionary [figure 3, arrow 5].
5 Check the glosses listed alongside the entry number 961 [figure 3, arrow 4]. Keep in mind those glosses which seem as if they may be similar in meaning to your original English word.
6 Find these glosses in the alphabetical order of the *English (Guide to meaning)* section [figure 4, arrow 1].
7 For each gloss, check which parts of the explanation of the meaning carry the number 961 [figure 4, arrow 2].
8 Look at these explanations [figure 4, arrow 3], and the related example sentences, to see whether this item seems to be a suitable alternative to your original English word.
9 Repeat the steps 5–8 for the entry number 962.

Query
I'm a fluent user of BSL and I know some English. I'm reading a book and I find a word which I know with one meaning: I want to check whether it has any other meanings I should know about. What do I do?

1 In the *English (Guide to meaning)* section of the book, find the English word in the alphabetical listing [figure 4, arrow 1]. Let's suppose it is 'check'.
2 Read the explanations [figure 4, arrow 3] of the meanings of 'check', and see which of them match the meaning you have in mind.
3 Ignoring those parts of the explanation of the meanings of 'check' which match the meaning you already know, you can see what other meanings 'check' has by looking at other parts of the explanation [figure 4, arrow 3].
4 If you would like to make sure that you understand the explanations by seeing the BSL signs which have the same meanings, look at the reference numbers alongside the new (to you) senses of 'check' [figure 4, arrow 2]. Suppose 961 is one of them.
5 Look for 961 in the column of entry numbers on the right-hand side of the right-hand pages in the *BSL* section of the Dictionary [figure 3, arrow 5].
5 Find your original English word 'check' amongst the glosses listed alongside the entry number 961 [figure 3, arrow 4].
6 If the gloss has a superscript number (^{1}, ^{2}, ^{3}, or ^{4}) beside it, read the relevant note [figure 3, arrow 6] and keep in mind the changes in production it demands.
7 Look at the sign entry photograph numbered 961 on the facing page [figure 3, arrow 2].
8 Compare the photograph (and notation) with the production guide information numbered 961 on the right-hand page [figure 3, arrow 3]. Taking into account any changes specified in the notes (step 6 above), you should now be able to recognise or produce the sign.

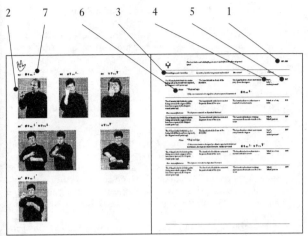

figure 3. **BSL section**

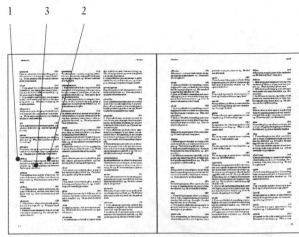

figure 4. **English (Guide to meaning) section**

Query

I'm a fluent user of BSL and I know some English. I'm writing a translation into English of a video in BSL. I can't think of a good way to translate one of the signs. What do I do?

1 Using the handshape table on pages xvii–xix, decide what the right handshape (if you are right-handed: left if you are left-handed) of the sign is [figure 1, arrow 1]. Let's suppose it is a ᰛ handshape. Note the first handshape in the handshape family [figure 1, arrow 2].

2 Decide whether the sign starts as a 'single dez' (one-handed), 'manual tab' (two-handed, one had moves) or 'double dez' (two-handed, both move) sign. Let's suppose it is a 'single dez' sign.

3 In the *BSL* section of the book, find the first page of the ᰛ handshape family signs [figure 2].

4 On this page, you can check which sign entry is the first 'single dez' sign with a ᰛ handshape [figure 2, arrow 1]. Let's suppose it is number 961.

5 In the *BSL* section, by checking the entry numbers on the top right hand corner of the right-handed page [figure 3, arrow 1], you can find the page where you need to start looking.

6 When you find the page with entry 961, start here to look at the photographs on the left-hand pages (and glosses on the right-hand pages, if you have an idea of the sign's meaning) until you see a sign which matches your recollections. Suppose it is entry 962 [figure 3, arrow 2].

7 On the right-hand side of the page opposite the photograph of entry 962, you will find the entry number 962 alongside a list of glosses matching this sign [figure 3, arrow 4].

8 Ignoring those items marked with superscript numbers ([1,2,3,4]), see which of these glosses are appropriate for the meaning you have in mind.

9 Find the appropriate glosses in the alphabetical order of the *English (Guide to meaning)* section [figure 4, arrow 1].

10 See where the number 962 is listed alongside the meanings given for these headwords [figure 4, arrow 2].

11 From the explanations [figure 4, arrow 3] and example sentences that appear under various headwords alongside the reference number 962, you will be able to work out which of the possible glosses is most suitable as a translation of the BSL sign in the context of your video.

Query

I'm a fluent user of BSL and I know some English. I'm writing a letter and I can't remember how to spell a certain word. I know what it means, and I know what sign to use in BSL. What do I do?

If you are fairly confident about the spelling, you could just use the *English (Guide to meaning)* section of this book as if it were an ordinary English Language Dictionary, and look it up in the alphabetical listing of entries. On the other hand, you could do it this way:

1 Make the BSL sign you would use as a translation of this English word.

2 Using the handshape table on pages xxii–xix, decide what the right handshape (if you are right-handed: left if you are left-handed) of the sign is [figure 1, arrow 1]. Let's suppose it is a ᰛ handshape. Note the first handshape in the handshape family [figure 1, arrow 2].

3 Decide whether the sign starts as a 'single dez' (one-handed), 'manual tab' (two-handed, one had moves) or 'double dez' (two-handed, both move) sign. Let's suppose it is a 'single dez' sign.

4 In the *BSL* section of the book, find the first page of the ᰛ handshape family signs [figure 2].

5 On this page, you can check which sign entry is the first 'single dez' sign with a ᰛ handshape [figure 2, arrow 1]. Let's suppose it is number 961.

6 In the *BSL* section, by checking the entry numbers on the top right hand corner of the right-handed page [figure 3, arrow 1], you can find the page where you need to start looking.

7 When you find the page with entry 961, start here to look at the photographs on the left-hand pages (and glosses on the right-hand pages, if you have an idea of the sign's meaning) until you see a sign which matches your recollections. Suppose it is entry 962 [figure 3, arrow 2].

8 On the right-hand side of the page opposite the photograph of entry 962, you will find the entry number 962 alongside a list of glosses matching this sign [figure 3, arrow 4].

9 See which of these glosses gives the English word you are looking for. Check the spelling.

Query

I'm a fluent user of English, and I know some BSL. There's a certain sign I've seen two or three times, but I can't exactly work out how to produce it. What do I do?

1 Using the handshape table on pages xvii–xix, decide what the right handshape (if you are right-handed: left if you are left-handed) of the sign is [figure 1, arrow 1]. Let's suppose it is a ᖷ handshape. Note the first handshape in the handshape family [figure 1, arrow 2].

2 Decide whether the sign starts as a 'single dez' (one-handed), 'manual tab' (two-handed, one had moves) or 'double dez' (two-handed, both move) sign. Let's suppose it is a 'single dez' sign.

3 In the *BSL* section of the book, find the first page of the ᖷ handshape family signs [figure 2].

4 On this page, you can check which sign entry is the first 'single dez' sign with a ᖷ handshape [figure 2, arrow 1]. Let's suppose it is number 961.

5 In the *BSL* section, by checking the entry numbers on the top right hand corner of the right-handed page [figure 3, arrow 1], you can find the page where you need to start looking.

6 When you find the page with entry 961, start here to look at the photographs on the left-hand pages (and glosses on the right-hand pages, if you have an idea of the sign's meaning) until you see a sign which matches your recollections. Suppose it is entry 962 [figure 3, arrow 2].

7 On the page opposite the photograph of entry 962, you will find—also marked by the number 962—the production guide to this sign [figure 3, arrow 3].

8 Using both the photograph and the production guide, you should be able to get a clear idea of how the sign is produced.

Query
I'm a fluent user of English and I know some BSL. I'm trying to translate a story from English into BSL and there's one word I don't know at all. What do I do?

1 In the *English (Guide to meaning)* section of the book, find the English word in the alphabetical listing [figure 4, arrow 1]. Let's suppose it is 'check'.

2 Read the explanations of the meanings of 'check' [figure 4, arrow 3]: using any clues the context of the story gives you, try to work out which of the meanings fits.

3 If you would like to confirm your understanding of the meaning, you can look at the BSL signs which share this meaning. Look at the reference numbers alongside the meaning which you feel is appropriate [figure 4, arrow 2]. Suppose 961 is one of them.

4 Find your original English word 'check' amongst the glosses listed alongside the entry number 961 [figure 3, arrow 4].

5 If the gloss has a superscript number (^{1}, ^{2}, ^{3}, or ^{4}) beside it, read the relevant note [figure 3, arrow 6] and keep in mind the changes in production it demands.

6 Look at the sign entry photograph numbered 961 on the facing page [figure 3, arrow 2].

7 Compare the photograph (and notation) with the production guide information numbered 961 on the right-hand page [figure 3, arrow 3]. Taking into account any changes specified in the notes (step 6), you should now be able to recognise/produce the sign.

Query
I'm a fluent user of English, and I know some BSL. I have a video in BSL and there's one sign I don't understand. What do I do?

1 Using the handshape table on pages xiv-xvi, decide what the right handshape (if you are right-handed: left if you are left-handed) of the sign is [figure 1, arrow 1]. Let's suppose it is a ᖷ handshape.

Note the first handshape in the handshape family [figure 1, arrow 2].

2 Decide whether the sign starts as a 'single dez' (one-handed), 'manual tab' (two-handed, one had moves) or 'double dez' (two-handed, both move) sign. Let's suppose it is a 'single dez' sign.

3 In the *BSL* section of the book, find the first page of the ᖷ handshape family signs [figure 2].

4 On this page, you can check which sign entry is the first 'single dez' sign with a ᖷ handshape [figure 2, arrow 1]. Let's suppose it is number 961.

5 In the *BSL* section, by checking the entry numbers on the top right hand corner of the right-handed page [figure 3, arrow 1], you can find the page where you need to start looking.

6 When you find the page with entry 961, start here to look at the photographs on the left-hand pages (and glosses on the right-hand pages, if you have an idea of the sign's meaning) until you see a sign which matches your recollections. Suppose it is entry 962 [figure 3, arrow 2].

7 On the right-hand side of the page opposite the photograph of entry 962, you will find the entry number 962 alongside a list of glosses matching this sign [figure 3, arrow 4].

8 Ignoring those glosses marked with superscript numbers (^{1}, ^{2}, ^{3}, ^{4}), see which of these glosses seem to be appropriate for the sign in the context in which it appears in your video.

9 Find the appropriate glosses in the alphabetical order of the *English (Guide to meaning)* section [figure 4, arrow 1].

10 See where the number 962 is listed alongside the meanings given for these headwords [figure 4, arrow 2].

11 The explanations of the meaning [figure 4, arrow 3], with their example sentences, tell you what the sign means in various contexts. Decide which of these is an appropriate equivalent.

Query
I'm a fluent user of English and I know some BSL. I'm sending a video letter. I know what I want to say (I've got notes in English) but there's one bit where I can't think of a BSL sign to fit. What do I do?

1 In the *English (Guide to meaning)* section of the book, find the English word in the alphabetical listing [figure 4, arrow 1]. Let's suppose it is 'check'.

2 Read the explanations [figure 4, arrow 3] of the meanings of 'check', and see which of them match the meaning you have in mind.

3 See which reference numbers [figure 4, arrow 2] are listed alongside the matching explanations. Suppose you find the numbers 961 and 962.

4 Look for 961 in the column of entry numbers on the right-hand side of the right-hand pages in the *BSL* section of the Dictionary [figure 3, arrow 5].

5 Find your original English word 'check' amongst the glosses listed alongside the entry number 961 [figure 3, arrow 4].

6 If the gloss has a superscript number (^{1}, ^{2}, ^{3}, or ^{4}) beside it, read the relevant note [figure 3, arrow 6] and keep in mind the changes in production it demands.

7 Look at the sign entry photograph numbered 961 on the facing page [figure 3, arrow 2].

8 If you know the notation system, check the notation for information about the production of the sign [figure 3, arrow 7].

9 Compare the photograph (and notation) with the production guide information numbered 961 on the right-hand page [figure 3, arrow 3]. Taking into account any changes specified in the notes (step 6), you should now be able to recognise/produce the sign.

THE VISUAL WORLD OF BRITISH SIGN LANGUAGE: AN INTRODUCTION
Mary Brennan

This introduction has several aims: firstly, it seeks to provide the reader with a general introduction to the nature of British Sign Language (BSL) and to the community of people who use this language; secondly, it aims to familiarise the reader with the nature of BSL words and with the creative lexical potential of the language, and, thirdly, it aims to provide a summary of the main features of the grammar of BSL.

The second aim clearly has special importance within the context of a dictionary, since it includes both a description of the established words of the language and an account of the enormous set of resources available to the signer for the on-going automatic creation of 'new' words. The vocabulary of BSL, the vocabulary used every day by signers, is not simply a set of individual signs which can be listed in a dictionary. It is not even simply a very large set of such signs. The vocabulary of BSL is made up also of meaningful parts which can be combined together in numerous different ways to provide a virtually inexhaustible set of words. This potential for creating vocabulary anew, as needed, contributes to the lexical richness of the language and provides a remarkable flexibility for the user.

Before exploring the lexical resources of BSL in more detail, it is necessary to focus firstly on the people who use this language and then on some general characteristics of the language itself.

The Deaf community and its language

The community

BSL is the language of the Deaf community in Britain. Fairly obviously, the Deaf community consists of people who have a profound hearing loss, often from birth. Less obviously perhaps, it also includes people with varying degrees of hearing loss as well as, possibly, people with no hearing loss at all, i.e. hearing people. Such people become members of the Deaf community either because they are born into a Deaf family or because they identify strongly with the community through the use of its language and through entering into its cultural life. The Deaf community is scattered throughout the country, but nevertheless has a strong coherence and sense of common identity. Often, membership of the community is the strongest allegiance felt by its members.

It will probably already have become clear that the term "Deaf" as it is used here refers more to membership of a particular linguistic and cultural grouping than it does to the physical condition of deafness. Certainly, most community members do have some hearing loss. However, often fellow members have no idea of the extent or nature of the deafness concerned. This is unimportant within the context of the Deaf community; what is more important is that Deaf people share a common cultural heritage, a common language, common life experiences and a common sense of identity.*

Throughout this account, the convention of referring to members of the Deaf community by using 'Deaf' with a capital 'D' and referring to people with a hearing loss by using 'deaf' with a lower case 'd' will be used. This convention was originally suggested by James Woodward (1972) and developed by Carol Padden (1980). Of course, the same person can be viewed as both Deaf and deaf, depending upon the perspective taken. Although, as Padden and Humphries (1988) point out, there can be some difficulty in applying the terms, they do provide a way of focussing in on the linguistic and cultural grouping of the Deaf community as distinct from the population of people who happen to have a hearing loss.

This way of viewing Deaf people and their lives is in sharp contrast to the pathological model traditionally accepted by hearing professionals. The recent account by the neurologist and author Oliver Sacks of his own discovery of the existence of the Deaf community in the U.S.A. provides a telling insight into the (sometimes inadvertent) ignorance which can lie behind such an approach: "Prior to reading Lane's[†] book I had seen the few deaf patients under my care in purely medical terms—as 'diseased ears' or 'biologically impaired'. After reading it, I started to see them in a different light, especially when I would catch sight of three or four

* See Brien (1981), Ladd (1981), Lawson (1981), Brennan (1987)), Miles (1988) and Taylor and Bishop (1991).

[†] Lane, H. (1984): *When the Mind Hears: A History of the Deaf*. Random House, New York (Penguin Books, 1988). Lane's book is a history of the Deaf community in the United States. The author takes on the role of Laurent Clerc, a French Deaf person who was a leading figure in the development of the American signing community. Lane takes an uncompromising approach to the oppression of sign language and his account has provoked considerable discussion in the U.S.A. and elsewhere.

of them signing, full of an intensity, an animation, I had failed to see before. Only then did I start thinking of them not as deaf but as Deaf, as members of a different linguistic community." (Sacks, 1989, p. 3)

As we shall see, other groups have more actively propounded the pathological approach, seeing Deaf people as handicapped, psychologically impaired and linguistically inadequate.* By seeing Deaf people only within the context of impairment, hearing people have all too often failed to recognise the reality of the British Deaf community.

The role of BSL

What then are the common elements of Deaf life and culture? One seemingly essential element is the use of BSL as the preferred language for social interaction. Lilian Lawson has suggested that "a native knowledge of sign language" appears to be the "principal identifying characteristic" of members of the community.†

In fact, the question of what exactly constitutes 'native knowledge' is somewhat problematic since only a very small proportion of Deaf people have access to BSL from birth. Most deaf children are not born into families where BSL is the first language of parents and siblings. This is because approximately ninety per cent of deaf children are born to hearing parents, approximately five per cent have one hearing and one deaf parent and only around five per cent are born into a family where both parents are deaf.¶

Most children of Deaf parents will acquire BSL naturally within the context of the family. This applies to both deaf and hearing children. However, the extent to which the hearing children develop and maintain competence in BSL varies considerably according to individual circumstances, experiences and attitudes. Once the hearing child begins to develop English, this may influence the manner and extent of BSL usage. However, it would be unusual for hearing children of Deaf parents not to make some use of BSL.

Those deaf children born into hearing families will not usually acquire BSL, or indeed English, at the normal age of acquisition. Hearing parents have usually had little or no contact with the Deaf community before the birth of their deaf child. Professionals, such as medical consultants, teachers of deaf children, psychologists and audiologists, have typically counselled parents to aim primarily at the development of spoken language skills in their children. Guidance programmes rarely make use of Deaf personnel and many parents of deaf children have no contact at all with the Deaf community or its language. Recently the more widespread recognition of the existence of the Deaf community and an increasing understanding of the nature of BSL have brought about some changes in both professional and family attitudes. A number of professionals now attempt to facilitate early access to sign language and some parents now actively seek to learn BSL and to provide an environment in which their children can develop signing competence. Nevertheless, only a very small proportion of deaf children of hearing parents are likely to be exposed to BSL within the first few years of their lives.

One potential route to sign language development for such children might appear to be within the education system. However, while BSL is now used within several higher and further education institutions, its use at primary and secondary school level is still rare.‡ There are very few Deaf teachers of the deaf and the number of education authorities and schools actively pursuing a language policy which includes BSL remains very low. The reduction in the number of residential schools for deaf children, where children from different backgrounds are able to mix and form signing communities of their own, has also limited the opportunities for deaf children to develop and exploit BSL.

The route to BSL usage thus varies considerably from child to child. A small number of deaf children may acquire BSL through exposure to the language at home and in contact with the Deaf community; others may develop BSL during the early school years through contact with signing peers, while others may not learn BSL until they are in their teens or once they have left school. Such varied paths to competence in BSL may lead to specific variations in language use and possibly even differences in assimilation into the Deaf community.§

The preference for BSL does not necessarily exclude the

---

* See Brennan (1976), Woodward (1982), Ladd (1981), Brien (1981), Brennan (1987) and Kyle (1987) for critical discussions of the pathological approach.
† Lawson (1981, p. 167).
¶ Precise statistics concerning the deaf population as a whole are difficult to obtain. However, the estimates provided here seem to be widely accepted.
‡ The explicitly bilingual policies adopted by, for example, the Hearing Impaired Service in Leeds (Pickersgill, 1990) and the Royal School for the Deaf in Derby remain exceptional.
§ Research on American Sign Language (ASL) usage by Elissa Newport and colleagues suggests that late learners, i.e. those learning ASL after the age of puberty, may be less likely to manipulate the complex productive morphology of the language: "The highly analysed morphology...is largely a property of the sign competence of only second generation deaf, those who learn ASL as a native language in infancy." (Newport, 1982, p. 481). See also Woodward (1973).

use of English, even within the Deaf community itself, but BSL inevitably takes on a primary role within Deaf culture. This is not surprising when we realise that BSL is undoubtedly the language which deaf children can acquire most easily. If deaf children are exposed to BSL early enough, then they will acquire this language in the normal way, just as French children develop the French language or Vietnamese children develop Vietnamese.*

Educational experience

The Rejection of BSL

Within the Deaf community, there is a common educational experience which seems to permeate every aspect of Deaf culture. The overall experience is essentially negative although, ironically, it has had certain positive effects. The very fact that BSL has not been used in schools means that Deaf people live with the reality that within their major educational experiences they have been denied the use of their preferred language. Almost any Deaf person has a fund of stories and descriptions of both the humorous and tragic aspects of this denial. Many jokes and anecdotes relate to what are seen as the bizarre antics of hearing people trying to teach Deaf people to speak. It is, above all, this educational experience which seems to provide the sense that many Deaf people have that hearing people belong to a different and alien culture.

This shared sense of oppression of language, and hence of human potential, is at the very heart of British Deaf culture. Yet it could be argued that this very experience of common oppression actually serves to provide Deaf people with an even stronger sense of common identity. Of course, this is something which is not unusual within minority language communities. However, what adds a special poignancy to the Deaf situation is the inherent difficulty of acquiring English. It is not simply that Deaf people prefer BSL to English, as many Scots Gaelic, Welsh or Irish speakers may prefer their own languages to English: it is that Deaf people are not in a position to acquire English in the usual way. Hence the singular power of Deaf people's adherence to their language.

Historically, there have been several phases within the educational experiences of Deaf people. Leaving aside iso-

lated examples, the beginnings of deaf education can be traced to the schools founded by Thomas Braidwood in Scotland and England in the second half of the eighteenth century. The Braidwood family dominated deaf education for over half a century. While they were extremely secretive about their methods, the impression given at the time was that they adopted a wholly 'oral' approach, that is to say they focussed on the development of speech in their pupils and taught through the medium of spoken English. However, evidence suggests that the Braidwood method actually included natural gesture, signing and finger spelling (see below, pp. 92–94) as well as spoken and written English.

The nineteenth century saw the establishment of over thirty schools for the deaf[†] and it seems likely that sign language was used in many schools. Indeed Kyle (1987) quotes evidence to suggest that there were no purely oral deaf establishments in the U.K. by the mid 1800s. The attitude to sign language must have been very positive for, as Kyle and Woll point out, "...all through the 19th century there was consistent and repeated expression of the value of signs to the mental life of deaf people." (Kyle and Woll, 1985, p. 56) During this period there were many Deaf teachers of deaf children. However, with the notorious Congress of Milan in 1880, when educators rejected the use of signing and demanded the implementation of oral methods within deaf education, the situation for deaf children changed dramatically. The focus was on the development of speech, often to the detriment of language and almost always to the detriment of genuine education. This emphasis was reinforced by the Royal Commission report of 1889 which recommended that children should be "taught to speak and lip-read on the pure oral system". School records from this period show that Deaf teachers were removed from their posts and deliberately replaced by hearing teachers who could not sign. Although some schools did retain sign language usage well into the new century and although finger spelling was actively encouraged in some areas, particularly in Scotland, the pattern was set for the major part of the next century: sign language was not an acceptable part of the education system.

This predominantly oral approach eventually led to the establishment of training courses for hearing teachers of deaf children. The training of such teachers in the middle

---

* For discussion of sign language acquisition see Bellugi and Klima (1972), Deuchar (1984, ch. 7) Kyle and Woll (1985, ch. 4) Wilbur (1987, ch. 8) articles in Woll (1989), Volterra and Erting (1990), Edmondson and Karlsson (1990) and Prillwitz and Vollhaber (1990).

† For accounts of the history of deaf education see Savage, Evans and Savage (1981), Kyle and Woll (1985, ch. 3), Kyle (1987), McLaughlin (1987) and Jackson (1990). For accounts relating to Europe and America see Lane (1988) and Sacks (1989).

years of this century was dominated by the oralist philosophy, particularly as expounded by Sir Alexander and Lady Ewing * within the Department of Audiology and Education of the Deaf at Manchester University. As Manchester was for a time the only training institution within the U.K., it took a lead in training numerous overseas students, particularly from Commonwealth countries. Hence the pervasive influence of the oralist philosophy in many Commonwealth countries as well as in the U.K. itself. Even now, 110 years after the Congress of Milan, there are no training courses specifically aimed at qualifying Deaf teachers, fluent in BSL, to teach deaf children using the language which they can access most easily and directly, namely BSL.

Residential schools

The other major factor within deaf education has been the existence of residential schools for deaf children. During the first half of the twentieth century, children would be sent to residential school from a very early age, often below the age of five. However, in the later part of the century residence was usually confined to the secondary years. Until the relatively recent increase in 'units for hearing impaired children' (which became more common in the 1960s and 70s) and the more recent advent of integration approaches (influenced by government policy and the Warnock Report of 1978) most Deaf people had some experience of residential schools.

The fascinating irony is that while many Deaf people feel they have suffered oppression because of the official school policies which denied them the right to use BSL, and hence often also the possibility of genuine access to the curriculum, they also see residential schools as having provided them with a genuine Deaf community. Whatever the policies within the classroom, and whatever the rules about signing ouside it, deaf children always seem to have managed to create opportunities to communicate using sign language. The sheer delight of being able to communicate with ease with their peers, and sometimes with Deaf personnel who often formed part of the ancillary staff, must have provided a telling contrast with the harsh realities of the classroom. The experience of residential school remains a significant part of the overall Deaf experience. Such schools have probably played a major role in ensuring the continuity of sign language and the passing on of BSL from

one generation to another. In particular, the schools have facilitated the passing on of BSL to children whose parents are hearing rather than deaf.

Current practice

The present school experience of deaf children varies considerably. Residential schools still exist, although the number of boarders is greatly reduced overall. Most deaf children will attend day school: in practice, this may mean the local primary school, a hearing-impaired unit or a special school for deaf children. Policies may differ considerably from setting to setting. Some educators use a purely oral approach with no access at all to sign language; some see signing as permissible outside the classroom or for older children; some exploit a form of signing which makes use of individual signs from BSL but attempts to structure them in a way that fits with the grammatical structure of English rather than BSL (various versions exist: Signed English; British Signed English; Sign Supported English—see further pp. 92–94). A small number of educators make as much use of BSL as is possible within the context of limited resources, the most scarce resource being qualified Deaf teachers.

Inevitably the changing patterns of deaf education will have implications for the structure and culture of the Deaf community. Already, there are more and more young Deaf people who do not have the experience of Deaf residential schools. It is interesting to note that there is a very strong demand within the Deaf community for the retention of residential schools and for an increase in their number. Whatever other arguments may exist against such a policy, the prevailing Deaf view is that a residential school provides a community where the child can interact with peers in a manner uninhibited by linguistic problems.

Deaf clubs

If residential schools in the past provided an initiation into Deaf culture, particularly for those deaf children who did not come from Deaf families, Deaf clubs and centres have provided a focus for the cultural life of local Deaf communities. Many of these centres originated in the nineteenth century as benevolent centres or societies run by 'missioners for the deaf'.[†] These were mainly hearing people who were concerned with both the spiritual and the temporal welfare of deaf people. However, Jackson (1990)

---

* See Ewing and Ewing (1964).

† For an account of the work of the missioners see Firth (1989), and for a more detailed account of the growth of Deaf centres, societies and clubs see Lysons (1979) and Jackson (1990).

demonstrates that Deaf people themselves also played an active role in the inauguration and development of these centres. The establishment of the schools for deaf children had given Deaf people a taste of community life: the clubs and centres were a means of allowing the community to flourish and develop. Many of these centres later evolved to become the focus of social service provision for deaf people as well as the home of Deaf clubs. The social service element is normally the responsibility of the local authority which may provide these services quite separately or through existing deaf societies. Thus 'deaf centres' may often be the location of both the social service provision and the local Deaf club. The former will typically be run by hearing professionals while the latter is increasingly, although not always, run by the local Deaf community itself. The last twenty years or so has seen a major increase in the participation of Deaf people in the running of these clubs. This increase in control of their own organisations has been part of a wider growth in community consciousness and confidence, encouraged to a considerable extent by the growing awareness that BSL is a legitimate and fully functional language. Deaf people have begun the process of empowerment which will, no doubt, lead in time to a much greater control not just of the social aspects of their community but of other fundamental areas such as education and employment training.

Many of the activities which are initiated in Deaf clubs play an important part in the lives of Deaf people. These activities include a range of social, sporting and religious functions. Many Deaf centres still retain a link with the Christian ministries established by the missioners for the deaf. Such links have resulted in the tradition of Deaf choirs: groups of Deaf people who sign in unison to existing English hymns. While some Deaf people see these as relying too much on English and ignoring the full poetic potential of BSL, others enjoy the opportunity to be involved in a religious performance. It is likely that with the increasing acceptance of BSL, such performances will evolve and adapt, just as indeed newer forms of worship are evolving in which BSL usage has a central role.

The signing of songs and hymns is an activity often encouraged and enjoyed by hearing people who are either members of the Deaf community or closely associated with it. While such activities can be seen as hearing or English-based, they are also clearly a symptom of the coming together of two cultures. Young people often enjoy the possibilities of taking part in rock and pop culture through signing and there are adventurous groups who seek to combine the two mediums in new and exciting ways.* Another major type of activity supported by the Deaf clubs is that of sport. Most clubs have sporting histories which go back into the nineteenth century. These activities have played an important part in developing a sense of both a local and a national Deaf community. At the local level, local teams inevitably engender a sense of pride and a sense of local identity. At a national level, they have ensured that Deaf people, travelling as members or supporters of their local teams, have met and mixed with Deaf people from many different geographical areas. Again this has given Deaf people a recognition that the Deaf community is wider than the confines of their own local grouping.†

The British Deaf Association

While there are several organisations concerned with deaf people in the U.K.,¶ the British Deaf Association (BDA) is undoubtedly the major Deaf organisation. The BDA was founded in 1890 ‡ at the beginning of a decade which Peter Jackson describes as "the most remarkable in British Deaf history—no other decade, with the possible exception of the 1980s, saw the social status of deaf people held so high in public esteem." (Jackson, 1990, p. 121) There is some irony in the fact that this decade saw the decline in Deaf involvement in schools for deaf children, while at the same time the Deaf community itself went from strength to strength.

From the very beginning, the BDA was opposed to oralist philosophies and committed to furthering the use of BSL (even though this title was not used at that time).§ However, the fight against the oral approach was waged

---

*See for example Thompson and Janes (1991).
† See Jackson (1990) for the history and importance of sporting activities.
¶ Major examples include the Royal National Institute for Deaf People (RNID), the National Deaf Children's Society (NDCS) and the British Association of the Hard of Hearing (BAHOH).
‡ According to Grant (1990) and Jackson (1990), the BDA was founded by a Deaf Irishman, Francis McGinn, with the support of two other leading Deaf men of the period, George Healey from Liverpool and William Agnew from Glasgow. It was originally called the British Deaf and Dumb Association: the word "dumb" was dropped from its title in 1970.
§ The title British Sign Language, BSL, was first used by linguists on the basis of the analogy with other sign languages, such as American Sign Language, Swedish Sign Language, etc. (see Brennan, 1975 and 1976). In the early years of its use, the term BSL did cause some consternation within the Deaf community, being mistakenly thought of as a new artificial sign system or regarded as an imposition from the hearing world. However, in recent years it has gained wide acceptance and is the focus for campaigns and demands by the Deaf community.

somewhat spasmodically and it has only been in the last fifteen years or so that the BDA has played a major role in developing support for BSL. Whether this was because of domination at the top by hearing people as Ladd (1988) suggests, lack of knowledge about the language, or the effects of on-going oppression remains unclear. What is undoubtedly true is that initially through the efforts of Allan B. Hayhurst, and subsequently through the official policies and actions of the organisation, the BDA has played an increasingly important role in the furthering of BSL recognition. Its co-operation with other European Deaf organisations in 1989 led to the official recognition by the European Parliament of the sign languages of its member states.

The BDA also has an important role in providing a forum for debate for Deaf people and also an opportunity to institutionalise and formalise the structure of the Deaf community. As the major representative organisation, it must respond to pressures from its own members as well as presenting their views on the larger platform of public and political debate. The democratic processes involved mean that Deaf people at a local level may participate in the structures of the organisation. Thus, at its best, the BDA is not simply an organisation 'out there' but a focus of action in the local community.

Other aspects of cultural life

One very important aspect of Deaf culture is comparable to what is known in other minority groups as a strong 'oral' tradition. This term usually refers to the handing down of stories, myths, poems and so on by word of mouth. Such traditions are often important in language communities where there is no written form of the community language(s). Such traditions are of course the basis for many of the early classics of English literature.

Within the Deaf community, there is a strong tradition of story-telling and joke-telling. In both cases, there is a delight in exploiting the resources of the language and manipulating these to dramatic effect. Often hearing 'incomers' who feel they can communicate with Deaf people reasonably well are both staggered and fascinated by the complexities of such performances. Here indeed the signers exploit to the full the visual imagery which is such an integral part of BSL. As in other communities, some individuals seem to have a particular talent for story-telling

and these people are in high demand at social functions.

The community is now also seeing some formalising of this signing tradition through the development of BSL poetry. The foremost BSL poet, Dorothy Miles, creates poetry not only in BSL but also in English and ASL.* Some of her poems are specifically created so that they work 'both ways', i.e. in sign language and English. Such poetry demonstrates that a gifted artist can modify, stretch and manipulate the language to remarkable effect.

It is fascinating to note that alongside this very strong BSL-based aspect of Deaf culture, there are other traditions which are rather more English-based. Thus while drama and drama competitions are an important part of the cultural activities of many Deaf clubs, the actual performances have frequently used a form of signing strongly influenced by English. Many productions have been of plays written by hearing people and in the past there was relatively little use of BSL or recognition of genuinely Deaf themes. In recent years this has begun to change as Deaf people have gained confidence in the notion that BSL is a language fit for anything—including drama and poetry. Recent productions have not only used BSL but have tackled themes which go to the very heart of the Deaf experience.† To the outsider, it may seem odd that there should have been any reticence at all about the use of BSL. However, it cannot be stressed strongly enough that English is presented to the Deaf person as the ultimate goal. Very often, even those who take a relatively liberal approach to 'signing' see it as a means to an end and the end is fluency in English.

BSL has survived primarily within the context of social interaction within families and Deaf centres. That it has survived at all is remarkable enough: the current flourishing of BSL in a range of art forms including drama, poetry, comedy and satire is itself a mark of the new confidence and pride which Deaf people are finding in their own language and culture.

Membership of the Deaf community

Research into the nature of the British Deaf community and its culture remains at a very early stage. Nevertheless, several aspects of community structure are already the subject of considerable debate. One primary question concerns the issue of membership of the community. Who are the members of the Deaf community? Are there different levels of membership? Can we distinguish 'core' members? Are

---

* Miles, D. (1976): *Poetry in Sign Language.* Joyce Publications, California.

† See for example the play "The Last Flickering Light of Hope" by Ian Townsley, which won the BDA's 1989 National Drama Competition.

hearing people excluded by definition? Such matters remain controversial. Moreover, it is only relatively recently that Deaf people themselves have begun to examine such questions and develop their own analyses and accounts 'from the inside'.

One particular descriptive model of community membership, developed by Baker and Cokely (1980) with respect to the American Deaf community, has provided the starting point for several accounts of the British situation.* Baker and Cokely recognise four different paths to community membership: audiological, political, linguistic and social. What may seem to be the most obvious pathway, the audiological, is not by itself a sufficient criterion for membership. People with a hearing loss may opt in to the community, but if they do so they will normally make use of its language and enter into its social life. The political pathway to membership involves active involvement in the political structures of the community, such as the representational structures within the BDA. Fluency in BSL and participation in the social life of the community may also provide potential entry points.

The Baker and Cokely model also assumes that attitude plays an important part. A person may have a hearing loss or even high level BSL skills, yet attitudinally may separate themself from the Deaf community. Some individuals who have felt uncomfortable with being Deaf, perhaps during their teens, come to what they then often see as their 'natural' home at a later period. Paddy Ladd provides a marvellous insight into the two attitudes of separating and belonging in his memoir (Ladd, 1981). His experience of integration required that, in effect, he denied his deafness: "You're not deaf: you're just a normal person who can't hear. But if I am normal, then why can't I act normally with others, or do their things...The real me is imprisoned in ice. And no tears on earth can melt it." (Ladd, 1981, p. 413)

Eventually through contact with the Deaf community all the negative associations of being deaf are replaced with a new realisation: "But I am deaf. So why worry? *That's it...I am Deaf*! What does it mean now. It means something good at last...I had always been taught that lipreading and hearing aids were adequate, yet only now could I realise that they were, at best, crutches. They were not legs. It became clear that my legs were in fact sign language. It seemed as if I had spent all of my time on crutches, when I could have had legs..." (Ladd, 1981, pp. 415–416)

As Kyle and Woll demonstrate in their adaptation of the Baker and Cokely model, being a member of the Deaf community involves an opting in on the part of the individual and it is precisely this opting in process which Ladd describes. Membership also requires an acceptance on the part of the other members of the community. Kyle and Woll argue that "...it is probably the commitment and sharing which represents the membership criterion, not the deafness, nor even language, per se." (Kyle and Woll, 1985, p. 22)

The preference for the use of BSL within the Deaf community means that on the whole people who become deafened in later life tend not to become members of the Deaf community as such. Not surprisingly, the preferred language of such people is English. However, there is the potential for some change in this situation as deafened people become more aware of the existence of BSL and as both groups develop common aims, such as the extension of English subtitles on television and greater access to information.

There are perhaps two key issues concerning membership of the Deaf community. The first relates to whether it is possible to distinguish a core group who occupy a central role in the structure and maintenance of the community, particularly in respect of the transmission of language and culture from one generation to another. The second concerns the somewhat ambiguous status of hearing people.

A core group?

As indicated earlier, only a very small proportion of deaf children are born into Deaf families. Such children are able to acquire their first language, BSL, and absorb the culture of the Deaf community simply through their family environment. Linguistic and cultural transmission operates for these children as it does for children in other language communities. In contrast, the deaf child of hearing parents rarely has direct access to BSL and to the community of BSL users, at least in the early years. Development of BSL competence and involvement in Deaf culture will usually begin to occur during the school years, sometimes much later. The transmission of language and culture is thus most probably mediated by peers, i.e. Deaf children of Deaf parents, outside the home context. It remains a matter of debate whether the smaller group should be seen as having a central role in the political and social life of the Deaf community. Some argue that there may be dangers in defining an elite within the community and imputing linguistic superiority to this small proportion of Deaf people. Others suggest that

---

* See for example Brien (1981) and Kyle and Woll (1985).

to ignore the significant differences between the two groups is to deny important aspects of Deaf life and tradition.

Hearing people

The role of hearing people is equally controversial. While for the most part, hearing people are clearly outside the community, there are two groups who could claim eligibility. The first is made up of hearing children of Deaf parents. Indeed it may be more accurate to speak of hearing children from Deaf families, as often the Deaf connection goes beyond parents to brothers and sisters and the extended family of aunts, uncles, grandparents, etcetera. As suggested earlier, such children may well acquire competence in BSL long before their deaf peers in hearing families. They are often involved in Deaf activities from an early age. This direct immersion in the life of the Deaf community is beautifully captured in this anecdote told by Padden and Humphries: "...we turn now to the story of Joe, the youngest child of a Deaf family on a farm in the heart of Indiana. Joe told us, 'I never knew I was hearing until I was six. I never suspected that I was different from my parents and siblings'." As Padden and Humphries observe, "This is not a case of pretended deafness; Joe did not fail to hear, but simply understood sound in a way he could reconcile with the experiences of his family...The most striking observation hearing children of Deaf parents make about their early years is that it never occurs to them until they are older that there is anything unusual about their abilities. For young children immersed in the world of their families, there is not yet space for contradictions." (Padden and Humphries, 1988, pp. 22–23) Given such early total involvement, it may seem surprising that there should be any doubt at all about membership.

Yet such doubts have been expressed. Lawson (1981) in her model of the Deaf community appears to exclude hearing children completely. Baker and Cokely suggest that individuals with a hearing loss "are accepted by and identify with the Community at a much deeper level" than hearing people, even hearing people with comparable linguistic skills. Similarly, Padden and Humphries accept that hearing children of Deaf parents constitute a special problem. They comment that stories of such children "involve conflicting sentiments that reveal the complexity of the rules for categorization and identity." (Padden and Humphries, 1988, p. 49) However, Ladd (1988b) not only suggests that

hearing people can be members of the British Deaf community, but predicts an increase in involvement as more and more hearing family members and associates of Deaf people learn BSL.

While there seems to be a strong case for community membership of hearing people born into Deaf families, the potential for full acceptance in respect of hearing people without such a background appears more limited at the present time.* In the past, the most likely candidates, hearing parents of deaf children, have rarely either tried to enter into the life of the community or indeed been accepted into it. Professionals involved with Deaf people have often sought to participate fully in the community and culture, but there can be difficulties. Often Deaf people are wary of individuals changing roles, one moment being the professional earning a living through the provision of services to the Deaf community, the next being a friend and fellow member of the community. At the same time, there can be an expectation on the part of Deaf people that such hearing professionals should both respect and be familiar with the culture of the Deaf community.

Perhaps the major factor which separates out hearing people from deaf, or even hearing, children of Deaf parents, is the different life experience of deaf members of the community. Padden and Humphries describe in fascinating detail the development of the world view of the deaf child. The child, like any other child, draws upon the information available to 'make sense' of the world. The kind of cognitive processes involved are comparable to those of other children, but the hypotheses formed will be very different. One further anecdote from the Padden and Humphries account captures the nature of the child's reasoning: "Imagine Jim sitting in a room near a door. Suddenly his mother appears, walking purposefully to the door. She opens a door, and there is a visitor waiting on the doorstep. But if the child opens the door at another time, odds are that there will be no visitor there. How does the child who does not hear the doorbell, understand what the stimulus is for the odd behaviour of opening a door and finding someone standing there? We can only guess. We know only that Jim assumed other people had powers not yet discernible to him, such as better lipreading skills." (Padden and Humphries, 1988, p. 21)

The authors demonstrate all too clearly that such an anecdote reveals not a 'naive' view of the world, but "the

---

* It has been suggested, for example in Bienvenu (1987), that Deaf-hearing interaction occurs within the context of a 'third' culture, which draws features from both the Deaf and hearing cultures, and develops new patterns of interaction.

unfolding of the human symbolic capacity". It is perhaps only now, as Deaf people begin to gain the confidence to express their own cultural experience, both within and outside the Deaf community, that a genuine understanding of difference can develop. Similarly, because hearing children of Deaf parents have not faced the linguistic barriers faced by their deaf peers, they can perhaps never fully participate in the shared sense of oppression that seems, at least for the present, to be an integral part of the total Deaf experience.

The Deaf community from the inside

If one looks at historical records, it is indeed possible to find accounts of the Deaf experience from the inside, from within the community itself. However, these "voices from a culture", to borrow the title of the Padden and Humphries account, have often been isolated or gone unnoticed. Now, at last, Deaf people are providing insights through their own sharing of ideas and experiences and through their own analyses of the lives of Deaf people.

One important aspect of this development lies in the contribution to sociological, linguistic and psychological research which is being made by Deaf people, sometimes in collaboration with hearing people. The major BSL projects within the U.K. have employed Deaf people and several important sociological studies have involved or been undertaken by Deaf researchers.* Often such people have not only played an essential role in the collection of data, but have brought unique insights to the analysis of this data.

As well as these more academic contributions, we can learn simply from the direct anecdotes and comments told by Deaf people. Some of these accounts have been produced in written form but undoubtedly the most direct are those expressed in BSL itself.† Such accounts can be found in signed form in the series of programmes produced by Tyne Tees Television called "Signs of our Times" (1991-2). The series encouraged Deaf people to sign for themselves on some of the central areas of their lives. It thus provided a unique insight into the heart of the Deaf community.

It is exactly this kind of insight which is required if we are to succeed in understanding the nature of the Deaf community.

Conclusion

There are numerous other aspects of Deaf life and culture which it is impossible to describe in detail here. What we can stress is that Deaf people are able to engage in rich and rewarding social interaction through the use of BSL. The language has survived through the vitality of the Deaf community rather than through acceptance and encouragement by the wider hearing community. Now, towards the end of the twentieth century, we are beginning to see real changes in attitudes and policies: whether these changes will be sufficient to see the use of BSL in all levels of education remains to be seen. Just as most research demonstrates that we have many under-functioning Deaf people, i.e. Deaf people who are not given the employment and life opportunities which they are clearly capable of undertaking, so it could be argued that BSL is an under-functioning language. It clearly has the internal resources to meet a full range of communicative functions: it is linguistic policy rather than linguistic potential which prevents this.

The language

The natural and preferred language of Deaf people in Britain is British Sign Language (BSL). It is the most natural language in that it can be acquired directly by deaf children, if they are given access to the language through contact with signing peers or adults. It is the preferred language of Deaf people precisely because it can be used with ease and efficiency within the Deaf community. BSL is a visual-gestural system: it is perceived visually and produced by means of bodily gesture. It would seem that both aspects of this description have influenced the ways in which the language has evolved over time.

Human gesture

We are all familiar with the communicative use of human gesture. However, hearing people are usually more familiar with gesture produced as an accompaniment to spoken language than with gesture used as the primary medium of language.

Rhythmic gesture

If we watch almost any spoken conversation we can note the occurrence of particular types of movement of the hands

---

*Kyle and Allsop (1982), Jackson (1986), Kyle and Pullen (1988) and Jones and Pullen (1990).
† An important collection of the personal experiences of d/Deaf people which makes use of English translations from BSL, as well as direct written contributions, can be found in Taylor and Bishop (1991). See also Lee (1992).

Use of gestures by Neil Kinnock.
(photographs by Dennis Thorpe; the Guardian, 13 May 1989)

and arms, together with facial expressions and actions of the head, shoulders and body. All of these actions may be said to be 'meaningful' in context. However this does not imply that such gestures are 'lexical': they cannot be regarded as equivalent to words. More usually, the gestures serve to emphasise the content of what is being said. Desmond Morris has labelled one such group of actions *baton* gestures: like the baton in a conductor's hand, these gestures beat time, but here it is to "the rhythm of spoken thoughts", rather than to the rhythm of music (Morris, 1978, p. 56).

However, the many different types of baton gestures used suggests that the form of the gesture itself may be significant. The speaker may use a range of different handshapes in different positions. The hand may be closed tightly into a fist, held fully open and flat, bent so that thumbtip and fingertips touch or bent into a fist with one finger extended. These and a host of other possible handshapes appear to reflect a particular mood or attitude. They may even be said to give metaphorical expression to the type of idea expressed. Thus what Morris calls the *precision grip*—in which the thumbtip and index fingertip touch so as to form a closed circle—appears to reflect "an urge on the part of the speaker to express himself delicately and with great exactness." (Morris, 1978, p. 58) The precision of the handshape is a physical manifestation of the precision intended by the speaker. Other factors may also be important. Even hand orientation can be significant: the upward palms may suggest pleading, while the palms facing outwards (away from the producer) may suggest pushing away or rejecting.

Symbolic gesture

A recent study of French natural gesture* reveals that many of the gestures accompanying speech are 'motivated' in that they are a physical representation of some abstract thought or intention. The author is able to perceive symbolic links between types of movements and notions such as honesty, confusion and stability. Many of the symbolic links suggested by Calbris are echoed in work on sign language undertaken by Brennan (1990). Thus Calbris suggests that "conflict is represented by two antagonistic entities, the two hands." A directly comparable symbolism is built into BSL where both physical opposition (two people standing opposite each other) and symbolic opposition are represented by signs which involve the two hands in opposition to each other, as in **face to face** (sign 434)[1†], **quarrel** (sign 915)[2] and **conflict** (sign 924)[3]. In contrast, the two hands coming together can suggest harmony or unity of intention as in BSL **same** (sign 424)[4]. The potential symbolic power which we can see in human gesture generally is exploited to a much greater degree in the sign languages of the world.

While the gestures which accompany speech clearly play a different communicative role from the gestures which make up human sign languages, both systems share common formational elements. Some gestures are made by the hands, others are produced by other body articulators, such as the head. We can note that some manual gestures, like some signs, require two active hands, while in others a single hand is sufficient. Many different handshapes may be used and these may involve quite precise configurations. The position and orientation of the hand(s) and the actual movement produced may all be significant. There is often also a matching of the behaviour of the hands, the manual articulators, with the behaviour of the head, face and body,

---

1. Ø G⊤⋏ G⌐⋏ᵩ ˣᵡˣ
   ₋ᵢ

3. Ø ï⋏⊥ ï⋏⊥ ˣ·

2. Ø I>⋏ I<⋏ ꙍˣ
   ₋ᵀₓ

4. Ø G⋈⊥ᵢ G⋈⊥ ˣˣ

---

* Calbris (1990).

† A sign number in brackets after a gloss (e.g. **face to face**), refers to the entry number of this sign in the *BSL* section of this Dictionary. The reference numbers (¹, ², ³, etc.) refer to the notation given in the footnotes on each page.

the non-manual articulators.

The actions which accompany speech thus provide a hint of the communicative potential available within the gestural medium. They demonstrate that, as with sound, contrastive and distinctive patterns may be produced. It is possible to discern sub-components or gestural building blocks, which can be combined to produce specific meaningful gestures. Nevertheless, it is clear that the gestures which accompany speech are highly personalised and idiosyncratic. One individual may develop a tendency to use the same few emphatic gestures again and again. There is no requirement that the gestures be identical with those used by any other person. In contrast, the actions used within a sign language require particular gestures to take on specific meanings for a whole community.

The 'V' sign, as produced by a smiling Dalai Lama and by the son of a Palestinian fighter.
(both photographs AP, 1982)

Semantic gestures

There are some gestures used by hearing people which appear to have a more definite content. Both the so-called 'thumbs up' gesture and the 'Victory-V' sign can be said to have definite, though somewhat generalised, meanings within the United Kingdom. The 'thumbs up' gesture is used to indicate a positive attitude and to express approval or support, while the 'Victory-V' sign is used as a gesture of celebration. Both gestures involve the use of quite specific handshapes and actions linked to particular meanings. The conventional nature of these links is shown by the fact that other communities may use comparable forms in quite different ways. Thus Morris (1978) notes that the 'upward thumb jerk' is an obscene gesture in Sardinia. Such negative connotations would be lost on someone familiar with the meaning attached to 'thumbs up' in Britain. It may be that the increase in media communications between different countries is leading to a universalisation of certain gestures. The 'Victory-V' sign, for example, has been used in a wide range of contexts to show defiance as well as victory. It was widely used in the countries of Eastern Europe during the period of momentous political change in 1989 and 1990. In many situations of conflict, it seems to function as much as a gesture of solidarity and hope as of actual victory. In the U.K. a gesture very similar in form, using the V hand formation but with the palm towards the signer and performed with an upward action, is recognised as being obscene and pejorative. The existence of the more positive 'Victory-V' sign, together with the use of alternative obscene gestures in other countries, probably militates against the more widespread usage of the obscene V sign.

Even a cursory glance at the nature and use of human gesture within non-Deaf communities demonstrates the communicative potential of the gestural medium. It is clearly possible to develop contrastive gestures which can carry meaning. Some of these gestures may be compared to the words of human language, in that they have internal structure and conventional links with meanings. However, for the most part such gestures are highly restricted in number, function and operation. There are probably fewer than 10 such gestures regularly used within the United Kingdom. They typically have somewhat generalised meanings and they do not normally combine together to form structures comparable to sentences.

Mime

One other form of gestural activity familiar among non-signing communities is mime. This has been used as an art form in many countries for hundreds, possibly thousands of years. In Britain it also forms part of popular culture as in the traditional game of 'charades' and the television programme 'Give us a Clue'. Mime involves a copying or mimicry of real-life activities without the presence of the real-life objects and persons normally involved. The mime artist may act out the process of riding a bike, going to bed or driving a bus without any props other than her or his own gestures and body movements. Such miming does share some of the features which are also present in human sign languages. Often the mime artist uses handshapes and actions appropriate to the handling of the object concerned: a closed fist to show the grasping of a narrow or cylindrical object, such as a ski pole or the handle of a kettle; a contact between the bent index finger and thumb to show the handling of a fine or delicate object, such as a necklace or a piece of string; fully open and spread hands to indicate the grasping of a large flat-sided object, such as a cardboard box. This use of appropriate handling handshapes is also exploited in a highly sophisticated form in British Sign Language.*

The mime artist also makes use of space and spatial patterns. S/he will place an imagined object at a particular point in space and use various techniques such as eye-gaze, pointing, and directed movement to refer back to this located object. The artist may, for example, place an imagined vase on a table, pour water into the vase and place flowers in it, all by using appropriate handling handshapes at the relevant location in space. BSL takes this locational potential and builds it into a system, indeed a set of systems, which operate as part of the grammar of the language.

However, it would be false to imagine that BSL is simply a sophisticated form of miming. It is obvious that mimed communication of the type seen both in games and in the theatre is too demanding of time and space to operate as an efficient communication system in daily life. The mime artist rarely stands or sits still, but walks around the stage re-creating the spatial scenarios s/he wishes to portray. Similarly the process of re-enacting a particular activity may involve a considerable amount of time. If the artist wishes to convey the meaning expressed by the sentence "I over-indulged last night by eating an enormous meal" an elaborate replay of the activity involved would be required. Such an elaboration may be amusing or fascinating to watch, but it would hardly be efficient within the context of an ordinary conversation. In contrast, sign languages can exploit the potential of space and gesture while honing the medium into a fast and efficient linguistic tool. The remnants of mimicry and spatial patterning are ever-present as a source of creativity in the language, but they are exploited within the confines of a highly structured and highly complex linguistic system.

Alternative sign languages

Besides the primary sign languages of Deaf people (that is those languages which have developed as the primary means of communication in Deaf communities) systems of signing which provide an alternative communication system to spoken languages have also been noted in a number of societies.

Several detailed studies are available of the signing used by the native people of North and South America and Australia. The work of Adam Kendon (1988) has revealed what he terms a "general disposition" on the part of Aboriginal communities to use sign. In some cases, such as amongst the Waramangu and the Warlpiri, there is a custom that women who have been bereaved of specific close relatives, such as a husband or child, will enter into a period during which sign replaces speech. According to Kendon, this period can last for as long as two years. However, Kendon's work also suggests that there may be other more subtle cultural reasons for choosing gestural rather than spoken communication. These reasons appear to be tied into the encoding of different types of social relationship through the choice of one medium rather than another (see Kendon, 1988).

There is also a long tradition within the contemplative orders of monasticism of a rule of silence. This rule has required almost total silence in some monastic communities and long periods of silence in others. There are accounts of the aspects of this gestural communication ranging from the Venerable Bede's eighth century account of a numeral system and the recently translated and republished "Monasteriales Indicia" from the eleventh century, through various manuscripts explaining aspects of the sign system for other monks, to the modern day account of Cistercian signing in America.†

It is quite clear when we look at the accounts of signs from these signing communities that they exploit the gestural medium in ways that are comparable to what happens within Deaf signing communities. Indeed, it could be argued that most of the different types of lexical item which are found in Deaf signing communities have a visual echo in these alternative sign systems. There are one- and two-handed signs; they exploit specific handshapes, positions on or near the body and use a range of different movements. Moreover, they exploit some of the same classifying functions that we shall see in the sections on BSL classifiers. Thus the handshapes may represent size and shape features of the referent as in the Plains Indian depiction of the ears and horn of buffalo using two Ġ hands (index finger and thumb extended): each hand is placed at either side of the head, with fingertips touching and the thumbs wiggle to represent the movement of the ears. "Monasteriales Indicia" shows the use of a handling handshape for the ringing of a bell to represent the meaning 'deacon'. Other signs appear to be arbitrary, while still others are complex compound forms which are a literal translation from the spoken language.

---

* See *Handling classifiers*, pp. 47.
† See Venerable Bede in Sebeok and Sebeok (1987), Banham (1992), Barakat (1975), Sebeok and Sebeok (1978, vols. 1 and 2), Sebeok and Sebeok (1987) and Stokoe (1988).

It is clear that these communities exploit certain aspects of the potential of the gestural medium. Yet, presumably because they are alternative, rather than primary, systems of communication, they have developed somewhat differently from Deaf sign languages. Certainly within monastic signing as described in the available literature, there is no hint of the complex grammatical patterning that we find, for example, in BSL.

Signed language

Gestural communication comes into its own in the Deaf sign languages of the world. While written accounts * of the enormous range of human languages have recognised the existence of thousands of spoken languages, they have largely ignored sign languages. Yet such languages appear to have evolved naturally, over time, wherever communities of Deaf people have emerged.

It is only since the advent of sign language research in the 1950s and the development of descriptive accounts of several different sign languages, that linguists themselves have become more aware of the phenomenon of human sign language. The publication in 1960 of William C. Stokoe's "Sign Language Structure: An Outline of the Visual Communication Systems of the American Deaf" represented the first major contribution to what is now the burgeoning field of sign language studies. Since that time an increasing amount of information has become available on other sign languages.

Signs

Sign languages make use of individual words, usually known as the signs of the language, which are organised into grammatical systems. These signs can be analysed into smaller formational gestural units, just as the spoken words of English can be broken down into regularly occurring units of sound. In BSL, as in English, the words themselves may be composed of more than one unit of meaning. Such compound and complex signs are an important part of the lexical resources of the language. The words of BSL are organised into larger structural units such as phrases, clauses and sentences. These larger units may perform a range of different functions such as the expression of questions, negatives, conditionals and so on.

Thus, although sign languages exploit a different linguistic medium from spoken languages, they appear to make use of comparable lexical and grammatical patterning. Nevertheless, there are several characteristics which, although not unique to sign languages, appear to have a special focus within the structure of the language.

Simultaneity

While sign languages exploit both sequential and simultaneous patterning, the nature and extent of simultaneity has been the focus of much debate amongst sign linguists. The earliest linguistic account of the internal structure of signs, developed by Stokoe in relation to American Sign Language (ASL), described signs as segmentable into specific aspects. According to Stokoe, the three aspects of handshape(s), position and motion were produced simultaneously by the signer. Stokoe's account is particularly important in alerting linguists to the fact that the words of ASL do indeed have internal structure. It is also clear that the nature of these internal components means that some degree of simultaneous production is necessary. Thus it would be impossible to produce a handshape, then a position and then a movement. Even though these elements might change in the course of the sign production, there is always and inevitably simultaneity. This view of the structure of signs has been echoed in descriptions of many sign languages, including those of BSL.[†]

In more recent years, several analysts have suggested that signs are also sequentially organised. The most influential account has been that of Liddell and Johnson (1985) who propose that most signs can be viewed as sequences of M (movement) and H(hold) elements. Other linguists have suggested that it is possible to analyse signs into syllables and nuclei. To a large extent, the formalism and theoretical debates surrounding this issue are outside the scope of this Dictionary. The broader question of whether sign words are somehow more simultaneous than spoken words still awaits further evidence. At the very least, it is clear that there is a very high degree of simultaneity within the sign word.

At the *morphological* [¶] level, commentators have noted the resistance of sign languages to processes of sequential segmentation such as *affixation*.[‡]

Instead, through the use of the dimensions of space and movement, additional meanings are superimposed or over-

---

* See, for example, Voegelin and Voegelin (1973) and Ruhlen (1976).
[†] See Brennan et al. (1984), Deuchar (1984) and Kyle and Woll (1985).
[¶] See pp. 120 for glossary of technical terms.

[‡] See, for example, Klima and Bellugi (1979), Supalla (1982) and Brennan (1990a).

laid upon the unmarked forms. A single sign can take several such overlaid modifications resulting in a highly elaborated complex form which simultaneously expresses several different aspects of meaning. Klima and Bellugi's account of such patterning in relation to ASL provides remarkable evidence of the potential for simultaneous patterning within sign language morphology. Recent work on BSL word-formation (Brennan, 1990a) also suggests that BSL may be able to exploit a process of simultaneous compounding inherently impossible within spoken languages. Nevertheless, linear, sequential patterning is not totally absent. Sequential compounds of the type found in many spoken languages, also occur in BSL, ASL and other sign languages.*

The *syntactic* level is also the focus of a complex and creative interaction between simultaneous and sequential patterning. Signers have two hands, each able to express separate units of meaning, and non-manual articulators, such as the eyes, mouth, face, head and shoulders, which are all also capable of conveying meaning. Sign languages exploit this potential in highly structured ways. Sentences cannot be viewed merely as linear sequences, even linear sequences with hierarchical patterning. Moreover, because the signer can also use space to locate referents, grammatical relations such as subject and object can be expressed without reliance on sign order alone. Once again, while simultaneity is clearly also a feature of spoken languages, especially through the operation of such systems as tone, intonation and stress, the linguistic medium of sign language does provide considerable scope for the operation of simultaneous patterning. The precise nature of this patterning within BSL will be explored more fully in the relevant sections below.†

Spatial patterning

A further major property of human sign languages is the direct exploitation of space for the representation of meaning. Gestures are not simply produced or articulated, they may also be 'located' in the space around the signer's body. In practice, this signing space is limited. Signing space is used in different ways, depending upon the particular linguistic level concerned. The space around the signer, as well as positions on the signer's body, may be used to distinguish formational elements below the level of the word: the *phonemic* use of space. Verbs may begin and end at different points in space to show different types of agreement, such as subject or object agreement: *morphological* use of space. Signing space may also be used for specific types of reference and indexation: the *syntactic* or *discourse* use of space.

Whilst this spatial resource is not directly available in spoken languages, current evidence suggests that similar types of linguistic constraints operate across language modalities. This means that on closer examination, the grammatical systems of sign languages are probably more, rather than less, like the other languages of the world. Details concerning the systematic use of space in BSL will be presented in the relevant sections below.

Links between form and meaning

There is often an expectation, both on the part of linguists and non-specialists, that the form which a sign takes will have some link with its meaning. Such an expectation is rarely present in relation to spoken languages. We do not ask why the sequence of sounds used in the English word "cat" is appropriate to its meaning. Rather, the expectation is that there will be no particular 'motivation' involved: the word-form is purely arbitrary. Of course, it may be possible to trace the form back to some other linguistic origin—Indo-European, Icelandic, Latin, French or whatever—but there is no expectation that even the earlier forms will demonstrate some perceivable link between form and meaning. However, in relation to sign languages there is a general expectation that the meaning 'cat' will be expressed by a gestural sign which has some formational link with real cats. Several sign languages encode the meaning 'cat' by the use of signs which can be said to represent the whiskers of a cat: BSL, ASL, Australian Sign Language (Auslan) and Irish Sign Language (ISL) all use such forms (see, for example, sign 889)[5]. However, it is worth noting that despite this link, the signs in the different sign languages have different formational properties. They are all made near the mouth, but use different handshapes (**5** , **F** , **G** and **G**) and involve different movements; in addition, some are one-handed while others are two-handed. Moreover, all of these sign

---

5. ⌴ F̄⃗>ʌ ₁ₓ F̄⃗ᴏ⊥ x̌

---

* See, for example, Klima and Bellugi (1979), Wallin (1983) and Brennan (1990a and b).

† For further discussions of simultaneity and sequentiality in sign lan-

guage, see Siple (1982), Boyes-Braem (1986), Brennan (1986) and Padden (1988).

languages have other ways of encoding the meaning 'cat', either through focusing on different physical properties of cats or by exploiting the ways in which humans interact with cats. Thus other signs may focus on the cat's tail or paws or on a human stroking a cat.

One of the continuing debates within sign language studies is whether *iconicity*, that is, the principled, perceivable link between linguistic form and meaning, is more pervasive in sign languages than in spoken languages. A full examination of this issue would require detailed elaboration of the nature of iconicity within a range of languages. As with simultaneity, it may be that iconicity has been under-estimated in spoken language and over-estimated in sign language. Nevertheless, within the account of BSL words presented in the next section, it will be possible to demonstrate a range of form-meaning links. It will be suggested that, on current evidence, BSL does exhibit a greater degree of iconicity than a language such as English. Such iconic links can be used as 'hooks' for learning on the part of the student and as potential for creativity on the part of the signer.

Unique sign languages

Another common expectation is that there is likely to be a single, world-wide sign language, rather than distinct and separate languages, within the different Deaf communities. There is, of course, no comparable expectation of a single, world-wide spoken language. Again, it can be difficult to fathom the reason for such an expectation. Its basis may relate back to the supposed iconic character of sign language. If sign-forms are linked to their meanings, then perhaps the same types of link will be used in more than one community. Thus it seems that some signs 'look like' or resemble what they mean. If this is so, then the nature of the resemblances may be common across languages. However, several factors militate against such commonality of patterning. Firstly, and obviously, not all signs relate to objects. It is difficult for a sign-form to resemble what it means if the meaning is abstract. Secondly, as we have already seen with 'cat', even where a relationship of resemblance occurs, different languages may choose to encode different aspects of resemblance. Finally, and most importantly, even where the same physical feature is encoded within the sign, the final form will be constrained by the linguistic structures which operate in that specific language. In particular, the form will be affected by the specific formational components, such as handshape, which happen to be used, just as the forms of English words are constrained by the particular sound contrasts which operate in the language. The expectation of universality tends to ignore the specific properties of different linguistic systems.

It seems clear then that unique sign languages evolve in different geographical locations. Given that these languages are not only typically distinct from one another but from the spoken languages of the particular area, it is important not to assume that the geographic linguistic boundaries will be identical with those occurring in respect of the associated speech communities. Thus the Republic of Ireland, the U.S.A. and the U.K. all share a common spoken language, English, but three quite separate and mutually unintelligible sign languages are used in these three countries. Sometimes, for historical reasons, there are closer links than might be expected between two different sign language communities. The fact that Thomas Gallaudet introduced the 'systematic sign system' developed by the Abbé de l'Epée into the United States in the eighteenth century means that today's American Sign Language has much closer links with French Sign Language (LSF) than with BSL (see Lane, 1984). Similarly, because of the close political relationship (through the British Commonwealth) between Australia, New Zealand and Britain, the sign languages of these countries share many common features. Inevitably, languages change and adapt as they are affected by internal and external influences. Even where signs betray some historical similarity, they tend to diverge over time. Because sign languages share a common modality, the visual-gestural modality, they may indeed share certain types of patterning. However, as with all living human languages, they are constantly subject to change and evolutionary processes.

Words of BSL

This section will examine the lexical resources of BSL. It will look firstly at what is here termed the *established lexicon*: those words of the language which are already clearly established and which can be listed in a dictionary. The second sub-section will deal with the resources of the *productive lexicon*: those units of meaning which can be combined productively to create words as required. A third sub-section on the *expanding lexicon* will examine how the lexical re-

6. **sign**　　　　　7. **that's right**　　　　8. **bang one's head against a brick wall**

sources of the language develop and change over time. The final sub-section will explore some of the *implications* for teaching and learning BSL of the particular types of lexical patterning found in BSL.

The established lexicon

The words of BSL are commonly known as *signs*. Despite the difference in terminology, the signs of sign languages do function in ways which are comparable to the words of spoken languages. Unfortunately, because our image of 'the word' is closely tied to spoken, and especially written forms, there is sometimes a reluctance to regard signs as words. However, as we shall see, signed language words behave very much like spoken language words, although there are, of course, some interesting differences.

There are several different ways of looking at words in BSL: we can examine them in terms of the building blocks that are used to produce the signs: the *formational parameters*. We can also examine them in terms of the number of *meaningful components* which they contain: the *morphological* structure of words. We can also explore the *relationships between words and meaning*. These three ways of approaching words will form the basis of the three main subdivisions of this section.

Formational structure

What do signs look like? The answer to this question relates to how signs are made or produced by the signer. What does

the signer actually do? What kind of gestural activity does she or he produce? We can begin to answer this question by sorting BSL signs into three main formational types:

manual signs:	signs which are made with the hands: for example, **sign** (sign1067) [6]
non-manual signs:	signs which are made with other parts of the body, excluding the hands: for example, **that's right** [7*]
multi-channel signs:	signs which are made with the hands and with other parts of the body: for example, **bang one's head against a brick wall** [8]

Numerically, manual signs are the most frequent type within BSL vocabulary, followed by multi-channel signs. Independent non-manual signs are very rare. Instead, non-manual markers, which can be seen as meaningful units or morphemes, function as additions to independent BSL signs or as markers of syntactic functions such as negation and questions. It seems that in BSL, as in most of the other sign languages which have so far been studied, there is a strong tendency to exploit non-manual features more fully for grammatical rather than for lexical purposes.

Manual signs

Manual signs, as the name suggests, are produced by movements of the hands and arms. Again we can see a division into three main categories, based upon the nature of the in-

---

6.　Ø 5>⊥ ¦ 5<⊥ ⌄̅	8.　∩ Ƨʊ< ˣ·

* Non-manual signs do not carry notations, since these are designed to indicate movements of the hands and arms only. Prototype symbol

systems for classifying and recording BSL non-manual features have been developed: see, for instance, Colville et al. (1984).

9. **remind**　　　　10. **definite**　　　　11. **administer**　　　　12. **number**

volvement of one or both hands:

single dez signs:	signs involving one hand: for example, **remind** (sign 1562)[9]
manual tab signs:	signs involving two hands, but with only one hand functioning as the active articulator: for example, **definite** (sign 1323)[10]
double dez signs:	signs involving two hands acting in a symmetrical or complementary fashion: for example, **administer** (sign 272)[11]

Signs are produced in time and space and, like the grammar of BSL, they can be analysed in terms of both sequential, linear patterning and complex, simultaneous, multi-layered patterning.

One of the great contributions of the work of William C. Stokoe, the pioneer of sign language research in the 1950s and 60s, was to recognise that the gestural actions or signs used by Deaf people actually had internal structure. They could be analysed into recurring component parts. Indeed, just as thousands of English words can be produced using a very small inventory of speech sounds, approximately forty-four, so the signs of American Sign Language could all be produced using a relatively small number of component parts. In looking at manual signs, Stokoe isolated three main aspects of the action of the sign; a specific *handshape*

(or handshapes) to which Stokoe gave the name *dezignation*, typically abbreviated to *dez*; a particular *location* of the hand(s), termed the *tabulation*, abbreviated to *tab* and a particular *movement*, termed the *signation* and abbreviated to *sig*. While it may seem unnecessary to make use of the additional technical terms *dez*, *tab* and *sig* when referring to the notions of handshape, position and movement, the terms do serve a useful purpose: they allow us to focus on these aspects as parameters within the formational structure of a sign. 'Position', for example, can function at different levels within BSL: it can be used as part of syntactic or discourse patterning, for example to express relationships between different referents. However, when the term *tab* is used, we know immediately that we are focusing on position as one of the basic parameters of the production of individual signs.

We can begin to explore the nature and functioning of these major parameters by looking firstly at some quite simple manual signs. The sign **number**[12] is made with one hand, i.e. it is a single dez sign. It is produced by placing the closed fist in front of the chin and tapping the chin twice. The closed fist is one of approximately fifty-seven significant handshapes of BSL. In fact, this handshape, which is labelled an **A** handshape within the transcription system used here, * is one of the most frequent in the language. We can contrast the sign **number** with the sign **aunt**[13] which makes use of a different handshape, but is otherwise produced in exactly the same way. Both signs are articulated in front of the chin and involve a repeated contact with the

---

9. Ø B̈⊥ʌ ˚ⁱ·

10. ‾ Bɑ> B<ʌ ᴧˣ v

11. Ø Âɑ⊥, Âɑ⊥ ˚ɪᴠ·

12. ∪ A⊤ʌ ˣ·

*See *How to use the Dictionary* section, pp. xvii to xxi.

13. aunt

chin. The handshapes used, labelled **A** and **V̈**, are two of the significant handshapes of the language.

One of the ways in which we can discern whether a particular handshape is significant or not is to see whether the substitution of one handshape for another can bring about a change in meaning. We are familiar with the notion that in English spoken words are made up of smaller units. These are not meaningful in themselves but the substitution of one unit for another can bring about a change in meaning. One of the difficulties of discussing this on paper is that we can be misled as to the number of sounds in any given word by the vagaries of the English spelling system. This is one of the reasons why dictionaries and other accounts of words often make use of a *transcription* or *notation system* which directly reflects the sound system. The following examples from English are presented both in traditional spelling and in the notation system developed by the International Phonetic Association (IPA). If we look at the following pairs of English words, we can see that each pair is distinguished by a single sound:

cat	–	bat	kæt	:	bæt
bat	–	bit	bæt	:	bɪt
bit	–	bill	bɪt	:	bɪl
bill	–	bin	bɪl	:	bɪn
bin	–	bone	bɪn	:	bəun
bone	–	boat	bəun	:	bəut

Ignoring the spelling system, and focusing only on the spoken forms, we can see that these are all what are technically termed *minimal pairs*: the items in each pair are distinguished from each other by a single sound. These sounds are contrastive in the language. Sometimes, the actual phonetic difference between two sounds is very slight. Indeed there are other phonetic differences which occur in speech but which are not contrastive within English. There are different 'l' and 'k' sounds in English, in part dependent upon their position in words. These differences are a potential source of contrastive difference which English happens not to exploit, but other languages may. Every spoken language extracts from the vast potential of spoken sounds a set of sound contrasts and builds them into a linguistic system.

Exactly the same kind of process occurs in sign languages. There is enormous gestural potential. We can produce a great number of different configurations with our hands and perform a wide range of movements. We also know that there is idiosyncratic variation in the shape and flexibility of hands, just as there is in relation to the vocal tract. Gestural linguistic systems abstract away from this variation to arrive at a set of significant gestural actions. In the case of signed language, we are dealing with sets of contrastive handshapes, positions and movements. As we shall see below, there are other contrastive elements as well. However, we will focus first on what have frequently been seen as the major parameters of BSL sign production.

Using the process of citing pairs of signs which are distinguished only by a specific handshape, location or movement, it has been possible to arrive at an inventory of these components, just as we can arrive at an inventory of the sounds of English.

Handshape or dez

The significant handshapes of BSL are those which bring about a change in meaning. The main body of this this dictionary distinguishes fifty-seven separate, contrastive handshape configurations, which we can technically describe as handshape *phonemes* or *cheremes*.* When we look at illustrations of these handshapes (see the listing on pp. xvii to xix of the *How to use the Dictionary* section), we can see that they are more or less different from one another

---

13. ∪ V̈ᴛʌ ˣ ˙

---

*Because of the oddity of using a technical term deriving from the Greek word for 'sound', Stokoe coined a new term *chereme*, linked to the Greek word for 'hand'. However, perhaps because linguists want to show that there are systematic similarities, despite differences in substance, between spoken and signed language, sign linguists frequently make use of the term *phoneme* and related terms such as *phonemic, phonetic, phonology*, etcetera. See glossary for more specific information.

on the basis of a number of features. These features include whether the finger joints are bent or not, whether there is bending at the palm knuckles, whether the fingers are spread or held together, whether the thumb is held at right angles to the fingers, parallel to the fingers or across the palm or closed fingers. Some linguists prefer to give a feature specification for each handshape, so that for each handshape they would specify whether there was bending of the finger joints, whether the fingers were spread and so on. The kind of labelling used in this dictionary, provides a holistic label for each handshape, although there is a partial nod to the existence of handshape features. This labelling derives from Stokoe's original work on ASL and work undertaken by BSL sign linguists in the late 1970s and early 1980s.*

ASL has a one-handed finger spelling system and some of the handshapes used within this finger spelling system also belong to the inventory of contrastive handshapes used within ASL signs. The closed fist hand represented the letter **a**, the fully open flat hand with fingers together represented **b**, the closed fist with index finger extended expressed the letter **g** and so on. The decision to use a closely related labelling system for BSL, despite the fact that there was no link between the British finger spelling system and the handshape labels, was influenced by the desire to make transcriptions of BSL signs as accessible as possible to an international as well as a national readership. However, it is probably best to think of these labels as relatively arbitrary: the closed fist happens to have been given the label **A**, although it could have been called Z or 1 or @. What is important is that when we see the label **A** in the context of BSL words, we know that this refers to the closed fist handshape. Because these labels are arbitrary for British users, it is necessary to learn or at least to become familiar with these handshape labels to use this dictionary with ease (just as we have to explicitly learn the English alphabet). Experience suggests that this can be achieved in a very short time and is obviously made easier by regular use of the system.

As suggested above, there is a hint of a feature analysis in the labelling of BSL handshapes. This is because work in the 1980s † attempted to develop some overall consistency in the use of so-called diacritics. These were separate smaller symbols, usually placed above a handshape symbol, to give a more precise indication of the hand configuration. Originally, these symbols were used especially where there was no equivalent finger spelling label for the handshape. Thus while it was possible to borrow the labels **G** and **V** for the handshapes in which the index finger was extended from the closed fist and the two fingers were extended from the closed fist, there were no equivalent labels for closely related handshapes in which the extended fingers were extended and bent. Such bending was indicated by Stokoe by the use of three short lines above the handshape label. The handshape table on pp. xvii to xix of the *How to use the Dictionary* section, presents twenty-two families of handshapes, with each member of the family listed under the appropriate diacritic. Thus all handshapes listed in the second column, headed by a dot, involve the extension of the thumb: **Ȧ** 'with a dot' is the closed fist with thumb extended; **Ġ** 'with a dot' has the index finger extended from the closed fist and the thumb extended. Similarly, the fifth column is headed by the diacritic 'three small vertical lines': all handshapes listed in this column involve bending of the finger joints. **G̈** 'with three small vertical lines' has the index finger extended from the closed fist and bent at the finger joints. The seventh column makes use of two sets of diacritics: in this case, **G̈̇** 'with a dot and three small vertical lines' means that the the index finger is extended from the closed fist and bent and the thumb is also extended. This system of basic handshape labels and additional diacritics allows all of the contrastive handshapes of BSL to be given a label.¶

If we look at the illustrations of the signs **have to** [14] and **die** [15] and the signs **bird** [16] and **talk** [17], we can see that, like **aunt** and **number** earlier, they are identical except for the handshapes. There can still be some variation in the production of these handshapes amongst individual signers. We could imagine variants of the **H** handshapes used in **die** relating to the precise position of the thumbs and the bent ring and little fingers. If these fingers and the thumbs actually touched at the tips, then the resulting handshape would seem odd, but would not bring about a change of meaning. We could, however, imagine a sign language in which this is a contrastive handshape. Some linguists have noted a distinction between unmarked and marked handshapes. The unmarked ones are those which are regarded as being maximally distinct geometrical shapes, such as the compact, solid closed fist, the fully open and spread hand, **5**; the fully extended, flat hand **B**; the extended index finger hand, **G**;

---

* See Bristol Sign Language Group (1979) and Brennan et al. (1980 and 1984).
† Particularly Brennan et al. (1984).

¶ Further details of the labelling system can be found in the *How to use the Dictionary* section and in Brennan et al. (1984), especially pp. 73–76.

14. have to

15. die

16. bird

17. talk

the curved hand, **c** and the circular hand, **o**.* These handshapes have been described as the most frequently occurring and the first to be used by children acquiring the language. Such handshapes can be contrasted with the marked handshapes which involve more complex articulations. Certainly, within this dictionary, several of the unmarked handshapes, especially **A**, **B**, **5** and **G** are represented by many more entries than marked handshapes such as **Y**, **Ч**, **Ö** and **R**. There is also evidence that young children learning BSL substitute the physically simpler unmarked forms for the more complex configurations in the early stages of acquisition. However, other factors besides geometrical and physical simplicity may be relevant to the frequency of handshape usage in the language. Some handshapes, for example, have a range of important *classifier* functions, indicating the size and shape of objects or the handling of objects (see further pp. 46–67). In a language such as BSL which exploits this potential for the creation of new signs, classifying handshapes may play a major role in the language. Other factors may also affect handshape frequency. In several parts of the U.K., there are BSL varieties which have been strongly influenced by Irish Sign Language and one-handed Irish finger spelling. These varieties occur, for example, in Manchester, Liverpool and Glasgow where there are groups of Catholic Deaf people who have been influenced by Irish signing through schooling. In the Glasgow Catholic Deaf community, it is possible to observe signs which derive from initial letter finger spelled forms: the handshape **R** represents the letter **r**, the handshape **Ч** the letter **h**, the handshape **A** s the letter **s** and the handshape **Y** the letter **y**. It is interesting to observe that as well as the derived initial letter signs discussed on p. 94, these handshapes generally seem to have wider distribution within the lexicon used amongst Catholic signers. Within this community, the sign **kettle** [18] is produced with the **Ч** handshape, although other communities in the same geographical area use an **A** handshape. It is as if the presence of these handshapes in finger spelling loan signs encourages their wider use within BSL vocabulary.

Position or tab

For the non-signer, the notion of a set of contrastive BSL handshapes may seem reasonably easy to observe. It may be less obvious that BSL exploits a set of significant locations on and around the body. However, just as we can draw up an inventory of the significant handshapes of BSL, we can also compile a list of the significant positions or tabs in which the hands are placed. In order to arrive at such a listing, it is necessary to go through the same kind of process as with handshapes. We need to discover whether changing the position of the hand(s) can bring about either a change of meaning or produce a nonsense sign. Just as we can find

14. ∅ B>∧ B<∧ $\overset{\cap}{\perp}$

15. ∅ H>∧ H<∧ $\overset{\cap}{\perp}$

16. ⌣ $\bar{\bar{\mathsf{G}}}$⊥∧ $^{\sharp\,[\hat{6}]}$ ·

17. ⌣ $\bar{\bar{\mathsf{B}}}$⊥∧ $^{\sharp\,[\hat{6}]}$ ·

18. ∅ Ч⊥∧ $\overset{\cap}{<}$

* See Battison (1974 and 1978).

19. name

20. afternoon

21. seem

22. thank you

minimal pairs of signs which are identical except for the choice of handshapes, so we can find minimal pairs of signs which are alike in every respect except their position on or near the body. The signs **name**[19] and **afternoon**[20] both make use of the н handshape and involve a twisting action away from the body. The only difference in the production of the two signs is that **name** begins at the forehead while **afternoon** begins at the chin. Sometimes positions which are physically close to each other are nevertheless distinctive. Thus the nose and mouth are contrastive locations in BSL as illustrated in the signs **seem**[21] and **thank you**[22]. Even the so-called trunk, i.e. the area roughly from shoulders to waist can be divided into upper and lower sections which can operate contrastively as in the signs **sorry**[23] and **delicious**[24]. We can see from these examples that the signs of BSL make use of positions on or near the signer's body. The area in which signs are produced, sometimes called the *signing space*, extends from approximately just above the head to the waist, and in width from elbow to elbow when the arms are held loosely bent. There are some other possible positions for signs outside this space, but these positions are rarely used. Thus many signs relating to sexu-

ality were probably originally produced in the area below the waist: signs such as **penis**[25], **vagina**[26], **condom**[27] and **erection**[28] may all be produced below the waist. However, in many varieties of signing, particularly formal varieties, these signs are actually articulated higher up in what is termed *neutral space*. Obviously, the signer is free to make use of the more explicit location for effect. Similarly, a sign such as **boot** (sign148)[29] would seem to require the tab 'leg', but the position is usually raised, so that within this dictionary it is given the tab 'hip' which includes the upper thighs. There are very rare instances of signs with a location on or near the back of the body. Some of these are deictic signs which merely point to a physical area, such as the bottom. The sign **squirrel** (sign 1674)[30] can be produced with the right hand placed behind the body in the lower hip region, but it is more typically signed at lower trunk level, as in the illustration. Thus despite the fact that position can be influenced by real-world physical locations, there is a strong pull towards locating all signs within a more restricted signing space.

Neutral space is one of the most frequent locations for BSL signs. This is the area in front of the signer's body, ap-

---

19. ∩ Hтʌ ˣᵚ⊥

20. ∪ Hтʌ ˣᵚ⊥

21. ⊔ Bтʌ ₒ↓∨

22. ◡ Bтʌ ₒ↓∨

23. [] Bт< ₒ⊚≷˙

24. ⊔ Bт< ₒ⊚≷∨˙

25. G̈ʊ>ᵖ ₓ G̈ʊ< ∅

26. ∅ Ġ>⊥ ₁ₓ Ġ<⊥ ∅

27. G>⊥ ₁ₓ F<⊥ ᵀˣᵀ

28. ∅ G<∨ ⁿ∧

29. н̄ A>∨ ₁ A<∨ ∧<∧ˣ∨ˣ

30. ʃ Cʊ⊥ >ᵃ∧ᵃ

23. sorry

24. delicious

29. boots

30. squirrel

31. walk

senses; the mouth is associated with speech and food and the forehead area is conventionally associated with thought. Thus, although the physical spatial difference between a mouth and a chin tab may be very slight, such a difference is significant in the language.

Movement or sig

Perhaps the most complex of the parameters of sign formation is that of movement, also termed sig.* As Stokoe has suggested, the movement of signs would present a bewildering maze if we were not able to apply the notion of significant contrast to this complex array of gestural activity. Of course, some signs may use relatively simple movements, but others may employ complex simultaneous and sequential movement.

Analyses of BSL movement have shown that it is possible to distinguish several broad categories of movement with sets of contrasts internally within these categories. Different choices from more than one category may then be brought together in individual signs. In order to demonstrate this, we will focus first on the broad categories of movement.

Some signs involve movements along one of three axes: vertical directional movements involve the contrasts up, down, and up and down; movements along the bilateral axis involve the contrasts right, left and side to side and movements along the horizontal depth axis involve the contrasts towards the signer, away from the signer and to and fro. Examples of directional movement include movement away in **walk** [31], movement down in **never** (p. 25 [48]) and side to side

proximately at mid to lower chest height, where the hands move easily and naturally. The precise location within the signing space will be conditioned by other features such as the orientation of the hands and the relationship between the two hands. Signs which are executed in space, without contact with the body, are usually given a neutral space location if the sign occurs below shoulder level, and a whole head location if they occur above shoulder level. A full list of the other tab options can be found on p. xx of the *How to use the Dictionary* section. It will be clear from this list that the head and body can, in effect, be divided into sets of different positions. Despite the relatively small area of the head compared to the rest of the body, ten different positions are cited on the head. This is presumably because of the physical and conventional significance of different parts of the head and face: the eyes, nose, mouth and ears are associated with the

31. Ø V̈ɔ⊥

*As with the handshape parameter, various feature analyses have been developed for the movement parameter. A useful discussion of these, particularly relating to ASL, but relevant also to BSL, can be found in Wilbur (1987).

42. separate

44. join

48. never

49. cabbage

movement in **iron** (sign 7) [32].

A further major category is what is termed *manner* of movement. Manner of movement relates not so much to the spatial route taken by the hands as to the action or actions of the hands themselves. The hand may twist or bend in space; different parts of the hands may articulate different types of movement. There may be repeated bending of the finger joints as in **spider** (p. 48 [203]), repeated bending of the hand at the palm knuckles as in **donkey** (sign 1462) [33], a twisting action as in **from** [34], a wiggling action of the fingers as in **walk** (sign 784) [35], an opening action as in **sun** (p. 68 [270]) or a closing action as in **finish** (sign 1552) [36].

Circular movement seems to straddle the boundary between direction and manner. It always involves some kind of directionality executed on one of three possible planes. The sign **fairground** (sign 108) [37] involves circular movement in the horizontal plane; **cycle** (sign 92) [38] involves circular movement in the vertical plane at right angles to the signer's body and the sign **suspicious** (sign 919) [39] involves circular movement in the vertical plane parallel to the signer's body.*

A further feature of movement is *contact*. This may occur either between the two hands (see further under *interaction* below) or between the hand(s) and some other part of the body. There are, in fact, several different types of contact. Contact can occur as a separate feature of movement, as in the sign **number** (p. 18 [12]). However, it frequently co-occurs with other features of movement. In a sign such as **sorry** (p. 22 [23]), the circular movement is produced while the hand maintains contact with the upper chest: this is known as *maintaining contact*. In some signs, one part of the hand retains contact with the tab, but the rest of the hand executes usually either a twisting or a nodding action, as in the sign **theatre** (sign 968) [40]: this is known as *holding contact*. A further type of contact, known as *brushing contact* can be seen in the sign **girl** (sign 339) [41]. For information on how to notate such signs, see *How to use the Dictionary* section, p. xxii.

In two-handed signs the movement parameter may involve *interaction* between the two hands. The hands may separate as in **separate** [42], approach each other as in **meet** (sign 434) [43], interlock or come together as in **join** [44], change

32. Ø A⊤v

33. ∩ B⊥∧ B⊥∧

34. Ø Bɑ⊥

35. Ø V̈ɒ⊥

36. Ø B̄⊥∧ B̄⊥∧ #[ᵬᵬ]

37. Ø Ā⊤> ₓ A⊤<⊤

38. Ø Aɒ⊥ | Aɒ⊥v

39. ∩ Ï⊤∧v

40. B̄ɑ> ₓ પɒ⊤z

41. Ƹ G⊥∧⊥

* See *How to Use the Dictionary* section, p. xxii for further clarification and explanation of the different planes.

50. but

51. what

52. tomorrow

53. yesterday

places as in **substitute** (sign 1164)[45], contact each other as in **same** (p. 28[70]), partially or wholly cross over each other as in **dark** (sign 1072)[46] and one hand may go into the space provided by the other (usually curved) hand as in **inside** (sign 1614)[47].

Signs may involve a *repetition* of all or some features of movement. Repetition can be recognised as the only significant difference between the signs **never**[48] and **cabbage**[49]. Signs which are produced by actions of the two hands may produce the relevant movements in a completely symmetrical fashion or the hands may alternate. In **administer** (p. 18[11]) both hands move to and fro, but one hand is moving towards the signer while the other is moving away from the signer: similarly in **cycle** (p.24[38]) both hands perform a downward circular movement, but they do so in an alternating fashion.

As with the other major formational parameters of the sign, we can arrive at a listing of the significant movements by a process of substitution within pairs of signs. The sign

but[50] involves a single nodding movement to the right while the sign **what**[51] involves a side to side nodding movement: the only manual difference between the two is the direction of the movement. Similarly, the sign **tomorrow**[52] involves a nodding movement away from the signer, while the sign **yesterday**[53] involves a nodding movement towards the signer (in some versions this action may end in contact with the signer's body).

As suggested by Brennan et al,* despite the enormous emphasis on simultaneous production, signs do occur in time as well as space and thus do have a beginning, a middle and an end. If we 'freeze' a sign in space and time we will be able to capture some expression of the relevant parameters of handshape, position and movement. Clearly, the movement parameter cannot be executed without the existence of a handshape and the hand must be positioned somewhere. So there is always and inevitably simultaneity in sign production.

However, it will be clear from both the signs illustrated

42. Ø FT> ɪ FㅗΛ

43. Ø GTΛ GㅗΛ

44. Ø F̄T> ǀ F̄ㅗΛ

45. Ø ʃ5̈ㅇㅗ ʃ5̈ㅇㅗ

46. Ọ 5TΛ 5TΛ

47. B̄>ㅗ B̈ㅇㅗ

48. ĀT> ǀ B<ㅗ

49. ĀT> ǀ B<ㅗ

50. Ø GㅗΛ

51. Ø GㅗΛ

52. З G̈TΛ

53. З G̈TΛ

* See Brennan et al. (1984, p. 174).

here and the positioning of the sig symbols within the notation system, that the movement features of BSL signs may operate simultaneously or sequentially. When the notation symbols occur vertically, one underneath the other, then the different movement features occur simultaneously; when they occur horizontally, one after the other in a linear sequence, then the individual movement features occur one after the other. In the signs **thank you** (p. 22[22]) and **seem** (p. 22[21]) the hands simultaneously move away from the signer and down; in **spider** (p. 48[203]) the hand moves down and at the same time the fingers wiggle. Sometimes there can be quite complex simultaneous patterning. In **crowd milling around** (p. 64[261]), the two hands perform an alternating circular movement in the horizontal plane while, at the same time, the fingers wiggle. This is an ongoing movement. In other signs, sequential patterning is more important: both **name** (p. 22[19]) and **afternoon** (p. 22[20]) have an initial contact followed sequentially by a twisting action directed away from the signer.

The above account of BSL movement suggests that although it is possible to find minimal pairs of signs which will support the list of movement options exemplified in the sig listing on p. xxi of the *How to use the Dictionary* section, in most cases we are dealing with a complex set of movement features which combine to provide the specific movement parameter choices in any given sign.

Other parameters of sign production

Stokoe's original account of ASL signs focused on the major parameters of handshape, location and movement. However, Stokoe was also aware of the potential importance of other factors, particularly the orientation of the hands. Within the first dictionary of a sign language ever published, the *Dictionary of American Sign Language* (Stokoe et al., revised ed. 1976), additional information was provided relating to orientation. However, such information was not seen as essential for every sign. Work on BSL sign structure suggests that three further types of information are relevant to sign production: *orientation*, *hand arrangement* and *point and place of contact*.

Orientation

Orientation (usually known as ori within accounts of sign notation) concerns the relationship of the hand(s) to the signer's body. If we choose a particular handshape—for example, the flat handshape **B**—and position it in neutral space, it is clear that we can hold the hand in a number of different relationships to the signer's body: the hand may be held with the palm facing up and the fingers pointing away from the signer, as in **arise** (sign 1201)[54]; the palm may face down with the fingers pointing away from the signer, as in **child** (sign 1211)[55]; the palm may be held towards the signer with the fingers pointing down, as in **absent** (sign 1220)[56] and the palm may face away from the signer with the fingers pointing up, as in **hang on** (sign 1222)[57]. From a descriptive point of view, it seems essential to provide information about hand orientation, for example, in a dictionary such as this; otherwise, the reader may produce a completely unrecognisable form of the sign. Moreover, it is clear that, as in the above examples, two types of information are essential: information about the direction of the palm and information about the direction of the fingers. One of the difficulties in respect of finger orientation is that, because there is such a range of hand configurations, the fingers themselves may be held in a range of positions—for example, straight, bent, closed into the fist or bent at the palm knuckles. In order to cope with such variation, the distinctions elaborated in the *How to use the Dictionary* section refer to the direction of the fingers once the handshape (whatever it might be) is opened flat. Thus, to check the finger orientation of a closed fist, the hand is held still and the hand is opened flat. In a sign such as **iron** (p. 24[32]), the finger orientation is down, because if the hand was held in position but opened flat, the fingers would point down; in contrast, the finger orientation of **your** (sign 9)[58] is up, because if the hand were opened the fingers would point up.

The status of orientation as a clearly separate parameter of sign production, on a par with the three major parameters distinguished earlier, has been the subject of heated debate.* This is in part because the selection of different

---

54. Ø Bɑ⊥ ^

55. Ø Bᴅ⊥ °ᵥ

56. Ø B⊤ᵥ ⁿ⊥

57. Ø B⊥ʌ °⊥·

58. Ø A⊥ʌ °⊥

*See for example the discussions in Brennan et al. (1984), Deuchar (1984), Stokoe (1978) and Wilbur (1979).

65. think   66. see   68. bank

orientation options can be rather more variable than other options. In the **G** and **G̈** chapters of the *BSL* section of this dictionary, a number of compound signs are listed which have **think** as the first element. In some of these compound signs, the first element has the hand facing the signer with the fingers pointing up, as in **can't believe** (sign 315)[59] and **stupid** (sign 316)[60]; in others, the orientation of the **think** component has the palm facing left and the fingers up as in **ill** (sign 318)[61] and **epidemic** (sign 319)[62]. A similar set of possibilities can be found in signs which have **see** as the first component of a compound: **evidence** (sign 330)[63] has the palm towards and fingers up, while **find** (sign 332)[64] has the palm left and fingers up. In all of these cases then, palm orientation seems to be variable. It could be argued that this variability is due to the occurrence of these forms within compounds: there is plenty of evidence that the first part of the sign undergoes modification in relation to the second part. However, even in the simple forms of **think**[65] and **see**[66] there seems to be considerable variation in use. The choice of which palm orientation to select as typical within the citation form is more or less arbitrary.

There is one other set of signs which shows considerable variation in orientation choices. These are manual tab signs (see p. 18) where the dominant (here cited as the right) hand performs an action on or in relation to the stationary non-dominant (left) hand. In the sign **commandments** (sign 402)[67], the palm faces up and the fingers point away from the signer. However, some signers may typically produce these signs with the palm up and the fingers pointing right. Here, then, finger orientation appears variable. However, what must remain constant is the orientation relationship between the two hands. The right index finger is placed at right angles to the fingers of the left hand, so that if the finger orientation changes for the left hand, there must be a complementary change in the right hand. If the fingers of the left hand point to the right, then the fingers of the right hand must point away from the signer (rather than left). In fact, there are numerous possible realisations of finger orientation in such examples, with the orientation of the right hand always adjusting so that the orientation relationship between the two hands is correct for that sign.

Despite such variability, orientation choices can still be regarded as descriptively important. Moreover, it is possible to distinguish otherwise identical signs purely on the basis of orientation. The signs **bank**[68] and **print** (p. 28[69]) are identical except for the palm orientation of the right

---

59. ∩ G⊤ʌ ˣ ᵛ [ᴮ] // ̄Bɑ⊥ B<⊥ ᵛˣʌ a̧

60. ∩ G⊤ʌ ˣ ᵛ [ʌ] ≠ // A̲⊤> A⊤< ᵒ˙ʌˣ

61. ∩ G<ʌ ˣ // ̄G⊤> G<⊥ᵩ ˣ ʌ̊ ˣ

62. ∩ G<ʌ ˣ // ̄G⊤> G<⊥ᵩ ˣ ʌ̊ ˣ // Ø 5ᴖ⊥ 5ᴖ⊥ ⊥÷

63. Ц G⊤ʌ ˣ⊥ᵛ // ̄Bɑ⊥ Bɑ⊥ ᵛˣ

64. Ц G<ʌ ˣ ᵛ // Ø (̄5̈>⊥ ˣ 5̈<⊥ ᵗˣ˙) >

65. ∩ G⊤ʌ ˣ⊥̊

66. Ц G⊤ʌ ˣ⊥

67. ̄Bɑ⊥ ₗ G⊤< ⁽ˣ˙⁾ᵀ

68. ̄Bɑ> A<⊥ ᵛˣɑ̊ ʌ

69. print

70. same

71. thing

hand: in **bank** the palm is facing left at the beginning of the sign; in **print** the palm is facing down. The sign pairs **same**[70] and **thing**[71] and **brother**[72] and **engine**[73] are distinguished by the combined realisations of palm and finger orientation: in **same** the palms face down and the fingers point away from the signer; in **thing** the palms face the signer and the fingers point up. Similarly, in **brother** the palms face each other (the right palm faces left and the left palm faces right) and the fingers (if the hands were held open and flat) point away from the signer; in **engine** the palms face towards the signer and the fingers point up. Thus orientation features, rather than handshape, position or movement are significant within these pairs of signs.

Hand arrangement

This parameter plays a role in signs which involve two hands, either double dez signs, where both hands are active, or manual tab signs, where one hand is stationary while the other hand performs some action in relation to it. Hand arrangement choices concern the relationship between the two hands at the beginning of a sign. We may see the neutral choice as being the arrangement of the two hands in respect to each other once the other parameter choices, including orientation, have been made. Many of the notations of signs involving two hands in this dictionary do not provide additional information on hand arrangements. In signs such as **idle** (sign 667)[74] and **assess** (sign 1367)[75], the two hands are placed in what can be seen as their most natural position, taking account of the particular handshape, position, movement and orientation involved. The hands are not particularly close together or touching, for example. However, other signs do exhibit special hand arrangement features. It has been possible to distinguish such features as the hands being held side by side as in **bargain** (sign 1387)[76]; the hands contacting each other as in **waste of time** (sign 1355)[77]; the right hand held above the left as in **empty** (sign 1321)[78]; the left hand held above the right as in **grill** (sign 1334)[79]; the right hand held behind (i.e. nearer the body than) the left as in **hide** (sign 1469)[80]; the left hand held behind the right as in **box** (sign 1458)[81]; one hand held

69. $\overline{\text{Ba}}$> A$\text{ʊ}\bot$ $\overset{\text{v x o}}{\wedge}$

70. Ø G$\text{ʊ}\bot$ ‚ G$\text{ʊ}\bot$ $^{\text{x .}}$

71. Ø G$\top\wedge$ ‚ G$\top\wedge$ $^{\text{x .}}$

72. Ø A>$\bot$ ‚ A<$\bot$ $\overset{\text{o}}{\underset{\text{x}}{\text{z}}}$·

73. Ø A$\top\wedge$ ‚ A$\top\wedge$ $\overset{\text{o}}{\underset{\text{x}}{\text{z}}}$·

74. Ø $\ddot{\text{A}}$a$\bot$ $\ddot{\text{A}}$a$\bot$ $\overset{\text{o}}{\text{v}}$·

75. Ø Ba$\bot$ Ba$\bot$ $^{\wedge\wedge}$·

76. Ø $\overline{\text{Ba}}$> ‚ Ba< $^{\text{IN ·}}$

77. $\overline{\text{B}}\top$> $_\text{x}$ B<$\bot$ $\overset{\text{n}}{\underset{\text{x}}{\text{v}}}$

78. $\overline{\text{Ba}}$> Bʊ< $^{\text{v x}}$

79. $\overline{\text{B}\text{ʊ}}$> Ba$\bot_\text{?}$ $^{\bot}$

80. $\subset$ B>$\wedge$ $_\text{x}$ B<$\wedge_\text{?}$ $^{\emptyset}$

81. Ø B>$\bot_\text{?}$ B<$\bot$ $\overset{\text{o o o}}{\underset{\text{x}}{\overset{\vee\wedge\vee}{\text{n}}}}$

72. brother

73. engine

85. parallel

86. follow

88. problem

89. best

inside the other as in **drown** (sign 1548)[82]; the two hands crossed as in **dawn** (sign 1467) [83]; and the two hands interlinking as in **wrestling** (sign 1736)[84].

As with orientation, it is possible to distinguish minimal pairs of signs on the basis of hand arrangement alone, although often we are dealing with a combination of such features. The signs **parallel**[85] and **follow**[86] share all the same choices of handshape, position, movement and orientation but differ in hand arrangement: **parallel** has the hands held side by side at the onset of the sign; **follow** has

the right hand held behind the left with the index finger of the right hand contacting the left hand.

Point and place of contact

The term *point of contact* is often used as a cover term for two different sets of choices. However, it is useful to separate out these two areas. We therefore distinguish here *point of contact* which relates to the part of the active hand which makes contact, either with the other hand or with some other part of the body, and the *place of contact*, the area of the hand or body which is touched by the active hand.

If we look at a selection of examples from the *BSL* section of this dictionary, it will be clear very quickly that different parts of the hand(s) are involved in contact. This will be conditioned very much by the actual dez realisation, i.e. the choice of handshape, but it will also be affected by the choices made from the other parameters, particularly location and orientaion. In the **Ȧ** section, we can see that even though there is extension of the thumb, it is not only the thumb which makes contact. In fact, different parts of the thumb and different parts of the closed hand may act as the contacting surface. In **know** (sign 168)[87] and **problem** (sign 208)[88], the thumbtip is the point of contact; in **best** (sign 192)[89] and **better** (sign 193)[90], the side of the thumb

82. $\bar{\text{B}}$>⊥ ◉ $\bar{\text{B}}$ɑ⊥ #[ɓ]

83. Ɔ $\acute{\text{J}}$ Bᴛ> ∓ $\acute{\text{J}}$ Bᴛ< ᴅ∧

84. Ø $\bar{\text{E}}$ɑ> ⊥ Eʊ< ᶻ˙ᶻ˙

85. Ø Gʊ⊥ ⫶ Gʊ⊥ ⊥

86. Ø Gʊ⊥ Gʊ⊥ᵩ ⊥

87. ∩ Ȧ<∧ ×˙

88. B>⊥ ⫶ Ȧʊ⊥ ×˙

89. $\bar{\text{Ȧ}}$>⊥ ⫶ Ȧʊ⊥ᵩ ⊥×⊥

90. Ȧ>⊥ ⫶ Ȧʊ⊥ᵩ ⊥×⊥˙

95. **marry**

makes contact; in **accurate** (sign 197)[91] and **always** (sign 204)[92], the heel of the palm, backs of the closed fingers and edge of the thumb make contact; in **fantastic** (sign 206)[93], it is the little finger edge and palm edge which make contact. We can see a similar range of choices in respect of other handshapes. Point of contact information is clearly an important part of sign description. Brennan et al. (1984) suggest that·for many signs point of contact can be predicted from the realisation of other parameter choices. However, this is clearly not always the case. For this reason, some researchers, such as Kyle and Woll (1985), have chosen to provide point of contact information within their sign notation system. They include such specifications as 'tip of thumb', 'base of index finger', 'thumb edge of hand', 'little finger edge of hand', 'palm surface of hand' and 'back surface of hand'. *

Place of contact relates to the precise area of the hand or body which is contacted. Again, in many cases, it is possible to predict the approximate area from the choice of the other formational parameters. The sign **problem** (p. 29[88]) involves contact approximately in the middle of the palm: a contact on the extended fingers would seem decidedly odd, although the sign would still be recognisable. In some cases, place of contact may be even more specific: the sign **answer**

(sign 370)[94] requires that the place of contact is the inside of the extended thumb; **marry** (sign 895)[95] requires that the place of contact is the edges of the fourth finger; **chat** (sign 380)[96] has the active dominant **G** hand contacting the manual tab **G** which is held below the right hand: the place of contact is the thumb edge of the left hand. In contrast, **automatic** (sign 383)[97] which has the hands in a similar orientation and hand arrangement, has the upper edge of the left index finger as the place of contact. By using the notation symbols developed by Kyle and Woll, it is possible to provide information on place of contact where the place is on the other hand. Indeed, Kyle and Woll use contact symbols as a regular part of their system (where contact occurs), not as an optional extra. A more limited system for notating both point and place of contact is used in this dictionary: the only specific elements of the hand referred to are the specific digits (thumb and fingers) and the spaces between the digits (see *How to use the Dictionary* section, p. xxi). Although Brennan et al. (1984) also developed a systematic use of diacritics to indicate more precise locations on the chest and shoulders, certain types of patterning are assumed both within the notation system and on the part of the user. Thus it is assumed that body contact occurs on the same side as the active hand unless otherwise specified: for example, a sign such as **look** (sign 755)[98] will be produced by a right handed signer at the right eye. Surprisingly, such signs can be transferred to the other side of the face or body, although the motivation for such transfer is not always clear.

Types of manual sign

As indicated on p. 17, there are three main types of manual sign. All of these types have been illustrated in the previous pages. In single dez signs, the non-dominant hand plays no role at all. In double dez signs, both hands have an equal role to play: both hands act as articulators and they either have exactly the same handshape, orientation and movement, or they have complementary realisations of these parameters. The orientation, for example, may be identical as in **cycle**

---

91. B̄ɑ> Ȧʊ⊥ᵛˣ

92. B̄ɑ> ₓ Ȧʊ⊥ᐟ ᐧˣ

93. B̄ɑ> Ȧ<⊥ ᵛˣᴧ ⵢ ⱥ

94. Ȧ>⊥ ₁ Gᴛ< $\begin{pmatrix} \circ\circ \\ T\,\Lambda \\ \times\times \\ \Lambda \end{pmatrix}$ ·

95. °5ʊ> ᵢₓ F̄ʊ⊥ ⱨˣ

96. Ḡᴛ> G<⊥ ˣ ·

97. Ḡᴛ> G<⊥ᵩ ⁽ᵛˣᴧ ⁾

98. ⊔ ᵉV<ᴧ ˣ⊥

*See Kyle and Woll (1985, ch. 5) for more detail.

(p. 24 [38]) or the hands may face each other as in **cold** (sign 118) [99]. Both hands may perform exactly the same movement simultaneously, as in **ski** (sign 120) [100] or they may produce identical actions alternately, as in **athlete** (sign 121) [101]. In **swim** (sign 1410) [102], the hands make complementary circular movements, with the right hand moving rightwards as the left hand moves leftwards. There is a strong pull towards such symmetry in double dez signs. However, signs do occur in which both hands move but without this symmetry. The sign **avoid** (sign 72) [103] makes use of two different handshapes, G and A, and both hands move away from the signer. Even more unusually, the sign **porridge** (sign 723) [104] not only has two different handshapes, but two completely different movements, a crumbling action with the left hand and a stirring action with the right hand. The rarity of this type of example demonstrates the typical symmetry of double dez signs. Manual tab signs involve the non-dominant hand acting as the location or tab for the dominant, active hand. In many cases, there is contact as in **bank** (p. 27 [68]) and **print** (p. 28 [69]); in other cases, the dominant hand acts in relation to the non-dominant hand, but without contact. In **underground train** (sign 414) [105] the G hand moves away under the stationary left B̌ hand; in **environment** (sign 1017) [106] the right 5 hand moves around the stationary left Ǧ hand.

In some rare instances, there may be what is termed a double tab: in these cases, an essentially manual tab sign is placed at some other location: **telescope** (p. 67 [268]) has the two O hands placed in front of the right eye, but only the right hand moves. More typically, these manual tab signs are located in the area in front of the body.

Citation forms and signs in context

The citation form of a sign is the form of the sign when it is produced in isolation. Citation forms of words, whether spoken or signed, are what we typically find in dictionaries. It is, of course, crucial to realise that neither speakers nor signers use citation forms in everyday life: we do not speak in citation forms and we do not sign in citation forms. If we did, we would sound and look decidedly odd. Rather, cita-

tion forms are an abstraction away from those forms which occur in everday usage. Yet citation forms are useful. It would be virtually impossible to produce a dictionary which presented all the forms of an individual word in actual usage. This is because the actual production of a sign or a spoken word is affected by the surrounding language. In English, there are processes such as elision and assimilation which alter the phonetic production of a spoken word. In "not that", the 't' sound at the end of "not" may be incorporated into the 'th' sound at the beginning of "that". The clause "you can have mine" will typically be realised as / jʊ kŋ ˌhæm ˋmaɪn /. Similar kinds of processes occur in BSL. In signs involving body contact in citation form, the hands may approach the tab without actually making contact. A sign which has a tab in neutral space may be given a raised location if it occurs immediately after a sign with a head tab; handshape production may be influenced by the following handshape as the hand 'gets ready for' the next sign, and so forth. These processes can also be seen at work in compound forms, where the first element in the compound is affected by the form of the second element (see pp. 36–37 for further discussion and illustration). It is essential that users of this dictionary recognise the difference between signs in context and the abstract 'artificial' status of isolated citation forms.

Non-manual signs

As the name suggests, non-manual signs are produced by parts of the body other than the hands. Non-manual features are actions of the head, face or body which are exploited in some way within the grammar and lexis of BSL. Whilst such features play a major role within the syntax of BSL, they may also have some function within BSL vocabulary. They occur particularly in multi-channel signs, but also as separate meaningful units which can be added to signs (non-manual morphemes) and more rarely as individual signs in their own right.

Given the physical features of the face, and the potential range of actions they can produce, it is not surprising that facial expression of various kinds together with movements

---

99. Ø A>⊥ A<⊥ ˣ·
  (ᵖᵥ)·

100. Ø A>⊥ A<⊥ ᵀᵥ

101. Ø A>⊥ A<⊥ ᵉᴺ·ᵥ

102. Ø B⊙⊥ ‖ B⊙⊥ ᵉ·÷

103. Ø Ḡ⊙> ₓ ꓛOA⊥Λₚ ᵒ·

104. Ø Ĥ⊙> ᵐ Ḧ⊙⊥ ᵉ<

105. Ḇ⊙Λ G⊙⊥ₚ ⊥

106. Ḡα⊥ 5⊙⊥ₚ ᵉ<ᵀ

107. **that's right**   108. **oh, my God**   **109. bang one's head against a brick wall**

of the whole head constitute the main set of non-manual features. Other actions of the body may also be involved, including movements of the shoulders and the central trunk of the body. Thus, the body may twist right or left, lean forwards or back and the shoulders may hunch, shrug or droop. The illustrations on pp. xxiv to xxvi of the *How to use the Dictionary* section give some indication of the range of facial expressions and head movements which can be used significantly in the language. Fairly obviously, these include movements and actions of the eyes and mouth and, perhaps more surprisingly, actions of the nose and cheeks. The human face is highly mobile and contains numerous muscles which can generate a great array of different actions and combinations of actions. *The Facial Action Coding System* (Ekman and Friesen, 1978), for example, recognises forty-six separate action units relating to the actions of the different muscles of the face. The business of deciding which of these elements is significant in any given linguistic context is extremely complex. However, it does seem clear that although the potential is available for the vocabulary of the language to make use of words that are constructed only of non-manual elements, this rarely happens.

Those non-manual signs that do occur usually express questions, negations, general responses or attitudes. The signer may use non-manual question markers such as furrowed brows and hunched shoulders or raised eyebrows and open mouth to indicate a questioning attitude. Similarly, the signer may use the negative headshake without any additional manual sign. Most of these non-manual signs seem to have an interactional function: they rarely, if ever, occur as content words. We do not find non-manual signs

meaning 'cat', 'tomato', 'abstract', 'supervisor' or 'economical'; we do find non-manual signs meaning 'yes', 'no', 'I know', 'that's right', 'is that right?' and 'I agree'. Some of these signs operate in a similar way to the general non-manual gestures found in the spoken language community in the U.K.: both signers and speakers use a head shake to express negation, a head nod to express agreement and a shoulder shrug to express lack of concern or knowledge. However, speakers would not typically use the kind of sign illustrated above and glossed as **that's right**[107]. Here the signer is using very small and specific non-manual features, such as nose puckering and a backward head nod. Although such non-manual resources could have been exploited more abundantly to create many non-manual signs, in fact, the language uses this potential only to a very limited extent. Instead non-manual features co-occur with manual actions, both within the wider lexicon and within BSL syntax.

Multi-channel signs

Multi-channel signs are made with the hands and with other parts of the body; they exploit both manual and non-manual actions. A distinguishing characteristic of multi-channel signs is that the non-manual components are compulsory: they are an inherent part of the sign. In the sign **oh my God**[108] the non-manual features involve lip-rounding, sucking in of air, slightly sucked in cheeks and furrowed brows; **bang one's head against a brick wall** [109] involves the lips stretched wide and the teeth showing in what is sometimes called the 'ee' mouthshape (as if saying "ee"). These non-manual components are not just added on, but occur regularly as part of the sign's production.

108. ∪ ⁵⁵TΛ ⱽ   109. ∩ Gᴑ<

Lexical items may be distinguished from one another purely on the basis of non-manual features. Entry 230 of this dictionary cites three signs with precisely the same manual components, but different non-manual features: **smart** (sign 230)[110] has neutral non-manual features; **can't be bothered** (sign 230, note 1)[111] requires tongue protrusion and a forward head tilt and **fed up** (sign 230, note 2)[112] requires the lips stretched and the corners of the mouth turned down.

Of course, as we can see in relation to both manual and multi-channel signs, there may well be differences between the citation form of a sign presented in a dictionary and its production in real life interaction (see discussion on p. 31). Moreover, because non-manual features may also co-occur with individual lexical items to express such functions as negation, questions, topic-comment and emphasis, it can be difficult to sort out just what the role of the specific non-manual features might be in any given context. It is therefore necessary to examine a number of occurrences of the same sign and to monitor whether the same features are regularly present and what factors can affect their ocurrence. Lawson's account of multi-channel signs in BSL (Lawson, 1983) and the set of video examples presented in *Sign: An Introduction to British Sign Language* (Edinburgh BSL Project, 1983) are based on exactly this type of analysis. These accounts tend to extract what is seen as a single dominant non-manual feature, even though several such features may co-occur.

This dictionary contains a substantial number of multi-channel signs. Pages xxiv to xxvi of the *How to use the Dictionary* section provide a listing of the individual non-manual features employed and specific signs which exploit the particular non-manual features concerned. A close examination of these examples will demonstrate the regular co-occurrence of certain categories of non-manual feature. We can see, for example, that tongue protrusion is often accompanied by a puckering of the nose and that widening of the eyes often co-occurs with the opening wide of the mouth. Moreover, although we can regard these combinations as essentially arbitrary, it is possible, in some cases at least, to discern similarities of meaning amongst signs which share comparable non-manual features. Several signs, for example, are given glosses relating to the attitude of boredom: **bore one to tears** (sign 759)[113], **bore one to tears** (sign 779)[114] and **bored stiff** (sign 1137)[115] all involve quite different manual components, involving three different handshapes, yet they share the common non-manual components of tongue protrusion and nose-wrinkling. In fact, if we look at other signs which involve these same non-manual features, we can see that they frequently have some unpleasant or negative connotation as in **crummy** (sign 825)[116], **clapped out** (sign 812)[117], **cut down to size** (sign 57)[118] and **gullible** (sign 58)[119]. Similarly, the wide opening of the mouth and eyes frequently occurs in signs which have meanings associated with astonishment as in **amazed** (sign 725)[120] and **amazed** (sign 831)[121]: again the manual components of these signs are quite different. What we can begin to notice is a similarity between the non-manual components which function as obligatory, inherent elements of some words of the language and non-manual units of meaning which are optional. These units of meaning, or non-manual morphemes (see pp. 73–76), often have an adverbial or adjectival function and can be added to manual signs.* The sign **ease** (sign 1495)[122] makes use of a manual

110, 111, 112. [] Ȧ>ʌ Ȧ<ʌ ˣ

113. ∪ V̌ᴛʌ ˣ

114. ∪ ᵉⁱV̈ᴛ< ˣ

115. ◌ ʃ̇5̈<ʌ ⁿ⊥

116. ⊔ ᵉV̈ᴛ< ˣ // ⁱV̈ᴛ> , ⁱV̈ᴛ< ˣ ·

117. ⊔ V̈ᴛʌ

118. Ɠʊ> ₓ ʃAᴛʌ₉

119. Ḡᴛ> ʃAᴛʌ₉ (ⁿ⊥)ˣ

120. ∅ H̤ɑᴛ ₓ H̤ʊᴛ

121. ◌ V̈ᴛʌ V̈ᴛʌ

122. ⎡ Ḃʊ> Ḃʊ< ˣ

*These non-manual adverbials are discussed in more detail on pp. 73–76.

123. **saunter**

127. **could have happened**

128. **because**

component involving two Ḃ hands and a non-manual component which has the features 'head tilt to one side' and 'lips pushed slightly forward'. Exactly the same non-manual component functions as a non-manual adverbial meaning 'with ease' which can be added to verbs: this can be seen for example in the illustration of **saunter**[123]. Despite such links, many combinations cannot be predicted on the basis of meaning and should be viewed as unpredictable, arbitrary components of sign formation.

An examination of the multi-channel signs in this dictionary will reveal that they typically express functions associated with verbs, adverbials or adjectives. They very rarely function as nouns in the language. The original corpus of over two hundred examples examined by the Edinburgh BSL Project (1984) included no noun forms at all. Similarly, within this dictionary there are very few noun forms which have compulsory non-manual features. In most cases, the noun form appears to be derived from the verb. The noun **kite** (sign 126)[124] probably derives from **fly a kite** (sign 126)[125]: eye-gaze upwards is required. Similarly, **javelin** (sign 19)[126] requires eye-gaze following the movement of the hands as if watching the javelin in flight. This type of non-manual feature frequently relates to some copying or imitation of real life physical action: we would actually look up when flying a kite and watch the line of flight when throwing a javelin. However, what can be seen as the central type of multi-channel sign does not exhibit such links. Instead, combinations of non-manual features are exploited in an essentially arbitrary fashion.

It has been suggested in the past that multi-channel signs may constitute a specific grouping in the language because they are difficult to translate into English. However, this is to view BSL in its relationship to English, rather than in its own terms. Nevertheless, the experience of providing glosses for the multi-channel signs in this dictionary does suggest that it is very often difficult to encapsulate their full meaning within English glosses. This may be because, as suggested above, they often express verbal or adverbial meaning relating to states and attitudes. In other cases, the reason may be that their function is grammatically complex. The sign glossed as **could have happened**[127] is typically used either immediately before or after a verb: it suggests that the action of the verb could or might have happened, but did not actually occur. The sign glossed as **because**[128] functions in a way comparable to the English conjunction "because", but it would not always be appropriate to use this term in a translation of the sign. It is virtually impossible to provide an appropriate glossing of the signs tentatively glossed as **be**[129] and **exist** or **there**[130]. They are used with what has been termed an 'existential function' (Hughes,

123. Ø V̈ɒ⊥ ⊥ᶻ

124, 125. Ø Ā>⊥ A<⊥ ⊤˅˚·

126. ○ ✓A<∧ ⊥ᴰ [5]

127. B̄a> 5̿a⊥ # ˅ [B̂] ×

128. Ø 5⊤> 5⊤< ᴰ⊣3ᵡ

129. Ø Ȧ⊥∧ ˚3z·

130. Ø 5ɒ⊥ ᵒ

129. **be**

130. **there**

Brennan and Colville, 1984). Both are frequently translated into English by some form of the verb 'to be' and/or by locative words and phrases, such as 'there', 'over there', 'outside', 'up here'. Both signs seem to include an existential component, suggesting that something 'is' or 'exists', but a locative component is also implied. Thus multi-channel signs may be complex in terms of both their formational structure and their linguistic function.

Morphological structure

So far we have examined the individual words of BSL, the signs of the language, in terms of their formational structure. We have seen that signs can be broken down into smaller elements which have no meaning in themselves, but whose substitution can bring about a change of meaning. The extended little finger, a circular movement, a position on the chest, puffed out cheeks, narrowed eyes—all of these, and many more, are elements which are used to construct BSL signs. However, this picture of the sign as created of purely arbitrary units does not tell the whole story: signs can, in some cases, be broken down into smaller units which do have meaning and the relationship between the form of a sign and what it represents is not always purely arbitrary. In the next two sub-sections we will explore both of these aspects of sign construction.

Units of meaning

How can the sign be broken down into smaller units of meaning? We are certainly familiar with the notion that English words can be composed of several units of meaning. English words such as "anti-inflationary", "declamping", "computerisation", "multi-media", "post-binary", "inter-departmental", "brainstorm" and "mailshot" conform to our expectations that English words can be separated out

into units of meaning. What is more, we can recognise that such units may recur in other words: we know we can add "anti" to a whole host of forms, usually nouns and adjectives, as in "anti-vivisectionist", "anti-freeze", "anti-war" and "anti-ballistic". These units of meaning are known technically as *morphemes*. Some of these morphemes can stand by themselves and fuction as words in their own right: thus "freeze" and "war" in the above examples can function both as individual words and as units within a word.

Some BSL signs are like "freeze" and "war": they are single units of meaning, i.e. single morphemes, and they cannot be broken down into smaller units of meaning. However, other signs can be regarded as analysable into smaller meaningful components. All of the English examples given above involve some kind of linear sequencing: we can add bits on to the beginning and end of words to create other words. However, we are dealing with two different types of sequential process: the first is what is technically known as *affixation* and the second is *compounding*. In affixation, the affixes themselves, the bits that get added on, do function as morphemes in that they do have regular meanings. However, they are so-called *bound morphemes* in that they must always be stuck to something else: they cannot stand alone. So morphemes like "anti-", "de-", "-ary" and "-ish" are of this type. Some of these bound morphemes act as prefixes: we add them on at the beginning of a word. Others act as suffixes: we add them on to the ends of words. Compounding is somewhat different to affixation although it still exploits linear sequencing. In compounding, *free morphemes*, those that are capable of standing alone as words, are combined to produce new forms. Compounding in English produces forms such as "babysit", "mailshot", "busybody" and "brainstorm".

When we look carefully at some of the signs within the established lexicon—for example, those signs listed in the *BSL* section of this dictionary—we can see that some of them involve more than one morpheme. However, we can also note that sequential affixation plays a very limited role, if any, in the language. The major type of patterning which we can observe is compounding. Once again, there is a major difference between English and BSL: where English makes use only of linear, sequential compounds, BSL makes use of both sequential and simultaneous compounding. There is no particular reason why BSL does not exploit sequential affixation. It might be argued that the language favours simultaneous patterning over sequential, but this ignores the fact that considerable use is made of sequential compounding. There are some candidates for affixation:

132. exaggerate |think+add|

133. rumour |say+talk|

these are primarily certain of the negative markers discussed under negation in the grammar section (pp. 110–130). However, as we shall see, even these seem somewhat dubious as true affixes in that, in all cases, they seem able to occur in isolation as free morphemes.

Sequential compounding

Sequential compounding involves the combining of two separate free morphemes to create a word with a different meaning. However, in true compounds, we do not simply produce these two components as if they were separate words occurring in a specific order. Rather, a number of predictable formational changes can be specified. Such modification of the components of compounds is familiar from English compounds where we see different patterning of stress between the free forms in isolation and their occurrence within a compound. In BSL sequential compounds, we can note the following kinds of change: the movement in the first part tends to be shortened or omitted; the second part tends to have added stress; if the second part makes use of the non-dominant hand as a base, this tends to 'take up its position' during the production of the first part of the compound; the transition between the two parts ends be more fluid and smooth than between two separate words; the compound sign tends to have a similar duration to a simple sign, rather than the duration of two separate words.*

Many BSL compounds have a first component with a head or face tab: a substantial number have **think, see** or **say** as the first element. When these signs occur in isolation, they tend to have a movement away from the signer. However, in most compound forms this movement is either greatly reduced or omitted completely. In **recommend** (sign 504) [131], which can be seen as deriving from **think + suggest**, the away movement of **think** is absent and the index finger merely touches the forehead. The same can be said of the first components in **exaggerate** |**think+add**| [132], **rumour** |**say+talk**| [133], and **believe** |**think+true**| (sign 514) [134]. In **believe**, the hand begins the downward movement required in the second part of the sign immediately after contact is made with the forehead. (As indicated earlier, some linguists have recently developed a more sequential account of sign production. According to such accounts, the process just explained would be seen as deletion of the movement segment of the first sign. See the work of Liddell and Johnson, cited in the bibliography, and discussion in Wilbur, 1989.)

In many compounds we can note that the second sign of a compound is given additional stress. This may involve an increased muscular tension and/or a final hold that is longer than usual. Within ASL compounds, it seems that where repetition occurs in the second sign, this is frequently omitted (see Klima and Bellugi, 1979, p. 216). While this can

---

131. ∩ G̈ᴛ∧ $^{×}$ // ∅ Bɑ⊥ ˌ Bɑ⊥ $^{⊥}$

132. ▽ Gᴛ∧ $^{×}$ // B̄ᴛ> B̈<⊥ ^{ᴠ}

133. ▽ G<∧ $^{×}$ // ∅ B̄̄>∧ B̄<∧ $^{(‡ [ɓ]·)}$

134. ∩ G̈<∧ $^{× ᴠ [ʙ]}$ // B̄ɑ> B<⊥ $^{ᴠ ×}$

*See Klima and Bellugi (1979) for discussion of these patterns in ASL; Brennan (1990a and b) for discussion of BSL compounds; and Liddell (1984) for alternative accounts of compounding processes.

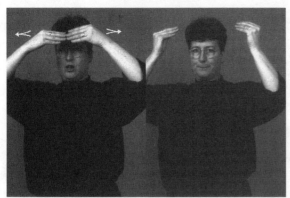

141. **slipped my mind**

happen in some BSL compounds, the more normal pattern seems to be that the repetition is retained but the sign is held longer in space. This is the case, for example, in **remember |think+value|** (sign 513) [135], **remember |think+keep|** (sign 513, note*) [136] and **tend |see+value|** (sign 333) [137]. Some signs require the repetition to be retained in the second sign, because this is an inflected form of the sign. The second part of **exaggerate** is not simply **add**, but **keep on adding**: the sign is inflected for aspect (see *Grammar* section, pp. 104–108). Similarly, the second part of **rumour** is not simply **talk**, but **many people talking incessantly**: here the repetition is required to give the compound its meaning. A substantial number of compounds use manual tab signs in second position. In these cases, the left hand is almost always brought into readiness at the onset of the production of the compound. This can be seen in the illustrations of **exaggerate** (p. 36 [132]) and **rumour** (p. 36 [133]). This anticipation on the part of the left hand means that there is no delay in the production of the second part of the compound. The anticipation works along with the reduction in movement of the first sign to promote a fluidity of transition between the two signs.

A further anticipatory characteristic can be found in the tendency of the hand configuration of the first part to adapt towards the handshape of the second part. The first part in **rumour** is glossed as **say** and is transcribed as being pro-

duced with a **G** handshape. However, if we look at the illustration we can see that this is not the typical production of the **G** handshape. Instead of being closed into a fist, the three fingers and thumb are bunched together. This is in anticipation of the **B̄** handshape which is required in the second part of the compound. In some cases, a completely different handshape may be used. The handshape **Ÿ** rarely occurs except in compound sign forms. The signs **check** (sign 961) [138] and **experiment** (sign 962) [139] seem to derive from **see+perhaps**. Rather than using the simple **G** handshape in the first component, the **Ÿ** handshape anticipates the **Y** dez that is required in the second part of the compound. The result is a form which combines features of the two different hand configurations.

A further characteristic which encourages fluidity in the transition between the two elements of the compound is that where the first part begins at head level, the second part (if it is normally produced in neutral space) is given a heightened position. This can be seen in the production of the **add** component of **exaggerate**.

Work on sign duration suggests that despite the fact that two signs are brought together in a compound, the kinds of anticipatory and reduction processes described above mean that the overall time taken to produce the compound sign is shorter than required for the production of the two signs separately within a phrase (see, for example, Klima and Bellugi, 1979).

There is some evidence that there may be a limit on the number of components within sequential compounds. In theory, it would be possible to string together more than two parts: in practice, this rarely occurs, except where the third element is simultaneous (see below). Moreover, there is some tendency for compounds to so reduce the first component that it is eventually lost. We have, in effect, a process of compounding which allows the language to expand, but also a contrary process which militates against retaining unnecessary, redundant information. We can thus see a sign such as **slipped my mind** being produced either as in entry 508 [140] with the first component **mind** articulated at the head or as in the illustration above [141] where the **disappear**

135. ∩ G̈<ʌ $^{x\ \vee}_{\perp}$ // B̄ɑ> B̈ɒ⊥ ^{x} ·

136. ∩ G̈<ʌ $^{x\ \vee}_{\perp}$ // Āɑ> Aɒ⊥ ^{x} ·

137. ⊔ G<ʌ $^{x\ \perp}_{\vee}$ // B̄ɑ> B̈ɒ⊥ ^{x} ·

138. ⊔ ᵉŸ<ʌ $^{x\ \perp\ [\vee]}_{\vee\ \#}$ // B̄ɑ> Y<⊥ $^{o}_{\omega}$ ·

139. ⊔ ᵉŸ<ʌ $^{o}_{\perp\ [\vee]}_{N\ \#}$ $\left(^{o}_{\omega}·\right)$ $_{\perp}$

140. ∩ G̈<ʌ ^{x} // ∅ B̄ɑ⊥ ⊚ B̄ɑ⊥ $^{÷\ [ᴮ̃ᴮ̃]}_{x\ \#}$

141. ∩ B̄>⊥ $_{\mid x}$ B̄<⊥ $^{÷\ [ᴮ̃ᴮ̃]}_{\#}$

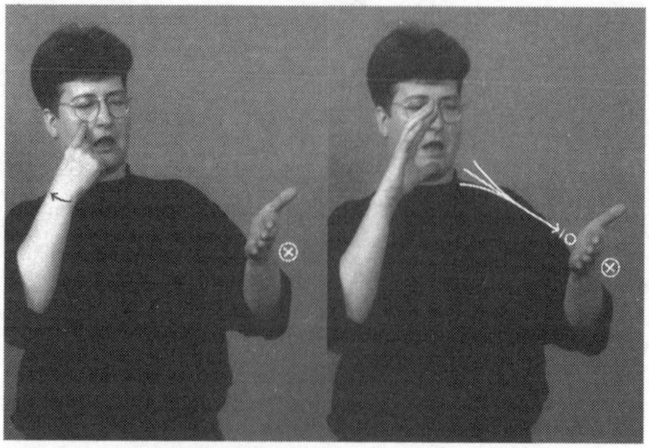

142. **catch sight of | see+catch |**

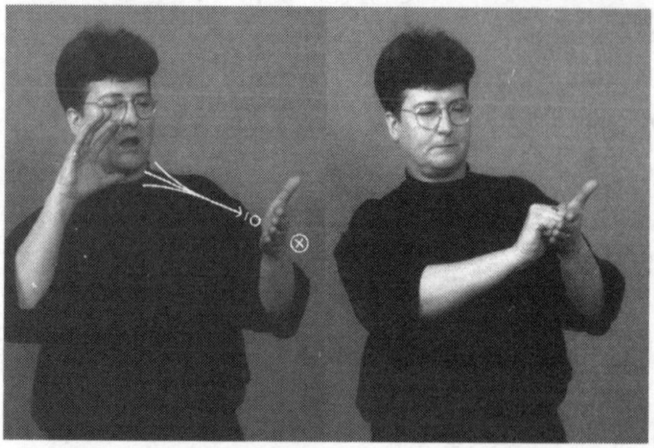

143. **catch sight of | see+catch |**

component is raised to head level and the first component is omitted entirely. A similar reduction can be seen in **catch sight of | see+catch |** which may be produced with the first component **see** [142] in first position or with the right **5** hand at eye level, ready to produce the second part of the compound [143].

Simultaneous compounding

Much of the research on compounds in sign languages has focused on sequential compounding. However, research on BSL (Brennan, 1990a and b) suggests that there is a second kind of compounding which plays an important part in the language. Like sequential compounding, simultaneous compounding brings together two independent signs that can occur as signs in their own right. However, because the signer has two hands, rather than having to produce these two signs sequentially, one after the other, the signer can express one element with one hand and the second element with the other hand. Of course, this inevitably means that there are changes to the forms of the component signs. However, as we have already seen, modification of the production of the component signs is also typical of sequential compounding. It would seem on the evidence available at the moment, that simultaneous compounding is unique to signed language: it has not been found in spoken language. The classic example of a simultaneous compound is the sign **Minicom** (sign 1019) [144]. A Minicom is a device which allows typed messages to be transmitted along a telephone line. The user fits the telephone receiver into a position on top of a keyboard. Messages are then typed and received via a digital display. The simultaneous compound sign which has developed to express this meaning combines two signs, **type** (sign 1043) [145] and **telephone** (sign 944) [146]. We can notice several points about the form of this compound. It is constructed as a manual tab sign: the non-dominant hand stays still while the dominant hand acts in relation to it; the non-dominant (here the left) hand has to articulate a sign, **telephone**, normally produced by the dominant (here the right) hand; the sign **telephone** is removed from its normal tab position beside the cheek; the sign **type**, normally a two-handed form is produced by one hand; the movement of the sign **type** is reduced (in respect to one of its possible productions, see entry 1043, note †) [147].

If we look at the signs **toss and turn | flat surface+legs |** [148] and **barber | person+ cut |** [149], we can see similarities in form. Both signs are manual tab signs. The right hand performs the action while the left hand stays still. Virtually all of the signs that can be viewed as simultaneous compounds can be characterised as manual tab signs: thus **underground train** (p. 31 [105]), **spacecraft** (sign

---

142. ⊔ GTʌ × // B̄T> ׀ 5⊥ʌ ⊥̇ > < # ×

143. B̄T> ׀ 5⊥ʌ ⊥̇ > < # [A] ×

144. Y̲ɑ⊥ 5ɑ⊥

145. Ø 5ɑ⊥ ׀ 5ɑ⊥

146. ⊃ ᵃYT< ×

147. Ø 5ɑ⊥ ׀ 5ɑ⊥ ᴺᴺ·

148. B̄a⊥ Vɑ⊥ (aɑ)· ×

149. G>ʌ VT< ʌ × ʌ # [H]·

144. **Minicom**

145. **toss and turn**

149. **barber**

405)[150], **mount** (sign 796)[151] and **trampoline** (sign 801)[152] are all manual tab signs. Perhaps more importantly, they are also classifier forms. As we shall see, classifiers are morphemes which categorise referents according to such features as size and shape and how humans handle objects (see further, pp. 46–67). Classifiers are expressed in BSL by means of specific handshapes which are said to have 'generalised' meanings: the **B** hand may represent flat surfaces, the **V** hand legs and the **G** hand long narrow objects. Thus **underground train** derives from | **curved surface+long narrow object** | ; **missile** from | **flat surface+long narrow object** | ; **mount** from | **long narrow object+legs** | and **trampoline** from | **flat surface+legs** |. An examination of the illustrations in the classifier table presented on pp. 53–67 reveals a number of examples of these simultaneous compound forms, including **pestle** (p. 53[226]), **carve** (p. 53[227]), **magnifying glass** (p. 53[228]), **drunk** (p. 60[247]), **clothes peg** (p. 60[249]) and **tea bag** (p. 62[253]).

Sequential-simultaneous compounds

The third, rather surprising, type of compounding process in BSL combines the two types of process described above. In the following examples, we have a sequential compound in which the second element can itself be viewed as a simultaneous compound: we thus have three units of meaning within the single sign. **Evidence** (sign 330)[153] is made up of | **see+paper+indicate** | ; **report** (sign 349)[154] is made up of | **say+paper+indicate** |. In virtually all of the exam-

ples cited in the literature (e.g. Brennan, 1990a), the second simultaneous compound makes use of the flat surface form **B**, usually interpreted as 'paper'. While such forms do seem to be limited in the language, their existence shows the inherent potential available for the creation of new forms (see further, pp. 86–91).

Meanings and compounds

There has been some discussion amongst researchers as to whether we should regard simultaneous compounds (whether occurring by themselves or as the second element in sequential-simultaneous forms) as full compounds. The concern centres around the generalised meaning of the individual morphemes concerned. We do not know, for example, what the more specific meaning of the flat surface morpheme **B** is until it occurs in a particular compound. Thus it may mean 'ground' (as in **drunk** | **bent legs+flat surface** |), 'paper' (as in **magnifying glass** | **hold narrow handle+flat surface** | , 'canvas sheet' (as in **trampoline** | **legs+flat surface** |), or 'bed' (as in **toss and turn** | **flat surface+legs** |). While this remains a controversial matter, it is worth noting that this type of 're-interpretation in context' is part of the process of understanding many lexical forms, both in BSL and in English. If we look at the initial components 'black' and 'red' in the following English examples, we can see that it is unhelpful to rely on a single interpretation of these words in order to understand their role in these combined forms. In

150. B꜌> ₓ G<ʌ₉ ^

151. Ḡ>⊥ ᵢ V̈<⊥ ᵨ°<

152. B̄ɑ> ₓ V̈꜌⊥ ^ ˙

153. ⊔ G⊤ʌ ˣ⊥ᵥ // B̄ɑ⊥ Bɑ⊥ ᵛˣ

154. ꜌ G⊤ʌ ˣᵛ[ᴮ]⊥□ // B̄ɑ> Bɑ⊥ ᵀˣ⊤

"blackbird", "black sheep", "black market", "red eye" (a Canadian drink of beer and tomato juice), "redneck", "red admiral" and "redleg", we have to understand the specialised meaning of the term as a whole, rather than relying on a literal interpretation of the component parts. In several of these examples, the colour terms do not refer literally to colours. We talk about a female "blackbird", even though it is brown in colour; similarly, a person who is labelled a "redneck" or a "redleg" (both disparaging terms) does not necessarily exhibit such physical features as a red neck or red legs. This leads us to a particularly important fact concerning compounds: the meanings of compound forms are not necessarily directly predictable from their component parts.

It may be useful to think of two types of compound forms. In many cases, we have what can be seen as literal combinations: these include such forms as "bus station", "bedroom" and "wedding dress" in English and **earache** |**ear+sore**| (sign 343)[155], **simultaneous** |**same+time**| (sign 425)[156], **sign language** |**sign+language**| (sign 1068)[157] and **bank book** |**bank+book**| (sign 60)[158] in BSL. In all of these cases, the meaning is directly predictable from the component parts. In other cases, the meanings cannot be determined solely on the basis of the internal components (even though we may be able to appreciate the motivation for these forms). These are sometimes called true compounds. BSL examples include **recommend** |**think+suggest**| (sign 504)[158], **slipped my mind** |**think+disappear**| (p. 37[141]), **bear in mind** |**think+value**| (p. 37[135]), **flatter** |**person+stroke**| (p. 89[419]) and **emphasise** |**person+hit frequently**| (p. 89[416]). These forms function in a similar way to the English examples "henpecked", "headstrong", "easy-going", "free-thinker" and "jailbird". We may be so familiar with such examples that it is hard to realise that they are not entirely predictable in meaning.

It is also worth noting that not everything that looks like a compound necessarily is one. Compounds always involve the combining of two (or more) units of meaning which are themselves capable of occurring as independent words. If we cannot isolate such units of meaning at all, then it is un-

likely that we are dealing with a compound. The signs **in case** (sign 359)[159] and **can't be bothered** (sign 361)[160] look formationally rather like compounds. The transcription divides the sign into two parts and there are two separate tabs, in each case at the chin in the first part of the sign and below the left shoulder in the second part of the sign. The reason we cannot regard these forms as compounds is that it is not possible to ascribe any separate meaning to the two parts of the sign. Instead, we should probably treat these signs as having comparable structure to the English words "control" and "infer". These words have two syllables, but, at least in modern English, only one morpheme: thus English does not have independent words "fer" or "trol". Similarly we cannot give any separate meaning to the form in which the **5** hand is placed below the shoulder (in the second part of **in case**) or the index finger contacts the chin (as in the first parts of **in case** and **can't be bothered**).

In this section we have focused on compounds within the established lexicon. Compounding is also a highly productive process for expanding the vocabulary of the language (see p. 89).

Other multi-morphemic forms

This section has been concerned with analysing signs into smaller units of meaning. As we shall see in later sections, there are other types of multi-morpheme forms. These are created 'as required' within what is termed here the *productive lexicon*. Because this plays such an important part in the language, it is discussed in considerable detail in its own section (see pp. 45–86).

It is also worth noting that so far we have only been discussing what might be termed *lexical* morphemes and have ignored the operation of units of meaning which have a more grammatical function: these are sometimes known as *inflectional* morphemes. Grammatical categories such as aspect and agreement may be expressed by inflectional morphemes. The component **keep on adding** which occurred as the second element of **exaggerate** (p. 36[132]) can be seen as an inflected form expressing one possible option of aspect. Such forms are elaborated in the third major section of this introduction relating to the grammar of BSL.

---

155. ꓷ ᴳ<ʌ ˣ ∥∥ Ø 5ᴛ< ⁿ·

156. Ø ᴳᴕ⊥ ┊ ᴳᴕ⊥ ˣ̊ˣ̊ ∥∥ ꝋ̄ ᴳᴕ< ˣ

157. Ø 5>⊥ ┊ 5<⊥ ⊥ɴ· ∥∥ ʙᴛ> ˣ ʙᴛ<ꜞ >ˣ

158. ʙ̄ᴕ⊥ ᴀᴛ< ᵛˣ ∥∥ Ø ʙ>⊥ ɪˣ ʙ<⊥ ᵃ

159. ∪ ᴳ<ʌ ˣ ∥∥ >⌐ 5ᴛ< ˣ

160. ∪ ᴳ<ʌ ˣ̊ᵥ ∥∥ >⌐ ᴳᴕʌ ˣ

Relationships between form and meaning

"Arbitrariness is...atypical of the BSL lexicon." (Brennan, 1990a, p. 35) This claim will certainly seem rather extraordinary to linguists who concur with the general and traditional view that "arbitrariness is typical of the lexicon." (Anderson, 1985, p.4) However, as suggested earlier, the claim does accord with a general expectation on the part of non-signers and perhaps also signers. This would not in itself, of course, validate the claim. In this sub-section, this claim is explored in more detail and different types of relationship between the form of a sign and what it means are suggested.

We have already discussed the words of BSL, the signs of the language, in terms of the arbitrary components of which they are composed. In the section headed *Formational structure* (p. 17) it was claimed that each sign language extracts from the visual-gestural medium different formational components such as handshapes, positions and movements to create its own signs. There is plenty of evidence that different sign languages have different inventories of such building blocks, although there is also some evidence that certain components regularly occur across sign languages: this is true for example of the unmarked handshapes mentioned on pp. 20–21.

If we think of the words of English, we can recognise that for the most part they are composed of arbitrary elements. Moreover, the word taken as a whole stands in an arbitrary relationship to what it represents. Indeed arbitrariness has been presented as a defining property of human language. * Part of the reason for setting considerable store by the notion of arbitrariness is that it has been seen as promoting "semiotic versatility and adaptability of the system" (Lyons, 1977, vol. 1, p.71) A rather cruder way of putting this would be to suggest that non-arbitrary forms may drag the language down and make it less flexible and capable of expansion. There are several different types of contrast which may be used when discussing form-meaning relationships. Hockett (1958), for example, stressed the contrast between *iconic* forms and *arbitrary* forms. If a linguistic signal could be regarded as geometrically similar to what it stood for, then it was regarded as iconic: everything else was arbitrary. The terms *iconic* and *iconicity* are used frequently in the

sign language literature. Perhaps the most useful definition that has emerged (based on the discussion in Boyes-Braem, 1986) is that iconicity always involves some perceivable link between form and meaning. However, the nature and type of link may vary: there may be several different ways in which the forms of words can be linked with their meanings. Some discussions of iconicity in signed language seem to imply that iconicity in sign languages usually involves some kind of pictorial relationship: the sign is somehow an icon or picture of the meaning. Because of this association with 'pictorial', it may be better to use the term *iconic* for one specific type of principled link between form and meaning (what will be termed below the relationship of resemblance) and to use the term *motivated*, originally used by Saussure, to refer to all form-meaning relationships which are non-arbitrary.

Another way of thinking about the motivated-arbitrary contrast is to say that when we look at the majority of BSL signs we can see some underlying motivation for the way they are made: we can see, in part at least, the reason why the sign has developed this particular shape or formational structure. In contrast, if we look at the majority of English words we can see no such motivation. If we pull words out of the air at random—"pig", "computer", "delicious", "remote", "yet"— we can see that they are purely arbitrary. The word "pig" does not sound like a pig; the word "computer" does not sound like a computer. Of course, English does have some motivated forms: the most frequently quoted examples make use of onomatopoeia and sound symbolism. Onomatopoeic words are said to be imitative: the sound of the word imitates what it means, as in "hiss" or "buzz". In sound symbolism, particular sounds or sound sequences are said to symbolise their meanings: the sound sequence 'sl' is said to be symbolic of unpleasantness in the English words "slimy", "slither" and "sloth".

Both of these notions can help us in looking at BSL words. There are signs which imitate what they represent and there are signs which somehow symbolise what they represent. Let us look firstly, however, at some signs which do seem to be purely arbitrary. If we look at the signs **exist** (p. 34[130]), **could have happened** (p. 34[127]), **can** (sign 477)[161] and **address** (sign 964)[162], it is hard to see any particular motivation underlying the forms of the signs. There

161. ○ Ḡ⊤∧ ⊥[ɑ̂] ∨ #

162. [] ʊ⊤< ○ x̃ˑ

*See Saussure (1916), Hockett (1958) and the discussion in Lyons (1977, vol. 1, p. 71).

164. **punk hairstyle**

167. **understand (grasp)**

are a considerable number of such signs in the language, although it is suggested here that they form a minority of BSL signs. However, if we look at the signs **cycle** (p. 24[38]), **elephant** (sign 1668)[163], **punk hairstyle**[164], **snooker** (sign 70)[165] **bake** (sign 99)[166], **understand (grasp)**[167], **love** (sign 235)[168] **criticise** (sign 916)[169], **irritable** (sign 1185)[170], **suspicious** (p. 24[39]) and **theory**[171], we gain a rather different impression about the relationship between signs and their meanings. It is suggested here that, in all of these cases, there is a motivated link between the form of the sign and what it means. This may be relatively unsurprising in signs which represent objects, but perhaps more surprising in signs which express emotions, and abstract concepts. The suggestion here is that while all of these signs are non-arbitrary, and therefore motivated, they exhibit different types of form–meaning relationship.

The first type of relationship between form and meaning is that of *resemblance*. The form of the sign in some way re-

sembles or looks like what it means: this is what is termed here an *iconic relationship*. The resemblance can take several different forms. The sign may in some way copy the physical features of what it represents. Thus the form might present an outline of the object as in **cheque** (sign 953)[172] and **window** (sign 441)[173]; it may depict the overall shape of the object as in **t.v. aerial** (p. 63[257]) and **tree** (sign 1026)[174]; it may extract some significant physical feature such as the trunk of an elephant or the tail of a rat and allow this to stand for the whole object as in **elephant**[163] and **rat** (sign 571)[175]. The sign may resemble what it means by imitating the action referred to in the sign: the hands imitate the action of the legs in **cycle** (p.24[38]), the action of knitting needles in **knitting** (sign 376)[176] and the action of wings in **butterfly** (sign 1659)[177]. Some signs involve more than one of these copying devices: **knitting** makes use of two G handshapes which indicate the size and shape of needles as well as imitating the action involved; **butterfly** gives us some idea of

163. Ꝋ C<ʌ $^{\overset{\circ}{\overset{v}{\underset{v}{\perp}}\overset{@}{\perp}}}$

164. ◌̄ E<ʌ $^{\overset{\tau\;[5]}{\underset{\Box}{\times}}}$

165. Ḃ℧< A℧⊥ᵩ $^{\overset{\circ}{\overset{v@}{v}}}$

166. ∅ Aᴛʌ Aᴛʌ $^{\overset{\circ}{\vphantom{x}}\!{\scriptstyle\circ\!\!\!\times}}$

167. ∩ ⏙5⊥ʌ $^{\overset{\circ}{\underset{\#}{\perp}}[ʌ]}$

168. ⌐ Ȧ⊥ʌ Ȧ⊥ʌ $^{\overset{\overset{\wedge}{\times}}{\underset{v}{\perp}}}$

169. ∅ I>ʌ , I<ʌ $^{\overset{@\sim\cdot}{\underset{v}{\tau}}}$

170. [] ⏙5ᴛ< $^{\overset{\overset{\wedge}{\cdot}}{\underset{\wedge}{\times}}}$

171. ∪ 5℧< $^{\overset{\underset{\bar{\scriptscriptstyle\Xi}}{\circ}\cdot}{}}$

172. ∅ Y℧> Y℧< $^{\div}$

173. ∅ G⊥ʌ , G⊥ʌ $^{\overset{\div\binom{\eta}{\underset{v}{\perp}}℧<}{}}$

174. B̄℧> ₓ ∫5<ʌ $^{\overset{\circ}{\underset{z}{\omega}}\cdot}$

175. ∅ G̈<⊥ $^{\binom{\eta}{\perp}\cdot}$

176. Ḡ℧> ₓ G℧⊥ᵩ $^{\overset{\scriptscriptstyle\Xi\cdot}{\times}}$

177. ∅ Ḃᴛ> ₓ Ḃᴛ< $^{\binom{\overset{\circ}{m}\cdot}{\wedge}}$

169. **criticise**   171. **theory**

the size and shape of the wings as well as the actions they make. Many signs do not copy the size and shape of the object itself, but instead copy how humans interact with the particular object. In particular, such signs copy how we handle objects. An **A** hand may indicate an object we would· grip with the clenched fist, as in **briefcase** (sign 15)[178]; an **F** handshape can indicate a small object which we would hold between the index finger and thumb as in **teabag** (p. 62[253]). A glance through the **A** chapter of the *BSL* section of this dictionary will reveal that a significant proportion of entries in this section, approximately thirty per cent, derive from this imitation of a handling action. Such examples may be seen as deriving from productive classifier forms. *

The second type of relationship suggested here is that of *conventional association*: certain elements of sign structure are associated with particular kinds of meaning. These associations are specific to the language and are not necessarily found in other languages. In BSL, we can note two major handshapes and two major locations which carry such associative links. The **A** handshape is associated with meanings

related to 'goodness': it is used for pleasing or positive actions, attitudes and attributes in signs such as **good** (sign 164)[179], **praise** (sign 225)[180], **best** (p. 29[89]) and **fantastic** (p. 30[93]). In contrast, the **I** handshape (and the closely related **ï**) is associated with meanings related to 'badness' and is used for negative meanings such as **bad** (sign 904)[181], **appalling** (sign 914)[182], **quarrel** (p. 11[2]) and **criticise**[169]. Almost all of the entries in the **I** and **ï** sections of this Dictionary exhibit this association. The few which do not are mainly derived from fingerspelling. There is one example of a tracing usage, but the strength of the negative association probably militates against other uses of this handshape. It is worth stressing that this link is a convention within BSL: in ASL, for example, the **I** handshape does not carry such negative associations. Thus an ASL sign closely related in form to the BSL sign **suspicious** (sign 919)[184]can be glossed as **idea** or **concept**: although both signs use the **I** handshape, there is no hint of any negative association in the ASL sign. The head location, particularly the forehead, is associated in BSL with meanings related to thought and cognitive processes generally. The sign **suspicious** thus makes use of two conventional links: the 'bad' **I** handshape and the link between the forehead and thought (in this case, negative or suspicious thought). It is extremely rare to find examples of BSL signs relating in any way to cognition which do not use the head-thought association. Thus the signs **consider** (sign 313)[184], **idea** (sign 314)[185] **assume** (sign 510)[186] and **theory** (p. 42[171]) all make use of the forehead location. A further conventional association exploited in BSL is that between the chest and emotions. Many signs relating to feelings and emotions have a chest tab. Examples include **feel** (sign 965)[187], **envious** (sign 1184)[188], **irritable** (p. 42[170]) and **anger** (sign 1195)[189]. All of these conventional associations appear to remain productive in the language:

178. Ø A<v $\overset{\circ}{\underset{v}{\cdot}}$

179. Ø A<⊥ $\overset{\circ}{\underset{⊥}{\cdot}}$

180. Ø Ȧ>⊥ , Ȧ<⊥ $\overset{⊥ ∾ \cdot}{v}$

181. Ø I<∧ $\overset{⊥}{v}$

182. Ø I>∧ I<∧ $\overset{\circ \cdot}{⊥ \cdot}$

183. ∩ ïт∧ $\overset{@ \cdot}{v}$

184. ∩ Gт∧ $\overset{\overset{\circ}{@}}{\underset{v}{<}}$

185. ∩ Gт∧ $^{× ⊥}$

186. ∩ Ḡ<∧ $\overset{\overset{\circ}{@}}{\underset{v}{⊥}}$

187. ⌐K ४т< $\overset{\circ \cdot}{\underset{×}{×}}$

188. [] 5̈т< $\overset{>}{×}$

189. [] 5̈т> 5̈т< $\overset{∧ ɑ}{\underset{∧}{×}}$

*See further p. 47.

we can expect that new signs will exploit such links (see further pp. 85–86).

The third type of form-meaning relationship suggested here is that of *transference*. This occurs in what have been described as *metaphor-based* signs (Brennan, 1990a and b and Wilbur, 1987). While this notion is discussed further (see pp. 68–73) within the context of the productive lexicon, such forms do also seem to be built into the established lexicon. There is frequently a strong intuition amongst signers that even signs with highly abstract referents show some link between form and meaning. Work on metaphor in spoken language has demonstrated that metaphor permeates our everday language: it is so much a part of our language usage, that we do not need to think about it. We only do so when a different or unusual metaphor is exploited. Several major pieces of work by Lakoff and associates (see Lakoff references in the bibliography) have demonstrated that one of the major categories of metaphor used in spoken language is spatial metaphor. It is suggested here that spatial metaphor is also used in signed language, but here it is actually realised through gestural activity occurring in space. Spatial metaphor in signed language therefore has an increased potential.

"The essence of metaphor is understanding one kind of thing in terms of another." (Lakoff and Johnson, 1980, p. 5) This is also the case in relation to understanding how metaphor works in BSL. The concept of 'doubt' or 'uncertainty' is presented in terms of the 'wavering' of the hands: the mental uncertainty or fluctuation is re-presented in spatial terms as a physical fluctuation. Thus **unsure** (sign 982)[190] involves a repeated up and down twisting movement of the **5** hand. This is almost identical to the gesture used by hearing people, which could be given the English translation of "so-so" or "dubious". The sign **doubt** (sign 1368)[191] involves an alternating up and down movement of the two **B** hands: the alternation of the hands is a physical re-presentation of the alternation in the mind. Interestingly, the head tilt which usually accompanies the manual component can also be viewed in this way. If the form of the signs relating to 'uncertainty' and 'doubt' were purely arbitrary, then we might just as well expect symmetrical, firm, direct movements to express this type of meaning. Not only is this not

193. **negotiate**

the case for BSL, but a perusal of sign books and dictionaries of other sign languages suggests that this is not the case for them either. The ASL signs **maybe** and **doubtful**, for example, both involve the same alternation as the BSL signs (see Stokoe et al., 1976, p. 144). It is not claimed here that all sign languages will exploit exactly the same metaphors, although there does seem to be some commonality of patterning which would be worth exploring.

One of the most helpful ways of clueing into the use of metaphors in BSL is to keep in mind the 'as if' relationship. The language operates, for example, as if ideas and achievements could be grasped in **understand** (grasp) (p. 42[167]); as if thought were a set of lines as in **theory** (p. 42[171]); as if interaction involved a physical to-ing and fro-ing as in **communication** (sign 1685, part two)[192] and as if negotiation actually involved a physical interchanging of position as in **negotiate**[193]. Thus, **understand** (grasp) is produced by performing a grasping action at the head: a two-handed form may be used which involves the hands, slowly and alternately, performing grasping actions to suggest 'gradually getting hold of ideas'. English happens to use very similar metaphors: "Now I've grasped what you mean", "Have you got hold of that idea?" English also happens to exploit the 'lines' metaphor where thought is presented in terms of a set of lines: "Do you follow my line of thought?" In BSL, this 'lines' metaphor can be seen in the sign **theory**. The sign **mull over**[194] uses an almost identical manual component, but produced more slowly and accompanied by a pushing

190. Ø 5ᴅ⊥ ⁰ᵚ·

191. Ø Bɑ⊥ Bɑ⊥ ᶺᶺ·

192. Ø Ğ>ᴧ ˌ Ğ<ᴧ ᴵᴺ·

193. Ø 5ɑ> 5ɑ< ᴵᴺ·

194. ∩ 5ᴅ> 5ᴅ< ᵚᴺ·

195. porcupine

196. people filing

197. smell

forward of the lips and a head tilt.

While this account of a metaphorical relationship remains somewhat controversial, it does provide a further explanation of the intuition that the majority of signs in BSL are in some sense motivated. Moreover, this metaphorical potential can be exploited within the productive lexicon and can be used to expand the lexical resources of the language (see pp. 85–86 and pp. 86–91).

In thinking about the relationship between form and meaning in BSL, it is helpful to avoid what Boyes-Braem has described as "..a confusion between characteristics of the referent (abstract, concrete, etc.) and the relationship between the form of the sign and its referent..." (Boyes-Braem, 1986, p. 68) We are dealing then with two different types of contrast: the contrast between concrete and abstract in respect of referents and the contrast between motivated and arbitrary in respect of form-meaning relationships. Although concrete referents, such as objects, are often expressed by motivated signs, we cannot make the simple assumption that this will always be the case. Nor can we assume that abstract referents, such as 'doubt' and 'truth' will always be expressed by non-motivated, arbitrary forms. The inter-relationships between these two sets of contrasts are far more complex.

The meanings 'porcupine' and 'people filing' can be seen as having concrete referents; 'smell' can be regarded as technically concrete in that it can be perceived by the senses, while 'thought' is clearly abstract. The BSL signs which express these meanings are all motivated, but in different ways, even though they all share the physical feature of the use of the **5** hand: **porcupine**[195] uses the spread fingers to resemble the spines of a porcupine; **people filing**[196] uses the upright fingers to resemble or depict a number of upright persons (see also discussion on p.49); both **smell**[197] and **theory** (p. 42[171]) operate as if smell and thought could be seen as lines. The use of such relationships, even for abstract meanings, is one of the major differences between the patterning of BSL and English.

The productive or the DIY lexicon

Individuals learning BSL are often bemused by the fact that, despite becoming familiar with hundreds, even thousands of individual BSL signs, they find it extremely difficult to understand real life BSL interactions. As with learning any other language, this may be because they know some vocabulary, but very little of the grammar of the language. However, a major problem is that very often learners have been introduced to only one kind of vocabulary: what has sometimes been called the *frozen lexicon* . The term *frozen* suggests that items within this word-list are completely fixed in form. Over time, they have become hardened into specific signs which are now unchanging. Here, because the term *frozen* seems rather too strong in its connotations of complete preservation and lack of change, the term *established* has been used instead. We can think of these established words as ' ready made', 'off the shelf' lexical items. They are already in existence: the signer simply

195. ⴾ Gↄ> ₓ A⊥<ᵩ ᚾ [5]
                        ˄
                      ₓ
                      □

196. ∅ 5>ᴧ 5<ᴧᵩ (°)
                    (⊥ ·)
                    (₂)

197. ⊔ 5ↄ< ᵒ·
            ₸

has to pluck them from her/his mental lexicon and place them in appropriate lexical contexts. These are the kind of signs we have been describing in the previous pages under the heading of the *established lexicon*.

However, there is another major category of BSL vocabulary which the native signer manipulates with consummate ease and which the learner must clue into if s/he is ever to make full sense of the language. This is what has been called the *productive* lexicon. The term *productive* focuses on the creative dimension of this type of lexical usage. The signer, in a sense, creates words as they are needed and in doing so may produce combinations which have never actually been used before, but which are fully understandable and meaningful in context. The signer is able to draw upon enormous resources in order to activate this creative process. In any given sample of BSL usage, there is likely to be a significant percentage of signs which have been created or re-created, on the spot, as required. Some types of discourse, such as story-telling and jokes, are likely to have a preponderance of this type of vocabulary. Of course, this does not mean that the signer simply creates signs in a totally idiosyncratic way. Rather the signer exploits the potential of the lexical resources available in a systematic way.

We are dealing, in effect, with a kind of *do-it-yourself* or *DIY* lexicon. All DIY experts know that to produce a finished item you must firstly have the appropriate components and secondly the know-how to put them together. In this section, we explore the nature of the resources available for the active creation of words. The BSL DIY expert has available a large set of meaningful units, i.e. morphemes of different types. These units of meaning, which include handshape, location and movement morphemes, as well as non-manual morphemes, are assembled by the signer to create the particular meaning required.

Classifiers

The first category of meaningful components which we shall describe is that of *classifiers*. The term *classifier* is not particularly familiar to users of English, mainly because English makes very limited use of classifier forms. However, there are many languages in the world which can be labelled *classifier languages* because of the important role played by classifiers in their grammars. Examples of classifier languages include Cantonese, Mandarin Chinese, Thai, Navajo and Vietnamese (see for example Allan, 1977 and Craig, 1986). Classifiers are linguistic units which indicate what kind of group or category a particular referent belongs to. They mark out what is referred to as belonging, for example, to the class of animate entities, the class of humans, the class of round things, the class of flat things, the class of vehicles and so on.

There are numerous possibilities for classification, although there seems to be a surprising similarity in the categories of classification used across languages. Thus, while it may not be surprising to discover that sign languages use features such as size and shape for grouping real world items, it is perhaps more surprising to find that the majority of spoken classifier languages also make use of size and shape as a basis of classification. In a language such as Mandarin Chinese, a book would be classified as a flat object. Thus "one book" and "three books" would be translated into Mandarin as "i ben shu" and "san ben shu" with "ben" being a classifier meaning 'flat object'.* BSL may also use a classifier for flat objects when referring to books, although as we shall see there is flexibility built into the system so that classification is not absolute. The same object may be classified in several different ways.†

Classifiers are expressed in BSL by means of the handshape. It is the handshape which tells us which class a referent belongs to: whether it is round, flat, long and thin, human, a vehicle and so on. However, the situation is rather more complex. This is both because the same handshape can express different types of classifier meaning, and because a specific category may be expressed by more than one classifying handshape: the B handshape can function as a size and shape classifier, a handling classifier, an instrumental classifier and a touch classifier. Almost all of the handshapes of BSL can express at least one type of classifier function: some, like B, express several different functions. Moreover, a specific class within a category may be expressed by more than one handshape. Round objects within the size and shape category, can be expressed by an A handshape, an O handshape, an F handshape and a V̈ handshape. It is this type of richness which provides the user with such enormous potential within the productive lexicon. However, this richness may also appear incredibly complex to the learner. In order to elucidate the complexity involved, it will be helpful firstly to establish the different types of classifier categories.

---

*Lyons (1977, p. 461).
† See Craig (1986) for a useful collection of papers dealing with classification and Lakoff (1986) for discussion of some of the complex processes involved in assigning entities to specific categories.

Size and shape specifiers or SASSes

SASSes are classifiers which tell us something about the physical features of objects, specifically their size and shape. It will become clear from the examples that are presented here, that classifiers in BSL are almost always motivated in the sense discussed on p. 41. The relationship involved in respect of SASSes is that of resemblance: the shape of the handshape resembles the shape of the object. Thus flat objects are represented by flat handshapes such as B, H, and Wm; round objects are represented by the circle formed by the fingers and thumb in O and by the circle formed by the index finger and thumb in F; solid, compact, round or spherical objects are represented by the compact hand A; narrow objects are expressed by single finger handshapes such as G and I; bent objects are expressed by handshapes in which one or more fingers are bent, such as G̈, Ḧ, V̈; curved objects are expressed by curved (bent at the palm knuckles) handshapes such as Ḃ and so on. We do not typically find that the classifiers of spoken language are similarly motivated: rather they are arbitrary morphemes. Of course, sign languages (as opposed to spoken languages) have the appropriate physical resources with which to copy information on size and shape. In that sense, it is not at all surprising that the relationship of resemblance occurs.

Tracing size and shape classifiers

Tracing classifiers are closely linked to SASSes. Here the hands are used to trace the size and shape either of the overall object or of some significant feature of the object. The term is sometimes used only for the tracing of geometric shapes, particularly by the G handshape, for example to show the outline of a square, a room, or a window. Here the term is used somewhat more widely to include those forms in which the handshape itself gives a clue to shape, but the hands nevertheless trace the size and positioning of the object. Thus the C handshape can both indicate the cylindrical nature of an elephant's trunk, a swan's neck and cathedral pillars and indicate their overall shape (e.g. curved) and position.

Handling classifiers

Handling classifiers categorise objects in terms of how humans handle them. The shape of the handshape thus represents not the shape of the objects as such, but the shape of the hands themselves when they handle different categories of object. The closed fist A is used to indicate the gripping of narrow, cylindrical objects such as ski poles and

a snooker cue, or the handle of a bag, a case, or a jug. The Â handshape is used when more control is required for example in handling a key, a racquet, a hammer or drum sticks. The F handshape and the Ĝ handshape are used to indicate the handling of tiny or delicate objects such as items of jewellery, pills, thread and pins. The 5̈, V̇ and V̈ handshapes are used in relation to round or compact objects such as knobs, handles, taps, earphones, and jar lids.

Instrumental classifiers

Instrumental classifiers are similar to SASSes in that they class instruments, such as tools, utensils or other implements, in terms of the physical features of size and shape. The H handshape is used for long narrow instruments, such as items of cutlery, particularly knives; the V handshape is used for instruments which have two narrow extensions, such as scissors and compasses or forks; the 5̈ handshape is used for instruments which have several, long narrow bent extensions or prongs, such as a mechanical grabber or a grass rake.

Touch classifiers

Here classification is based on the manner in which objects may be *touched*. The shape of the handshape thus represents, not the shape of the objects as such, but the shape of the hands themselves both when they touch different categories of object and when they touch the same type of objects in different ways. Objects may be touched by the tips of the fingers of the 5 or 5̈ hand as in playing the piano, using a keyboard or reading braille; they may be touched by the tip of the thumb as in pressing a doorbell, putting on a sticking plaster and putting in ear plugs; they may be touched by the tip of the index finger as in using a push-button telephone or a remote control device. While these classifiers may be seen as very similar to handling classifiers (indeed the boundary between the two is not always easy to draw), the main difference is that in touch classifiers the object is viewed as being touched rather than handled, moved or placed (see examples in classifier table, pp. 53–67).

Handshape inventory and classifiers

The classifier table lists forty four handshapes of BSL which express at least one of these classifier usages. Some are used for the five different types of classifier function so far described; many express several of these functions and others have a much more limited use, expressing only one type of classifier function. Handshapes which do not appear to express any classifier function or which do so very rarely

198. sea lion

200. carry a pile…

201. guillotine

202. stroke a small animal

203. spider

204. Rubik's cube

205. mechanical grabber

206. scratch

are omitted from the table. The **B** handshape, for example, expresses each of the different classifier functions: it operates as a SASS (representing flippers which stand for the whole animal) in **sea lion**[198]; a tracing size and shape classifier in **basin** (sign 1374)[199]; a handling classifier in **carry a pile of flat objects**[200]; an instrumental classifier in **guillotine**[201] and a touch classifier in **stroke a small animal**[202]. As we shall see, **B** also operates within the semantic classifier set relating to vehicles (see pp.49–50). Similarly, the **5̄**

handshape operates as a SASS to indicate objects with many long narrow bent extensions as in **spider**[203]; a handling classifier as in **Rubik's cube**[204]; an instrumental classifier as in **mechanical grabber**[205] and a touch classifier as in **scratch**[206]. This listing reveals the richness of classifier usage within BSL. It also demonstrates that if learners want to develop fluency in the use of BSL lexis, they must tune into this abundant source of lexical creativity.

198. Ø B<⊥ ; B>⊥ $\overset{\text{ɒ ∾ ·}}{z}$

199. Ø Bɑ⊥ ; Bɑ⊥ $\overset{\div \omega}{\underset{\wedge}{x}}$

200. Ø B̄ɑ> Bʊ< $\overset{\text{°}}{\text{∾ ·}}$

201. B̄⊤> B⊤< $\overset{\text{˙ v x}}{}$

202. Ā̄ʊ⊥ Bʊ< $\overset{\text{⊤ ·}}{\underset{\top}{x}}$

203. Ø 5̈ʊ⊥ $\overset{(\overset{m}{v}\text{·})}{}$

204. Ø 5̈ɑ> 5̈ʊ⊥ $\overset{\text{ɒ ∾ ·}}{z}$

205. Ḡ⊤> ₓ ✓ 5̈ʊ⊥ᵩ $\overset{\text{x}}{\underset{\wedge}{\text{ɒ}}}$

206. ✓ 5̈⊤v $\overset{\text{⊤ ·}}{x}$

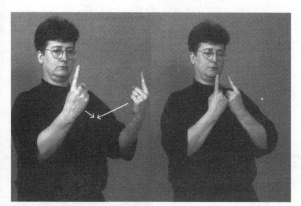

207. two persons approaching

208. one person separating...   **209. process**

211. tailback

Major semantic classifier sets: person, people and vehicle

Earlier accounts of BSL classifiers tended to focus on the functioning of what are known as the *person*, *people* and *vehicle* classifiers. There is little doubt that these classifiers do occur with considerable frequency in the language, although they function along with the wide range of other classifier options described above and in the classifier table on pp. 53–67. These classifiers are sometimes known as *semantic* classifiers because they group objects in terms of specific semantic features other than those already mentioned, such as size and shape. They are also sometimes viewed as arbitrary, in that their form is not necessarily related to their meaning. However, most users do see some link between form and meaning and these

classifiers are listed in the classifier table, partly for convenience, under the size and shape heading. Although not all persons are long and narrow, it is suggested that BSL categorises them in this way. People can be viewed as several long, narrow objects and vehicles as typically longer than they are wide. However, it is worth stressing that for the most part the focus is on these handshapes as representing these major semantic categories rather than as focusing on their size and shape.

The *person* classifier is expressed by the **G** handshape. In this function, the handshape is sometimes referred to as '**G** up' because the finger is typically pointing up. In **two persons approaching me**[207] and **one person separating from another**[208] each hand expresses the person classifier. The *people* classifier is expressed by the **5** handshape or **5̈** handshape. Interestingly enough, it can be realised by the **5** hand either with upward finger orientation as in **people filing** (p. 45[196]) or with the palms facing down and the fingers pointing either away from the signer or right and left as in **crowd milling about** (p. 67[261]). The **5** handshape may also open out from the closed **O** or **A** handshape. This usage is comparable to the way in which the **A** hand opens to a **5** to express the size and shape function as in **punk hairstyle** (p. 42[164]) and **porcupine** (p. 45[195]). However, it can also be used to give emphasis to particular kinds of rhythmic movement such as marching or processing as in **process**[209].

The *vehicle* classifier is expressed by the **B** handshape. In **overtake**[210] and **tailback**[211] it can occur with palm down

207. Ø G⊤∧ G⊤∧ $\overset{\text{т}}{\underset{\text{x}}{}}$

208. G⊤∧ G⊥∧ᵩ $^{>⊥}$

209. Ø A⌐⊥ A⌐⊥ᵩ $^{\perp}_{\square}$ [5 5]˙

210. B⌐⊥ B⌐⊥ᵩ $^{>⊥<}$

211. B⌐⊥ ₓ B⌐⊥ᵩ $\left(\begin{smallmatrix} o \\ n \\ n \\ \tau \\ > \end{smallmatrix} \cdot \right)$

213. **car coming to…**   214. **paragraph**   215. **thick-soled shoe**   216. **pillars in a cathedral**

orientation; or in palm to the side (left) orientation as in **car park** (sign 1392, note 1)[212] and **car coming to an abrupt halt**[213]. The use of these classifiers in different types of verbs and nouns is discussed further on pp. 76–78.

Classifiers and the real world

So far, classifiers have been discussed as though there is a direct relationship between real world actions and objects and what occurs in BSL. However, this is not strictly the case. There is some abstraction away from real world phenomena, even though the language does reflect these. Handling classifiers do reflect how we actually handle objects, but they do so as if we always used very specific handshapes. We may regularly hold tiny objects between the thumb and index finger, but the hand does not necessarily form an **F** or a **Ĝ** configuration: the language acts as if it does. So handling classifiers fit with and conform to the specific set of handshapes found in the language. Of course, it may be that the language has evolved these specific handshapes in part to reflect the human handling function. Nevertheless, while all of the sign languages studied so far do make use of classifier forms, they do not all have precisely the same set of relationships between handling functions and particular handshapes.

In a similar way, although size and shape classifiers reflect the size and shape of objects, there is kind of two-way approximation to reality. The hands themselves can only approximate to the shapes they represent because they are restricted both by the physical limitations of their anatomy and the constraints of the linguistic system of handshape contrasts. Similarly, objects which are in many respects different in size and shape, may be categorised as belonging to the same group. Thus the **C** handshape is used as a size and shape classifier in the signs **paragraph**[214] and **thick-soled shoe**[215]. In reality, the soles of shoes and paragraphs are rather different from each other in size and shape, yet we can see the motivation for the choice of classifier. The tracing size and shape classifier **C** is used for objects as various as a train carriage, **pillars in a cathedral**[216], cables, an elephant's trunk, a can of beer, a giraffe's neck, railway carriages and a **squirrel's tail** (p. 22[30]). Again, there are major differences in the actual size and shape of these objects, yet they are treated as if they have some feature, presumably cylindricalness, in common. The **G** SASS classifier may be used for objects as different as a cigarette, an underground train, a telegraph pole and a missile.

In fact, signers seem to operate with and switch between two different scales of reference (see Mandel, 1977 and Schick, 1990). In the real-world scale, it is assumed that objects represented by classifiers are represented at more-or-less life size: a cigarette as represented by a **G** hand, is more or less the length of an index finger. In contrast, model-scale gives a signer "…a long-range perspective point to look down on a scene rather than participating in it." (Schick, 1990, p. 32) This is sometimes referred to within the British tradition as *close* and *distant* focus (see

212. Ø (B̄ɑ> B<⊥ °ᵛ× ·) >

213. Bɑ> × B<⊥

214. B⊤∧ C<∧₉ ×

215. B̄ʊ> C⊥∧ ×

216. Ø C>⊥ C<⊥ (∧·) ⊥

217. **horse galloping** 218. **two heads look up** 219. **flush a toilet** 220. **flush a toilet**

Brennan and Colville, 1984). As Schick suggests, by their very nature, handling classifiers operate within the real-world scale, whereas size and shape specifiers can operate within both scales. The signer will change from one scale to another, sometimes zooming in to provide a close up view, at other times pulling back to provide a 'long shot' on the action. The impact of such changes in perspective can be compelling and, almost by definition, extremely difficult to convey in translation from BSL to English.

Verbs, nouns and adjectives

Classifiers can take on different types of role within the grammar of the language. They can operate, for example, in both noun and verb forms and participate in the expression of plurality and extent (see pp. 102–104 in the *Grammar* section). We shall explore this further below. Initially, it is worth stressing that in looking at the many examples in the classifier table on pp. 53–67, we need to keep in mind the potential for most of the items listed to operate in both noun and verb forms, even though they may be listed as one or the other. The **A** SASS can be used as the nouns meaning 'head', 'hoof' or 'pestle' or may function in verb forms such as **horse galloping**[217] or **two heads look up**[218]. The handling classifier **ᵇ̈** may be used as the noun 'Rubik's cube' or for the verb 'handle a Rubik's cube'; the handling classifier **Â** may be used for the noun 'key' or the verb 'to open with a key'. The instrumental classifier **V** may be used for the noun 'scissors' or the verb 'to cut with scissors' . This ability to take on different syntactic roles ensures that classifiers play

a major role in the language.

There has been some discussion in relation to other sign languages as to whether the word-class 'adjective' is used in these languages (see , for example, Bergman, 1983 and 1986). Although BSL does appear to have separate items which can function as adjectives, for example colour terms, there is some evidence that even these function predominantly as adjectival predicates, acting like verbs. What we can note in respect of classifier usage in BSL is that the very existence of classifying handshapes militates against the need for additional separate adjectives. There is a much more limited use for adjectives meaning 'narrow', 'round', 'curved' and 'flat' if this information is already built into the noun and verb forms through the use of classifying handshapes. What is more, the language tends to give such information as a matter of course, rather than adding it on as an optional extra. This can be demonstrated by the everyday activity of flushing a toilet. The signs meaning 'flushing a toilet' can vary according to the specific device used to activate this process: a handling **A** classifier may be used to show the pulling of a chain[219] or the depressing of a lever[220]; a handling **V̈** classifier may be used to show the pulling of a round lever which is typically gripped by the bent fingers (page 52[221]); an **Ȧ** touch classifier handshape may be used to indicate the pressing of a button (page 52[222]); **B** and **B̈** handling classifiers may be used to show the pressing of a lever with the whole hand (page 52[223]) or fingertips (page 52[224]) and a **B** SASS classifier may be used to indicate the pressing of a lever with the foot (page 52[225]). All of these classifiers

217. Ø Ā⊅⊥ A⊅⊥ₚ ᵛ

218. Ø A⊅⊥ A⊅⊥ ᵖ∧

219. Ọ A<⊥ ᵛ

220. Ø A⊅⊥ ω<

221. flush a toilet

222. flush a toilet

223. flush a toilet

224. flush a toilet

225. flush a toilet

will be produced in an appropriate position in relation to an imaginary toilet. It may well be that there is a regular established sign in the language which the signer may use in all instances, just as the same sign can be used for 'kettle', even though some kettles may have a handle on the top of the kettle and others at the side. However, the signer can choose to mirror real-life differences and this reflection of physical variation is typical of much BSL usage. It seems that because the language has this potential built into it, the signer exploits these possibilities on a regular basis. Thus the signer gives information about size and shape or how objects are handled as a matter of course. If the signer refers to walking into a building or opening a cupboard, s/he will typically also provide specific information about the type of doors involved: swing doors, double doors, automatic doors, doors that open to the side, doors with press button opening devices, doors with round handles, doors with long narrow handles and so on. For native users of English, this may seem very strange as they are used to adding such information only when they feel it is needed. BSL, however, tends to encode this information automatically and the signer homes in on significant physical features. It is worth stressing that these features are significant within the context of the language. BSL happens not to encode information about colour on a regular, automatic basis: it does encode information about size and shape.

221. Ø V̈ᴛᴠ ° ^

222. Ø Ȧᴛᴠ ° ⊥

223. Ø Bᴅ< ° ᵛ

224. Ø B̈⊥ʌ ° ᵛ

225. Ø Bᴅ⊥ ° ᵛ

Classifier table

Classifier handshape	A

Size and shape — round or spherical objects; compact or solid objects;
horse galloping (p. 51 [217]), **ball, head, hoof, jaw**

Tracing size and shape

Handling — hold narrow and/or cylindrical objects; hold handles;
shake prison bars , snooker cue, jug, briefcase

Instrumental — instruments with round, spherical or solid base;
pestle [226], **polo stick, croquet hammer, mallet, poss stick**

Touch — actions of the closed fist;
boxer (sign 82), **knock, tap, hit, punch**

226. pestle

Classifier handshape	Ȧ

Size and shape — small, compact object with short upright extension;
vinegar (sign 205), **oil shaker, vinegar bottle, candle**

Tracing size and shape — tracing outlines of shapes;
obese (sign 214), **straight line, arc, braces, curve of stomach**

Handling — holding tool with blade or cutting component;
potato peeler (sign 210), **razor, carving tool**

Instrumental — instruments with blade;
carve [227], **razor, scalpel, knife, penknife, stanley knife**

Touch — touching small items or areas with thumb;
doorbell (sign 162), **sticking plaster, push button, ear plugs**

227. carve

Classifier handshape	Â

Size and shape

Tracing size and shape

Handling — holding narrow cylindrical objects, narrow flat objects and small objects: particularly used for objects needing fine control;
magnifying glass [228], **hammer, drumsticks, racquet, key**

Instrumental

Touch

228. magnifying glass

226. B̄a> ₓ Aᴛv ᵡ³ⱽ   227. C̄>⊥ ¡ Ȧ⊥ʌ ᵀᵂᴰᴛ⊥   228. B̄a> Â<⊥₉ (ʸᴬ⊥ᴛ) ·

Classifier handshape	**G**

Size and shape	objects which are relatively long and thin, often cylindrical: the person classifier occupies a major paradigm of its own; **cigarette**[229], **leg, missile, penis, tube train**
Tracing size and shape	index fingers trace size, shape or outline of shapes and objects; **window** (sign 441), **square, triangle, lightning**
Handling	holding objects on tip of index finger; **contact lens, plates** (as in spinning plates)
Instrumental	instruments with long narrow, often cylindrical, component; **compass** (sign 403), **rowel, knitting needles, compass needle**
Touch	actions of the index finger **get at** (sign 444), **prod, poke, press/push buttons**

229. cigarette

Classifier handshape	**Ġ**

Size and shape	objects with one long and one short extension at right angles; **walking stick, set square**
Tracing size and shape	tracing dimensions, particularly depth of items, e.g. on body; **briefs** (sign 742), **bikini, bra, pants**
Handling	(usually combines with instrumental function) holding items with long narrow extension; **petrol** (sign 462), **gun, electric drill, staple gun, video camera**
Instrumental	(usually combines with handling function) instruments with long narrow extensions; **gun** (sign 463)[230], **electric drill, staple gun**
Touch	

230. gun

Classifier handshape	**Ĝ**

Size and shape	triangular or wedge-shaped objects; **beak, wedge, bow** (two hands)
Tracing size and shape	used with initial opening action to trace position and shape of objects; **ear ring, collar, cuffs**
Handling	holding small, tiny or delicate objects or relatively flat items; **pill** (sign 476)[231], **capsule, jewellery, audiotape, paper**
Instrumental	instruments with wedge-shaped or triangular components (rare); **wedge**
Touch	

231. pill

229. ⌒ G♈< ˣₘᵐ ·

230. Ø °Ġ<⊥ (°ₙ⌃ₘ)

231. B̄ɑ> Ĝ♈⊥ ˣ(°ₜ⌃) // ⌒ Ĝ⊤< ˣ

Classifier handshape	$\bar{\bar{\text{G}}}$

Size and shape	objects with two parallel surfaces; **bird** (sign 479), **beak, clothes peg, paper clip**
Tracing size and shape	tracing the position and size of narrow objects or sections; **layer** (e.g. of custard on a trifle)[232], **envelope, rim, border, subtitles**
Handling	holding shallow, flat items; **audiotape, shallow box, shallow book**
Instrumental	instruments with two parallel flat surfaces; **paper clip, clothes peg**
Touch	

232. **layer**

Classifier handshape	$\ddot{\text{G}}$

Size and shape	objects which are relatively long and thin, often cylindrical: the person classifier occupies a major paradigm of its own; **kick** (sign 546), **leg, missile, pole, tube train**
Tracing size and shape	index fingers trace size, shape or outline of shapes and objects; **certificate** (sign 562), **roundabout, disc, wheel, saucer**
Handling	holding objects on tip of index finger; **contact lens, plates** (as in spinning plates)
Instrumental	instruments with long narrow, often cylindrical, component; **compass** (sign 443), **dowel, knitting needle, dibber, compass needle**
Touch	actions of the index finger; **push button telephone**[233], **prod, poke, press/push buttons**

233. **push button telephone**

Classifier handshape	$\ddot{\text{G}}$

Size and shape	bent or curved objects; **sitting with legs apart**[234], **bent legs, hooked nose, hearing aid**
Tracing size and shape	to trace position and size of (often uneven) lines; **tears** (sign 574), **cracks, zig-zag patterning**
Handling	handling objects with bent index finger; **ring pull** (sign 592), **circular aperture**
Instrumental	instruments with a hooked component; **caravan** (sign 597), **butcher's hook, crane hook, towing hook**
Touch	

234. **sitting with legs apart**

Classifier handshape	G̈

Size and shape used primarily as a tracing size and shape classifier

Tracing size and shape to trace the position and size of narrow flat objects;
tie (sign 605), **belt, braces, bill**

Handling handling cylindrical objects or objects whose use requires a squeezing action;
shotgun (sign 609)[235], **hose, torch, toothpaste, filler**

Instrumental

Touch

235. shotgun

Classifier handshape	Ĝ

Size and shape

Tracing size and shape used with opening and closing action to trace position and shape;
moon (sign 616), **segment, earrings**

Handling handling of tiny objects or writing implements;
chalk (sign 615)[236], **bit, earmould, pen, biro**

Instrumental instruments which can be handled by the thumb and index finger
(see handling classifiers)

Touch

236. chalk

Classifier handshape	G̈

Size and shape curved or bent objects;
parrot (sign 639), **curved beak, cock, woodpecker, bent legs**

Tracing size and shape tracing of narrow, sometimes cylindrical objects and shapes, such as
a cross;
swan (sign 642)[237], **railings, coat hanger, swan's neck, cross**

Handling handling small object or object with press down attachment;
whistle (sign 641), **aerosol spray, perfume, breath freshener**

Instrumental instrument with curved or bent component (rare: other options
such as G̈ typically used)

Touch

237. swan

235. Ø (G̈ɑ⊥ ᵉG̈<⊥ ᵐ)⊤̇ᵥ̇   236. Ø Ĝ⊥ʌ (ᵒᵥ̊.)   237. π G̈⊤< ᷤ̂᷍

Classifier handshape	**ʎ**
Size and shape	rare: ɢ would normally be preferred in all functions
Tracing size and shape	objects which are relatively long and thin, often cylindrical:(including persons); **horn of unicorn, pole, post, horn**
Handling	handling of tiny objects with fingertip: rare; **contact lens**[238]
Instrumental	long narrow instruments: rare
Touch	

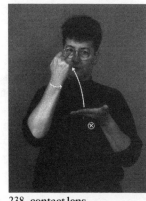

238. **contact lens**

Classifier handshape	**R**
Size and shape	long narrow objects interwined; **rope**[239]**, braids, ringlets**
Tracing size and shape	
Handling	holding items between index and middle fingers; **chopsticks**
Instrumental	instruments with narrow intertwined components: rare
Touch	

239. **rope**

Classifier handshape	**H**
Size and shape	straight narrow objects; **dormitory**[240]**, bed, bench, ears of rabbits, legs of animals**
Tracing size and shape	tracing position and shape of objects; **corridor** (sign 697)**, bridge, river, path, chef's hat**
Handling	
Instrumental	long narrow instruments, especially relating to cutlery; **knife** (sign 689)**, spoon, cutlery, spurtle**
Touch	

240. **dormitory**

238. ᘞ Ḃɑ> Ӱʊ⊥ $\overset{\overset{a}{\top}}{\lambda}$ 239. Ø Rᴛ> ‚ R⊥< $\overset{\omega\cdot}{\div}$ 240. Ø H⊃⊥ ‚ H⊃⊥ $\overset{(\overset{o}{\underset{v}{}}\cdot)}{\div}$

Classifier handshape	H̄

Size and shape	objects with two parallel surfaces; **duck** (sign 711), **hair slide, beaks of duck, goose, swan**
Tracing size and shape	tracing the dimensions of narrow objects and sections; **moustache** (sign 715)[241], **banana, sausages, layer, rim**
Handling	holding shallow, flat items; **pie dish, audiotape, shallow box**
Instrumental	instruments with two parallel flat surfaces; **paper clip, clothes peg, microphone clip**
Touch	

241. **moustache**

Classifier handshape	Ḧ

Size and shape	straight narrow objects; **animal walking**[242], **legs of animals, legs of humans, ears of animals**
Tracing size and shape	tracing position and shape of objects; **scarf** (sign 731), **house, bridge**
Handling	long narrow instruments, especially relating to cutlery; **dessert spoon** (sign 732), **spoon, knife, paint brush, spurtle**
Instrumental	
Touch	

242. **animal walking**

Classifier handshape	Ḧ

Size and shape	bent, narrow objects; **sit** (sign 734)[243], **legs, inverted commas, thick eyebrows**
Tracing size and shape	to trace position and size of (often uneven) lines : rare (ö more usual)
Handling	handling objects with bent index and middle finger; **elastic** (sign 735), **elasticated material, circular aperture**
Instrumental	instruments with a hooked component: a rare alternative to Ğ
Touch	

243. **sit**

---

241. ⌒ H̄>ʌ H̄<ʌ ^ᴅᵛ_±ꞎ   242. ∅ Ḧʊ⊥ Ḧʊ⊥ ᵀᴺ·   243. ‾Ḧʊ> Ḧ⊥ʌₒ ⊥ᴅˣ

Classifier handshape	V

Size and shape	objects with two fixed but moveable long narrow extensions and wedge shaped objects; **compasses** (sign 773), **legs, scissors, medal** (ribbons), **glasses**
Tracing size and shape	tracing the size, position and outline of narrow objects; **mayor** (sign 793), **stripes, ribbons, collar, chain of office**
Handling	handling objects between the extended index and middle fingers; **smoke** (sign 757)[244], **cigarette, cigar**
Instrumental	instruments with two fixed but moveable extensions; **scissors** (sign 752), **compasses, fork**
Touch	

244. smoke

Classifier handshape	V̄

Size and shape	object with parallel surfaces, one wider than the other; **badge** (sign 781), **brooch, slide, hair clip, paper clip**
Tracing size and shape	handling of narrow object with extension; **hypodermic** (sign 782)[245], **syringe, inject, vaccinate, take blood**
Handling	instruments with parallel surfaces, one wider than the other: rare
Instrumental	rare
Touch	

245. hypodermic

Classifier handshape	V̈

Size and shape	objects with two fixed but moveable long narrow extensions and wedge shaped objects; **walk**[246], **legs** (highly productive), **earrings, medal** (ribbons), **glasses**
Tracing size and shape	tracing the size, position and outline of narrow objects; **police** (sign 795), **stripes, ribbons, collar, chain of office**
Handling	handling objects between the extended index and middle fingers; **smoke** (sign 575), **cigarette, cigar**
Instrumental	instruments with two fixed but moveable extensions; **scissors** (sign 752), **compasses, fork**
Touch	

246. walk

244. ᴐ Vᴛʌ ˣ˙ 245. ↳ V̄ɑ< ⊤[ᴋ]ˣ 246. ∅ V̈ᴅ⊥ ⚲˙

Classifier handshape	V̈

Size and shape	objects with two fixed, but moveable bent extensions; bent objects; **drunk**[247], **legs** (highly productive), **trolley wires, inverted commas**
Tracing size and shape	tracing the position, size and outline of stripes or lines, especially uneven lines: rare
Handling	handling of objects by the two bent fingers; **tube** (safety strap in tube train) (sign 807), **circular aperture**
Instrumental	instruments with two, possibly bent, extensions; **fork, prongs, double hook**
Touch	touch with two bent fingers: rare

247. **drunk**

Classifier handshape	V̈̈

Size and shape	round or spherical objects or objects with three bent narrow extensions; **spiral of coins**[248], **badge, watch, stone, claws**
Tracing size and shape	tracing, usually by a twisting action, a circular shape; swelling or bump shown by outward movement; **owl** (sign 832), **circular markings, brooch, panda, bump**
Handling	handling of round, spherical or uneven objects; **can't believe one's eyes** (sign 831), **chess player, stone, eyes** (metaphorical handling)
Instrumental	instrument with three bent prongs; **mechanical claw**
Touch	rare

248. **spiral of coins**

Classifier handshape	K

Size and shape	objects with two narrow extensions and wedge shaped objects; **decoration** (sign 835), **medal** (ribbons), **turkey**
Tracing size and shape	tracing the size, position and outline of narrow objects; alternative to V in **stripes, ribbons**
Handling	rare
Instrumental	instruments with two narrow extensions; **clothes peg** (sign 836)[249], **paper clip**
Touch	

249. **clothes peg**

247. B̄ɑ⊥ ₓ V̈τν ꞰꞰ   248. V̈ɑ⊥ V̈ɑ⊥ (꞉)   249. Ø (Ḡτ> Kɔ⊥ °·) >

Classifier handshape	**W** 
Size and shape	objects with three narrow extensions or objects viewed as lines; **streams of traffic, shipyard**
Tracing size and shape	tracing of three parallel lines or stripes; **sergeant**[250]
Handling	
Instrumental	instruments with three or more extensions; **toasting fork, garden fork**
Touch	

250. sergeant

Classifier handshape	**Wm** 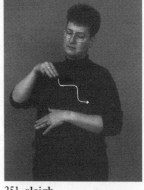
Size and shape	relatively narrow flat objects; **sleigh**[251]**, bench, sledge, table, ticket**
Tracing size and shape	to trace the position and size of stripes or shapes; **bless, stripes, lines, strips, cross**
Handling	
Instrumental	instruments with relatively narrow, flat component; **small spade, hand trowel**
Touch	

251. sleigh

Classifier handshape	**4**
Size and shape	objects with four, several or many long narrow extensions; several persons; **team** (sign 840)[252]**, comb, panel, group**
Tracing size and shape	rare
Handling	
Instrumental	instruments with four, several or many extensions; **garden fork** (sign 839)**, comb, rake**
Touch	

252. team

---

250. ⌐ Ẅт< V ^
> >
X X

251. Ø Wmт°⊥ (z ·)
V
⊥

252. Ø °4⊥∧ ₁x °4⊥∧ (°÷ω̃т) т x
х

Classifier handshape	**F**

Size and shape	small round objects; **button, coin, small hole, washer**
Tracing size and shape	tracing the position and size of cylindrical objects; **degree** (sign 875), **rod, pole, pipe, roll of paper**
Handling	handling of very small or delicate objects; **teabag**[253], **needle, seed, matchstick, stockings**
Instrumental	instruments which have a circular or cylindrical component; **stethoscope, eyeglass, rawl plug**
Touch	

253. teabag

Classifier handshape	**F̄**

Size and shape	
Tracing size and shape	
Handling	infrequent: used in place of **F** for slightly thicker objects or for particular type of handling; **marry** (sign 895)[254], **wedding ring, engagement ring**
Instrumental	
Touch	

254. marry

Classifier handshape	**I , Ï**

Size and shape	small narrow objects; **small penis**
Tracing size and shape	tracing of size and position of small narrow objects; **sheep** (sign 929)[255], **horns**
Handling	
Instrumental	small narrow instrument; **poison** (sign 912), **spoon, small stirring implement**
Touch	

255. sheep

---

253. C>⊥ F̌ɤ⊥ °̌·   254. °5ɤ> ıx F̄ɤ⊥ ×̌   255. ∩ Ïτʌ Ïτʌ °̌ᵥ

Classifier handshape	Y	

Size and shape	solid objects with extensions at each side or each end; **typetalk** [256], **teapot, aeroplane, horns, telephone**
Tracing size and shape	tracing the position, size and outline of narrow objects; **cheque** (sign 953), **envelope, card, programme, leaflet**
Handling	handling of solid items with extensions at either end; **telephone** (sign 944), **pay phone, pipe, kettle, acoustic modem**
Instrumental	instruments which have a narrow extension and are grasped by the closed fingers: infrequent substitute for A or G; **stirring implement**
Touch	

256. typetalk

Classifier handshape	Ч	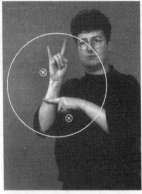

Size and shape	objects with two vertical extensions; **television aerial** [257], **goalposts, horns, aerial**
Tracing size and shape	tracing the position, size and outline of rectangular area; **football pitch, sports arena, playing field**
Handling	rare
Instrumental	rare
Touch	

257. aerial

Classifier handshape	8, 8̇, 8̂	

Size and shape	rare use for narrow objects, including persons; **wasp sting, cork, person, sting**
Tracing size and shape	
Handling	handling of small or delicate items; 8̂ used for handling sticky substances; **hand over coins** [258], **ring, earring, necklace, pin**
Instrumental	rare
Touch	touch small area or touch delicately; **Christ** (wounds of) (sign 966), **pulse**

258. hand over coins

---

256. Y⊤> ¦ Y⊤<ᵖ ⊥⊥
                   ><

257. Ϭ♡> ₓ Ч⊥Λᵖ ∅

258. ∅ ४ɑ> ४ɑ< ⊥

Classifier handshape	**5**

Size and shape   objects with many long extensions;
crowd congregating [259], **porcupine, punk hairstyle, eyelashes**

Tracing size and shape   tracing the position and size of stripes and lines and of (usually) undulating surfaces;
sea (sign 1045), **stripes, mesh, countryside, field**

Handling   handling large flat-sided or bulky items;
carry heavy machine, carry large box

Instrumental   instruments with several or many long narrow extensions;
garden rake, car wash brushes, grinding machine

Touch   actions of the whole hands, the palms and the fingers;
Minicom, bounce, knead plasticene, type, remote control

259. crowd congregating

Classifier handshape	**5̄**

Size and shape   cone-shaped objects;
wolf (sign 1094) [260], **nozzle, snout, nose, witch's hat**

Tracing size and shape   tracing the position and size of curved, cone-shaped or cylindrical objects;
bottom (sign 1106), **marrow, aubergine, melon**

Handling   handling curved, cone-shaped, cube-shaped or cylindrical objects;
shuffle playing cards (sign 1099), **playing cards, collecting tin**

Instrumental   cone-shaped instruments;
respirator, dust mask, gas mask

Touch   rare

260. wolf

Classifier handshape	**5̈**

Size and shape   objects with many long extensions; people; objects of indeterminate shape;
crowd milling about (sign 1056) [261], **assembly, furniture**

Tracing size and shape   tracing the position and size of stripes and lines;
screeds of writing, lines, graph paper

Handling   handling curved items or flat items with fingertips;
netball (sign 1108), **coconut, ball**

Instrumental   instruments with several or many long narrow extensions;
garden rake, combine harvester, car wash brushes

Touch   actions of the fingers;
play the piano (sign1118), **deaf-blind alphabet, keyboard**

261. crowd milling about

---

259. ∅ 5>ʌ 5<ʌ

260. ○ 5̄⊤ʌ

261. ∅ 5ℸ> ⎸ 5ℸ<

Classifier handshape	**5̈**

Size and shape	objects with several or many long narrow bent extensions; circular objects; objects of indeterminate shape; **spider** (p. 48[203]), **claws, crown, bruise, island**
Tracing size and shape	tracing the position of several lines or stripes; indicationg position of spots or small marks; tracing position of indeterminate shape; **mottled** (sign 1157), **stripes, lines, freckles, beard**
Handling	handling of relatively large, round or spherical objects or objects which fit into and/or can be manipulated by the clawed hands; **Rubik's cube** (p. 48[204]), **headphones, tap, jar lid, gas mask**
Instrumental	instruments with several or many long narrow bent extensions; **mechanical grabber** (p. 48[205]), **rake, combine harvester**
Touch	actions of the fingers, especially the fingertips; **scratch**[262], **scrape, gash, tear at, claw at**

262. scratch

Classifier handshape	**B**

Size and shape	vehicle classifier; objects with flat surfaces; **tailback** (p. 49[211]), **car park, table, wall**
Tracing size and shape	tracing the position and size of objects with flat or smooth surfaces; **basin** (sign 1418), **ground, vase, globe, slide**
Handling	handling flat items or piles of flat items; **carry pile of towels, pile of videotapes, pile of books** (p. 48[200])
Instrumental	flat instruments; **guillotine**[263], **spade, slicer, paintbrush, saw**
Touch	actions of the whole hand; **stroke** (p. 89[420]), **rub, pat, hit, shove**

263. guillotine

Classifier handshape	**B̂**

Size and shape	triangular or wedge-shaped objects; **emu, beak, wedge**
Tracing size and shape	used with initial opening action to trace position and shape of objects; **water melon** (sign 1550), **moustache, beard, cuffs**
Handling	holding flat objects, handling powdery substances; **frisbee** (sign 1498)[264], **bedspread, hat, cash, ashes**
Instrumental	instruments with wedge-shaped or triangular components (rare); **wedge**
Touch	

264. frisbee

Classifier handshape	B̄̄	

Size and shape objects with two parallel surfaces;
swan, **beaks of large birds**, **paper holder**

Tracing size and shape tracing the position, shape and dimensions of narrow sections; with
Ḃ in second position to indicate cone or wedge-shaped objects;
layer (e.g. of custard on a trifle)[265], **layer**, **border**, **snout**, **melon**

Handling holding shallow, usually flat items;
hat (sign 1530), **audiotape**, **wad of money**, **cardboard**

Instrumental instruments with two parallel flat surfaces;
clamp

Touch

265. layer

Classifier handshape	B̈	

Size and shape flat surfaces, usually at above shoulder height; bent smooth surfaces;
yacht[266], **ceiling**, **shelf**, **wings**, **bowl**

Tracing size and shape tracing the position and size of objects with smooth but curved surfaces;
basin (sign 1628), **globe**, **urn**, **bowl**, **pot**

Handling handling of curved items or delicate items of indeterminate shape;
rugby (sign 1589), **ball**, **holding small animal**

Instrumental flat or curved instruments, especially sharp edged implements;
dig (sign 1565), **guillotine**, **spade**, **plough**, **mechanical excavator**

Touch

266. yacht

Classifier handshape	C	

Size and shape curved or cylindrical objects; chunks of material;
glasses piled on top of each other[267], **mug**, **glass**, **can**, **chunk of text**

Tracing size and shape tracing of position and size of curved objects;
pillars opposite each other (p. 50[216]), **pillars**, **cables**, **elephant's trunk**, **train carriages**

Handling handling of curved or cylindrical objects or chunks of material;
sauce (sign 1662), **glass**, **sauce bottle**, **pepper pot**, **wad of money**

Instrumental curved or cylindrical instruments;
wheel spanner, **scoop**, **mechanical grabber**

Touch

267. glasses piled...

265. Ø B̄⊥∧ , B̄⊥∧ $\overset{(\div x)}{\underset{T}{\omega}}$ 266. Ø (B↻> ₓ √B̈<∧ᵩ $\overset{\omega}{T}$)$^{⊥\overset{⊥}{<}}$ 267. C̄>⊥ ₓ C<⊥ ∧

Classifier handshape	O

Size and shape   round, spherical or cylindrical objects;
telescope[268], **lens, binoculars, sunrise, berry**

Tracing size and shape   tracing size and position of cylindrical objects;
pole (p. 104[560]), **pipe, tube, rod, mast**

Handling   handling narrow cylindrical objects or spherical objects;
bowls (sign 1713), **javelin, spear, pipe, rod**

Instrumental   round, spherical or cylindrical instruments;
stethoscope, microscope, periscope, binoculars

Touch

268. **telescope**

Classifier handshape	E , Ė

Size and shape

Tracing size and shape

Handling   handling of small items and instruments requiring leverage action;
portable telephone[269], **nail brush, discus, plyers, dominoes**

Instrumental   graspingor rubbing actions of fingers;
grapple (sign 1736), **grasp, scratch, scrape, rub**

Touch

269. **portable telephone**

268. ʮ $\left(\text{O>∧}_? \times \text{O<∧} \begin{smallmatrix} n \\ < \\ x \end{smallmatrix} \cdot \right)$ 269. ⊃ E<∧ ø

270. **sun**

271. **floodlights**

272. **lighthouse**

277. **chimney**

Metaphor-based signs

We have already seen (*Form and Meaning* section, pp. 44–45) that some signs bear a metaphorical relationship to their meanings. This was discussed earlier in terms of the 'as if' relationship: the sign **understand** (p. 42 [167]) operates as if thought were something that could be grasped. Here it is suggested that as well as the classifier morphemes discussed above, there are other classes of morphemes which also have generalised meanings. It is possible to recognise a range of *metaphor sets*, i.e. classes of morpheme which express different underlying metaphors. Items from one set will occur in signs which share some aspect of this underlying metaphor, even though they may express what seem to be very different meanings. Classifiers bring together referents which generally share some common physical feature (such as flatness or roundness): metaphor morphemes bring together meanings which can be expressed by the same underlying metaphor. In order to explore this notion further and to demonstrate its importance within the productive lexicon, it will be useful to exemplify some major metaphor sets within the language.

Major metaphor sets: handshape pairs

One major set makes use of what is termed here the *emanate*

or *emit* metaphor. The notions of emanation and emission are closely related: both involve a 'flowing forth' from a source. In BSL this meaning is expressed by the circular handshape **O** or the closed fist **A** (representing the source) opening into either a fully spread **5** or **5̈** handshape, representing the coming forth. Perhaps the best (or 'prototypical') example is the BSL sign **sun** [270] which is performed with the closed fist **A** hand (or **O** hand) held at above the head level while the hand produces an opening action. It is not surprising to see this same unit of meaning expressed in other signs which relate to 'light', such as **floodlights** [271] **floods of tears** (p.85 [393]) and **lighthouse** [272], **lamp** (sign 1698) [273] and **traffic lights** (sign 1702) [274]. However, we can also recognise the same morpheme in the following signs: **volcano** (sign 1715) [275], **transmit** (p. 88 [411]), , **shower** (sign 1706) [276], **chimney** (sign 1719) [277] and **peacock** (sign 1729, note 1) [278].

Section **O** of the *BSL* section of this dictionary will reveal further examples. If we look at some of the meanings of the relevant signs presented both here and in that section, it may initially seem hard to imagine that they share some common component of meaning. We may not usually think of the meanings 'magic', 'shower', 'fart', 'peacock', 'microwave oven', 'steam', 'scald', and 'transmit' as having much

270. $\overline{\cap}$ A<∧ $\overset{\cap\ [\ddot{5}]}{\square}$

271. $\overline{\cap}$ A◡⊥ A◡⊥ $\square$ [55]

272. $\overline{B}$◡> ₓ ʃ○⊥∧ $\left(\overset{\cap\ [5]}{\underset{\square}{\bot}} \overset{\omega}{\underset{<}{\cap}} \overset{\cap\ [O]}{\underset{\#}{T}} \overset{\omega}{\underset{\bot}{}} \right)$·

273. ∅ ○◡⊥ $\square$ [5̈]·

274. ∅ ○⊤∧ $\left(\overset{○}{\underset{\square}{T}} \overset{[5̈]}{\underset{\vee}{}} · \right)$

275. B◡∧ ₁ₓ ○◠⊥ $\overset{∧\ [5̈]}{\square}$

276. $\overline{\cap}$ ○◡< $\overset{\cap\ [5]}{\underset{\square}{\vee}}$·

277. C>⊥ ⊙ ʃ○◠⊥ $\square$ [5̈]·

278. ∅ ○⊥∧ ₁ₓ ○⊥∧ $\overset{∧\ [55]}{\underset{\square}{\div}}$

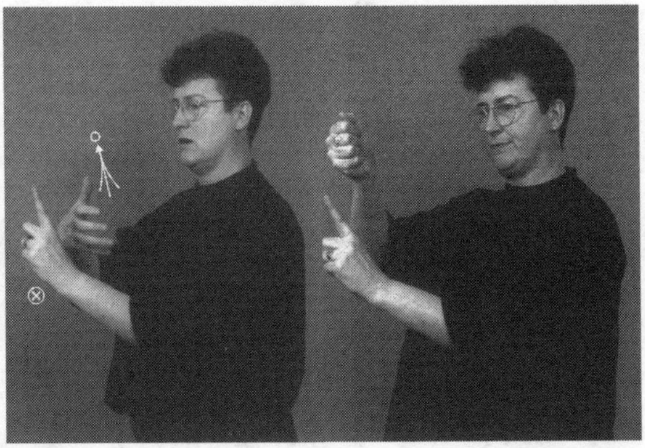

283. **achieve**

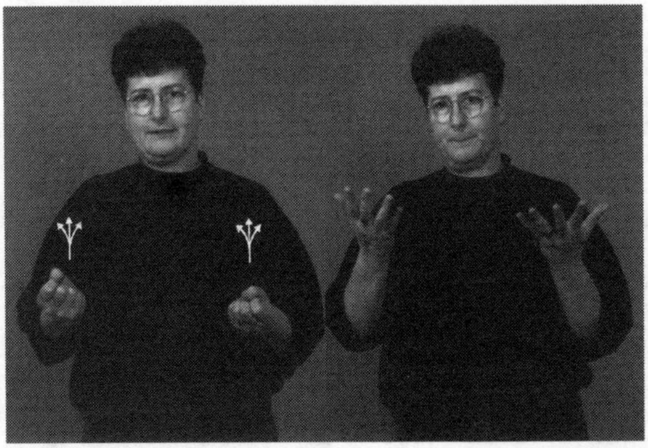

284. **give up**

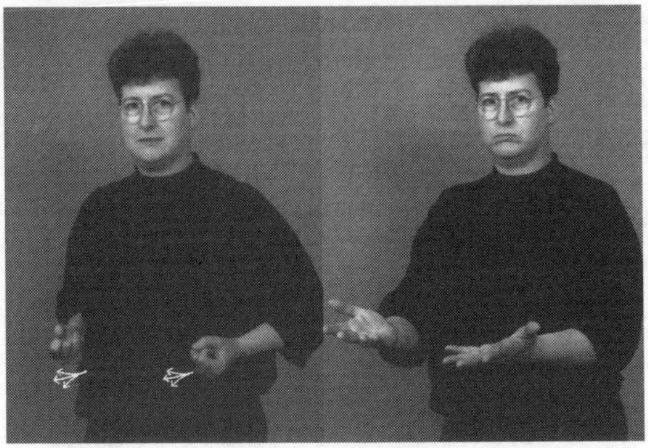

285. **spend**

in common. However, the claim here is that they all share the notion of 'emission' which can be expressed in BSL by the particular handshape pairs **O** → **5** and **A** → **5**.

On p. 44, it was suggested that BSL makes use of a *grasp* metaphor which is expressed by the handshape pair **5** → **A**: the hand closes as if actually grasping or getting hold of something. The language then operates as if both objects and more abstract notions such as 'ideas' and 'aims' can be grasped. We can grasp or get hold of an idea as in **understand** (p.42 [167]) or get hold of money as in **deduct** (sign 1159) [279], get hold of a person in **adopt** (sign 984) [280], take over a country or someone else's ideas in **take over** (sign 1171) [281] and get hold of something visually as in **catch sight of** (p.38 [143]). One of the signs meaning 'aim' makes use the left **G** hand representing the goal and the **B** hand, placed nearer the signer, moving towards the **G** hand, i.e. towards the goal (sign 1299) [282]. The achievement of the aim is expressed by a similar sign, but in this case the right hand performs a grasping action close to the **A** hand: **achieve** [283].

An opposite kind of action is used for meanings associated with *giving up* or *getting rid of*. Like the emit set of metaphors, the give up set involves the opening of the **O** or **A** hand to a **5** hand. However, there is usually also some kind of directional movement involved, such as downward or upward movement. The sign **give up** [284], in the sense of admitting defeat, uses the **A** → **5** opening action with a firm upward movement and a backward head nod; **spend** [285] uses an accompanying outward movement to indicate getting rid of money; **retire** (sign 236) [286] involves an outward movement away from the signer and **rebel** (sign 89) [287] involves an upward twisting movement.

The *copy/absorb* set of metaphors also involves a closing

279. B⊤> 5̈ɒ⊥ ∨×∨#

280. Ø 5ɒ⊥ °⊤<# [A]

281. Ø 5̈⊥∧ ı 5̈⊥∧ °⊥# [AA]

282. G>∧ B<∧ (ɒ⊥)⊥

283. G>∧ 5⊤< °∧# [A]

284. Ø Aɑ⊥ Aɑ⊥ ∧□ [55]

285. ⌊⌋ Aɑ⊥ Aɑ⊥ ×⊥□ [55]

286. ⌈⌉ Ȧ>∧ Ȧ<∧ ×⊥∨□ [55]

287. Ø Aɒ⊥ Aɒ⊥ ω̇÷)(∧ ∨□ [55]

288. **copy**

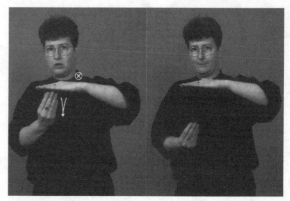

289. **photocopy**

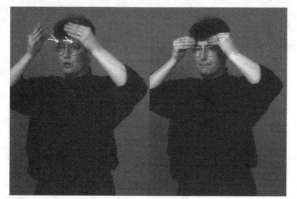

290. **learn**

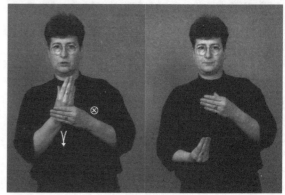

292. **drown**

action, but here the action begins with either the $\bar{\bar{\mathsf{B}}}$ or $\bar{\bar{5}}$ handshape and closes to a $\hat{\mathsf{B}}$ handshape: this action is almost always accompanied by a steady directional movement. The hand usually moves away from the source of what is being copied or absorbed. Thus the left **B** hand occurs as a non-specified source in the relatively neutral sign **copy** [288]; in **photocopy** [289], the orientation and hand arrangement indicate the nature of the copying; in **learn** [290], the absorption is viewed as some kind of cognitive process and therefore occurs at head level.

The *disappear/drown* grouping can be regarded as a subset of the absorb set. In this group the meanings involved

include total absorption to the point of disappearance as in **disappear** (sign 1548, note 2) [291]; being absorbed by water as in **drown** [292]; **lost for words** (sign 1548, note 1) [293] and ideas being sucked from the mind as in **slipped my mind** (p. 37 [141]). As with the other metaphor sets illustrated so far, the copy/absorb set appears to be currently productive in the language.

Other relevant morphemes expressed by handshape actions include the *elicit* morpheme, which uses the **v** flexing to a $\ddot{\mathsf{V}}$ in a repeated action ($\mathsf{G} \rightarrow \ddot{\mathsf{G}}$ is sometimes used instead). It occurs in a range of signs relating to extracting information or money and soliciting information or people,

288. $\mathsf{B}{>}\wedge \;\; _{\mathsf{I}\mathsf{X}} \;\; \bar{\bar{\mathsf{B}}}{<}\wedge \;\; {}^{>\,[\hat{\mathsf{B}}]}_{\#}$

289. $\underline{\mathsf{B}}{\smallsmile}{>} \;\; \bar{\bar{\mathsf{B}}}{<}\perp \;\; {}^{\vee\,[\hat{\mathsf{B}}]}_{\#}$

290. $\cap \;\; \bar{\bar{\mathsf{B}}}{>}\perp \;\; \bar{\bar{\mathsf{B}}}{<}\perp \;\; {}^{\top\,[\hat{\mathsf{B}}\,\hat{\mathsf{B}}]}_{\#}$

291. $\mathsf{L}\mathsf{I} \;\; \mathsf{G}{<}\wedge \;\; {}^{\times\perp}_{\vee} \;\; {/\!/} \;\; \bar{\bar{\mathsf{B}}}{>}\perp \;\; _{\odot} \;\; \bar{\bar{\mathsf{B}}}\alpha\perp \;\; {}^{\vee\,[\hat{\mathsf{B}}]}_{\#}$

292. $\mathsf{C}{>}\perp \;\; _{\odot} \;\; \bar{\bar{\mathsf{B}}}\alpha\perp \;\; {}^{\vee\,[\hat{\mathsf{B}}]}_{\#}$

293. $\bar{\bar{\mathsf{B}}}{>}\perp \;\; _{\odot} \;\; \bar{\bar{\mathsf{B}}}\alpha\perp \;\; {}^{\vee\,[\hat{\mathsf{B}}\,\hat{\mathsf{B}}]}_{\#}$

as in **exploit** (sign 774)[294]. The *shimmer* morpheme involves the **B** or **5** hand producing short twisting actions as in **shimmer** (sign 1057)[295]; the *pulsation* metaphor has the fingers wiggling as in **digital watch**[296] and the *blossom* morpheme involves a gradual opening of the **O** hand to **5̄** as in **blossom** (sign 1718)[297].

Major metaphor sets: movements

All of the metaphor sets described so far have been expressed by specific handshape pairs. However, different types of movement and positioning of the hands can also be linked to different types of meaning in a regular manner. As with the examples given so far, this does not imply that all instances of the specific movement-position pattern can necessarily be regarded as morphemic but the potential is there to be exploited. Interestingly, the suggestion that BSL movement and position patterns may express regular metaphorical relationships is echoed in recent work on semiotics. Calbris (1990) has suggested that French gestures (those that accompany spoken French in France) can be described in a similar manner. All of the examples mentioned here for BSL happen to have some kind of corollary in the French gesture system. This suggests that it may be worth exploring whether there is a common universal basis for such links.

It is no surprise that there is a structured correspondence between the positioning of the body articulators and certain categories of spatial dimension. Proximity of objects is shown by nearness of the hands to each other or to the body; physical separation or distance is expressed by a physical separation of the two hands or hands and body. Locative relations such as 'under', 'above', 'beside', 'one behind the other' and so on are shown by positionings of the hands to mirror these relationships. Although this is obvious to both signers and non-signers, and in a sense expected, it nevertheless reveals one further aspect of the way in which

the signs of BSL are motivated (see earlier discussion, pp. 41–45). However, the language can take this simulation several stages further by exploiting positional relationships to express spatialisation metaphors. In their account of metaphors in English, Lakoff and Johnson (1980) point out that the language makes use of spatialisation metaphors on a regular daily basis. We take it for granted that high status is up, low status is down; more is up, less is down; having control is up, being subject to control is down. BSL uses many similar spatialisation metaphors, but they are actually expressed in space and they can be built into the form of an individual sign by using appropriate choices from the movement, orientation and hand arrangement parameters. For reasons of space, it will not be possible to illustrate all the different types of spatialisation metaphor in BSL. However, several different examples will be presented in order to give some sense of the pervasive use of such metaphor within the language.

Within the *opposition* metaphor set, the notions of opposition and conflict are represented by the physical opposition of the two hands. The intensity of the opposition is then further emphasised by alternating and/or repeated movement. This is a highly productive metaphor set in BSL and can be seen in such signs as **argue** (sign 437)[298], **controversy** (sign 564)[299], **politics** (sign 886)[300], **war** (sign 1120)[301] and many more. In fact, this metaphorical relationship is so strong that very few signs relating to conflict do not exploit it in some way.

The *change* metaphor set makes use of the physical changing of the position of the hands to express the abstract notion of 'change'. The abstract alternation is most typically expressed by a physical alternation: examples include **adapt** (sign 276)[302], **alter** (sign 432)[303], **modify** and **changeable** (sign 955)[304] which all involve an alternating movement. The *substitute* set can be seen as closely related. Here the hands typically cross or interchange. This physical

---

294. Ø V̄ɑ⊥ Vᴏ⊥ ᵐ̄ᴛ

295. Ø 5>∧ 5<∧ $\left(\begin{smallmatrix} \circ \\ \omega \\ z \\ \wedge \end{smallmatrix}\cdot\right)$

296. ᴖ 5̈ɑ< ˣₒ

297. C>⊥ ₒ Oɑ⊥ ˣₒ□ [5̄]

298. Ø Gᴛ> ᵢ Gᴛ< ˚∧∧·

299. Ø G̈>⊥ G̈<⊥ ᶻ·

300. Ø F>⊥ ᵢ F<⊥ ˚∧∧·

301. Ø 5̈>∧ 5̈<∧ ᶻ·

302. Ø Āᴛ> Âᴛ< ᵉ∧ᴛᵥ

303. Ø Gᴛ∧ ₓ G⊥∧ₚ ˣ

304. Ø Y>⊥ ᵢ Y<∧ $\left(\begin{smallmatrix} \omega\wedge \\ \wedge \\ > \end{smallmatrix}\cdot\right)$

318. **working class**   319. **upper middle class**

transference of each hand to the other's original position mirrors the transference embodied in the meaning of the sign. Examples include **change over** (sign 446)[305], **replace** (sign 889)[306], and **exchange** (sign 1389)[307].

Interaction between two people is expressed by the physical to-ing and fro-ing of the two hands, with alternating movement representing the turn-taking involved. This can be seen in such signs as **conversation** (sign 458)[308], **negotiate** (p. 44 [193]), **dialogue** (sign 1387)[309] and **communication** (p. 44 [192]). These signs, which involve the notion of a two way interaction, can be contrasted with signs which involve a one way flow of ideas or information: the one way flow is mirrored by the single direction of the movement as in **tell a story** (sign 455)[310], **blame** (sign 439)[311], **announce** (sign 456)[312] and **command** (sign 303)[313]. Again

it is hard to imagine signs involving interaction being produced with a single movement or signs involving a one way flow involving a to and fro alternating movement. The motivated nature of these forms is fairly obvious: given the physical potential of the gestural system, it would be surprising if the language did not exploit such contrasts.

Status metaphors involve the differential placing of the two hands in relation to each other to mirror the equal or differential standing of individuals or groups. This can be seen in the sign **equal** (sign 1406)[314] where the hands start together and then separate in an arc to take up equivalent positions in space; **unequal** (sign 1639)[315] where the hands start together, but one moves up and the other down; **inferior** (sign 1340)[316] where the dominant hand moves to a position below the non-dominant hand and **superior** (sign 1342)[317] where the dominant hand is placed above the non-dominant. Various signs relating to socio-economic class make use of the non-dominant lower arm and **B** hand, from elbow to fingertips, as a basis for locating the dominant hand: the position, higher or lower on the arm or hand, reflects the position in society as in **working class** [318] and **upper middle class** [319].

Other signs which exploit comparable positional metaphors are **oppress** (sign 1364)[320] in which the dominant hand is held above the non-dominant and presses it downwards; **advocate** (sign 229, note 3)[321] where the right hand takes up a position behind and touching the left and both move forwards; **setback** (sign 1641)[322] where the two hands move back (towards the body); **exclude** (sign 1616)[323]

---

305. Ø ⌐G>∧ ⌐G<∧ ⊤×

306. Ø F>⊥ ₁ F<⊥₉ ''

307. Ø Bɑ> Bɑ<₉ ''

308. ⌣ G>∧ G<∧ ᴵᴺ·

309. Ø B̄ɑ> ₁ Bɑ< ᴵᴺ·

310. ∪ G⊤∧ ₁ G⊤∧ ⊥ᵥ ⍀ᴺ·

311. Ø G⊤⊥ ₁ G<⊥ ₒ⟩ᵢ

312. ⌣ G⊤> G⊤< ×(ⁿ⊥÷⊥)

313. Ø G⊥∧ (ⁿ⊥ᵥ<)

314. Ø Ḃʊ⊥ ₁ Ḃʊ⊥ ÷

315. Ø B̈>∧₉ ∧ B̈<∧ ᵛₒ

316. B̄ʊ> Bʊ< ₒₒₒ>ᵛ<

317. B̲ʊ> Bʊ< ₒₒₒ>∧<

318. ⌐ᵛ B̲>∧₉ Bʊ< ×·

319. B̲>∧₉ Bʊ< ×·

320. Ø G̈ɑ⊥ ₓ Bʊ⊥ ᵛ

321. A>⊥ A<⊥₉ ⊥× ⫽ Ø Ȧ>⊥ ₓ Ȧ<⊥₉ ⊥

325. 'th'

where the right hand pushes away from the left and **divorce** (sign 1634) [324] where the two hands are placed together but then separate.

Like classifiers, metaphorical morphemes expressed both by handshape pairs and movement-position combinations constitute a major resource for creating signs within the productive lexicon. They also enter into processes which allow the expansion of the established lexicon. Their usage within these contexts will be discussed further on pp. 85–88.

Non-manual morphemes

As we have already seen, BSL makes use of a range of non-manual actions within the established lexicon. These occur somewhat rarely as individual non-manual signs (see pp. 31–32) and much more frequently as components within multi-channel signs (see pp. 32–35). While it has been suggested that non-manual free forms, i.e. non-manual signals operating independently as the carriers of lexical meaning, are infrequent, there is plenty of evidence of the existence of non-manual bound morphemes. Such morphemes can be added on to either established forms or forms created through productive processes. They therefore constitute a further set of lexical resources for the user.

In this section, we present an account of the main non-manual morphemes which have been noted by researchers.* As with the other classes of morpheme outlined here, there is no claim that this is a fully comprehensive account. As we study the language in more depth, we will no doubt discover further examples of such morphemes and be able to elaborate their function in more detail.

Most of the non-manual components of meaning established so far typically take on an adverbial function in the language. Some can also take on an intensifying function in respect of adjectives or classifier forms. In examining these non-manual morphemes, it will be useful to establish both the form of the morpheme, i.e. the particular non-manual feature or combinations involved, and the semantic content of the form. Once again, we are dealing with rather generalised meanings which can, in some cases, be difficult to elaborate. Several of the examples mentioned here appear to have equivalents in other sign languages: again, it will be fascinating in future to see whether any universal basis for such similarities can be discerned. This is especially worth considering, given that work in semiotics suggests comparable non-manual actions may occur as accompaniments to speech (see Calbris, 1990).

A convention has been established within the wider sign language literature of giving abbreviated labels to some of these non-manual adverbials. Where appropriate, the same labels will be applied here. Although these labels sometimes relate to lip patterns and are expressed in terms of spoken language mouth shapes such as "ee", there is no suggestion at all that these forms relate to English. On the contrary, such forms are completely independent of English and this labelling is merely used as a convenient device.

The 'th' adverbial [325] has the dominant feature of tongue protrusion. In fact, the tip of the tongue is held between the teeth, as if the signer were about to produce the sound sequence "th" [θ]. Other non-manual actions may also co-occur with this tongue protrusion: probably the chief amongst these is a puckering of the nose. This non-manual morpheme 'th' expresses meanings such as 'boring' and 'unpleasant'. If added to an established sign like **work** (sign 1345) [326], it may mean that the work involved was boring or not very enjoyable. It may also be used to give the impression that something is 'incredibly easy' or 'no problem': however, even here, the connotation is somewhat negative

---

322. ∅ B̈>⊥ B̈<⊥ °°
ʌ̂ ̌

323. B̈ɑ>ₗ B̈ʊ< >

* Much of the material in this section is based on published and unpublished material from the Edinburgh BSL Research Project, in

324. ∅ B̈ʊ> ₗₓ B̈ʊ< ÷

326. ‾B⊤⊥ B⊤⊥ ×·

particular work carried out by Lilian Lawson, Gerry Hughes and Martin Colville.

328. 'sh'   331. 'ee'   333. 'puffed cheeks'

or pejorative. Thus it may be used by someone who is boasting about something being too easy. Interestingly, the same non-manual signal occurs as an inherent component of the multi-channel sign **doddle** [327].

The BSL non-manual adverbial meaning 'at ease' or 'without effort' was mentioned earlier (p. 34) in respect of the non-manual signal in which the head is typically tilted to one side and the lips are pushed forward. This seems to be comparable to the non-manual adverb labelled 'mm' and noted by researchers in relation to ASL and SSL.* This can be seen, for example, in the sign **saunter** (p. 34[123]). The semantic content of this sign is 'walking in no particular direction in a casual manner'. The sign has three meaningful components corresponding to the different aspects of this meaning: the legs classifier; a variable movement path (see further p. 76) and the non-manual component 'with ease'. As we have seen in relation to compounding, it is only once the whole word is assembled that the particular results of bringing together these specific meaningful units can be appreciated. The 'mm' or 'at ease' adverbial is used frequently by BSL users. One other view of this adverbial is that it carries the meaning 'normally' or 'in the normal or proper fashion'.† Such an interpretation is also appropriate for many instances of its usage in BSL. When added to **drive** it can mean something like 'just driving along' (i.e. in the normal way). Which of the possible meanings is uppermost depends to a large extent on the nature of the other components with which it co-occurs.

The non-manual signal in which the lips are pushed forward and air is expelled through the mouth as if producing the sound 'sh' [ʃ], occurs within the multi-channel sign which is glossed here as **exist**. The same non-manual signal occurs in a non-manual adverbial labelled 'sh'[328] and having the function of stressing occurrence or existence. Thus it can be added to the sign **die** (sign 699)[329] to mean '(the person) really did die' or to the sign **that** (sign 310)[330] to mean 'it really is that one'. In these instances, the manual components are usually produced with a short repeated movement. The non-manual adverbial labelled 'ee'[331] has the lips stretched wide and the teeth showing. It usually has the meaning of 'with great effort or intensity'. It often co-occurs with the aspectual inflections meaning 'to go on for a long time' and 'to happen again and again'. It can also act as an intensifier to stress some aspect of the sign's meaning. When added to **expect** (sign 188)[332] it means 'expect at any moment'. It can also function in a comparable manner to 'sh' to stress existence and occurrence as in 'it really is that one'. In such instances, there is often an accompanying head nod, too.

Several further intensifiers occur frequently in BSL. Two make use of actions of the cheeks. The first usually labelled 'puffed cheeks'[333] involves a puffing out of the cheeks, together with, in some cases, an exhalation of air through the vibrating lips. The second, sometimes labelled

---

327. ○ B̂⊤∧ ᵒ̵I

330. Ø G<⊥ ᵒ̵⋛

329. Ø H>∧ H<∧ ⁿ̵I

332. ⌐⌐ᐸ À<⊥ ˣ ·

* See Liddell (1980), Baker-Shenk (1983) and Bergman (1983).
† See discussion in Coerts (1992, ch. 2).

336. 'open wide' 339. 'drawn in lips' 340. 'puckered nose' 341. 'downward droop...'

'oo' involves a sucking in of the cheeks and an accompanying sucking in of air through the rounded lips. There seems to be no absolute division between the function of these two adverbials. The 'oo' form seems to occur most frequently within signs which have inherently unpleasant or negative meanings such as 'really terrible' and 'absolutely impossible'. When the 'puffed cheeks' adverbial is added to verbs such as **work** (p. 73[326]) or **try** (sign 374)[334] it usually means 'with great effort' and/or 'over a long time'. This adverbial therefore frequently occurs along with inflections for durative aspect (see *Grammar* section, p. 106). It is also used as an intensifier in expressions of extent or plurality with meanings such as 'a huge box'. It can be added to time expressions to stress length of time as in **long ago** (sign 1480)[335]. A third intensifier is labelled the 'head turn'. Here the head usually turns away from the location of the sign and tilts downwards. Although this head position is the dominant feature, it may appear with sucked in cheeks, puffed cheeks and/or furrowed brows. It is often used when signs such as **work** and **try** (see above) are inflected for aspect.

Several ASL researchers have drawn attention to an adverbial which they label as 'cheek-shoulder' or 'cs' for short. This involves a bringing together of the shoulder and cheek, through raising and bringing forward the shoulder and turning the cheek and mouth towards the shoulder. Coerts (1992) describes the essential meaning of this adverbial as 'proximity', i.e. 'close in time or space'. It can function in a similar way to 'ee' when added to the verb **expect**: the form would then mean 'expect something to occur at any moment'. Perhaps because BSL also has other adverbials

which express this same meaning, 'cs' may not occur quite as frequently in BSL as it seems to in ASL.

The 'open wide' adverbial[336] is used to express the meaning 'astonishment'. The form typically consists of a wide open mouth and wide open eyes, usually with raised eyebrows. As we have already seen (p. 33), it is an inherent element of some multi-channel signs relating to surprise and amazement. Added to a verb such as **look**[337], it gives the meaning 'to look in astonishment'. However, it does sometimes function as an independent free morpheme within syntax, for example, to allow the signer to comment on an action. Thus the form **the person came towards me**[338] could be articulated with an accompanying open wide adverbial sign so that the utterance would mean something like 'I watched in amazement as the person came towards me'. In this instance, the adverbial is not part of the sign **look**, but a separate, independent adverbial sign within the sentence.

There are several further non-manual signals which appear to have adverbial functions, although it can be quite difficult to provide a precise account of the meanings involved. The adverbial 'drawn-in lips'[339] appears to be mean something like 'put up with', although other non-manual signals such as a forward-side head tilt may be necessary to provide this meaning fully. The 'puckered nose' adverbial[340] can suggest some negative connotation, although more precise characterisation of this feature is difficult. The 'downward droop of the mouth' adverbial[341] also usually has similar negative connotations. However, these last three examples may occur more frequently across stretches of sign

334. Gᴏ⊥ ᵢ Gᴏ⊥ᵩ ⊥·ˣ⊥

335. ⁱ̌ᴵ Bᴛ> Bᴛ<ᵩ ᴰᴺ·ᵉᵀᵥ

337. ⊔ V<ʌ ˣ⊥

338. ∅ Gᴛʌ ᵀ

utterance to express moods or attitude.

In this section, our main focus has been on non-manual signals which can be regarded as units of meaning: such morphemes are part of the resources of the productive lexicon and can combine with other morphemes to produce multi-morphemic words of BSL.

Movement and location morphemes

Work on American Sign Language, particularly that undertaken by McDonald (1982), Supalla (1982 and 1986) and Schick (1990), has revealed the operation of what have been termed *verbs of motion and location* within ASL. These are essentially multi-morphemic verbs which combine classifier forms with movement morphemes to produce a huge variety of possible forms within the productive lexicon. Supalla refers to these morphemes technically as movement *roots*. There is some controversy in the literature as to whether the classifier or the movement morpheme should be regarded as the stem to which the other category of morpheme is added. A more recent account by Schick (1990) provides a somewhat different description of the functioning of movement morphemes within productive morphology. Supalla distinguished three different predicate types: existence, location and movement. Thus a classifier form accompanied by zero movement, i.e. holding the hand static expressed the notion 'this X exists' as in the utterance 'this vehicle exists'. In the second type, the classifier handshape is accompanied by a stamping action: the hand 'bounces' downward, ending with a firm hold. When used with the vehicle classifier it would mean something like 'a vehicle is located in this position'. In these two cases, the location of the hand does not change. In the third category, called *motion roots*, the hand changes location following different movement paths or in different manners. The types of movement involved include moving from one place to another (in a linear fashion); moving through an arc; moving in a circle; swinging and turning upside down. Supalla suggests that these are separate movement morphemes which can combine sequentially or simultaneously. Schick's account gives more recognition to the role of visual imagery in ASL and to that extent is rather more in line with the kind of perspective offered here. She proposes three different types of morpheme: movement through space (MOV); a stylised imitation of real world action (IMIT) and a single point in space (DOT). Schick is then able to show how these different morphemes operate in different kinds of ways with the different classes of classifier to produce a range of possible constructions.

The following description of BSL predicates is influenced by both of the above accounts, but is somewhat different from both in terms of emphasis and terminology. (In some cases, the terminological changes are made merely to fit with descriptive categories used within the BSL literature and tradition.) Within the account of classifiers presented on pp. 46–47, six different types of classifier are established: semantic classifiers; size and shape classifiers; size and shape tracing classifiers; handling classifiers; instrumental classifiers; and touch classifiers. For the purposes of elaborating how movement and location morphemes can interact with classifiers so as to express different kinds of grammatical information, it will be useful to collapse these into three broad categories: semantic classifiers, SASS classifiers (including tracing and instrumental) and handling classifiers (including touch). There are differences in functioning which could be handled in a more elaborate account, although some of these differences have yet to be researched.

The following categories specify different types of movement and/or location morphemes. In their primary functions, they combine with the different categories of classifier to produce a range of different types of predicate in BSL. We can distinguish the following categories of movement/location morphemes in BSL. The *existence* category of movement morphemes simply focuses on the existence or presence of a referent (which is typically expressed by a classifier). Its location as such is not emphasised. This category is expressed by zero movement.

The *be located* category of movement morphemes tells us that something is located in a particular place: the focus is on the location. This category is expressed by a stamping action. The *path* category of movement morphemes (termed MOV by Schick, 1990) indicates path movement, i.e. the hand moving from one point of space to another. This movement may be in a straight path, an arc or a circular path. The path category is expressed through directional movements. The *imitation* morpheme provides "a stylised imitation of real-world action." (Schick, 1990, p.17) Here the focus is on manner of action, such as 'turning upside down'. This category is typically expressed by changes in the orientation of the hand and other choices of manner of movement as outlined on pp. 23–26. The *extent* category of morphemes provides information on the extent of the object. Tracing SASSes can thus seen as combinations of a SASS morpheme and an extent morpheme.

There may be many different choices of morpheme within specific categories, particularly the last three.

342. **one person separated from another**

Moreover, different choices may combine internally, within categories, and in some cases across categories, resulting in highly complex forms. The separation out of the two categories of 'existence' and 'be located' morphemes follows Supalla (1982) who distinguishes a *hold root* which means 'be stationary' and a *contact root* which means 'be located'. Schick (1990) collapses these into one category which she labels DOT and which refers to a single point in space.

Clearly the two are very closely related: location implies existence and vice versa. The difference is one of focus. Although the existence morpheme is classed as a movement morpheme, it is typically expressed by zero movement: the hand is merely held in space. This morpheme is often attached to the classifier which is functioning as the affected object or location within an utterance: in **one person separated from another** [342], the left hand person is simply 'there'; the other person carries out the action. In **one vehicle crashes into another** [343], the left hand typically takes on the role of the object, i.e. that which is affected by the action. The 'be located' morpheme is often used when establishing referents in space. Thus when describing an accident the signer may locate a vehicle to the left of the signing space, another vehicle to the right and behind (i.e. two predicates meaning 'vehicle located here') and then use forms involving movement and/or imitation morphemes to show how they interact with each other.

Probably the most controversial aspect of the Schick model which has been adopted here is the use of the *imitation* (IMIT) category. She describes this as "...a prototypical idealisation or distillation of real-world activity, but not an imitation or complete analogue image of it."

(Schick, 1990, p. 18) Simply by using this label, Schick recognises the motivation underlying specific morphemes. However, we have already seen that classifier morphemes which are obviously motivated nevertheless conform to and are constrained by the phonological (cherological) structure of the language. In a similar way, the movement and location morphemes are constrained by aspects of the movement phonology of BSL. The table below presents some indication of the potential of the system.

existence	semantic:	a person is stationary
	SASS:	a round thing is stationary
	handling:	I hold a round thing
be located	semantic:	a person is located in this position
	SASS:	a round thing is located in this position
	handling:	I place a round thing in this position
path	semantic:	a person moves in a straight line
	SASS:	a round thing moves in an arc
	handling:	I move a round thing in a straight line
imitation	semantic:	a person rolls over from side to side
	SASS:	a round thing moves in an erratic fashion
	handling:	I unscrew a jar lid
extent	semantic:	—
	SASS:	1. a thin pole of approximately this length; 2. a thin pole of indefinite length
	handling:	—

Once we realise that we can substitute a whole range of classifier and movement/location morpheme choices in these positions, we begin to develop some idea of the power of the morphological patterning of the language. One further important aspect of Schick's account of classifier predicates in ASL is her outlining of some of the major functions of these forms within morphology and syntax. While the reader is referred to Schick (1990) for further elaboration, it is worth noting some key insights. Semantic classifiers typically operate as intransitive verbs expressing

342. BꞰⱢ BꞰⱢⱭ ⱶˣ

343. Ø AⱢⱭ , AⱢⱭ ⱶ

344. **car headlights**   345. **airport landing lights**   346. **tail lights**   347. **thought transfer**

the grammatical relations 'subject' and 'verb' with optional locative information: for example, 'a person approaches', or 'a car moves (to the right)'. In contrast, handling classifiers typically act as transitive verbs expressing the relations of verb and object, with the subject implied and locative information optional: for example, 'I (usually the signer, unless otherwise specified) move a round thing (from the table and put it on the floor)'.

Movement and location morphemes thus provide an essential set of options for creating classifier predicates and, as we shall see further below, nominals in BSL.

Classes of imitative location morphemes

If we look at how and where classifier and metaphor based forms are placed, we begin to realise that there is probably an equivalent to the IMIT category proposed for movement, but in this case for location. In this *imitative location* category, handshapes are placed with reference to what Liddell (1992) has called *surrogate* objects. In other words, the signer acts as if a specific object were present and locates the hand(s) with reference to that object. The signer may use a touch or handling classifier to indicate pressing or dialling numbers on a phone. Here the left hand may be used as a base, but this is not compulsory. However, the signer will typically locate the classifying handshape with reference to the imagined object. In this way, we typically know whether the signer is using a wall phone, a table phone or a mobile phone. Similarly, if the signer uses a handling classifier predicate to indicate moving a round thing from X to Y, we

will typically know whether X is relatively high or low in relation to the signer, for example if the object is moved from a high shelf to a low shelf. If we use the metaphor-based *emit* morpheme to indicate car headlights, then the two hand will take up a position in front of the body [344]; if we use the same morpheme for relatively low traffic lights, then we can show these in relation to ourselves or in relation to each other. If we use the reduced *emit* morpheme (using $\hat{H} \rightarrow \bar{V}$ rather than $O \rightarrow 5$ to show, for example, either smaller lights or lights at a distance) we can place these to show the position of **airport landing lights** [345] or in relation to an aircraft which is moving away from us, i.e. as the **tail lights** of such an aircraft [346]. The language exploits such possibilities, whilst nevertheless restricting the use of signing space and the inventory of handshape morphemes.

Such imitation of real-world location has to be distinguished from the conventionalised locations discussed on pp. 43–44. This latter type combines productively primarily with metaphor-based morphemes. Thus **thought transfer** [347] combines the conventional location of the head (conventionally associated with cognition), the lines metaphor and the interaction movement metaphor to express the meaning of 'two way thought transfer'. (The choice of metaphor movement could be changed to indicate a one way flow of information.) We are thus able to distinguish several different types of location morpheme including referential location (placing referents in space), imitative location and conventional location.

344. Ø A⊥∧ ¦ A⊥∧ ⁿ[55]

345. Ø O⊓⊥ O⊓⊥ (□[55]·)⊥

346. O Ĥ⊤∧ Ĥ⊤∧ (□[V̊V̊]·)⊥

347. ∩ 5̄ʊ> ¦ 5ʊ<ʔ ⊥∩·

348. walk   349. walk

Summary of resources

So far then, we have seen that the BSL signer has a powerful set of lexical resources available: powerful because the signer can generate exactly what is required in a particular context by appropriate manipulation of the creative potential of the lexicon. These resources include classifier morphemes, metaphor-based morphemes, movement morphemes, location morphemes and non-manual morphemes. A glance at the classifier table on pp. 53–67 will give some indication of the richness of these resources. In the discussion of movement morphemes (on pp. 76–78), we began to see how the signer can combine items from these morpheme categories to produce an incalculable number of words within the productive lexicon. The resources can be exploited in different ways in different contexts. Thus the signer has a remarkable degree of flexibility: the signer may simply choose words from the established lexicon; he/she can add units of meaning to these established words, to create new lexical items; and the signer may combine items from the different sets of morpheme listed above, again to create new forms. In all of these cases, the signer may then choose, or be required by the grammar, to add specific inflectional morphemes to these lexical forms (see pp. 100–113).

The notion of 'new'can be somewhat problematic in this context. Linguists very often stress the creativity of syntax: we frequently produce 'new' sentences that no-one has ever seen or heard before: we cope with these because of our knowledge of the syntactic resources of the language involved. Of course, someone else may have uttered a particular sentence before, but we do not know this and it might be difficult to discover if this were the

case or not. The English sentence "Lexicographers work best on a diet of strong beer and cheese sandwiches", is a perfectly comprehensible sentence of English, but there is a strong likelihood that it has never been uttered before. Word-formation has generally been regarded as a less creative process and indeed even within BSL the generative powers of syntax are probably considerably greater than the lexical generation processes. Nevertheless, many of the words of BSL are like the above sentence: they may have never been produced in quite that way before, yet they are clearly comprehensible.

We can begin to get some idea of the range of possibilities involved by exploring some examples. We shall look firstly at some examples which add morphemes to words from the established lexicon and then at combinations from the productive lexicon.

Options within the established lexicon

As we have seen (pp. 50–51), one of the features of BSL which is particularly fascinating for the watcher and learner is the way in which the signer can provide a range of different perspectives. Some of the options associated with close and distant focus or frame of reference may be present within the established lexicon, while others are created anew for the particular effect. What is almost always true is that we are able to note a frequent manipulation of visual imagery and visual effect; the signer plays with the possibilities of viewing the world in different kinds of ways—a fact which is not particularly surprising within a visual language.

If we asked a signer to produce a sign to express the meaning 'walk', the most likely response would be a sign using the right **v** hand. In one version, **walk**[348] the hand would be bent at the palm knuckles, held in front of the body and the hand would move away from the signer with the two extended fingers moving to and fro alternatively. This is also, interestingly enough, what non-signers often do when asked to make up a sign for the notion of walking. There are several other manual signs which make use of a **v** configuration, i.e. the handshape in which the first two fingers are extended and bent as in **walk**[349]. In these cases, the bending is not semantically 'salient': we are not expected to imagine that a person is actually walking with both knees bent. This contrasts with a sign like **drunk** (p. 80[350]) where the focus is again on the legs but where the combination of the handshape and action suggests an inability to stand up

---

348. Ø V̈ᴏ⊥   ꝏ·⊥

349. Bɑ⊥ V̈ᴛᴠ   ⊥·×

| 350. drunk | 351. walk | 352. walk | 354. walk |

straight: a meaning captured by the English colloquialism "legless". It seems that signers have an ongoing ability to decide what visual information should be regarded as salient in any given sign.

Walking does not simply involve actions of the legs. The signer can choose to focus in on other elements of the bodily action. If the feet are chosen as the central focal point, the signer may use a sign involving the two flat **B** hands moving forward in an alternating manner, **walk**[351]. Obviously the action can vary depending on the type of walking involved, e.g. 'walking away', 'walking upstairs', 'walking very quietly', etcetera. Such changes may be depicted through modifications of the movements of the hands and the head and body. An alternative sign, which also focuses on the feet, makes use of the two **Ö** hands, **walk**[352]. The choice of handshape together with accompanying liprounding would indicate that the action involves walking either on tip-toe or on very high heels.

Other signs which could be glossed as **walk** may focus on the actions of the upper part of the body. In several of these signs, the central focus is on the shoulders and arms, although clearly the head is also important. The sign in which the hands are clenched into fists and the shoulders make an alternating forward action, **walk**[353], is often used to indicate walking in a determined fashion. One version of this, in which the chest is thrust forward, the head held back and the hands and arms held more tensely, may be

used to indicate a massive person walking. The sign in which the two **5** hands move in an alternating fashion at chest level, **walk**[354], is often used to express a more casual or nonchalant kind of walking. Once again the facial expression is also important in distinguishing nuances of meaning. Further options are available. The signer may choose to focus on the hands at shoulder level, as in the action of holding the straps of a rucksack or satchel: the walking action is shown primarily by the alternating forward movement of the shoulders, **walk**[355].

Modifications of established signs

All of the above signs could be said to be part of the established lexicon. Yet these signs can themselves be further modified to show the manner, location and direction of walking. Some of these modifications may be regarded as resulting from the application of grammatical rather than lexical morphemes. This is a somewhat technical question as the boundaries between these two classes is not always easy to draw. Leaving aside the theoretical questions involved here, we can recognise that the addition of appropriate modifications can result in dozens, possibly hundreds, of different forms.

In the English language we typically have two options for providing manner and location information: either we choose a verb which in itself includes the type of information we wish to express or we add an appropriate adverb or

---

350. B̄ɑⳐ ₓ V̈ₜᵥ ᵡᵇₓₜ₃

351. Ø BᴅⳐ BᴅⳐ ⊥ᴎ·

352. Ø G̈ᴅⳐ G̈ᴅⳐ ⊥ᴎ·

353. Ø Aₜ> Aₜ< ⊥ᴎ·

354. Ø 5>ʌ 5<ʌ ᴅᴎᵥᵢ

355. ⌐⌐ Ȧₜ> Ȧₜ< ˣᴎ·ᵢ

356. **struggling along**   357. **sauntering**   358. **creeping warily**   359. **marching defiantly**

adverbial phrase. English has a set of lexical items related to the action of walking. The set includes such items as "walk", "stride", "stroll", "saunter", "march" and "creep". However, this set alone would not provide sufficient choice for the English user, hence the frequent use of adverbial elements as in "walk upstairs", "stroll nonchalantly", "march along the road", "stride determinedly across the room", "creep quietly along the corridor", "wander carelessly across the road" etcetera. It could be argued that words like 'saunter' and 'stroll' have an adverbial element built into them. The words themselves tell us how the individual walked. In BSL, there is always the potential to build this type of information into the sign itself. This is achieved by using the type of non-manual modifiers presented on pp. 73–76 and by modifying the orientation, location and movement of the manual sign.

The addition of tongue protrusion together with a downward droop of the shoulders to the above manual forms would suggest walking with difficulty or in an exhausted manner, e.g. **struggling along** [356]. The use of a short side to side and away movement of the V̈ handshape together with the head raised, a short side to side action of the head and the lips pushed forward would suggest walking in a casual manner, e.g. **sauntering** [357].

The use of the two flat **B** hands together with the head pushed forward and a slow side to side action of the head and eyes would indicate **creeping warily** [358], while the use of the closed fists in a relatively fast alternating action, together with head and shoulders thrust back would indicate **marching defiantly** [359]. Thus even with what we might

think of as the established manual signs, it is still possible to vary the manner of production and add non-manual components in such a way as to create a much wider selection of options than might be obvious at first sight.

Productive options

Such flexibility and creativity come into full force within what we have termed the *productive lexicon*. Here we have the potential of using a whole range of classifiers along with other relevant choices to create forms which suit the communication needs of the moment. In the next set of examples we shall retain the notion of 'walking' as the central semantic element, but demonstrate the choices available to the signer. Most of the examples given below are taken from real examples of story-telling and joke-telling by Deaf people.

A signer describing a giant chasing after a young girl made use of the two forearms and G̈ hands together with the non-manual feature 'drawn in lips' to produce the sign **running with huge strides** (page 82[360]). Signers telling stories about animals, frequently distinguish between animal and person referents. Again we can see this with meanings linked to 'walk'. The two Ḧ hands are often used to depict the front legs and paws of a four-legged animal. This immediately provides us with sets of choices similar to those above, but here the handshapes indicate that it is an animal that is walking warily or carelessly or hurriedly etcetera. To show the basic action of walking, the two Ḧ hands make an alternating action towards the body: the body of the signer becomes, as it were, the body of the ani-

356.  Baⵍ V̈тv ⊤/× ·

357. Ø V̈ⵍ z/⊥

358. Ø Bⵍ Bⵍ ⊥∿·

359. Ø Aт> Aт< ⊥∿·

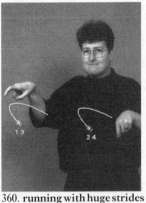

360. **running with huge strides** 361. **animal walking**

362. **animal running** 363. **animal running**

364. **animal walking** 366. **horse trotting**

mal, **animal walking** [361]. However, the signer can vary this perspective by placing the two Ḧ hands one behind the other and then making simultaneous movements towards the body: this form is typically used when the signer wishes to show the animal moving very fast, i.e. running rather than walking, **animal running** [362]. The signer may also choose to exploit the V̈ handshape rather than the Ḧ handshape as in **animal running** [363].

The fact that we are talking about a four-legged animal does not mean that Ḧ Ḧ or V̈ V̈ are the only choices. If a large animal such as an elephant or a hippopotamus is referred to, then the lower arms and closed fists ⌐A ⌐A are used to repre-

sent the legs of the animal, **animal walking** [364], although the basic alternating movement would be comparable to that in previous examples. Of course the signer may choose to exploit this particular manual component for special effect with reference to animals which are much smaller in size than elephants or hippopotamuses. The signer may choose this form to refer to a particularly large cat, especially if wishing to contrast its size with some less formidable specimen. In complete contrast, the use of the two G̈ hands could refer to very small animals such as **mice scuttling away** [365].

The lower arm and closed fist pair ⌐A ⌐A can also be found in signs relating to the movement of a horse. In such examples, the arms are held less vertically. Here the closed fists represent the horse's hooves: the range of movements available can express the various types of action expressed by such English words as "trot" (**horse trotting** [366]), "canter" and "gallop". In such examples, both the manner of movement and the accompanying rhythm are particularly important.

If an animal has claws, then the signer may choose to focus on this feature. Here the two SASS classifiers 5̈ 5̈ would be used to show, for example, a **tiger** or a **lion walking** [367]. Once again, while we can say that some particular choices are more likely for one animal rather than another, the signer may choose to surprise the watcher by a possible but

360. ∅ G̈⊥ʌ G̈⊥ʌ ᵈ ᴺ· / ⊥

361. ∅ Ḧʊ⊥ Ḧʊ⊥ ᵀᴺ·

362. ∅ Ḧʊ⊥ Ḧʊ⊥₉ ᵈ· / ᵀ

363. ∅ V̈ʊ⊥ V̈ʊ⊥₉ ᵈ· / ᵀ

364. ∅ ⌐Aᴛᵥ ⌐Aᴛᵥ ᵀᴺ·

365. ∅ G̈ʊ⊥ G̈ʊ⊥ (ᵀᴺ·) / ⊥

366. ∅ Aʊ⊥ Aʊ⊥ ᵈ ᴺ· / ᵀ

367. **tiger** or **lion walking**   368. **penguin waddling**   371. **sitting with legs crossed**   375. **splayed**

less likely option. In the case of a cat, Ħ Ħ may be the most likely, but 5̈ 5̈, G̈ G̈, V̈ V̈ and ╱A ╱A are also possible. Once we begin to recognise the different types of physical feature involved in say a **penguin waddling**[368], a **spider walking**[369] and a **seal shuffling**[370], then we realise that the classifiers of BSL provide the potential for focusing in on these visually contrastive elements.

In the above examples, we have concentrated primarily on the notions of 'walking' and 'running'. If we extend this only slightly to meanings related to 'standing', 'getting up', 'sitting down', 'lying down' and 'falling', it should become immediately obvious that other new sets of possibilities open up. It would be virtually impossible to list the sets of options fully as, once again, the signer is able to choose to focus on different salient elements.

The following examples give a hint of the possibilities available. **sitting with legs crossed**[371] and **sitting with legs dangling**[372] both make use of the two G̈ hands as legs classifiers. In one case the extended index fingers will actually be crossed; in the other the hands will move to and fro imitating the action of the legs. Both of these contrast with the established signs **sit**[373] and **sit**[374]. Similarly, the sign glossed as **splayed**[375] was used by a signer to refer to a dead bird splattered on the ground. The sign uses the legs classi-

fiers G̈ G̈ together with the non-manual component 'tongue protrusion' (symbolised by 'th') which here indicates unpleasantness. The same non-manual component was used in a sign denoting the somewhat haphazard swinging action of a parrot on a perch: here the V̈ legs classifier was used (**parrot swinging on perch**[376]). In all of these cases, the signer decides to focus on the legs as the salient element, although other choices would clearly have been possible.

We can contrast these examples with choices relating to the meanings 'fall' and 'dive'. The established signs **fall** (p. 84[378]) and **dive** (p. 84[379]) relating to these meanings clearly derive from the V legs classifiers. However, examples have been noted where the lower arm and closed fist (╱A) component was used instead of the V component. In a sign which could be glossed as **his whole body fell with a thud** (page 84[380]), the A hand and lower arm were held vertically and then bent forward from the elbow in a bending action. In a comparable example, a signer referred to a huge being diving into the sea by using the lower arm and closed fist (╱A) component with a downward bending action. The resulting sign focuses on the bulk of the giant figure and on the stiffness of the diving action (**huge being dives** (p. 84[381])). Again the signer exploits the resources available within the productive lexicon to provide a particular kind of focus or

367. Ø 5̈ʊ⊥ 5̈ʊ⊥ ⊥ᴎ·

368. ⊔ Bʊ⊥ Bʊ⊥ ˣᴎ· ᴅᴎ

369. Ø 5̈ʊ⊥ ˢᵀᐳ

370. [] Bʊ⊥ Bʊ⊥ ˣᴎ· ᴵ

371. G̈ʊ⊥ G̈⊲⊥ ᵛ ᵒˣ

372. Ø G̈ʊ⊥ G̈ʊ⊥ ᵀᴎ·

373. Ø H⊳ʌ H⊲ʌ ᵒᵛ

374. Ø Aʊ⊥ Aʊ⊥ ᵒᵛ

375. Ø G̈ʊ⊥ G̈ʊʌ ᴅᵵᴎ

376. Ø (G⊃ᐳ ₓ V̈ʊ⊥ ᴅᵀ·)ᴵ

380. **his whole body…** 382. **sleigh winding…** 383. **cars somersaulting** 386. **nervous**

visual image. It may seem that the kind of flexibility we have referred to above is unlikely to apply to what we might think of as the most strongly established meaning-form links, as exemplified by the vehicle classifier. Yet despite the frequency of the use of the **B** handshape to express movements and actions of vehicles, other choices are also exploited by signers. One signer, referring to a sleigh moving swiftly down a long and winding hill, made use of the handshapes **B**, **H** and **G** to refer to the sleigh. It was as if the narrower handshapes, **H** and **G**, were more appropriate for showing the movements of the sleigh at a distance (**sleigh winding downhill** [382]). Similarly, several signers describing a film of a motor racing grand prix also used **H** and **G** classifiers when referring to the cars speeding round the track, interweaving amongst each other and in a couple of cases somersaulting (**cars somersaulting** [383]) into the air. These choices provided the watcher with a different perspective.

One American researcher, Scott Liddell, examining lexical imagery in American Sign Language has recently suggested that signers make use of what he terms "an enhanced semantic image." (Liddell, 1992) It is as if there is a twoway process: the choice of image (in the above examples, the classifier choice) provides a particular way of viewing the meaning, while at the same time the actual image (the classifier) can only be fully appreciated once the meaning is

known. The **V̌** handshape combined with a swinging action may be used to express such different meanings as 'dancing' (**dance** [384]) and 'a person hanging by the neck' (**hang** [385]). We can only interpret the image appropriately once we have the context, at which point the image can enhance the meaning. This exploitation of imagery is a central generating force within the BSL lexicon.

Sometimes the signer can substitute one component for another within what are normally regarded as established signs in order to create a particular effect. The sign glossed as **nervous** [386] makes use of two **G̈** hands, presumably deriving from a legs classifier form. One signer chose to replace this with two **H** hands when signing about a nervous cat [387]. The same signer also replaced the usual **B̈** handshapes with **Ḧ Ḧ** to mean (**animal**) **withdraw** [388].

Sometimes the signer makes choices which are appropriate, but which have a particularly strong impact because they are unusual within the context. The sign **carry a pile of coins** (p. 63 [258]) was used by a signer when telling a joke. The humour was enhanced by the precariousness of the action as revealed in the choice of handling classifier. The metaphorically extended, classifier-based form **glance to the left** [389] or variations, such as **glance furtively** (**V̈ V̈** at the eyes, plus shoulder hunch and lips pushed forward) and **gradually have ones eyes drawn to the right in in-**

378. $\overline{\text{B̌ʊ>}}$ ₓ V̈ʊ⊥ $\overset{\text{ɑ}}{\underset{\text{ϱ}}{>}}$

379. Ø V̈ʊ⊥ $\overset{\text{ɑv}}{\underset{\text{ϱ}}{}}$

380. Ø ✓ʌⲦʌ $\overset{\text{v̊ v̊}}{\cdot}$

381. Ø ✓ʌ⌐ʌ $\overset{\text{v}}{<}$

382. Ø Gʊ< $\overset{\left(\overset{\text{ɳ}}{\text{z}}\right)}{\underset{<}{\text{v}}}$

383. Ø Hʊ⊥ Hʊ⊥ $\overset{\text{ɑⲚ} \cdot}{\underset{⊥}{}}$

384. Ø V̈Ⲧ> V̈Ⲧ< $\overset{\left(\overset{\text{ɳ v}}{\text{z}} \cdot\right)}{}$

385. Ø V̈ʊ⊥ $\overset{\text{ɳ}}{\text{z}}$

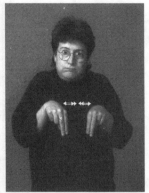

387. **animal nervous**

388. **animal withdraw**

390. **car travelling fast**

393. **floods of tears**

394. **drip**

395. **sweat**

creasing amazement (V̈ V̈ handshapes at the eyes and the open wide adverbial morpheme plus an aspectual inflection) may be used instead of the established sign **look** (p. 50[98]). The signer may indicate the speed of a vehicle by making the non-dominant **B** classifier the active articulator, instead of the normally expected dominant hand which expresses the vehicle classifier. Thus **car travelling very fast**[390] draws our attention to a particular visual image: 'it was as if the ground were moving beneath the car'. One signer used a similar form, but with an *emit* metaphor instead of the

ground, to show a speed boat throwing up spray as it raced through the water. The **car travelling fast** example may be regarded as becoming so frequent as to be eligible for inclusion in the established lexicon (see pp. 86–91 in respect of the expanding lexicon), while the speed boat example is clearly a productive formation. Most of the examples given so far have exploited classifier forms. However, the signer can also use metaphor-based forms in a productive manner. One of the most common established signs meaning 'cry' makes use of the two **G** hands moving down the cheeks with the two index fingers bending as in **cry** (sign 453)[391]. Several related forms are also common, including a sign in which the hands move sharply away from the signer while the fingers flex (sign 453, note 1)[392]. In this sign, the hands retain the same orientation of the palms towards the signer. However, signs have also been observed which exploit a different set of productive possibilities. One signer used the two **O** hands placed at the eyes and opening to two **5** hands to express the meaning 'floods of tears'[393] in a productive exploitation of the *emit* metaphor. BSL makes use of a version of the 'emit' metaphor which uses the handshape pair Ĝ Ĝ. which means 'to emit in a single thin stream'. A modified form occurs in the established signs meaning **drip**[394] and **sweat**[395] where the emission can be seen as intermittent. In the sign glossed

386. Ø G̈ʊ⊥ G̈ʊ⊥ ᵒ˙ ⤬ ˙

387. Ø Ḧʊ⊥ Ḧʊ⊥ ᵒ˙ ⤬ ˙

388. Ø Ḧʊ⊥ , Ḧʊ⊥ ᵒ T

389. ⊔ V̈ᴛʌ V̈ᴛʌ ᵂ ˢ ᵒ ˂

390. ‾ Bʊ˃ ˚ ⤬ ⤬ B˂⊥ ᵒ Ø

391. ⊔ Gᴛʌ Gᴛʌ ᵛᴺ˙ ⤬ ˅

392. ⊔ Gᴛʌ Gᴛʌ ᵚ ⤬ ᵚ

393. ⊔ A⊥ʌ A⊥ʌ ᴨ [ₛₛ] T ᵒ

394. Ø Ĝʊ⊥ ᵒ [d̃]

395. ∩ Ĝʊ˃ Ĝʊ˂ ᴨ [d̃d̃] ᴺ˙ ˅ ᵒ

396. jet of tears

here as **jet of tears**[396] the signer uses this form in a single movement to mean 'someone burst into tears'. The image suggests two single jets of tears bursting forth from the eyes. A comparable sign has been seen with the fingers placed at each side of the mouth to mean **emitting jets of saliva**[397]. As will be obvious from these glosses, it can be difficult to find concise English translations which directly correspond to such forms.

Once we begin to focus on a metaphor such as 'emission' we can see its use in a whole range of forms: to sign about a gritter lorry spewing out grit we could use a vehicle classifier form plus *emit*; for 'a huge chimney spewing out smoke', we can exploit the forearm plus closed fist combination; for 'a car emitting exhaust fumes', we can locate and orientate the *emit* metaphor with respect to an imaginary car; for the notion of 'effluent being discharged into a river' we can combine the *emit* metaphor, the conventional I handshape and the non-manual adverbial 'th'. Again we can see that these forms are typically motivated, not merely arbitrary.

Expanding the lexicon

The lexicon of BSL is constantly changing. New signs are added and existing signs may take on new functions or become obsolete. The major changes are those which occur within the established lexicon and at the interface between the productive and established lexicons. In examining the

processes of change within BSL vocabulary, we have to keep in mind that the productive lexicon is by its very nature dynamic and changeable; in contrast, the established lexicon is relatively stable. However, the very dynamism of the productive lexicon can throw up forms which are candidates for a process of stabilisation.

Establishment of productive forms

It is helpful to distinguish two major categories within the productive lexicon: signs which must always be created anew as required, such as verbs of motion and location and creative combinations which may be used for particular kinds of effect or to meet new demands. This latter type, in particular, are potential candidates for stabilisation within the established lexicon.

We can see this by comparing several forms which all use the A SASS classifier for a round object, here relating to the human head. The signs **feel small**[398] and **gullible**[399] both appear to derive from the metaphorical extension in meaning of classifier-based productive forms: **feel small** involves the A hand moving down below the surface represented by the G hand: the meaning is comparable to the English phrase "I wish the ground could have swallowed me up". **gullible** has the A hand (i.e. the head) nodding forward in an exaggerated movement and the non-manual component 'th' and could be literally paraphrased as 'nodding acceptance in a foolish manner'. While we can see the likely origins of these two signs as being within the productive lexicon, they have become stabilised as 'off the shelf' forms which relate in a regular way to specific meanings. In contrast, one signer was observed producing the form **keep hitting a barrier**[400] which can be seen as consisting of a B SASS handshape, representing a flat barrier or obstacle and a round SASS classifier A representing a head: the position and movement indicates the head banging against the barrier and the iterative aspectual inflection (see pp. 106–107) indicates this action occurring again and again: the literal action of continually banging one's head against an obstacle was used with metaphorical extension to express the notion of constantly being thwarted. The signer created this sign from the resources available within the productive lexicon,

396. ʊ Ĝ⊥ʌ Ĝ⊥ʌ ᶯ⊥□ [ɔ̃ɔ̃]

397. ᴐ Ĝ⊥ʌ Ĝ⊥ʌ ᶯ⊥□ [ɔ̃ɔ̃]

398. Gꜿ> ₓ ∫A⊥ʌ₉ ᵀˣˣᵀ

399. Ḡ⊤> ∫A⊥ʌ₉ (ᶯ⊥)ˣ ᵛ⊥

400. B⊤> A⊥ʌ₉ ᶯ⊥ˣᶯ⊥·

401. wash clothes

402. wash clothes

403. wash clothes

404. wash clothes

405. wash clothes

406. wash clothes

even though there is an established sign available with almost identical meaning, i.e. **bang one's head against a brick wall** (p. 17[8]). Clearly there is potential for the productive forms to move over into the established lexicon.

These examples also reveal one further important aspect of word-formation in BSL: new forms, especially those deriving from the productive lexicon, are typically motivated—there is, initially at least, some link between their form and what they mean. It is relatively rare to find new words in the language which are purely arbitrary. The signs illustrated on this page all relate to the action of washing clothes. Their meanings can be elaborated as follows:

'wash clothes by grasping part of the fabric in each hand and rubbing the two surfaces of the fabric against each other'[401]; 'wash clothes by holding a washboard with one hand and rubbing the grasped material up and down against the washboard'[402]; 'wash clothes by grasping a pounding instrument with both hands and beating the clothes repeatedly'[403]; 'wash clothes by using a manually operated machine with a gyrating action'[404]; 'wash clothes by using a washing machine with two tubs each involving a gyrating action'[405]; 'wash clothes using an automatic washing machine with one tub using a gyrating action'[406]. These forms provide a kind of visual history of ways of washing clothes over the past one hundred years. In a language such as English, we are not surprised to find different words occurring at different periods. However, we do not expect the words themselves to mirror directly what they represent: in BSL, such visual reflection is the norm.

There are numerous other comparable sets of items. Some older signers may still use a sign meaning 'telephone' which involves the two **A** hands, acting as handling classifiers, with one hand placed in front of the mouth and the other at the ear to represent the holding of the mouthpiece and ear piece separately. In the last fifty or so years, the more typical sign choice has been **telephone** (sign 944)[407] where the widespread use of a telephone apparatus involving an 'all in one' receiver led to the comparable use of the

---

401. A⍺> ₓ Aᴐ< $\overset{\text{I}}{\underset{\text{x}}{\cdot}}$

402. Ø Aᴛᵥ Aᴛᵥ $\overset{\text{o}}{\text{v}}\cdot$

403. Ø A̅ᴛ> Aᴛ< $\overset{}{\text{v}}\cdot$

404. Ø A<⊥ $\left(\begin{smallmatrix}\text{T}⊥\\>< \end{smallmatrix}\right)\cdot$

405. Ø Bᴛᵥ Bᴛᵥ $\overset{@}{\underset{\div}{\cdot}}$

406. Ø B<⊥ $\overset{@}{\underset{\text{v}}{\gtrless}}\cdot$

407. ᴐ ᵃYᴛ< ˣ

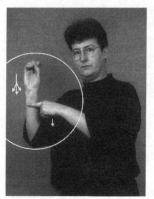

408. **portable telephone**   409. **portable telephone**   410. **tv programme**   411. **transmit**

'all in one' handshape, **Y**. In more recent years, the invention of the portable telephone has led to the development of further new signs. The illustrations above show two signs which both express the meaning 'portable telephone': in the first[408] the signer uses a grasping ꝋ̈ hand to express the holding of the hand set and a further handling classifier, **F**, to show the action of extending the aerial; the second sign[409] shows the signer holding the handset to the ear. In some cases, the signer uses a combination of these two forms. Indeed, currently, several different forms co-exist to express the meaning 'portable telephone'. Several of these involve multiple affixation and/or compounding. They thus seem to straddle the boundary of the two lexicons. It is likely that the longer, more elaborated options will reduce to more concise forms and that a more compressed sign will eventually be adopted as the general 'off the shelf' item. This still leaves open the option of other, sometimes more descriptive, forms being created as required within the productive lexicon. We can anticipate that one of these will become more regularly used and thence established in the language. This would be the form which signers would present if asked for the sign which referred to this particular type of object.

The newly established signs may exploit any of the different types of relationship discussed on pp. 41–45 and any of the different sets of morphemes discussed on pp. 73–77. The sign **typetalk** (p. 63[256]), for example, refers to a newly established service which allows deaf people to converse over a distance, through an intermediary, with a hearing person. The exchange involves text communication between the deaf person and intermediary and spoken conversation between the intermediary and the hearing person. The sign makes use of a double articulation of the **Y** SASS classifier (referring to two telephone receivers) and a metaphorical movement morpheme expressing the notion 'relay'. The *emit* metaphor is exploited by the signs **tv programme**[410] and **transmit**[411]. Such recently developed signs reveal the inbuilt categorisation processes of the language. English, for example, happens to use the same word "programme" for a theatre programme, a programme of events, a radio programme and a television programme. In contrast, BSL uses a deictic (i.e. pointing) image, as in pointing to items on a list in order to express the notion of a 'written programme' (**programme** (sign 196)[412]) and an 'emit' metaphor to express the notion of a 'television programme', which involves the emission of electrical signals.

Numerous other signs appear to be in the process of becoming incorporated into the established lexicon. Relatively recent examples include the following: conventional handshapes or locations are used to express the notion of **advocate** (p. 72[32]); a conventional location, the *lines* metaphor and the *exchange* metaphor combine to express **thought transfer** (p. 78[347]); two **B** SASS classifier forms are used in **fax machine**[413]; a V̈ handling classifier at the ear is used in **cochlear implant**[414].

408. ꝋ̈a>₉ Fa< ⊥

409. ꝰ E<ʌ ∅

410. ∅ (G̅ʋ> ₓ ✓o⊥ʌ₉ □[5]) ᵛ

411. ∅ (G̅ʋ> ₓ ✓o⊥ʌ₉ ⁿ□[5]) ⊥°

412. B̅a⊥ Åʋ⊥ (ⁿʌᴛ·)

413. B̅ʋ> Bᴛᵛ ⊥ⁿ·

415. hit

416. emphasis

417. naive

422. paternalistic

Compounding

As indicated on p. 36, compounding is a process which brings together two independent signs in the language to create new words with different meanings. The technical difference between compounds and the multi-morphemic signs originating in the productive lexicon is that while the meaningful components of compounds can occur by themselves as independent words, this is not necessarily the case with the multi-morphemic forms. However, as the status of some of these forms remains unclear the boundary between compounding and what might be thought of as multi-layered simultaneous affixation remains somewhat fuzzy. This is particularly the case with respect to what have been termed here *simultaneous compounds*. Nevertheless, compounding is clearly a way of expanding the lexicon. An account of the nature of compounding in BSL, some of the reduction processes involved in their production and specific illustrative examples can be found on pp. 36–40.

Lexical extension

Lexical extension is a further means of expanding the lexical resources of the language. There are probably several different types of process involved. In some cases, there is

simply a broadening or extending of the meanings covered by the sign; in other cases, the form itself alters slightly. Very often, there is a metaphorical basis for the extension involved: for example, a physical action is used to symbolise a more abstract notion.

The sign **hit**[415] which uses a single sharp action has both a literal meaning ('to strike someone with the hand') and an extended meaning ('to make an impact'). A further extension in meaning and form can be found in the closely related sign **emphasise**[416]: the literal meaning of 'hit a person' is extended to meanings such as 'emphasise', 'put pressure on someone' 'get at' and 'lobby'. The derived form uses short repeated movement and the non-manual signals of the head thrust slightly forward. Additional non-manual signals (shrugged shoulders, drawn in lips) and repetition are also involved in the derivation of **naive**[417] from **don't know** (sign 1568)[418]. Similarly, **flatter**[419] is extended from the sign **stroke**[420]: the derived form makes use of both a slow repeated form of the manual component of **stroke** and the 'th' non-manual component. The same non-manual signal, with its negative connotations is added to a repeated form of **shame** (sign 1215)[421] to produce the meaning **paternalistic**[422] and to a repeated form of **respect** (sign 1461)[423] to produce **sycophantic** (page 90)[424]. These and many other

---

414. ⊃ V̈<ʌ   ○̌

415. G>ʌ A<⊥₉   ⊥×

416. G>ʌ A<⊥₉   ⊥×·

417. ○ B̈⊤ʌ B̈⊤ʌ   ÷̊

418. ∩ B̈⊤ʌ   ×(⊓̪) ⌄̪⊥

419. G>ʌ B<⊥₉   ᴍ·×ᴍ

420. G>ʌ B<⊥₉   ᴍ<·×ᴍ<

421. ∅ B⌐⊥   @̪⌄̪

422. ∅ B⌐⊥   @̪⊥⌄

423. ∩ ✓B⊤ʌ ✓B⊤ʌ   ⊓÷

430. **dissident**

437. **to film with…**

438. **video camera**

examples demonstrate a lexicalisation of specific aspectual options (see *Grammar* section, pp. 104–108 for discussion of aspect). The following examples all have the inherent or built in choice of regular aspect, which can be interpreted as 'to do something regularly'. We can thus see a systematic relationship between such pairs of BSL signs as **pay**[425] and **mortgage**[426] which is literally 'pay money regularly'; **receive**[427] and **alimony** (sign 1008)[428], literally 'receive regularly' and **refuse** (sign 56)[429] and **dissident**[430], literally 'refuse regularly'.

A cursory examination of the *BSL* section of this dictionary will reveal many more examples of lexical, often semantic, extension. In some cases we are dealing with a relationship between an object, an action performed with the object and a person performing the action. Thus sign 601[431] can be used to mean the noun 'torch', the verb 'to shine a torch' and 'usherette' (someone who regularly shines a torch); sign 90[432] can be used to mean the noun 'canoe', the

verb 'to canoe' and the agentive noun 'canoeist' i.e. a person who canoes. Similar relationships can be seen in sign 66[433] which can mean 'lever', 'to pull a lever' and 'barmaid' (someone who regularly pulls a lever) and sign 234[434] which can mean 'rucksack', 'to hike' (i.e. typically walk with a rucksack) and 'hiker' (person who regularly hikes). In some cases there may be some systematic differences in form. Thus there is some evidence that there are formational differences between many noun-verb pairs in BSL. These differences are comparable to those noted for ASL by Newport and Supalla (1979), i.e. the hand usually moves steadily for the verb but in a restrained manner for the noun form. The verb **to lock with a key** (sign 250, note 1)[435] is usually performed with a single continuous twisting movement; the noun **key** (sign 250)[436] often exploits a repeated to and fro action; the verb **to film with a video camera**[437] usually involves a single continuous arc movement, while the noun **video camera**[438] frequently uses a short repeated

424. ∩ ⌡Bᴛ∧ ⌡Bᴛ∧ $\frac{n\cdot}{\div}$

425. B̄ɑ⊥ Â<v ⌄ˣ

426. B̄ɑ⊥ Â<v ⌄ˣ·

427. ⌐ 5ɑ< $\frac{\circ}{T}$[∧]x

428. ⌐ 5ɑ< $\left(\frac{\circ}{T}[∧]x\right)$·

429. ∫ Ḡ⋁> ₓ Aᴛ∧₉ ⋗̇

430. B̄⋁> ₓ ⌡A<∧ ⊥̇

431. ∅ G̈<v ᶻ·

432. ∅ A⋁⊥ A⋁⊥ $\left(\begin{smallmatrix}\odot N\\\updownarrow V\\X\\\Xi\\N\end{smallmatrix}\right)$·

433. ∫ B̄⋁>₉ Aᴛ< $\frac{\circ}{\dot{o}}$·

434. ⌐ Ȧᴛ> Ȧᴛ< $\frac{xN\cdot}{\Xi}$

435. ∅ Â⋁⊥ ᵃ

436. ∅ Â<⊥ $\frac{\circ}{Z}$·

437. ∅ Gᴛ> ₓ Ġ<⊥ $\frac{>}{\Xi}$

438. ∅ Ḡᴛ> ₓ Ġ<⊥ ᵛ·

441. **placard**   443. **campaign**

downward movement; the sign **to open a drawer** [439] involves a continuous movement towards the body, while **drawer** [440] may be produced with short repeated to and fro movements. However, the reader will discover that such clear distinctions are not necessarily made within the *BSL* section. This is because Deaf informants felt strongly that such distinctions were not compulsory and not necessarily made on a regular basis. This is clearly an area where more observational data is required before any general claims can be made. What we can see is that if a particular noun enters the language, signers may derive a verb form, which is either identical in form, but extended in meaning, or different in both form and function. Of course, the difference in verb and noun forms will also be revealed by the addition of appropriate inflections (see *Grammar* section pp. 104–113). This is comparable to the form "fish" in English: we only know whether we are dealing with a noun or a verb because of context and/or because of the additions of appropriate inflections such as '-ed' and '-ing'. It is also worth remembering that the process of conversion, i.e. the conversion of a noun to a verb or vice versa, can operate hand in hand with semantic extension. Thus we have the set **placard** [441], **to**

carry a **placard** [442] which results from a process of conversion, and **campaign** [443] which results from a process of metaphorical semantic extension. The complex interaction of the processes of word-formation in BSL combines to produce a massive potential for the creation of new words.

Lexical borrowing

Borrowing from other sign languages

So far the focus has been on expanding the lexicon through internal word-formation processes. However, BSL also makes use of borrowings from other sign languages. Such borrowings are currently on the increase because of the greater international mobility of Deaf people and the increasing opportunities to see Deaf people from other countries on television and even in the cinema. Many of the earlier borrowings were linked with international meetings of Deaf people, particularly those involving the World Federation of the Deaf. Such borrowings often relate to names of countries and cities and topics of central importance within the wider international Deaf community. Thus signs such as **New York** (sign 952) [444], **Austria** (sign 821) [445] and **Brussels** (sign 822) [446] are all borrowings of this type. An historically important phase of development occurred with the beginning of formal international conferences on sign languages. These began for U.K. participants in the late 1970s and resulted in the borrowings of terms such as **language** (sign 1068, second part) [447] from Swedish Sign Language, **language** [448] and **linguistics** [449] from ASL and **aspect** (p. 120) from Swedish Sign Language. At the time of these borrowings, the established BSL sign **language** [450] was produced at the mouth and therefore seemed to imply a focus on the spoken language. The borrowed forms either allowed an emphasis on the written language or, because of the arbitrary nature of the sign to British users, a more generalised meaning which was not linked to one specific type

439. Ø A⍺⊥ A⍺⊥ ᵀ

440. Ø A⍺⊥ A⍺⊥ ⁺ᴵ

441. Ø A̅ᴛ> ₓ Aᴛ< ᵒᵛ·

442. Ø A̅ᴛ> ₓ Aᴛ< ⊥

443. Ø A̅ᴛ> ₓ Aᴛ< ᵒᴵ·

444. B̅⍺> ₓ Y̆ᴏ⊥ ᶻₓˣ·

445. Ø V̈ᴏ∧ ∓ₓ V̈ᴏ∧ ᵐ·

446. Ø V̈ᴛ> ₗ V̈ᴛ< ˣ·

447. Bᴛ> ₓ Bᴛ<₎ ˃ˣ

448. Ø Ġ⊥∧ ₗ Ġ⊥∧ ⁽ᵛ÷̇⁾

449. Ø Ġᴛ∧ ₗ Ġᴛ∧ ⁽ω̇÷⁾

450. ◡ Gᴛ∧ ⊥

language. One interesting technical example is the BSL sign for the term *classifier* (p. 122): this is actually the ASL classifier for vehicle which has come to stand for the whole class of classifiers in BSL. Of course, signers are not necessarily aware of the origins of such signs. Signs such as **recognise**[451] and **impressive**[452] from ASL and **attitude** (sign 1249)[453] from DSL are frequently used without any awareness of their origins in other sign languages. This is comparable to the situation for many English speakers who have little awareness of the borrowings they use on an everyday basis. More recently there has been much greater contact amongst signers from many different countries and we can anticipate that borrowings will increase.

Borrowings from English

BSL exists within the context of a wider English-using community. Members of the Deaf community themselves are typically bi-lingual: there are very few signers, if any, who do not make some use of English. Of course, the written medium of English provides the most ready and useful access to English for most Deaf people. The use of text telephones has provided a boost to the use of English amongst Deaf people and there is some evidence that Deaf English * constitutes a distinctive language variety. Regrettably, very little work has been done on the Deaf person's perception or view of English: we can expect it to be very different from that of the hearing user. A Deaf person's notion of what English is like will have been formed primarily by the written language and to some extent by lip-reading in direct interactions. Ordinary, everyday colloquial English has probably been least accessible to Deaf people as it is rarely written, although the increased use of subtitling on television is helping to improve this situation. What we can say is that the Deaf person's experience of English is a visual experience and we can anticipate that aspects of this experience will be encoded into the primary visual language of Deaf people, BSL.

It is also the case that contact varieties, involving elements of both BSL and English, have developed both through the mixing of Deaf and hearing people and through the interaction of Deaf people with other d/Deaf people from widely varied linguistic backgrounds. Thus the age of

access to and acquisition of BSL varies enormously from signer to signer, depending upon family, educational and social circumstances. A comparable situation applies with respect to the learning of English. Moreover, as well as the naturally evolving contact varieties, several contrived systems, which also make use of elements from both BSL and English, have been developed over the last twenty years. Systems such as Signed English (SE) and Signed Exact English (SEE) are geared to presenting English to deaf children. This type of sign system typically makes use of literal sign word—English word correspondences and draws its vocabulary almost entirely from the established lexicon. Because SE and SEE typically use spoken English simultaneously with gestural production, it is normally only the manual components of signs which can be produced. Thus multi-channel signs and non-manual signs are excluded from SEE, almost by definition. SEE is also geared to present the syntax and morphology of English in visual, usually manual, form and therefore inevitably cuts across the spatial and simultaneous patterning that occurs in BSL. The terms Sign Supported English (SSE) or Pidgin Sign English (PSE) are sometimes used for the naturally occurring contact varieties, although the former is also used to refer to the use of signs in a merely supportive role, with English as the dominant language.

The nature and function of mixed and contact varieties is highly complex and deserving of further study. Within the context of the BSL lexicon, we can see English as a further source of borrowing: here instead of borrowing from other sign languages, the language borrows from the written and spoken language with which it is in daily contact. It is therefore not surprising that there is substantially more borrowing from English, with which the language has been in daily contact for hundreds of years, than from ASL or SSL, where the contact has been intermittent and partial.

Fingerspelling

One very obvious way in which to borrow items from English is to make use of fingerspelt forms. As described in the BSL section, fingerspelling is a way of representing the letters of written English. It is probably used by all

---

451. G>ʌ B<⊥ᵩ Ṫ

452. ∅ (B>⊥ ₁ₓ Ȧ⋅⊥)ᵀ

453. Ц Bтʌ ×ω̊ ⊥

*This term is used here in the positive sense of a distinctive variety which is worth studying and describing; it is not used in the sense of 'problem English' as is sometimes the case with respect to the educational literature.

signers, although the manner and extent of usage may vary considerably from signer to signer. The British fingerspelling system is based on a two-handed alphabet (see Kyle and Woll, 1985, for historical details). However, some signing communities in the U.K. have also been influenced by fingerspelling systems which exploit one-handed alphabets. The most important of these is the Irish one-handed alphabet.

While we may regard any use of a fingerspelt word as a (possibly one-off) borrowing, some researchers have suggested that in many cases we are dealing with what may more appropriately be viewed as a type of code-switching (Sutton-Spence, Woll and Allsop, 1990). According to this view, there is a distinction to be made between those forms which, as it were, represent English and those which have become established within the language.

One of the difficulties in making this distinction is that fingerspelt items are rarely articulated as independent sequences of letters: almost always, as used by fluent BSL signers, the fingerspelt item is articulated and 'read back' as a holistic movement-shape. Some research on the use of one-handed fingerspelling in ASL (Akamatsu, 1982) has even suggested that signers may be able to produce appropriate movement-shapes for fingerspelt items yet be unable to spell the specific English word concerned. This suggests that such fingerspelt forms have already begun a process of assimilation into the language. Colville (1983 and forthcoming) has found that almost one hundred distinctive letter shapes are used for the twenty-six letters of the English alphabet. Such handshapes appear to have developed naturally through processes of economy and efficiency, which initially allow easy movement from one letter to another and gradually lead to the distinctive fingerspelt shapes of individual words (see the *Fingerspelling in BSL* section for examples of this type of patterning). Battison (1978) suggests that when fingerspelt forms are restructured through such processes as the deletion of the medial letters

and the addition of more sign-like movements, we are dealing with loan words rather than merely fingerspelt English words: these items have in effect become part of the established sign lexicon. In BSL we can find such examples in **club**[454], **project**[455], **about**[456] and **Celtic**[457] where there is an almost total reduction of the vowels and changes in orientation and positioning of the other letters. Each form is articulated in a single flowing movement.

Initialisation

One of the major ways in which fingerspelt items can become lexicalised is through the process of initialisation resulting in what are here called *initial letter handshape signs* and elsewhere initial dez signs (see the Introductions to the BSL handshapes in the *BSL* section for examples of handshapes which are used in this way).

In these examples, the initial letter of the English word is articulated by the appropriate handshape(s) and a specific movement pattern is produced so that the fingerspelt sign looks like (and conforms to) other signs of the language. Colville (1979) noted three types of initialised signs: those which articulate the initial letter in the normal way, but add a repetition of the movement as in **America** (sign 370)[458] and **government** (sign 50)[459]; those which add other types of arbitrary movement to the initial letter articulation such as **Wales** (sign 837)[560] and **qualification** (sign 598)[461] and those which exploit what Colville calls an *iconic movement*. It would seem that the choice of movement within this last group is not merely arbitrary, but motivated. The sign **gold** (sign 125)[462] involves an initial contact, as for the letter **g**, but then the hands open to **5** hands and separate. A comparable form is used for **silver** (sign 913)[463], but here the initial handshapes and position are the same as those used for the manual alphabet form of **s**; the second component of these signs appears to be one possible rendition of the *glitter* morpheme. The sign **recommend** (sign 599)[464] uses the letter **r** and both hands move forward in what appears to be a moti-

---

454. 5>⊥ ╷ °Ḡ<⊥ [symbols] // O>⊥ ╷ O<⊥ ×

455. °5>⊥ ╷× °G<⊥ [symbols]

456. ᵃ5>⊥ ╷ Ḡ<⊥ [symbols]

457. ⁱ5>⊥ ╷ °Ḡ<⊥ [symbols]

458. Ȧ>⊥ ╷ GT< [symbols]

459. A̅T> AT< ×·

460. ∅ W⊥∧ [symbols]

461. ∅ F>⊥ ₓ Ḡʊ< [symbols]

462. ∅ A>⊥ ₓ A<⊥ [symbols] [55]

463. ∅ I T> ₓ I ʊ⊥ [symbols] [55]

vated movement, i.e. as if giving or offering something to another person. BSL also uses other types of loan signs which have their roots in fingerspelt forms. These include abbreviated forms of various types, such as the signs for Birmingham (**b-m**) and Glasgow (**g-w**), which use the initial and final letters of the English word; initials such as **b-b-c** (BBC) and **w-f-d** (WFD) and acronyms such as **v-a-t** (VAT). Colville has suggested that the manual alphabet forms which are traditionally presented on fingerspelling charts and the like are almost always only used within abbreviations. For further discussion and examples see the works already cited in this section.

ISL loan signs

Because of the influence of Irish Sign Language in relation to some Catholic Deaf communities—for example, through the presence of members of Irish religious orders or Irish priests in schools and Deaf centres—initial letter signs which have their roots in the one-handed Irish fingerspelling system occur in areas such as Manchester, Liverpool, London and Glasgow. Many of these signs are so assimilated into the BSL varieties used within these communities that the users are not aware of their fingerspelling roots. Moreover, because, in some cases, the handshapes used either do not otherwise occur in BSL or occur only rarely, there has been a strong tendency for such signs to adapt towards the BSL phonological system. Thus the Irish sign **ready**[465] uses an R handshape on the upper arm: most BSL signers who use this sign, now use an H handshape which is both phonetically simpler and more common within the language. The Irish manual alphabet letters **f** and **g** are very similar in formation: the **g** is identical to the F handshape in this Dictionary (and identical to **f** in the American manual alphabet) while **f** is the same formation, but with the thumb touching the middle section of the bent index finger. The initial letter **g** loan signs, such as **goal**[466] and **green**[467] have generally retained the original handshape, which 'fits in' with the BSL system. In contrast, loan signs like **football**[468] and **for**[469], have adapted towards the BSL F handshape. Irish Sign Language also makes use of initial letter handshape signs within name signs and some of these have been borrowed into some BSL varieties. Thus loan sign forms exist for such names as **Gerry**[470], **Jeff**[471], **Thomas**[472] and **Margaret**[473].

ASL loan signs

In recent years, with increased contact between the American and British Deaf communities, some initial letter signs from ASL have been borrowed into BSL. These are frequently names which have some cultural relevance for the Deaf community, such as **Kendall** (School for the Deaf)[474] and **Hartford**[475] as well as names of cities such as **New York** (p. 91[444]) and **Washington**[476]. Other examples include **philosophy**[477] and **no**[478]. The ASL sign **I love you**[479] has been borrowed into many sign languages, including BSL, and has a particular function within public gatherings of Deaf people where it is used to show affirmation and support for one another. It has also developed as a sign of greeting, again especially within international contexts.

Mouth patterns

Many signers make some use of English-related *mouth pat-*

---

464. Ø B̄a⊥ ₁ₓ G̈⊤< °⊥

465. \ R⊤< ˅ₓ

466. Ø F⊥∧ ᶻω

467. √ Fʊ⊥ ˃

568. Ø F<⊥ ω≈ ·

469. F̄ >⊥ F<⊥ ˅ₓ

470. ∩ F<∧ °ω ·

471. ˅Π Ïa< ˄ₓ˃

472. Π Â<∧ ₓ ·

473. Ø Wmʊ∧ ₁ Wmʊ∧ ₓ ·

474. B>∧ ₁ K<∧ ˅ₓ ·

475. Ø H⊥∧ ˅ ·

476. [] W⊤∧ (°@⊥˅⊥ ·)

477. ∩ K⊤< °ᴅ≈ ·

478. Ø H̄⊥∧ # [A] ·

479. Ø Ẏ⊥∧ ⊥

terns while signing. These can be distinguished from the type of non-manual components which have already been discussed in previous sections. Unfortunately there has been relatively little work on when and why signers exploit such mouth patterns within BSL. What is clear is that there is considerable variation from signer to signer and even within the usage of individual signers. Research on other sign languages* has pointed out that such mouth patterns (sometimes known in the literature as *word-pictures*) frequently differ in form from the equivalent mouth patterns within the spoken language. The typical mouth pattern accompanying one of the signs glossed as **finish** (see p. 107[572]) makes use of a form which could be represented as 'f-sh'; as with the fingerspelt forms, there is reduction of the medial vowels and some modification of the initial and final (mouth-)shapes. For most signers these forms will be produced without any actual sound, although vocalisation may occur in particular situations.

Mouth pattern appears to be used within the BSL lexicons in a number of different ways. In many cases, it serves to disambiguate signs whose meanings might otherwise be confused with signs which have the same manual components. Mouth pattern frequently accompanies fingerspelt forms. This may be because the same manual form can often be used for a range of different meanings. Within this dictionary, entry 50 (p. 93[495]), which derives from the manual alphabet form **g**, is glossed as **garage**, **geography**, **government** and **guarantee** and entry 770[480] has the glosses **vegetable**, **vegetarian**, **virgin** and **vodka**. While it is quite likely that the context itself will ensure that there is no ambiguity, the mouthpattern helps to ensure this. However, it is worth noting that the mouth pattern itself may be considerably removed in form from the English word it derives from. Schermer (1990) found that certain categories of what she terms *spoken components* within Dutch signing were hardly recognisable without the accompanying sign. In some cases the meaning is only understood if both manual and non-manual, here mouth pattern, components are present. Indeed within some accounts (see Coerts, 1992) the mouth pattern is actually treated as a non-manual component at the phonological level which happens to function as the distinguishing component in respect of otherwise identical pairs of signs. While this may be true of some BSL signs, the use of mouth patterns is subject to considerable variation. It is therefore difficult to decide to what extent mouth pattern functions as part of the formational structure of individual signs and to what extent it is an optional extra, dependent upon situational factors. There are some indications that mouth patterns most typically accompany nouns and verbs and are much more frequent in established, rather than productive forms.

In some cases, the signer may produce one lexical item on the lips (through an English-based mouth pattern) and another on the hands simultaneously. Thus the meaning 'Is the artwork finished?' could be expressed by the signer articulating the sign meaning 'artwork' with the right hand, using appropriate questioning non-manual signals (eyebrow raising, eye widening and head in forward side tilt) and producing the mouth pattern 'f-sh'. We could therefore consider the form 'f-sh' as having been borrowed from English and being capable of expressing meaning by itself, i.e. without a related manual form meaning 'finish'.

Literal borrowings

BSL may also borrow English vocabulary through a process of literal translation. In these cases, the phonological or morphological components which are used are clearly part of BSL, but the lexical form derives from English. We can see this very clearly in various forms meaning 'brainwash' which can be seen as literal combinations of the signs **brain**[481] and **wash** (p. 87[401]). This can be compared to the form **brainwash**[482] which uses morphemes from within BSL itself. Similarly, the form **mouse**[483] is sometimes used for a computer mouse, even though the language also makes use of a handling classifier form[484] for the same meaning. The literal borrowings are usually highly controversial and awareness of their use has heightened since the increase in BSL research and the involvement of Deaf people in teach-

480. 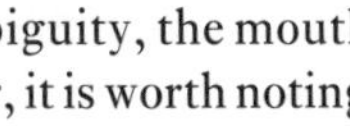

481. 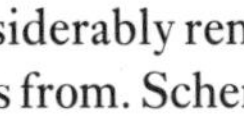

482. 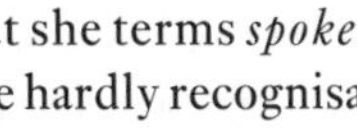

483. 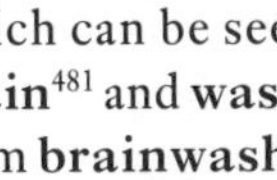

484. 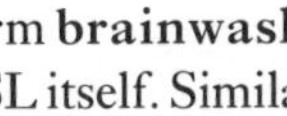

*See for example, Vogt Svendsen 1983 and 1985; Schroeder, 1985, Schermer, 1990 and Coerts, 1992

ing their own language. For many signers, these forms represent unacceptable usage, yet there is no doubt that they do occur amongst BSL users. In some cases, the sign has become such a part of the language, that it no longer arouses strong feelings. The sign **stand firm** (sign 804)[485] clearly derives from English, yet its classifier basis probably makes it more acceptable as a BSL sign.

Many name signs, including the names of people and places, are closely linked with a literal translation of all or part of the English name as can be seen in sign 642 (p. 56[237]) which is used to mean both 'swan' and 'Swansea' and sign 1094 (p. 64[260]) which is used to mean both 'wolf' and 'Wolverhampton'. Other name signs may be sign translations of English words which are viewed as being similar in form to some part of the English name, as in **live** (sign 964)[486] for "Clive" and **key** (p. 90[436]) for "Kay": such forms are regarded as fully acceptable within the Deaf community.

Implications for the BSL teacher and learner

Within this account of the words of BSL, we have seen that BSL has a rich assortment of lexical resources available to the signer. It is clearly essential that those learning the language are given access to this wide range of resources and that learners are helped to clue into the different types of motivation which underlies much of the structure of BSL words.

In the past, the teaching of BSL vocabulary tended to focus on the most frozen forms of the established lexicon. Hearing learners were introduced to the form **people** (sign 482)[487] very early, but were rarely taught the much more frequent productive use of the **5** hand 'people' classifier (see p. 49). This was probably in part because teachers of BSL were pressurised by hearing learners to give them 'the sign' for a specific English word and also because teachers of BSL had not themselves had the opportunity to study the nature of BSL lexical structure. The norms that were imposed from the outside for teaching the language were therefore accepted as appropriate.

What kind of factors should we keep in mind when teaching and learning the language? In looking back through the information provided in this section, we can see that learners need to be aware of the structural properties of signs, including the fact that some signs require the use of non-manual components as well as manual. They need to be aware that signs can be composed of several meaningful bits, the morphemes of the language, which can recur in other signs. Learners can be encouraged to tune in to the relationships between form and meaning that are built into the language. Most importantly of all they can be given access to the considerable potential of the productive lexicon and become aware of the different ways in which the vocabulary of the language is constantly expanding and changing.

Vocabulary usage is very much to do with making choices which either suit the context or have a particular kind of impact. As with any other language, it is important that learners make such choices within particular parameters of the specific language concerned. It is no good 'thinking in English' and then choosing a frozen established sign from the established lexicon to fit the English word one has in one's head. Once one enters into the visual and symbolic world of BSL, then a whole range of different kinds of options and nuances are possible.

Even within the established lexicon, different choices can give different focus or effect. Thus BSL has several different signs which can be given the gloss **evidence**: sign 326[488] is a compound of **see** and **witness**; sign 330[489] is a combination of **see** and **show on paper**. A further possible sign involves **see** plus **demonstrate**[490]. The signer can make a choice depending upon the kind of focus s/he wishes to choose, for example, whether reference is made to written evidence, the evidence of a witness or demonstrable evidence. This kind of information happens to be built into the structure of these particular BSL signs. Similarly, the meaning 'proposal' (in the sense of putting forward an idea) can be expressed by a fingerspelling based sign **proposal**[491], a compound involving **say** and **show on paper** (sign 349)[492] and a

---

485. Ø B̄ɑ>ₓ V̈ʊ⊥ °͘

486. [] ᶘᴛ< ͦₓ̇N̊ ·

487. ∪ Ḡᴛ< V̊ₓ // ∪ G<ʌ ᶘ

488. ⊔ Gᴛʌ ˣ // B̄ʊ>ₓ J̇B<ʌ ∅

489. ⊔ Gᴛʌ ˣ⊥V // B̄ɑ⊥ Bɑ⊥ ᵛˣ

490. ⊔ Gᴛʌ Gᴛʌ ˣ⊥ // Ø Bɑ⊥ Bɑ⊥ ⁽ᵛ·⁾÷

491. Ø (G>⊥ Ĝ<⊥)⊥

494. **smell**

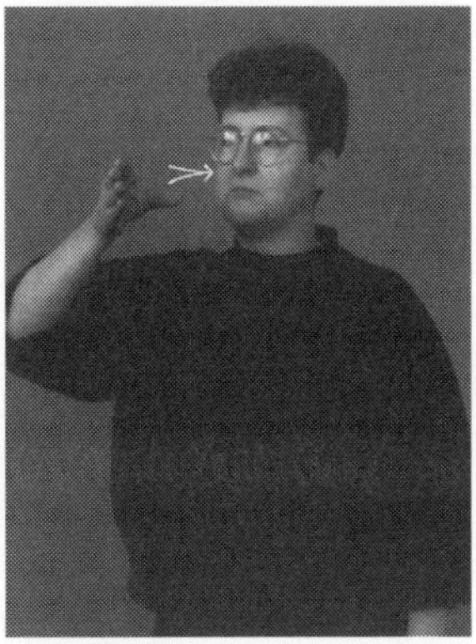

495. **smell**

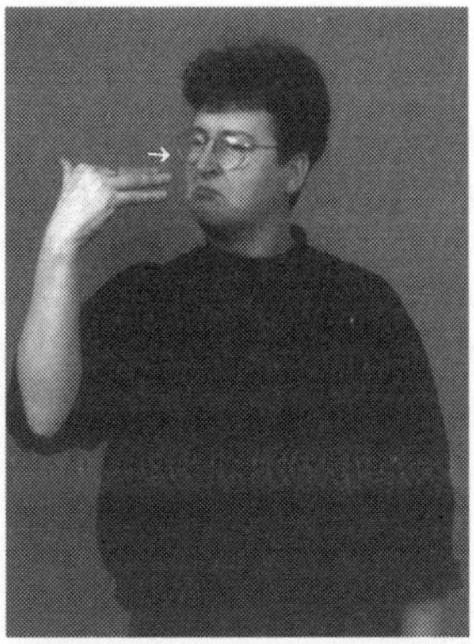

496. **smell**

497. **strong breath**

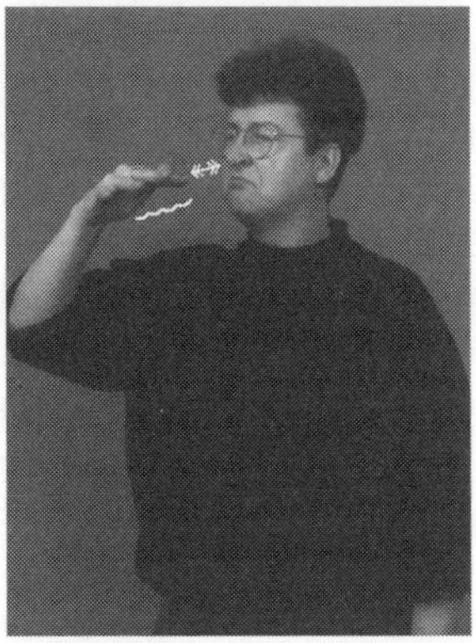

498. **smell**

compound involving **say** and **suggestion**[493]. Again the signer can make the choice which best fits the particular intent of the utterance.

Often the choice relates to specific images which are conveyed by the individual sign. BSL has several different signs meaning 'smell'. In **smell**[494] the focus is on the sniffing action typical of animals when they are actively 'on the scent' of something; **smell**[495] makes use of the *absorb* morpheme: the smell is actively inhaled by the nostrils. This sign is often used when the signer wishes to show the enjoyment of a particular aroma; **smell**[496] makes use of the *lines* metaphor: the action again suggests that the lines of smell are being taken in by the nose. Whether this is pleasurable or not will be revealed by the non-manual features. The same image is used in the sign **strong breath**[497], but here the 'lines' of odour are moving outwards away from the signer. In **smell**[498] the *lines* metaphor is again used, but here the wiggling of the fingers suggests that the odour is hovering in the vicinity and is only intermittently discerned. Again, facial expression will indicate whether the odour is pleasant or not. The fluent signer makes choices from such sets of signs, often automatically and without conscious effort, sometimes more deliberately for conscious effect as in sign poetry and story telling.

There are numerous such lexical sets in BSL. The notions of 'fear' and 'anxiety' can be expressed by a range of signs. Some, such as **scared stiff** (sign 947)[499] and **afraid** (sign 1180)[500] already contain inherent non-manual components; others can be modified by the use of additional non-manual features.

Again we can choose different types of image to suit the focus of the message: **anxious** (sign 539)[501] and **anx-**

---

492. ◡ GTA ×V⊥□ [B] // // B̄a> Ba⊥ T×T

493. ◡ GTA × // // Ø Ba⊥ Ba⊥ ⊥

494. ⊔ ḦTA ×

495. ⊔ B̿<⊥ T[B̂]× #

496. ⊔ 5̈TA °T

497. ◡ 5̈⊥A °⊥

498. ⊔ 5ʊ< ·

499. ⊻ J̇Y<A ×D⊥

500. [] 5̄̈T> 5̈T< × ·

501. >[] G̈<A ×m ·

ious (sign 539, note *) [502] both use the image of the heart beating fast; **nervous** (p. 84 [386]) uses the image of the legs shaking and **anxious** (sign 1144) [503] uses the image of churning emotions. Several different signs can be used to indicate that one's mind is empty: the sign **empty** [504] can simply be relocated at the head; the *drown* metaphor can be used as in **slipped my mind** (p. 37 [144]) The signer can also choose to show the deliberate emptying of the mind by using a combination of the *grasp* and *drop* metaphors as in **emptied my mind** [505]: here the signer is using the same symbolic image as in the sign **abortion** (sign 1009) [506]. These and many more examples demonstrate that learners must be helped to move away from simple 'BSL sign–English word' correspondences towards an appreciation of the BSL system within its own terms.

Readers of this dictionary who are themselves learners are asked to take special note of the information about the function of individual handshapes which is given at the beginning of each handshape chapter within the BSL section. This information should be supported by the detailed information provided in the classifier table on pp. 53–67. By using this information, you will begin to recognise that many of the signs which you see on an everyday basis are constructed from elements within the productive lexicon. Once you begin to see the operation of such semantic classifiers as the 'person', 'people' and 'vehicle' classifiers and also recognise how the same handshape can act as a size and shape specifier, a handling classifier, a touch classifier and so on, you should find that a whole new area of BSL structure is opened up. When you begin to recognise that signers are also frequently shifting perspective, from model world to real world, from close to distant focus, then again the visual relationships which are encoded in the lexicon will begin to make sense.

Meaning of BSL words

Finally, we should not expect that meaning in BSL will be encoded within specific lexical items in precisely the same way as it is in English. Thus BSL has two signs which may

be translated by the English word "alimony": **alimony** (p. 90 [428]) means literally 'to receive payments on a regular basis'; **alimony** (sign 1507, note 1) [507] means literally 'to make payments on a regular basis'. This difference is encoded in the lexicon of BSL in a way that is not the case in respect of English. The meanings 'anorak', 'hood' and 'monk' are expressed in BSL by the same sign form (sign 287) [508]. Although we would find it odd for "monk" also to mean anorak in English, once we are tuned into the types of categorisation which occur in BSL, there is nothing surprising at all to find the three meanings expressed by a form which is derived from a handling classifier. Again while English makes use of the same form "engaged" to express the meanings 'pledged to be married' and 'telephone line in use', BSL makes use of two quite different forms with different underlying motivation: **engaged** [509] is linked to the visual image of betrothal, the engagement ring; **engaged** (sign 47) [510] is linked to the notion of 'being tied down or bound', 'unable to free oneself' and in BSL covers other meanings such as 'captive', 'prison' and 'slavery'. Again while we can see the basis of both types of categorisation, there is no point in expecting both languages to categorise meaning in this way.

Homonymy

Learners of BSL are sometimes taken aback by particular examples of homonyms which occur in the language. A homonym involves the same form being used for different meanings. In English, the form "pupil" is used to mean both 'a student who is taught by a teacher' and 'the dark circular aperture at the centre of the iris in the eye'. The term 'iris' is used for 'the coloured muscular diaphragm that surrounds the pupil of the eye', for 'plants with flowers which have brightly coloured petals composed of three petals and three sepals', for 'a rare poetic name for a rainbow' and as a girls name. Many of the most common words in English have a wide range of different meanings and grammatical functions. We can see this by noting the meaning and function of "down" in the following English sentences: "Moses came

---

502. ⁾[] G̈ᴛ< ×·

503. [] 5̈ᴛ< ×

504. B̄ɑ⊥ Bʊ< ⊥ₓ

505. ∩ 5ʊ< ∧ [o] □ [s]

506. ⊔ 5⊥< ×⊥[ß] // ∅ B̂ʊ⊥ ○̌□[s]

507. B̄ɑ> B̂ᴛᴠ

508. ⌐¹ Âᴛ∧ Âᴛ∧

509. ⁰5̌ʊ> ᵢₓ F̄ʊ⊥ // 5̄ʊ> 5ʊ⊥

510. ɑ Âɑ> ≠ ʊÂʊ⊥

down from the mountain"; "Frances went down with the flu"; "We require an immediate down payment"; "The leaves are covered in a soft white down"; "He's feeling a bit down about his exam results"; "Patrick comes from County Down" and "Canterbury lies close to the southern downs". We do not find it at all extraordinary that we have to re-interpret the meaning of "down" in each of these sentences according to both its grammatical function and the context in which it occurs. This is also what happens in respect of BSL homonyms. Some may seem very odd collections indeed: entry 257 [511] covers the meanings 'butcher', 'impudent' and 'nude'; entry 815 [512] is used for the meanings 'aunt', 'battery', electric', 'uncle' and 'niece' and entry 133 [513] for the meanings 'brother' and 'milk'. However, we do not expect confusions to occur when expressing meanings such as 'Pass the milk' and 'How old is your brother?' any more than we are confused by "pane" and "pain" in such contexts as "I've a pain in my stomach" and "We had to have a new pane fitted". Where there is any likelihood of real confusion within BSL, the signer can minimise the ambiguity, for example, by exploiting clarifying mechanisms, such as additional mouth-pattern, using forms from the productive lexicon and making additional or alternative choices from the established BSL lexicon. In order to make the most of BSL vocabulary, teachers and learners need to become aware of the range of resources available and the complex ways in which these can interact to produce an almost incalculable number of BSL lexical items.

The grammar of BSL

The focus of this account of the nature of BSL has been mainly on the lexical resources available to the signer. This section provides a brief overview of the grammatical context in which these resources are exploited. A fully comprehensive account of the grammar of BSL would require a major volume in its own right, even given the relatively limited nature of the research to date. The aim here is to provide a summary account of some of the main types of grammatical patterning which relate to the internal structure of words. Where appropriate, reference will be given to relevant, sometimes more detailed accounts. Some of these will relate to other sign languages: although we cannot make direct inferences about the structure of BSL from findings in respect of other sign languages, such information can often provide a hint as to the types of patterning which may occur.

Traditional grammatical accounts of languages such as English, Latin and French make a distinction between *inflection* and *syntax*. Inflection is typically concerned with changes in the structure of words required by the grammar. Thus within grammatical descriptions of English, certain types of affix, such as plural '-s' or past tense -'ed', i.e. affixes which signal particular grammatical relationships, will be elaborated within what is sometimes called *inflectional mor-*

phology. In contrast, syntax is concerned with the rules which govern the combining of words into sentences or, within so-called *transformational grammars*, the rules which allow the generation of well-formed syntactic structures. In BSL, inflectional morphology is concerned with the regular ways in which the words of BSL, i.e. signs, can be modified to express specific grammatical categories such as number and aspect. BSL syntax specifies the rules for combining BSL signs into larger units of organisation, such as clauses and sentences and deals with grammatical operations that occur above the word level, such as the expression of question forms and topic-comment structures. In practice, these two areas of grammatical organisation are closely inter-related and inter-dependent. In both cases, we need to keep in mind the interaction of manual and non-manual patterning and the inter-relationship between multi-layered simultaneous structuring and linear, sequential structuring.

Within this brief survey of grammatical structure in BSL, there will be a focus on morphological patterning, with only limited reference to syntactic patterning. However, as it is not possible to make an absolute division between the two types of organisation, the elaboration of different aspects of grammatical structure in BSL will be

511. 3 $\hat{A}_{<\wedge}$ $^{(\frac{\pi}{z}\cdot)}$

512. $\cup$ $\ddot{V}_{T\wedge}$ $^{\times\cdot}$

513. $\emptyset$ $A_{>\perp}$ $_{\times}$ $A_{<\perp}$ $^{\frac{N N\cdot}{\times}}$

presented under specific category headings such as *number*, *aspect* and *negation*. When looking at inflectional morphology, wherever possible information will be given on the *form* of the inflection (for example a particular type of movement) and the *function* of the inflection, i.e. its role in the language. In English the form '-s' is used for the function of expressing the plural; in BSL, the form reduplication (repeated movement) is used for the function of expressing plurality. To understand BSL inflectional morphology we need to understand both the form and the function of the inflections concerned. In most cases, a name will be given for the specific inflection. Wherever possible the names will have some currency within sign linguistics, for example they may have been used in the description of the inflectional morphology of other sign languages.

Word classes in BSL

BSL makes use of some of the main word classes found in other human languages, including nouns, verbs, adjectives, adverbs and conjunctions. However, word class categorisation is not always straightforward, especially as the same form may incorporate information which in other languages might be expressed by several different word classes. We have already seen (p. 51) that adjectives are less likely to occur as separate items in BSL because attributive information, for example relating to the size and shape of objects, can be built into the verb (or predicate) form. Similarly, information that would in English be given within a separate noun form, can be built into certain verb forms in BSL through the incorporation of a classifying handshape.

Number in BSL

How does BSL express the grammatical category of *number*? In particular, does the language show contrasts such as singular, dual and plural? Is the marking of the cat-

egory of number required within certain word-classes such as nouns and verbs? While further studies are needed in relation to this and most other areas of BSL grammar, we can make some generalisations. BSL uses several different methods to mean 'more than one'. These include the use of quantifying signs with or without repetition of the relevant noun form; reduplication of or within noun signs; double articulation; repetition of classifier forms; number incorporation and repetition within verb forms.

Quantifying signs

BSL has available a number of quantifiers such as **lots** (sign 1053)[514], **many** (sign 1722)[515], **few** (sign 618)[516], **some** (sign 1496)[517], **different** (sign 429)[518] (literally 'some or many different') and **various** (sign 447)[519]. Number signs (see the *Numbers in BSL* section) may also be used as quantifiers. A quantifying expression may function as the single marker of plurality, usually occurring after the noun form. The use of quantifying expressions appears to be common in BSL and almost any noun can be pluralised in this way. However, a quantifier is particularly likely to occur when the other means of indicating plurality are not available. Quantifiers may also co-occur with other markers of plurality. The quantifiers themselves may be modified through non-manual intensifiers: the 'puffed cheeks' intensifier can be added to **many** to mean 'very many'; the 'rounded lips' intensifier can be added to **few** to mean 'very few'.

Pronouns

Some of the pronouns of BSL are given separate entries in this dictionary. However, when we look at the plural forms of pronouns, we can see three main types of patterning: the use of a smooth, arc movement in signs like **you** (i.e. 'all of you')[520] and **they** ('all of them')[521]; the use of a repeated stabbing or chopping movement as in **you** (i.e. 'each of you individually')[522] and **they** ('each of them individually')[523] and the use of alternating stabbing movements made at ran-

---

514. Ø 5⊤>ₗ 5⊤< ⚇

515. Ø Oа⊥ᵢ Oа⊥ ⚇ [55]

516. Ø Ĝ<⊥ ⚇ [A]

517. Ø B̂а< ᵐ

518. Ø °G⩑⊥ ᵢₓ °G⩑⊥ ⚇

519. Ø (G>⊥ ᵢₓ G<⋏ ⚇)⚇

520. Ø G⊤< ⚇

521. Ø Gᴠ< ⚇

522. Ø G<⊥ (⚇)

523. Ø Gᴠ⊥ (⚇)

dom positions in space as in **you, you, you and you**[524] and **her, him, him and her**[525]. For convenience these three inflections can be referred to as *sweep*, *all individuated* and *random*. They can be viewed as plural inflections which are applied to the basic forms **you** (sign 293)[526] and **him/her** (sign 310)[527]. It is particularly tempting to view the plural pronouns in this way because, as we shall see, these three types of inflection are mirrored in the number agreement rules within BSL verbs and also have some corollary in the patterning of classifier-based plural forms. BSL also makes use of number incorporation within pronouns to give such meanings as **we (two)** (sign 760)[528], **you both** (sign 783)[529], **three of us**[530] and **four of you**[531]. Number incorporation is used in certain time adverbials, such as **two days ago** (sign 756)[532], **in a fortnight's time** (sign 763)[533] and **last week**, literally 'seven days ago' (sign 902)[534].

Changes within the noun

In some cases, plurality is shown through reduplication, i.e. repetition of all or part of the noun form. This reduplication may be articulated at different points within the signing space: this type of articulation can be interpreted as 'several/ many in no particular arrangement': it can therefore be seen as the application of the *random* inflection with respect to nouns. Alternatively, the reduplicated sign may reflect a specific spatial organisation, such as 'in rows' or 'one behind the other' using the equivalent to the *sweep* and *in rows* inflections (see further below). However, in the ma-

jority of such cases, classifier-based forms will be preferred. Some signs may take both an unmarked, i.e. more usual, plural inflection and more marked forms: in **children** (sign 1216)[535] the expected plural involves a repeated downward movement to the right. Marked forms of **child** +*plural* can include: specification of number as in **three children**[536], or the addition of the *sweep* inflection which results in the meaning **lots of/many children**[537]. Some nouns which have a body location also allow reduplication for plurality. Thus the noun **man** (sign 1539)[538] uses a simple repeated downward movement in the plural form **men**[539]. In a complex or compound sign, it is typically only the final component which is repeated: thus **several reports** would involve the repetition of the second part of the compound, **show on paper**, articulated (in a horizontal line) at two different points in space. The first part of the compound **say** is only articulated once: **reports**+*plural*[540]. Nouns such as **address** which have a repeated form in the singular do not appear to take any explicit marking for plural. Unfortunately, we do not yet have sufficient information available on this area of the grammar to know when and whether repetition for plurality is required in noun forms. There is little doubt that such modifications do occur: just what triggers their presence or absence remains unclear. Double articulation, where a one-handed sign is produced in an alternating fashion by two hands can be seen as a particular realisation of the *random* inflection: thus if **plane** (sign 932)[541] is articulated by both hands in turn it becomes **many planes**[542].

524. ∅ G>⊥ G<⊥ (⊥∿·)÷

534. ∪ °7⊤∧ ×°×
                 ⊤

525. ∅ G⊽⊥ G⊽⊥ (⊥∿·)÷

535. ∅ B⊽⊥ °°°ᵛᴧᵛ
                >

526. ∅ G⊽⊥ °⊥

536. ∅ B⊽⊥ (ᵛᵛᵛ)>

527. ∅ G<⊥ °⊥>

537. ∅ B⊽⊥ °ᵛ>

528. [] V⍺< °⊥·

538. ∪ B̄⍺< ᵛ°ᵛ[ʙ] ⊥⊥×#

529. ∅ V̈⍺⊥ °z·

539. ∪ B̄⍺< ᵛ°ᵛ[ʙ] ⊥⊥×#

530. ∅ W⊤∧ ℮⊤

540. ◡ G⊤∧ ×ᵛ[ʙ]⊥□ // ∅ (B̄⍺> B⍺⊥ ⁻×⊤) >·

531. ∅ 4⊤∧ >

541. ∅ Y⊽∧ ᴧ<

532. 3 ⁱV⊤∧ ×ᵐ×⊤

542. ∅ Y⊽> Y⊽< ᴧ∿·÷

533. Ḡ⊤⊥ × V⊽⊥ ⊥>×

543. **many books in a row**

544. **many books in a row**

545. **individual pencils...**

547. **many books in rows...**

Classifier forms

The most frequent way of indicating plurality with respect to concrete nouns is to replace the noun by a related classifier form and add one or more plural inflections. Some classifiers are themselves inherently plural and plurality is built into their usage. Such forms include the **5** people classifier, the **5** many classifier (meaning 'many items', such as planes and cattle) and forms for persons including 'two persons' (**V**), 'three persons' (**W**), and 'four persons' (**4**).

The plural forms of singular classifiers almost always include inherent information about location. The main plural inflections used with classifier forms are: 'in a row/pile'— shown by smooth directional movement, usually with the two hands separating (the *sweep* inflection) for example, **many books in a row** [543]; 'in a row/pile, with benchmark'— the non-dominant hand acts as a benchmark while the other hand produces a smooth directional movement (the *sweep with benchmark* inflection)—for example, **many books in a row** [544]; 'in a row/pile (with or without benchmark), individuated'—the hand (or hands) indicates the individual items, by a chopping action (usually down or away) or a twisting movement, as the hand(s) produces a directional movement (the *individuated* inflection)—for example, **individual pencils in a row** [545]; 'at different levels (individual rows)'—the hand(s) produce one or more of the above inflections at different levels in space, with each

articulation beginning anew (the *levels* inflection)—for example, **rows of books at different levels** [546])—'at different levels (ongoing)'—the hands produce the *sweep* inflection in an ongoing movement in a 'z' shape, to show many items at different levels (the *ongoing sweep* inflection)—for example, **many books in rows at different levels** [547])—'in no particular arrangement'—the hands produce alternating chopping or twisting movements (the *random* inflection)—for example, **houses dotted about** [548].

As can be seen from the illustrations above the signer first chooses the classifier form which fits the object and then chooses one of a limited number of ways to pluralise the form. The signer typically uses a SASS classifier: for example, a **G** SASS in relation to narrow objects, for example pencils; an **H** classifier to indicate narrow objects, for example beds; a **B** classifier in relation to flat objects such as folders and magazines. The signer can choose to focus on the individual items by using the repeated chopping or twisting movement of the *individuated* inflection. Of course, this same set of inflections can operate within the vertical as well as the horizontal planes, as in **pile of flat objects** [549] which uses the *individuated* inflection, and **pile of cups** [550] which uses the *sweep* inflection.

The *random* inflection can be used to indicate that there are several or many items but in no particular arrangement: here the two hands typically produce alternating movements. The signer may decide to place emphasis on the

---

543. Ø B>∧ ¦ B<∧ ÷

544. B>∧ ¦ B<∧ >

545. G⊙⊥ ¦ G⊙⊥ $\binom{\circ}{\underset{>}{\vee}}$

546. B>∧ ¦ B<∧ $\overset{(\underset{>}{\cdot})}{\vee}$

547. B>∧ ¦ B<∧ $\overset{(\underset{z}{\cdot})}{\vee}$

548. Ø $\ddot{5}$⊙⊥ $\ddot{5}$⊙⊥ $\binom{\circ}{\underset{\div}{\mathrm{i}\sim}\cdot}$

549. **pile of flat objects**   550. **pile of cups**

random nature of the plurality by adding an adverbial. Thus the signer may use the **B** flat SASS classifier plus the *random* modulation and the 'th' adverbial to mean **papers scattered all over the place** [551]. Plural forms can be lexicalised in the language so that they become 'off the shelf' items within the established lexicon as in **dormitory** (p. 57 [240]) which derives from the plural form SASS classifier **long narrow item** +*inviduated* inflection meaning literally 'many long narrow items (beds) in a row'. This is comparable to the established signs in which aspect has been lexicalised, discussed on p. 90.

Number agreement in verb forms

There is currently very little information about the extent to which verbs are required to agree with plural nouns, plural pronouns, quantifiers or classifiers, especially when these occur in subject position. In a sentence meaning 'many people (55 classifier) arrive', we do not expect the verb 'arrive' itself to indicate plurality. However, in 'many people flee' the sign **flee** (sign 415) [552] is likely to show repetition. It may involve the right hand simply repeating its normal movement, which can be regarded either as a neutral plural form or carrying the implicit information that people are fleeing in the same direction. Alternatively, the whole sign can be repeated at several, usually three, points in space. This lat-

ter usage seems to mean 'many people flee in different directions'. Again there is no information yet as to whether such a form is ever required by the surrounding linguistic environment. This latter usage seems to mean 'many people flee in different directions'.

Other verbs can be inflected to agree with plural objects, although in many cases we are dealing not only with plurality, but with location too. The addition of a smooth arc-like movement to a verb can indicate agreement with a plural object as in **I help them** [553]. This is comparable to the *sweep* inflection in nouns and pronouns: it indicates several or many as a group. The addition of several separate forward movements is comparable to the *individuated* inflection above and means here 'each one of several' as in **I help each of you** [554]. Similarly the addition of the *all of several/many* inflection, (the arc movement) to **look at** means **look at several/many**; the addition of the *several or many individually* modulation to **look at** means to **look at each of many in turn**. *

Form	sweeping arc movement
Meaning	all of several/many
Form	several forward chopping movements
Meaning	several or many individually
Form	several alternating forward chopping movements
Meaning	a random selection of several/many

Extent

Information about the *extent* of objects (for example, how long, short, wide or deep they are) can be expressed in BSL through a set of options which are in many ways comparable to those available for number. In both cases, classifier forms play a major role.

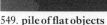

549. $\overline{\text{B}}$ᴅ> Bᴅ< $\left(\begin{smallmatrix} \circ \\ \vee \\ \wedge \end{smallmatrix} \cdot\right)$

550. $\overline{\text{C}}$>⊥ × C<⊥ ^

551. ∅ Bɑ⊥ Bɑ⊥ $\left(\begin{smallmatrix} \circ \\ \vee \, ℵ \\ \div \end{smallmatrix} \cdot\right)$

552. $\underline{\ddot{\text{B}}}$>ʌ Gᴅ⊥₉ $\begin{smallmatrix} ⊥ \\ \times \\ ⊥ \end{smallmatrix}$

553. ∅ $\left(\overline{\text{Bɑ}}> \, × \, \text{A}<⊥\right)^{\begin{smallmatrix} \tau⊥ \\ >> \end{smallmatrix}}$

554. ∅ $\left(\overline{\text{Bɑ}}> \, × \, \text{A}<⊥\right)^{\left(\begin{smallmatrix} \circ \cdot \\ ⊥ \\ > \end{smallmatrix}\right)}$

*For discussion of plurality see Wilbur, 1989, Kyle and Woll, 1985, Deuchar, 1984, Klima and Bellugi, 1979 and Baker and Cokely, 1980.

Qualifiers of extent

As with quantifiers in respect of plurality, a number of individual qualifying signs are available for the expression of extent. Such forms as **big** (sign 1064)[555], **long** (sign 1454)[556] and **wee** (sign 1574)[557] can be used. As with quantifiers, extent qualifiers may function as the single marker of extent, usually occurring after the noun form. Extent qualifiers may also be further modified or stressed through the use of non-manual intensifiers: the 'puffed cheeks' intensifier can be added to **big** to mean' very big' and the 'rounded lips' intensifier can be added to **little** (sign 1574)[558] to mean 'very little'.

Changes within the noun

In some cases, encoding for extent can be built into the form of nouns themselves. This is typically the case where the noun form probably derives from a SAS classifier. Nouns such as **tent** (sign 1394)[559] and **basin** (p. 48[199]) can be modified to show a relatively small or large tent or basin. The hands simply delineate a smaller or larger area.

Classifier forms

As indicated earlier (p. 47), many classifiers in BSL can be used as what are termed *tracing classifiers*. They can trace the shape and extent of objects. Usually the classifier gives some indication of the shape of the item, i.e. whether it is flat, cylindrical, curved and so on. The movement gives an indication of the approximate extent and the overall configuration. The two **F** hands may separate to show a **pole** of indefinite length[560]; this can be thought of as the general *extent* morpheme or what Schick describes as MOV(see p. 76); one hand may be used as a benchmark while the other produces the tracing movement. If the tracing hand (or hands) does not come to an abrupt halt, the extent indicated is indefinite. If there is end-marking, the meaning is 'something of approximately this dimension'. A configuration morpheme can also be added to show the overall configuration.

An elephant's trunk and a cathedral pillar can both be depicted using a **c** SASS classifier for cylindrical object and an *extent* morpheme to show approximate length. However, 'elephant's trunk' will require a *configuration* morpheme meaning 'curved', while 'pillar' will require a *configuration* morpheme meaning 'straight'.*

Verb inflections in BSL

One way of categorising verbs in BSL is to class them according to the kinds of inflection they can take. Some verbs take no inflections at all, while others may accept several different types. However, work on BSL verbs is not at a point which would allow us to make absolutely definitive claims. It is often easy to ascribe group membership for the central members of a category, but less easy with those that seem to occur at the boundaries between categories. The following account is therefore an attempt to bring together some key points from research to date.

Invariant verbs

Some verbs in BSL do not take any inflections at all. Verbs such as **know** (p. 29[87]), **love**[561] and **live** (p. 96[486]) do not accept inflections for aspect, person or number. The form of the sign can be modified to some extent: the sign **know** can be produced with a firm movement or with a repeated movement; the sign **love** can be articulated with a longer hold and with greater muscular tension. These changes from the citation form appear to have an *emphatic* function: they stress the semantic content of the verbs concerned. While it might be possible that such modifications function as inflections, the general consensus is that these are patterns of emphasis which may occur across a whole range of sign word classes and are therefore best described by the rather looser term *modification*.

Aspectual verbs

Many verbs in BSL can be inflected for *temporal aspect*. The

---

555. Ø 5>⊥ ¡ 5<⊥ ᴬ÷ᵛ

556. Ø B>⊥ ¡ B<⊥ ÷

557. Ɔ B̈<ʌ ᵛ·

558. Ø B>⊥ B<⊥ ˣ·

*For further discussion of extent see Schick (1990).

559. Ø Bʊʌ ₓ Bʊʌ ÷

560. Ø F̄>⊥ F>⊥ ᷈ɴ

561. [] B⊤> ₓ∓ B⊤< ᵀˣ

grammatical category of aspect is probably less familiar to users of English than the related grammatical category of *tense*. This is because while tense is typically encoded within English verbs, aspect has only minimal encoding. In contrast, BSL regularly incorporates aspectual information within the form of the verb, but only incorporates information on tense in a very few examples.

The grammatical category of *temporal aspect* is, as the name suggests, connected with time. Tense is what is termed a *deictic category*: it allows us to point to specific moments or periods in time and thus to place an event in time. Aspect does not do this. Rather aspect expresses how we wish to view an action in respect of time. Thus we might place an event (such as swimming) at a particular point in time (for example, yesterday). However, we can still view that event temporally in different ways: we can see it as complete – 'Yesterday, I swam': we can view it as ongoing or in process – 'Yesterday, I was swimming (when...)' or we can view it as about to start – 'Yesterday I was just about to start swimming (when...)'. There are different ways of looking at the same event from a temporal perspective. Thus aspectual choices allow us to focus on an event as completed, ongoing, stretching over a period of time, happening again and again, occurring gradually, occurring bit by bit, just starting, just about to start (but not starting) and just about to finish.

In English, some aspectual choices can be made by changing the form of the verb (more accurately the verb phrase as often two verbs are involved, an auxiliary and a main verb). The two kinds of aspect which are most familiar to users of English are probably *continuous* or *progressive* aspect and *perfect*(ive) aspect as in "he is walking" (progressive aspect) and "she has walked" (perfective aspect).

In both English and BSL the exact meaning conveyed by the choice of aspect is affected by the type of verb concerned. All verbs (and some adjectives) have what might be termed *inherent aspect*. This simply means that they have some idea of time already built into them. We can recognise a basic distinction between *stative* and *dynamic* verbs. Stative verbs denote states rather than activities and in English they do not normally take progressive aspect. The non-dynamic nature of the English verb "know" can be seen in the oddity of the sentence "I am knowing the answer": this is strange because the so-called progressive inflection in English cannot be added to stative verbs. As we have already

seen, the BSL verb **know** (p. 29 [87]) is an invariant verb and does not inflect at all for aspect, while **analyse** (sign 776) [562] is a dynamic verb which can take aspectual inflections.

Dynamic verbs can be divided into two further groups: *durative* and *punctual*. As the names imply, durative verbs carry with them the idea of happening over a period of time, while punctual verbs are momentary events which have no temporal duration. The notions of 'walking', 'singing', and 'talking' imply activities that stretch over some time, while 'kick', 'hit' and 'jump' are momentary actions. Linguists have developed more complex categorisations of verb types, but these basic distinctions allow us to recognise that when we add aspectual meanings to verbs, the end result will be different depending upon the original inherent aspect of the verb. In BSL, unlike English, most aspectual meanings (though not all) can be expressed by changes to the movement of the verb. (In English, we often have to add other words and phrases.) As with other areas of BSL morphology, we can recognise that different changes in form, again here particularly changes in type of movement, can bring about regular changes in meaning. The following kinds of change in the movement of the sign are relevant to an understanding of aspect:

reduplication	This may be slow or fast.
end marking	A slight pause at the end of an articulation of the movement of a sign. When combined with reduplication, this may produce an arc-like movement.
initial hold	The onset of the sign is held in space. The sign may be cut off at this point or produced, depending on the aspectual choice.
hold	The sign is held in space for a longer time than normal.
elongation	The sign takes up more space (and sometimes more time).
tenseness	The sign is produced with extra muscular tension.
steps	The movement of the sign is articulated in 'steps' or bits.
speed	The sign may be articulated more slowly or quickly than usual.

562. Ø V⋅ʊ> , V⋅ʊ<

563. **waited a long time**

564. **always goes**

565. **waited for ages and ages**

566. **went again and again…**

By adding these types of movement to BSL signs we can bring about changes of meaning related to aspect. Two of the most frequently used movement changes are slow reduplication and fast reduplication. Bergman (1982) has shown that these movements will bring about different types of meaning depending on the nature of the verb. They can be characterised as follows:

look+*aspect/ durational*[569] meaning 'keep on looking for ages'. Elongation is usually used along with other movement features to stress the aspectual choice (see **cry** below). Movement 'in steps' can be used to show something occurring incrementally, i.e. bit by bit as in **dark**+*aspect/ incremental*[570] meaning 'get darker by degrees'. The normal movement of a sign may be made more slowly in order to ex-

Movement Change	*Durative Verb* e.g. **wait**	*Punctual Verb* e.g. **go**
Fast Reduplication	*Durational Aspect* **waited a long time**[563]	*Habitual Aspect* (he) **always goes** (on a Friday)[564]
Slow Reduplication	*Continuative Aspect* **waited for ages and ages and ages**[565]	*Iterative Aspect* (he) **went again and again and again**[566]

End-marking is often used to emphasise continuative and iterative aspect. The result can be to give a circular or arc-like movement to signs not normally signed in this way, e.g. **cry**+*continuative+end-marking*[567].

Initial hold may be used to express what is called *inceptive* aspect, i.e. 'something is about to happen but does not' or simply to show that 'something has just started to happen' as in **sign**+*aspect/ inceptive*[568]: this may be used in such meanings as "I was just about to start signing when the lights went out." A sign may be held in space for an extra period of time to stress duration or continuation as in

press something happening gradually as in **fall asleep**+*aspect/ gradual*[571] meaning 'gradually fall asleep'.

Aspectual inflections can be overlaid, one on top of the other, to give quite complex forms: **cry**+*aspect/ continuative, elongated, end-marked* can be translated as something like "keep on crying and crying for ages and ages". Certain inflections can be quite clearly defined in terms of their form and function and specific names have been developed for these. The *iterative* inflection involves a slow repeated movement, usually with end-marking and has the function of iteration, meaning 'something occurring

---

563. Ø B̈ɒ⊥ B̈ɒ⊥ ˇ·

564. Ø B<⊥ ⸰⊥·

565. Ø B̈ɒ⊥ B̈ɒ⊥ ⸰@·⊥ˇ

566. Ø B<⊥ ⸰@·⊥ˇ

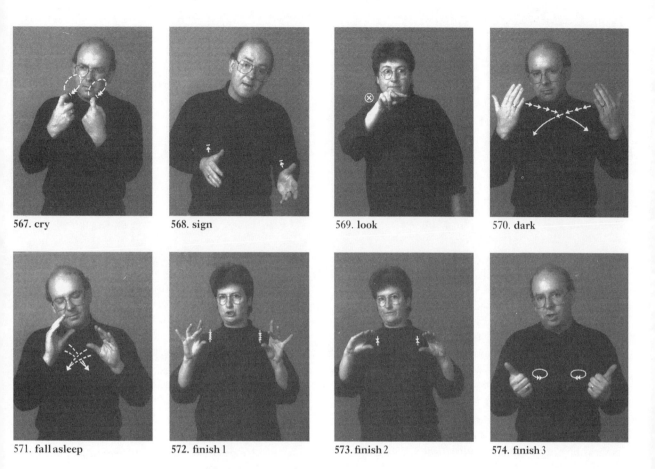

567. cry

568. sign

569. look

570. dark

571. fall asleep

572. finish 1

573. finish 2

574. finish 3

again and again and again'. However, in some cases, the precise relationship between form and function is not yet fully clear: in these cases it is helpful practice to specify the actual form of the movement changes within the transcription of the sign.

BSL has one other set of markers relating to aspect: these are completion markers. There are at least six of these in regular use: the first five are glossed here as **finish**, the sixth is glossed as **been**. These glosses relate both to the glosses Deaf people themselves use for these signs and to the modified mouthpatterns which typically accompany them. The signs are **finish 1**[572], **finish 2**[573], **finish 3**[574], **finish 4**[575], **finish 5**[576] and **been**[577] (see also page 108). There is some regional distribution of these markers, with **finish 3** being

567. Ц Gⱅʌ Gⱅʌ

568. ∅ 5>⊥ 5<⊥

569. ○ V̈⊥ʌ ∅

570. ○ J̓ʙⱅʌ J̓ʙⱅʌ

571. ○ B̿>ʌ B̿<ʌ₎

572. ∅ 8̄⊥ʌ 8̄⊥ʌ

573. ∅ B̄⊥ʌ B̄⊥ʌ

574. ∅ A̓ⱅ> A̓ⱅ<

575. finish 4

576. finish 5

577. been

578. see+been

much more common in England than Scotland. However, most signers will use more than one of these. There is currently little information on when one form is used in in preference to another. Gregory and Llewellyn-Jones (1992) present information on one signer's use of what appear to be variations of **finish** 3. They demonstrate that the function of **finish** can be complex, with slightly different realisations depending upon the specific meanings. Thus in choosing to use a particular form the signer "has to indicate whether the completion is total or partial, whether it is an individual act which is completed or a sequence of acts, and whether the sign **finish** is used to imply another related act will follow. It also has a phatic use which may be stylistic and used more by some speakers than others." (Gregory and Llewellyn-Jones, 1992, p. 30) These completion markers are treated somewhat differently from other markers of aspect because they occur sequentially with the verb, usually following the verb. They appear to function as sequential affixes, as in **see+been**[578] meaning 'have seen (already)', but may also occur in isolation especially in response to questions. Their status therefore remains unclear.

While BSL, like ASL and some other sign languages, has a particularly rich morphology in relation to aspect, it remains unclear whether there are any obligatory linguistic contexts in which specific aspectual choices are required.

Although learners of BSL are usually unfamiliar with the terminology associated with aspect, they often find it relatively easy to tune into the kinds of movement changes and related meanings described above. This may be because they appear motivated, i.e. they make some kind of symbolic sense.

Directional verbs

BSL has several different ways of indicating the grammatical roles of nouns in sentences. The notions of 'subject', 'object' and 'indirect object' are important in BSL, just as they are in other languages. We want to know who does what to whom in BSL sentences, just as we do in English sentences. One of the ways in which BSL expresses this information is through verb inflections which are expressed through changes in directional movement. Thus as used here, and generally within sign language studies in the U.K., *directional* within the context of *directional verbs*, refers to directional movement options which provide information on the arguments of the verb, i.e. subject, direct object and indirect object.

As there are different levels of complexity involved here, it is worth looking firstly at a relatively straightforward example. In understanding this example, we have to keep in mind the way in which signers exploit the signing space and the typical locations used for first, second and third persons: the spatial location of the first person is the signer and that of the addressee the second person. Other spatial locations may represent third person referents. Directional verbs can be said to agree with these locations. Changes in the starting point and end point of directional (or path) movement indicate who is carrying out the action (i.e. who is the subject)

---

575. Ø Ȧᴛ> Ȧᴛ< $\substack{\cap \\ \ddagger \\ \cdot \sqcup}$

576. Ø Ȧᴛ> Ȧᴛ< $\substack{\cap \\ \cap \sqcup \\ \ddagger}$

577. Ø Bᴛʌ Bᴛʌ $\substack{\cap \\ \ddagger \\ \cdot \sqcup}$

578. ⊔ Gᴛʌ $^{×}$ ∥∥ Ø 5ᴛʌ 5ᴛʌ ^{ʋ}

580. you help me   582. you criticise me   584. you visit me   586. you tease me

and who or what is affected by the action (the object). The verb sign meaning 'help' is usually given an away movement in its citation form. However, this is slightly misleading because the away movement actually tells us that the full meaning of the form is 'I help you' or 'I (the signer or role taken on by the signer) help you (the addressee) or her/him (some third person referent or referents)'. In this and the majority of other directional verbs, the starting point of the movement agrees with the subject and the end point agrees with either the object or the indirect object.

When we look more carefully at BSL verbs which show subject-object agreement, we can see that other types of patterning, as well as changes in directional movement may be employed. The precise form which these agreeing verbs take depends very much on the formational sign types to which they belong. Single and double dez signs which occur in neutral space are most likely to exploit directional movement. Manual tab signs frequently require changes in orientation. Brennan and Colville (1984) divide directional verbs into seven main groups on the basis of the different changes in formational parameters involved. The following examples will give some idea of the range of parameters involved.

Group one

These are the verbs which have a neutral space tab. The verbs usually have a movement away in their citation form. The form **help me** is expressed by a simple change in directional movement; e.g. **I help you**[579]; **you help me**[580].

Group two

These verbs are produced in neutral space, they have movement away in their citation forms and change both direction and orientation in the marked form; e.g. **I criticise you**[581]; **you criticise me**[582].

Group three

These are formationally manual tab signs. In this group the non-dominant hand stays still and the dominant hand changes both its movement and orientation; e.g. **I visit you**[583]; **you visit me**[584].

Group four

This group also consists of manual tab signs. In this group the dominant hand normally changes both movement and direction, and the non-dominant hand changes its orientation; e.g. **I tease you**[585]; **you tease me**[586].

Group five

Some verbs incorporate information about subject and object, not by changing the direction of movement but by locating the sign at a relatively shorter distance from the

579. Ø B̄ɑ> ₓ A<⊥

580. Ø B̄ɑ> ₓ A<⊥

581. Ø I>ʌ ₁ I<ʌ

582. Ø ïɑ⊥ ₁ ïɑ⊥

583. B̈ʊ>₎ B̈ʊ⊥

584. B̈ʊ>₎ B̈Tʌ

585. Ḡ>⊥ Vʊ⊥

586. Ḡ̈Tʌ V̈T<

587. you stab me

589. you ignore me

592. you phone me

body. Again formationally these are usually manual tab signs. Closeness to the body indicates 'me' as the object; e.g. **I stab you**[587]; **you stab me**[588].

Group six

These signs normally have contact with the body in their citation form. This contact is retained in the marked form but the hand moves away from the body and then moves towards the body to contact the signer; e.g. in **I ignore you**[589] the hand simply moves away from the ear; in **you ignore me**[590] the sign begins with contact on the ear; the hand moves away and then comes back towards the signer to touch the signer's chest.

Group seven

Some signs can be, as it were, converted into directional verbs by the addition of a sign which can itself be directionalised. Thus **telephone** may be converted in this manner by adding the sign **respond**, but in ear position[591], so we literally have the options **telephone+I respond to you**[592] and **telephone+you respond to me**[593].

As used within this account, directional verbs typically have animate subjects and objects.

Locative and locatables

Some verbs can modify one or more of their parameters to express *locative* information, i.e. where the action of the verb occurs. *Locative* verbs are verbs such as **paint** (sign 716)[593] and **clean** (sign 4)[594]. Typically they will be oriented towards an imaginary object which is then affected by the action of the verb. Thus we can change orientation to show 'paint a car', 'paint the ceiling', 'paint the wall', 'paint my face' and so on. These verbs are different from what are termed *verbs of movement and location* which provide information as to where and how referents move and where referents are located.

Signs such as **shave** (sign 256)[595] and **operation** (sign 190)[596] are *locatables* which can be moved to different locations on the body to show for example 'ear operation', 'heart operation' and so on. The related verb sign may be modified to show 'operating in a specific location'.

Negation

Negation makes it possible for us to deny, reject, oppose or contradict specific meanings. Grammatical processes of *ne-*

587. B>⊥ ¦ Å𝜊⊥ ˙<ˣ

588. [] (B>⊥ ¦ Å𝜊⊥ <ˣ)

589. ⊃ G⊥ʌ

590. ⊃ G𝜊< // [] Ğ⊤< ˣ

591. 3 Y⊤< // Ø G>ʌ G<ʌ

592. 3 Y⊤< // [] G>ʌ G<ʌ ˣ⊤ˣ

593. Ø Ḧ𝜊⊥

594. Ø Å𝜊⊥

595. 3 Â⊤ʌ ˣ

596. Ц Å𝜊< ˣ

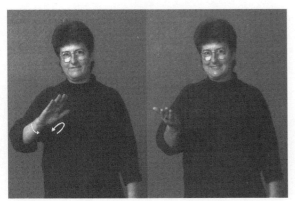

597. neg 3   598. see+neg 3   599. neg 4

gation allow us to produce negative sentences or clauses, rather than positive ones. BSL has a number of different *negative markers* which provide the user with a range of options for expressing negation. The choices a user makes may depend upon the type of discourse, the linguistic context, the particular focus or emphasis and the precise negative meaning the user wishes to convey.

At least some of these negative markers appear to have the status of inflectional affixes. However, negation does seem to straddle the boundary of syntax and morphology. One main criterion for regarding the negative markers as morphological concerns the prosodic nature of the combined verb and *neg* forms: the two components can seem to blend into a single unified sign. However, a counter factor is that the neg elements seem to be able to move around into different positions and have the potential to stand alone. Neg markers frequently occur as responses within interactions (see Brennan, 1990a and Dahl, 1979 for relevant discussion). Whatever the case, BSL clearly has a rich set of options for the expression of negation. This allows different nuances to be expressed by the different neg markers.

Probably the most obvious marker of negation in BSL is **neg** 1, the negative headshake. This consists of a repeated short side-to-side movement of the head. This action is sometimes accompanied by other non-manual activities such as furrowed brows, nose wrinkling and rounded or curved-down lips. However, the headshake is the dominant and essential action. In its most typical usage the negative headshake negates an otherwise positive word, clause or sentence. In such cases, the negated stretch of language does

not contain a separate negative manual sign. The negative headshake as the sole marker of negation is used frequently in topic-comment structures and responses.

Neg 1 can also be used along with other manual signs expressing negation in order to add emphasis. However, it is probable that in most examples of this type a negative head turn **neg** 2 is used instead. In this case, the head is turned away, either to the left or right, and holds this position during the first part of the manual sign. (A tilt position may also be used.) The head then turns to its natural forward position. This action often mirrors the rhythmic action of the manual sign when produced in an emphatic form. This involves a 'hold' or pause at the beginning of the sign sequence before the hands continue the action.

Neg 3 [597], in which the flat hand begins in the palm down position and then twists so that the palm faces up, is one of the most frequently used markers of negation. It occurs in a one-handed and a two-handed form and is usually accompanied by a specific mouthpattern. This begins with the top teeth touching the lower lip and is followed by an opening and slight stretching of the lips as in the sound sequence 'vee'. **Neg** 3 can occur either as a separate item within the clause or attached to the verb form. In the latter case, the usual movement of the verb is modified. In **see+neg** 3 [598] the away movement of **see** is not produced: instead the **G** hand changes to a **B** immediately after contact and then twists upward. The final action is more or less level with the face rather than lower down in neutral space. **Neg** 3 is often used to mean denial of presence or possession.

Neg 4 [599] also involves both a manual and a non-manual

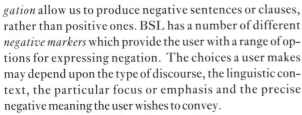

597. ∅ B⌐⊥ $\substack{\wedge\ \vee \\ <\ > \\ a}$

599. ⌣ J̇B⊤< $\substack{\sqcap \\ \wedge}$

598. ⊔ G<∧ $^{\times}$ ∥⟋ ○ B⊥∧ ^{a}

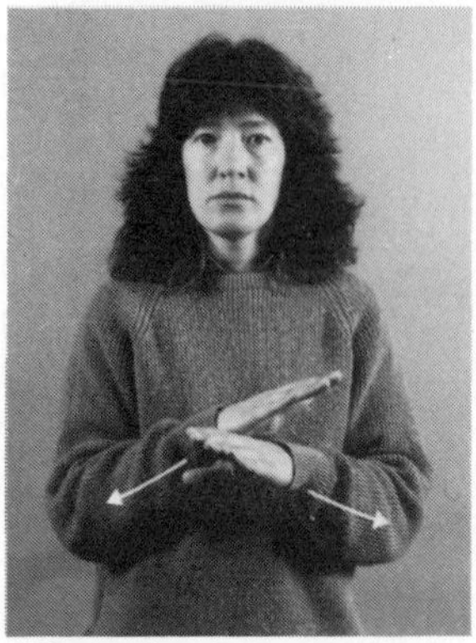
600. **neg 5**

601. **neg 6**

602. **neg 7**

603. **neg 8**

604. neg 9

element. The lips are pressed together and drawn back at the start of the sign. As the B hand moves in front of the mouth, the mouth opens sharply with the lips rounded. This form appears to convey a similar set of meanings to **neg** 3. It may occur either immediately before or after the verb. It can also occur at the end of a stretch of utterance to negate all that has gone before.

Neg 5 [600] appears only to occur as a separate item. It is frequently used in contexts involving instructions or commands. There is no single non-manual feature associated with this form. However, as it is often used in contexts requiring emphasis, it is often used with the negative head turn. It is also often used in contexts where spoken English is 'reported' within the signing, i.e. when indicating what a speaker has said. In such cases the word-order is English-based.

Neg 6 [601] is also used frequently in English-based contexts, although for some signers it has a wider usage. It almost always occurs directly before the verb which is negated.

Neg 7 [602] and **neg** 8 [603] are sometimes translated by the English words 'nothing' and 'nobody'. Indeed the signer may use a lip-pattern based on one of these English words while producing the sign. In some cases, although not always, such a translation is appropriate

There are two separate negative markers, **neg** 9 [604] and **neg** 10 (sign 111) [605] which express the meaning 'not yet'. Both involve combined manual and non-manual activity and can be used as a separate marker of negation or attached to the verb. They can be placed either before or after the item to be negated or at the end of a stretch of utterance.

Neg 11 [606] uses a B handshape with side to side action. It is frequently used for narrative purposes after a rhetorical question such as "Do we want to abolish residential schools? Not at all!" It also occurs frequently as a response in direct interactions. It does not appear to have the status of an affix since it is often articulated quite separately from the verb form.

Neg 12 [607] does occur as an affix. It is not particularly common, but when used seems to imply that it was accidental that something did not occur. Thus when added to a sign meaning '**see**' it means 'missed it', 'didn't catch it'. Several

600. Ø √Bɒ⊥ ∓ₓ √Bɒ< ÷

601. ⊻ Ȧ<∧ ⊥̊⊥̊ ×∨

602. Ø F>∧ F<∧ z̊ ·

603. Ø O>∧ O<∧ z̊ ∾ ·

604. Ø 5̈ɑ⊥ 5̈ɑ⊥ ∨̊ ·

605. Ø A⊥∧ A⊥∧ x̊ ·

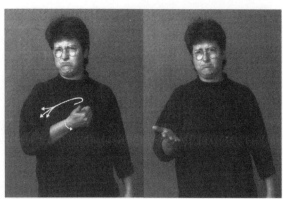

606. neg 11   607. neg 12   608. **no good**

609. **not bad**

signs in BSL make use of negative incorporation: the negative inflection appears to be embedded in the form of the sign as in the signs **no good**[608] and **not bad**[609].

The wider grammatical context

The various types of morphological patterning that we find within BSL operate within the context of a spatially realised grammar. As we have already seen, grammatical information can be encoded in the language both sequentially and simultaneously. Hence morphemes expressing perfective aspect and morphemes expressing negation occur in linear sequence; morphemes expressing other types of aspect and and number occur within multi-layered simultanous structures. In a comparable way, the syntax of BSL exploits both linear sequencing and spatial organisation. Both are essential to the workings of the language.

Non-manual and manual features interact across stretches of utterances to provide a framework for the expression of different types of grammatical relationships. One of the current tasks within BSL sign linguistics is to provide a more adequate account of the criteria for distinguishing syntactic units such as *clause* and *sentence*. Within English, there is a tendency to take such units for granted. However, many of the same problems occur in distinguishing the units of spoken English. With BSL, however, there is no danger of falling back on definitions and criteria which have their basis in the written language. What is clear is that non-manual features play a crucial role: these features include eye-gaze, head movement, eyebrow raising and the whole host of non-manual signals mentioned in the *How to use the Dictionary* section of this dictionary.

Non-manual features also play a crucial role in the expression of some of the main types of sentence and clause patterning. Thus the different kinds of question form in BSL, i.e yes-no questions, wh questions, rhetorical questions and tag questions, are distinguished from one another primarily by non-manual features relating to the position of the eyebrows and head position. Topic marking in BSL, as used in topic-comment structure, requires the use of head tilt, raised eyebrows and eye-gaze towards the addressee. Similarly eye-gaze and body shift are crucially important to the expression of what is sometimes termed *role-shift*, where the signer takes on different roles within the discourse.

606. ∅ B⊥∧ $\overset{o}{\underset{z}{n}}$ ·

607. ∅ B⊥∧ $\overset{n}{v}$

608. ∅ Å<⊥ $\overset{o}{\underset{\square}{\overset{<}{\overset{>}{\top}}}}$ [s]

609. ∅ I⊥∧ $\overset{o}{\underset{\square}{\square}}$ [s]

Such non-manual patterning typically co-occurs with manual patterning so that there is always a level of simultaneous patterning.

The kind of inflectional morphological patterning that we have seen in this last section can only work because of the way in which BSL syntax makes use of space. Signs can be established at specific locations within the signing space. Reference can be made back to these locations through eye-gaze and deictic signs and verbs can be made to agree with these loci. This same type of spatial organisation can be used to express locative relationships and, where appropriate, symbolic realtionships such as those of status, power and control.

Nevertheless, in syntax as in morphology, linear, sequential patterning also has a place. The fact that BSL uses both agreement inflections and non-manual features such as eye-gaze to relate to objects, does not mean that there is no role at all for word-order patterning. The limited evidence that is available with respect to the ordering of clause elements suggests that BSL may well be a subject-verb-object (SVO) language, even though it does also make use of topic-comment structures.

The words of BSL which are themselves structured both sequentially and simultaneously enter into different kinds of grammatical process within the areas of syntax and morphology. The learner wishing to exploit the lexical resources of BSL which have been explored in some detail in the central part of this account, will need to become familiar not only with the vocabulary of the language, but with its grammar also.

Conclusion

This exploration into the nature and structure of BSL has had as its central focus the lexical resources of British Sign Language. These resources provide Deaf people with a wealth of possibilities for the creative manipulation of their own language and demonstrate the enormous potential of visual-gestural linguistic systems.

Bibliography

Ahlgren, I. and Bergman, B. (1990): Preliminaries on narrative discourse in Swedish Sign Language, in: Prillwitz, S. and Vollhaber, T. (eds.): *Current Trends in European Sign Language Research*. Signum Press, Hamburg.

Akamatsu, C.T. (1982): *The Acquisition of Fingerspelling in Pre-school Children*. Ph.D. Dissertation. University of Rochester, Rochester.

Allan, K. (1977) Classifiers, in: *Language 53*.

Anderson, S.R. (1985): Typological distinctions in word formation, in: Shopen, T. (ed.): *Language Typology and Syntactic Description vol. 3*. Cambridge University Press, Cambridge.

Baker, C. and Cokely, D. (1980): *American Sign Language: A Teacher's Resource Text on Grammar and Culture*. T.J. Publishers, Silver Spring, Md.

Baker-Shenk, C. (1983): *A Microanalysis of the Nonmanual Components of Questions in American Sign Language*. Unpublished Ph.D. Dissertation. University of California, Berkeley, Ca.

Banham, D. (1992): *Monasteriales Indicia*. Anglo Saxon Books

Barakat, R.A. (1975): *The Cistercian Sign Language: A study in Non-verbal Communicaton*. Cistercian Publications, Kalamazoo, Michigan.

Battison, R.M. (1974): Phonological deletion in American Sign Language, in: *Sign Language Studies 5*.

Battison, R.M. (1978): *Lexical Borrowing in American Sign Language*. Linstok Press, Silver Spring, Md.

Bellugi, U. and Klima, E. (1972): The roots of language in the sign talk of the deaf, in: *Psychology Today 6*.

Bellugi, U., Lillo-Martin, D., O'Grady, L. and Van Hoek, K. (1990): The development of spatialized syntactic mechanisms, in: Edmondson, W.H. and Karlsson, F. (eds.): *Papers from the Fourth International Symposium on Sign Language Research*. Signum Press, Hamburg.

Bergman, B. (1978): *On Motivated Signs in the Swedish Sign Language*. Studia Linguistica.

Bergman, B. (1983): Verbs and adjectives: morphological processes in Swedish Sign Language, in: Kyle, J.G. and Woll, B. (eds.): *Language in Sign: An International Perspective on Sign Language*. Croom Helm, London.

Bergman, B. (1986): A comparison between some static sentences in Swedish Sign Language and in English, in: Tervoort, B.T. (ed.): *Signs of Life: Proceedings of the Second European Congress on Sign Language Research*. University of Amsterdam, Amsterdam.

Bergman, B. (1990): Grammaticalization of location, in: Edmondson, W.H. and Karlsson, F. (eds.): *Papers from the Fourth International Symposium on Sign Language Research*. Signum Press, Hamburg.

Bienvenu, M.J. (1987): Third culture: working together, in: *Journal of Interpretation, vol. 4*. RID Publications, Rockville, Md.

Bos, H. (1990): Person and location marking in SLN: some implications of a spatially expressed syntactic system, in: Prillwitz, S. and Vollhaber, T. (eds.): *Current Trends in European Sign Language Research: Proceedings of the 3rd European Congres on Sign Language Research*. Signum Press, Hamburg.

Boyes-Braem, P. (1981): *Features of the Handshape in ASL*. Ph.D. Dissertation. University of California, Berkeley.

Boyes-Braem, P. (1986): Two aspects of psycholinguistic research: iconicity and temporal structure, in: Tervoort, B.T. (ed.): *Signs of Life: Proceedings of the Second European Congress on Sign Language Research*. Institute of Linguistics, University of Amsterdam, Amsterdam.

Boyes-Braem, P., Fournier, M.L., Rickli, F., Corazza, S., Franchi, M.L. and Volterra, V. (1987): A comparison of techniques for expressing semantic roles and locative relations in two different sign languages, in: Edmondson, W.H. and Karlsson, F. (eds.): *Papers from the Fourth International Symposium on Sign Language Research*. Signum Press, Hamburg.

Brennan, M. (1975): Can deaf children acquire language? An evaluation of linguistic principles in deaf education, in: *American Annals of the Deaf, October 1975*. (reprinted as Brennan, 1976).

Brennan, M. (1976): Can deaf children acquire language? An evaluation of linguistic principles in deaf education, in: *The British Deaf News*.

Brennan, M. (1986): Linguistic perspectives, in: Tervoort, B.T. (ed.): *Signs of Life: Proceedings of the Second European Congress on Sign Language Research*. Institute of Linguistics, University of Amsterdam, Amsterdam.

Brennan, M. (1987): British Sign Language: the language of the Deaf community, in: Booth, T. and Swann, W. (eds.): *Including Pupils with Disabilities: Curricula for All*. Open University Press, Milton Keynes.

Brennan, M. (1990a): *Word Formation in British Sign Language*. University of Stockholm, Stockholm.

Brennan, M. (1990b): Productive morphology in British Sign Language, in: Prillwitz, S. and Vollhaber, T. (eds.): *Current Trends in European Sign Language Research: Proceedings of the 3rd European Congress on Sign Language Research*. Signum Press, Hamburg.

Brennan, M. and Colville, M.D. (1984): *Final Report to Economic and Social Research Council*. ESRC, London.

Brennan, M., Colville, M.D. and Lawson, L.K. (1980): *Words in Hand: A Structural Analysis of the Signs of British Sign Language*. Moray House College of Education, Edinburgh.

Brennan, M., Colville, M.D. Lawson, L.K. and Hughes, G. (1984): *Words in Hand: A Structural Analysis of the Signs of British Sign Language* (second edition). Moray House College of Education, Edinburgh.

Brien, D. (1981): Is there a Deaf culture available to the young deaf person? Paper presented to the National Council of Social Workers with the Deaf.

Bristol Sign Language Group (1979): *Coding British Sign Language: Proceedings of the Sign Language Notation Workshop, Newcastle, 11th-13th May 1979*. Bristol Sign Language Group, Bristol.

Calbris (1990): *The Semiotics of French Gestures*. Indian University Press, Bloomington.

Coerts, J. (1992): *Nonmanual Grammatical Markers: An Analysis of Interrogatives, Negations and Topicalisations in Sign Language of the Netherlands*. University of Amsterdam, Amsterdam.

Colville, M.D. (1979): Loan signs from finger spelled words. Paper presented at the NATO Advanced Summer Institute on Sign Language Research, Copenhagen, August 1979.

Colville, M.D. (1984): Patterns of fingerspelling. Paper presented at SIGN '84 Conference, Edinburgh.

Colville, M.D. (forthcoming): Signs of fingerspelling.

Colville, M.D., Hughes, G. and Brennan, M. (1984): Edinburgh non-manual coding system. Working paper 1, Edinburgh BSL Project. Moray House College of Education, Edinburgh.

Craig, C. (1986): *Noun Classes and Categorisation*. John Benjamin Publishing Company, Amsterdam.

Dahl, H. (1979): *Typology of Sentence Negation*. Mouton Publishers, The Hague.

Deuchar, M. (1983): Is British Sign Language an SVO Language?, in: Kyle, J.G. and Woll, B. (eds.): *Language in Sign: An International Perspective on Sign Language*. Croom Helm, London.

Deuchar, M. (1984): *British Sign Language*. Routledge and Kegan Paul, London.

Deuchar, M. (1985): Implications of sign language research for linguistic theory, in: Stokoe, W.C. and Volterra, V. (eds.): *SLR '83: Proceedings of the 3rd International Symposium on Sign Language Research*. Linstok Press, Silver Spring, Md.

Edinburgh BSL Project (1983): *Sign: An Introduction to British Sign Language (BSL)*. Videotape series. Moray House College of Education, Edinburgh.

Edinburgh BSL Project (1984): *Non-manual features in BSL*. Working Paper 4. Moray House College of Education, Edinburgh.

Edmondson, W.H. and Karlsson, F. (eds.) (1990): *SLR '87: Papers from the Fourth International Symposium on Sign Language Research. International Studies on Sign Language and the Communication of the Deaf, vol. 10*. Signum Press, Hamburg.

Ekman, P. and Friesen, W. (1978): *Facial Action Coding System*. Consulting Psychologists Press, Palo Alto, CA.

Engberg-Pedersen, E. (1985): The use of space with verbs in Danish Sign Language, in: Tervoort, B.T. (ed.) *Signs of Life: Proceedings of the Second European Congress on Sign Language Research*. Institute of Linguistics, University of Amsterdam, Amsterdam.

Ewing, Sir A. and Ewing, E.L. (1964): *Teaching Deaf Children to Talk*. Manchester University Press, Manchester.

Firth, G.C. (1989): *Chosen Vessels*. Sydney Road, Exeter.

Fischer, S.D. and Siple, P. (eds.) (1990): *Theoretical Issues in Sign Language Research, vol. 1: Linguistics*. University of Chicago Press, Chicago.

Friedman, L.A. (1977): *On the Other Hand: New Perspectives on American Sign Language*. Academic Press, New York.

Gimson A.C. (1962): *An Introduction to the Pronunciation of English*. Edward Arnold, London.

Grant, B. (1990): *The Deaf Advance: A History of The British Deaf Association*. Pentland Press, Edinburgh.

Gregory, S. and Llewellyn-Jones, M. (1992): The development of temporal reference in British Sign Language, in: *Signpost, spring 1992*.

Hacking, I. (1990) Signing, in: *London Review of Books, 5th April*.

Hockett, C.F. (1958): *A Course in Modern Linguistics*. Macmillan, New York.

Hughes, G., Brennan, M. and Colville, M.(1984): Talking about existence in British Sign Language, in: Loncke, F., Boyes-Braem, P. and Lebrun, Y. (eds.): *Recent Research on European Sign Language*. Swets and Zeitlinger, Lisse.

Jackson, P.W. (1986): Interim Report on a Sociological Study of the Deaf Community. Paper presented to the 1986 B.D.A. Congress. B.D.A./University of Durham.

Jackson, P. W. (1990): *Britain's Deaf Heritage*. Pentland Press, Edinburgh.

Johnson, S. (1755) *Dictionary of the English Language*. Knapton, London.

Johnston, T. (1989) *Auslan Dictionary: A Dictionary of the Sign Language of the Australian Deaf Community*. Deafness Resources, Australia.

Jones, L. and Pullen, G. (1990): *Inside We Are All Equal: A Social Policy Survey of Deaf People in the European Community*. ECRS, London.

Kendon, A. (1988): *Sign Languages of Aboriginal Australia: Cultural, Semiotic and Communicative Perspectives*. Cambridge University Press, Cambridge.

Klima, E. and Bellugi, U. (1979): *The Signs of Language*. Harvard University Press, Cambridge, Mass.

Kyle, J.G. (1986): Deaf people and minority groups in the U.K., in: Tervoort, B.T. (ed.) *Signs of Life: Proceedings of the Second European Congress on Sign Language Research*. Institute of Linguistics, University of Amsterdam, Amsterdam.

Kyle, J.G. (1987): Deaf people from school to society, in: Taylor, I.G. (ed.): *Proceedings of International Congress of the Education of the Deaf*. Croom Helm, London.

Kyle, J.G. (1990): The Deaf community: culture, custom and tradition, in: Prillwitz, S. and Vollhaber, T. (eds.): *Sign Language: Research and Application*. Signum Press, Hamburg.

Kyle, J.G. and Allsop, L. (1982): *Deaf People and the Community: Final Report to Nuffield*. Bristol University School of Education, Bristol.

Kyle, J.G. and Pullen, G. (1988): Cultures in contact: deaf and hearing people, in: *Disability, Handicap and Society*.

Kyle, J.G. and Woll, B. (eds.)(1983): *Language in Sign: An International Perspective on Sign Language*. Croom Helm, London.

Kyle, J.G. and Woll, B. (1985): *Sign Language: The Study of Deaf People and Their Language*. Cambridge University Press, Cambridge.

Ladd, P. (1981): Making plans for Nigel: the erosion of identity by mainstreaming, in: Taylor, G. and Bishop, J. (eds.) (1990): *Being Deaf: The Experience of Deafness*. Pinter Publishers, London.

Ladd, P. (1988a): Hearing-impaired or British Sign Language users? Social policies and the Deaf community, in: *Disability, Handicap and Society, vol.3 no.2*.

Ladd, P. (1988b): The modern Deaf community, in: Miles, D.: *British Sign Language: A Beginner's Guide*. .BBC Books, London.

Lakoff, G. (1986): Classifiers as a reflection of mind, in: Craig, C. (ed.): *Noun Classes and Categorization*. John Benjamins Publishing Company, Amsterdam.

Lakoff, G. (1987): *Women, Fire, and Dangerous Things: What Categories Reveal about the Mind*. University of Chicago Press, Chicago.

Lakoff, G. and Johnson, M. (1980): *Metaphors We Live By*. University of Chicago Press, Chicago.

Lakoff, G. and Turner, M. (1989): *More than Cool Reason: A Field Guide to Poetic Metaphor*. University of Chicago Press, Chicago.

Landau, S.I. (1989): *Dictionaries: The Art and Craft of Lexicography*. Cambridge University Press, Cambridge.

Lane, H. (1984): *When the Mind Hears: A History of the Deaf*. Random House, New York.

Lane, H. (1988): The failure of Deaf education. Paper given at Northeastern University, Boston.

Lawson, L.K. (1981): The role of Sign in the Structure of the Deaf Community, in: Woll, B., Kyle, J.G., Deuchar, M. (eds.). *Perspectives on British Sign Language and Deafness*. Croom Helm, London.

Lawson, L. K. (1983): Multi-channel signs, in: Kyle, J.G. and Woll, B. (eds.): *Language in Sign*. Croom Helm, London.

Lee (1992): *Deaf Liberation*. National Union of the Deaf, Middlesex.

Liddell, S.K. (1978): Nonmanual signals and relative clauses in ASL, in: Siple, P. (ed.): *Understanding Language Through Sign Language Research*. Academic Press, London.

Liddell, S.K. (1980): *American Sign Language Syntax*. Mouton, The Hague.

Liddell, S.K. (1984): Think and Believe: Sequentiality in American Sign Language, in: *Language 60*.

Liddell, S.K. (1985): British signs and linguistic theory: a review of Deuchar: British Sign Language, in: *Sign Language Studies 46*.

Liddell, S.K. (1992): Paths to lexical imagery. Unpublished manuscript. Gallaudet University, Washington D.C.

Liddell, S.K. (1992): Tokens and surrogates. Paper presented at the 5th International Symposium on Sign Language Research, Salamanca.

Liddell, S.K. and Johnson, R.E. (1985): *American Sign Language: The Phonological Base*. Gallaudet College, Washington.

Lyons, J. (1977): *Semantics: Volumes 1 and 2*. Cambridge University Press, Cambridge.

Lysons, K. (1979): The Development of Local Voluntary Societies for Adult Deaf Persons in England, in: *The British Deaf News*.

McDonald, B. (1982): *Aspects of the American Sign Language Predicate System*. Ph.D. Thesis, University of Buffalo.

McDonald, B. (1985): Productive and frozen lexicon in ASL: an old problem revisited, in: Stokoe, W.C. and Volterra, V. (eds.): *SLR '83: Proceedings of the 3rd International Symposium on Sign Language Research*. Linstok Press, Silver Spring, Md.

McLaughlin, M.G. (1987): *History of the Education of the Deaf in England and Wales*. Private publication, Liverpool.

Mandel, M. (1977): Iconic devices in American Sign Language, in: Friedman, L. (ed.): *On the Other Hand: New Perspectives in American Sign Language*. Academic Press, New York.

Miles, D. (1976): *Poetry in Sign Language*. Joyce Publications, Northridge, Ca.

Miles, D. (1988): *British Sign Language: A Beginners Guide*. BBC Books, London.

Morris, D. (1978): *Manwatching: A Field Guide to Human Behaviour*. Triad Panther, St. Albans.

Newport, E.L. (1982): Task specificity in language learning: evidence from speech perception and American Sign Language, in: Wanner, E. and Gleitman, L.R. (eds.): *Language Acquisition: The State of the Art*. University Press, Cambridge.

Newport, E.L. and Supalla, T. (1980): The structure of language: clues from the acquisition of signed and spoken language, in: Bellugi, U. and Studdert-Kennedy, M. (eds.): *Signed and Spoken Language: Biological Constraints on Linguistic Form*. Verlag Chemie, Berlin.

Padden, C. (1980): The Deaf community and the culture of Deaf people, in : Baker, C. and Battison, R (eds.): *Sign Language and the Deaf Community: Essays in Honour of William C. Stokoe*. National Association of the Deaf, Silver Spring, Md.

Padden, C. (1988): Grammatical theory and signed languages, in: Newmeijer, F.J. (ed.): *Linguistics: The Cambridge Survey, vol. 2: Linguistic Theory: Extensions and Implications*. Cambridge University Press, Cambridge.

Padden, C. and Humphries, T. (1988): *Deaf in America: Voices from a Culture*. Harvard University Press, Cambridge, Mass.

Pickersgill, M. (1990): Bilingualism and the education of deaf children, parts 1 and 2, in: *Deafness and Development, vol. 1 issues 1–2*.

Prillwitz, S. and Vollhaber, T. (1990): *Current Trends in European Sign Language Research*: *Proceedings of the 3rd European Congress on Sign Language Research*. Signum Press, Hamburg.

Ruhlen, M. (1976): *A Guide to the Languages of the World*. Stanford University, Paolo Alto, Ca.

Sacks, O. (1989): *Seeing Voices*. Picador, London.

Saussure, F. (1916): *Cours de Linguistique Générale*. Payot, Paris.

Savage, R.D., Evans, L. and Savage, J.F. (1981): *Psychology and Communication in Deaf Children*. Grune and Stratton, Sydney.

Schermer, T.M. (1990): *In Search of a Language*. Eburon Publisher, The Netherlands.

Schick, B.S. (1990): Classifier predicates in American Sign Language, in: *International Journal of Sign Linguistics, vol. 1, no. 1*.

Schroeder, O. (1985) A problem in phonological description, in: Stokoe, W.C. and Volterra, V. (eds.): *SLR '83: Proceedings of the 3rd International Symposium on Sign Language Research*. Linstok Press, Silver Spring, Md.

Sebeok, D.J.U. and Sebeok, T.A. (1978): *Aboriginal Sign Languages of the Americas and Australia, volumes 1 and 2*. Plenum Press, London.

Sebeok, D.J.U. and Sebeok, T.A. (1987): *Monastic Sign Languages*. Mouton de Gruyter, New York.

Sinclair, J. (ed.) (1987): *Collins COBUILD English Language Dictionary*. Collins, London.

Sinclair, J. (ed.) (1988): *Collins COBUILD Essential English Dictionary*. Collins, London.

Siple, P. (1982): Signed language and linguistic theory, in: Obler, L. and Menn, L. (eds.): *Exceptional Language and Linguistics*. Academic Press, New York.

Siple, P. and Fischer, S.D. (1991): *Theoretical Issues in Sign Language Research vol. 2: Psychology*. University of Chicago Press, Chicago.

Sternberg, M. (1981): *American Sign Language: A Comprehensive Dictionary*. Harper and Row, New York.

Stokoe, W.C. (1960): *Sign Language Structure: an Outline of the Visual Communication Systems of the American Deaf*. University of Buffalo, Occasional papers 8.

Stokoe, W.C. (1972): *Semiotics and Human Sign Languages*. Mouton, The Hague.

Stokoe, W.C. (1978): *Sign Language Structure* (revised edition). Linstok Press, Silver Spring, Md.

Stokoe, W.C. (1988): Approaching monastic sign language: a review of Sebeok and Sebeok, in: *Sign Language Studies 58*. Linstok Press, Silver Spring, Md.

Stokoe, W.C., Casterline, D.C. and Croneberg, C.G. (1965): *A Dictionary of American Sign Language on Linguistic Principles*. Gallaudet College Press, Washington; (Revised 1976) Linstok Press, Silver Spring, Md.

Stokoe, W.C. and Volterra, V. (1985): *SLR '83: Proceedings of the 3rd International Symposium on Sign Language Research*. Linstok Press, Silver Spring, Md.

Supalla, T. (1982): *Structure and Acquisition of Verbs of Motion and Location in American Sign Language*. Doctoral dissertation, University of California, San Diego.

Supalla, T. (1986): The classifier system in American Sign Language, in: Craig, C. (ed.): *Noun Classes and Categorization*. John Benjamin Publishing Company, Amsterdam.

Supalla, T. and Newport, E.L. (1978): How many seats in a chair? The derivation of nouns and verbs in American Sign Language, in: Siple, P. (ed.): *Understanding Language Through Sign Language Research*. Academic Press, New York.

Sutton-Spence, R., Woll, B. and Allsop, L.K. (1990): Variation and recent change in fingerspelling in British Sign Language, in: *Language Variation and Change 2*. Cambridge University Press, Cambridge.

Suwanarat, M. et al. (1986): *Thai Sign Language Dictionary*. National Association of the Deaf in Thailand and the Human Assistance Programme, Thailand.

Taylor, G. and Bishop, J. (eds.) (1991): *Being Deaf: The Experience of Deafness*. Pinter Publishers, London.

Tervoort, B. T. (1986): *Signs of Life: Proceedings of the Second European Congress on Sign Language Research*. Institute of Linguistics, University of Amsterdam, Amsterdam.

Thompson, C. and Janes, L.(1991): Sign singer, in: Taylor, G. and Bishop, J. (eds.): *Being Deaf: The Experience of Deafness*. Pinter Publishers, London.

Tyne Tees Television (1991): *Signs of Our Times*. Television series.

Voegelin and Voegelin (1973): *Index of the World's Languages*. Washington D.C. Dept. of Health, Education and Welfare, Office of Education, Bureau of Research.

Volterra, V. and Erting, C.J. (eds.) (1990): *From Gesture to Language in Hearing and Deaf Children*. Springer Verlag, Berlin.

Vogt-Svendsen, M. (1978): Eye gaze in Norwegian Sign Language interrogatives, in: Edmondson, W.H. and Karlsson, F. (eds.): *Papers from the Fourth International Symposium on Sign Language Research*. Signum Press, Hamburg.

Vogt-Svendsen, M. (1983): Lip movements in Norwegian Sign Language, in: Kyle, J.G. and Woll, B. (eds.)(1983): *Language in Sign: An International Perspective on Sign Language*. Croom Helm, London.

Vogt-Svendsen, M. (1984): Word-pictures in Norwegian Sign Language : a preliminary analysis, in: *Working Papers in Linguistics*. University of Trondheim, Trondheim.

Wallin, L. (1983): Compounds in Swedish Sign Language, in: Kyle, J.G. and Woll, B. (eds.): *Language in Sign*. Croom Helm, London.

Wilbur, R.B. (1979): *American Sign Language and Sign Systems*. University Park Press, Baltimore, Md.

Wilbur, R.B. (1987): *American Sign Language: Linguistic and Applied Dimensions* (second edition). Little, Brown and Co., Boston, Mass.

Wilbur, R.B. (1989): Metaphors in American Sign Language and English, in: Edmondson, W.H. and Karlsson, F. (eds.): *Papers from the Fourth International Symposium on Sign Language Research*. Signum Press, Hamburg.

Woll, B. (1981): Question structure in British Sign Language, in: Woll, B., Kyle, J.G. and Deuchar, M. (eds.): *Perspectives on British Sign Language and Deafness*. Croom Helm, London.

Woll, B. (ed.) (1989): *Language Development and Sign Language: Papers from the Seminar on Language Development and Sign Language*. International Sign Linguistics Association, Bristol.

Woodward, J. (1972): Implications for sociolinguistic research among the deaf, in: *Sign Language Studies 1*.

Woodward, J. (1973): Some characteristics of Pidgin Sign English, in: *Sign Language Studies 3*.

Woodward, J. (1982): How you gonna get to heaven if you can't talk with Jesus: the educational establishment vs the Deaf community, in: Woodward, J.: *How You Gonna Get To Heaven If You Can't Talk With Jesus: On Depathologizing Deafness*. T.J. Publishers, Silver Spring, Md.

World Federation of the Deaf (1975): *Gestuno: International Sign Language of the Deaf*. British Deaf Association (for the WFD), Carlisle.

Worswick, C. (1982): *Interrogatives in British Sign Language*. Unpublished manuscript, BSL Research Project, Edinburgh.

Glossary

610. arbitrary

611. aspect

arbitrary

Description

The $\bar{5}$ hand is held with the palm facing up (if the hand were opened, the fingers would point towards the signer). The hand is held at head height in front of the body. The hand twists at the wrist, so that the fingers point away from the signer, while closing (forming an F hand); the hand then moves down.

Definition

A type of relationship between form and meaning in which there is no physical correspondence between the entities in the real world and the forms which represent them. An arbitrary sign in BSL is one which bears no physical correspondence to what it represents. This is in contrast to motivated signs (see under **iconic**).
pp. 41–42

aspect

Description

The left G hand is held with the palm facing right; the right V̌ hand is held with the palm facing away from the signer (if the hands were opened, the fingers would all point up). The hands are held in front of the body; the right hand is held nearer to the signer than the left hand. The right hand moves away from the signer and, at the same time, to the right while bending to the left at the wrist.

Definition

A grammatical category, usually marked in verbs, which allows the user to view an event from different temporal perspectives. The same event may be viewed as completed, ongoing, of long duration, happening again and again, just about to happen and so on. Aspectual verbs in BSL are those which can be inflected for aspect.
pp.104–108

610. Ø $\bar{5}$ɑт $\overset{\omega\ [\text{F}]\vee}{\underset{\#}{\perp}}$

611. G>ʌ V̈⊥ʌ̩ $\overset{\text{n}}{\underset{\vee}{\overset{\vee}{\underset{\perp}{\vee}}}}$

612. **bodyshift**

613. **citation form**

bodyshift

Description

Two 5̄ hands are held with the palms facing towards the signer (if the hands were opened, the left fingers would point to the right and the right fingers would point to the left). The hands are held with the fingertips touching the front of the shoulders. No movement. NMF: the shoulders move forward and back alternately.

Definition

A movement of the signer's upper body, usually perceived as a twisting movement of the shoulders. This particular non–manual action can have several different functions in the language, but is particularly important as an indicator of role–shift.

citation form

Description

The left v hand is held with the palm facing right, the right v hand is held with the palm facing left (if the hands were opened, the fingers would all point away from the signer). The hands are held side by side in front of the signer. The extended fingers flex while the hands make a short movement towards the signer.

Definition

The form of a sign or spoken word when it is cited or articulated in isolation, rather than within ordinary interaction. Dictionaries typically list citation forms. Such forms are abstractions away from real world usage: the sign (or spoken word) within connected discourse will be subject to modifications relating to the contexts in which it occurs.

p. 31

---

612. ⌐ 5̄ₜ> 5̄ₜ< ×

613. ∅ V>⊥ ' V<⊥ ᵀₘ°

614. **classifier**

615. **compound**

classifier

Description

The v̇ hand is held with the palm facing left (if the hand were opened, the fingers would point away from the signer). The hand is held in front of the body. The hand makes several short, sharp movements, bending up and down at the wrist.

Definition

Classifiers are linguistic units which indicate what kind of group or category a particular referent belongs to. They may signal that an item belongs to the class of humans, the class of vehicles, the class of round things, the class of flat things and so on. BSL classifiers are expressed in BSL by means of the handshape and are usually motivated: the configuration of the hand has some link with what it represents. So the class of flat objects is represented by a flat handshape. Several different categories of classifier are found in BSL. Almost every handshape in the language can express at least one of these categories: some handshapes express several. This results in a very rich system of classifier options.
pp. 46–67

compound

Description

Two 5 hands are held with the palms facing down and the fingers pointing away from the signer. The hands are held side by side in front of the body; the left hand is held higher than the right hand. The hands twist at the wrists, so that the palms face towards each other while closing (forming two ɓ hands); the movement ends with the fingertips all touching.

Definition

A compound is a word which consists of two free morphemes which can themselves function as separate words of the language. The meaning of the resulting form may not be directly predictable from the component parts, for example, in BSL the combination **see+never** produces a sign which can be glossed as **strange**. BSL has two main types of compounds: sequential compounds combine two separate signs in linear sequence, one after the other as in |**think+add**| **exaggerate** (pp. 36–38); simultaneous compounds combine the two separate morphemes simultaneously, by articulating one morpheme with one hand and the other morpheme with the other hand as in |**telephone+type**| **text telephone** (pp. 38–39). Compounding is a highly productive process in BSL.
pp. 36–39

614. Ø v̇<⊥ ᴅ̊·̇/ɴ

615. Ø 5⊽⊥ , 5⊽⊥ (ω/ẋ/#)[ɓɓ]×

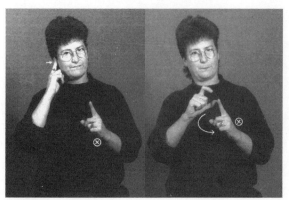

616. **Deaf community**

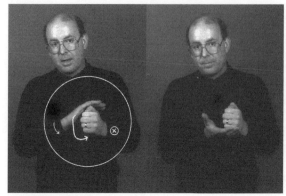

617. **dez handshape**

Deaf community

Description

The н hand is held with the palm facing left (if the hand were opened, the fingers would point up). The hand is held with the extended fingers beside the ear. The pads of the extended fingers touch the ear.

The left ɢ hand is held with the palm facing right (if the hand were opened, the fingers would point up). The right ɢ̆ hand is held with the palm facing left (if the hand were opened, the fingers would point up). The hands are held in front of the body; the right hand is held nearer to the signer than the left hand. The right hand moves to the right and, at the same time, away from the signer and then moves to the left.

Definition

A group of people who see themselves as sharing a common sign language, heritage and Deaf identity. Members typically have some kind of hearing loss, but this is not seen as the most important criterion of membership. Participation in the life and culture of the community and commitment to furthering the interests of the group are considered of central importance.

pp. 2–10

dez handshape

Description

The left ᴀ hand is held with the palm facing right (if the hand were opened, the fingers would point away from the signer); the right ʙ hand is held with the palm facing down and the fingers pointing to the left. The hands are held in front of the body; the right hand rests on the left hand. The right hand moves down across the left knuckles, twisting at the wrist, while maintaining contact with the left fingers throughout; the movement ends with the right palm facing up and the left hand held on the right fingers.

Definition

Dez, which is short for dezignation, is the technical term (also glossed as **handshape**) used when handshape functions as one of the major aspects of the structure of individual signs. Within this context, the different handshapes can function as separate dez phonemes. BSL makes use of approximately 57 different dezes which can be used contrastively in the language.

pp. 19–21

---

616. ⊃ H<ʌ × // G>ʌ Ğ<ʌ₉ ⊥<
        // >

617. A̅>⊥ × Bʊ< ᵛ
                  ₓ

618. **directional verb**

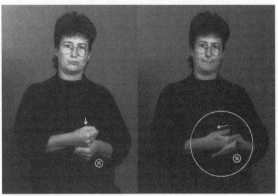

619. **grammar**

directional verb

Description

The B hand is held with the palm facing left and the fingers pointing up. The hand is held in front of the face. The hand moves away from the signer and then twists at the wrist, so that the palm faces right before moving back towards the signer.

Definition

A directional verb is one in which the movement conveys information about the subject and/or object and/or indirect object of the verb. Within many of these verbs, it is the direction of movement which conveys such information, hence the name directional. In others, the same information can be conveyed by changes in orientation and position, as well as, or instead of direction. The BSL signs **help** and **explain** are both directional verbs.
pp. 108–110

grammar

Description

Two A hands are held with the palms facing towards the signer (if the hands were opened, the left fingers would point to the right and the right fingers would point to the left). The hands are held in front of the body; the right hand is held above the left hand. The right hand makes a short downward movement to touch the left hand.
The left B hand is held with the palm facing towards the signer and the fingers pointing to the right; the right Ḃ hand is held with the palm facing left (if the hand were opened, the fingers would point away from the signer). The hands are held in front of the body; the backs of the right fingers rest against the left palm. The right hand moves to the right, maintaining contact with the left hand throughout.

Definition

A central term within linguistics, but one which is used in several different ways, depending upon the theoretical perspective of the linguist. Within traditional language studies, grammar is used as a generic term to cover the areas of inflection and syntax (see separate entries). Within generative accounts, a grammar consists of a limited set of rules which allow a signer or speaker to produce and understand an unlimited set of possible utterances. A major task within linguistics is to provide an account of the general principles which underlie the grammars of specific languages, including sign languages.
pp. 99–114

618. ⊙ B<ʌ ⊥ωт
>

619. ⦰ Ā⊤> A⊤< ᵒ ᵛx // B⊤> x Ḃ<⊥ᵩ >
x

620. iconic

621. inflection

iconic

Description

The ɕ hand is held with the palm facing left (if the hand were opened, the fingers would point up). The hand is held with the index fingertip touching the cheek below the eye. The hand moves down and away from the signer while changing (forming a v̌ hand) and then makes a short movement towards the signer.

Definition

The term iconic is used in two main ways within the sign linguistics literature: it is used for any type of relationship between form and meaning in which there is a perceivable correspondence between the entities in the real world and the forms which represent them. Within the account of form-meaning relationships presented here, the term *motivated* has been used for this wider meaning, while iconicity has been reserved for one particular type of motivated relationship: that of resemblance. Therefore, an iconic sign in BSL is one which in some ways resembles what it represents. The sign **butterfly** resembles an actual butterfly, both in terms of its overall shape and the action produced by the hands, which can be said to imitate the actions of a butterfly's wings.

pp. 42–43

inflection

Description

The left ĉ hand is held with the palm facing up; the right ĉ hand is held with the palm facing down (if the hands were opened, the left fingers would point away from the signer and the right fingers would point to the left). The hands are held in front of the body; the right hand is held on the left hand. The hands change places, maintaining contact throughout.

Definition

An inflection is a regular change of form, applied to a specific word class (or to a sub group within a word class) which brings about a regular change of meaning. Inflectional morphemes provide information on grammatical categories such as number and aspect. In BSL, inflections very often involve changes in movement: examples include aspectual inflections, such as *continuative* (p.106) and plural inflections, such as the *sweep* inflection (p. 101). There remains some doubt as to whether all of these forms can be regarded as full inflections: in particular, it is not always possible to indicate the precise grammatical contexts in which particular forms are required or to view them as fully productive., i.e. as always applying in certain conditions. For this reason, some sign linguists prefer to use the looser term *modulation* for such changes.

p. 99

620. Ʊ ɕ<ʌ

621. Ø ĉɑ⊥ × ĉʊ<

622. linguistics

623. linguistics

linguistics

Description

The left B hand is held with the palm facing towards the signer and the fingers pointing to the right; the right B̊ hand is held with the palm facing left (if the hand were opened the fingers would point away from the signer). The hands are held in front of the body; the backs of the right fingers rest against the left palm. The right hand moves to the right, brushing across the left palm and then bends upwards at the wrist while changing (forming a c hand).

Definition

Within the twentieth century, linguistics has developed as the scientific study of human language. Linguistics is centrally concerned with the underlying laws or principles which govern the patterning of all human language. However, like most disciplines, linguistics has a theoretical branch and an applied branch. Since the 1960s, initially inspired by the work of Noam Chomsky, both of these areas have expanded enormously. Sign linguistics is concerned with the scientific study of the sign languages of the world. Sign linguists are keen to discern whether the same universal properties which have been proposed in relation to spoken languages, also operate in respect of sign languages. Applied sign linguistics work in such areas as sign language acquisition, sign language teaching and sign language variation is beginning to provide new insights and new information of relevance to the Deaf community.

linguistics

Description

The left F hand is held with the palm facing right; the right F hand is held with the palm facing left (if the hands were opened the fingers would all point away from the signer). The hands are held side by side in front of the body with the thumb and index finger tips all touching. The hands make alternate short up and down bending movements at the wrists while moving apart throughout.

Definition

Within the twentieth century, linguistics has developed as the scientific study of human language. Linguistics is centrally concerned with the underlying laws or principles which govern the patterning of all human language. However, like most disciplines, linguistics has a theoretical branch and an applied branch. Since the 1960s, initially inspired by the work of Noam Chomsky, both of these areas have expanded enormously. Sign linguistics is concerned with the scientific study of the sign languages of the world. Sign linguists are keen to discern whether the same universal properties which have been proposed in relation to spoken languages, also operate in respect of sign languages. Applied sign linguistics work in such areas as sign language acquisition, sign language teaching and sign language variation is beginning to provide new insights and new information of relevance to the Deaf community.

622. B⊤> ₓ B̊<⊥ᵩ

623. ∅ F>⊥ ᵢₓ F<⊥

624. location

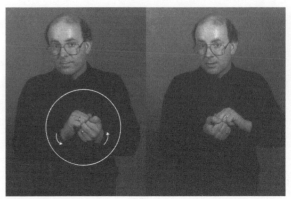

625. modulation

location

Description

The **B** hand is held with the palm facing down and the fingers pointing to the left. The hand is held in front of the forehead. The side of the hand touches the forehead before moving down to the chin.
The **B** hand is held in the palm facing down and the fingers pointing to the left. The hand is held in front of the chest. The side of the hand touches the chest.

Definition

This same sign can also be glossed as **position** and **tabulation** or **tab**. Location, in the sense expressed by this sign, functions as one of the major aspects of the structure of individual signs. Within this context, the different locations on the head, face, body and in front of the body, can function as separate tab phonemes which can be used contrastively in the language.
pp. 21–23

modulation

Description

The left **A** hand is held with the palm facing up; the right **A** hand is held with the palm facing down (if the hands were opened, the left fingers would point away from the signer and the right fingers would point to the left). The hands are held in front of the body; the right hand is held on the left hand. The hands change places, maintaining contact throughout.

Definition

A change in the form of a sign which brings about a regular change in meaning. This term is sometimes used in the literature as directly equivalent to inflection. However, because the status of some of these changes is not always clear, the term modulation appears to have developed as a looser, more general term. It may be helpful to make the following distinctions: *modification* relates to any alteration of a sign's citation form, whether or not this alteration is applied on a regular basis; *modulation* involves changing the forms of signs in regular ways to express specific sets of meanings, but without necessarily claiming that these changes can be regarded as full inflections; *inflections* also involve changes in the form of signs to bring about regular changes of meaning, but belong to a limited set of options, are fully productive, express grammatical meaning and do not change the word-class of the signs to which they apply.

---

624. ◌ B⅊< ˣᵛˣ ∥ [] B⅊< ˣ

625. Ø Ā⅁⊥ ₓ A⅊< ⁝

626. morpheme

627. morphology

morpheme

Description

The left ᴳ hand is held with the palm facing down (if the hand were opened, the fingers would point away from the signer). The right ᴮ̄ hand is held with the palm facing up (if the hand were opened, the fingers would point to the left). The hands are held side by side in front of the body. The right hand makes a short movement to the left while closing (forming a ᴮ̂ hand); the movement ends with the backs of the right fingers touching the left index finger.

Definition

A morpheme is the smallest unit of meaning within grammatical theory and description. Words in BSL consist of one or more morphemes. Some morphemes, known as *free* morphemes, can stand by themselves as independent words in the language. Others, known as *bound* morphemes, cannot occur independently: they must always be tied to some other morpheme or morphemes. Affixes in BSL and English are typically bound morphemes: in BSL they may be added simultaneously or, more rarely, sequentially. In BSL, **die** (p. 21) is a single free morpheme functioning as an independent word of the language; **see** and **catch** are free morphemes which can combine to form the compound **catch sight of** (p. 142); **wait for ages and ages and ages** (p. 106, sign 565) consists of a free morpheme **wait**, and a bound morpheme, *continuative aspect*.
pp. 35–40

morphology

Description

The left ᴳ hand is held with the palm facing down (if the hand were opened, the fingers would point away from the signer). The right ᴮ̄ hand is held with the palm facing up (if the hand were opened, the fingers would point to the left). The right hand makes a short movement to the left while closing (forming a ᴮ̂ hand) ending with the backs of the right fingers touching the left index finger; the movement is repeated.

Definition

Morphology is concerned with the internal structure of words. In particular, it is concerned to elaborate the processes for combining different units of meaning, i.e. morphemes, within single words. Traditionally, a distinction is made between *derivational* morphology, which relates to the ways in which morphemes can combine to produce new lexical items and *inflectional* morphology, which is concerned with the ways in which words are required to change in order to express particular kinds of grammatical information. This distinction is not absolute. BSL has a rich morphological structure, both in terms of the resources and processes available for the production of new words and in terms of the types of inflection carried by specific word classes, particularly nouns and verbs.
p. 99

626. Gᴖ⊥ , ᴮ̄ɑ< ^{≶ [ᴮ]×}

627. Gᴖ⊥ , ᴮ̄ɑ< ^{∘≶ [ᴮ]× ·}

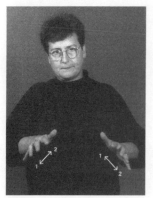

628. movement

629. multi-channel

movement

Description

Two 5 hands are held with the palms facing down and the fingers pointing away from the signer. The hands are held in front of the body. The hands move towards and away from the signer alternately and, at the same time, from side to side.

Definition

This same sign can also be glossed as **signation** or **sig**. Movement, in the sense expressed by this sign, functions as one of the major aspects of the structure of individual signs. Within this context, many different types of movement can either function separately as separate sig phonemes or can combine to provide further sig phonemes.
pp. 23–26

multi-channel

Description

The left B̄ hand is held with the palm facing right; the right B̄ hand is held with the palm facing left (if the hands were opened the fingers would all point up). The hands are held in front of the head. The hands move down, away from the signer and, at the same time, twist at the wrists, so that the palms face up while moving towards each other and closing (forming two B̂ hands). The movement ends with the hands touching.

Definition

Multi-channel is a term used to describe those BSL signs which include both manual and non-manual features in their citation form. Thus multi-channel signs always involve some action of the hands and some other bodily action(s). The particular non-manual component of a specific sign may be quite complex, involving several different non-manual features or simple, involving only one non-manual feature.
pp.32–35

628. Ø 5⌄⊥ 5⌄⊥ ÷⊥ᴎ

629. ◯ B̄>ᴧ B̄<ᴧ ᴠ[B̂B̂]×/ᵖ/◌⊥×/#

630. non-manual features

631. notation

non-manual features

Description

The left Â hand is held with the palm facing right; the right Â hand is held with the palm facing left (if the hands were opened, the fingers would all point up). The hands are held in front of the face. The hands move up and down alternately several times.

Definition

Non-manual features are actions produced by any part of the body other than the hands. They include actions of the eyes, mouth, cheeks, face, head, shoulders and torso. Non-manual features have different types of function within the structure of the language: they can operate at the phonological level as non-manual components of multi-channel signs (pp. 32–35); they can operate rather infrequently at the lexical level as full signs (pp.32–33); they can operate at the morphological level as non-manual adverbial morphemes which can be added to established signs or used to create productive forms (pp. 73–76) and they can operate at the syntactic level to signal processes operating at clause or sentence level, such as questions and topic-comment structures.
pp.113–114

notation

Description

The left ♀ hand is held with the palm facing right; the right ♀ hand is held with the palm facing left (if the hands were opened, the fingers would all point up). The hands are held in front of the body. The hands make several short twisting movements towards and away from the signer at the wrists.

Definition

Notation systems make use of special symbols and conventions to allow the graphic representation of sign language or spoken language. The English words "notation" and "transcription" are used almost interchangeably, although transcription is used particularly frequently in relation to phonemic or phonetic transcription. This dictionary uses a particular transcription system, with its own symbols and conventions, to represent manual signs. Other comparable systems are used within the sign language literature. Systems have also been developed to allow graphic representation of non-manual information, spatial information and prosodic information, such as speed and rhythm of signing. Specialised notation is also used within sign linguistics to express particular types of linguistic analysis, for example, within the analysis of multi-morphemic forms.

630. ○ Â>ʌ Â<ʌ ᴎᴎ·

631. ∅ ♀>ʌ ♀<ʌ ♀̊·

632. **phoneme**

633. **phonetics**

phoneme

Description

The left G hand is held with the palm facing down (if the hand were opened, the fingers would point away from the signer). The right 4 hand is held with the palm facing down and the fingers pointing to the left. The hands are held in front of the body; the right fingertips are held above the left index finger. The right fingers touch the left index finger.

Definition

A phoneme can be described as the minimal unit within linguistic sound systems. Phonemes can be seen as distinctive, in that the substitution of one phoneme for another will bring about a change of meaning. When used within sign linguistics, the term relates to the distinctive gestural units of a sign language. In BSL, we can distinguish different types of gestural phoneme, including dez, tab and sig phonemes. Thus the substitution of one dez (handshape) phoneme for another will either produce another sign with a different meaning or a nonsense sign. The term **chereme**, coined by W.C. Stokoe and deriving from the Greek word for 'hand', is sometimes used instead of phoneme within sign linguistics. While it seems odd to use any sound-related terminology within sign linguistics, some linguists argue that by doing so it is possible to show links amongst the comparable levels of organisation. The counter argument is that such usage may obscure any real difference in organisation which may occur.

pp. 18–19

phonetics

Description

The left F hand is held with the palm facing right; the right F hand is held with the palm facing left (if the hands were opened the fingers would all point up). The hands are held side by side in front of the body with the thumb and index finger tips all touching. The right hand makes a short movement up, at the same time, to the right, before moving firmly down and, at the same time away from the signer.

Definition

The study of the characteristics of human sound-making, especially those sounds which are used in speech. Sound can be studied in terms of its production (articulatory phonetics), its physical properties (acoustic phonetics) and how it is perceived and interpreted by the ear and brain (auditory phonetics). When applied to the study of sign languages, phonetics is concerned with the characteristics of human gestural activity: again this can be studied in terms of the articulation of gesture, the physical properties of human gesture and the manner in which gesture is perceived and interpreted by the eye and the brain. The term **cheretics**, coined by W.C. Stokoe and deriving from the Greek word meaning 'hand', is sometimes used instead of phonetics within sign linguistics.

---

632. G̅ʊ⊥ 4ʊ< ˣ

633. F>⊥ ₁ₓ F<⊥ ⸦⸧

634. phonology

635. placement

phonology

Description

The left ɢ hand is held with the palm facing down (if the hand were opened, the fingers would point away from the signer). The right 4 hand is held with the palm facing down and the fingers pointing to the left. The hands are held in front of the body; the right fingertips are held above the left index finger. The right fingers wiggle so that the fingertips tap the left index finger several times.

Definition

The study of the way in which sound can be organised into the different systems of linguistic patterning within human language. Phonologists are keen to discern general principles or rules which underlie all phonological systems, as well as describing the more specific rules which operate within a specific language. When applied to the study of sign languages, phonology is concerned with the ways in which human gestural activity can be organised into different types of linguistic patterning, as well as with a description of the particular gestural organisation within a specific language. The term **cherology**, coined by W.C. Stokoe and deriving from the Greek word for 'hand', is sometimes used instead of phonology within sign linguistics.

placement

Description

Two 5 hands are held with the palms facing down (if the hands were opened, the fingers would all point away from the signer). The hands are held in front of the body. The left hand makes a short, firm movement down and away from the signer and, at the same time, to the left; the right hand then makes a short, firm movement down and away from the signer and, at the same time, to the right.

Definition

Placement is used in relation to the placing or establishing of signs in space. The signer locates or places particular referents within the signing space in different types of relationship with the signer and with the other referents. Some linguists describe this in terms of the establishment of a spatial *locus* (literally 'the place where something occurs') or *loci* ('the places where things occur'). Once a locus has been established in space, the signer may use various means, including eye-gaze and directional verbs, to refer back to this place. Therefore placement has an important grammatical function in the language. The signer may use the specific category of 'be located' morphemes to establish referents in space.

pp. 76–78

634. Ġ̄ᴏ⊥ 4ᴏ< ᵡ

635. ∅ 5̈ᴏ⊥ 5̈ᴏ⊥ ᵞ

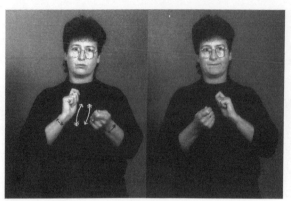

636. **roleshift**

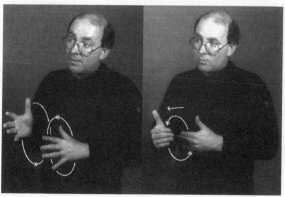

637. **sign order**

roleshift

Description

The left Â hand is held with the palm facing right; the right Â hand is held with the palm facing left (if the hands were opened, the left fingers would point away from the signer and the right fingers would point up). The hands are held side by side in front of the body. The hands change places several times.

Definition

This is a general term which relates to the signer taking on different roles within the discourse. This may be indicated by body shift and eye gaze: once the signer has indicated a change of role, everything that is signed is produced as if it were from that person's perspective. Thus role shift allows the signer to make use of what is sometimes called 'direct address'. Typically, the signer also takes on key aspects of the other person's character, as portrayed in the discourse. *p. 113*

sign order

Description

The left 5 hand is held with the palm facing right and the fingers pointing away from the signer; the right 5 hand is held with the palm facing left and the fingers pointing away from the signer. The hands are held side by side in front of the body. The hands make alternate clockwise circles in the vertical plane at right angles to the signer's body. The left ᴃ hand is held with the palm facing right; the right ᴃ hand is held with the palm facing left (if the hands were opened, the fingers would all point away from the signer). The hands are held in front of the body; the left hand is held nearer to the signer than the right hand. The hands make alternate circles in the vertical plane at right angles to the signer's body, while moving away from the signer throughout.

Definition

Sign order refers to the type of patterning usually expressed by the term word-order. Within spoken languages, speakers may make use of different types of ordering at clause level (e.g. subject–verb–object; subject–object–verb) and phrase level (e.g. adjective-noun; noun-adjective). Within sign languages, such linear ordering may also be important. However, linear ordering also interacts with spatial and simultaneous patterning to provide quite complex sets of relationships amongst signs. *p. 114*

636. ∅ Â>⊥ ¦ Â<∧ ·˙·

637. ∅ 5>⊥ ¦ 5<⊥ ᵉⁿ· ⊥ᵛ // ∅ ᴃ>⊥₉ ᴃ<⊥ (ᵉⁿ· ⊥ᵛ ⊥)

638. syntax

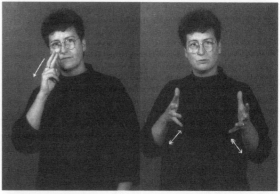

639. visual-gestural

syntax

Description

The left ꜰ hand is held with the palm facing right; the right ꜰ hand is held with the palm facing left (if the hands were opened, the left fingers would point away from the signer and the right fingers would point up). The hands are held in front of the body with the thumbs and index fingers linked together. The hands change places twice while moving to the right throughout.

Definition

Syntax is concerned with the rules which govern the combining of words into sentences or, within transformational grammars, the rules which allow the generation of well-formed syntactic structures. BSL syntax makes use of both manual and non-manual structure, simultaneous and sequential patterning and spatial as well as linear arrangement. The rules of BSL syntax allow for the generation of different types of clauses and sentences and the operation of different types of processes such as the formation of questions, commands, negation and topic-comment structures.

pp. 99–100

visual-gestural

Description

The ᴠ hand is held with the palm facing left (if the hand were opened, the fingers would point up). The hand is held with the index fingertip touching the cheek below the eye. The hand moves away from the signer and, at the same time, down. The left ꜱ hand is held with the palm facing right and the fingers pointing away from the signer; the right ꜱ hand is held with the palm facing left and the fingers pointing away from the signer. The hands are held in front of the body. The hands make alternate movements towards and away from the signer while moving from side to side.

Definition

Visual-gestural is the description given to the type of of linguistic medium used by sign languages. There are several functionally distinct dimensions in which a language may be produced: these include the oral-aural medium of spoken languages and the visual-gestural medium of sign languages. The description relates to the two complementary aspects of language use: production and perception. A sign language such as BSL is produced gesturally by movements of the hands, arms, face, head and body: the basic 'stuff' from which the language is formed is gesture. The language is perceived visually. One of the major areas of speculation within sign linguistics concerns whether the visual-gestural medium imposes particular constraints on the types of organisation available within the language.

p. 14

---

638. Ø F>⊥ ꜰ F<∧ ˙>

639. ⊔ V<∧ ˣ⊥ᵥ ∥∥ Ø 5>⊥ 5<⊥ (ᴵᴢ∩)·

3

BSL SECTION

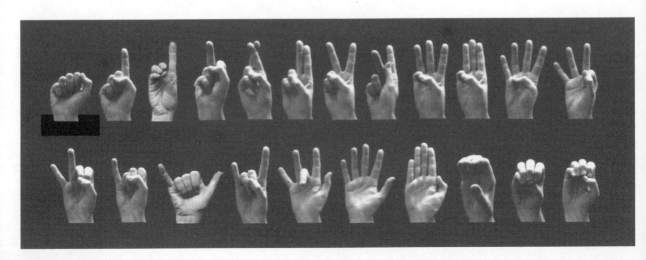

A

Handshape	Handshape description	Type	Sign entries	
A	Fist handshape in which the thumb is usually held against the side of the index finger.	Single dez	1	−42
		Manual tab	43	−71
		Double dez	72	−153
Á	The thumb is extended from the fist.	Single dez	154	−191
		Manual tab	192	−210
		Double dez	211	−237
Â	The bent index finger is extended from the fist, enclosing the top of the extended thumb.	Single dez	238	−262
		Manual tab	263	−269
		Double dez	270	−292

1 Ø Aɑ⊥ ⁺ᵒ̇ᵥ

2 Ø Aʊ⊥ ᵛᵛ̇ɑ

3 Ø Aʊ⊥ ᶻ·

4 Ø Aʊ⊥ ᵛ⁺ᵒ̇ᵒ·

5 Ø A⊤ʌ ·ᵕ⁺ᵥ

Fist handshape in which the thumb is usually held against the side of the index finger.

The **A** handshape has two main *variants*: the thumb may be held touching the side of the index finger or resting across the fingers. The choice is partly individual, but may also depend on the form of the sign. Where there is contact involving the index finger side of the hand as in **cough** (sign 36) and **coffee** (sign 53), the thumb is held out of the way, i.e. across the fingers.

A has several different *classifier* functions in the productive lexicon and also appears as a classifying element in established signs:

– it is used as a *size and shape* classifier to represent round or spherical objects such as a ball as in **bounce of a ball** (sign 62) or a person's head as in **feel small** (sign 57). It can combine with the lower arm to represent the leg and foot of a large animal (downward orientation of the fingers) or the head and body of a person (upward orientation of the fingers);

– it is used as a *handling* classifier to indicate the handling of long, narrow, cylindrical objects, such as a snooker cue in **snooker** (sign 70) or

a ski pole in **ski** (sign 120), or shorter, narrow objects such as handles, as in **jug** (sign 8) or **case** (sign 15);

– it can be used as an *instrumental* classifier to represent implements, tools or utensils with a solid, round or cylindrical end, such as a polo hammer, croquet mallet or a large pestle;

– it can be used as a *touch* classifier to indicate the action of the fist(s) in meanings such as **hit** (sign 69) and **thump** (sign 69).

A expresses the letter **a** in the Irish and American manual alphabets. As such, it is used in initial letter handshape signs borrowed from Irish Sign Language (ISL) and American Sign Language (ASL). Examples include **assist** from ISL and **Atlanta** from ASL (see *Introduction*).

The variant in which the thumb is held across the bent fingers (sometimes known as the **As** variant) expresses the letter **s** in the Irish and American manual alphabets. As such, it occurs in initial letter handshape signs such as **shop** from ISL and **state** from ASL (see *Introduction*).

Handshape and orientation	Location, hand arrangement and contact	Movement	Glosses	
The **A** hand is held with the palm facing up (if the hand were opened, the fingers would point away from the signer).	The hand is held in front of the body.	The hand makes a short, firm movement away from the signer and, at the same time, down.	grip* hang onto hold* hold onto hold tight keep*	1
Notes * This sign may be produced using a ⍟ handshape which closes (forming an **A** hand) as the hand moves.				
The **A** hand is held with the palm facing down (if the hand were opened, the fingers would point away from the signer).	The hand is held in front of the body.	The hand moves firmly down and to the left while twisting at the wrist, so that the palm faces up.	compulsory mandatory must obligatory ought should pity[1] regret[1] shame[1] should have[1] blast[2] damn[2]	2
Notes 1 If the lips are pressed together and the eyes are narrowed, the sign produced is **pity, regret, shame, should have**. 2 If the lips are stretched, and the eyes narrowed, the sign produced is **blast, damn**.				
The **A** hand is held with the palm facing down (if the hand were opened, the fingers would point away from the signer).	The hand is held in front of the body.	The hand moves from side to side several times.	knit with a knitting machine knitting machine	3
The **A** hand is held with the palm facing down (if the hand were opened, the fingers would point away from the signer).	The hand is held in front of the body.	The hand makes small clockwise circles in the horizontal plane.	clean cleaner cleaning cloth polish Saturday*	4
Notes * Regional sign.				
The A hand is held with the palm facing towards the signer (if the hand were opened, the fingers would point up).	The hand is held in front of the body.	The hand twists firmly at the wrist, so that the palm faces away from the signer, while moving to the right.	denial deny no refusal refuse turn[1] turn away[1] rebel[2] rebellion[2]	5
Non-manual features The brows are furrowed and the head shakes slightly.				
Notes 1 If the non-manual features are not present the sign produced is **turn, turn away**. 2 If the movement is large the sign produced is **rebel, rebellion**.				

6   Ø   ʲAⱯ∧ °ᴺ⊤

7   Ø   AⱯ∨ °ᶻ·

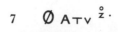

8   Ø   AⱯ< °ᴰ∨

9   Ø   A⊥∧ °⊥

10   Ø   A⊥∧ °⊤

11   Ø   A⊥∧ °∨

A

Fist handshape in which the thumb is usually held against the side of the index finger.

Handshape and orientation	Location, hand arrangement and contact	Movement	Glosses	
The **A** hand is held with the palm facing towards the signer (if the hand were opened, the fingers would point up).	The hand is held in front of the body.	The hand makes a short, firm movement towards the signer, bending from the elbow.	energy might Pernod power powerful strength strong	6
The **A** hand is held with the palm facing towards the signer (if the hand were opened, the fingers would point down).	The hand is held in front of the body.	The hand makes several short movements from side to side.	iron (to iron) ironing press iron (an iron)[1]	7

Notes   1 If the hand makes a single short movement from side to side, the sign produced is **iron (an iron)**.   Ø A⊤∨ $\overset{\circ}{z}$

The **A** hand is held with the palm facing towards the signer (if the hand were opened, the fingers would point to the left).	The hand is held in front of the body.	The hand makes a short downward bending movement from the wrist.	container with
			  a handle
			jug
			pour from a container
			  with a handle/ jug/
			  teapot
			teapot
				8

The **A** hand is held with the palm facing away from the signer (if the hand were opened, the fingers would point up).	The hand is held in front of the body.	The hand makes a short movement away from the signer.	belong to you *singular* * your *singular* your own *singular* yours *singular* *	9

Non-manual features   The eyegaze is usually directed in line with the hand movement.

Notes   * This sign may be produced with a repeated movement.   Ø A⊥∧ $\overset{\circ}{\underset{.}{\imath}}$

The **A** hand is held with the palm facing away from the signer (if the hand were opened, the fingers would point up).	The hand is held in front of the body.	The hand makes a short, firm movement towards the signer.	communism communist feminism feminist militant radical Russia Russian socialism * socialist * Soviet Soviet Union U.S.S.R.	10

Notes   * This sign may be produced with the hand making several short twisting movements from side to side at the wrist.   Ø A⊥∧ $\overset{\circ}{\underset{z}{\omega}}$

The **A** hand is held with the palm facing away from the signer (if the hand were opened, the fingers would point up).	The hand is held in front of the body and at an angle, so that the palm is turned to the right.	The hand makes a short movement to the right and, at the same time, away from the signer.	belong to
			  her/him/it/
			    them *singular* *
			her *
			her/his/its/
			    their own *singular* *
			hers *
			his *
			its *
			their *singular* *
			theirs *singular* *
				11

Notes   * This sign may be produced with a repeated movement.   Ø A⊥∧ $\overset{\circ}{\underset{.}{>}}$

12 Ø A⊥∧ $\begin{pmatrix} \dot{\omega} \\ \vee \\ \vee \end{pmatrix}$

13 Ø A⊥∧ $\overset{>}{\underset{\top}{\overset{\circ}{>}}}$

14 Ø A⊥∧ $\overset{\circ}{\underset{>}{\overset{\iota}{\top}}}$

15 Ø A<∨ $\overset{\circ}{\vee}\cdot$

16 Ø A<⊥ $\begin{pmatrix} \cap \\ < \\ \top \end{pmatrix}$

17 Ø A<⊥ $\overset{\overset{\circ}{@}}{\underset{\vee}{\top}}\cdot$

18 ○ A⊤∧ $\overset{@}{\underset{<}{\vee}}\cdot$

19 ○ ʝA<∧ $\overset{\cap}{\underset{\square}{\top}}$ [s]

[142]

A

Fist handshape in which the thumb is usually held against the side of the index finger.

Handshape and orientation	Location, hand arrangement and contact	Movement	Glosses	
The **A** hand is held with the palm facing away from the signer (if the hand were opened, the fingers would point up).	The hand is held in front of the body.	The hand moves sharply down and to the left while twisting at the wrist, so that the palm faces left.	play squash squash squash player squash racquet	12
The **A** hand is held with the palm facing away from the signer (if the hand were opened, the fingers would point up).	The hand is held in front of the body at an angle so that the palm is turned to the right.	The hand moves to the right and towards the signer in an arc.	belong to them *plural* their *plural* their own *plural* theirs *plural*	13
Non-manual features The eyegaze may be directed in line with the hand movement.				
The **A** hand is held with the palm facing away from the signer (if the hand were opened, the fingers would point up).	The hand is held in front of the body.	The hand moves to the right in an arc.	belong to you *plural* your *plural* your own *plural* yours *plural*	14
Non-manual features The eyegaze is usually directed in line with the hand movement.				

The **A** hand is held with the palm facing left (if the hand were opened, the fingers would point down).	The hand is held at the side of the body.	The hand makes two short downward movements.	bag
			baggage
			briefcase
			bucket
			carry a bag/briefcase/
			   bucket/case/pail/
			   suitcase
			case
			luggage
			pail
			shopping*
			suitcase
				15

Notes * Regional sign.				
The **A** hand is held with the palm facing left (if the hand were opened, the fingers would point away from the signer).	The hand is held in front of the body.	The hand bends to the left at the wrist while moving towards the signer.	cupboard open a cupboard	16
The **A** hand is held with the palm facing left (if the hand were opened, the fingers would point away from the signer).	The hand is held in front of the body.	The hand makes small clockwise circles in the vertical plane at right angles to the signer's body.	railway* railway station* train*	17
Notes * This sign may also be produced with the hand making a short movement away from the signer. Ø A<⊥				
The **A** hand is held with the palm facing towards the signer (if the hand were opened, the fingers would point up).	The hand is held in front of the face.	The hand makes anticlockwise circles in the vertical plane parallel to the signer's body.	Africa African Afro- Black Black person	18
The **A** hand is held with the palm facing left (if the hand were opened, the fingers would point up).	The hand is held beside the head.	The hand moves away from the signer with the arm bending at the elbow, and, at the same time, opens (forming a **5** hand).	javelin javelin thrower spear throw a javelin/ spear	19
Non-manual features The eyegaze is directed in line with the hand movement.				

20 ⊔ A<∧ ˅<@˅<˅@ °
˅<@˅<˅@

21 Ǝ A⊥< ˚ᴼ

22 Ǝ A<∧ ˅×⊥˅
⊥×⊥˅

23 Ǝ A<∧ ×·

24 Ǝ A<∧ ᵀ··
˅

25 Ǝ A<∧ ×⊥[ₛ]
□

26 ◡ A⊤< (ᵂ⊤)
∧

27 ◡ A<∧ °·
˅

28 ∪ A⊤∧ ˅×
˅

[144]

Handshape and orientation	Location, hand arrangement and contact	Movement	Glosses	
The **A** hand is held with the palm facing left (if the hand were opened, the fingers would point up).	The hand is held in front of the nose.	The hand makes small anticlockwise circles in the vertical plane parallel to the signer's body, brushing the nose in completing each circle.	pig (animal) pork greed[1] greedy[1] pig[1] selfish[1]	20

Notes   1 If the nose is wrinkled and the brows are furrowed, the sign produced is **greed, greedy, pig** *(see entry 2 in the English section)*, **selfish**.

The **A** hand is held with the palm facing away from the signer (if the hand were opened, the fingers would point to the left).	The hand is held with the knuckles against the cheek.	The hand twists away from the signer at the wrist, so that the palm faces down; the knuckles maintain contact with the cheek throughout.	after bone* rock* shall† will† would†	21

Notes   * Regional sign.

       † This sign may also be produced using an **Á** handshape.   ℈ Á⊥ʌ ˣₒ

The **A** hand is held with the palm facing left (if the hand were opened, the fingers would point up).	The hand is held beside the cheek.	The hand moves away from the signer and, at the same time, down, so that the knuckles brush across the cheek.	black Blackpool[1] prostitute[2] prostitution[2]	22

Notes   1 If the hand moves towards and away from the signer several times with the knuckles maintaining contact with the cheek throughout, the sign produced is **Blackpool**.   ℈ A<ʌ

       2 If the hand makes two small clockwise circles with the knuckles maintaining contact with the cheek throughout, the sign produced is **prostitute, prostitution**.   ℈ A<ʌ

The **A** hand is held with the palm facing left (if the hand were opened, the fingers would point up).	The hand is held beside the cheek.	The knuckles tap the cheek twice.	address* live*	23

Notes   * Regional sign.

The **A** hand is held with the palm facing left (if the hand were opened, the fingers would point up).	The hand is held beside the head.	The hand moves down and, at the same time, towards the signer; the movement is repeated.	brush one's hair hairbrush	24
The **A** hand is held with the palm facing left (if the hand were opened, the fingers would point up).	The hand is held with the knuckles touching the cheek.	The hand moves away from the signer while opening (forming a **5** hand).	refusal refuse will not won't would not wouldn't	25

The **A** hand is held with the palm facing towards the signer (if the hand were opened, the fingers would point to the left).	The hand is held in front of the chin.	The hand twists towards the signer at the wrist while moving up.	drink from a glass
			    with a handle/
			    mug/tankard
			 glass with a handle
			 mug
			 tankard
				26

The **A** hand is held with the palm facing left (if the hand were opened, the fingers would point up).	The hand is held in front of the mouth.	The hand makes two short downward movements.	eat ice cream eat an ice cream cone/cornet ice cream ice cream cone ice cream cornet	27

Non-manual features   The mouth is open with the tongue tip resting on the lower lip.

The **A** hand is held with the palm facing towards the signer (if the hand were opened, the fingers would point up).	The hand is held in front of the chin.	The hand moves down, so that the knuckles brush the chin.	cold fridge refrigerator	28

29 U AТʌ ᵛᵛ // Ø A<⊥ ⁽ᴫ⁽ᴛ⁾

30 U AТʌ ˣ·

31 U A<ʌ ᵒᵀᵛˣᵀᵥ

32 [] Aᴐ< ˣ⊥>ᴛˣ

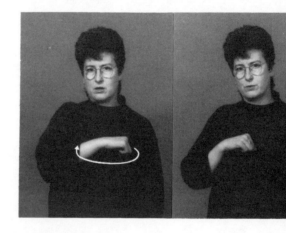

33 [] Aᴛ< ˣ

34 [] Aᴛ< @ᵛᵛˣ

35 [] Aᴛ< ˣ·

A

Fist handshape in which the thumb is usually held against the side of the index finger.

Handshape and orientation	Location, hand arrangement and contact	Movement	Glosses	
The **A** hand is held with the palm facing towards the signer (if the hand were opened, the fingers would point up).	The hand is held in front of the chin.	The hand moves down, so that the knuckles brush the chin.	fridge open a fridge/ refrigerator refrigerator	29
The **A** hand is held with the palm facing left (if the hand were opened, the fingers would point away from the signer).	The hand is held in front of the body.	The hand bends to the left at the wrist, while moving towards the signer.		
The **A** hand is held with the palm facing towards the signer (if the hand were opened, the fingers would point up).	The hand is held in front of the chin.	The knuckles tap the chin twice.	date figure(s) mathematics maths number	30
The **A** hand is held with the palm facing left (if the hand were opened, the fingers would point up).	The hand is held in front of the chin.	The hand moves towards the signer and, at the same time, down, so that the knuckles brush the chin; the movement is repeated.	greed greedy selfish	31

Non-manual features   The nose is wrinkled and the brows are furrowed.

The **A** hand is held with the palm facing down (if the hand were opened, the fingers would point to the left).	The hand is held resting against the left side of the chest.	The hand moves to the right in an arc; the movement ends with the hand touching the right side of the chest.	belong to us* our* our own* ours*	32

    Notes   * This sign may be produced with the hand moving from the right side of the chest to the left in an arc.

[] A ɒ < ˣ⊥<⊤ˣ

The **A** hand is held with the palm facing towards the signer (if the hand were opened, the fingers would point to the left).	The hand is held in front of the chest.	The hand touches the chest.	belong to me mine my my own	33
The **A** hand is held with the palm facing towards the signer (if the hand were opened, the fingers would point to the left).	The hand is held resting against the chest.	The hand makes an anticlockwise circle in the vertical plane parallel to the signer's body, maintaining contact with the chest throughout.	apologise apology regret sorrow sorry	34

Non-manual features   The head is tilted to one side and the lips are pressed together.

The **A** hand is held with the palm facing towards the signer (if the hand were opened, the fingers would point to the left).	The hand is held in front of the chest.	The knuckles tap the chest twice.	belong to me confess confession fault (my fault) mine my own repent repentance	35

36 [] A<∧ ×·

37 ⌐⌐< A⊤< ×·

38 ⱶ ⌡A<⊥ <×·

39 ⌐⌐ A⍺⊥ $\left(\begin{smallmatrix} \circ \\ \vee \end{smallmatrix} \times\right)$·

40 ⌐⌐ A⍺< ×·

41 ⌐⌐ A⊤< $\begin{smallmatrix} \circ \\ \sim \\ \times \end{smallmatrix}$·

42 ⌡ A⍺< ×·

43 ‾A⍺⊥ ⌐ ⌡A⍀∧ $\begin{smallmatrix} \circ \\ n \\ < \end{smallmatrix}$·

Fist handshape in which the thumb is usually held against the side of the index finger.

Handshape and orientation	Location, hand arrangement and contact	Movement	Glosses	
The **A** hand is held with the palm facing left (if the hand were opened, the fingers would point up).	The hand is held in front of the chest.	The hand taps the chest twice.	**cough**	36
The **A** hand is held with the palm facing towards the signer (if the hand were opened, the fingers would point to the left).	The hand is held in front of the right side of the upper chest.	The knuckles tap the chest twice.	**Canada** **Canadian**	37
The **A** hand is held with the palm facing left (if the hand were opened, the fingers would point away from the signer).	The hand is held in front of the body; the right elbow is held away from the side of the body.	The elbow touches the side of the body; the movement is repeated.	**Scot** **Scotland** **Scottish**	38
The **A** hand is held with the palm facing up (if the hand were opened, the fingers would point away from the signer).	The hand is held beside the waist.	The hand makes a short firm movement down and, at the same time, to the left, so that the hand touches the side of the waist; the movement is repeated.	**fault (someone's own fault)** **serves someone right**	39

Non-manual features   The brows are furrowed, the nose is wrinkled and the lips are rounded and pushed forward with the mouth open wide.

The **A** hand is held with the palm facing up (if the hand were opened, the fingers would point to the left).	The hand is held in front of the waist.	The side of the hand taps the waist twice.	**greed *** **greedy *** **selfish ***	40

Non-manual features   The nose is wrinkled and the brows are furrowed.

Notes   * Regional sign.

The **A** hand is held with the palm facing towards the signer (if the hand were opened, the fingers would point to the left).	The hand rests against the stomach.	The hand moves up and down several times; the knuckles maintain contact with the stomach throughout.	**Hungarian *** **Hungary *** **hunger *** **hungry *** **famished *¹** **ravenous *¹** **starve *¹** **starving *¹**	41

Notes   * Regional sign.

   1 If the eyes are narrowed and the lips are tightly rounded, the sign produced is **famished, ravenous, starve, starving.**

The **A** hand is held with the palm facing up (if the hand were opened, the fingers would point to the left).	The hand is held beneath the left elbow; the left arm is positioned across the chest.	The right knuckles tap the left elbow twice.	**bone**	42
The left **A** hand is held with the palm facing up; the right **A** hand is held with the palm facing down (if the hands were opened, the left fingers would point away from the signer and the right fingers would point up).	The hands are held side by side in front of the body; the right hand is held higher than the left hand, and at an angle so that the palm is turned to the left.	The right hand makes several short movements down and to the left, with the arm bending at the elbow.	**sex *** **sex (have sex) *** **sexual intercourse *** **sexual intercourse (have sexual intercourse) ***	43

Note   * This sign may be produced with both hands moving.

$$\emptyset \ \bar{\jmath A}\alpha\perp \ , \ \dot{\jmath}A\partial\wedge \ \substack{\circ \\ \cap \\ \times \\ N} \cdot$$

44 Aa>₁ₓ Aa<$^{\wedge}_{\top}{}^{\vee}_{>}$ // Ø A>ʌ A<ʌ $^{\circ}_{\vee}$

45 Āa>ₓ Aʊ⊥ $^{z\cdot}_{x}$

46 Āa>ₓ Aʊ⊥ $^{@}_{\substack{<\\ \top \\ x}}{}^{\cdot}$

47 aĀa>≠ ÖAʊ⊥ $^{\circ}_{\substack{\vee\\x}}$

48 Āa>ₓ Aʊ< $^{n}_{\substack{\perp\\x}}$

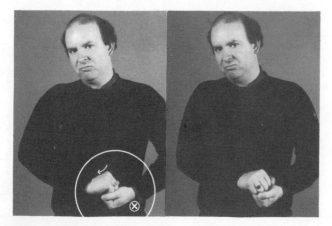

A

Fist handshape in which the thumb is usually held against the side of the index finger.

Handshape and orientation	Location, hand arrangement and contact	Movement	Glosses	
Two **A** hands are held with the palms facing up (if the hands were opened, the left fingers would point to the right and the right fingers would point to the left).	The hands are held in front of the body with the knuckles touching.	The right hand moves up and towards the signer and, at the same time, to the right and then makes a short downward movement.	deckchair * folding chair *	44
The left **A** hand is held with the palm facing right; the right **A** hand is held with the palm facing left (if the hands were opened, the fingers would all point up).	The hands are held in front of the body.	The hands make a short downward movement.		

Notes * This sign can be produced with the two parts reversed.   Ø A>∧ A<∧ ⌄̊ ∥⁄∥ A⍺> ₁ₓ A⍺<⌄̊̂⊤

The left **A** hand is held with the palm facing up; the right **A** hand is held with the palm facing down (if the hands were opened, the left fingers would point to the right and the right fingers would point away from the signer).	The hands are held in front of the body; the right hand rests on the left hand.	The right hand moves from side to side several times; the right knuckles maintain contact with the left knuckles throughout.	wash wash by hand washing	45
The left **A** hand is held with the palm facing up; the right **A** hand is held with the palm facing down (if the hands were opened, the left fingers would point to the right and the right fingers would point away from the signer).	The hands are held in front of the body; the right hand rests on the left hand.	The right hand makes anticlockwise circles in the horizontal plane; the right knuckles maintain contact with the left knuckles throughout.	chew chew up	46

Non-manual features   The lower jaw moves from side to side and up and down; the lips are closed throughout.

The left **A** hand is held with the palm facing up; the right **A** hand is held with the palm facing down (if the hands were opened, the left fingers would point to the right and the right fingers would point away from the signer).	The hands are held crossed over in front of the body; the right hand is held above the left hand.	The right hand makes a short, firm, downward movement, so that the wrists touch.	captive engaged fix gaol imprison jail prison prisoner slave slavery	47
The left **A** hand is held with the palm facing up; the right **A** hand is held with the palm facing down (if the hands were opened, the left fingers would point to the right, and the right fingers would to the left).	The hands are held in front of the body; the right hand rests on the left hand.	The right hand bends away from the signer at the wrist, maintaining contact with the left hand throughout.	avenge* get one's own back* revenge* vengeance*	48

Non-manual features   The mouth is closed and the lips are pushed forward.

Notes * Regional sign.

49 A⊃>ₓ A⊃⊥ᵩ ᵗ³ᵛᵀ

50 Ā⊤> A⊤< ˣ˙

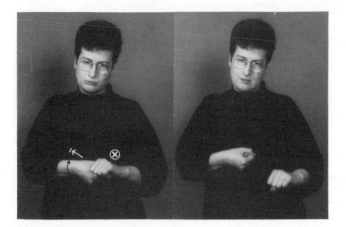

51 A̱⊤> A⊤< ᵒˑᵛˣ

52 Ā⊤>ₓ A<⊥ ˙ⁱ□ [5]

53 Ā⊤>ₓ A<⊥ ᵒ@ˑᵛᵀˣ

54 A>∧ᵩ A<∧ ˣ˙

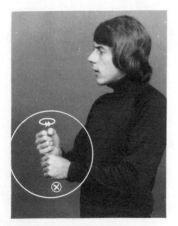

Handshape and orientation	Location, hand arrangement and contact	Movement	Glosses	
Two **A** hands are held with the palms facing down (if the hands were opened, the left fingers would point to the right, and the right fingers would point away from the signer).	The hands are held in front of the body; the right hand is held nearer to the signer than the left hand, and the hands are touching.	The right hand makes a short, firm movement towards the signer while twisting at the wrist, so that the palm faces left.	cracker pull a cracker	49
Two **A** hands are held with the palms facing towards the signer (if the hands were opened, the left fingers would point to the right, and the right fingers would point to the left).	The hands are held in front of the body; the right hand is held above the left hand.	The right hand taps the left hand twice.	garage geography government guarantee Guinness bugger [1]	50

Notes 1 If the eyebrows are furrowed, the sign produced is **bugger**.

Two **A** hands are held with the palms facing towards the signer (if the hands were opened, the left fingers would point to the right and the right fingers would point to the left).	The hands are held in front of the body; the right hand is held below the left hand.	The right hand makes a short, firm, upward movement to touch the left hand.	rubbish* stupid*	51

Notes * Regional sign.

The left **A** hand is held with the palm facing towards the signer; the right **A** hand is held with the palm facing left (if the hands were opened, the left fingers would point to the right, and the right fingers would point away from the signer).	The hands are held in front of the body; the right hand rests on the left hand.	The right hand moves firmly away from the signer while opening (forming a **5** hand).	pull someone's leg* wind someone up*	52

Non-manual features The nose is wrinkled and the top teeth are touching the lower lip; as the hand moves, the mouth opens with the lips stretched.

Notes * Directional verb.

The left **A** hand is held with the palm facing towards the signer; the right **A** hand is held with the palm facing left (if the hands were opened, the left fingers would point to the right and the right fingers would point away from the signer).	The hands are held in front of the body; the right hand rests on the left hand.	The right hand makes anticlockwise circles in the horizontal plane, maintaining contact with the left hand throughout.	coffee grind grinder	53
The left **A** hand is held with the palm facing right; the right **A** hand is held with the palm facing left (if the hands were opened, the fingers would all point up).	The hands are held in front of the body; the left hand is held nearer to the signer than the right hand.	The right hand taps the left hand twice.	advertise* promote* propaganda* publicise* publicity*	54

Notes * The following notes apply to all glosses:-

This sign may be produced with the palms facing down (if the hands were opened, the left fingers would point to the right and the right fingers would point to the left).

This sign may be produced with the right hand moving away from the signer repeatedly, brushing the left knuckles.

A⊃>₉ A⊃< ×·

A>∧ ₁ A<∧ ⊥̽

55 $\overline{A}>\perp \ A<\perp \ ^{<}_{\times ^{<}.}$

56 $\sqrt{\overline{G}\upsilon}>_{\times} \ A\top\wedge_{9} \ ^{.\overset{\omega}{>}}$

57 $G\upsilon>_{\times} \ \sqrt{A\perp\wedge_{9}} \ ^{\overset{\vee}{_{\top}}\overset{\times}{_{\vee}}}_{\top}$

58 $\overline{G}\top> \ \sqrt{A\perp\wedge_{9}} \ \overset{\binom{\cap}{\perp}}{\underset{\perp}{\vee}}{}^{\times}$

59 $\overset{..}{5}\alpha\perp \ A<\wedge_{9} \ \binom{\cap}{\perp}$

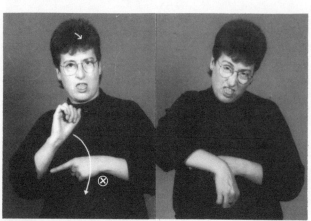

[154]

A

Fist handshape in which the thumb is usually held against the side of the index finger.

Handshape and orientation	Location, hand arrangement and contact	Movement	Glosses	
The left **A** hand is held with the palm facing right; the right **A** hand is held with the palm facing left (if the hands were opened, the fingers would all point away from the signer).	The hands are held side by side in front of the body; the right hand is held higher than the left hand.	The right hand moves to the left, brushing across the left hand; the movement is repeated.	fix mend repair dog[1]	55

Notes   1   If the movement is changed to a short, repeated brushing movement, the sign produced is **dog**. This is a regional sign.

$$\overline{A}>\!\!\perp \ A<\!\!\perp \ \overset{\circ}{\underset{\times}{<}}\cdot$$

The left **G** hand is held with the palm facing down (if the hand were opened, the fingers would point to the right). The right **A** hand is held with the palm facing towards the signer (if the hand were opened, the fingers would point up).	The hands are held in front of the body; the right hand is held above the left hand, with the left index finger against the right forearm.	The right hand twists firmly at the wrist, so that the palm faces away from the signer.	denial deny refusal refuse turn[1] turn away[1] rebel[2] rebellion[2]	56

Non-manual features   The brows are furrowed and the head shakes slightly.

Notes   1   If the non-manual feature is not present, the sign produced is **turn, turn away**.

      2   If the movement is large, with the right forearm brushing the left index finger, the sign produced is **rebel, rebellion**.

$$/G\,\mho>\ A\top\wedge_{\varphi}\ \overset{\cdot}{\underset{\wedge\times\Im}{\Im}}$$

The left **G** hand is held with the palm facing down (if the hand were opened, the fingers would point to the right). The right **A** hand is held with the palm facing away from the signer (if the hand were opened, the fingers would point up).	The hands are held in front of the body; the left index fingertip is held touching the front of the right forearm.	The right hand moves down and, at the same time, towards the signer, so that the right forearm and wrist brush the left index fingertip.	cut down to size small (feel small) words (eat one's words) words (swallow one's words)	57

Non-manual features   The nose is wrinkled and the tongue protrudes between the teeth.

The left **G** hand is held with the palm facing towards the signer (if the hand were opened, the fingers would point to the right). The right **A** hand is held with the palm facing away from the signer (if the hand were opened, the fingers would point up).	The hands are held in front of the body; the right hand is held higher and nearer to the signer than the left hand.	The right hand bends away from the signer at the wrist, while moving down and away from the signer; the movement ends with the left index finger touching the right forearm.	fall for a lie/trick * 58 gullible sucker swallow a statement/ story *	

Non-manual features   The tongue protrudes between the top teeth and the lower lip; as the hand moves, the head nods forward and the nose wrinkles.

Notes   *   Directional verb.

The left **5̈** hand is held with the palm facing up (if the hand were opened, the fingers would point away from the signer). The right **A** hand is held with the palm facing left (if the hand were opened, the fingers would point up).	The left hand is held in front of the body; the right hand is held in front of the right shoulder.	The right hand bends away from the signer at the wrist while moving away from the signer.	tennis* serve with a tennis racquet[1]	59

Notes   *   This sign may be produced using one hand only.

$$\emptyset \ A<\wedge \ \overset{(\overset{\cap}{\underset{\perp}{}})}{}$$

      1   If a left **O** hand is used, which makes a short upward movement while opening (forming a **5̈** hand) before the right hand movement, the sign produced is **serve with a tennis racquet**.

$$\emptyset \ \overline{O}\,\mathrm{Q}\!\perp\!\overset{\wedge}{\underset{\Box}{\circ}}{}^{[\text{5̈}]}\ A<\wedge_{\varphi}\overset{\emptyset}{/\!/}\ \overline{\overline{\text{5̈}}}\,\mathrm{Q}\!\perp\ A<\wedge_{\varphi}\overset{(\overset{\cap}{\underset{\perp}{}})}{}$$

60 $\overline{B}a\bot$ $A\top< ^{\vee\times}$ // Ø $B>\bot_{1\times}$ $B<\bot^a$

61 $\overline{B}a> A\sigma\bot \overset{\circ @\times}{\underset{\vee}{>}}$

62 $\overline{B}a> A\sigma\bot \overset{\vee\times\wedge\circ}{\underset{\bot}{>}}$

63 $\overline{B}a> \sigma A\bot\wedge \overset{\times\wedge}{\bot}$

64 $\overline{B}a> A<\vee ^{\vee\times}$

[156]

A

Fist handshape in which the thumb is usually held against the side of the index finger.

Handshape and orientation	Location, hand arrangement and contact	Movement	Glosses	
The left **B** hand is held with the palm facing up and the fingers pointing away from the signer; the right **A** hand is held with the palm facing towards the signer (if the hand were opened, the fingers would point to the left).	The hands are held in front of the body; the right hand is held above the left hand.	The right hand moves down to touch the left palm.	bankbook passport	60
The left **B** hand is held with the palm facing right and the fingers pointing away from the signer; the right **B** hand is held with the palm facing left and the fingers pointing away from the signer.	The hands are held in front of the body with the palms touching.	The hands twist apart at the wrists, so that the palms face up.		
The left **B** hand is held with the palm facing up and the fingers pointing to the right; the right **A** hand is held with the palm facing down (if the hand were opened, the fingers would point away from the signer).	The hands are held in front of the body; the right hand is held above the left hand.	The right hand makes a small clockwise circle in the vertical plane parallel to the signer's body, and then comes to rest on the left palm.	accurate* confirm* correct* proper* put right* right*	61

Non-manual features The head is tilted forward.

Notes * This sign may be produced with the right knuckles brushing the left palm in making the circular movement.

B ɑ> A ʋ⊥

The left **B** hand is held with the palm facing up and the fingers pointing to the right; the right **A** hand is held with the palm facing down (if the hand were opened, the fingers would point away from the signer).	The hands are held in front of the body; the right hand is held above the left hand.	The right hand moves down and taps the left palm before making a short movement up and to the right, while moving away from the signer.	bounce (of a round object)	62
The left **B** hand is held with the palm facing up and the fingers pointing to the right; the right **A** hand is held with the palm facing away from the signer (if the hand were opened, the fingers would point up).	The hands are held in front of the body; the right hand is held above the left hand.	The heel of the right hand touches the left palm and then the hand moves up and, at the same time, away from the signer.	character characteristic culture belong to you *singular*[1] your *singular*[1] yours *singular*[1] belong to her/him/it/ them *singular*[2] her[2] her/his/its/ their own *singular*[2] hers[2] his[2] its[2] their *singular*[2] theirs *singular*[2]	63

Notes 1 The eyegaze is usually directed in line with the hand movement.
2 The eyegaze may be directed in line with the hand movement.

The left **B** hand is held with the palm facing up and the fingers pointing to the right; the right **A** hand is held with the palm facing left (if the hand were opened, the fingers would point down).	The hands are held in front of the body; the right hand is held above the left hand.	The right hand moves down; the movement ends with the right knuckles held against the left palm.	hit the bottom/ floor/ground	64

65   B̄ɑ> A<⊥ $^{°}_{ɑ}$ˇ×$^{°}_{>}$

66   B̄ʊ>ᵩ A⊤< $^{°}_{ʊ}$⊤·

67   B>⊥ ₁× Aɑ< $^{ρ}_{×}$

68   B̄>⊥ ₁ Aʊ< $^{∩}_{∨}$$^{∨}_{×}$$^{∩}_{∨}$

69   B>⊥ A⊤< $^{·}_{<}$×

Fist handshape in which the thumb is usually held against the side of the index finger.

Handshape and orientation	Location, hand arrangement and contact	Movement	Glosses
The left B hand is held with the palm facing up and the fingers pointing to the right; the right A hand is held with the palm facing left (if the hand were opened, the fingers would point away from the signer).	The hands are held in front of the body; the right hand is held above the left hand.	The right hand makes a short downward movement to touch the left palm and then makes a short movement to the right while twisting at the wrist, so that the palm faces up.	bank **65** dole endorse endorsement frank * passport stamp * unemployment benefit

Notes   * This sign may be produced with the right hand touching the left palm and then making a short movement to the right before touching the palm again.

$$B\alpha> \ A<\perp \ (^{x}_{>}\cdot)$$

The left B hand is held with the palm facing down and the fingers pointing to the right; the right A hand is held with the palm facing towards the signer (if the hand were opened, the fingers would point to the left).	The left arm is positioned across the body; the left hand is held lower and nearer to the signer than the right hand.	The right hand makes a short movement towards the signer while twisting at the wrist, so that the palm faces down; the movement is repeated.	bar * **66** barmaid * barman * pub * public house * beer (pull a measure of beer) [1] beer (draught beer) [2]

Notes   * This sign can be produced using one hand only.

$$\emptyset \ A\top< \ ^{\top}_{\circ}\cdot$$

   1 If a left C hand is used and there is a single, slow movement, the sign produced is **pull a measure of beer**.

$$\sqrt{C}>\perp_? \ A\top< \ ^{\top}_{\circ}$$

   2 If a left C hand is used and there is a single short movement, the sign produced is **draught beer**.

$$\sqrt{C}>\perp_? \ A\top< \ ^{\top}_{\circ}$$

The left B hand is held with the palm facing right and the fingers pointing away from the signer; the right A hand is held with the palm facing up (if the hand were opened, the fingers would point to the left).	The hands are held side by side in front of the body; the right knuckles are held against the left palm.	The right hand twists towards the signer at the wrist, so that the palm faces down; the right knuckles maintain contact with the left palm throughout.	lock **67** lock and key (under lock and key) lock in lock out lock up
The left B hand is held with the palm facing right and the fingers pointing away from the signer; the right A hand is held with the palm facing down (if the hand were opened, the fingers would point to the left).	The hands are held side by side in front of the body; the right hand is held higher than the left hand.	The right hand bends sharply downwards from the wrist, so that the knuckles brush across the left palm.	firm **68** hard stubborn tough

Non-manual features   The eyes are narrowed.

The left B hand is held with the palm facing right and the fingers pointing away from the signer; the right A hand is held with the palm facing towards the signer (if the hand were opened, the fingers would point to the left).	The hands are held in front of the body.	The right hand moves sharply to the left, so that the right knuckles touch the left palm.	bump into **69** crash hit run into hit (with one's fist) *[1] thump *[1]

Non-manual features   The cheeks are puffed out.

Notes   * Directional verb.

   1 If the right hand moves sharply to the left and then down, so that the right knuckles brush the left palm, the sign produced is **hit (with one's fist), thump**.

$$B>\perp \ A\top< \ ^{\cdot}_{\vee}{}^{\vee}_{\vee}$$

70 Ḃɤ< Aɤ⊥ᵩ ^oè_v ·

71 C̄ɤ⊥ ₁ A<⊥ᵩ (T̅ᵥ) ·

72 Ø Ḡɤ> ₓ ƆA⊥ᴧᵩ ĭ

73 Ø Aɑ⊥ Aɑ⊥ ᵀ

A *Fist handshape in which the thumb is usually held against the side of the index finger.*

Handshape and orientation	Location, hand arrangement and contact	Movement	Glosses

The left **Ḃ** hand is held with the palm facing down and the fingers pointing to the left; the right **A** hand is held with the palm facing down (if the hand were opened, the fingers would point away from the signer). | The hands are held in front of the body; the right hand is held nearer to the signer than the left hand. | The right hand makes small clockwise circles in the vertical plane parallel to the signer's body. | play snooker
snooker
snooker player
billiards[1]
billiards player[1]
play billiards[1]
play pool[2]
pool[2]
pool player[2]

70

Notes 1 If the left fingers point away from the signer and the right hand makes a firm movement to the left and, at the same time, away from the signer, the sign produced is **billiards, billiards player, play billiards**.

$$\dot{B}\text{o}\bot \ A\text{o}\bot_{\varrho} \ \overset{\cdot}{\underset{<}{}}$$

2 If the left fingers point away from the signer and the right hand is held with the palm facing up (so that the fingers, if opened, would point towards the signer), and the right hand bends to the left at the wrist several times, the sign produced is **play pool, pool, pool player**.

$$\dot{B}\text{o}\bot \ A\text{a}\top_{\varrho} \ \overset{n\,\cdot}{\underset{<}{}}$$

The left **C** hand is held with the palm facing down; the right **A** hand is held with the palm facing left (if the hands were opened, the fingers would all point away from the signer). | The hands are held side by side in front of the body; the right hand is held higher and nearer to the signer than the left hand. | The right hand moves down and, at the same time, away from the signer and then up and, at the same time, towards the signer; the movements are repeated. | saw *
saw a piece of wood *

71

Notes * This sign can also be produced with a left **A** handshape.

$$\overline{A}\text{o}\bot_{\scriptstyle |} \ A<\bot_{\varrho} \ \overset{\text{I}\,\cdot}{\underset{N}{}}$$

The left **G** hand is held with the palm facing down (if the hand were opened, the fingers would point to the right). The right **A** hand is held with the palm facing away from the signer (if the hand were opened, the fingers would point up). | The hands are held in front of the body; the side of the left index finger is held against the right wrist. | The hands remain together and make a short, firm movement away from the signer. | avoid *
block *
defence
defend *
defender
prevent *
prevention
protect *
protection
protector
resist *
resistance
birth control[1]

72

Notes * Directional verb.

1 This sign may be used as the first part of a compound sign meaning **birth control** (see 1386 for the second part of the sign).

$$\emptyset \ \text{G}\text{o}> \ _\times \ \text{o}A\bot\wedge_{\varrho} \ \overset{\cdot\,\circ}{\underset{}{\text{I}}} \ /\!/$$

$$\emptyset \ \underline{B}\text{a}> \ _\times \ B\text{a}< \ ^{z\,\cdot} \ /\!/$$

Two **A** hands are held with the palms facing up (if the hands were opened, the fingers would all point away from the signer). | The hands are held in front of the body. | The hands move towards the signer. | drawer *
open a drawer *

73

Notes * This sign may be produced using one hand only.

$$\emptyset \ A\text{a}\bot \ ^\top$$

74 Ø Aa⊥ Aa⊥ $\left(\frac{\circ}{Z}{\sim}\right)$ ·

75 Ø ʝAa⊥ ʝAa⊥ $\overset{\cdot}{\underset{\wedge}{D}}$

76 Ø Aa⊥ ₁× Aa⊥ $\overset{\circ}{\underset{\wedge}{\perp}}$ ·

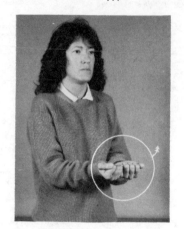

77 Ø Āa⊥ × Aʊ⊥ $\overset{\circ\ \circ}{\underset{\perp}{\wedge\ \vee}}$

78 Ø Āa> × Aʊ⊥ $^{\top}$

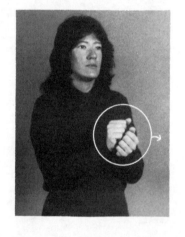

79 Ø Āa> × Aʊ⊥ $\begin{pmatrix}\cdot\ \cdot \\ \times \\ \perp \end{pmatrix}$

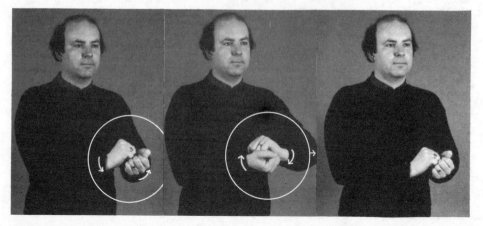

A

Fist handshape in which the thumb is usually held against the side of the index finger.

Handshape and orientation	Location, hand arrangement and contact	Movement	Glosses	
Two **A** hands are held with the palms facing up (if the hands were opened, the fingers would all point away from the signer).	The hands are held in front of the body.	The hands make short movements towards and away from the signer alternately while moving from side to side; the movements are repeated.	bus drive a bus/ juggernaut/ large vehicle/lorry/ truck/van driver of a bus/ juggernaut/ large vehicle/lorry/ truck/van juggernaut large vehicle lorry truck van	74
Two **A** hands are held with the palms facing up (if the hands were opened, the fingers would all point away from the signer).	The hands are held in front of the body.	The hands move firmly towards the signer and, at the same time, upwards, with the arms bending at the elbows.	energy might power powerful strength strong	75
Two **A** hands are held with the palms facing up (if the hands were opened, the fingers would all point away from the signer).	The hands are held in front of the body with the sides of the little fingers held together.	The hands remain together and make a short movement up and, at the same time, away from the signer; the movement is repeated.	play volleyball volleyball volleyball player	76
The left **A** hand is held with the palm facing up; the right **A** hand is held with the palm facing down (if the hands were opened, the fingers would all point away from the signer). *Notes* * Directional verb.	The hands are held in front of the body; the right hand is held on the left hand.	The hands remain together and move away from the signer in a short arc.	hire out * lend * lender	77
The left **A** hand is held with the palm facing up; the right **A** hand is held with the palm facing down (if the hands were opened, the left fingers would point to the right and the right fingers would point away from the signer). *Notes* * Directional verb.	The hands are held in front of the body; the right hand is held on the left hand.	The hands remain together and move towards the signer.	borrow* borrower hire* loan*	78
The left **A** hand is held with the palm facing up; the right **A** hand is held with the palm facing down (if the hands were opened, the left fingers would point to the right, and the right fingers would point away from the signer).	The hands are held in front of the body; the right hand rests on the left hand.	The hands change places twice (so that the knuckles brush together each time), while moving away from the signer throughout.	billiards	79

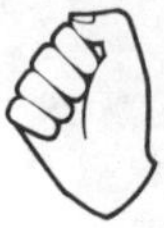

80 Ø ʊĀɑ > ∓× Aʊ⊥ ⁰̣ᵥ

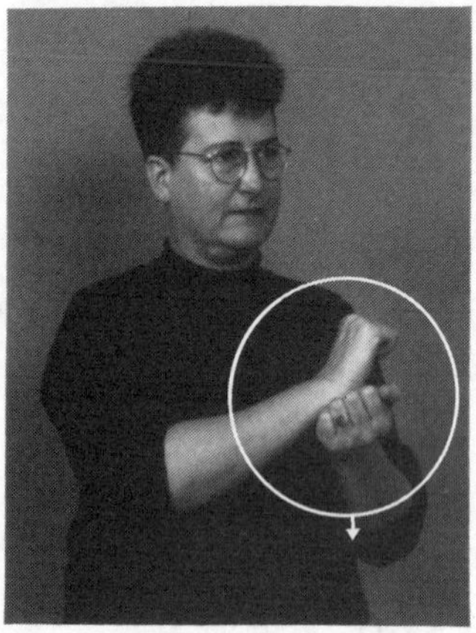

81 Ø ɑAɑ > ∓× ʊAʊ⊥ ω̇ ÷ ▫ [55]

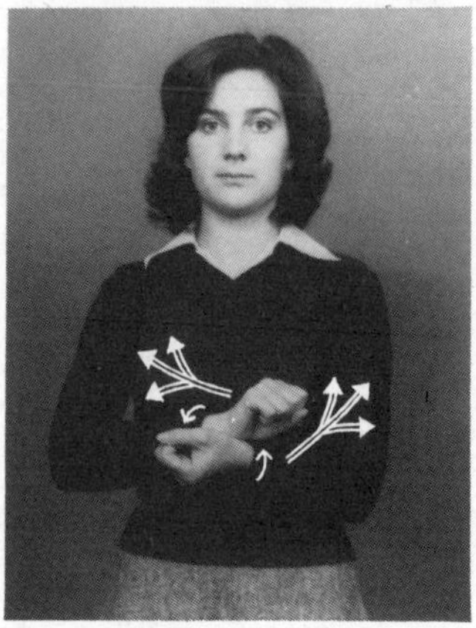

82 Ø Āʊʌ Aʊʌ ᵩ ⊥ᵥ ⊚∾·

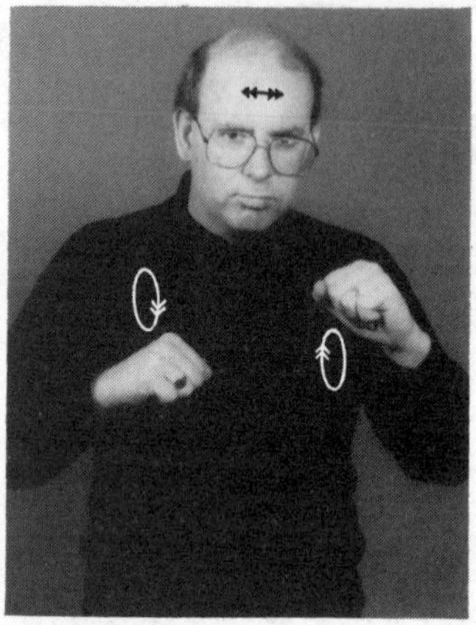

83 Ø A̲ʊʌ × Aʊʌ (·,·) ^

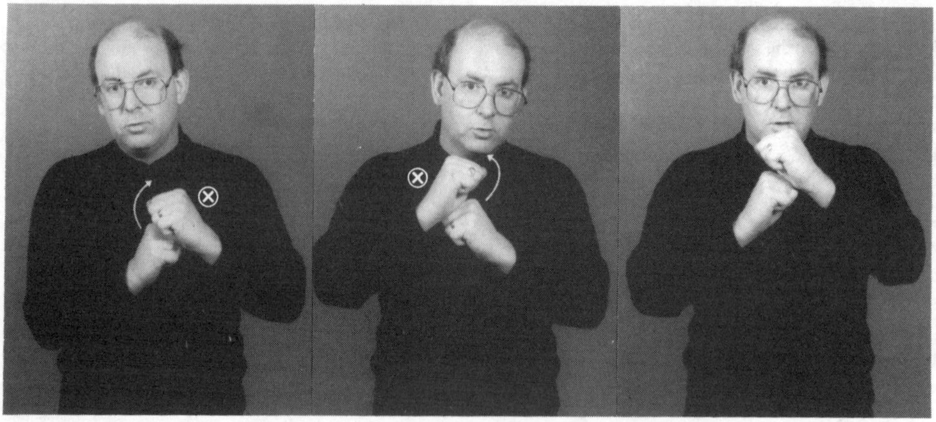

84 Ø Aʊ⊥ Aʊ⊥ ⊥

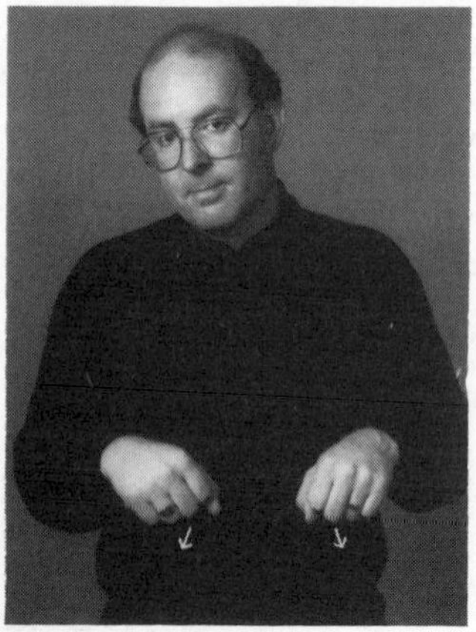

85 Ø Aʊ⊥ Aʊ⊥ ⊥

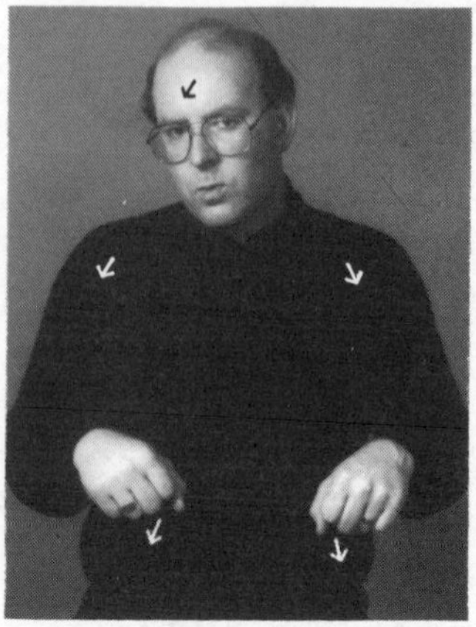

Handshape and orientation	Location, hand arrangement and contact	Movement	Glosses	
The left **A** hand is held with the palm facing up; the right **A** hand is held with the palm facing down (if the hands were opened, the left fingers would point to the right and the right fingers would point away from the signer).	The hands are held crossed over in front of the body; the right wrist is held on the left wrist.	The hands remain together and make a short, firm downward movement.	block jam stick stuck trap	80
The left **A** hand is held with the palm facing up; the right **A** hand is held with the palm facing down (if the hands were opened, the left fingers would point to the right and the right fingers would point away from the signer).	The hands are held crossed over in front of the body; the right wrist is held on the left wrist.	The hands move sharply apart while twisting at the wrists and, at the same time, opening (forming two **5** hands, with the palms facing towards each other and the fingers all pointing up).	free freedom liberate[1] liberation[1] release[1]	81

Notes   1   If the hands make a short downward movement before moving apart and, at the same time, away from the signer with the palms facing up, the sign produced is **liberate, liberation, release.**

Ø ⟨symbols⟩

Two **A** hands are held with the palms facing down (if the hands were opened, the fingers would all point up).	The hands are held in front of the body and at an angle, so that the palms are turned towards each other; the right hand is held higher and nearer to the signer than the left hand.	The hands make alternate small clockwise circles in the vertical plane at right angles to the signer's body.	box* boxer* boxing*	82

Non-manual features   The head makes short movements from side to side.

Notes   *   The following notes apply to all glosses:

This sign may be produced with the hands making two short movements down and, at the same time, away from the signer.   Ø ⟨symbols⟩

This sign may be produced with the hands making two short movements away from the signer, with a short downward movement between the two.   Ø ⟨symbols⟩

Two **A** hands are held with the palms facing down (if the hands were opened, the fingers would all point up).	The hands are held in front of the body and at an angle, so that the palms are turned towards each other; the left hand is held on the right hand.	The hands change places twice, while moving up throughout.	structure	83
Two **A** hands are held with the palms facing down (if the hands were opened, the fingers would all point away from the signer).	The hands are held in front of the body.	The hands move away from the signer.	pram push a pram/ pushchair/ trolley pushchair trolley	84

Two **Ⳁ** hands are held with the palms facing down (if the hands were opened, the fingers would all point away from the signer).	The hands are held in front of the body.	The hands move away from the signer.	lawnmower
			  (mechanically
			  operated lawnmower)
			mow with a
			  mechanically operated
			  lawnmower
			lawnmower (manually
			  operated lawnmower)[1]
			mow with a manually
			  operated lawnmower[1]
				85

Non-manual features   The shoulders and head move forward.

Notes   1   If the movement is changed so that the hands move towards and away from the signer several times, the sign produced is **lawnmower (manually operated lawnmower), mow with a manually operated lawnmower.**   Ø ⟨symbols⟩

86　∅ ᴧᴐ⊥ ᴧᴐ⊥ ̊˅

87　∅ ᴧᴐ⊥ ᴧᴐ⊥ ˖̊˙˅

88　∅ ᴧᴐ⊥ ᴧᴐ⊥ ⁓̇˖̊˅

89　∅ ᴧᴐ⊥ ᴧᴐ⊥ ̇ω÷ [55] ⁓̇˖̊˅□

90　∅ ᴧᴐ⊥ ᴧᴐ⊥ (⁓̇@˖̇ᴧ˖̇x᷍3z)·

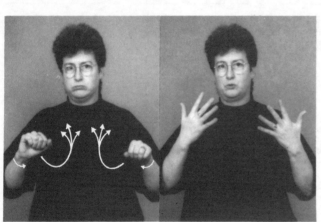

91　∅ /ᴧᴐ⊥ /ᴧᴐ⊥ ̊˅

92　∅ ᴧᴐ⊥ ¦ ᴧᴐ⊥ ⁓̇@⊥˅

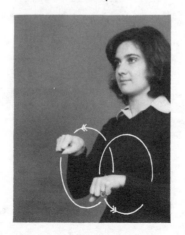

Handshape and orientation	Location, hand arrangement and contact	Movement	Glosses	
Two **A** hands are held with the palms facing down (if the hands were opened, the fingers would all point away from the signer).	The hands are held in front of the body.	The hands make a short downward movement.	chair chairman chairperson chairwoman preside president seat sit	86
Two **A** hands are held with the palms facing down (if the hands were opened, the fingers would all point away from the signer).	The hands are held in front of the body.	The hands make a short, firm movement down and towards each other.	abbreviate abbreviation brief less minimum short shortage	87
Two **A** hands are held with the palms facing down (if the hands were opened, the fingers would all point away from the signer).	The hands are held in front of the body.	The hands make alternate circles (the left hand moves clockwise, the right hand moves anticlockwise) in the vertical plane parallel to the signer's body.	clean cleaner cleaning domestic housework spring-clean spring-cleaning	88
Two **A** hands are held with the palms facing down (if the hands were opened, the fingers would all point away from the signer).	The hands are held in front of the body.	The hands twist towards each other at the wrists while moving down, and then move up and apart while opening (forming two **5** hands).	rebel rebellion revolt, revolution riot uprising finish[1] fresh[1]	89

Non-manual features   The cheeks are puffed out and then the mouth opens slightly as the hands move.

Notes   1 If the cheeks are not puffed out and the lips are rounded and pushed forward, the sign produced is **finish, fresh**. This is a regional sign.

Two **A** hands are held with the palms facing down (if the hands were opened, the fingers would all point away from the signer).	The hands are held in front of the body.	The hands make alternate clockwise circles in the vertical plane at right angles to the signer's body, moving towards each other each time they move away from the signer; the hands twist from side to side at the wrists throughout.	canoe canoeing paddle a canoe	90
Two **A** hands are held with the palms facing down (if the hands were opened, the fingers would all point away from the signer).	The hands are held in front of the body with the elbows raised at the sides of the body.	The hands and elbows make a short downward movement.	armchair easychair sit in an armchair/ easychair	91
Two **A** hands are held with the palms facing down (if the hands were opened, the fingers would all point away from the signer).	The hands are held side by side in front of the body.	The hands make alternate clockwise circles in the vertical plane at right angles to the signer's body.	bicycle bike cycle cycling cyclist pedal ride a bicycle/bike	92

93 ∅ A⍝⊥ ₁ A⍝⊥ $\overset{e}{\underset{v}{\uparrow}}$ $\overset{~}{\cdot}$ // ∅ Ö>⊥ Ö<⊥ $\overset{e}{\underset{v}{\uparrow}}$ 94 ∅ A⍝⊥ ₁ₓ A⍝⊥ $\overset{°}{\underset{÷}{3}}$

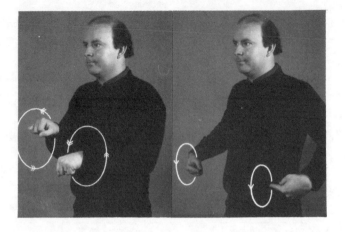

95 ∅ A⍝⊥ ₁ₓ A⍝⊥ $\overset{e}{\underset{÷}{\underset{v}{\top}}}$ $\cdot$ 96 ∅ A⍝> A⍝< $\overset{°}{v}$ $\cdot$ 97 ∅ A⍝> ₁ A⍝< $\overset{°}{v}$

98 ∅ A⍝⊥ $\overset{°}{\wedge}$ ⌁A<⊥₉ $\overset{°}{\wedge}$ 99 ∅ A⊤∧ A⊤∧ $\overset{⍝}{\underset{x}{}}$ $\cdot$ 100 ∅ A⊤∧ A⊤∧ $\overset{(NN)}{z}$ $\cdot$

A

Fist handshape in which the thumb is usually held against the side of the index finger.

Handshape and orientation	Location, hand arrangement and contact	Movement	Glosses	
Two **A** hands are held with the palms facing down (if the hands were opened, the fingers would all point away from the signer).	The hands are held side by side in front of the body.	The hands make alternate clockwise circles in the vertical plane at right angles to the signer's body.	**tricycle** **trike**	93
The left **Ġ** hand is held with the palm facing right; the right **Ġ** hand is held with the palm facing left (if the hands were opened, the fingers would all point away from the signer).	The hands are held in front of the body.	The hands make a clockwise circle in the vertical plane at right angles to the signer's body.		
Two **A** hands are held with the palms facing down (if the hands were opened, the fingers would all point away from the signer).	The hands are held side by side in front of the body with the sides of the index fingers touching.	The hands make a short twisting movement at the wrists, so that the hands move apart and the palms face towards each other.	**break** **broke** **fracture** **snap**	94
Two **A** hands are held with the palms facing down (if the hands were opened, the fingers would all point away from the signer).	The hands are held in front of the body with the sides of the index fingers touching.	The hands make anticlockwise circles in the vertical plane at right angles to the signer's body, moving apart each time they move towards the signer.	**oars** **row** **rowing** **rowing boat** **scull**	95
Two **A** hands are held with the palms facing down (if the hands were opened, the left fingers would point to the right and the right fingers would point to the left).	The hands are held in front of the body and at an angle, so that the fingers are turned away from the signer.	The hands make two short downward movements.	**wait** * **wait and see**	96

Notes   * This sign can be produced using one hand only.   Ø A⌐< °v̌ ·

Two **A** hands are held with the palms facing down (if the hands were opened, the left fingers would point to the right and the right fingers would point to the left).	The hands are held side by side in front of the body.	The hands make a short downward movement.	**chair** **chairman** **chairperson** **chairwoman** **preside** **president** **seat** **sit**	97
The left **A** hand is held with the palm facing down; the right **A** hand is held with the palm facing left (if the hands were opened, the fingers would all point away from the signer).	The hands are held in front of the body; the right hand is held nearer to the signer than the left hand.	The right hand makes a short upward movement, so that the right elbow moves up and away from the body; at the same time, the left hand makes a short downward movement.	**water with a watering can** **watering can**	98
Two **A** hands are held with the palms facing towards the signer (if the hands were opened, the fingers would all point up).	The hands are held in front of the body.	The hands twist towards each other from the wrists, so that the palms face down; the movement is repeated.	**bake** **baker** **bakery** **baking** **knead**	99
Two **A** hands are held with the palms facing towards the signer (if the hands were opened, the fingers would all point up).	The hands are held in front of the body.	The hands move up and down alternately while moving from side to side; the movements are repeated.	**car** **drive a car/small vehicle/van** **driver of a car/small vehicle/van** **small vehicle** **van**	100

101 $\emptyset$ A⊤∧ A⊤∧$^{(NN)}_{Z}$ · $\frac{}{//}$ $\overline{B}$a⊥ B⊤<$^{(x\cdot)}_{⊥}$

102 $\emptyset$ A⊤∧ A⊥∧$^{(N)}_{÷}$

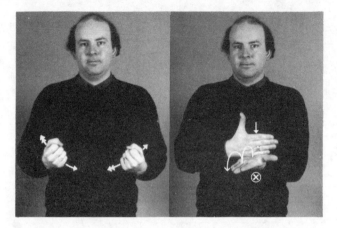

103 $\emptyset$ A⊤> A⊤<$^{\dot{x}x}$

104 $\emptyset$ $\overline{A}$⊤> A⊤<$^{\overset{\circ}{\omega}}_{⊥}$·

105 $\emptyset$ $\overline{A}$⊤> ₁ A⊤<$^{\dot{<}}_{\dot{v}}$ $\frac{}{//}$ G☞> V⊤v$_{\varsigma}$ $^{(N)\overset{\circ}{⊥}}_{<\dot{v}}$ $\overset{}{a}$

106 $\emptyset$ $\overline{A}$⊤> ₓ A⊤<$^{\overset{\circ}{v}}$·

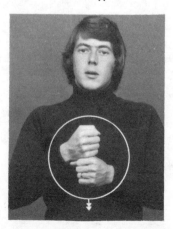

Handshape and orientation	Location, hand arrangement and contact	Movement	Glosses	
Two **A** hands are held with the palms facing towards the signer (if the hands were opened, the fingers would all point up).	The hands are held in front of the body.	The hands move up and down alternately while moving from side to side; the movements are repeated.	**car park**	**101**
The left **B** hand is held with the palm facing up and the fingers pointing away from the signer; the right **B** hand is held with the palm facing towards the signer and the fingers pointing to the left.	The hands are held in front of the body; the side of the right hand rests across the left palm.	The right hand moves away from the signer, tapping the left palm several times.		
The left **A** hand is held with the palm facing the signer; the right **A** hand is held with the palm facing away from the signer (if the hands were opened, the fingers would all point up).	The hands are held in front of the body; the right hand is held higher than the left hand.	The hands bend away from the signer at the wrists; at the same time, the left hand moves down while the right hand moves up.	**binman** **dustman** **empty a dustbin** **refuse collector**	**102**
Non-manual features The body moves forward.				
Two **A** hands are held with the palms facing towards the signer (if the hands were opened, the left fingers would point to the right and the right fingers would point to the left).	The hands are held in front of the body.	The hands move firmly towards each other, so that the knuckles touch.	**accident** **collide** **collision** **crash**	**103**
Non-manual features The cheeks are puffed out.				
Two **A** hands are held with the palms facing towards the signer (if the hands were opened, the left fingers would point to the right and the right fingers would point to the left).	The hands are held in front of the body; the right hand is held above the left hand.	The hands make a short movement away from the signer while twisting at the wrists, so that the palms face down; the movement is repeated.	**broom** **labourer** **long- handled brush** **sweep** **sweeper**	**104**
Two **A** hands are held with the palms facing towards the signer (if the hands were opened, the left fingers would point to the right and the right fingers would point to the left).	The hands are held side by side in front of the body; the right hand is held higher than the left hand.	The hands make a firm movement down and, at the same time, to the left.	**pole vault** **pole vaulter**	**105**
The left **G** hand is held with the palm facing down (if the hand were opened, the fingers would point to the right). The right **V** hand is held with the palm facing towards the signer (if the hand were opened, the fingers would point down).	The hands are held in front of the body; the right hand is held nearer to the signer than the left hand.	The right hand bends to the left at the wrist while moving to the right and, at the same time, twisting at the wrist, so that the palm faces up; the hand then makes a short movement down and, at the same time, away from the signer.		
Two **A** hands are held with the palms facing towards the signer (if the hands were opened, the left fingers would point to the right and the right fingers would point to the left).	The hands are held in front of the body; the right hand is held on the left hand.	The hands remain together and make a short downward movement; the movement is repeated.	**bellringer** **bellringing** **cathedral** **chapel** **church** **kirk** **ring a bell with a rope** **toll a bell with a rope** **verger**	**106**

107 Ø $\overline{A}$T> $_\times$ AT< $\overset{\circ}{\underset{\perp}{}}$ ·

108 Ø $\overline{A}$T> $_\times$ AT< $\overset{@}{\underset{\top}{<}}$ ·

109 Ø $\jmath$ $\overline{A}$T> $_\times$ $\jmath$AT< $\left(\overset{\dot{\cap}}{\underset{\circ}{\perp}}\right)$

110 Ø AT> $_|$ AT< $\overset{\dot{\div}}{\underset{\vee}{}}$

111 Ø A$\perp$∧ A$\perp$∧ $\overset{\circ}{\times}$ ·

112 Ø A$\perp$∧ A$\perp$∧ $\left(\overset{@}{\underset{\top}{\overset{\top}{\underset{\times}{\vee}}}}\right)^{\sim}$ ·

A *Fist handshape in which the thumb is usually held against the side of the index finger.*

Handshape and orientation	Location, hand arrangement and contact	Movement	Glosses	
Two **A** hands are held with the palms facing towards the signer (if the hands were opened, the left fingers would point to the right and the right fingers would point to the left).	The hands are held in front of the body; the right hand is held on the left hand.	The hands remain together and make two short movements down and, at the same time, away from the signer.	**horse** **ride a horse** **rodeo**	107
Two **A** hands are held with the palms facing towards the signer (if the hands were opened, the left fingers would point to the right and the right fingers would point to the left).	The hands are held in front of the body; the right hand is held on the left hand.	The hands remain together and make anticlockwise circles in the horizontal plane.	**fair** **fairground** **funfair** **stir**[1] **stirrer**[1]	108

Notes   1   If the eyes are narrowed, the nose is wrinkled and the lips are stretched, the sign produced is **stir, stirrer**.

Two **A** hands are held with the palms facing towards the signer (if the hands were opened, the left fingers would point to the right and the right fingers would point to the left).	The hands are held in front of the body; the right hand rests on the left hand.	The hands move firmly away from the signer, with the arms bending at the elbows, while twisting at the wrists, so that both palms face down.	**ban*** **disallow*** **forbid*** **not allow*** **prohibit*** **taboo***	109

Non-manual features   The lips are pressed together and the brows are slightly furrowed.

Notes   * This sign can be produced using two **I** hands.

$$\varnothing \; \textit{J} \, \bar{\textsf{I}} \, {\textsf{T}} {>} \;_{\times} \, \textit{J} \, \textsf{I} \, {\textsf{T}} {<} \, \left(\begin{smallmatrix} \dot{n} \\ \bar{o} \end{smallmatrix}\right)$$

Two **A** hands are held with the palms facing towards the signer (if the hands were opened, the left fingers would point to the right and the right fingers would point to the left).	The hands are held side by side in front of the body.	The hands make circles (the left hand moves anticlockwise, the right hand moves clockwise) in the vertical plane parallel to the signer's body; the movements are repeated.	**devoted*** **faithful*** **steadfast***	110

Non-manual features   The cheeks are puffed out.

Notes   * Regional sign.

Two **A** hands are held with the palms facing away from the signer (if the hands were opened, the fingers would all point up).	The hands are held in front of the body.	The hands make several short movements towards each other.	**before*** **not yet*** **still not***	111

Non-manual features   The mouth is open, the lips are pushed forward and the head shakes slightly.

Notes   * This sign may be produced using one hand only.

$$\varnothing \; \textsf{A} {\perp} {\wedge} \; \overset{\circ}{\textit{z}} \cdot$$

Two **A** hands are held with the palms facing away from the signer (if the hands were opened, the fingers would all point up).	The hands are held in front of the body.	The hands make alternate anticlockwise circles in the vertical plane at right angles to the signer's body, while moving towards each other and, at the same time, towards the signer.	**back off** **defend** **defensive** **fend off** **resist** **resistance** **retreat** **struggle** **ward off**	112

Non-manual features   The shoulders move back.

113 Ø A⊥∧ ¦ A⊥∧؟ $\begin{pmatrix} {}^{\circ}_{\wedge}\ {}_{\square}\ [55]\ {}^{D}_{\perp}\ {}^{\circ}_{\wedge}\ {}^{D}_{\wedge} \\ {}_{\mp} \end{pmatrix}$

114 Ø ∫A>∧ ∫A<∧ ˚ᵛ

115 Ø ∫A>∧ ∫A<∧ ˚ᵛ ∥ Ø Υↄ> ¦ Υↄ< ÷

116 Ø ∫A>∧ ∫A<∧ ˚ᵛ ∥ Ø Cↄ⊥ ¦ Cↄ⊥ ÷

117 Ø ∫A>ᵛ ∫A<ᵛ ⊥

[174]

Handshape and orientation	Location, hand arrangement and contact	Movement	Glosses	
Two **A** hands are held with the palms facing away from the signer (if the hands were opened, the fingers would all point up).	The hands are held in front of the body; the right hand is held nearer to the signer than the left hand.	The hands, moving away from the signer and to the left throughout, make a short upward movement, while opening (forming two **5** hands), and then bend away from the signer at the wrists before making a short upward bending movement at the wrists.	surf waves	113
The left **A** hand is held with the palm facing right; the right **A** hand is held with the palm facing left (if the hands were opened, the fingers would all point up).	The hands are held in front of the body, with the elbows raised.	The hands and elbows make a short downward movement.	chair chairman chairperson chairwoman preside seat sit	114
The left **A** hand is held with the palm facing right; the right **A** hand is held with the palm facing left (if the hands were opened, the fingers would all point up).	The hands are held in front of the body; the elbows are raised at the sides of the body.	The hands and elbows make a short downward movement.	couch settee sit on a couch/settee/ sofa sofa	115
Two **Y** hands are held with the palms facing down (if the hands were opened, the left fingers would point to the right and the right fingers would point to the left).	The hands are held side by side in front of the body.	The hands move apart.		
The left **A** hand is held with the palm facing right; the right **A** hand is held with the palm facing left (if the hands were opened, the fingers would all point up).	The hands are held in front of the body; the elbows are raised at the sides of the body.	The hands and elbows make a short downward movement.	couch settee sit on a couch/settee/ sofa sofa	116
Two **C** hands are held with the palms facing down (if the hands were opened, the fingers would all point away from the signer).	The hands are held side by side in front of the body.	The hands move apart.		
The left **A** hand is held with the palm facing right; the right **A** hand is held with the palm facing left (if the hands were opened, the fingers would all point down).	The hands are held in front of the body; the elbows are held out from the sides of the body.	The hands move away from the signer.	cart push a cart/ wheelbarrow wheelbarrow	117

118　∅ A>⊥ A<⊥ ᵒˣ·

119　∅ A>⊥ A<⊥ ᵒˣ·

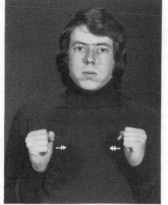

120　∅ A>⊥ A<⊥ ⁽ᴰ⁾·

121　∅ A>⊥ A<⊥ ᵉᴺ·

122　∅ ⟍A>⊥ ⟍A<⊥ ᴰᴵ

123　∅ ⟋A>⊥ ⟋A<⊥ ᴵᴺ·

124　∅ ‾A>⊥ ‚A<⊥ ⁺ˣ⁺

[176]

Handshape and orientation	Location, hand arrangement and contact	Movement	Glosses	
The left **A** hand is held with the palm facing right; the right **A** hand is held with the palm facing left (if the hands were opened, the fingers would all point away from the signer).	The hands are held in front of the body.	The hands make several short movements towards each other.	cold (very cold) freezing [1] shiver [1] chill [2] chilly [2] cool [2]	118

Non-manual features The cheeks are puffed out.

Notes 1 If the cheeks are not puffed out and the lips are stretched, the sign produced is **freezing, shiver.**

2 If the cheeks are not puffed out and the lips are rounded, the sign produced is **chill, chilly, cool.**

The left **A** hand is held with the palm facing right; the right **A** hand is held with the palm facing left (if the hands were opened, the fingers would all point away from the signer).	The hands are held in front of the body.	The hands make several short, firm movements towards each other.	cold winter wintry	119

Non-manual features The shoulders are hunched.

The left **A** hand is held with the palm facing right; the right **A** hand is held with the palm facing left (if the hands were opened, the fingers would all point away from the signer).	The hands are held in front of the body.	The hands bend down at the wrists while moving down and towards the signer; the movement is repeated.	ski skier skiing	120

The left **A** hand is held with the palm facing right; the right **A** hand is held with the palm facing left (if the hands were opened, the fingers would all point away from the signer).	The hands are held in front of the body.	The hands make alternate clockwise circles in the vertical plane at right angles to the signer's body.	athlete athletics run runner running	121

The left **A** hand is held with the palm facing right; the right **A** hand is held with the palm facing left (if the hands were opened, the fingers would all point away from the signer).	The hands are held in front of the body.	The hands move towards and away from the signer several times, with the arms bending from the shoulders.	park with swings swing	122

The left **A** hand is held with the palm facing right; the right **A** hand is held with the palm facing left (if the hands were opened, the fingers would all point away from the signer).	The hands are held in front of the body.	The hands move towards and away from the signer several times alternately.	hike hiker hiking ramble rambler rambling walk walker walking	123

Non-manual features The shoulders move back and forward alternately.

The left **A** hand is held with the palm facing right; the right **A** hand is held with the palm facing left (if the hands were opened, the fingers would all point up).	The hands are held side by side in front of the body; the right hand is held higher than the left hand.	The hands cross over so that the right hand brushes across the top of the left hand; the hands then uncross, moving sharply apart.	bang* blast* bomb* burst* explode* explosion*	124

Non-manual features The cheeks are puffed out.

Notes * This sign may be produced with the hands opening (forming two **5** hands) as they move firmly apart.

$$\emptyset \ \overline{A} \!>\!\perp \ , \ A \!<\!\perp \ \substack{\mp \div [55] \\ \times \square \\ \mp}$$

125 Ø Ā>⊥ ₓ A<⊥ ÷̥̊⬚[55]

126 Ø Ā>⊥ᵩ A<⊥ ᵥ̊ᵀ·

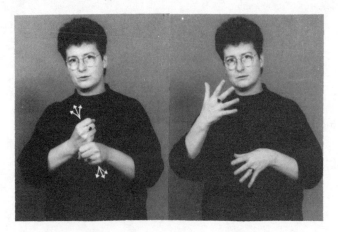

127 Ø Ā>⊥ᵩ A<⊥ ᵥ̌ᵀ·

128 Ø A>⊥ᵢ A<⊥ ˣˣ

129 Ø A>⊥ᵢ A<⊥ ̊ᶰᶰ·

130 Ø A>⊥ᵢ A<⊥ ˣ÷̥⬚[55]

131 Ø A>⊥ᵢₓ A<⊥ ̊ᵢᵥ·

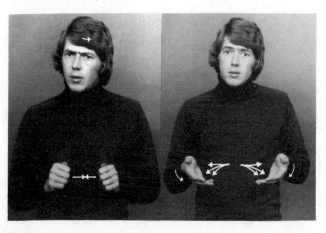

Handshape and orientation	Location, hand arrangement and contact	Movement	Glosses	
The left **A** hand is held with the palm facing right; the right **A** hand is held with the palm facing left (if the hands were opened, the fingers would all point away from the signer).	The hands are held in front of the body; the right hand rests on the left hand.	The left hand makes a short downward movement while the right hand makes a short upward movement and, at the same time, the hands open (forming two **5** hands).	gold golden	125
The left **A** hand is held with the palm facing right; the right **A** hand is held with the palm facing left (if the hands were opened, the fingers would all point away from the signer).	The hands are held in front of the body; the left hand is held lower and nearer to the signer than the right hand.	The hands make two short movements down and, at the same time, towards the signer.	fly a kite kite	126
Non-manual features The eyegaze is directed up and forwards.				
The left **A** hand is held with the palm facing right; the right **A** hand is held with the palm facing left (if the hands were opened, the fingers would all point away from the signer).	The hands are held in front of the body; the left hand is held lower and nearer to the signer than the right hand.	The hands move down and to the left and, at the same time, towards the signer; the movement is repeated.	gondola gondolier punt	127
The left **A** hand is held with the palm facing right; the right **A** hand is held with the palm facing left (if the hands were opened, the fingers would all point away from the signer).	The hands are held side by side in front of the body.	The hands move towards each other, so that the knuckles touch.	appointment book commitment engagement pact accord[1] agree[1] agreement[1] appropriate[1] compatible[1] in accord[1] suit[1] suitable[1]	128
Notes 1 If the head nods and the lips are pressed together, the sign produced is **accord, agree, agreement, appropriate, compatible, in accord, suit, suitable.**				
The left **A** hand is held with the palm facing right; the right **A** hand is held with the palm facing left (if the hands were opened, the fingers would all point away from the signer).	The hands are held side by side in front of the body.	The hands make alternate short up and down movements.	milk*	129
Notes * This sign may be produced using two **C** hands which close (forming **A** hands) as they move down alternately.		$\emptyset$ C >⊥ C <⊥ $\overset{\circ}{\#}\overset{v}{[AA]} \sim \cdot$		
The left **A** hand is held with the palm facing right; the right **A** hand is held with the palm facing left (if the hands were opened, the fingers would all point away from the signer).	The hands are held side by side in front of the body.	The knuckles touch and then the hands move apart, twisting at the wrists, so that the palms face up, while opening (forming two **5** hands).	disagree disagreement discord inappropriate incompatible unsuitable	130
Non-manual features The lips are pressed together and the corners of the mouth are turned down; the head is turned slightly to the side.				
The left **A** hand is held with the palm facing right; the right **A** hand is held with the palm facing left (if the hands were opened, the fingers would all point away from the signer).	The hands are held side by side in front of the body with the knuckles held together.	The hands remain together and make two short movements down and, at the same time, away from the signer.	precious valuable value worth	131

132 Ø A>⊥ ×A<⊥ $\overset{(\overset{\omega}{\sim})}{\div}$

133 Ø A>⊥ ×A<⊥ $\overset{\sim\sim\cdot}{×}$

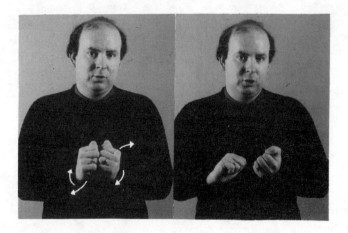

134 Ø A>⊥ A<⊥₉ $\overset{°\cdot}{⊥}$

135 ⌣ A>∧ ×A<∧₉ $\overset{\div[55]}{⊡}$

136 [] A⊤∨ A⊤∨ ×∨×

137 [] A⊤> A⊤< $\overset{\sim\cdot}{×}$

138 [] A⊤> A⊤< $^{(×I)\sim\cdot}$

Fist handshape in which the thumb is usually held against the side of the index finger.

Handshape and orientation	Location, hand arrangement and contact	Movement	Glosses	
The left A hand is held with the palm facing right; the right A hand is held with the palm facing left (if the hands were opened, the fingers would all point away from the signer).	The hands are held side by side in front of the body with the knuckles touching.	The hands move apart (the left hand moves away from the signer and the right hand moves towards the signer) while twisting at the wrists, so that the left palm faces down and the right palm faces up.	athletics sport sports	132
The left A hand is held with the palm facing right; the right A hand is held with the palm facing left (if the hands were opened, the fingers would all point away from the signer).	The hands are held side by side in front of the body with the knuckles touching.	The hands move up and down alternately several times with the knuckles rubbing across each other.	brother* milk	133

Notes * This sign may be produced with the hands moving towards and away from the signer alternately.

$$\emptyset \ \ \text{A>} \wedge \ _{\times} \ \text{A<} \wedge \ ^{\text{I} \sim \cdot}_{\times}$$

The left A hand is held with the palm facing right; the right A hand is held with the palm facing left (if the hands were opened, the fingers would all point away from the signer).	The hands are held in front of the body; the right hand is held nearer to the signer than the left hand.	The hands make two short, firm movements away from the signer.	cabinetmaker carpenter carpentry joiner joinery plane woodwork	134
The left A hand is held with the palm facing right; the right A hand is held with the palm facing left (if the hands were opened, the fingers would all point up).	The hands are held in front of the mouth and chin; the right hand is held nearer to the signer than the left hand, and the sides of the hands are touching.	The hands move apart and away from the signer while opening (forming two 5 hands).	balloon blow up a balloon inflate a balloon	135

Non-manual features The cheeks are puffed out.

Two A hands are held with the palms facing towards the signer (if the hands were opened, the fingers would all point down).	The hands are held in front of the chest.	The hands touch the upper chest and then move down before touching the lower chest.	jersey
			jumper
			put on a jersey/
			  jumper/pullover/
			  sweater
			pullover
			sweater
				136

Two A hands are held with the palms facing towards the signer (if the hands were opened, the left fingers would point to the right and the right fingers would point to the left).	The hands are held with the knuckles resting against the chest.	The hands move up and down several times, maintaining contact with the chest throughout.	bath* bathroom*	137

Notes * This sign may be produced using two B hands.

$$[] \ \ \text{B} \top \text{>} \ \text{B} \top \text{<} \ ^{\sim \cdot}_{\times}$$

Two A hands are held with the palms facing towards the signer (if the hands were opened, the left fingers would point to the right and the right fingers would point to the left).	The hands are held in front of the chest.	The hands make alternate movements towards and away from the signer, touching the chest in completing each movement.	ape* gorilla* Tarzan*	138

Non-manual features The mouth is closed with the lips pushed forward.

Notes * This sign may be produced without the alternation of the movements.

$$[] \ \ \text{A} \top \text{>} \ \text{A} \top \text{<} \ ^{(\times \text{I}) \cdot}$$

139 [] A>⊥ A<⊥ $_T^{\mp\times}$

140 ⌐⌐ A⊤∧, A⊤∧ $_\times^{\overset{\circ}{\wedge}}$

141 ⌐⌐ √A⊤∧ $_{\times\mp}$ √A⊤∧ $\left(\overset{\circ}{_T^D}\times\right)$

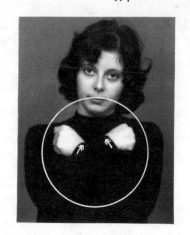

142 ⌐⌐ A⊥∧ A⊥∧ $\overset{\circ}{_⊥}\cdot$

143 ⌐⌐ A>∧ A<∧ $^{(\times\mathbb{I})\sim}\cdot$

144 ⌐⌐ A>⊥ A<⊥ $^{\times\times}$

145 ⌐⌐< A>∧ $_\times$ A<∧, $\overset{\circ}{_\vee}\cdot$

A

Fist handshape in which the thumb is usually held against the side of the index finger.

Handshape and orientation	Location, hand arrangement and contact	Movement	Glosses	
The left **A** hand is held with the palm facing right; the right **A** hand is held with the palm facing left (if the hands were opened, the fingers would all point away from the signer).	The hands are held in front of the chest.	The hands move towards the signer while crossing over; the movement ends with the knuckles touching the chest.	embrace hug cuddle[1] cuddly[1]	**139**

Notes   1   If the hands, already crossed over, are held against the chest, and the body makes short twisting movements from side to side, the sign produced is **cuddle, cuddly**.

$$[] \; A \!>\!\perp \; {}_{\neq x} \; A \!<\!\perp \;\; {}^{x}$$

Two **A** hands are held with the palms facing towards the signer (if the hands were opened, the fingers would all point up).	The hands are held side by side with the knuckles resting against the upper chest.	The hands make a short upward movement, maintaining contact with the chest throughout.	bedclothes blanket snuggle up under a blanket/the bedclothes	**140**

Notes   1   If the eyes are narrowed, the shoulders move backwards and forwards alternately, and the corners of the mouth are turned up, the sign produced is **snuggle up under a blanket/ the bedclothes**.

Two **A** hands are held with the palms facing towards the signer (if the hands were opened, the fingers would all point up).	The hands are held crossed over in front of the chest.	The hands make a short bending movement towards the signer at the wrists, to touch the upper chest; the movement is repeated.	bear* teddy bear* cuddle[1] cuddly[1]	**141**

Notes   *   This sign may be produced using two **5̈** hands.

        1   If the shoulders move back and forward alternately, the sign produced is **cuddle, cuddly**.

$$\lceil\rceil \; \sqrt{5̈} \top \wedge \; {}_{x\neq} \; \sqrt{5̈} \top \wedge \left({}^{\circ}_{\top}{}^{x}\right)\!\cdot$$

Two **A** hands are held with the palms facing away from the signer (if the hands were opened, the fingers would all point up).	The hands are held above the shoulders.	The hands make two short movements up and, at the same time, away from the signer.	weightlifter weightlifting	**142**

The left **A** hand is held with the palm facing right; the right **A** hand is held with the palm facing left (if the hands were opened, the fingers would all point up).	The hands are held against the upper chest.	The hands make alternate movements towards and away from the signer, touching the chest in completing each movement; the movements are repeated.	act* acting* actor* actress* bathtowel* drama* miles† performance* play* station*† theatre* towel*	**143**

Notes   *   This sign may be produced without the hands touching the body (**towel** is typically produced in this way).

        †   Regional sign.

$$\emptyset \; A \!>\!\wedge \; A \!<\!\wedge \;\; {}^{\mathsf{I} \wedge}\!\cdot$$

The left **A** hand is held with the palm facing right; the right **A** hand is held with the palm facing left (if the hands were opened, the fingers would all point away from the signer).	The hands are held in front of the sides of the upper chest.	The hands move towards each other, and then meet, touching the middle of the upper chest.	coat overcoat put on a coat/an overcoat	**144**

The left **A** hand is held with the palm facing right; the right **A** hand is held with the palm facing left (if the hands were opened, the fingers would all point up).	The hands are held in front of the right shoulder; the right hand is held nearer to the signer than the left hand, with the left hand held against the side of the right hand.	The hands make two short downward movements.	carry something over one's shoulder* Father Christmas postman* postwoman* Santa Claus	**145**

Non-manual features   The right shoulder is slightly hunched.

Notes   *   This sign may be produced using one hand only.

$$\lceil\rceil^{<} \; A \!<\!\wedge \;\; {}^{\circ}_{\vee}\!\cdot$$

146 ⊔ A>⊥ A<⊥ ˣⁱ̊ˣˣ

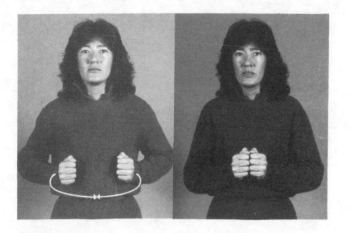

147 ⋈ A⊤v A⊤v ˣ̂

148 ⋈ A>v ₁ A<v ˣ̂v̂ˣ̂

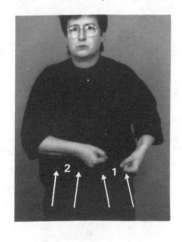

149 [∫A⊤v ⊙ ∫A⊥ʌ ⁽ˆˇ⁾·

150 ∅ B̄ɑ>ₓ A<⊥ ⊥

151 ∅ Bʊ>ₓ A⊤< v̊

A *Fist handshape in which the thumb is usually held against the side of the index finger.*

Handshape and orientation	Location, hand arrangement and contact	Movement	Glosses
The left **A** hand is held with the palm facing right; the right **A** hand is held with the palm facing left (if the hands were opened, the fingers would all point away from the signer).	The hands are held resting against the sides of the lower chest.	The hands make a short movement away from the signer and then move towards each other; the movement ends with the knuckles touching.	birthday* 146
Notes * Regional sign.			
Two **A** hands are held with the palms facing towards the signer (if the hands were opened, the fingers would all point down).	The hands are held resting against the front of the hips.	The hands move up, maintaining contact with the body throughout.	jeans 147 put on jeans/tights/ trousers tights trousers
The left **A** hand is held with the palm facing right; the right **A** hand is held with the palm facing left (if the hands were opened, the fingers would all point down).	The hands are held side by side resting against the right thigh.	The hands move up, maintaining contact with the right side of the waist; they then move across to the left thigh and repeat the movement.	boots 148 put on boots/ wellingtons wellingtons
The left **A** hand is held with the palm facing towards the signer; the right **A** hand is held with the palm facing away from the signer (if the hands were opened, the left fingers would point down and the right fingers would point up).	The left hand is held at the left side of the chest; the right hand is held at the right side of the head; the elbows are held away from the body.	The hands move up and, at the same time, to the right, and then down and, at the same time, to the left; the movements are repeated.	bath 149 bathroom bathtowel dry oneself with a towel/ bathtowel towel
The left **B** hand is held with the palm facing up and the fingers pointing to the right; the right **A** hand is held with the palm facing left (if the hand were opened, the fingers would point away from the signer).	The hands are held in front of the body; the right hand is held on the left palm.	The hands remain together and move away from the signer.	aid* 150 assist* assistance assistant help* helper support* supporter
Notes * Directional verb.			
The left **B** hand is held with the palm facing down and the fingers pointing to the right; the right **A** hand is held with the palm facing towards the signer (if the hand were opened, the fingers would point to the left).	The hands are held in front of the body; the right hand is held on the back of the left hand.	The hands remain together and make a short downward movement.	base* 151 basic* basis* constitute* constitution* establish* establishment* form* found* foundation* founder* launch* set up*
Notes * This sign may be produced with a right **Ȧ** hand.	Ø B⌐> × Ȧ⊤< °		

152 Ø <u>B</u>ʊ>ₓ A<ʌ ̊ʌ   153 Ø B̈ɑ>, A<v ᵛ<ᵂₜ<

154 Ø Ȧʊ⊤ ᵃ   155 Ø Ȧʊ⊤ ᵛᵂ

Handshape and orientation	Location, hand arrangement and contact	Movement	Glosses	
The left **⫟B** hand is held with the palm facing down and the fingers pointing to the right; the right **A** hand is held with the palm facing left (if the hand were opened, the fingers would point up).	The hands are held in front of the body; the right knuckles are held against the left palm.	The hands remain together and make a short upwards movement.	**hold up** **prop** **support** **ceiling**[1] **limit**[1] **maximum**[1]	152

Notes 1 If the movement is changed so that the right hand moves up until it meets the left palm, the sign produced is **ceiling, limit, maximum.**

$$\underline{B\,\text{ʊ}>\;A<\wedge}\quad {}^{\circ}_{\wedge\times}$$

The left **B̈** hand is held with the palm facing up (if the hand were opened, the fingers would point to the right). The right **A** hand is held with the palm facing left (if the hand were opened, the fingers would point down).	The hands are held side by side in front of the body; the right hand is held higher than the left hand.	The hands make a short movement down and to the left, and then twist towards the signer and, at the same time, to the left at the wrists.	**dig** **garden** **gardener** **dig a hole**[1] **dig up**[1] **shovel**[1] **spade**[1]	153

Notes 1 If a left **A** handshape is used and the movement is changed so that the left hand moves up and towards the signer as the right hand twists, the sign produced is **dig a hole, dig up, shovel, spade.**

$$\emptyset\quad \text{j}\,\overline{A}\,\text{a}>{}^{\circ}_{<\intercal}\!\!\overset{\vee}{}^{\wedge}\;,\;A<\wedge\;{}^{\circ}_{<\intercal}\!\!\overset{\vee}{}^{\omega}$$

The thumb is extended from the fist.

À has several different *classifier* functions in the productive lexicon and also appears as a classifying element in established signs:
- it has a limited use as a *size and shape* classifier to represent small, stocky items with a short extension such as a vinegar bottle, as in **vinegar** (sign 205);
- it has limited use as a *tracing size and shape* classifier to indicate the shape or outline of objects;
- it seems only to be used as a *handling* classifier when an *instrumental* function is also involved, as in **potato peeler** (sign 210). Here both the holding of the implement and the cutting edge seem to be represented in the one handshape;
- it is used as an *instrumental* classifier to indicate implements, tools or utensils which have a short sharp blade, as in **operation** (signs 173 and 190);
- it is used as a *touch* classifier to indicate the touching of small items or areas, as in **press a doorbell** (sign 162) and **put on a sticking plaster** (sign 191). The action involved has often been extended for use in the related noun forms, e.g. **doorbell** (sign 162) and **sticking plaster** (sign 191);
- two-handed forms can be used to express *extent*, particularly the length, depth and height of objects such as buildings, rooms and columns.

This handshape has a *symbolic* value in many signs in that it is associated with positive meanings or 'goodness'. This usage can be seen in signs such as **good** (sign 164), **wisdom** (sign 166), **excellent** (sign 213) and **praise** (sign 226). **À** contrasts with the **I** handshape which has an opposing symbolic value relating to 'badness'.

The **À** handshape can also be seen as having a *deictic* (pointing) function in a number of signs, for example, **programme** (sign 196) where the derivation is based on the extended thumb pointing in turn to items on a piece of paper, and **neighbour** (sign 154) where the extended thumb indicates an area to the right of the signer.

Handshape and orientation	Location, hand arrangement and contact	Movement	Glosses	
The **À** hand is held with the palm facing down (if the hand were opened, the fingers would point away from the signer).	The hand is held in front of the body.	The hand twists at the wrist, so that the palm faces up.	**after** **neighbour** **next** **next door** **then**	154
The **À** hand is held with the palm facing down (if the hand were opened, the fingers would point away from the signer).	The hand is held in front of the body.	The hand twists to the right at the wrist, so that the thumb points up.	**good** **great**	155

156 Ø Ȧʊ⊥ $\binom{n}{v}$

157 Ø Ȧʊ⊥ $\binom{°}{\lambda\lambda}$

158 Ø ɟȦʊ⊥ $\overset{\dot{n}}{\lambda}$

159 Ø Ȧ⊤< ᵐ·

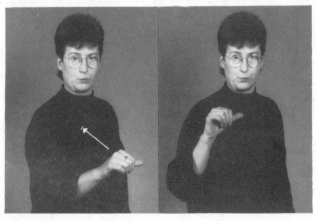

160 Ø ɟȦ⊤< $\overset{\dot{n}}{>}$

161 Ø Ȧ⊥ʌ $\overset{°\dot{3}\dot{N}}{}$

162 Ø Ȧ<⊥ $\overset{°}{\lambda}$

Å The thumb is extended from the fist.

156-162

Handshape and orientation	Location, hand arrangement and contact	Movement	Glosses	
The **Å** hand is held with the palm facing down (if the hand were opened, the fingers would point away from the signer).	The hand is held in front of the body.	The hand bends down at the wrist; the movement is repeated several times, with the hand moving away from the signer throughout.	order * procedure * sequence * series * turn (in turn) *	156

Notes   * This sign may be produced using two hands moving alternately.

$$\emptyset \quad \dot{A}\text{ɔ⊥} \text{ }, \text{ } \dot{A}\text{ɔ⊥}^{\left(\begin{smallmatrix}ᴅ\sim\cdot\\\vee\\⊤\end{smallmatrix}\right)}$$

The **Å** hand is held with the palm facing down (if the hand were opened, the fingers would point away from the signer).	The hand is held in front of the body.	The hand makes a short twisting movement to the right at the wrist, so that the palm faces left; the movement is repeated several times, with the hand moving to the right throughout.	neighbours * order procedure sequence series turn (in turn)	157

Notes   * This sign can be produced using two hands moving apart.

$$\emptyset \quad \dot{A}\text{ɔ⊥} \text{ } \dot{A}\text{ɔ⊥}^{\left(\begin{smallmatrix}\circ\\\omega\\+\\\div\end{smallmatrix}\cdot\right)}$$

The **Å** hand is held with the palm facing down (if the hand were opened, the fingers would point away from the signer).	The hand is held in front of the body.	The hand moves firmly up and, at the same time, towards the signer, bending from the elbow.	expert skill whizz	158

Non-manual features   The lips are tightly rounded.

The **Å** hand is held with the palm facing towards the signer (if the hand were opened, the fingers would point to the left).	The hand is held in front of the body.	The thumb flexes twice.	lighter	159

The **Å** hand is held with the palm facing towards the signer (if the hand were opened, the fingers would point to the left).	The hand is held in front of the body.	The hand makes a firm movement to the right, bending at the elbow, so that the movement ends with the thumb pointing to the right.	bike (on your bike) * bugger off * clear off * get lost * get out * piss off * scram * sod off *	160

Non-manual features   The brows are furrowed.
Notes   * This sign may be produced with a repeated movement.

$$\emptyset \quad \acute{J}\dot{A}\text{⊤<}^{\dot{\tilde{\,}}}_{\check{>}}\cdot$$

The **Å** hand is held with the palm facing away from the signer (if the hand were opened, the fingers would point up).	The hand is held in front of the body.	The hand makes small, sharp movements from side to side at the wrist.	be exist still there	161

Non-manual features   The lips are rounded and pushed forward.

The **Å** hand is held with the palm facing left (if the hand were opened, the fingers would point away from the signer).	The hand is held in front of the body.	The hand makes a short movement away from the signer.	doorbell operating button press a doorbell/ an operating button ring a doorbell	162

163 Ø Ȧ<⊥ ⃘ͦ // Ø O℧⊥ □[ʒ]·

164 Ø Ȧ<⊥ ⃘ͦ

165 Ø Ȧ<⊥ ᵛ°ᵛₒ·

166 ∩ Ȧ℧< ᴰ⊥ᵥ

167 ∩ Ȧ⊥ʌ ˣ⊥ᵥ // B⊥ʌ₉ x B⊤< ᵛ°ᵛ@·ₓ

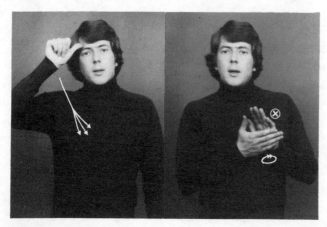

168 ∩ Ȧ<ʌ ˣ·

The thumb is extended from the fist.

Handshape and orientation	Location, hand arrangement and contact	Movement	Glosses	
The Å hand is held with the palm facing left (if the hand were opened, the fingers would point away from the signer).	The hand is held in front of the body.	The hand makes a short movement away from the signer.	**flashing doorbell** **press a flashing doorbell** **ring a flashing doorbell**	163
The O hand is held with the palm facing down (if the hand were opened, the fingers would point away from the signer).	The hand is held at shoulder height in front of the body.	The hand opens (forming a $\ddot{5}$ hand) several times.		
The Å hand is held with the palm facing left (if the hand were opened, the fingers would point away from the signer).	The hand is held in front of the body.	The hand makes a short, firm movement away from the signer.	**good** **great** **hello**[†] **all right?**[*1]	164

Notes * This sign may be produced with a repeated movement.

$\emptyset$ Å<⊥ $\overset{\circ}{\mathring{\text{ı}}}$ ·

† This sign can be produced with a **5** hand (palm facing away from the signer, fingers pointing up) which closes (forming an Å hand) while twisting at the wrist, so that the palm faces left.

$\emptyset$ 5⊥∧ $\overset{\omega}{\underset{\#}{\gtrless}}$ [∧]

1 If the eyebrows are raised, the sign produced is **all right?**

The Å hand is held with the palm facing left (if the hand were opened, the fingers would point away from the signer).	The hand is held in front of the body.	The hand makes two small clockwise circles in the vertical plane parallel to the signer's body.	**all right*** **fine*** **OK*** **okay***	165

Notes * This sign may be produced using two hands; the right hand moves clockwise, the left hand moves anticlockwise.

$\emptyset$ Å>⊥ Å<⊥ $\overset{\circ}{\underset{\vee}{\overset{@}{\div}}}$ ·

The Å hand is held with the palm facing left (if the hand were opened, the fingers would point away from the signer).	The hand is held in front of the forehead.	The hand moves to the left while bending away from the signer at the wrist.	**academic** **bright** **clever** **gifted** **intelligence** **intelligent** **wisdom** **wise**	166
The Å hand is held with the palm facing away from the signer (if the hand were opened, the fingers would point up).	The hand is held with the thumbtip touching the right side of the forehead.	The hand moves down and away from the signer while opening (forming a **B** hand).	**know what** someone means **understand what** someone means	167
The left **B** hand is held with the palm facing away from the signer and the fingers pointing up; the right **B** hand is held with the palm facing towards the signer and the fingers pointing to the left.	The hands are held in front of the body; the right fingers rest against the left palm.	The right hand makes anticlockwise circles in the vertical plane parallel to the signer's body, maintaining contact with the left palm throughout.		

Notes * The second part of this sign may be produced (with the left palm facing up, and the right palm facing down) with the right hand making clockwise circles in the horizontal plane, maintaining contact with the left palm.

∩ Å⊥∧ × // $\overline{\text{B}}$⊓⊥ × B℧< $\overset{@}{\underset{×}{\overset{·}{\gtrless}}}$

The Å hand is held with the palm facing left (if the hand were opened, the fingers would point up).	The hand is held in front of the forehead.	The thumbtip taps the forehead twice.	**aware** **know** **knowledge**	168

Non-manual features   The head is tilted forward slightly.

169 ∩ Ȧ<ʌ ˣ⊥ᵥ // ∅ G<⊥ °ᵢ

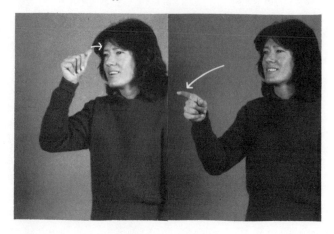

170 ∩ Ȧ<ʌ ˣ⊥ᵥ // B̄⊤⊥ B<ʌₒ

171 ∩ Ȧ<ʌ⁽ᵛ˄>⟩

172 Ʒ Ȧᴅ< ᵛₓ

173 Ʒ Ȧ<ʌ ᵛₓ

Å *The thumb is extended from the fist.*

Handshape and orientation	Location, hand arrangement and contact	Movement	Glosses
The **Å** hand is held with the palm facing left (if the hand were opened, the fingers would point up).	The hand is held in front of the forehead.	The thumbtip touches the forehead; the hand then moves away from the signer and downwards while changing to form a **G** hand.	know someone/ something* recognise someone/ something* **169**

Notes   * The following notes apply to all glosses:-

Directional verb.

This sign may be produced with a short movement away from the signer as the index finger opens (forming a **Ġ** hand).   ∩   Å<ʌ   ×ᵒₚ[ġ] ⊥ □

| The **Å** hand is held with the palm facing left (if the hand were opened, the fingers would point up). | The hand is held with the thumbtip touching the forehead. | The hand moves down while opening (forming a **B** hand). | experience authority¹ experienced¹ expert¹ knowledgeable¹ **170** |
| The left **B** hand is held with the palm facing towards the signer and the fingers pointing away from the signer; the right **B** hand is held with the palm facing left and the fingers pointing up. | The hands are held in front of the body; the right hand is held higher and nearer to the signer than the left hand, and the left hand is held at an angle, so that the fingers are turned to the right. | The right hand bends to the left at the wrist while moving down, so that the fingertips brush across the left palm. | |

Notes   1   If the cheeks are puffed out, the sign produced is **authority, experienced, expert, knowledgeable.**

| The **Å** hand is held with the palm facing left (if the hand were opened, the fingers would point up). | The hand is held with the thumbtip touching the forehead. | The thumbtip draws a cross on the forehead; the thumbtip maintains contact with the forehead throughout. | baptise* baptism* Catholic christen* christening* Christian Roman Catholic **171** |

Notes   * This sign may be produced using a **Ġ** hand.   ∩   Ġ⊤ʌ   (ᵛʌ>) ×

| The **Å** hand is held with the palm facing down (if the hand were opened, the fingers would point to the left). | The hand is held with the thumbtip touching the cheek. | The hand moves down; the thumbtip maintains contact with the cheek throughout. | cheat crafty sly **172** |

Non-manual features   The eyes are narrowed and the head is pushed forward.

| The **Å** hand is held with the palm facing left (if the hand were opened, the fingers would point up). | The hand is held with the thumbtip touching the right cheek. | The hand moves down; the thumbtip maintains contact with the cheek throughout. | hospital* mauve* operate on the face† operation on the face† purple* scar on the face† surgery (facial surgery) **173** |

Notes   * Regional sign.

† The hand is located at the appropriate part of the face.

174 ⌣ Ȧт< ˣ // ‾Ɓɑ> Ȧɿ⊥ ˣᵛ

175 ⌣ Ȧ<⊥ ˣᵛ

176 ∪ Ȧɤ< ˣ⊥>ω̇

177 ∪ Ȧт< ˣ·

178 ∪ Ȧт< ˣ ᵛ·

179 ∪ Ȧт< ˣᵛ·ᵥ

180 ∪ Ȧ<ʌ ˣ(ⁿ⊥̇)

[194]

Handshape and orientation	Location, hand arrangement and contact	Movement	Glosses	
The **Å** hand is held with the palm facing towards the signer (if the hand were opened, the fingers would point to the left).	The hand is held with the thumb in front of the mouth and chin.	The thumbtip touches the mouth.	insurance letter mail stamp	174
The left **B** hand is held with the palm facing up and the fingers pointing to the right; the right **Å** is held with the palm facing down (if the hand were opened, the fingers would point away from the signer).	The hands are held in front of the body; the right hand is held above the left hand.	The right hand moves down, so that the right thumb touches the left palm.		
The **Å** hand is held with the palm facing left (if the hand were opened, the fingers would point away from the signer).	The hand is held with the thumbtip touching the left side of the chin.	The hand moves to the right; the thumb maintains contact with the chin throughout.	appetising delicious lovely nice sweet tasty	175
The **Å** hand is held with the palm facing down (if the hand were opened, the fingers would point to the left).	The hand is held with the thumbtip touching the chin.	The hand moves to the right (with the thumbtip maintaining contact with the chin throughout), and then moves firmly away from the signer while twisting at the wrist, so that the palm faces away from the signer.	fault (someone's own fault) serves someone right	176

Non-manual features   The tongue tip is held between the lower lip and the bottom teeth; the nose wrinkles and the eyes narrow.

The **Å** hand is held with the palm facing towards the signer (if the hand were opened, the fingers would point to the left).	The hand is held with the thumb in front of the chin.	The side of the thumb taps the chin twice.	prefer preference	177
The **Å** hand is held with the palm facing towards the signer (if the hand were opened, the fingers would point to the left).	The hand is held with the side of the thumb touching the chin.	The hand moves down, with the thumb maintaining contact with the chin; the movement is repeated.	man* use useful	178

Notes   * Regional sign.

The **Å** hand is held with the palm facing towards the signer (if the hand were opened, the fingers would point to the left).	The hand is held in front of the chin.	The hand moves down, so that the thumb brushes the chin; the movement is repeated.	endure grin and bear it patience patient perseverance persevere put up with tolerance tolerate	179

Non-manual features   The shoulders are hunched, the brows are slightly furrowed and the lips are pressed together.

The **Å** hand is held with the palm facing left (if the hand were opened, the fingers would point up).	The hand is held with the thumbtip touching the chin.	The hand bends firmly away from the signer from the wrist, while moving away from the signer.	fault (someone's own fault) serves someone right	180

Non-manual features   The tongue tip is held between the lower lip and the bottom teeth and the nose is wrinkled.

181 ∪ Å<⊥ ᵒᵥ̇ₓ·

182 ⊆ ⌐Å<∧ ˣ♭⊥

 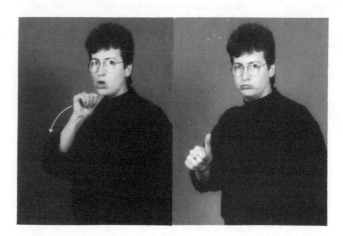

183 ⊆ Å<⊥ ˣ⊥ᵥ̇ ∥ B̄ɑ> B<⊥ ᵥ̇ₓ

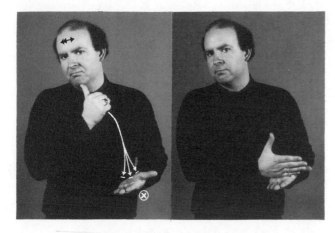

184 ⫪ Å<⊥ ·ᵂ⊤ᵥ·   185 [] Åɒ⊥ ˣ⊥ᵥˣᵥ⊤

[196]

The thumb is extended from the fist.

Handshape and orientation	Location, hand arrangement and contact	Movement	Glosses	
The Å hand is held with the palm facing left (if the hand were opened, the fingers would point away from the signer).	The hand is held with the back of the thumb touching the chin.	The hand makes a short downward movement with the back of the thumb maintaining contact with the chin; the movement is repeated.	endure grin and bear it patience patient perseverance persevere put up with tolerance tolerate	181
Non-manual features The lips are closed and drawn back.				
The Å hand is held with the palm facing left (if the hand were opened, the fingers would point up).	The hand is held with the thumbtip touching the underside of the chin.	The hand moves down and, at the same time, away from the signer, bending from the elbow.	purpose (on purpose) sure (make sure)	182
Non-manual features The mouth is open, and then closes with the cheeks puffed out as the hand moves.				
The Å hand is held with the palm facing left (if the hand were opened, the fingers would point away from the signer).	The hand is held with the thumbtip touching the underside of the chin.	The hand moves down and, at the same time, away from the signer while opening (forming a **B** hand).	not sure not true not trust	183
The left **B** hand is held with the palm facing up and the fingers pointing to the right; the right **B** hand is held with the palm facing left and the fingers pointing away from the signer.	The hands are held in front of the body; the right hand is held above the left hand.	The right hand moves firmly down to touch the left palm.		
Non-manual features The head shakes.				
The Å hand is held with the palm facing left (if the hand were opened, the fingers would point away from the signer).	The hand is held in front and to the left of the neck.	The hand twists at the wrist, so that the palm faces towards the signer, while moving sharply to the right.	abbatoir * cut one's throat * murder * slaughter * slaughterhouse * suicide * suicide (commit suicide) *	184
Notes * This sign may be produced with the hand moving sharply to the right maintaining contact with the neck throughout.				
The Å hand is held with the palm facing down (if the hand were opened, the fingers would point away from the signer).	The hand is held with the back of the thumb touching the chest.	The hand moves down and away from the signer, and then down and towards the signer; the movement ends with the back of the thumb touching the lower chest.	capitalism capitalist farm farmer paunch pot belly	185

186 [ ] ȦⲦ< ᵖˣ
T

187 ⌈ᴷ Ȧᴅ< ᵉᵀᵛˣᵉᵀᵛ

188 ⌈ᴷ Ȧ<⟂ ˣ˙
11

189] ȦⲦ< ˆˣˣ

190 ⎣⎦ Ȧᴅ< ˣᵛᵛ°
ˣˣ

191 ō̄ ȦⲦᵛ ˃ᵛᵛ
ˣˣ

The thumb is extended from the fist.

Handshape and orientation	Location, hand arrangement and contact	Movement	Glosses
The **Ȧ** hand is held with the palm facing left (if the hand were opened, the fingers would point away from the signer).	The hand is held in front of the chest.	The hand moves towards the signer while twisting at the wrist, so that the palm faces down; the movement ends with the thumbtip touching the chest.	after you 186 next (my go next) next (my turn next)
The **Ȧ** hand is held with the palm facing down (if the hand were opened, the fingers would point to the left). *Non-manual features* The right cheek is puffed out.	The hand is held in front of the right side of the upper chest.	The hand makes anticlockwise circles in the vertical plane at right angles to the signer's body; the thumbtip brushes the side of the chest in completing each circle.	already 187 fast quick
The **Ȧ** hand is held with the palm facing left (if the hand were opened, the fingers would point away from the signer). *Non-manual features* The lips are stretched.	The hand is held in front of the right side of the upper chest.	The back of the thumb taps the side of the chest twice.	about to 188 anticipate anticipation expect expectation going to imminent intend intention
The **Ȧ** hand is held with the palm facing towards the signer (if the hand were opened, the fingers would point to the left).	The hand is held with the knuckles resting against the lower chest.	The hand moves upwards, maintaining contact with the chest throughout.	morning* 189 good morning*[1]

Notes   * The following notes apply to all glosses:

Regional sign.

This sign can be produced using two hands.

$$[] \quad \dot{A}_{T>} \quad \dot{A}_{T<} \quad {}^{\wedge}_{\times}$$

1 If the movement is changed so that the hand moves upwards, brushing the chest, and then moves firmly away from the signer, the sign produced is **good morning**.

$$] \quad \dot{A}_{T<} \quad {}^{\wedge \; \dot{\imath}}_{\times \; \wedge}$$

The **Ȧ** hand is held with the palm facing down (if the hand were opened, the fingers would point to the left). *Notes* * The hand is located at the appropriate part of the body.	The hand is held in front of the waist, with the thumbtip touching the body.	The hand makes a short movement down and, at the same time, to the right, maintaining contact with the body throughout.	appendicectomy 190 operate * operation * scar on the side of the stomach * surgery *

The **Ȧ** hand is held with the palm facing towards the signer (if the hand were opened, the fingers would point down).
 	
Notes   * The hand is located at the appropriate part of the body.
	The left hand is positioned in front of the body with the palm facing down; the pad of the right thumb rests on the back of the left hand.	The right hand moves to the right and then down; the thumb maintains contact with the back of the left hand throughout.	plaster 191
			put a plaster/sticking
			  plaster on the back
			  of the hand
			put on a plaster/
			  sticking plaster *
			sticking plaster

192 $\overline{\dot{A}}{>}{\perp}$ ¡ $\dot{A}\,\upsilon{\perp}$၃ $\overset{\perp}{\underset{\perp}{\times}}$

193 $\overline{\dot{A}}{>}{\perp}$ ¡ $\dot{A}\,\upsilon{\perp}$၃ $\overset{\perp}{\underset{\perp}{\times}}\cdot$

194 $\dot{A}{>}{\perp}$ ¡ $\dot{A}\,\upsilon{\perp}$ ᵃ

195 $5{>}{\perp}$ ¡ $\dot{A}\,\upsilon{\perp}$ $\overset{\omega\cdot}{\underset{\wedge}{\times}}$

196 $\overline{B}\alpha{\perp}$ $\dot{A}\,\upsilon{\perp}$ $\left(\overset{\circ}{\underset{\wedge}{\overset{n}{_T}}}\cdot\right)$

197 $\overline{B}\alpha{>}$ $\dot{A}\,\upsilon{\perp}$ ˅ˣ

[200]

Handshape and orientation	Location, hand arrangement and contact	Movement	Glosses	
The left **Á** hand is held with the palm facing right; the right **Á** hand is held with the palm facing down (if the hands were opened, the fingers would all point away from the signer).	The hands are held side by side in front of the body; the right hand is held higher and nearer to the signer than the left hand.	The right hand moves away from the signer, so that the right thumb brushes along the left thumb.	**best**	192
The left **Á** hand is held with the palm facing right; the right **Á** hand is held with the palm facing down (if the hands were opened, the fingers would all point away from the signer).	The hands are held side by side in front of the body; the right hand is held higher and nearer to the signer than the left hand.	The right hand moves away from the signer, so that the right thumb brushes along the left thumb; the movement is repeated.	**better** improve [1] **improvement** [1]	193

Notes   1   If both hands move away from the signer, and the repeated brushing movement of the right hand is short and sharp, the sign produced is **improve, improvement**.

$$\varnothing \; \left(\overline{\text{Á}} \text{>v} \; \text{Áɒ⊥}_9 \; {}^{\substack{\text{o.} \\ \frac{1}{x} \\ \frac{1}{1}}} \right) \perp$$

| The left **Á** hand is held with the palm facing right; the right **Á** hand is held with the palm facing down (if the hands were opened, the fingers would all point away from the signer). | The hands are held side by side in front of the body. | The right hand twists at the wrist, so that the palm faces up. | **beside** **neighbour** **next** **next door** **then** | 194 |
| The left **5** hand is held with the palm facing right and the fingers pointing away from the signer; the right **Á** hand is held with the palm facing down (if the hand were opened, the fingers would point away from the signer). | The hands are held side by side in front of the body. | The right hand twists up at the wrist, so that the thumbtip brushes the left palm; the movement is repeated. | **wood** **wooden** actually [1] in fact [1] | 195 |

Notes   1   If the right hand moves towards the signer with the thumbtip maintaining contact with the left palm throughout, the sign produced is **actually, in fact**.

$$\text{5>⊥} \; {}_{\text{ix}} \; \text{Áɒ⊥} \; {}^{\substack{\text{o} \\ \top \\ x}}$$

| The left **B** hand is held with the palm facing up and the fingers pointing away from the signer; the right **Á** hand is held with the palm facing down (if the hand were opened, the fingers would point away from the signer). | The hands are held in front of the body; the right hand is held above the left hand. | The right hand bends upwards in a short movement from the wrist; the movement is repeated several times with the hand moving towards the signer throughout. | **agenda*** **list*** **order*** **procedure*** **programme*** **sequence*** **series*** | 196 |

Notes   *   The following notes apply to all glosses:

This sign may be produced with the right hand only.

$$\varnothing \; \text{Áɒ⊥} \; {}^{\left(\substack{\text{o} \\ \text{ɒ} \\ \wedge \\ \top} \cdot \right)}$$

The sign may be produced with the right thumb touching the left palm several times as the hand moves towards the signer.

$$\overline{\text{Bɒ⊥}} \; \text{Áɒ⊥} \; {}^{\left(\substack{\text{o} \\ \top x \\ \top} \cdot \right)}$$

| The left **B** hand is held with the palm facing up and the fingers pointing to the right; the right **Á** hand is held with the palm facing down (if the hand were opened, the fingers would point away from the signer). | The hands are held in front of the body; the right hand is held above the left hand. | The right hand moves down; the movement ends with the right hand held against the left palm. | **accurate** **confirm** **correct** **proper** **put right** **right** | 197 |

198 $\overline{\text{B}}$a> Ȧʊ⊥ ˣ·

199 $\overline{\text{B}}$a> Ȧᴖ⊥ ·ˣ

200 $\overline{\text{B}}$a> Ȧʊ⊥ $\overset{\overset{\circ}{@}\dot{\times}}{\underset{>}{\perp}}$

201 $\overline{\text{B}}$a> Ȧᴖ⊥ $\overset{\overset{\circ}{@}\overset{\circ}{v}\times}{\underset{>}{\perp}}$

202 $\overline{\text{B}}$a> Ȧʊ⊥ $\overset{\overset{\circ}{@}\overset{\circ}{v}\times}{\underset{>}{\perp}}$ // Ø $\overline{\text{B}}$a> ₓ Ba< $\overset{\wedge}{\top}$

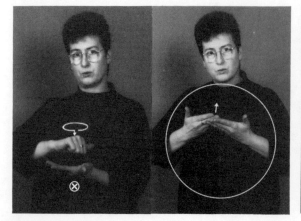

203 $\overline{\text{B}}$a> Ȧʊ⊥ $\overset{\overset{\circ}{@}\overset{\circ}{v}\times}{\underset{>}{\perp}}$ // Ø B>⊥ ₁ₓ B<⊥ ᵃ

The thumb is extended from the fist.

Handshape and orientation	Location, hand arrangement and contact	Movement	Glosses	
The left **B** hand is held with the palm facing up and the fingers pointing to the right; the right **Á** hand is held with the palm facing down (if the hand were opened, the fingers would point away from the signer).	The hands are held in front of the body; the right hand is held above the left hand.	The right knuckles tap the left palm twice.	acceptable good enough prefer preference well (may as well) will do	198

Non-manual features   The mouth is closed and the lips are pushed slightly forward.

The left **B** hand is held with the palm facing up and the fingers pointing to the right; the right **Á** hand is held with the palm facing down (if the hand were opened, the fingers would point away from the signer).	The hands are held in front of the body; the right hand is held above the left hand.	The right knuckles tap the left palm twice.	keep preserve reserve value	199
The left **B** hand is held with the palm facing up and the fingers pointing to the right; the right **Á** hand is held with the palm facing down (if the hand were opened, the fingers would point away from the signer).	The hands are held in front of the body; the right hand is held above the left hand.	The right hand makes a small clockwise circle in the horizontal plane and then moves firmly down to touch the left palm.	accurate confirm correct proper put right right	200
The left **B** hand is held with the palm facing up and the fingers pointing to the right; the right **Á** hand is held with the palm facing down (if the hand were opened, the fingers would point away from the signer).	The hands are held in front of the body; the right hand is held above the left hand.	The right hand makes a small clockwise circle in the horizontal plane and then makes a short downward movement to touch the left palm.	consecrate holy sanctify	201
The left **B** hand is held with the palm facing up and the fingers pointing to the right; the right **Á** hand is held with the palm facing down (if the hand were opened, the fingers would point away from the signer).	The hands are held in front of the body; the right hand is held above the left hand.	The right hand makes a small clockwise circle in the horizontal plane and then makes a short downward movement to touch the left palm.	holy communion	202
The left **B** hand is held with the palm facing up and the fingers pointing to the right; the right **B** hand is held with the palm facing up and the fingers pointing to the left.	The hands are held in front of the body; the right fingers are held on the left fingers.	The hands remain together and move up and, at the same time, towards the signer.		
The left **B** hand is held with the palm facing up and the fingers pointing to the right; the right **Á** hand is held with the palm facing down (if the hand were opened, the fingers would point away from the signer).	The hands are held in front of the body; the right hand is held above the left hand.	The right hand makes a small clockwise circle in the horizontal plane and then makes a short downward movement to touch the left palm.	bible * holy bible * holy book* scripture *	203
The left **B** hand is held with the palm facing right and the fingers pointing away from the signer; the right **B** hand is held with the palm facing left and the fingers pointing away from the signer.	The hands are held in front of the body with the palms together.	The hands twist at the wrists, so that the palms face up.		

Notes   * The second part of this sign may be produced with a repeated movement.

Bɑ> Áɒ⊥ ⊥> ⁰⁰ᵉᵛˣ // //

Ø B>⊥ ₁ₓ B<⊥ ᵃ˙

204 $\overline{B}a> {}_x \dot{A}\sigma\bot \,{}^>_x$

205 $\overline{B}a> {}_\prime \dot{A}\bot\wedge \,{}^o_{\overset{v}{<}}\cdot$

206 $\overline{B}a> \dot{A}<\bot \,{}^{\overset{v \times \wedge}{\overset{>}{a}}}$

207 $B\top> {}_x \dot{A}\top<_{\scriptscriptstyle?} \,{}^>_x$

208 $B>\bot {}_\prime \dot{A}\sigma\bot \,{}^{x\cdot}$

209 $B>\bot {}_\prime \dot{A}\top< \,{}^{\overset{v}{v}}$

The thumb is extended from the fist.

Handshape and orientation	Location, hand arrangement and contact	Movement	Glosses	
The left **B** hand is held with the palm facing up and the fingers pointing to the right; the right **A** hand is held with the palm facing down (if the hand were opened, the fingers would point away from the signer).	The hands are held in front of the body; the right knuckles rest on the left palm.	The right hand moves to the right, maintaining contact with the left palm throughout.	always frequent habitual normal ordinary regular usual	204
The left **B** hand is held with the palm facing up and the fingers pointing to the right; the right **A** hand is held with the palm facing away from the signer (if the hand were opened, the fingers would point up).	The hands are held side by side in front of the body; the right hand is held higher than the left hand.	The right hand makes a short movement down and, at the same time, to the left; the movement is repeated several times.	sprinkle vinegar vinegar oil[1] pour oil[1]	205

Notes   1   If the right hand is held above the left hand with the palm facing away from the signer and the thumb pointing down, and the hand makes a small anticlockwise circle in the horizontal plane, the sign produced is **oil, pour oil**.

$$\overline{}\quad B\alpha> \;\mid\; \dot{A}\bot<\;{}^{\circ}_{\textstyle{<\atop \scriptstyle 1}}$$

The left **B** hand is held with the palm facing up and the fingers pointing to the right; the right **A** hand is held with the palm facing left (if the hand were opened, the fingers would point away from the signer).	The hands are held in front of the body; the right hand is held above the left hand.	The right hand moves down to touch the left palm and then moves up and to the right while twisting at the wrist, so that the palm faces up.	fantastic terrific	206

Non-manual features   The nose is wrinkled and the top teeth are touching the lower lip; the mouth opens so that the lips are stretched.

The left **B** hand is held with the palm facing towards the signer and the fingers pointing to the right; the right **A** hand is held with the palm facing towards the signer (if the hand were opened, the fingers would point to the left).	The hands are held in front of the body; the back of the right hand rests against the left palm.	The right hand moves to the right with the back of the hand maintaining contact with the left palm throughout.	always* frequent* habitual* normal* ordinary* regular* usual*	207

Notes   *   This sign can be produced with the right knuckles maintaining contact with the left palm as the right hand moves to the right.

$$B\top> \;{}_{\times}\; \dot{A}<\bot_{\varphi}\;{}^{\textstyle >}_{\textstyle \times}$$

The left **B** hand is held with the palm facing right and the fingers pointing away from the signer; the right **A** hand is held with the palm facing down (if the hand were opened, the fingers would point away from the signer).	The hands are held side by side in front of the body.	The right thumbtip taps the centre of the left palm twice.	difficult difficulty hard problem	208
The left **B** hand is held with the palm facing right and the fingers pointing away from the signer; the right **A** hand is held with the palm facing towards the signer (if the hand were opened, the fingers would point to the left).	The hands are held side by side in front of the body.	The right hand moves down, so that the right knuckles brush across the left palm.	begin beginner commence initial initiate launch original originate start	209

210 Ca⊥, Ȧⲧⴸ $\left(\frac{n}{\top}\right)$˙

211 Ø Ȧɑ⊥ Ȧɑ⊥ ⱴ̊

212 Ø Ȧⴸ⊥ Ȧⴸ⊥ ⱴ̊

213 Ø Ȧⴸ⊥ Ȧⴸ⊥ ⸓̇

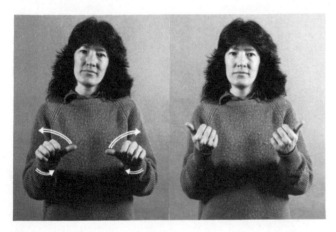

214 Ø Ȧⴸ⊥ ｜ Ȧⴸ⊥ ⸓̊⊤

215 Ø Ȧⴸ⊥ ｜ Ȧⴸ⊥ ⸓ⱴ̊

Handshape and orientation	Location, hand arrangement and contact	Movement	Glosses	
The left Ċ hand is held with the palm facing up (if the hand were opened, the fingers would point away from the signer). The right Ȧ hand is held with the palm facing towards the signer (if the hand were opened, the fingers would point down).	The hands are held in front of the body; the left hand is held nearer to the signer than the right hand.	The right hand bends away from the signer at the wrist while moving towards the signer; the movement is repeated.	peel a round vegetable/ fruit with a peeler * peel potatoes/spuds * peeler * potato * spud *	210

Notes   * This sign may also be produced using two G̈ hands.

G̈αⱢ, G̈ᴛⱽ ⁽ᵑ₊₁⁾˙

| Two Ȧ hands are held with the palms facing up (if the hands were opened, the fingers would all point away from the signer). | The hands are held in front of the body. | The hands make a short downward movement while twisting firmly at the wrists, so that the palms face down. | achieve <br> achievement <br> succeed <br> success <br> successful | 211 |

| Two Ȧ hands are held with the palms facing down (if the hands are opened, the fingers would all point away from the signer). | The hands are held in front of the body. | The hands make a short firm downward movement. | adopt *
 adoption <br> approval <br> approve *
 bless *
 blessing <br> confirm *
 confirmation | 212 |

Notes   * Directional verb.

| Two Ȧ hands are held with the palms facing down (if the hands were opened, the fingers would all point away from the signer). | The hands are held in front of the body. | The hands twist sharply apart at the wrists, so that the palms face up. | excellent *†
 fantastic *†
 fine *
 great *†
 marvellous *†
 smashing *†
 superb *†
 very good *†
 brainwave [1]
 genius [1] | 213 |

Non-manual features   The lips are pressed together and stretched.

Notes   * This sign can be produced using one hand only.

Ø ȦɔⱢ ᵚ˃˙

   † This sign may be produced without the lips pressed together and stretched but with the cheeks puffed out.

   1 This sign (using one or both hands) may be used as the second part of a compound sign meaning **brainwave, genius** (see 511 Note 1 for the first part of the sign).

∩ G̈<ʌ ˣ ∥ Ø ȦɔⱢ ᵚ˃˙   or

∩ G̈<ʌ ˣ ∥ Ø ȦɔⱢ ȦɔⱢ ᵚ˦˙

| Two Ȧ hands are held with the palms facing down (if the hands were opened, the fingers would all point away from the signer). | The hands are held side by side in front of the body. | The hands move apart and then make a short movement towards the signer. | fat <br> stout <br> obese [1]
 obesity [1] | 214 |

Notes   1 If the cheeks are puffed out, the sign produced is **obese, obesity.**

| Two Ȧ hands are held with the palms facing down (if the hands were opened, the fingers would all point away from the signer). | The hands are held side by side in front of the body. | The hands make a clockwise circle in the vertical plane at right angles to the signer's body, ending with a short, firm downward movement. | all right *
 bless <br> complete *
 completion *
 conclude *
 conclusion *
 OK <br> okay <br> safe * | 215 |

Notes   * This sign may be produced with the hands making circles (the left hand moves anticlockwise, the right hand moves clockwise) in the vertical plane parallel to the signer's body, ending with a short firm downward movement.

Ø ȦɔⱢ , ȦɔⱢ ᵒᵉᵥ˦

216 Ø ȦT∧ ȦT∧ $\overset{\overset{.}{\lor}}{o}$

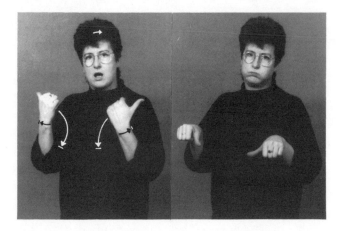

217 Ø ȦT∨ ᵢ ȦT∨ᵧ $\overset{(\overset{o}{⊥}\overset{o\cdot}{\lor}\sim\cdot)}{}$

218 Ø ȦT> ȦT< $\overset{\overset{.}{⊥}\cdot}{}$

219 Ø Ȧ⊥∧ ᵢ Ȧ⊥∧ $\overset{\overset{o}{\sim}\sim\cdot}{}$

220 Ø Ȧ>⊥ Ȧ<⊥ $\overset{\overset{.}{⊥}}{}$

221 Ø Ȧ>⊥ Ȧ<⊥ $\overset{\overset{@}{\lor}\cdot}{}$

222 Ø Ȧ>⊥ Ȧ<⊥ $\overset{x\div[55]}{\overset{o}{\square}}$

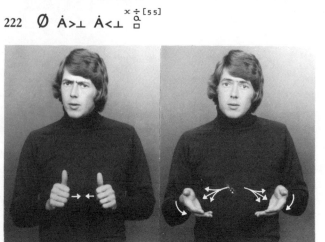

Handshape and orientation	Location, hand arrangement and contact	Movement	Glosses	
Two **Ȧ** hands are held with the palms facing towards the signer (if the hands were opened, the fingers would all point up).	The hands are held in front of the body.	The hands move down while twisting firmly at the wrists, so that the palms face down.	eventually * finally * got it * last (at last) * manage *	216

Non-manual features   The mouth is open; as the hands move, the head tilts to one side and the mouth closes with the cheeks puffed out.

     Notes   * This sign may be produced using one hand only.   Ø Ȧⲧ∧ ⱴ̇

| Two **Ȧ** hands are held with the palms facing towards the signer (if the hands were opened, the fingers would all point down). | The hands are held side by side in front of the body; the right hand is held nearer to the signer than the left hand. | The hands alternately make a short movement away from the signer and then a short, firm downward movement; the movements are repeated with the hands moving away from the signer throughout. | jigsaw
jigsaw puzzle
put a jigsaw/
  jigsaw puzzle
  together | 217 |
| Two **Ȧ** hands are held with the palms facing towards the signer (if the hands were opened, the left fingers would point to the right and the right fingers would point to the left). | The hands are held in front of the body. | The hands make two short movements away from the signer. | acceptable *
all right *
average *
do (will do) *
fair *
passable * | 218 |

Non-manual features   The head is tilted to the right and the nose is wrinkled.

     Notes   * This sign can be produced using one hand only.   Ø Ȧⲧ< ⁱ̊·

Two **Ȧ** hands are held with the palms facing away from the signer (if the hands were opened, the fingers would all point up).	The hands are held side by side in front of the body.	The hands make alternate short up and down movements.	league results	219
The left **Ȧ** hand is held with the palm facing right; the right **Ȧ** hand is held with the palm facing left (if the hands were opened, the fingers would all point away from the signer).	The hands are held in front of the body.	The hands make a short, firm movement away from the signer.	excellent fantastic fine great marvellous smashing superb very good	220
The left **Ȧ** hand is held with the palm facing right; the right **Ȧ** hand is held with the palm facing left (if the hands were opened, the fingers would all point away from the signer).	The hands are held in front of the body.	The hands make circles (the left hand moves anticlockwise, the right hand moves clockwise) in the vertical plane parallel to the signer's body.	complete * completion * conclude * conclusion * finish *	221

     Notes   * This sign may be produced using one hand only.   Ø Ȧ<⊥ ⱴ̊·

| The left **Ȧ** hand is held with the palm facing right; the right **Ȧ** hand is held with the palm facing left (if the hands were opened, the fingers would all point away from the signer). | The hands are held in front of the body. | The hands move towards each other and then move apart while twisting at the wrists so that the palms face up and, at the same time, opening (forming two **5** hands). | ineffectual *
no good *
useless * | 222 |

Non-manual features   Appropriate negative non-manual features must be used.

     Notes   * This sign may be produced using one hand only.   Ø Ȧ<⊥ ^{< > [5]}

223 Ø Ȧ>⊥ Ȧ<⊥ $\overset{\circ}{{}^{\perp}}(\overset{\vee}{{}_{\text{T}}}_{\perp})\overset{\circ}{{}^{\perp}}$

224 Ø Ȧ>⊥ ₁ Ȧ<⊥ ˣ·

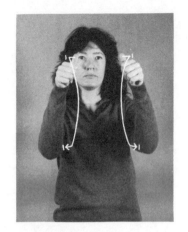

225 Ø Ȧ>⊥ ₁ Ȧ<⊥ $\overset{@N·}{\underset{\text{v}}{\perp}}$

226 Ø Ȧ>⊥ ₁ Ȧ<⊥ $\overset{@N·}{\underset{\text{v}}{\perp}}$

227 Ø Ȧ>⊥ ₁ˣ Ȧ<⊥ $\overset{@}{\underset{>}{\perp}}$

228 Ø Ȧ>⊥ ˣ Ȧ<⊥₉ $\overset{\div}{\perp}$

[210]

The thumb is extended from the fist.

Handshape and orientation	Location, hand arrangement and contact	Movement	Glosses	
The left **Å** hand is held with the palm facing right; the right **Å** hand is held with the palm facing left (if the hands were opened, the fingers would all point away from the signer).	The hands are held in front of the body.	The hands make a short, firm movement away from the signer and then move down and towards the signer in an arc before making another short, firm movement away from the signer.	**notice** **notice board** **poster** **put up a notice/** **poster**	223
The left **Å** hand is held with the palm facing right; the right **Å** hand is held with the palm facing left (if the hands were opened, the fingers would all point away from the signer).	The hands are held side by side in front of the body.	The knuckles tap together twice.	**colleague** **friend** **mate** **pal** **paper***	224

    Notes   * Regional sign.

The left **Å** hand is held with the palm facing right; the right **Å** hand is held with the palm facing left (if the hands were opened, the fingers would all point away from the signer).	The hands are held side by side in front of the body.	The hands make alternate clockwise circles in the vertical plane at right angles to the signer's body.	**admire*** **congratulate*** **congratulations** **favourite** **fond (be fond of)*** **glorify*** **honour*** **popular** **praise***	225

    Notes   * Directional verb.

The left **Å** hand is held with the palm facing right; the right **Å** hand is held with the palm facing left (if the hands were opened, the fingers would all point away from the signer).	The hands are held side by side at head height in front of the body.	The hands make alternate clockwise circles in the vertical plane at right angles to the signer's body.	**glorify*** **honour*** **praise***	226

  Non-manual features   The eyegaze is directed up and forward.

    Notes   * Directional verb.

The left **Å** hand is held with the palm facing right; the right **Å** hand is held with the palm facing left (if the hands were opened, the fingers would all point away from the signer).	The hands are held in front of the body with the knuckles held together.	The hands remain together and make a clockwise circle in the horizontal plane.	**agree*** **agreement*** **agreement** **(in agreement)*** **associates*** **consensus*** **favour (in favour)*** **fellowship***	227

    Notes   * This sign may be produced with an anticlockwise circling movement.

Ø Å>⊥ ₓ Å<⊥ ⫸

The left **Å** hand is held with the palm facing right; the right **Å** hand is held with the palm facing left (if the hands were opened, the fingers would all point away from the signer).	The hands are held in front of the body; the right hand is held nearer to the signer than the left hand with the right knuckles touching the base of the left thumb.	The right hand moves towards the signer, and, at the same time, the left hand moves away from the signer.	**company** **factory** **firm**	228

229 Ø Ȧ>⊥ Ȧ<⊥, ᵒ˙ᵢ˙

230 [] Ȧ>ʌ Ȧ<ʌ ˇₓ

231 [] Ȧ>⊥ Ȧ<⊥ ˣᵒˇ÷[ᵇᵇ]ₓω̲

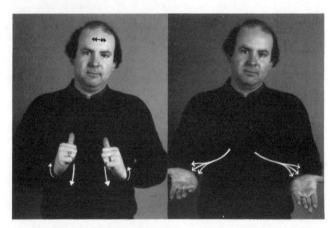

232 [] Ȧ>⊥ Ȧ<⊥ @ₜ✕@ₜᴎ˙

[212]

Handshape and orientation	Location, hand arrangement and contact	Movement	Glosses
The left **Å** hand is held with the palm facing right; the right **Å** hand is held with the palm facing left (if the hands were opened, the fingers would all point away from the signer).	The hands are held in front of the body; the right hand is held nearer to the signer than the left hand.	The hands make two short, firm movements away from the signer.	encourage * encouragement fan support *¹ supporter ¹ back up *² favour *² advocacy ³ advocate *³ 229

Notes * Directional verb.

1 If the hands are held side by side, and the movement is not repeated, the sign produced is **support, supporter**.

$$\emptyset \quad \dot{A}{>}\bot \;{}_{|}\; \dot{A}{<}\bot \quad \overset{\circ\cdot}{\bot}$$

2 If the knuckles of the right hand are held against the heel of the left hand, and the movement is not repeated, the sign produced is **back up, favour**.

$$\emptyset \quad \dot{A}{>}\bot \;{}_{x}\; A{<}\bot_{\wp} \quad \overset{\circ\cdot}{\bot}$$

3 If the right hand moves away from the signer to touch the left hand, and then the hands remain together while moving firmly away from the signer, the sign produced is **advocacy, advocate**.

$$A{>}\bot \; A{<}\bot_{\wp} \;\overset{\bot x}{\mathbin{/\!/}}\; \emptyset \; \dot{A}{>}\bot \;{}_{x}\; \dot{A}{<}\bot_{\wp} \quad \overset{\cdot}{\bot}$$

The left **Å** hand is held with the palm facing right; the right **Å** hand is held with the palm left (if the hands were opened, the fingers would all point up).	The hands are held with the thumbtips touching the sides of the chest.	The hands move down; the thumbtips maintain contact with the chest throughout.	smart * suit * well-dressed * cannot be bothered †¹ can't be bothered †¹ tired †¹ fed up †² 230

Notes * This sign may be produced using two **Y** hands.

$$\ulcorner \quad Y{>}\wedge \; Y{<}\wedge \quad \overset{\vee}{x}$$

† This sign may be produced using one hand only.

$$[\,]^{<} \quad \dot{A}{<}\wedge \quad \overset{\vee}{x}$$

1 If the tongue protrudes between the teeth and the head tilts forward, the sign produced is **cannot be bothered, can't be bothered, tired**.

2 If the lips are stretched, and the corners of the mouth are turned down, the sign produced is **fed up**.

The left **Å** hand is held with the palm facing right; the right **Å** hand is held with the palm facing left (if the hands were opened, the fingers would all point away from the signer).	The hands are held with the thumb tips touching the chest.	The hands make a short downward movement, maintaining contact with the chest, and then twist apart and away from the signer while opening (forming two **Ḃ** hands) so that the palms face up.	unfit* unwell* 231

Non-manual features The brows are furrowed and the head shakes slightly.

Notes * This sign may be produced using one hand only.

$$[\,] \quad \dot{A}{<}\bot \quad \overset{\overset{\circ}{\vee}\,>\,[\text{ß}]}{\underset{\square}{x\,\omega}}$$

The left **Å** hand is held with the palm facing right; the right **Å** hand is held with the palm facing left (if the hands were opened, the fingers would all point away from the signer).	The hands are held in front of the chest.	The hands make alternate anticlockwise circles in the vertical plane at right angles to the signer's body, so that the thumbs brush the chest in completing each circle.	pride proud boast¹ boastful¹ brag¹ poser¹ poseur¹ show off¹ show-off¹ 232

Notes 1 If the head tilts back, and the hands make alternate downward movements, maintaining contact with the chest through each movement, the sign produced is **boast, boastful, brag, poser, poseur, show off, show-off**.

$$[\,] \quad \dot{A}{>}\bot \; \dot{A}{<}\bot \quad \overset{\vee\wedge\,\cdot}{x}$$

233　[] Ȧ>⊥ Ȧ<⊥ $^{(ᑎ×)^{ᑎ}}_{ᣥ}$　　234　⌐⌐ ȦT> ȦT< $^{×ᑎ}_{ᥳ}$ ·

235　⌐⌐ Ȧ⊥ᣥ Ȧ⊥ᣥ $^{°⊥}_{ᣥᣥ}$　　236　⌐⌐ Ȧ>ᣥ Ȧ<ᣥ $^{×⊥[ss]}_{ᄆ}$

237　⌐⌐ Ȧᖷ⊥ Ȧᖷ⊥ $^{×}_{ᑎ}$

[214]

The thumb is extended from the fist.

Handshape and orientation	Location, hand arrangement and contact	Movement	Glosses	
The left **Å** hand is held with the palm facing right; the right **Å** hand is held with the palm facing left (if the hands were opened, the fingers would all point away from the signer).	The hands are held in front of the chest.	The hands make alternate movements towards the signer, so that the backs of the thumbs touch the chest; the movements are repeated.	boast boastful brag poser poseur show off show-off	233
Non-manual features The eyes are narrowed and the cheeks are puffed out.				
Two **Å** hands are held with the palms facing towards the signer (if the hands were opened, the left fingers would point to the right, and the right fingers would point to the left).	The hands are held against the upper chest.	The shoulders move forward and back alternately several times; the hands are held against the upper chest throughout.	hike hiker hiking ramble rambler rambling backpack[1] rucksack[1] duffle bag[2] satchel[2] shoulder-bag[2]	234

Notes 1 If the hands are held against the chest and the elbows bend in towards the body several times, the sign produced is **backpack, rucksack**.

        2 If only one hand is used, the sign produced is **duffle bag, satchel, shoulder-bag**.

$$\ulcorner 1\,\ \dot{J}\dot{A}\tau\!\!> \ \dot{J}\dot{A}\tau\!\!< \ \begin{smallmatrix}x&\cdot\\ \tiny\Box\\ \tau\end{smallmatrix}$$

$$\ulcorner 1\!\!< \ \dot{J}\dot{A}\tau\!\!< \ \begin{smallmatrix}x&\cdot\\ \tiny\Box\\ \tau\end{smallmatrix}$$

Two **Å** hands are held with the palms facing away from the signer (if the hands were opened, the fingers would all point up).	The hands are held in front of the upper chest.	The hands make a short upward movement, brushing the chest, and then move firmly down and, at the same time, away from the signer.	adore* favour* favourite fond (be fond of)* love*	235
Notes * Directional verb.				
The left **Å** hand is held with the palm facing right; the right **Å** hand is held with the palm facing left (if the hands were opened, the fingers would all point up).	The hands are held with the backs of the thumbs resting against the chest.	The hands move away from the signer and downwards while opening (forming two **5** hands).	relax* relaxation* retire* retired* retirement*	236

$$\ulcorner 1\quad \dot{A}\!\!<\!\!\wedge \ \begin{smallmatrix}x&\perp&[5]\\ &v\\ &\Box\end{smallmatrix}$$

Notes * This sign may be produced using one hand only.				
Two **Å** hands are held with the palms facing down (if the hands were opened, the fingers would all point away from the signer).	The hands are held with the backs of the thumbs against the waist.	The hands bend down from the wrists; the thumbs are held against the waist throughout.	hunger hungry	237

238 Ø Âɑ⊥ ᵒ͘⊥˙

239 Ø Âɑ< ᵒ͘⊥˙

240 Ø Âʊ< ꞷ͘⊤˄

241 Ø Â⊤v ᵒ͘z˙

242 Ø Â⊥˄ ᴅ͘⊥˙

The Â handshape has three main *variants*: the most frequent variant is the one in which the thumb is held straight, as in **cement** (sign 252) and **administer** (sign 272); a second variant has the thumb slightly bent with the thumb edge held slightly lower on the index finger, as in **almost** (sign 238) and **marbles** (sign 246): this variant is used most frequently in signs involving a flicking action; a third variant, used especially in signs which involve a pinching action, has a small gap between the thumb and index finger, as in **bare** (sign 257).

Â has one primary *classifier* function within the productive lexicon and appears as a classifying component in established signs:

– it is used as a *handling* classifier to indicate the handling of narrow, cylindrical objects and narrow, flat objects as well as the narrow, cylindrical or flat components of larger objects. Examples include **briefcase** (sign 247), **badminton racquet** (sign 245), **hammer** (sign 251) and **drumsticks** (sign 277). It may be used for small objects whose use typically involves fine, controlled action, as in **rubber** (sign 243) and **key** (sign 250). It may also be used for flat materials such as paper and cloth, as in the signs **magazine** (sign 283) and **anorak** (sign 287).

The choice between Â and **A** in the productive lexicon is usually linked to the perceived extent of the control required in handling specific objects: objects associated with actions requiring more finely controlled movements usually use Â rather than **A**.

Â expresses the letter **t** of the Irish manual alphabet. As such it occurs in initial letter handshape signs borrowed from Irish Sign Language such as **tea** and **terrible** (see *Introduction*).

Handshape and orientation	Location, hand arrangement and contact	Movement	Glosses	
The Â hand is held with the palm facing up (if the hand were opened, the fingers would point away from the signer).	The hand is held in front of the body.	The hand makes two short movements away from the signer.	**almost** **nearly**	**238**
Non-manual features The eyes are narrowed.				
The Â hand is held with the palm facing up (if the hand were opened, the fingers would point to the left).	The hand is held in front of the body.	The hand makes two short movements away from the signer.	**cook** **cooker** **cookery** **cooking** **feed** * **fry** **frying pan** **fry up** **saucepan**	**239**
Notes * Directional verb.				
The Â hand is held with the palm facing down (if the hand were opened, the fingers would point to the left).	The hand is held in front of the body.	The hand twists at the wrist, so that the palm faces towards the signer, while moving up; the movement is repeated.	**cereal** **dessert** **dessert spoon** **eat cereal/dessert/ porridge/pudding/ sweet with a dessert spoon** **eat soup with a soup spoon** **eat with a dessert spoon / soup spoon** **porridge** **pudding** **soup** **soup spoon** **sweet**	**240**
The Â hand is held with the palm facing towards the signer (if the hand were opened, the fingers would point down).	The hand is held in front of the body.	The hand makes several short movements from side to side, bending at the wrist.	**hand bell** **president** **ring a hand bell**	**241**
The Â hand is held with the palm facing away from the signer (if the hand were opened, the fingers would point up).	The hand is held in front of the body.	The hand bends firmly away from the signer at the wrist; the movement is repeated.	**auction** **auctioneer** **court** **gavel** *	**242**
Notes * This sign may be produced with a G̈ hand.		Ø G̈⊥⋀ T̈		

243 Ø Â⊥ʌ $\overset{\overset{o}{n}}{z}$ ·

244 Ø Â<ʌ $\overset{n}{\underset{v}{\perp}}$

245 Ø Â<ʌ $\overset{\overset{o}{n}}{\perp}$ ·

246 Ø Â<v $\overset{\cdot}{\square}$[A]

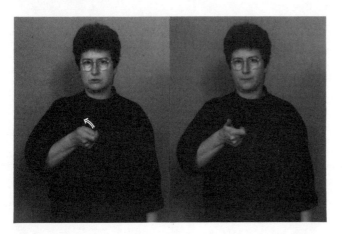

247 Ø Â<v $\overset{\wedge}{\cdot}$ ·

248 Ø Â<v $\overset{\overline{\underline{I}}}{N}$ ·

249 Ø Â<⊥ $\overset{\overset{o}{\cdot}}{<}$

250 Ø Â<⊥ $\overset{\overset{\omega o}{z}}{\cdot}$ ·

[218]

Â The bent index finger is extended from the fist, enclosing the top of the extended thumb.

243-250

Handshape and orientation	Location, hand arrangement and contact	Movement	Glosses	
The Â hand is held with the palm facing away from the signer (if the hand were opened, the fingers would point up).	The hand is held in front of the body.	The hand makes several short, sharp movements from side to side, bending at the wrist.	erase eraser rub out rubber	243
The Â hand is held with the palm facing left (if the hand were opened, the fingers would point up).	The hand is held in front of the body.	The hand bends away from the signer at the wrist while moving down.	appeal* ban* booked* lay off* pay off* prosecute* prosecution redundant (make redundant)* sue* suspend* suspension*	244

    Notes   * Directional verb.

The Â hand is held with the palm facing left (if the hand were opened, the fingers would point up).	The hand is held in front of the body.	The hand makes a short bending movement away from the signer at the wrist; the movement is repeated.	badminton badminton player badminton racquet play badminton	245
The Â hand is held with the palm facing left (if the the hand were opened, the fingers would point down).	The hand is held in front of the body.	The thumb flicks open sharply (forming an Â hand).	marble play marbles* marbles¹	246

    Notes   * This sign may be produced with a repeated movement.   ∅ Â<v □ [A] ·

                1 This sign is produced with a repeated movement.   ∅ Â<v □ [A] ·

The Â hand is held with the palm facing left (if the hand were opened, the fingers would point down).	The hand is held in front of the body.	The hand makes two short upward movements.	briefcase carry a briefcase/ handbag handbag	247
The Â hand is held with the palm facing left (if the hand were opened, the fingers would point down).	The hand is held in front of the body.	The hand moves down and, at the same time, away from the signer and then up and, at the same time, towards the signer; the movements are repeated.	hoover vacuum vacuum cleaner poke¹ poker¹ stoke¹	248

    Notes   1 If the movement is changed to a repeated movement down and, at the same time, away from the the signer, the sign produced is **poke, poker, stoke.**   ∅ Â<v ⊥v ·

The Â hand is held with the palm facing left (if the hand were opened, the fingers would point away from the signer).	The hand is held in front of the body.	The hand moves firmly to the left while twisting at the wrist, so that the palm faces up.	hit with a rounders bat/small bat play rounders rounders rounders bat small bat	249
The Â hand is held with the palm facing left (if the hand were opened, the fingers would point away from the signer).	The hand is held in front of the body.	The hand makes several short twisting movements from side to side at the wrist.	key lock with a key¹ unlock with a key²	250

    Notes   1 If the hand is held with the palm facing down and twists at the wrist, so that the palm faces up, the sign produced is **lock with a key.**   ∅ Â⌐⊥ ª

                2 If the hand is held with the palm facing up and twists at the wrist so that the palm faces down, the sign produced is **unlock with a key.**   ∅ Âª⊥ ᵒ

251 Ø Â<⊥ $\overset{\cdot}{\underset{v}{\square}}$

252 Ø Â<⊥ $^{<v>}$

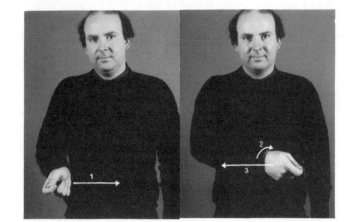

253 ̄∩ Â<∧ $\overset{\square}{\underset{\top}{\cdot}}$

254 ∩ Â<∧ $\overset{\circ}{v}$

255 ○ Â<∧ $\overset{\overset{e}{\circ}\cdot}{\underset{\top}{<}}$

256 Ǝ Â⊤∧ $\overset{v\cdot}{x}$

257 Ǝ Â<∧ $^{(\frac{\pi}{z}\cdot)}$

Â

The bent index finger is extended from the fist, enclosing the top of the extended thumb.

Handshape and orientation	Location, hand arrangement and contact	Movement	Glosses	
The **Â** hand is held with the palm facing left (if the hand were opened, the fingers would point away from the signer).	The hand is held in front of the body.	The hand bends sharply downwards from the wrist; the movement is repeated.	**hammer**	251
The **Â** hand is held with the palm facing left (if the hand were opened, the fingers would point away from the signer).	The hand is held in front of the body.	The hand moves to the left and then twists at the wrist, so that the palm faces down, before moving back to the right.	**bricklayer** **cement**	252
The **Â** hand is held with the palm facing left (if the hand were opened, the fingers would point up).	The hand is held beside the forehead.	The hand bends towards the signer from the wrist; the movement is repeated.	**comb** **comb one's hair**	253
The **Â** hand is held with the palm facing left (if the hand were opened, the fingers would point up).	The hand is held in front of the forehead.	The hand makes a short downward movement.	**cap** **Council for the Advancement of Communication with Deaf People (C.A.C.D.P.)** **change roles**[1] **switch hats**[1]	254

Notes 1 If the sign is produced using two hands in which the right hand bends away from the signer and the left hand bends towards the signer from the wrist alternately, the sign produced is **change roles, switch hats**.

$$\cap \ \hat{A}>\wedge \ _| \ \hat{A}<\wedge \ {\binom{D}{T}_{\times}}^{\sim \cdot}$$

The **Â** hand is held with the palm facing left (if the hand were opened, the fingers would point up).	The hand is held at head height in front of the body.	The hand makes small anticlockwise circles in the horizontal plane.	**achieve** **achievement** **alleluia** **hallelujah** **Italian** **Italy** **succeed** **success** **successful** **win** **cheer**[1] **hooray**[1]	255

Notes 1 If the mouth is open wide, the sign produced is **cheer, hooray**.

The **Â** hand is held with the palm facing towards the signer (if the hand were opened, the fingers would point up).	The hand is held with the back of the index finger resting against the cheek.	The hand moves down, maintaining contact with the cheek; the movement is repeated.	**razor** **razor blade** **shave with a razor**	256
The **Â** hand is held with the palm facing left (if the hand were opened, the fingers would point up).	The hand is held with the thumb and index finger pinching the cheek.	The hand moves from side to side, holding the cheek throughout.	**bare*** **beef** **butcher** **cheek** **cheeky** **flesh*** **impudent** **insult** **meat** **naked*** **nude***	257

Notes * This sign may be produced with no movement.

$$3 \ \hat{A}<\wedge \ ^{\mathbb{x}}$$

258 ⌣ Âᴅ< $\overset{\circ}{z}$·

259 ⌣ ÂT< $\overset{\circ}{v}$

260 ⌣ Â⊥ʌ ×$\overset{\circ}{\underset{⊥}{ᴅ}}$·

261 ˃ᴦ⌐ Â<ʌ $\overset{\omega}{\underset{×}{T}}$·

262 ⸜₉Â˃T $\overset{\overset{\omega@}{˅}}{˅}$·

263 ‾AT˃₉ Â˃T $\left(\overset{˅}{\underset{˃}{\land}}\right)$·

264 Âᴅ⊥ Âᴅ⊥ $\overset{(\overset{\omega}{˂})·}{}$

265 ‾ÂT˃ × ÂT< ^

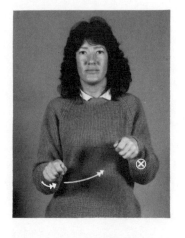

[222]

Â *The bent index finger is extended from the fist, enclosing the top of the extended thumb.*

Handshape and orientation	Location, hand arrangement and contact	Movement	Glosses	
The **Â** hand is held with the palm facing down (if the hand were opened, the fingers would point to the left).	The hand is held in front of the mouth.	The hand makes several short movements from side to side.	brush one's teeth * toothpaste * toothbrush [1]	258

Notes   * This sign may be produced with several short up and down movements.

⌣ Âↄ< ᴺ̊.

     1 If the movement is repeated once only, the sign produced is **toothbrush.**

The **Â** hand is held with the palm facing towards the signer (if the hand were opened, the fingers would point to the left).	The hand is held in front of the mouth.	The hand makes a short, sharp downward movement.	dentist extraction extract a tooth	259
The **Â** hand is held with the palm facing away from the signer (if the hand were opened, the fingers would point up).	The hand is held with the back of the index finger touching the mouth.	The hand makes two short bending movements away from the signer at the wrist.	budgerigar budgie	260
The **Â** hand is held with the palm facing left (if the hand were opened, the fingers would point up).	The hand is held resting against the left side of the upper chest.	The hand twists at the wrist, so that the palm faces towards the signer, maintaining contact with the chest; the movement is repeated.	detective prostitute [1]	261

Notes   1 If the hand is held at the left shoulder, the sign produced is **prostitute.**

ˠ1 Â<ʌ ᵂᵀ×.

The **Â** hand is held with the palm facing right (if the hand were opened, the fingers would point towards the signer).	The hand is held in front of the left arm; the left elbow is bent and held away from the body.	The hand makes anticlockwise circles, twisting at the wrist, in the vertical plane parallel to the signer's body.	beat with a whisk cook cookery cooking mix with a whisk whisk	262
The left **A** hand is held with the palm facing towards the signer (if the hand were opened, the fingers would point to the right). The right **Â** hand is held with the palm facing right (if the hand were opened, the fingers would point towards the signer).	The hands are held in front of the body; the left hand is held lower and nearer to the signer than the right hand.	The right hand moves down while bending up at the wrist; the movement is repeated twice with the hand moving to the right throughout.	peel a banana	263
Two **Â** hands are held with the palms facing down (if the hands were opened, the fingers would all point away from the signer).	The hands are held in front of the body.	The right hand moves to the left while twisting at the wrist, so that the palm faces left; the movement is repeated.	dustpan and brush sweep up with a dustpan and brush	264
Two **Â** hands are held with the palms facing towards the signer (if the hands were opened, the left fingers would point to the right and the right fingers would point to the left).	The hands are held in front of the body; the right hand rests on the left hand.	The right hand moves up.	brolly open a brolly/ parasol/umbrella parasol umbrella	265

266 $\underline{\hat{A}}>V_?$ ₁× $\hat{A}<V$ ⁿ_<

267 $\overline{\hat{G}}>\perp$ $\hat{A}<\perp_?$ $\overset{.}{\underset{V}{n}}\cdot$

268 $\overline{B}a\perp$ $\hat{A}\upsilon\perp$ ^{o.}_{V×}

269 $\overline{B}a>$ $\jmath\hat{A}<\wedge_?$ [.]_{⊥×n⊥}

270 Ø $\hat{A}a\perp$ $\hat{A}a\perp$ ^o_⊥_V·

271 Ø $\hat{A}a\perp$ $\hat{A}a\perp$ ^{@.}_{⊥×}_V

Â *The bent index finger is extended from the fist, enclosing the top of the extended thumb.*

Handshape and orientation	Location, hand arrangement and contact	Movement	Glosses	
The left Â hand is held with the palm facing right; the right Â hand is held with the palm facing left (if the hands were opened, the fingers would all point down).	The hands are held side by side in front of the body; the left index finger and thumb are held against the heel of the right hand.	The right hand bends to the left at the wrist; the hands are held together throughout.	**putt** **putter**	266
The left **G** hand is held with the palm facing right (if the hand were opened, the fingers would point away from the signer). The right Â hand is held with the palm facing left (if the hand were opened, the fingers would point away from the signer).	The hands are held in front of the body; the right hand is held higher and nearer to the signer than the left hand.	The right hand bends firmly down from the wrist; the movement is repeated.	**hammer** **hammer a nail/** **tack with a hammer***	267

Notes   * This sign may be produced with a left **F** hand.

$$\overline{\text{F}} \gt \!\!\perp\ \hat{\text{A}} \lt\!\!\perp_{\varrho}\ \overset{\cdot}{\underset{v}{\scriptstyle D}}\cdot$$

The left **B** hand is held with the palm facing up and the fingers pointing away from the signer; the right Â hand is held with the palm facing down (if the hand were opened, the fingers would point away from the signer).	The hands are held in front of the body; the right hand is held above the left hand.	The right hand makes a short firm downward movement to touch the left palm.	**market*** **marketing*†** **sale*** **sell***	268

Notes   * The following notes apply to all glosses:

This sign may be produced using a right **G̈** hand.

$$\overline{\text{B}}\alpha\!\perp\ \ddot{\text{G}}\text{ʊ}\!\perp\ \overset{\overset{\circ\circ}{v}}{}_{x}$$

This sign may be produced with a repeated movement.

$$\overline{\text{B}}\alpha\!\perp\ \hat{\text{A}}\text{ʊ}\!\perp\ (\overset{\overset{\circ\circ}{v}}{}_{x})\cdot\ \text{or}$$
$$\overline{\text{B}}\alpha\!\perp\ \ddot{\text{G}}\text{ʊ}\!\perp\ (\overset{\overset{\circ\circ}{v}}{}_{x})\cdot$$

† This sign may be produced with both hands moving to the right throughout.

$$\emptyset\left(\overline{\text{B}}\alpha\!\perp\ \hat{\text{A}}\text{ʊ}\!\perp\ (\overset{\overset{\circ\circ}{v}}{}_{x})\cdot\right)\!\gt\ \text{or}$$
$$\emptyset\left(\overline{\text{B}}\alpha\!\perp\ \ddot{\text{G}}\text{ʊ}\!\perp\ (\overset{\overset{\circ\circ}{v}}{}_{x})\cdot\right)\!\gt$$

The left **B** hand is held with the palm facing up and the fingers pointing to the right; the right Â hand is held with the palm facing left (if the hand were opened, the fingers would point up).	The hands are held in front of the body; the right hand is held higher and nearer to the signer than the left hand.	The right hand moves sharply down and away from the signer with the arm bending at the elbow, so that the right index finger brushes the side of the left palm.	**beat with a**
			   cane/strap*†
			 cane*†
			 hit with a cane/
			   strap*†
			 penalty*
			 punish*†
			 punishment*
			 strap*†
				269

Notes   * This sign may be produced with the right palm initially facing away from the signer.

$$\overline{\text{B}}\alpha\gt\ \dot{\text{J}}\hat{\text{A}}\!\perp\!\wedge_{\varrho}\ \overset{\cdot}{\underset{\underset{v}{\overset{x}{v}}}{\overset{v}{D}}}$$

† Directional verb.

Two Â hands are held with the palms facing up (if the hands were opened, the fingers would all point away from the signer).	The hands are held in front of the body.	The hands make several short movements down and, at the same time, away from the signer.	**revise** **revision** **study** **swot**	270

Non-manual features   The head is tilted forward and the eye gaze is directed towards the hands.

Two Â hands are held with palms facing up (if the hands were opened, the fingers would all point away from the signer).	The hands are held in front of the body.	The hands make clockwise circles in the vertical plane at right angles to the signer's body, moving towards each other each time they move away from the signer.	**skipping rope** **skip with a** **skipping rope**	271

272 Ø Âa⊥ ¡ Âa⊥ $\overset{\circ}{\overset{I}{\sim}}$ ·

273 Ø Âa⊥ ¡ Âa<˛ $\overset{\top}{>}$

274 Ø Âa> Âa< $\overset{\circ}{\text{¡}}$ ·

275 Ø Â⊤> Âa⊥ $<\overset{\circ}{\overset{\lessgtr}{\vee}}$

276 Ø $\overline{\text{Â}}$⊤> Â⊤< $\overset{@\sim}{\overset{\top}{\vee}}$

277 Ø Â⊤> ¡ Â⊤< $\overset{D\sim}{\overset{}{\vee}}$·

Â *The bent index finger is extended from the fist, enclosing the top of the extended thumb.*

Handshape and orientation	Location, hand arrangement and contact	Movement	Glosses	
Two **Â** hands are held with the palms facing up (if the hands were opened, the fingers would all point away from the signer).	The hands are held side by side in front of the body.	The hands make alternate short movements towards and away from the signer.	administer administration administrator control controller deal with direct director govern governor manage management manager produce producer manipulate[1] manipulator[1]	272
Notes 1 If the tongue tip is pushed into the cheek or protrudes between the lips and the eyes are narrowed, the sign produced is **manipulate, manipulator**.				
Two **Â** hands are held with the palms facing up (if the hands were opened, the left fingers would point away from the signer and the right fingers would point to the left).	The hands are held side by side in front of the body; the right hand is held nearer to the signer than the left hand.	The hands move towards the signer and, at the same time, to the right.	pull* tug* drag[1] haul[1] tug-of-war[1] heave[2]	273
Notes * This sign may be produced using one hand only.		$\emptyset$ $\hat{A}a< \overset{T}{>}$		
1 If the shoulders move back, the eyes are narrowed and the lips are stretched, the sign produced is **drag, haul, tug-of-war**.				
2 If the hands move up and towards the signer while moving to the right, and at the same time, the body moves back and the lips are stretched, the sign produced is **heave**.		$\emptyset$ $\hat{A}a\perp$, $\hat{A}a<_{\wp}$ $\overset{T}{\underset{\wedge}{>}}$		
Two **Â** hands are held with the palms facing up (if the hands were opened, the left fingers would point to the right and the right fingers would point to the left).	The hands are held in front of the body at an angle, so that the fingers are turned away from the signer.	The hands make two short movements away from the signer.	charge cook cooker cookery cooking feed*	274
Notes * Directional verb.				
The left **Â** hand is held with the palm facing towards the signer; the right **Â** hand is held with the palm facing up (if the hands were opened, the left fingers would point to the right and the right fingers would point away from the signer).	The hands are held in front of the body.	The hands move to the left and then make a short movement down and, at the same time, to the left.	bring* fetch*	275
Notes * Directional verb.				
Two **Â** hands are held with the palms facing towards the signer (if the hands were opened, the left fingers would point to the right and the right fingers would point to the left).	The hands are held in front of the body; the left hand is held above the right hand.	The hands make an anticlockwise circle in the vertical plane at right angles to the signer's body.	adapt* adaptation* alter* alteration* amend* amendment* become* change*	276
Notes * This sign may also be produced using two **A** hands.		$\emptyset$ $\overline{A}\top> A\top< \overset{\mathscr{e}\,\mathscr{N}}{\underset{v}{\top}}$		
Two **Â** hands are held with the palms facing towards the signer (if the hands were opened, the left fingers would point to the right and the right fingers would point to the left).	The hands are held side by side in front of the body.	The hands bend down alternately from the wrist; the movements are repeated several times.	drum drummer drumsticks	277

278　Ø　Â⊥ʌ　Â⊥ʌ　˟̥·

279　Ø　Ā̄>ʌ९　Â<ʌ　ᴰ̩·

280　Ø　Ā̄>⊥९　Â<ʌ　ᴰ̩·　//　Ā̄>⊥　F⊥<　̩ᵒ

281　Ø　Â>ʌ　Â<ʌ　ᴰ̩·

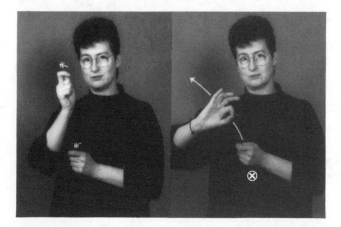

282　Ø　<u>Â</u>>v　ı　Â<v　ᵒ̥z

283　Ø　Â>⊥　ı　Â<⊥　ᵃ·

284　Ø　Â>⊥　ıx　Â<⊥　^ȝ÷

Â

The bent index finger is extended from the fist, enclosing the top of the extended thumb.

Handshape and orientation	Location, hand arrangement and contact	Movement	Glosses	
Two **Â** hands are held with the palms facing away from the signer (if the hands were opened, the fingers would all point up).	The hands are held in front of the body.	The hands make two short movements towards each other.	curtains*	278
Notes * This sign may be produced using one hand only, typically when referring to a single **curtain**.		Ø Â⊥∧ ⬠˙		
The left **Â** hand is held with the palm facing right; the right **Â** hand is held with the palm facing left (if the hands were opened, the left fingers would point away from the signer and the right fingers would point up).	The hands are held side by side in front of the body; the left hand is held lower and nearer to the signer than the right hand.	The hands make a short bending movement away from the signer at the wrists; the movement is repeated.	angler angling fish fisherman fishing	279
The left **Â** hand is held with the palm facing right; the right **Â** hand is held with the palm facing left (if the hands were opened, the left fingers would point away from the signer and the right fingers would point up).	The hands are held in front of the body; the left hand is held lower and nearer to the signer than the right hand.	The hands make a short bending movement away from the signer at the wrists; the movement is repeated.	fishing rod	280
The left **Â** hand is held with the palm facing right (if the hand were opened, the fingers would point away from the signer). The right **F** hand is held with the palm facing away from the signer (if the hand were opened, the fingers would point to the left).	The hands are held in front of the body; the right hand is held above the left hand.	The right hand moves up and away from the signer while twisting at the wrist, so that the palm faces down.		
The left **Â** hand is held with the palm facing right; the right **Â** hand is held with the palm facing left (if the hands were opened, the fingers would all point up).	The hands are held in front of the body.	The hands bend away from the signer at the wrists; the movement is repeated.	horse-drawn carriage sledge pulled by animals sleigh pulled by animals	281
The left **Â** hand is held with the palm facing right; the right **Â** hand is held with the palm facing left (if the hands were opened, the fingers would all point down).	The hands are held side by side in front of the body; the left hand is held higher than the right hand.	The hands make a short movement from side to side, bending at the wrists.	cricket* cricket bat* cricketer* hockey hockey player hockey stick play cricket* play hockey putt[1] putter[1]	282
Notes * This sign may be produced with the left palm facing towards the signer and the right palm facing away from the signer and the hands making a short, firm movement away from the signer.		Ø Ā⊤∨ ⏐ Â⊥∨ ˚|		
1 If the eye gaze is directed towards the hands and the hands make a short movement to the right and then move to the left, the sign produced is **putt, putter**.		Ø Ā>∨ ⏐ Â<∨ ˚<		
The left **Â** hand is held with the palm facing right; the right **Â** hand is held with the palm facing left (if the hands were opened, the fingers would all point away from the signer).	The hands are held side by side in front of the body.	The hands twist at the wrists, so that the palms face up; the movement is repeated.	comic journal magazine periodical	283
The left **Â** hand is held with the palm facing right; the right **Â** hand is held with the palm facing left (if the hands were opened, the fingers would all point away from the signer).	The hands are held side by side in front of the body with the knuckles touching.	The hands move up and apart while twisting at the wrists, so that the palms face up.	newspaper*	284
Notes * This sign can be produced using two **A** hands.		Ø A>⊥ ₁ₓ A<⊥ ÷∧		

285 Ø Â>⊥ ₁ₓ Â<⊥ $\overset{\wedge}{\underset{\div}{\omega}}$ // B̄ɑ⊥ Ğ̈ʋ⊥ $\overset{\circ}{>}$

286 [] Â⊤∧ Â⊤∧ $\overset{\times\, n}{\underset{\times}{\underset{\vee}{}}}$ // Âɑ>₉ Âɑ< $\overset{@\, \bot}{\underset{\vee}{\bot}}$

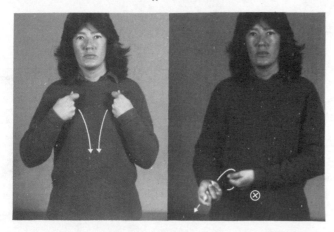

287 ⌐1 Â⊤∧ Â⊤∧ $\overset{\circ}{\underset{\bot}{n}}$ 288 ⌐1 Â⊤> Â⊤< $\overset{\times\, \overset{\circ}{\times}\, \times}{\vee}$

[230]

Â

The bent index finger is extended from the fist, enclosing the top of the extended thumb.

Handshape and orientation	Location, hand arrangement and contact	Movement	Glosses
The left **Â** hand is held with the palm facing right; the right **Â** hand is held with the palm facing left (if the hands were opened, the fingers would all point away from the signer).	The hands are held side by side in front of the body with the knuckles touching.	The hands move up and apart while twisting at the wrists, so that the palms face up.	newspaper 285 article newspaper column
The left **B** hand is held with the palm facing up and the fingers pointing away from the signer; the right **č** hand is held with the palm facing down (if the hand were opened, the fingers would point away from the signer).	The hands are held in front of the body; the right hand is held above the left hand.	The right hand makes a short movement to the right.	
Two **Â** hands are held with the palms facing towards the signer (if the hands were opened, the fingers would all point up).	The hands are held resting against the upper chest.	The hands move down and, at the same time, bend towards each other from the wrists.	bathrobe 286 dressing gown put on a bathrobe/ dressing gown
Two **Â** hands are held with the palms facing up (if the hands were opened, the left fingers would point to the right and the right fingers would point to the left).	The hands are held in front of the waist; the left hand is held nearer to the signer than the right hand.	The right hand makes a clockwise circle in the vertical plane at right angles to the signer's body (moving around the left hand) and then moves down and, at the same time, away from the signer.	
Two **Â** hands are held with the palms facing towards the signer (if the hands were opened, the fingers would all point up).	The hands are held in front of the shoulders.	The hands make a short bending movement away from the signer from the wrists.	anorak 287 hood hood (put up a hood) monk

Two **Â** hands are held with the palms facing towards the signer (if the hands were opened, the left fingers would point to the right and the right fingers would point to the left).	The hands are held with the knuckles resting against the sides of the upper chest.	The hands make a short movement down and, at the same time, towards each other; the movement ends with the hands touching the centre of the chest together.	coat 288
			  (lightweight coat)
			jacket
			mac
			mackintosh
			put on a coat
			  (lightweight coat)/
			  jacket/mac/
			  mackintosh

289 ⌐⌐ Â>ʌ Â<ʌ ˣⁿ↓ᵥ

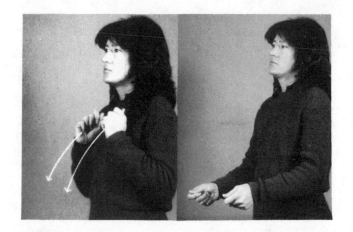

290 ⌐⊤ Ā̄ɔ> <ᵥᵥₐ ⌐ ʃÂ<ʌ९ ⁿ↓ᵥ

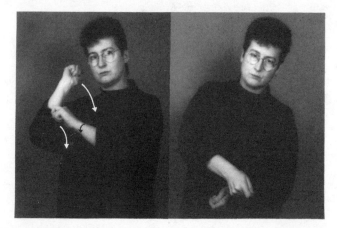

291 ⌐⌐ ÂɔⱢ ⌐ ÂɔⱢ ⁿᵥ÷⊤ˣ

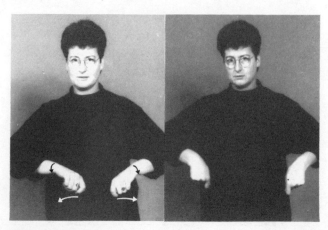

292 Ø 5⊥ʌ Â⊥ʌ ˚ⁿ⊥·

[232]

The bent index finger is extended from the fist, enclosing the top of the extended thumb.

Handshape and orientation	Location, hand arrangement and contact	Movement	Glosses	
The left Â hand is held with the palm facing right; the right Â hand is held with the palm facing left (if the hands were opened, the fingers would all point up). *Notes* * This sign may be produced using one hand only.	The hands are held with the backs of the thumbs resting against the upper chest.	The hands bend away from the signer at the wrists while moving down.	give up* quit* resign* resignation*	**289**
The left Â hand is held with the palm facing down; the right Â hand is held with the palm facing left (if the hands were opened, the left fingers would point to the right and the right fingers would point up). *Non-manual features* The right shoulder is hunched as the hands move.	The hands are held side by side in front of the right side of the upper chest; the right hand is held higher and nearer to the signer than the left hand.	The left hand moves down and to the left while twisting at the wrist so that the palm faces up; at the same time, the right hand moves down, bending away from the signer from the elbow.	judo throw someone/ something over one's shoulder	**290**
Two Â hands are held with the palms facing down (if the hands were opened, the fingers would all point away from the signer).	The hands are held side by side in front of the waist, at an angle so that the fingers are turned towards each other.	The hands move apart and towards the signer while bending down at the wrists; the movement ends with the hands touching the sides of the waist.	apron	**291**
The left 5 hand is held with the palm facing away from the signer and the fingers pointing up; the right Â hand is held with the palm facing away from the signer (if the hand were opened, the fingers would point up).	The hands are held in front of the body.	The hands make a short bending movement away from the signer at the wrists; the movement is repeated.	fairy	**292**

ㄒㄒ< Â<ʌ × n ⊥ v

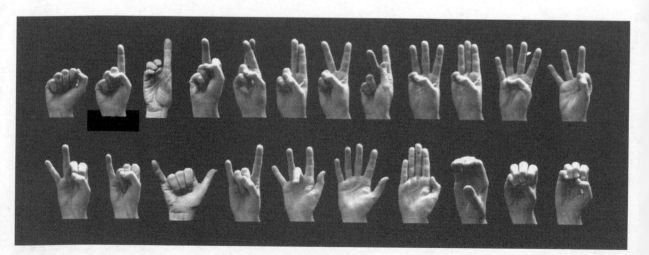

G

Handshape	Handshape description	Type	Sign entries
G	The index finger is extended from the fist.	Single dez Manual tab Double dez	293 − 369 370 − 417 418 − 459
Ġ	The index finger and thumb are extended from the fist.	Single dez Manual tab Double dez	460 − 469 470 − 473
Ĝ	The index finger and thumb are extended from the fist so that the pad of the thumb is touching the pad of the index finger.	Single dez Manual tab Double dez	474 − 475 476
Ḡ	The extended index finger, bent at the palm knuckle, and extended thumb are held parallel to each other.	Single dez Manual tab Double dez	477 − 483 484 − 485 486 − 490
G̈	The index finger is extended from the fist and bent at the palm knuckle.	Single dez Manual tab Double dez	491 − 544 545 − 555 556 − 569
G̈	The bent index finger is extended from the fist.	Single dez Manual tab Double dez	570 − 585 586 − 593 594 − 600
G̈	The thumb and bent index finger are extended from the fist.	Single dez Manual tab Double dez	601 − 605 606 607 − 611
Ĝ	The bent index finger is extended from the fist so that the pad of the index finger touches the tip of the thumb.	Single dez Manual tab Double dez	612 − 626 627 − 630 631 − 633
G̈	The bent index finger and bent thumb are extended from the fist in the shape of a "C".	Single dez Manual tab Double dez	634 − 647 648 − 650 651 − 661

293 Ø G⌐⊤ ˚

294 Ø G⌐< ˚

295 Ø G⊤ʌ ⊤

296 Ø G⊤ʌ ˚ʌ·

297 Ø G⊤ʌ ˚@˚<⊤

The main *variant* of **G** is **G̈**. In some cases **G̈** is required by the physical constraints of the sign production. In other cases the use of **G** or **G̈** depends on personal choice. (See also separate entry for **G̈**.)

G has several different *classifier* functions in the productive lexicon and also appears as a classifying element in established signs:

- the **G** *person* classifier plays a range of roles in the language, featuring in verbs of motion and location, such as **approach** (sign 295) and **face to face** (sign 434) and in simultaneous compound forms such as **oppress** (sign 1364);
- it is used as a *size and shape* classifier to represent relatively long, thin and typically cylindrical objects. Examples include **missile** (sign 405) and **underground train** (sign 414); **G** can be seen as contrasting with **H**, **Wm** and **B** in showing different degrees of width;
- it is used as a *tracing size and shape* classifier, the index finger tracing the size and shape of objects in space, for example, for geometric shapes such as triangles, circles and squares as in the signs **mainframe computer** (sign 420) and **window** (sign 441);
- it is used as a *point* classifier to indicate objects which are perceived as small specks or points, as in **stars** (sign 449);

- it is used as a *handling* classifier to indicate objects which may be balanced on the fingertip, as in a juggler spinning plates;
- it is used as an *instrumental* classifier to represent long, narrow tools, utensils or implements such as knitting needles in **knitting** (sign 376) and a needle in **compass** (sign 403);
- it is used as a *touch* classifier for actions and objects which involve pressing a small area, as in a push-button telephone; to indicate prodding or poking persons or things and for metaphorical extensions of such actions, as in the signs **get at** (sign 444) and **provoke** (sign 444).

G also has a major role in *deictic* signs where **G** is used to point to referents, as in the signs **eye** (sign 325) and **throat** (sign 365). It is also used for *pronominal reference* as in the signs **you** (sign 293) and **her** (sign 310) and for *location* signs such as **up** (sign 296).

G also expresses the right-hand component of several letters of the British manual alphabet, including all the vowels, **a, e, i, o, u** and the letters **j, l, t, x** and **y**. It occurs in initial letter handshape signs such as **answer** (sign 370), **uncle** (sign 393), **toilet** (sign 395) and **year** (sign 416).

G also expresses the letter **g** in the American manual alphabet. As such, it is used in initial letter handshape signs borrowed from American Sign Language such as **guilty** (see *Introduction*).

Handshape and orientation	Location, hand arrangement and contact	Movement	Glosses	
The **G** hand is held with the palm facing down (if the hand were opened, the fingers would point away from the signer).	The hand is held in front of the body.	The hand makes a short movement away from the signer.	**you**	293
The **G** hand is held with the palm facing down (if the hand were opened, the fingers would point to the left).	The hand is held in front of the body.	The hand makes a firm movement away from the signer.	**first**	294
The **G** hand is held with the palm facing towards the signer (if the hands were opened, the fingers would point up).	The hand is held in front of the body.	The hand moves towards the signer.	**approach*** come **come back** **draw near*** **move towards*** **return** **come here**[1]	295
Notes * Directional verb. 1 If the hand remains stationary and the index finger flexes twice, the sign produced is **come here**.		Ø G⊤∧ ᵐ·		
The **G** hand is held with the palm facing towards the signer (if the hand were opened, the fingers would point up).	The hand is held in front of the body.	The hand makes two short upward movements.	**north***† **up***† **upstairs***†	296
Notes * This sign may be produced with a **G̈** hand with the palm facing up (if the hand were opened, the fingers would point away from the signer).		Ø G̈α⊥ ˚∧·		
† This sign may be produced with a single upward movement (**up** is typically produced in this way).		Ø G⊤∧ ˚∧ or Ø G̈α⊥ ˚∧		
The **G** hand is held with the palm facing towards the signer (if the hand were opened, the fingers would point up).	The hand is held in front of the body.	The hand makes small anticlockwise circles in the horizontal plane.	**anybody** **anyone** **somebody** **someone**	297

298 Ø G⊤∨ $\overset{\overset{\circ}{_ё}\cdot}{_>^⊤}$

299 Ø G⊤< $\overset{(\overset{\circ}{∧}\overset{\circ}{⊥}\overset{\circ}{∨}\cdot)}{}$

300 Ø G⊥∧ $\overset{п}{>}$

301 Ø G⊥∧ $\overset{\dot{ω}}{⊤}$

302 Ø G⊥∧ $\overset{(\overset{\dot{ω}}{⊤})}{∧}$

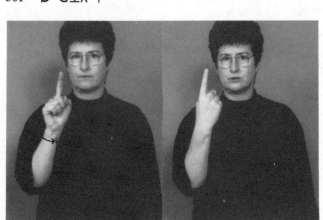

303 Ø G⊥∧ $\overset{(\overset{п}{⊥})}{∨}$

304 Ø G⊥∧ $\overset{(\overset{\dot{z}}{∨}\cdot)}{}$

[238]

Handshape and orientation	Location, hand arrangement and contact	Movement	Glosses	
The **G** hand is held with the palm facing towards the signer (if the hand were opened, the fingers would point down).	The hand is held in front of the body.	The hand makes several small, sharp clockwise circles in the horizontal plane.	spin spinning top	298

The **G** hand is held with the palm facing towards the signer (if the hand were opened, the fingers would point to the left).	The hand is held in front of the body.	The hand moves away from the signer in a series of short arcs.	now and then*
			occasional*
			occasion
			  (on occasion)*
			time (from time to
			  time)*
			while
			  (once in a while)*
				299

Notes   * This sign may be produced using a **B̈** hand.

$$\emptyset \quad \ddot{B}{<}\perp \; ({}^{\times}_{\wedge}{}^{\circ}_{\perp}{}^{\circ}_{\vee}\cdot)$$

The **G** hand is held with the palm facing away from the signer (if the hand were opened, the fingers would point up).	The hand is held in front of the body.	The hand bends to the right from the wrist.	afterwards* later* then while (in a while)*	300

Notes   * This sign may be produced with a short, repeated movement.

$$\emptyset \quad G{\perp}{\wedge} \; {}^{\cap}_{>}$$

The **G** hand is held with the palm facing away from the signer (if the hand were opened, the fingers would point up).	The hand is held in front of the body.	The hand twists firmly at the wrist, so that the palm faces towards the signer.	first one o'clock	301
The **G** hand is held with the palm facing away from the signer (if the hand were opened, the fingers would point up).	The hand is held in front of the body.	The hand moves firmly up and, at the same time, twists at the wrist, so that the palm faces towards the signer.	above all first initial original primary priority	302
The **G** hand is held with the palm facing away from the signer (if the hand were opened, the fingers would point up).	The hand is held in front of the body.	The hand bends sharply away from the signer at the wrist, while moving down and to the left.	call for charge command order summon	303
The **G** hand is held with the palm facing away from the signer (if the hand were opened, the fingers would point up).	The hand is held in front of the body.	The hand moves sharply down while moving from side to side several times.	lightning people* thunder electric[1] electricity[1]	304

Notes   * Regional sign.

1   If the movement is short, the sign produced is **electric, electricity**.

$$\emptyset \quad G{\perp}{\wedge} \; ({}^{\circ}_{\vee}{}^{z}\cdot)$$

305 Ø G⊥∧ $\overset{(\dot{z}\,\cdot)}{\lor}$ // Ø 5ʊ⊥ 5ʊ⊥ $\overset{(\overset{o}{z}\,\cdot)}{⊥}$　　　　306 Ø G∨⊥∧ $\overset{\overset{n}{o}\cdot}{z}$

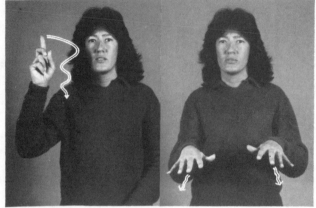

307 Ø G<∧ $\overset{o}{⊥}$　　　　308 Ø G<∧ $\overset{\overset{n}{o}\cdot}{⊥}$

309 Ø G<∧ $\overset{\overset{\omega\,[5]}{\lor}}{\square}$　　　　310 Ø G<⊥ $\overset{o}{\underset{\lor}{⊥}}$

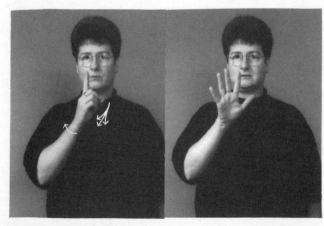

Handshape and orientation	Location, hand arrangement and contact	Movement	Glosses	
The **G** hand is held with the palm facing away from the signer (if the hand were opened, the fingers would point up).	The hand is held in front of the body.	The hand moves sharply down, while moving from side to side several times.	**thunder and lightning thunderstorm**	305
Two **5** hands are held with the palms facing down and the fingers pointing away from the signer.	The hands are held in front of the body.	The hands make short, sharp movements from side to side while moving away from the signer.		
Non-manual features The lips vibrate.				
The **G** hand is held with the palm facing away from the signer (if the hand were opened, the fingers would point up).	The hand is held in front of the body.	The hand makes several short sharp bending movements from side to side at the wrist.	**what? why?***	306
Non-manual features Non-manual features appropriate for questions must be used.				
Notes * Regional sign.				
The **G** hand is held with the palm facing left (if the hand were opened, the fingers would point up).	The hand is held in front of the body.	The hand makes a short, firm movement away from the signer.	**but however**	307
The **G** hand is held with the palm facing left (if the hand were opened, the fingers would point up).	The hand is held in front of the body.	The hand makes a short, firm movement away from the signer, bending at the wrist; the movement is repeated.	**rebuke* scold* tell off* tick off* warn***	308
Non-manual features The brows are furrowed.				
Notes * Directional verb.				
The **G** hand is held with the palm facing left (if the hand were opened, the fingers would point up).	The hand is held in front of the body.	The hand twists at the wrist, so that the palm faces away from the signer, while opening (forming a **5** hand).	**once only**	309
The **G** hand is held with the palm facing left (if the hand were opened, the fingers would point away from the signer).	The hand is held in front and to the right of the body, at an angle, so that the index finger is turned slightly to the right.	The hand makes a short movement away from the signer and, at the same time, to the right.	**he her him it she that this**	310

311　⌒ G<⊥ $\overset{\dot{D}}{\wedge}$

312　∩ Gʊ< $\overset{×⊥}{\vee}$ // ∅ $\overline{\overline{5}}$a> $\ddot{5}$ʊ< $\overset{3÷}{\mathsf{H}}$

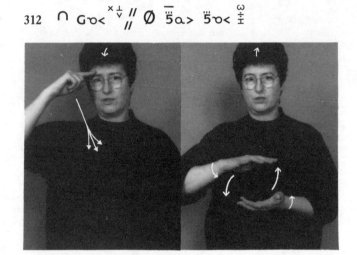

313　∩ G⊤∧ $\overset{\overset{\circ}{@}}{\underset{\vee}{<}}$

314　∩ G⊤∧ ×⊥

315　∩ G⊤∧ $\overset{×\underset{\square}{\vee[B]}}{}$ // $\overline{\mathsf{B}}$a⊥ B<⊥ $\overset{\vee×∧}{\underset{a}{>}}$

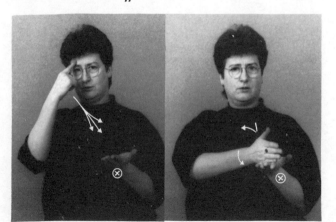

Handshape and orientation	Location, hand arrangement and contact	Movement	Glosses	
The **G** hand is held with the palm facing left (if the hand were opened, the fingers would point away from the signer).	The hand is held in front of the top of the head.	The hand bends up from the wrist.	deity* god*	311

Non-manual features   The eye gaze is directed up and to the right.

       Notes   * This sign may be produced with the index finger pointing up and the hand making a short, firm movement away from the signer.

$$\overline{\cap} \quad \text{G<}\wedge \quad \overset{\circ}{\underset{\perp}{\cdot}}$$

The **G** hand is held with the palm facing down (if the hand were opened, the fingers would point to the left).	The hand is held with the index fingertip held against the side of the forehead.	The hand moves down and away from the signer while opening (forming a **5̈** hand).	disorient disorientate disorientation screw up throw	312

Non-manual features   The head tilts forward.

The left **5̈** hand is held with the palm facing up (if the hand were opened, the fingers would point to the right). The right **5̈** hand is held with the palm facing down (if the hand were opened, the fingers would point to the left).	The hands are held in front of the body; the right hand is held above the left hand.	The right hand twists away from the signer (so that the palm faces left) while the left hand twists towards the signer (so that the palm faces right).		

Non-manual features   The head tilts back.

The **G** hand is held with the palm facing towards the signer (if the hand were opened, the fingers would point up).	The hand is held with the index finger in front of the forehead.	The hand makes small anticlockwise circles in the vertical plane parallel to the signer's body.	consider* consideration* deliberate* deliberation* imagine* mull over* philosopher* philosophy* ponder* puzzle* reflect* reflection* think* thinker* thought* wonder*	313

Non-manual features   The head is tilted to the right and the brows are furrowed.

       Notes   * This sign may also be produced using a **G̈** hand.

$$\cap \quad \text{G̈}\top\wedge \quad \overset{\circ}{\underset{\vee}{\overset{@}{<}}}\,\cdot$$

The **G** hand is held with the palm facing towards the signer (if the hand were opened, the fingers would point up).	The hand is held with the index fingertip touching the forehead.	The hand moves away from the signer.	idea notion suggest suggestion think	314

The **G** hand is held with the palm facing towards the signer (if the hand were opened, the fingers would point up).	The hand is held with the index fingertip touching the forehead.	The hand moves down and, at the same time, opens (forming a **B** hand).	cannot believe can't believe do not believe don't believe	315

The left **B** hand is held with the palm facing up and the fingers pointing away from the signer; the right **B** hand is held with the palm facing left and the fingers pointing away from the signer.	The hands are held in front of the body; the right hand is held above the left hand.	The right hand moves down, so that the side of the hand touches the left palm; the right hand then moves up and to the right while twisting at the wrist, so that the palm faces up.		

Non-manual features   Appropriate negative non-manual features must be used.

316 ∩ G⊤∧ ^{x v[A]}# // A̲⊤> A⊤< ^{°̊∧x}

317 ∩ G<∧ ^x

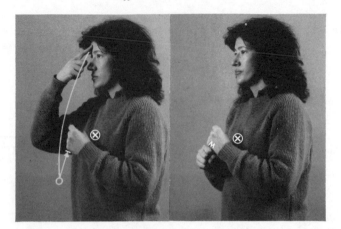

318 ∩ G<∧ ^x // G̅⊤> G<⊥_ρ ^{x∧̊x}

319 ∩ G<∧ ^x // G̅⊤> G<⊥_ρ ^{x∧̊x} // ∅ 5ʋ⊥ 5ʋ⊥ [÷]

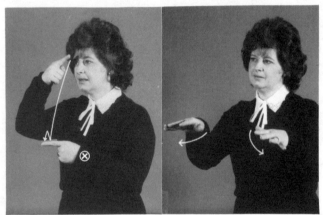

320 ∩ G<∧ ^{x(ω̊⊤∨)⊤x}
⊥

321 ∩ G<⊤ ^{°̊ρ}

Handshape and orientation	Location, hand arrangement and contact	Movement	Glosses	
The **G** hand is held with the palm facing towards the signer (if the hand were opened, the fingers would point up).	The hand is held with the index fingertip touching the forehead.	The hand moves down while closing (forming an **A** hand).	daft dumb fool ignorant stupid thick as two short planks wally	316
Two **A** hands are held with the palms facing towards the signer (if the hands were opened, the left fingers would point to the right and the right fingers would point to the left).	The hands are held in front of the body; the left hand is held above the right hand.	The right hand makes a short, firm upward movement; the movement ends with the right hand held against the left hand.		
The **G** hand is held with the palm facing left (if the hand were opened, the fingers would point up).	The hand is held in front of the forehead.	The side of the hand touches the forehead.	German* Germany*	317

Notes   * The following notes apply to all glosses:

This sign may be produced with the palm facing away from the signer.   ∩ G⊥∧ ˣ

This sign may be produced with a repeated movement.   ∩ G<∧ ˣ·   or   ∩ G⊥∧ ˣ·

Handshape and orientation	Location, hand arrangement and contact	Movement	Glosses	
The left **G** hand is held with the palm facing towards the signer; the right **G** hand is held with the palm facing left (if the hands were opened, the left fingers would point to the right and the right fingers would point up).	The left hand is held in front of the body; the right hand is held with the index fingertip touching the forehead.	The right hand moves down, so that the right index finger touches the left index finger and then makes a short upward movement before touching the left index finger again.	ill illness invalid poorly sick unwell	318
The left **G** hand is held with the palm facing towards the signer; the right **G** hand is held with the palm facing left (if the hands were opened, the left fingers would point to the right and the right fingers would point up).	The left hand is held in front of the body; the right hand is held with the index fingertip touching the forehead.	The right hand moves down, so that the right index finger touches the left index finger and then makes a short upward movement before touching the left index finger again.	epidemic	319
Two **5** hands are held with the palms facing down and the fingers pointing away from the signer.	The hands are held in front of the body.	The hands move apart and, at the same time, away from the signer.		
The **G** hand is held with the palm facing left (if the hand were opened, the fingers would point up).	The hand is held with the index fingertip touching the side of the forehead.	The hand makes a short movement away from the signer and to the left while twisting at the wrist (so that the palm faces towards the signer); the hand then moves back towards the signer, so that the index fingertip touches the left side of the forehead.	chauffeur guard keeper warden	320
The **G** hand is held with the palm facing left (if the hand were opened, the fingers would point towards the signer).	The hand is held with the index fingertip touching the middle of the forehead.	The hand twists at the wrist, so that the palm faces down; the index fingertip maintains contact with the forehead throughout.	Hindu* India* Indian* Pakistan* Pakistani* tilak*†	321

Notes   * This sign may be produced using a **G̈** hand with a short, repeated twisting movement from side to side.   ∩ G̈⊤∧ ˣ·_ω˟

     † This sign may be produced using a **ช** hand with a short, repeated twisting movement from side to side.   ∩ ช⊤∧ ˣ·_ω˟

322 Ỏ Gᴛʌ ˅ // Ø ı<ʌ ᵒ̣

323 Ỏ Gᴛʌ ᵌ@⌄ᵗ

324 Ỏ Gᴛʌ ˣ˅ˣ

325 Ц Gᴛʌ ˣ

326 Ц Gᴛʌ ˣ // B̄ʊ> ˣ ʲB<ʌ ᵒ̸

Handshape and orientation	Location, hand arrangement and contact	Movement	Glosses	
The **G** hand is held with the palm facing towards the signer (if the hand were opened, the fingers would point up).	The hand is held in front of the face.	The hand moves down and then twists at the wrist (so that the palm faces left) while changing (forming an **I** hand); the hand then makes a short, sharp movement away from the signer.	ugly	322

Non-manual features	The eyes are narrowed and the nose is wrinkled.			

The **G** hand is held with the palm facing towards the signer (if the hand were opened, the fingers would point up).	The hand is held beside the head.	The hand makes anticlockwise circles in the horizontal plane, twisting from the wrist.	fan helicopter[1] dizzy*[2] spin*[2] swim*[2] vertigo*[2]	323

Notes   * This sign may be produced with the lips rounded.

   1 If the hand is held at head height in front of the body, the sign produced is **helicopter**.

Ø G⊤∧ ⌃

   2 If the tongue protrudes slightly between the teeth, the sign produced is **dizzy, spin, swim, vertigo**.

The **C** hand is held with the palm facing towards the signer (if the hand were opened, the fingers would point up).	The hand is held with the index fingertip touching the forehead.	The hand moves down and then the index fingertip touches the chin.	face toilet* image[1] profile[1]	324

Notes   * Regional sign.

   1 If the hand moves down with the index fingertip maintaining contact with the face throughout, the sign produced is **image, profile**.

Ⓒ G⊤∧ ˅×

The **C** hand is held with the palm facing towards the signer (if the hand were opened, the fingers would point up).	The hand is held with the index finger in front of the cheek.	The index fingertip touches the cheek below the eye.	eye	325

The **G** hand is held with the palm facing towards the signer (if the hand were opened, the fingers would point up).	The hand is held with the index finger in front of the cheek.	The index fingertip touches the cheek below the eye.	evidence proof witness	326

The left **B** hand is held with the palm facing down and the fingers pointing to the right; the right **B** hand is held with the palm facing left and the fingers pointing up.	The hands are held in front of the body; the left fingertips are held against the right elbow.	No movement.		

327 L G⊤∧ ˣ ·

328 L G⊤∧ ˣ⊥ᵥ // Ø 5⊤< ᵒ˚∧#[∧]

329 L G⊤∧ ˣ⊥ᵥ // Ø Bɑ⊥ ǀ Bɑ⊥ ᴺᴺ·

330 L G⊤∧ ˣ⊥ᵥ // ‾Bɑ⊥ Bɑ⊥ ᵛˣ

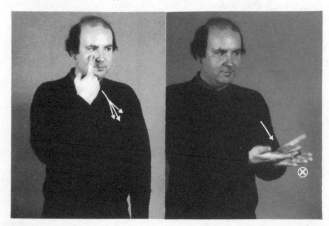

Handshape and orientation	Location, hand arrangement and contact	Movement	Glosses	
The **G** hand is held with the palm facing towards the signer (if the hand were opened, the fingers would point up).	The hand is held with the index finger in front of the cheek.	The index fingertip taps the cheek below the eye.	look (have a look) look out see (let's see) see (let us see) look [1] see [1] sight [1]	327

Notes   1 If the hand is held with the index fingertip resting against the cheek below the eye and makes a short movement away from the signer, the sign produced is **look, see, sight**.   Ʊ G⊤∧ ×≗

The **G** hand is held with the palm facing towards the signer (if the hand were opened, the fingers would point up).	The hand is held with the index fingertip touching the cheek below the eye.	The hand moves down and away from the signer while opening (forming a **5** hand); the hand then makes a short sharp upward movement while closing (forming an **A** hand).	discover discovery find find out locate	328
The **G** hand is held with the palm facing towards the signer (if the hand were opened, the fingers would point up).	The hand is held with the index fingertip touching the cheek below the eye.	The hand moves down and away from the signer while opening (forming a **B** hand).	assess * assessment * estimate * estimation * evaluate * evaluation *	329
Two **B** hands are held with the palms facing down and the fingers pointing away from the signer.	The hands are held side by side in front of the body.	The hands make alternate short up and down movements.		

Notes   * The second part of this sign may be produced with the palms facing up.   Ʊ G⊤∧ × ∥ Ø Bɑ⊥ , Bɑ⊥ ≈̊

The **G** hand is held with the palm facing towards the signer (if the hand were opened, the fingers would point up).	The hand is held with the index fingertip touching the cheek below the eye.	The hand moves down and, at the same time, away from the signer while opening (forming a **B** hand).	evidence fact proof	330
Two **B** hands are held with the palms facing up and the fingers pointing away from the signer.	The hands are held in front of the body; the right hand is held above the left hand.	The right hand moves down; the movement ends with the back of the right hand held against the left palm.		

331 $\text{LI}\ \text{G<}\wedge\ {}^{\perp}\ {}^{//}_{//}\ 5\top>\ 5\text{<}\perp_{\varrho}\ {}^{\mathbb{I}}$

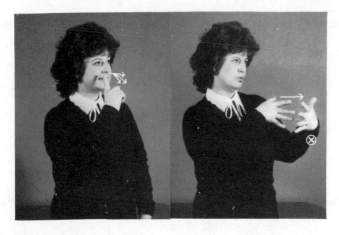

332 $\text{LI}\ \text{G<}\wedge\ {}^{\times\vee}\ {}^{//}_{//}\ \emptyset\ \left(\overline{\ddot{5}}\text{>}\perp\ {}_{\times}\ \ddot{5}\text{<}\perp\ {}^{@}_{\substack{<\\\top\\\times}}\cdot\right)\text{>}$

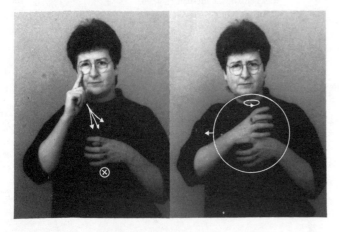

333 $\text{LI}\ \text{G<}\wedge\ {}^{\times\perp}_{\vee}\ {}^{//}_{//}\ \overline{\ddot{B}}\alpha\text{>}\ \ddot{B}\eth\perp\ {}^{\times\cdot}$

Handshape and orientation	Location, hand arrangement and contact	Movement	Glosses	
The **G** hand is held with the palm facing left (if the hand were opened, the fingers would point up).	The hand is held with the index fingertip in front of the eye.	The hand moves away from the signer while opening (forming a **5** hand).	**glass*** **see through** **transparent**	331
The left **5** hand is held with the palm facing towards the signer and the fingers pointing to the right; the right **5** hand is held with the palm facing left and the fingers pointing away from the signer.	The hands are held in front of the body; the right hand is held nearer to the signer than the left hand.	The right hand moves away from the signer, so that the right fingers interlock with the left fingers.		
Notes * Regional sign.				
The **G** hand is held with the palm facing left (if the hand were opened, the fingers would point up).	The hand is held with the index fingertip touching the cheek below the eye.	The hand moves down while opening (forming a **5** hand).	**find** **hunt** **hunter** **look for** **search** **seek**	332
The left **5̈** hand is held with the palm facing right; the right **5̈** hand is held with the palm facing left (if the hands were opened, the fingers would all point away from the signer).	The hands are held in front of the body; the right hand rests on the side of the left hand.	The hands move to the right and, at the same time, the right hand makes anticlockwise circles in the horizontal plane, maintaining contact with the left hand throughout.		
The **G** hand is held with the palm facing left (if the hand were opened, the fingers would point up).	The hand is held with the index fingertip touching the cheek.	The hand moves down and, at the same time, away from the signer while opening (forming a **B** hand).	**care** **look after** **tend**	333
The left **B̈** hand is held with the palm facing up; the right **B̈** hand is held with the palm facing down (if the hands were opened, the left fingers would point to the right and the right fingers would point away from the signer).	The hands are held in front of the body; the right hand is held above the left hand.	The right hand taps the left hand twice.		

334 Ц GⲦᴧ ˣ·

335 Ц GⲦᴧ ˣ⤮

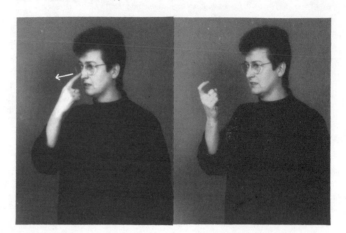

336 З GⲦᴧ ˣ⤮ // ˈḂ>⊥ Gꙷꙷ⊥ᵩ ˅ˣ

337 З GⲦᴧ ˣᵐ // ΓΊ< G̈Ⲧᴧ ˣ

338 З G⊥ᴧ ⤮

339 З G⊥ᴧ ⤮·

Handshape and orientation	Location, hand arrangement and contact	Movement	Glosses	
The **G** hand is held with the palm facing towards the signer (if the hand were opened, the fingers would point up).	The hand is held with the index fingertip in front of the nose.	The index fingertip taps the nose twice.	inquisitive nosey nosey-parker pry	334
Non-manual features The eyes are narrowed.				
The right **G** hand is held with the palm facing towards the signer (if the hand were opened, the fingers would point up).	The hand is held with the index fingertip touching the nose.	The hand makes a short movement away from the signer and, at the same time, the index finger bends.	ability* able* can* capable* could* feasible* possible* possibly* potential*	335
Notes * This sign may be produced with a repeated flexing of the index finger.		○ G⊤ʌ ᵐ·		
The **G** hand is held with the palm facing towards the signer (if the hand were opened, the fingers would point up).	The hand is held with index fingertip touching the right cheek.	The hand moves down and away from the signer while twisting at the wrist, so that the palm faces down.	year (last year)	336
The left **Ḃ** hand is held with the palm facing right and the fingers pointing away from the signer; the right **G** hand is held with the palm facing down (if the hand were opened, the fingers would point away from the signer).	The hands are held in front of the body; the right hand is held higher and nearer to the signer than the left hand.	The right hand moves down, so that the index fingertip touches the base of the left thumb.		
The **G** hand is held with the palm facing towards the signer (if the hand were opened, the fingers would point up).	The hand is held with the index fingertip touching the cheek.	The hand moves towards the signer and down while the index finger bends at the palm knuckle; the movement ends with the index fingertip touching the right shoulder.	yesterday	337
The **G** hand is held with the palm facing away from the signer (if the hand were opened, the fingers would point up).	The hand is held beside the cheek.	The hand makes a short movement away from the signer, so that the side of the index finger brushes the cheek.	yesterday*	338
Notes * Regional sign.				
The **G** hand is held with the palm facing away from the signer (if the hand were opened, the fingers would point up).	The hand is held with the index finger beside the cheek.	The hand makes a short movement away from the signer, so that the side of the index finger brushes across the cheek; the movement is repeated.	always* female feminine girl girlfriend lady lass woman	339
Notes * Regional sign.				

340 3 G<∧ ×·

341 3 G<∧ ×ᵈ[5]ᵥ□

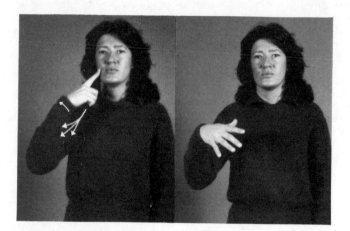

342 ⊃ G<∧ ×// // ⌣ G<∧ ×·

343 ⊃ G<∧ ×// // Ø 5T< ᵒᴅ~·

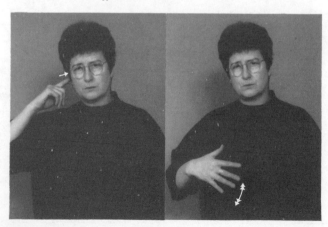

Handshape and orientation	Location, hand arrangement and contact	Movement	Glosses	
The **G** hand is held with the palm facing left (if the hand were opened, the fingers would point up).	The hand is held with the index finger beside the cheek.	The side of the index finger taps the cheek twice.	**always***†	340

      Notes   * Regional sign.

                     † This sign can also be produced with the palm facing away from the signer.   3 G⊥∧ ×·

The **G** hand is held with the palm facing left (if the hand were opened, the fingers would point up).	The hand is held with the index fingertip touching the cheek.	The hand moves down while twisting at the wrist, so that the palm faces down and, at the same time, opens (forming a **5** hand).	**accustomed** **au fait** **familiar** **used to**	341
The **G** hand is held with the palm facing left (if the hand were opened, the fingers would point up).	The hand is held with the index finger beside the ear.	The index fingertip touches the ear; the hand then moves across the cheek and the index fingertip taps the mouth twice.	**hearing** **hearing person**	342

Non-manual features   The lips are rounded.

The **G** hand is held with the palm facing left (if the hand were opened, the fingers would point up).	The hand is held with the index fingertip beside the ear.	The index fingertip touches the ear.	**earache** **toothache**[1]	343
The **5** hand is held with the palm facing towards the signer (if the hand were opened, the fingers would point to the left).	The hand is held in front of the body.	The hand makes several short up and down bending movements from the wrist.		

Non-manual features   The brows are furrowed and the lips rounded.

      Notes   1 The first part of this sign may be located at various parts of the body: e.g. if located at the mouth, the sign produced is **toothache**.   ⌣ G̈⊤∧ × // // ∅ 5⊤< °ᴺ·

344　⊃ G<Λ $^{×ω\dot{n}}_{\underset{>}{\perp\perp}}$

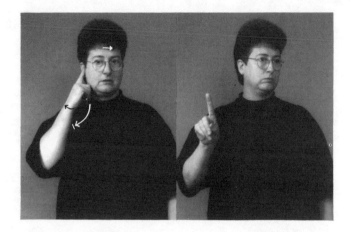

345　⌣ GTΛ $^{×}_{//}$ $^{//}$ Ø ȦT< $^{\dot{○}}_{\perp}$

346　⌣ GTΛ $^{\overset{○×}{3}\dot{}}_{N}$

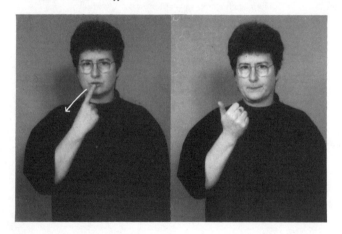

347　⌣ GTΛ $^{×}_{\perp}$

348　⌣ GTΛ $^{\overset{×}{\underset{3}{\overset{\perp}{v}}}\dot{○}}$

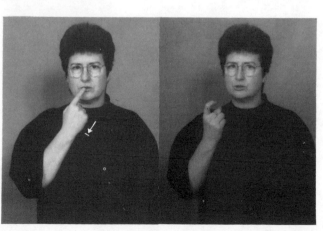

Handshape and orientation	Location, hand arrangement and contact	Movement	Glosses
The **G** hand is held with the palm facing left (if the hand were opened, the fingers would point up).	The hand is held with the index fingertip touching the ear.	The hand twists away from the signer and then bends firmly away from the signer and, at the same time, to the right from the wrist.	ignore *† **344** pay no attention *† take no notice *†

Non-manual features   The mouth opens with a slight puff of air, and the head turns to the left.

Notes   * Directional verb.

     † This sign may also be produced with the hand held with the palm facing away from the signer, and then bending firmly away from the signer and to the right from the wrist.

The **G** hand is held with the palm facing **towards** the signer (if the hand were opened, the fingers would point up).	The hand is held with the index fingertip resting against the lips.	The hand moves away from the signer while changing (forming an **Ȧ** hand).	appetising **345** delicious lovely nice sweet tasty

Notes   * This sign may be produced using a **Ġ** hand which moves away from the signer while closing (forming a **Ġ̈** hand).

The **G** hand is held with the palm facing towards the signer (if the hand were opened, the fingers would point up).	The hand is held with the index fingertip resting against the lower lip.	The hand makes several short twisting movements at the wrist; the index fingertip is held against the lower lip throughout.	confectionery * **346** sweet *

Notes   * The following notes apply to all glosses:

This sign may be produced using a **Ĝ̂** hand.

This sign may be produced using a **G̈** hand.

The **G** hand is held with the palm facing towards the signer (if the hand were opened, the fingers would point up).	The hand is held with the index fingertip touching the lower lip.	The hand moves away from the signer.	comment * **347** mention * say * state * statement tell *

Notes   * Directional verb.

The **G** hand is held with the palm facing towards the signer (if the hand were opened, the fingers would point up).	The hand is held with the index fingertip touching the mouth.	The hand makes a short, firm movement down and away from the signer while the index finger bends (forming a **G̈** hand).	crimson **348** red * scarlet

Notes   * This sign may be produced with a short repeated movement.

349 ⌣ Gᴛʌ ^{×ᵛ[ʙ]}_{⊥□} // ‾Bɑ> Bɑ⊥ ^ᴛ_ᴛ

350 ⌣ Gᴛʌ ^{×(ω)}⊥ ω̇⊤

351 ⌣ Gᴛʌ ^{×v̊□[5]ʌ}

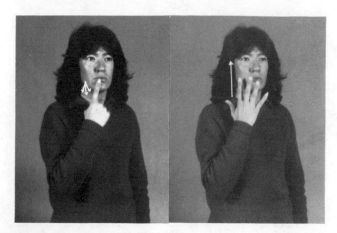

352 ⌣ G<ʌ [×]

Handshape and orientation	Location, hand arrangement and contact	Movement	Glosses	
The left **B** hand is held with the palm facing up and the fingers pointing away from the signer; the right **G** hand is held with the palm facing towards the signer (if the hand were opened, the fingers would point up).	The left hand is held in front of the body; the right hand is held with the index fingertip touching the mouth.	The right hand moves away from the signer and, at the same time, down while opening (forming a **B** hand).	**paper,** **written proposal** **written report** **written statement**	**349**
The left **B** hand is held with the palm facing up and the fingers pointing to the right; the right **B** hand is held with the palm facing up and the fingers pointing away from the signer.	The hands are held in front of the body; the right hand is held above the left hand.	The right hand moves towards the signer with the back of the right hand brushing across the left palm.		
The **G** hand is held with the palm facing towards the signer (if the hand were opened, the fingers would point up).	The hand is held with the index fingertip touching the lower lip.	The hand moves away from the signer while twisting at the wrist, so that the palm faces away from the signer; the hand then twists sharply back towards the signer at the wrist.	**call for*** **command** **demand*** **order** **summon***	**350**

Notes   *   This sign may also be produced with the hand held in front of the body.   Ø G⊤ʌ $\overset{\circ}{\underset{⊤}{\overset{\iota\,\cdot}{\omega}}}$

Handshape and orientation	Location, hand arrangement and contact	Movement	Glosses	
The **G** hand is held with the palm facing towards the signer (if the hand were opened, the fingers would point up).	The hand is held with the index fingertip touching the lower lip.	The hand makes a short downward movement and then opens (forming a **5** hand) before moving up.	**blush** **embarrass** **embarrassed** **embarrassment** **red-faced**	**351**
The **G** hand is held with the palm facing left (if the hand were opened, the fingers would point up).	The hand is held with the index finger in front of the mouth.	The side of the index finger touches the mouth.	**hush*** **quiet (be quiet)*** **sh*** **silent (be silent)***	**352**

Non-manual features   The lips are rounded and pushed forward.

Notes   *   This sign may be produced with the lips pressed together.

353　⌒ G<ʌ ×// Ø Ḡ⊥ʌ , G⊥ʌ₉‿

354　⌒ G<ʌ ×// Ø F⊥ʌ ₁× F⊥ʌ ÷

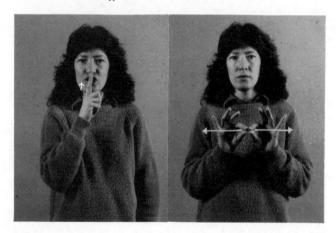

355　⌒ G<ʌ ×⊥// Ø B̿⊥ʌ (#[ɓ]↓)　　　　356　⌒ G<ʌ ×ṅ↓ᵥ

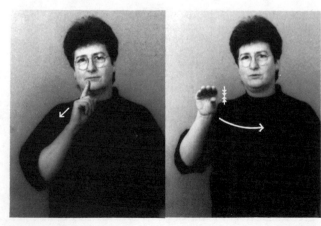　　　

Handshape and orientation	Location, hand arrangement and contact	Movement	Glosses	
The left **G** hand is held with the palm facing away from the signer; the right **G** hand is held with the palm facing left (if the hands were opened, the fingers would all point up).	The left hand is held in front of the body; the right hand is held with the side of the index fingertip touching the chin.	The right hand twists at the wrist, so that the palm faces away from the signer.	**refer** * **referent** [1]	353
Two **G** hands are held with the palms facing away from the signer (if the hands were opened, the fingers would all point up).	The hands are held side by side in front of the body; the right hand is held higher and nearer to the signer than the left hand.	The hands bend away from the signer at the wrists.		

Notes   * Directional verb.

1 If the left hand is held still throughout, with the index finger pointing up, and the right hand bends away from the signer at the wrist, the sign produced is **referent**.

$\smile$ G<∧ × // $\overline{\text{G}⊥∧}$, G⊥∧ʅ

The **G** hand is held with the palm facing left (if the hand were opened, the fingers would point up).	The hand is held with the index finger in front of the mouth.	The side of the index finger touches the mouth.	**hush** * **quiet** * **quiet (be quiet)** * **sh** * **silence** * **silent** * **silent (be silent)** *	354
Two **F** hands are held with the palms facing away from the signer (if the hands were opened, the fingers would all point up).	The hands are held in front of the body with the index fingers and thumbs touching.	The hands move apart.		

Non-manual features   The lips are rounded and pushed forward.

Notes   * This sign may be produced with the lips pressed together.

The **G** hand is held with the palm facing left (if the hand were opened, the fingers would point up).	The hand is held with the index fingertip touching the lower lip.	The hand moves away from the signer.	**gossip** * **rumour** *	355
The **B̄** hand is held with the palm facing away from the signer (if the hand were opened, the fingers would point up).	The hand is held in front of the body.	The hand moves away from the signer and to the left in an arc; at the same time, the fingers and thumb close (forming a **B̂** hand) repeatedly.		

Notes   * This sign may be produced without the first part, in which case the **B̄** hand moves in an arc from the side of the mouth.

$\smile$ B̄<∧ × (# [ɓ] ⋮)

The **G** hand is held with the palm facing left (if the hand were opened, the fingers would point up).	The hand is held with the index fingertip touching the chin.	The hand bends firmly away from the signer at the wrist while moving down.	**call for** * **command** * **instruct** * **instruction** * **order** *	356

Notes   * Directional verb.

357 ⊃ G<ʌ ×⊥[ʙ]□ᵥ̌ // ‾Bɑ> B<⊥ ᵛ×

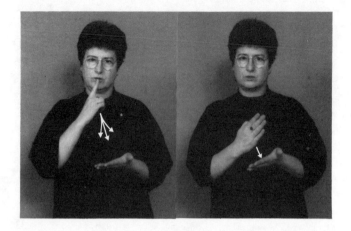

358 ∪ GⳆʌ ×

359 ∪ G<ʌ × // >Γ1 5Ⳇ< ×

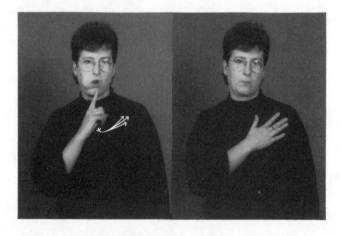

360 ∪ G<ʌ <ᵪˑ

361 ∪ G<ʌ ×⊥°ᵥ // >Γ1 GꞶʌ ×

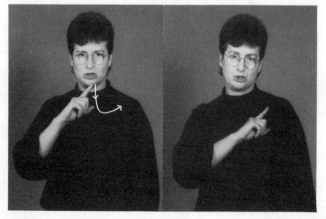

Handshape and orientation	Location, hand arrangement and contact	Movement	Glosses	
The **G** hand is held with the palm facing left (if the hand were opened, the fingers would point up).	The hand is held with the index fingertip touching the mouth.	The hand moves down and away from the signer while opening (forming a **B** hand).	honest promise swear truth	357
The left **B** hand is held with the palm facing up and the fingers pointing to the right; the right **B** hand is held with the palm facing left and the fingers pointing away from the signer.	The hands are held in front of the body; the right hand is held above the left hand.	The right hand moves down; the movement ends with the side of the right hand touching the left palm.		
The **G** hand is held with the palm facing towards the signer (if the hand were opened, the fingers would point up).	The hand is held with the index finger beside the chin.	The index fingertip touches the side of the chin.	day* daily*[1] everyday*[1]	358

Notes   * Regional sign.

1 If the movement is repeated, the sign produced is **daily, everyday**.   ∪ G⊤ʌ ˣ˙

The **G** hand is held with the palm facing left (if the hand were opened, the fingers would point up).	The hand is held with the index fingertip touching the chin.	The hand makes a short downward movement while opening (forming a **5** hand); the hand then moves to the left and, at the same time, towards the signer; the movement ends with the palm held against the left side of the upper chest.	case (in case)	359

Non-manual features   The lips are rounded and the tongue tip is pushed into the right cheek; as the hand moves, the tongue moves back into the mouth and the lips close.

The **G** hand is held with the palm facing left (if the hand were opened, the fingers would point up).	The hand is held with the index finger in front of the chin.	The hand moves to the left so that the side of the index finger brushes across the chin; the movement is repeated.	girl lass	360
The **G** hand is held with the palm facing left (if the hand were opened, the fingers would point up).	The hand is held with the index fingertip touching the chin.	The hand makes a short movement down and, at the same time, away from the signer; the side of the hand then touches the left side of the upper chest.	cannot be bothered can't be bothered landed with stuck with	361

Non-manual features   The lips are rounded and pushed forward.

362 ∪ G<∧ ×∨[5]
           ⊞

363 ∪ G<∧ ×ω[∧] ⸛
           ⊥⊥   ∨
           ∨#

364 ∪ G<∧ °×3⊤

365 π G⊤∧ ×·

366 π G⊥< ×̇
           ○

Handshape and orientation	Location, hand arrangement and contact	Movement	Glosses
The **G** hand is held with the palm facing left (if the hand were opened, the fingers would point up).	The hand is held with the index fingertip touching the side of the chin.	The hand moves down and away from the signer while opening (forming a **5** hand).	doddle* easy* no problem* simple* straightforward*	362

Notes   * This sign may also be produced using a **Y** hand.

∪   Y<∧   x ∨ [5] ⊥ ᗐ

| The **G** hand is held with the palm facing left (if the hand were opened, the fingers would point up). | The hand is held with the index fingertip touching the side of the chin. | The hand moves down and away from the signer, twisting at the wrist, so that the palm faces away from the signer, while closing (forming an **A** hand); the hand then continues in a short, firm movement down and, at the same time, away from the signer. | accustomed
always
custom
habit
habit (be in the habit)
tendency
tendency (have a
   tendency) | 363 |
| The **G** hand is held with the palm facing left (if the hand were opened, the fingers would point up). | The hand is held with the index fingertip touching the underside of the chin. | The hand twists towards the signer at the wrist; the index fingertip is held against the chin throughout. | bashful
coy
shy | 364 |

Non-manual features   The head tilts to one side.

| The **G** hand is held with the palm facing towards the signer (if the hand were opened, the fingers would point up). | The hand is held with the index finger in front of the neck. | The index fingertip taps the neck twice. | throat
voice | 365 |
| The **G** hand is held with the palm facing towards the signer (if the hand were opened, the fingers would point to the left). | The hand is held with the index fingertip against the neck. | The hand twists firmly at the wrist, so that the palm faces left; the index fingertip is held against the neck throughout. | kill
brutal[1]
brutality[1]
cruel[1]
cruelty[1]
harsh[1] | 366 |

Notes   1 If the brows are furrowed, the eyes are narrowed and the lips rounded, the sign produced is **brutal, brutality, cruel, cruelty, harsh.**

367 Π GꙨ< ᵛᴵᶜˣᴾ

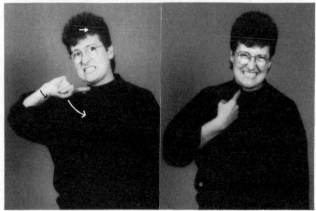

368 ᐟꓚ Gʊʌ ˣ˙

369 ʊ Gʊ< ˣ˙

370 Å>ꓕᵨ x Gʊ< ˣˣ

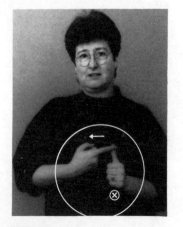

371 Å>ꓕᵨ x Gɑ< ˣˣ

372 Gʊʌ Gʊʌᵨ ˣ

Handshape and orientation	Location, hand arrangement and contact	Movement	Glosses
The **G** hand is held with the palm facing away from the signer (if the hand were opened, the fingers would point to the left).	The hand is held with the index fingertip held against the neck.	The hand moves away from the signer and to the left while twisting at the wrist so that the palm faces down; the index fingertip is held against the neck throughout.	**kill oneself to do something work one's guts out** 367

Non-manual features   The lips are stretched and the head tilts to the left with the eyes narrowing as the hand twists.

The **G** hand is held with the palm facing down (if the hand were opened, the fingers would point up).	The hand is held in front of the left side of the upper chest, at an angle so that the index finger is turned to the left.	The index finger taps the left side of the upper chest twice.	**why?** **because**[1] **reason**[1] 368

Non-manual features   Non-manual features appropriate for questions must be used.

Notes   1   If the non-manual features are not present, the sign produced is **because, reason**.

The **G** hand is held with the palm facing down (if the hand were opened, the fingers would point to the left).	The left forearm is positioned in front of the body (with the palm facing down); the right index finger is held above the left wrist.	The right index fingertip taps the left wrist several times.	**time** **what time?**[1] 369

Notes   1   If the eyebrows are raised, the sign produced is **what time?**

The left **Á** hand is held with the palm facing right (if the hand were opened, the fingers would point away from the signer). The right **G** hand is held with the palm facing up (if the hand were opened, the fingers would point to the left).	The hands are held side by side in front of the body, with the right index fingertip touching the top of the left thumb pad.	The right hand moves to the right, so that the side of the right index finger brushes across the pad of the left thumb.	**cut one's thumb** 370 **cut on one's thumb** **cut**[1] **cut oneself**[1]

Notes   1 The right hand is located at the appropriate part of the body.

$$\text{Á}>\bot_\varphi \; \text{x} \; \text{Ga}< \overset{>}{\underset{>}{\times}}$$

The left **Á** hand is held with the palm facing right (if the hand were opened, the fingers would point away from the signer). The right **G** hand is held with the palm facing towards the signer (if the hand were opened, the fingers would point to the left).	The hands are held side by side in front of the body, with the right index finger held further away from the signer than the left thumb.	The right hand makes a short movement towards the signer and then up so that the index finger brushes the pad of the left thumb; the movement is repeated.	**alcoholic*** 371 **America*** **American*** **answer*** **automatic*** **reply***

Notes   *   The movement may be changed so that the right hand makes small clockwise circles in the vertical plane at right angles to the signer's body, with the right index finger brushing the left thumb in making each circle.

$$\text{Á}>\bot \; | \; \text{GT}< \overset{\cdot}{\underset{\vee}{...}}$$

Two **G** hands are held with the palms facing down (if the hands were opened, the fingers would all point up).	The hands are held in front of the body at an angle so that the index fingers are turned towards each other.	The middle knuckle of the right index finger touches the middle knuckle of the left index finger.	**multiplication** 372 **multiply** **times**

373   G⌒⊥ ˌ G⌒⊥ₚ $\frac{\perp}{\top}^{\times}$ 374   G⌒⊥ ˌ G⌒⊥ₚ $\frac{\perp}{\top}^{\times}$˙

375   Ḡ⌒> ˌ G⌒⊥ $\overset{\vee}{\underset{\vee}{}}$ 376   Ḡ⌒> ₓ G⌒⊥ₚ $\overset{\times}{\underset{\perp}{}}$˙   377   Ḡ⊤⊥ ₓ G⌒⊥ $\overset{\times}{\underset{\times}{\perp}}$

378   Ḡ⊤⊥ ₓ G⊤⊥ $\overset{\times}{\underset{\text{N}}{}}$ 379   G⊤> ˌ G⊤∧ₚ

 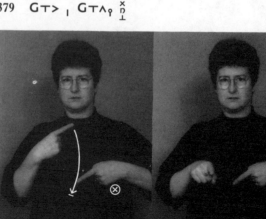

[268]

Handshape and orientation	Location, hand arrangement and contact	Movement	Glosses	
Two **G** hands are held with the palms facing down (if the hands were opened, the fingers would all point away from the signer).	The hands are held side by side in front of the body; the right hand is held nearer to the signer than the left hand.	The right hand moves away from the signer, so that the side of the right index finger brushes the side of the left index finger.	attempt effort (make an effort) majority most mostly try	373
Two **G** hands are held with the palms facing down (if the hands were opened, the fingers would all point away from the signer).	The hands are held side by side in front of the body; the right hand is held nearer to the signer than the left hand.	The right hand moves away from the signer, so that the side of the right index finger brushes the side of the left index finger; the movement is repeated.	attempt attempted effort (make an effort) try	374
Two **G** hands are held with the palms facing down (if the hands were opened, the left fingers would point to the right and the right fingers would point away from the signer).	The hands are held side by side in front of the body; the right hand is held higher than the left hand.	The right hand moves down, so that the right index finger brushes the left index fingertip.	fine * † penalty	375

Notes   * Directional verb.

† This sign may also be produced with the right hand held below the left hand (with the palm facing up) and then moving up and towards the signer, so that the right index fingertip brushes the left index fingertip.

G̲ɔ> Gɑ⊥ᵨ ^T×>T

Two **G** hands are held with the palms facing down (if the hands were opened, the left fingers would point to the right and the right fingers would point away from the signer).	The hands are held in front of the body; the right index finger rests across the left index finger.	The right hand makes two short movements towards and away from the signer; the right index finger maintains contact with the left index finger throughout.	knit with knitting needles knitting	376
The left **G** hand is held with the palm facing towards the signer; the right **G** hand is held with the palm facing down (if the hands were opened, the fingers would all point away from the signer).	The hands are held in front of the body; the left hand is held at an angle so that the palm is turned to the right and the right hand rests on the left hand.	The right hand moves away from the signer and, at the same time, to the right maintaining contact with the left hand throughout.	week (following week) week (next week)	377
Two **G** hands are held with the palms facing towards the signer (if the hands were opened, the fingers would all point away from the signer).	The hands are held in front of the body with the fingers turned towards each other so that the right index finger rests across the left index finger.	The right hand moves towards and away from the signer, and at the same time, from side to side; the movement is repeated several times with the index fingers maintaining contact throughout.	England English	378
Two **G** hands are held with the palms facing towards the signer (if the hands were opened, the left fingers would point to the right and the right fingers would point up).	The hands are held side by side in front of the body; the right hand is held nearer to the signer than the left hand and the left hand is held at an angle so that the index finger is turned upwards.	The right hand bends firmly away from the signer from the wrist so that the right index finger brushes the left index fingertip.	boot out * dismiss * dismissal fire * kick out * sack * suspend * suspension	379

Notes   * Directional verb.

380 $\overline{G}\text{T}>\ G<\bot\ ^{\times}\cdot$ 381 $\overline{G}\text{T}>\ _\times\ G<\bot\ \overset{<}{\times}$

382 $\overline{G}\text{T}>\ _\times\ G<\bot_?\ \overset{\dot{\text{T}}}{\square}{}^{[5]}$ 383 $\overline{G}\text{T}>\ G<\bot_?\ {}^{(\vee\,\dot{\times}\,\wedge)}$

384 $\overline{G}\text{T}>\ G<\bot_?\ ^{\times}\cdot$

Handshape and orientation	Location, hand arrangement and contact	Movement	Glosses	
The left **G** hand is held with the palm facing towards the signer; the right **G** hand is held with the palm facing left (if the hands were opened, the left fingers would point to the right and the right fingers would point away from the signer).	The hands are held in front of the body; the right hand is held above the left hand.	The right hand taps the left hand twice.	chat * comment * † conversation * converse * discuss * discussion * mention * † speak * talk *	380

Notes   * This sign may be produced using two **V** hands.

$$\overline{V}\tau> \ V<\perp \ ^{\times} \cdot$$

     † This sign may be used as the second part of a compound sign which also means **comment, mention** (see 347 for the first part of the sign).

$$\cup \ G<\wedge \ {}^{\times}_{\vee}{}^{\perp} \ // \ \overline{G}\tau> \ G<\perp \ ^{\times} \cdot$$

The left **G** hand is held with the palm facing towards the signer; the right **G** hand is held with the palm facing left (if the hands were opened, the left fingers would point to the right and the right fingers would point away from the signer).	The hands are held in front of the body; the right hand rests on the left index finger.	The right hand moves towards the signer and to the left, maintaining contact with the left hand throughout.	week (last week) week (one week ago)	381
The left **G** hand is held with the palm facing towards the signer; the right **G** hand is held with the palm facing left (if the hands were opened, the left fingers would point to the right, and the right fingers would point away from the signer).	The hands are held in front of the body with the right index finger resting across the left index finger.	The right hand moves sharply towards the signer and, at the same time, opens (forming a **5** hand).	fast quick sharp speed	382
The left **G** hand is held with the palm facing towards the signer; the right **G** hand is held with the palm facing left (if the hands were opened, the left fingers would point to the right and the right fingers would point away from the signer).	The hands are held in front of the body; the right index finger is held above the left index finger.	The right hand moves sharply down, so that the right index finger touches the left index finger, and then moves back up.	automatic early emergency fast haste immediate quick sudden urgent	383
The left **G** hand is held with the palm facing right; the right **G** hand is held with the palm facing left, (if the hands were opened, the left fingers would point to the right and the right fingers would point away from the signer).	The hands are held side by side in front of the body, at an angle so that the right index finger is held above the left index finger.	The side of the right index finger taps the side of the left index finger several times.	fast hurry hurry up quick (be quick) soon (as soon as possible) speed up emergency [1] urgent [2]	384

Notes   1 If the eyes are opened wide, the sign produced is **emergency**.

     2 If the brows are furrowed, the sign produced is **urgent**.

385 G⊥∧ₚ x G⊤∧ ᵒᵢ

386 G>∧ x Gʊ< ᶺᵛᵢ⊥

387 G>∧ x Gʊ<ₚ ˣ̆

388 G>∧ x Gʊ<ₚ ᵒₙˣ·

389 G>∧ Gʊ<ₚ ˣ

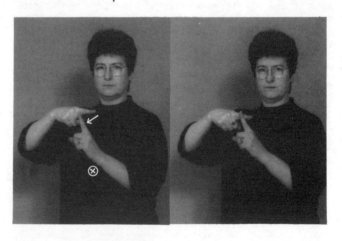

390 G>∧ ₁x G<⊥ ᐟ

391 ᐟV⊤>₁ Gʊ⊥ₚ ˣ·

Handshape and orientation	Location, hand arrangement and contact	Movement	Glosses	
The left **G** hand is held with the palm facing away from the signer; the right **G** hand is held with the palm facing towards the signer (if the hands were opened, the fingers would all point up).	The hands are held in front of the body; the left hand is held nearer to the signer than the right hand, with the closed fingers touching.	The right hand moves away from the signer.	close* near* across[1] opposite[1]	385

Notes   *   This sign can also be produced with the right hand moving towards the signer, and the movement ending with the closed fingers touching.

$$G⊥∧_? \quad G⊤∧ \quad ^{⊤×}$$

1   If the movement is changed so that the right hand moves away from the signer in a short arc, the sign produced is **across, opposite**.

$$G⊥∧_? \quad × \quad G⊤∧ \quad ^{°\,°·}_{∧\,∨}_⊥$$

The left **G** hand is held with the palm facing right; the right **G** hand is held with the palm facing down (if the hands were opened, the fingers would point up).	The hands are held in front of the body with the tips of the index fingers touching.	The right hand moves up and, at the same time, away from the signer and then continues to move away from the signer while moving down.	satellite (beam by satellite) satellite (communication satellite) satellite (transmit by satellite)	386
The left **G** hand is held with the palm facing right; the right **G** hand is held with the palm facing down (if the hands were opened, the left fingers would point up and the right fingers would point to the left).	The hands are held in front of the body; the right hand is held nearer to the signer than the left hand, and the side of the right index finger rests against the side of the left index finger.	The right hand moves to the right; the right index finger maintains contact with the left index finger throughout.	half	387
The left **G** hand is held with the palm facing right; the right **G** hand is held with the palm facing down (if the hands were opened, the left fingers would point up and the right fingers would point to the left).	The hands are held in front of the body; the right hand is held nearer to the signer than the left hand with the side of the right index finger touching the side of the left index finger.	The right hand makes short up and down movements; the right index finger maintains contact with the left index finger throughout.	temperature	388
The left **G** hand is held with the palm facing right; the right **G** hand is held with the palm facing down (if the hands were opened, the left fingers would point up and the right fingers would point to the left).	The hands are held in front of the body; the right hand is held nearer to the signer than the left hand.	The index fingers touch at the middle knuckle forming a cross.	plus positive[1]	389

Notes   1   If the movement is repeated, the sign produced is **positive**.

$$G>∧ \quad G℧<_? \quad ^{×·} \quad \text{or} \quad G℧> \quad G<∧_? \quad ^{×·}$$

| The left **G** hand is held with the palm facing right; the right **G** hand is held with the palm facing left (if the hands were opened, the left fingers would point up and the right fingers would point away from the signer). | The hands are held side by side with the index fingertips touching. | The right hand moves to the right. | sentence | 390 |
| The left **V** hand is held with the palm facing towards the signer (if the hand were opened the fingers would point to the right). The right **G** hand is held with the palm facing down (if the hand were opened, the fingers would point away from the signer). | The hands are held side by side in front of the body; the right hand is held nearer to the signer than the left hand. | The right index fingertip taps the left middle fingertip twice. | another other second secondly | 391 |

392　V̈ʊ⊥ႇ GT< ˣ˙

393　ᵘ5>⊥ ˌ Gʊ⊥ ˣ˙

394　5>⊥ ˌ GT< ˣ // 5>⊥ ˌ V<ʌ ˣ

395　5>⊥ ˌ GT< ˣ˙

396　ᵉ5>⊥ ˌ GT< ˣ

397　²5>⊥ ˌ GT< °̇

Handshape and orientation	Location, hand arrangement and contact	Movement	Glosses	
The left **V** hand is held with the palm facing down (if the hand were opened the fingers would point away from the signer). The right **G** hand is held with the palm facing towards the signer (if the hand were opened, the fingers would point to the left).	The hands are held in front of the body; the left hand is held nearer to the signer than the right hand.	The right index fingertip taps the backs of the left index and middle fingers twice.	**AIDS** **person with AIDS**	392
The left **5** hand is held with the palm facing right and the fingers pointing away from the signer; the right **G** hand is held with the palm facing down (if the hand were opened, the fingers would point away from the signer).	The hands are held side by side in front of the body.	The right index fingertip taps the left little fingertip twice.	**uncle** **university**	393
The left **5** hand is held with the palm facing up and the fingers pointing away from the signer; the right **G** hand is held with the palm facing towards the signer (if the hand were opened, the fingers would point to the left).	The hands are held side by side in front of the body.	The right index fingertip touches the side of the left palm.	**T.V.** **television** **telly** satellite T.V. [1] satellite television [1]	394
The left **5** hand is held with the palm facing up and the fingers pointing away from the signer; the right **V** hand is held with the palm facing left and the extended fingers pointing up.	The hands are held side by side in front of the body; the left hand is held at an angle so that the palm is turned to the left.	The extended fingers of the right hand touch the left palm.		

Notes 1 This sign may be used as the second part of a compound sign meaning **satellite T.V.**, **satellite television** (see 386 for the first part of the sign).

$$G{>}\wedge \ _{\times} \ G\text{ʊ}{<} \ \overset{\wedge \ \curlyvee}{{\perp}{\perp}} \ /\!/ $$
$$5{>}{\perp} \ _| \ G{\top}{<} \ ^{\times} \ /\!/ \ 5{>}{\perp} \ _| \ V{<}\wedge \ ^{\times}$$

The left **5** hand is held with the palm facing right and the fingers pointing away from the signer; The right **G** hand is held with the palm facing towards the signer (if the hand were opened, the fingers would point to the left).	The hands are held side by side in front of the body.	The right index fingertip taps the side of the left palm twice.	**sober** * **teetotal** **teetotaller** **toilet**	395

Notes * Regional sign.

The left **5** hand is held with the palm facing right and the fingers pointing away from the signer; the right **G** hand is held with the palm facing towards the signer (if the hand were opened, the fingers would point to the left).	The hands are held side by side in front of the body; the left index finger is bent at the palm knuckle.	The right index fingertip touches the left index fingertip.	**east**	396
The left **5** hand is held with the palm facing right and the fingers pointing away from the signer; the right **G** hand is held with the palm facing towards the signer (if the hand were opened, the fingers would point to the left).	The hands are held side by side in front of the body.	The right index finger moves sharply between the left index and middle fingers.	**goal** **puncture** [1]	397

Notes 1 If the cheeks are slightly puffed out and then the mouth opens a little with a puff of air, the sign produced is **puncture**.

398 B̄α⊥ Gᴜᴌ⊥ $\overset{\text{n}}{\text{v}}$

399 B̄α⊥ | Gᴜ< ˣ

400 B̄α⊥ | Gᴛᴧ $^{\binom{\text{n x}}{<}\cdot}$

401 B̄α⊥ | Gᴛ< $\overset{\cdot}{\text{v}}$ˣ

402 B̄α⊥ | Gᴛ< $^{\binom{\text{x}\,\cdot}{\text{ᴛ}}}$

403 B̄α> ˣ G<⊥ $^{\overset{\text{o}}{\underset{\text{z}}{\text{n}}}}$ ˣ ·

[276]

Handshape and orientation	Location, hand arrangement and contact	Movement	Glosses	
The left **B** hand is held with the palm facing up and the fingers pointing away from the signer; the right **G** hand is held with the palm facing down (if the hand were opened, the fingers would point away from the signer).	The hands are held in front of the body; the right hand is held above the left hand.	The right hand bends sharply downwards from the wrist, so that the index finger passes over the left palm.	charge*	398

| | | *Notes* | * Directional verb. | | |
| | | This sign can be produced using one hand only. | | |

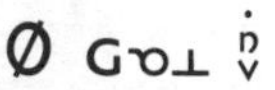

$$\emptyset \quad \text{G} \delta \text{L} \quad \overset{.}{\underset{\vee}{\text{P}}}$$

| The left **B** hand is held with the palm facing up and the fingers pointing away from the signer; the right **G** hand is held with the palm facing down (if the hand were opened, the fingers would point to the left). | The hands are held side by side in front of the body; the right hand is held higher than the left hand. | The right index finger touches the left palm. | pound* | 399 |

Notes * Regional sign.

| The left **B** hand is held with the palm facing up and the fingers pointing away from the signer; the right **G** hand is held with the palm facing towards the signer (if the hand were opened, the fingers would point up). | The hands are held side by side in front of the body; the right hand is held higher than the left hand. | The right hand bends to the left from the wrist, so that the right index finger touches the left palm; the movement is repeated. | commandment | 400 |

| The left **B** hand is held with the palm facing up and the fingers pointing away from the signer; the right **G** hand is held with the palm facing towards the signer (if the hand were opened, the fingers would point to the left). | The hands are held side by side in front of the body; the right hand is held higher than the left hand. | The right hand moves firmly down until the side of the right index finger touches the left palm. | decide* decision* decree definite law principle rule ruling | 401 |

Notes * This sign may be used as the second part of a compound sign which also means **decide, decision** (see 511 Note 1 for the first part of the sign).

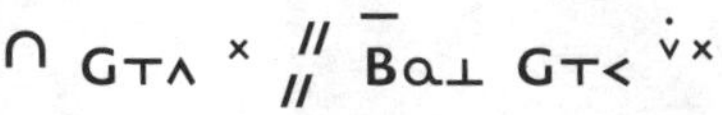

$$\cap \quad \text{G} \tau \wedge \quad ^\times \quad \overset{//}{//} \quad \overline{\text{B}} \text{a} \bot \quad \text{G} \tau < \quad \overset{\vee \times}{}$$

| The left **B** hand is held with the palm facing up and the fingers pointing away from the signer; the right **G** hand is held with the palm facing towards the signer (if the hand were opened, the fingers would point to the left). | The hands are held side by side in front of the body; the right index finger is held above the left palm. | The right index finger taps the palm several times, while the right hand moves towards the signer throughout. | commandments constitution legislate legislation policy principles regulations rules | 402 |

| The left **B** hand is held with the palm facing up and the fingers pointing to the right; the right **G** hand is held with the palm facing left (if the hand were opened, the fingers would point away from the signer). | The hands are held in front of the body; the right hand is held on the left palm. | The right hand bends from side to side from the wrist, maintaining contact with the left palm throughout. | compass gauge meter navigate navigator orienteering | 403 |

404 $\overline{B}\text{ʊ}> \text{ʃG⊤ʌ}^{\binom{n\,x}{<}\cdot}$ 405 $B\text{ʊ}> _{x} G<\text{ʌ}_?\ ^{\wedge}$

406 $\underline{B}⊤⊥_|\ G⊤<^{\overset{\circ}{\underset{v}{@}}\cdot}$ 407 $B⊥\text{ʌ}_?\ G\text{ʊ}<^{\,x\,\cdot}$

408 $B>\text{ʌ}_|\ G\text{ʊ}\text{ʌ}^{\,x\,\cdot}$ 409 $B>\text{ʌ}_{|x}\ G⊥\text{ʌ}^{\,\overset{n}{\underset{x}{\top}}}$

The index finger is extended from the fist.

Handshape and orientation	Location, hand arrangement and contact	Movement	Glosses	
The left **B** hand is held with the palm facing down and the fingers pointing to the right; the right **G** hand is held with the palm facing towards the signer (if the hand were opened, the fingers would point up).	The left arm is positioned across the body; the right elbow is held against the left fingertips.	The right arm bends to the left from the elbow, so that the right hand touches the left forearm; the movement is repeated, with the right elbow held against the left fingertips throughout.	barrier	404
The left **B** hand is held with the palm facing down and the fingers pointing to the right; the right **G** hand is held with the palm facing left (if the hand were opened, the fingers would point up).	The hands are held in front of the body; the right hand is held nearer to the signer, resting against the side of the left hand.	The right hand moves up.	space spacecraft spaceship launch pad [1] missile [2] rocket [2] blast off [3] launch [3] lift off [3]	405

Notes 1 If there is no movement, the sign produced is **launch pad**.

$$B\text{ʊ}> \quad_{\times} \quad G{<}\wedge_\wp \quad^{\emptyset}$$

2 If the right index finger points and moves firmly away from the signer, the sign produced is **missile, rocket**.

$$B\text{ʊ}> \quad_{\times} \quad G{<}\perp_\wp \quad^{\dot{\perp}}$$

3 If the cheeks are puffed out and the eyes are narrowed, the sign produced is **blast off, launch, lift off**.

The left **B** hand is held with the palm facing towards the signer and the fingers pointing away from the signer; the right **G** hand is held with the palm facing towards the signer (if the hand were opened, the fingers would point to the left).	The hands are held side by side in front of the body; the left hand is held higher than the right hand.	The right hand makes small clockwise circles in the vertical plane at right angles to the signer's body.	propeller (of a boat)	406
The left **B** hand is held with the palm facing away from the signer and the fingers pointing up; the right **G** hand is held with the palm facing down (if the hand were opened, the fingers would point to the left).	The hands are held in front of the body; the left hand is held nearer to the signer than the right hand.	The right index finger taps the left palm twice.	negative	407
The left **B** hand is held with the palm facing right and the fingers pointing up; the right **G** hand is held with the palm facing down (if the hand were opened, the fingers would point up).	The hands are held side by side in front of the body; the right hand is held at an angle, so that the index finger is turned away from the signer.	The side of the right index finger taps the left palm twice.	alarm alarm clock electric bell [1] ring of an electric bell [1]	408

Notes 1 If the movement is repeated several times, the sign produced is **electric bell, ring of an electric bell**.

The left **B** hand is held with the palm facing right and the fingers pointing up; the right **G** hand is held with the palm facing away from the signer (if the hand were opened, the fingers would point up).	The hands are held side by side in front of the body with the side of the right index finger resting against the left palm.	The right hand bends away from the signer from the wrist, maintaining contact with the left palm throughout.	late overdue	409

410 B>ʌ ₁x G⊥ʌ $^{ᑎ}_{×}$$^{ᑎ}_{×}$
$_{⊥}$$_{v}$

411 B>ʌ ₁x G⊥ʌ $^{ᑎ}_{×}$$^{ω}_{×}$
$_{⊤}$

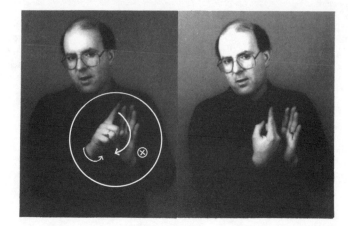

412 B>ʌ ₁x G<⊥ $^{ᑎ}_{×}$
^{ʌ}

413 B>⊥ ₁ Gၒ< $^{⊤}_{×}$$^{o}_{v}$$^{v}_{×}$$^{v}_{v}$
$_{⊤}$$_{×}$$_{⊤}$$_{⊤}$

414 B̈ၒʌ Gၒ⊥ၡ $^{⊥}$

415 B̲̈>ʌ Gၒ⊥ၡ $^{⊥}_{×}$
$_{⊤}$

416 ˈB̊ၒ⊥ × Gၒ⊥ၡ $^{o}_{×}$
$_{⊤}$

[280]

Handshape and orientation	Location, hand arrangement and contact	Movement	Glosses	
The left **B** hand is held with the palm facing right and the fingers pointing up; the right **G** hand is held with the palm facing away from the signer (if the hand were opened, the fingers would point up).	The hands are held side by side in front of the body, with the side of the right index finger resting against the left palm.	The right hand bends away from the signer and then down from the wrist, maintaining contact with the right palm throughout.	clock* time* what time?[1]	410

Notes   * This sign may be produced with a right **Ġ** handshape.

$$B{>}\wedge \ _{IX} \ \dot{G}{\perp}\wedge \ ^{D\ D}_{\perp\ V}$$

   1 If the right index finger bends up and down at the palm knuckle and the eyebrows are raised, the sign produced is **what time?**

$$B{>}\wedge \ _{IX} \ G{\perp}\wedge \ ^{m.}_{\sim} \quad \text{or} \quad B{>}\wedge \ _{IX} \ \dot{G}{\perp}\wedge \ ^{m.}_{\sim}$$

The left **B** hand is held with the palm facing right and the fingers pointing up; the right **G** hand is held with the palm facing away from the signer (if the hand were opened, the fingers would point up).	The hands are held in front of the body; the right index finger rests against the left palm.	The right hand bends away from the signer and then down at the wrist; the right hand then twists towards the signer (so that the palm faces towards the signer and the index finger points up); the right hand maintains contact with the left palm throughout.	hour	411
The left **B** hand is held with the palm facing right and the fingers pointing up; the right **G** hand is held with the palm facing left (if the hand were opened, the fingers would point away from the signer).	The hands are held side by side in front of the body; the closed right fingers are held against the left palm.	The right hand bends up from the wrist; the closed right fingers maintain contact with the left palm throughout.	early	412
The left **B** hand is held with the palm facing right and the fingers pointing away from the signer; the right **G** hand is held with the palm facing down (if the hand were opened, the fingers would point to the left).	The hands are held side by side in front of the body.	The right index finger draws a cross on the left palm.	ballot ban call off cancel cancellation censor elect election vote	413
The left **B̈** hand is held with the palm facing down (if the hand were opened, the fingers would point up). The right **G** hand is held with the palm facing down (if the hand were opened, the fingers would point away from the signer).	The hands are held in front of the body; the right hand is held lower and nearer to the signer than the left hand and the left hand is held at an angle, so that the palm is turned to the right.	The right hand moves away from the signer.	metro subway tube tunnel underground underground train	414
The left **B̈** hand is held with the palm facing right (if the hand were opened, the fingers would point up). The right **G** hand is held with the palm facing down (if the hand were opened, the fingers would point away from the signer).	The hands are held in front of the body; the right hand is held lower and nearer to the signer than the left hand.	The right hand moves away from the signer, so that the back of the right index finger brushes across the left palm.	abscond escape escapee flee run away truant[1] truant (play truant)[1]	415

Notes   1 If the movement is repeated, the sign produced is **truant, play truant.**

$$\ddot{B}{>}\wedge \ G{\cap}{\perp}_\varphi \ ^{\perp\ .}_{x}_{\perp}$$

The left **B̈** hand is held with the palm facing down and the fingers pointing away from the signer; the right **G** hand is held with the palm facing down (if the hand were opened, the fingers would point away from the signer).	The hands are held in front of the body; the right index fingertip rests on the base of the left thumb.	The right hand makes a short movement towards the signer, maintaining contact with the left hand throughout.	year	416

417 ˈB̄>⊥ Gᴜᴸ⊥ₚ ᵒₓᵀ·

418 ∅ Ḡɑ⊥ Gᴜᴸ⊥ ᵉᴺ·

419 ∅ Ḡɑ⊥ Gᴜᴸ⊥ ᵉᴺ // ∅ 5>ʌ 5<ʌ (ᵒ ᴧ ᴧ ᴅ)

420 ∅ Gᴜᴸ⊥ Gᴜᴸ⊥ ᵉ·

421 ∅ Gᴜᴸ⊥ Gᴜᴸ⊥ ᴅᵃ

422 ∅ Gᴜᴸ⊥ˌ Gᴜᴸ⊥ ⊥

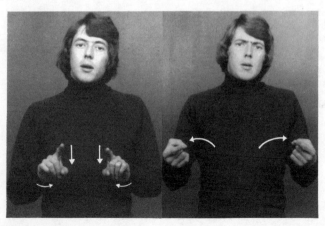

Handshape and orientation	Location, hand arrangement and contact	Movement	Glosses	
The left Ḃ hand is held with the palm facing right and the fingers pointing away from the signer; the right **G** hand is held with the palm facing down (if the hand were opened, the fingers would point away from the signer).	The hands are held in front of the body; the right index finger is held above the left hand.	The right hand makes a short movement towards the signer, so that the tip of the right index finger brushes the base of the left thumb; the movement is repeated.	**paper** **years** **yellow** **yoghurt** **young** **year** [1]	**417**

Notes   1 If the right hand makes a short downward movement, so that the index finger touches the base of the left thumb, the sign produced is **year**.   ˈB̄>⊥   G⌒⊥ₚ   ᵒᵥˣ

Handshape and orientation	Location, hand arrangement and contact	Movement	Glosses	
The left **G** hand is held with the palm facing up; the right **G** hand is held with the palm facing down (if the hands were opened, the fingers would all point away from the signer).	The hands are held in front of the body; the right hand is held above the left hand.	The hands make alternate clockwise circles in the horizontal plane.	**conference** **congress** **convention** **meeting**	**418**
The left **G** hand is held with the palm facing up; the right **G** hand is held with the palm facing down (if the hands were opened, the fingers would all point away from the signer).	The hands are held in front of the body; the right hand is held above the left hand.	The hands make alternate clockwise circles in the horizontal plane.	**conference** **congress** **convention** **meeting**	**419**
The left **5** hand is held with the palm facing right and the fingers pointing up; the right **5** hand is held with the palm facing left and the fingers pointing up.	The hands are held in front of the body.	The hands make a short movement up and towards each other while bending towards each other at the wrists.		
The left **G** hand is held with the palm facing right; the right **G** hand is held with the palm facing left (if the hands were opened, the fingers would all point away from the signer).	The hands are held in front of the body.	The hands make two anticlockwise circles in the vertical plane parallel to the signer's body.	**mainframe** **computer**	**420**
Two **G** hands are held with the palms facing down (if the hands were opened, the fingers would all point away from the signer).	The hands are held in front of the body.	The hands move down, bending from the wrists, and then twist at the wrists, so that the palms face up.	**cannot** * **can't** * **could not** * **couldn't** * **impossible** * **incapable** * **unable** *	**421**

Non-manual features   Appropriate negative non-manual features must be used.

Notes   * The following notes apply to all glosses:

     This sign may be produced using one hand only.   Ø   G⌒⊥   ⁿᵃᵥ

     This sign may be produced with the movement beginning in front of the face.   Ↄ   G<ʌ   ⁿᵃ_ᵢ

     This sign may be produced with the movement beginning from the forehead.   ∩   G<ʌ   ⁿᵃ_ᵢ

Handshape and orientation	Location, hand arrangement and contact	Movement	Glosses	
Two **G** hands are held with the palms facing down (if the hands were opened, the fingers would all point away from the signer).	The hands are held side by side in front of the body.	The hands move away from the signer.	**parallel** **side by side**	**422**

423 Ø Gᴠ⊥ ¦ Gᴠ⊥ ˣ ·

424 Ø Gᴠ⊥ ¦ Gᴠ⊥ ˣˣ

425 Ø Gᴠ⊥ ¦ Gᴠ⊥ ˣˣ⌣ ∧ // ᴒ Gᴠ< ˣ

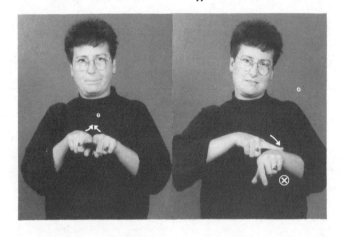

426 Ø Gᴠ⊥ ¦ Gᴠ⊥ ⁽ˣˣ÷·⁾

427 Ø Gᴠ⊥ ¦ Gᴠ⊥ ⁽ᴺᴺ÷·⁾

428 Ø Gᴠ⊥ ¦ Gᴠ⊥ ⁽ˣ∧ˣ÷·⁾

Handshape and orientation	Location, hand arrangement and contact	Movement	Glosses	
Two **G** hands are held with the palms facing down (if the hands were opened, the fingers would all point away from the signer).	The hands are held side by side in front of the body.	The sides of the index fingers tap together twice.	also as…as as well as like same similar too	423
Two **G** hands are held with the palms facing down (if the hands were opened, the fingers would all point away from the signer).	The hands are held side by side in front of the body.	The hands move towards each other; the movement ends with the sides of the index fingers touching.	like same alike[1] identical[1]	424

Notes 1 If the sign begins with the palms facing up and then turning over before moving towards each other, and finally touching, the sign produced is **alike, identical**. — Ø Gɑ⊥ ¦ Gɑ⊥ ᵛˣˣ

Two **G** hands are held with the palms facing down (if the hands were opened, the fingers would all point away from the signer).	The hands are held side by side in front of the body.	The hands make a short movement towards each other and then a short upward movement with the index fingers held together.	simultaneous time (at the same time)	425
The right **G** hand is held with the palm facing down (if the hand were opened, the fingers would point to the left).	The left hand is positioned in front of the body with the palm facing down; the right index finger is held above the left wrist.	The right index fingertip touches the left wrist.		
Two **G** hands are held with the palms facing down (if the hands were opened, the fingers would all point away from the signer).	The hands are held side by side in front of the body.	The hands twist at the wrists, so that the palms face towards each other; the movement is repeated several times with the hands moving apart throughout.	assorted assortment diverse etc et cetera kinds (all kinds of) range selection sorts (all sorts of) variation variety various	426
Two **G** hands are held with the palms facing down (if the hands were opened, the fingers would all point away from the signer).	The hands are held side by side in front of the body.	The hands move up and down alternately several times while moving apart throughout.	assorted assortment diverse etc et cetera kinds (all kinds of) range selection sorts (all sorts of) variation variety various	427
Two **G** hands are held with the palms facing down (if the hands were opened, the fingers would all point away from the signer).	The hands are held side by side in front of the body.	The hands move up and, at the same time, towards each other, and then move down with the index fingers held together, before finally moving apart; the movement is repeated several times with the hands moving to the right throughout.	pattern	428

429 Ø ᵉGᴜ⊥ ₁x ᵉGᴜ⊥ ⁺̣

430 Ø Gᴜ⊥ x Gᴜ⊥ᵨ ⊤

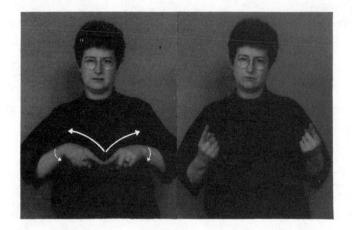

431 Ø Gᴜ⊥ Gᴜ⊥ᵨ ˙᾿

432 Ø Gᴛᴧ x G⊥ᴧᵨ ˙ₓ

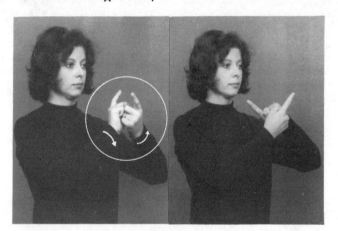

433 Ø Gᴛᴧ G⊥ᴧᵨ ˙ω̇

434 Ø Gᴛᴧ G⊥ᴧᵨ ˣˣ̣

Handshape and orientation	Location, hand arrangement and contact	Movement	Glosses	
Two Ḡ hands are held with the palms facing down (if the hands were opened, the fingers would all point away from the signer).	The hands are held side by side in front of the body, with the index fingertips touching.	The hands move apart and, at the same time, twist at the wrists, so that the palms face up.	differ difference different	429
Two **G** hands are held with the palms facing down (if the hands were opened, the fingers would all point away from the signer).	The hands are held in front of the body; the right hand is held nearer to the signer with the right index finger tip held against the left wrist.	The hands remain together and move away from the signer.	follow go along with stick to stick with chase[1] tail[1]	430

Notes 1 If the hands make short movements from side to side while moving away from the signer, the sign produced is **chase, tail**. Ø GⱱⱵ × GⱱⱵ⸴ $\left(\begin{smallmatrix}o\\z\end{smallmatrix}.\right)$

| Two **G** hands are held with the palms facing down (if the hands were opened, the fingers would all point away from the signer). | The hands are held in front of the body; the right hand is held nearer to the signer than the left hand. | The left hand moves towards the signer; the right hand moves to the right and then left, while moving away from the signer throughout. | overtake[*†§] | 431 |

Notes * This sign, when referring to vehicles, may be produced using two **B** hands. Ø BⱱⱵ BⱱⱵ⸴ ··

† This sign, when referring to vehicles, may be produced using two **B** hands (with the left palm facing right and the right palm facing left). Ø B>Ⱶ B<Ⱶ⸴ ··

§ This sign, when referring to people, may be produced with the palms facing away from the signer (if the hands were opened, the fingers would all point up). Ø GⱵΛ GⱵΛ⸴ ··

| The left **G** hand is held with the palm facing towards the signer; the right **G** hand is held with the palm facing away from the signer (if the hands were opened, the fingers would all point up). | The hands are held in front of the body with the knuckles of the closed fingers touching. | The hands change places; the knuckles maintain contact with each other throughout. | alter
alteration
change
conversion
convert
revenge[1] | 432 |

Notes 1 If the hands move away from the signer throughout, the sign produced is **revenge**. Ø GΤΛ × GⱵΛ $\begin{smallmatrix}Ⱶ\\×\end{smallmatrix}$

| The left **G** hand is held with the palm facing towards the signer; the right **G** hand is held with the palm facing away from the signer (if the hands were opened, the fingers would all point up). | The hands are held in front of the body; the right hand is held nearer to the signer than the left hand. | The hands change places, twisting at the wrists, so that the left palm faces away from the signer and the right palm faces towards the signer. | reply[*†]
respond[*†]
response[†] | 433 |

Notes * Directional verb.

† This sign may be produced with the hands held side by side. Ø GΤΛ ¦ GⱵΛ⸴ ··ω

| The left **G** hand is held with the palm facing towards the signer; the right **G** hand is held with the palm facing away from the signer (if the hands were opened, the fingers would all point up). | The hands are held in front of the body; the right hand is held nearer to the signer than the left hand. | The left hand moves towards the signer and, at the same time, the right hand moves away from the signer until the knuckles meet. | face to face
meet
approach[1]
before[1]
close[1]
near[1] | 434 |

Notes 1 If the left hand does not move and the right hand moves away from the signer, the sign produced is **approach, before, close, near**. GΤΛ GⱵΛ⸴ Ⱶ

435   Ø G⊤⊥ G⊤⊥ $\overset{x}{\underset{\perp}{}}$

436   Ø $\overline{\text{G}}$⊤> ₁ G⊤< $\overset{\mp}{\underset{x}{}}$

437   Ø G⊤> ₁ G⊤< $\overset{\overset{\circ}{\sim}\sim}{\cdot}$

438   Ø G⊤> ₁ₓ G⊤< $\overset{\text{n}}{\underset{\perp}{}}$

439   Ø G⊤⊥ ₁ G<⊥ $\overset{\overset{\circ}{>}}{\underset{\perp}{}}$

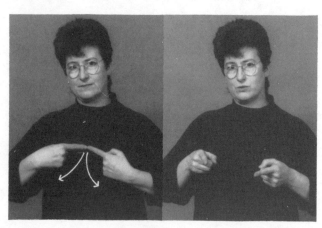

440   Ø G⊥∧₉ ₓ G⊤∧ $\overset{\ddagger}{\mp}$

441   Ø G⊥∧ ₁ G⊥∧ $\overset{\div(\overset{\text{n}}{\underset{\vee}{\perp}})x}{}$

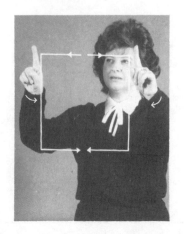

[288]

Handshape and orientation	Location, hand arrangement and contact	Movement	Glosses	
Two **G** hands are held with the palms facing towards the signer (if the hands were opened, the fingers would all point away from the signer).	The hands are held in front of the body at an angle, so that the index fingers are turned towards each other.	The hands move away from the signer and, at the same time, towards each other.	converge convergence	435
Two **G** hands are held with the palms facing towards the signer (if the hands were opened, the left fingers would point to the right and the right fingers would point to the left).	The hands are held side by side in front of the body; the right hand is held higher than the left hand.	The hands cross over, with the right hand brushing the top of the left hand.	err error miss mistake wrong misunderstand[1] misunderstanding[1]	436

Non-manual features   The lips are pressed together.

Notes   1 This sign may be used as the second part of a compound sign which also means **misunderstand, misunderstanding** (see 511 Note 1 for the first part of the sign).

$$\cap \ G\tau\wedge \ ^{\times} \ \overset{//}{/\!/} \ \varnothing \ \overline{G\tau >} \ _{|} \ G\tau < \ ^{\overline{\times}}$$

Two **G** hands are held with the palms facing towards the signer (if the hands were opened, the left fingers would point to the right and the right fingers would point to the left).	The hands are held side by side in front of the body.	The hands make alternate short up and down movements.	argue argument debate dispute fight	437

Non-manual features   The head is pushed forward and the brows are furrowed.

Two **G** hands are held with the palms facing towards the signer (if the hands were opened, the left fingers would point to the right and the right fingers would point to the left).	The hands are held side by side in front of the body with the index fingertips touching.	The hands bend away from the signer from the wrists.	divorce divorced divorcee	438
The left **G** hand is held with the palm facing towards the signer; the right **G** hand is held with the palm facing left (if the hands were opened, the fingers would all point away from the signer).	The hands are held side by side in front of the body at an angle, so that the fingers are turned to the right.	The hands make a short movement away from the signer and, at the same time, to the right.	accusation accuse* blame* accused[1]	439

Non-manual features   The eyes are narrowed and the brows are furrowed.

Notes   * Directional verb

1 If the non-manual feature is not present, the sign produced is **accused**.

The left **G** hand is held with the palm facing away from the signer; the right **G** hand is held with the palm facing towards the signer (if the hands were opened, the fingers would all point up).	The hands are held in front of the body; the left hand is held nearer to the signer than the right hand, with the closed right fingers resting against the closed left fingers.	The left hand moves towards the signer and, at the same time, the right hand moves away from the signer.	facing opposite	440
Two **G** hands are held with the palms facing away from the signer (if the hands were opened, the fingers would all point up).	The hands are held side by side in front of the body.	The hands move apart and then bend away from the signer at the wrists while moving down, before finally moving back towards each other.	frame picture window	441

442　Ø G⊥∧ G⊥∧₉ ⊥

443　Ø G>⊥ G<⊥ ∧°₁∨

444　Ø G>⊥ ₁ G<⊥₉ °₁·

445　Ø G>⊥ ₁× G<⊥ (ᵑ÷₁÷)

446　Ø √G>∧ √G<∧ ≠×

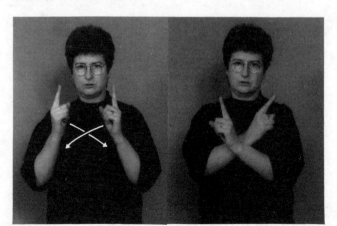

Handshape and orientation	Location, hand arrangement and contact	Movement	Glosses	
Two ꞬG hands are held with the palms facing away from the signer (if the hands were opened, the fingers would all point up).	The hands are held in front of the body; the right hand is held nearer to the signer than the left hand.	The hands move away from the signer.	bodyguard follow* minder shadow* stick to stick with trainee precede [1] chase *[2] tail *[2]	442

Notes   * Directional verb.

1 If the left hand is held nearer to the signer than the right hand, the sign produced is **precede**.

$$\emptyset \quad G\!\perp\!\wedge_\varrho \quad G\!\perp\!\wedge \quad {}^\perp$$

2 If the hands move away from the signer while making short movements from side to side, the sign produced is **chase, tail**.

$$\emptyset \quad G\!\perp\!\wedge \quad G\!\perp\!\wedge_\varrho \quad {\binom{\circ}{\overline{z}\,.}}_\perp$$

| The left **G** hand is held with the palm facing right; the right **G** hand is held with the palm facing left (if the hands were opened, the fingers would all point away from the signer). | The hands are held in front of the body. | The hands move away from the signer in an arc. | appoint* appointee appointment elect* election nominate* nomination nominee propose* | 443 |

Notes   * Directional verb.

| The left **G** hand is held with the palm facing right; the right **G** hand is held with the palm facing left (if the hands were opened, the fingers would all point away from the signer). | The hands are held side by side in front of the body; the right hand is held nearer to the signer than the left hand. | The hands make two short movements away from the signer. | get at* goad* provoke* taunt* tease* | 444 |

Non-manual features   The eyes are narrowed, the nose is wrinkled and the lips are stretched.

Notes   * Directional verb.

| The left **G** hand is held with the palm facing right; the right **G** hand is held with the palm facing left (if the hands were opened, the fingers would all point away from the signer). | The hands are held side by side in front of the body with the thumbs touching. | The hands move apart and away from the signer while bending apart at the wrists. | diverge | 445 |

Notes   * This sign may be produced with the palms facing down.

$$\emptyset \quad G\!\eth\!\perp \quad {}_{I}x \quad G\!\eth\!\perp \quad {\binom{\textnormal{n}}{\div}}_\div$$

| The left **G** hand is held with the palm facing right; the right **G** hand is held with the palm facing left (if the hands were opened, the fingers would all point up). | The hands are held in front of the body. | The hands cross over; the movement ends with the forearms touching. | change over changeover exchange substitute substitution swap switch | 446 |

447　Ø （G>⊥ ₁x G<∧ ⁿ⊥x ·）ᐳ

448　∩ G>∧ G<∧ (ω⊥x)ˣ

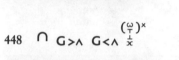

449　Ŏ G⊥∧ G⊤∧ °₁~·

450　Ŏ G>⊥ G<⊥ ·ᴅ∧

451　Ц G⊤∧ G⊤∧ °₊x

Handshape and orientation	Location, hand arrangement and contact	Movement	Glosses	
The left **G** hand is held with the palm facing right; the right **G** hand is held with the palm facing left (if the hands were opened, the left fingers would point away from the signer and the right fingers would point up).	The hands are held in front of the body with the closed fingers touching.	The right hand bends away from the signer at the wrist, maintaining contact with the left hand throughout; the movement is repeated several times while the hands move to the right.	assorted assortment diverse etc et cetera kinds (all kinds of) range selection sorts (all sorts of) variation variety various	447

Notes * The following notes apply to all glosses:

This sign may be produced with both hands bending down at the wrists several times as the hands move to the right.

$$\emptyset \left(G{>}\wedge \; _{|x} \; G{<}\wedge \; {}^{x}_{\underset{\perp}{\overset{D}{\,}}} \right)^{>}$$

This sign may be produced with the hands bending up and down several times alternately at the wrists as the hands move to the right.

$$\emptyset \left(G{>}\perp \; _{|x} \; G{<}\wedge \; {}^{\ddots}_{x} \right)^{>}$$

The left **G** hand is held with the palm facing right; the right **G** hand is held with the palm facing left (if the hands were opened, the fingers would all point up).	The hands are held at the side of the head.	The hands move away from the signer and towards each other while twisting at the wrists (so that the palms face towards the signer); the movement ends with the sides of the hands touching.	college university Mexican[1] Mexico[1] sombrero[1]	448

Notes 1 If the movement is larger, the sign produced is **Mexican, Mexico, sombrero.**

Two **G** hands are held with the palms facing away from the signer (if the hands were opened, the fingers would all point up).	The hands are held on either side of the face.	The hands make alternate short movements up and, at the same time, away from the signer.	stars	449

The left **G** hand is held with the palm facing right; the right **G** hand is held with the palm facing left (if the hands were opened, the fingers would all point away from the signer).	The hands are held on either side of the face.	The hands bend sharply up and towards the signer from the wrists; the movement is repeated.	authority * boss * charge (in charge) * chief * depends * † director * employer * head * headmaster * headmistress * headteacher * lord * manager * manageress * master * mistress * principal * bossy[1]	450

Notes * This sign may be produced using one hand only.

† Regional sign.

1 If the nose is wrinkled, the sign produced is **bossy.**

$$\circlearrowright \; G{<}\perp \; {}^{\overset{\cdot}{D}}_{\wedge}$$

Two **G** hands are held with the palms facing towards the signer (if the hands were opened, the fingers would all point up).	The hands are held with the index fingertips touching the face beside the eyes.	The hands make a short movement apart; the index fingertips maintain contact with the face throughout.	China * Chinese * Japan * Japanese * Korea * Korean *	451

Notes * This sign may be produced with two ** G̈** hands, which make a short twisting movement at the wrists, so that the palms face towards the signer.

$$\sqcup \; \ddot{G}{>}\wedge \; \ddot{G}{<}\wedge \; {}^{x\overset{\circ}{\underset{\div}{\omega}}}$$

452 ⊔ Gᴛ∧ Gᴛ∧ $^{\times}_{\overset{\perp}{\underset{m}{\vee}}}$

453 ⊔ Gᴛ∧ Gᴛ∧ $^{\overset{\vee\wedge\cdot}{\times}}_{\vee}$

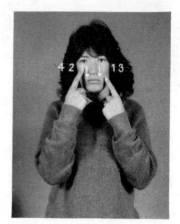

454 ⊔ G>∧ G<∧ $^{\overset{\times\mathring{\omega}}{\underset{\overset{\div}{\vee}}{\perp}}}$

455 ⊔ Gᴛ∧ ₁ Gᴛ∧ $^{\overset{e\wedge\cdot}{\perp}}_{\vee}$

456 ⌣ Gᴛ> Gᴛ< $^{\times\left(\overset{\cap}{\underset{\div}{\perp}}\right)}$

457 ⌣ G>∧ G<∧ $^{\overset{\mathring{\circ}}{\underset{\div}{\vee}}}$

[294]

Handshape and orientation	Location, hand arrangement and contact	Movement	Glosses	
Two G hands are held with the palms facing towards the signer (if the hands were opened, the fingers would all point up).	The hands are held with the index fingertips touching the cheeks below the eyes.	The hands move down and away from the signer while the index fingers flex.	care * care (with care) * expect * † beware [1] care (take care) [1] careful [1]	452

      Notes   * This sign may be produced using one hand only.

          † Regional Sign.

          1 If the head is tilted forward and the brows are furrowed, the sign produced is **beware, careful, take care.**

          Ⅱ G⊤ʌ

| Two G hands are held with the palms facing towards the signer (if the hands were opened, the fingers would all point up). | The hands are held with the index fingertips pointing to the eyes. | The hands move down alternately, so that the index fingers brush the cheeks; the movements are repeated. | cry * †
crying * †
tears * †
weep * †
cry baby [1]
tears (burst into tears) [1] | 453 |

  Non-manual features   The corners of the mouth are turned down.

      Notes   * This sign may be produced using one hand only.   Ⅱ G⊤ʌ

          † This sign may be produced with the index fingers flexing several times so that the index fingertips brush the cheeks. (The sign may also be produced using one hand only).   Ⅱ G⊤ʌ G⊤ʌ or Ⅱ G⊤ʌ

          1 If the hands move sharply away from the signer while the index fingers flex, the sign produced is **cry baby, burst into tears.**

          Ⅱ G⊤ʌ G⊤ʌ

| The left G hand is held with the palm facing right; the right G hand is held with the palm facing left (if the hands were opened, the fingers would all point up). | The hands are held with the index fingertips touching the face beside the eyes. | The hands twist at the wrists, so that the palms face towards the signer while making a short movement up and apart. | China
Chinese
Japan
Japanese
Korea
Korean | 454 |

| Two G hands are held with the palms facing towards the signer (if the hands were opened, the fingers would all point up). | The hands are held side by side in front of the chin. | The hands make alternate clockwise circles in the vertical plane at right angles to the signer's body. | inform *
information
relate an event/
  a story *
story
tell *
tell about an event/
  a story * | 455 |

      Notes   * Directional verb.

| Two G hands are held with the palms facing towards the signer (if the hands were opened, the left fingers would point to the right and the right fingers would point to the left). | The hands are held with the index fingertips touching the chin. | The hands bend away from the signer at the wrists while moving apart and away from the signer. | announce
announcement
declaration, declare
decree, order
proclaim
proclamation
pronounce
pronouncement
public
publicize | 456 |

| The left G hand is held with the palm facing right, the right G hand is held with the palm facing left (if the hands were opened, the fingers would all point up). | The hands are held side by side in front of the mouth. | The hands make two short movements away from the signer and, at the same time, down and apart. | instruct * †
instructor
teach * †
teacher
tutor (a tutor)
tutor (to tutor) * † | 457 |

      Notes   * Directional verb.

          † This sign may be produced with a single movement.

          ⊍ G>ʌ G<ʌ

458 ⌣ G>ʌ G<ʌ ᴵᴺ˙

459 Ø G̈>⊥ ¦ G⊤< °⁺

460 Ø Ġɑ⊥ ⁽ᵍ ˙⁾
          ⁽ᵛ⁾
          ⁽ᵛ⊤⁾
          ˄

G *The index finger is extended from the fist.*

Handshape and orientation	Location, hand arrangement and contact	Movement	Glosses	
The left **G** hand is held with the palm facing right; the right **G** hand is held with the palm facing left (if the hands were opened, the fingers would all point up).	The hands are held with the index fingers in front of the chin.	The hands move towards and away from the signer alternately several times.	conversation converse dialogue discuss discussion interview	458
The left **Ġ** hand is held with the palm facing right (if the hand were opened, the fingers would point away from the signer). The right **G** hand is held with the palm facing towards the signer (if the hand were opened, the fingers would point to the left).	The hands are held side by side in front of the left side of the body.	The hands make a short, firm movement apart.	opponent oppose opposite opposition	459

Non-manual features The eyes are narrowed and the lips are pressed together.

Ġ *The index finger and thumb are extended from the fist.*

In the most frequent realisation of **Ġ**, the thumb is extended so that it is virtually at right angles to the extended index finger. However, some signs require a *variant* in which the thumb is positioned nearer to the closed fingers, as in **leaf** (sign 471). A further variant has some bending at the palm knuckles, as in **frequent** (sign 473). This final variant could be phonetically transcribed as **Ğ**.

Ġ appears to have rather limited use within the productive lexicon and as a classifying component in established signs:

– it has the potential for use as a *size and shape* classifier to represent objects with one long and one short extension such as walking sticks or certain types of tools, for example a set square. However, there is a more general tendency in the language for such items to be indicated through the use of *handling* classifiers (e.g. **A** and **Â**) rather than *size and shape* classifiers;

– in a small number of cases, the use of **Ġ** combines *size and shape* specification and *handling* and / or *instrumental* functions. In **hand gun** (sign 463), the closed fingers represent the handling of the weapon, while the index finger appears to represent both the barrel and, when the movement occurs, the action of the finger on the trigger; similarly in **petrol** (sign 462), the extended finger represents the long, cylindrical nozzle of the pump and the closed fingers indicate the grasping of the handle. Comparable uses can be seen in a range of tools such as **electric drill**, **welding gun** and **staple gun** (see *Introduction*);

– it can be used to express *extent*, for example, in depicting stripes of a particular width. A comparable function can be seen in the signs **briefs** (sign 472) and **bikini** (sign 472) where the location indicates the depth of the garment on the body.

Ġ is used in both the Irish and American manual alphabets to express the letter l. As such, it is used in borrowed initial letter handshape signs from Irish Sign Language (ISL) and American Sign Language (ASL). The combined effects of the pictorial link between the upper case letter L and the **Ġ** handshape and the presence of borrowed signs using this form have also led to the development of indigenous BSL forms which exploit this link. Examples include **Liverpool** (sign 464) from ISL, **language** (see *Introduction*) from ASL and **lesbian** (sign 464) developed within BSL.

Handshape and orientation	Location, hand arrangement and contact	Movement	Glosses	
The **Ġ** hand is held with the palm facing up (if the hand were opened, the fingers would point away from the signer).	The hand is held in front of the body.	The hand moves up and away from the signer and, at the same time, makes clockwise circles in the vertical plane parallel to the signer's body.	distance* distant* far* faraway* far-off* long* remote*	460

Non-manual features The lips are rounded.

Notes * This sign may also be produced with a slow movement up and, at the same time, away from the signer; the cheeks are puffed out.

Ø Ġ<⊥ $\overset{\perp}{\wedge}$

461 Ø Ġ⊤v $\begin{pmatrix} \overset{o}{\underset{>}{@}} \\ i \end{pmatrix}$ v

462 Ø Ġ⊤< $\overset{n}{\underset{<}{v}}$

463 Ø ᵉĠ<⊤ $\begin{pmatrix} \overset{o}{n} \\ \underset{m}{\wedge} \end{pmatrix}$

464 Ø Ġ<⊤ $\overset{o}{\underset{z}{\tilde{\omega}}}$ ˙

465 Ц Ġ⊤< $\overset{>\#[\wedge]}{x}$

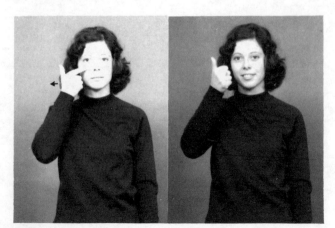

Ġ

The index finger and thumb are extended from the fist.

Handshape and orientation	Location, hand arrangement and contact	Movement	Glosses	
The Ġ hand is held with the palm facing towards the signer (if the hand were opened, the fingers would point down).	The hand is held in front of the body.	The hand, moving downwards, makes a small clockwise circle in the horizontal plane, and then continues straight down.	deep* depth* deep[1]	461

Notes   * The following notes apply to all glosses:

> This sign can be produced with a straight downward movement.
>
> Ø ĠTv ˅
>
> This sign can also be produced with a left **B** hand held in front of the body (the left palm faces down and the fingers point to the right) and nearer to the signer than the right hand.
>
> Bʊ>ᵩ × ĠTv ˅
>
> 1 If the left **B** hand is held in front of the body with the palm facing down and the fingers pointing to the right, and the right hand moves down and to the left and, at the same time, towards the signer, the sign produced is **deep** *(see entry 2 in the English section).*
>
> Bʊ>ᵩ ĠTv ˅ᵀ˂

| The Ġ hand is held with the palm facing towards the signer (if the hand were opened, the fingers would point to the left). | The hand is held in front of the body. | The hand bends down at the wrist while moving to the left. | filling station
oil
petrol
petrol (put petrol in a petrol tank/container)
petrol station
service station
water with a small watering can[1]
watering can (small watering can)[1] | 462 |

Notes   1 If the hand bends down at the wrist and then makes a clockwise circle in the horizontal plane, the sign produced is **small watering can, water with a small watering can.**

> Ø ĠT˂ ᴰᵉ˅ᵀ˃

| The Ġ hand is held with the palm facing left (if the hand were opened, the fingers would point away from the signer). | The hand is held in front of the body. | The index finger flexes while the hand bends up at the wrist. | fire a hand gun/pistol/revolver*†§
hand gun
pistol
revolver
shoot with a hand gun/pistol/revolver*†§
shot of a hand gun/pistol/revolver †§
shooting[1]
shooting with a hand gun/pistol/revolver[1] | 463 |

Notes   * Directional verb.

> † This sign may be produced with the hand moving firmly towards the signer as the index finger flexes.
>
> Ø ᵉĠ˂⊥ ˙ᵀᴹ
>
> § This sign may be produced with the hand moving firmly away from the signer as the index finger flexes.
>
> Ø ᵉĠ˂⊥ ˙ᵢᴹ
>
> 1 If the hand bends up at the wrist as the index finger flexes, and the movement is repeated, the sign produced is **shooting, shooting with a hand gun/pistol/revolver.**
>
> Ø ᵉĠ˂⊥ (ᴰˆᴹ)·

| The Ġ hand is held with the palm facing left (if the hand were opened, the fingers would point away from the signer). | The hand is held in front of the body at an angle, so that the index finger is turned up. | The hand makes several short twisting movements from side to side at the wrist. | lesbian
Liverpool
Liverpudlian | 464 |

| The Ġ hand is held with the palm facing towards the signer (if the hand were opened, the fingers would point to the left). | The hand is held with the index fingertip touching the face just below the right eye. | The index fingertip moves to the right, across the cheek, and then closes into the hand (forming an Ȧ hand). | lovely
nice
pretty
sweet
young*
youth* | 465 |

Notes   * Regional sign.

466　⊔ Ġ⊤< ˣω̣̇

467　⊔ Ġ⊤< ˣ⊥ [ʌ] ˚⊥ ·
　　　　　　　＃ ᵛ ᵛ

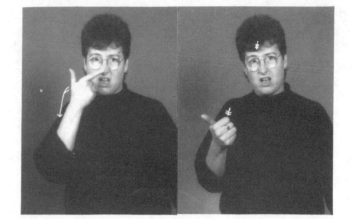

468　◡ Ġ⊤< ˣ⊥̣＃ [ʌ]

469　⌐1< Ġ⊤< ˚ᵛˣᵛ ·

470　∅ Ā⊤> ˣ Ġ<⊥ ⁻>

471　∅ Ġ>⊥ ₁ˣ Ġ<⊥ ÷ [ô̂ô̂]
　　　　　　　　　　　　　＃ ᵛ

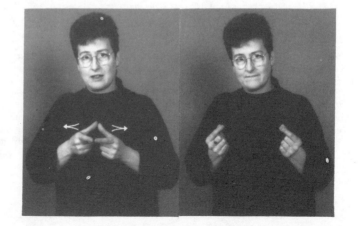

Handshape and orientation	Location, hand arrangement and contact	Movement	Glosses	
The Ġ hand is held with the palm facing towards the signer (if the hand were opened, the fingers would point to the left).	The hand is held with the thumbtip touching the nose.	The hand twists sharply away from the signer at the wrist, so that the palm faces down.	**fortunate** **fortune** **good luck** **luck** **lucky**	466
The Ġ hand is held with the palm facing towards the signer (if the hand were opened, the fingers would point to the left).	The hand is held with the index fingertip touching the nose.	The hand moves down and away from the signer while closing (forming an Ȧ hand); the hand then makes two short movements down and, at the same time, away from the signer.	**great** **nice (very nice too)** **thanks a lot** **thanks very much**	467

Non-manual features   The brows are slightly furrowed, the nose is wrinkled and the mouth is open; the head nods twice as the hand moves.

The Ġ hand is held with the palm facing towards the signer (if the hand were opened, the fingers would point to the left).	The hand is held with the index fingertip touching the chin.	The hand makes a short movement away from the signer and, at the same time, closes (forming an Ȧ hand).	**appetising** * **delicious** * **lovely** * **nice** * **sweet** * **tasty** *	468

Notes   * This sign may also be produced with the index fingertip moving to the right, brushing across the chin, while closing (forming an Ȧ hand) before the hand moves away from the signer.

⊍ Ġ⊤< $\overset{\dot{\downarrow}}{}$# [A]

The Ġ hand is held with the palm facing towards the signer (if the hand were opened, the fingers would point to the left).	The hand is held in front of the right side of the chest.	The hand makes a short downward movement, so that the thumbtip brushes the side of the upper chest; the movement is repeated.	**what for?** **why?**[1] **what's the point?**[2]	469

Non-manual features   The brows are furrowed and the head tilts slightly to the right.

Notes   1 If the thumbtip taps the side of the upper chest twice, the sign produced is **why?**

⌐⌐ Ġʊ< × ·

       2 If the brows are furrowed, the nose is wrinkled and the mouth is open, the sign produced is **what's the point?** This is a regional sign.

The left Ȧ hand is held with the palm facing towards the signer (if the hand were opened, the fingers would point to the right). The right Ġ hand is held with the palm facing left (if the hand were opened, the fingers would point away from the signer).	The hands are held in front of the body; the right hand is held against the back of the left hand.	The hands remain together and move away from the signer and, at the same time, to the right.	**cameraman** **camera person** **film with a film/ television/video camera** * **shoot with a film/ television/video camera** * **film/ television/ video camera** [1]	470

Notes   * Directional verb.

       1 If the hands remain together and make two short, downward movements, the sign produced is **film/ television/video camera.**

∅ Ā⊤> × Ġ<⊥ $\overset{\circ}{\vee}$ ·

The left Ġ hand is held with the palm facing right; the right Ġ hand is held with the palm facing left (if the hands were opened, the fingers would point away from the signer).	The hands are held in front of the body at an angle, so that the thumbtips and index fingertips are touching.	The hands move apart while the thumbs and index fingers close (forming two Ĝ hands).	**leaf**	471

472 Ⱨ Ġⲧⱴ ¦ Ġⲧⱴ ×̇

473 Ø Ġ>⟂ Ġ<⟂ ⁰̇ᵥ

474 ΓⲔ ĜⲧⱯ ×ⁿₜₘ

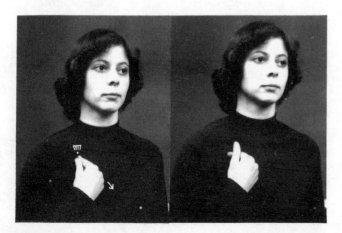

475 ΓⲔ Ĝⲧ< ᵒᵥ×ᵥ

The index finger and thumb are extended from the fist.

Handshape and orientation	Location, hand arrangement and contact	Movement	Glosses	
Two Ġ hands are held with the palms facing towards the signer (if the hands were opened, the fingers would all point down).	The hands are held side by side with the thumbs and index fingertips touching the waist.	The hands move apart, maintaining contact with the waist throughout.	**briefs** **knickers** **pants** **underpants** **bikini**¹	472

Notes   1   If the movement is produced across the chest and then repeated at the waist, the sign produced is **bikini**.

[] Ġᴛⱽ ꞁ Ġᴛⱽ ÷× ∥ ⊦ Ġᴛⱽ ꞁ Ġᴛⱽ ÷×

The left Ġ hand is held with the palm facing right; the right Ġ hand is held with the palm facing towards the signer (if the hands were opened, the left fingers would point to the right and the right fingers would point to the left).	The hands are held in front of the body.	The hands make several short movements down and, at the same time, away from the signer.	**frequent*** **loads*** **lot*** **lots*** **many*** **much*** **numerous*** **often*** **too many*** **too much***	473

Notes   *   This sign may be produced with the hands moving apart throughout.

Ø Ġ>⊥ Ġ<⊥ $\left(\substack{\circ\\v}\cdot\right)$ ÷

The index finger and thumb are extended from the fist so that the pad of the thumb is touching the pad of the index finger.

This handshape does occur independently in a number of signs, but it occurs primarily as the second handshape in signs which involve a closing action and have Ḡ as the initial handshape. Examples include **ability** (sign 477), **have the nerve** (sign 478), **bird** (sign 479) and **choice** (sign 487). Less frequently, it is used as the initial handshape in signs involving Ĝ opening to Ḡ, or some other open handshape: **awake** may be produced with the closed handshape Ĝ, as shown in sign 633, or with Ĝ as the initial handshape.

Ĝ has two main *classifier* functions in the productive lexicon and is used as a classifying element in established signs:
– it is used as a *size and shape* classifier to represent triangular or wedge-like shapes such as beaks and bows (using two hands);
– it is used as a *handling* classifier to indicate the handling of tiny or delicate objects such as jewellery or tablets as in **pill** (sign 476) and **capsule** (sign 476); it is also used to refer to the handling of small, flat objects such as audiotapes and pieces of card or paper.

Handshape and orientation	Location, hand arrangement and contact	Movement	Glosses	
The Ĝ hand is held with the palm facing towards the signer (if the hand were opened, the fingers would point up).	The hand is held with the thumb and index finger tips touching the right side of the upper chest.	The hand makes a short bending movement away from the signer from the wrist and, at the same time, the thumb rubs along the side of the index finger.	**grey***	474

Notes   *   Regional sign.

The Ĝ hand is held with the palm facing towards the signer (if the hand were opened, the fingers would point to the left).	The hand is held in front of the right side of the upper chest.	The hand makes a short downward movement, so that the thumb and index finger tips brush the chest; the movement is repeated.	**white***	475

Notes   *   This sign may also be produced using an **F** handshape.

ꞁˈ Fᴛ< $\substack{\circ\\x\\v}\cdot$

476 $\overline{B}\alpha\!> \hat{G}\!\sigma\!\perp \!^{\times(\stackrel{\omega}{\stackrel{\top}{\wedge}})}$ $/\!/$ $\cup$ $\hat{G}\!\top\!< ^{\times}$

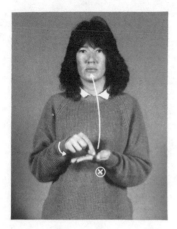

477 $\bigcirc$ $\overline{\overline{G}}\!\top\!\wedge \!^{\perp\,[\hat{a}]}_{\stackrel{\vee}{\#}}$

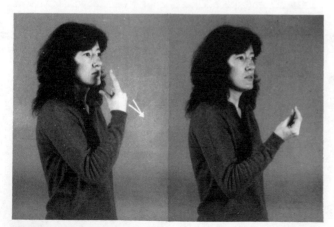

The index finger and thumb are extended from the fist so that the pad of the thumb is touching the pad of the index finger.

Handshape and orientation	Location, hand arrangement and contact	Movement	Glosses	
The left **B** hand is held with the palm facing up and the fingers pointing to the right; the right **Ĝ** hand is held with the palm facing down (if the hand were opened, the fingers would point away from the signer).	The hands are held in front of the body; the right thumb and index finger tips rest on the left palm.	The right hand moves up while twisting at the wrist so that the palm faces towards the signer; the movement ends with the right thumb and index finger tips touching the mouth.	capsule pill tablet take a capsule/ pill / tablet	476

The extended index finger, bent at the palm knuckle, and extended thumb are held parallel to each other.

The main *variation* in the production of Ḡ concerns the size of the gap between the index finger and thumb.

Ḡ has several different *classifier* functions within the productive lexicon and also appears as a classifying element in established signs:

– it is used as a *size and shape* classifier to represent objects with two parallel, flat surfaces such as a beak, as in **bird** (sign 479);

– it is used as a *tracing size and shape* classifier to indicate flat, narrow or shallow objects, as in **candle** (sign 484) and **ruler** (sign 486). It may also be used to depict a narrow rim, border, layer or chunk, as in **layer of custard** (see *Introduction*) and **chunk of text** (see *Introduction*). Ḡ is sometimes used contrastively with H̄ and B̄ in this function;

– it is used to show *extent*, for example, one-handed forms may show relative depth or thickness and two-handed forms may indicate length, width or height.

Handshape and orientation	Location, hand arrangement and contact	Movement	Glosses	
The Ḡ hand is held with the palm facing towards the signer (if the hand were opened, the fingers would point up).	The hand is held in front of the face.	The hand moves down and away from the signer while the index finger and thumb close (forming a Ĝ hand).	ability* able* can* capable* could* feasible* possible* possibly* potential*	477

Notes   * This sign may be produced using a repeated closing movement (**possibly** is typically produced in this way).   ○ Ḡ⊤∧   ⽌ [ĝ] ·

478 ◐ Ḡ⊤ʌ ⁺ᵥ[ĝ]⁺꜀#

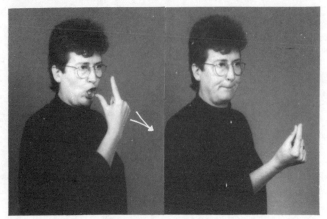

479 ◡ Ḡ⊥ʌ ˣ[ĝ]⁼# ·

480 ◡ Ḡ<ʌ ᴍᵥ°

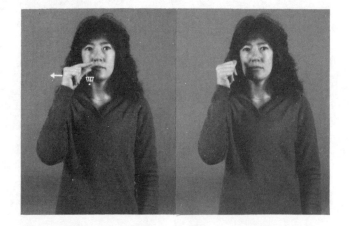

481 ◡ Ḡ<ʌ ᴍꞷ⊤

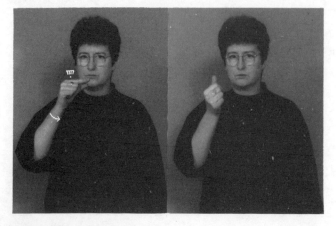

G̿

The extended index finger, bent at the palm knuckle, and extended thumb are held parallel to each other.

Handshape and orientation	Location, hand arrangement and contact	Movement	Glosses	
The G̿ hand is held with the palm facing towards the signer (if the hand were opened, the fingers would point up).	The hand is held in front of the face.	The hand moves down and away from the signer while the index finger and thumb close (forming a Ĝ hand).	**brass cheek** **brass neck** **brass nerve** **have the nerve**	478
Non-manual features The lips are rounded and pushed forward; the mouth closes with the lips drawn back as the hand moves away from the signer.				
The G̿ hand is held with the palm facing away from the signer (if the hand were opened, the fingers would point up).	The back of the hand is held against the side of the mouth.	The finger and thumb close (forming a Ĝ hand); the movement is repeated, with the hand held against the side of the mouth throughout.	**bird** **chicken**	479
The G̿ hand is held with the palm facing left (if the hand were opened, the fingers would point up).	The hand is held with the index finger and thumb in front of the mouth.	The hand makes a short movement to the right and, at the same time, the thumb rubs across the pad of the index finger.	**France*** **French*** **moustache***	480
Notes * This sign may also be produced using an F̿ hand.		⌣ F̿<∧ ⠿		
The G̿ hand is held with the palm facing left (if the hand were opened, the fingers would point up).	The hand is held in front of the chin.	The hand twists at the wrist (so that the palm faces towards the signer) and, at the same time, the thumb rubs across the pad of the index finger.	**brown***†§	481
Notes * Regional sign.				
† This sign may also be produced using an H̿ handshape.		⌣ H̿<∧ ⠿		
§ This sign may also be produced using a B̿ handshape.		⌣ B̿<∧ ⠿		

482 ∪ Ḡ⊤< $\overset{\circ}{\underset{x}{v}}$ // ∪ G<∧ $\overset{\top}{\underset{v}{\underset{<}{\underset{x}{\underset{\top}{v}}}}}$

483 ∪ Ḡ⊤< $\overset{(v\overset{\circ}{v}\overset{}{v}[\hat{a}])}{\underset{x\#}{\bot\bot}}$.

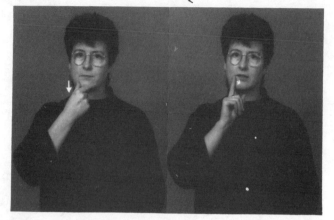

484 Ḡ>⊥ ₁x Ḡ<⊥ ∧

485 G̈ɑ⊥ ᴈ Ḡɔ⊥ $\overset{\circ}{\underset{\bot}{}}$.

486 ∅ Ḡɔ⊥ | Ḡɔ⊥ ÷

487 ∅ Ḡ⊥∧ Ḡ⊥∧ $\overset{\top[\hat{a}\hat{a}]\sim}{\#}$

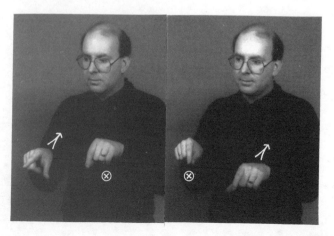

G̿

The extended index finger, bent at the palm knuckle, and extended thumb are held parallel to each other.

Handshape and orientation	Location, hand arrangement and contact	Movement	Glosses	
The G̿ hand is held with the palm facing towards the signer (if the hand were opened, the fingers would point to the left).	The hand is held with the index finger and thumb touching the sides of the chin.	The hand makes a short downward movement, maintaining contact with the chin.	folk* human* human being* people* population* public*	482
The G hand is held with the palm facing left (if the hand were opened, the fingers would point up).	The hand is held with the side of the index finger touching the side of the chin.	The hand moves away from the signer and, at the same time, down and to the left, with the side of the index finger brushing the side of the chin.		

Notes   * This sign may be produced with the two parts of the sign reversed.

$$\text{U } \text{G}{<}{\wedge} \; {\overset{\underset{\underset{\underset{<}{\vee}}{\perp}}{\underset{\times}{\overset{<}{\times}}}}{\overset{\top}{\vee}}} \; // \; \text{U } \text{G̿}\top{<} \quad {\overset{\vee\,\vee}{\times}}^{[\hat{c}]}_{\#}$$

The G̿ hand is held with the palm facing towards the signer (if the hand were opened, the fingers would point to the left).	The hand is held with the index finger and thumb touching the sides of the chin.	The hand moves down, maintaining contact with the chin; the hand then continues to make a short downward movement while closing (forming a Ĝ hand); the movement is repeated.	boy boyfriend lad	483
The left G̿ hand is held with the palm facing right; the right G̿ hand is held with the palm facing left (if the hands were opened, the fingers would all point away from the signer).	The hands are held side by side in front of the body with the right index finger and thumb tips resting on the left index finger and thumb tips.	The right hand moves up.	candle test tube	484
The left G̈ hand is held with the palm facing up; the right G̿ hand is held with the palm facing down (if the hands were opened, the fingers would all point away from the signer).	The hands are held in front of the body; the right hand is held above the left hand, with the left index fingertip held between the right thumb and index finger.	The right hand, holding the left index finger throughout, makes two short movements towards and away from the signer.	weak wimp	485

Non-manual features   The eyes are narrowed and the head tilts to one side.

Two G̿ hands are held with the palm facing down (if the hands were opened, the fingers would all point away from the signer).	The hands are held side by side in front of the body.	The hands move apart.	ruler	486
Two G̿ hands are held with the palms facing away from the signer (if the hands were opened, the fingers would all point up).	The hands are held in front of the body.	The right hand moves towards the signer, while closing (forming a Ĝ hand); the movement is repeated by the left hand.	choice* choose*† elect*† election* pick*† select*† selection* selective*¹	487

Notes   * The following notes apply to all glosses:

This sign may also be produced using two F̿ hands.

$$\varnothing \; \overline{\overline{F}}{\perp}{\wedge} \; \overline{\overline{F}}{\perp}{\wedge} \quad {\overset{\top[FF]}{\#}}{\sim}$$

This sign may be produced using one hand only.

$$\varnothing \; \overline{\overline{F}}{\perp}{\wedge} \; {\overset{\top[F]}{\#}} \quad \text{or} \quad \varnothing \; \overline{\overline{G}}{\perp}{\wedge} \; {\overset{\top[\hat{c}]}{\#}}$$

† Directional verb.

1 If the movement is slow, the sign produced is **selective**.

488 Ø $\overline{\overline{G}}$⊥∧ ǀ $\overline{\overline{G}}$⊥∧ ÷   489 Ø $\overline{\overline{G}}$⊥∧ ǀx $\overline{\overline{G}}$⊥∧ ÷·   490 ⌐⌐ $\overline{\overline{G}}$⊤> $\overline{\overline{G}}$⊤< $\overset{\circ}{\underset{\#}{\bot}}$ [ĝĝ]

491 Ø $\ddot{G}$α⊥ ᵠ // ·$\dot{B}$⊥∧ Gʊ∧ᵨ ˣ   492 Ø $\ddot{G}$α⊥ $\binom{\circ}{>}$·

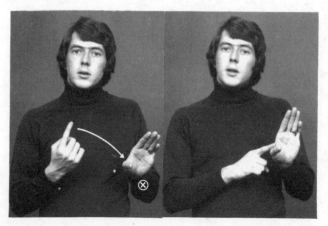 

G̿ *The extended index finger, bent at the palm knuckle, and extended thumb are held parallel to each other.*

Handshape and orientation	Location, hand arrangement and contact	Movement	Glosses	
Two G̿ hands are held with the palms facing away from the signer (if the hands were opened, the fingers would all point up).	The hands are held side by side in front of the body.	The hands move apart.	**envelope** **post card**	488
Two G̿ hands are held with the palms facing away from the signer (if the hands were opened, the fingers would all point up).	The hands are held side by side in front of the body with the thumb tips and the finger tips touching.	The hands move apart; the movement is repeated.	**subtitles**	489
Two G̿ hands are held with the palms facing towards the signer (if the hands were opened, the left fingers would point to the right, and the right fingers would point to the left).	The hands are held with the thumb and index finger tips touching the upper chest.	The hands make a short movement away from the signer while the fingers and thumbs close (forming two Ĝ hands).	**collar** **shirt**	490

G̈ *The index finger is extended from the fist and bent at the palm knuckle.*

The main *variant* of G̈ is **G**. In some cases G̈ is required by the physical constraints of the sign production. In other cases the use of G̈ or **G** depends on personal choice. (See also separate entry for **G**.)

G̈ has several different *classifier* functions in the productive lexicon and also appears as a classifying element in established signs:

- G̈ may function as a *person* classifier, but it is used less frequently than **G**: it is lexicalised in such forms as **loner** (sign 555);
- it is used as a *size and shape* classifier to represent relatively long, thin and typically cylindrical objects such as **missile** (sign 405) and legs as in **kick** (sign 546); **G** can be seen as contrasting with Ḧ, Ẅm and B̈ in showing different degrees of width;
- it is frequently used as a *tracing size and shape* classifier, the index finger tracing the size and shape of objects in space, for example for geometric shapes such as circles, squares and triangles as in **wheel** (sign 503) and **room** (sign 559);
- it is used as a *point* classifier to indicate objects which are perceived as small specks or points, as in **stars** (sign 449);
- it is used as a *handling* classifier to indicate objects which may be balanced on the fingertip, as in a juggler spinning plates;
- it is used as an *instrumental* classifier to indicate long, narrow instruments, tools or utensils such as a knife or sharp blade;
- it is used as a *touch* classifier for actions and objects which involve pressing a small area, as in a push-button telephone; to indicate prodding or poking persons or things and for metaphorical extensions of such actions as in the signs **abuse** (sign 558) and **taunt** (sign 558).

G̈ also has a *deictic* (pointing) function in signs such as **brain** (sign 511) and **taste** (sign 523). It is also used for *pronominal reference*, as in the sign **they** (sign 500) and for *location* signs such as **here** (sign 497).

G̈ may be used instead of **G** to express the right-hand component of several letters of the British manual alphabet, including all the vowels, **a, e, i, o, u** and the letters **j, l, t, x** and **y**. As such, it can occur in initial letter handshape signs such as **answer** (sign 370) and **year** (sign 416).

Handshape and orientation	Location, hand arrangement and contact	Movement	Glosses	
The right G̈ hand is held with the palm facing up (if the hand were opened, the fingers would point away from the signer).	The hand is held in front of the body.	No movement.	**year** (one year)	491
The left Ḃ hand is held with the palm facing away from the signer and the fingers pointing up; the right **G** hand is held with the palm facing down (if the hand were opened, the fingers would point up).	The hands are held in front of the body; the right hand is held nearer to the signer than the left hand and at an angle, so that the index finger is turned away from the signer.	The right index finger touches the base of the left thumb.		
The G̈ hand is held with the palm facing up (if the hand were opened, the fingers would point away from the signer).	The hand is held in front of the body.	The hand makes several short movements away from the signer while moving to the right throughout.	**each** **individual** **individually**	492

493 Ø Ö⍺⊥ $\overset{\overset{e}{e}}{\underset{v}{\cdot}}$

494 Ø Ö⍺⊥ $\overset{\overset{e}{e}}{\underset{<}{\cdot}}$

495 Ø Ö⍥⊥ $\overset{\top}{v}$

496 Ø Ö⍺⊥ $\overset{@}{\underset{\top}{>}}$

497 Ø Ö⍥⊥ $\overset{\circ}{\underset{\cdot}{v}}$

498 Ø Ö⊤< $\overset{\omega\text{-}}{\cdot}$

499 Ø Ö⊥∧ $\overset{(\overset{n}{\top})}{\top}$ // $\overline{\text{B}}$>⊥ G⍥⊥ʔ $\overset{vx}{}$

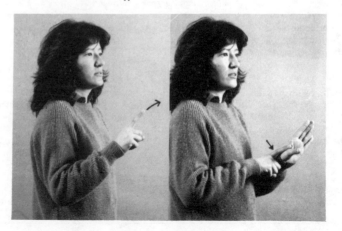

Handshape and orientation	Location, hand arrangement and contact	Movement	Glosses	
The **G̈** hand is held with the palm facing up (if the hand were opened, the fingers would point away from the signer).	The hand is held in front of the body.	The hand makes small clockwise circles in the vertical plane at right angles to the signer's body.	herself himself itself personal personally yourself	493
The **G̈** hand is held with the palm facing up (if the hand were opened, the fingers would point away from the signer).	The hand is held in front of the body.	The hand makes small anticlockwise circles in the horizontal plane.	who?	494

Non-manual features — Non-manual features appropriate for questions must be used; the lips are rounded.

The **G̈** hand is held with the palm facing down (if the hand were opened, the fingers would point away from the signer).	The hand is held in front of the body at an angle, so that the index finger is turned away from the signer.	The hand moves down and, at the same time, away from the signer.	that there this that one [1] this one [1] that is the one [2] that's the one [2] this is the one [2]	495

Non-manual features — The eyegaze is usually in line with the hand movement.

Notes

1 If the movement is short and repeated, the sign produced is **that one, this one**.

2 If the movement is short and repeated and the lips are stretched, the sign produced is **that is the one, that's the one, this is the one.**

Ø G̈ɔ⊥ ¦°.

The **G̈** hand is held with the palm facing down (if the hand were opened, the fingers would point away from the signer).	The hand is held in front of the body.	The hand makes a clockwise circle in the horizontal plane.	circle hole puddle round roundabout	496
The **G̈** hand is held with the palm facing down (if the hand were opened, the fingers would point away from the signer).	The hand is held in front of the body.	The hand makes two short downward movements.	down * downstairs * here *† south * this *†	497

Notes — * This sign may be produced with a single downwards movement. (**down** is typically produced in this way).

Ø G̈ɔ⊥ ˅

† This sign may be produced using two hands.

Ø G̈ɔ⊥ G̈ɔ⊥ ˅. or Ø G̈ɔ⊥ G̈ɔ⊥ ˅°

The **G̈** hand is held with the palm facing towards the signer (if the hand were opened, the fingers would point to the left).	The hand is held in front of the body.	The hand twists away from the signer from the wrist, so that the index finger points away from the signer.	go go away go (off you go) send send for get lost [1]	498

Notes — 1 If the movement is sharp, and the eyes are narrowed and lips stretched, the sign produced is **get lost**.

Ø G⊤< ˙ω̣

The **G̈** hand is held with the palm facing away from the signer (if the hand were opened, the fingers would point up).	The hand is held in front of the body.	The hand moves away from the signer while bending away from the signer at the wrist.	year (next year)	499
The left **B̈** hand is held with the palm facing right and the fingers pointing away from the signer; the right **G** hand is held with the palm facing down (if the hand were opened, the fingers would point away from the signer).	The hands are held in front of the body; the right hand is held higher and nearer to the signer than the left hand.	The right hand moves down, so that the index fingertip touches the base of the left thumb.		

500　Ø Ġ⊥∧ $\binom{\cap}{\substack{>\\>}}$

501　Ø Ġ⊥∧ $(\substack{\perp < \overset{\circ}{\mathsf{i}} > \perp \\ \mathsf{v}})$

502　Ø Ġ⊥∧ $>(\substack{\wedge \perp \forall \perp \\ < \quad \top})$

503　Ø Ġ<⊥ $\overset{@}{\underset{\mathsf{v}}{\perp}}$

504　∩ ĠT∧ × // Ø B⍺⊥ ¦ B⍺⊥ ⊥

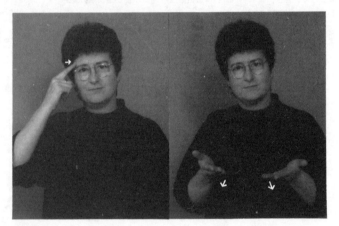

505　∩ ĠT∧ ×$\overset{\circ}{\underset{\mathsf{m}}{\perp}}$

Handshape and orientation	Location, hand arrangement and contact	Movement	Glosses	
The G̈ hand is held with the palm facing away from the signer (if the hand were opened, the fingers would point up).	The hand is held in front of the body at an angle, so that the index finger is turned to the left.	The hand moves to the right and, at the same time, bends to the right at the wrist.	them these they those you *plural*	**500**
The G̈ hand is held with the palm facing away from the signer (if the hand were opened, the fingers would point up).	The hand is held in front of the body.	The hand (making short movements throughout) moves away from the signer, then down and to the left before moving away from the signer and then to the right, before finally making a third movement away from the signer.	therefore	**501**
The G̈ hand is held with the palm facing away from the signer (if the hand were opened, the fingers would point up).	The hand is held in front of the body.	The hand moves to the right and then makes a short movement up, and at the same time, to the left; the hand makes a short movement away from the signer before moving down and making another short movement away from the signer.	divide division	**502**
The G̈ hand is held with the palm facing left (if the hand were opened, the fingers would point away from the signer).	The hand is held in front of the body.	The hand makes a clockwise circle in the vertical plane at right angles to the signer's body.	tyre wheel rotate[1] spin[1] turn[1] drive a tractor[2] tractor[2] tractor driver[2]	**503**

     Notes   1 If the movement is repeated, the sign produced is **rotate, spin, turn.**

$$\varnothing \ \ddot{G}{<}{\perp}\ \overset{@}{\underset{\vee}{\top}}\cdot$$

          2 If both hands are used and the lips are closed and pushed forward, the sign may be used as the second part of a compound sign (see 74 for the first part of the sign) meaning **drive a tractor, tractor, tractor driver.**

$$\varnothing \ A{\alpha}{\perp}\ A{\alpha}{\perp}\ \overset{\text{I N}}{\underset{Z}{}}\cdot \ \ /\!/ \ \ \varnothing \ \ddot{G}{>}{\perp}\ \ddot{G}{<}{\perp}\ \overset{@}{\underset{\perp}{}}$$

The G̈ hand is held with the palm facing towards the signer (if the hand were opened, the fingers would point up).	The hand is held with the index finger in front of the forehead.	The index fingertip touches the side of the forehead.	put forward an idea/ recommendation/ suggestion* recommend* suggest* suggestion*	**504**
Two B hands are held with the palms facing up and the fingers pointing away from the signer.	The hands are held side by side in front of the body.	The hands move away from the signer.		

     Notes   * The following notes apply to all glosses:

          The first part of this compound sign may be replaced with sign 347.

          This sign may be produced without the first part.

$$\smile \ G{\top}{\wedge}\ \overset{\times}{\perp}\ \ /\!/ \ \ \varnothing \ B{\alpha}{\perp}\ {}_{|}\ B{\alpha}{\perp}\ {}^{\perp}$$
$$\varnothing \ B{\alpha}{\perp}\ {}_{|}\ B{\alpha}{\perp}\ {}^{\perp}$$

The G̈ hand is held with the palm facing towards the signer (if the hand were opened, the fingers would point up).	The hand is held with the fingertip touching the forehead.	The hand moves away from the signer and, at the same time, the index finger flexes.	anticipate anticipation expect expectation expecting*	**505**

     Notes   * Regional sign.

506 ∩ G̈⊥< ×·

507 ∩ G̈<∧ ×⊥∨ // ꝯ 8̄ꝯ< ×·

508 ∩ G̈<∧ ×⊥∨ // ∅ B̄ɑ⊥ ⊙ B̄ɑ⊥ ·÷×÷# [ɓɓ]

509 ∩ G̈<∧ ×̇×

510 ∩ G̈<∧ ⊥̊̇∨

511 ∩ G̈<∧ ×·

[316]

Handshape and orientation	Location, hand arrangement and contact	Movement	Glosses
The Ö hand is held with the palm facing away from the signer (if the hand were opened, the fingers would point to the left).	The hand is held in front of the forehead with the index finger turned to the right.	The back of the hand taps the forehead twice.	bang one's head 506 against a brick wall
Non-manual features The teeth are clenched, the lips are stretched and the brows are slightly furrowed.			
The Ö hand is held with the palm facing left (if the hand were opened, the fingers would point up).	The hand is held with the index fingertip touching the side of the forehead.	The hand moves down and away from the signer while opening (forming a ŏ hand).	psychiatrist 507 psychiatry
The right 8̄ hand is held with the palm facing down (if the hand were opened, the fingers would point to the left).	The hand is held above the left wrist which is positioned in front of the body with the palm facing down.	The thumb and middle fingertips tap the back of the left wrist twice.	
The Ö hand is held with the palm facing left (if the hand were opened, the fingers would point up).	The hand is held with the index fingertip touching the side of the forehead.	The hand moves down and away from the signer while opening (forming a B̄ hand).	blank (go blank) 508 escape one forget mind (go from one's mind) mind (slip one's mind)
Two B̄ hands are held with the palms facing up (if the hands were opened, the fingers would all point away from the signer).	The hands are held in front of the body, angled towards each other so that the right fingers are held between the left fingers and the thumb.	The hands move sharply apart, so that the fingers brush together, while closing (forming two B̄ hands).	
Non-manual features The eyes close and the lips become slightly rounded.			
The Ö hand is held with the palm facing left (if the hand were opened, the fingers would point up).	The hand is held with the side of the index finger resting against the forehead.	The hand moves to the right; the side of the index finger maintains contact with the forehead throughout.	girl* 509 lass*
Notes * Regional sign.			
The Ö hand is held with the palm facing left (if the hand were opened, the fingers would point up).	The hand is held in front and to the right of the forehead.	The hand makes small clockwise circles in the vertical plane at right angles to the signer's body.	assume 510 assumption presume presumption suppose supposition
Non-manual features The eyebrows are raised.			
The Ö hand is held with the palm facing left (if the hand were opened, the fingers would point up).	The hand is held with the index finger beside the forehead.	The index finger taps the side of the forehead twice.	brain 511 mind think[1] intelligent[2] sensible[2] daft[3]

Notes 1 If the brows are furrowed, and the movement is not repeated, the sign produced is **think**.

∩ Ö<ʌ ˣ

2 If the brows are raised, the sign produced is **intelligent, sensible**.

3 If the hand is held with the palm facing towards the signer and makes two short movements towards the signer, the sign produced is **daft**.

∩ Öтʌ ⊤̥˙

512 ∩ G̈<∧ ⊥ˣᵛ // B̄a> Ba⊥ ⁽ᵒᵥ̌ₓ⁾.

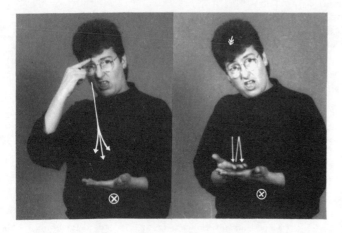

513 ∩ G̈<∧ ⊥ˣᵛ // B̄a> B̈ʊ⊥ ˣ·

514 ∩ G̈<∧ ⊡ˣᵛ⁽ᴮ⁾ // B̄a> B<⊥ ᵛˣ

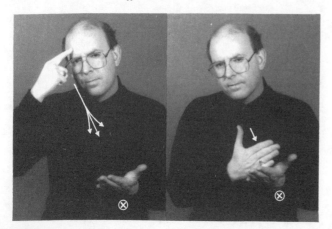

Handshape and orientation	Location, hand arrangement and contact	Movement	Glosses
The **G̈** hand is held with the palm facing left (if the hand were opened, the fingers would point up).	The hand is held with the index fingertip touching the forehead.	The hand moves down and, at the same time, away from the signer while opening (forming a **B** hand).	committed **512** (be committed to) devoted (be devoted to) think a lot of worship
The left **B** hand is held with the palm facing up and the fingers pointing to the right; the right **B** hand is held with the palm facing up and the fingers pointing away from the signer.	The hands are held in front of the body; the right hand is held above the left hand.	The right hand makes a short downward movement, so that the back of the right hand touches the left palm; the movement is repeated.	

Non-manual features   The brows are slightly furrowed, the nose is wrinkled and the mouth is open with the tongue protruding slightly; the head nods as the right hand moves up and down.

The **G̈** hand is held with the palm facing left (if the hand were opened, the fingers would point up).	The hand is held with the index fingertip touching the side of the forehead.	The hand moves down and, at the same time, away from the signer while opening (forming a **B̈** hand).	memorise * **513** memory * mind (bear in mind) * mind (keep in mind) * remember * remembrance (in remembrance) * ¹
The left **B̈** hand is held with the palm facing up; the right **B̈** hand is held with the palm facing down (if the hands were opened, the left fingers would point to the right and the right fingers would point away from the signer).	The hands are held in front of the body; the right hand is held above the left hand.	The right hand taps the left hand twice.	

Notes   * The second part of the sign may be produced using two **A** hands.

1 If the lips are pressed together and the head tilts to the right, the sign produced is **in remembrance**.

∩ G̈<ʌ ˣ ᵛ_ᴛ // ‾ Aɑ> Aɔ⊥ ˣ·

The **G̈** hand is held with the palm facing left (if the hand were opened, the fingers would point up).	The hand is held with the index fingertip touching the side of the forehead.	The hand moves down while opening (forming a **B** hand).	believe * **514** believer * convinced *
The left **B** hand is held with the palm facing up and the fingers pointing to the right; the right **B** hand is held with the palm facing left and the fingers pointing away from the signer.	The hands are held in front of the body; the right hand is held above the left hand.	The right hand moves down; the movement ends with the side of the right hand touching the left palm.	

Notes   * The first part of this sign may also be produced using a **G** hand.

∩ G<ʌ ˣ ᵛ [B]

515 ∩ Ü<ʌ $\overset{\times}{\left(\begin{smallmatrix} n \\ @ \\ \downarrow \\ \vee \end{smallmatrix}\right)}$ᐧ

516 Ц Üтʌ $\overset{\times\,\overset{\downarrow}{\imath}}{\underset{\varpi}{\vee}}$

517 Ц Ü<ʌ ×

518 Ц Ü<ʌ $\overset{\dot{\times}}{\underset{\tau}{\varpi}}$

519 Э Üтʌ $\overset{\times\,n}{\underset{\perp}{}}$

520 Э Ü<ʌ ×ᐧ

521 Ɔ Ü<ʌ $\overset{\cdot}{\left(\begin{smallmatrix} @ \\ \downarrow \\ \vee \end{smallmatrix}\right)}$

The index finger is extended from the fist and bent at the palm knuckle.

Handshape and orientation	Location, hand arrangement and contact	Movement	Glosses	
The **G̈** hand is held with the palm facing left (if the hand were opened, the fingers would point up).	The hand is held with the index fingertip touching the side of the forehead.	The hand makes small clockwise circles in the vertical plane at right angles to the signer's body, bending at the wrist and, at the same time, moves upwards and to the right.	absurd * ludicrous * nonsense * ridiculous * rubbish *	515

Notes   * This sign may be produced with the eyes narrowed and the nose wrinkled.

The **G̈** hand is held with the palm facing towards the signer (if the hand were opened, the fingers would point up).	The hand is held with the index fingertip touching the nose.	The hand moves sharply down and away from the signer while the index finger flexes.	coincidence just so spot on	516

Non-manual features   The lips are drawn back and pressed together; as the hand moves, the mouth opens with the lips stretched and, at the same time, the nose wrinkles.

The **G̈** hand is held with the palm facing left (if the hand were opened, the fingers would point up).	The hand is held with the index finger in front of the nose.	The head moves sharply forward.	sneeze	517

The **G̈** hand is held with the palm facing left (if the hand were opened, the fingers would point up).	The hand is held with the index fingertip against the side of the nose.	The hand twists firmly at the wrist, so that the palm faces towards the signer; the index fingertip is held against the nose throughout.	pig pig (animal) * mouse [1]	518

Non-manual features   The nose is wrinkled.

Notes   * This sign may be produced without the non-manual feature and without a firm movement *(see entry 1 in the English section).*

⨆ G̈<ʌ ×ω̇⊤

1 If the non-manual features are not present and the movement is repeated, the sign produced is **mouse**.

⨆ G̈<ʌ (×°ω̇ᴴ·)

The **G̈** hand is held with the palm facing towards the signer (if the hand were opened, the fingers would point up).	The hand is held with the index fingertip touching the cheek.	The hand bends away from the signer from the wrist.	day (following day) day (next day) tomorrow	519

The **G̈** hand is held with the palm facing left (if the hand were opened, the fingers would point up).	The hand is held beside the cheek.	The index finger taps the cheek twice.	easy no problem simple soft straightforward doddle [1] gentle [2] tender [2]	520

Notes   1 If the cheeks are puffed out, the sign produced is **doddle**.

2 If the eyes are narrowed, and the brows slightly furrowed, the sign produced is **gentle, tender**.

The **G̈** hand is held with the palm facing left (if the hand were opened, the fingers would point up).	The hand is held beside the head.	The hand makes clockwise circles in the vertical plane parallel to the side of the head while moving to the right throughout.	din *† loud *† noise *† noisy *† sound London [1]	521

Notes   * This sign may be produced without movement to the right.

⊃ G̈<ʌ ℮⊥ᵥ·

† This sign may be produced using two hands.

⊃ G̈>ʌ G̈<ʌ (℮⊥ᵥ~·÷)

1 This sign must be produced without movement to the right.

⊃ G̈<ʌ ℮⊥ᵥ·

522 ⌣ G̈т⋀ ˣⱽ⊥ // ⁻5̈ɔ⊥ ˣ 5̈ɔ⊥ (↻̊↓ₓ)

523 ⌣ G̈т⋀ ˣ·

524 ⌣ G̈<⋀ ↻̊@↓ⱽ

525 ⌣ G̈<⋀ ˣ⊥#[ı]↻̊↑

Ö

The index finger is extended from the fist and bent at the palm knuckle.

Handshape and orientation	Location, hand arrangement and contact	Movement	Glosses	
The Ö hand is held with the palm facing towards the signer (if the hand were opened, the fingers would point up).	The hand is held in front of the mouth and chin.	The index finger touches the lower lip and then moves down and away from the signer while opening (forming a 5 hand).	blood* bleed*	522
Two 5 hands are held with the palms facing down (if the hands were opened, the fingers would all point away from the signer).	The hands are held in front of the body; the right hand is held above the left hand with the right fingertips touching the back of the left hand.	The right hand moves away from the signer and, at the same time, down; the right fingertips wriggle, tapping the back of the left hand throughout.		

Notes   * The second part of this sign may be produced with the right hand moving down and, at the same time, away from the signer, brushing across the back of the left hand (**blood** is typically produced in this way).

⊃ Ӫ⊤∧ × // ⁻5○⊥ 5○⊥ ᵞ↓×↓⊤↓

The Ö hand is held with the palm facing towards the signer (if the hand were opened, the fingers would point up).	The hand is held in front of the chin.	The index fingertip taps the lips twice.	taste	523
The Ö hand is held with the palm facing left (if the hand were opened, the fingers would point up).	The hand is held with the index finger in front of the mouth.	The hand makes small clockwise circles in the vertical plane at right angles to the signer's body.	pronounce pronunciation speech Peterborough[1] posh[1] snob[1] snobbish[1]	524

Notes   * Regional sign.

     1 If the index finger is held in front of the nose, and brushes the tip of the nose in completing each circle, the sign produced is **Peterborough, posh, snob, snobbish.**

⊔ Ӫ<∧ ○@⊥ᵥ×@⊥ᵥ .

The Ö hand is held with the palm facing left (if the hand were opened, the fingers would point up).	The hand is held with the index fingertip touching the corner of the mouth.	The hand moves away from the signer while changing (forming an I hand).	bitter sour tart	525

Non-manual features   The eyes are narrowed and the head tilts back slightly.

526 ∪ Ğтʌ ×ᐧ₃ᴠ→ᐁ

527 ∪ Ğ<ʌ ᐸ×

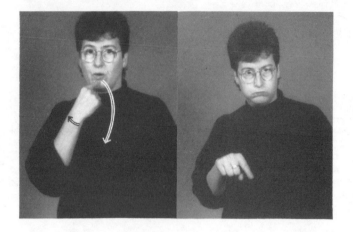

528 ∪ Ğ<ʌ ᐳ×ᐯ

529 ∪ Ğ<ʌ ×°ᐧ

530 π Ğтʌ ×ᐧ

531 π Ğтʌ ×ᐧ

532 π Ğтʌ ᵀ×

533 [] Ğɑ< ×ᐯ

Handshape and orientation	Location, hand arrangement and contact	Movement	Glosses	
The **Ġ** hand is held with the palm facing towards the signer (if the hand were opened, the fingers would point up).	The hand is held with the index fingertip touching the chin.	The hand twists sharply to the left at the wrist while moving down and away from the signer.	get someone to do something* take advantage of someone*	526

Non-manual features The lips are rounded; as the hand moves, the mouth closes with the cheeks puffed out.

Notes * Directional verb.

The **Ġ** hand is held with the palm facing left (if the hand were opened, the fingers would point up).	The hand is held with the side of the index fingertip resting against the chin.	The hand moves to the left; the side of the index finger maintains contact with the chin throughout.	bully cruel cruelty	527

Non-manual features The brows are furrowed.

The **Ġ** hand is held with the palm facing left (if the hand were opened, the fingers would point up).	The hand is held in front of the chin.	The hand moves to the right, so that the side of the index finger brushes across the chin.	fib* fibber* liar* lie* Russia* Russian*	528

Notes * This sign may be produced with a repeated movement.

$$\cup \;\; \ddot{G}{<}{\wedge} \;\; \overset{>\,\cdot}{\underset{>}{\times}}$$

The **Ġ** hand is held with the palm facing left (if the hand were opened, the fingers would point up).	The hand is held with the side of the index finger touching the chin.	The hand moves to the left, maintaining contact with the chin; the movement is repeated.	boy*† boyish*† red*† Russia† Russian†	529

Notes * Regional sign.

† This sign may be produced with a single movement.

$$\cup \;\; \ddot{G}{<}{\wedge} \;\; \overset{\circ}{\underset{\times}{\vee}}$$

The **Ġ** hand is held with the palm facing towards the signer (if the hand were opened, the fingers would point up).	The hand is held beside the neck.	The index fingertip taps the neck twice.	beef butcher meat	530

The **Ġ** hand is held with the palm facing towards the signer (if the hand were opened, the fingers would point up).	The hand is held in front of the neck.	The index fingertip taps the neck several times.	contain oneself face (keep a straight face) laughter (suppress one's laughter)	531

The **Ġ** hand is held with the palm facing towards the signer (if the hand were opened, the fingers would point up).	The hand is held beside the neck.	The hand moves towards the signer; the movement ends with the index fingertip touching the neck.	kill meat	532

The **Ġ** hand is held with the palm facing up (if the hand were opened, the fingers would point to the left).	The hand is held against the chest.	The hand moves down, maintaining contact with the chest throughout.	alone individual lone loner personal sole independent [1]	533

Notes 1 If the movement ends with a firm movement away from the signer, the sign produced is **independent**.

$$[\,] \;\; \ddot{G}a{<} \;\; \overset{\iota}{\underset{\times}{\vee}}$$

534 [] Ö̈α< _×ᵛᵒᵉᵀᵛ·

535 [] Ö̈ᴐ< ×ᵛ

536 [] Ö̈ᴐ< ×ᵛ⁄⁄ ⁻Aα> × Aᴐᴛ ×ᵛᵒᵉᵀᵛ·

537 [] Ö̈ᴛ< ×

538 [] Ö̈ᴛ< ᵀᵒᵛᵒᵛ×

539 ˟[] Ö̈<ʌ ×ᵐ·

Handshape and orientation	Location, hand arrangement and contact	Movement	Glosses	
The **G̈** hand is held with the palm facing up (if the hand were opened, the fingers would point to the left).	The hand is held in front of the chest.	The hand makes small anticlockwise circles in the vertical plane at right angles to the signer's body, brushing the chest in completing each circle.	alone independent individual lone loner myself personal personally sole	534
The **G̈** hand is held with the palm facing down (if the hand were opened, the fingers would point to the left).	The hand is held against the chest.	The hand moves down, maintaining contact with the chest throughout.	swallow	535
The **G̈** hand is held with the palm facing down (if the hand were opened, the fingers would point to the left).	The hand is held against the chest.	The hand moves down, maintaining contact with the chest throughout.	digest digestion	536
The left **A** hand is held with the palm facing up; the right **A** hand is held with the palm facing down (if the hands were opened, the left fingers would point to the right and the right fingers would point away from the signer).	The hands are held in front of the body; the right hand rests on the left hand.	The right hand makes anticlockwise circles in the horizontal plane, maintaining contact with the left hand throughout.		
The **G̈** hand is held with the palm facing towards the signer (if the hand were opened, the fingers would point to the left).	The hand is held in front of the chest.	The index fingertip touches the chest.	I me	537
The **G̈** hand is held with the palm facing towards the signer (if the hand were opened, the fingers would point to the left).	The hand is held in front of the body.	The hand moves towards the signer while twisting at the wrist, so that the palm faces down; the hand then makes a short downward movement before continuing to move down, maintaining contact with the chest.	fall for a lie/trick gullible sucker swallow a statement/story	538

Non-manual features	The mouth is open with the tongue protruding slightly; the mouth closes as the tongue is drawn in and, at the same time, the head nods slightly.			

| The **G̈** hand is held with the palm facing left (if the hand were opened, the fingers would point up). | The hand is held against the left side of the chest. | The index finger bends up and down from the palm knuckle several times. | anxious* apprehensive* nervous* scared | 539 |

Non-manual features	The eyes are narrowed and the lips are pressed together.	
Notes	* This sign may be produced using a **G̈** hand with the palm facing towards the signer; the index finger taps the left side of the chest several times.	ʔ] G̈⊤< × ·

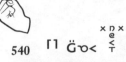

540 ⌐⌐ Ö⌒⊃< ˣⁿˣ
　　　　　　　　@
　　　　　　　　<⊤

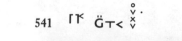

541 ⌐⊬ ÖT< °˅˅
　　　　　　　　˅.

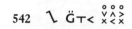

542 ⅄ ÖT< °°°
　　　　　　　˅^>
　　　　　　　ˣ<ˣ

543 ⌐ Ö⌒⊤ <˂
　　　　　　　ˣ⊤

544 ⌐ₒ Ö⌒< ˅ˣˣ˅
　　　　　　　　˅<˅

545 ‾A⌒> ˣ Ö⌒⊤ ⊤°>
　　　　　　　　　　ˣ⊥˂
　　　　　　　　　　ˣ<ˣ

546 G⊤> Ö⌒⊤ₒ ⁿˣⁿ.
　　　　　　　　　⊤ˣⁿ⊤

[328]

Handshape and orientation	Location, hand arrangement and contact	Movement	Glosses	
The Ġ hand is held with the palm facing down (if the hand were opened, the fingers would point to the left).	The hand is held with the index fingertip touching the chest.	The hand makes an anticlockwise circle in the horizontal plane, bending at the wrist; the movement ends with the index fingertip again touching the chest.	us* we*	540

Notes   * This sign may be produced with the hand making a clockwise circle in the horizontal plane.

The Ġ hand is held with the palm facing towards the signer (if the hand were opened, the fingers would point to the left).	The hand is held in front of the right side of the upper chest.	The hand makes a short downward movement, so that the index fingertip brushes the side of the upper chest; the movement is repeated.	white*	541

Notes   * This sign can also be produced using an **F** handshape.

The Ġ hand is held with the palm facing towards the signer (if the hand were opened, the fingers would point to the left).	The hand is held with the index fingertip touching the left upper arm.	The right index finger draws a small cross on the left upper arm; the index fingertip maintains contact with the arm throughout.	ambulance* ambulanceman* ambulancewoman* first aid* hospital* nurse* Red Cross*	542

Notes   * This sign may also be produced using an Ȧ hand.

The Ġ hand is held with the palm facing down (if the hand were opened, the fingers would point away from the signer).	The right index fingertip rests on the back of the left forearm, which is positioned across the body.	The right hand moves slowly to the left; the right index fingertip maintains contact with the left arm throughout.	long slow ages[1] an age[1]	543

Notes   1 If the eyes are narrowed and the cheeks are puffed out, the sign produced is **ages, an age**.

The Ġ hand is held with the palm facing down (if the hand were opened, the fingers would point to the left).	The left forearm is positioned at an angle across the chest; the right hand is held further away from the signer than the left arm.	The right hand moves down and, at the same time, to the left, brushing along the left forearm.	bankrupt debt (in debt) impoverished liquidate poverty	544

The left **A** hand is held with the palm facing down (if the hand were opened, the fingers would point to the right). The right Ġ hand is held with the palm facing down (if the hand were opened, the fingers would point away from the signer).	The hands are held in front of the body; the right hand is held above the left hand, with the right index fingertip touching the back of the left hand.	The right index finger draws a cross on the back of the left hand.	Easter	545

The left **G** hand is held with the palm facing towards the signer (if the hand were opened, the fingers would point to the right). The right Ġ hand is held with the palm facing down (if the hand were opened, the fingers would point away from the signer).	The hands are held in front of the body; the right hand is held nearer to the signer than the left hand.	The right hand bends sharply away from the signer from the wrist, so that the right index fingertip brushes the left index fingertip.	ban* boot out* dismiss* dismissal fire* kick* kick out* sack* suspend* suspension	546

Notes   * Directional verb.

547 $\overline{\ddot{G}}>\perp {}_{I}\times \ddot{G}<\perp {}_{\overset{@}{\underset{v}{\bot}}}$ ·

548 $\overline{\ddot{G}}>\perp {}_{I}\times \ddot{G}<\perp {}_{\overset{@}{\underset{v}{\top}}}{}^{\times}$

549 $\overline{\ddot{G}}>\perp {}_{I}\times \ddot{G}<\perp {}_{\overset{@}{\underset{v}{\bot}}}{}^{\times}$

550 $\ddot{G}>\perp {}_{I} \ddot{G}<\perp {}_{\overset{(@}{\underset{v}{\bot}})}{}_{>}$

551 $5>\perp {}_{I} \ddot{G}\top< {}^{\overset{o}{\times}\overset{I}{\times}\overset{a}{\times}v}_{}$

552 $\overline{B}a> \ddot{G}\sigma\perp {}_{\overset{@}{\underset{\top}{>}}}$

553 $\underline{B}\top> \ddot{G}a\perp {}_{\varphi}{}^{\overset{\wedge}{\times}}_{\wedge}$

Handshape and orientation	Location, hand arrangement and contact	Movement	Glosses
The left **G̈** hand is held with the palm facing right; the right **G̈** hand is held with the palm facing left (if the hands were opened, the fingers would all point away from the signer).	The hands are held side by side in front of the body; the right index finger rests on the left index finger.	The right hand makes several clockwise circles in the vertical plane at right angles to the signer's body, moving around the left index finger.	annual year (every year) yearly	547
The left **G̈** hand is held with the palm facing right; the right **G̈** hand is held with the palm facing left (if the hands were opened, the fingers would all point away from the signer).	The hands are held side by side in front of the body; the right index finger rests on the left index finger.	The right hand makes an anticlockwise circle in the vertical plane at right angles to the signer's body; the movement ends with the right index finger touching the left index finger.	year before year (last year) year (previous year)	548
The left **G̈** hand is held with the palm facing right; the right **G̈** hand is held with the palm facing left (if the hands were opened, the fingers would all point away from the signer).	The hands are held side by side in front of the body; the right index finger rests on the left index finger.	The right hand makes a clockwise circle in the vertical plane at right angles to the signer's body; the movement ends with the right index finger touching the left index finger.	year (following year) year (next year) year (one year after) year (one year later)	549
Two **G̈** hands are held with the palms facing towards the signer (if the hands were opened, the left fingers would point to the right and the right fingers would point to left).	The hands are held side by side in front of the body.	The right hand moves to the right while making clockwise circles in the vertical plane at right angles to the signer's body.	eternal everlasting forever	550

Non-manual features   The cheeks are puffed out.

The left **5** hand is held with the palm facing right and the fingers pointing away from the signer; the right **G̈** hand is held with the palm facing towards the signer (if the hand were opened, the fingers would point to the left).	The hands are held side by side in front of the body.	The right hand makes a short movement away from the signer and then turns, so that the palm faces up, and finally moves down; the right index fingertip brushes across the left fingers throughout.	and so forth and so on etc et cetera others several flirt[1] promiscuous[2]	551

Notes   1 If the eyes are narrowed, the sign produced is **flirt**.

2 If the eyes are narrowed and the cheeks are puffed out, the sign produced is **promiscuous**.

The left **B** hand is held with the palm facing up and the fingers pointing to the right; the right **G̈** hand is held with the palm facing down (if the hand were opened, the fingers would point away from the signer).	The hands are held in front of the body; the right hand is held above the left hand.	The right hand makes a clockwise circle in the horizontal plane.	disc plate record	552
The left **B** hand is held with the palm facing towards the signer and the fingers pointing to the right; the right **G̈** hand is held with the palm facing up (if the hands were opened, the fingers would point away from the signer).	The hands are held in front of the body; the right hand is held lower and nearer to the signer than the left hand.	The right hand moves up, so that the back of the right index finger brushes across the left palm.	appear arise crop up happen occur rise show up high flier[1] sudden[2] suddenly[2]	553

Notes   1 If the movement is changed, so that the right hand continues to move upwards while the forearm brushes across the left palm, the sign produced is **high flier**.

B⊤> √G̈α⊥ᵨ ‸ẍ‸

2 If the movement is sharp, the sign produced is **sudden**, **suddenly**.

B⊤> G̈α⊥ ‸ẍ‸

554 B̄a> G̈ʊ⊥ ⊥̇°̌   555 O>⊥ ⊙ G̈a⊥ ^vı̇   556 Ø G̈a⊥ ¡ G̈a⊥ ×·

557 Ø G̈aʊ⊥ ¡ G̈aʊ⊥ ⊥̇v̌@ᴎ·   558 Ø G̈ʊ⋀ G̈ʊ⋀ ⊥̇ẋᴎ·   559 Ø G̈ʊ⊥ ¡ G̈ʊ⊥ ÷⊥⊥

560 Ø G̈ʊ⊥ ¡ ⊥a⊥ ⊥̇ṗ·   561 Ø G̈ʊ⊥ ¡ G̈ʊ⊥ ·ᴎᴎ̊v

[332]

The index finger is extended from the fist and bent at the palm knuckle.

Handshape and orientation	Location, hand arrangement and contact	Movement	Glosses	
The left **B̈** hand is held with the palm facing up (if the hand were opened, the fingers would point to the right). The right **Ğ** hand is held with the palm facing down (if the hand were opened, the fingers would point away from the signer).	The hands are held in front of the body; the right hand is held above the left hand.	The right hand makes a small clockwise circle in the horizontal plane.	saucer	554
The left **O** hand is held with the palm facing right; the right **Ğ** hand is held with the palm facing up (if the hand were opened, the fingers would all point away from the signer).	The hands are held in front of the body; the right index finger is held between the left fingers and thumb.	The right hand moves down and then makes a short movement away from the signer.	alone independence independent individual isolate isolation lone loner single sole	555
Two **Ğ** hands are held with the palms facing up (if the hands were opened, the fingers would all point away from the signer).	The hands are held side by side in front of the body.	The hands tap together twice.	device item object something thing	556
Two **Ğ** hands are held with the palms facing up (if the hands were opened, the fingers would all point away from the signer).	The hands are held side by side in front of the body.	The hands make alternate clockwise circles in the vertical plane at right angles to the signer's body.	themselves yourselves	557
Two **Ğ** hands are held with the palms facing down (if the hands were opened, the fingers would all point up).	The hands are held in front of the body at an angle, so that the palms are turned away from the signer.	The hands make alternate firm movements down and away from the signer and, at the same time, towards each other; the movements are repeated.	abuse* provoke* taunt* torture*	558
Non-manual features The lips are stretched.				
Notes * Directional verb.				
Two **Ğ** hands are held with the palms facing down (if the hands were opened, the fingers would all point away from the signer).	The hands are held side by side in front of the body.	The hands move apart and then towards the signer.	room studio	559
Two **Ğ** hands are held with the palms facing down (if the hands were opened, the fingers would all point away from the signer).	The hands are held side by side in front of the body.	The hands bend firmly away from the signer from the wrists several times.	encourage* encouragement persuade* persuasion urge*	560
Non-manual features The lips are pressed together.				
Notes * Directional verb.				
Two **Ğ** hands are held with the palms facing down (if the hands were opened, the fingers would all point away from the signer).	The hands are held side by side in front of the body.	The hands move up and down alternately several times.	disability disabled disabled person handicap handicapped person with disability	561

562 Ø G̈⊥ʌ ¦ G̈⊥ʌ ÷ᵛˣ

563 Ø G̈>⊥ G̈<⊥ ˙ˣ

564 Ø G̈>⊥ G̈<⊥ ᶻ˙

565 Ø G̈>⊥ G̈<⊥ (˚ˣᵥ˙)

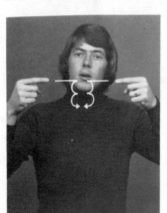

566 Ø G̈̄>⊥ ¦ G̈<⊥ (˚℮⊥ᵥ⊥∼˙)

567 ∩ G̈⊤ʌ G̈⊤ʌ ˚Ɪ∼˙

568 ∩ G̈>ʌ G̈<ʌ ˣ˙

569 [] G̈ɑ⊥ ¦ G̈ɑ⊥ ˚℮⊤ᵥˣ℮⊤ᵥ∼˙

G̈

The index finger is extended from the fist and bent at the palm knuckle.

Handshape and orientation	Location, hand arrangement and contact	Movement	Glosses	
Two G̈ hands are held with the palms facing away from the signer (if the hands were opened, the fingers would all point up).	The hands are held side by side in front of the body.	The hands move apart and then down before finally moving back towards each other.	**certificate** **chart** **diagram** **paper** **picture** **poster** **square**	562
The left G̈ hand is held with the palm facing right; the right G̈ hand is held with the palm facing left (if the hands were opened, the fingers would all point away from the signer).	The hands are held in front of the body.	The hands move firmly towards each other.	**clash** **enemy**	563
The left G̈ hand is held with the palm facing right; the right G̈ hand is held with the palm facing left (if the hands were opened, the fingers would all point away from the signer).	The hands are held in front of the body.	The hands move from side to side several times.	**controversial** **controversy** **debate** **dispute**	564
The left G̈ hand is held with the palm facing right; the right G̈ hand is held with the palm facing left (if the hands were opened, the fingers would all point away from the signer).	The hands are held in front of the body.	The hands make a short movement towards each other; the movement is repeated several times with the hands moving down throughout.	**competition** **fixtures** **tournament**	565
The left G̈ hand is held with the palm facing right; the right G̈ hand is held with the palm facing left (if the hands were opened, the fingers would all point away from the signer).	The hands are held side by side in front of the body; the right index finger is held above the left index finger.	The hands make alternate small clockwise circles in the vertical plane at right angles to the signer's body, while moving away from the signer throughout.	**forever** **roll** **tumble** **rotate**[1] **forward roll**[2] **somersault**[2]	566

Notes   1   If the hands make circles without moving forward, the sign produced is **rotate**.

$$\emptyset \;\; \ddot{G}{>}\!\perp \;_| \;\; \ddot{G}{<}\!\perp \left(\begin{smallmatrix} \circ \\ @ \\ \perp \\ \vee \end{smallmatrix} \!\sim\! \cdot \right)$$

2   If the hands make a single larger circle, the sign produced is **forward roll, somersault**.

$$\emptyset \;\; \ddot{G}{>}\!\perp \;_| \;\; \ddot{G}{<}\!\perp \begin{smallmatrix} @ \\ \perp \\ \vee \end{smallmatrix}$$

Two G̈ hands are held with the palms facing towards the signer (if the hands were opened, the fingers would all point up).	The hands are held with the index fingers at either side of the forehead.	The hands make alternate short movements towards and away from the signer.	**anxious** **concern** **worry**	567

Non-manual features   The brows are furrowed.

The left G̈ hand is held with the palm facing right; the right G̈ hand is held with the palm facing left (if the hands were opened, the fingers would all point up).	The hands are held at the sides of the forehead.	The hands make several short movements towards each other.	**headache** **migraine**	568

Non-manual features   The brows are furrowed and the eyes are narrowed.

Two G̈ hands are held with the palms facing up (if the hands were opened, the fingers would all point away from the signer).	The hands are held side by side in front of the chest.	The hands make alternate small anticlockwise circles in the vertical plane at right angles to the signer's body, brushing the chest in completing each circle.	**ourselves**	569

570 Ø G̈ɑ⊥ ᵀ

571 Ø G̈<⊥ ⁽ᵐ⁓·⁾⊥

572 Ö G̈⊤ʌ ᵐ·

573 Ö G̈<ʌ ˣᵛˣ

There is some *variation* in the degree of bending of the index finger, for example, the finger is relatively loosely bent in a sign such as **Finland** (sign 581) and tightly bent in **envy** (sign 580) and **kitchen** (sign 588).
Ğ has several different *classifier* functions in the productive lexicon and also appears as a classifying element in established signs:

– it is used as a *size and shape* classifier to represent hook-shaped objects, such as **hooked nose** (sign 577) and **hook** (sign 589), small, curved objects, such as **hearing aid** (sign 578), small, long, narrow objects, such as **caterpillar** (sign 587) and the tails of mice and rats as in **rodent** (sign 571). It is also used as a classifier for legs, usually bent legs, as in **sit with legs apart** (see *Introduction*) and **chase** (sign 595);

– Ğ is also used as a *tracing size and shape* classifier to represent lines, especially wavy lines for example to depict uneven cracks or the path of tears trickling down the cheeks, as in **crack** (see *Introduction*) and **tears** (sign 574);

– it is used as a *handling* classifier to indicate objects which may be grasped by the bent index finger, such as the circular aperture of a sliding window or the ring–pull of a can as in **can** (sign 592); two-handed forms are used to indicate the holding of elasticated material;

– it is used as an *instrumental* classifier to indicate implements, tools or utensils with a hooked component such as a towing hook, as in **caravan** (sign 597);

– it is used as a *touch* classifier to indicate scratching or knocking actions or objects associated with such actions, as in **boiled egg** (sign 586);

– one- and two-handed forms may be used to show *extent* or *quantity*, as in **many hearing aids lying side by side** (see *Introduction*).

Ğ is the right-hand component of two letters of the British manual alphabet, **k** and **r** (see *Introduction*). As such, it occurs in initial letter handshape signs such as **kitchen** (sign 588) and **recommend** (sign 599). It also expresses the letter **x** in the Irish and American manual alphabets. As such, it has the potential to be used in borrowed initial letter handshape signs from Irish Sign Language and American Sign Language. However, presumably because of the infrequency of **x** in initial position in English words, such borrowing has not been noted.

Handshape and orientation	Location, hand arrangement and contact	Movement	Glosses	
The Ğ hand is held with the palm facing up (if the hand were opened, the fingers would point away from the signer).	The hand is held in front of the body.	The hand moves towards the signer.	approach* come come back draw near* move towards* return	570
Notes * Directional verb.				
The Ğ hand is held with the palm facing left (if the hand were opened, the fingers would point away from the signer).	The hand is held in front of the body.	The index finger flexes several times while the hand moves away from the signer.	mouse* rat* rodent* slug worm	571
Notes * Regional sign.				
The Ğ hand is held with the palm facing towards the signer (if the hand were opened, the fingers would point up).	The hand is held in front of the face.	The index finger flexes twice.	ability able can capable could feasible possible possibly potential	572
Non-manual features The lips are pressed together.				
The Ğ hand is held with the palm facing left (if the hand were opened, the fingers would point up).	The hand is held with the side of the index finger touching the forehead.	The hand moves down and then the side of the index finger touches the chin.	**Portugal** **Portuguese**	573

574 ⊔ G̈⊤ʌ ×̥°·

575 ⊔ G̈<ʌ ×·

576 ⊔ G̈<ʌ ×·

577 ⊔ G̈<ʌ ×ⁿᵢ

578 ⊃ G̈⊤ʌ ⁿ⊤ₓ

579 ⊃ G̈⊤ʌ ×ᵥᵐ // Ḡa⊤ 5̈ᴜ< ⁿᵢ

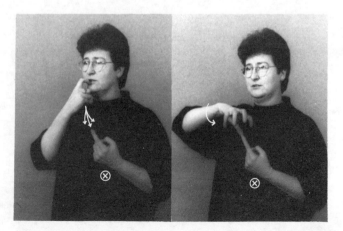

Handshape and orientation	Location, hand arrangement and contact	Movement	Glosses	
The G̈ hand is held with the palm facing towards the signer (if the hand were opened, the fingers would point up).	The hand is held with the index fingertip touching the cheek below the right eye.	The index fingertip flexes, maintaining contact with the cheek; the movement is repeated.	**onion** **cry**[1] **tears**[2]	574

Notes   1   If the corners of the mouth are turned down, the sign produced is **cry**.

      2   If the finger does not flex, the sign produced is **tears**.   ⊔   G̈⊤∧   ᵒᵥₓ ·

| The G̈ hand is held with the palm facing left (if the hand were opened, the fingers would point up). | The hand is held in front of the cheek. | The side of the index fingertip taps the face beneath the eye twice. | **glass***
 window*
 careful
   (be careful)*†[1]
 watch out*†[1] | 575 |

Notes   *   Regional sign.

      †   This sign can be produced using a G̈̈ hand.   ⊔   ᵃG̈<⊥   ×·

      1   If the eyes are narrowed and the brows are furrowed, the sign produced is **be careful, watch out**.

| The G̈ hand is held with the palm facing left (if the hand were opened, the fingers would point up). | The hand is held so that the crook of the index finger rests across the nose. | The index finger taps the nose twice. | **sister*** | 576 |

Notes   *   The following notes apply to the gloss:

This sign may be produced with the palm initially facing down; the hand bends up at the wrist with the index finger maintaining contact with the nose throughout. This is a regional sign.   ⊔   G̈ᴅ<   ⊓∧ₓ

This sign may be produced with a G̈̂ hand; the index finger rests against the nose and then the hand makes a short movement to the right while opening (forming a G̈ hand). This is a regional sign.   ⊔   G̈̂<∧   ×ᵒ□ [ǎ]

| The G̈ hand is held with the palm facing left (if the hand were opened, the fingers would point up). | The hand is held with the side of the index finger touching the nose. | The hand bends away from the signer at the wrist. | **Jew**
 nose (hooked nose) | 577 |

| The G̈ hand is held with the palm facing away from the signer (if the hand were opened, the fingers would point up). | The hand is held with the index fingertip touching the top of the ear. | The hand bends towards the signer at the wrist, maintaining contact with the ear throughout. | **hearing aid**
   (behind the ear
   hearing aid) | 578 |

| The G̈ hand is held with the palm facing towards the signer (if the hand were opened, the fingers would point up). | The hand is held with the index fingertip touching the mouth. | The hand moves down while opening (forming a 5̈ hand). | **tomato**
 raspberry[1]
 strawberry[1] | 579 |

| The left G̈ hand is held with the palm facing up (if the hand were opened, the fingers would point away from the signer). The right 5̈ hand is held with palm facing down (if the hand were opened, the fingers would point to the left). | The hands are held in front of the body; the right hand is held above the left hand. | The right hand bends away from the signer at the wrist. | | |

Notes   1   If the right handshape (in the second part of the sign) is changed to an Ḧ handshape, the sign produced is **raspberry, strawberry**.   ⌣   G̈⊤∧ ×⊥ᵥꟽ   //   G̈ɑ⊥ Ḧᴅ<   ⊓

580 ⌢ G̈<ʌ ⌀

581 ∪ G̈⊤ʌ ×·

582 ∪ G̈⊤ʌ ×· ⫽⫽ ⌀ A⊥ʌ _{<e}·

583 ∪ G̈<ʌ ×̌×·

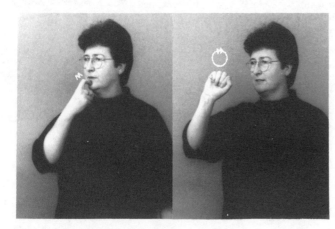

584 ⌣ G̈⊥< (×̃·)

Handshape and orientation	Location, hand arrangement and contact	Movement	Glosses	
The **G̈** hand is held with the palm facing left (if the hand were opened, the fingers would point up).	The hand is held in front of the mouth.	The index finger taps the front teeth.	envy* jealous* jealousy*	580

Non-manual features The mouth is open.

Notes * The following notes apply to all glosses:

This sign may be produced with the index finger being held between the front teeth.

⏝ G̈<ʌ ⊙

This sign may be produced with the index finger being held between the front teeth while the hand makes two short movements from side to side.

⏝ G̈<ʌ ^(⊙ ˣ/z ·)

| The **G̈** hand is held with the palm facing towards the signer (if the hand were opened, the fingers would point up). | The hand is held with the index finger in front of the chin. | The index fingertip taps the chin twice. | Finland
Finn
Finnish
glass*
window*
metal[1]
steel[1]
stone[1]
tin[1] | 581 |

Notes * Regional sign.

1 If the lips are stretched, the sign produced is **metal, steel, stone, tin.**

| The **G̈** hand is held with the palm facing towards the signer (if the hand were opened, the fingers would point up). | The hand is held with the index finger in front of the chin. | The index fingertip taps the chin twice. | clean a window *
window cleaner * | 582 |

| The **A** hand is held with the palm facing away from the signer (if the hand were opened, the fingers would point up). | The hand is held in front of the body. | The hand makes anticlockwise circles in the vertical plane parallel to the signer's body. | | |

Notes * The following notes apply to all glosses:

Regional sign.

The second part of this sign may be used as the second part of a compound sign (see 441 for the first part) also meaning **clean a window, window cleaner.**

∅ G̈⊥ʌ ¦ G̈⊥ʌ ÷ᵛˣ // ∅ A⊥ʌ ^(⊚<ᵛ ·) //

| The **G̈** hand is held with the palm facing left (if the hand were opened, the fingers would point up). | The hand is held with the index finger in front of the chin. | The hand makes a short downward movement, so that the side of the index finger brushes the chin; the movement is repeated. | chocolate * †
dinner * †
envy *
jealous *
jealousy * | 583 |

Notes * Regional sign.

† This sign can also be produced with a tapping movement.

∪ G̈<ʌ ˣ·

| The **G̈** hand is held with the palm facing away from the signer (if the hand were opened, the fingers would point to the left). | The hand is held with the side of the index finger against the underside of the chin. | The hand makes several short up and down movements; the index finger is held against the chin throughout. | bully *
daring *
frightening *
terrifying *
threatening * | 584 |

Non-manual features The cheeks are puffed out and the brows are furrowed.

Notes * Regional sign.

585 ⊔ G̈⊥< ⁰ˣⁿₙ ·

586 ‾A>⊥ G̈<⊥₎ ˣ·

587 G⊥∧ ₗₓ G̈<∧ ⁹ˆₓ

588 G>∧ ₗ G̈⊤< ˣ·

589 ‾G̈ɑ> G̈⊥∧₎ ⊞

590 ‾G̈ʊ> G̈ɑ⊥₎ ^∨⊛ˣ<∨⊛ ·

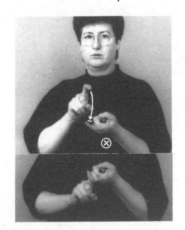

591 °5ʊ> ₗ G̈<⊥ ⁰ˣₚ <∨ˆ

592 ‾5>⊥ G̈ʊ⊥ ⁿᵥ

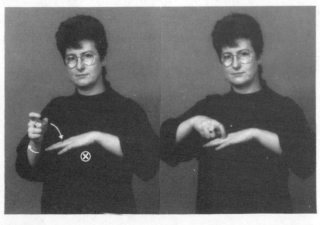

[342]

Handshape and orientation	Location, hand arrangement and contact	Movement	Glosses	
The G̈ hand is held with the palm facing away from the signer (if the hand were opened, the fingers would point to the left).	The hand is held with the side of the index finger against the underside of the chin.	The hand makes several short up and down movements bending from the wrist; the index finger is held against the chin throughout.	awesome* awful* dreadful* fearsome* terrible*	585
Non-manual features The lips are rounded and the brows are furrowed.				
The left A hand is held with the palm facing right; the right G̈ hand is held with the palm facing left (if the hands were opened, the fingers would all point away from the signer).	The hands are held in front of the body; the right index finger is held above the left hand.	The side of the right index finger taps the left hand twice.	egg (boiled egg) crack the top of a boiled egg	586
The left G hand is held with the palm facing away from the signer; the right G̈ hand is held with the palm facing left (if the hands were opened, the fingers would all point up).	The hands are held side by side in front of the body; the right fingertip rests against the side of the left index finger.	The right hand moves slowly up, maintaining contact with the left index finger; the right index finger wiggles throughout.	caterpillar caterpillar crawling up a thin object	587
The left G hand is held with the palm facing right (if the hand were opened, the fingers would point up). The right G̈ hand is held with the palm facing towards the signer (if the hand were opened, the fingers would point to the left).	The hands are held side by side in front of the body.	The middle knuckle of the right index finger taps the middle of the left index finger twice.	kitchen	588
The left G̈ hand is held with the palm facing up; the right G̈ hand is held with the palm facing away from the signer (if the hands were opened, the left fingers would point to the right and the right fingers would point up).	The hands are held in front of the body; the right hand is held higher and nearer to the signer than the left hand.	The right hand moves firmly down, so that the index fingers link together.	hook hook (hang on a hook)	589
The left G̈ hand is held with the palm facing down; the right G̈ hand is held with the palm facing up (if the hands were opened, the left fingers would point to the right and the right fingers would point away from the signer).	The hands are held in front of the body; the right index finger is held above the left index finger.	The right hand makes clockwise circles in the vertical plane parallel to the signer's body; the right index finger brushes the left index finger in completing each circle.	nothing special nothing to write home about ordinary	590
Non-manual features The nose is wrinkled and the tongue protrudes between the teeth.				
The left 5 hand is held with the palm facing down and the fingers pointing to the right; the right G̈ hand is held with the palm facing left (if the hand were opened, the fingers would point away from the signer).	The hands are held side by side in front of the body; the right hand is held higher than the left hand.	The right hand makes a short movement down to the left and, at the same time, twists at the wrist, so that the palm faces down; the movement ends with the right index fingertip touching the left ring finger.	engaged engagement fiancé fiancée	591

The left 5̈ hand is held with the palm facing right; the right G̈ hand is held with the palm facing down (if the hands were opened, the fingers would all point away from the signer).	The hands are held in front of the body; the right index finger is held above the left hand.	The right hand bends up at the wrist.	can with a ring-
			  pull
			open a can with a ring-
			  pull
			ring-pull
				592

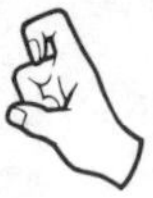

593 B>∧ ɪx G̈ɒ⊥ (ᵐ·) ⊥ x

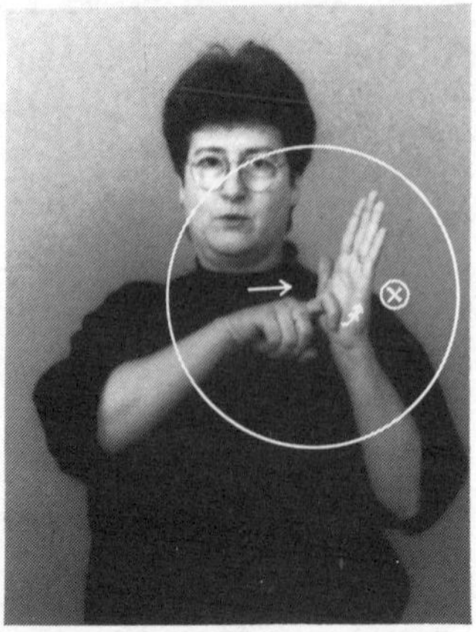

594 Ø G̈ɑ> ɪ G̈ɒ⊥ ° ∨

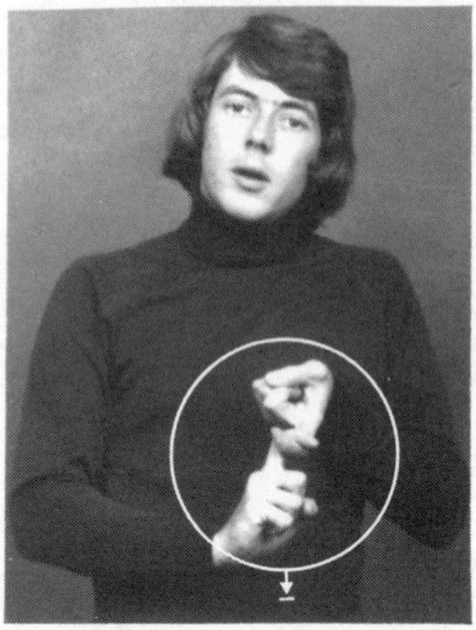

595 Ø G̈ɒ⊥ G̈ɒ⊥ₒ (ᵐ·) ⊥

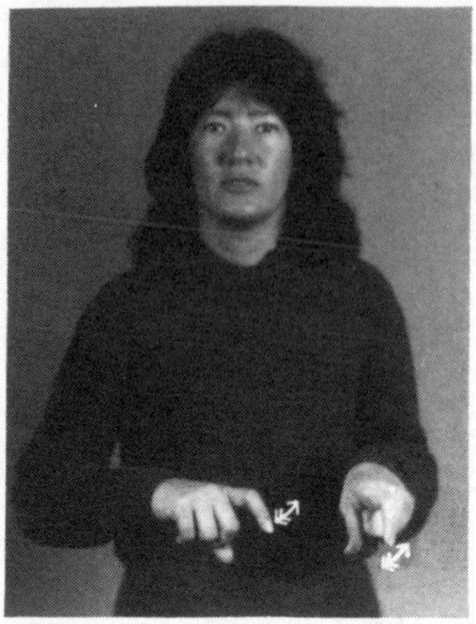

596 Ø G̈>⊥ ɪ G̈⊥∨ ° ⊥

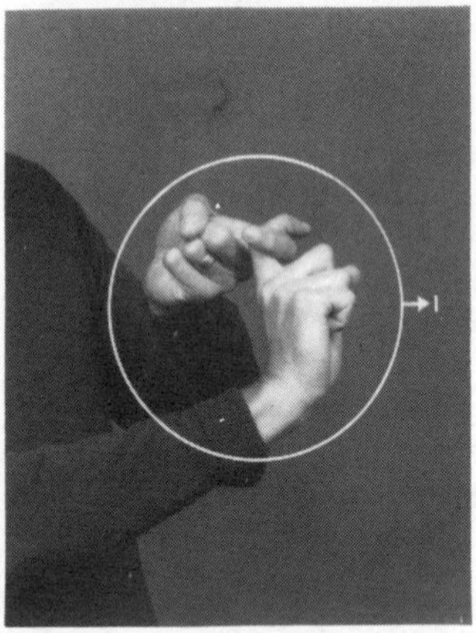

597 Ø F>⊥ ɪ G̈ɒ< >

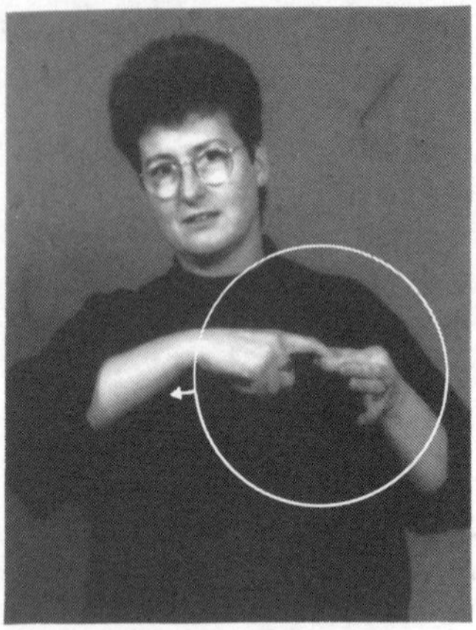

598 Ø F>⊥ ɪ G̈ɒ< ° ∨

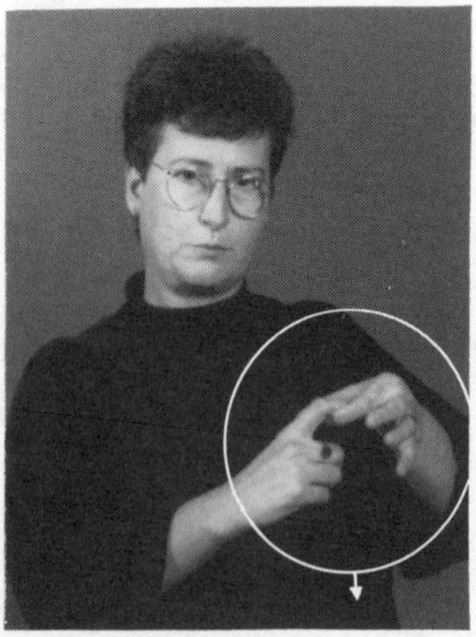

599 Ø B̄ɑ⊥ ɪx G̈⊤< ° ⊥

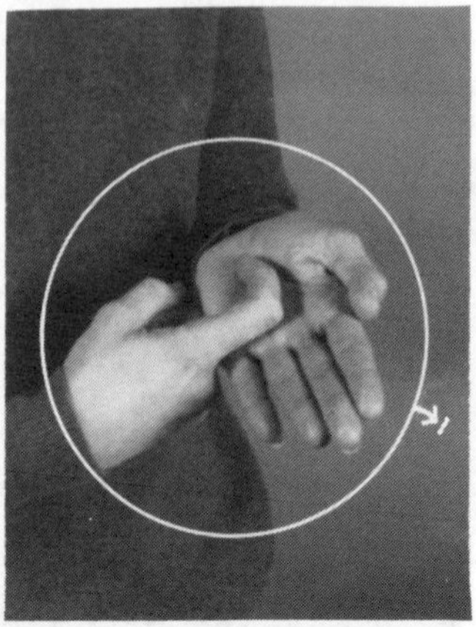

Handshape and orientation	Location, hand arrangement and contact	Movement	Glosses	
The left **B** hand is held with the palm facing right and the fingers pointing up; the right **G̈** hand is held with the palm facing down (if the hand were opened, the fingers would point away from the signer).	The hands are held side by side in front of the body; the side of the right index finger rests against the left palm.	The right index finger flexes several times while the hand moves away from the signer, maintaining contact with the left palm throughout.	**maggot** **maggot/worm** **crawling** **worm**	593
The left **G̈** hand is held with the palm facing up; the right **G̈** hand is held with the palm facing down (if the hands were opened, the left fingers would point to the right, and the right fingers would point away from the signer).	The hands are held in front of the body with the index fingers linked together.	The hands make a short, firm, downward movement.	**commit** **commitment** **depend** **dependent** **firm** **fix** **fixed** **reliable** **rely** **remain** **stay**	594
Two **G̈** hands are held with the palms facing down (if the hands were opened, the fingers would all point away from the signer).	The hands are held in front of the body; the right hand is held nearer to the signer than the left hand.	The hands move away from the signer while the index fingers flex several times.	**chase*** **pursue*** **pursuit*** **run after***	595
Notes * Directional verb.				
The left **G̈** hand is held with the palm facing right; the right **G̈** hand is held with the palm facing away from the signer (if the hands were opened, the left fingers would point away from the signer and the right fingers would point up).	The hands are held in front of the body with the index fingers linked together.	The hands remain together and make a short, firm movement away from the signer.	**firm** **fix** **fixed**	596
The left **F** hand is held with the palm facing right (if the hand were opened, the fingers would point away from the signer). The right **G̈** hand is held with the palm facing down (if the hand were opened, the fingers would point to the left).	The hands are held in front of the body with the right index finger linked together with the left thumb and index finger.	The hands remain together and move to the right.	**caravan** **tow** **tow a caravan**	597
The left **F** hand is held with the palm facing right (if the hand were opened, the fingers would point away from the signer). The right **G̈** hand is held with the palm facing down (if the hand were opened, the fingers would point to the left).	The hands are held in front of the body with the right index finger linked together with the left thumb and index finger.	The hands remain together and make a short downward movement.	**qualification** **qualify**	598
The left **B** hand is held with the palm facing up and the fingers pointing away from the signer; the right **G̈** hand is held with the palm facing towards the signer (if the hand were opened, the fingers would point to the left).	The hands are held side by side in front of the body; the right index finger is held on the left palm.	The hands remain together and make a short, firm movement away from the signer.	**recommend*** **recommendation**	599
Notes * Directional verb.				

600 Ø (B̲ɔ> × G̈ɔ⊥ ᵐ·)⊥

601 Ø G̈<v ᶻ·

G *The bent index finger is extended from the fist.*

Handshape and orientation	Location, hand arrangement and contact	Movement	Glosses
The left **B** hand is held with the palm facing down (if the hand were opened, the fingers would point to the right). The right **G** hand is held with the palm facing down (if the hand were opened, the fingers would point away from the signer).	The hands are held in front of the body; the left palm is held against the back of the right hand.	The hands remain together while moving away from the signer; the right index finger flexes repeatedly throughout.	**snail** **600** **snail crawling** **tortoise** **tortoise walking**

G *The thumb and bent index finger are extended from the fist.*

G has two main *classifier* functions in the productive lexicon and also appears as a classifying element in established signs:
– it is used as a *tracing size and shape* classifier to represent objects which are straight and relatively narrow. Usually, at least one of the hands moves so as to trace the imagined length of the object, as in **tie** (sign 605), **bill** (sign 607) and **belt** (sign 611) and the tongue in **blether** (see *Introduction*);

– it is used as a *handling* classifier to indicate the handling of cylindrical objects such as **torch** (sign 601) and **hose** (sign 601), small, rectangular objects such as **ticket** (sign 607) or objects whose use requires a squeezing action, as in **squeeze toothpaste from a tube onto a toothbrush** (sign 606). Two-handed forms may be used for longer, oblong or cylindrical objects such as **rifle** (sign 609) or **shotgun** (sign 609).

Handshape and orientation	Location, hand arrangement and contact	Movement	Glosses
The **G** hand is held with the palm facing left (if the hand were opened, the fingers would point down).	The hand is held in front of the body.	The hand moves from side to side several times.	**flashlight** **601** **torch** **torchlight** **usherette** **hose**[1]
Notes 1 A larger movement is typically used for **hose**.			

602 ⊔ G̈⊤∧ ×°⊥[Ă]˙⊥[Ġ]
　　　　　　　　#　∨　˙
　　　　　　　　　 ₒ
　　　　　　　　　 □

603 ⌣ ʃĠ⊤< ×ⁿ⊥

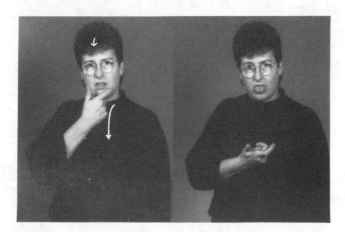

604 ⌣ ʃG̈⊤< ×ⁿ⊥

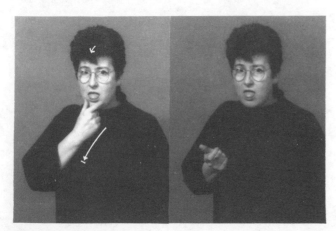

Handshape and orientation	Location, hand arrangement and contact	Movement	Glosses
The **G̈** hand is held with the palm facing towards the signer (if the hand were opened, the fingers would point up).	The hand is held with the index finger and thumb touching the nose.	The hand makes a short movement away from the signer while the thumb and index finger close (forming an **Â** hand); the hand then twists sharply down and away from the signer from the wrist, so that the palm faces down and, at the same time, the index finger and thumb open (forming a **Ġ** hand).	could not **602** care less * couldn't care less * do not care a damn * don't care a damn * do not give a damn * don't give a damn *

Non-manual features   The brows are slightly furrowed, the nose is wrinkled and the tongue tip protrudes slightly between the top teeth and the lower lip.

        Notes   * Directional verb.

The **G̈** hand is held with the palm facing towards the signer (if the hand were opened, the fingers would point to the left).	The hand is held with the index finger and thumb tips touching the chin.	The hand moves down and, at the same time, away from the signer, bending from the elbow.	blether **603** chatterbox

Non-manual features   The tongue protrudes between the top teeth and the lower lip and the eyes are narrowed; the head tilts forward.

The **G̈** hand is held with the palm facing towards the signer (if the hand were opened, the fingers would point to the left).	The hand is held with the thumb and index fingertips touching the chin.	The hand moves firmly down and away from the signer, bending from the elbow.	amazed **604** flabbergasted gobsmacked staggered

Non-manual features   The mouth is open with the tongue protruding slightly; as the hand moves, the eyes open wide with the eyebrows raised and the head is pushed forward.

605   [] G̈т< ^ˇₓ

606   ÂT>₁ G̈тv ^{>[Ā]}#

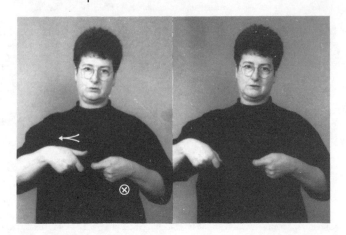

607   Ø G̈т> [˚]^ G̈⊥>₎ [˚]ᵛ

608   Ø G̈>⊥ ₁ G̈<⊥ ^{ᵉ∾·}⊥ᵛ

609   Ø (G̲̈⍺⊥ ᵉG̈<⊥₎ ᵐ)⊤̇ᵛ

Handshape and orientation	Location, hand arrangement and contact	Movement	Glosses	
The G̈ hand is held with the palm facing towards the signer (if the hand were opened, the fingers would point to the left).	The hand is held with the thumb and index fingertips touching the chin.	The hand moves down; the thumb and index finger tips maintain contact with the chest throughout.	character identity personality tie*	**605**

    Notes * This sign may be produced with the hand touching the upper chest and then moving down before touching the lower chest.   [] G̈⊤< ×∨×

The left Â hand is held with the palm facing towards the signer (if the hand were opened, the fingers would point to the right). The right G̈ hand is held with the palm facing towards the signer (if the hand were opened, the fingers would point down).	The hands are held side by side in front of the body.	The right hand moves to the right, and, at the same time, closes (forming an Â hand).	squeeze something from a tube onto a small implement squeeze toothpaste from a tube onto a toothbrush	**606**
The left G̈ hand is held with the palm facing towards the signer; the right G̈ hand is held with the palm facing away from the signer (if the hands were opened, the fingers would all point to the right).	The hands are held in front of the body at an angle, so that the fingers are turned away from the signer; the right hand is held nearer to the signer than the left hand.	The left hand makes a short upward movement while the right hand makes a short downward movement.	bill card list pass pocket diary prescription receipt slip ticket	**607**
The left G̈ hand is held with the palm facing right; the right G̈ hand is held with the palm facing left (if the hands were opened, the fingers would all point away from the signer).	The hands are held side by side in front of the body.	The hands make alternate clockwise circles in the vertical plane at right angles to the signer's body.	engine* machine* machinery* motor*	**608**

    Notes * Regional sign.

The left G̈ hand is held with the palm facing up; the right G̈ hand is held with the palm facing left (if the hands were opened, the fingers would all point away from the signer).	The hands are held in front of the body; the right hand is held lower and nearer to the signer than the left hand.	The right index finger flexes and, at the same time, the hands make a firm movement down and towards the signer.	fire a rifle/shotgun shoot with a rifle/shotgun shot of a rifle/shotgun shooting with a rifle/shotgun [1] rifle* [2] shotgun* [2]	**609**

Non-manual features The eyes are narrowed, the head is tilted to the right and the eye gaze is directed in line with the hands.

    Notes * This sign may be produced without movement of the right index finger.   Ø G̲̈ɑ⊥ ᵉG̈<⊥ᵨ ᵀ∨

        1 If the movement of the hands is short and repeated, and the right index finger flexes with each movement of the hands, the sign produced is **shooting with a rifle/shotgun**.   Ø (G̲̈ɑ⊥ ᵉG̈<⊥ᵨ ᵐ·) ᵒᵀ∨·

        2 If the non-manual features are not present and the hands make a short, firm movement towards the signer the sign produced is **rifle, shotgun**.   Ø G̈ɑ⊥ G̈<⊥ᵨ ᵒᵀ

610   ◯ G̈ᴛ> G̈ᴛ< ^{⊚ᴎ·}⁣_{↓ᵥ÷}

611   ⊔ G̈ᴛᵥ G̈ᴛᵥ ˣˣˣ

612   ∅ Ĝɑ⊥ ᵂ

613   ∅ Ĝɑ⊥ ᵒᶻ·

Handshape and orientation	Location, hand arrangement and contact	Movement	Glosses	
Two **G̈** hands are held with the palms facing towards the signer (if the hands were opened, the left fingers would point to the right and the right fingers would point to the left).	The hands are held in front of the head.	The hands make alternate clockwise circles in the vertical plane at right angles to the signer's body, moving apart each time they move away from the head.	**find** **hunt** **hunter** **look for** **search** **seek**	**610**
Non-manual features	The brows are furrowed, the eyegaze is directed down and forward, and the head moves from side to side several times.			
Two **G̈** hands are held with the palms facing towards the signer (if the hands were opened, the fingers would all point down).	The hands are held against the waist.	The hands move towards each other and then meet touching the middle of the waist.	**belt**	**611**

The bent index finger is extended from the fist so that the pad of the index finger touches the tip of the thumb.

Ĝ is used primarily as a *handling* classifier within the productive lexicon and as a classifying element in established signs:
– it is used to indicate objects which are so tiny they can be held by the tips of index finger and thumb, as in **bit** (sign 612) and **earmould** (sign 623);

– it is used as an *instrumental* classifier for small or fine instruments, implements or tools such as **pen** (sign 614) and **chalk** (sign 615). Several signs make use of the handling of a pen component, for example **author** (sign 628), **write** (sign 628), **ballot** (sign 629) and **bingo** (sign 629).

Handshape and orientation	Location, hand arrangement and contact	Movement	Glosses	
The **Ĝ** hand is held with the palm facing up (if the hand were opened, the fingers would point away from the signer).	The hand is held in front of the body.	The pads of the thumb and index finger rub together several times.	**almost*** **bit*** **few*** **insignificant*** **little*** **minor*** **nearly*** **tiny*** **some***[1]	**612**
Non-manual features	The eyes are narrowed and the corners of the mouth are turned down.			
Notes	* This sign may also be produced using an **Â** hand.	Ø Âɑ⊥ ᵂ		
	1 If the non-manual feature is not present, the sign produced is **some**.			
The **Ĝ** hand is held with the palm facing up (if the hand were opened, the fingers would point away from the signer).	The hand is held in front of the body.	The hand makes several short movements from side to side.	**borrow*** **hire*** **temporary***	**613**
Notes	* This sign may be produced using an **Â** hand.	Ø Âɑ⊥ ᶻ·		

614　∅　Ĝ◡⊤ (◦̣ ᴅ ·)
　　　　　　　 ͮ
　　　　　　　 >

615　∅　Ĝ⊤ᴧ (◦̣ ·)
　　　　　　　 ͮ
　　　　　　　 >

616　∅　Ĝ⊤ᴧ (ᴅ)[ǧ] ͮ [ĉ]
　　　　　 □ > ♯
　　　　　 ͮ
　　　　　 □

617　∅　Ĝ<⊤ ˙□ [ᴧ]

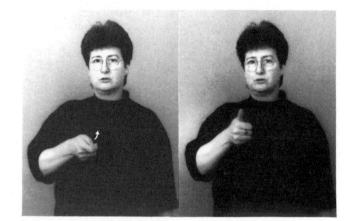

618　∅　Ĝ<⊤ ˙ᴅ [ᴧ]
　　　　　 ͮ
　　　　　 □

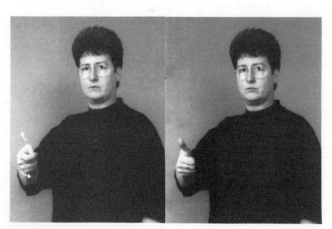

The bent index finger is extended from the fist so that the pad of the index finger touches the tip of the thumb.

Handshape and orientation	Location, hand arrangement and contact	Movement	Glosses	

The Ĝ hand is held with the palm facing down (if the hand were opened, the fingers would point away from the signer).	The hand is held in front of the body.	The hand moves to the right and, at the same time, makes short up and down bending movements at the wrist.	ballpoint pen
			biro
			office
			pen
			pencil
			sign one's name
			write with a
			   ballpoint pen/
			   biro/pen/pencil
			write
				614

The Ĝ hand is held with the palm facing away from the signer (if the hand were opened, the fingers would point up).	The hand is held in front of the body.	The hand makes several short up and down movements while moving to the right throughout.	chalk
			write on a
			   blackboard with
			   chalk
			write on an upright
			   surface
				615

The Ĝ hand is held with the palm facing away from the signer (if the hand were opened, the fingers would point up).	The hand is held in front of the body.	The hand bends to the right from the wrist and moves down while the index finger and thumb open (forming a G̈ hand); the downward movement then continues while the index finger and thumb close (forming a Ĝ hand).	moon Pakistan Pakistani	616
The Ĝ hand is held with the palm facing left (if the hand were opened, the fingers would point away from the signer).	The hand is held in front of the body.	The thumb flicks up (forming an Å hand).	cheap early captain [1] toss a coin [1]	617

    Notes   1 If the movement is changed so that the hand makes a short upward movement while the thumb flicks up, the sign produced is **captain, toss a coin**.

    Ø Ĝ<⊥ ⋀̊ [A]

| The Ĝ hand is held with the palm facing left (if the hand were opened, the fingers would point away from the signer). | The hand is held in front of the body. | The thumb flicks up (forming an Å hand) and, at the same time, the hand bends down at the wrist. | few*
insignificant*
little*
minor*
rare
rather
seldom
tiny*
almost [1]
nearly [1] | 618 |

    Notes   * This sign can be produced with the pad of the thumb rubbing across the pad of the index finger several times.

    Ø Ĝ<⊥ ᵐ ·

    1 If the palm faces up and the hand makes a short, repeated movement away from the signer, the sign produced is **almost, nearly**.

    Ø Ĝɑ⊥ ᵢ̊ ·

    If the palm faces up and the movement is changed to a short firm movement away from the signer, the sign produced is also **almost, nearly**.

    Ø Ĝɑ⊥ ᵢ̊

619 ∩ Ĝ̂T∧ ⁰̣ː [G]

620 Ш Ĝ̂<∧ ˣ ω̂̇ ˣ
        T
        <

621 Ʒ Ĝ̂T∧ (ⁿ)[ɞ]
                T
                ☐

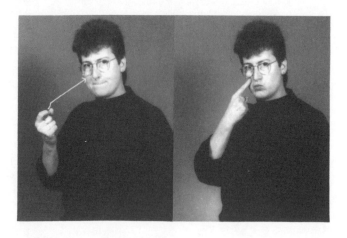

622 Ʒ Ĝ̂<⊥ ˅ˣ

623 ⊃ Ĝ̂<∧ ω̇ˣ
              ✗

624 ⊃ Ĝ̂<∧ ⁿ̇˅

[356]

The bent index finger is extended from the fist so that the pad of the index finger touches the tip of the thumb.

Handshape and orientation	Location, hand arrangement and contact	Movement	Glosses	
The Ĝ hand is held with the palm facing towards the signer (if the hand were opened, the fingers would point up).	The hand is held in front of the forehead.	The index finger straightens sharply (forming a G hand) while the hand makes a short movement away from the signer.	**idea** **notion** **realise** **initiative**[1] **invent**[1] **invention**[1]	619

Notes   1   If the eyebrows are raised as the hand moves, the sign produced is **initiative, invent, invention.**

The Ĝ hand is held with the palm facing left (if the hand were opened, the fingers would point up).	The hand is held with the thumb and index finger tips touching the side of the nose.	The hand twists at the wrist (so that the palm faces towards the signer) while making a short movement to the left; the movement ends with the index finger and thumb tips touching the left side of the nose.	**flower***† **garden**† **snuff**†	620

Notes   *   This sign may be produced with a repeated movement.

$$\sqcup \ \ \hat{\tilde{G}}{<}{\wedge} \left({}^{\times}_{<}{}^{\overset{\circ}{\underset{\mathsf{T}}{\omega}}}{}^{\times} \right)\cdot$$

Notes   †   This sign may be produced using an **F** handshape.

$$\sqcup \ \ \mathsf{F}{<}{\wedge} \ {}^{\times}_{<}{}^{\overset{\circ}{\underset{\mathsf{T}}{\omega}}}{}^{\times} \quad \text{or} \quad \sqcup \ \ \mathsf{F}{<}{\wedge} \left({}^{\times}_{<}{}^{\overset{\circ}{\underset{\mathsf{T}}{\omega}}}{}^{\times} \right)\cdot$$

The Ĝ hand is held with the palm facing towards the signer (if the hand were opened, the fingers would point up).	The hand is held in front of the face.	The hand bends towards the signer from the wrist while opening (forming a Ĝ hand) and, at the same time, moving towards the signer, so that the index fingertip touches the cheek.	**see through** **suss**	621

Non-manual features   The lips are drawn back and pressed together; the mouth opens, with a sharp puff of air, so that the lips are rounded.

The Ĝ hand is held with the palm facing left (if the hand were opened, the fingers would point away from the signer).	The hand is held with the index finger and thumb tips touching the cheek.	The hand moves down, maintaining contact with the cheek throughout.	**just***† **shit**[1]	622

Notes   *   Regional sign.

Notes   †   This sign may be produced using an **F** handshape.

$$3 \ \ \mathsf{F}{<}{\perp} \ {}^{\vee}_{\cdot}{}^{\times}$$

Notes   1   If the handshape is changed to a V̈ handshape (if the hand were opened, the fingers would point up), the sign produced is **shit.**

$$3 \ \ \ddot{\mathsf{V}}{<}{\wedge} \ {}^{\vee}_{\cdot}{}^{\times}$$

The Ĝ hand is held with the palm facing left (if the hand were opened, the fingers would point up).	The index finger and thumb tips are held against the ear.	The hand twists away from the signer at the wrist; the index finger and thumb tips are held against the ear throughout.	**earmould*** **hearing aid (body worn hearing aid)***	623

Notes   *   This sign may be produced with a repeated movement.

$$\supset \ \ \hat{\tilde{G}}{<}{\wedge} \ {}^{\omega}_{\times}{}^{\cdot}_{\downarrow}$$

The Ĝ hand is held with the palm facing left (if the hand were opened, the fingers would point up).	The hand is held beside the ear.	The hand makes a short bending movement to the left from the wrist; the movement is repeated.	**yellow***	624

Notes   *   Regional sign.

625 ⌄ $\widehat{\overset{\frown}{G}}$⊤∧ $\overset{\cdot}{\square}$ [ɢ] .

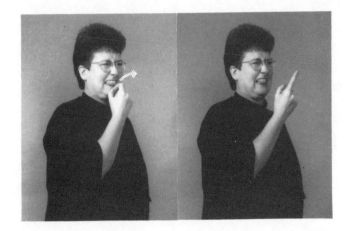

626 ∪ $\widehat{\overset{\frown}{G}}$<∧ $\overset{\overset{\circ}{ð}}{\underset{\square}{<}}$ [ᷰ]

627 G>⊤ ¦ $\widehat{\overset{\frown}{G}}$<∧ $\overset{\overset{\circ}{\underset{\times}{\bot}}}{\cdot}$.

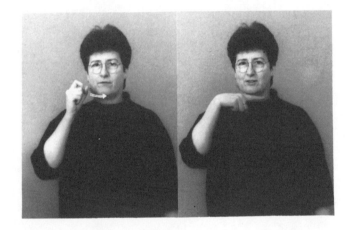

628 $\overline{B}$a> $\widehat{\overset{\frown}{G}}$⊤ɔ $\overset{>}{\underset{<}{\times}}$.

629 $\overline{B}$a> $\widehat{\overset{\frown}{G}}$ɔ⊤ $\overset{<\overset{\circ}{\bot}>}{\underset{\times}{\top}}$⊤×

630 $\underline{B}$⊤>ͦ $\widehat{\overset{\frown}{G}}$a⊤ $\overset{\overset{\cdot}{n}\ [ǎ]\ \times}{\underset{\square}{\wedge}}$

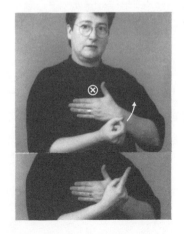

The bent index finger is extended from the fist so that the pad of the index finger touches the tip of the thumb.

Handshape and orientation	Location, hand arrangement and contact	Movement	Glosses	
The **Ĝ** hand is held with the palm facing towards the signer (if the hand were opened, the fingers would point up).	The hand is held in front of the mouth and chin.	The index finger straightens sharply (forming a **G** hand); the movement is repeated.	grass informer inform on sneak telltale tell tales	625
Non-manual features The tongue protrudes between the teeth and the nose is wrinkled.				
The **Ĝ** hand is held with the palm facing left (if the hand were opened, the fingers would point up).	The hand is held at the side of the chin.	The hand makes a short, sharp bending movement to the left from the wrist and, at the same time, the index finger opens (forming a **Ḡ** hand).	funny odd peculiar strange weird	626
Non-manual features The brows are furrowed and the nose is wrinkled.				
The left **G** hand is held with the palm facing right; the right **Ĝ** hand is held with the palm facing left (if the hands were opened, the left fingers would point away from the signer and the right fingers would point up).	The hands are held side by side in front of the body.	The right hand makes a short movement away from the signer, so that the right thumb and index finger tips brush along the left index finger; the movement is repeated.	paper point[1]	627

Notes 1 If the right thumb and index finger tips are held against the left index fingertip, and the right hand bends away from the signer at the wrist, with the fingertips held together throughout, the sign produced is **point**.

$$\text{G>}\bot \ _{\text{IX}} \ \hat{\hat{\text{G}}}\text{<}\wedge \ _{\bot}^{\overset{\times}{\text{D}}}$$

The left **B** hand is held with the palm facing up and the fingers pointing to the right; the right **Ĝ** hand is held with the palm facing down (if the hand were opened, the fingers would point away from the signer).	The hands are held in front of the body; the right hand is held above the left hand.	The right hand moves to the right, brushing across the left palm; the movement is repeated.	author notes notetaker notetaking scribe secretary write writer scribble[1]	628

Notes 1 If the right hand makes short movements from side to side and, at the same time, moves towards the signer, maintaining contact with the left palm throughout, the sign produced is **scribble**.

$$\overline{\text{B}}\text{a>} \ _{\times} \ \hat{\hat{\text{G}}}\text{ɒ}\bot \ \overset{(\overset{\text{o}}{\underset{\text{T}}{\text{z}}}.)}{\times}$$

The left **B** hand is held with the palm facing up and the fingers pointing to the right; the right **Ĝ** hand is held with the palm facing down (if the hand were opened, the fingers would point away from the signer).	The hands are held in front of the body; the right hand is held above the left hand.	The right thumb and index finger tips draw a cross on the left palm.	ballot bingo cancel censor elect election vote	629
The left **B** hand is held with the palm facing towards the signer and the fingers pointing to the right; the right **Ĝ** hand is held with the palm facing up (if the hand were opened, the fingers would point away from the signer).	The hands are held in front of the body; the left hand is held above the right hand.	The right hand moves up, bending from the wrist, while the index finger straightens (forming a **Ḡ** hand); the movement ends with the right wrist touching the side of the left hand.	appear chance crop up happen occur opportunity show up sudden[1] suddenly[1] funny[2] odd[2] peculiar[2] strange[2] weird[2]	630

Notes 1 If the movement is sharp, the sign produced is **sudden, suddenly**.

$$\underline{\text{B}}\text{ᴛ>}_{\text{ç}} \ \hat{\hat{\text{G}}}\text{ɑ}\bot \ \overset{\underset{\square}{\wedge}}{}$$

2 If the brows are furrowed, the sign produced is **funny, odd, peculiar, strange, weird**.

631 Ø Ĝ⌄⊥ Ĝ⌄⊥ $\overset{\wedge[GG]\sim \cdot}{\overset{\wedge}{\square}}$

632 ○ Ḡ̿⊥⌃ ₁ Ĝ̂⊥⌃₉ $\overset{(ᵑ)[GG]}{\overset{⊥}{\square}}$

633 ⊔ Ĝ̂>⌃ Ĝ̂<⌃ $\overset{\circ \div [ǒǒ]}{\square}$

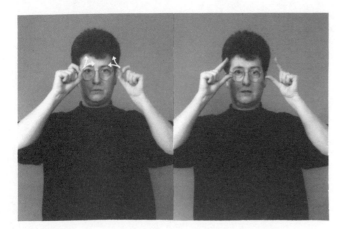

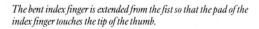

Handshape and orientation	Location, hand arrangement and contact	Movement	Glosses	
Two Ĝ hands are held with the palms facing up (if the hands were opened, the fingers would all point away from the signer).	The hands are held in front of the body.	The hands move up while opening (forming a G hand); the movements are repeated alternately several times.	**fireworks**	631
Two Ĝ hands are held with the palms facing away from the signer (if the hands were opened, the fingers would all point up).	The hands are held side by side in front of the head; the right hand is held higher and nearer to the signer than the left hand.	The hands bend away from the signer at the wrists while moving away from the signer and, at the same time, opening (forming two G hands).	**blame***	632

Non-manual features   The eyes are narrowed and the brows furrowed.

Notes   * Directional verb.

The left Ĝ hand is held with the palm facing right; the right Ĝ hand is held with the palm facing left (if the hands were opened, the fingers would all point up).	The hands are held with the fingers beside the eyes.	The hands make a short movement apart and, at the same time, the index finger and thumb of each hand open (forming two Ḡ hands).	**aware** **awareness** **awake**[1] **wake up**[1]	633

Notes   1 If the eyes are closed and then open as the hands move, the sign produced is **awake** *(see entry 2 in the English section)*, **wake up** *(see entries 1 and 2 in the English section)*.

634 Ø $\overset{\ddot{=}}{G}_{\perp\wedge}$ $\overset{(\,\overset{o}{z}\,.)}{\vee}$

635 Ø $\overset{\ddot{=}}{G}_{\perp>}$ $^{\vee}$

636 Ø $\overset{\ddot{=}}{G}_{\perp>}$ $\overset{\vee\,\omega\,>}{\underset{\wedge}{<}}$

č̆ has several different *classifier* functions in the productive lexicon and is used as a classifying element in established signs:
– it is used as a *size and shape* classifier to represent curved or bent objects such as a curved beak in **parrot** (sign 639) and bent legs in **cycle** (sign 654);
– it can be used as a *tracing size and shape* classifier to represent narrow objects of varying lengths such as a swan's neck in **swan** (sign 642), a clerical collar in **clergy** (sign 643), **bars** (sign 657), **ticket** (sign 658) and **horizontal stripes** (sign 660). It may also be used to indicate a rim or layer, as in **layer of custard** (see *Introduction*);
– it may be used as a *handling* classifer to indicate small objects held between thumb and index finger such as **whistle** (sign 641) or cylindrical objects with a press-down attachment as in **aerosol** (sign 634) and **deodorant spray** (sign 634);
– it may be used to show *extent* as in **small** (sign 637) and a measure of spirits as in **short** (sign 650). One- and two-handed forms can show

quantity such as many, long, narrow objects, as in **railings** (sign 657) and **bones** (sign 660).

This handshape expresses the letter **c** of the British manual alphabet. As such, it occurs in initial letter handshape signs such as **confidence** (sign 646) and **course** (sign 648), as well as in signs derived from abbreviated English forms such as **county council** (sign 638) and **Coca Cola** (sign 638). The letter **c** is expressed in the Irish and American manual alphabets by the **C** handshape rather than č̆. The interplay between these two forms means that in some borrowed initial letter handshape signs č̆ and **C** may be interchangeable, at least for some signers. Examples include **committee** (see *Introduction*) and **coffee** (sign 638). In a few examples, **C** is required rather than č̆, as in **curriculum** and **copyright** (see *Introduction*).

This handshape also expresses the right-hand component of the British manual aphabet letter **d** and thus occurs in initial letter handshape signs such as **daddy** (sign 649) and **daughter** (sign 649).

Handshape and orientation	Location, hand arrangement and contact	Movement	Glosses	
The č̆ hand is held with the palm facing away from the signer (if the hand were opened, the fingers would point up).	The hand is held in front of the body.	The hand makes several short movements from side to side while moving down, and then moves straight down.	aerosol graffiti spray with an aerosol * deodorant [1] spray deodorant * [1] hairspray [2] spray hairspray * [2] breath freshener [3] spray breath freshener * [3] perfume [4] spray perfume * [4]	634
Notes * Directional verb.				
	1 If the hand is held at the left side of the body with the palm facing towards the signer and the hand moves from side to side repeatedly, the sign produced is **deodorant**, **spray deodorant**.	⊃⌐ č̆⊤ʌ °ᴢ·		
	2 If the hand is held beside the head with the palm facing left, and the hand moves towards and away from the signer repeatedly, the sign produced is **hairspray**, **spray hairspray**.	○ č̆<ʌ °ʜ·		
	3 If the hand is held in front of the wide open mouth with the palm facing towards the signer, and the finger flexes, the sign produced is **breath freshener**, **spray breath freshener**.	◡ č̆⊤ʌ ᴍ		
	4 If the hand is held in front of the neck with the palm facing towards the signer, and the index finger flexes and the hand then moves to the left before the index finger flexes again, the sign produced is **perfume**, **spray perfume**.	π č̆⊤ʌ ᴍ<ᴍ		
The right č̆ hand is held with the palm facing away from the signer (if the hand were opened, the fingers would point to the right).	The hand is held in front of the body.	The hand moves down.	individual person student	635
The č̆ hand is held with the palm facing away from the signer (if the hand were opened, the fingers would point to the right).	The hand is held in front of the body.	The hand makes a cross.	cross	636

637 Ø G̈<ʌ ᵒ

638 Ø G̈<ʌ ᵒ₃ᴴ·

639 ○ G̈⊥ʌ ᵒᴵ·

640 ○ G̈ᴑ⊥ ᵒᴺ·

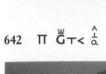

641 ○ G̈⊤< ×

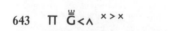

642 π G̈⊤< ᴧᴑ

643 π G̈<ʌ ×>×

644 [] G̈⊤< ×̌

[364]

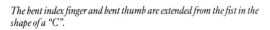

The bent index finger and bent thumb are extended from the fist in the shape of a "C".

Handshape and orientation	Location, hand arrangement and contact	Movement	Glosses	
The Ğ hand is held with the palm facing left (if the hand were opened, the fingers would point up).	The hand is held in front of the body.	No movement.	bit little small small part small piece tiny	637
The Ğ hand is held with the palm facing left (if the hand were opened, the fingers would point up).	The hand is held in front of the body.	The hand makes several very short twisting movements towards and away from the signer at the wrist.	coffee Coca Cola [1] county council [1]	638

Notes 1 If the hand makes a short, firm movement away from the signer and then a short, firm movement to the right, the sign produced is **Coca Cola, county council**.

$$Ø \quad \overset{\underset{\smile}{}}{G}_{<\wedge} \quad \overset{\circ\cdot}{\llcorner>}$$

The Ğ hand is held with the palm facing away from the signer (if the hand were opened, the fingers would point up).	The hand is held in front of the face.	The hand makes a short bending movement away from the signer from the wrist; the movement is repeated.	cock hen parrot peck turkey woodpecker	639
The Ğ hand is held with the palm facing down (if the hand were opened, the fingers would point away from the signer).	The hand is held in front of the mouth.	The hand makes several short up and down movements, bending from the wrist.	turkey	640
The Ğ hand is held with the palm facing towards the signer (if the hand were opened, the fingers would point to the left).	The hand is held in front of the mouth and chin.	The index finger and thumb touch the lower lip.	blow a whistle * whistle * referee *†[1] umpire *†[1]	641

Non-manual features The lips are rounded.

Notes * This sign may be produced using a Ğ̈ hand.

$$\smile \quad \overset{\cdot\cdot}{G}_{T<} \quad ^{\times}$$

† This sign may be produced using an Ḧ hand which taps the lower lip twice.

$$\smile \quad \overset{\cdot\cdot}{H}_{T\wedge} \quad ^{\times\cdot}$$

1 If the index finger and thumb tips tap the lower lip twice, the sign produced is **referee, umpire**.

$$\smile \quad \overset{\cdot\cdot}{G}_{T<} \quad ^{\times\cdot} \quad \text{or} \quad \smile \quad \overset{\cdot\cdot}{G}_{T<} \quad ^{\times\cdot}$$

The Ğ hand is held with the palm facing towards the signer (if the hand were opened, the fingers would point to the left).	The hand is held in front of the neck.	The hand moves up and away from the signer and, at the same time, twists at the wrist, so that the palm faces up.	neck of an ostrich/a swan ostrich swan	642
The Ğ hand is held with the palm facing left (if the hand were opened, the fingers would point up).	The hand is held in front of the neck.	The index finger and thumb tips touch the left side of the neck; the hand then moves to the right and touches the right side of the neck.	clergy * clergyman * clerical collar * dog-collar * minister of religion * priest * vicar *	643

Notes * This sign may be produced using two hands.

$$\Pi \quad \overset{\underset{\smile}{}}{G}_{>\wedge} \mid \overset{\underset{\smile}{}}{G}_{<\wedge} \quad ^{\times\div\times}$$

The Ğ hand is held with the palm facing towards the signer (if the hand were opened, the fingers would point to the left).	The hand is held with the index finger and thumb tips touching the chest.	The hand moves down, maintaining contact with the chest throughout.	character identity personality	644

645　[]　G̈ᴛ< ˣ(ᴅ)ˣˬ
　　　　　　 　 ^
　　　　　　　 <

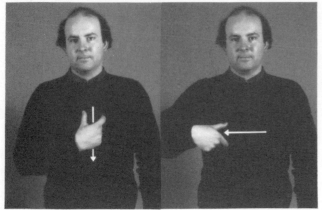

646　[]　G̈<ʌ ˣ·

647　ˀΓ1　G̈ᴛ< ˟ᵛˣᵒ

648　G̈ʊ> ˣ G̈⊥ʌ ˣᵛ

649　G>ʌ ¦ G̈<ʌ ˣ·

650　G>ʌ ¦ G̈<ʌᵩ ᵀˣᵀ

651　∅　G̈ʊ⊥ G̈ʊ⊥ ᵒᵛ

The bent index finger and bent thumb are extended from the fist in the shape of a "C".

Handshape and orientation	Location, hand arrangement and contact	Movement	Glosses	
The **Ğ** hand is held with the palm facing towards the signer (if the hand were opened, the fingers would point to the left).	The hand is held with the index finger and thumb tips touching the chest.	The hand draws a cross on the chest, maintaining contact with the chest throughout.	**Swiss** **Switzerland**	645
The **Ğ** hand is held with the palm facing left (if the hand were opened, the fingers would point up).	The hand is held in front of the chest.	The side of the hand taps the chest twice.	**confidence** **confident** **gain confidence**[1] **lose confidence**[2]	646

Notes 1 If the hand makes a short upward movement, maintaining contact with the chest throughout, the sign produced is **gain confidence**.

2 If the hand makes a short downward movement, maintaining contact with the chest throughout, the sign produced is **lose confidence**.

The **Ğ** hand is held with the palm facing towards the signer (if the hand were opened, the fingers would point to the left).	The hand is held with the index finger and thumb tips resting against the left side of the upper chest.	The hand makes a short movement to the right, maintaining contact with the chest throughout.	**badge** **committee member** **delegate** **official** **steward** **supervisor**	647
The left **G** hand is held with the palm facing down (if the hand were opened, the fingers would point to the right). The right **Ğ** hand is held with the palm facing away from the signer (if the hand were opened, the fingers would point up).	The hands are held in front of the body; the right hand rests on the back of the left hand.	The right hand moves to the right, maintaining contact with the left hand throughout.	**course**	648
The left **G** hand is held with the palm facing right; the right **Ğ** hand is held with the palm facing left (if the hands were opened, the fingers would all point up).	The hands are held side by side in front of the body at an angle, so that the fingers are all turned away from the signer.	The right index finger and thumb tips tap the left index finger twice.	**dad** **daddy** **daughter**	649
The left **G** hand is held with the palm facing right; the right **Ğ** hand is held with palm facing left (if the hands were opened, the fingers would all point up).	The hands are held side by side in front of the body; the right hand is held nearer to the signer than the left hand.	The right hand moves away from the signer, so that the right thumb and index finger tips brush the left index finger.	**short** **whiskey** **whisky**	650
Two **Ğ** hands are held with the palms facing down (if the hands were opened, the fingers would all point away from the signer).	The hands are held in front of the body.	The hands make a short, firm downward movement.	**remain*** **stay*** **still*** **Exeter**[1] **Leeds**[1]	651

Notes * This sign may be produced using one hand only.

1 If the hands make a longer, repeated movement, the sign produced is **Exeter, Leeds**. This is a regional sign.

652 Ø G̈ʊ⊥ G̈ʊ⊥ ᐟ⊥

653 Ø G̈ʊ⊥ ˌ G̈ʊ⊥ ÷#[ôô]

654 Ø G̈ʊ⊥ ˌ G̈ʊ⊥ @÷⊥∨ⁿ·

655 Ø G̈ʊ⊥ ₁ₓ G̈ʊ⊥ ÷

656 Ø G̈⊥ʌ ˌ G̈⊥ʌ ÷

657 Ø G̈⊥< ˌ G̈⊥> ⁽ᵛ·⁾÷

658 Ø G̈>⊥ ₁ₓ G̈<⊥ ÷ᵒ

659 ◯ (G̈>ʌ ᵉG̈<ʌ ᵐ·) ø

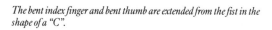

Handshape and orientation	Location, hand arrangement and contact	Movement	Glosses
Two G̈ hands are held with the palms facing down (if the hands were opened, the fingers would all point away from the signer).	The hands are held in front of the body.	The hands move to the right and, at the same time, away from the signer.	**carry on** * **consistent** * **constant** * **continuation** * **continue** * **permanent** * **remain** * **stay** * **stay on** * **still** *	652
Notes * This sign can be produced using one hand only.			
Two G̈ hands are held with the palms facing down (if the hands were opened, the fingers would all point away from the signer).	The hands are held side by side in front of the body.	The hands move apart, and, at the same time, the thumbs and index fingers close (forming two G̈ hands).	**bacon** **rasher of bacon**	653
Two G̈ hands are held with the palms facing down (if the hands were opened, the fingers would all point away from the signer).	The hands are held side by side in front of the body.	The hands make alternate clockwise circles in the vertical plane at right angles to the signer's body.	**bicycle** **bicycle (to bicycle)** * **bike** **cycle** **cycle (to cycle)** * **cycling** * **cyclist** **pedal** * **ride a bicycle/bike** *	654
Notes * This sign may be produced with the hands moving up and down alternately several times.			
Two G̈ hands are held with the palms facing down (if the hands were opened, the fingers would all point away from the signer).	The hands are held side by side in front of the body with the sides of the index fingers touching.	The hands move apart.	**cheque** **cheque book**	655
Two G̈ hands are held with the palms facing away from the signer (if the hands were opened, the fingers would all point up).	The hands are held side by side in front of the body.	The hands move apart.	**coat hanger**	656
Two G̈ hands are held with the palms facing away from the signer (if the hands were opened, the left fingers would point to the left and the right fingers would point to the right).	The hands are held side by side in front of the body.	The hands move down and then apart before repeating the downward movement.	**bars** **cage** **posts** **railings**	657
The left G̈ hand is held with the palm facing right; the right G̈ hand is held with the palm facing left (if the hands were opened, the fingers would all point away from the signer).	The hands are held side by side in front of the body with the index fingertips and the thumbtips touching.	The hands make a short movement apart.	**card** **pass** **receipt** **slip** **ticket**	658
The left G̈ hand is held with the palm facing right; the right G̈ hand is held with the palm facing left (if the hands were opened, the fingers would all point up).	The hands are held at eye level in front of the face.	The right index finger flexes twice.	**camera** * **photograph** * **photographer** * **picture** * **snap** * **snapshot** *	659

Notes   * The following notes apply to all glosses:

This sign may be produced using two G̈ hands.

This sign may be produced using one hand only.

660 [] G̈ᴛᵥ ₁ G̈ᴛᵥ (÷·)
            (x̌ᵥ)

661 ⌈1 G̈ᴛ> G̈ᴛ< ᵒ·
                 x̌

The bent index finger and bent thumb are extended from the fist in the shape of a "C".

Handshape and orientation	Location, hand arrangement and contact	Movement	Glosses	
Two Ğ hands are held with the palms facing towards the signer (if the hands were opened, the fingers would all point down).	The hands are held side by side in front of the body with the fingertips touching the chest.	The hands move apart, maintaining contact with the chest; the movement is repeated several times, each time below the previous movement.	bones hoops † horizontal stripes † ribcage ribs * skeleton	660
Notes * This sign can be produced using one hand only.		] Ğτv (≳ ·/ x̌)		
† This sign can be produced using one hand only, if the movement is across the whole chest each time.		[] Ğτv (≳ ·/ x̌)		
Two Ğ hands are held with the palms facing towards the signer (if the hands were opened, the left fingers would point to the right, and the right fingers would point to the left).	The hands are held with the index finger and thumb tips touching the upper chest.	The hands make a short downward movement, maintaining contact with the chest throughout; the movement is repeated.	missioner to the deaf social worker welfare welfare officer	661

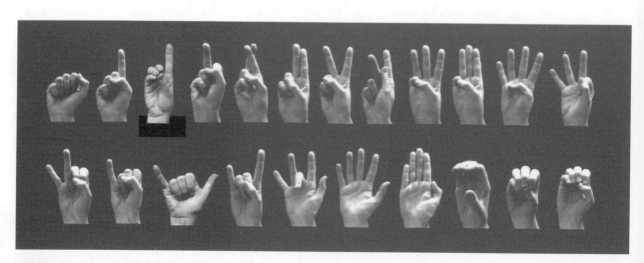

Gd

Handshape	Handshape description	Type	Sign entries
Gd	The index finger is extended with the thumb and other fingers touching at the tips to form a circle.	Single dez Manual tab Double dez	662

662   ⊔ Gd<ʌ ˇ×

Gd

The index finger is extended with the thumb and other fingers touching at the tips to form a circle.

662

This handshape is used very rarely in BSL. However, as this handshape expresses the letter **d** in the Irish and American manual alphabets, it is used in initial letter handshape signs which are borrowed from Irish Sign Language (ISL) and American Sign Language (ASL). Examples include **do** and **daughter** from ISL and **Dallas** from ASL (see *Introduction*).

Handshape and orientation	*Location, hand arrangement and contact*	*Movement*	*Glosses*	
The **Gd** hand is held with the palm facing left (if the hand were opened, the fingers would point up).	The hand is held with the side of the index fingertip touching the nose.	The hand moves down, maintaining contact with the nose.	**pink***	662

Notes * The following notes apply to this sign:

This sign may be produced using a Ψ hand. ⊔ Ψ<∧ ∨×

This sign may also be produced using a **Gd** hand, which makes a short movement to the left, so that the index fingertip brushes the nose; the movement is repeated. ⊔ Gd<∧ °<×< ·

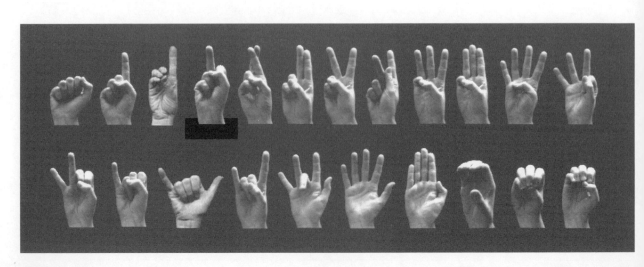

Handshape	Handshape description	Type	Sign entries
Ӽ	The middle finger is extended from the fist and bent at the palm knuckle.	Single dez Manual tab Double dez	663 – 666 667 – 668

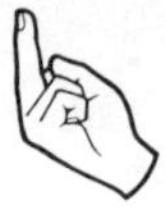

663 ∩ Ẍ⊤∧ ⊤̊·

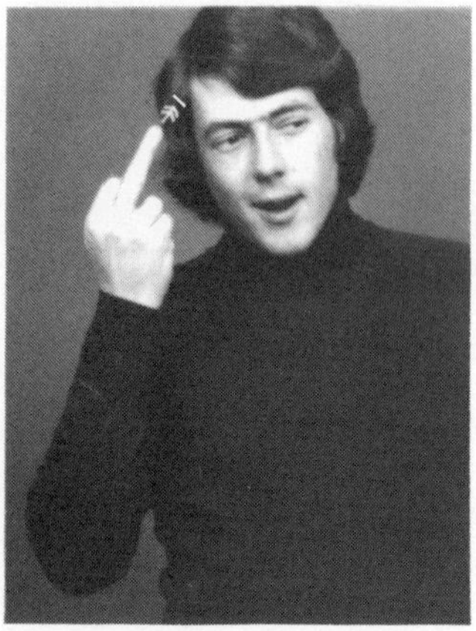

664 ⊔ Ẍ⊤∧ × ∥ Ẍɑ⊥ Ẍ⊥∧ₒ ×·

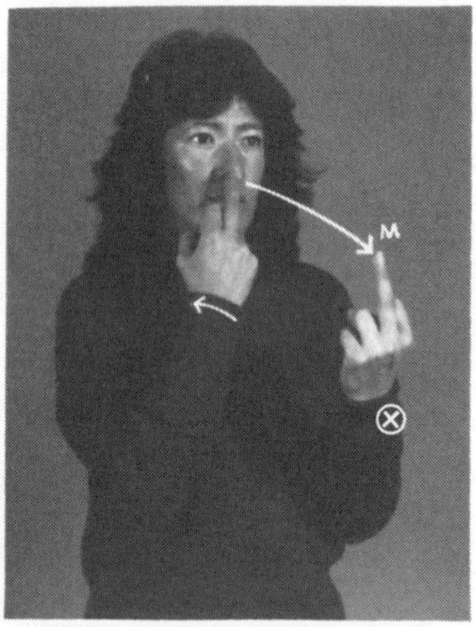

665 ⊔ Ẍ⊤∧ ×ᵛ ∥ [] Ẍ⊤∧ ×

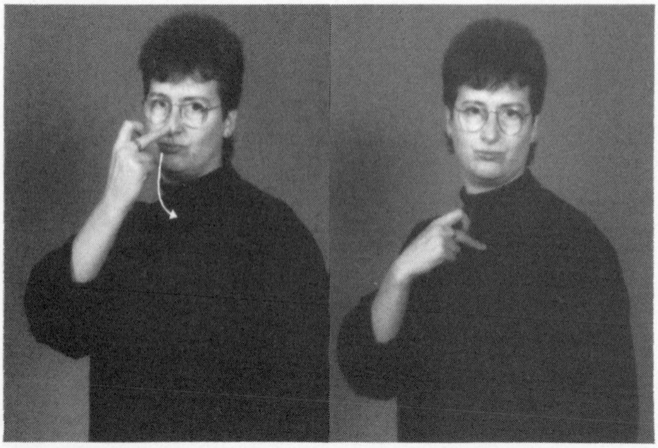

The middle finger is extended from the fist and bent at the palm knuckle.

The main variant of Ä is ʌ, the form in which the hand is held straight rather than bent at the palm knuckles. The choice of Ä or ʌ depends primarily on individual physical characteristics (some people find it physically impossible to produce the straight form ʌ), rather than phonological requirements.

This handshape may be used in BSL signs without the obscene connotations found in the hearing community and within other sign languages, such as American Sign Language, although as such usage is now familiar to members of the British Deaf community, the handshape can be deliberately exploited in this way.

ʌ has some *classifier* functions in the productive lexicon and is used as a classifying component in established signs:

– it has limited use as a *person* classifier. This may be the origin of its use

for the non-dominant hand in **mock** (sign 664). It may also replace **G** or **Ġ** in signs where the non-dominant hand is a person classsifier, as in **oppress** (sign 1364);

– it is used as a *size and shape* classifier to represent long, thin objects, such as the horn of a unicorn;

– it may be used as a *handling* classifier to indicate tiny objects which are handled by the fingertip, such as **contact lens** (see *Introduction*);

– it may be used as an *instrumental* classifier to indicate straight, narrow implements, tools or utensils. However, **G** would normally be preferred.

Ä also has some *deictic* (pointing) functions, for example in pointing to items on a page, as in **correct** (sign 666).

Handshape and orientation	Location, hand arrangement and contact	Movement	Glosses	
The left Ä hand is held with the palm facing towards the signer (if the hand were opened, the fingers would point up).	The hand is held in front and to the side of the forehead.	The hand makes two short, firm movements towards the signer.	comedian comic daft fool foolish idiot idiotic silly	663
Non-manual features The lips are stretched and the nose is wrinkled.				
The left Ä hand is held with the palm facing up; the right Ä hand is held with the palm facing towards the signer (if the hands were opened, the left fingers would point away from the signer, and the right fingers would point up).	The left hand is held in front of the body; the right hand is held with the middle fingertip touching the nose.	The right hand moves away from the signer, twisting at the wrist, so that the palm faces away from the signer; the right middle fingertip then taps the left middle fingertip twice.	artificial* fake* false* imitation* mock* pretend* pseudo*	664
Notes * This sign may be produced using one hand only; the right hand is held with the middle fingertip touching the nose before twisting away from the signer from the wrist.		⊔ Äaⱶ $^{×ω}_{⊥}$		
The Ä hand is held with the palm facing towards the signer (if the hand were opened, the fingers would point up).	The hand is held with the middle fingertip touching the nose.	The hand moves down and then towards the signer, so that the middle fingertip touches the chest.	have someone on* pull someone's leg* string someone along*	665
Non-manual features The lips are pushed forward and pressed together and the brows are slightly furrowed.				
Notes * Directional verb.				

666 ⌒ ÄTʌ ˣ⊻ᵛᵒ⌐ // ∅ (5̄ɑ> Ӭᴠ⊥ ᵖᵛˣᵖᵛ .)ˀ

667 ∅ Ӭɑ⊥ Ӭᴛⓥ ᵒᵛ.

668 ∅ Ӭɑ⊥ Ӭᴛⓥ ᵉᵛ.

The middle finger is extended from the fist and bent at the palm knuckle.

Handshape and orientation	Location, hand arrangement and contact	Movement	Glosses	
The **Ẍ** hand is held with the palm facing towards the signer (if the hand were opened, the fingers would point up).	The hand is held with the middle fingertip touching the chin.	The hand moves down and away from the signer while twisting at the wrist, so that the palm faces down.	criticise criticism find fault correct [1] correction [1]	666
The left **5** hand is held with the palm facing up and the fingers pointing to the right; the right **Ẍ** hand is held with the palm facing down (if the hand were opened, the fingers would point away from the signer).	The hands are held in front of the body; the right hand is held above the left hand.	The right hand bends down at the wrist, so that the middle fingertip brushes across the left palm; the movement is repeated several times with both hands moving to the right throughout.		

Non-manual features   The nose is slightly wrinkled and the tongue tip protrudes between the top teeth and the lower lip.

Notes   1 If the movement in the second part of the sign is not repeated, the sign produced is **correct, correction**.

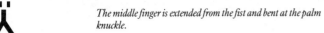

Two **Ẍ** hands are held with the palms facing up (if the hands were opened, the fingers would all point away from the signer).	The hands are held in front of the body.	The hands make two short downward movements.	idle lazy	667

Non-manual features   The tip of the tongue protrudes between the teeth.

Two **Ẍ** hands are held with the palms facing up (if the hands were opened, the fingers would all point away from the signer).	The hands are held in front of the body.	The hands make circles (the left hand moves anticlockwise, the right hand moves clockwise) in the vertical plane parallel to the signer's body.	dole (on the dole)* holiday* idle* lazy* unemployed* unemployment* vacation*	668

Notes   * This sign can be produced using one hand only.

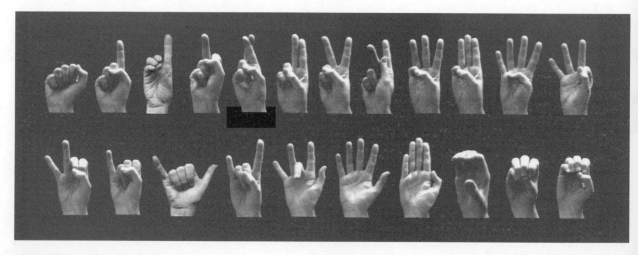

R

Handshape	Handshape description	Type	Sign entries
R	The index and middle fingers are extended from the fist and crossed.	Single dez Manual tab Double dez	669

669 Ø RⅬ∧ RⅬ∧ ⁱ

This handshape is used very rarely in BSL. However, as this handshape expresses the letter **r** in the Irish and American manual alphabets, it is used in initial letter signs borrowed from Irish Sign Language (ISL) and American Sign Language (ASL). Examples include **ready** and **religion** from ISL and **Rochester** from ASL (see *Introduction*).

Handshape and orientation	Location, hand arrangement and contact	Movement	Glosses	
Two **R** hands are held with the palms facing away from the signer (if the hands were opened, the fingers would all point up).	The hands are held in front of the body.	The hands make a short movement away from the signer.	hope* pray* wish*	669

Notes * This sign can be produced using one hand only.

Ø R⅃ʌ ⚬̣

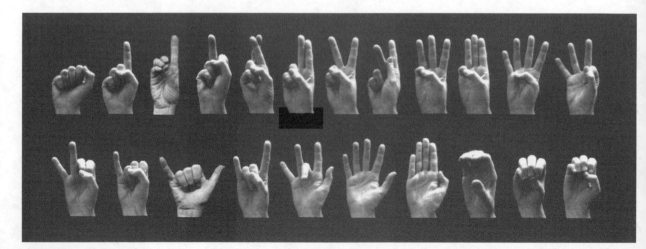

H

Handshape	Handshape description	Type	Sign entries
H	The index and middle fingers are extended from the fist and held together.	Single dez Manual tab Double dez	670 – 681 682 – 691 692 – 709
H̄	The index and middle fingers (held together) are extended from the fist and bent at the palm knuckles; the extended thumb is held parallel to the extended fingers.	Single dez Manual tab Double dez	710 – 711 712 – 715
Ḣ	The index and middle fingers (held together) are extended from the fist and bent at the palm knuckles.	Single dez Manual tab Double dez	716 – 718 719 – 722 723 – 732
Ḧ	The bent index and middle fingers (held together) are extended from the fist.	Single dez Manual tab Double dez	 733 – 734 735 – 737
Ĥ	The bent index and middle fingers (held together) and bent thumb are extended from the fist and touch at the tips.	Single dez Manual tab Double dez	738 – 741 742 – 743 744 – 745

670 Ø Hɑ⊥ $\overset{\circ}{z}$ ·

671 Ø H⊥ʌ $\overset{\circ}{\underset{z}{n}}$ ·

672 Ø H⊥ʌ $\begin{pmatrix}\overset{\circ}{\underset{\vee}{n}}\cdot\end{pmatrix}$

673 Ø H<⊥ $\overset{\circ\;\circ\;\circ}{\underset{<}{\vee\;\wedge\;>}}$

The index and middle fingers are extended from the fist and held together.

The main *variant* of H is Ḧ in which there is bending at the palm knuckles. In some cases, these two forms are interchangeable; in others, the H form is required.

H has several different *classifier* functions within the productive lexicon and appears as a classifying element in established signs:

– it is used as a *size and shape* classifier to indicate straight, narrow objects such as beds, benches, narrow tables, the ears of certain animals as in **hare** (sign 705) and the legs of animals, such as dogs, cats and rabbits (see *Introduction*); H can be seen as contrasting with G, Wm and B in showing different degrees of width;

– it is used as a *tracing size and shape* classifier to indicate the outline of long and/or tall objects, as in **corridor** (sign 697), **bridge** (sign 700), **river** (sign 703) and **chef's hat** (sign 706);

– it is used as an *instrumental* classifier to indicate narrow implements, tools or utensils, as in **cutlery** (sign 686) and **spread with a knife** (sign 689);

– it is used to express *extent* or *quantity*, as in the two-handed forms **beds in a row, benches lined up one behind the other** (see *Introduction*).

H is used in the British manual alphabet as the right-hand component of the letters f and n. As such, it is used in initial letter handshape signs such as **father** (sign 684), **family** (sign 695), **north** (sign 687) and **natural** (sign 688). It also expresses the letter h in the American manual alphabet. As such, it has the potential to be used in initial letter handshape signs borrowed from American Sign Language (ASL) such as **Hartford** (see *Introduction*).

Handshape and orientation	Location, hand arrangement and contact	Movement	Glosses	
The H hand is held with the palm facing up (if the hand were opened, the fingers would point away from the signer).	The hand is held in front of the body.	The hand makes short movements from side to side.	sugar sprinkle from a spoon [1] sprinkle sugar from a spoon [1]	670
Notes 1 If the hand makes short movements from side to side while moving towards the signer in an arc, the sign produced is **sprinkle from a spoon, sprinkle sugar from a spoon.**		Ø Hɑ⊥ $\left(\begin{smallmatrix} \circ \\ z \\ \bot \\ < \end{smallmatrix} \cdot\right)$		
The H hand is held with the palm facing away from the signer (if the hand were opened, the fingers would point up).	The hand is held in front of the body.	The hand makes several short bending movements from side to side from the wrist.	school*†	671
Notes * Regional sign.				
† This sign may be produced using two hands.		Ø H⊥ʌ H⊥ʌ $\begin{smallmatrix} \circ \\ n \\ x \end{smallmatrix} \cdot$		
The H hand is held with the palm facing away from the signer (if the hand were opened, the fingers would point up).	The hand is held in front of the body.	The hand makes several short bending movements from side to side from the wrist while moving down throughout.	school*†	672
Notes * Regional sign.				
† This sign may be produced using two hands.		Ø H⊥ʌ H⊥ʌ $\left(\begin{smallmatrix} \circ \\ n \\ x \\ v \end{smallmatrix} \cdot\right)$		
The H hand is held with the palm facing left (if the hand were opened, the fingers would point away from the signer).	The hand is held in front of the body.	The hand draws a cross.	bless* consecrate* sanctify*	673
Notes * Directional verb.				

674 ∩ Hↄ< $^{×ω}_{⊤}$

675 ○ H⊤ʌ $^{ωח}_{≤<}_{>⊤}$

676 Ц H<ʌ $^{×}·$

677 ⊃ H<ʌ $^{×}$

678 ⊃ H<ʌ $^{×}$ ⫽ ⊾ H⊤ʌ $^{×}$

H

The index and middle fingers are extended from the fist and held together.

Handshape and orientation	Location, hand arrangement and contact	Movement	Glosses	
The **H** hand is held with the palm facing down (if the hand were opened, the fingers would point to the left).	The hand is held with the tips of the extended fingers touching the side of the forehead.	The hand moves away from the signer while twisting at the wrist, so that the palm faces away from the signer.	**call** **name**	674
The **H** hand is held with the palm facing towards the signer (if the hand were opened, the fingers would point up).	The hand is held in front of the face.	The hand moves to the right while twisting at the wrist, so that the palm faces away from the signer; the hand then bends to the left at the wrist while moving towards the signer, so that the movement ends with the extended fingers behind the head.	**hypocrite** **two-faced**	675
The **H** hand is held with the palm facing left (if the hand were opened, the fingers would point up).	The hand is held with the extended fingers alongside the nose.	The tips of the extended fingers tap the side of the nose twice.	**posh** **smart** **tidy***	676
Notes * Regional sign.				
The **H** hand is held with the palm facing left (if the hand were opened, the fingers would point up).	The hand is held beside the ear.	The tips of the extended fingers touch the ear.	**Deaf*** **Deaf person*** **deaf** **deaf person**	677
Notes * This sign may be produced with the cheeks puffed out.				
The **H** hand is held with the palm facing left (if the hand were opened, the fingers would point up).	The hand is held with the tips of the extended fingers touching the ear.	The hand moves down and to the left and, at the same time, away from the signer while twisting at the wrist, so that the palm faces towards the signer; the movement ends with the tips of the extended fingers touching the chin.	**Deaf*** **Deaf person*** **deaf and dumb** **deaf without speech**	678
Notes * This sign may be produced with the cheeks puffed out.				

679 ꓔ H<ʌ ˣ // Ц V̈ᴛʌ ˚ᴈ̇ᴎ ·

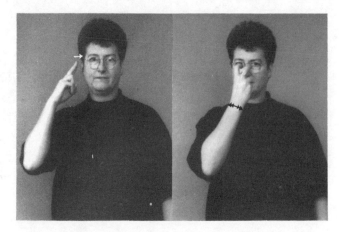

680 ꓴ Hᴛʌ ˣ // B̄ɑ> Hʊᴛ ˇˣ

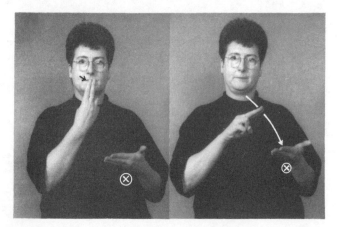

681 ꓴ Hᴛʌ ˣᴩᴛᵥ // H̄ɑ> Hʊᴛ ˣ

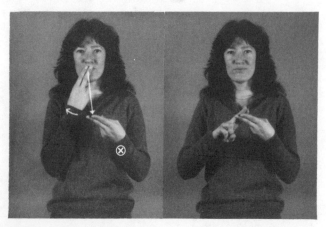

682 Āᴛ> ı Hɑᴛ ˟ˣˇ

[392]

The index and middle fingers are extended from the fist and held together.

Handshape and orientation	Location, hand arrangement and contact	Movement	Glosses	
The **H** hand is held with the palm facing left (if the hand were opened, the fingers would point up).	The hand is held beside the ear.	The index and middle fingertips touch the ear.	deaf-blind deaf-blind person	679
The **V̈** hand is held with the palm facing towards the signer (if the hand were opened, the fingers would point up).	The hand is held in front of the face.	The hand makes short twisting movements from side to side at the wrist.		
The **H** hand is held with the palm facing towards the signer (if the hand were opened, the fingers would point up).	The hand is held with the extended fingers in front of the mouth and chin.	The tips of the extended fingers touch the mouth.	insurance* stamp	680
The left **B** hand is held with the palm facing up and the fingers pointing to the right; the right **H** hand is held with the palm facing down (if the hand were opened, the fingers would point away from the signer).	The hands are held in front of the body; the right fingers are held above the left hand.	The right hand moves down, so that the extended fingers touch the left palm.		

Notes   * Regional sign.

The left **H** hand is held with the palm facing up; the right **H** hand is held with the palm facing towards the signer (if the hands were opened, the left fingers would point to the right and the right fingers would point up).	The left hand is held in front of the body; the right hand is held with the extended fingers in front of the mouth.	The tips of the extended right fingers touch the lips; the hand then twists down and, at the same time, away from the signer, so that the palm faces down; the extended right fingertips then touch the extended left fingertips.	kiss peck[1]	681

Notes   1 If the hands move apart after touching (the left hand moves down, the right hand moves up), the sign produced is **peck**.   ⌣ H⊤∧ // Hɑ> Hʊ⊥

The left **A** hand is held with the palm facing towards the signer (if the hand were opened, the fingers would point to the right). The right **H** hand is held with the palm facing up (if the hand were opened, the fingers would point away from the signer).	The hands are held side by side in front of the body; the right hand is held higher than the left hand.	The right hand moves to the left, so that the backs of the right index and middle fingers brush across the side of the left index finger and thumb.	egg (boiled egg) cut the top off a boiled egg	682

683 H̄ʊ⊥ x Hʊ< $^{H.}_{x}$

684 H̄ʊ> Hʊ⊥ $^{x.}$

685 H̄ʊ> Hʊ⊥ $^{o}_{<⊥x}$

686 H̄>⊥ x H<⊥ $^{H.}_{x}$

687 5̄a> Hʊ⊥ ^{x}

688 B̄a⊥ Hʊ< $^{x.}$

689 B̄a⊥ H⊤< $^{⊤.}_{x}$

[394]

H

The index and middle fingers are extended from the fist and held together.

Handshape and orientation	Location, hand arrangement and contact	Movement	Glosses	
Two **H** hands are held with the palms facing down (if the hands were opened, the left fingers would point away from the signer and the right fingers would point to the left).	The hands are held in front of the body; the extended right fingers rest across the extended left fingers.	The right hand moves towards and away from the signer several times, maintaining contact with the left fingers throughout.	walk*	683

Notes   * Regional sign.

Two **H** hands are held with the palms facing down (if the hands were opened, the left fingers would point to the right and the right fingers would point away from the signer).	The hands are held in front of the body; the extended right fingers are held above the extended left fingers.	The right fingers tap the left fingers twice.	dad daddy father	684
Two **H** hands are held with the palms facing down (if the hands were opened, the left fingers would point to the right, and the right fingers would point away from the signer).	The hands are held in front of the body; the extended right fingers rest on the extended left fingers.	The right hand makes small anticlockwise circles in the horizontal plane; the extended right fingers maintain contact with the extended left fingers throughout.	Friday blank[1] free[1]	685

Notes   1   If the movement is changed so that the right hand moves to the right with the extended right fingers brushing along the back of the extended left fingers, the sign produced is **blank, free**.

$$H \smallsmile> \ H \smallsmile \perp \ {}^{>}_{x}{}^{>}_{v}$$

The left **H** hand is held with the palm facing right; the right **H** hand is held with the palm facing left (if the hands were opened, the fingers would all point away from the signer).	The hands are held in front of the body at an angle, so that the extended right fingers rest across the extended left fingers.	The right hand moves towards and away from the signer several times, so that the side of the right middle finger maintains contact with the side of the left index finger throughout.	cutlery dinner knife meal restaurant Sheffield	686
The left **5** hand is held with the palm facing up and the fingers pointing to the right; the right **H** hand is held with the palm facing down (if the hand were opened, the fingers would point away from the signer).	The hands are held in front of the body; the extended fingers of the right hand are held above the left palm.	The right hand moves down, so that the extended right fingers touch the left palm.	north	687
The left **B** hand is held with the palm facing up and the fingers pointing away from the signer; the right **H** hand is held with the palm facing down (if the hand were opened, the fingers would point to the left).	The hands are held in front of the body; the extended fingers of the right hand are held above the left palm.	The right fingers tap the left palm twice.	natural normal	688

The left **B** hand is held with the palm facing up and the fingers pointing away from the signer; the right **H** hand is held with the palm facing towards the signer (if the hand were opened, the fingers would point to the left).	The hands are held in front of the body; the side of the right middle finger rests on the left palm.	The right hand moves towards the signer, maintaining contact with the left palm; the movement is repeated.	butter
			margarine
			marge
			spread with a knife
			paste[1]
			paté[1]
			spread butter/
			  margarine/marge/
			  paste/paté with
			  a knife[1]
				689

Notes   1   If the right hand is held with the palm facing down, the sign produced is **paste, paté, spread butter/ margarine/marge/paste/paté with a knife**.

$$B \alpha \perp \ H \smallsmile< \ {}^{\top}_{x}{}^{\cdot}$$

690 B>⊥ ₁ₓ H⩊⊥ $\overset{\circ}{\underset{x}{\bot}}$·

691 √ B̈ɑ> H⩊< $\overset{\circ\circ\circ}{\underset{<}{\overset{\wedge}{\underset{\top}{\top}}}}$

692 Ø H̄ɑ⊥ ₓ Hɑ⊥ $\overset{\circ}{\bot}$

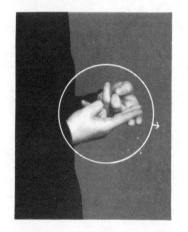

693 Ø H⩊∧ ₁ₓ H⩊∧ $\overset{\div}{\vee}$

694 Ø H⩊∧ ₁ₓ H⩊∧ $\overset{\div}{\underset{\bot}{\pi}}$

695 Ø H̄⩊> ₓ H⩊⊥ $\overset{x@⊥}{\underset{\vee}{\cdot}}$

696 Ø H⊤> ₁ₓ H⊤< $\overset{\pi}{\bot}$

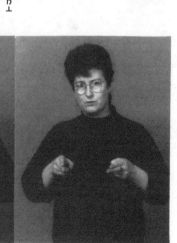

[396]

The index and middle fingers are extended from the fist and held together.

Handshape and orientation	Location, hand arrangement and contact	Movement	Glosses	
The left **B** hand is held with the palm facing right and the fingers pointing away from the signer; the right **H** hand is held with the palm facing down (if the hand were opened, the fingers would point away from the signer).	The hands are held side by side in front of the body; the side of the right index finger rests against the left palm.	The right hand makes a short movement away from the signer, maintaining contact with the left palm; the movement is repeated.	exam examination test	690
The left **B̈** hand is held with the palm facing up (if the hand were opened, the fingers would point to the right). The right **H** hand is held with the palm facing down (if the hand were opened, the fingers would point to the left).	The left hand is held in front of the body; the right hand is held above the left forearm.	The right hand draws a cross above the left forearm.	baptise baptism christen christening	691
Two **H** hands are held with the palms facing up (if the hands were opened, the fingers would all point away from the signer).	The hands are held in front of the body, angled towards each other with the extended right fingers held on the extended left fingers.	The hands remain together and make a short movement away from the signer.	ferry go by ferry ride transport elevator[1] go up by elevator/lift[1] lift[1] escalator[2] go up by escalator[2]	692

Notes   1   If the hands remain together and make a short upward movement, the sign produced is **elevator, go up by elevator/ lift, lift.**

$$\emptyset \quad \overline{H\alpha\bot} \quad _x \quad H\alpha\bot \quad \overset{\circ}{\wedge}$$

           2   If the hands remain together and make a short movement up and, at the same time, away from the signer, the sign produced is **escalator, go up by escalator.**

$$\emptyset \quad \overline{H\alpha\bot} \quad _x \quad H\alpha\bot \quad \overset{\circ}{\underset{\bot}{\wedge}}$$

| Two **H** hands are held with the palms facing down (if the hands were opened, the fingers would all point up). | The hands are held side by side in front of the body, angled towards each other so that the tips of the extended fingers are touching. | The hands move down and, at the same time, apart. | camp*
tent* | 693 |

Notes   *   This sign may also be produced using two **B** hands.

$$\emptyset \quad B\sigma\wedge \quad _{|x} \quad B\sigma\wedge \quad \overset{\div}{\vee}$$

| Two **H** hands are held with the palms facing down (if the hands were opened, the fingers would all point up). | The hands are held side by side in front of the body at an angle, so that the tips of the extended fingers are touching. | The hands move apart while bending away from the signer from the wrists. | house
home[1]
visit*[1] | 694 |

Notes   * Directional verb.

           1   If two **Ḧ** hands are used, bending away from the signer from the wrists while the extended fingers straighten at the palm knuckles (forming two **H** hands), the sign produced is **home, visit.**

$$\emptyset \quad \ddot{H}{>}\wedge \quad _{|x} \quad \ddot{H}{<}\wedge \quad \overset{(\overset{n}{\underset{\bot}{)}}}{\underset{m}{}}$$

| Two **H** hands are held with the palms facing down (if the hands were opened, the left fingers would point to the right, and the right fingers would point away from the signer). | The hands are held in front of the body; the extended right fingers are held on the extended left fingers. | The hands remain together and make clockwise circles in the horizontal plane. | family | 695 |
| Two **H** hands are held with the palms facing towards the signer (if the hands were opened, the left fingers would point to the right, and the right fingers would point to the left). | The hands are held side by side in front of the body with the middle fingertips touching. | The hands bend away from the signer from the wrists. | divorce
divorced
divorcee | 696 |

697 Ø H>ʌ H<ʌ ⊥

698 Ø H>ʌ H<ʌ ˇ

699 Ø H>ʌ H<ʌ ⊥ⁿ

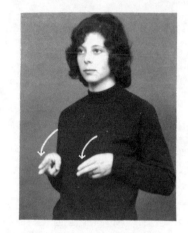

700 Ø H>ʌ | H<ʌ $\binom{n}{\overset{\wedge}{\perp}}\binom{n}{\overset{v}{\perp}}$

701 Ø H>ʌ | H<ʌ $\overset{n}{\underset{\perp}{H}}$~·

702 Ø H>v | H<v $\binom{n}{\perp}$

703 Ø H>v | H<v $\binom{o}{\overset{z}{\perp}}·)$

704 Ø H>⊥ | H<⊥ $\binom{n}{\overset{\wedge}{\underset{x}{x}}}\overset{\overset{o}{x}}{\overset{x}{\wedge}}$

[398]

The index and middle fingers are extended from the fist and held together.

Handshape and orientation	Location, hand arrangement and contact	Movement	Glosses	
The left **H** hand is held with the palm facing right; the right **H** hand is held with the palm facing left (if the hands were opened, the fingers would all point up).	The hands are held in front of the body.	The hands move away from the signer.	corridor* hall*	697

Notes   * This sign may also be produced using two **B** hands.

$$\varnothing \quad B{>}\wedge \quad B{<}\wedge \quad {\perp}$$

The left **H** hand is held with the palm facing right; the right **H** hand is held with the palm facing left (if the hands were opened, the fingers would all point up).	The hands are held in front of the body.	The hands make a short downward movement.	seat* sit*	698

Notes   * Regional sign.

The left **H** hand is held with the palm facing right; the right **H** hand is held with the palm facing left (if the hands were opened, the fingers would all point up).	The hands are held in front of the body.	The hands bend away from the signer at the wrists.	dead* death* die* dying*[1]	699

Notes   1 If the movement is slow, the sign produced is **dying**.

          * This sign may be produced using one hand only.

$$\varnothing \quad H{<}\wedge \quad {\perp}$$

The left **H** hand is held with the palm facing right; the right **H** hand is held with the palm facing left (if the hands were opened, the fingers would all point up).	The hands are held side by side in front of the body at an angle, so that the fingers are turned away from the signer.	The hands move up and away from the signer while bending away from the signer at the wrists; the hands then continue to move away from the signer while bending down at the wrists.	bridge	700
The left **H** hand is held with the palm facing right; the right **H** hand is held with the palm facing left (if the hands were opened, the fingers would all point up).	The hands are held side by side in front of the body.	The hands make alternate short bending movements towards and away from the signer at the wrists; the movements are repeated.	interpret interpreter	701
The left **H** hand is held with the palm facing right; the right **H** hand is held with the palm facing left (if the hands were opened, the fingers would all point down).	The hands are held side by side in front of the body.	The hands bend away from the signer at the wrists while moving away from the signer.	avenue method path road street style system track way	702
The left **H** hand is held with the palm facing right; the right **H** hand is held with the palm facing left (if the hands were opened, the fingers would all point down).	The hands are held side by side in front of the body at an angle, so that the fingers are turned away from the signer.	The hands make several short movements from side to side while moving away from the signer throughout.	canal river stream waterway	703
The left **H** hand is held with the palm facing right; the right **H** hand is held with the palm facing left (if the hand were opened, the fingers would all point away from the signer).	The hands are held side by side in front of the body.	The hands move up and towards each other while bending at the wrists, so that the extended fingers point up; the hands then continue to make a short upward movement, with the tips of the extended fingers held together.	Paris tower	704

705 ∩ H⊥ʌ H⊥ʌ ^{ɯ·}

706 ∩ H>ʌ H<ʌ ^{x ʌ ɯ ÷ x}

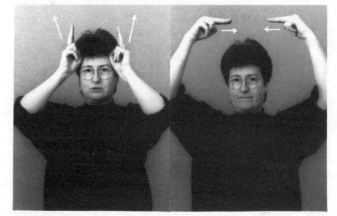

707 Ɔ H>ʌ H<ʌ ^{ɴ·}_Ⅱ

708 Γ͡ l H⊤> ₁x H⊤<ᵨ [⊤]

709 ⊔ H>⊥ ₁ H<⊥ ^{ɴ<ɴ}

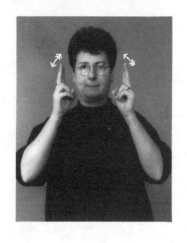

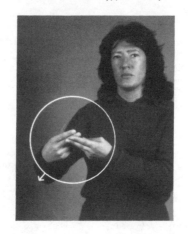

H

The index and middle fingers are extended from the fist and held together.

Handshape and orientation	Location, hand arrangement and contact	Movement	Glosses	
Two **H** hands are held with the palms facing away from the signer (if the hands were opened, the fingers would all point up).	The hands are held in front and to the sides of the forehead.	The extended fingers bend at the palm knuckles several times.	hare* rabbit*	705

Notes   * This sign can be produced using two **Ḧ** hands.

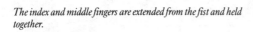

The left **H** hand is held with the palm facing right; the right **H** hand is held with the palm facing left (if the hands were opened, the fingers would all point up).	The hands are held with the backs of the thumbs touching the sides of the forehead.	The hands move up and, at the same time, apart; the extended fingers then bend towards each other from the palm knuckles while the hands move towards each other.	chef* chef's hat*	706

Notes   * This sign may also be produced with the hands moving up and, at the same time, apart.

The left **H** hand is held with the palm facing right; the right **H** hand is held with the palm facing left (if the hands were opened, the fingers would all point up).	The hands are held in front of the face.	The hands bend towards and away from the signer alternately from the wrists.	motorway	707
Two **H** hands are held with the palms facing towards the signer (if the hands were opened, the left fingers would point to the right and the right fingers would point to the left).	The hands are held side by side in front of the right shoulder at an angle, so that the fingers are turned up; the backs of the extended right fingers are held against the pads of the extended left fingers.	The hands remain together and move down and, at the same time, away from the signer.	tradition	708
The left **H** hand is held with the palm facing right; the right **H** hand is held with the palm facing left (if the hands were opened, the fingers would all point down).	The hands are held side by side in front of the right side of the waist.	The hands bend down from the wrists; the movement is then repeated in front of the left side of the waist.	slacks trousers	709

710　⊔ H̄⊤∧ ×⊥[A] V #

711　⊃ H̄⊥∧ #[A]·

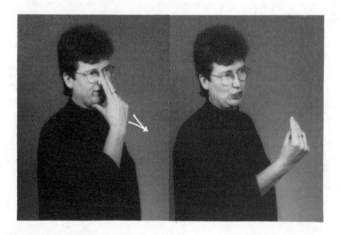

712　∅ H̄ɑ⊥ ⊙ H̄ɑ⊥ ⊞ ᵛ⌄

713　∅ H̄>∧ ₁× H̄<∧ ÷[AA] ᵛ #

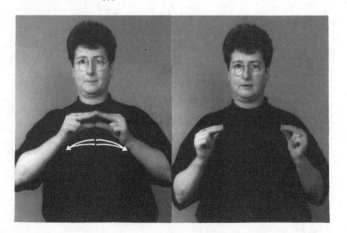

The index and middle fingers (held together) are extended from the fist and bent at the palm knuckles; the extended thumb is held parallel to the extended fingers.

The main *variation* in the production of H̄ concerns the size of the gap between the two extended fingers and the thumb: in **enjoy** (sign 710) the gap is relatively wide, in **handlebar moustache** (sign 715) it is quite narrow.

H̄ has several different *classifier* functions within the productive lexicon and also appears as a classifying element in established signs:

– it is used as a *size and shape* classifier to represent small, narrow objects or objects with two parallel, flat surfaces such as beaks, as in **duck** (sign 711) and **goose** (sign 711); it is also used to indicate flat, narrow or shallow objects and in this function can be used in contrast with Ḡ and B̄ to show varying degrees of width;

– it is used as a *tracing size and shape* classifier to trace the outline of narrow objects as in **banana** (sign 713), **sausages** (sign 714) and **han**-dlebar moustache (sign 715). It is also used in a comparable way to indicate a layer, rim, strip or chunk of something, as in **layer of cus-tard** (see *Introduction*) and **chunk of text** (see *Introduction*). H̄ is sometimes used contrastively with Ḡ and B̄ in this function;

– it is used as a *handling* classifier to indicate small, shallow objects such as an audiotape or, in the two-handed versions, long or wide, shallow objects such as a tray;

– it is used as an *instrumental* classifier for implements, tools or utensils with parallel extensions such as a clothes peg, a paper clip, a microphone clip and a hair slide;

– the gap between fingers and thumb may be used to indicate *extent*, usually to indicate relative shallowness.

Handshape and orientation	Location, hand arrangement and contact	Movement	Glosses	
The H̄ hand is held with the palm facing towards the signer (if the hand were opened, the fingers would point up).	The hand is held with the index and middle fingertips touching the nose.	The hand moves down and away from the signer and, at the same time, the thumb and extended fingers close (forming an Ĥ hand).	**enjoy** **fun** **like**	**710**
Non-manual features	The nose is wrinkled and the upper teeth are touching the lower lip; the nose then relaxes and the mouth opens with the lips rounded and pushed forward.			
The H̄ hand is held with the palm facing away from the signer (if the hand were opened, the fingers would point up).	The hand is held in front of the mouth and chin.	The tips of the thumb and extended fingers close (forming an Ĥ hand); the movement is repeated.	**duck*** **goose*** **swan** **Swansea**	**711**
Notes	* This sign may also be produced using a B̄ handshape. ⌣ B̄⊤∧ ⧺ [ɓ] ·			
The left H̄ hand is held with the palm facing right; the right H̄ hand is held with the palm facing up (if the hands were opened, the fingers would all point away from the signer).	The hands are held in front of the body at an angle, so that the extended right fingers are held between the extended left fingers and thumb.	The hands move away from the signer and to the left and, at the same time, the fingers and thumbs grasp each other.	**accompany** someone **go with someone** **partner someone** **partner**[1]	**712**
Notes	1 If the hands are held with the extended fingers and thumbs linked together, and then remain together while making short movements from side to side, the sign produced is **partner**. Ø H̄α⊥ ₓ H̄α⊥ ẑ·			
The left H̄ hand is held with the palm facing right; the right H̄ hand is held with the palm facing left (if the hands were opened, the fingers would all point up).	The hands are held in front of the body with the thumbtips and the tips of the extended fingers touching.	The hands move down and apart and, at the same time, the tips of the thumbs and extended fingers come together (forming two Ĥ hands).	**banana**	**713**

714 Ø H̄>∧ ₁ₓ H̄<∧ ^(÷# [AA]·)
÷

715 ⌣ H̄>∧ H̄<∧ ^{n v [AA]}
^÷
#

The index and middle fingers (held together) are extended from the fist and bent at the palm knuckles; the extended thumb is held parallel to the extended fingers.

Handshape and orientation	Location, hand arrangement and contact	Movement	Glosses	
The left Ḧ hand is held with the palm facing right; the right Ḧ hand is held with the palm facing left (if the hands were opened, the fingers would all point up).	The hands are held side by side in front of the body with the tips of the thumbs and extended fingers touching.	The hands move apart while closing (forming two Ĥ hands); the movement is repeated several times with the hands moving apart throughout.	**sausages**	714
The left Ḧ hand is held with the palm facing right; the right Ḧ hand is held with the palm facing left (if the hands were opened, the fingers would all point up).	The hands are held with the extended fingers in front of the mouth.	The hands bend up at the wrists and then move down and apart while the fingers and thumbs close (forming two Ĥ hands).	**handlebar moustache** walrus [1]	715

Notes   1 This sign may be used as the first part of a compound sign meaning **walrus** (see 1404 for the second part of the sign).

$$\cup \quad \bar{\mathsf{H}}{>}\wedge \quad \bar{\mathsf{H}}{<}\wedge \quad {}^{\cap\;\vee\;[\mathsf{AA}]}_{\wedge\;\div\;\#} \quad /\!/$$
$$\varnothing \quad \mathsf{B}\!\mathsf{v}\!\perp \quad \mathsf{B}\!\mathsf{v}\!\perp \quad {}^{\circ}_{\ominus\;\mathsf{N}\;\cdot}_{\perp\;\vee}$$

716 Ø Ḧʋ⊥ ᴴ ·

717 Ø Ḧʋ⊥ ⁽⊥ᵛ̠⊥⁾

The main *variant* of Ḧ is H where there is no bending at the palm knuckles. In some cases, the two forms are interchangeable; in others, Ḧ is required.

Ḧ has several different *classifier* functions in the productive lexicon and is used as a classifying element in established signs:

– it is used as a *size and shape* classifier to represent small, narrow objects such as the ears of certain animals as in **hare** (sign 705) and the legs of animals as in **dog** (sign 726) and **dog begging** (sign 726). It is also used for human legs, as in **dive** (sign 722). It is used within many verbs of motion and location such as **animal running, animal prowling, animal skulking** and **person walking with stealth** (see *Introduction*); Ḧ can be seen as contrasting with Ǧ, Ẅm and B̈ in showing different degrees of width;

– it is used as a *tracing size and shape* classifier to indicate the shape or outline of narrow objects, as in **scarf** (sign 731). This tracing usage can also be seen in signs for **house** and **House of Commons** (see *Introduction*);

– it is used as an *instrumental* classifier to indicate long, narrow implements, tools or utensils such as a narrow paintbrush in **paint** (sign 716), a wooden spoon or spurtle in **make porridge** (sign 723) and cutlery of various kinds as in **dinner** (sign 730) and **eat with a dessert spoon** or **soup spoon** (sign 732);

– several signs indicating putting information on paper or other flat surface seem to combine an *instrumental* function (writing with a narrow implement) and a *deictic* (pointing) function, pointing to the positioning of the written information. Examples include **list** (sign 720), **make notes** (sign 720), **contract** (sign 721), **signature** (sign 721), **book-keeping** (sign 727) and **fill in a form** (sign 727);

– it is used to indicate *quantity* or *extent*. Two-handed forms may be used to show a number of narrow objects, such as **many seats in a row, seats one behind the other, seats in tiers** (see *Introduction*). Two-handed forms can show small or decreasing amounts as in **decrease** (sign 728) and **less** (sign 728) and, when the movement is reversed, larger or increasing amounts.

Handshape and orientation	Location, hand arrangement and contact	Movement	Glosses	
The Ḧ hand is held with the palm facing down (if the hand were opened, the fingers would point away from the signer).	The hand is held in front of the body.	The hand bends towards and away from the signer at the wrist several times.	**paint**	716
The Ḧ hand is held with the palm facing down (if the hand were opened, the fingers would point away from the signer).	The hand is held in front of the body.	The hand bends away from the signer, then down, then away from the signer again from the wrist, while moving to the right throughout.	**Norway Norwegian**	717

718 凵 Ḧ⊤ʌ ᵚ͓˙

719 H̄>ʌ Ḧ<ʌ₉ ⌄⌄⊤

720 B̄ɑ> Ḧʊ⊤ (⌄⊤˙)

721 B̄ɑ> Ḧʊ⊤₉ ⌄⊤ˣ

722 B̄>ʌ ×Ḧʊ< (ᵕ⌄□)⁽ᵛ⁾

723 ∅ Ĥʊ> ᵚ Ḧʊ⊤ ⊤⌄@

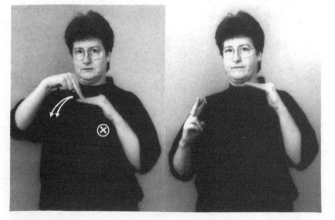

The index and middle fingers (held together) are extended from the fist and bent at the palm knuckles.

Handshape and orientation	Location, hand arrangement and contact	Movement	Glosses	
The Ḧ hand is held with the palm facing towards the signer (if the hand were opened, the fingers would point up).	The hand is held with the fingers in front of the nose.	The extended fingers bend down from the palm knuckles, brushing the nose; the movement is repeated.	evening*† night*† good evening¹ good night¹	718

Notes   * This sign may be produced with a single movement.

       † This sign may also be produced using an Ḣ hand.

       1   If an Ḣ hand is used, touching the nose and then moving away from the signer while closing (forming an Ȧ hand), the sign produced is **good evening, good night**.

| The left Ḧ hand is held with the palm facing right; the right Ḧ hand is held with the palm facing left (if the hands were opened, the fingers would all point up). | The hands are held in front of the body; the right hand is held higher and nearer to the signer than the left hand. | The right hand moves down and, at the same time, away from the signer, so that the extended right fingers brush across the extended left fingers. | afternoon* | 719 |

Notes   * Regional sign.

| The left **B** hand is held with the palm facing up and the fingers pointing to the right; the right Ḣ hand is held with the palm facing down (if the hand were opened, the fingers would point away from the signer). | The hands are held in front of the body; the right hand is held above the left hand. | The right hand makes a series of short downward movements while moving down and towards the signer throughout. | list make notes minutes note down notes take notes written record written statement | 720 |

| The left **B** hand is held with the palm facing up and the fingers pointing to the right; the right Ḣ hand is held with the palm facing down (if the hand were opened, the fingers would point away from the signer). | The hands are held in front of the body; the right hand is held higher and nearer to the signer than the left hand. | The right hand makes a short movement down and, at the same time, away from the signer, so that the right index and middle fingertips touch the left palm. | contract, make a note of signature sign for sign in sign on sign one's name take a note of witness someone's signature | 721 |

| The left **B̈** hand is held with the palm facing right (if the hand were opened, the fingers would point up). The right Ḣ hand is held with the palm facing down (if the hand were opened, the fingers would point to the left). | The hands are held in front of the body; the right index and middle fingertips are held touching the backs of the left index and middle fingertips. | The right hand bends up at the wrist while moving down and, at the same time, opening (forming a **V** hand). | dive diver diving diving board | 722 |

| The left Ḣ hand is held with the palm facing down (if the hand were opened, the fingers would point to the right). The right Ḣ hand is held with the palm facing down (if the hand were opened, the fingers would point away from the signer). | The hands are held in front of the body; the left hand is held above the right hand. | The left thumb rubs from side to side across the pads of the left fingers; at the same time, the right hand makes a clockwise circle in the horizontal plane. | make porridge* porridge* stir and sprinkle | 723 |

Notes   * Regional sign.

724 Ø Ḧɔ⊥ ¦ Ḧɔ⊥ $_{\overline{\text{H}}\text{x}}^{\text{H}\sim}$ ·

725 Ø H̄ɔ⊥ ₓ Ḧɔ⊥ $_{\div\text{N}}^{\text{o}\text{n}}$

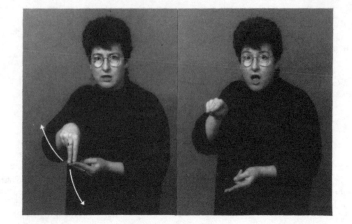

726 Ø Ḧɔ⊥ TɔḦ $^{\text{o}}_{\text{v}}$ ·

727 Ø Ḧ⊥ʌ ¦ Ḧ⊥ʌ $^{(\frac{\text{o}}{\text{l}}\text{·})}_{\text{v}}$

728 Ø Ḧ>ʌ Ḧ<ʌ $^{\text{o}}_{\text{v}}$

729 Ø Ḧ>⊥ Ḧ<⊥ $_{\text{v}}^{\omega\text{N}}$ ·

[410]

The index and middle fingers (held together) are extended from the fist and bent at the palm knuckles.

Handshape and orientation	Location, hand arrangement and contact	Movement	Glosses	
Two Ḧ hands are held with the palms facing up (if the hands were opened, the fingers would all point away from the signer).	The hands are held side by side in front of the body at an angle, so that the extended fingers are turned towards each other.	The hands move towards and away from the signer alternately, so that the extended fingers brush together; the movements are repeated.	news	724
The left Ḧ hand is held with the palm facing up; the right Ḧ hand is held with the palm facing down (if the hands were opened, the fingers would all point away from the signer).	The hands are held in front of the body; the right hand is held above the left hand, and the tips of the extended fingers are touching.	The right hand bends sharply up from the wrist and, at the same time, the left hand bends sharply down from the wrist.	amazed flabbergasted gobsmacked staggered	725
Non-manual features The mouth is open; as the hands move, the shoulders hunch and the head is pushed forward while the eyes and mouth are opened wide with the eyebrows raised.				
Two Ḧ hands are held with the palms facing down (if the hands were opened, the fingers would all point away from the signer).	The hands are held in front of the body.	The hands make two short downward movements.	dog dog begging	726
Two Ḧ hands are held with the palms facing away from the signer (if the hands were opened, the fingers would all point up).	The hands are held side by side in front of the body.	The hands make several short movements away from the signer, while moving down throughout.	accountant *§ accounts *§ bookkeeper *§ bookkeeping *§ fill in a form *†	727

Notes   * This sign may be produced with the lips rounded.

    † This sign may also be produced using two V̈ hands.   Ø V̈⊥∧ , V̈⊥∧ $\binom{\substack{o\\ \top}}{v}$

    § This sign may be produced with the hands bending up at the wrists while moving up and away from the signer.   Ø Ḧↄ⊥ , Ḧↄ⊥ $\binom{\substack{o\\ ∩}}{\substack{∧\\ \top}}$

The left Ḧ hand is held with the palm facing right; the right Ḧ hand is held with the palm facing left (if the hands were opened, the fingers would all point up).	The hands are held in front of the body at an angle, so that the fingers are turned upwards.	The hands make a short movement down and, at the same time, towards each other.	decrease * few * fewer * less * lessen * lesser * minimise * minimum * reduce * reduction * small * smaller *	728

Notes   * This sign may be produced with a firm movement (the sign for **fewer, lesser, smaller** is typically produced in this way).   Ø Ḧ>∧ Ḧ<∧ $\substack{o\cdot\\ x\\ v}$

The left Ḧ hand is held with the palm facing right; the right Ḧ hand is held with the palm facing left (if the hands were opened, the fingers would all point away from the signer).	The hands are held in front of the body.	The hands move down while twisting away from the signer at the wrist; the movements are repeated several times alternately.	autumn leaves (falling leaves)	729

730　○ Ḧ>ʌ Ḧ<ʌ $\overset{\nwarrow\nearrow\cdot}{\text{I}}$

731　Π Ḧ>ʌ | Ḧ<ʌ $\overset{\overset{\circ}{\underset{\vee}{@}}N÷}{}$

732　○ $\left(\overline{\text{B}}\text{a> } Ḧ\text{a<} \overset{\wedge\cdot}{\top} \right)$

The index and middle fingers (held together) are extended from the fist and bent at the palm knuckles.

Handshape and orientation	Location, hand arrangement and contact	Movement	Glosses
The left Ḧ hand is held with the palm facing right; the right Ḧ hand is held with the palm facing left (if the hands were opened, the fingers would all point up).	The hands are held in front of the mouth.	The hands move up and towards the signer and then down and away from the signer alternately several times.	dinner **730** lunch meal restaurant
The left Ḧ hand is held with the palm facing right; the right Ḧ hand is held with the palm facing left (if the hands were opened, the fingers would all point up).	The hands are held side by side beside the neck.	The hands make alternate small clockwise circles in the vertical plane at right angles to the signer's body and then move apart.	nurse **731** Salvation Army scarf

The left **B** hand is held with the palm facing up and the fingers pointing to the right; the right Ḧ hand is held with the palm facing up (if the hand were opened, the fingers would point to the left).	The hands are held side by side in front of the body; the right hand is held higher than the left hand, and at an angle, so that the palm is turned to the left.	The right hand moves up and towards the signer's mouth; the movement is repeated.	cereal* **732**
			dessert*
			eat cereal/dessert/
			  porridge/pudding/
			  soup/sweet*
			eat with a dessert
			  spoon/soup spoon*
			porridge*
			pudding*
			soup*
			sweet*

Notes   * This sign can be produced using one hand only.

⌣ Ḧɑ< ᵀ̂˙

733 $\overline{G}$ʊ> ₓ Ḧʊ⊤ $^{(ꞏ)[v]\,{}^{o}_{\overline{v}}}_{\substack{+\\A\\□}}$

734 $\overline{H}$ʊ> Ḧ⊥ʌ૧ $^{ꞏ\,ᵪ}_{⊤}$

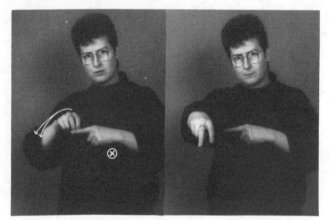

735 Ø Ḧɑ>₁ Ḧɑ< $^{÷ꞏ}$

736 Ø $\overline{H}$ɑ> Ḧʊ⊤ $^{@ᴎꞏ}_{\lessgtr⊤}$

737 Ø Ḧ>ʌ Ḧ<ʌ $^{(ꞏ)}_{\substack{ᴧ\\ᵪ}}$

The bent index and middle fingers (held together) are extended from the fist.

Ḧ has several different *classifier* functions in the productive lexicon and is used as a classifying element in established signs:

– it is used as a *size and shape* classifier to represent bent, narrow objects such as bent legs in **long jump** (sign 733) and **sit** (sign 734). However, it is used as a legs classifier even where there is no particular focus on the bending of the legs as in **roam** (sign 736) and **prowl** (sign 736);

– it is used as a *handling* classifier to indicate the handling of stretch or elasticated material, as in **elastic** (sign 735);

– it is used to indicate *quantity* and *extent*. It can show a number of items, as in **many people sitting in rows** and **several people sitting one behind the other**. Two-handed forms can show *extent*, particularly the extent of long, narrow, curved objects, such as the extent of a hedge or the size of a cooking dish.

Handshape and orientation	Location, hand arrangement and contact	Movement	Glosses	
The left **G** hand is held with the palm facing down (if the hand were opened, the fingers would point to the right). The right **Ḧ** hand is held with the palm facing down (if the hand were opened, the fingers would point away from the signer).	The hands are held in front of the body; the right index and middle fingertips rest on the left index finger.	The right hand moves up and away from the signer while bending down at the wrist and, at the same time, opening (forming a **V** hand); the hand then makes a short movement down and, at the same time, away from the signer.	long jump long jumper	733
The left **H** hand is held with the palm facing down (if the hand were opened, the fingers would point to the right). The right **Ḧ** hand is held with the palm facing away from the signer (if the hand were opened, the fingers would point up).	The hands are held in front of the body; the right hand is held higher and nearer to the signer than the left hand.	The right hand bends away from the signer from the wrist, so that the bent fingers hook over the extended left fingers.	chair seat sit	734
Two **Ḧ** hands are held with the palms facing up (if the hands were opened, the left fingers would point to the right and the right fingers would point to the left).	The hands are held side by side in front of the body.	The hands move apart twice.	elastic elastic band	735
The left **Ḧ** hand is held with the palm facing up; the right **Ḧ** hand is held with the palm facing down (if the hands were opened, the left fingers would point to the right and the right fingers would point away from the signer).	The hands are held in front of the body; the right hand is held above the left hand.	The hands make alternate anticlockwise circles in the horizontal plane; the movements are repeated several times.	circulate circus roam roundabout prowl[1]	736

Notes   1   If the shoulders are hunched and the head is pushed forward, the eyes are narrowed and the movement is slow, the sign produced is **prowl**.

The left **Ḧ** hand is held with the palm facing right; the right **Ḧ** hand is held with the palm facing left (if the hands were opened, the fingers would all point up).	The hands are held in front of the body.	The extended fingers flex several times while the hands move up and, at the same time, towards each other.	castle* Newcastle*	737

Notes   * This sign may be produced using two **V̈** hands.

$$\varnothing \quad \ddot{V}{>}{\wedge} \quad \ddot{V}{<}{\wedge} \quad \overset{(\text{\tiny ᴍ}\,\cdot)}{\underset{x}{\wedge}}$$

738　Ø Ĥ⊥ʌ $\overset{\overset{\cdot}{\omega}}{\underset{\square}{\mathsf{T}}}$ [v]　　　　　　　　739　Ø Ĥ⊥ʌ $\left(\overset{[\breve{v}]}{\underset{>}{\overset{\mathsf{n}}{\underset{\square}{\underline{1}}}}}\cdot\right)$

740　Ц Ĥ⊤ʌ $\overset{\overset{\mathsf{o}}{\underset{\square}{\times}}}{\underset{\square}{\underline{1}}}$ [v]·

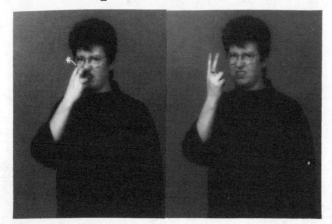

The bent index and middle fingers (held together) and bent thumb are
extended from the fist and touch at the tips.

The main *variants* of Ĥ relate to the degree of bending of the index and middle fingers and the related positioning of the thumb. In some cases, the bending is relatively loose, so that the fingers and thumb create a clear circular formation. In other cases, there is very little space between the fingers and the palm.

Despite the circular formation mentioned, which could make it appropriate for use as a *size and shape* classifier, Ĥ seems to be used infrequently with *classifier* functions (although its use in **bow tie** (sign 745)

may be seen as indicating the central knot of the tie). It occurs in the lexicon primarily in signs involving an opening action from Ĥ to **V**. All of the signs cited here are of this type. The precise function of this opening action may vary: it may be seen as giving *emphasis* to the action, as in the sharp, shooting out of a snake's tongue in **snake** (sign 741); it may have a *symbolic* function, expressing meanings such as 'emit' or 'spread', as in **stars** (sign 744) or it may be purely arbitrary.

Handshape and orientation	Location, hand arrangement and contact	Movement	Glosses	
The Ĥ hand is held with the palm facing away from the signer (if the hand were opened, the fingers would point up).	The hand is held in front of the body.	The hand twists sharply at the wrist so that the palm faces towards the signer and, at the same time, the index and middle fingers open (forming a **V** hand).	midday midnight noon twelve o'clock	738
The Ĥ hand is held with the palm facing away from the signer (if the hand were opened, the fingers would point up).	The hand is held in front of the body.	The hand bends away from the signer from the wrist while opening (forming a **V̄** hand); the movement is repeated several times with the hand moving to the right throughout.	tour travel trip walkabout walk[1]	739

Notes   1   If the hand opens (forming a **V̄** hand) while making a short bending movement away from the signer at the wrist, and the movement is repeated several times with the hand moving away from the signer throughout, the sign produced is **walk**.

$$\emptyset \quad \hat{\tilde{H}}_{\perp\wedge} \begin{pmatrix} \overset{\circ}{\underset{\square}{\sqcap}} {}^{[\text{v̄}]} & \cdot \\ {}_{\perp} & \end{pmatrix}$$

The Ĥ hand is held with the palm facing towards the signer (if the hand were opened, the fingers would point up).	The hand is held with the fingers in front of the nose.	The hand makes a short movement away from the signer while opening (forming a **V** hand), so that the index and middle fingertips brush the nose; the movement is repeated.	clapped out lousy pathetic rotten rubbish tatty useless	740

Non-manual features   The eyes are narrowed, the nose is wrinkled and the tongue tip protrudes between the teeth.

741 ○ Ĥ⊥ʌ $\overset{(\overset{o}{\underset{z}{}}.)[\triangledown]}{\underset{\square}{\bot}}$

742 Gᴛ> Ĥↄ⊥ᵩ $\overset{\overset{\circ}{\underset{\square}{\bot}}[v]\overset{\circ}{\underset{\bot}{}}}{}$

743 Ğ>⊥ Ĥↄ⊥ᵩ $\overset{\overset{\wedge}{\underset{\square}{\bot}}[v]v}{}$

744 ○ Ĥ⊥ʌ Ĥ⊥ʌ $\overset{\overset{\circ}{\underset{\square}{}}[\triangledown\triangledown]\sim\cdot}{}$

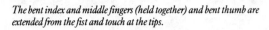

*The bent index and middle fingers (held together) and bent thumb are
extended from the fist and touch at the tips.*

Handshape and orientation	Location, hand arrangement and contact	Movement	Glosses	
The Ĥ hand is held with the palm facing away from the signer (if the hand were opened, the fingers would point up).	The hand is held with the back of the hand resting against the mouth and chin.	The hand moves away from the signer and, at the same time, makes short movements from side to side, while the fingers open (forming a V̄ hand).	**snake**	741

Non-manual features   The tongue protrudes slightly between the teeth.

The left **G** hand is held with the palm facing towards the signer (if the hand were opened, the fingers would point to the right). The right Ĥ hand is held with the palm facing down (if the hand were opened, the fingers would point away from the signer).	The hands are held in front of the body; the right hand is held nearer to the signer than the left hand.	The right hand makes a short movement up and away from the signer while opening (forming a **V** hand); the hand then makes a short movement down and, at the same time, away from the signer.	**clear** (an obstacle) **jump over** **leap over**	742
The left **G̈** hand is held with the palm facing right; the right Ĥ hand is held with the palm facing down (if the hands were opened, the fingers would all point away from the signer).	The hands are held in front of the body; the right hand is held nearer to the signer than the left hand.	The right hand moves up and away from the signer while opening (forming a **V** hand) and, at the same time, turning over, so that the palm faces up; the hand then moves down.	**high-jump** **high-jumper**	743

Non-manual features   The eyes are opened wide and the cheeks are slightly puffed out.

Two Ĥ hands are held with the palms facing away from the signer (if the hands were opened, the fingers would all point up).	The hands are held in front and to the sides of the head.	The hands make alternate short upward movements while opening (forming two V̄ hands); the movements are repeated several times.	**stars** **stars**[1]	744

Notes   1 If one hand only is used, the sign produced is **stars**
(see entry 2 in the English section).

$$Ø \quad \hat{H}_{⊥∧} \quad {}^{\circ}_{∧} {}^{\circ}_{□} [\bar{v}]$$

745 Π Ĥ⊤> ₁ Ĥ⊤< ÷̥̊ [vv]

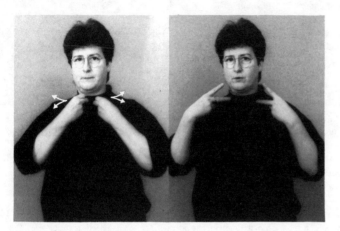

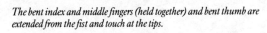

The bent index and middle fingers (held together) and bent thumb are extended from the fist and touch at the tips.

Handshape and orientation	Location, hand arrangement and contact	Movement	Glosses	
Two Ĥ hands are held with the palms facing towards the signer (if the hands were opened, the left fingers would point to the right and the right fingers would point to the left).	The hands are held side by side in front of the neck.	The hands make a short movement apart, and, at the same time, the extended fingers open (forming two **V** hands).	**bouncer** **bow tie**	745

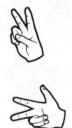

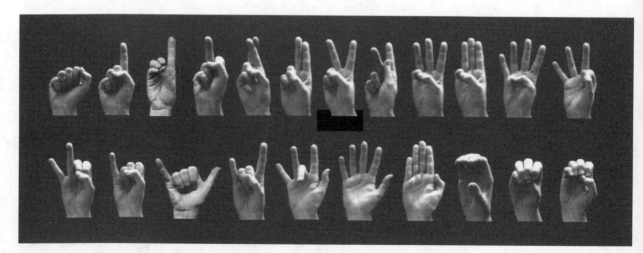

V

Handshape	Handshape description	Type	Sign entries
V	The index and middle fingers are extended from the fist and spread apart.	Single dez Manual tab Double dez	746 – 762 763 – 773 774 – 777
V̇	The index finger, middle finger and thumb are extended from the fist and spread apart.	Single dez Manual tab Double dez	778 – 780
V̄	The index and middle fingers (spread apart) are extended from the fist and bent at the palm knuckles; the extended thumb is held parallel to the extended fingers.	Single dez Manual tab Double dez	781 – 782
V̈	The index and middle fingers (spread apart) are extended from the fist and bent at the palm knuckles.	Single dez Manual tab Double dez	783 – 795 796 – 802 803 – 804
V̈	The bent index and middle fingers are extended from the fist and spread apart.	Single dez Manual tab Double dez	805 – 816 817 – 820 821 – 824
V̈	The thumb and the bent index and middle fingers are extended from the fist and spread apart.	Single dez Manual tab Double dez	825
V̈	The bent index and middle fingers and bent thumb are extended from the fist and spread apart; the thumb is held parallel to the index finger.	Single dez Manual tab Double dez	826 – 829 830 831 – 832

746 Ø Vɑ< ↕ⁿᵥ

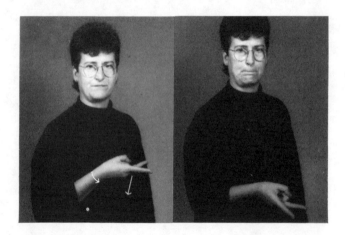

747 Ø VɑT (⟂ᴺᴼ·)

748 Ø Vɑ< ⟂

749 Ø V⟂ʌ ⊹ω·

750 Ø V<ʌ ᵀʌ

V

The index and middle fingers are extended from the fist and spread apart.

The main *variant* of V is V̈, where the fingers are bent at the palm knuckles. In some cases, V̈ is required by the physical constraints of the sign production. In other cases, the use of V or V̈ depends on personal choice. (See also separate entry for V̈). Further *variants* of V involve one or other of the extended fingers being held slightly behind the other. Such variants can be seen in **don't give a damn** (sign 746), **day before yesterday** (sign 756) and **another** (sign 767).

V has several different *classifier* functions in the established lexicon and is used as a classifying element in established signs:

– it is used as a *size and shape* classifier to represent two narrow, fixed but moveable extensions, particularly human legs, and thereby persons. Many items associated with the V *legs* classifier are given in this dictionary under V̈. However, some of these may also occur with a straight V: examples include **fall** (sign 786) and **lie** (sign 802). It is also used to indicate wedge-shaped or narrow objects, such as **spectacles** (sign 754);

– it is also used as a *tracing size and shape* classifier to trace the outline and positioning of strips, ribbons, collars and stripes, as in a clerical collar (of the type used by Church of Scotland ministers) and the stripes, indicating rank, of the armed forces and the police. V̈ may

also be used in such examples, see **mayor** (sign 793), **officer** (sign 794) and **police** (sign 795);

– it has a specialised use to indicate *duality* or 'two–ness'. This can be seen primarily in two sets of signs, those relating to eyes and those relating to the number 2. Examples relating to the two eyes include **look around** (sign 747), **observe** (sign 755), **read** (sign 771) and **surveillance** (sign 777). Among many examples linked with the number 2 are **second** (sign 748), **fortnight** (sign 750), **two days ago** (sign 756) and **both of us** (sign 760);

– it is used infrequently as a *handling* classifier to indicate the handling of narrow objects. The most common examples of this usage are **cigarette** (sign 757) and **smoke** (sign 757);

– it is used as an *instrumental* classifier to indicate implements, tools or utensils which have two narrow, joined but moveable extensions, such as **scissors** (sign 752) and **compass** (sign 773).

V expresses the right-hand component of the letter v of the British manual alphabet and also expresses the v in the Irish and American one-handed alphabets. It occurs in a number of initial letter handshape signs, such as **vegetable** (sign 770), **virgin** (sign 770), **vodka** (sign 770) and **video** (sign 775).

Handshape and orientation	Location, hand arrangement and contact	Movement	Glosses	
The V hand is held with the palm facing up (if the hand were opened, the fingers would point to the left).	The hand is held in front of the body.	The hand bends away from the signer at the wrist while moving down.	do not care a damn don't care a damn do not give a damn don't give a damn to hell with	746
Non-manual features The upper teeth are touching the lower lip; the mouth closes, with the lips drawn back, as the hand moves down.				
The V hand is held with the palm facing down (if the hand were opened, the fingers would point away from the signer).	The hand is held in front of the body.	The hand makes several short bending movements from side to side at the wrist, while moving away from the signer throughout.	go sightseeing look around sightseeing tour	747
The V hand is held with the palm facing down (if the hand were opened, the fingers would point to the left).	The hand is held in front of the body.	The hand moves away from the signer.	fortnight second weeks (two weeks)	748
The V hand is held with the palm facing away from the signer (if the hand were opened, the fingers would point up).	The hand is held in front of the body.	The hand twists firmly at the wrist, so that the palm faces towards the signer.	second * two o'clock *	749
Notes * This sign may be produced with a repeated movement. Ø V⊥∧ ⸚·				
The V hand is held with the palm facing left (if the hand were opened, the fingers would point up).	The hand is held in front of the shoulder.	The hand moves towards the signer and, at the same time, up.	fortnight ago * weeks (two weeks ago) *	750
Notes * Regional sign.				

751 Ø V<⊥ ᴰᵥ·

752 Ø V<⊥ #[ʜ]·

753 Ц ᵉV⊤ʌ ˣ // Ḡ>ʌ V𝔯⊥ᵩ ⊥ᴵ/ᵥ

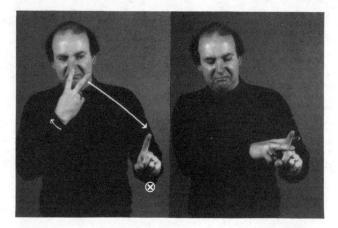

754 Ц ⁱV⊤< ˣ·

V

The index and middle fingers are extended from the fist and spread apart.

Handshape and orientation	Location, hand arrangement and contact	Movement	Glosses	
The **V** hand is held with the palm facing left (if the hand were opened, the fingers would point away from the signer).	The hand is held in front of the body.	The hand bends down from the wrist twice.	**again** **frequent** **often** **repeat** **repetition**	751
The **V** hand is held with the palm facing left (if the hand were opened, the fingers would point away from the signer).	The hand is held in front of the body.	The index and middle fingers close (forming an **H** hand) several times.	**scissors** **cut**[1,2] **edit**[3] **barber**[4,6] **hairdresser**[4,6] **cut back**[5] **cut off**[5] **disconnect**[5]	752

Notes

1 If the movement is not repeated, the sign produced is **cut** *(see entry 1 in the English section)*.

$$\emptyset \quad V<\perp \quad \text{\# [H]}$$

2 If the hand moves away from the signer while the index and middle fingers close repeatedly, the sign produced is **cut** *(see entry 2 in the English section)*.

$$\emptyset \quad V<\perp \quad \left(\text{\# [H]} \cdot \right)_{\perp}$$

3 If two **V** hands are held side by side and move to the right while closing (forming two **H** hands) and the movement is repeated, the sign produced is **edit**.

$$\emptyset \quad V>\perp {}_{\shortmid} V<\perp \quad \left({}^{>}_{\text{\#}} {}^{\text{[HH]}}\right) \cdot$$

4 If the hand is held beside the head (with the palm facing left and the extended fingers pointing up), and bends repeatedly towards the signer at the wrist while closing (forming an **H** hand), the sign produced is **barber, hairdresser**.

$$\circ \quad V<\wedge \quad {}^{\text{n [H]}}_{\substack{\text{T}\\\text{\#}}} \cdot$$

5 If the left **G** hand is held in front of the body (with the palm facing towards the signer and the index finger pointing right) and the **V** hand makes a firm movement down and away from the signer while closing (forming an **H** hand), the sign produced is **cut back, cut off, disconnect**.

$$\underline{\ } \quad G\top> \quad V<\perp_{\wp} \quad {}^{\text{v [H]}}_{\substack{\perp\\\text{\#}}}$$

6 If the left **G** hand is held in front of the body (with the palm facing down and the extended fingers pointing up) and the right hand moves up and away from the signer, brushing the left index finger several times, the sign produced is **barber, hairdresser**.

$$G\circlearrowright\wedge \quad V\circlearrowright<_{\wp} \quad {}^{\wedge}_{\substack{\perp\\ \text{x}\\ \wedge}}\cdot$$

The **V** hand is held with the palm facing towards the signer (if the hand were opened, the fingers would point up).	The hand is held with the extended fingers in front of the nose.	The index fingertip touches the nose.	**betray*** **deceive*** **fool*** **trick***	753
The left **G** hand is held with the palm facing left (if the hand were opened, the fingers would point up). The right **V** hand is held with the palm facing down (if the hand were opened, the fingers would point away from the signer).	The hands are held in front of the body; the right hand is held higher and nearer to the signer than the left hand.	The right hand moves away from the signer, so that the left index finger is held between the right index and middle fingers.		

Non-manual features The lips are pressed together and the corners of the mouth are turned down.

Notes * Directional verb.

The **V** hand is held with the palm facing towards the signer (if the hand were opened, the fingers would point to the left).	The hand is held beside the eye.	The middle fingertip taps the cheek beneath the eye twice.	**glasses*** **optician*** **Preston specs*** **spectacles***	754

Notes * This sign may be produced using two hands.

$$\sqcup \quad {}^{\text{i}}V\top> \; {}^{\text{i}}V\top< \quad {}^{\text{x}}\cdot$$

755 ⊔ ᵉV<ʌ ˣ⊥

756 Ʒ ⁱVтʌ ˣ⊤ᵐˣ

757 ◡ Vтʌ ˣ·

758 ◡ ⁱVт< ˣ(°@⊥V>⊤·)

759 ⊔ Vтʌ ˣˣ

760 [] Vɑ< °⊥·

761 ⊽ Vʊ< (ˣ°⊤·)

V

The index and middle fingers are extended from the fist and spread apart.

Handshape and orientation	Location, hand arrangement and contact	Movement	Glosses	
The **V** hand is held with the palm facing left (if the hand were opened, the fingers would point up).	The hand is held with the index fingertip touching the cheek.	The hand moves away from the signer.	eyesight look * observation observe * observer see * sight view * viewer vision watch * notice [1] have a look [2]	755

Notes   * Directional verb.

     1   If the movement is short and firm, the sign produced is **notice**.   ⊔ ᵉV<ʌ ×ᵒ⊥

     2   If the index fingertip taps the cheek below the eye several times, the sign produced is **have a look**.   ⊔ ᵉV<ʌ ×·

The **V** hand is held with the palm facing towards the signer (if the hand were opened, the fingers would point up).	The hand is held with the middle fingertip touching the right cheek.	The hand moves towards the signer while the middle finger bends at the palm knuckles; the movement ends with the middle finger touching the right shoulder.	day before yesterday days (two days ago)	756
The **V** hand is held with the palm facing towards the signer (if the hand were opened, the fingers would point up).	The hand is held with the extended fingers in front of the mouth and chin.	The tips of the extended fingers tap the mouth twice.	cigarette fag smoke smoke a cigarette/fag smoking	757
The **V** hand is held with the palm facing towards the signer (if the hand were opened, the fingers would point to the left).	The hand is held with the middle fingertip touching the chin.	The hand moves up and away from the signer and, at the same time, to the right while making small clockwise circles in the vertical plane at right angles to the signer's body.	carol * carol singer * hymn * sing * singer * song *	758

Notes   * This sign may be produced using two hands.   ⌣ ʲVᴛ> ʲVᴛ<

The **V** hand is held with the palm facing towards the signer (if the hand were opened, the fingers would point up).	The hand is held with the extended fingers on either side of the nose.	The hand moves slowly down; the index and middle fingertips maintain contact with the lower face throughout.	bore one stiff bore one to death bore one to tears	759

Non-manual features   The nose is wrinkled and the tongue protrudes between the top teeth and the lower lip.

The **V** hand is held with the palm facing up (if the hand were opened, the fingers would point to the left).	The hand is held in front of the chest.	The hand makes two short movements towards and away from the signer.	both of us pair of us two of us us (two) we (two)	760
The **V** hand is held with the palm facing down (if the hand were opened, the fingers would point to the left).	The right hand is held above the left forearm, which is positioned in front of the body.	The hand makes a series of short movements towards the signer; the tips of the extended fingers touch the left forearm at the end of each movement.	Carlisle	761

762 $\overline{}\sqrt{}$ V⊤< $\overset{\circ \times}{\underset{v}{\alpha}}$

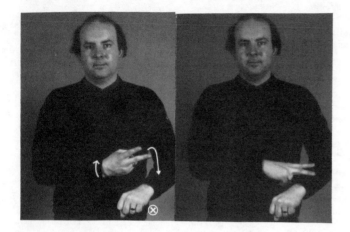

763 $\overline{}$ G⊤⊥ x Vʊ⊥ $\overset{\vee \perp}{\underset{x}{}}$

764 $\overline{}$ G⊤> x V<⊥ $\overset{<}{\underset{x}{\vee}}$

765 $\overline{}$ G>⊥ Vʊ⊥ρ $\overset{\perp \cdot}{\underset{x}{\perp}}$

766 V⊤ʌ x Vʊʌρ $\overset{\alpha \times}{}$

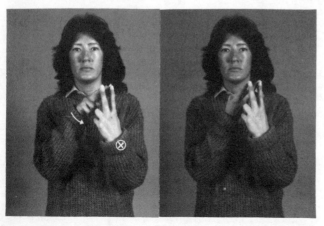

767 ¡V̇ɑ⊥ρ ¡ ¡V⊤< $\overset{\circ \cdot}{\underset{v}{\overset{\times}{\times}}}$

The index and middle fingers are extended from the fist and spread apart.

Handshape and orientation	Location, hand arrangement and contact	Movement	Glosses	
The **V** hand is held with the palm facing towards the signer (if the hand were opened, the fingers would point to the left).	The hand is held above the left forearm which is positioned in front of the body.	The right hand moves down while twisting at the wrist, so that the palm faces down; the movement ends with the right index and middle fingertips touching the left forearm.	foreman gaffer supervisor	762

The left **G** hand is held with the palm facing towards the signer; the right **V** hand is held with the palm facing down (if the hands were opened, the fingers would all point away from the signer).	The hands are held in front of the body; the right hand rests on the left hand.	The right hand moves away from the signer and, at the same time, to the right, maintaining contact with the left hand throughout.	fortnight *
			fortnight later *
			fortnight (in a
			  fortnight's time) *
			week after next *
			weeks (in two
			  week's time) *
			weeks (two weeks) *
			weeks (two
			  weeks later) *
				763

Notes   * This sign may be produced using one hand only.

$$\emptyset \quad \text{V} \text{ɔ⊥} \quad {}^{\perp}_{>}$$

The left **G** hand is held with the palm facing towards the signer (if the hand were opened, the fingers would point to the right). The right **V** hand is held with the palm facing left (if the hand were opened, the fingers would point away from the signer).	The hands are held in front of the body; the right hand rests on the left index finger.	The right hand moves to the left, maintaining contact with the left hand throughout.	fortnight ago weeks (two weeks ago)	764
The left **G** hand is held with the palm facing right; the right **V** hand is held with the palm facing down (if the hands were opened, the fingers would all point away from the signer).	The hands are held in front of the body; the right hand is held higher and nearer to the signer than the left hand.	The right hand moves away from the signer, brushing along the left index finger; the movement is repeated.	fool * have someone on * joke joker kid * play a joke on * pull someone's leg * tease * jeer *[1] mock *[1] ridicule *[1] taunt *[1]	765

Notes   * Directional verb.

      1   If the eyes are narrowed and the tongue protrudes between the teeth, the sign produced is **jeer, mock, ridicule, taunt**.

The left **V** hand is held with the palm facing towards the signer; the right **V** hand is held with the palm facing down (if the hands were opened, the fingers would all point up).	The hands are held in front of the body; the right hand is held nearer to the signer than the left hand and at an angle, so that the right index and middle fingertips rest against the left index and middle fingertips.	The right hand turns over, so that the palm faces up; the movement ends with the index and middle fingers touching each other again.	substitute substitution swap switch	766
The left **V̇** hand is held with the palm facing up (if the hand were opened, the fingers would point away from the signer). The right **V** hand is held with the palm facing towards the signer (if the hand were opened, the fingers would point to the left).	The hands are held side by side in front of the body; the left hand is held nearer to the signer than the right hand.	The right hand makes a short upward movement, so that the right middle fingertip brushes the left middle fingertip; the movement is repeated.	another else other	767

768 5>⊥ ¦ V⌢<ₓ^ω^ₓ⊥

769 B̄ɑ> V⌢⊥^n_v

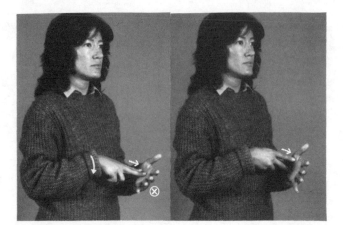

770 B̄ɑ> V⌢⊥ ˣ˙

771 B⊤> V⌢∧ᵨ ᵒ_z͜ᵥ ˙

772 B>⊥ ¦ V⌢< ˣ˙

773 B>⊥ ¦ₓ ᵉV⌢< ˣ³ᵥ ˙

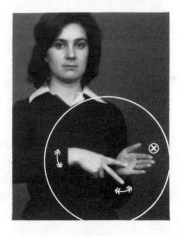

The index and middle fingers are extended from the fist and spread apart.

Handshape and orientation	Location, hand arrangement and contact	Movement	Glosses	
The left **5** hand is held with the palm facing right and the fingers pointing away from the signer; the right **V** hand is held with the palm facing down (if the hand were opened, the fingers would point to the left).	The hands are held side by side in front of the body.	The right index and middle fingertips touch the left palm; the right hand then twists at the wrist, so that the palm faces towards the signer, and then the index and middle fingertips touch the left palm again.	design * designer * devise * intend * intention * organisation * organise * organiser * plan * planner * strategy *	768

Notes   * The following notes apply to all glosses:

This sign may also be produced as the second part of a compound sign (see 511 Note 1 for the first part of the sign).

$$\cap \ \ddot{G}\tau\wedge \ ^{\times} \ \ /\!/ \ 5>\perp \ , \ V\sigma< \ ^{\times\omega\times}_{\perp}$$

This sign may also be produced with a left **B** handshape.

$$B>\perp \ , \ V\sigma< \ ^{\times\omega\times}_{\perp}$$

| The left **B** hand is held with the palm facing up and the fingers pointing to the right; the right **V** hand is held with the palm facing down (if the hand were opened, the fingers would point away from the signer). | The hands are held in front of the body; the right hand is held above the left hand. | The right hand bends down from the wrist. | check a document read a document scan a document skim a document | 769 |
| The left **B** hand is held with the palm facing up and the fingers pointing to the right; the right **V** hand is held with the palm facing down (if the hand were opened, the fingers would point away from the signer). | The hands are held in front of the body; the extended right fingers are held above the left hand. | The extended right fingers tap the left palm twice. | vegetable vegetarian virgin vodka versus [1] | 770 |

Notes   1 If the movement is not repeated, the sign produced is **versus**. $B\alpha> \ V\sigma\perp \ ^{\times}$

The left **B** hand is held with the palm facing towards the signer and the fingers pointing to the right; the right **V** hand is held with the palm facing down (if the hand were opened, the fingers would point up).	The hands are held in front of the body; the right hand is held nearer to the signer than the left hand and at an angle, so that the fingers are turned away from the signer.	The right hand makes short movements from side to side while moving down throughout.	read read a document	771
The left **B** hand is held with the palm facing right and the fingers pointing away from the signer; the right **V** hand is held with the palm facing down (if the hand were opened, the fingers would point to the left).	The hands are held side by side in front of the body.	The right index and middle fingertips tap the left palm twice.	fork toast	772
The left **B** hand is held with the palm facing right and the fingers pointing away from the signer; the right **V** hand is held with the palm facing down (if the hand were opened, the fingers would point to the left).	The hands are held side by side in front of the body; the right index fingertip is held against the left palm.	The right hand twists up and down from the wrist several times; the right index fingertip is held against the left palm throughout.	compass *	773

Notes   * This sign may be produced with a right **Ġ** hand.

$$B>\perp \ _{1\times} \ ^{a}\dot{G}\sigma\perp \ ^{\times}_{\tilde{N}}$$

774 Ø V̄ɑ⊥ Vʊ⊥ $\overset{⫿}{\text{⊤}}$

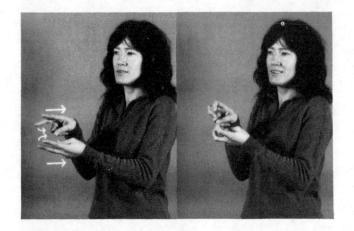

775 Ø Vʊ∨ Vʊ∨ $\overset{ⓔ.}{\text{⊥∨}}$

776 Ø Vʊ> ¡ Vʊ< $\overset{ᵒᵛ.}{\text{÷ɰ}}$

777 Ø V̄⊤⊥ ≠× V⊤⊥ $\overset{ᵒ.}{\text{∨}}$

V

The index and middle fingers are extended from the fist and spread apart.

Handshape and orientation	Location, hand arrangement and contact	Movement	Glosses	
The left **V** hand is held with the palm facing up; the right **V** hand is held with the palm facing down (if the hands were opened, the fingers would all point away from the signer).	The hands are held in front of the body; the right hand is held above the left hand.	The hands move towards the signer and, at the same time, the extended fingers flex.	attract * † attraction † elicit * † § extract * † extraction † exploit * † [1]	774

Notes   * Directional verb.

     † This sign may be produced using two **G** hands.

     § This sign may be produced with a repeated movement.

     1 If the tongue protrudes between the teeth, the nose is wrinkled and the movement is repeated, the sign produced is **exploit**.

Two **V** hands are held with the palms facing down (if the hands were opened, the fingers would all point down).	The hands are held in front of the body at an angle, so that the fingers are turned away from the signer.	The hands make clockwise circles in the horizontal plane.	video video cassette video recorder video tape	775
Two **V** hands are held with the palms facing down (if the hands were opened, the left fingers would point to the right and the right fingers would point to the left).	The hands are held side by side in front of the body.	The hands make a short movement down and apart and, at the same time, the extended fingers flex; the movement is repeated.	analyse * analysis analyst examine * explanation explore * explorer investigate * investigation investigator research researcher survey	776

Notes   * Directional verb.

Two **V** hands are held with the palms facing towards the signer (if the hands were opened, the fingers would all point away from the signer).	The hands are held in front of the body at an angle, so that the right fingers are turned to the left and the left fingers are turned to the right; the right hand is held on the left hand.	The hands remain together and make a short movement down and, at the same time, away from the signer.	guard * guardian look after * monitor * protect * protection protector supervise * supervision supervisor watch over * surveillance [1]	777

Notes   * Directional verb.

     1 If the hands remain together and make a clockwise circle in the horizontal plane, the sign produced is **surveillance**.

778 ∩ V̇<∧(ω̇ẋᵒ/ɴ·)

779 ∪ ᵉⁱV̇ᴛ< ˣ>

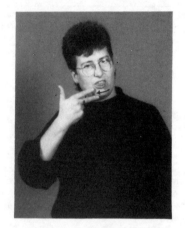

780 [] V̇ᴛ<(ɴ̇ᴅᵒ·/ᴢˣ)

V̇

The index finger, middle finger and thumb are extended from the fist and spread apart.

V̇ is used infrequently in the lexicon. It has a limited function as a *size and shape* classifier for objects with three extensions or for objects with jagged edges. Thus it is used to indicate the serrated outgrowth on the heads of certain birds as in **cockscomb** (sign 778). It is also used in number systems to indicate numbers involving **3** or **8** and this function is lexicalised in signs such as **the three of us** (see *Introduction*).

Handshape and orientation	Location, hand arrangement and contact	Movement	Glosses	
The V̇ hand is held with the palm facing left (if the hand were opened, the fingers would point up).	The hand is held with the thumbtip against the forehead.	The hand makes several short twisting movements from side to side at the wrist; the thumbtip is held against the forehead throughout.	**cock** **cockscomb** **hen**	778
The V̇ hand is held with the palm facing towards the signer (if the hand were opened, the fingers would point to the left).	The hand is held with the index and middle fingertips touching the chin.	The hand moves to the right; the index and middle fingertips maintain contact with the chin throughout.	**bore one stiff** **bore one to death** **bore one to tears**	779

Non-manual features The nose is wrinkled and the tongue protrudes between the teeth.

The V̇ hand is held with the palm facing towards the signer (if the hand were opened, the fingers would point to the left).	The hand is held with the extended fingers resting against the chest.	The hand bends up and down twice at the wrist while moving to the right; the fingertips maintain contact with the chest throughout.	**Dane** **Danish** **Denmark**	780

781 ＞⌐1 V̄<ᴧ ≠[A]

782 ⌐ V̄ɑ< ᵒ·T<≠[ᴋ]×

The index and middle fingers (spread apart) are extended from the fist and bent at the palm knuckles; the extended thumb is held parallel to the extended fingers.

V̄ is used infrequently in the lexicon. It has limited classifier functions. It appears to combine *size and shape* and *handling* functions in **badge** (sign 781) and has a *handling* function in **hypodermic** (sign 782).

Handshape and orientation	Location, hand arrangement and contact	Movement	Glosses	
The V̄ hand is held with the palm facing left (if the hand were opened, the fingers would point up).	The hand is held in front of the left side of the upper chest.	The extended fingers and thumb close (forming an Ĥ hand).	badge brooch	781
The V̄ hand is held with the palm facing up (if the hand were opened, the fingers would point to the left).	The hand is held in front of the left upper arm.	The hand moves firmly towards the signer and to the left while the extended fingers and thumb close (forming a K hand); the movement ends with the hand touching the left upper arm.	drug hypodermic inject injection innoculate innoculation jab syringe vaccinate vaccination drug abuser[1] drug addict[1] drugs[1] junkie[1] blood sample[2] take blood[2]	782

Notes   1 If the movement is repeated, the sign produced is **drug abuser, drug addict, drugs, junkie.**

2 If the right hand rests against the side of the left forearm and then moves to the right while closing (forming a K hand), the sign produced is **blood sample, take blood.**

783 Ø V̈ɑ⊥ $\overset{\circ}{\underset{z}{\cdot}}$

784 Ø V̈ɔ⊥ $\overset{\circ}{\underset{\check{}}{\cdot}}$

785 Ø ⌐V̈⊥∧ $\overset{\cdot}{\underset{<}{\underset{\top}{\overline{}}}}$

786 Ø V̈⊥∧ $\overset{\circ}{\vee}$

The index and middle fingers (spread apart) are extended from the fist and bent at the palm knuckles.

The main variant of V̈ is V, where the fingers are held straight, rather than bent at the palm knuckles. In some cases, V̈ is required by the physical constraints of the sign production. In other cases, the use of V̈ or V depends on personal choice. (See also separate entry for V).

V̈ has several different *classifier* functions in the established lexicon and is used as a classifying element in established signs:

– it is used as a *size and shape* classifier to represent two narrow, joined but moveable extensions, particularly human legs, and thereby persons. The V̈ *legs* classifier is highly productive. Examples of its use in the established lexicon include **walk** (sign 784), **mount** (sign 796), **fall over** (sign 799) and **lie down** (sign 802). It may also express other long, narrow items as in **earrings** (sign 790);

– it is also used as a *tracing size and shape* classifier to trace the outline and positioning of stripes (including those indicating rank), strips, ribbons and collars. Examples include **mayor** (sign 793), **officer** (sign 794) and **police** (sign 795);

– it has a specialised use to indicate *duality* or 'two–ness'. This can be seen primarily in two sets of signs, those relating to eyes and those relating to the number 2. Examples relating to the two eyes include **look** (sign 788) and **gaze** (sign 788). Examples incorporating the number 2 include **both** (sign 783), **two days later** (sign 789) and **in two years' time** (sign 798).

– it is used infrequently as a *handling* classifier to indicate the handling of narrow objects. The most common examples of this usage are **cigarette** (sign 757) and **smoke** (sign 757) which may use V̈ or V;

– it is used as an *instrumental* classifier to indicate implements, tools or utensils which have two narrow, joined but moveable extensions, such as **scissors** (sign 752) and **compass** (sign 773) which may use V̈ or V.

It expresses the right-hand component of the letter v of the British manual alphabet and also expresses the v in the Irish and American one-handed alphabets. It occurs in a number of initial letter handshape signs, such as **vegetable** (sign 770), **virgin** (sign 770), **vodka** (sign 770) and **video** (sign 775) which may use V̈ or V.

Handshape and orientation	Location, hand arrangement and contact	Movement	Glosses	
The V̈ hand is held with the palm facing up (if the hand were opened, the fingers would point away from the signer).	The hand is held in front of the body.	The hand makes two short movements from side to side.	both (you both) couple pair	783
The V̈ hand is held with the palm facing down (if the hand were opened, the fingers would point away from the signer).	The hand is held in front of the body.	The extended fingers wiggle and, at the same time, the hand moves away from the signer.	walk	784
The V̈ hand is held with the palm facing away from the signer (if the hand were opened, the fingers would point up).	The hand is held in front of the body at an angle, so that the palm is turned to the left.	The hand makes a firm movement away from the signer and, at the same time, to the left, with the arm bending from the elbow.	get knotted * get stuffed * to hell with *	785
Non-manual features The brows are furrowed, the nose is wrinkled and the top teeth are touching the lower lip; the mouth opens with the lips stretched and the teeth clenched, and the eye gaze is directed in line with the movement.				
Notes * Directional verb.				
The V̈ hand is held with the palm facing away from the signer (if the hand were opened, the fingers would point up).	The hand is held in front of the body.	The hand moves down while twisting at the wrist, so that the palm faces up.	drop fall	786

787 ○ V̈ᴛʌ ⚬̇ω̇z̥·

788 ○ V̈⊥ʌ ⚬̣̇

789 Ɜ ⁱV̈ᴛʌ ˣᴨ̄⊥

790 ⊃ V̈ơ< ⚬̇ω̇н̥·

791 ◡ V̈<ʌ ⚬̇ω̇⊥·

792 π V̈ᴛʌ ˣ

793 [] V̈ᴛ< ˇˇ̌ˣˣ̌

794 ˇᴦ1 V̈ᴛʌ (⚬̌ˣ)·

The index and middle fingers (spread apart) are extended from the fist and bent at the palm knuckles.

Handshape and orientation	Location, hand arrangement and contact	Movement	Glosses	
The **V̈** hand is held with the palm facing towards the signer (if the hand were opened, the fingers would point up).	The hand is held in front of the face.	The hand makes short twisting movements from side to side from the wrist.	blind as a bat miss	787

Non-manual features   The tongue protrudes between the teeth.

The **V̈** hand is held with the palm facing away from the signer (if the hand were opened, the fingers would point up).	The hand is held in front of the face.	The hand makes a short movement away from the signer.	look * see * watch * gaze * 1 observation 1 observe 1 observer 1 spectator 1 stare * 1 view * 1 viewer 1	788

Notes   * Directional verb.

1 If the hand moves and is then held still, the sign produced is **gaze, observation, observe, observer, spectator, stare, view, viewer.**   ⌒ V̈⊥ʌ ˚⊥ø

The **V̈** hand is held with the palm facing towards the signer (if the hand were opened, the fingers would point up).	The hand is held with the middle fingertip touching the right cheek.	The hand bends away from the signer from the wrist.	day after tomorrow days (two days later) days (two days' time)	789
The **V̈** hand is held with the palm facing down (if the hand were opened, the fingers would point to the left).	The hand is held beside the ear.	The hand makes short twisting movements towards and away from the signer from the wrist.	cherry earrings	790
The **V̈** hand is held with the palm facing left (if the hand were opened, the fingers would point up).	The hand is held in front of the chin.	The hand twists away from the signer at the wrist; the movement is repeated.	pear *	791

Notes   * This sign may be produced with the hand making a repeated movement to the left, so that the index finger brushes across the chin each time.   ⌣ V̈<ʌ ˟˟˟< ˚

The **V̈** hand is held with the palm facing towards the signer (if the hand were opened, the fingers would point up).	The hand is held with the fingers in front of the neck.	The index and middle fingertips touch the neck.	disappoint disappointment frustrate * frustration * miss †	792

Non-manual features   The lips are pressed together and the corners of the mouth are turned down.

Notes   * This sign may be produced with a repeated movement.   π V̈⊤ʌ ˟·

† Regional sign.

The **V̈** hand is held with the palm facing towards the signer (if the hand were opened, the fingers would point to the left).	The hand is held with the tips of the extended fingers touching the left side of the upper chest.	The hand moves down and to the right, and then up and to the right, maintaining contact with the chest throughout.	civic council councillor mayor mayoress	793
The **V̈** hand is held with the palm facing towards the signer (if the hand were opened, the fingers would point up).	The hand is held with the extended fingers above the left shoulder.	The hand makes a short downward movement, so that the tips of the fingers touch the left shoulder; the movement is repeated.	officer	794

Notes   This sign may also be produced using a **V̈** handshape.   Π V̈⊤⊥ (˚v̈x)·

795 ō̄ V̈ɔ⊥ ᵀₓ

796 Ḡ>⊥ ¹ V̈<⊥ ⁿᵖᵥ

797 Ḡ>⊥ ₁ₓ V̈<⊥ ᵉˣᵀᵥ

798 G̈>⊥ ₁ₓ V̈<⊥ ᵉˣᵥᵥ

799 B̄ɑ⊥ ₓ V̈ɔ⊥ ⁿᵥₒ ᵛ

800 B̄ɑ> ₓ V̈ɔ⊥ ᵒ

801 B̄ɑ> ₓ V̈ɔ⊥ ^·

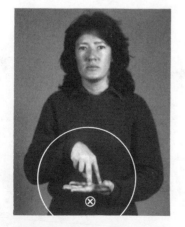

[444]

V

The index and middle fingers (spread apart) are extended from the fist and bent at the palm knuckles.

Handshape and orientation	Location, hand arrangement and contact	Movement	Glosses	
The **V̈** hand is held with the palm facing down (if the hand were opened, the fingers would point away from the signer).	The left hand is held in front of the body with the palm facing down; the right hand is held with the tips of the extended fingers resting on the left wrist.	The right hand moves towards the signer; the extended right fingers maintain contact with the left wrist throughout.	constable* police* policeman* police officer* policewoman*	795

Notes * The following notes apply to all glosses:

This sign may be produced with a **V** handshape; the index and middle fingertips tap the left wrist twice.

This sign may be produced with a **V** handshape; the extended fingers flex, so that the tips of the fingers brush the left wrist; the movement is repeated.

The left **G** hand is held with the palm facing right; the right **V̈** hand is held with the palm facing left (if the hands were opened, the fingers would all point away from the signer).	The hands are held side by side in front of the body; the right hand is held higher than the left hand.	The right hand twists down and, at the same time, to the left from the wrist; the movement ends with the left index finger held between the extended right fingers.	get on mount	796
The left **G̈** hand is held with the palm facing right; the right **V̈** hand is held with the palm facing left (if the hands were opened, the fingers would all point away from the signer).	The hands are held side by side in front of the body; the right middle finger rests on the left index finger.	The right hand makes an anti-clockwise circle in the vertical plane at right angles to the signer's body, moving around the left index finger; the movement ends with the right middle finger touching the left index finger.	year before last years (two years ago)	797
The left **G̈** hand is held with the palm facing right; the right **V̈** hand is held with the palm facing left (if the hands were opened, the fingers would all point away from the signer).	The hands are held side by side in front of the body; the right middle finger rests on the left index finger.	The right hand makes a clockwise circle in the vertical plane at right angles to the signer's body, moving around the left index finger; the movement ends with the right middle finger touching the left index finger.	year after next years (in two years' time) years (two years later)	798
The left **B** hand is held with the palm facing up and the fingers pointing away from the signer; the right **V̈** hand is held with the palm facing down (if the hand were opened, the fingers would point away from the signer).	The hands are held in front of the body; the right index and middle fingertips rest on the left palm.	The right hand twists at the wrist, so that the palm faces up, while moving to the right and, at the same time, the extended fingers straighten (forming a **V** hand).	collapse faint fall over	799
The left **B** hand is held with the palm facing up and the fingers pointing to the right; the right **V̈** hand is held with the palm facing down (if the hand were opened, the fingers would point away from the signer).	The hands are held in front of the body; the right index and middle fingertips are held on the left palm.	No movement.	stand wait	800
The left **B** hand is held with the palm facing up and the fingers pointing to the right; the right **V̈** hand is held with the palm facing down (if the hand were opened, the fingers would point away from the signer).	The hands are held in front of the body; the tips of the extended right fingers rest on the left palm.	The right hand moves up and then returns to touch the left palm; the movement is repeated.	bounce on a trampoline trampoline	801

802 $\overline{B}\alpha> {}_x \ddot{V}<v {}^{>}_x$

803 $\emptyset \ddot{V}>\perp \mid \ddot{V}<\perp {}^{n<n}_{v\ v}$

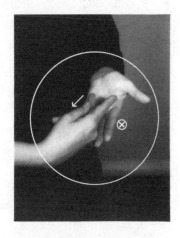

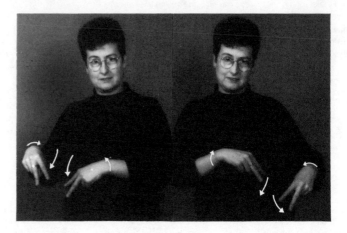

804 $\emptyset \overline{B}\alpha> {}_x \ddot{V}\sigma\perp {}^{\circ}_{v}$

The index and middle fingers (spread apart) are extended from the fist and bent at the palm knuckles.

Handshape and orientation	Location, hand arrangement and contact	Movement	Glosses	
The left **B** hand is held with the palm facing up and the fingers pointing to the right; the right V̈ hand is held with the palm facing up (if the hand were opened, the fingers would point to the left).	The hands are held in front of the body; the backs of the extended right fingers rest on the left palm.	The right hand moves to the right, maintaining contact with the left palm throughout.	lie lie down	802
The left V̈ hand is held with the palm facing right; the right V̈ hand is held with the palm facing left (if the hands were opened, the fingers would all point away from the signer).	The hands are held side by side in front of the body.	The hands bend down at the wrists and then move to the left before bending down again at the wrists.	dance dancer dancing	803

Non-manual features   The head tilts to the right and then to the left.

The left **B** hand is held with the palm facing up and the fingers pointing to the right; the right V̈ hand is held with the palm facing down (if the hand were opened, the fingers would point away from the signer).	The hands are held in front of the body; the right index and middle fingertips are held on the left palm.	The hands remain together and make a short, firm, downward movement.	adamant determined independent stand firm stubborn take a stand	804

805 Ø V̈ɔ⊥ ⱥ̂

806 Ø V̈ɔ⊥ ⱥ̆

807 Ø V̈<∧ ⱥ̊

808 ⊔ V̈⊤∧ ⱬ̊˙

The bent index and middle fingers are extended from the fist and spread apart.

The main *variants* of V̈ relate to the degree of bending of the index and middle fingers. The fingers may be relatively loosely bent, as in **aged** (sign 810) and **evening** (sign 811). In other cases, the fingers may be tightly bent, as in **clapped out** (sign 812) and **kneel** (sign 824).

V̈ has several different *classifier* functions in the established lexicon and is used as a classifying element in established signs:

– it is used as a *size and shape* classifier to represent two narrow, bent, fixed but moveable extensions, particularly human legs, and thereby persons. As with Ḧ, there is no necessary focus on bent legs when V̈ is used as the V̈ *legs* classifier. Examples include **go upstairs** (sign 805), **disembark** (sign 818) and **drunk** (sign 819). It is also used to show the bent extensions of the overhead trolley in **bus** (sign 807) and the curved punctuation marks in **inverted commas** (sign 823);

– it has a specialised use to indicate what may be termed *duality* or 'two-

ness'. This can be seen primarily in signs relating to the eyes, as in **blind** (sign 809) and **lipread** (sign 814);

– it is also used as a *tracing size and shape* classifier to trace the outline and positioning of stripes or lines, especially where these are irregular in form. V̈ could be used to show markings, as seen, for example, on the faces of certain ardent football fans;

– it is used as a *handling* classifier where objects are held by the two bent fingers, for example, the safety straps in a tube train, as in **tube** (sign 807);

– it is used as an *instrumental* classifier to indicate implements, tools or utensils which have two, possibly bent, narrow, fixed but moveable extensions. Thus it may be used to refer to a fork, even though the prongs are not bent, possibly to emphasise that the prongs are stuck in another object. This is probably the basis of the sign **potato** (sign 817).

Handshape and orientation	Location, hand arrangement and contact	Movement	Glosses	
The V̈ hand is held with the palm facing down (if the hand were opened, the fingers would point away from the signer).	The hand is held in front of the body.	The hand moves up and away from the signer and, at the same time, the extended fingers wiggle.	**go upstairs** * **stairs** * **walk upstairs** * **escalator** [1] **go up by escalator** [1]	805
Notes * This sign may be produced with a series of short movements away from the signer and, at the same time, up.		Ø V̈ɔ⊥ (ᵒᴅ V ᴧ ⊥)		
1 If the movement is slow, and the fingers do not wiggle, the sign produced is **escalator, go up by escalator**.		Ø V̈ɔ⊥ ᴧ⊥		
The V̈ hand is held with the palm facing down (if the hand were opened, the fingers would point away from the signer).	The hand is held in front of the body.	The hand moves down and away from the signer and, at the same time, the extended fingers wiggle.	**go downstairs** * **stairs** * **walk downstairs** * **escalator** [1] **go down by escalator** [1]	806
Notes * This sign may be produced with a series of short movements away from the signer and, at the same time, down.		Ø V̈ɔ⊥ (ᵒᴅ V ⊥)		
1 If the movement is slow, and the fingers do not wiggle, the sign produced is **escalator, go down by escalator**.		Ø V̈ɔ⊥ v⊥		
The V̈ hand is held with the palm facing left (if the hand were opened, the fingers would point up).	The hand is held in front of the shoulder.	The hand makes a short movement away from the signer.	**bus** * **metro** *[1] **subway** *[1] **tube** *[1] **underground** *[1] **underground train** *[1]	807
Notes * Regional sign.				
1 If the movement is changed to a short repeated downward movement, the sign produced is **metro, subway, tube, underground, underground train**.		Ø V̈<ᴧ ᵒv·		
The V̈ hand is held with the palm facing towards the signer (if the hand were opened, the fingers would point up).	The hand is held with the extended fingers in front of the eyes.	The hand makes two short movements from side to side.	**blind as a bat** **miss**	808
Non-manual features The lips are rounded and pushed forward.				

809 ⊔ Ü⊤ʌ ^ω̇z

810 ⊔ Ü⊤ʌ ^v̊

811 ⊔ Ü⊤ʌ ^ẋ·

812 ⊔ Ü⊤ʌ ^e@o̊<ᴧx⊤⊥

813 ⊔ eÜ<ʌ ^x○:o<ᴠ⊥<

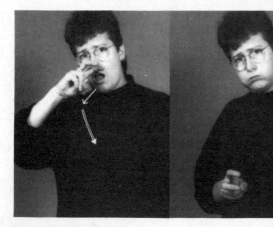

814 ⌣ Ü⊤ʌ ^<@o̊<

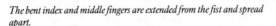

The bent index and middle fingers are extended from the fist and spread apart.

Handshape and orientation	Location, hand arrangement and contact	Movement	Glosses	
The V̈ hand is held with the palm facing towards the signer (if the hand were opened, the fingers would point up).	The hand is held with the extended fingers in front of the eyes.	The hand makes short twisting movements from side to side at the wrist.	blind blind person	809
The V̈ hand is held with the palm facing towards the signer (if the hand were opened, the fingers would point up).	The hand is held with the extended fingers in front of the nose.	The hand makes a short downward movement.	aged * † ageing * † dark * † elderly * † evening * † night * † old * † tonight * †	810

Notes   * This sign may be produced with the hand bending towards the signer from the wrist.   ⊔ V̈ㅜʌ ᴅ�

† This sign may be produced with a repeated movement.   ⊔ V̈ㅜʌ or ⊔ V̈ㅜʌ

The V̈ hand is held with the palm facing towards the signer (if the hand were opened, the fingers would point up).	The hand is held with the bent fingers in front of the nose.	The index and middle fingertips tap the nose twice.	evening * tonight * night *	811

Notes   * Regional sign.   ⊔ V̈ㅜʌ ˣ

The V̈ hand is held with the palm facing towards the signer (if the hand were opened, the fingers would point up).	The hand is held with the fingers in front of the nose.	The hand makes two small clockwise circles in the vertical plane at right angles to the signer's body; the index and middle fingertips brush the nose in completing each circle.	clapped out lousy pathetic rotten rubbish tacky tatty useless	812

Non-manual features   The eyes are narrowed, the nose is wrinkled and the tongue tip protrudes between the teeth.

The V̈ hand is held with the palm facing left (if the hand were opened, the fingers would point up).	The hand is held with the index finger touching the tip of the nose.	The hand makes a short movement away from the signer and, at the same time, to the right and then moves sharply down and, at the same time, to the left.	loads lots	813

Non-manual features   The mouth is open and then the cheeks puff out; the brows are furrowed throughout.

The V̈ hand is held with the palm facing towards the signer (if the hand were opened, the fingers would point up).	The hand is held with the extended fingers in front of the mouth.	The hand makes small anti-clockwise circles in the vertical plane parallel to the signer's body.	lipread * lipreader * lipspeak * lipspeaker * oral * oralism * oralist *	814

Notes   * This sign may be produced with a repeated movement.   ⏝ V̈ㅜʌ

815 ∪ Ⓥᴛᴧ ˣ˙

816 π Ⓥᴛᴧ ˣ˙

817 A̅ʊ⊥ Ⓥʊ< ˣ˙

818 A̅ᴛ> ˣ Ⓥᴛ⊥ ᵢⱽ

819 B̅ɑ> ˣ Ⓥʊ⊥ ⱽ⊥@ˣ˙

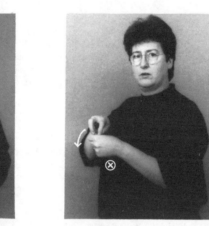

820 ∕ B̅ʊ> ˣ Ⓥʊ< ^⌄ˣ⌵ᴇ

V

The bent index and middle fingers are extended from the fist and spread apart.

Handshape and orientation	Location, hand arrangement and contact	Movement	Glosses	
The V̈ hand is held with the palm facing towards the signer (if the hand were opened, the fingers would point up).	The hand is held in front of the chin.	The index and middle fingertips tap the chin twice.	aunt battery electric electricity uncle niece¹	815

Notes 1 If the middle and index fingertips are held against the chin, and the hand makes short twisting movements from side to side at the wrist, the sign produced is **niece**.

$$\cup \ddot{V}_{T\wedge}\left(\substack{\times \\ \circ \\ \omega \\ z}\cdot\right)$$

The V̈ hand is held with the palm facing towards the signer (if the hand were opened, the fingers would point up).	The hand is held in front of the neck.	The tips of the extended fingers tap the neck several times.	contain oneself keep a straight face suppress one's laughter	816

Non-manual features The shoulders are hunched, the eyebrows are raised and the eyes are open wide; the lips are pressed together and the cheeks slightly puffed out.

The left **A** hand is held with the palm facing down (if the hand were opened, the fingers would point away from the signer). The right V̈ hand is held with the palm facing down (if the hand were opened, the fingers would point to the left).	The hands are held in front of the body; the right hand is held above the left hand.	The right index and middle fingertips tap the back of the left hand twice.	Ireland Irish potato	817
The left **A** hand is held with the palm facing towards the signer (if the hand were opened, the fingers would point to the right). The right V̈ hand is held with the palm facing down (if the hand were opened, the fingers would point away from the signer).	The hands are held in front of the body; the right hand is held above the left hand with the tips of the extended fingers resting on the left hand.	The right hand makes a short movement away from the signer and then down.	alight* disembark* get off* get out*	818

Notes * This sign may be produced with a left Ḧ handshape.

$$\bar{\ddot{H}}_{>\perp} \times \ddot{V}_{\mho\perp} \stackrel{\circ\circ}{\perp_{\vee}}$$

The left **B** hand is held with the palm facing up and the fingers pointing to the right; the right V̈ hand is held with the palm facing down (if the hand were opened, the fingers would point away from the signer).	The hands are held in front of the body; the right index and middle fingertips are held on the left palm.	The right hand makes clockwise circles in the horizontal plane; the index and middle fingertips are held against the left palm throughout.	drunk inebriated intoxicated legless	819
The left **B** hand is held with the palm facing down and the fingers pointing to the right; the right V̈ hand is held with the palm facing down (if the hand were opened, the fingers would point to the left).	The hands are held in front of the body; the right middle and index fingertips rest on the back of the left hand.	The right hand moves up and to the left while the extended fingers open; the hand then moves down, so that the tips of the extended fingers touch the left forearm.	frog frog hopping frog jumping toad toad hopping toad jumping	820

821 Ø V̈ꝋᴧ ⊤x V̈ꝋᴧ ᵐ·

822 Ø V̈⊤> ، V̈⊤< ×·

823 Ø V̈⊥ᴧ V̈⊥ᴧ ⸰ᴈ̊x

824 Ø B̄ɑ> × V̈⊤ᴠ ᵛ̊

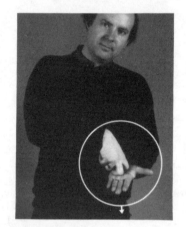

The bent index and middle fingers are extended from the fist and spread apart.

Handshape and orientation	Location, hand arrangement and contact	Movement	Glosses	
Two V̈ hands are held with the palms facing down (if the hands were opened, the fingers would all point up).	The hands are held crossed over in front of the body with the sides of the wrists held together.	The extended fingers flex twice.	**Austria** **Austrian**	821
Two V̈ hands are held with the palms facing towards the signer (if the hands were opened, the left fingers would point to the right and the right fingers would point to the left).	The hands are held side by side in front of the body.	The knuckles of the extended fingers tap together twice.	**Brussels**	822
Two V̈ hands are held with the palms facing away from the signer (if the hands were opened, the fingers would all point up).	The hands are held in front of the body.	The hands make a short twisting movement at the wrists, so that the palms face towards each other.	**entitled** * **inverted commas** * **quote** * **title** * **quasi** *[1] **so-called** *[1] **terminology** *[1]	823

Notes   * The following notes apply to all glosses:

This sign may be produced with the extended fingers flexing.   ∅ V̈⊥ʌ V̈⊥ʌ ᵐ or ∅ V̈⊥ʌ V̈⊥ʌ ᵐ·

This sign may be produced with the palms facing towards each other.   ∅ V̈>ʌ V̈<ʌ ᵐ or ∅ V̈>ʌ V̈<ʌ ᵐ·

1 If the movement is repeated, the sign produced is **quasi, so-called, terminology.**   ∅ V̈⊥ʌ V̈⊥ʌ ⨳·

| The left **B** hand is held with the palm facing up and the fingers pointing to the right; the right **V̈** hand is held with the palm facing towards the signer (if the hand were opened, the fingers would point down). | The hands are held in front of the body; the knuckles of the right index and middle fingers are held on the left palm. | The hands remain together and make a short downward movement. | **kneel**
grovel [1] | 824 |

Notes   1 If the knuckles of the extended right fingers rest on the left palm and then move away from the signer, maintaining contact with the left palm throughout, the sign produced is **grovel.**

B̄ɑ> ₓ V̈⊤∨ ˣ

825 ⊔ ^eV̈τ< × // V̈τ> ı V̈τ< × ·

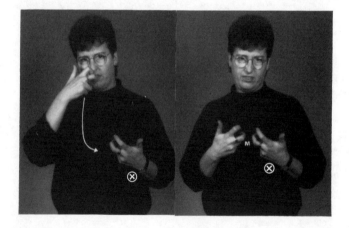

This is a relatively rare handshape. It is used as a *handling* classifier within the productive lexicon and as a classifying element in established signs:
– it is used as a *handling* classifier to indicate the handling of spherical or curved objects, such as a tenpin bowling ball. It may also be used instead of **C**, for example, in **apple** (sign 1695).

Handshape and orientation	Location, hand arrangement and contact	Movement	Glosses	
The right 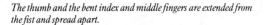 hand is held with the palm facing towards the signer (if the hand were opened, the fingers would point to the left).	The hand is held with the index finger touching the nose.	The hand moves down and, at the same time, away from the signer.	clapped out crummy lousy rotten rubbish	825
Two V̈ hands are held with the palms facing towards the signer (if the hands were opened, the left fingers would point to the right and the right fingers would point to the left).	The hands are held side by side in front of the body.	The right middle finger taps the left middle finger twice.	tacky tatty	

Non-manual features The brows are slightly furrowed, the nose is wrinkled and the lips are pushed forward with the tongue tip protruding between the top teeth and the lower lip.

826 Ø V̈ʊ⊥ ⊥̊V̊⊥̊V̊
           ∧ > ∧ <

827 ⊔ V̈⊤∧ ∩̊
               <

828 ˃⌐1 V̈⊤< × ·

829 ʊ V̈ʊ< ̊v ×

The bent index and middle fingers and bent thumb are extended from the fist in the shape of a "C"; the thumb is held parallel to the index finger.

The main *variants* of Ⅴ relate to the degree of bending of the index and middle fingers. The fingers may be relatively loosely bent as in **draughts** (sign 826) or relatively tightly bent as in **badge** (sign 828). Ⅴ has several different *classifier* functions in the established lexicon and is used as a classifying element in established signs:

– it is used as a *size and shape* classifier to represent round or spherical objects, as in **badge** (sign 828), **watch** (sign 829) and **stone** (the first

part of sign 830). It is also used to depict three narrow, bent extensions, such as the claws of birds;

– it is used as a *handling* classifier for round, spherical or chunky items, as in **draughts** (sign 826), **chess player** (sign 826) and **can't believe one's eyes** (sign 831) where there is metaphorical holding of the eyes (see *Introduction*).

Handshape and orientation	Location, hand arrangement and contact	Movement	Glosses	
The Ⅴ hand is held with the palm facing down (if the hand were opened, the fingers would point away from the signer).	The hand is held in front of the body.	The hand moves up and to the right in a short arc, and then up and to the left in a short arc, while moving away from the signer throughout.	draughts draughts player play draughts chess[1] chess player[1] play chess[1]	826
Notes　1 If two Ⅴ hands are used, moving towards and away from the signer alternately, the sign produced is **chess, chess player, play chess.**				
The Ⅴ hand is held with the palm facing towards the signer (if the hand were opened, the fingers would point up).	The hand is held in front of the nose.	The hand makes a short bending movement to the left at the wrist.	circus* clown*	827
Notes　* The following notes apply to all glosses:				
This sign may be produced with the palm facing left and the wrist twisting towards the signer.				
This sign may be produced using a 5 handshape.				
The Ⅴ hand is held with the palm facing towards the signer (if the hand were opened, the fingers would point to the left).	The hand is held in front of the left side of the upper chest.	The tips of the extended fingers and thumb tap the chest twice.	badge* brooch* committee* shop steward* steward* union* union member*	828
Notes　* This sign may be produced with the hand bending to the left from the wrist, so that the thumb and fingertips maintain contact with the chest throughout.				
The Ⅴ hand is held with the palm facing down (if the hand were opened, the fingers would point to the left).	The left forearm is positioned in front of the body (with the palm facing down); the right fingers are held above the left wrist.	The right index and middle fingertips make a short downward movement to touch the left wrist.	watch wristwatch	829

830 Gт>⌐₁ V̈<ʌ ₊ω̥ // Ø ⁵ᴅ⊥ ⁵ᴅ⊥ ˇᵛ·

831 Ö V̈⊤ʌ V̈⊤ʌ ᵒᵛ∩⊥

832 Ö V̈⊤ʌ V̈⊤ʌ ³ˣ·

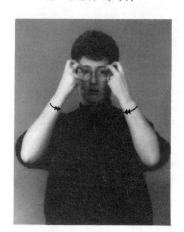

The bent index and middle fingers and bent thumb are extended from the fist in the shape of a "C"; the thumb is held parallel to the index finger.

Handshape and orientation	Location, hand arrangement and contact	Movement	Glosses	
The left **G** hand is held with the palm facing towards the signer (if the hand were opened, the fingers would point to the right). The right **V̈** hand is held with the palm facing left (if the hand were opened, the fingers would point up).	The hands are held side by side in front of the body.	The right hand makes a short twisting movement away from the signer from the wrist.	hail hailstones hailstorm	830
Two **5̈** hands are held with palms facing down (if the hands were opened, the fingers would all point away from the signer).	The hands are held in front of the body; the right hand is held higher than the left hand.	The hands move down and, at the same time, to the left; the movement is repeated.		
Non-manual features The cheeks are puffed out.				

Two **V̈** hands are held with the palms facing towards the signer (if the hands were opened, the fingers would all point up).	The hands are held with the bent fingers in front of the eyes.	The hands make a short downward movement while bending away from the signer at the wrists.	amazed
			cannot believe
			  one's eyes
			can't believe
			  one's eyes
			flabbergasted
			staggered
				831

Non-manual features The mouth is open with the tongue protruding slightly; as the hands move, the shoulders hunch and the head is pushed forward while the eyes open wide with the eyebrows raised.				
Two **V̈** hands are held with the palms facing towards the signer (if the hands were opened, the fingers would all point up).	The hands are held in front of the face.	The hands twist towards each other from the wrists several times.	owl	832

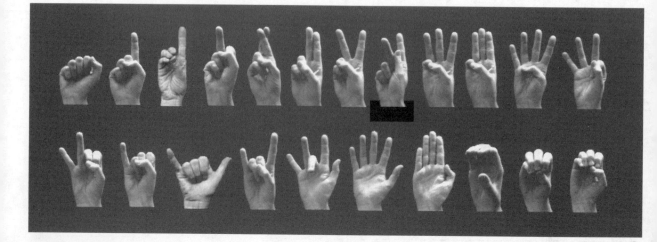

K

Handshape	Handshape description	Type	Sign entries
K	The thumb, index finger and middle finger are extended from the fist; the middle finger is bent at the palm knuckle and the pad of the thumb touches the middle joint of the middle finger.	Single dez Manual tab Double dez	833 – 835 836

833 Ø K<ʌ ᵚ

834 ⊑ Kʊ< ˣᴈ̇ᴴ

835 ˒ꟼ Kʊ< ˣ·

836 Ø (G̅ᴛ> Kʊ⊥ ⊙·)˒

K

*The thumb, index finger and middle finger are extended from the fist;
the middle finger is bent at the palm knuckle and the pad of the thumb
touches the middle joint of the middle finger.*

K could be seen as a variant of V̈. However, in the signs listed here, the thumb is either held out of the way of the extended fingers or touching the middle finger. K has comparable functions to V̈ as a *classifier* in the productive lexicon and as a classifying component of established signs:
– it is used as a *size and shape* classifier to indicate wedge-shaped objects or objects with two extensions, as in the fleshy outgrowth on a turkey's neck in **turkey** (sign 834) and the ribbons and medals of **decoration** (sign 835);

– it can be used as an *instrumental* classifier for tools, utensils or implements with two hinged extensions such as clothes pegs in **peg out on a line** (sign 836).

As K expresses the letters **k** and **p** of the American manual alphabet, it has some use in initial letter signs borrowed from American Sign Language, as in **Kendall School** and **philosophy** (see *Introduction*).

Handshape and orientation	Location, hand arrangement and contact	Movement	Glosses	
The K hand is held with the palm facing left (if the hand were opened, the fingers would all point up).	The hand is held in front of the body.	The pad of the thumb rubs across the pad of the middle finger; the movement is repeated.	**taxi**	833
The K hand is held with the palm facing down (if the hand were opened, the fingers would point to the left).	The back of the hand is held against the underside of the chin.	The hand twists towards and away from the signer at the wrist; the movement is repeated several times with the back of the hand held against the chin throughout.	**turkey**	834
The K hand is held with the palm facing down (if the hand were opened, the fingers would point to the left).	The hand is held in front of the left side of the upper chest.	The hand taps the chest twice.	**decoration medal**	835
The left G hand is held with the palm facing towards the signer (if the hand were opened, the fingers would point to the right). The right K hand is held with the palm facing down (if the hand were opened, the fingers would point away from the signer).	The hands are held in front of the body; the right hand is held above the left hand.	The right hand moves down, so that the left index finger is held between the right index and middle fingers; the movement is repeated several times, with the hands moving to the right throughout.	**clothes line hang on a clothes line/line hang out line peg out on a clothes line/line**	836

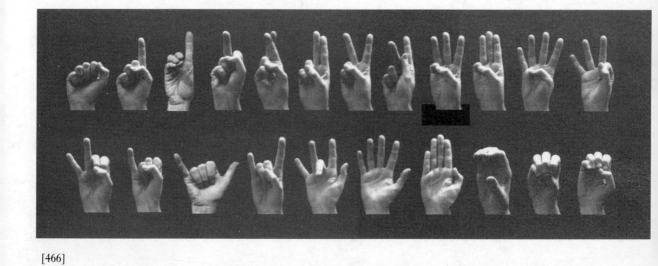

W

Handshape	Handshape description	Type	Sign entries
W	The index, middle and ring fingers are extended and spread apart.	Single dez Manual tab Double dez	837

837   Ø W⊥ʌ ᵛᵒₘᵛ

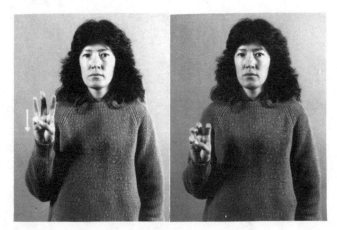

This is an infrequent handshape except for its use in initial letter handshape signs.

It has limited classifier functions in the productive lexicon and in established signs:

- it is used as a *size and shape* classifier to indicate objects with three or several narrow extensions or to represent objects viewed as lines, as in **streams of traffic** (see *Introduction*) and the Scottish sign **shipyard** (see *Introduction*);
- it is used as a *tracing size and shape* classifier to trace the position and shape of stripes or lines, as in **sergeant** (see *Introduction*);
- it is used as an *instrumental* classifier for tools, utensils or implements with three or more extensions or prongs, as in a three-pronged toasting fork.

W expresses the letter **w** in the Irish and American manual alphabets. As such, it is used for initial letter handshape signs borrowed from Irish Sign Language (ISL) and American Sign Language (ASL). Examples include **wine** and **will** from ISL and **Washington** (DC) from ASL. **Wales** (sign 837) appears to be an indigenous form.

Handshape and orientation	*Location, hand arrangement and contact*	*Movement*	*Glosses*	
The **W** hand is held with the palm facing away from the signer (if the hand were opened, the fingers would point up).	The hand is held in front of the body.	The hand makes a short downward movement and, at the same time, the fingers bend.	**Wales** **Welsh**	837

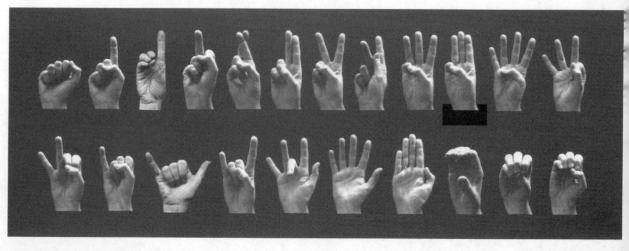

Wm

Handshape	Handshape description	Type	Sign entries
Wm	The index, middle and ring fingers are extended and held together.	Single dez Manual tab Double dez	838

838   B⍺⊥ Wmʊ< ˣ ˙

Wm has some use as a *size and shape* classifier to indicate relatively narrow, flat items, such as a sledge, table or bench. It can be seen as contrasting with G, H and B in showing different degrees of width. It is also used as a *tracing size and shape* classifier, for example to trace the shape of a cross in the sign bless (see *Introduction*).

Wm expresses the right-hand component of the letter m of the British manual alphabet. As such, it occurs in initial letter handshape signs such as mother (sign 838) and mad (see *Introduction*). Wm also ex-

presses the letter p of the Irish manual alphabet. As such, it occurs in initial letter handshape signs such as Irish Sign Language (ISL) influenced name signs, for example Patrick and Patricia (see *Introduction*). When bent at the palm knuckles, Wm also expresses the letter m of the Irish and American manual alphabets. As such, it occurs in borrowed initial letter handshape signs, such as ISL influenced name signs, for example Mary and Michael (see *Introduction*).

Handshape and orientation	Location, hand arrangement and contact	Movement	Glosses	
The left B hand is held with the palm facing up and the fingers pointing away from the signer; the right Wm hand is held with the palm facing down (if the hand were opened, the fingers would point to the left).	The hands are held in front of the body; the extended right fingers are held above the left palm.	The extended right fingers tap the left palm twice.	mam * mammy * mother * mum * mummy * parent(s)¹	838

Notes	* This sign may be produced using two B hands.	B̄ɑ⊥ Bʊ< ˣ˙
	1 This sign may be used as the first part of a compound sign meaning parent(s) (see 684 for the second part of the sign); the movements are not repeated.	B̄ɑ⊥ Wmʊ< ˣ ∥ H̄ʊ> Hʊ⊥ ˣ

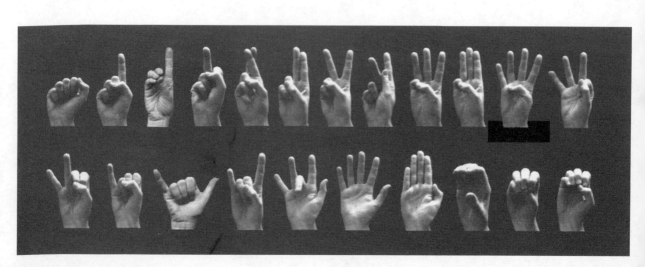

4

Handshape	Handshape description	Type	Sign entries
4	The hand is held flat with the fingers spread apart and the thumb held across the palm.	Single dez Manual tab	839
		Double dez	840

839 Ø 4 ɑ⊥ $\overset{\top}{\underset{\circ}{\vee}}$

840 Ø ᵉ4⊥ʌ ₁ₓ ᵉ4⊥ʌ $\overset{(\overset{\circ}{\div})\top\times}{\underset{\top}{\omega}\times}$

4 is used infrequently in the language.

– It has some use as a *size and shape* classifier to represent objects with several long, narrow extensions. In this usage it contrasts with the **G**, **V**, **W** and **5** handshapes. It has a specialised, but limited use as a *people* classifier (again contrasting with **G**, one person, and **5**, several or many people). This usage can be seen in **group** (sign 840) and **team** (sign 840). Comparable forms may be used for **panel**, **teams** and **platform presenters** (see *Introduction*);

– it is used as an *instrumental* classifier for implements, tools or utensils with several long, narrow extensions or prongs as in **fork** (sign 839) and **rake** (see *Introduction*);

– it is used to express *quantity* or *extent* as in rows and rows of people.

4 expresses the number **4** in several BSL number systems. This usage is lexicalised in sign such as **the four of us** (see *Introduction*).

Handshape and orientation	Location, hand arrangement and contact	Movement	Glosses	
The **4** hand is held with the palm facing up and the fingers pointing away from the signer.	The hand is held in front of the body.	The hand moves down and away from the signer while twisting at the wrist, so that the palm faces down.	dig with a fork fork	839
Two **4** hands are held with the palms facing away from the signer and the fingers pointing up.	The hands are held side by side in front of the body with the index fingertips touching.	The hands make a short movement apart while twisting at the wrists, so that the palms face towards the signer; the hands then move towards each other and, at the same time, away from the signer; the movement ends with the little fingers touching.	class group team party	840

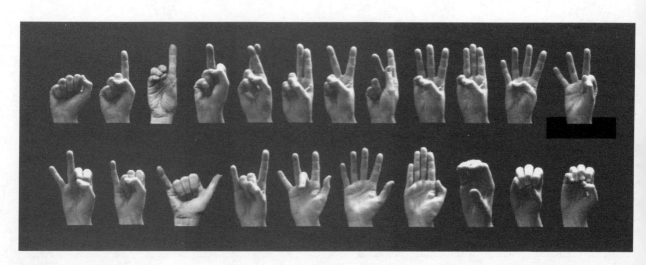

F

Handshape	Handshape description	Type	Sign entries
F	The fingers and thumb are extended and spread apart; the index finger is bent at the palm knuckle with the pad of the thumb touching the pad of the index finger.	Single dez Manual tab Double dez	841 – 863 864 – 873 874 – 892
F̄	The fingers and thumb are extended and spread apart; the index finger is bent at the palm knuckle and the thumb is held parallel to the index finger.	Single dez Manual tab Double dez	893 – 894 895 – 897 898 – 899

841 Ø Fᴄⱱ⊥ ³ⱽ

842 Ø Fᴄⱱ⊥ °ᵢ∘ᵥ

843 Ø Fᴄⱱ⊥ (°ᵥ·)
_>

844 Ø Fᴄⱱ⊥ (°ᴈᵥ·)

F

The fingers and thumb are extended and spread apart; the index finger is bent at the palm knuckle with the pad of the thumb touching the pad of the index finger.

The most common realisation of **F** is that described above. However, in a few examples the extended fingers may be held together, not spread, as in some regional signs from North–East England, such as **drive** and **mouse** (see *Introduction*) and signs derived from the letter **g** of the Irish manual alphabet (see further below).

Further *variants* relate to the nature of the contact between the index finger and thumb. In some signs, instead of forming a circle, the space is flattened and the index finger and thumb form a wedge-shape. This can be seen in the signs **breathalyse** (sign 857) and **advantage** (sign 861). **F** has several different *classifier* functions in the productive lexicon and also appears as a classifying element in established signs:

– it is used as a *size and shape* classifier to represent small, round objects, such as coins and buttons. In **Olympics** (sign 881) it represents the interlocking circles of the Olympic logo. It may also be used to indicate cylindrical objects such as a rod, a pole or a roll of paper as in **degree** (sign 875);

– it has a major use as a *handling* classifier to indicate small, delicate objects such as seeds, jewellery and flowers; objects which are long and thin, such as thread and wire and objects which are held with precision (such as darts) or gingerly (such as smelly socks). The many examples in this section include **needle** (sign 841), **seeds** (sign 843), **darts** (sign 854), **strike a match** (sign 873) and **wire** (sign 888);

– it is used as an *instrumental* classifier to represent implements, tools or utensils which have a circular component, such as a stethoscope;

– it is used to show *quantity* such as a number of small, round objects lying in rows or a number of small, round objects piled one on top of the other and *extent*, as in the length of a vertical, cylindrical object or a short, vertical rod.

The form with closed, extended fingers expresses the letter **g** of the Irish manual alphabet and the form with closed, extended fingers and thumb touching the middle of the index finger expresses the letter **f** of the Irish manual aphabet. As such, it occurs in initial letter handshape signs borrowed from Irish Sign Language such as **for** and **green** and initial letter name signs such as **Gerry** (see *Introduction*).

F also expresses the letter **f** of the American manual alphabet. As such, it occurs in initial letter handshape signs borrowed from American Sign Language such as **French** (see *Introduction*).

F is also the same as an old form of the letter **q** of the British manual alphabet. Some current BSL signs, such as **question** (sign 848), derive from older initial letter handshape signs.

Handshape and orientation	Location, hand arrangement and contact	Movement	Glosses	
The **F** hand is held with the palm facing down (if the hand were opened, the fingers would point away from the signer).	The hand is held in front of the body.	The hand twists to the left from the wrist.	**needle** **pin**	841
The **F** hand is held with the palm facing down (if the hand were opened, the fingers would point away from the signer).	The hand is held in front of the body.	The hand makes a small clockwise circle in the horizontal plane.	**stir with a** **teaspoon*** **teaspoon***	842
Notes * This sign may be produced with the hand making a small anticlockwise circle in the horizontal plane.		$\emptyset$ FɔꞱ		
The **F** hand is held with the palm facing down (if the hand were opened, the fingers would point away from the signer).	The hand is held in front of the body.	The hand makes several short downward movements while moving to the right throughout.	**plant*** **seed*** **seeds***[1] **sow***[1]	843
Notes * This sign may be produced using a ĝ hand.		$\emptyset$ ĜɔꞱ		
1 If the thumb tip rubs across the pad of the index finger several times with the hand moving to the right throughout, the sign produced is **seeds, sow**.		$\emptyset$ FɔꞱ or $\emptyset$ ĜɔꞱ		
The **F** hand is held with the palm facing down (if the hand were opened, the fingers would point away from the signer).	The hand is held in front of the body.	The hand moves to the left, while making short twisting movements from side to side at the wrist.	**sew** **tack**	844

845　Ø F⊤< ⊥

846　Ø F⊥∧ ⌄̊

847　Ø F<∧ ⊥̥̊⌄

848　Ø F<∧ <̥̊⌄

849　Ø F<⊥ ⌄̥̊

The fingers and thumb are extended and spread apart; the index finger is bent at the palm knuckle with the pad of the thumb touching the pad of the index finger.

Handshape and orientation	Location, hand arrangement and contact	Movement	Glosses	
The **F** hand is held with the palm facing towards the signer (if the hand were opened, the fingers would point to the left).	The hand is held in front of the chest.	The hand moves away from the signer.	incline † inclination invitation invite † select † selection voluntary [1] volunteer [1] attract * † [2] lure * † [2] tempt * † [2] temptation * [2]	845
Notes * This sign may be produced using two hands.				
† Directional verb.				
1 If the movement of the hand is from in front of the shoulder, the sign produced is **voluntary, volunteer**.				
2 If the mouth is open with the tongue resting on the lower lip, the sign produced is **attract, lure, tempt, temptation**.				
The **F** hand is held with the palm facing away from the signer (if the hand were opened, the fingers would point up).	The hand is held in front of the body.	The hand makes a short downward movement.	switch * switch on * switch off [1]	846
Notes * The following notes apply to all glosses:				
This sign may be produced with the hand bending up at the wrist while moving down.				
This sign may also be produced with a ĝ handshape.				
1 If the hand makes a short upward movement, the sign produced is **switch off**.				
The **F** hand is held with the palm facing left (if the hand were opened, the fingers would point up).	The hand is held in front of the body.	The hand makes a short firm movement away from the signer and, at the same time, down.	accurate exact meticulous perfect precise, proper stickler, strict joking (you must be joking) [1] kidding (you're kidding) [1] serious (you can't be serious) [1]	847
Notes 1 If the mouth is closed and the lips are stretched, the brows are furrowed and the eyes are narrowed, the sign produced is **you can't be serious, you must be joking, you're kidding**.				
The **F** hand is held with the palm facing left (if the hand were opened, the fingers would point up).	The hand is held in front of the body.	The hand makes a small anticlockwise circle in the vertical plane parallel to the signer's body.	enquire * † query * † cross-examine * † [1] cross-examination † [1] interview * † [1] investigate * † [1] investigation † [1] proof † [1] question * † [1]	848
Non-manual features Non-manual features appropriate for questions must be used.				
Notes * Directional verb.				
† Regional sign.				
1 If the movement is repeated, the sign produced is **cross-examine, cross-examination, interview, investigate, investigation, question** (see entry 2 in the English section), **proof**.				
The **F** hand is held with the palm facing left (if the hand were opened, the fingers would point away from the signer).	The hand is held in front of the body.	The hand makes a short, firm downward movement.	accurate exact meticulous perfect precise proper stickler, strict	849
Non-manual features The head is tilted slightly forward and to the right, and the lips are stretched.				

850   ∅   F<⊥ $^{ꓥ}_{ꓥ}$ 851   ⊓̄   F<ꓥ $^{○×·}_{3H}$

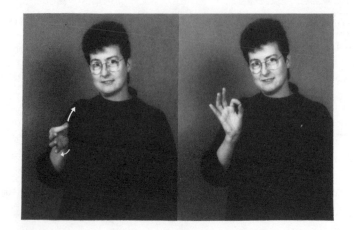

852   ⊓   F⊤< $^{×○}_{⊥ꓦ}$ 853   ⊓   F<ꓥ $^{○·}_{3H}$

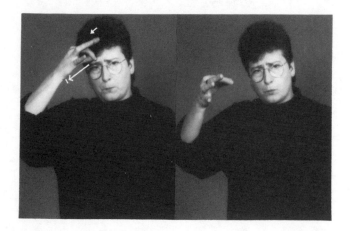

854   ◯   F<ꓥ $^{○}_{□}$ [5]·   855   ⊔   F⊤ꓥ $^{×3·}_{P}$

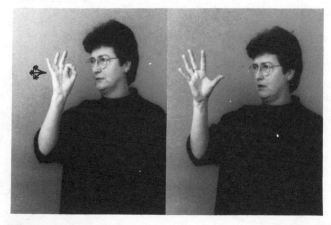

The fingers and thumb are extended and spread apart; the index finger is bent at the palm knuckle with the pad of the thumb touching the pad of the index finger.

Handshape and orientation	Location, hand arrangement and contact	Movement	Glosses	
The **F** hand is held with the palm facing left (if the hand were opened, the fingers would point away from the signer).	The hand is held in front of the body.	The hand bends up from the wrist.	café coffee cup cup of coffee/tea cuppa drink a cup of coffee/tea drink coffee/tea drink from a cup tea	850
Notes This sign may be produced with the hand held in front of the mouth.				
The **F** hand is held with the palm facing left (if the hand were opened, the fingers would point up).	The hand is held beside the top of the head, with the index finger and thumb tips touching the head.	The hand makes several short twisting movements towards and away from the signer at the wrist; the index finger and thumb tips are held against the head throughout.	hair	851
Notes * This sign may also be produced using an Â handshape.				
The **F** hand is held with the palm facing towards the signer (if the hand were opened, the fingers would point to the left).	The hand is held with the thumb and index finger tips touching the forehead.	The hand makes a short, firm movement down and, at the same time, away from the signer.	accurate exact meticulous perfect precise proper stickler strict supposed to happen *	852
Non-manual features The lips are stretched and the head tilts to the right, with the eyes narrowing as the hand twists. * Regional sign.				
The **F** hand is held with the palm facing left (if the hand were opened, the fingers would point up).	The hand is held in front and to the side of the forehead.	The hand makes short twisting movements towards and away from the signer at the wrist.	comedy * † comic * † committee * council *	853
Notes * This sign may be produced with the thumb and index fingertips held against the side of the forehead throughout. † Regional sign.				
The **F** hand is held with the palm facing left (if the hand were opened, the fingers would point up).	The hand is held in front of the face.	The hand makes a short movement away from the signer while opening (forming a **5** hand); the movement is repeated.	darts * darts player * play darts *	854
Notes * This sign may also be produced using an **O** hand.				
The **F** hand is held with the palm facing towards the signer (if the hand were opened, the fingers would point up).	The hand is held with the index finger and thumb tips touching the nose.	The hand twists away from the signer from the wrist; the movement ends with the palm facing down.	few hardly anyone hardly anything	855
Non-manual features The brows are slightly furrowed, the nose is wrinkled and the tongue tip protrudes between the top teeth and the lower lip.				

856 ⊔ F⊤< $\overset{\times}{\underset{v}{\perp}}$ 857 ⌣ F<ʌ $\overset{\times}{}$ 858 ⌣ F<ʌ $\overset{\times<\times}{\underset{\top}{\omega}}$

859 ⌣ F⊤< $\overset{\overset{\circ}{v}}{\underset{v}{\times}}$ 860 π F⊤< $^{(\times\mathtt{I})\cdot}$ 861 ⌐⌐< Fᴏ< $\overset{\overset{\circ}{v}}{\times}$

862 ⊔⌐< F⊤v $\overset{\times(\overset{n}{\underset{\perp}{}})\overset{\circ}{v}}{}$ 863 ᓂ Fᴏ⊥ $\overset{\mathtt{I}\times}{\underset{z}{z}}$

[486]

The fingers and thumb are extended and spread apart; the index finger is bent at the palm knuckle with the pad of the thumb touching the pad of the index finger.

Handshape and orientation	Location, hand arrangement and contact	Movement	Glosses	
The **F** hand is held with the palm facing towards the signer (if the hand were opened, the fingers would point to the left).	The hand is held with the index finger and thumb tips touching the nose.	The hand moves down and, at the same time, away from the signer.	fall for a lie/trick gullible sucker swallow a statement/story	856
Non-manual features The nose is slightly wrinkled and the tongue protrudes between the top teeth and the lower lip.				
The **F** hand is held with the palm facing left (if the hand were opened, the fingers would point up).	The hand is held in front of the mouth.	The thumb and index fingertips touch the lips.	breathalyse * breathalyser *	857
Non-manual features The cheeks puff out.				
Notes * This sign may be produced using two hands.		⌣ F >∧ ₓ F <∧_ρ ˣ		
The **F** hand is held with the palm facing left (if the hand were opened, the fingers would point up).	The hand is held beside the mouth.	The thumb and index finger tips touch the right side of the mouth; the hand then moves to the left while twisting at the wrist, so that the palm faces towards the signer, before the thumb and index finger tips touch the left side of the mouth.	flower garden	858
The **F** hand is held with the palm facing towards the signer (if the hand were opened, the fingers would point to the left).	The hand is held in front of the chin.	The hand makes a short downward movement, so that the thumb and index finger tips brush the chin; the movement is repeated.	few † tidy * visit * visitor *	859
Notes * Regional sign; the three meanings are associated with three different regions. † This sign can be produced using a ĝ hand.		∪ Ĝ⊤<		
The **F** hand is held with the palm facing towards the signer (if the hand were opened, the fingers would point to the left).	The hand is held in front of the neck.	The thumb and index finger tips touch the neck and then the hand moves away from the signer; the movement is repeated.	apprehensive risk risky	860
Non-manual features The lips are stretched with the teeth clenched, the eyebrows are raised and the head is pushed forward.				
The **F** hand is held with the palm facing down (if the hand were opened, the fingers would point to the left).	The hand is held with the index finger and thumb tips touching the right side of the upper chest.	The hand makes a short downward movement, maintaining contact with the chest throughout.	advantage benefit gain profit take advantage of something	861
The **F** hand is held with the palm facing towards the signer (if the hand were opened, the fingers would point down).	The hand is held with the index finger and thumb tips touching the right side of the waist.	The hand bends away from the signer at the wrist while moving away from the signer, and then makes a short downward movement.	donate * donation donor give a donation/ gratuity/tip * gratuity tip *	862
Notes * Directional verb.				
The right **F** hand is held with the palm facing down (if the hand were opened, the fingers would point away from the signer).	The left hand is positioned in front of the body; the right thumb and index finger tips pinch the back of the left hand.	The right hand makes short movements from side to side, holding the back of the left hand throughout.	flesh skin	863

864 A>⊥ | F<⊥၉ °⊤□[5]

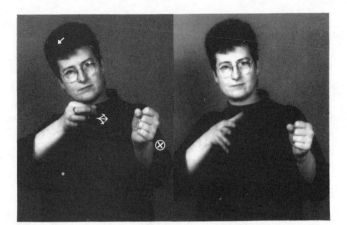

865 Å⊤> | F<⊥ <ᵥ@ₓ<ᵥ@ₒ

866 G>∧ ₁ₓ F<∧ ^ˣ

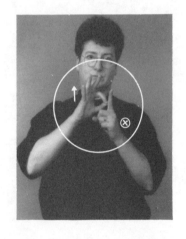

867 G>∧ ₁ₓ F<∧ ˣ᷂⊥

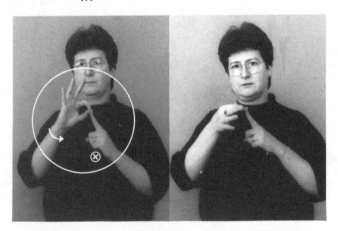

868 Ḡ>⊥ | F<∧ ⊥ᵛˣᵥ·

869 F̄>⊥ | F𝒪⊥ <ᵥ@ₒ·

F

The fingers and thumb are extended and spread apart; the index finger is bent at the palm knuckle with the pad of the thumb touching the pad of the index finger.

864-869

Handshape and orientation	Location, hand arrangement and contact	Movement	Glosses	
The left **A** hand is held with the palm facing right; the right **F** hand is held with the palm facing left (if the hands were opened, the fingers would all point away from the signer).	The hands are held side by side in front of the body; the right hand is held nearer to the signer than the left hand.	The right hand makes a short movement towards the signer and then opens (forming a **5** hand).	archer archery bow bow and arrow shoot an arrow with a bow	864

Non-manual features The eyes are narrowed and the head is tilted to the right.

The left **A** hand is held with the palm facing towards the signer (if the hand were opened, the fingers would point to the right). The right **F** hand is held with the palm facing left (if the hand were opened, the fingers would point away from the signer).	The hands are held side by side in front of the body.	The right hand makes small clockwise circles in the vertical plane parallel to the signer's body; the right thumb and index finger tips brush the left thumb in completing each circle.	court case enquiry interview query question trial	865
The left **G** hand is held with the palm facing right; the right **F** hand is held with the palm facing left (if the hands were opened, the fingers would all point up).	The hands are held side by side in front of the body; the right index finger and thumb tips are touching the base of the left index finger.	The right hand moves up, maintaining contact with the left index finger throughout.	improve improvement promote[1] promotion[1]	866

Notes 1 If the right finger and thumb tips touch the base of the left index finger and then move up before touching the tip of the finger, the sign produced is **promote, promotion.**

$$\text{G} \text{>} \wedge \;_{|}\; \text{F} \text{<} \wedge \quad {}^{\times}\overset{\circ}{\wedge}{}^{\times}$$

The left **G** hand is held with the palm facing right; the right **F** hand is held wit the palm facing left (if the hands were opened, the fingers would all point up).	The hands are held side by side in front of the body; the right thumb and index finger tips are held against the left index fingertip.	The right hand twists down and, at the same time, away from the signer at the wrist; the right thumb and index finger tips maintain contact with the left index fingertip throughout.	point*	867

Notes * This sign may be produced using a right **ĝ** hand.

$$\text{G} \text{>} \wedge \;_{|\times}\; \hat{\text{G}} \text{<} \wedge \quad \overset{\times}{\underset{\perp}{\omega}}$$

The left **G** hand is held with the palm facing right (if the hand were opened, the fingers would point away from the signer). The right **F** hand is held with the palm facing left (if the hand were opened, the fingers would point up).	The hands are held side by side in front of the body; the left hand is held higher than the right hand and the right index finger is turned upwards.	The right hand moves away from the signer and, at the same time, down, so that the right thumb and index finger tips brush the tip of the left index finger; the movement is repeated.	detail fussy meticulous nitpicking pernickety[1] stickler[1] strict[1] minutiae[2] pedantic[2]	868

Non-manual features The lips are tightly rounded and the nose is slightly wrinkled.

Notes 1 If the movement is not repeated, the sign produced is **pernickety, stickler, strict.**

$$\overline{\text{G}} \text{>} \perp \;_{|}\; \text{F} \text{<} \wedge \quad \overset{\perp}{\underset{\perp}{\overset{\times}{\vee}}}$$

2 If the movement is repeated several times, the sign produced is **minutiae, pedantic.**

The left **F** hand is held with the palm facing right; the right **F** hand is held with the palm facing down (if the hands were opened, the fingers would all point away from the signer).	The hands are held side by side in front of the body; the right hand is held higher than the left hand.	The right hand makes small clockwise circles in the vertical plane parallel to the signer's body.	darn embroider embroidery sew sewing stitch	869

870 $\overline{B}a> Fʊ< \overset{ω⊤·}{_∧}$

871 $\overline{B}a> _x F⊥∧_ρ \overset{⊥}{^∧}$

872 $\overline{B}a>_| \sqrt{F}<⊥ \overset{n}{^∧}$

873 $\overline{\hat{B}}>⊥_ρ | Fʊ< \overset{ω⊤×ω⊤}{⊤}$

874 $\emptyset\ Fʊ⊥\ Fʊ⊥ \overset{⊥(\overset{n}{^∧⊤})\overset{°}{ᵛ}}{}$

875 $\emptyset\ Fʊ⊥ _{|x} Fʊ⊥ \overset{÷}{}$

876 $\emptyset\ F⊤ᵛ | F⊤ᵛ \overset{∧}{}$

The fingers and thumb are extended and spread apart; the index finger is bent at the palm knuckle with the pad of the thumb touching the pad of the index finger.

Handshape and orientation	Location, hand arrangement and contact	Movement	Glosses	
The left **B** hand is held with the palm facing up and the fingers pointing to the right; the right **F** hand is held the palm facing down (if the hand were opened, the fingers would point to the left).	The hands are held in front of the body; the right hand is held above the left hand.	The right hand moves up while twisting at the wrist, so that the palm faces towards the signer; the movement is repeated.	chips * crisps † eat chips * eat crisps †	870

Notes * This sign may be produced with a left **B̄** handshape.

$$\overline{\overline{B}}α> \quad F℧< \quad {}^{ω}_{\top} {}^{\cdot}_{\wedge}$$

† This sign may be produced with a left **B̄** handshape with the palm facing right (the fingers, if straight, would point away from the signer).

$$\overline{\overline{B}}>\!\!\top \quad F℧< \quad {}^{ω}_{\top}{}^{\cdot}_{\wedge}$$

The left **B** hand is held with the palm facing up and the fingers pointing to the right; the right **F** hand is held held with the palm facing away from the signer (if the hand were opened, the fingers would point up).	The hands are held in front of the body; the right index finger and thumb tips rest on the left palm.	The right hand moves away from the signer and, at the same time, up.	donate * donation donor give a donation/ gratuity/tip * gratuity tip *	871

Notes * Directional verb.

$$\emptyset \quad F\!\perp\!\wedge \quad {}^{\wedge}_{\perp}$$

The left **B** hand is held with the palm facing up and the fingers pointing to the right; the right **F** hand is held with the palm facing left (if the hands were opened, the fingers would point away from the signer).	The hands are held side by side in front of the body; the right hand is held higher than the left hand.	The right arm bends up from the elbow.	cup and saucer cup of tea cuppa drink a cup of tea drink from a cup drink tea, tea	872
The left **b̂** hand is held with the palm facing right (if the hand were opened, the fingers would point away from the signer). The right **F** hand is held with the palm facing down (if the hand were opened, the fingers would point to the left).	The hands are held side by side in front of the body; the left hand is held lower and nearer to the signer than the right hand.	The right hand twists towards the signer from the wrist, so that the index finger and thumb tips brush the left index finger; the movement ends with the right palm facing towards the signer.	light a match match strike a match	873

Two **F** hands are held with the palms facing down (if the hands were opened, the fingers would all point away from the signer).	The hands are held in front of the body.	The hands make a short movement away from the signer and then bend up at the wrists, while moving towards the signer, before making a short downward movement.	sheet
			spread out a
			  sheet/tablecloth
			tablecloth
			unfold a piece
			  of material
				874

Two **F** hands are held with the palms facing down (if the hands were opened, the fingers would all point away from the signer).	The hands are held side by side in front of the body with the thumb and index finger tips all touching.	The hands move apart.	degree diploma	875
Two **F** hands are held with the palms facing towards the signer (if the hands were opened, the fingers would all point down).	The hands are held side by side in front of the body.	The hands make a short upward movement.	socks * nylons †¹ put on nylons/ stockings †¹ stockings †¹	876

Notes * This sign may be produced with a repeated movement.

$$\emptyset \quad F\top\!\vee {}_{|} F\top\!\vee \quad {}^{\circ}_{\wedge}{}^{\cdot}$$

† This sign may be produced with a longer movement in which the thumb and index finger tips maintain contact with the thigh throughout.

$$\emptyset \quad F\top\!\vee {}_{|} F\top\!\vee \quad {}^{\wedge}$$

1 If the movement is not short, the sign produced is **nylons, put on nylons/stockings, stockings.**

$$! \quad F\top\!\vee {}_{|} F\top\!\vee \quad {}^{\hat{\times}}$$

877 Ø F⊥ʌ F⊥ʌ $_{Z}^{H}$∿·

878 Ø F⊥ʌ F⊥ʌ $(_{X÷}^{∧∨})$·

879 Ø F⊥ʌ ₁ₓ F⊥ʌ $_{∨}^{÷}$

880 Ø F>ʌ F<ʌ $_{⊥}^{°}$

881 Ø F>⊥ ⅒ Fↄ< $^{□[FF]·ₐ⅒}$

882 Ø F>⊥ ⅒ F<ʌ $_{∨}^{@}$

The fingers and thumb are extended and spread apart; the index finger is bent at the palm knuckle with the pad of the thumb touching the pad of the index finger.

Handshape and orientation	Location, hand arrangement and contact	Movement	Glosses	
Two F hands are held with the palms facing away from the signer (if the hands were opened, the fingers would all point up).	The hands are held in front of the body.	The hands make alternate movements towards and away from the signer at an angle; the movements are repeated.	dance dancer dancing party	877
Two F hands are held with the palms facing away from the signer (if the hands were opened, the fingers would all point up).	The hands are held in front of the body.	The hands move up and, at the same time, towards each other and then down and, at the same time, apart; the movements are repeated.	music* orchestra* conduct a choir/ orchestra*¹ conductor*¹	878

Notes   * This sign may be produced using one hand only.

$$\emptyset \quad F{\perp}{\wedge} \;\overset{N\cdot}{z} \quad \text{or} \quad \emptyset \quad G{\text{ɔ}}{\perp} \;\overset{N\cdot}{z}$$

   1 If the handshapes are changed to two **G** hands with the palms facing down and the extended fingers pointing away from the signer, the sign produced is **conduct a choir/orchestra, conductor**.

$$\emptyset \quad G{\text{ɔ}}{\perp} \quad G{\text{ɔ}}{\perp} \;\overset{(\overset{\wedge}{\underset{\div}{x}}\overset{\vee}{})\cdot}{}$$

Two F hands are held with the palms facing away from the signer (if the hands were opened, the fingers would all point up).	The hands are held side by side in front of the body, with the tips of the thumbs and index fingers all touching.	The hands move slowly down and, at the same time, apart.	peace peaceful quiet silence silent still	879
The left F hand is held with the palm facing right; the right F hand is held with the palm facing left (if the hands were opened, the fingers would all point up).	The hands are held in front of the body.	The hands make a short, firm movement away from the signer.	exquisite superb excellent¹ perfect¹	880

Non-manual features   The eyes are narrowed and the lips are stretched.

Notes   1 If the movement is repeated, the sign produced is **excellent, perfect**.

$$\emptyset \quad F{>}{\wedge} \quad F{<}{\wedge} \;\overset{\circ}{\underset{\;}{\mathsf{I}}}\cdot$$

The left F hand is held with the palm facing right; the right F hand is held with the palm facing down (if the hands were opened, the left fingers would point away from the signer and the right fingers would point to the left).	The hands are held side by side in front of the body with the thumbs and index fingers forming interlinking circles.	The hands change places.	Olympic Games Olympics	881
The left F hand is held with the palm facing right; the right F hand is held with the palm facing left (if the hands were opened, the left fingers would point away from the signer, and the right fingers would point up).	The hands are held in front of the body with the thumbs and index fingers forming interlinking circles.	The hands remain together and make a clockwise circle in the horizontal plane.	associate association co-operate co-operation co-ordinate co-ordination co-ordinator union unite	882

883 Ø F>⊥ ⌶ F<∧ ⌶·

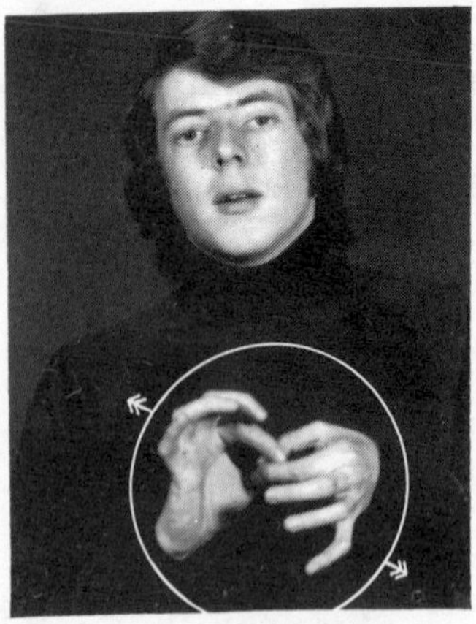

884 Ø F>⊥ ⌶ F<∧ ÷□ [55]

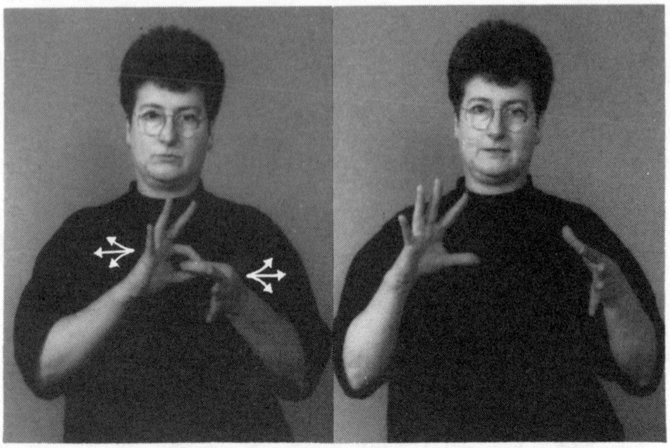

885 Ø F>⊥ ı F<⊥ °^⊥ °v

886 Ø F>⊥ ı F<⊥ °~~·

887 Ø F>⊥ ı F<⊥ (°@⊥v÷ ~) ÷

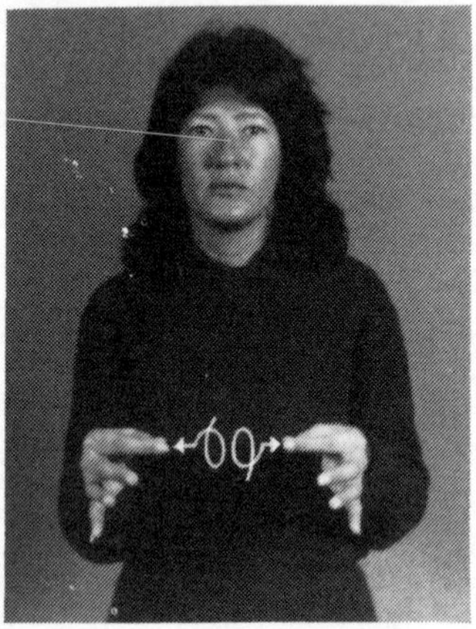

888 Ø F>⊥ ıx F<⊥ ÷

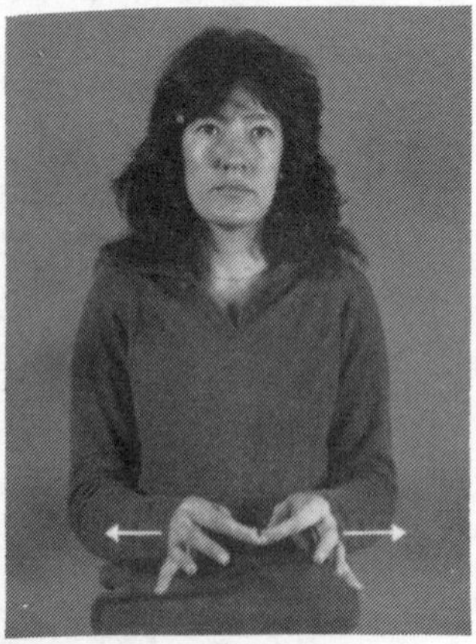

889 Ø F>⊥ ı F<⊥ɂ ʿʾ

The fingers and thumb are extended and spread apart; the index finger is bent at the palm knuckle with the pad of the thumb touching the pad of the index finger.

Handshape and orientation	Location, hand arrangement and contact	Movement	Glosses	
The left **F** hand is held with the palm facing right; the right **F** hand is held with the palm facing left (if the hands were opened, the left fingers would point away from the signer and the right fingers would point up).	The hands are held in front of the body with the index fingers and thumbs interlinked.	The hands remain together and move towards and away from the signer twice.	connect connection co-operate co-operation co-ordinate co-ordination interact interaction liaise liaison relate related relation relationship	883
The left **F** hand is held with the palm facing right; the right **F** hand is held with the palm facing left (if the hands were opened, the left fingers would point away from the signer and the right fingers would point up).	The hands are held in front of the body with the thumb and index fingers forming interlinking circles.	The hands move apart and, at the same time, open (forming two **5** hands).	free release breakaway[1] break away[1] disassociate[1] dissociate[1]	884

Notes 1 If the movement is changed, so that the right hand opens while moving to the right, the sign produced is **breakaway, break away, disassociate, dissociate.**   F >⊥ ᵢ F <∧ $^{>\,[s]}_{□}$

The left **F** hand is held with the palm facing right; the right **F** hand is held with the palm facing left (if the hands were opened, the fingers would all point away from the signer).	The hands are held side by side in front of the body.	The hands move away from the signer in an arc.	defer deferment delay postpone postponement put back put off advance[1] advancement[1] bring forward[1]	885

Notes 1 If the movement is in an arc towards the signer, the sign produced is **advance, advancement, bring forward.**   Ø F >⊥ ᵢ F <⊥ $^{°\;°}_{∧\;∨}$

The left **F** hand is held with the palm facing right; the right **F** hand is held with the palm facing left (if the hands were opened, the fingers would all point away from the signer).	The hands are held side by side in front of the body.	The hands make alternate short up and down movements.	politician politics	886
The left **F** hand is held with the palm facing right; the right **F** hand is held with the palm facing left (if the hands were opened, the fingers would all point away from the signer).	The hands are held side by side in front of the body.	The hands make alternate small clockwise circles in the vertical plane at right angles to the signer's body, while moving apart, and then continue to move straight apart.	knot lace tie tie up	887
The left **F** hand is held with the palm facing right; the right **F** hand is held with the palm facing left (if the hands were opened, the fingers would all point away from the signer).	The hands are held side by side in front of the body with the thumb and index finger tips all touching.	The hands move apart.	measure string wire	888
The left **F** hand is held with the palm facing right; the right **F** hand is held with the palm facing left (if the hands were opened, the fingers would all point away from the signer).	The hands are held side by side in front of the body; the right hand is held nearer to the signer than the left hand.	The hands change places.	replace replacement substitute substitution swap switch	889

890 Ø F>⊥ ¦ F<⊥₉ $\overset{(\mathbb{I}\sim)\cdot}{z}$

491 ○ F̄>ʌ ¦ F<ʌ $\overset{\circ\cdot}{\underset{v}{\perp}}$

892 Ø 5̄⊤> ¦ F<ʌ ᵒ̸

The fingers and thumb are extended and spread apart; the index finger is bent at the palm knuckle with the pad of the thumb touching the pad of the index finger.

Handshape and orientation	Location, hand arrangement and contact	Movement	Glosses	
The left **F** hand is held with the palm facing right; the right **F** hand is held with the palm facing left (if the hands were opened, the fingers would all point away from the signer).	The hands are held side by side in front of the body; the right hand is held nearer to the signer than the left hand.	The hands move towards and away from the signer alternately while moving from side to side; the movements are repeated.	ice-skate* ice-skater* ice-skating*	890

Non-manual features   The body moves from side to side.

Notes   * This sign may also be produced using two **B** hands. $\emptyset \quad B{>}\perp \mid B{<}\perp_{\wp} {\left(\frac{\mathbb{I}^{\wedge}}{\mathbb{Z}}\right)} \cdot$

The left **F** hand is held with the palm facing right; the right **F** hand is held with the palm facing left (if the hands were opened, the fingers would all point up).	The hands are held side by side in front of the face; the right hand is held higher than the left hand.	The hands make a short, firm movement away from the signer and, at the same time, down.	accurate exact meticulous perfect precise proper stickler strict	891

Non-manual features   The lips are tightly rounded.

The left **5** hand is held with the palm facing towards the signer and the fingers pointing to the right; the right **F** hand is held with the palm facing left (if the hand were opened, the fingers would point up).	The hands are held side by side in front of the body; the right hand is held above the left hand.	No movement.	ballroom dancer ballroom dancing	892

Non-manual features   The body twists from side to side from the waist.

893 ⊔ F̄⊤< ˣ

894 π F̄⊤< ˣ⊙̇⊤ᵥ# [F]

895 °⅃℧> ₁ₓ F̄℧⊤ ˟˟

The fingers and thumb are extended and spread apart; the index finger is bent at the palm knuckle and the thumb is held parallel to the index finger.

F̄ is used primarily for handling and symbolic functions.

Its use as a *handling* classifier can be seen in the signs relating to marriage, such as **marry** (sign 895), **wedding** (sign 896) and **spouse** (sign 897), where the handshape relates to the handling of a wedding ring. It is also sometimes used as a substitute for F where the focus is on the actual act of getting hold of or picking up a small or delicate object.

The two-handed forms which begin with two F̄ handshapes and then link as two F handshapes can be seen as having a *symbolic* function expressing meanings related to coming together as in **affiliate** (sign 898) and **join** (sign 898).

Handshape and orientation	Location, hand arrangement and contact	Movement	Glosses	
The F̄ hand is held with the palm facing towards the signer (if the hand were opened, the fingers would point to the left).	The hand is held with the index finger and thumb tips touching the nose.	No movement.	bull* pong*¹ stench*¹ stink*¹	893

	Notes	* The following notes apply to all glosses.	
		This sign may be produced using a Ğ handshape.	⊔ Ğ⊤< ˣ
		This sign may be produced using an Â handshape.	⊔ Â⊤< ˣ
		1 If the index finger and thumb tips hold the nose, the nose is wrinkled and the eyes are narrowed, the sign produced is **pong, stench, stink**.	⊔ F̄⊤< ˣ or ⊔ Ğ⊤< ˣ or ⊔ Â⊤< ˣ

The F̄ hand is held with the palm facing towards the signer (if the hand were opened, the fingers would point to the left).	The hand is held with the thumb and index finger tips touching the neck.	The hand makes a short, sharp movement down and, at the same time, away from the signer, while the index finger and thumb close (forming an F hand).	thank God thank goodness thank heavens	894

	Non-manual features	The tongue protrudes between the lips and is then drawn in sharply , so that the mouth closes as the hand moves.

The left 5 hand is held with the palm facing down and the fingers pointing to the right; the right F̄ hand is held with the palm facing down (if the hand were opened, the fingers would point away from the signer).	The hands are held side by side in front of the body with the right thumb and index finger tips touching the left ring finger.	The right hand makes a short movement to the left with the right index finger and thumb tips maintaining contact with the left ring finger throughout.	marry* ring*	895

	Notes	* This sign may also be produced using a right ŏ hand.	°5⊃> ₁ₓ ŏ⊃⊥ ˣ°̥

896 °5ᴎ> ₁× F̄ᴎ⊤ ˣ⌄ᴧ[ᴮ]ˣ

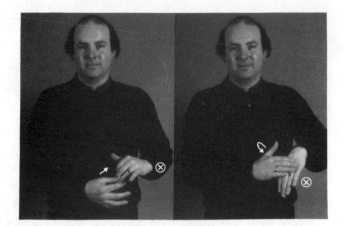

897 °5ᴎ> ₁× F̄<⊥ ˣ⌄̊·

898 Ø F̄>⊥ ₁ F̄<ᴧ ˣ⌶

899 ⌣ F̄>ᴧ F̄<ᴧ ⁺[ꜰꜰ]#

The fingers and thumb are extended and spread apart; the index finger is bent at the palm knuckle and the thumb is held parallel to the index finger.

Handshape and orientation	Location, hand arrangement and contact	Movement	Glosses	
The left **5** hand is held with the palm facing down and the fingers pointing to the right; the right **F̄** hand is held with the palm facing down (if the hand were opened, the fingers would point away from the signer).	The hands are held in front of the body with the right index finger and thumb touching the left ring finger.	The right hand makes a short movement to the left, so that the index finger and thumb of the right hand move along the left ring finger. The right hand then moves up and, at the same time, opens (forming a **B** hand) and finally moves down to rest across the back of the left hand.	**marriage*** **married*** **wedding***	896
Notes	* This sign may also be produced using a right **8** hand.	°5ᴖ> ₁x 8̄ᴖ⊥ <ʌ[ʙ]x x□		
The left **5** hand is held with the palm facing down and the fingers pointing to the right; the right **F̄** hand is held held with the palm facing left (if the hand were opened, the fingers would point away from the signer).	The hands are held side by side in front of the body; the right index finger and thumb tips are touching the left ring finger.	The right hand makes a short movement to the left, with the right index finger and thumb tips maintaining contact with the left ring finger; the movement is repeated.	**husband*** **spouse*** **wedding*** **wife***	897
Notes	* This sign may also be produced using a right **8** hand.	°5ᴖ> ₁x 8̄<⊥ °<x·		
The left **F̄** hand is held with the palm facing right; the right **F̄** hand is held with the palm facing left (if the hands were opened, the left fingers would point away from the signer, and the right fingers would point up).	The hands are held side by side in front of the body.	The hands move towards each other and then the fingers and thumbs link together.	affiliate affiliation associate association attach attachment connect connection contact go home* home* join link member relate[1] related[1] relation[1] relationship[1]	898
Notes	* Regional sign. 1 If the movement ends with a short, repeated movement from side to side, the sign produced is **relate, related, relation, relationship**.	Ø F̄>⊥ ₁ F̄<ʌ xɪᶻ̥·		
The left **F̄** hand is held with the palm facing left; the right **F̄** hand is held with the palm facing right (if the hands were opened, the fingers would all point up).	The hands are held with the index fingers and thumbs in front of the mouth.	The hands move apart while the index fingers and thumbs close (forming two **F** hands).	cat cat's whiskers moustache whiskers	899

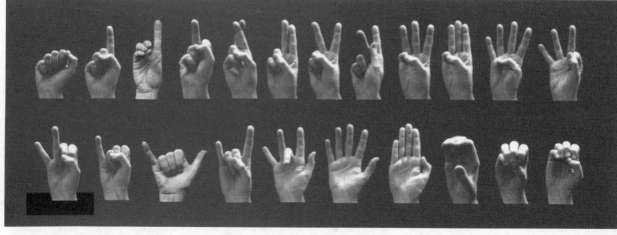

7

Handshape	Handshape description	Type	Sign entries
7	The ring and little fingers are extended from the fist and spread apart.	Single dez Manual tab Double dez	900 – 902

900　∪ °7⊤∧ ×·

901　∪ °7⊤∧ ×⊥

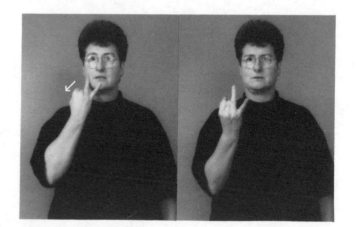

902　∪ °7⊤∧ ×ᵥ̊×
　　　　　　　⊤

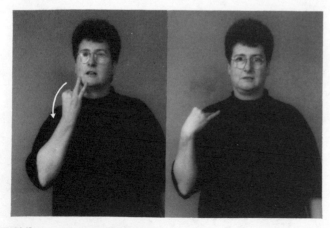

7 is used rarely in the language. As its name suggests, this form is used to represent the number **7** in several of the number systems used in the UK. It has been lexicalised in forms relating to a seven day period, i.e. a week. Examples include **every week** (sign 900), **next week** (sign 901) and **last week** (sign 902).

Handshape and orientation	Location, hand arrangement and contact	Movement	Glosses	
The **7** hand is held with the palm facing towards the signer (if the hand were opened, the fingers would point up).	The hand is held beside the chin.	The ring fingertip taps the side of the chin several times.	week (every week)* weekly*	900

    Notes   * The following notes apply to all glosses:

      Regional sign.

      This sign may also be produced using a ġ hand.   U ᵉĠ⊤ʌ ˣ·

The **7** hand is held with the palm facing towards the signer (if the hand were opened, the fingers would point up).	The hand is held with the ring fingertip touching the side of the chin.	The hand moves away from the signer.	week (following week)* week (in a week's time)* week (next week)*	901

    Notes   * The following notes apply to all glosses:

      Regional sign.

      This sign may also be produced using a ġ hand.   U ᵉĠ⊤ʌ ˣ⊥

The **7** hand is held with the palm facing towards the signer (if the hand were opened, the fingers would point up).	The hand is held with the ring fingertip touching the side of the chin.	The hand makes a short movement down and towards the signer; the movement ends with the fingertips touching the right shoulder.	week before* week (last week)* week (one week ago)*	902

    Notes   * The following notes apply to all glosses:

      Regional sign.

      This sign may also be produced using a ġ hand.   U ᵉĠ⊤ʌ ˣᵛˣ

      This sign may be produced without the final contact.   U ᵉĠ⊤ʌ ˣᵛ or U °7⊤ʌ ˣᵛ

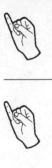

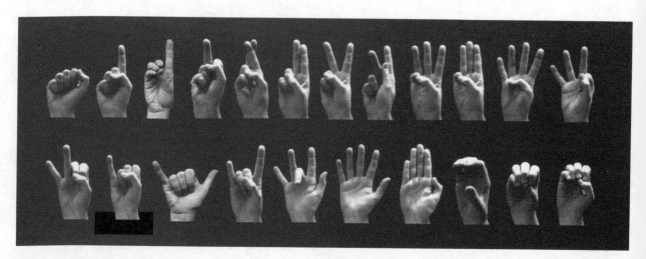

I

Handshape	Handshape description	Type	Sign entries
I	The little finger is extended from the fist.	Single dez	903 – 906
		Manual tab	907 – 912
		Double dez	913 – 918
Ï	The little finger is extended from the fist and bent at the palm knuckle.	Single dez	919 – 922
		Manual tab	923
		Double dez	924 – 931

903 Ø | ⊥∧ $\substack{\varrho \\ \square}$ [5]

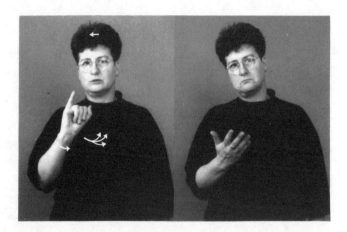

904 Ø | <∧ $\substack{\perp \\ \vee}$

905 ⊃ | ⊤∧ $\substack{× \perp \\ \vee}$

906 ✓ | ⊤< $\substack{> \\ ×}$

The main *variant* of l is ï in which there is bending at the palm knuckles. In some cases, ï is required by the physical constraints of the sign production. In other cases the use of l or ï depends on personal choice. (See also separate entry for ï.)

l has limited *classifier* functions within the productive lexicon and as a classifying component in established signs:
– it is used as a *size and shape* classifier to represent small, narrow objects;
– it is used as a *tracing size and shape* classifier to indicate small, curved, narrow objects such as curled horns in **sheep** (sign 929);
– it is used as an *instrumental* classifier to represent implements, tools or utensils which are short and narrow, such as a short stick or small spoon, as in the sign **poison** (sign 912).

There is a conventional association within BSL linking the l handshape with meanings relating to 'badness'. Virtually all of the signs listed in this section have such negative associations. This link has probably limited the use of l in other functions, such as classifier use. The 'bad' association remains dominant in the language and new forms which exploit this link are likely to occur. The numerous examples in this section include **bad** (sign 904), **discrimination** (sign 909), **evil** (sign 910), **appalling** (sign 914), **quarrel** (sign 915) and **criticise** (sign 916). In this usage, l contrasts with the handshape Å which has an opposing symbolic value relating to 'goodness'.

This handshape, or a *variant* in which the little finger is bent, also expresses the right-hand component of the letter **s** of the British manual alphabet. As such, it occurs in initial letter handshape signs such as **south** (sign 908) and **silver** (sign 913). This handshape also expresses the letters **i** and (with a twisting movement) **j** of the American and Irish manual alphabets. As such, it occurs in Irish influenced initial letter signs, especially name signs, for example **Ian** and **Jeff** (see *Introduction*). Other borrowings may be limited, especially as American Sign Language does not share the association between this handshape and 'badness' (see *Introduction* for further discussion).

Handshape and orientation	*Location, hand arrangement and contact*	*Movement*	*Glosses*	
The l hand is held with the palm facing away from the signer (if the hand were opened, the fingers would point up).	The hand is held in front of the body.	The hand twists at the wrist, so that the palm faces up, while opening (forming a **5** hand).	not bad not so bad not too bad	903
Non-manual features The corners of the mouth are turned down, and the head tilts to the right.				

The l hand is held with the palm facing left (if the hand were opened, the fingers would point up).	The hand is held in front of the body.	The hand moves away from the signer and, at the same time, downwards.	appalling†
			awful†
			bad†
			be awful/bad/
			  dreadful/
			  terrible/wicked *†
			dreadful†
			horrible†
			terrible†
			wicked†
			pity[1]
			shame[1]
				904

Non-manual features Appropriate negative non-manual features must be used.				
Notes * Directional verb.				
† This sign may be produced with a short repeated movement from side to side.				
1 If the head is tilted forward, and the hand moves down and then up while twisting sharply to the left from the wrist throughout, the sign produced is **pity**, **shame**.				
The l hand is held with the palm facing towards the signer (if the hand were opened, the fingers would point up).	The hand is held with the little fingertip touching the mouth.	The hand moves down and, at the same time, away from the signer.	blaspheme blast curse damn swear	905
Non-manual features The brows are furrowed.				
The l hand is held with the palm facing towards the signer (if the hand were opened, the fingers would point to the left).	The hand is held resting on the left forearm.	The hand moves to the right, maintaining contact with the left forearm throughout.	feeble * weak *	906
Notes * This sign may be produced on the upper arm.				

$$\emptyset \quad l_{<\wedge} \overset{o}{z}\cdot$$

$$\emptyset \quad l_{<\wedge} \overset{(\dot{\omega}_{<})}{_{\vee\wedge}}$$

$$\lambda \quad l\tau_{<} \overset{\vee}{\times}$$

907 $\overline{\mathsf{I}}\mathsf{T>}\;_\mathsf{x}\;\mathsf{I<\bot}\,{}^{\mathsf{o}}_{\substack{@\\<\mathsf{T}\\\mathsf{x}}}\cdot$

908 ${}^{\mathsf{u}}\mathsf{5>\bot}\;_{|}\;\mathsf{I\sigma<}\;{}^{\mathsf{x}}$

909 $\overline{\mathsf{B}}\mathsf{a\bot}\;\mathsf{I}\mathsf{T<}\;{}^{\bot}_{\substack{\mathsf{x}\\\bot}}$

910 $\overline{\mathsf{B}}\mathsf{a\bot}\;\mathsf{I}\mathsf{T<}\;{}^{\mathsf{x}}\cdot$

911 $\overline{\mathsf{B}}\mathsf{a>}\;_\mathsf{x}\;\mathsf{I<\bot}\,{}_{\substack{@\\<\mathsf{T}\\\mathsf{x}}}$

912 $\mathsf{O\sigma\bot}\;_{|@}\;\mathsf{I}\mathsf{T<}\;{}_{\substack{@\\<\mathsf{T}\\\mathsf{x}}}\cdot$

Handshape and orientation	Location, hand arrangement and contact	Movement	Glosses	
The left I hand is held with the palm facing towards the signer; the right I hand is held with the palm facing left (if the hands were opened, the left fingers would point to the right and the right fingers would point away from the signer).	The hands are held in front of the body; the right hand rests on the left hand.	The right hand makes small anti-clockwise circles in the horizontal plane, maintaining contact with the left hand throughout.	grey	907
The left 5 hand is held with the palm facing right and the fingers pointing away from the signer; the right I hand is held with the palm facing down (if the hand were opened, the fingers would point to the left).	The hands are held side by side in front of the body.	The right little finger touches the left little finger.	south *	908

Notes   * This sign may be produced in front of the waist with the left palm facing towards the signer and the right palm facing down; the right little finger is held against the left little finger and the hands make a short downward movement.

$$\emptyset \quad {}^{u}5{\scriptstyle\top}{\scriptstyle>} \times \text{I}\,{\scriptstyle\text{o}\perp}{}_{\varrho} \quad {}^{\text{o}}_{\text{v}}$$

| The left B hand is held with the palm facing up and the fingers pointing away from the signer; the right I hand is held with the palm facing towards the signer (if the hand were opened, the fingers would point to the left). | The hands are held in front of the body; the right hand is held above the left hand. | The right hand moves away from the signer, brushing across the left palm. | discriminate * discrimination object * objection oppose * opposition protest * reject * rejection | 909 |

Non-manual features   The brows are furrowed.

Notes   * Directional verb.

| The left B hand is held with the palm facing up and the fingers pointing away from the signer; the right I hand is held with the palm facing towards the signer (if the hand were opened, the fingers would point to the left). | The hands are held in front of the body; the right hand is held above the left hand. | The side of the right hand taps the left palm twice. | evil fault sin wrong what's the matter? [1] what's wrong? [1] | 910 |

Notes   1 If the eyebrows are raised, the sign produced is **what's the matter?, what's wrong?**.

| The left B hand is held with the palm facing up and the fingers pointing to the right; the right I hand is held with the palm facing left (if the hand were opened, the fingers would point away from the signer). | The hands are held in front of the body, with the right little finger resting on the left palm. | The right hand makes an anti-clockwise circle in the horizontal plane; the side of the little finger maintains contact with the left hand throughout. | appalling awful dreadful horrible inferior poor rotten rubbish shoddy sin terrible | 911 |

Non-manual features   The corners of the closed mouth are turned down and the nose is wrinkled.

| The left O hand is held with the palm facing down (if the hand were opened, the fingers would point away from the signer). The right I hand is held with the palm facing towards the signer (if the hand were opened, the fingers would point to the left). | The hands are held side by side in front of the body, with the right little finger inside the circle formed by the left thumb and fingers. | The right hand makes clockwise circles in the vertical plane at right angles to the signer's body; the right little finger maintains contact with the left hand throughout. | chemist medicine pharmacist pharmacy poison | 912 |

913 Ø | ⊤ > × | ↻ ⊥ ₉ $\overset{\wedge[55]}{\square}$

914 Ø | > ∧ | < ∧ $\overset{\circ\cdot}{\perp}$

915 Ø | > ∧ | < ∧ $\overset{\dot\omega×}{\underset{×}{\top}}$

916 Ø | > ∧ ₁ | < ∧ $\overset{@\wedge\cdot}{\underset{v}{\perp}}$

917 Ø | > ∧ ╤× | < ∧ $\overset{v}{\underset{\perp}{\div}}$

918 Ø | > ⊥ | < ⊥ $\overset{×╤÷}{}$

Handshape and orientation	Location, hand arrangement and contact	Movement	Glosses	
The left I hand is held with the palm facing towards the signer; the right I hand is held with the palm facing down (if the hands were opened, the left fingers would point to the right and the left fingers would point away from the signer).	The hands are held in front of the body; the right hand is held nearer to the signer than the left hand, with the right little finger resting on the left little finger.	The hands move apart (the left hand makes a short movement away from the signer, the right hand makes a short movement towards the signer) while opening (forming two **5** hands).	silver	913
The left I hand is held with the palm facing right; the right I hand is held with the palm facing left (if the hands were opened, the fingers would all point up).	The hands are held in front of the body.	The hands make two short firm movements away from the signer.	appalling †§ awful †§ bad critical *†§ danger dangerous dreadful *§ evil † grave *†§ horrible *§ serious *†§ severe * terrible †§ unfortunate unlucky wicked *§	914

Non-manual features Appropriate negative non-manual features must be used.

Notes * This sign may be produced with a single movement.   Ø I >∧ I <∧ ⊥

† This sign may be produced with a repeated short movement towards the signer.   Ø I >∧ I <∧

§ This sign may be produced with the hands making several short movements towards each other.   Ø I >∧ I <∧

| The left I hand is held with the palm facing right; the right I hand is held with the palm facing left (if the hands were opened, the fingers would all point up). | The hands are held in front of the body. | The hands twist at the wrists, so that the palms face towards the signer, while moving firmly towards each other; the movement ends with the sides of the little fingers touching. | clash fall out quarrel row | 915 |
| The left I hand is held with the palm facing right; the right I hand is held with the palm facing left (if the hands were opened, the fingers would all point up). | The hands are held side by side in front of the body. | The hands make alternate clockwise circles in the vertical plane at right angles to the signer's body. | critic criticise * criticism blame *[1,2] | 916 |

Notes * Directional verb.

1 If the hands make a short repeated movement away from the signer, the sign produced is **blame** *(see entry 1 in the English section).*   Ø I >∧ ₁ I <∧

2 If the hands make a firm movement away from the signer, the sign produced is **blame** *(see entry 2 in the English section).*   Ø I >∧ ₁ I <∧

| The left I hand is held with the palm facing right; the right I hand is held with the palm facing left (if the hands were opened, the fingers would all point up). | The hands are held crossed over in front of the body with the sides of the wrists touching. | The hands uncross, moving down and apart and, at the same time, away from the signer. | ban disallow forbid not allow prohibit taboo | 917 |

Non-manual features Appropriate negative non-manual features must be used.

| The left I hand is held with the palm facing right; the right I hand is held with the palm facing left (if the hands were opened, the fingers would all point away from the signer). | The hands are held in front of the body. | The hands move towards each other and then cross over before moving firmly apart. | appalling awful dreadful horrible terrible unfortunate wicked | 918 |

Non-manual features Appropriate negative non-manual features must be used.

919 ∩ ï⊤∧ $\overset{\overset{\circ}{e}}{\underset{v}{<}}$

920 [] ï α< $\overset{×}{\cdot}$

921 [] ï α< $\overset{\overset{@}{\cdot}}{\underset{×}{<}}$

922 ⌈⌉ ï α< $^{×>×}$

923 $\overline{ï}$ >⊥ ¦ ï <⊥ $\overset{v}{\underset{v}{×}}$

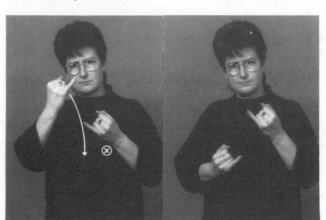

The main *variant* of ï is ı in which there is no bending at the palm knuckles. In some cases, ı is required by the physical constraints of the sign production. In other cases, the use of ï or ı depends on personal choice. (See also separate entry for ı .)

ï has limited *classifier* functions within the productive lexicon and as a classifying component in established signs:

– it is used as a *size and shape* classifier to represent small, narrow objects;

– it is used as a *tracing size and shape* classifier to indicate small, curved, narrow objects such as curled horns in **sheep** (sign 929);

– it is used as an *instrumental* classifier to represent implements, tools or utensils which are short and narrow, such as a short stick or small spoon, as in the sign **poison** (sign 912).

There is a conventional association within BSL linking the ï handshape with meanings relating to 'badness'. Virtually all of the signs listed in this section have such negative associations. This link has probably limited the use of ï in other functions, such as classifier use. The 'bad' association remains dominant in the language and new forms which exploit this link are likely to occur. The numerous examples in this section include **suspect** (sign 919), **blame** (sign 920), **fail** (sign 923), **argue** (sign 924), **spoil** (sign 925) and **deteriorate** (sign 926). In this usage, ï contrasts with the handshape Á which has an opposing symbolic value relating to 'goodness'.

This handshape, or a *variant* in which the little finger is bent, also expresses the right hand component of the letter **s** of the British manual alphabet. As such, it occurs in initial letter handshape signs such as **south** (sign 908) and **silver** (sign 913). This handshape also expresses the letters **i** and (with a twisting movement) **j** of the American and Irish manual alphabets. As such, it occurs in Irish influenced initial letter signs, especially name signs, for example **Ian** and **Jeff** (see *Introduction*). Other borrowings may be limited, especially as American Sign Language does not share the asociation between this handshape and 'badness' (see *Introduction* for further discussion).

Handshape and orientation	Location, hand arrangement and contact	Movement	Glosses	
The ï hand is held with the palm facing towards the signer (if the hand were opened, the fingers would point up).	The hand is held in front and to the side of the forehead.	The hand makes small anticlockwise circles in the vertical plane parallel to the signer's body.	suspect suspicious wary	919
Non-manual features The eyes are narrowed and the brows are furrowed.				
The ï hand is held with the palm facing up (if the hand were opened, the fingers would point to the left).	The hand is held in front of the chest.	The side of the hand taps the chest twice.	blame* confess confession fault (my fault) guilt guilty sorry wrong	920
Non-manual features The mouth is slightly turned down at the corners, and the head is slightly tilted to one side.				
Notes * Directional verb.				
The ï hand is held with the palm facing up (if the hand were opened, the fingers would point to the left).	The hand is held with the side of the index finger resting against the chest.	The hand makes anticlockwise circles in the vertical plane parallel to the signer's body; the side of the little finger maintains contact with the chest throughout.	apologise apology regret sorrow sorry	921
The ï hand is held with the palm facing up (if the hand were opened, the fingers would point to the left).	The hand is held in front of the left side of the upper chest.	The side of the little finger touches the left side of the chest; the hand then moves to the right before touching the right side of the chest.	insurance*	922
Notes * Regional sign.				
The left ï hand is held with the palm facing right; the right ï hand is held with the palm facing left (if the hands were opened, the fingers would all point away from the signer).	The hands are held side by side in front of the body; the right hand is held higher than the left hand.	The right hand moves down, so that the tip of the right little finger brushes the tip of the left little finger.	fail last worst	923
Non-manual features The brows are furrowed.				

924 Ø ï α⊥ ï α⊥ $\overset{\circ}{x}$ ·

925 Ø ï α⊥ ı ï α⊥ $\overset{\circ}{o}$

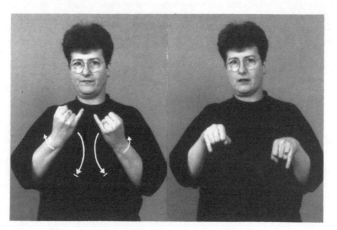

926 Ø ï α⊥ ı ï α⊥ $\overset{\div}{v}$

927 Ø ï α⊥ ⪱x ï α⊥ $\overset{\div}{v}$

928 Ø ⌐ï⊤> ⌐ï⊤< $\overset{(\overset{.}{D})^{\sim}·}{\overset{\div}{\underset{\perp}{\wedge}}}$

Handshape and orientation	Location, hand arrangement and contact	Movement	Glosses	
Two ï hands are held with the palms facing up (if the hands were opened, the fingers would all point away from the signer).	The hands are held in front of the body.	The hands make a short movement towards each other; the movement is repeated.	argue* argument battle conflict fight* quarrel* squabble* enemy [1]	924

Non-manual features   The cheeks are slightly puffed out.

Notes   * This sign may be produced with the hands moving firmly towards each other and touching; the movement is repeated.

$$\emptyset \quad \ddot{\text{ï}}\text{a}\perp \,_{\text{ı}}\, \ddot{\text{ï}}\text{a}\perp ^{(\ddot{x}x)}\cdot$$

1 If the lips are stretched, the sign produced is **enemy**.

Two ï hands are held with the palms facing up (if the hands were opened, the fingers would all point away from the signer).	The hands are held side by side in front of the body.	The hands turn over firmly, so that the palms face down.	fail* failure* spoil* how dare you? [1] watch it! [1] have someone on [2]	925

Notes   * This sign may be produced using one hand only.

$$\emptyset \quad \ddot{\text{ï}}\text{a}\perp {}^{\dot{\text{o}}}$$

1 If one hand only is used, and the movement is changed, so that the handshape changes (forming a **G** hand) as the hand turns over, and the cheeks are puffed out, the sign produced is **how dare you?, watch it!**

$$\emptyset \quad \ddot{\text{ï}}\text{a}\perp {}^{\dot{\text{o}}}_{\square}{}^{[\text{G}]}$$

2 If the sign is produced as in note 1, but the cheeks are not puffed out, and the mouth is curved up, the sign produced is **have someone on**.

Two ï hands are held with the palms facing up (if the hands were opened, the fingers would all point away from the signer).	The hands are held side by side in front of the body.	The hands move slowly down and, at the same time, apart.	deteriorate worsen	926

Two ï hands are held with the palms facing up (if the hands were opened, the fingers would all point away from the signer).	The hands are held in front of the body, angled towards each other, so that the little fingers are crossed.	The hands make a short movement downwards and, at the same time, apart.	worse worsen*	927

Non-manual features   The brows are furrowed.

Notes   * This sign may be produced with the movement repeated several times, with the hands moving down throughout.

$$\emptyset \quad \ddot{\text{ï}}\text{a}\perp \,_{\mp x}\, \ddot{\text{ï}}\text{a}\perp ^{\left(\substack{\text{o}\\ \div\\ \text{v}}\cdot\right)}$$

Two ï hands are held with the palms facing towards the signer (if the hands were opened, the left fingers would point to the right and the right fingers would point to the left).	The hands are held in front of the body.	The hands bend alternately away from each other from the elbows, while moving firmly up and away from the signer; the movements are repeated.	bang one's head against a brick wall	928

Non-manual features   The lips are drawn back against the teeth and the brows are furrowed; the mouth opens and closes several times.

929 ∩ ïτʌ ïτʌ $\overset{@}{\underset{v}{\perp}}$

930 [] ïα> ïα< $\overset{v}{x}$

931 [] ïα> ïα< $\overset{\overset{o}{v}}{x}\cdot$

Handshape and orientation	Location, hand arrangement and contact	Movement	Glosses	
Two ï hands are held with the palms facing towards the signer (if the hands were opened, the fingers would all point up).	The hands are held at either side of the forehead.	The hands make a clockwise circle in the vertical plane, parallel to the side of the head.	sheep*	929

Notes * This sign may be produced using one hand only.

∩ ï⊤∧ ⊥̅ᵥᵉ

Two ï hands are held with the palms facing up (if the hands were opened, the left fingers would point to the right and the right fingers would point to the left).	The hands are held with the sides of the little fingers resting against the chest.	The hands move down slowly, maintaining contact with the chest throughout.	exhausted tired weary worn-out	930

Non-manual features The cheeks are puffed out.

Two ï hands are held with the palms facing up (if the hands were opened, the left fingers would point to the right and the right fingers would point to the left).	The hands are held with the sides of the little fingers resting against the chest.	The hands make a short downward movement, maintaining contact with the chest; the movement is repeated.	ill* poorly* sick* unwell*	931

Notes * This sign can be produced using one hand only.

] ïα< ᵛ̊ₓ ·

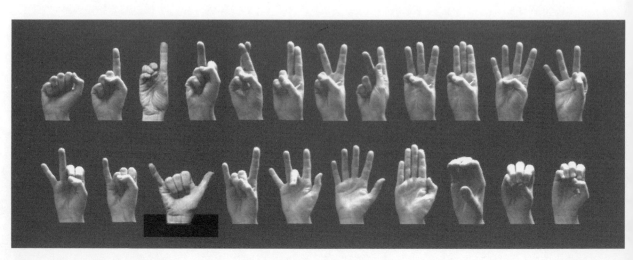

Y

Handshape	Handshape description	Type	Sign entries
Y	The little finger and thumb are extended from the fist.	Single dez	932 – 947
		Manual tab	948 – 952
		Double dez	953 – 957

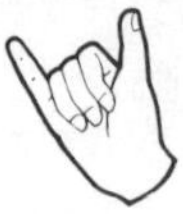

932 Ø Yɑ∧ ^<

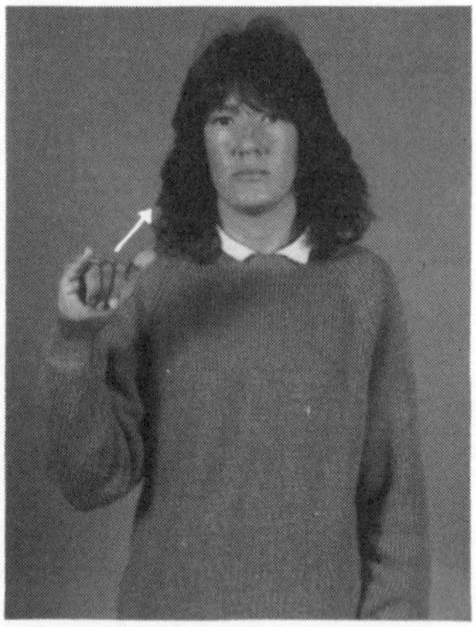

933 Ø Yɑ⊥ °z ·

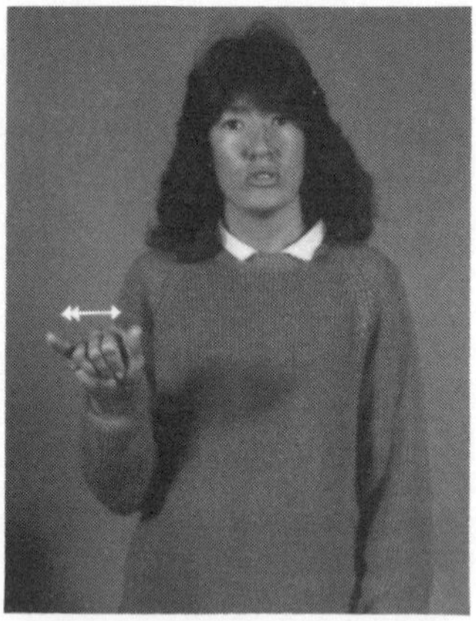

934 Ø Yɑ⊥ °⊥v ·

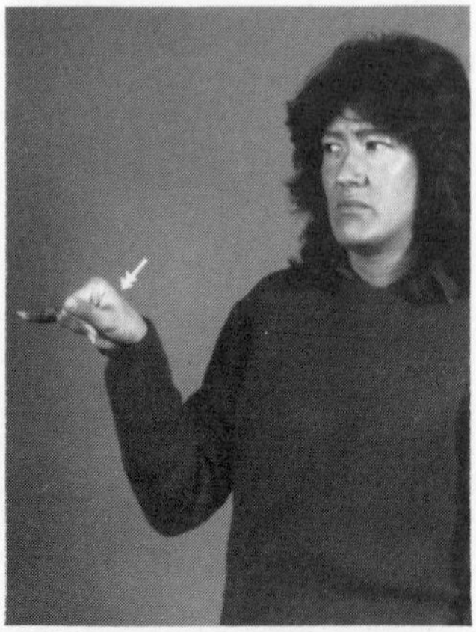

935 Ø Y⊤∧ ⊃<

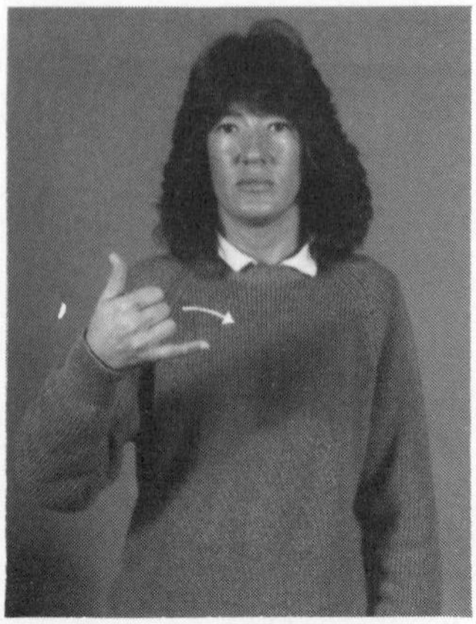

The little finger and thumb are extended from the fist.

Y has several different _classifier_ functions in the productive lexicon and also appears as a classifying component in established signs:
- it is used as a _size and shape_ classifier to represent objects with an extension at each side, or each end. The primary example of this is the use of Y in forms relating to aeroplane such as **plane** (sign 932), **fly by plane** (sign 949), **airport** (sign 950) and **runway** (sign 951). Other uses of Y as a _size and shape_ classifier can be seen in forms relating to horns such as **devil** (sign 939) and **cow** (sign 956);
- it is used as a _tracing size and shape_ classifier to trace (with two Y hands) the outline of oblong items, as in **cheque** (sign 953) and **envelope** (sign 953);
- it is used as a _handling_ classifier. In some examples, the form seems to combine a _handling_ function, indicated by the bent middle fingers, and a _size and shape_ function, indicated by the extended thumb and index finger. This seems to be the case in signs relating to telephone such as **acoustic modem** (sign 936), **pay phone** (sign 942) and **phone** (sign 944). A comparable usage can be seen in **kettle** (sign 935) and **pipe** (sign 946);
- it is used as an _instrumental_ classifier to represent implements, tools or utensils which have a narrow extension and are grasped by the closed

fingers. This seems to have limited use, but is sometimes used as an alternative to **A** or **I** in signs where the meaning involves a stirring or circular action;
- it can be used to show the _extent_ of narrow objects, such as the length of a border around a room.

A number of signs using Y seem to derive from the negative use of **I**. In most cases the Y appears to result from an anticipation of the **I** handshape in the second part of the sign, as in **take advantage of someone** (sign 940) and **try it on** (sign 941).

The inclusion in one handshape of the form relating to 'goodness', **A**, and the form relating to 'badness', **I**, leads to a further form-meaning link which may be termed 'ambivalence'. This is sometimes stressed further by the form of movement involved in the sign. Such meanings are expressed in, for example, **maybe** (sign 937), **whichever** (sign 938), and **inconsistent** (sign 955).

Y expresses the letter y within the Irish and American manual alphabets. As such, it is used in initial letter handshape signs borrowed from Irish Sign language (ISL) and American Sign Language (ASL), for example **yes** (see _Introduction_) from ISL and **New York** (sign 952) from ASL.

Handshape and orientation	Location, hand arrangement and contact	Movement	Glosses	
The Y hand is held with the palm facing down (if the hand were opened, the fingers would point up).	The hand is held in front of the body, at an angle, so that the fingers are turned to the left.	The hand moves up and, at the same time, to the left.	aeroplane air force airline flight fly in an aeroplane/ plane plane	932
The Y hand is held with the palm facing down (if the hand were opened, the fingers would point away from the signer).	The hand is held in front of the body.	The hand makes several short movements from side to side.	which? either [1]	933
Non-manual features Non-manual features appropriate for questions must be used.				
Notes 1 If the non-manual features are not present, the sign produced is **either**.				
The Y hand is held with the palm facing down (if the hand were opened, the fingers would point away from the signer).	The hand is held in front of the body.	The hand makes two short movements down and, at the same time, away from the signer.	be suspicious/ wary * suspect * suspicious wary	934
Non-manual features The eyes are narrowed, the brows are furrowed and the mouth is turned down at the corners.				
Notes * Directional verb.				

The Y hand is held with the palm facing towards the signer (if the hand were opened, the fingers would point up).	The hand is held in front of the body.	The hand bends to the left from the the wrist.	container with
			   a handle
			kettle *
			teapot *
			pour from a container
			   with a handle/
			   kettle/teapot [1]
				935

Notes * This sign may be produced with a repeated movement. 1 If the movement is slow, the sign produced is **pour from a container with a handle/kettle/teapot**.		Ø YTΛ �		

936 Ø Υ⊤v ⟂̇

937 Ø Υ<⊥ ⚬ẑ·

938 Ø Υ<⊥ (⚬ẑ·/>)

939 ∩ Υ⊥ʌ ×

940 Ц Υ<ʌ ×⊥ᵥ

941 Ʒ ᵃΥɔʌ ·3↑×3↑ᵥ

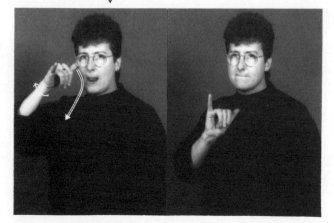

[524]

Y

The little finger and thumb are extended from the fist.

Handshape and orientation	Location, hand arrangement and contact	Movement	Glosses	
The Y hand is held with the palm facing towards the signer (if the hand were opened, the fingers would point down).	The hand is held in front of the body.	The hand makes a short downward movement.	kettle acoustic modem [1]	936

Notes 1 If the left **B** hand is held in front of the body (with the palm facing up and the fingers pointing to the right) and the right **Y** hand moves down to touch the left palm, the sign produced is **acoustic modem**.

Ba> Ytv

The Y hand is held with the palm facing left (if the hand were opened, the fingers would point away from the signer).	The hand is held in front of the body.	The hand makes several short twisting movements from side to side at the wrist.	maybe perhaps possible possibly	937
The Y hand is held with the palm facing left (if the hand were opened, the fingers would point away from the signer).	The hand is held in front of the body.	The hand moves to the right, while making short twisting movements from side to side at the wrist.	any anybody anyone whichever	938
The Y hand is held with the palm facing away from the signer (if the hand were opened, the fingers would point up).	The hand is held in front of the forehead.	The back of the hand touches the forehead.	devil* evil* hell* Satan*	939

Notes * This sign may also be produced with a **Ꮞ** handshape, held with the palm facing down, and bending up at the wrist to touch the forehead.

∩ Ʇɔ⊥

The Y hand is held with the palm facing left (if the hand were opened, the fingers would point up).	The hand is held with the thumbtip touching the nose.	The hand moves down and, at the same time, away from the signer.	take advantage of someone*	940

Non-manual features The tongue protrudes between the teeth and the nose is wrinkled.

Notes * Directional verb.

The Y hand is held with the palm facing down (if the hand were opened, the fingers would point up).	The hand is held beside the cheek at an angle, so that the palm is turned to the left.	The hand twists away from the signer at the wrist while moving down sharply, with the thumbtip brushing across the cheek.	creep toady try it on	941

Non-manual features The eyes are narrowed and the mouth is open with the tongue tip touching the upper lip; the tongue is sharply drawn in (so that the mouth closes) as the hand moves.

942 З ᵃY⊤< ×ǂ ∥ ∅ Ĝ⊥ʌ ⁿ[ᵟ]·

943 З ᵃY<ʌ ǂ·

944 ꓛ ᵃY⊤< ×

945 ꑼ Y<ʌ (ᵒᵑ⊤)

946 ꑼ Y<ʌ ×·

947 ꒙ ꓹY<ʌ ×ⁿǂ

948 Ḡ⊤> Y⌐⊥ᵩ ᶻ·

Y

The little finger and thumb are extended from the fist.

Handshape and orientation	Location, hand arrangement and contact	Movement	Glosses	
The Y hand is held with the palm facing towards the signer (if the hand were opened, the fingers would point to the left).	The hand is held with the thumbtip touching the cheek.	The hand makes a short movement away from the signer.	pay phone	942
The Ḡ hand is held with the palm facing away from the signer (if the hand were opened, the fingers would point up).	The hand is held in front of the body.	The hand makes a short bending movement away from the signer at the wrist, while the thumb and index finger open (forming a Ḡ hand).		
The Y hand is held with the palm facing left (if the hand were opened, the fingers would point up).	The hand is held with the thumb beside the cheek.	The hand makes a short movement away from the signer, so that the thumbtip brushes the cheek; the movement is repeated.	water*	943

Notes * Regional sign.

The Y hand is held with the palm facing towards the signer (if the hand were opened, the fingers would point to the left).	The hand is held beside the ear.	The thumb touches the ear.	phone phone call telephone telephone call toilet call by phone/ telephone [1] phone [1] telephone [1]	944

Notes 1 If the thumb touches the ear and then the hand moves away from the signer, the sign produced is **call by phone/telephone, phone** *(see entry 3 in the English section)*, **telephone** *(see entry 2 in the English section)*. This is a directional verb.

⊃ ᵃY⊤< ˣ⊥

The Y hand is held with the palm facing left (if the hand were opened, the fingers would point up).	The hand is held in front of the mouth and chin.	The hand moves towards the signer while bending slightly towards the signer from the wrist.	wine	945
The Y hand is held with the palm facing left (if the hand were opened, the fingers would point up).	The hand is held in front of the mouth and chin.	The hand moves towards the signer, so that the thumbtip touches the lips; the movement is repeated.	pipe pipe tobacco smoke a pipe pipe [1] plumber [1] radiator [1]	946

Notes 1 If the thumbtip touches the cheek, the sign produced is **pipe** *(see entry 2 in the English section)*, **plumber, radiator**. This is a regional sign.

3 Y<ʌ ˣ·

The Y hand is held with the palm facing left (if the hand were opened, the fingers would point up).	The hand is held with the tip of the thumb touching the underside of the chin.	The hand moves down and away from the signer, with the arm bending away from the signer.	scared stiff scared to death terrified	947

Non-manual features The lips are rounded and then the cheeks puff out.

The left Ġ hand is held with the palm facing towards the signer (if the hand were opened, the fingers would point to the right). The right Y hand is held with the palm facing down (if the hand were opened, the fingers would point away from the signer).	The hands are held in front of the body; the right hand is held higher and nearer to the signer than the left hand.	The right hand makes several short movements from side to side.	either* which of two? *[1]	948

Notes * This sign may also be produced with a left V̈ hand.

V̈a⊥ Yɔ⊥ᵩ ᶻ·

1 If non-manual features appropriate to questions are used, the sign produced is **which of two?**

[527]

949 $\overline{B}a\perp \times Y\sigma\perp \overset{\wedge}{_\perp}$

950 $\overline{B}a\perp Y\sigma< \overset{\vee x}{<}$

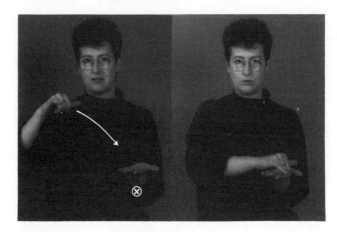

951 $\overline{B}a\perp \times Y\sigma< \overset{<}{x}$

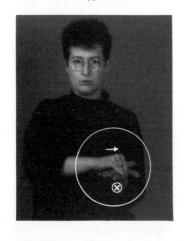

952 $\overline{B}a> \times Y\sigma\perp \overset{z.}{x}$

953 $\emptyset \ Y\sigma> Y\sigma< \div$

954 $\emptyset \ Y\perp\wedge \ Y\perp\wedge \overset{\omega .}{\tau}$

[528]

Handshape and orientation	Location, hand arrangement and contact	Movement	Glosses	
The left **B** hand is held with the palm facing up and the fingers pointing away from the signer; the right **Y** hand is held with the palm facing down (if the hand were opened, the fingers would point away from the signer).	The hands are held in front of the body; the right hand rests on the left palm.	The right hand moves up and, at the same time, away from the signer.	fly by aeroplane/ plane take off in an aeroplane/plane takeoff of an aeroplane/plane	949
The left **B** hand is held with the palm facing up and the fingers pointing away from the signer; the right **Y** hand is held with the palm facing down (if the hand were opened, the fingers would point to the left).	The hands are held in front of the body; the right hand is held higher than the left hand.	The right hand moves down and, at the same time, to the left; the movement ends with the right hand held on the left palm.	airport land in an aeroplane/plane landing of an aeroplane/plane touch down in an aeroplane/plane touchdown of an aeroplane/plane	950
The left **B** hand is held with the palm facing up and the fingers pointing away from the signer; the right **Y** hand is held with the palm facing down (if the hand were opened, the fingers would point to the left).	The hands are held in front of the body; the right hand rests on the left palm.	The right hand moves to the left, maintaining contact with the left palm throughout.	runway taxi in an aeroplane/plane	951
The left **B** hand is held with the palm facing up and the fingers pointing to the right; the right **Y** hand is held with the palm facing down (if the hand were opened, the fingers would point away from the signer).	The hands are held in front of the body; the right hand rests on the left palm.	The right hand moves from side to side several times, maintaining contact with the left palm throughout.	New York shop * shopping *	952

Notes * Regional sign.

Two **Y** hands are held with the palms facing down (if the hands were opened, the left fingers would point to the right, and the right fingers would point to the left).	The hands are held side by side in front of the body.	The hands move apart.	cheque cheque book envelope	953
The left **Y** hand is held with the palm facing right; the right **Y** hand is held with the palm facing left (if the hands were opened, the fingers would all point up).	The hands are held in front of the body.	The hands twist at the wrists, so that the palms face towards the signer; the movement is repeated.	celebrate celebration have fun party social leisure [1] recreation [1] knees up * † [2] paint the town red * † [2] rave up * † [2] shindig * † [2]	954

Notes * This sign may be produced with the hands moving up while twisting towards each other several times at the wrists.

$$\emptyset \quad Y\perp\wedge \quad Y\perp\wedge \quad \left(\begin{smallmatrix}\omega \cdot \\ \times \\ \wedge\end{smallmatrix}\right)$$

† This sign may be produced with the hands moving up, apart and away from the signer while twisting towards each other several times at the wrists.

$$\emptyset \quad Y\perp\wedge \quad Y\perp\wedge \quad \begin{smallmatrix}(\omega \cdot)\\ \times \\ \div \\ \perp\end{smallmatrix}$$

1 If the cheeks are puffed out, the sign produced is **leisure, recreation.**

2 Appropriate non-manual features must be used with this sign; these might include puffed cheeks, narrowed eyes, lips pushed forward, rounded lips, opened mouth.

955 Ø Y>⊥ ¦ Y<∧ $\binom{\omega N\cdot}{N}_>$ 956 ∩ Y>∧ Y<∧ $^{x\omega}_\perp$

957 ⌐ Y⊃∧ Y⊃∧ ˣ

Handshape and orientation	Location, hand arrangement and contact	Movement	Glosses	
The left Y hand is held with the palm facing right; the right Y hand is held with the palm facing left (if the hands were opened, the left fingers would point away from the signer, and the right fingers would point up).	The hands are held side by side in front of the body.	The hands twist up and down alternately from the wrists, while moving to the right throughout.	**changeable** **inconsistent** **infrequent** **irregular** **sometimes**[1]	955

Notes 1 If there is no movement to the right, the sign produced is **sometimes.**

$$\varnothing \quad Y_{>\perp} \ , \ Y_{<\wedge} \ {}^{\omega N \cdot}_{N}$$

The left Y hand is held with the palm facing right; the right Y hand is held with the palm facing left (if the hands were opened, the fingers would all point up).	The hands are held with the thumbs touching the sides of the forehead.	The hands make a short movement away from the signer while twisting at the wrists, so that the palms face away from the signer.	**bull*** **cattle*** **cow*** **horns*** **wicked***†	956

Notes * This sign may be produced using one hand only.

† Regional sign.

$$\cap \quad Y_{<\wedge} \ {}^{x \omega}_{\perp}$$

Two Y hands are held with the palms facing down (if the hands were opened, the fingers would all point up).	The hands are held in front of the upper chest at an angle, so that the palms are turned towards each other.	The thumbtips touch the sides of the upper chest.	**boss***† **company*** **employer***† **firm*** **manager***† **manageress***† **owner***† **bossy***[1]	957

Notes * This sign may be produced using one hand only.

† This sign may be produced with a repeated movement.

$$\ulcorner \mathsf{T}^< \quad Y_{\mho\wedge} \ {}^x$$

$$\ulcorner \urcorner \quad Y_{\mho\wedge} \ Y_{\mho\wedge} \ {}^{x \cdot}$$

or $\ulcorner \mathsf{T}^< \quad Y_{\mho\wedge} \ {}^{x \cdot}$

1 If the movement is repeated and the nose is wrinkled, the sign produced is **bossy.**

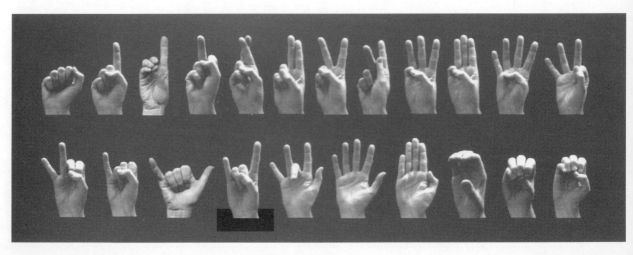

Handshape	Handshape description	Type	Sign entries
५	The index and little fingers are extended from the fist.	Single dez Manual tab Double dez	958 – 959 960
५	The index and little fingers and thumb are extended from the fist.	Single dez Manual tab Double dez	961 – 962

958 ∪ ⅄<ʌ $\overset{\dot{\times}\times 3}{\top}$

959 ∪ ⅄<ʌ $\overset{\times\perp[5]}{\underset{\square}{\vee}}$

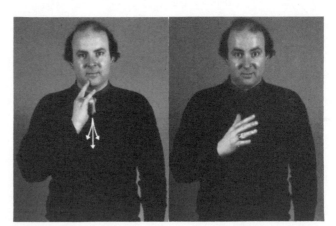

960 ∪ ⅄>ʌ ⅄<ʌ $\overset{\times\dot{\vee}[55]}{\underset{\square}{\overset{\perp}{\rho}}}$

Ч has two main *variants*. In the form shown here, the non-extended fingers are closed in against the palm, with the thumb held against the back of these fingers. A variant form has the two middle fingers held touching the tip of the thumb: this can be transcribed as Ŷ.

Ч has several different *classifier* functions in the productive lexicon and also appears as a classifying component in established signs:

– it is used as a *size and shape* classifier to represent objects with two vertical extensions such as a television aerial and goal posts. It is also used to represent horns, as in the sign **devil** (sign 939 note);

– it has limited use in some areas as a *handling* classifier. In some examples the form seems to combine a *handling* function, indicated by the bent middle fingers, and a *size and shape* function, indicated by the extended index and little fingers. Thus Ч can be used instead of Y in the sign **kettle** (sign 935);

– it can be used to show *extent*, for example, to show the extent of an area with goal posts at either end, such as a rugby pitch or football pitch.

A number of signs using Ч seem to derive from a process of assimiliation. The sign **bitter** (sign 958) is derived from a compound form **taste⌢bad**: rather than using the simple G hand in the first part of the sign, the handshape anticipates the I form required in the second part (see *Introduction* for further discusssion).

Ч expresses the letter **h** of the Irish manual alphabet. As such, it occurs in initial letter handshape signs borrowed from Irish Sign Language. These include **holy** and **hurry up** (see *Introduction*).

The form in which the two middle fingers and thumb touch at the fingertips is sometimes used with the generic meaning of 'animal'. This form has possibly been borrowed from the Paget–Gorman Sign System (see *Introduction*), although it is also well known in the wider hearing community as a way of representing animals, for example, in shadow games played with young children.

Handshape and orientation	*Location, hand arrangement and contact*	*Movement*	*Glosses*	
The Ч hand is held with the palm facing left (if the hand were opened, the fingers would point up).	The hand is held with the index fingertip against the side of the chin.	The hand makes a short, sharp twist at the wrist, so that the palm faces towards the signer; the index fingertip is held against the side of the chin throughout.	**bitter** **sour** **tart**	958
Non-manual features The brows are furrowed, the eyes are narrowed, and the lips are tightly rounded.				
The Ч hand is held with the palm facing left (if the hand were opened, the fingers would point up).	The hand is held with the index fingertip touching the side of the chin.	The hand moves down and away from the signer while opening (forming a **5** hand).	**just*** **plain*** **simple*** **unexciting*** **unimpressive***	959
Notes * Regional sign.				
The left Ч hand is held with the palm facing right; the right Ч hand is held with the palm facing left (if the hands were opened, the fingers would all point up).	The hands are held with the index fingertips touching the sides of the chin.	The hands move firmly down and away from the signer, twisting at the wrists, so that the palms face down and, at the same time, opening (forming two **5** hands).	**amazing*** **dramatic*** **fantastic*** **great*** **marvellous*** **wonderful***	960
Notes * This sign can be produced using one hand only.				

961 ⊔ ᵉ⸰Ψ<ʌ $\overset{\times\perp[\gamma]}{\underset{\#}{v}}$ // $\overset{-}{Bɑ>}$ Y<⊥ $\overset{\overset{\circ}{\tilde{\omega}\cdot}}{z}$

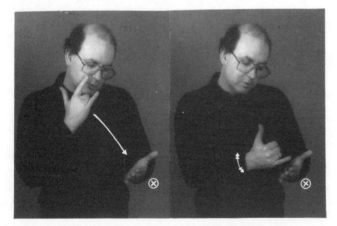

962 ⊔ ᵉ⸰Ψ<ʌ $\overset{\overset{\circ}{\perp[\gamma]}}{\underset{\#}{v}}\left(\overset{\overset{\circ}{\tilde{\omega}\cdot}}{\underset{\perp}{z}}\right)$

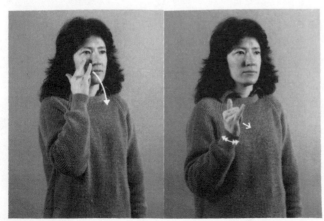

This form results primarily from processes of assimilation. Signs 961 and 962 seem to be derived from a compound form **see⌒perhaps**. Rather than using the **G** handshape for the first part of the compound, the handshape ⍦ anticipates the **Y** handshape which is required in the second part of the sign. This is a rarely used handshape and only seems to occur in such assimilated forms and a few borrowed signs. This form, derived from the American manual alphabet letters **i, l** and **y**, is used in the American sign **I love you** which has been borrowed from American Sign Language (see *Introduction*).

Handshape and orientation	Location, hand arrangement and contact	Movement	Glosses	
The right ⍦ hand is held with the palm facing left (if the hand were opened, the fingers would point up).	The hand is held with the index finger touching the cheek below the eye.	The hand moves down and away from the signer and, at the same time, the index finger closes (forming a ⍦ hand).	check a document examine a document inspect a document review a document	**961**
The left **B** hand is held with the palm facing up and the fingers pointing to the right; the right **Y** hand is held with the palm facing left (if the hand were opened, the fingers would point away from the signer).	The hands are held in front of the body; the right hand is held above the left hand.	The right hand makes several short twisting movements from side to side at the wrist.		

Non-manual features   The eye gaze is directed towards the left hand.

The ⍦ hand is held with the palm facing left (if the hand were opened, the fingers would point up).	The hand is held with the index fingertip touching the cheek below the eye.	The hand makes a short movement down and away from the signer and, at the same time, the index finger closes (forming a **Y** hand); the hand then continues to move away from the signer, while making short twisting movements at the wrist.	check* examine* examiner* experiment* inspect* inspector test* trial* try out* survey[1] surveyor[1]	**962**

Notes   * This sign may be produced using two hands.

1 If two hands are used, moving down and away from the signer and then to the left, the sign produced is **survey, surveyor**.

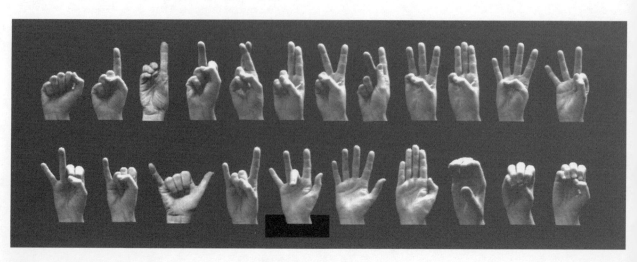

Handshape	Handshape description	Type	Sign entries
୪	The fingers and thumb are extended and spread apart; the middle finger is bent at the palm knuckle.	Single dez Manual tab Double dez	963 – 965 966 – 969
୪̂	The fingers and thumb are extended and spread apart; the middle finger is bent at the palm knuckle with the pad of the thumb touching the pad of the middle finger.	Single dez Manual tab Double dez	970 – 972 973
୪̿	The fingers and thumb are extended and spread apart; the middle finger is bent at the palm knuckle and the thumb is held parallel to the middle finger.	Single dez Manual tab Double dez	974 – 975 976

963 Ø ४⊥ʌ ^o⊤

964 [] ४⊤< ^oᴺ_x·

965 ⌐ᛕ ४⊤< ^o^_x_x^·

The fingers and thumb are extended and spread part; the middle finger is bent at the palm knuckle.

The ଞ handshape shows some *variation* in the degree of bending of the middle finger: in some signs, such as **empty** (sign 963) a relatively straight variant is used; in others, such as **address** (sign 964) a more bent variant is required.

This sign has some *symbolic* functions within the lexicon. The fact that the central finger of the hand is the main articulator makes it symbolically appropriate for meanings such as **centre** (sign 967) and **middle** (sign 967).

It is also symbolically associated with meanings related to feelings and sensitivity as in **feel** (sign 965) and **sensitive** (sign 965). This set of meanings may be a metaphoric extension from its use as a *touch* classifier for small or delicate areas (see below for further discussion).

ଞ has some *classifier* functions within the productive lexicon and is used as a classifying component in established signs:

– it is used as a *size and shape* classifier to indicate narrow objects, such as a cork in **lemonade** (sign 969). Its use in **theatre** (sign 968) may derive from the use of ଞ as a *person* classifier i.e. a person on stage, but such usage appears to be rare within the productive lexicon;

– it operates as a *handling* or *touch* classifier to indicate the handling or touching of small items, small areas or objects which require delicate contact. This seems to be the basis of the sign **Christ** (sign 966) where each middle finger is used to contact the centre of the opposite palm, i.e. the positioning of the wounds in Christ's hands. It is also used to indicate the small mark on the foreheads of Hindu women, as in **tilak** (sign 321 note).

Handshape and orientation	Location, hand arrangement and contact	Movement	Glosses	
The ଞ hand is held with the palm facing away from the signer (if the hand were opened, the fingers would point up).	The hand is held in front of the body.	The hand makes a short movement away from the signer.	empty* ignore*† leave out*† nothing*	963
Non-manual features The tongue tip protrudes between rounded lips and is drawn in sharply as the hand moves.				
Notes * Regional sign.				
† Directional verb.				
The ଞ hand is held with the palm facing towards the signer (if the hand were opened, the fingers would point to the left).	The hand is held with the middle fingertip touching the chest.	The hand makes two short up and down movements; the middle fingertip maintains contact with the chest throughout.	address alive life live toilet	964
The ଞ hand is held with the palm facing towards the signer (if the hand were opened, the fingers would point to the left).	The hand is held in front of the right side of the upper chest.	The hand makes a short upward movement, so that the middle fingertip brushes the chest; the movement is repeated.	feel* sensitive* feel fine*¹ feel good*¹ feel awful*² feel ill*²	965

Notes   * This sign may be produced using two hands.

୮୮ ଞт> ଞт< ଡ଼

1 This sign (with a single brushing movement) may be used as the first part of a compound sign meaning **feel fine, feel good, feel well** (see 164 and 220 respectively for the second part of the sign).

୮୮ᐸ ଞт< ⅂⅂ Ø Åт< ⁱ or

୮୮ ଞт> ଞт< ⅂⅂ Ø Åт> Åт< ⁱ

2 This sign (with a single brushing movement) may be used as the first part of a compound sign meaning **feel awful, feel ill,** (see 904 and 914 respectively for the second part of the sign, produced with a short movement away from the signer).

୮୮ᐠ ଞт< ⅂⅂ Ø I<ʌ ⁱ or

୮୮ ଞт> ଞт< ⅂⅂ Ø I>ʌ I<ʌ ⁱ

966 5>ʌ ˌ ୪<ʌ ˣ ⫽ ୪>ʌ ˣ ˌ 5<ʌ

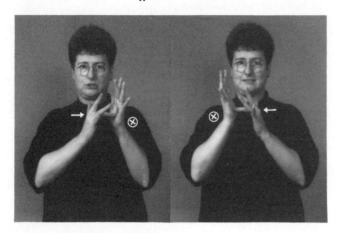

967 B̄ɑ> ୪ʊ⊥ ˣˈ

968 B̄ʊ> ˣ ୪ʊ⊥ ᶻ³ˣ°ᵒ

969 Ō⊤> ⊙ ୪ʊ⊥ ᴬᵒ□ [5] ⫽ Ō⊤> 5ʊ⊥ ᵛˣᵒˈ

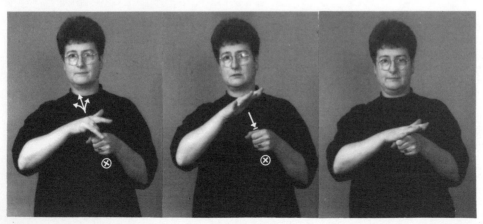

The fingers and thumb are extended and spread part; the middle finger is bent at the palm knuckle.

966-969

Handshape and orientation	Location, hand arrangement and contact	Movement	Glosses	
The left **5** hand is held with the palm facing right and the fingers pointing up; the right **8** hand is held with the palm facing left (if the hand were opened, the fingers would point up).	The hands are held side by side in front of the body.	The right middle fingertip touches the left palm.	**Christ** **Christian** **Jesus** bible [1]	966
The left **8** hand is held with the palm facing right (if the hand were opened, the finger would point up). The right **5** hand is held with the palm facing left and the fingers pointing up.	The hands are held side by side in front of the body.	The left middle fingertip touches the right palm.		

Notes   1 This sign may be used as the first part of a compound sign meaning **bible** (see 1456 for the second part of the sign).

$$5{>}{\wedge}\;_{|}\;\;8{<}{\wedge}\;^{\times}\;\rlap{/}{/}\;\;8{>}{\wedge}\;^{\times}\;_{|}\;\;5{<}{\wedge}\;\rlap{/}{/}$$

$$\varnothing\;\;B{>}{\perp}\;_{|\times}\;B{<}{\perp}\;^{\overset{\times}{\alpha}}$$

The left **B** hand is held with the palm facing up and the fingers pointing to the right; the right **8** hand is held with the palm facing down (if the hand were opened, the fingers would point away from the signer).	The hands are held in front of the body; the right hand is held above the left hand.	The tip of the right middle finger taps the left palm twice.	central centre middle Midlands	967
The left **B** hand is held with the palm facing down and the fingers pointing to the right; the right **8** hand is held with the palm facing down (if the hand were opened, the fingers would point away from the signer).	The hands are held in front of the body; the right middle fingertip is held against the back of the left hand.	The right hand makes short twisting movements from side to side at the wrist; the right middle fingertip is held against the back of the left hand throughout.	drama * play * show * theatre *	968

Notes   * Regional sign.

The left **O** hand is held with the palm facing towards the signer (if the hand were opened, the fingers would point to the right). The right **8** hand is held with the palm facing down (if the hand were opened, the fingers would point away from the signer).	The hands are held in front of the body; the middle finger of the right hand is held between the left thumb and middle fingers.	The right hand makes a short upward movement while opening (forming a **5** hand).	fizzy drink lemonade pop blast [1] bloody [1] damn [1] fuck [2]	969
The left **O** hand is held with the palm facing towards the signer (if the hand were opened, the fingers would point to the right). The right **5** hand is held with the palm facing down and the fingers pointing away from the signer.	The hands are held in front of the body; the right hand is held above the left hand.	The right hand makes a short, firm downward movement; the movement ends with the right palm held on the left hand.		

Notes   1 If the lips are stretched, the sign produced is **blast, bloody, damn**.

            2 If the top teeth are held on the lower lip, the sign produced is **fuck**.

970   Ø   8ᴅⱢ   □̇ [5]

971   Ø   8⊥ᴧ $\left(\begin{smallmatrix}\dot{n}\\\downarrow\\\lor\\□\end{smallmatrix}\right)$ [5]

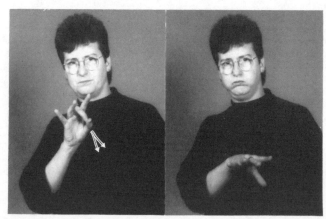

972   ˃⅂⌐   8⊤< $\left(\times\begin{smallmatrix}°ⁱ\\\downarrow\\□\end{smallmatrix}[5]\right)$.

973   Ø   8˃ᴠ   8<ᴠ   □ [88].

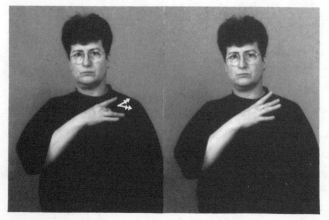

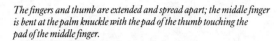

The fingers and thumb are extended and spread apart; the middle finger is bent at the palm knuckle with the pad of the thumb touching the pad of the middle finger.

970-973

8 is used in signs requiring an opening or flicking action. There are two main variants: contact may initially be made between the very edge of the thumbtip and fingertip, as in **contempt** (sign 970) and **Ireland** (sign 972); in the second variant, the contact is between the pads of the thumb and middle finger, as in **sticky** (sign 973).

This handshape seems to have limited *classifier* use within the productive lexicon and within established signs:

– it may be used as a *handling* or *touch* classifier to indicate the handling of sticky substances, as in **sticky** (sign 973), or to indicate the flicking

away of tiny objects. Signs such as **dismiss** (sign 970) and **reject** (sign 970) may be seen as metaphorical extensions of this meaning. This handshape expresses the letter **k** of the Irish manual alphabet. As such it has the potential to occur in initial letter handshape signs borrowed from Irish Sign Language. However, perhaps because of the infrequency of this handshape within BSL generally, such borrowings seem to be rare except in Irish influenced name signs such as **Kevin** (see *Introduction*).

Handshape and orientation		Location, hand arrangement and contact	Movement	Glosses	
The 8 hand is held with the palm facing down (if the hand were opened, the fingers would point away from the signer).		The hand is held in front of the body.	The middle finger and thumb flick open (forming a 5 hand).	contempt † disdain * † dismiss * † reject * † show contempt/ disdain *	970
Non-manual features	The nose is wrinkled and the corners of the mouth are turned down.				
Notes	* Directional verb.				
	† This sign may be produced with the hand bending firmly away from the signer from the wrist, while opening (forming a 5 hand).		Ø 8⊥∧		
The 8 hand is held with the palm facing away from the signer (if the hand were opened, the fingers would point up).		The hand is held in front of the body.	The hand bends sharply away from the signer at the wrist while moving down and, at the same time, opening (forming a 5 hand).	could not care less couldn't care less do not care a damn don't care a damn do not give a damn don't give a damn have no time for not on your life	971
Non-manual features	The brows are furrowed and the cheeks are puffed out.				
The 8 hand is held with the palm facing towards the signer (if the hand were opened, the fingers would point to the left).		The hand is held with the back of the thumb touching the left side of the upper chest.	The hand makes a short movement away from the signer, while the middle finger and thumb open sharply (forming a 5̄ hand); the movement is repeated.	Ireland Irish	972
The left 8 hand is held with the palm facing right; the right 8 hand is held with the palm facing left (if the hands were opened, the fingers would all point down).		The hands are held in front of the body.	The thumbs and index fingers open (forming two 8 hands) and close; the movement is repeated several times.	sticky tacky	973
Notes	This sign may be produced using one hand only.		Ø 8<∨		

974 ℧ 𝄃̄oⲧ ˣ ·

975 ℧ 𝄃̄oⲧ ˣᵃ [s]

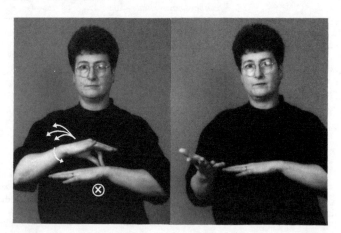

976 ∅ 𝄃̄⊥ʌ 𝄃̄⊥ʌ #[88] ·

The fingers and thumb are extended and spread apart; the middle finger is bent at the palm knuckle and the thumb is held parallel to the middle finger.

ŏ̄ is used rarely in the lexicon. Like ŏ it may be used as a *handling* or *touch* classifier to indicate the contacting of small or delicate areas, as in the delicate contact required to take a pulse: see **doctor** (sign 974). This handshape is sometimes used instead of **F** for the handling of delicate items, such as jewellery.

Handshape and orientation	Location, hand arrangement and contact	Movement	Glosses	
The right ŏ̄ hand is held with the palm facing down (if the hand were opened, the fingers would point away from the signer).	The left hand is held in front of the body with the palm facing down; the right thumb and middle finger tips rest on the left wrist.	The right middle finger and thumb tips tap the left wrist twice.	**doctor** **medical**	974
The right ŏ̄ hand is held with the palm facing down (if the hand were opened, the fingers would point away from the signer).	The left hand is held in front of the body with the palm facing down; the right thumb and middle finger tips rest on the left wrist.	The hand twists at the wrist, so that the palm faces up, while opening (forming a **5** hand).	**trade** **professional**[1] **qualified**[1] **skilled**[1]	975

Notes 1 If an ŏ handshape is used, making a short upward movement while opening (forming a **5** hand), the sign produced is **professional, qualified, skilled**.

ʋ ŏ̄ɒ⊥ ×ᴬ° [5]

Two ŏ̄ hands are held with the palms facing away from the signer (if the hands were opened, the fingers would all point up).	The hands are held in front of the body.	The thumb and middle fingertips close, (forming two ŏ hands); the movement is repeated.	**complete*** **completion*** **conclude*** **conclusion*** **finish***	976

Notes * Regional sign.

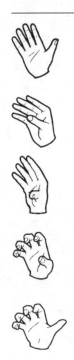

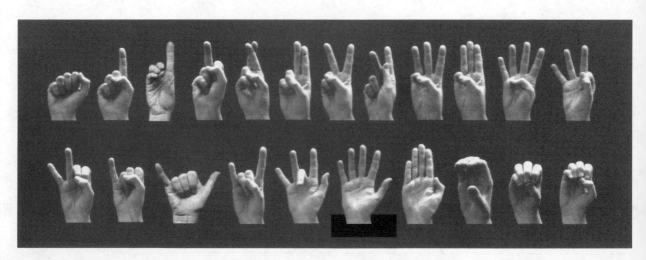

5

Handshape	Handshape description	Type	Sign entries
5	The hand is held flat with the fingers and thumb spread apart.	Single dez Manual tab Double dez	977 – 1013 1014 – 1027 1028 – 1089
5̄	The extended fingers (spread apart) are bent at the palm knuckles with the extended thumb held parallel to the fingers.	Single dez Manual tab Double dez	1090 – 1097 1098 – 1099 1100 – 1107
5̈	The hand is held flat with the fingers and thumb spread apart and bent at the palm knuckles.	Single dez Manual tab Double dez	1108 – 1110 1111 – 1112 1113 – 1122
5̈	The bent fingers and bent thumb are extended and spread apart.	Single dez Manual tab Double dez	1123 – 1148 1149 – 1160 1161 – 1180
5̤	The extended fingers (spread apart) are bent and the thumb is extended.	Single dez Manual tab Double dez	1181 – 1188 1189 1190 – 1200

977 Ø 5ᴅ⊥ ᵉ

978 Ø 5ᴅ⊥ ⁀<ᴛ

979 Ø 5ᴅ⊥ ˚ᵛ·

980 Ø 5ᴅ⊥ ⁽ᴺ·⁾>

981 Ø 5ᴅ⊥ ⁽˚ᴺ·⁾>

982 Ø 5ᴅ⊥ ˚ω·ᴺ

5 is one of the most frequent handshapes used within BSL. In some uses, **5̈**, where the fingers are bent at the palm knuckles, may be used instead of **5**. However, **5** is normally used in most of the examples cited in this section.

5 has several different *classifier* functions in the productive lexicon and is used as a classifying element in established signs:

– it is used as a *people* classifier to indicate several or many people as in **queue** (sign 1024) and **audience** (sign 1049) and is frequently used in verbs of motion or location involving people (see *Introduction*);

– it is used as a *size and shape* classifier to represent several long, thin things or objects with several or many long, narrow extensions such as the branches of a tree and the antler of deer, as in **tree** (sign 1026) and **antlers** (sign 1071). It is used to indicate lines or stripes. Two-handed forms are used to indicate the intersecting lines of graph paper, timetables and netting. It is also used to indicate objects of large, indeterminate shape, such as **furniture** (sign 1038); it may be used to indicate many pairs of eyes, as in **stare** (see *Introduction*);

– it is used as a *tracing size and shape* classifier to trace the outline and shape of objects or areas perceived either as flat or having an uneven surface, as in **countryside** (sign 980) and **sea** (sign 981);

– it is used as a *handling* classifier to indicate the handling of large items such as a large box or a pile of heavy, flat items;

– it is used as an *instrumental* classifier to represent implements, tools or utensils with several long, narrow extensions, such as a rake, the brushes of a car wash or the spiked units of a combine harvester;

– it is used as a *touch* classifier to indicate actions of the whole hand(s) such as patting, pushing and hitting as in **bounce a ball** (sign 979), actions of the palms such as kneading plasticine as in **plasticine** (sign 1020) and to indicate actions of the fingers such as hitting keys in **text telephone** (sign 1019) and **type** (sign 1043);

– it is used to indicate the *extent* of large areas or objects as in **enormous** (sign 1064) and to indicate depth as in **high tide** (sign 1047). It is also used to express *quantity*, particularly to indicate multiplicity, as in **numerous** (sign 1053);

5 also has a *deictic* (pointing) function, as in **there** (sign 977).

5 expresses both the right-hand and left-hand components of the letter **w** of the British manual alphabet. As such, it occurs in initial letter handshape signs such as **west** (sign 1048) and **worth** (sign 1050).

5 also has a wide range of symbolic functions within the lexicon (see *Introduction*).

Handshape and orientation	Location, hand arrangement and contact	Movement	Glosses	
The **5** hand is held with the palm facing down and the fingers pointing away from the signer.	The hand is held in front of the body.	The fingers wiggle.	be exist still there	977
Non-manual features The lips are rounded and pushed forward.				
The **5** hand is held with the palm facing down and the fingers pointing away from the signer.	The hand is held in front of the body.	The hand makes an anticlockwise circle in the horizontal plane.	general overall	978
The **5** hand is held with the palm facing down and the fingers pointing away from the signer.	The hand is held in front of the body.	The hand makes two short downward movements.	basketball basketball player bounce a ball/ basketball play basketball	979
The **5** hand is held with the palm facing down and the fingers pointing away from the signer.	The hand is held in front of the body.	The hand makes several up and down movements while moving to the right throughout.	countryside hills waves	980
The **5** hand is held with the palm facing down and the fingers pointing away from the signer.	The hand is held in front of the body.	The hand moves to the right while making short up and down movements throughout.	ocean sea water	981
The **5** hand is held with the palm facing down and the fingers pointing away from the signer.	The hand is held in front of the body.	The hand makes several short up and down twisting movements at the wrist.	average fair maybe so-so not sure[1] unsure[1]	982
Non-manual features The mouth is closed with the lips pushed forward.				
Notes 1 If the mouth is closed with the lips pushed forward and the eyebrows are slightly furrowed, the sign produced is **not sure, unsure**.				

983 Ø 5ᴅ⊥ ⊥̬@·

984 Ø 5ᴅ⊥ ⊥̬°<# [A]

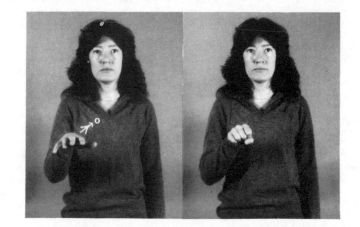

985 Ø 5ᴅ⊥ (°ω·)̬>

986 Ø 5ᴅ⊥ (°ω·)̬> // Ø G̈ᴅ⊥ ⊥̬>@

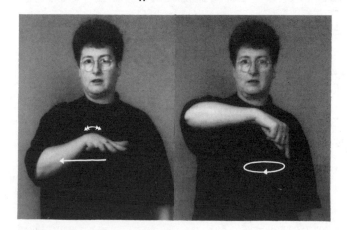

987 Ø ɪ⁵5ᴅ⊥ ᴖ̬>

988 Ø 5⊥ᴧ ℓ

Handshape and orientation	Location, hand arrangement and contact	Movement	Glosses	
The **5** hand is held with the palm facing down and the fingers pointing away from the signer.	The hand is held in front of the body.	The hand makes anticlockwise circles in the horizontal plane.	area*† family* local*† locality*† location*† place*† region*† regional* situation* somewhere*† about*†[1] approximate*[1]	983

Notes   * This sign may be produced with the hand making clockwise circles in the horizontal plane.

Ø 5ᴖ⊥ (diagram)

    † This sign may be produced with the palm facing away from the signer and the fingers pointing up; the hand makes circles in the vertical plane parallel to the signer's body.

Ø 5⊥ʌ (diagram)

or Ø 5⊥ʌ (diagram)

    1 If the mouth is closed and the lips are pushed forward slightly, the sign produced is **about, approximate.**

| The **5** hand is held with the palm facing down and the fingers pointing away from the signer. | The hand is held in front of the body. | The hand makes a short movement towards the signer and to the left, while closing (forming an **A** hand). | adopt* adoption pinch* take* grab*[1] seize*[1] snatch*[1] | 984 |

Notes   * Directional verb.

    1 If the movement is sharp, the sign produced is **grab, seize, snatch.**

Ø 5ᴖ⊥ (diagram) [A]

| The **5** hand is held with the palm facing down and the fingers pointing away from the signer. | The hand is held in front of the body. | The hand moves to the right and, at the same time, makes small up and down twisting movements at the wrist. | bumpy* uneven ripple[1] | 985 |

Notes   * This sign may be produced with a short, firm twist to the right at the wrist, repeated several times as the hand moves to the right.

    1 If the lips are tightly rounded, the sign produced is **ripple.**

Ø 5ᴖ⊥ (diagram)

| The **5** hand is held with the palm facing down and the fingers pointing away from the signer. | The hand is held in front of the body. | The hand moves to the right while making short up and down twisting movements at the wrist. | lake loch pond | 986 |

| The **Ğ** hand is held with the palm facing down (if the hand were opened, the fingers would point away from the signer). | The hand is held in front of the body. | The hand makes a clockwise circle in the horizontal plane. | | |

| The **5** hand is held with the palm facing down and the fingers pointing away from the signer. | The hand is held in front of the body. | The hand moves to the left and towards the signer in an arc, with the arm bending from the elbow. | all every everybody everyone everything everywhere | 987 |

| The **5** hand is held with the palm facing towards the signer and the fingers pointing up. | The hand is held in front of the body. | The fingers wiggle. | how many? how much? | 988 |

Non-manual features   The eyebrows are raised.

989 Ø 5⊤< °ṅ·
N

990 Ø 5⊥ʌ °e·
V

991 Ø 5⊥ʌ °ṅ·
Z

992 ∩ 5<ʌ ∧̇
⊤

993 Ọ 5⊤ʌ °⊤

994 Ц 5ʊ< ℓ̇
<

995 Ц 5⊤ʌ ℓ̇
x

996 Ц 5<ʌ ˣṅ̇
⊥
V

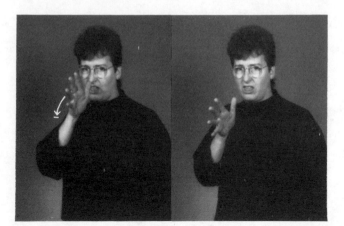

[554]

Handshape and orientation	Location, hand arrangement and contact	Movement	Glosses	
The 5 hand is held with the palm facing towards the signer and the fingers pointing to the left.	The hand is held in front of the body.	The hand makes several short up and down bending movements from the wrist.	hurt † pain † painful † sore † Brighton [1] costly [2] dear [2] expensive [2] amazing * [3] gosh * [3] stunning * [3] wow * [3]	989

Non-manual features The lips are rounded.

Notes * This sign may be produced using two hands.

$\emptyset$ 5т> 5т<

† This sign may be produced using two hands, making alternate movements.

$\emptyset$ 5т> 5т<

1 If the non-manual features are not present, the sign produced is **Brighton**.

2 If the cheeks are slightly puffed out, the sign produced is **costly**, **dear**, **expensive**.

3 If the lips are rounded and the eyebrows are raised, the sign produced is **amazing**, **gosh**, **stunning**, **wow**.

The 5 hand is held with the palm facing away from the signer and the fingers pointing up.	The hand is held in front of the body.	The hand makes an anticlockwise circle in the vertical plane parallel to the signer's body.	colour	990
The 5 hand is held with the palm facing away from the signer and the fingers pointing up.	The hand is held at head height in front of the body.	The hand makes several short, sharp bending movements from side to side at the wrist.	bye cheerio goodbye hello	991
The 5 hand is held with the palm facing left and the fingers pointing up.	The hand is held in front of the face.	The hand moves firmly up and, at the same time, towards the signer, so that the thumbtip approaches the forehead.	horrible nasty terrible ugly	992

Non-manual features The cheeks puff out and, at the same time, the eyes narrow.

| The 5 hand is held with the palm facing towards the signer and the fingers pointing up. | The hand is held in front of the face. | The hand makes a short, firm movement towards the signer. | ashamed
embarrass
embarrassed
embarrassment
shame | 993 |

Non-manual features The head tilts forward and the lips are pressed together.

| The 5 hand is held with the palm facing down and the fingers pointing to the left. | The hand is held beside the nose. | The fingers wiggle and, at the same time, the hand moves to the left. | aroma
scent
smell
waft
water [1] | 994 |

Notes 1 If the location is changed, so that the hand moves across the mouth and chin, the sign produced is **water**. This is a regional sign.

∪ 5◦<

| The 5 hand is held with the palm facing towards the signer and the fingers pointing up. | The hand is held with the fingertips in front of the nose. | The fingers wiggle, tapping the nose. | age
how old? [1] | 995 |

Notes 1 If the brows are raised or furrowed, the sign produced is **how old?**

| The 5 hand is held with the palm facing left and the fingers pointing up. | The hand is held with the thumbtip touching the nose. | The hand bends firmly away from the signer at the wrist, while moving down. | take advantage of someone/something * | 996 |

Non-manual features The eyes are narrowed, the nose is wrinkled and the tongue tip protrudes between the top teeth and the lower lip.

Notes * Directional verb.

997　Ӡ 5<ʌ ˣ

998　⌣ 5ᴛʌ ˣ ∥ B̄ɑ> I<⊥ ˅ˣ

999　∪ 5ʋ< ˣ

1000　∪ 5ʋ< ˣ ∥ B̄ʋ> 5̈ʋ⊥ ˣ·

1001　∪ 5<ʌ ˣ ∥ B̄ɑ> C⊥ʌ ˅<

Handshape and orientation	Location, hand arrangement and contact	Movement	Glosses	
The **5** hand is held with the palm facing left and the fingers pointing up.	The hand is held with the fingers beside the right cheek.	The fingers wiggle, tapping the cheek repeatedly.	**when?** **time**[1]	**997**

Non-manual features   Non-manual features appropriate for questions must be used.

Notes   1 If the non-manual features are not present, the sign produced is **time**. This is a regional sign.

The left **B** hand is held with the palm facing up and the fingers pointing to the right; the right **5** hand is held with the palm facing towards the signer and the fingers pointing up.	The left hand is held in front of the body; the right hand is held with the fingertips touching the chin.	The right hand moves down while closing (forming an **I** hand); the movement ends with the right hand held against the left palm.	**wrong** **confess**[1] **confession**[1] **fault**[1] **faulty**[1]	**998**

Notes   1 If the movement of the **I** hand onto the left palm is repeated, the sign produced is **confess, confession, fault, faulty**.

$$\cup\ \ 5\text{T}\wedge\ ^{\times}\ {}^{\prime\prime}_{\prime\prime}\ \overline{\text{B}\alpha}{\rangle}\ \text{I}{\langle}{\perp}\ ^{(\vee\times)\cdot}$$

The **5** hand is held with the palm facing down and the fingers pointing to the left.	The hand is held with the thumbtip against the chin.	The fingers wiggle.	**fish** **fisherman** **fishmonger**	**999**
The **5** hand is held with the palm facing down and the fingers pointing to the left.	The hand is held with the thumbtip against the chin.	The fingers wiggle; the thumbtip is held against the chin throughout.	**fishcake**	**1000**
The left **B** hand is held with the palm facing down and the fingers pointing to the right; the right **5̈** hand is held with the palm facing down (if the hand were opened, the fingers would point away from the signer).	The hands are held in front of the body; the right hand is held above the left hand.	The right fingertips tap the back of the left hand twice.		

Notes   * The second part of this sign may be produced with the left palm facing up.

$$\cup\ \ 5\text{v}{\langle}\ ^{\times}_{2}\ {}^{\prime\prime}_{\prime\prime}\ \overline{\text{B}\alpha}{\rangle}\ \ddot{5}\text{v}{\perp}\ ^{\times\cdot}$$

The **5** hand is held with the palm facing left and the fingers pointing up.	The hand is held with the thumbtip against the chin.	The fingers wiggle; the thumbtip is held against the chin throughout.	**fish and chips**	**1001**
The left **B** hand is held with the palm facing up and the fingers pointing to the right; the right **C** hand is held with the palm facing away from the signer (if the hand were opened, the fingers would point up).	The hands are held in front of the body; the right hand is held above the left hand.	The right hand makes a short movement down and, at the same time, to the left; the movement is repeated.		

1002 ⊓ 5ᴚ< $^{×ॐ}_{⊥}$

1003 [] ª5ᴚ< $^{×⊚×}_{∨∨}$·

1004 [] 5⊤ʌ $^{×⊥[ɢ]}_{#}$

1005 [] 5⊤< $^{°°}_{×}$$^{×⊤}_{∨}$$_{ᴅ}$

Handshape and orientation	Location, hand arrangement and contact	Movement	Glosses	
The 5 hand is held with the palm facing down and the fingers pointing to the left.	The hand is held with the index fingertip against the side of the neck.	The hand twists away from the signer; the index finger is held against the neck throughout.	awful disgusting dreadful horrible horrid revolting terrible	1002
Non-manual features The brows are slightly furrowed, the nose is wrinkled and the tongue protrudes between the top teeth and the lower lip.				
The 5 hand is held with the palm facing down and the fingers pointing to the left.	The hand is held with the thumbtip against the chest.	The hand makes anticlockwise circles in the vertical plane parallel to the signer's body; the thumbtip is held against the chest throughout.	delay put off time (take one's time)	1003
Non-manual features The tongue protrudes between the teeth, and the head is tilted slightly to one side.				
The 5 hand is held with the palm facing towards the signer and the fingers pointing up.	The hand is held in front of the chest.	The palm touches the chest and then the hand moves away from the signer while closing (forming a G hand).	like (if you like) please yourself suit yourself up to you want (if you want) wish (if you wish)	1004
The 5 hand is held with the palm facing towards the signer and the fingers pointing to the left.	The hand is held resting against the chest.	The hand makes a short upward movement brushing the chest, and then makes a short movement away from the signer while twisting at the wrist, so that the palm faces up.	dislike do not like don't like	1005

Non-manual features   The nose is wrinkled and the brows are slightly furrowed.

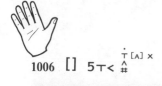

1006 [] 5⊤< $\overset{\dot{\top}^{[A]}×}{\overset{\wedge}{\#}}$

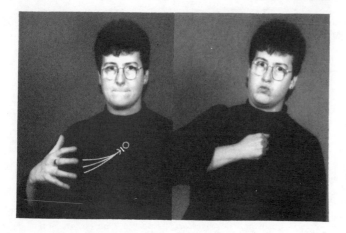

1007 [] 5⊤< $\overset{\overset{\circ}{\wedge}\overset{\omega}{\top}\overset{\top}{\vee}}{\overset{\times}{\vee}\overset{\top}{\circ}}$

1008 └┘< 5ɑ< $\begin{pmatrix}\overset{\circ}{\top}^{[A]}× \\ \overset{<}{\#}\end{pmatrix}$ ·

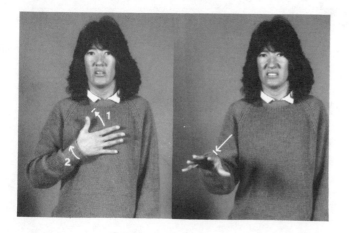

1009 └┘ 5⊤< $\overset{×\dot{\top}^{[B]}}{\#}$ // $\emptyset$ $\hat{B}$ɔ⊤ $\overset{\circ}{\square}^{[5]}$

1010 ⌐⊤< 5ɣ< $\overset{×}{\varphi}$

Handshape and orientation	Location, hand arrangement and contact	Movement	Glosses	
The 5 hand is held with the palm facing towards the signer and the fingers pointing to the left.	The hand is held in front of the chest.	The hand moves firmly up and towards the signer while closing (forming an A hand); the movement ends with the hand held against the chest.	scared stiff scared to death terrified	**1006**

Non-manual features The lips are closed and drawn back; as the hand moves, the body moves back, the eyes open wide and the mouth opens with a sharp puff of air, so that the lips are rounded.

The 5 hand is held with the palm facing towards the signer and the fingers pointing to the left.	The hand is held with the palm resting against the chest.	The hand makes a firm upward movement, brushing the chest, and then twists away from the signer from the wrist (so that the palm faces down and the fingers point away from the signer) before making a firm movement down and, at the same time, away from the signer.	cannot bear can't bear cannot stand can't stand detest disgust hate loathe	**1007**

Non-manual features Appropriate non-manual features must be used.

The 5 hand is held with the palm facing up and the fingers pointing to the left.	The hand is held in front of the waist.	The hand moves towards the signer and to the left while closing (forming an A hand); the movement ends with the hand touching the body, and is then repeated.	alimony benefit dole grant income maintenance pension salary wage	**1008**

The 5 hand is held with the palm facing towards the signer and the fingers pointing to the left.	The hand is held with the fingers resting against the lower chest.	The hand moves firmly away from the signer and, at the same time, closes (forming a B̂ hand).	abort
			abortion
			abortion
			  (have an abortion)
			hysterectomy (have
			  an hysterectomy)
			hysterectomy
				1009

The B̂ hand is held with the palm facing down (if the hand were opened, the fingers would point away from the signer).	The hand is held in front of the body.	The hand makes a short downward movement and, at the same time, opens (forming a 5̄ hand).		

The 5 hand is held with the palm facing down and the fingers pointing to the left.	The hand is held with the thumbtip against the right side of the upper chest.	The fingers wiggle; the thumbtip is held against the side of the upper chest throughout.	loads * lot * lots * many * much * numerous *	**1010**

Non-manual features The right cheek is puffed out.

Notes * Regional sign.

1011 Ў1 ᵃ5ᴕ< $\overset{\circ}{\underset{\vee}{3}}$>×$\overset{\cdot}{3}$>

1012 ⌐⌐ 5ɑ< $\overset{\mathsf{T\,[\wedge]}}{\#}$

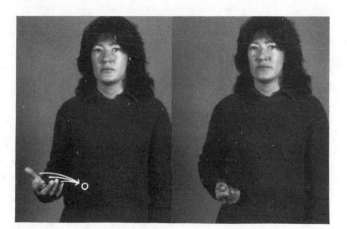

1013 ⌐⌐ 5⊤< ×$\overset{\circ}{\perp}$

1014 $\overline{\mathsf{G}}$⊤> ₁× 5⊥∧ᵨ $\overset{\circ}{\underset{\mathsf{Z}}{\mathsf{n}}}$·

1015 $\overline{\mathsf{G}}$ ⊤> ₁× 5⊥∧ᵨ ᵉ

 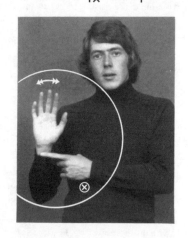 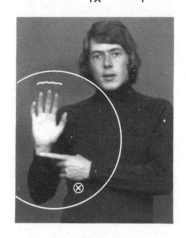

1016 $\overline{\mathsf{G}}$>⊥ 5ᴕ⊥ᵨ $\overset{\perp}{\underset{\perp}{×}}$·

1017 $\overline{\overline{\mathsf{G}}}$ɑ⊥ 5ᴕ⊥ᵨ $\overset{@}{\underset{\mathsf{T}}{<}}$

[562]

Handshape and orientation	Location, hand arrangement and contact	Movement	Glosses	
The 5 hand is held with the palm facing towards the signer and the fingers pointing to the left.	The hand is held in front of the left side of the upper chest.	The hand makes a short downward twisting movement at the wrist, so that the thumbtip brushes the side of the chest; the movement is repeated.	maid* servant* waiter* waitress*	1011

Notes   * This sign may be produced on the right side of the chest.

The 5 hand is held with the palm facing up and the fingers pointing to the left.	The hand is held beside the waist.	The hand moves towards the signer and, at the same time, closes (forming an A hand).	accept* get* receive*	1012

Notes   * This sign may be produced using two hands.

The 5 hand is held with the palm facing towards the signer and the fingers pointing to the left.	The hand is held resting against the lower chest.	The hand makes a short movement away from the signer.	expecting pregnant	1013

The left G hand is held with the palm facing towards the signer (if the hand were opened, the fingers would point to the right). The right 5 hand is held with the palm facing away from the signer and the fingers pointing up.	The hands are held in front of the body; the left index fingertip is held against the front of the right wrist.	The right hand makes several short bending movements from side to side at the wrist.	cinema* film* movie* picture* pictures* programme*	1014

Notes   * This sign may be produced with both hands moving down throughout.

The left G hand is held with the palm facing towards the signer (if the hands were opened, the fingers would point to the right). The right 5 hand is held with the palm facing away from the signer and the fingers pointing up.	The hands are held in front of the body; the left index fingertip is held against the front of the right wrist.	The fingers wiggle.	calendar* date*	1015

Notes   * Regional sign.

The left G hand is held with the palm facing right (if the hand were opened, the fingers would point away from the signer). The right 5 hand is held with the palm facing down and the fingers pointing away from the signer.	The hands are held in front of the body; the right hand is held higher than the left hand.	The right hand moves away from the signer, so that the right palm brushes along the left index finger; the movement is repeated several times.	fool*† have someone on* joke† joker† kid* play a joke on* pull someone's leg* tease*† jeer*†¹ mock*†¹ ridicule*†¹ taunt*†¹	1016

Notes   * Directional verb.

† This sign may be produced using one hand only.

1 If the eyes are narrowed and the tongue protrudes between the teeth, the sign produced is **jeer, mock, ridicule, taunt**.

The left Ġ hand is held with the palm facing up (if the hand were opened, the fingers would point away from the signer). The right 5 hand is held with the palm facing down and the fingers pointing away from the signer.	The hands are held in front of the body; the right hand is held higher and nearer to the signer than the left hand.	The right hand makes a large anticlockwise circle in the horizontal plane.	environment national majority¹	1017

Notes   1 If the cheeks are puffed out, the sign produced is **majority**.

1018 G̈ɑ⊥ 5ᴛᴅ⊥, ⊥<@o°

1019 Y⊥ᴅ 5ᴅ⊥ ᵒ

1020 5ɑ⊥ ₓ 5ᴅ< ⊥<@°

1021 5ᴅ⊥ ₓ 5ᴅ⊥ ⊥ₓ

1022 5ᴅ> 5ᴅ⊥ ⊥<(⊓<⊥<

1023 5⊤> ∓ 5<⊥ ×·

Handshape and orientation	Location, hand arrangement and contact	Movement	Glosses	
The left Ğ hand is held with the palm facing up (if the hand were opened, the fingers would point away from the signer). The right 5 hand is held with the palm facing down and the fingers pointing away from the signer.	The hands are held in front of the body; the right hand is held higher and nearer to the signer than the left hand.	The right hand makes a small anti-clockwise circle in the horizontal plane.	area* around* family* local* locality* location* neighbourhood* place* region* regional* situation* somewhere* surrounding*	1018
Notes * This sign may be produced with a repeated movement.				
The left Y hand is held with the palm facing down (if the hand were opened, the fingers would point away from the signer). The right 5 hand is held with the palm facing down and the fingers pointing away from the signer.	The hands are held in front of the body; the left hand is held above the right hand.	The right fingers wiggle.	Deaf Communicating Terminal (DCT) Minicom telephone by Deaf Communicating Terminal/minicom/ vistel/text telephone text telephone Vistel	1019
The left 5 hand is held with the palm facing up and the fingers pointing away from the signer; the right 5 hand is held with the palm facing down and the fingers pointing to the left.	The hands are held in front of the body; the right hand rests on the left hand.	The right hand makes anticlockwise circles in the horizontal plane, maintaining contact with the left palm throughout.	dirt* dirty* filth* filthy* grime* grimy* plasticine unclean*	1020
Notes * This sign may be produced with the lips stretched and the nose wrinkled.				
Two 5 hands are held with the palms facing down and the fingers pointing away from the signer.	The hands are held in front of the body; the right hand is held higher and nearer to the signer than the left hand.	The right hand moves away from the signer, maintaining contact with the back of the left hand throughout.	influence* persuade*[1] persuasion[1] flow[2]	1021
Notes * Directional verb.				
1 If the movement is repeated, the sign produced is **persuade, persuasion.**				
2 If the right hand makes short movements from side to side while moving away from the signer, maintaining contact with the back of the left hand throughout, the sign produced is **flow.**				
The left 5 hand is held with the palm facing down and the fingers pointing to the right; the right 5 hand is held with the palm facing down and the fingers pointing away from the signer.	The hands are held in front of the body; the right hand is held higher than the left hand.	The right hand moves away from the signer and to the left, before bending to the left at the wrist while moving to the left and towards the signer.	field meadow pasture	1022
The left 5 hand is held with the palm facing towards the signer and the fingers pointing to the right; the right 5 hand is held with the palm facing left and the fingers pointing away from the signer.	The hands are held crossed over in front of the body; the right hand is held higher than the left hand.	The right wrist taps the left wrist twice.	green	1023

1024 5>∧ ₓ 5<∧₉ ᵀ

1025 √B℧> ₓ 5⊥∧₉ ˣ̌

1026 B̄℧> ₓ j̇5<∧ ⍥̇ℤ

1027 C̄a⊥ 5℧< ⎛∘⎞· ⎝⌃⎠

1028 ∅ 5a⊥ 5a⊥ ˅̊

1029 ∅ 5a⊥ 5a⊥ ÷̇˅

Handshape and orientation	Location, hand arrangement and contact	Movement	Glosses	
The left 5 hand is held with the palm facing right and the fingers pointing up; the right 5 hand is held with the palm facing left and the fingers pointing up.	The hands are held in front of the body; the right hand is held nearer to the signer than the left hand, with the side of the right little finger touching the side of the left index finger.	The right hand moves towards the signer.	line* line up* queue*	1024

Notes   * The following notes apply to all glosses:

This sign may also be produced using two 4 hands.

$$4 >\wedge \quad _\times \quad 4 <\wedge_\varphi \quad ^\top$$

This sign may be produced with the left hand moving away from the signer as the right hand moves towards the signer.

$$\emptyset \quad 5 >\wedge \quad _\times \quad 5 <\wedge_\varphi \quad ^{\div}_{\top}$$

$$\text{or} \quad \emptyset \quad 4 >\wedge \quad _\times \quad 4 <\wedge_\varphi \quad ^{\div}_{\top}$$

The left B hand is held with the palm facing down and the fingers pointing to the right; the right 5 hand is held with the palm facing away from the signer and the fingers pointing up.	The left arm is positioned across the body; the right hand is held nearer to the signer than the left hand, with the right wrist held against the side of the left forearm.	The right hand moves to the right; the right wrist maintains contact with the side of the left arm throughout.	bushes hedge	1025
The left B hand is held with the palm facing down and the fingers pointing to the right; the right 5 hand is held with the palm facing left and the fingers pointing up.	The left arm is positioned across the body; the right elbow is held on the back of the left hand.	The right hand makes several short twisting movements from side to side at the wrist.	tree forest[1] wood[1]	1026

Notes   1 If the hand movement is maintained while the body twists from left to right from the waist, the sign produced is **forest, wood.**

The left Ċ hand is held with the palm facing up (if the hand were opened, the fingers would point away from the signer). The right 5 hand is held with the palm facing down and the fingers pointing to the left.	The hands are held in front of the body; the right fingers are held above the left palm.	The right hand makes small clockwise circles in the horizontal plane; the right fingers wiggle throughout.	calculate using a calculator calculator	1027
Two 5 hands are held with the palms facing up and the fingers pointing away from the signer.	The hands are held in front of the body.	The hands make a short downward movement.	heavy*†	1028

Non-manual features   The brows are furrowed.

Notes   * This sign may be produced using one hand only.

$$\emptyset \quad 5 a \perp \quad \overset{\circ}{\vee}$$

† This sign may be produced with a repeated movement.

$$\emptyset \quad 5 a \perp \quad 5 a \perp \quad \overset{\circ}{\vee}\cdot \quad \text{or} \quad \emptyset \quad 5 a \perp \quad \overset{\circ}{\vee}\cdot$$

Two 5 hands are held with the palms facing up and the fingers pointing away from the signer.	The hands are held in front of the body.	The hands make circles (the left hand moves anticlockwise, the right hand moves clockwise) in the vertical plane parallel to the signer's body.	game play cheer up[1]	1029

Notes   1 If the head is tilted forward, and the brows are slightly furrowed, the sign produced is **cheer up.**

1030 Ø 5α⊥ 5α⊥ ⚲⋮v̇

1031 Ø 5̄α⊥ 5ʊ< ⋰⊤ₓ

1032 Ø 5̄α> ₓ 5ʊ⊥ ⋰ₓ

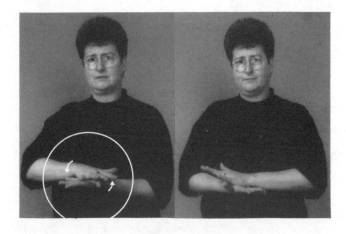

1033 Ø 5ʊʌ 5ʊʌ °v[ʌʌ]ω✕# // Ø A⊤ʌ A⊤ʌ °⊥

1034 Ø 5ʊ⊥ 5ʊ⊥ ^

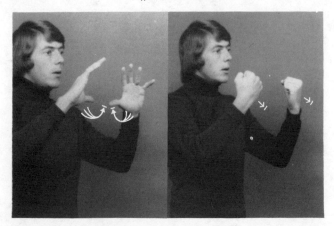

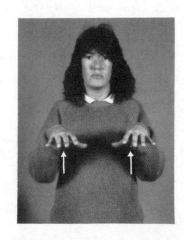

Handshape and orientation	Location, hand arrangement and contact	Movement	Glosses	
Two 5 hands are held with the palms facing up and the fingers pointing away from the signer.	The hands are held in front of the body.	The hands make small circles in the vertical plane, parallel to the signer's body (the left hand moves anti-clockwise, the right hand moves clockwise).	where? *†	1030

Non-manual features   Non-manual features for questions must be used.

Notes   * This sign can be produced using one hand only.

Ø   5ɑ⊥   ⌄

† This sign may be produced with the hands making a short movement towards each other and then apart; the movement is repeated.

Ø   5ɑ⊥   5ɑ⊥   x·

The left 5 hand is held with the palm facing up and the fingers pointing away from the signer; the right 5 hand is held with the palm facing down and the fingers pointing to the left.	The hands are held in front of the body; the right hand is held above the left hand.	The hands change places while twisting, so that the palms rub firmly against each other; the movement ends with the heels of the hands touching.	bankrupt corrupt damage destroy devastate ruin sabotage spoil vandalise wreck upside down [1]	1031

Non-manual features   The cheeks are puffed out.

Notes   1 If the tongue protrudes between the teeth, the sign produced is **upside down.**

The left 5 hand is held with the palm facing up and the fingers pointing to the right; the right 5 hand is held with the palm facing down and the fingers pointing away from the signer.	The hands are held in front of the body with the heels of the hands together.	The hands twist from the wrists, so that the left palm faces down and the right palm faces up; the palms maintain contact throughout.	bankrupt corrupt damage destroy devastate ruin sabotage spoil vandalise wreck	1032
Two 5 hands are held with the palms facing down and the fingers pointing up.	The hands are held in front of the body at an angle, so that the palms are turned towards each other.	The hands move firmly down and, at the same time, twist at the wrists, so that the palms face towards the signer, while closing (forming two A hands); the hands then make a short, firm movement away from the signer.	Almighty Almighty God	1033
Two 5 hands are held with the palms facing down and the fingers pointing away from the signer.	The hands are held in front of the body.	The hands move up.	flood overflow [1]	1034

Note   1 If the hands move up and then apart and, at the same time, away from the signer, the sign produced is **overflow.**

Ø   5ɒ⊥   5ɒ⊥   ^⊤÷

1035 Ø 5ᴖ⊥ 5ᴖ⊥ $\overset{\varrho}{\vee}$

1036 Ø 5ᴖ⊥ 5ᴖ⊥ $\overset{\circ}{\underset{\wedge}{\top}}$

1037 Ø 5ᴖ⊥ 5ᴖ⊥ $\overset{\circ}{\vee}\cdot$

1038 Ø 5ᴖ⊥ 5ᴖ⊥ $\overset{(\overset{\circ}{\vee}\cdot)}{\div}$

1039 Ø 5ᴖ⊥ 5ᴖ⊥ $\overset{(\overset{\circ}{z}\cdot)}{\top}$

1040 Ø 5ᴖ⊥ 5ᴖ⊥ $\overset{\circ}{\underset{\top}{I\wedge}}\cdot$

Handshape and orientation	Location, hand arrangement and contact	Movement	Glosses	
Two **5** hands are held with the palms facing down and the fingers pointing away from the signer.	The hands are held in front of the body.	The hands move slowly down and, at the same time, the fingers wiggle.	snow snowfall	1035

Two **5** hands are held with the palms facing down and the fingers pointing away from the signer.	The hands are held in front of the body.	The hands make a short, firm movement up and, at the same time, towards the signer.	regret
			  something
			wish something
			  had not happened
			sorry something
			  has happened
				1036

Non-manual features   The mouth is open.

Two **5** hands are held with the palms facing down and the fingers pointing away from the signer.	The hands are held in front of the body.	The hands make two short downward movements.	Belfast Britain British Great Britain here settle settle down take it easy calm down [1]	1037

Notes   1 If the movement is slower, the sign produced is **calm down**.

Two **5** hands are held with the palms facing down and the fingers pointing away from the signer.	The hands are held in front of the body.	The hands make several short downward movements while moving apart throughout.	furniture	1038
Two **5** hands are held with the palms facing down and the fingers pointing away from the signer.	The hands are held in front of the body.	The hands make short, sharp movements from side to side while moving away from the signer.	earthquake * tremor * vibrate *	1039

Non-manual features   The lips vibrate together.

Notes   * This sign may be produced with the cheeks slightly puffed out instead of the lips vibrating together.

Two **5** hands are held with the palms facing down and the fingers pointing away from the signer.	The hands are held in front of the body.	The hands make alternate short movements towards and away from the signer.	move shake [1] wobble [2] jelly [3] quiver [3] earthquake [4] tremor * [4] vibrate * [4]	1040

Notes   * This sign may be produced with the cheeks slightly puffed out instead of the lips vibrating.

1 If the cheeks are slightly puffed out, the sign produced is **shake**.

2 If the tongue protrudes between the teeth, the sign produced is **wobble**.

3 If the lips are rounded and the movements are not alternate, the sign produced is **jelly, quiver**.

4 If the lips vibrate together, the sign produced is **earthquake, tremor, vibrate**.

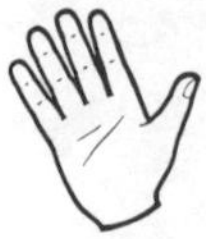

1041 Ø 5̄ɑ⊥ 5ɑ⊥ ≷·

1042 Ø 5̄ɑ⊥ ǀ 5ɑ⊥

1043 Ø 5ɑ⊥ ǀ 5ɑ⊥

1044 Ø 5ɑ⊥ ǀ 5ɑ⊥ ÷

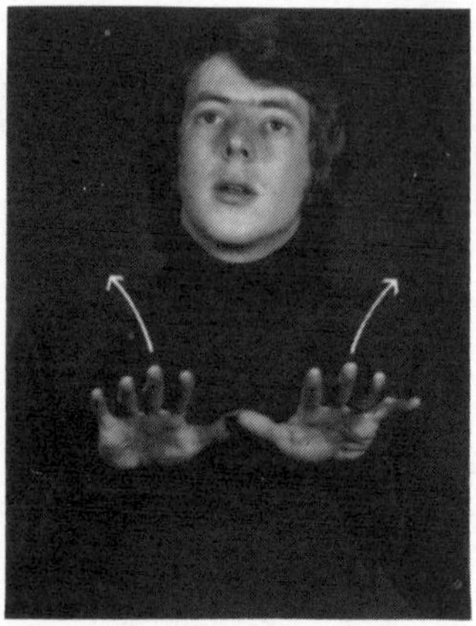

1045 Ø 5ɑ⊥ ǀ 5ɑ⊥

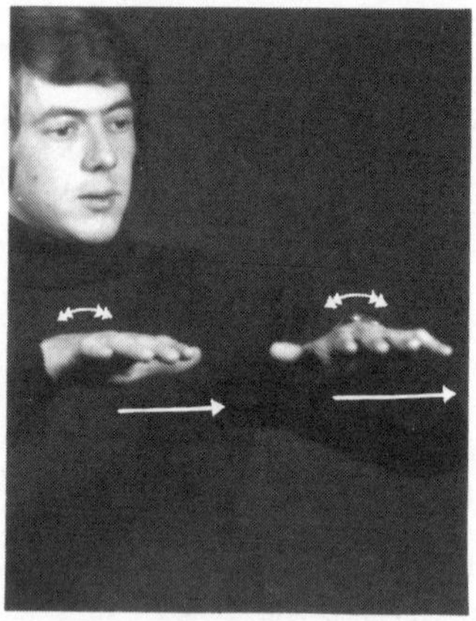

1046 Ø 5ɑ⊥ ǀ 5ɑ⊥

1047 Ø 5ɑ⊥ ǀ 5ɑ⊥ ˅

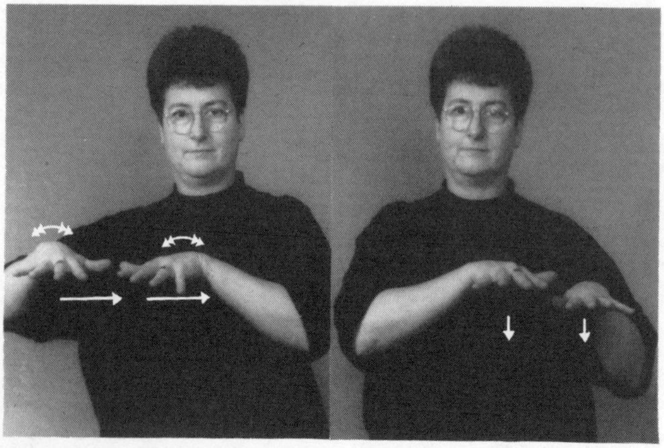

Handshape and orientation	Location, hand arrangement and contact	Movement	Glosses	
Two **5** hands are held with the palms facing down and the fingers pointing away from the signer.	The hands are held in front of the body; the right hand is held higher than the left hand.	The hands move down and, at the same time, to the left; the movement is repeated.	rain	1041
Two **5** hands are held with the palms facing down and the fingers pointing away from the signer.	The hands are held side by side in front of the body; the right hand is held higher than the left hand.	The hand moves up and, at the same time, towards the signer with the fingers flexing and wiggling throughout; the movement is repeated.	cast a spell hypnosis hypnotise hypnotist spell	1042

Non-manual features   The head tilts to the right and the eyes are narrowed.

Handshape and orientation	Location, hand arrangement and contact	Movement	Glosses	
Two **5** hands are held with the palms facing down and the fingers pointing away from the signer.	The hands are held side by side in front of the body.	The fingers wiggle.	computer keyboard † keyboard operator † office † secretary † type * † typewriter † typist †	1043

     Notes   * This sign may be produced with the hands moving down while the fingers wiggle.

           † This sign may be produced with the hands moving up and down alternately while the fingers wiggle.

$$\varnothing \ \ 5\,\widehat{}\!\perp \ , \ 5\,\widehat{}\!\perp \ \overset{\vee}{\underset{\wedge}{}}$$

$$\varnothing \ \ 5\,\widehat{}\!\perp \ , \ 5\,\widehat{}\!\perp \ \overset{\wedge\wedge}{\underset{\wedge}{}}\cdot$$

Handshape and orientation	Location, hand arrangement and contact	Movement	Glosses	
Two **5** hands are held with the palms facing down and the fingers pointing away from the signer.	The hands are held side by side in front of the body.	The hands move away from the signer and, at the same time, apart.	common national spread universal widespread epidemic [1]	1044

     Notes   1 This sign may be used as the second part of a compound sign meaning **epidemic** (see 931 for the first part of the sign).

$$[] \ \ \ddot{\imath}\,a> \ \ddot{\imath}\,a< \ \overset{\circ}{\underset{\times}{\vee}}\cdot \ /\!/ \\ /\!/$$

$$\varnothing \ \ 5\,\widehat{}\!\perp \ , \ 5\,\widehat{}\!\perp \ \overset{\perp}{\div}$$

Handshape and orientation	Location, hand arrangement and contact	Movement	Glosses	
Two **5** hands are held with the palms facing down and the fingers pointing away from the signer.	The hands are held side by side in front of the body.	The hands move to the left, while making small up and down twisting movements at the wrists throughout.	ocean * sea * water * waves *	1045

     Notes   * This sign may be produced with the hands moving apart while twisting at the wrists.

$$\varnothing \ \ 5\,\widehat{}\!\perp \ , \ 5\,\widehat{}\!\perp \ \left(\overset{\circ}{\underset{\div}{\omega}}\cdot\right)$$

Handshape and orientation	Location, hand arrangement and contact	Movement	Glosses	
Two **5** hands are held with the palms facing down and the fingers pointing away from the signer.	The hands are held side by side in front of the body.	The hands make short up and down twisting movements at the wrists while moving apart and, at the same time, away from the signer.	country countryside desert	1046
Two **5** hands are held with the palms facing down and the fingers pointing away from the signer.	The hands are held side by side in front of the body.	The hands move to the left while making small up and down twisting movements at the wrists; the hands then move down.	ebb tide low tide high tide [1]	1047

     Notes   1 If the final movement of the hands is upwards, the sign produced is **high tide**.

$$\varnothing \ \ 5\,\widehat{}\!\perp \ , \ 5\,\widehat{}\!\perp \ \left(\overset{\circ}{\underset{<}{\omega}}\cdot\right)\wedge$$

1048 ∅ 5ᴕ>ᵢ 5ᴕ< ᴵ

1049 ∅ 5ᴛ∧ 5ᴛ∧ ᴰᵀ↓ₘ

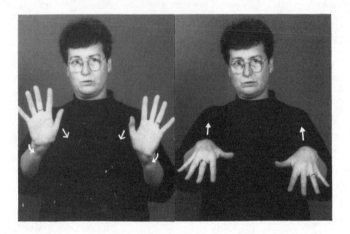

1050 ∅ 5ᴛ⊥ ᴵ 5ᴛ⊥ °↓∨

1051 ∅ 5ᴛ⊥ ᴵ 5ᴛ⊥ °<↑ᴛ

1052 ∅ 5ᴛ> 5ᴛ< ᴰᴺ·

1053 ∅ 5ᴛ>ᵢ 5ᴛ< ♀÷

1054 ∅ 5ᴛ>ᵢ 5ᴛ< ♀ᴺ·ᴺᴵ

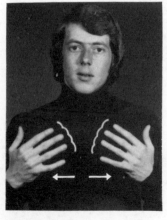

Handshape and orientation	Location, hand arrangement and contact	Movement	Glosses	
The left 5 hand is held with the palm facing down and the fingers pointing to the right; the right 5 hand is held with the palm facing down and the fingers pointing to the left.	The hands are held side by side in front of the body at an angle, so that the palms are turned towards each other.	The hands move towards each other, so that the fingers link together.	week west *	1048

Notes   * This sign may be produced with the hands held in front of the left side of the body.

Two 5 hands are held with the palms facing away from the signer and the fingers pointing up.	The hands are held in front of the body.	The hands bend away from the signer at the wrists, and then move up and towards the signer while the fingers bend at the palm knuckles.	audience	1049
Two 5 hands are held with the palms facing towards the signer and the fingers pointing away from the signer.	The hands are held in front of the body at an angle, so that the palms are turned towards each other; the fingers are held linked together.	The hands remain together and make a short movement away from the signer and, at the same time, down.	worth	1050
Two 5 hands are held with the palms facing towards the signer and the fingers pointing away from the signer.	The hands are held in front of the body with the palms turned towards each other and the fingers linked together.	The hands remain together and make a small clockwise circle in the horizontal plane.	America American The States United States of America USA	1051
The left 5 hand is held with the palm facing towards the signer and the fingers pointing to the right; the right 5 hand is held with the palm facing towards the signer and the fingers pointing to the left.	The hands are held in front of the body.	The hands bend up and down from the wrists several times alternately.	hurt injure injury pain painful sore suffer	1052

Non-manual features   Appropriate negative non-manual features must be used.

The left 5 hand is held with the palm facing towards the signer and the fingers pointing to the right; the right 5 hand is held with the palm facing towards the signer and the fingers pointing to the left.	The hands are held side by side in front of the body.	The hands move apart and, at the same time, the fingers wiggle.	loads lot lots many much numerous too many too much	1053

Non-manual features   The cheeks are puffed out.

The left 5 hand is held with the palm facing towards the signer and the fingers pointing to the right; the right 5 hand is held with the palm facing towards the signer and the fingers pointing to the left.	The hands are held side by side in front of the body.	The hands move up and away from the signer and then down and towards the signer alternately, with the fingers wiggling throughout; the movements are repeated.	accountant accounts add up arithmetic calculate figures finance mathematician mathematics maths results scores statistician statistics sums add *[1] add up to *[1] count *[1]	1054

Notes   * This sign may be produced with the hands making a single movement up and away from the signer, while the fingers wiggle.

   1 If the hands do not move alternately, the sign produced is **add, add up to, count.**

$\emptyset$ 5⊤> ⎸   5⊤< $\overset{\text{o}}{\underset{\perp}{\wedge}}$

$\emptyset$ 5⊤> ⎸   5⊤< $\overset{\text{o·}}{\underset{\mathrm{I}}{\mathrm{N}}}$

1055 ∅ 5⊤> ╷ 5⊤< $^{\substack{♀\,∿\,·\\ I}}$ // ∅ Ö⊥∧ ╷ Ö⊥∧ $^{÷∨×}$

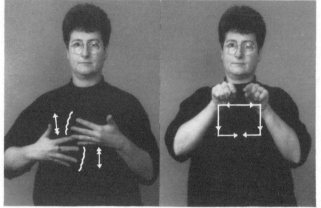

1056 ∅ 5>∧ 5<∧ $\left(\substack{○\\∧\\×\\∪\\×}\right)$

1057 ∅ 5>∧ 5<∧ $\left(\substack{○\\ω\\z\\·\\∧}\right)$

1058 ∅ 5>∧ 5<∧ $^{∿∿·}$

1059 ∅ 5>∧ 5<∧ $^{\substack{□\,∿\,·\\I}}$

1060 ∅ 5>∧ ╷ 5<∧ $^{\substack{(♀)\,∿\,·\\∿}}$

1061 ∅ 5>⊥ 5<⊥ $^{\substack{×\,ℯ\,×\\∧÷∧\\∨}}$

[576]

Handshape and orientation	Location, hand arrangement and contact	Movement	Glosses	
The left 5 hand is held with the palm facing towards the signer and the fingers pointing to the right; the right 5 hand is held with the palm facing towards the signer and the fingers pointing to the left.	The hands are held side by side in front of the body.	The hands move up and away from the signer and then down and towards the signer alternately with the fingers wiggling throughout; the movements are repeated.	balance sheet	1055
Two ŏ hand are held with the palms facing away from the signer (if the hands were opened, the fingers would all point up).	The hands are held side by side in front of the body.	The hands move apart and then down before finally moving back towards each other.		
The left 5 hand is held with the palm facing right and the fingers pointing up; the right 5 hand is held with the palm facing left and the fingers pointing up.	The hands are held in front of the body.	The hands make a short movement up and towards each other, while bending towards each other at the wrists.	attendance crowd gathering turnout	1056
The left 5 hand is held with the palm facing right and the fingers pointing up; the right 5 hand is held with the palm facing left and the fingers pointing up.	The hands are held in front of the body.	The hands move up and, at the same time, make several short twisting movements from side to side at the wrists.	gleam glitter gloss glossy shimmer shine shiny sparkle	1057
The left 5 hand is held with the palm facing right and the fingers pointing up; the right 5 hand is held with the palm facing left and the fingers pointing up.	The hands are held in front of the body.	The hands move up and down alternately twice.	five-a-side*	1058

Notes   * This sign may be modified according to number, e.g. **six-a-side**.

$\emptyset$ $|>\wedge$ $|<\wedge$ $^{\wedge\wedge}\cdot$

The left 5 hand is held with the palm facing right and the fingers pointing up; the right 5 hand is held with the palm facing left and the fingers pointing up.	The hands are held side by side in front of the body.	The hands bend towards and away from the signer alternately from the wrists.	traffic motorway [1]	1059

Notes   1 If the hands make alternate short bending movements towards and away from the signer from the wrists, the sign produced is **motorway**.

The left 5 hand is held with the palm facing right and the fingers pointing up; the right 5 hand is held with the palm facing left and the fingers pointing up.	The hands are held side by side in front of the body.	The hands move up and down several times alternately, with the fingers wiggling throughout.	burn fire flames	1060
The left 5 hand is held with the palm facing right and the fingers pointing away from the signer; the right 5 hand is held with the palm facing left and the fingers pointing away from the signer.	The hands are held in front of the body.	The hands move up and towards each other and then make circles (the left hand moves anticlockwise, the right hand moves clockwise) in the vertical plane parallel to the signer's body, before finally continuing to move up and towards each other.	blaze bonfire large fire smoke	1061

Non-manual features   The cheeks are puffed out.

1062 Ø $\overline{5>\perp}$ × 5<⊥ $\overset{\overset{o}{\uparrow}}{\underset{\#}{\top}}$[AA]

1063 Ø 5>⊥ ¦ 5<⊥ $^{(\overset{o}{\div}.)}$

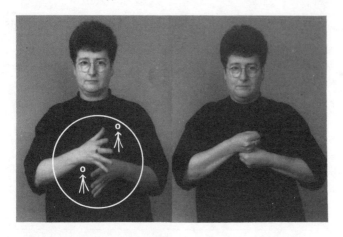

1064 Ø 5>⊥ ¦ 5<⊥ $^{\overset{o}{\wedge}\overset{o\cdot}{\div}\vee}$

1065 Ø 5>⊥ ¦ 5<⊥ $^{\overset{\cap\wedge\cdot}{\wedge}}$ // Ø Bʊ⊥ ¦ Bʊ⊥ ÷

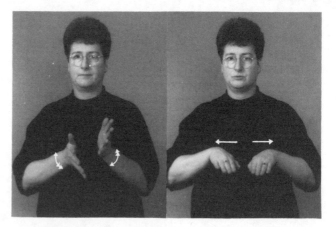

1066 Ø 5>⊥ ¦ 5<⊥ $^{\overset{\wedge\wedge\cdot}{\underset{\wedge}{\times}}}$

1067 Ø 5>⊥ ¦ 5<⊥ $^{\overset{\omega\wedge\cdot}{\sqcap}}$

[578]

Handshape and orientation	Location, hand arrangement and contact	Movement	Glosses	
The left 5 hand is held with the palm facing right and the fingers pointing away from the signer; the right 5 hand is held with the palm facing left and the fingers pointing away from the signer.	The hands are held in front of the body; the right hand is held on the side of the left hand.	The hands remain together and move towards the signer while closing (forming two A hands).	feelings (bottle up one's feelings) restrain oneself toilet (desperate to go to the toilet)	1062
The left 5 hand is held with the palm facing right and the fingers pointing away from the signer; the right 5 hand is held with the palm facing left and the fingers pointing away from the signer.	The hands are held side by side in front of the body.	The hands move apart in two stages.	develop expand grow increase	1063
The left 5 hand is held with the palm facing right and the fingers pointing away from the signer; the right 5 hand is held with the palm facing left and the fingers pointing away from the signer.	The hands are held side by side in front of the body.	The hands make a short upward movement and then move apart before making a short, firm downwards movement.	big enormous great large major majority	1064
The left 5 hand is held with the palm facing right and the fingers pointing away from the signer; the right 5 hand is held with the palm facing left and the fingers pointing away from the signer.	The hands are held side by side in front of the body.	The hands bend up and down from the wrists several times alternately.	playground	1065
Two B hands are held with the palms facing down and the fingers pointing away from the signer.	The hands are held side by side in front of the body.	The hands move apart.		
The left 5 hand is held with the palm facing right and the fingers pointing away from the signer; the right 5 hand is held with the palm facing left and the fingers pointing away from the signer.	The hands are held in front of the body.	The hands move up and down alternately, so that the palms brush together; the movements are repeated several times.	game play	1066
The left 5 hand is held with the palm facing right and the fingers pointing away from the signer; the right 5 hand is held with the palm facing left and the fingers pointing away from the signer.	The hands are held side by side in front of the body.	The hands make alternate clockwise circles in the vertical plane at right angles to the signer's body.	sign* sign language*	1067

Notes   * This sign may be produced with the hands making alternate short, sharp movements towards and away from the signer, twisting from the wrists.

Ø 5>∧ ┊ 5<∧ $\overset{\overset{\circ}{\omega N}}{H}$ ·

1068 Ø 5>⊥ ; 5<⊥ ↓ᵛ @∾· // B⊤> ₓ B⊤<₉ ˣₓ

1069 Ø 5>⊥ ; 5<⊥ ⁽ω⁾ₙₙ ∾·

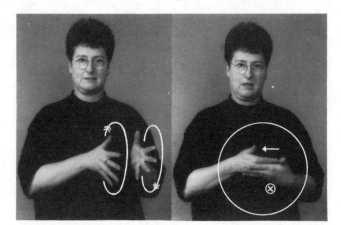

1070 ⊓̄ 5⊥ʌ 5⊥ʌ ⁰ω̇z·

1071 ∩ 5⊥ʌ 5⊥ʌ ˣ⁽⁰⊥÷÷·⁾

1072 ◡ 5⊤ʌ 5⊤ʌ ˣᵛ≠

1073 ◡ 5⊤ʌ 5⊤ʌ ⁰⊓⊤·

Handshape and orientation	Location, hand arrangement and contact	Movement	Glosses	
The left **5** hand is held with the palm facing right and the fingers pointing away from the signer; the right **5** hand is held with the palm facing left and the fingers pointing away from the signer.	The hands are held side by side in front of the body.	The hands make alternate clockwise circles in the vertical plane at right angles to the signer's body.	sign language	1068
The left **B** hand is held with the palm facing towards the signer and the fingers pointing to the right; the right **B** hand is held with the palm facing towards the signer and the fingers pointing to the left.	The hands are held in front of the body; the backs of the right fingers rest against the left palm.	The right hand moves to the right, maintaining contact with the left palm throughout.		
The left **5** hand is held with the palm facing right and the fingers pointing away from the signer; the right **5** hand is held with the palm facing left and the fingers pointing away from the signer.	The hands are held side by side in front of the body.	The hands move up and down alternately while twisting up and down alternately from the wrists.	crawl crawler flatter flatterer suck up to	1069

Non-manual features   The head is tilted forward and to one side, and the tongue protrudes between the top teeth and the lower lip.

Two **5** hands are held with the palms facing away from the signer and the fingers pointing up.	The hands are held above and to the sides of the head.	The hands make several short, sharp twisting movements from side to side at the wrists.	applaud applause	1070
Two **5** hands are held with the palms facing away from the signer and the fingers pointing up.	The hands are held with the thumbtips touching the sides of the forehead.	The hands move apart and, at the same time, away from the signer in two short stages.	antlers deer reindeer	1071
Two **5** hands are held with the palms facing towards the signer and the fingers pointing up.	The hands are held in front of the face.	The hands move down and, at the same time, towards each other, crossing over in front of the face.	cloud dark darken dim dull dusk fog mist overcast	1072

Non-manual features   The eyes are narrowed.

Two **5** hands are held with the palms facing towards the signer and the fingers pointing up.	The hands are held in front and to the sides of the face.	The hands make a short bending movement towards the signer from the wrists; the movement is repeated several times.	weather * wind * wind blowing windy *	1073

Non-manual features   The lips are rounded.

Notes   * This sign may be produced using one hand only.

$$\bigcirc \quad 5\top\wedge \quad \overset{\circ}{\underset{\top}{n}} \cdot$$

1074 ○ 5⊤∧ 5⊤∧ $^{@N·}_{×_V}$

1075 ○ 5⊥∧ 5⊥∧ $^{×_V}_{≠}$

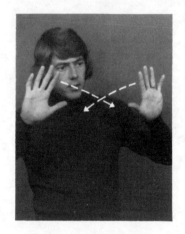

1076 ○ 5>∧ 5<∧ $^{°}_{÷·}$

1077 ○ 5>∧ 5<∧ $^{∩}_{⊤·}$

1078 [] 5⊤> 5⊤< $^{V}_{×}$

1079 [] 5⊤> 5⊤< $^{∩·}_{×V}$

[582]

Handshape and orientation	Location, hand arrangement and contact	Movement	Glosses	
Two **5** hands are held with the palms facing towards the signer and the fingers pointing up.	The hands are held in front of the face.	The hands make alternate circles (the left hand moves clockwise, the right hand moves anticlockwise) in the vertical plane parallel to the signer's body.	confused * dizzy *[1] faint [2] busy [3]	1074

Notes * This sign can be produced using one hand only.

1 If the eyes are opened wide and the upper body moves backwards and forwards, the sign produced is **dizzy**.

2 If the eyes are narrowed and the upper body moves backwards and forwards, the sign produced is **faint**.

3 If the non-manual features are not present, the sign produced is **busy**. This is a regional sign.

Two **5** hands are held with the palms facing away from the signer and the fingers pointing up.	The hands are held in front and to the sides of the face.	The hands move slowly down and, at the same time, towards each other, crossing over in front of the face.	dim fog haze mist	1075

Non-manual features The eyes are narrowed.

The left **5** hand is held with the palm facing right and the fingers pointing up; the right **5** hand is held with the palm facing left and the fingers pointing up.	The hands are held at either side of the face.	The hands make a short movement apart; the movement is repeated.	conceited * know-all * bighead * arrogant *[1]	1076

Notes * This sign may be produced with a single movement.

1 If the nose is wrinkled and the corners of the mouth are turned down, the sign produced is **arrogant**.

The left **5** hand is held with the palm facing right and the fingers pointing up; the right **5** hand is held with the palm facing left and the fingers pointing up.	The hands are held at either side of the face.	The hands bend towards the signer from the wrists; the movement is repeated.	careless lucky * mean [1] miser [1] miserly [1] selfish [1] tight [1]	1077

Notes * Regional sign.

1 If the lips are rounded and pushed forward, the sign produced is **mean, miser, miserly, selfish, tight**.

The left **5** hand is held with the palm facing towards the signer and the fingers pointing to the right; the right **5** hand is held with the palm facing towards the signer and the fingers pointing to the left.	The hands are held with the fingers resting against the chest.	The hands move down, maintaining contact with the chest throughout.	body * wear *	1078

Notes * This sign may be produced using one hand only.

The left **5** hand is held with the palm facing towards the signer and the fingers pointing to the right; the right **5** hand is held with the palm facing towards the signer and the fingers pointing to the left.	The hands are held with the fingertips resting against the chest.	The hands bend up and down repeatedly at the wrists; the fingers maintain contact with the chest throughout.	pyjamas *	1079

Notes * This sign may be produced using two **v** hands.

1080 [] 5т> 5т< ×⊥

1081 [] 5т> 5т< ᵛ·

1082 [] 5т> 5т< ∧ ○
                  × ÷
                  × ∧

1083 [] 5т> 5т< ᵘᵖ
                  × ÷
                  ×
                  ᵛ

1084 [] ¯5т> 5т< ∧ ○
                  × ⊥

[584]

Handshape and orientation	Location, hand arrangement and contact	Movement	Glosses	
The left 5 hand is held with the palm facing towards the signer and the fingers pointing to the right; the right 5 hand is held with the palm facing towards the signer and the fingers pointing to the left.	The hands are held with the fingertips resting against the chest.	The hands move firmly away from the signer.	amaze amazement astonish astonishment horrify shock startle startling surprise	1080

Non-manual features   The mouth opens.

The left 5 hand is held with the palm facing towards the signer and the fingers pointing to the right; the right 5 hand is held with the palm facing towards the signer and the fingers pointing to the left.	The hands are held with the fingertips resting against the chest.	The hands move down, maintaining contact with the chest; the movement is repeated.	clothes clothing dress dress up[1] dressed[1,2]	1081

Notes   1 If the hands move alternately, the sign produced is **dressed** (*see entry 1 in the English section*), **dress up.**

$$[] \ 5\top> \ 5\top< \ ^{v\cap \cdot}_{x}$$

2 If the movement is not repeated, the sign produced is **dressed** (*see entry 2 in the English section*).

$$[] \ 5\top> \ 5\top< \ ^{v}_{x}$$

The left 5 hand is held with the palm facing towards the signer and the fingers pointing to the right; the right 5 hand is held with the palm facing towards the signer and the fingers pointing to the left.	The hands are held with the fingertips resting against the chest.	The hands move up and then make a short movement up and, at the same time, apart, maintaining contact with the chest throughout.	emotion* † emotional* † feel* feeling* sense* sensation*	1082

Notes   * The following notes apply to all glosses:

This sign may be produced using one hand only.

$$[] \ 5\top< \ ^{\wedge \ \circ}_{x \ \wedge}$$

This sign may also be produced using one or two 8 hands.

$$[] \ 8\top> \ 8\top< \ ^{\wedge \div}_{x \ \wedge} \ \text{or} \ [] \ 8\top< \ ^{\wedge \ \circ}_{x \ \wedge}$$

† This sign may be produced with a repeated movement.

$$[] \ 5\top> \ 5\top< \left(^{\wedge \ \circ}_{x \ \wedge} \right)^{\cdot} \ \text{or} \ [] \ 5\top< \left(^{\wedge \ \circ}_{x \ \wedge} \right)^{\cdot}$$

The left 5 hand is held with the palm facing towards the signer and the fingers pointing to the right; the right 5 hand is held with the palm facing towards the signer and the fingers pointing to the left.	The hands are held in front of the chest.	The hands move down, brushing the chest, before moving apart while twisting at the wrists, so that the palms face down.	dress* frock* wear* dress up[1]	1083

Notes   * This sign may be produced with the palms facing up and twisting to face down while the hands move down.

$$[] \ 5\alpha> \ 5\alpha< \ ^{v}_{p}{}^{v}_{x}{}^{p}_{d}$$

1 If the movement is repeated with the hands moving alternately, the sign produced is **dress up.**

$$[] \ 5\top> \ 5\top< \ ^{v\cap \cdot}_{x \div}$$

The left 5 hand is held with the palm facing towards the signer and the fingers pointing to the right; the right 5 hand is held with the palm facing towards the signer and the fingers pointing to the left.	The hands are held with the fingers resting against the chest; the left hand is held below the right hand.	The hands make a short upward movement, maintaining contact with the chest, and then move away from the signer while twisting at the wrists, so that the palms face up.	express	1084

1085 [] $\overline{5\top>}$ 5⊤< $\overset{\circ}{\underset{\#}{\overset{\top[AA]×}{\wedge}}}$

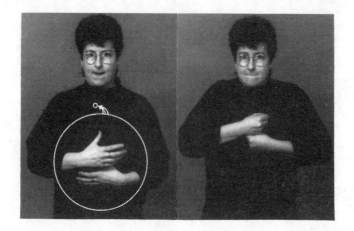

1086 ⌐⌐ 5ʊ> 5ʊ< $\overset{×}{\underset{\circ}{}}$

1087 ⌐⌐ 5ʊ> 5ʊ< $\overset{\circ\omega}{\underset{\wedge}{\overset{×}{\top}}}$

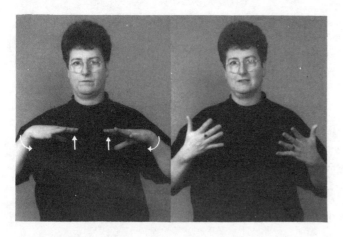

1088 ⌐⌐ 5ʊ> 5ʊ< $\overset{\circ\omega}{\underset{\omega<}{\overset{×}{<}}}$

1089 Ӈ 5⊤∨ ⌐ 5⊤∨ $^{×>×}$

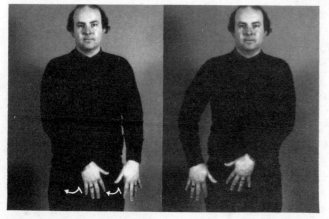

[586]

Handshape and orientation	Location, hand arrangement and contact	Movement	Glosses	
The left 5 hand is held with the palm facing towards the signer and the fingers pointing to the right; the right 5 hand is held with the palm facing towards the signer and the fingers pointing to the left.	The hands are held in front of the chest; the right hand is held above the left hand.	The hands make a short movement up and towards the signer while closing (forming two A hands); the movement ends with the hands touching the chest.	contain oneself keep a straight face suppress one's laughter	1085

Non-manual features   The eyebrows are slightly raised and the lips are pulled back against the teeth; as the hands move, the mouth closes, so that the lips are pressed together.

The left 5 hand is held with the palm facing down and the fingers pointing to the right; the right 5 hand is held with the palm facing down and the fingers pointing to the left.	The hands are held with the thumbtips against the upper chest.	The fingers wiggle; the thumbtips are held against the upper chest throughout.	break* holiday* leisure* relax* relaxation*	1086

Notes   * This sign may be produced using one hand only.

$$ \lceil \check{1} \quad 5\text{-}0< \quad \overset{\times}{\underset{2}{}} $$

The left 5 hand is held with the palm facing down and the fingers pointing to the right; the right 5 hand is held with the palm facing down and the fingers pointing to the left.	The hands are held in front of the upper chest.	The hands make a short upward movement (so that the thumbtips brush the chest) and then twist from the wrists, so that the palms face towards the signer.	free* freedom*	1087

Notes   * This sign may be produced using one hand only.

$$ \lceil \check{1} \quad 5\text{-}0< \quad \overset{\wedge \omega}{\underset{\wedge}{\times \perp}} $$

The left 5 hand is held with the palm facing down and the fingers pointing to the right; the right 5 hand is held with the palm facing down and the fingers pointing to the left.	The hands are held in front of the upper chest.	The hands make a short upward movement while twisting at the wrists, so that the thumbtips brush the upper chest; the movement is repeated.	already* preparation* prepare* ready*	1088

Notes   * The following notes apply to all glosses:

This sign can be produced without the upward movement, so that the thumbtips tap the chest twice.

$$ \lceil 1 \quad 5\text{-}0> \quad 5\text{-}0< \quad \overset{\times}{}\cdot $$

This sign may be produced using one hand only.

$$ \lceil \check{1} \quad 5\text{-}0< \quad \overset{\omega \cdot}{\underset{\wedge}{\times}} \quad \text{or} \quad \lceil \check{1} \quad 5\text{-}0< \quad \overset{\times}{}\cdot $$

Two 5 hands are held with the palms facing towards the signer and the fingers pointing down.	The hands are held side by side in front of the left side of the waist.	The hands touch the waist and then move to the right before touching the waist again.	kilt	1089

1090 Ø $\overline{\overline{5}}$Ɔ⊥ $\overset{\cdot}{\underset{\#}{\overset{\cap}{\wedge}}}$[ʌ]

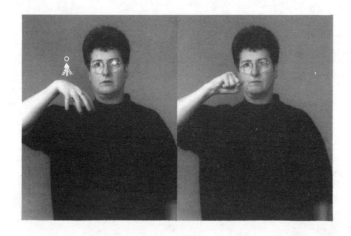

1091 Ø $\overline{\overline{5}}$<⊥ $\overset{\circ}{z}$.

1092 ∩ $\overline{\overline{5}}$Ɔ⊥ $\overset{\cap}{\underset{\square}{\overset{[ß]}{\underset{\times}{\overset{>}{\underset{<}{\overset{\cap}{\underset{\square}{\overset{[s]}{}}}}}}}}$

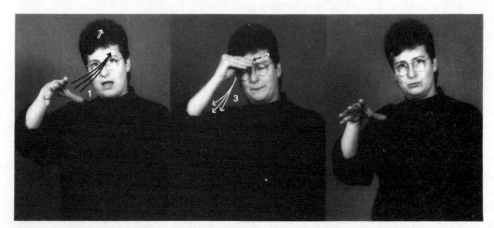

The extended fingers (spread apart) are bent at the palm knuckles with
the extended thumb held parallel to the fingers.

$\bar{5}$ has several different *classifier* functions in the productive lexicon and is used as a classifying element in established signs:
– when accompanied by a closing action it is used as a *size and shape* classifier to represent pointed or cone-shaped objects such as a nozzle, a large nose or the snout of an animal, as in **wolf** (sign 1094);
– it can be used as a *tracing size and shape* classifier to trace the outline and shape of curved objects, as in **bottom** (sign 1106);
– it is used as a *handling* classifier to indicate the handling of cylindrical objects such as a tin as in **collecting tin** (sign 1091) and cuboid objects such as a pack of cards, as in **playing cards** (sign 1099).

$\bar{5}$ also has a range of *symbolic* functions within the lexicon. The $\bar{\bar{5}}$ handshape forms the first part of a handshape pair in which the open $\bar{\bar{5}}$ hand closes to a $\hat{B}$ handshape. This handshape pair has the generalised meanings of 'copy' or 'absorb' (see *Introduction*). As such it occurs in a range of signs which are linked with these meanings. Examples include **copy** (sign 1093), **photo** (sign 1093), **absorb** (sign 1102) and **soak up** (sign 1102). This meaning can also be expressed by the $\bar{\bar{B}} \to \hat{B}$ handshape pair. The same handshape pairs can also express meanings related to 'disappear' (see *Introduction*), as in **fade away** (sign 1100) and **fizzle out** (sign 1100).

Handshape and orientation	Location, hand arrangement and contact	Movement	Glosses	
The $\bar{5}$ hand is held with the palm facing down (if the hand were opened, the fingers would point away from the signer).	The hand is held at head height in front of the body.	The hand bends sharply upwards from the wrist while closing (forming an **A** hand).	switch off a lamp/light	1090
The $\bar{5}$ hand is held with the palm facing left (if the hand were opened, the fingers would point away from the signer).	The hand is held in front of the body.	The hand makes several short movements from side to side.	shake collect with a collecting tin [1] collecting tin [1] flag day [2]	1091

Notes 1 If the movement is changed to a short, repeated up and down movement, the sign produced is **collect with a collecting tin, collecting tin**.

$$\emptyset \quad \bar{5}_{<\perp} \quad \overset{\circ}{\underset{N}{\cdot}}$$

2 If the movement is changed to a short, repeated up and down movement, with the hand moving to the right throughout, the sign produced is **flag day**.

$$\emptyset \quad \bar{5}_{<\perp} \quad \left(\overset{\circ}{\underset{N}{\cdot}}\right)$$

The $\bar{5}$ hand is held with the palm facing down (if the hand were opened, the fingers would point away from the signer).	The hand is held in front of the face.	The hand bends to the left from the wrist while closing (forming a $\hat{B}$ hand); the hand then moves to the right, maintaining contact with the forehead, before finally bending away from the signer while opening (forming a **5** hand).	catch someone off guard catch someone on the hop taken aback	1092

Non-manual features The mouth and the eyes close and the head moves sharply back as the hand moves towards the signer; the cheeks then puff out slightly and the eyes open as the hand moves away from the signer.

1093 ○ =5⊤∧ ⊥̥°[ḅ]
#

1094 ○ =5⊤∧ ⊥̥°[ḅ]
#

1095 ○ =5⊤∧ ⊼<[ḅ]⊥
⌄

1096 3 =5⊤< ×⌄°[ḅ]
>
#

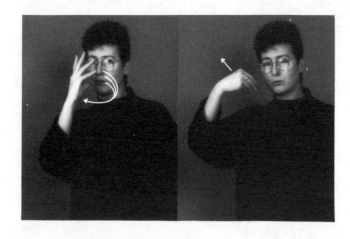

1097 3 =5<∧ ×⌄[ḅ]·
#

1098 B⌐> =5⌐⊥ ⌄[ḅ]×
#

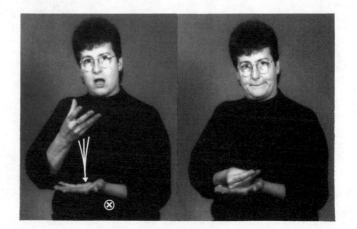

The extended fingers (spread apart) are bent at the palm knuckles with the extended thumb held parallel to the fingers.

Handshape and orientation	Location, hand arrangement and contact	Movement	Glosses	
The 5̄ hand is held with the palm facing towards the signer (if the hand were opened, the fingers would point up).	The hand is held in front of the face.	The hand makes a short movement away from the signer while closing (forming a ɓ̂ hand).	copy * photo * photograph *	1093

    Notes   * Directional verb.

The 5̄ hand is held with the palm facing towards the signer (if the hand were opened, the fingers would point up).	The hand is held in front of the face.	The hand moves away from the signer while closing (forming a ɓ̂ hand).	wolf Wolverhampton	1094

    Non-manual features   The head is pushed forward.

The 5̄ hand is held with the palm facing towards the signer (if the hand were opened, the fingers would point up).	The hand is held in front of the face.	The hand bends to the left at the wrist while closing (forming a ɓ̂ hand), and then moves up and, at the same time, away from the signer.	Holy Ghost soul spirit	1095

The 5̄ hand is held with the palm facing towards the signer (if the hand were opened, the fingers would point to the left).	The hand is held with the fingertips touching the cheek.	The hand makes a short movement down and to the right while closing (forming a ɓ̂ hand).	oops * oops sorry *	1096

    Non-manual features   The lips are slightly rounded; as the hand moves, the mouth closes with the right cheek puffed out.

    Notes   * Regional sign.

The 5̄ hand is held with the palm facing left (if the hand were opened, the fingers would point up).	The hand is held with the fingertips touching the cheek.	The hand moves down while closing (forming a ɓ̂ hand); the movement is repeated.	sugar *	1097

    Notes   * The following notes apply to the gloss:

        Regional sign.

        This sign may be produced using an H̄ hand which closes (forming an Ĥ hand).

$$3 \ \bar{H}_T{<} \ {\overset{\times}{} \overset{\circ}{\underset{>}{\vee}} \overset{[A]}{}} \ {\#}$$

The left B hand is held with the palm facing up and the fingers pointing to the right; the right 5̄ hand is held with the palm facing up (if the hand were opened, the fingers would point away from the signer).	The hands are held in front of the body; the right hand is held above the left hand.	The right hand moves down while closing (forming a ɓ̂ hand); the movement ends with the back of the right hand held on the left palm.	could have happened might have happened	1098

    Non-manual features   The mouth closes (so that the lips are pressed together) as the hand moves.

1099 C̄α> 5̿<⊥ ˇv̊.

1100 ∅ 5̿α⊥ 5̿α⊥ ᵚ

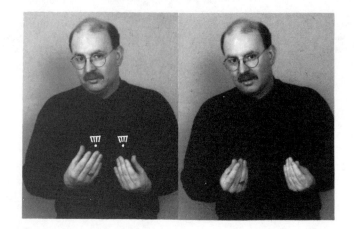

1101 ∅ 5̿α⊥ 5̿α⊥ ˣ[oo]ˣ#

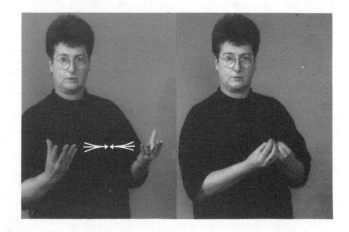

1102 ∅ 5̿ʊ⊥ 5̿ʊ⊥ ˣ[b̄b̄]T#

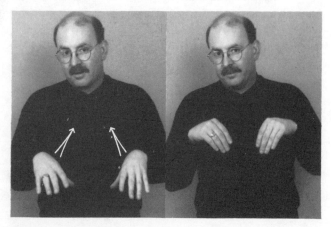

The extended fingers (spread apart) are bent at the palm knuckles with the extended thumb held parallel to the fingers.

Handshape and orientation	Location, hand arrangement and contact	Movement	Glosses	
The left **c** hand is held with the palm facing up (if the hand were opened, the fingers would point to the right). The right **5̄** hand is held with the palm facing left (if the hand were opened, the fingers would point away from the signer).	The hands are held in front of the body; the right hand is held above the left hand.	The right hand makes a short movement down and, at the same time, to the left; the movement is repeated.	card player play cards playing cards shuffle playing cards	**1099**
Two **5̄** hands are held with the palms facing up (if the hands were opened, the fingers would all point away from the signer).	The hands are held in front of the body.	The thumbs rub across the pads of the fingers.	dry * dry up * fade away [1] fizzle out [1]	**1100**

Notes   * This sign can be produced using one hand only.

$\emptyset \quad \bar{\bar{5}}_{\text{α}\perp} \quad ^{\text{ш}}$

1 If the hands move slowly apart throughout, the sign produced is **fade away, fizzle out**.

$\emptyset \quad \bar{\bar{5}}_{\text{α}\perp} \quad \bar{\bar{5}}_{\text{α}\perp} \quad ^{\text{ш}}_{\div}$

Two **5̄** hands are held with the palms facing up (if the hands were opened, the fingers would all point away from the signer).	The hands are held in front of the body.	The hands move towards each other and, at the same time, close (forming two **o** hands); the movement ends with the fingertips touching.	altogether coalition combination combine compound together	**1101**
Two **5̄** hands are held with the palms facing down (if the hands were opened, the fingers would all point away from the signer).	The hands are held in front of the body.	The hands move towards each other and towards the signer while closing (forming two **b̂** hands).	absorb * soak up * suck *	**1102**

Non-manual features   The lips are rounded and close with a sharp intake of breath as the hands move.

Notes   * This sign can be produced using one hand only.

$\emptyset \quad \bar{\bar{5}}_{\text{o}\perp} \quad ^{\text{т [b̂]}}_{\#}$

1103 Ø $\overline{\overline{5}}$ʊ⊥ ˌ $\overline{5}$ʊ⊥ˌ $^{\cdot\cdot[AA]}_{\substack{x\cdot x \\ \#}}$

1104 Ø $\overline{5}$ʊ⊥ ˌ $\overline{\overline{5}}$ʊ⊥ $^{\div x[\check{B}\check{B}]x}_{\substack{v\# \\ a}}$

1105 Ø $\overline{\overline{5}}$⊤v $\overline{5}$⊤v $^{n[AA]}_{\substack{\perp \\ \#}}$

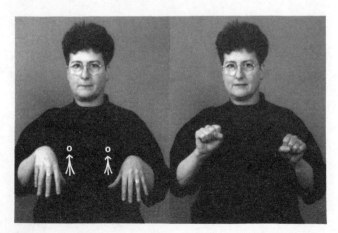

The extended fingers (spread apart) are bent at the palm knuckles with the extended thumb held parallel to the fingers.

Handshape and orientation	Location, hand arrangement and contact	Movement	Glosses
Two 5̄ hands are held with the palms facing down (if the hands were opened, the fingers would all point away from the signer).	The hands are held side by side in front of the body; the right hand is held higher and nearer to the signer than the left hand.	The left hand moves up and towards the signer while closing (forming an A hand) and, at the same time, the right hand moves down and away from the signer while closing (forming an A hand); the sides of the hands brush as they pass.	**wring someone's neck** 1103
Non-manual features The brows are furrowed, the nose is wrinkled and the top teeth are touching the lower lip; as the hands move, the mouth opens and then closes with the lips stretched and the teeth clenched.			
Two 5̄ hands are held with the palms facing down (if the hands were opened, the fingers would all point away from the signer).	The hands are held side by side in front of the body.	The hands move down and apart while twisting at the wrists, so that the palms face up, and then move towards each other while closing (forming two B̂ hands); the movement ends with the hands touching.	**all complete everything whole** 1104
Two 5̄ hands are held with the palms facing towards the signer (if the hands were opened, the fingers would all point down).	The hands are held in front of the body.	The hands bend away from the signer at the wrists while closing (forming two A hands).	**begin* commence* start*** 1105

    Notes   * This sign may be produced using one hand only.

$$\emptyset \quad \bar{\bar{5}}\top\vee \quad \overset{\text{D [A]}}{\underset{\#}{\perp}}$$

1106 Ø $\overline{\overline{5}}$>⊥ ┆ $\overline{\overline{5}}$<⊥ $\overset{\overset{D}{\wedge}}{\underset{\vee}{\downarrow}}$ // $\overline{\overline{5}}$>∧ ┆ $\overset{\ddot{m}}{\vee}$α⊥ $\overset{o}{\underset{D}{\vee}}$

1107 Ø $\overline{\overline{5}}$>⊥ ┆ $\overline{\overline{5}}$<⊥ $\overset{\div[\bar{B}\bar{B}]}{\#}$ ·

5

The extended fingers (spread apart) are bent at the palm knuckles with the extended thumb held parallel to the fingers.

Handshape and orientation	Location, hand arrangement and contact	Movement	Glosses	
The left 5̄ hand is held with the palm facing right; the right 5̄ hand is held with the palm facing left (if the hands were opened, the fingers would all point away from the signer).	The hands are held side by side in front of the body.	The hands bend up at the wrists while moving down and away from the signer.	anus, arse [1] backside [1] bottom [1] bum [1]	**1106**
The left 5̄ hand is held with the palm facing right (if the hand were opened, the fingers would point up). The right V̈ hand is held with the palm facing up (if the hand were opened, the fingers would point away from the signer).	The hands are held side by side in front of the body; the left hand is held higher than the right hand.	The right hand makes a short bending movement to the left at the wrist.		

Notes   1 If the second part of the compound is omitted, the sign produced is **arse, backside, bottom, bum**.

$$\emptyset \quad \bar{\bar{5}}{>}{\perp} \;,\; \bar{\bar{5}}{<}{\perp} \; {\overset{\curvearrowright}{\underset{\vee}{\wedge}}}$$

The left 5̄ hand is held with the palm facing right; the right 5̄ hand is held with the palm facing left (if the hands were opened, the fingers would all point away from the signer).	The hands are held side by side in front of the body.	The hands move apart while closing (forming two ᵬ hands); the movement is repeated.	wool woollen	**1107**

1108 Ø 5̈⊥⊤ ⋔̊·

1109 ⊔ 5̈⊤ʌ ⋔̊⊤

1110 ⊃ 5̈<ʌ ⋓̊·

5

The hand is held flat with the fingers and thumb spread apart; the fingers are bent at the palm knuckles.

5̈ is a relatively frequent handshape within BSL. In some uses, it may occur as a variant of **5**, although 5̈ is normally required in most of the examples cited in this section.

5̈ has several different *classifier* functions in the productive lexicon and is used as a classifying element in established signs:

– it is used as a *people* classifier to indicate several or many people as in **crowd** (sign 1056), **assembly** (sign 1119) and **congress** (sign 1119) and in verbs of motion or location involving people (see *Introduction*);

– it is used as a *size and shape* classifier to represent several long, thin things or objects with several or many long, narrow extensions such as eyelashes and teeth. It is used to indicate lines or stripes such as the stripes on an animal or clothing and lines of writing, as in **screeds** (see *Introduction*). Two-handed forms are used to indicate the intersecting lines of graph paper, timetables and netting. It is also used to indicate objects of large, indeterminate shape, such as **furniture** (sign 1036); it may be used to indicate many pairs of eyes as in **stare** (see *Introduction*) or **astonished** (see *Introduction*);

– it is used as a *handling* classifier to indicate the handling of large items such as a ball, as in **netball** (sign 1108);

– it is used as an *instrumental* classifier to represent implements, tools or utensils with several long, narrow extensions, such as a rake or the spiked units of a combine harvester;

– it is used as a *touch* classifier to indicate actions of the fingers such as hitting keys in **play the piano** (sign 1118), feeling raised print as in **braille** (sign 1112) and touching another person's hand as in **deaf–blind alphabet** (sign 1112);

– it may be used to indicate the *extent* of objects and areas, although **5** would be the more usual choice.

5̈ has a range of *symbolic* functions within the lexicon, although again **5** is used more frequently in these functions than 5̈. Many of these functions arise from metaphoric extensions of the size and shape link with 'lines': this is extended to lines of sound, vibration, odour, liquid (rivulets), sensation and thought. See, for example, **odour** (sign 1109) and **baptise** (sign 1111).

Handshape and orientation	Location, hand arrangement and contact	Movement	Glosses	
The 5̈ hand is held with the palm facing away from the signer (if the hand were opened, the fingers would point towards the signer).	The hand is held at head height in front of the body at an angle, so that the palm is turned up.	The hand makes a short movement up and, at the same time, away from the signer; the movement is repeated.	netball netball player play netball	1108
Non-manual features The eye gaze is directed forward and up.				
The 5̈ hand is held with the palm facing towards the signer (if the hand were opened, the fingers would point up).	The hand is held in front of the body with the fingers pointing to the nose.	The hand moves upwards and towards the signer and, at the same time, the fingers wiggle.	fumes smelly odour [1] stench [1] smell [1,2] inhale [2] exhaust fumes [3] petrol fumes [3]	1109
Non-manual features The nose is wrinkled.				
Notes 1 If the movement is changed to a firm movement up and, at the same time, towards the signer, the sign produced is **odour, smell** *(see entries 1 and 2 in the English section)*, **stench**.		⊔ 5̈⊤∧ ⌃⊤		
2 If the non-manual feature is not present, the sign produced is **inhale, smell** *(see entry 3 in the English section)*.				
3 If the movement is towards the open mouth, the sign produced is **exhaust fumes, petrol fumes**.		⌣ 5̈⊤∧ ⌃⊤		
The 5̈ hand is held with the palm facing left (if the hand were opened, the fingers would point up).	The hand is held beside the head.	The hand makes several short twisting movements to the left at the wrist.	custard* yellow*	1110
Notes * Regional sign.				

1111 √ ⊼5т> 5̈т<ᵧ ᵒ·

1112 B̅α> 5̈ʊ⊥ ⁹ᶻₓ·

1113 Ø 5̈α⊥ 5̈α⊥ ᵒᵧ̈ᵢ·

1114 Ø ⊼5̈α> 5̈ʊ⊥ ⁼ᵀ

1115 Ø 5̈ʊ⊥ 5̈ʊ⊥ ᵃ

5 *The hand is held flat with the fingers and thumb spread apart; the fingers are bent at the palm knuckles.*

Handshape and orientation	Location, hand arrangement and contact	Movement	Glosses	
The left 5 hand is held with the palm facing towards the signer and the fingers pointing to the right; the right 5 hand is held with the palm facing towards the signer (if the hand were opened, the fingers would point to the left).	The hands are held in front of the body; the right hand is held higher and nearer to the signer than the left hand.	The right hand twists from the wrist, so that the palm faces down; the movement is repeated.	baptise * baptism * christen * christening *	1111

Notes   * Regional sign.

| The left B hand is held with the palm facing up and the fingers pointing to the right; the right 5 hand is held with the palm facing down (if the hand were opened, the fingers would point away from the signer). | The hands are held in front of the body; the right fingers rest on the left palm. | The right fingers wiggle and, at the same time, the right hand moves from side to side twice, maintaining contact with the left palm throughout. | braille *
 deaf-blind alphabet [1]
 deaf-blind manual alphabet [1]
 fingerspell using the deaf-blind alphabet [1] | 1112 |

Notes   * This sign may be produced with the right hand making clockwise circles in the horizontal plane.

$$\text{B}\alpha > \ddot{5}\text{o}\perp \; {}^{\circ}_{\times}{}^{\underset{\wedge}{\vee}}_{T}{}^{\cdot}$$

           1 If a right 5 handshape is used, making clockwise circles in the horizontal plane, the sign produced is **deaf-blind alphabet, deaf-blind manual alphabet, fingerspell using the deaf-blind alphabet**.

$$\text{B}\alpha > \ddot{5}\text{o}\perp \; {}^{\circ}_{\times}{}^{\underset{\wedge}{\vee}}_{T}{}^{\cdot}$$

| Two 5 hands are held with the palms facing up (if the hands were opened, the fingers would all point away from the signer). | The hands are held in front of the body. | The hands make two short, firm movements down and, at the same time, away from the signer. | not yet * | 1113 |

Non-manual features   The brows are slightly furrowed and the mouth is open with the tongue tip protruding slightly.

Notes   * Regional sign.

| The left 5 hand is held with the palm facing up; the right 5 hand is held with the palm facing down (if the hands were opened, the left fingers would point to the right and the right fingers would point away from the signer). | The hands are held in front of the body; the right hand is held above the left hand. | The hands make alternate anti-clockwise circles in the horizontal plane. | complicate <br> confuse <br> confused <br> complex *[1]
 complicated *[1]
 jumble [2]
 mix-up [2] | 1114 |

Notes   * This sign may be produced using two 5 hands.

$$\emptyset \; \bar{\ddot{5}}\alpha > \ddot{5}\text{o}\perp \; {}^{@}_{T}{}^{N}_{<}$$

           1 If the brows are furrowed, the sign produced is **complex, complicated**.

           2 If the tongue protrudes between the teeth, the sign produced is **jumble, mix-up**.

| Two 5 hands are held with the palms facing down (if the hands were opened, the fingers would all point away from the signer). | The hands are held in front of the body. | The hands twist at the wrists, so that the palms face up. | feeble <br> weak | 1115 |

Non-manual features   The head nods forward as the hands move.

1116 Ø 5̈ᴕ⊥ 5̈ᴕ⊥ ^{T̄ᴟ}

1117 Ø 5̈ᴕ⊥ 5̈ᴕ⊥ ^{ω̇·}

1118 Ø 5̈ᴕ⊥ 5̈ᴕ⊥ ^{♀̇·}

1119 Ø 5̈>ʌ 5̈<ʌ ^(ꓵ)_(x̊)

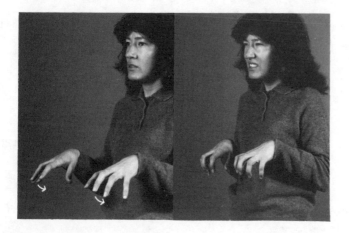

1120 Ø 5̈>ʌ 5̈<ʌ ^{z·}

1121 Ø 5̈>ʌ 5̈<ʌ ^{x̊·}

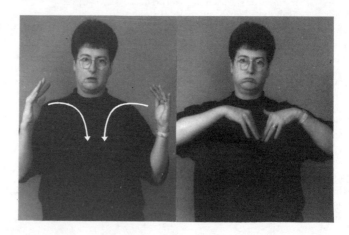

1122 ⊔ 5̈ɑ> 5̈ɑ< ^{(T̊x)·}

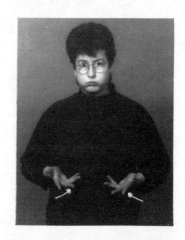

5   *The hand is held flat with the fingers and thumb spread apart; the fingers are bent at the palm knuckles.*

Handshape and orientation	Location, hand arrangement and contact	Movement	Glosses	
Two 5 hands are held with the palms facing down (if the hands were opened, the fingers would all point away from the signer).	The hands are held in front of the body.	The hands move towards the signer and, at the same time, the fingers flex tightly.	mean* miser* miserly* selfish* tight* freeze*[1] frosty*[1] frozen*[1] ice*[1] icy*[1] set*[1]	1116
Non-manual features The mouth is open with the teeth clenched and the lips stretched, and the eyes are narrowed.				
Notes * This sign may be produced using one hand only.				
1 If the non-manual features are not present, the sign produced is **freeze, frosty, frozen, ice, icy, set**.		Ø 5̈ʊ⊥		
Two 5 hands are held with the palms facing down (if the hands were opened, the fingers would all point away from the signer).	The hands are held in front of the body.	The hands twist apart from the wrists several times.	feeble weak nervous[1]	1117
Notes 1 If the movement is changed, so that the hand makes short, repeated twisting movements from side to side, the sign produced is **nervous**.		Ø 5̈ʊ⊥ 5̈ʊ⊥		
Two 5 hands are held with the palms facing down (if the hands were opened, the fingers would all point away from the signer).	The hands are held in front of the body.	The hands move towards each other, and then apart several times; the fingers wiggle throughout.	music* pianist* piano* play the piano*	1118
Notes * This sign may be produced with two 5 hands held side by side, and moving from side to side with the fingers wiggling throughout.		Ø 5ʊ⊥ , 5ʊ⊥		
The left 5 hand is held with the palm facing right; the right 5 hand is held with the palm facing left (if the hands were opened, the fingers would all point up).	The hands are held in front of the body.	The hands bend towards each other from the wrists, while moving towards each other.	assemble assembly attend attendance congregate congress meet	1119
Non-manual features The cheeks are puffed out.				
The left 5 hand is held with the palm facing right; the right 5 hand is held with the palm facing left (if the hands were opened, the fingers would all point up).	The hands are held at shoulder height in front of the body.	The hands move from side to side several times.	battle conflict game match war	1120
The left 5 hand is held with the palm facing right; the right 5 hand is held with the palm facing left (if the hands were opened, the fingers would all point up).	The hands are held in front of the body.	The hands make a short movement towards each other; the movement is repeated.	battle conflict war game[1] match[1]	1121
Notes 1 If the movement is not repeated, the sign produced is **game, match**.		Ø 5̈>ʌ 5̈<ʌ		
Two 5 hands are held with the palms facing up (if the hands were opened, the left fingers would point to the right and the right fingers would point to the left).	The hands are held in front of the waist.	The hands make a short movement towards the signer, so that the sides of the hands touch the waist; the movement is repeated.	do not care a damn don't care a damn do not give a damn don't give a damn too bad tough	1122
Non-manual features The cheeks are puffed out.				

1123 Ø 5̈ɑⲦ ^ᗂ

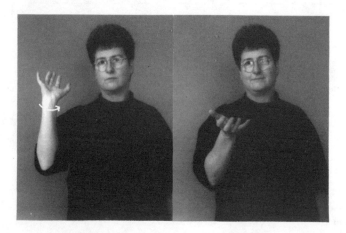

1124 Ø 5̈ɑⲦ ^{#[ʌ]}

1125 Ø 5̈ʊⲦ ^ᵛ

1126 Ø 5̈ʊⲦ (ᵈᵥⲦ)

5̈ has several different *classifier* functions in the productive lexicon and is used as a classifying element in established signs:

— it is used as a *size and shape* classifier to represent several or many long, bent, thin things or objects with several or many long, bent, narrow extensions. It may be used to indicate bent legs, as in **spider** (sign 1148), claws, as in **crab** (see *Introduction*) and **animal** (sign 1168) and teeth, as in **bite** (sign 1129). It may be used to indicate circular objects or objects of indeterminate shape, as in **crown** (sign 1131) and **stone** (sign 1149). It is used to indicate large areas or large objects of indeterminate shape, as in **place** (sign 1125), **building** (sign 1127), **island** (sign 1127) and **suburbs** (sign 1152). The fingertips are used to show many small marks or dots, as in **mottled** (sign 1157) and **freckles** (sign 1177). It may also be used to indicate marks such as scratches, stripes or lines, as in lines of rain in **downpour** (sign 1165);

— it is used as a *tracing size and shape* classifier to trace the outline and shape of objects such as a beard in **Hebrew** (sign 1141);

— it is used as a *handling* classifier to indicate the handling of relatively large, round items such as a jar or tin lid, a dial, a handle, taps, headphones, as in **turn on a tap** (sign 1128) and **audiology** (sign 1178). It may also be used for the handling of cubes or other objects which can fit into the clawed hands, as in **Rubik's cube** (see *Introduction*) and to indicate the carrying of flat objects, such as a tray, by the fingertips, as in **waitress** (sign 1123);

— it is used as an *instrumental* classifier to indicate implements, tools or utensils with several long, narrow, bent extensions, such as a comb, a grass rake, or the spiked units of a combine harvester, see for example **rake** (sign 1126);

— it is used as a *touch* classifier to indicate actions of the fingertips, such as scraping or scratching. It is used in a similar way to indicate the scraping actions of the claws of animals, for example **monkey** (see *Introduction*). It is also used for verbs indicating touching or working sticky substances such as clay or dough;

— it is used to indicate the *extent* of large, spheroid objects such as an aubergine or melon.

5̈ also has a range of *symbolic* functions within the lexicon (see *Introduction*).

Handshape and orientation	Location, hand arrangement and contact	Movement	Glosses	
The 5̈ hand is held with the palm facing up (if the hand were opened, the fingers would point towards the signer).	The hand is held in front of the shoulder.	The hand twists away from the signer at the wrist.	waiter waitress	1123
The 5̈ hand is held with the palm facing up (if the hand were opened, the fingers would point away from the signer).	The hand is held in front of the body.	The hand closes (forming an A hand).	can get have hold against possess is there [1] there is [1] hold [2] hold on [2] hold onto [2]	1124
Notes 1 If an E hand is used and the movement is sharp and repeated, while the top teeth close repeatedly against the lower lip, the sign produced is **is there, there is**.		Ø E ⌒⊥ ⁛[A]·		
2 If the palm faces down and the hand closes firmly, the sign produced is **hold, hold on, hold onto**.		Ø 5̈⌒⊥ ⁛[A]·		
The 5̈ hand is held with the palm facing down (if the hand were opened, the fingers would point away from the signer).	The hand is held in front of the body.	The hand makes a short downward movement.	place town	1125
The 5̈ hand is held with the palm facing down (if the hand were opened, the fingers would point away from the signer).	The hand is held in front of the body.	The hand bends down at the wrist while moving sharply towards the signer.	nick pinch shoplifter shoplifting steal thief rake [1] rob [2] robber [2] robbery [2]	1126
Notes 1 If the hand makes several movements towards the signer, the sign produced is **rake**.		Ø 5̈⌒⊥ ⊤·		
2 If two hands are used, the sign produced is **rob, robber, robbery**.		Ø 5̈⌒⊥ 5̈⌒⊥ (ᵥᵀ)		

1127 Ø ⍥5ʊ⊥ ⊥°ᵛ   1128 Ø ⍥5ʊ⊥ ᵒⁿᵤ·

1129 Ø ⍥5⊤ʌ ⊥[ᴇ]⁄#

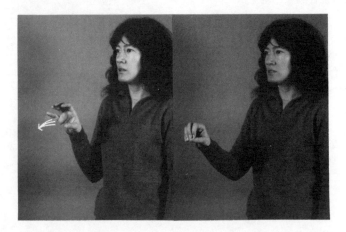

1130 Ø ⍥5<⊥ <[ʌ]⁄#

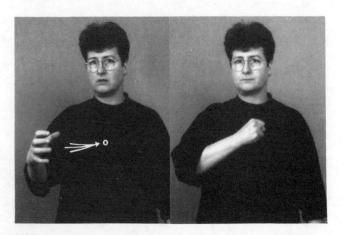

1131 ⌐ ⍥5ʊ< ˣ

[606]

Handshape and orientation	Location, hand arrangement and contact	Movement	Glosses	
The 5̈ hand is held with the palm facing down (if the hand were opened, the fingers would point away from the signer).	The hand is held in front of the body.	The hand moves away from the signer and then makes a short downward movement.	building island place town	1127
The 5̈ hand is held with the palm facing down (if the hand were opened, the fingers would point away from the signer).	The hand is held in front of the body.	The hand makes several short bending movements from side to side at the wrist.	tap* tap (turn on a tap)*[1] tap (turn off a tap)*[2]	1128

Notes   * This sign may be produced using a v̈ handshape.

Ø v̈↻⊥ ⁿ>

1 If the hand bends to the left from the wrist, the sign produced is **turn on a tap**.

Ø 5̈↻⊥ ⁿ<   or   Ø v̈↻⊥ ⁿ<

2 If the hand is held so that the fingers (if straight) would point to the left, and bends away from the signer from the wrist, the sign produced is **turn off a tap**.

Ø 5̈↻< ⊥ⁿ   or   Ø v̈↻< ⊥ⁿ

The 5̈ hand is held with the palm facing away from the signer (if the hand were opened, the fingers would point up).	The hand is held in front of the body.	The hand moves away from the signer while closing (forming an E hand).	bite*† snap*†	1129

Non-manual features   The nose is wrinkled, the lips are stretched and the teeth are clenched.

Notes   * Directional verb.

Ø 5̈⊥∧ ⊥[o]
#

† This sign may be produced with the hand closing (forming an O hand).

The 5̈ hand is held with the palm facing left (if the hand were opened, the fingers would point away from the signer).	The hand is held in front of the body.	The hand moves to the left while closing (forming an A hand).	achieve achievement adopt adoption get obtain grab[1] snatch[1] get[2] see[2]	1130

Notes   1 If the movement is sharp, the sign produced is **grab**, **snatch**.

Ø 5̈<⊥ <[∧]
#

2 If the mouth is open and the head nods, the sign produced is **get** (*see entry 3 in the English section*), **see**.

The 5̈ hand is held with the palm facing down (if the hand were opened, the fingers would point to the left).	The hand is held above the head.	The fingertips touch the top of the head.	crown government king prince princess queen royal	1131

1132 ∩ ⸚5⊤ʌ ˣ⊤ᵥ₎

1133 ○ ⸚5⊤ʌ ˣ

1134 ○ ⸚5⊤ʌ ᵖ₍

1135 ○ ⸚5⊤ʌ ᵐ·

1136 ○ ⸚5<ʌ ₕⁿₒ·

1137 ○ ∫⸚5<ʌ ᵖᵀ

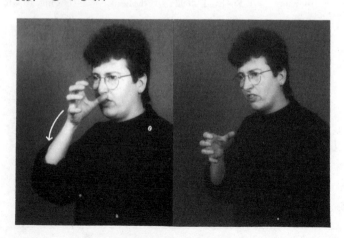

Handshape and orientation	Location, hand arrangement and contact	Movement	Glosses	
The 5̈ hand is held with the palm facing towards the signer (if the hand were opened, the fingers would point up).	The hand is held with the fingertips touching the forehead.	The hand moves down and away from the signer and, at the same time, to the right.	cannot be bothered can't be bothered cannot face it can't face it	1132
Non-manual features The nose is wrinkled and the top teeth are touching the lower lip; the nose then relaxes as the mouth opens, so that the lips are rounded.				
The 5̈ hand is held with the palm facing towards the signer (if the hand were opened, the fingers would point up).	The hand is held in front of the face.	The fingertips touch the face around the nose.	anaesthetic anaesthetise * gas * gas mask	1133
Notes * Directional verb.				
The 5̈ hand is held with the palm facing towards the signer (if the hand were opened, the fingers would point up).	The hand is held beside the face.	The hand bends to the left from the wrist.	concern * worry *	1134
Non-manual features The brows are furrowed.				
Notes * The following notes apply to all glosses: This sign can be produced with two hands. This sign may be produced with the lips stretched.		Ø 5̈⊤∧ 5̈⊤∧ ⌒		
The 5̈ hand is held with the palm facing towards the signer (if the hand were opened, the fingers would point up).	The hand is held in front of the face.	The fingers flex twice.	crabby crotchety grumpy miserable moody sulk frown[1] scowl[1]	1135
Non-manual features The nose is wrinkled, the brows are furrowed and the lips are pressed together.				
Notes 1 If the hand moves firmly away from the signer while the fingers flex, the sign produced is **frown, scowl**.		◯ 5̈⊤∧ ⊥		
The 5̈ hand is held with the palm facing left (if the hand were opened, the fingers would point up).	The hand is held beside the head.	The hand makes several short bending movements towards and away from the signer at the wrist.	accident error mistake sorry	1136
The 5̈ hand is held with the palm facing left (if the hand were opened, the fingers would point up).	The hand is held in front of the face.	The hand bends away from the signer with the arm moving from the elbow.	bored stiff bored to death bored to tears	1137
Non-manual features The nose is slightly wrinkled and the tongue protrudes between the teeth.				

1138 ⊔ 5̈<ʌ ˣ⊥ᵥ

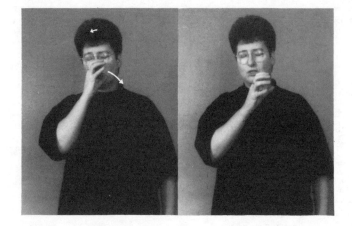

1139 ⊃ 5̈⊤< ˂°@˙ᵥ

1140 ⊃ 5̈<ʌ ᵐ˙

1141 ∪ 5̈⊤ʌ ˣ°⊥ᵥ

1142 [] 5̈⊤< ᵑᵥˣ

1143 [] 5̈⊤< ˣ˙

The bent fingers and bent thumb are extended and spread apart.

Handshape and orientation	Location, hand arrangement and contact	Movement	Glosses	
The 5̈ hand is held with the palm facing left (if the hand were opened, the fingers would point up).	The hand is held with the side of the index finger touching the nose.	The hand moves down and, at the same time, away from the signer.	asleep (fast asleep) asleep (sound asleep) oversleep sleep (deep sleep) sleep like a log lonely [1] lie in [2] snooze [2] snore [2]	1138
Non-manual features The head is tilted to one side, the eyes are closed and the mouth is open with the tongue tip resting on the lower lip.				
Notes 1 If the eyes are open and the tongue protrudes between the teeth, the sign produced is **lonely**. This is a regional sign. 2 If the head is tilted to one side, the eyes are closed and the lips are rounded and pushed forward, the sign produced is **lie in, snooze, snore**.				
The 5̈ hand is held with the palm facing towards the signer (if the hand were opened, the fingers would point to the left).	The hand is held in front of the mouth.	The hand makes small anticlockwise circles in the vertical plane parallel to the signer's body.	warm	1139
The 5̈ hand is held with the palm facing left (if the hand were opened, the fingers would point up).	The hand is held in front of the mouth.	The fingers flex twice.	orange *†	1140
Notes * This sign may be produced with the palm facing away from the signer. † This sign may also be produced with a 5̈ hand closing (forming an ∧ hand) several times.				
The 5̈ hand is held with the palm facing towards the signer (if the hand were opened, the fingers would point up).	The hand is held with the fingertips touching the chin.	The hand makes a short movement down and, at the same time, away from the signer.	Hebraic Hebrew Israel Israeli Jew Jewish	1141
The 5̈ hand is held with the palm facing towards the signer (if the hand were opened, the fingers would point to the left).	The hand is held with the fingertips resting against the chest.	The hand bends down at the wrist; the fingertips maintain contact with the chest throughout.	mayor mayoress president provost	1142
The 5̈ hand is held with the palm facing towards the signer (if the hand were opened, the fingers would point to the left).	The hand is held in front of the chest.	The fingertips tap the chest twice.	afraid * fear * fearful * frighten * scare * terrified * coward [1] really? [2] surprised [2]	1143
Non-manual features The eyes are opened wide and the shoulders move back.				
Notes * This sign may be produced with the lips stretched, the eyes opened wide and the body moving back. 1 If the nose is wrinkled, the sign produced is **coward**. 2 If the eyebrows are raised, the corners of the mouth are turned down and the body moves forward, the sign produced is **really?, surprised**.				

1144 [] 5̈т< $\overset{@}{\underset{x}{<}}$

1145 $\overset{.}{\underline{J}}$ 5̈α< $^{×}$ ·

1146 $\overset{.}{J}_{\varphi}$ 5̈т< $\overset{°}{\underset{x}{<}}$ ·

1147 $\overline{/}$ 5̈ᴕ< $\overset{n}{\underset{x}{⊥}}$

1148 $\overline{/}$ 5̈ᴕ< $\binom{2}{x}_{<}$

1149 $\overline{A}$ᴕ>₁ 5̈<ʌ $\overset{n}{⊥}$·

1150 Gт>₁ 5̈<ʌ $\overset{ω⊥}{}$

Handshape and orientation	Location, hand arrangement and contact	Movement	Glosses
The 5̈ hand is held with the palm facing towards the signer (if the hand were opened, the fingers would point to the left).	The hand is held with the fingertips resting against the chest.	The hand makes an anticlockwise circle in the vertical plane parallel with the signer's body, maintaining contact with the chest throughout.	**butterflies** 1144 **in one's stomach** * **unease** * **uneasy** * **anxiety** *[1] **anxious** *[1] **apprehension** *[1] **apprehensive** *[1] **worried** *[1] **worry** *[1] **nausea** *[2] **nauseous** *[2] **queasy** *[2]

Non-manual features The eyes are narrowed and the mouth is open with the tongue tip resting on the lower lip.

Notes * This sign may be produced with the hand touching the stomach.

1 If the non-manual features are changed, so that the lips are stretched, the sign produced is **anxiety, anxious, apprehension, apprehensive, worried, worry**.

2 This sign may be produced with the cheeks puffed out.

LʃJ 5̈τ< ⊻⊻×@

| The 5̈ hand is held with the palm facing up (if the hand were opened, the fingers would point to the left). | The hand is held below the left elbow. | The right fingertips tap the left elbow twice. | **biscuit** 1145 |

| The 5̈ hand is held with the palm facing towards the signer (if the hand were opened, the fingers would point to the left). | The hand is held with the fingertips touching the left elbow. | The hand makes a short movement to the right maintaining contact with the left forearm; the movement is repeated. | **poor** 1146 **poverty** **brown** [1] **common** [2] **scruffy** [2] |

Notes 1 If the movement is not repeated, the sign produced is **brown**. This is a regional sign.

2 If the nose is wrinkled, the sign produced is **common, scruffy**.

Ʃ˳ 5̈τ< ⊻⊻×°

| The 5̈ hand is held with the palm facing down (if the hand were opened, the fingers would point to the left). | The hand is held with the fingertips resting on the left forearm, which is positioned across the body. | The hand bends away from the signer at the wrist; the fingertips maintain contact with the left forearm throughout. | **bruise** * 1147 **bruise on one's arm** * |

Notes * This sign may be located at the appropriate part of the body.

| The 5̈ hand is held with the palm facing down (if the hand were opened, the fingers would point to the left). | The hand is held resting on the left forearm, which is positioned across the body. | The right hand moves to the left and, at the same time, the fingers wiggle, maintaining contact with the left forearm throughout. | **beetle** 1148 **beetle/insect/spider crawling** **insect** **spider** |

| The left A hand is held with the palm facing down (if the hand were opened, the fingers would point to the right). The right 5̈ hand is held with the palm facing left (if the hand were opened, the fingers would point up). | The hands are held side by side in front of the body; the right hand is held higher than the left hand. | The right hand bends away from the signer from the wrist twice. | **gem** 1149 **jewel** **stone** |

| The left G hand is held with the palm facing towards the signer (if the hand were opened, the fingers would point to the right). The right 5̈ hand is held with the palm facing left (if the hand were opened, the fingers would point away from the signer). | The hands are held side by side in front of the body. | The right hand twists away from the signer at the wrist. | **coal** 1150 **rock** **stone** |

1151 5̄ɑ⊥ 5̈ʊ⊥ ᵀₓ

1152 5̈ʊ> ₁ 5̈ʊ⊥₉ (°ᵈᵛ·)>⊥<

1153 B̄ɑ⊥₉ 5̈ʊ∧ ᵀᵥ#[ᴧ]ˣ

1154 B̄ɑ> 5̈ʊ⊥ ᵑ>

1155 B̄ɑ> ₁ 5̈<⊥ (<ˣ<)[ᴧ]#

1156 B̄ʊ> 5̈ʊ⊥ ˣ·

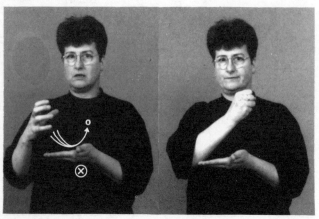

Handshape and orientation	Location, hand arrangement and contact	Movement	Glosses	
The left 5 hand is held with the palm facing up and the fingers pointing away from the signer; the right 5̈ hand is held with the palm facing down (if the hand were opened, the fingers would point away from the signer).	The hands are held in front of the body, with the right fingertips resting on the left palm.	The right hand moves towards the signer; the right fingertips maintain contact with the left palm throughout.	nick* pinch* rake* rob* robber* robbery* shoplifter* shoplifting* steal* thief*	1151

Notes   * The following notes apply to all glosses:

    This sign may be produced with a short repeated movement.

    This sign may be produced using one hand only.

$$\overline{5\alpha\bot} \;\; \ddot{5}\!\!\sigma\bot \;\; {}^{\circ}_{\underset{x}{\top}}\cdot$$

$$\emptyset \;\; \ddot{5}\!\!\sigma\bot \;{}^{\top} \; \text{or} \; \emptyset \;\; \ddot{5}\!\!\sigma\bot \;{}^{\circ}_{\top}\cdot$$

The left 5̈ hand...				
Two 5̈ hands are held with the palms facing down (if the hands were opened, the left fingers would point to the right and the right fingers would point away from the signer).	The hands are held side by side in front of the body; the right hand is held nearer to the signer than the left hand.	The right hand makes a short downward bending movement at the wrist; the movement is repeated several times while the hand moves to the right, away from the signer and then to the left.	suburbs	1152
The left B hand is held with the palm facing up and the fingers pointing away from the signer; the right 5̈ hand is held with the palm facing down (if the hand were opened, the fingers would point up).	The hands are held in front of the body; the right hand is held above the left hand at an angle, so that the palm is turned away from the signer.	The right hand moves down and towards the signer while closing (forming an A hand); the movement ends with the right hand held on the left palm.	catch catch[1]	1153

Notes   1 If the left 5 hand is used, and the hands both move towards the signer as the right hand movement continues, and the movement ends with the hands closing (the left hand forms a 5̈ hand, the right hand forms an E hand), the sign produced is **catch** *(see entry 2 in the English section).*

$$\emptyset \left(\overline{5\alpha\bot}_{\varsigma} \; \ddot{5}\!\!\sigma\wedge \; {}^{\cap}_{\underset{\vee}{\bot}} \right)^{\top[\ddot{5}\text{E}]}_{\#}$$

The left B hand is held with the palm facing up and the fingers pointing to the right; the right 5̈ hand is held with the palm facing down (if the hand were opened, the fingers would point away from the signer).	The hands are held in front of the body; the right hand is held above the left hand.	The right hand bends to the right at the wrist.	bun* cake (small cake)* pie (small pie)* roll* scone*	1154

Notes   * This sign may be produced with the right fingertips touching the left palm.

$$\overline{B\alpha>} \; \ddot{5}\!\!\sigma\bot \; {}^{\cap}_{\underset{x}{>}}$$

The left B hand is held with the palm facing up and the fingers pointing to the right; the right 5̈ hand is held with the palm facing left (if the hand were opened, the fingers would point away from the signer).	The hands are held side by side in front of the body; the right hand is held higher than the left hand.	The right hand moves to the left, brushing across the left palm and, at the same time, closes (forming an A hand).	achieve achievement gain win	1155
The left B hand is held with the palm facing down and the fingers pointing to the right; the right 5̈ hand is held with the palm facing down (if the hand were opened, the fingers would point away from the signer).	The hands are held in front of the body; the right hand is held above the left hand.	The tips of the right fingers tap the back of the left hand twice.	bun cake (small cake) pie (small pie) roll scone	1156

1157 $\overline{B}ʊ>\,_x\,\ddot{5}ʊ<\,{\binom{\circ_x.}{>}}$

1158 $\overline{B}ʊ>_?\,\ddot{5}⊤ʌ\,^v$

1159 $B⊤>\,\ddot{5}ʊ⊥_?\,{\overset{v\,[ʌ]}{\underset{\#}{\overset{x}{v}}}}$

1160 $\overline{\hat{B}}ɑ>\,\ddot{5}ʊ⊥\,{\overset{\omega\,.}{>}}$

1161 $\varnothing\,\overline{\ddot{5}}ɑ>\,\ddot{5}ʊ<\,{}^{\prime\prime}$

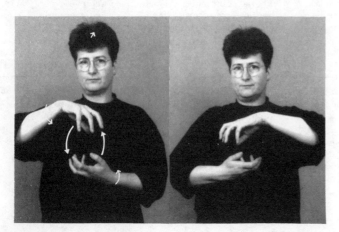

The bent fingers and bent thumb are extended and spread apart.

Handshape and orientation	Location, hand arrangement and contact	Movement	Glosses	
The left B hand is held with the palm facing down and the fingers pointing to the right; the right 5̈ hand is held with the palm facing down (if the hand were opened, the fingers would point to the left).	The hands are held in front of the body with the right fingertips resting on the back of the left hand.	The right fingertips tap the back of the left hand several times, with the right hand moving to the right throughout.	mottled* dappled*¹ flecked*¹ embossed*²	1157

Non-manual features   The cheeks are slightly puffed out and the nose is wrinkled.

Notes   * The right hand is located as appropriate.

1 If the non-manual features are changed, so that the lips are rounded, the sign produced is **dappled, flecked**.

2 If the right hand is held above the left hand and moves to the right, while making short up and down bending movements at the wrist, the sign produced is **embossed**. $\overline{\text{B}}\upsilon> \ddot{5}\upsilon< \left(\begin{smallmatrix} \circ \\ \text{D} \\ \sim \\ > \end{smallmatrix} \right)$

The left B hand is held with the palm facing down and the fingers pointing to the right; the right 5̈ hand is held with the palm facing towards the signer (if the hand were opened, the fingers would point up).	The hands are held in front of the body; the left hand is held lower and nearer to the signer than the right hand.	The right hand moves slowly down.	sunset sun sets sun sinks	1158
The left B hand is held with the palm facing towards the signer and the fingers pointing to the right; the right 5̈ hand is held with the palm facing down (if the hand were opened, the fingers would point away from the signer).	The hands are held in front of the body; the right hand is held nearer to the signer than the left hand.	The right hand moves down, brushing across the left palm and, at the same time, closes (forming an A hand).	deduct deduction discount subtract subtraction take away withdraw	1159
The left B̂ hand is held with the palm facing up (if the hand were opened, the fingers would point to the right). The right 5̈ hand is held with the palm facing down (if the hand were opened, the fingers would point away from the signer).	The hands are held in front of the body; the right hand is held above the left hand.	The right hand twists to the right at the wrist; the movement is repeated.	squeeze squeezer	1160
The left 5̈ hand is held with the palm facing up; the right 5̈ hand is held with the palm facing down (if the hands were opened, the left fingers would point to the right and the right fingers would point to the left).	The hands are held in front of the body; the right hand is held above the left hand.	The hands change places.	upside down topsy turvy¹	1161

Non-manual features   The tongue protrudes between the teeth and the head tilts back.

Notes   1 If the hands move away from the signer throughout, the sign produced is **topsy turvy**. $\emptyset \ \overline{\ddot{5}}\upsilon> \ddot{5}\upsilon< \ \overset{\cdot\cdot}{\iota}$

1162 Ø 5̈ᴕ⊥ 5̈ᴕ⊥ ᴎˣ[ᴏᴏ]ˣ⌗

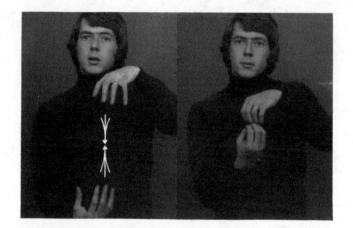

1163 Ø 5̈ᴕ⊥ 5̈ᴕ⊥ ˚ᴇ↓ᴎ·

1164 Ø ⁄5̈ᴕ⊥ ⁄5̈ᴕ⊥ ∓ˣ

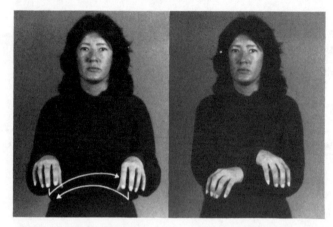

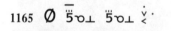

1165 Ø 5̄ᴕ⊥ 5̈ᴕ⊥ ᵛ<·

1166 Ø 5̈ᴕ⊥ ₁ 5̈ᴕ⊥ ᴅˣ·

Handshape and orientation	Location, hand arrangement and contact	Movement	Glosses	

The left 5̈ hand is held with the palm facing down; the right 5̈ hand is held with the palm facing up (if the hands were opened, the fingers would all point away from the signer).	The hands are held in front of the body; the left hand is held above the right hand.	The hands move towards each other and, at the same time, close (forming two o hands); the movement ends with the fingertips touching.	add
			addition
			add up
			add up to conclusion
			  (in conclusion)
			summary
			  (in summary)
			sum up
			total
			tot up
				1162

Two 5̈ hands are held with the palms facing down (if the hands were opened, the fingers would all point away from the signer).	The hands are held in front of the body.	The hands make alternate small clockwise circles in the vertical plane at right angles to the signer's body.	investigate investigator rake rummage search	1163
Two 5̈ hands are held with the palms facing down (if the hands were opened, the fingers would all point away from the signer).	The hands are held in front of the body.	The hands cross over; the movement ends with the right forearm resting on the left forearm.	replace replacement substitute substitution swap switch	1164
Two 5̈ hands are held with the palms facing down (if the hands were opened, the fingers would all point away from the signer).	The hands are held in front of the body; the right hand is held higher than the left hand.	The hands move firmly down and, at the same time, to the left; the movement is repeated.	downpour rain (heavy rain) raining cats and dogs rainstorm	1165
Non-manual features The cheeks are puffed out.				
Two 5̈ hands are held with the palms facing down (if the hands were opened, the fingers would all point away from the signer).	The hands are held side by side in front of the body.	The hands bend towards each other from the wrists several times.	taps taps (turn on taps)	1166

Notes   This sign can also be produced using two v̈ hands.

Ø v̈ɒ⊥ ، v̈ɒ⊥ x

1167 Ø 5̈ɔ⊥ ¦ 5̈ɔ⊥ $\binom{\overset{\circ}{\omega}\cdot}{\div}$

1168 Ø 5̈ɔ⊥ ¦ 5̈ɔ⊥ $\overset{@ N\,\cdot}{\underset{v}{\bot}}$

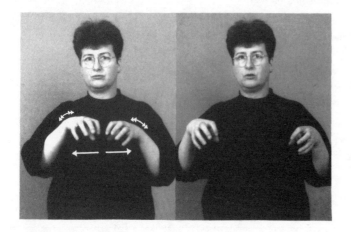

1169 Ø 5̈ɔ⊥ ¦ 5̈ɔ⊥ $\overset{@ N\,\cdot}{\underset{v}{\bot}}$ // [] G̈⊤v ¦ G̈⊤v $\binom{\div\,\cdot}{\overset{}{x}}$

1170 Ø 5̈⊥ʌ 5̈⊥ʌ $\overset{@}{\underset{v}{x}}\cdot$

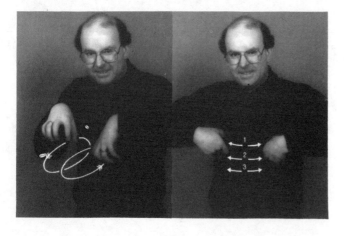

1171 Ø 5̈⊥ʌ ¦ 5̈⊥ʌ $\overset{\circ}{\underset{\#}{\bot}}$[ʌ ʌ]

1172 Ø 5̈⊥ʌ ¦ 5̈⊥ʌ $\overset{@ N\,\cdot}{\underset{v}{x}}$

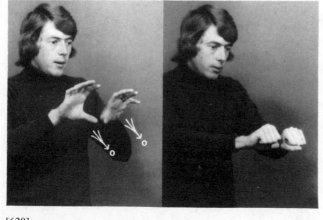

Handshape and orientation	Location, hand arrangement and contact	Movement	Glosses	
Two 5̈ hands are held with the palms facing down (if the hands were opened, the fingers would all point away from the signer).	The hands are held side by side in front of the body.	The hands move apart, while making small up and down twisting movements at the wrists.	**rockery** **rocks**	1167
Two 5̈ hands are held with the palms facing down (if the hands were opened, the fingers would all point away from the signer).	The hands are held side by side in front of the body.	The hands make alternate clockwise circles in the vertical plane at right angles to the signer's body.	**animal** **crawl** **lion**	1168
Two 5̈ hands are held with the palms facing down (if the hands were opened, the fingers would all point away from the signer).	The hands are held side by side in front of the body.	The hands make alternate clockwise circles in the vertical plane at right angles to the signer's body.	**tiger**	1169
Two č hands are held with the palms facing towards the signer (if the hands were opened, the fingers would all point down).	The hands are held side by side with the index finger and thumb tips touching the chest.	The hands move apart, maintaining contact with the chest; the movement is repeated several times, each time below the previous movement.		

Non-manual features The lips are stretched and the nose is wrinkled.

Handshape and orientation	Location, hand arrangement and contact	Movement	Glosses	
Two 5̈ hands are held with the palms facing away from the signer (if the hands were opened, the fingers would all point up).	The hands are held at head height in front of the body.	The hands make circles (the left hand moves clockwise, the right hand moves anticlockwise) in the vertical plane parallel to the signer's body.	**cloud** **cloudy**	1170
Two 5̈ hands are held with the palms facing away from the signer (if the hands were opened, the fingers would all point up).	The hands are held side by side in front of the body.	The hands make a short movement away from the signer while closing (forming two A hands).	**arrest** *† **capture** *† **catch** *† **grab** *† **seize** *† **take over** †	1171

Notes * Directional verb.

† This sign may be produced using one hand only.

Ø 5̈⊥∧ ⊥°[A]

Handshape and orientation	Location, hand arrangement and contact	Movement	Glosses	
Two 5̈ hands are held with the palms facing away from the signer (if the hands were opened, the fingers would all point up).	The hands are held side by side in front of the body.	The hands make alternate circles (the left hand moves clockwise, the right hand moves anticlockwise) in the vertical plane parallel to the signer's body.	**colour** **colourful** **complex**[1] **complicate**[1] **complicated**[1]	1172

Notes 1 If the brows are furrowed and the lips are pressed together, the sign produced is **complex, complicate, complicated.**

1173 Ø 5̈⊥ʌ 5̈⊥ʌ, $\overset{@N\cdot}{\underset{v}{\lessgtr}}$

1174 Ø 5̈>⊥ , 5̈<⊥ $\overset{♀}{×}$

1175 Ø 5̈>⊥ , 5̈<⊥ $\overset{(\omega)}{\underset{÷}{H}}$

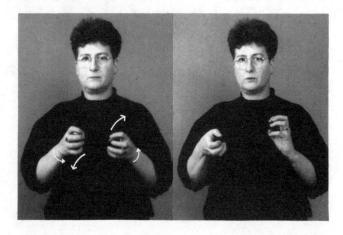

1176 Ø 5̈>⊥ , 5̈<⊥ ×ˣ

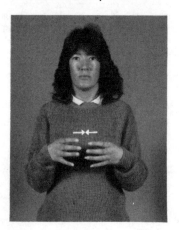

1177 ◡ 5̈⊤ʌ 5̈⊤ʌ $\overset{(×\cdot)}{v}$

1178 ⊃ 5̈>ʌ 5̈<ʌ $\overset{o}{\underset{H}{.}}$

Handshape and orientation	Location, hand arrangement and contact	Movement	Glosses	
Two 5̈ hands are held with the palms facing away from the signer (if the hands were opened, the fingers would all point up).	The hands are held in front of the body; the right hand is held nearer to the signer than the left hand.	The hands make alternate anti-clockwise circles in the vertical plane parallel to the signer's body.	pattern	1173
The left 5̈ hand is held with the palm facing right; the right 5̈ hand is held with the palm facing left (if the hands were opened, the fingers would all point away from the signer).	The hands are held side by side in front of the body.	The fingers wiggle, so that the fingertips maintain contact throughout.	British manual alphabet fingerspell two-handed alphabet spell[1]	1174

Notes   1 If the hands move to the right throughout, the sign produced is **spell**.

$$\varnothing \quad \ddot{5}>\!\!\perp \, | \, \ddot{5}<\!\!\perp \, \overset{\mathbf{x}}{\underset{\mathbf{x}}{\gtrless}}$$

| The left 5̈ hand is held with the palm facing right; the right 5̈ hand is held with the palm facing left (if the hands were opened, the fingers would all point away from the signer). | The hands are held side by side in front of the body. | The left hand twists towards the signer while the right hand twists away from the signer and, at the same time, the hands move apart. | bone* | 1175 |

Notes   * This sign can also be produced using two V̈ hands.

$$\varnothing \quad \ddot{V}>\!\!\perp \, | \, \ddot{V}<\!\!\perp \, \overset{(\frac{\omega}{H})}{\div}$$

| The left 5̈ hand is held with the palm facing right; the right 5̈ hand is held with the palm facing left (if the hands were opened, the fingers would all point away from the signer). | The hands are held side by side in front of the body. | The hands move towards each other, so that the fingertips touch. | body class group party | 1176 |
| Two 5̈ hands are held with the palms facing towards the signer (if the hands were opened, the fingers would all point up). | The hands are held in front of the face. | The fingertips tap the face several times and, at the same time, the hands move down. | chicken pox* measles* freckles*[1] | 1177 |

Notes   * This sign may be produced using one hand only.

$$3 \quad \ddot{5}\top\!\!\wedge \, \overset{(\mathbf{x} \, \cdot)}{\underset{\mathbf{v}}{}}$$

      1 If the fingers wiggle while the hands move down, the sign produced is **freckles**.

$$\mathbf{O} \quad \ddot{5}\top\!\!\wedge \, \ddot{5}\top\!\!\wedge \, \overset{(\mathbf{x} \, \cdot)}{\underset{\mathbf{v}}{}} \, \text{or} \, 3 \, \ddot{5}\top\!\!\wedge \, \overset{(\mathbf{x} \, \cdot)}{\underset{\mathbf{v}}{}}$$

| The left 5̈ hand is held with the palm facing right; the right 5̈ hand is held with the palm facing left (if the hands were opened, the fingers would all point up). | The hands are held beside the ears. | The hands make several short twisting movements towards and away from the signer at the wrists. | audiologist* audiology* radio* wireless* | 1178 |

Notes   * This sign may be produced using one hand only.

$$\supset \quad \ddot{5}<\!\!\wedge \, \overset{\circ}{\underset{H}{\Box}} \cdot$$

1179 ∏ 5̈>ʌ 5̈<ʌ ÷

1180 [] 5̈⊤> 5̈⊤< ×·

1181 ⊔ ᵉ5̈⊤< × ⫽⫽ 5̈⊤> ₁ 5̈⊤< ×·

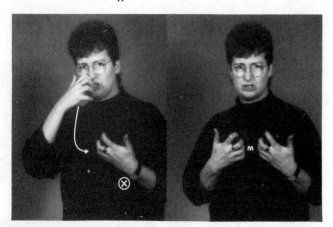

Handshape and orientation	Location, hand arrangement and contact	Movement	Glosses	
The left 5 hand is held with the palm facing right; the right 5 hand is held with the palm facing left (if the hands were opened, the fingers would all point up).	The hands are held at either side of the neck.	The hands make a short movement apart.	**mumps** **swollen glands**	1179

Non-manual features	The cheeks are puffed out.

Two 5 hands are held with the palms facing towards the signer (if the hands were opened, the left fingers would point to the right and the right fingers would point to the left).	The hands are held in front of the chest; the right hand is held above the left hand.	The fingertips tap the chest several times.	**afraid*** **fear*** **fearful*** **frighten*** **scare*** **terrified*** **coward**[1]	1180

Non-manual features	The eyes are opened wide and the body moves back.
Notes	* This sign may be produced with the lips stretched, the eyes opened wide, and the body moving back.
	1 If the nose is wrinkled, the sign produced is **coward**.

The thumb and bent fingers are extended and spread apart.

5 has several different *classifier* functions in the productive lexicon and is used as a classifying element in established signs:
- it is used as a *size and shape* classifier to represent several or many long, narrow, bent things such as teeth, as in **alligator** (sign 1190); when both hands are used in an interlocking manner, they can indicate the action of interlocking mechanisms or cogs, as in **equipment** (sign 1193) and **technology** (sign 1193); 5 may be used to indicate stripes or lines, as in lines of rain in **drizzle** (sign 1192);
- it is used as a *touch* classifier to indicate scraping or scratching, as in

scrape (sign 1189) and scratch (sign 1189).

Although 5 can express the above classifier functions, it occurs most commonly in signs relating to strong emotion. The handshape in these signs is usually accompanied by considerable muscular tension. In many cases, these signs are made on the chest: this location has a conventional association with emotions in BSL (see *Introduction*). Examples include **annoy** (sign 1185), **complain** (sign 1187), **frustration** (sign 1195), **furious** (sign 1196) and **aggressive** (sign 1198).

Handshape and orientation	Location, hand arrangement and contact	Movement	Glosses	
The 5 hand is held with the palm facing towards the signer (if the hand were opened, the fingers would point to the left).	The hand is held in front of the lower face.	The index finger touches the nose.	**crummy** **rotten** **tacky** **tatty**	1181
Two 5 hands are held with the palms facing towards the signer (if the hands were opened, the left fingers would point to the right and the right fingers would point to the left).	The hands are held side by side in front of the body.	The knuckles of the right hand tap the knuckles of the left hand twice.		

Non-manual features	The brows are slightly furrowed, the nose is wrinkled and the lips are rounded and pushed forward.

1182 ∪ 5̈T∧ ×·

1183 ⌒ 5̈T< ˇ°

1184 [] 5̈T< ˃×

1185 [] 5̈T< °×̂×̂·̂

1186 [] 5̈T< °×̂×̂·

1187] 5̈T< ˏ˃̂ᵖ̂·̂

1188 ⌇ 5̈T< ˇ×·

1189 ⁻5̇∟ 5̈ᴅ∟ ᴅˇᴛ×ᴅˇᴛ·

1190 ∅ ⁼5̇∟ 5̈ᴅ∟ (ᴺ×̂×)·

Handshape and orientation	Location, hand arrangement and contact	Movement	Glosses	
The 5̈ hand is held with the palm facing towards the signer (if the hand were opened, the fingers would point up).	The hand is held with the fingers in front of the chin.	The fingertips tap the chin several times.	**grin and bear it** **put up with** **tolerate**	1182
Non-manual features The lips are drawn in and pressed together and the brows are slightly furrowed.				
The 5̈ hand is held with the palm facing towards the signer (if the hand were opened, the fingers would point to the left).	The hand is held in front of the mouth and chin.	The hand makes a short, sharp movement to the right.	**heat** **hot** **summer**	1183
The 5̈ hand is held with the palm facing towards the signer (if the hand were opened, the fingers would point to the left).	The hand is held with the fingertips resting against the chest.	The hand moves to the right; the fingertips maintain contact with the chest throughout.	**envious** **envy** **jealous** **jealousy**	1184
The 5̈ hand is held with the palm facing towards the signer (if the hand were opened, the fingers would point to the left).	The hand is held in front of the chest.	The hand moves up, so that the fingertips brush the chest; the movement is repeated.	**aggravate*** **aggravation*** **annoy*** **annoyance*** **irritable*** **irritate*** **irritation*** **temper***	1185
Non-manual features The lips are stretched.				
Notes * This sign may be produced using two hands.		[] 5̈⊤> 5̈⊤<		
The 5̈ hand is held with the palm facing towards the signer (if the hand were opened, the fingers would point to the left).	The hand is held with the fingertips resting against the chest.	The hand makes several short up and down movements; the fingertips maintain contact with the chest throughout.	**alive** **interesting** **life** **live** **toilet**	1186
The 5̈ hand is held with the palm facing towards the signer (if the hand were opened, the fingers would point to the left).	The hand is held in front of the side of the chest.	The hand twists at the wrist, so that the palm faces up and, at the same time, moves up with the fingertips brushing the side of the chest; the movement is repeated.	**complain** **grumble** **moan** **temper**	1187
Non-manual features The brows are furrowed.				
The 5̈ hand is held with the palm facing towards the signer (if the hand were opened, the fingers would point to the left).	The hand is held with the fingertips resting against the left upper arm.	The hand moves down, maintaining contact with the left upper arm; the movement is repeated.	**impolite** **impudent** **rude**	1188
Non-manual features The mouth is closed and the nose is wrinkled.				
The left 5 hand is held with the palm facing up and the fingers pointing away from the signer; the right 5̈ hand is held with the palm facing down (if the hand were opened, the fingers would point away from the signer).	The hands are held in front of the body; the right hand is held above the left hand.	The right hand bends down at the wrist while moving sharply towards the signer, so that the right fingertips brush along the left palm.	**scrape** **scratch**	1189
The left 5̈ hand is held with the palm facing up; the right 5̈ hand is held with the palm facing down (if the hands were opened, the fingers would all point away from the signer).	The hands are held in front of the body; the right hand is held above the left hand.	The left hand moves up while the right hand moves down, so that the fingertips all touch; the movement is repeated.	**alligator** **crocodile**	1190
Non-manual features The nose is wrinkled and the mouth opens and shuts twice.				

1191 Ø 5̈a>¸ 5̈a< ×·

1192 Ø 5̈ɒ⊥ 5̈ɒ⊥ ᵛ·

1193 Ø 5̈⊤ʌ¸ 5̈⊤ʌ ˣ̈ˣ

1194 Ø (5̈ɒ⊥ 5̈⊥ʌ ᵛ)⊤

1195 [] 5̈⊤> 5̈⊤< ˣᵃ̂ˇ

1196 [] 5̈⊤> 5̈⊤< ᵒ̈·̂ˣ÷

The extended fingers (spread apart) are bent and the thumb is extended.

Handshape and orientation	Location, hand arrangement and contact	Movement	Glosses	
Two 5̈ hands are held with the palms facing up (if the hands were opened, the left fingers would point to the right and the right fingers would point to the left).	The hands are held side by side in front of the body.	The knuckles tap together twice.	how?*	1191

Non-manual features   Non-manual features appropriate for questions must be used.

Notes   * This sign may be produced with the palms facing towards the signer.

Ø   5̈т> ,   5̈т<   ×·

Two 5̈ hands are held with the palms facing down (if the hands were opened, the fingers would all point away from the signer).	The hands are held in front of the body.	The hands make several short downward movements.	drizzle light rain shower	1192

Non-manual features   The eyes are narrowed and the lips are tightly rounded.

Two 5̈ hands are held with the palms facing towards the signer (if the hands were opened, the fingers would all point up).	The hands are held side by side in front of the body.	The hands bend towards each other from the wrists, so that the fingers link together.	engineer engineering equipment machine mechanic mesh technician technology	1193

The left 5̈ hand is held with the palm facing up; the right 5̇ hand is held with the palm facing away from the signer (if the hands were opened, the left fingers would point away from the signer and the right fingers would point up).	The hands are held in front of the body; the right hand is held above the left hand.	The right hand bends down at the wrist, so that the palm faces down; the hands then move towards the signer.	collect inherit inheritance windfall	1194

Two 5̈ hands are held with the palms facing towards the signer (if the hands were opened, the left fingers would point to the right and the right fingers would point to the left).	The hands are held in front of the chest.	The hands move up, so that the fingertips brush the chest, and then twist away from the signer, so that the palms face up.	anger* angry* frustrated* frustration*	1195

Non-manual features   The brows are furrowed and the head nods forward.

Notes   * This sign may be produced using one hand only.

[]   5̈т<   ^ ᵃ
           ×
           ^

Two 5̈ hands are held with the palms facing towards the signer (if the hands were opened, the left fingers would point to the right and the right fingers would point to the left).	The hands are held with the fingertips resting against the chest.	The hands make a short sharp upward movement bending from the wrists and maintaining contact with the chest, and then continue to move sharply up and, at the same time, apart in front of the chest.	anger angry furious livid mad rage temper wild	1196

Non-manual features   The brows are furrowed and the cheeks are slightly puffed out.

1197 [] 5̈ᴛ> 5̈ᴛ< ᴺᴺ·ˣ

1198 [] 5̈ᴛ> 5̈ᴛ< ⎛·o⎞ ᴺ·
⎝ᴧ⊥⎠
ˣ
ᴧ

1199 [] 5̈ᴛ> 5̈ᴛ< ᴼᴺ·
⊥
ᵛ
ˣ
ᴼ
⊥

1200 ⌈⌉ 5̈ᴛᴧ 5̈ᴛᴧ ˣ⊥ [ᴧᴧ]
#

Handshape and orientation	Location, hand arrangement and contact	Movement	Glosses	
Two 5̈ hands are held with the palms facing towards the signer (if the hands were opened, the left fingers would point to the right and the right fingers would point to the left).	The hands are held with the fingertips resting against the chest.	The hands move up and down alternately several times, maintaining contact with the chest throughout.	eager enthusiasm enthusiastic excite excited interest interested keen stimulate zeal zest	1197
Non-manual features The eyes are opened wide.				
Two 5̈ hands are held with the palms facing towards the signer (if the hands were opened, the left fingers would point to the right and the right fingers would point to the left).	The hands are held in front of the chest.	The hands move firmly upwards (so that the fingertips brush the chest) and then make a short movement away from the signer; the movements are repeated several times alternately.	aggression * aggressive *	1198
Non-manual features The brows are furrowed, the nose is wrinkled and the corners of the mouth are turned down.				
Notes * This sign may be produced using one hand only.				

$$[] \quad \ddot{5}_{\top <} \left(\begin{smallmatrix} \cdot & \circ \cdot \\ \wedge & \bot \\ \wedge & \end{smallmatrix} \right) \cdot$$

Handshape and orientation	Location, hand arrangement and contact	Movement	Glosses	
Two 5̈ hands are held with the palms facing towards the signer (if the hands were opened, the left fingers would point to the right and the right fingers would point to the left).	The hands are held in front of the chest.	The hands make alternate clockwise circles in the vertical plane at right angles to the signer's body; the fingertips brush the chest in completing each circle.	complain frustrate frustrated frustration grumble moan	1199
Non-manual features The eyes are narrowed and the nose is wrinkled.				
Two 5̈ hands are held with the palms facing towards the signer (if the hands were opened, the fingers would all point up).	The hands are held at an angle, so that the fingers are turned towards each other; the fingertips rest against the upper chest.	The hands move firmly away from the signer while closing (forming two A hands).	bold * brave * bravery * courage * courageous * daring * heroic * valiant *	1200
Non-manual features The brows are furrowed and the eyes are narrowed.				
Notes * This sign may be produced using one hand only.				

$$[1] \quad \ddot{5}_{\top \wedge} \quad {}^{\times} \tfrac{\dot{\bot}}{\#} {}_{[\wedge\wedge]}$$

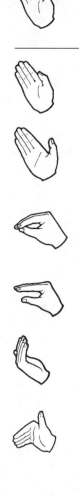

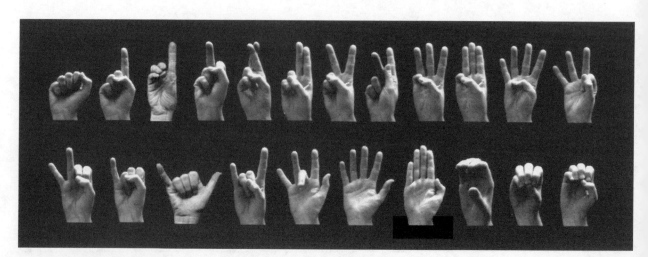

B

Handshape	Handshape description	Type	Sign entries
B	The hand is held flat with the fingers held together; the thumb is usually held against the side of the index finger.	Single dez Manual tab Double dez	1201 – 1289 1290 – 1363 1364 – 1486
Ḃ	The hand is held flat with the fingers held together and the thumb extended.	Single dez Manual tab Double dez	1487 – 1490 1491 – 1492 1493 – 1495
B̂	The extended fingers are held together and bent at the palm knuckles with the pad of the extended thumb touching the pad of the index and middle fingers.	Single dez Manual tab Double dez	1496 – 1501 1502 – 1512 1513 – 1527
B̿	The extended fingers are held together and bent at the palm knuckles with the extended thumb held parallel to the fingers.	Single dez Manual tab Double dez	1528 – 1544 1545 – 1548 1549 – 1559
̈B	The hand is held flat with the fingers held together and bent at the palm knuckles.	Single dez Manual tab Double dez	1560 – 1589 1590 – 1620 1621 – 1656
Ḅ̇	The hand is held flat with the fingers held together and bent at the palm knuckles, and the thumb is extended.	Single dez Manual tab Double dez	1657 1658 1659 – 1660

1201 Ø Ba⊥ ^

1202 Ø Ba⊥ ⊥

1203 Ø Ba⊥ ˚

1204 Ø Ba⊥ ˇ

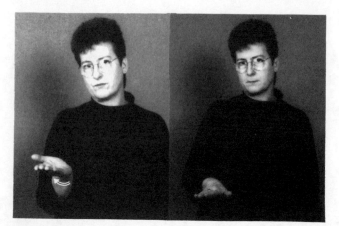

B is one of the most frequent handshapes used within BSL. The main *variation* which occurs relates to the positioning of the thumb, which may be held loosely at a slight angle to the fingers, across the palm or extended. As can be seen from the photographs in this section, the precise position often depends on the physical characteristics of the signer. Signs which do require the thumb to be extended are listed under **ḃ**.

B has several different *classifier* functions in the productive lexicon and is used as a classifying element in established signs:

- it is used as a *vehicle* classifier to represent vehicles such as cars, motorbikes, buses and boats. As such, it occurs in many verbs of motion and location relating to vehicles such as **car winding up hill** (see *Introduction*) and **car park** (sign 1392);
- it is used as a *size and shape* classifier to represent flat surfaces such as **wall** (sign 1227) and **table** (sign 1415). It is particularly used for flat, smooth surfaces which are longer than they are wide such as a sail, as in **yacht** (sign 1459); the **B** handshape can be seen as contrasting with **G**, **H** and **Wm** in showing different degrees of width.
- it is used as a *tracing size and shape* classifier to trace the outline of objects perceived as having flat and/or smooth sides or surfaces, as in **mountains** (sign 1236), **basin** (sign 1374), and **vase** (sign 1455);
- it is used as a *handling* classifier to indicate the holding of flat items or piles of flat-sided items, as in **hand over** (sign 1377);
- it is used as an *instrumental* classifier to represent flat implements, tools or utensils, as in **spade** (sign 1223) and **slice** (sign 1293);
- it is used as a *touch* classifier to indicate actions of the whole hand(s), as in **rub** (sign 1286), **stroke** (sign 1290) and **shove** (sign 1397);
- it is used to indicate *extent* or *quantity*, as in **shallow** (sign 1391) and **less** (sign 1393). One- and two-handed forms can express plurality, as in **flat items in a row** (see *Introduction*).

B also has a *deictic* (pointing) function, as in **get up** (sign 1201) and **get the attention of** (sign 1214). It is also used for *pronominal reference*, as in **them** (sign 1208) and for location signs such as **up** (sign 1201).

The **B** variant in which the thumb is held across the fingers expresses the letter **b** of the Irish and American manual alphabets. As such, it occurs in initial letter handshape signs borrowed from Irish Sign Language (ISL) and American Sign Language (ASL). Examples include **blue** from ISL and **Boston** from ASL (see *Introduction*). The **B** handshape in which the thumb is held loosely at the side of the fingers expresses the letter **l** of the Irish manual alphabet but borrowing of initial letter handshape signs from Irish Sign Language are rare.

Handshape and orientation	Location, hand arrangement and contact	Movement	Glosses	
The **B** hand is held with the palm facing up and the fingers pointing away from the signer.	The hand is held in front of the body.	The hand moves up.	arise get up lift raise rise stand up up	1201
The **B** hand is held with the palm facing up and the fingers pointing away from the signer.	The hand is held in front of the body.	The hand moves away from the signer.	grill oven put into an oven put under a grill toast	1202
The **B** hand is held with the palm facing up and the fingers pointing away from the signer.	The hand is held in front of the body.	The hand turns over sharply, so that the palm faces down.	from where from?[1]	1203

Notes   1 Appropriate non-manual features for a question must be used.

The **B** hand is held with the palm facing up and the fingers pointing away from the signer.	The hand is held in front of the body.	The hand moves down and, at the same time, to the left.	admit introduce invite welcome	1204

Non-manual features   The head tilts forward.

1205 Ø Bɑ⊥ ⊥̇˙ 1206 Ø Bɑ⊥ ˚ᵛ˙ ⊥

1207 Ø Bɑ⊥ (˚ᵛ<ᵛ<) 1208 Ø ⌡Bɑ< ᴅ̅⊥ 1209 Ø Bɒʌ ⊥̂

1210 Ø Bɒ⊥ ^ 1211 Ø Bɒ⊥ ᵛ 1212 Ø Bɒ⊥ ˙>

The hand is held flat with the fingers held together; the thumb is usually held against the side of the index finger.

Handshape and orientation	Location, hand arrangement and contact	Movement	Glosses	
The B hand is held with the palm facing up and the fingers pointing away from the signer.	The hand is held in front of the body.	The hand moves to the right and, at the same time, away from the signer.	delegate * give * hand * hand over * pass * pass on *	1205
Notes * Directional verb.				
The B hand is held with the palm facing up and the fingers pointing away from the signer.	The hand is held in front of the body.	The hand makes a short movement down and, at the same time, away from the signer; the movement is repeated.	beg beggar [1]	1206
Notes 1 If the movement is firm, the sign produced is **beggar**. Ø Bɑ⊥				
The B hand is held with the palm facing up and the fingers pointing away from the signer.	The hand is held in front of the body.	The hand moves down and, at the same time, to the left, in a series of short arcs.	custom generation hand down * hand on * hereditary heredity heritage inherit * inheritance pass down * tradition	1207
Notes * Directional verb.				
The B hand is held with the palm facing up and the fingers pointing to the left.	The hand is held in front of the body.	The hand bends away from the signer with the arm moving from the elbow.	them these they those you *(plural)*	1208
The B hand is held with the palm facing down and the fingers pointing up.	The hand is held in front of the body at an angle, so that the palm is turned away from the signer.	The hand moves up and, at the same time, away from the signer.	hill slope up upland upward ascend *†[1] ascent *†[1] steep *†[1] uphill [1]	1209

Notes   * This sign may be produced with the lips stretched.
     † This sign may be produced with the lips rounded, typically to indicate that a long distance is involved.
     1 If the cheeks are puffed out, the sign produced is **ascend, ascent, steep, uphill**.				

The B hand is held with the palm facing down and the fingers pointing away from the signer.	The hand is held in front of the body.	The hand moves up.	grow grow up high raise tall	1210
The B hand is held with the palm facing down and the fingers pointing away from the signer.	The hand is held beside the body at waist level.	The hand makes a short downward movement.	child kid low south toddler	1211
The B hand is held with the palm facing down and the fingers pointing away from the signer.	The hand is held in front of the body.	The hand makes a firm movement to the right.	flat level even [1] smooth [1]	1212
Notes 1 If the movement is slow, the sign produced is **even, smooth**. Ø Bɒ⊥ ›				

1213 Ø BƆ⊥ $\overset{\circ}{\vee}$.

1214 Ø BƆ⊥ $\overset{\overset{n}{\circ}}{\wedge}$.

1215 Ø BƆ⊥ $\overset{\overset{@}{\perp}}{\vee}$.

1216 Ø BƆ⊥ $\overset{\circ\ \circ\ \circ}{\overset{\vee\ \wedge\ \vee}{>}}$

1217 Ø BƆ< $\wedge$

1218 Ø BƆ< $\overset{\overset{+}{\omega+}}{\overset{\vee}{\wedge}}$

1219 Ø B⊤∧ $\overset{\overset{\cdot}{n}}{\overset{\vee}{\perp}}$

1220 Ø B⊤∨ $\overset{n}{\perp}$

The hand is held flat with the fingers held together; the thumb is usually held against the side of the index finger.

Handshape and orientation	Location, hand arrangement and contact	Movement	Glosses	
The **B** hand is held with the palm facing down and the fingers pointing away from the signer.	The hand is held in front of the body.	The hand makes two short downward movements.	bottom* little low* small south wee common[1] menial[2]	1213

Notes   * This sign may be produced using two hands.

     1 If the corners of the mouth are turned down, the sign produced is **common.**

     2 If the tongue protrudes between the teeth, the sign produced is **menial.**

Ø B⊅⊥ B⊅⊥   °ᵥ ·

The **B** hand is held with the palm facing down and the fingers pointing away from the signer.	The hand is held in front of the body.	The hand bends up and down from the wrist several times.	excuse me try to get the attention of hey!	1214

The **B** hand is held with the palm facing down and the fingers pointing away from the signer.	The hand is held in front of the body at an angle, so that the fingers are turned up.	The hand makes clockwise circles in the vertical plane at right angles to the signer's body.	merciful mercy pity poor shame sympathise* sympathy* paternalistic[1] patronise[1]	1215

Notes   * This sign may be used as the second part of a compound sign also meaning **sympathise, sympathy** (see 1276 for the first part of the sign).

     1 If the tongue protrudes between the teeth, the sign produced is **paternalistic, patronise.**

[] B⊤<   × //
        //

Ø B⊅⊥   ℮· / ᵥ

The **B** hand is held with the palm facing down and the fingers pointing away from the signer.	The hand is held beside the body at waist level.	The hand makes a short downward movement, moves to the right and then repeats the short downward movement.	children* infants* kids* toddlers*	1216

Notes   * The following notes apply to all glosses:

     This sign may be produced using two hands.

Ø B⊅⊥ B⊅⊥   ° ° °
             ᵥ ∧ ᵥ
             ÷

     The movement may be changed, so that the hand makes a short downward movement and then moves to the right; this sign typically refers to three or more children.

Ø B⊅⊥   °
        ᵥ >

The **B** hand is held with the palm facing down and the fingers pointing to the left.	The hand is held in front of the body.	The hand moves up.	big grown-up high tall	1217

The **B** hand is held with the palm facing down and the fingers pointing to the left.	The hand is held in front of the body.	The hand moves up and away from the signer while twisting at the wrist, so that the palm faces away from the signer, and then continues to move away from the signer with the palm facing down.	bank embankment hillside	1218

The **B** hand is held with the palm facing towards the signer and the fingers pointing up.	The hand is held in front of the body.	The hand moves down while bending firmly away from the signer at the wrist.	claim demand	1219

The **B** hand is held with the palm facing towards the signer and the fingers pointing down.	The hand is held in front of the body.	The hand bends away from the signer from the wrist.	absent away depart go leave	1220

1221 Ø B⊥ʌ [>]

1222 Ø B⊥ʌ ^{i.}

1223 Ø B⊥v ^{ẏ°}

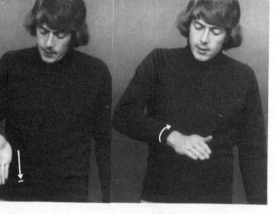

1224 Ø B<ʌ ^{ż.}

1225 Ø B<v ^ɒ

1226 Ø B<v ^(ωω⊤>)

1227 Ø B<⊥ ^ʌ

Handshape and orientation	Location, hand arrangement and contact	Movement	Glosses	
The **B** hand is held with the palm facing away from the signer and the fingers pointing up.	The hand is held in front of the body.	The hand moves to the right.	do not don't no refuse[1]	1221

Notes 1 If the head turns to the left, the sign produced is **refuse**.

The **B** hand is held with the palm facing away from the signer and the fingers pointing up.	The hand is held in front of the body.	The hand makes two short movements away from the signer.	hang on hold on wait	1222
The **B** hand is held with the palm facing away from the signer and the fingers pointing down.	The hand is held in front of the body.	The hand moves firmly down and, at the same time, away from the signer, and then turns over, so that the palm is facing down.	dig dig a hole dig with a spade spade	1223
The **B** hand is held with the palm facing left and the fingers pointing up.	The hand is held in front of the body.	The hand makes short movements from side to side.	about approximate between rough	1224
The **B** hand is held with the palm facing left and the fingers pointing down.	The hand is held in front of the body.	The hand bends away from the signer at the wrist.	go	1225
The **B** hand is held with the palm facing left and the fingers pointing down.	The hand is held in front of the body.	The hand twists at the wrist, so that the palm faces towards the signer and then to the right, while moving to the right throughout.	bay cove	1226
The **B** hand is held with the palm facing left and the fingers pointing away from the signer.	The hand is held in front of the body.	The hand moves up.	barrier * partition * screen * side * wall * wall off *	1227

Notes * This sign may be produced with the hand moving down.   Ø B<⊥ ˅

1228 Ø B<⊥ $\begin{pmatrix} \eta \\ z \\ \bot \end{pmatrix}$

1229 Ø B<⊥ $\overset{\bot}{\wedge}\overset{\circ}{\vee}$

1230 Ø B<⊥ $\overset{@}{\underset{\vee}{>}}\cdot$

1231 Ø B<⊥ $\overset{\cdot}{\underset{a}{>}}$

1232 Ø B<⊥ $\begin{pmatrix} \circ \\ \omega \\ z \\ \bot \end{pmatrix}$

1233 Ø B<⊥ $\begin{pmatrix} \circ & \circ & \circ \\ \wedge & > & \vee & \cdot \\ & > & & \end{pmatrix}$

1234 Ø ʝB<⊥ $\overset{\eta}{<}$

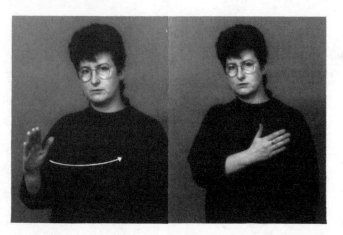

Handshape and orientation	Location, hand arrangement and contact	Movement	Glosses	
The **B** hand is held with the palm facing left and the fingers pointing away from the signer.	The hand is held in front of the body.	The hand bends from side to side at the wrist and, at the same time, moves away from the signer.	**zigzag** **evasive**[1] **roundabout**[1]	1228

Notes   1 If the tongue protrudes between the teeth, the sign produced is **evasive, roundabout.**

The **B** hand is held with the palm facing left and the fingers pointing away from the signer.	The hand is held in front of the body.	The hand moves away from the signer and, at the same time, upwards in an arc ending with a short downward movement.	**across** **go** **head** **travel**	1229
The **B** hand is held with the palm facing left and the fingers pointing away from the signer.	The hand is held in front of the body.	The hand makes clockwise circles in the vertical plane parallel to the signer's body.	**tumble dryer** **washing machine** **(front loading)** **spin dryer** **(front loading)**[1]	1230

Notes   1 If the movement is sharp, the sign produced is **spin dryer (front loading).**

Ø B<⊥ $\overset{\cdot}{\underset{\vee}{\overset{@}{\cdot}}}$ ·

The **B** hand is held with the palm facing left and the fingers pointing away from the signer.	The hand is held in front of the body.	The hand moves to the right while twisting sharply at the wrist, so that the palm faces up.	overturn	1231

Non-manual features   The cheeks puff out.

The **B** hand is held with the palm facing left and the fingers pointing away from the signer.	The hand is held in front of the body.	The hand moves away from the signer and, at the same time, makes small twisting movements from side to side at the wrist.	**fish** **swim**	1232
The **B** hand is held with the palm facing left and the fingers pointing away from the signer.	The hand is held in front of the body.	The hand moves to the right in a series of short arcs.	**intermittent*** **occasional*** **sporadic***	1233

Notes   * This sign may be produced using a **V** handshape and bending at the wrist.

Ø V<⊥ $\left(\overset{\circ}{\underset{\vee}{\overset{D}{\cdot}}}\right)$ ·

The **B** hand is held with the palm facing left and the fingers pointing away from the signer.	The hand is held in front of the body at an angle, so that the fingers are turned upwards.	The hand moves to the left, with the arm bending from the elbow, so that the movement ends with the palm facing towards the signer.	**all** **every** **everybody** **everyone** **everything** **everywhere**	1234

1235 ∅ B>⊥ $^{\wedge\omega\vee}_{><>}$

1236 ∅ B>⊥ $\left(^{\wedge\vee}_{?}{}^{\wedge\vee}_{\omega}\cdot\right)$

1237 ∅ B>< $^{\vee}_{<}$

1238 ∩ Bᴐ∧ $^{\times}_{\perp}{}^{\circ}$

1239 ∩ B⊤< $^{\times}_{\wedge}{}^{\perp}_{\vee}$ // ∅ B̄⊤> | B⊤< $^{\circ}_{\perp}$

1240 ∩ B<∧ $^{(\circ}_{\perp}{}^{\times)}.$

1241 ∩ B<∧ $^{\omega\circ}_{\vee}{}^{\geq}_{>}{}^{[A]}_{\times}{}^{\circ}_{\#}{}^{<}_{\vee}{}^{\times}$

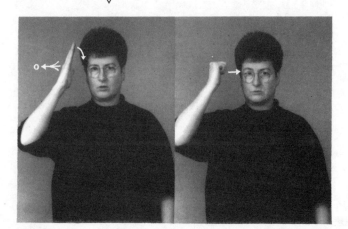

[644]

B

The hand is held flat with the fingers held together; the thumb is usually held against the side of the index finger.

Handshape and orientation	Location, hand arrangement and contact	Movement	Glosses	
The B hand is held with the palm facing right and the fingers pointing away from the signer.	The hand is held in front of the body.	The hand moves up and, at the same time, to the right, and then twists at the wrist, so that the palm faces left before moving down and, at the same time, to the right.	hill hump mound	1235
The B hand is held with the palm facing right and the fingers pointing away from the signer.	The hand is held in front of the body.	The hand moves up while twisting at the wrist, so that the palm faces down, and then down while twisting to the left at the wrist; the movements are repeated with the hand moving to the right throughout.	camel hills mountain range mountains	1236
The B hand is held with the palm facing right and the fingers pointing to the left.	The hand is held in front of the body at an angle, so that the palm is turned down.	The hand moves down and, at the same time, to the left.	chute down downward hill slide slide down a chute/ slide slope descend *†[1] descent *†[1] downhill [1] steep *†[1]	1237

Notes   * This sign may be produced with the lips stretched.

      † This sign may be produced with the lips rounded, typically to indicate that a long distance is involved.

      1 If the cheeks are puffed out, the sign produced is **descend, descent, downhill, steep.**

Handshape and orientation	Location, hand arrangement and contact	Movement	Glosses	
The B hand is held with the palm facing down and the fingers pointing up.	The hand is held (at an angle, so that the palm is turned to the left) with the side of the index finger touching the side of the forehead.	The hand makes a short firm movement away from the signer.	hello hi	1238
The B hand is held with the palm facing towards the signer and the fingers pointing to the left.	The hand is held with the fingertips touching the side of the forehead.	The hand moves down and, at the same time, away from the signer.	accommodation hotel lodge reside stay	1239
The left B hand is held with the palm facing towards the signer and the fingers pointing to the right; the right B hand is held with the palm facing towards the signer and the fingers pointing to the left.	The hands are held side by side in front of the body; the right hand is held higher than the left hand.	The hands make a short movement away from the signer while twisting at the wrists, so that the palms face down.		
The B hand is held with the palm facing left and the fingers pointing up.	The hand is held in front of the forehead at an angle, so that the fingers are turned to the left.	The hand makes a short, firm movement towards the signer, so that the side of the index finger touches the forehead; the movement is repeated.	danger dangerous hazard risk [1] risky [1] hazardous [2]	1240

     Notes   1 If the lips are rounded and there is a sharp intake of air, the sign produced is **risk, risky.**

           2 If the cheeks are puffed out, the sign produced is **hazardous.**

Handshape and orientation	Location, hand arrangement and contact	Movement	Glosses	
The B hand is held with the palm facing left and the fingers pointing up.	The hand is held beside the head.	The hand moves down and, at the same time, the fingers bend at the palm knuckles, so that the fingertips brush the side of the forehead; the hand then makes a short movement to the right while closing (forming an A hand) before moving to the left, so that the knuckles touch the side of the forehead.	Australia Australian	1241

1242 ○ BTΛ ᵀ

1243 ○ BTΛ ⊥ᵥ

1244 ○ BTΛ ⌃ᵥ@

1245 ○ BTΛ °ω̇N

1246 ○ B<Λ (ⁿ⊥)

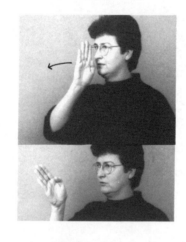

1247 ○ B<Λ ⁿᴴ·

1248 ○ B<Λ °ⁿᴴ·

1249 Ц BTΛ ˣω̇⊥

The hand is held flat with the fingers held together; the thumb is usually held against the side of the index finger.

Handshape and orientation	Location, hand arrangement and contact	Movement	Glosses	
The **B** hand is held with the palm facing towards the signer and the fingers pointing up.	The hand is held beside the head.	The hand moves towards the signer.	before former formerly* past* then	1242

Notes   * This sign may be produced with a repeated movement.   ○ B⊤∧ ⊤ ·

| The **B** hand is held with the palm facing towards the signer and the fingers pointing up. | The hand is held in front of the face. | The hand moves down and, at the same time, away from the signer. | apparent appear look as if look like seem | 1243 |
| The **B** hand is held with the palm facing towards the signer and the fingers pointing up. | The hand is held in front of the face. | The hand makes anticlockwise circles in the vertical plane parallel to the signer's body. | facecloth flannel wash* wash one's face with a facecloth/flannel | 1244 |

Notes   * This sign may be produced at appropriate locations on the body.

| The **B** hand is held with the palm facing towards the signer and the fingers pointing up. | The hand is held in front of the face. | The hand makes several small twisting movements from side to side at the wrist. | mirror reflection shimmer blue[1] purple[2] | 1245 |

Non-manual features   The eyegaze is directed towards the hand.

Notes   1 If the thumb is held across the palm and the palm faces left, the sign produced is **blue**. This is a regional sign.   ○ B<∧

   2 If the palm faces left and the hand moves up while twisting from side to side, the sign produced is **purple**. This is a regional sign.   ○ B<∧

| The **B** hand is held with the palm facing left and the fingers pointing up. | The hand is held in front of the face. | The hand moves away from the signer while bending away from the signer at the wrist. | direct go straight straight ahead straight on straight[1] | 1246 |

Notes   1 If the side of the index finger touches the nose before the hand moves away from the signer, the sign produced is **straight** (*see entry 3 in the English section*).   ○ B<∧

| The **B** hand is held with the palm facing left and the fingers pointing up. | The hand is held beside the head. | The hand bends towards and away from the signer from the wrist several times. | address lecture lecturer paper preach* preacher sermon speaker speech talk | 1247 |

Notes   * This sign may be produced using two hands.   ○ B>∧   B<∧

| The **B** hand is held with the palm facing left and the fingers pointing up. | The hand is held beside the head. | The hand makes two short movements towards and away from the signer, bending from the wrist. | fortunate fortunately luck luckily lucky careless[1] | 1248 |

Notes   1 If the tongue protrudes between the teeth, the sign produced is **careless**.

| The **B** hand is held with the palm facing towards the signer and the fingers pointing up. | The hand is held with the fingers touching the nose. | The hand twists away from the signer from the wrist, so that the palm faces away from the signer. | attitude | 1249 |

1250 Ⴇ B⊤ʌ ×ⱽ·

1251 Ⴇ B⊥ʌ ⊥×·

1252 Ⴇ B<ʌ ×ⁿⱽ // [] Ḃ◌< ×ⱽ
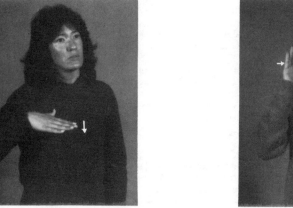

1253 ⊃ B⊥ʌ ×

1254 ⊃ B<ʌ ×

1255 ∪ B⊤ʌ ×·

1256 ∪ B<ʌ ×

[648]

The hand is held flat with the fingers held together; the thumb is usually held against the side of the index finger.

Handshape and orientation	Location, hand arrangement and contact	Movement	Glosses	
The B hand is held with the palm facing towards the signer and the fingers pointing up.	The hand is held beside the right cheek.	The fingers bend towards the signer from the palm knuckles, brushing the cheek; the movement is repeated.	before * earlier * just * recent * recently * previous *¹ previously *¹ while ago *¹ just now *² minutes ago *² seconds ago *²	1250

Non-manual features   The lips are stretched.

Notes   * This sign may be produced using a B̄ hand (closing to a B̂ hand). This is a regional sign.

1 If the mouth is closed with the lips pushed forward, the sign produced is **previous, previously, while ago**.

2 If the lips are stretched and the shoulders are hunched, the sign produced is **just now, minutes ago, seconds ago**.

The B hand is held with the palm facing away from the signer and the fingers pointing up.	The hand is held with the fingers beside the right cheek.	The hand moves away from the signer, brushing across the cheek; the movement is repeated.	before * Hartlepool *	1251

Notes   * Regional sign.

The B hand is held with the palm facing left and the fingers pointing up.	The hand is held against the side of the head.	The hand moves down and, at the same time, turns, so that the palm faces down and the fingers point to the left; the hand then continues to move down with the thumbtip brushing the chest.	nightdress nightgown nightie	1252

The B hand is held with the palm facing away from the signer and the fingers pointing up.	The hand is held beside the ear.	The side of the hand touches the head beside the ear.	hear listen	1253

Non-manual features   The head is turned to the left.

The B hand is held with the palm facing left and the fingers pointing up.	The hand is held against the side of the head.	No movement.	bed * bedroom * sleep *¹	1254

Non-manual features   The head is tilted to the right.

Notes   * This sign may be produced using two hands with the palms held together, and located at the side of the head.

1 If the eyes close, the sign produced is **sleep**.

The B hand is held with the palm facing towards the signer and the fingers pointing up.	The hand is held with the fingers in front of the chin.	The fingers tap the chin twice.	bore bored boring dull tedious uninteresting yawn	1255

Non-manual features   The mouth is open.

The B hand is held with the palm facing left and the fingers pointing up.	The hand is held with the side of the index finger resting against the nose.	The hand moves down, maintaining contact with the lower face throughout.	sad serious solemn subdued	1256

Non-manual features   The corners of the mouth are slightly turned down and the brows are slightly furrowed.

1257 ⌣ Bᴛ∧ ˣ⊥ᵥ // ɑ Bʊ⊥ ˣ⊥ᵥ@

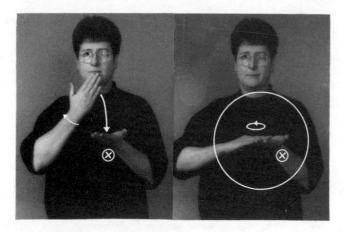

1258 ⌣ Bᴛ∧ ˣ⊥ᵥ // ‾Bɑ> Bʊ⊥

1259 ⌣ Bᴛ∧ ˣ⊥ᵥ // ‾Bɑ> Bʊ⊥ ˣˣ

1260 ⌣ Bᴛ∧ ˣⁿᵥ // [] Bᴛ< ˣˣ

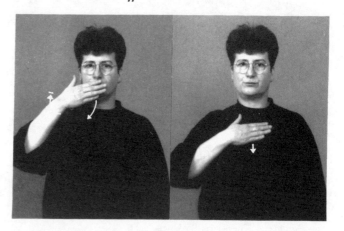

1261 ⌣ Bᴛ∧ ˣ⊥ᵥ

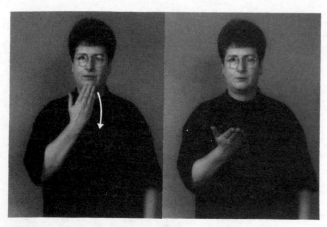

1262 ⌣ Bᴛ∧ ᶻ°·

[650]

The hand is held flat with the fingers held together; the thumb is usually held against the side of the index finger.

Handshape and orientation	Location, hand arrangement and contact	Movement	Glosses	
The right B hand is held with the palm facing towards the signer and the fingers pointing up.	The hand is held with the fingertips resting against the mouth and chin.	The hand moves down and, at the same time, away from the signer.	mauve* purple* violet*	1257
The right B hand is held with the palm facing down and the fingers pointing away from the signer.	The left hand is positioned in front of the body with the palm facing up; the right fingers rest on the left wrist.	The right hand makes an anti-clockwise circle in the horizontal plane, maintaining contact with the left wrist throughout.		

Notes * The following notes apply to all glosses:

Regional sign.

This sign may also be produced with the right hand making a circle on the back of the left hand.

The right B hand is held with the palm facing towards the signer and the fingers pointing up.	The hand is held with the fingertips resting against the mouth and chin.	The hand moves down and, at the same time, away from the signer.	burn	1258
The left B hand is held with the palm facing up and the fingers pointing to the right; the right B hand is held with the palm facing down and the fingers pointing away from the signer.	The hands are held in front of the body; the right hand is held above the left hand.	The right fingers touch the left palm.		
The right B hand is held with the palm facing towards the signer and the fingers pointing up.	The hand is held with the fingertips resting against the mouth and chin.	The hand moves down and, at the same time, away from the signer.	envelope seal an envelope excuse me [1] pardon me [1]	1259
The left B hand is held with the palm facing up and the fingers pointing to the right; the right B hand is held with the palm facing down and the fingers pointing away from the signer.	The hands are held in front of the body; the right hand is held above the left hand.	The right hand moves to the right, maintaining contact with the left palm throughout.		

Notes 1 If the movement in the second part of the sign is repeated, the sign produced is **excuse me, pardon me**.

The B hand is held with the palm facing towards the signer and the fingers pointing up.	The hand is held with the fingers touching the mouth and chin.	The hand bends firmly to the left at the wrist while moving down.	shut one up silence one	1260
The B hand is held with the palm facing towards the signer and the fingers pointing to the left.	The hand is held resting against the chest.	The hand moves down, maintaining contact with the chest throughout.		

Non-manual features The lips are pressed together.

The B hand is held with the palm facing towards the signer and the fingers pointing up.	The hand is held with the fingertips touching the mouth and chin.	The hand moves down and, at the same time, away from the signer.	grateful gratitude please* thank thanks thank you	1261

Notes * This sign may be produced with the fingers bending at the palm knuckles as the hand moves down and away from the signer.

The B hand is held with the palm facing towards the signer and the fingers pointing up.	The hand is held in front of the mouth.	The hand makes two short movements from side to side.	class* classroom* school*	1262

Notes * Regional sign.

1263 ⊃ ∮BⲦ⋀ ᗡ⋀×ᗡ

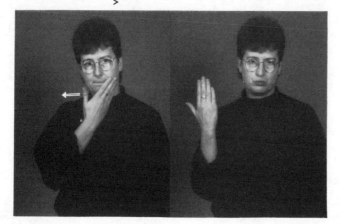

1264 ⊃ B<⋀ ×·

1265 ⊖ B<⋀ ×·

1266 ⊃ B<⋀ ×ᵛᵀ // B̄ᵒ> B<⋀ᵩ ×ᵛ⋀ᵒ

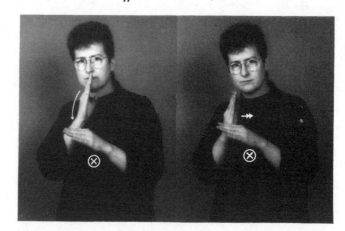

1267 ⊔ Bᵒ< ⁽⋀×⁾·

1268 Π BⲦ⋀ ᵚᴹᴹ·

1269 [ ] Bα⋀ ᵛ×

[652]

Handshape and orientation	Location, hand arrangement and contact	Movement	Glosses	
The **B** hand is held with the palm facing towards the signer and the fingers pointing up.	The hand is held with the fingers in front of the mouth.	The hand moves sharply to the right, so that the fingers brush across the lips.	**have not** **haven't** **nothing**	1263

Non-manual features   The lips are pressed together and drawn back; as the hand moves, the mouth opens sharply with the lips rounded.

The **B** hand is held with the palm facing left and the fingers pointing up.	The hand is held beside the mouth.	The side of the hand taps the side of the mouth twice.	**Belgian** **Belgium** **maybe*** **toilet***·	1264

Notes   * Regional sign.

The **B** hand is held with the palm facing left and the fingers pointing up.	The hand is held with the fingers in front of the mouth and chin.	The side of the hand taps the mouth and chin twice.	**period** **private** **secret***†	1265

Notes   * This sign may be produced with the hand bending towards the signer at the wrist, to touch the mouth and chin; the movement is repeated.

$$\smile \ B{<}\wedge \left(\begin{smallmatrix} \circ \\ \square \\ \mathsf{T} \end{smallmatrix} \times \right)\cdot$$

† This sign may be produced with the mouth open and the lips pushed forward.

The left **B** hand is held with the palm facing down and the fingers pointing to the right; the right **B** hand is held with the palm facing left and the fingers pointing up.	The left hand is held in front of the body; the right hand is held with the side of the index finger resting against the mouth and chin.	The right hand makes a short movement down and, at the same time, away from the signer, and then makes a short, repeated movement to the left, so that the side of the right hand brushes the left index finger.	**confidential** **hidden** **hide** **private** **secret**	1266
The **B** hand is held with the palm facing down and the fingers pointing to the left.	The hand is held under the chin.	The hand moves up, so that the backs of the fingers touch the underside of the chin; the movement is repeated.	**enough** **full** **full up** **sufficient**	1267
The **B** hand is held with the palm facing towards the signer and the fingers pointing up.	The hand is held in front of the neck.	The fingers bend at the palm knuckles, so that the fingertips brush the neck; the movement is repeated.	**thirsty** **water**	1268
The **B** hand is held with the palm facing up and the fingers pointing up.	The side of the hand rests against the left side of the chest; the hand is held at an angle, so that the fingers are turned to the left.	The hand moves down and to the right, maintaining contact with the chest throughout.	**insurance** **insure** **Protestant** **Yugoslav** **Yugoslavia** **Yugoslavian**	1269

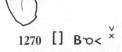

1270 [] B℧< ˣ̌

1271 [] B℧< ˣ̌̇

1272 [] B⊤< ˣ̌

1273 [] B⊤< ˣ·

1274 [] B⊤< ˣ̌ω⊤ // ∅ G⊥∧ ᵒᵈ·z

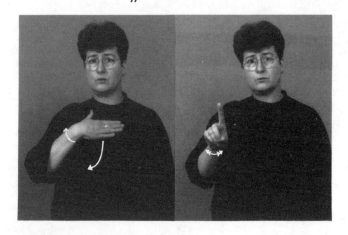

1275 [] B⊤< ˣ̌@·ᵛˣ

1276 ⟩[] B⊤< ˣ·

B

The hand is held flat with the fingers held together; the thumb is usually held against the side of the index finger.

Handshape and orientation	Location, hand arrangement and contact	Movement	Glosses	
The **B** hand is held with the palm facing down and the fingers pointing to the left.	The side of the hand rests against the chest.	The hand moves down, maintaining contact with the chest throughout.	depress depressed depressing depression down (feel down) sad	1270
Non-manual features The corners of the mouth are turned down and the shoulders sag.				
The **B** hand is held with the palm facing down and the fingers pointing to the left.	The hand is held in front of the chest.	The hand moves down with the side of the thumb brushing the chest; the movement is repeated.	content happy satisfaction satisfactory satisfy relief¹	1271
Non-manual features The lips are pressed together.				
Notes 1 If the movement is not repeated, the sign produced is **relief**.	[] Bꙮ< ˅˅			
The **B** hand is held with the palm facing towards the signer and the fingers pointing to the left.	The hand is held with the palm resting against the chest.	The hand moves slowly down, maintaining contact with the chest throughout.	calm gentle mild quiet put in one's place¹	1272
Notes 1 If the eyes are opened wide, the shoulders move back and the movement of the hand is firm, the sign produced is **put in one's place**.	[] B⊤< ˅×			
The **B** hand is held with the palm facing towards the signer and the fingers pointing to the left.	The hand is held in front of the chest.	The palm taps the chest twice.	front like	1273
The **B** hand is held with the palm facing towards the signer and the fingers pointing to the left.	The hand is held with the palm resting against the chest.	The hand moves down, maintaining contact with the chest, and then twists away from the signer, so that the palm faces down.	what do you want? what's the point?¹ what's up?²	1274
The **G** hand is held with the palm facing away from the signer (if the hand were opened, the fingers would point up).	The hand is held in front of the body.	The hand makes several short bending movements from side to side at the wrist.		
Non-manual features The eyebrows are raised.				
Notes 1 If the lips are pressed together and stretched, the sign produced is **what's the point?**				
2 If the brows are slightly furrowed and the mouth is open, the sign produced is **what's up?**				
The **B** hand is held with the palm facing towards the signer and the fingers pointing to the left.	The hand is held with the palm resting against the chest.	The hand makes anticlockwise circles in the vertical plane parallel to the signer's body, maintaining contact with the chest throughout.	appreciate appreciation glad happy please	1275
The **B** hand is held with the palm facing towards the singer and the fingers pointing to the left.	The hand is held in front of the left side of the chest.	The hand taps the left side of the chest twice.	heart*	1276
Notes * This sign may also be produced with a **Ġ** handshape.	ᐟ[] Ġ⊤< × ·			

1277 ⌈⌉ B<ʌ ˣ>ˣ

1278 ⌈Y̆⌉ Bтʌ ᵐ̥·

1279 ⌈Y̆⌉ Bтʌ @ᵀᵀᵥ

1280 >⌈⌉ Bᴜʌ ˣ·

1281 ⌉ B<⊥ ᵛᵢ̥ₐ ˣₒ

1282 ⌊⌋< Bтᵥ ᵛ̥ᵥ ˣ

1283 ᵢ̇ Bɑ< ˣ·

1284 ⎯⎯√ Bᴜ⊥ ˣˣ

1285 ⎯⎯√ Bᴜ⊥ ˣₓ(ₒ₃)ᵥ

B

The hand is held flat with the fingers held together; the thumb is usually held against the side of the index finger.

Handshape and orientation	Location, hand arrangement and contact	Movement	Glosses	
The **B** hand is held with the palm facing left and the fingers pointing up.	The hand is held in front of the left side of the upper chest.	The side of the hand touches the left side of the upper chest, and the hand then moves to the right before touching the right side of the upper chest.	armed forces army military soldier	1277
The **B** hand is held with the palm facing towards the signer and the fingers pointing up.	The hand is held in front of the shoulder.	The fingers make several short bending movements towards the signer from the palm knuckles.	breeze draught [1]	1278

Non-manual features   The lips are rounded.

Notes   1 If the eyes are narrowed, the sign produced is **draught**.

The **B** hand is held with the palm facing towards the signer and the fingers pointing up.	The hand is held in front of the shoulder.	The hand makes an anticlockwise circle in the vertical plane at right angles to the signer's body, and then moves back over the shoulder.	history past	1279
The **B** hand is held with the palm facing down and the fingers pointing up.	The hand is held in front of the left side of the chest at an angle, so that the fingers are turned to the left.	The side of the hand taps the left side of the upper chest twice.	Burwood Park School green park recreation ground school *	1280

Notes   * Regional sign.

The **B** hand is held with the palm facing left and the fingers pointing away from the signer.	The hand is held resting against the right side of the chest, at an angle, so that the fingers are turned to the left.	The hand moves down, maintaining contact with the chest, and then makes a short movement away from the signer while twisting at the wrist, so that the palm faces down.	desire hope need want wish	1281
The **B** hand is held with the palm facing towards the signer and the fingers pointing down.	The hand is held with the palm resting against the side of the waist.	The hand makes a short downward movement, maintaining contact with the side of the waist throughout.	pocket pocket money [1]	1282

Notes   1 If the palm taps the hip twice, the sign produced is **pocket money**.

Ḣ B⊤v ×·

The **B** hand is held with the palm facing up and the fingers pointing to the left.	The hand is held below the left elbow.	The palm taps the left elbow twice.	biscuit idle lazy	1283
The **B** hand is held with the palm facing down and the fingers pointing away from the signer.	The hand rests on the left forearm, which is positioned across the body.	The hand moves slowly to the left, maintaining contact with the left forearm throughout.	age ages long slow	1284
The **B** hand is held with the palm facing down and the fingers pointing away from the signer.	The left arm is positioned across the body; the right palm rests on the left forearm.	The hand moves to the left, maintaining contact with the left forearm and then makes a short upward movement, while twisting to the left at the wrist.	field garden grass green boot [1]	1285

⌐ ⊂ᴑ⊥ ×(°°)
ω<

Notes   1 If a right **C** handshape is used, the sign produced is **boot**.

1286 ⌐╵ Bʊ⊥ °⊚∨⊤ₓ ˙

1287 ╵₉ B⊤< ⊗∨∧∨ₓ

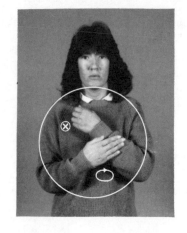

1288 ⁻◠ Bʊ⊥ ⊚∨⊤ₓ

1289 ⊔ B<∨ ×˙

1290 ⁻A⊍⊥₉ Bʊ< °⊤ₓ˙⊤

1291 A⊤∧ B⊥∧ ᵘ⊥

1292 ⁻A⊤> ₁ B<⊥ ∨ₓ˙∨

Handshape and orientation	Location, hand arrangement and contact	Movement	Glosses	

The **B** hand is held with the palm facing down and the fingers pointing away from the signer.	The hand is held resting on the left forearm, which is positioned in front of the body.	The hand makes small anticlockwise circles in the horizontal plane, maintaining contact with the left forearm throughout.	apply*
			apply to one's arm
			rub/rub into/
			  rub off/rub on
			  one's arm
			rub in*
			rub off*
			rub on*
				1286

Notes   * This sign may be located at the appropriate part of the body.

The **B** hand is held with the palm facing towards the signer and the fingers pointing to the left.	The hand is held resting against the left forearm, which is positioned across the chest.	The hand makes an anticlockwise circle in the vertical plane parallel to the signer's body, maintaining contact with the left forearm throughout.	brown*	1287

Notes   * Regional sign.

The **B** hand is held with the palm facing down and the fingers pointing away from the signer.	The left hand is positioned in front of the body, with the palm facing up; the right fingers rest on the left wrist.	The right hand makes an anticlockwise circle in the horizontal plane, maintaining contact with the left wrist throughout.	blue*	1288

Notes   * The following notes apply to this gloss:

This sign may be produced with the right hand making a circle on the left palm.

$$\overline{\text{B}\alpha>} \ \text{B}\text{ʊ}\botatop{\tiny @}{\tiny <}\text{}_{\tiny x}^{\tiny T}$$

This sign may be produced with the right hand making a circle on the back of the left hand.

$$\overline{\text{B}\text{ʊ}>} \ \text{B}\text{ʊ}\bot \ ^{@}_{x}$$

The **B** hand is held with the palm facing left and the fingers pointing down.	The hand is held beside the right hip.	The hand taps the hip twice.	dog*	1289

Notes   * Regional sign.

The left **A** hand is held with the palm facing down (if the hand were opened, the fingers would point away from the signer). The right **B** hand is held with the palm facing down and the fingers pointing to the left.	The hands are held in front of the body; the left hand is held lower and nearer to the signer than the right hand.	The right hand makes a short movement towards the signer, so that the fingers brush across the back of the left hand; the movement is repeated.	cat night stroke	1290
The left **A** hand is held with the palm facing towards the signer (if the hand were opened, the fingers would point up). The right **B** hand is held with the palm facing away from the signer and the fingers pointing up.	The hands are held in front of the body.	The right hand bends away from the signer from the wrist.	accelerate acceleration put one's foot down speed up	1291

Non-manual features   The cheeks are slightly puffed out.

The left **A** hand is held with the palm facing towards the signer (if the hand were opened, the fingers would point to the right). The right **B** hand is held with the palm facing left and the fingers pointing away from the signer.	The hands are held side by side in front of the body; the right hand is held higher than the left hand.	The right hand moves down, brushing the left knuckles; the movement is repeated.	cabbage	1292

1293 $\overline{A}>\perp_1$ B$\sigma\perp$ $\overset{<}{\underset{<}{x}}$

1294 $\overline{A}>\perp_{\varphi}$ B$\top<$ $\overset{v}{\underset{v}{x}}$

1295 $\underline{G}\sigma>$ $_x$ $\diagup$B$<$v $\overset{n}{\underset{<}{}}$

1296 G$\top\wedge$ B$<\perp_{\varphi}$ $\overset{\overset{o}{i}>n<}{\underset{\perp<}{}}$

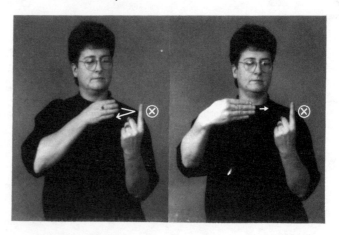

1297 $\overline{G}>\wedge$ $_{1x}$ αB$<\perp$ $\overset{x}{\underset{<}{n}}\cdot$

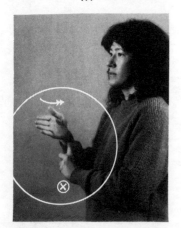

1298 $\overline{G}>\wedge$ B$\sigma<$ $\overset{o}{v}x$

Handshape and orientation	Location, hand arrangement and contact	Movement	Glosses	
The left **A** hand is held with the palm facing right (if the hand were opened, the fingers would point away from the signer). The right **B** hand is held with the palm facing down and the fingers pointing away from the signer.	The hands are held side by side in front of the body; the right hand is held higher than the left hand.	The right hand moves to the left, so that the right palm brushes the top of the left fist.	cover * full * chop [1] cut [1] slice [1]	1293

Notes   * This sign can also be produced with a right **A** hand which opens (forming a **5** hand) as it moves to the left, brushing across the left fist.

$$A{>}\bot \mid A\sigma\bot \begin{smallmatrix} <[5] \\ \times \\ < \\ \square \end{smallmatrix}$$

1 If the right hand is held with the palm facing up, the sign produced is **chop, cut, slice.**

$$A{>}\bot \mid B\sigma\bot \begin{smallmatrix} < \\ \times \\ < \end{smallmatrix}$$

The left **A** hand is held with the palm facing right (if the hand were opened, the fingers would point away from the signer). The right **B** hand is held with the palm facing towards the signer and the fingers pointing to the left.	The hands are held in front of the body; the left hand is held lower and nearer to the signer than the right hand.	The right hand moves down, so that the right fingers brush the left knuckles.	never	1294
The left **G** hand is held with the palm facing down (if the hand were opened, the fingers would point to the right). The right **B** hand is held with the palm facing left and the fingers pointing down.	The right hand is held in front of the body; the left arm is positioned across the body with the left index finger held against the right forearm.	The right hand bends to the left from the wrist.	cricket * cricket bat * cricketer * play cricket *	1295

Notes   * This sign may also be produced with the left index fingertip held against the right wrist.

$$G\sigma{>} {}_{\times} \alpha B{<}v \begin{smallmatrix} \cap \\ < \end{smallmatrix}$$

The left **G** hand is held with the palm facing towards the signer (if the hand were opened, the fingers would point up). The right **B** hand is held with the palm facing left and the fingers pointing away from the signer.	The hands are held in front of the body; the right hand is held nearer to the signer than the left hand.	The right hand makes a short movement away from the signer and, at the same time, to the right, before bending to the left from the wrist (so that the palm faces towards the signer) and then moving to the left.	diversion indirect roundabout	1296
The left **G** hand is held with the palm facing towards the signer (if the hand were opened, the fingers would point up). The right **B** hand is held with the palm facing left and the fingers pointing away from the signer.	The hands are held in front of the body; the left index fingertip is held against the wrist.	The right hand bends to the left from the wrist; the movement is repeated, with the left index finger held against the right wrist throughout.	flag flag flying	1297
The left **G** hand is held with the palm facing right (if the hand were opened, the fingers would point up). The right **B** hand is held with the palm facing down and the fingers pointing to the left.	The hands are held at head height in front of the body; the right hand is held above the left hand.	The right hand moves down, so that the right palm touches the left index fingertip.	important peak summit superior top V.I.P. ultimate [1]	1298

Notes   1 If the hands are held side by side, the right hand moves up before coming down to touch the left index fingertip, and the lips are pressed together, the sign produced is **ultimate.**

$$G{>}\wedge \mid B\sigma{<} \begin{smallmatrix} \wedge & \circ \\ & v & \times \\ < \end{smallmatrix}$$

1299 G̈>ʌ B<ʌ₉ $\binom{n}{\perp}$

1300 G̈ɑ⊥ Bʊ< ˣ˙

1301 ¯Iᴛ>₁ Bʊ⊥ ᵛˣ

1302 ¯I>⊥₉ Bᴛ< ᵛˣ

1303 ¯I>⊥ Bᴛ<₉ ⊥ᵛˣ

1304 ¯5ʊ> Bɑ⊥ $\begin{smallmatrix} T & \mathring{} & [ʌ] & \mathring{} & \\ \times & \wedge & & v & \times \\ \# & & & & \\ T & & & & \end{smallmatrix}$

1305 ²5ᴛʌ B<⊥₉ °

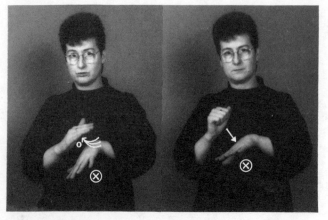

The hand is held flat with the fingers held together; the thumb is usually held against the side of the index finger.

Handshape and orientation	Location, hand arrangement and contact	Movement	Glosses	
The left G hand is held with the palm facing right (if the hand were opened, the fingers would point up). The right B hand is held with the palm facing left and the fingers pointing up.	The hands are held in front of the body; the right hand is held nearer to the signer than the left hand, and at an angle, so that the fingers are turned away from the signer.	The right hand moves away from the signer while bending away from the signer at the wrist.	aim direct point (to the point) target	1299
The left G hand is held with the palm facing up (if the hand were opened, the fingers would point away from the signer). The right B hand is held with the palm facing down and the fingers pointing to the left.	The hands are held in front of the body; the right hand is held above the left hand.	The right palm taps the left index finger twice.	crucial essential important vital	1300
The left I hand is held with the palm facing towards the signer (if the hand were opened, the fingers would point to the right). The right B hand is held with the palm facing down and the fingers pointing away from the signer.	The hands are held side by side in front of the body; the right hand is held with the right fingers above the left little finger.	The right hand moves down, so that the right fingers touch the left little finger.	final last	1301
The left I hand is held with the palm facing right (if the hand were opened, the fingers would point away from the signer). The right B hand is held with the palm facing towards the signer and the fingers pointing to the left.	The hands are held in front of the body; the right hand is held above the left little finger.	The right hand moves down, so that the edge of the hand touches the left little finger.	end * final * last *	1302

Notes * This sign may start with the right hand held above the left hand and end with the backs of the right fingers held on the left little finger.

$$\overline{\text{I}} >\!\!\perp \text{ B}\top< \quad \overset{\perp\,\text{v}\,\text{x}}{\text{a}}$$

The left I hand is held with the palm facing right (if the hand were opened, the fingers would point away from the signer). The right B hand is held with the palm facing towards the signer and the fingers pointing left.	The hands are held in front of the body; the right hand is held higher and nearer to the signer than the left hand.	The right hand moves away from the signer and then down, so that the side of the hand touches the left little finger.	end final last until weekend	1303
The left 5 hand is held with the palm facing down and the fingers pointing to the right; the right B hand is held with the palm facing down and the fingers pointing away from the signer.	The hands are held in front of the body; the right hand is held above the left hand.	The right hand moves towards the signer, brushing across the back of the left hand, and then makes a short upward movement while closing (forming an A hand); the hand then moves down to touch the back of the left hand.	Christmas Xmas	1304
The left 5 hand is held with the palm facing towards the signer and the fingers pointing up; the right B hand is held with the palm facing left and the fingers pointing away from the signer.	The hands are held in front of the body; the right hand is held nearer to the signer than the left hand.	The right hand moves away from the signer, so that the right hand is held between the left index and middle fingers.	access interfere interference interrupt interruption intervene intervention	1305

1306 B̲a⊥ ₁x B̲a⊥ $\begin{pmatrix} \circ \\ \vee \\ \vee \\ \vee \end{pmatrix}$

1307 B̄a> B̄a⊥ $^{\bar{\;}}_{\substack{\top \\ \times \\ \top}}$

1308 B̄a> ₓ B̄a< $^{>}_{\times}$

1309 B̄a⊥ ₁ B̄ʊʌ $^{\vee\;\times\;\perp}_{<\;\;\;a}$

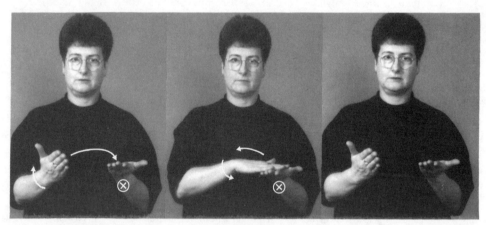

1310 B̄a⊥ B̄ʊ⊥ $^{\times\;\cdot}$

1311 B̄a⊥ B̄ʊ< $^{@}_{\substack{> \\ \perp \\ \times}}$ ·

1312 B̄a⊥ B̄ʊ< $^{\circ}_{\substack{\vee\;\times\;a\;\times}}$

[664]

Handshape and orientation	Location, hand arrangement and contact	Movement	Glosses	
Two **B** hands are held with the palms facing up and the fingers pointing away from the signer.	The hands are held side by side in front of the body with the sides of the little fingers touching.	The right hand makes a series of short movements down and, at the same time, to the right.	custom* generation* hand down* hand on* hereditary* heredity* heritage* inherit* inheritance* pass down* pass on* tradition*	1306
Notes * This sign can be produced using one hand only.		$\emptyset \quad B\alpha\perp \left(\begin{smallmatrix} \circ \\ > \\ \vee \\ > \\ \vee \end{smallmatrix} \cdot \right)$		
The left **B** hand is held with the palm facing up and the fingers pointing to the right; the right **B** hand is held with the palm facing up and the fingers pointing away from the signer.	The hands are held in front of the body; the right hand is held above the left hand.	The right hand moves towards the signer with the back of the right hand brushing across the left palm.	document written paper written proposal written report written statement	1307
The left **B** hand is held with the palm facing up and the fingers pointing to the right; the right **B** hand is held with the palm facing up and the fingers pointing to the left.	The hands are held in front of the body; the back of the right hand rests on the left palm.	The right hand moves to the right, maintaining contact with the left palm throughout.	language	1308
The left **B** hand is held with the palm facing up and the fingers pointing away from the signer; the right **B** hand is held with the palm facing down and the fingers pointing up.	The hands are held side by side in front of the body; the right hand is held higher than the left hand and at an angle, so that the fingers are turned to the left.	The right hand moves down and, at the same time, to the left, so that the right palm touches the left palm; the right hand then moves away from the signer and to the right, twisting at the wrist, so that the palm faces up.	advertise advertisement print printer publish publisher	1309
The left **B** hand is held with the palm facing up and the fingers pointing away from the signer; the right **B** hand is held with the palm facing down and the fingers pointing away from the signer.	The hands are held in front of the body; the right hand is held above the left hand.	The right palm taps the left palm twice.	lunch (packed lunch) sandwich	1310
The left **B** hand is held with the palm facing up and the fingers pointing away from the signer; the right **B** hand is held with the palm facing down and the fingers pointing to the left.	The hands are held in front of the body; the right fingers rest on the left palm.	The right hand makes clockwise circles in the horizontal plane, maintaining contact with the left palm throughout.	explain explanation mean* meaning* story	1311
Notes * This sign may be produced with the right hand making anticlockwise circles.		$\overline{} \quad B\alpha\perp \quad B\eth< \begin{smallmatrix} @ \\ < \\ \vee \\ \tau \\ \times \end{smallmatrix} \cdot$		
The left **B** hand is held with the palm facing up and the fingers pointing away from the signer; the right **B** hand is held with the palm facing down and the fingers pointing away from the signer.	The hands are held in front of the body; the right hand is held above the left hand.	The right hand moves down, so that the fingers touch the left palm; the hand then turns over, so that the palm faces up; the movement ends with the backs of the fingers touching the left palm.	bacon* fry	1312
Notes * Regional sign.				

1313 $\overline{B}a\perp \ _\times B\mho <\ ^\perp_\times$ 1314 $\overline{B}a\perp \ BT<\ ^\perp_\perp$ 1315 $\overline{B}a\perp \ BT<\ ^{(\times\cdot)}_\perp$

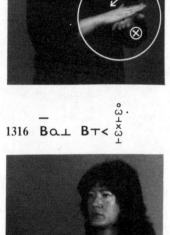
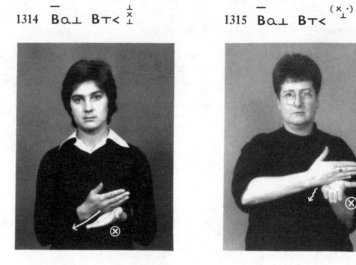

1316 $\overline{B}a\perp \ BT<\ ^{\circ\exists\perp}_{\perp\times\exists\perp}$ 1317 $\overline{B}a> \ Ba\perp \ ^{\vee\times}$

1318 $\overline{B}a> \ _|\ Ba\perp \ ^{\circ\times}_\circ$ 1319 $\overline{B}a> \ B\mho\perp \ ^{\vee\times a\times}$

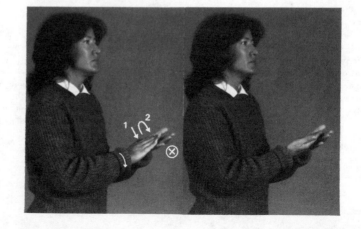

Handshape and orientation	Location, hand arrangement and contact	Movement	Glosses	
The left **B** hand is held with the palm facing up and the fingers pointing away from the signer; the right **B** hand is held with the palm facing down and the fingers pointing to the left.	The hands are held in front of the body; the right palm rests on the heel of the left hand.	The right hand moves away from the signer, maintaining contact with the left palm throughout.	clean* clear* wipe out [1]	1313

Notes   * This sign may be produced with the lips rounded.

       1 If the cheeks are puffed out, the sign produced is **wipe out.**

The left **B** hand is held with the palm facing up and the fingers pointing away from the signer; the right **B** hand is held with the palm facing towards the signer and the fingers pointing to the left.	The hands are held in front of the body; the right hand rests across the left palm.	The right hand moves away from the signer, brushing along the left palm.	clarity clean* clear pure purity clarify [1] cleanliness [1]	1314

Notes   * This sign may be produced with a repeated movement.

       1 This sign requires a repeated movement.

The left **B** hand is held with the palm facing up and the fingers pointing away from the signer; the right **B** hand is held with the palm facing towards the signer and the fingers pointing to the left.	The hands are held in front of the body; the side of the right hand rests across the left palm.	The right hand moves away from the signer, tapping the left palm several times.	rhubarb*	1315

Notes   * Regional sign.

The left **B** hand is held with the palm facing up and the fingers pointing away from the signer; the right **B** hand is held with the palm facing towards the signer and the fingers pointing to the left.	The hands are held in front of the body; the right hand is held above the left hand.	The right hand twists at the wrist while making a short movement away from the signer, so that the side of the hand brushes the left palm; the movement is repeated.	ping pong play ping pong/ table tennis table tennis table tennis player	1316

The left **B** hand is held with the palm facing up and the fingers pointing to the right; the right **B** hand is held with the palm facing up and the fingers pointing away from the signer.	The hands are held in front of the body; the right hand is held above the left hand.	The right hand moves down; the movement ends with the back of the right hand resting on the left palm.	depend lay on place put down put on claim [1] demand [1]	1317

Notes   1 If the movement is firm, the sign produced is **claim, demand.**

The left **B** hand is held with the palm facing up and the fingers pointing to the right; the right **B** hand is held with the palm facing up and the fingers pointing away from the signer.	The hands are held side by side in front of the body; the right hand is held higher than the left hand.	The right hand makes a short movement to the left while twisting at the wrist, so that the palm faces down; the right fingers then touch the left palm.	bet book buy cash deposit invest shares	1318

The left **B** hand is held with the palm facing up and the fingers pointing to the right; the right **B** hand is held with the palm facing down and the fingers pointing away from the signer.	The hands are held in front of the body; the right hand is held above the left hand.	The right hand makes a short downward movement, so that the right palm touches the left palm; the right hand then turns over (so that the palm faces up) and moves down again, so that the back of the right hand touches the left palm.	translate translation translator	1319

1320 B̄ɑ> Bʊ⊥ρ ⊥̇∧̇
x ⊥

1321 B̄ɑ> Bʊ< ∨x

1322 B̄ɑ> x Bʊ< ∧

1323 B̄ɑ> B<∧ ɔx
⊥

1324 B̄ɑ> x B<∨ <ᵐ>
x x

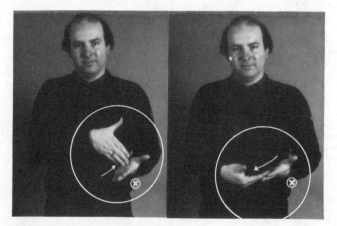

B

The hand is held flat with the fingers held together; the thumb is usually held against the side of the index finger.

Handshape and orientation	Location, hand arrangement and contact	Movement	Glosses	
The left B hand is held with the palm facing up and the fingers pointing to the right; the right B hand is held with the palm facing down and the fingers pointing away from the signer.	The hands are held in front of the body; the right hand is held higher and nearer to the signer than the left hand.	The right hand moves sharply away from the signer, brushing across the left palm, and then moves sharply up and, at the same time, away from the signer.	slip *† slippery *† skid [1]	1320

Notes   * This sign may be produced using one hand only.

$$\emptyset \quad B\sigma\perp \quad \overset{\circ\cdot\circ}{\underset{\wedge}{\overset{\square}{\top}}}$$

† This sign may also be produced using a right v̈ handshape.

$$\overline{\quad} \quad B\sigma> \quad \ddot{V}\sigma\perp_{\varrho} \quad \overset{\wedge}{\underset{\square}{\overset{\square}{\underset{\top}{\overset{\top}{\underset{\square}{x}}}}}}$$

1 If the right hand bends to the left at the wrist while moving away from the signer, so that the right palm brushes the left palm, the sign produced is **skid**.

$$\overline{\quad} \quad B\alpha> \quad B\sigma\perp_{\varrho} \quad \overset{\square}{\underset{<}{\overset{\square}{\underset{x}{\overset{x}{\underset{\perp}{v}}}}}}$$

| The left B hand is held with the palm facing up and the fingers pointing to the right; the right B hand is held with the palm facing down and the fingers pointing to the left. | The hands are held in front of the body at an angle, so that the fingers are turned away from the signer; the right hand is held above the left hand. | The right hand moves down onto the left hand. | empty flat flatten * | 1321 |

Notes   * This sign may be produced with the right hand moving down to touch the left palm and then bending firmly to the right at the wrist, maintaining contact with the left palm; the eyes are also narrowed and the tongue protrudes between the teeth.

$$\overline{\quad} \quad B\alpha> \quad B\sigma< \quad \overset{v\,x\,\square}{\underset{x}{\overset{>}{}}}$$

| The left B hand is held with the palm facing up and the fingers pointing to the right; the right B hand is held with the palm facing down and the fingers pointing to the left. | The hands are held in front of the body; the right palm rests on the left palm. | The right hand moves up. | accumulate pile up | 1322 |

Non-manual features   The cheeks are puffed out.

| The left B hand is held with the palm facing up and the fingers pointing to the right; the right B hand is held with the palm facing left and the fingers pointing up. | The hands are held in front of the body; the right hand is held above the left hand. | The right hand bends away from the signer from the wrist; the movement ends with the side of the hand held against the left palm. | definite factual half honest positive real sure true trust actually [1] honestly [1] positively [1] really [1] surely [1] truly [1] | 1323 |

Notes   1 If the movement is repeated, the sign produced is **actually, honestly, positively, really, surely, truly.**

$$\overline{\quad} \quad B\alpha> \quad B<\wedge \quad \overset{(\square\,x)\cdot}{\underset{\top}{}}$$

| The left B hand is held with the palm facing up and the fingers pointing to the right; the right B hand is held with the palm facing left and the fingers pointing down. | The hands are held in front of the body with the right fingertips touching the left palm. | The right hand moves to the left, maintaining contact with the left palm; the fingers then bend at the palm knuckles and the right hand moves to the right, with the backs of the right fingers maintaining contact with the the left palm. | glue * jam * marmalade * paste * spread * spread glue/jam/ marmalade/paste * | 1324 |

Notes   * This sign can also be produced with a right H handshape.

$$B\alpha> \quad _x H<v \quad \overset{<\square>}{\underset{x}{\overset{}{x}}}$$

1325 $\overline{B}a> B<\perp \overset{(\overset{x}{n}\cdot)}{>}$

1326 $\overline{B}a> _x B<\perp \overset{T}{x}$

1327 $\overline{B}a> _x B<\perp \overset{\text{I}\cdot}{x}$

1328 $\overline{B}a> _x B<\perp \overset{\circ\cdot}{\overset{3}{n}}$

1329 $\overline{B}\sigma\perp { }_| B\sigma\perp \overset{v}{v}$

1330 $B\sigma\perp { }_| B\sigma\perp_? \overset{\perp\cdot}{x}$

1331 $\sqrt{B}\sigma\perp B\sigma< \overset{\cdot,\cdot}{}$

[670]

The hand is held flat with the fingers held together; the thumb is usually held against the side of the index finger.

Handshape and orientation	*Location, hand arrangement and contact*	*Movement*	*Glosses*	
The left **B** hand is held with the palm facing up and the fingers pointing to the right; the right **B** hand is held with the palm facing left and the fingers pointing away from the signer.	The hands are held in front of the body; the right hand is held above the left hand.	The side of the right hand taps the left palm several times, while the right hand bends to the right from the wrist.	divide* portion out* share* share out* shares* split*	1325

Notes   * This sign may also be produced with the right hand touching the left palm twice.

$$ \overline{}\ B\alpha > \ B < \perp \quad \overset{\times\ \cap\ \times}{>} $$

| The left **B** hand is held with the palm facing up and the fingers pointing to the right; the right **B** hand is held with the palm facing left and the fingers pointing away from the signer. | The hands are held in front of the body; the right hand rests on the left palm. | The right hand moves towards the signer, maintaining contact with the left palm throughout. | half* part* partly* | 1326 |

Notes   * This sign may be produced with the right hand moving towards the signer and then to the right, while bending to the left at the wrist.

$$ \overline{}\ B\alpha > \ _\times \ B < \perp \quad \overset{(\top\ >)}{\underset{\times}{\cap}} $$

| The left **B** hand is held with the palm facing up and the fingers pointing to the right; the right **B** hand is held with the palm facing left and the fingers pointing away from the signer. | The hands are held in front of the body; the right hand rests on the left palm. | The right hand moves towards and away from the signer several times, maintaining contact with the left palm throughout. | bread loaf | 1327 |

| The left **B** hand is held with the palm facing up and the fingers pointing to the right; the right **B** hand is held with the palm facing left and the fingers pointing away from the signer. | The hands are held in front of the body; the side of the right hand is held against the left palm. | The right hand makes short twisting movements from side to side from the wrist; the side of the right hand is held against the left palm throughout. | doubtful hesitant uncertain unsure fry[1] | 1328 |

Non-manual features   The lips are pressed together and the brows are slightly furrowed.

Notes   1 If the twisting movement is not short, and the non-manual features are absent, the sign produced is **fry**.

$$ \overline{}\ B\alpha > \ _\times \ B < \perp \quad \overset{\omega\cdot}{\underset{z}{}} $$

| Two **B** hands are held with the palms facing down and the fingers pointing away from the signer. | The hands are held side by side in front of the body; the right hand is held higher than the left hand. | The right hand moves down, so that the side of the right thumb brushes the side of the left thumb. | decide decision pass verdict | 1329 |

| Two **B** hands are held with the palms facing down and the fingers pointing away from the signer. | The hands are held side by side in front of the body; the right hand is held nearer to the signer than the left hand. | The right hand moves away from the signer, so that the side of the right index finger brushes along the side of the left index finger; the movement is repeated. | learn* learner* practice* practise* rehearse* student* study* train* trainee* | 1330 |

Notes   * This sign may also be produced with the hands moving towards and away from the signer alternately several times, maintaining contact throughout.

$$ B\sigma \perp \ | \ B\sigma \perp_{\varrho} \quad \overset{\top\ \wedge\ \cdot}{\underset{\times}{}} $$

| The left **B** hand is held with the palm facing down and the fingers pointing away from the signer; the right **B** hand is held with the palm facing down and the fingers pointing to the left. | The hands are held in front of the body; the right hand is held above the left forearm. | The right fingers tap the left forearm twice. | left left-hand left-handed | 1331 |

1332 √B̄ʊ⊥ B⊤< ˣᵀˣ

1333 B̄ʊ> Bɑ⊥ °̌ˣ

1334 B̲ʊ> Bɑ⊥ₒ ⊥

1335 B̄ʊ> ₓ Bʊ⊥ ˃ˣ

1336 B̄ʊ> Bɑ⊥ ˃°̌˂ₐ

1337 B̄ʊ> ₓ Bʊ⊥ ˂°@ˣ ˣ˄˃

1338 B̲ʊ> ˣ· √Bɑ⊥

The hand is held flat with the fingers held together; the thumb is usually held against the side of the index finger.

Handshape and orientation	Location, hand arrangement and contact	Movement	Glosses	
The left **B** hand is held with the palm facing down and the fingers pointing away from the signer; the right **B** hand is held with the palm facing towards the signer and the fingers pointing to the left.	The hands are held in front of the body; the right hand is held resting on the back of the left hand.	The right hand makes a short movement towards the signer, before touching the left forearm.	before earlier early precede previous previously	1332
The left **B** hand is held with the palm facing down and the fingers pointing to the right; the right **B** hand is held with the palm facing up and the fingers pointing away from the signer.	The hands are held in front of the body; the right hand is held above the left hand.	The right hand moves down; the movement ends with the right hand held on the back of the left hand.	lay on on place on put down put on	1333
The left **B** hand is held with the palm facing down and the fingers pointing to the right; the right **B** hand is held with the palm facing up and the fingers pointing away from the signer.	The hands are held in front of the body; the right hand is held lower and nearer to the signer than the left hand.	The right hand moves away from the signer.	grill oven put into an oven put under a grill roast under	1334
The left **B** hand is held with the palm facing down and the fingers pointing to the right; the right **B** hand is held with the palm facing down and the fingers pointing away from the signer.	The hands are held in front of the body; the right hand is held above the left hand, with the right fingertips resting on the back of the left hand.	The right hand moves to the right, maintaining contact with the back of the left hand throughout.	surface* smooth[1]	1335

Notes   * This sign may be produced with a short, repeated movement.

$$\overline{B\eth>}\ B\eth\bot\ \overset{\circ}{\underset{\times}{\scriptstyle\vee}}\,\cdot$$

1 If the lips are rounded, the sign produced is **smooth**.

The left **B** hand is held with the palm facing down and the fingers pointing to the right; the right **B** hand is held with the palm facing down and the fingers pointing away from the signer.	The hands are held in front of the body; the right hand is held above the left hand.	The right hand moves to the right, and then turns over, so that the palm faces up, before moving to the left below the left hand.	slipper	1336
The left **B** hand is held with the palm facing down and the fingers pointing to the right; the right **B** hand is held with the palm facing down and the fingers pointing away from the signer.	The hands are held in front of the body; the right fingers rest on the left fingers.	The right hand makes a short movement to the left, maintaining contact with the left hand, and then makes a clockwise circle in the vertical plane parallel to the signer's body; the movement ends with the right hand held on the back of the left hand.	marriage married wedding	1337
The left **B** hand is held with the palm facing down and the fingers pointing to the right; the right **B** hand is held with the palm facing down and the fingers pointing away from the signer.	The right hand is held in front of the body; the left hand is held above the right forearm.	The left fingers tap the right forearm twice.	right right-hand right-handed	1338

1339 $\overline{B}ʊ> Bʊ< \overset{\overset{\circ}{\perp}\omega\check{}}{\tau}$

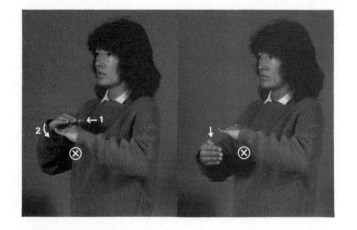

1340 $\overline{B}ʊ> Bʊ< \overset{\circ\circ\circ}{>\vee<}$

1341 $\underline{B}ʊ> Bʊ< \overset{\overset{\circledcirc}{<}\cdot}{\tau}$

1342 $\underline{B}ʊ> Bʊ< \overset{\circ\circ\circ}{>\wedge<}$

1343 $\underline{B}ʊ>_{|} Bʊ< \overset{\check{v}\cdot}{}$

1344 $\overline{B}ʊ>_{\times} \sqrt{}B<\wedge \overset{\phi}{}$

1345 $\overline{B}\tau\perp B\tau\perp \overset{\times\cdot}{}$

The hand is held flat with the fingers held together; the thumb is usually held against the side of the index finger.

Handshape and orientation	Location, hand arrangement and contact	Movement	Glosses	
The left **B** hand is held with the palm facing down and the fingers pointing to the right; the right **B** hand is held with the palm facing down and the fingers pointing to the left.	The hands are held in front of the body; the right hand is held above the left hand.	The right hand makes a short movement away from the signer, and then twists at the wrist, so that the palm faces towards the signer, before making a short downward movement.	kerb ledge step cliff[1] cliff edge[1]	1339

Notes 1 If the final downward movement is not short, the sign produced is **cliff, cliff edge**.

$$\overline{\text{B}\text{ʊ}>\ \ \text{B}\text{ʊ}<\ \ \overset{\circ}{\underset{\text{T}}{\text{⊥ω}}}\text{v}}$$

| The left **B** hand is held with the palm facing down and the fingers pointing to the right; the right **B** hand is held with the palm facing down and the fingers pointing to the left. | The hands are held in front of the body; the right hand is held above the left hand. | The right hand makes a short movement to the right and then down and under the left hand; the movement ends with the right hand held beneath the left hand. | below*
beneath*
inferior*
inferiority*
under*
underneath* | 1340 |

Notes * This sign may also be produced using two **B̈** hands.

$$\text{B̈}>\wedge\ \mid\ \text{B̈}<\wedge\ \ \overset{\circ\,\circ\,\circ}{>\text{v}<}$$

| The left **B** hand is held with the palm facing down and the fingers pointing to the right; the right **B** hand is held with the palm facing down and the fingers pointing to the left. | The hands are held in front of the body; the left hand is held above the right hand. | The right hand makes anticlockwise circles in the horizontal plane. | basement
below
beneath
bottom
cellar
internal
underneath
inferior[1]
inferiority[1] | 1341 |

Notes 1 If the corners of the mouth are turned down, the sign produced is **inferior, inferiority**.

| The left **B** hand is held with the palm facing down and the fingers pointing to the right; the right **B** hand is held with the palm facing down and the fingers pointing to the left. | The hands are held in front of the body; the left hand is held above the right hand. | The right hand makes a short movement to the right, and then up and over the left hand; the movement ends with the right hand held above the left hand. | above*
over*
superior*
superiority* | 1342 |

Notes * This sign may also be produced using two **B̈** hands.

$$\underline{\text{B̈}}>\wedge\ \mid\ \text{B̈}<\wedge\ \ \overset{\circ\,\circ\,\circ}{>\wedge<}$$

| The left **B** hand is held with the palm facing down and the fingers pointing to the right; the right **B** hand is held with the palm facing down and the fingers pointing to the left. | The hands are held side by side in front of the body; the left hand is held above the right hand. | The right hand makes two short downward movements. | below
beneath
bottom
inferior
inferiority
low | 1343 |

| The left **B** hand is held with the palm facing down and the fingers pointing to the right; the right **B** hand is held with the palm facing left and the fingers pointing up. | The hands are held in front of the body; the left fingertips are held against the right elbow. | No movement. | proof
prove
volunteer
vote
witness | 1344 |

| Two **B** hands are held with the palms facing towards the signer and the fingers pointing away from the signer. | The hands are held in front of the body with the palms turned towards each other; the right hand is held above the left hand. | The side of the right hand taps the side of the left hand twice. | business
career
job
labour
labourer
Labour Party
work
worker | 1345 |

1346 $\overline{B}\top\bot$ $B\top\bot$ $^{\times}\cdot$ $^{//}_{//}$ $\emptyset$ $\overline{B}a>_{\shortmid}$ $Ba<_{\wp}$ $^{IN\cdot}$

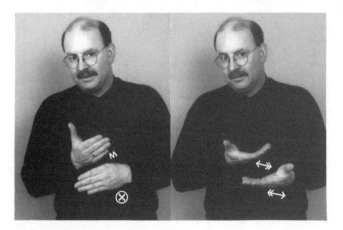

1347 $B\top>$ $B\cup\bot_{\wp}$ $^{\cap\cdot}_{\wedge}$

1348 $B\top>$ $B\top\wedge_{\wp}$ $^{\circ}_{\bot\times}$

1349 $\overline{B}\top>_{\wp}$ $_{\times}$ $B\top\vee$ $^{\vee\,\cap}_{\times\bot}_{\vee}$

1350 $\overline{B}\top>$ $B\top<$ $^{@\cdot}_{\bot}_{\vee}$

1351 $\overline{B}\top>$ $_{\times}$ $B\top<$ $^{\wedge\times}$

1352 $B\top>$ $_{\shortmid\times}$ $\dot{\jmath}B\top<$ $^{\cap}_{\bot}$

[676]

Handshape and orientation	Location, hand arrangement and contact	Movement	Glosses	
Two **B** hands are held with the palms facing towards the signer and the fingers pointing away from the signer.	The hands are held in front of the body at an angle, so that the fingers are turned towards each other; the right hand is held above the left hand.	The side of the right hand taps the side of the left hand twice.	**business trade**	1346
The left **B** hand is held with the palm facing up and the fingers pointing to the right; the right **B** hand is held with the palm facing up and the fingers pointing to the left.	The hands are held side by side in front of the body; the right hand is held higher than the left hand.	The hands move towards and away from the signer alternately several times.		
The left **B** hand is held with the palm facing towards the signer and the fingers pointing to the right; the right **B** hand is held with the palm facing down and the fingers pointing away from the signer.	The hands are held in front of the body; the right hand is held higher and nearer to the signer than the left hand.	The right hand bends up and down twice from the wrist.	**decorate decorator paint painter paper wallpaper**	1347
The left **B** hand is held with the palm facing towards the signer and the fingers pointing to the right; the right **B** hand is held with the palm facing towards the signer and the fingers pointing up.	The hands are held in front of the body; the right hand is held nearer to the signer than the left hand.	The right hand moves away from the signer, so that the backs of the right fingers touch the palm of the left hand.	**against** (an upright surface) **lean** (against an upright surface) **on** (an upright surface) **put on** (an upright surface)	1348
The left **B** hand is held with the palm facing towards the signer and the fingers pointing to the right; the right **B** hand is held with the palm facing towards the signer and the fingers pointing down.	The hands are held in front of the body; the left hand is held lower and nearer to the signer than the right hand with the pads of the right fingers touching the back of the left index finger.	The right hand moves down, maintaining contact with the left hand, and then continues to move down while bending away from the signer at the wrist.	**sled sledge toboggan**	1349
The left **B** hand is held with the palm facing towards the signer and the fingers pointing to the right; the right **B** hand is held with the palm facing towards the signer and the fingers pointing to the left.	The hands are held in front of the body; the right hand is held above the left hand.	The right hand makes clockwise circles in the vertical plane at right angles to the signer's body.	**bandage hospital** [1]	1350

Notes   1 If the hands make alternate circles in the vertical plane at right angles to the signer's body, the sign produced is **hospital**.

$$\emptyset \quad \overline{\text{B}\top>} \quad \text{B}\top< \quad {}^{@\sim\cdot}_{\substack{\perp\\ \vee}}$$

The left **B** hand is held with the palm facing towards the signer and the fingers pointing to the right; the right **B** hand is held with the palm facing towards the signer and the fingers pointing to the left.	The hands are held in front of the body; the side of the right hand rests on the side of the left hand.	The right hand moves up and then down; the movement ends with the side of the right hand resting on the side of the left hand.	**pantomime premiere window**	1351
The left **B** hand is held with the palm facing towards the signer and the fingers pointing to the right; the right **B** hand is held with the palm facing towards the signer and the fingers pointing to the left.	The hands are held side by side in front of the body with the middle fingertips touching.	The right hand bends away from the signer from the elbow.	**gate** * **open a gate** *	1352

Notes   * This sign may be produced with a repeated movement.

$$\text{B}\top> \quad {}_{\text{I}\times} \quad \dot{\text{J}}\text{B}\top< \quad {}^{\text{n}\cdot}_{\perp}$$

1353 B⊤>ᵩ B⊤<(°ᴅ×)·

1354 B̄⊤> B<⊥ ⊥×⊥·

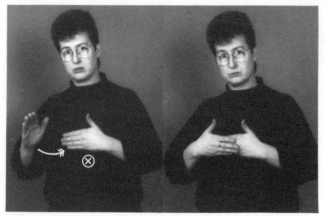

1355 B̄⊤> ₓ B<⊥ ᴅᵛ⊥ₓ

1356 B̄⊤> ₓ B<⊥ ᴅᵛ⊥ₓ

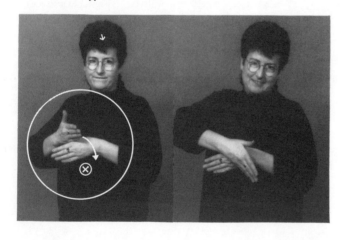

1357 B̄⊤> ₓ B<⊥ ᴴₓ·

1358 B⊤>ᵩ ₗ B<⊥ ᴅ<×

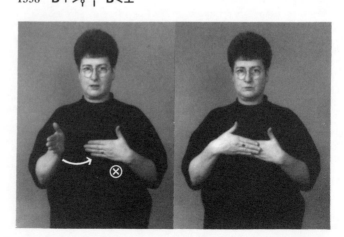

The hand is held flat with the fingers held together; the thumb is usually held against the side of the index finger.

Handshape and orientation	Location, hand arrangement and contact	Movement	Glosses	
The left **B** hand is held with the palm facing towards the signer and the fingers pointing to the right; the right **B** hand is held with the palm facing towards the signer and the fingers pointing to the left.	The hands are held in front of the body; the left hand is held nearer to the signer than the right hand.	The right hand makes a short bending movement towards the signer from the wrist, so that the right fingers touch the back of the left hand; the movement is repeated.	door gate (small gate)	1353
The left **B** hand is held with the palm facing towards the signer and the fingers pointing to the right; the right **B** hand is held with the palm facing left and the fingers pointing away from the signer.	The hands are held in front of the body; the right hand is held above the left hand.	The right hand moves away from the signer, so that the side of the right hand brushes the side of the left hand; the movement is repeated.	business busy * † effort (make an effort) * † industrious * † labour work	1354

Notes * This sign may be produced with the lips stretched.

† This sign may be produced with the cheeks slightly puffed out.

The left **B** hand is held with the palm facing towards the signer and the fingers pointing to the right; the right **B** hand is held with the palm facing left and the fingers pointing away from the signer.	The hands are held in front of the body; the side of the right hand rests across the side of the left hand.	The right hand bends down at the wrist while moving away from the signer, maintaining contact with the left hand throughout.	nothing (for nothing) waste of time	1355

Non-manual features The top teeth are touching the lower lip; the mouth then opens, so that the lips are stretched, and the head nods forward slightly.

The left **B** hand is held with the palm facing towards the signer and the fingers pointing to the right; the right **B** hand is held with the palm facing left and the fingers pointing away from the signer.	The hands are held in front of the body; the side of the right hand rests across the side of the left hand.	The right hand bends down at the wrist while moving away from the signer, maintaining contact with the left hand throughout.	busy hard-working industrious laborious overworked	1356

Non-manual features The cheeks are puffed out.

The left **B** hand is held with the palm facing towards the signer and the fingers pointing to the right; the right **B** hand is held with the palm facing left and the fingers pointing away from the signer.	The hands are held in front of the body; the right hand rests across the left hand.	The right hand moves towards and away from the signer several times, maintaining contact with the side of the left hand throughout.	wood *	1357

Notes * Regional sign.

The left **B** hand is held with the palm facing towards the signer and the fingers pointing to the right; the right **B** hand is held with the palm facing left and the fingers pointing away from the signer.	The hands are held side by side in front of the body; the left hand is held nearer to the signer than the right hand.	The right hand bends towards the signer from the wrist; the movement ends with the right fingers held against the back of the left hand.	close close/shut a door close/shut a small gate shut	1358

1359　B>⊥ ⌐ Bɑ⊥ ᵛ<ˣ

1360　B̄>⊥ ⌐ Bʊ⊥ ᵛˣᵛ³ᵛ<>

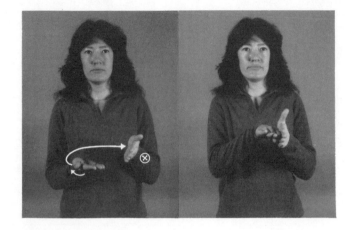

1361　'Ḃ>ʌ B<ʌₚ ˣ˙

1362　B̈ɑ> ˣ Bʊ⊥ @<⊥ˣ˙

1363　B̲̈>ʌ B<⊥ₚ ⊥

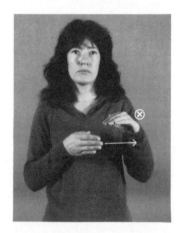

1364　∅ Ḡɑ⊥ ˣ Bʊ⊥ ᵛ

1365　∅ Ḡɑ> ˣ Bʊ< ᵛ

1366　∅ Bɑ⊥ Bɑ⊥ ˣ˙

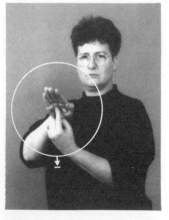

[680]

B

The hand is held flat with the fingers held together; the thumb is usually held against the side of the index finger.

Handshape and orientation	Location, hand arrangement and contact	Movement	Glosses	
The left B hand is held with the palm facing right and the fingers pointing away from the signer; the right B hand is held with the palm facing up and the fingers pointing away from the signer.	The hands are held in front of the body.	The right hand turns over, so that the palm faces down and then moves to the left; the movement ends with the side of the right hand touching the left palm.	close down shut down	1359
The left B hand is held with the palm facing right and the fingers pointing away from the signer; the right B hand is held with the palm facing down and the fingers pointing away from the signer.	The hands are held side by side in front of the body; the right hand is held higher than the left hand.	The right hand moves down, while twisting to the right at the wrist, so that the side of the right hand brushes across the left palm.	from about [1] decide [1] decision [1]	1360

Notes   1   If the movement is changed to a downward movement which brushes across the left palm, the sign produced is **about, decide, decision.**

The left B̌ hand is held with the palm facing right and the fingers pointing up; the right B hand is held with the palm facing left and the fingers pointing up.	The hands are held in front of the body; the right hand is held nearer to the signer than the left hand.	The side of the right hand taps the left hand (between the thumb and index finger) twice.	psychological psychologist psychology	1361
The left B̈ hand is held with the palm facing up (if the hand were opened, the fingers would point to the right). The right B hand is held with the palm facing down and the fingers pointing away from the signer.	The hands are held in front of the body; the right fingers rest on the left palm.	The right hand makes anticlockwise circles in the horizontal plane, maintaining contact with the left palm throughout.	soap	1362

The left B̈ hand is held with the palm facing right (if the hand were opened, the fingers would point up). The right B hand is held with the palm facing left and the fingers pointing away from the signer.	The hands are held in front of the body; the right hand is held lower and nearer to the signer than the left hand.	The right hand moves away from the signer.	car port
			drive/go through
			  a tunnel
			drive into a
			  car port/garage
			garage
			tunnel
				1363

The left G̈ hand is held with the palm facing up (if the hand were opened, the fingers would point away from the signer). The right B hand is held with the palm facing down and the fingers pointing away from the signer.	The hands are held in front of the body; the right hand is held above the left hand, with the left index fingertip held against the right palm.	The hands remain together and make a firm downward movement.	compel * dominate * emphasis emphasise * force * oppress * oppression overcome * reinforce * repress * repression stress * suppress *	1364

Notes   * Directional verb.

The left G̈ hand is held with the palm facing up (if the hand were opened, the fingers would point to the right). The right B hand is held with the palm facing down and the fingers pointing to the left.	The hands are held in front of the body; the left index fingertip is held against the right palm.	The hands remain together and make a short downward movement.	depress depressed depression down (feel down) sad	1365

Non-manual features   The lips are pressed together.

Two B hands are held with the palms facing up and the fingers pointing away from the signer.	The hands are held in front of the body.	The hands make a short movement towards each other; the movement is repeated.	today	1366

1367 Ø Ba⊥ Ba⊥ ∿∿·

1368 Ø Ba⊥ Ba⊥ ∿∿·

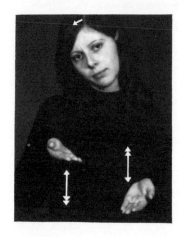

1369 Ø Ba⊥ Ba⊥ ⊐∿·

1370 Ø Ba⊥ Ba⊥ (∨∿·)⁄÷

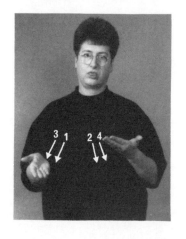

1371 Ø Ba⊥ ₁ Ba⊥ ÷

1372 Ø Ba⊥ ₁ Ba⊥ ⁰⁄∧

1373 Ø Ba⊥ ₁ Ba⊥ ∨÷

The hand is held flat with the fingers held together; the thumb is usually held against the side of the index finger.

Handshape and orientation	Location, hand arrangement and contact	Movement	Glosses	
Two **B** hands are held with the palms facing up and the fingers pointing away from the signer.	The hands are held in front of the body.	The hands move up and down alternately several times.	assess assessment assessor average balance compare comparison court evaluate evaluation judge judgement scales trial tribunal	1367 weigh weight weigh up
Two **B** hands are held with the palms facing up and the fingers pointing away from the signer. *Non-manual features* The lips are stretched and the head tilts to one side.	The hands are held in front of the body.	The hands move up and down alternately several times.	doubt doubtful hesitant maybe uncertain unsure	1368
Two **B** hands are held with the palms facing up and the fingers pointing away from the signer.	The hands are held in front of the body at an angle, so that the fingers are turned towards each other.	The hands move towards and away from the signer alternately several times.	serve services	1369
Two **B** hands are held with the palms facing up and the fingers pointing away from the signer. *Non-manual features* The tongue tip protrudes between the teeth. *Notes* 1 If the movement is changed, so that the hands do not move apart, the sign produced is **slipshod, sloppy**.	The hands are held in front of the body.	The hands move down and, at the same time, away from the signer alternately; the movements are repeated with the hands moving apart throughout.	disorder mess messy untidy slipshod [1] sloppy [1]	1370

Ø Ba⊥ , Ba⊥ ⌄ᴺ˙

Two **B** hands are held with the palms facing up and the fingers pointing away from the signer.	The hands are held side by side in front of the body.	The hands move apart.	compare comparison	1371
Two **B** hands are held with the palms facing up and the fingers pointing away from the signer. *Notes* * Directional verb. † This sign may be produced using one hand only.	The hands are held side by side in front of the body.	The hands make a short movement up and, at the same time, away from the signer.	gift † give * † give a gift/present * † offer * † present * †	1372

Ø Ba⊥ ⌀
⌃

Two **B** hands are held with the palms facing up and the fingers pointing away from the signer. *Notes* * Directional verb.	The hands are held side by side in front of the body.	The hands move down and then apart.	demonstrate demonstration demonstrator display exhibit exhibition expose open prove public show * show of presents	1373

1374 Ø Ba⊥ , Ba⊥ ÷ωᵪ∨

1375 Ø Ba⊥ , Ba⊥ ÷ωᵪ∧ // Ø 5̈ʊ⊥ , 5̈ʊ⊥ ᵑᵪ·

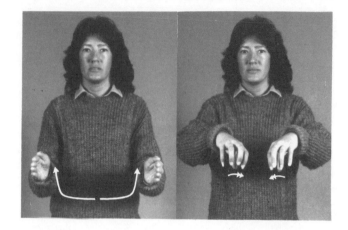

1376 Ø √Ba⊥ √Ba⊥ °ᵑ∨

1377 Ø Ba⊥ Bʊ< ⊥>

1378 Ø B̄a⊥ ₓ Bʊ< °∨

1379 Ø B̄ʊ⊥ B⊥∧ ø

1380 Ø B̄a> ₓ Ba⊥ °∧∨

The hand is held flat with the fingers held together; the thumb is usually held against the side of the index finger.

Handshape and orientation	Location, hand arrangement and contact	Movement	Glosses	
Two **B** hands are held with the palms facing up and the fingers pointing away from the signer.	The hands are held side by side in front of the body.	The hands move apart and then twist at the wrists (so that the palms face towards each other) while moving up.	basin bowl sink tub washbasin	1374
Two **B** hands are held with the palms facing up and the fingers pointing away from the signer.	The hands are held side by side in front of the body. ·	The hands move apart and then twist at the wrists (so that the palms face towards each other) while moving up.	washbasin *	1375
Two **5̈** hands are held with the palms facing down (if the hands were opened, the fingers would all point away from the signer).	The hands are held side by side in front of the body.	The hands bend towards each other from the wrist several times.		

Notes   * This sign may also be produced using two **v̈** hands for the second part.

$$\emptyset \ \ B\alpha\perp \ , \ B\alpha\perp \ {}^{\div\omega}_{\times} \ {}_{\wedge} \ // \ //$$

$$\emptyset \ \ \ddot{V}\sigma\perp \ , \ \ddot{V}\sigma\perp \ {}^{n\cdot}_{\times}$$

Two **B** hands are held with the palms facing up and the fingers pointing away from the signer.	The hands are held in front of the body.	The elbows bend, so that the hands make a short upward movement.	get up light raise rise	1376
The left **B** hand is held with the palm facing up and the fingers pointing to the right; the right **B** hand is held with the palm facing down and the fingers pointing to the left.	The hands are held in front of the body; the right hand is held above the left hand.	The hands move to the right and, at the same time, away from the signer.	deliver * dispatch * give * hand over *	1377

Notes   * Directional verb.

The left **B** hand is held with the palm facing up and the fingers pointing to the right; the right **B** hand is held with the palm facing down and the fingers pointing to the left.	The hands are held in front of the body; the right palm is held on the left palm.	The hands remain together and make a short, firm downward movement.	compress press crush[1] squash[1]	1378

Notes   1 If the movement is changed, so that the right hand bends firmly to the right at the wrist, maintaining contact with the left palm throughout, the sign produced is **crush, squash**.

$$B\alpha> \ {}_{\times} \ B\sigma< \ {}^{n\cdot}_{\times>}$$

The left **B** hand is held with the palm facing down and the fingers pointing away from the signer; the right **B** hand is held with the palm facing away from the signer and the fingers pointing up.	The left hand is held in front of the body; the right hand is held in front of the right shoulder.	No movement.	affirmation oath pledge swear swear in	1379
The left **B** hand is held with the palm facing up and the fingers pointing to the right; the right **B** hand is held with the palm facing up and the fingers pointing away from the signer.	The hands are held in front of the body; the right fingers are held on the left palm.	The hands remain together and make a short, firm downward movement.	depend dependence dependent beg[1] beggar[1] lie[2] sit[2]	1380

Notes   1 If the movement is changed to a short, repeated downward movement, the sign produced is **beg, beggar**.

$$\emptyset \ \ \overline{B\alpha>} \ {}_{\times} \ B\alpha\perp \ {}^{\circ\cdot}_{v}$$

2 If the movement is changed to a small repeated clockwise circle in the vertical plane at right angles to the signer's body, the sign produced is **lie, sit**.

$$\emptyset \ \ \overline{B\alpha>} \ {}_{\times} \ B\alpha\perp \ {}^{\circ\cdot}_{\odot\, v}$$

1381 Ø B̄a>ₓ Ba⊥ $\binom{\circ}{\sim}_>$

1382 Ø Ba> Ba< $\overset{п}{\perp}$

1383 Ø B̄a> Ba< $\overset{⊜ℕ·}{\underset{v}{\perp}}$

1384 Ø ʃB̄a> ʃBa< $\overset{п}{\underset{v}{\perp}}$

1385 Ø ʔB̄a>ₓ ʔBa< $\overset{\circ}{\underset{z}{}}·$

1386 Ø B̲a>ₓ Ba< $^{z·}$

B

The hand is held flat with the fingers held together; the thumb is usually held against the side of the index finger.

Handshape and orientation	Location, hand arrangement and contact	Movement	Glosses	
The left **B** hand is held with the palm facing up and the fingers pointing to the right; the right **B** hand is held with the palm facing up and the fingers pointing away from the signer.	The hands are held in front of the body; the right fingers are held on the left palm.	The hands remain together and make short up and down movements while moving to the right.	bob float	1381
The left **B** hand is held with the palm facing up and the fingers pointing to the right; the right **B** hand is held with the palm facing up and the fingers pointing to the left.	The hands are held in front of the body.	The hands bend away from the signer from the wrists.	but however nevertheless well	1382

The left **B** hand is held with the palm facing up and the fingers pointing to the right; the right **B** hand is held with the palm facing up and the fingers pointing to the left.	The hands are held in front of the body; the right hand is held above the left hand.	The hands make alternate clockwise circles in the vertical plane at right angles to the signer's body.	explain *
			explanation
			relate an event/
			    a story *
			story
			tell *
			tell about an event/
			    a story *
			reiterate * 1
				1383

Notes   * Directional verb.

1 If the right hand makes a firm downward movement in completing each circle and, at the same time, the head nods forward, the sign produced is **reiterate**.

The left **B** hand is held with the palm facing up and the fingers pointing to the right; the right **B** hand is held with the palm facing up and the fingers pointing to the left.	The hands are held in front of the body; the right hand is held above the left hand.	The hands move apart, bending from the elbows, while moving down.	demonstrate demonstration demonstrator display exhibit exhibition expose open prove public show * show of presents	1384

Notes   * Directional verb.

The left **B** hand is held with the palm facing up and the fingers pointing to the right; the right **B** hand is held with the palm facing up and the fingers pointing to the left.	The hands are held in front of the body; the back of the right hand is held against the left palm.	The hands remain together and make short movements from side to side from the shoulders.	cradle
			cradle a baby/
			    doll/infant
			rock
			rock a baby/
			    doll/infant
				1385

The left **B** hand is held with the palm facing up and the fingers pointing to the right; the right **B** hand is held with the palm facing up and the fingers pointing to the left.	The hands are held in front of the body; the left fingers are held on the right fingers.	The hands remain together and move from side to side twice.	baby * doll * infant *	1386

Notes   * This sign may be produced with the right fingers held on the left fingers.

$$\emptyset \quad \overline{Ba} > {}_\times Ba < {}^{z.}$$

1387 Ø B̄a>ₗ Ba<ᴵᴺ˙

1388 Ø Ba>ₗ Ba<ᴵᴺ˙ // Ø A>⊥ₗ A<⊥ˣ

1389 Ø Ba> Ba<₎ ˙˙

1390 Ø B̄a> Bʊ⊥ ⁺

1391 Ø B̄a> Bʊ<⊥

The hand is held flat with the fingers held together; the thumb is usually held against the side of the index finger.

Handshape and orientation	Location, hand arrangement and contact	Movement	Glosses	
The left **B** hand is held with the palm facing up and the fingers pointing to the right; the right **B** hand is held with the palm facing up and the fingers pointing to the left.	The hands are held side by side in front of the body; the right hand is held higher than the left hand.	The hands move towards and away from the signer alternately several times.	**bargain** **barter** **converse** **conversation** **correspond** **correspondence** **deal** **dealings** **debate** **dialogue** **diplomat** **diplomatic** **discuss** **discussion** **negotiate** **negotiations**	1387
The left **B** hand is held with the palm facing up and the fingers pointing to the right; the right **B** hand is held with the palm facing up and the fingers pointing to the left.	The hands are held side by side in front of the body.	The hands make alternate movements towards and away from the signer.	**compromise** **deal**	1388

Non-manual features The lips are closed and pushed slightly forward.

The left **A** hand is held with the palm facing right; the right **A** hand is held with the palm facing left (if the hands were opened, the fingers would all point away from the signer).	The hands are held side by side in front of the body.	The knuckles touch.		

Non-manual features The lips are pressed together and the head nods.

The left **B** hand is held with the palm facing up and the fingers pointing to the right; the right **B** hand is held with the palm facing up and the fingers pointing to the left.	The hands are held in front of the body; the right hand is held nearer to the signer than the left hand.	The hands change places.	**exchange*** **replace*** **replacement*** **substitute*** **substitution*** **swap*** **switch***	1389

Notes * This sign can also be produced with the initial and final hand positions reversed.

Ø Bɑ>ᵩ Bɑ< ``

The left **B** hand is held with the palm facing up and the fingers pointing to the right; the right **B** hand is held with the palm facing down and the fingers pointing away from the signer.	The hands are held in front of the body; the right hand is held above the left hand.	The right hand moves to the left, while the left hand moves to the right, so that the palms brush together; the movement is repeated.	**delight** **delighted** **enjoy** **enjoyable** **enjoyment** **happy** **pleased** **pleasure**	1390
The left **B** hand is held with the palm facing up and the fingers pointing to the right; the right **B** hand is held with the palm facing down and the fingers pointing to the left.	The hands are held in front of the body; the right hand is held above the left hand.	The hands move away from the signer.	**deliver*** **dispatch*** **give*** **hand over*** **shallow**	1391

Notes * Directional verb.

1392　Ø　B̄ɑ>　×　B<⊥ ⌄̥°

1393　Ø　Bʊʌ　Bʊʌ ⌄̥×

1394　Ø　Bʊʌ　Bʊʌ ᐱˣˣ

1395　Ø　Bʊʌ　Bʊʌ (°⌄⌄ˣˣ·)

1396　Ø　Bʊʌ ₁　Bʊʌ °

The hand is held flat with the fingers held together; the thumb is usually held against the side of the index finger.

Handshape and orientation	Location, hand arrangement and contact	Movement	Glosses	
The left **B** hand is held with the palm facing up and the fingers pointing to the right; the right **B** hand is held with the palm facing left and the fingers pointing away from the signer.	The hands are held in front of the body; the right hand is held on the left palm.	The hands remain together and make a short downward movement.	halt park stationary stop car park[1]	1392

Notes   1 If the right hand moves down to touch the left palm, and the movement is repeated several times as both hands move to the right, the sign produced is **car park**.

$$\emptyset \ \left[B\alpha > \ B<\perp \ {\binom{\circ}{\vee}}_{\times} \right) . \ \right] >$$

| Two **B** hands are held with the palms facing down and the fingers pointing up. | The hands are held in front of the body at an angle, so that the fingers are turned towards each other. | The hands move down and, at the same time, towards each other. | decrease
few
fewer
minimise
minimum
reduce
reduction[1]
shrink[1] | 1393 |

Notes   1 If the movement is changed, so that the heels of the hands move firmly towards each other and the raised elbows move firmly towards the body, the sign produced is **reduction, shrink**.

$$\emptyset \ \ \swarrow B\upsilon\wedge \ \ \swarrow B\upsilon\wedge \ \ \overset{\cdot\cdot}{\times}$$

| Two **B** hands are held with the palms facing down and the fingers pointing up. | The hands are held in front of the body at an angle, so that the fingers are turned towards each other. | The hands move towards each other and, at the same time, up; the movement ends with the fingertips touching. | mount
pyramid
tent[1]
fell[2]
mountain[2] | 1394 |

Notes   1 If the movement is reversed, the sign produced is **tent**.

$$\emptyset \ \ B\upsilon\wedge \ _\times \ B\upsilon\wedge \ \ \overset{\div}{\vee}$$

           2 If the hands move up and towards each other while making short twisting movements towards and away from the signer at the wrists, the sign produced is **fell, mountain**.

$$\emptyset \ \ B\upsilon\wedge \ \ B\upsilon\wedge \ \ {\binom{\circ}{\omega\mp\times}}_{\wedge} \times$$

| Two **B** hands are held with the palms facing down and the fingers pointing up. | The hands are held at an angle in front of the body, so that the fingers are turned towards each other. | The hands move down and, at the same time, towards each other in a series of short movements. | contract
contraction
decline
decrease
reduce
reduction
shrink
shrinkage
whittle down | 1395 |

Non-manual features   The lips are slightly rounded.

| Two **B** hands are held with the palms facing down and the fingers pointing up. | The hands are held side by side in front of the body at an angle, so that the fingers are turned away from the signer. | No movement. | fire
warm oneself
  before a fire | 1396 |

1397 Ø BᴖʌΙ BᴖʌΙ ⊥

1398 Ø Bᴖ⊥ Bᴖ⊥ ˣˣ

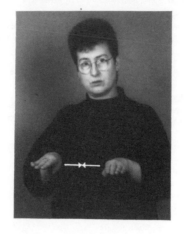

1399 Ø Bᴖ⊥ Bᴖ⊥ °̌·

1400 Ø Bᴖ⊥ Bᴖ⊥ °̌·

1401 Ø Bᴖ⊥ Bᴖ⊥ ↓°̇⊥

1402 Ø Bᴖ⊥ Bᴖ⊥ ᶜ(ω)̇⊥ˣ

1403 Ø Bᴖ⊥ Bᴖ⊥ ᴺᴺ·

1404 Ø Bᴖ⊥ Bᴖ⊥ ↓°̇ᴺ·

B

The hand is held flat with the fingers held together; the thumb is usually held against the side of the index finger.

Handshape and orientation	Location, hand arrangement and contact	Movement	Glosses	
Two **B** hands are held with the palms facing down and the fingers pointing up.	The hands are held side by side in front of the body at an angle, so that the palms are turned away from the signer.	The hands move away from the signer.	shove * push * 1 rebuff 2 resist 2	1397

Non-manual features   The body moves forward.

Notes   * This sign may be produced using one hand only, typically to indicate pushing or shoving a person.

Ø B⌐∧ ⊥

1 If the movement is repeated, the sign produced is **push**.

Ø B⌐∧ ͺ B⌐∧ ⊥˳

2 If the upper body moves back and the head twists to one side, the sign produced is **rebuff, resist.**

Two **B** hands are held with the palms facing down and the fingers pointing away from the signer.	The hands are held in front of the body.	The hands move towards each other; the movement ends with the sides of the index fingers touching.	close shut	1398
Two **B** hands are held with the palms facing down and the fingers pointing away from the signer.	The hands are held in front of the body.	The hands make two short downward movements.	Muslim obeisance	1399

Non-manual features   The head nods twice.

Two **B** hands are held with the palms facing down and the fingers pointing away from the signer.	The hands are held in front of the body.	The hands make two short downward movements.	calm down quiet (be quiet) take it easy take your time	1400

Non-manual features   The brows are slightly furrowed.

Two **B** hands are held with the palms facing down and the fingers pointing away from the signer.	The hands are held in front of the body.	The hands make two clockwise circles in the vertical plane at right angles to the signer's body.	comfort * compassion console *	1401

Notes   * Directional verb.

Two **B** hands are held with the palms facing down and the fingers pointing away from the signer.	The hands are held in front of the body.	The hands twist at the wrists (so that the palms face away from each other) while moving down and towards each other; the wrists then twist, so that the palms face down while the hands continue to move towards each other.	dale glen vale valley	1402
Two **B** hands are held with the palms facing down and the fingers pointing away from the signer.	The hands are held in front of the body.	The hands make alternate up and down movements.	seesaw	1403
Two **B** hands are held with the palms facing down and the fingers pointing away from the signer.	The hands are held in front of the body at an angle, so that the fingers are turned apart.	The hands make alternate small clockwise circles in the vertical plane at right angles to the signer's body.	seal	1404

Non-manual features   The shoulders move up and down alternately.

1405 Ø B̅ʊ⊥ ×ₓ Bʊ⊥ ᵐ̽

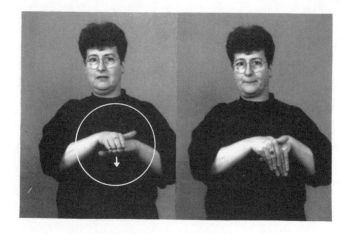

1406 Ø Bʊ⊥ ₁ Bʊ⊥ ÷

1407 Ø Bʊ⊥ ₁ Bʊ⊥ ⁺÷ // B̅ʊ> 5̈⊥ʌₒ ⁺̂

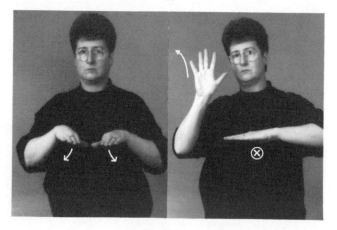

1408 Ø Bʊ⊥ ₁ Bʊ⊥ ᴵ·

1409 Ø Bʊ⊥ ₁ Bʊ⊥ ⁽ᵒ̂ᵒ̌₊÷⁾

1410 Ø Bʊ⊥ ₁ Bʊ⊥ ⁺⊙·÷

The hand is held flat with the fingers held together; the thumb is usually held against the side of the index finger.

Handshape and orientation	Location, hand arrangement and contact	Movement	Glosses	
Two **B** hands are held with the palms facing down and the fingers pointing away from the signer.	The hands are held in front of the body; the right palm is held on the back of the left hand.	The hands remain together while the fingers all bend at the palm knuckles.	disabled disabled person disability handicap handicapped handicapped person ballerina [1] ballet [1] ballet dancer [1]	1405

Notes   1   If the hands make a short movement up and towards the signer while the fingers bend, the sign produced is **ballerina, ballet, ballet dancer**.

$$\emptyset \quad B\text{ɔ⊥} \quad \times \quad B\text{ɔ⊥} \quad {}^{\text{o}}_{\substack{\text{x}\\\text{m}\\\text{t}\\\text{v}}}$$

Two **B** hands are held with the palms facing down and the fingers pointing away from the signer.	The hands are held side by side in front of the body.	The hands move apart.	equal equality fair fairness flat floor level platform shelf stage straight	1406
Two **B** hands are held with the palms facing down and the fingers pointing away from the signer.	The hands are held side by side in front of the body.	The hands make a short movement away from the signer and, at the same time, apart.	play water polo water polo water polo player	1407
The left **B** hand is held with the palm facing down and the fingers pointing to the right; the right **5̈** hand is held with the palm facing away from the signer (if the hand were opened, the fingers would point up).	The hands are held in front of the body; the right hand is held higher and nearer to the signer than the left hand.	The right hand moves up and, at the same time, away from the signer.		

Non-manual features   The body twists, so that the right shoulder moves forward.

Two **B** hands are held with the palms facing down and the fingers pointing away from the signer.	The hands are held side by side in front of the body.	The hands move towards and away from the signer twice.	rolling pin roll out	1408
Two **B** hands are held with the palms facing down and the fingers pointing away from the signer.	The hands are held side by side in front of the body.	The hands make a short upward movement and then a short downward movement, while moving apart throughout.	draw equal equality equivalent fair fairness just same	1409
Two **B** hands are held with the palms facing down and the fingers pointing away from the signer.	The hands are held side by side in front of the body.	The hands make circles (the left hand moves anticlockwise, the right hand moves clockwise) in the horizontal plane.	breast-stroke * swim * swimmer * swimming *	1410

Notes   *   This sign may also be produced with the left palm facing left and the right palm facing right.

$$\emptyset \quad B\text{<⊥} \quad , \quad B\text{ɔ⊥} \quad {}^{\text{@ .}}_{\substack{\text{⊥}\\\div}}$$

1411 Ø Bʊ⊥ | Bʊ⊥ ⊕⊥÷ · ∥ ∥ [ ] 5⊤> 5⊤< ^×

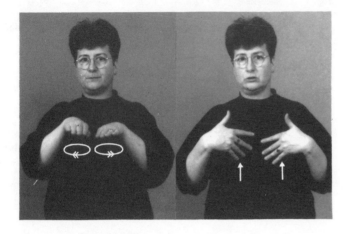

1412 Ø Bʊ⊥ | Bʊ⊥ ⊕⊥÷ · ∥ ∥ Ħ Ċ⊤∨ ×| Ċ⊤∨ ÷×

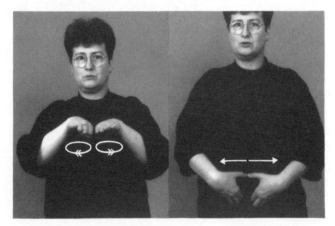

1413 Ø Bʊ⊥ | Bʊ⊥ ᴺ~·

1414 Ø Bʊ⊥ | Bʊ⊥ ᴺ~·

1415 Ø Bʊ⊥ ×| Bʊ⊥ ÷

The hand is held flat with the fingers held together; the thumb is usually held against the side of the index finger.

Handshape and orientation	Location, hand arrangement and contact	Movement	Glosses	
Two B hands are held with the palms facing down and the fingers pointing away from the signer.	The hands are held side by side in front of the body.	The hands make circles (the left hand moves anticlockwise, the right hand moves clockwise) in the horizontal plane.	bathing costume swimming costume swimsuit	1411
The left 5 hand is held with the palm facing towards the signer and the fingers pointing to the right; the right 5 hand is held with the palm facing towards the signer and the fingers pointing to the left.	The hands are held with the finger-tips touching the chest.	The hands move up, maintaining contact with the chest throughout.		
Two B hands are held with the palms facing down and the fingers pointing away from the signer.	The hands are held side by side in front of the body.	The hands make circles (the left hand moves anticlockwise, the right hand moves clockwise) in the horizontal plane.	swimming trunks	1412
Two Ċ hands are held with the palms facing towards the signer (if the hands were opened, the fingers would all point down).	The hands are held with the sides of the thumbtips touching and the fingertips all touching the waist.	The hands move apart; the fingertips maintain contact with the waist throughout.		
Two B hands are held with the palms facing down and the fingers pointing away from the signer.	The hands are held side by side in front of the body.	The hands make alternate short up and down movements.	assess assessment assessor average balance court evaluate evaluation judge judgement scales trial tribunal	1413
Two B hands are held with the palms facing down and the fingers pointing away from the signer.	The hands are held side by side in front of the body.	The hands bend up and down alternately from the wrists; the movements are repeated.	decorate decorator paper wallpaper	1414
Two B hands are held with the palms facing down and the fingers pointing away from the signer.	The hands are held side by side in front of the waist, with the sides of the index fingers touching.	The hands move apart.	carpet flat floor grass ground ground floor level linoleum platform table	1415

1416 Ø B⌒⊥ ₁ₓ B⌒⊥ [⊚]_⊥_∨

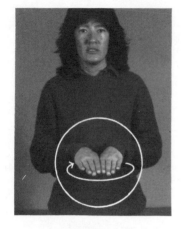

1417 Ø B⌒⊥ ₁ₓ B⌒⊥ ^{⊥<⊤}

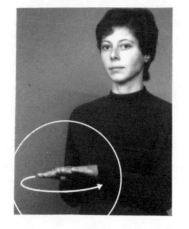

1418 Ø B⌒⊥ ₁ₓ B⌒⊥ ^{÷×ˣ}_{ᵥᵥ}_{ᵃᵛ}

1419 Ø B⌒⊥ ₁ B⌒⊥ᵩ [○]_{⊥˙}

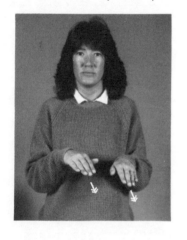

1420 Ø √B̄⌒⊥ ∓ₓ √B⌒< [÷]

1421 Ø B⌒< B⌒> [○]_{∿∿˙}

1422 Ø √B̄⌒> √B⌒< ^{⊤∿}_×_⊤

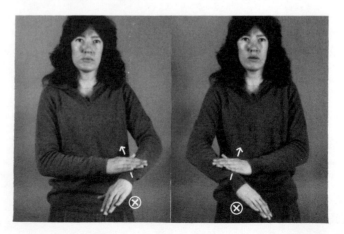

B

The hand is held flat with the fingers held together; the thumb is usually held against the side of the index finger.

Handshape and orientation	Location, hand arrangement and contact	Movement	Glosses	
Two B hands are held with the palms facing down and the fingers pointing away from the signer.	The hands are held side by side in front of the body with the sides of the index fingers held together.	The hands remain together and make a clockwise circle in the horizontal plane.	common consistent equal equality general identical same standard uniform	1416
Two B hands are held with the palms facing down and the fingers pointing away from the signer.	The hands are held side by side in front of the body with the sides of the index fingers held together.	The hands remain together and move in an arc away from the signer, then to the left, and finally back towards the signer.	common consistent equal equality general identical same standard uniform	1417
Two B hands are held with the palms facing down and the fingers pointing away from the signer.	The hands are held in front of the body with the sides of the index fingers touching.	The hands move apart and down while twisting at the wrists (so that the palms face up) and then continue to move down while moving towards each other; the movement ends with the sides of the little fingers touching.	ball earth football globe round sphere spherical world	1418
Two B hands are held with the palms facing down and the fingers pointing away from the signer.	The hands are held side by side in front of the body; the right hand is held nearer to the signer than the left hand.	The hands make two short movements away from the signer.	sew sewing machine sewing machinist	1419
The left B hand is held with the palm facing down and the fingers pointing away from the signer; the right B hand is held with the palm facing down and the fingers pointing to the left. *Non-manual features* The brows are furrowed.	The hands are held crossed over in front of the body with the right wrist resting on the back of the left hand.	The hands uncross and move firmly apart while the elbows move in towards the body; the movement ends with the fingers all pointing away from the signer.	do not don't finished forbid forbidden had enough no not not allowed ought not should not that's it	1420
The left B hand is held with the palm facing down and the fingers pointing to the left; the right B hand is held with the palm facing down and the fingers pointing to the right. *Non-manual features* The shoulders move up and down alternately.	The hands are held in front of the body.	The hands make alternate short up and down movements.	penguin penguin waddling waddle	1421
The left B hand is held with the palm facing down and the fingers pointing to the right; the right B hand is held with the palm facing down and the fingers pointing to the left. *Notes* * Regional sign.	The hands are held in front of the body; the right hand is held above the left forearm.	The right hand moves towards the signer, brushing across the left forearm; the left hand then moves towards the signer, brushing across the right forearm.	trouble*	1422

1423 Ø <u>B</u>ʊ>ͺ Bʊ< $\left(\begin{smallmatrix} m\sim \cdot \\ x \\ m \\ \wedge \end{smallmatrix}\right)$

1424 Ø $\overline{B}$⊤⊥ B⊤⊥ $^{x \div [BB]}_{a}$

1425 Ø B⊤⊥ ₁x B⊤⊥ ⊥

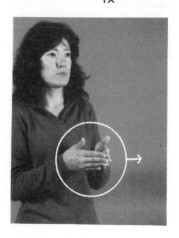

1426 Ø B⊤⊥ ₁x B⊤⊥ ⊥ // // <u>B</u>⊤⊥ ͺ G⊤< $^{\overset{o}{\underset{v}{\overset{e}{\perp}}}\cdot}$

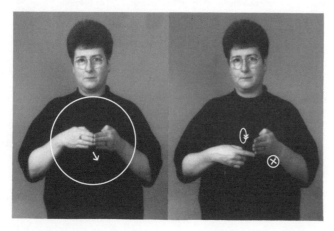

1427 Ø B⊤⊥ ₁x B⊤⊥ ⊥ // // Ø $\overline{B}$a> x B̈<⊥ $^{\overset{o}{⊤}}$

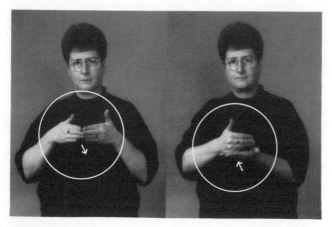

1428 Ø B⊤⊥ ₁x B⊤⊥ $^{\left(\begin{smallmatrix}o\\N\\\perp\end{smallmatrix}\right)}$

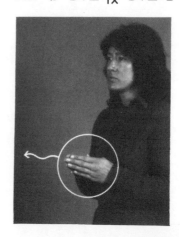

Handshape and orientation	Location, hand arrangement and contact	Movement	Glosses	
The left B hand is held with the palm facing down and the fingers pointing to the right; the right B hand is held with the palm facing down and the fingers pointing to the left.	The hands are held side by side in front of the body; the left fingers are held above the right fingers.	The hands bend alternately at the palm knuckles, so that the fingers brush together; the movements are repeated several times, with the hands moving upwards throughout.	build builder building build up construct	1423
Two B hands are held with the palms facing towards the signer and the fingers pointing away from the signer.	The hands are held in front of the body at an angle, so that the palms are turned towards each other; the right hand is held above the left hand.	The sides of the hands touch and then the hands move apart whilst twisting at the wrists, so that the palms face up.	out of work unemployed unemployment unwaged	1424

Non-manual features The head shakes slightly.

Two B hands are held with the palms facing towards the signer and the fingers pointing away from the signer.	The hands are held side by side in front of the body, angled towards each other, so that the fingertips are touching.	The fingertips remain together and the hands move away from the signer.	cruise liner liner/ship sailing sail sailing ship	1425
Two B hands are held with the palms facing towards the signer and the fingers pointing away from the signer.	The hands are held side by side in front of the body, angled towards each other, so that the fingertips are touching.	The fingertips remain together and the hands move away from the signer.	launch motorboat speedboat	1426
The left B hand is held with the palm facing towards the signer and the fingers pointing away from the signer; the right G hand is held with the palm facing towards the signer (if the hand were opened, the fingers would point to the left).	The hands are held side by side in front of the body; the left hand is held higher than the right hand.	The right hand makes small circles in the vertical plane at right angles to the signer's body.		
Two B hands are held with the palms facing towards the signer and the fingers pointing away from the signer.	The hands are held side by side in front of the body, angled towards each other, so that the fingertips are touching.	The fingertips remain together and the hands move away from the signer.	lifeboat rescue boat	1427
The left B hand is held with the palm facing up and the fingers pointing to the right; the right B̈ hand is held with the palm facing left (if the hand were opened, the fingers would point away from the signer).	The hands are held in front of the body; the right hand is held on the left palm.	The hands remain together and make a short movement towards the signer.		
Two B hands are held with the palms facing towards the signer and the fingers pointing away from the signer.	The hands are held side by side in front of the body, angled towards each other, so that the fingertips are touching.	The fingertips remain together and the hands make short up and down movements while moving away from the signer.	boat boat/ferry sailing ferry sail sailing	1428

1429 ∅ BT⊥ ₁× BT⊥ $_{\div}^{(\frac{n}{x})^x}$

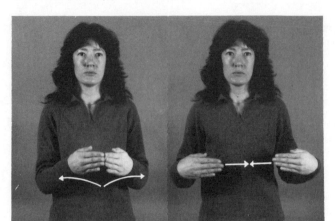

1430 ∅ BT> ₁× BT< $^{\frac{n}{\perp}}$

1431 ∅ BT> ₁× BT< $^{\frac{n}{\perp} \cdot}$

1432 ∅ BT> × BT< $^{\div}$

1433 ∅ BT>₉ ₁ BT< $^{\substack{N \cdot \\ H×H}}$

[702]

The hand is held flat with the fingers held together; the thumb is usually held against the side of the index finger.

Handshape and orientation	Location, hand arrangement and contact	Movement	Glosses	
Two **B** hands are held with the palms facing towards the signer and the fingers pointing away from the signer.	The hands are held side by side in front of the body, angled towards each other, so that the fingertips are touching.	The hands move apart and towards the signer while bending towards each other at the wrists, so that the palms face towards the signer; the hands then move towards each other.	snooker	1429
The left **B** hand is held with the palm facing towards the signer and the fingers pointing to the right; the right **B** hand is held with the palm facing towards the signer and the fingers pointing to the left.	The hands are held side by side in front of the body with the middle fingertips touching.	The hands bend away from the signer from the wrists.	launch open	1430
The left **B** hand is held with the palm facing towards the signer and the fingers pointing to the right; the right **B** hand is held with the palm facing towards the signer and the fingers pointing to the left.	The hands are held side by side in front of the body with the middle fingertips touching.	The hands bend away from and then towards the signer from the wrists; the movements are repeated.	doors (double doors) doors (double doors opening)[1] level crossing[1] level crossing opening[1]	1431

Notes   1 If the hands move away from the signer and apart, bending from the elbows, the sign produced is **double doors opening, level crossing, level crossing opening.**

$$\emptyset \quad \dot{J}\text{B}\top> {}_{1\times} \dot{J}\text{B}\top< \overset{\text{n}}{\perp}$$

The left **B** hand is held with the palm facing towards the signer and the fingers pointing to the right; the right **B** hand is held with the palm facing towards the signer and the fingers pointing to the left.	The hands are held side by side in front of the body with the middle fingertips touching.	The hands move apart.	automatic doors* automatic/sliding doors opening* border boundary frontier front line sliding doors*	1432

Notes   * This sign may be produced with the fingers all pointing up. $\emptyset \quad \text{B}\top\wedge \,{}_{\times}\, \text{B}\top\wedge \,\div$

The left **B** hand is held with the palm facing towards the signer and the fingers pointing to the right; the right **B** hand is held with the palm facing towards the signer and the fingers pointing to the left.	The hands are held side by side in front of the body; the left hand is held nearer to the signer than the right hand.	The hands make alternate bending movements towards and away from the signer from the wrists, so that the fingertips brush together in completing each movement.	administrate administration administrator all the same anyway arrange arrangement manage management manager never mind nevertheless organisation organise organiser sort out	1433

1434 ∅ B̄⊤> ⊥ᵒ B<∧ (ṅ⊤)

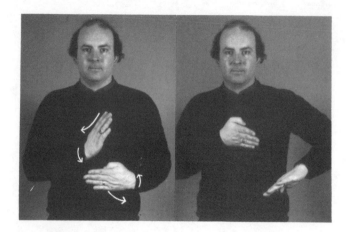

1435 ∅ B⊥∧ B⊥∧ ⊥°˙

1436 ∅ B⊥∧ ǀ B⊥∧ (ᵉ∿˙⊤∿⊤)

1437 ∅ B>∧ B<∧ ⊥ṅ˙

1438 ∅ B>∧ B<∧ ᵛₒ

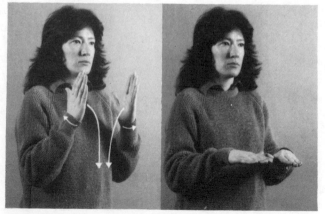

1439 ∅ B>∧ B<∧ ᶻ˙

The hand is held flat with the fingers held together; the thumb is usually held against the side of the index finger.

Handshape and orientation	Location, hand arrangement and contact	Movement	Glosses	
The left B hand is held with the palm facing towards the signer and the fingers pointing to the right; the right B hand is held with the palm facing left and the fingers pointing up.	The hands are held in front of the body; the right hand is held above the left hand.	The left hand moves away from the signer while twisting at the wrist, so that the palm faces down; at the same time, the right hand bends away from the signer at the wrist while moving towards the signer.	karate kung-fu martial arts	1434
Two B hands are held with the palms facing away from the signer and the fingers pointing up.	The hands are held in front of the body.	The hands make a short, firm movement away from the signer.	halt * stop * wait *† hang on *1 hold on *1 pause *1	1435

Notes   * This sign can be produced using one hand only.

$$\varnothing \quad B\perp\wedge \overset{\circ}{\underset{.}{\perp}}$$

† This sign can be produced with a repeated movement.

$$\varnothing \quad B\perp\wedge \quad B\perp\wedge \overset{\circ}{\underset{.}{\perp}} \cdot \text{ or}$$

$$\varnothing \quad B\perp\wedge \overset{\circ}{\underset{.}{\perp}} \cdot$$

1 If the movement is repeated, the sign produced is **hang on, hold on, pause.**

$$\varnothing \quad B\perp\wedge \quad B\perp\wedge \overset{\circ}{\underset{.}{\perp}} \cdot \text{ or } \varnothing \quad B\perp\wedge \overset{\circ}{\underset{.}{\perp}} \cdot$$

Handshape and orientation	Location, hand arrangement and contact	Movement	Glosses	
Two B hands are held with the palms facing away from the signer and the fingers pointing up.	The hands are held side by side in front of the body.	The hands make alternate anti-clockwise circles in the vertical plane at right angles to the signer's body, while moving towards the signer throughout.	disconcert embarrass feel uncomfortable fluster throw	1436

Non-manual features   The body moves back.

The left B hand is held with the palm facing right and the fingers pointing up; the right B hand is held with the palm facing left and the fingers pointing up.	The hands are held in front of the body.	The hands bend firmly away from the signer from the wrists.	compel compulsory have got to have to important must obligatory should	1437
The left B hand is held with the palm facing right and the fingers pointing up; the right B hand is held with the palm facing left and the fingers pointing up.	The hands are held in front of the body.	The hands move down while twisting at the wrists, so that the palms face down and the fingers all point away from the signer.	fold collapse 1 flop 2	1438

Notes   1 If the cheeks are puffed out, the sign produced is **collapse.**

2 If the tongue tip protrudes between the teeth, the sign produced is **flop.**

The left B hand is held with the palm facing right and the fingers pointing up; the right B hand is held with the palm facing left and the fingers pointing up.	The hands are held in front of the body.	The hands move from side to side several times.	gale storm stormy	1439

Non-manual features   The cheeks are puffed out and the eyes are narrowed.

1440 Ø B>∧ ⌐ B<∧ ˣ

1441 Ø B>∧ ₁× B<∧ ⊥̊

1442 Ø B>∧ ₁× B<∧ ⊥̊·

1443 Ø B>∨ B<∨ ⊥̌ₓₓ

1444 Ø B>∨ B<∨ $\binom{\cap}{\perp}$

1445 Ø B>⊥ ⌐ B<∧ ⁽ˣˣ⁾·

1446 Ø B>⊥ B<⊥ ˣ

1447 Ø B>⊥ B<⊥ ˚̌ᵛ

[706]

B

The hand is held flat with the fingers held together; the thumb is usually held against the side of the index finger.

Handshape and orientation	Location, hand arrangement and contact	Movement	Glosses	
The left **B** hand is held with the palm facing right and the fingers pointing up; the right **B** hand is held with the palm facing left and the fingers pointing up.	The hands are held side by side in front of the body.	The hands move towards each other, so that the palms touch.	chapel church kirk pray prayer Sunday*	1440

Notes   * This sign may be produced with a repeated movement. $\emptyset$ B>∧ , B<∧ ˣ˙

The left **B** hand is held with the palm facing right and the fingers pointing up; the right **B** hand is held with the palm facing left and the fingers pointing up.	The hands are held in front of the body with the palms together.	The hands remain together and make a short movement away from the signer.	pray prayer	1441
The left **B** hand is held with the palm facing right and the fingers pointing up; the right **B** hand is held with the palm facing left and the fingers pointing up.	The hands are held in front of the body with the palms together.	The hands remain together and make several short movements away from the signer.	pray prayer worship religion [1] religious [1]	1442

Notes   1 If the hands remain together and make two bending movements away from the signer at the wrists, the sign produced is **religion, religious**. $\emptyset$ B>∧ ᵢₓ B<∧ ⁿ˙

The left **B** hand is held with the palm facing right and the fingers pointing down; the right **B** hand is held with the palm facing left and the fingers pointing down.	The hands are held in front of the body at an angle, so that the fingers are turned towards each other.	The hands move down and away from the signer and, at the same time, towards each other.	burial bury funeral grave inter interment	1443
The left **B** hand is held with the palm facing right and the fingers pointing down; the right **B** hand is held with the palm facing left and the fingers pointing down.	The hands are held in front of the body.	The hands bend away from the signer at the wrists while moving away from the signer.	method path road street style system way	1444
The left **B** hand is held with the palm facing right and the fingers pointing away from the signer; the right **B** hand is held with the palm facing left and the fingers pointing up.	The hands are held side by side in front of the body.	The hands move towards each other, so that the palms touch; the movement is repeated several times.	applaud applause clap	1445
The left **B** hand is held with the palm facing right and the fingers pointing away from the signer; the right **B** hand is held with the palm facing left and the fingers pointing away from the signer.	The hands are held in front of the body.	The hands move towards each other.	limited short	1446
The left **B** hand is held with the palm facing right and the fingers pointing away from the signer; the right **B** hand is held with the palm facing left and the fingers pointing away from the signer.	The hands are held in front of the body.	The hands make a short, firm downward movement.	block chunk section unit	1447

1448　Ø　B>⊥　B<⊥ ˅̽⟋⟋ ⁻B⊤⊥ B⊤⊥ ˣ·

1449　Ø　B>⊥　B<⊥ ˅̽

1450　Ø　B>⊥　B<⊥ ˚̽·

1451　Ø　B>⊥　B<⊥ ⁿˣ̽

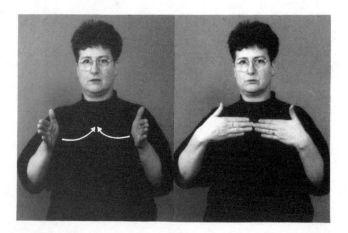

1452　Ø　B>⊥　B<⊥ @⊥̽˅·

1453　Ø　B>⊥ ၊ B<⊥ ˃

[708]

B

The hand is held flat with the fingers held together; the thumb is usually held against the side of the index finger.

Handshape and orientation	Location, hand arrangement and contact	Movement	Glosses	
The left **B** hand is held with the palm facing right and the fingers pointing away from the signer; the right **B** hand is held with the palm facing left and the fingers pointing away from the signer.	The hands are held in front of the body.	The hands move down and away from the signer and, at the same time, towards each other.	**conscientious*** **diligent***	1448

Non-manual features   The head is tilted forward.

Two **B** hands are held with the palms facing towards the signer and the fingers pointing away from the signer.	The hands are held in front of the body at an angle, so that the palms are turned towards each other; the right hand is held above the left hand.	The side of the right hand taps the side of the left hand several times.		

Notes   * This sign may be produced with the two parts reversed.

$$\overline{\text{B}\top\bot} \quad \text{B}\top\bot \quad {}^{\times}\cdot{}^{//}_{//} \quad \varnothing \quad \text{B}{>}\bot \quad \text{B}{<}\bot \quad {}^{\vee}_{\times}$$

The left **B** hand is held with the palm facing right and the fingers pointing away from the signer; the right **B** hand is held with the palm facing left and the fingers pointing away from the signer.	The hands are held in front of the body.	The hands move down and towards each other, while twisting at the wrists, so that the palms face up.	**introduce** **introduction**	1449
The left **B** hand is held with the palm facing right and the fingers pointing away from the signer; the right **B** hand is held with the palm facing left and the fingers pointing away from the signer.	The hands are held in front of the body.	The hands make a short repeated movement towards each other.	**little*** **narrow*** **small*** **tiny*** **wee***	1450

Non-manual features   The brows are slightly furrowed and the lips are tightly rounded.

Notes   * This sign may be produced with a single movement.

$$\varnothing \quad \text{B}{>}\bot \quad \text{B}{<}\bot \quad {}^{\circ}_{\times}$$

The left **B** hand is held with the palm facing right and the fingers pointing away from the signer; the right **B** hand is held with the palm facing left and the fingers pointing away from the signer.	The hands are held in front of the body.	The hands bend towards each other from the wrists; the movement ends with the fingertips touching.	**close** **doors (double doors closing)** **level crossing closing** **shut**	1451
The left **B** hand is held with the palm facing right and the fingers pointing away from the signer; the right **B** hand is held with the palm facing left and the fingers pointing away from the signer.	The hands are held in front of the body.	The hands make clockwise circles in the vertical plane at right angles to the signer's body.	**hospital**	1452
The left **B** hand is held with the palm facing right and the fingers pointing away from the signer; the right **B** hand is held with the palm facing left and the fingers pointing away from the signer.	The hands are held side by side in front of the body.	The hands move to the right.	**move** **shift** **lift**[1] **meanwhile**[1] **pick up**[1]	1453

Notes   1 If the movement is changed to a short upward movement, followed by a movement to the left and finally a short, downward movement, the sign produced is **lift, meanwhile, pick up.**

$$\varnothing \quad \text{B}{>}\bot \quad {}_{\textbar} \quad \text{B}{<}\bot \quad {}^{\circ}{}^{\wedge}{<}^{\circ}_{\vee}$$

1454 Ø B>⊥ ꞁ B<⊥ ⁝÷

1455 Ø B>⊥ ꞁ B<⊥ ^÷

1456 Ø B>⊥ ꞁx B<⊥ ᵒᵅ

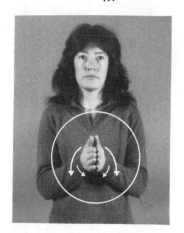

1457 Ø B>⊥ ꞁx B<⊥ $\binom{\circ}{\div}_{\alpha}$ // Ø B<∧ $\binom{\circ}{\stackrel{\cdot}{\stackrel{|}{>}}}$

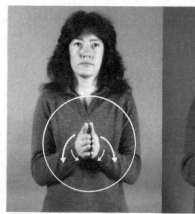  

1458 Ø B>⊥ꝑ B<⊥ $\stackrel{\stackrel{\circ\circ\circ}{\vee\wedge\vee}}{\stackrel{\cap}{\times}}$

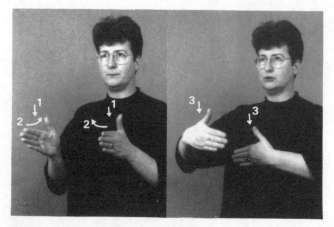

1459 Ø $\left(B\,\mho> \stackrel{\cap}{\perp} \times B<\wedge\!ꝑ \stackrel{\omega}{\top}\right)^{x}_{\stackrel{\perp}{\vee}}$

[710]

Handshape and orientation	Location, hand arrangement and contact	Movement	Glosses	
The left B hand is held with the palm facing right and the fingers pointing away from the signer; the right B hand is held with the palm facing left and the fingers pointing away from the signer.	The hands are held side by side in front of the body.	The hands move apart.	wide width* length† long†	1454

Notes   * This sign may be produced with the left hand held still in front of the body, while the right hand moves to the right.

    † This sign may be produced using two G hands.

$$\text{B}>\perp \, | \, \text{B}<\perp \,^{>}$$
$$\emptyset \;\; \text{G}>\perp \, | \, \text{G}<\perp \,^{\div}$$

The left B hand is held with the palm facing right and the fingers pointing away from the signer; the right B hand is held with the palm facing left and the fingers pointing away from the signer.	The hands are held side by side in front of the body.	The hands move up and, at the same time, apart.	vase	1455
The left B hand is held with the palm facing right and the fingers pointing away from the signer; the right B hand is held with the palm facing left and the fingers pointing away from the signer.	The hands are held side by side in front of the body with the palms together.	The hands twist apart at the wrists, so that the palms face up; the sides of the little fingers are held together throughout.	book* catalogue* dictionary* passport*	1456

Notes   * This sign may be produced with a repeated movement.

$$\emptyset \;\; \text{B}>\perp \, {}_{|x} \, \text{B}<\perp \,^{\overset{x}{\underset{}{\alpha}}\,\cdot}$$

The left B hand is held with the palm facing right and the fingers pointing away from the signer; the right B hand is held with the palm facing left and the fingers pointing away from the signer.	The hands are held in front of the body with the palms together.	The hands twist apart from the wrists, so that the palms face up.	bookcase library	1457
The B hand is held with the palm facing left and the fingers pointing up.	The hand is held in front of the body.	The hand makes several short movements away from the signer, while moving to the right throughout.		
The left B hand is held with the palm facing right and the fingers pointing away from the signer; the right B hand is held with the palm facing left and the fingers pointing away from the signer.	The hands are held in front of the body; the left hand is held nearer to the signer than the right hand.	The hands make a short downward movement, and then bend towards each other at the wrists while making a short upward movement; the hands then make a final short downward movement.	box carton package parcel room	1458
The left B hand is held with the palm facing down and the fingers pointing to the right; the right B hand is held with the palm facing left and the fingers pointing up.	The hands are held in front of the body; the side of the right wrist is held against the side of the left index finger.	The left hand bends away from the signer and, at the same time, the right hand twists at the wrist, so that the palm faces towards the signer; at the same time, the hands move away from the signer and to the left, with the side of the right wrist held against the side of the left index finger throughout.	sail sailing yacht yachting	1459

1460 ∩ Bʊʌ Bʊʌ $^{×ω}_{⊥}$

1461 ∩ ↓Bтʌ ↓Bтʌ $^{∩}_{÷}$

1462 ∩ B⊥ʌ B⊥ʌ $^{×}_{ε}·$

1463 ○ Bтʌ Bтʌ $^{°}_{ε}·$

1464 ○ ↓Bтʌ ↓Bтʌ $^{∩°}_{×}$

1465 ○ Bтʌ Bтʌ $_{♀}$ $^{∩×}_{×}$

The hand is held flat with the fingers held together; the thumb is usually held against the side of the index finger.

Handshape and orientation	Location, hand arrangement and contact	Movement	Glosses	
Two **B** hands are held with the palms facing down and the fingers pointing up.	The hands are held at an angle, so that the palms are turned slightly towards each other; the index fingertips rest against the sides of the forehead.	The hands move away from the signer while twisting at the wrists, so that the palms face away from the signer.	holiday*	1460

Notes   * The following notes apply to the gloss:

     Regional sign.

     This sign can be produced using one hand only.   ∩ Bɔ∧ ×ω⊥

Two **B** hands are held with the palms facing towards the signer and the fingers pointing up.	The hands are held with the fingers in front of the forehead.	The hands move down and away from the signer, bending from the elbows, while moving apart.	defer deference deferential homage honour honourable obedience obeisance obey respect worship	1461

Non-manual features   The head is tilted forward and the eyegaze is directed forward and down.

Two **B** hands are held with the palms facing away from the signer and the fingers pointing up.	The hands are held against the sides of the forehead.	The fingers bend away from the signer from the palm knuckles several times.	ass donkey mule fool[1] idiot[1]	1462

Notes   1 If one hand only is used, the sign produced is **fool, idiot**.   ∩ B⊥∧ ×ɯ·

Two **B** hands are held with the palms facing towards the signer and the fingers pointing up.	The hands are held in front and to the sides of the face.	The fingers make several short bending movements towards the signer from the palm knuckles.	air air (fresh air) outside weather breeze[1] cool[1]	1463

Notes   1 If the lips are rounded, the sign produced is **breeze, cool**.

Two **B** hands are held with the palms facing towards the signer and the fingers pointing up.	The hands are held in front and to the sides of the face.	The hands move slowly down and, at the same time, towards each other, bending from the elbows.	darken dusk evening twilight	1464

Non-manual features   The eyes are narrowed.

Two **B** hands are held with the palms facing towards the signer and the fingers pointing up.	The hands are held in front and to the sides of the face; the right hand is held nearer to the signer than the left hand.	The hands bend towards each other from the wrists; the movement ends with the backs of the right fingers touching the left palm.	dark evening night tonight	1465

1466 ○ Bꚋ> ×　Bꚋ<ᵩ ᵑ∧

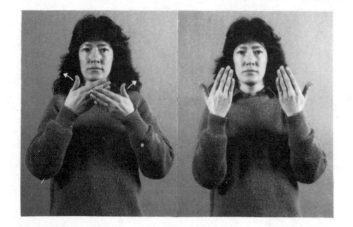

1467 ○ ِBꚋ> ∓ ِBꚋ< ᵑ∧

1468 ○ B>∧ B<∧ ˟÷[∧∧]⃛

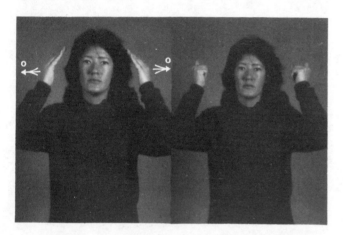

1469 ○ B>∧ × B<∧ᵩ ∅

1470 ◡ ⎛B◌∧ × B◌∧ᵩ ᵒᶻᶻ˟⎞

1471 ∪ Bꚋ∧ Bꚋ∧ ˟⟂ᵥ÷

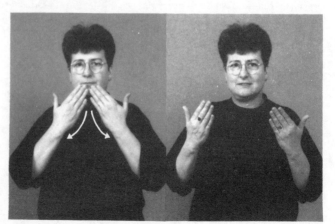

The hand is held flat with the fingers held together; the thumb is usually held against the side of the index finger.

Handshape and orientation	Location, hand arrangement and contact	Movement	Glosses	
The left **B** hand is held with the palm facing towards the signer and the fingers pointing to the right; the right **B** hand is held with the palm facing towards the signer and the fingers pointing to the left.	The hands are held in front of the face; the backs of the right fingers rest against the left palm.	The hands bend up from the wrists.	dawn day light	1466
The left **B** hand is held with the palm facing towards the signer and the fingers pointing to the right; the right **B** hand is held with the palm facing towards the signer and the fingers pointing to the left.	The hands are held crossed over in front of the face.	The hands move slowly up and, at the same time, apart, bending from the elbows.	dawn daybreak lighten	1467
The left **B** hand is held with the palm facing right and the fingers pointing up; the right **B** hand is held with the palm facing left and the fingers pointing up.	The hands are held with the fingertips touching the sides of the head.	The hands move apart while closing (forming two **A** hands).	Mexican Mexico	1468
The left **B** hand is held with the palm facing right and the fingers pointing up; the right **B** hand is held with the palm facing left and the fingers pointing up.	The hands are held in front of the face; the side of the right little finger is held against the side of the left index finger.	No movement.	hide hide and seek peek peep Peeping Tom spy voyeur	1469

Non-manual features   The head moves to the right twice.

Two **B** hands are held with the palms facing down and the fingers pointing up.	The hands are held in front of the mouth and chin at an angle, so that the palms are turned towards each other; the side of the right hand rests against the side of the left hand.	The right hand makes a short movement up and to the right and then down and to the left, maintaining contact with the side of the left index finger throughout; the movement is repeated several times.	secret* hide [1,2] confidence (in confidence) [2] confidential [2] private [2]	1470

Notes   * This sign can also be used as the second part of a compound sign meaning **secret** (see 347 for the first part of the sign).

   1 If the hands are held in front of the whole face, the sign produced is **hide**.

   2 If the hands are held in front of the body, so that the fingers point away from the signer, and the forearms are held against the sides of the chest, the sign produced is **confidential, hide** *(see entry 3 in the English section),* **in confidence, private.**

$$\cup \ \mathsf{G}{<}\wedge \ \substack{\times \perp \\ //} \ \substack{// \\ } \ \circlearrowleft \ \left(\mathsf{B}\eth\wedge \ \times \ \mathsf{B}\eth\wedge_\wp \ \substack{\mathsf{Z} \\ \mathsf{N} \\ \times} \substack{o \\ \cdot} \right)$$

$$\circlearrowleft \ \left(\mathsf{B}\eth\wedge \ \times \ \mathsf{B}\eth\wedge_\wp \ \substack{\mathsf{Z} \\ \mathsf{N} \\ \times} \substack{o \\ \cdot} \right)$$

$$[\ ] \ \left(\overline{\mathsf{B}}\top{>} \ \times \ \mathsf{B}{<}\perp \ \substack{\mathsf{Z} \\ \mathsf{H} \\ \times} \substack{o \\ \cdot} \right)$$

Two **B** hands are held with the palms facing towards the signer and the fingers pointing up.	The hands are held with the fingertips touching the chin.	The hands move down and away from the signer and, at the same time, apart.	appreciate* appreciation* grateful* gratitude* thank* thankful* thanks* thank you*	1471

Notes   * This sign may be produced using one hand only.

$$\cup \ \mathsf{B}\top\wedge \ \substack{\times \perp \\ \div \\ \vee}$$

1472 ∪ B>ʌ B<ʌ ÷

1473 [] B℧∧ ∓× B℧∧ ×·

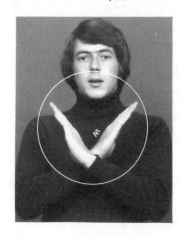

1474 [] B̄℧> B℧< ×·

1475 [] B⊤> B⊤<

1476 [] B⊤> B⊤<

1477 [] B⊤> × B⊤<⸴

1478 [] B>⊥ ǀ B<⊥

1479 ⌐⌐ B̄⊤> B⊤<

B

Handshape and orientation	Location, hand arrangement and contact	Movement	Glosses	
The left B hand is held with the palm facing right and the fingers pointing up; the right B hand is held with the palm facing left and the fingers pointing up.	The hands are held with the fingers in front of the chin.	The hands move firmly away from the signer and, at the same time, apart.	amazing * fantastic * marvel * marvellous * terrific * wonder * wonderful *	1472
Non-manual features The eyes are opened wide.				
Notes * This sign can be produced using one hand only.		∪ B<∧ ⊥⟩		
Two B hands are held with the palms facing down and the fingers pointing up.	The hands are held crossed over in front of the chest at an angle, so that the palms are turned away from each other; the wrists are held together.	The side of the right hand taps the chest twice; the wrists are held together throughout.	angel	1473
The left B hand is held with the palm facing down and the fingers pointing to the right; the right B hand is held with the palm facing down and the fingers pointing to the left.	The hands are held in front of the chest; the right hand is held above the left hand.	The sides of the hands tap the chest twice.	goalkeeper	1474
The left B hand is held with the palm facing towards the signer and the fingers pointing to the right; the right B hand is held with the palm facing towards the signer and the fingers pointing to the left.	The hands are held in front of the chest; the right hand is held above the left hand.	The hands make alternate anti-clockwise circles in the vertical plane at right angles to the signer's body, brushing the chest in making each circle.	behave behaviour manner manners	1475
The left B hand is held with the palm facing towards the signer and the fingers pointing to the right; the right B hand is held with the palm facing towards the signer and the fingers pointing to the left.	The hands are held in front of the chest; the right hand is held above the left hand.	The hands make alternate slow anticlockwise circles in the vertical plane at right angles to the signer's body, brushing the chest in making each circle.	calm meek modest patient tolerant tolerate	1476
Non-manual features The lips are pressed together and the head is tilted to one side.				
The left B hand is held with the palm facing towards the signer and the fingers pointing to the right; the right B hand is held with the palm facing towards the signer and the fingers pointing to the left.	The hands are held in front of the chest at an angle, so that the fingers are all turned up; the back of the right hand is held against the left palm.	The hands remain together and make a short movement towards the signer, so that the right palm touches the chest.	affection love	1477
The left B hand is held with the palm facing right and the fingers pointing away from the signer; the right B hand is held with the palm facing left and the fingers pointing away from the signer.	The hands are held side by side in front of the body with the wrists touching the chest.	The hands move down, maintaining contact with the body, and then make a short twist apart at the wrists (so that the palms are turned down) while continuing to move down.	slender slim thin	1478
The left B hand is held with the palm facing towards the signer and the fingers pointing to the right; the right B hand is held with the palm facing towards the signer and the fingers pointing to the left.	The hands are held in front of the right shoulder; the right hand is held above the left hand.	The hands make alternate clockwise circles in the vertical plane at right angles to the signer's body, while moving down and, at the same time, away from the signer.	centuries (over the centuries) history time (over time) time (through time) tradition	1479

1480 ꁍ̆ B⊤> B⊤<ₒ ᴺᴺ·
             ⓝ
             ⓔ
             ⊤
             ᵛ

1481 ꁍ̆ B⊤> B⊤<ₒ (ⓔᴺ·
                     ⊤
                     ᵛ
                     ⊤
                     ^)

1482 ⌐⌐ Bɑ> Bɑ< ˣˣ
                  ⊥

1483 ⌐⌐ B⊤ᵛ ₁ B⊤ᵛ ˣ>ˣ

1484 ⌐⌐ B⊤>ₒ B⊤< ˚·˚
                  ˣ ˣ

 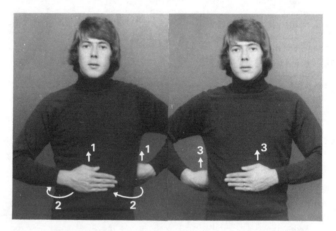

1485 Ⱶ Bᴑ⊤ Bᴑ⊤ ˣ˚
                  ⊥÷
                  ᵛ

1486 Ø B̄ᴑ⊤ ⊙ B⊤< ˂

 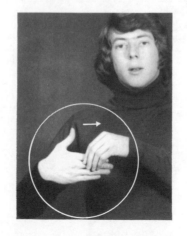

[718]

The hand is held flat with the fingers held together; the thumb is usually held against the side of the index finger.

Handshape and orientation	Location, hand arrangement and contact	Movement	Glosses	
The left B hand is held with the palm facing towards the signer and the fingers pointing to the right; the right B hand is held with the palm facing towards the signer and the fingers pointing to the left. *Non-manual features* The cheeks are puffed out.	The hands are held in front of the right shoulder.	The hands make alternate anticlockwise circles in the vertical plane at right angles to the signer's body, bending at the wrists.	age old ages bygone long ago past prehistoric prehistory time (once upon a time)	1480
The left B hand is held with the palm facing towards the signer and the fingers pointing to the right; the right B hand is held with the palm facing towards the signer and the fingers pointing to the left.	The hands are held in front of the right shoulder.	The hands make alternate anticlockwise circles in the vertical plane at right angles to the signer's body, while moving up and, at the same time, towards the signer.	historical history past time (once upon a time)	1481
The left B hand is held with the palm facing up and the fingers pointing to the right; the right B hand is held with the palm facing up and the fingers pointing to the left.	The hands are held with the sides of the little fingers touching the sides of the waist, and at an angle, so that the fingers are turned away from the signer.	The hands move away from the signer and, at the same time, towards each other.	birth birth (give birth) born	1482
Two B hands are held with the palms facing towards the signer and the fingers pointing down.	The hands are held side by side in front of the left side of the waist.	The fingertips touch the waist and then move to the right before touching the right side of the waist.	naval navy sailor	1483
The left B hand is held with the palm facing away from the signer and the fingers pointing to the right; the right B hand is held with the palm facing towards the signer and the fingers pointing to the left.	The back of the left hand is held against the signer's back; the right palm is held against the lower chest.	The hands make a short upward movement, and then change places before making another short upward movement.	naval navy sailor	1484
Two B hand are held with the palms facing down and the fingers pointing away from the signer.	The hands are held touching the sides of the waist at an angle, so that the fingers are turned down.	The hands make a short movement down, away from the signer and, at the same time, apart.	skirt	1485
The left B̄ hand is held with the palm facing down (if the hand were opened, the fingers would point away from the signer). The right B hand is held with the palm facing towards the signer and the fingers pointing to the left.	The hands are held in front of the body; the left fingers are holding the right fingers.	The hands remain together and move to the left.	guide lead leader	1486

1487 ○ Ḃ⊤< ᵛ °> [A]
       #

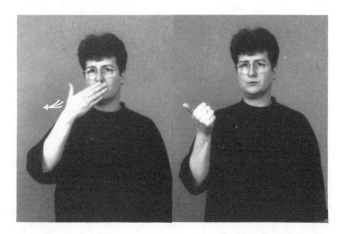

1488 ∪ Ḃ⊤< ×⊥[A] °⊥·
         ˅ ˅
         #

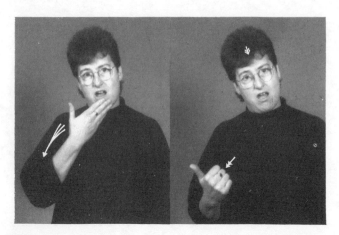

B

The hand is held flat with the fingers held together and the thumb extended.

Although Ḃ is one of the possible *variants* of **B**, it is required in some signs. Ḃ is essentially a conditional variant of **B** in that it is possible to specify the type of environment in which Ḃ rather than **B** is required. These are mainly compound signs and signs which involve contact with the extended thumb. In compounds such as **beautiful** (sign 1487), **charming** (sign 1488) and **generous** (sign 1489), the extended thumb of Ḃ anticipates the extended thumb of the handshape in the second part of the compound, in these cases Ȧ. Ḃ is also required in signs where the thumbs contact each other or some other part of the body, as in **desire** (sign 1490), **relax** (sign 1493) and **break** (sign 1495), where the tips of the extended thumbs make contact with the body.

Handshape and orientation	*Location, hand arrangement and contact*	*Movement*	*Glosses*	
The Ḃ hand is held with the palm facing towards the signer and the fingers pointing to the left.	The hand is held in front of the face.	The hand moves down, and then makes a short movement to the right while closing (forming an Ȧ hand).	beautiful beauty good looking handsome	**1487**
The Ḃ hand is held with the palm facing towards the signer and the fingers pointing to the left.	The hand is held with the fingertips touching the chin.	The hand moves down and away from the signer while closing (forming an Ȧ hand); the hand then makes a short repeated movement down and, at the same time, away from the signer.	charming nice (very nice too)	**1488**

Non-manual features   The brows are slightly furrowed, the nose is wrinkled and the mouth is open; the head nods twice as the hand moves.

1489 [] Ḃᴛ< ^{×⊥[A]}_#

1490 []ᐸ Ḃᴛ< ^{v ·}_v

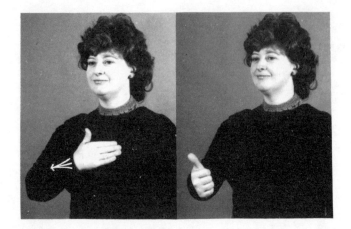

1491 B̄ᴛ> Ḃʊ⊥ ^{ω×}_ᐸ

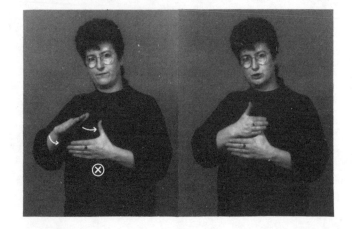

1492 B̄ᴛ> Ḃʊ⊥ ^{v×ω×}_ᐸ

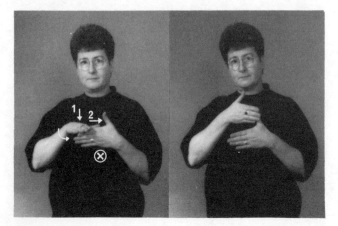

The hand is held flat with the fingers held together and the thumb extended.

Handshape and orientation	Location, hand arrangement and contact	Movement	Glosses	
The Ḃ hand is held with the palm facing towards the signer and the fingers pointing to the left.	The hand is held with the palm resting against the chest.	The hand moves away from the signer while closing (forming an Ȧ hand).	fine generous health kind kind-hearted obliging well	1489
The Ḃ hand is held with the palm facing towards the signer and the fingers pointing to the left.	The hand is held in front of the right side of the chest.	The hand moves down, brushing the side of the chest; the movement is repeated.	desire † necessary † ready *† need †¹ want †¹ wish †¹	1490

    Notes   * Regional sign.

          † This sign may be produced using a **5** hand.

$$[]^< \quad 5\top< \quad \overset{\vee}{\underset{\vee}{}} \cdot$$

          1 If the movement is not repeated, the sign produced is **need, want, wish.**

$$[]^< \quad \dot{B}\top< \quad \overset{\vee}{\underset{\vee}{}} \quad \text{or} \quad []^< \quad 5\top< \quad \overset{\vee}{\underset{\vee}{}}$$

The left Ḃ hand is held with the palm facing towards the signer and the fingers pointing to the right; the right Ḃ hand is held with the palm facing down and the fingers pointing away from the signer.	The hands are held in front of the body; the right hand is held above the left hand.	The right hand twists to the left at the wrist, so that the right fingers touch the left thumb.	first * initial original since	1491

    Notes   * This sign may be produced with the right hand moving to the left, so that the side of the hand touches the left thumb; the movement is repeated.

$$\dot{B}\top> \quad \dot{B}\text{ʊ}\bot^{(<\times)} \cdot$$

The left Ḃ hand is held with the palm facing towards the signer and the fingers pointing to the right; the right Ḃ hand is held with the palm facing down and the fingers pointing away from the signer.	The hands are held in front of the body; the right hand is held above the left hand.	The right hand moves down, so that the fingers touch the side of the left hand, and then twists to the left at the wrist, so that the fingers touch the left thumb.	account (on account of) because due to	1492

1493 [] Ḃʊ> Ḃʊ< ×ᵒ⊥

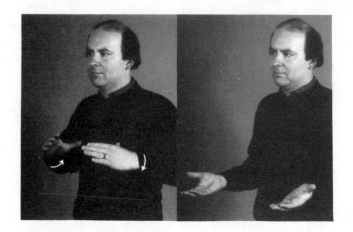

1494 [] Ḃᴛ>ᵢ Ḃᴛ< ×⊥[ÀÁ]#

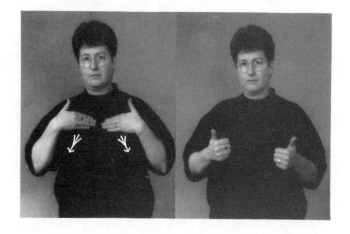

1495 ˹˺ Ḃʊ> Ḃʊ< ×

B

The hand is held flat with the fingers held together and the thumb extended.

Handshape and orientation	Location, hand arrangement and contact	Movement	Glosses	
The left ᏴB hand is held with the palm facing down and the fingers pointing to the right; the right ᏴB hand is held with the palm facing down and the fingers pointing to the left.	The hands are held with the thumb-tips touching the sides of the chest.	The hands move away from the signer while twisting at the wrists, so that the palms face up.	relax* relaxation*	1493

Notes   * This sign may be produced using one hand only.

$$] \quad \dot{B}\text{ʊ}< {}^{\times\, ᵃ}_{\perp}$$

The left ᏴB hand is held with the palm facing towards the signer and the fingers pointing to the right; the right ᏴB hand is held with the palm facing towards the signer and the fingers pointing to the left.	The hands are held side by side with the fingers resting against the chest.	The hands move away from the signer while closing (forming two Å hands).	fine* generous* health* kind* kind-hearted* obliging* well* how are you? *[1]	1494

Notes   * This sign may be produced using two ᏴB hands.

    1 If the eyebrows are raised, the sign produced is **how are you?**

$$[] \quad \dot{B}\top> \quad \dot{B}\top< {}^{\times\, \perp\, [AA]}_{\sharp}$$

The left ᏴB hand is held with the palm facing down and the fingers pointing to the right; the right ᏴB hand is held with the palm facing down and the fingers pointing to the left.	The hands are held in front of the upper chest.	The hands make a short movement towards the signer, so that the thumb-tips touch the sides of the upper chest.	break* comfortable* ease (at ease)* easy (take it easy)* holiday* leisure* relax* relaxation* rest*	1495

Non-manual features   The head is tilted to one side and the lips are pushed slightly forward.

Notes   * This sign may be produced using one hand only.

$$\ulcorner\urcorner^< \quad \dot{B}\text{ʊ}< {}^{\times}$$

1496 Ø B̂ɑ< ᵚ

1497 Ø B̂ᴥ⊥ ᵚ

1498 Ø B̂⊤< ᴖ[5] ⊥̸□

1499 Ø B̂⊥ʌ (ᴖ⊥̸)⊥

1500 ∩ B̂<ʌ □[B]ˣ

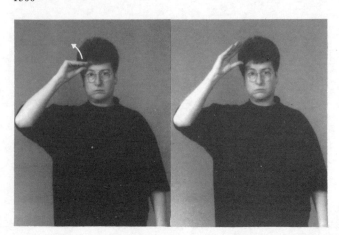

The extended fingers are held together and bent at the palm knuckles with the pad of the extended thumb touching the pads of the index and middle fingers.

B̂ has several different *classifier* functions within the productive lexicon and is used as a classifying handshape in established signs:
- it has the potential to be used as a *size and shape* classifier to represent wedge-shapes or flat-sided, pointed objects such as the beaks of large birds, as in **goose** (see *Introduction*) and **emu** (see *Introduction*);
- it has a major function as a *handling* classifier for indicating flat objects such as **frisbee** (sign 1498), **mail** (sign 1499), **bedspread** (sign 1521), **plastic** (sign 1523) and **hat** (sign 1525). The use of the B̂

hand in signs linked with the handling of money provides the basis of a large set of signs which have meanings related to money. The many examples in this section include **cash** (sign 1502), **finance** (sign 1503), **alimony** (sign 1504), **cost** (sign 1505), **bribe** (sign 1512) and **buy** (sign 1513). The B̂ handshape is also used for signs involving a crumbling action for meanings linked with crumbling or decomposition, as in **crumble** (sign 1497), **sprinkle** (sign 1497), **cremation** (sign 1514) and **ashes** (sign 1520).

Handshape and orientation	Location, hand arrangement and contact	Movement	Glosses	
The B̄ hand is held with the palm facing up (if the hand were opened, the fingers would point to the left).	The hand is held in front of the body.	The thumb rubs across the pads of the fingers.	few several some	1496
The B̄ hand is held with the palm facing down (if the hand were opened, the fingers would point away from the signer).	The hand is held in front of the body.	The thumb rubs from side to side across the pads of the fingers.	crumble* crumble a stock cube* salt*†§	1497
Notes * This sign can also be produced using an Ĥ handshape.	Ø Ĥ↶⊥ ▥		sprinkle*†§ sprinkle salt*†§	
† This sign may be produced with an F handshape.	Ø F↶⊥ ▥		sprinkle sugar* stock cube*	
§ This sign may be produced with an ⅋ handshape.	Ø ⅋↶⊥ ▥		sugar* pinch¹	
1 If an F handshape is used, the sign produced is **pinch**.	Ø F↶⊥ ▥			
The B̄ hand is held with the palm facing towards the signer (if the hand were opened, the fingers would point to the left).	The hand is held in front of the body.	The hand bends away from the signer from the wrist, while opening (forming a 5 hand).	frisbee throw* throw a frisbee* scatter¹	1498
Notes * Directional verb.				
1 If the movement is repeated several times while the hand moves to the right, the sign produced is **scatter**.	Ø B̂⊤< (ⁿ[5]·/⅄/>)			
The B̄ hand is held with the palm facing away from the signer (if the hand were opened, the fingers would point up).	The hand is held in front of the body.	The hand moves away from the signer and, at the same time, bends away from the signer at the wrist.	mail*† mail/post a letter*† post*†	1499
Notes * Directional verb.			postage†	
† This sign may be produced using an O hand which opens (forming a B̄ hand).	Ø O⊥∧ (ⁿ/⅄)[B̄]			
The B̄ hand is held with the palm facing left (if the hand were opened, the fingers would point up).	The hand is held with the thumb and index finger tips touching the side of the forehead.	The hand opens (forming a B̄ hand); the thumbtip is held against the forehead throughout.	academic bright brilliant clever	1500
Non-manual features The cheeks are puffed out.			intelligent learned smart	

1501 ⌒ B̂⊤∧ $\overset{\circ}{\top}$ ·

1502 $\overline{B\alpha\bot}$ B̂<∨ $\overset{\text{ш}}{}$ ·

1503 $\overline{B\alpha\bot}$ × B̂<∨ $\overset{\text{ш}}{\gtrless}$

1504 $\overline{B\alpha\bot}$ × B̂<∨ $\overset{\bot}{\underset{\bot}{\times}}$ ·

1505 $\overline{B\alpha\bot}$ × B̂<∨ $\overset{\wedge [\mathfrak{s}] \varrho}{\underset{\square}{\gtrless}}$

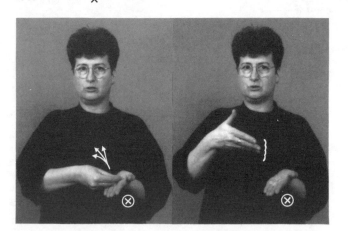

1506 B̄α⊥ × B̂<∨ $\overset{\bot [\mathfrak{s}] ·}{\underset{\square}{}}$

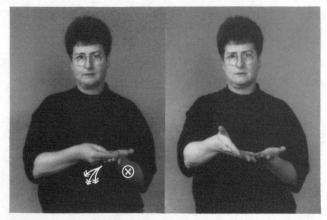

The extended fingers are held together and bent at the palm knuckles with the pad of the extended thumb touching the pads of the index and middle fingers.

Handshape and orientation	Location, hand arrangement and contact	Movement	Glosses	
The ƀ hand is held with the palm facing towards the signer (if the hand were opened, the fingers would point up).	The hand is held in front of the mouth and chin.	The hand makes two short movements towards the signer.	breakfast eat food lunch meal supper tea	1501
The left B hand is held with the palm facing up and the fingers pointing away from the signer; the right ƀ hand is held with the palm facing left (if the hand were opened, the fingers would point down).	The hands are held in front of the body; the right hand is held above the left hand.	The right thumb rubs across the pads of the right fingers twice.	cash currency finance funds money	1502
The left B hand is held with the palm facing up and the fingers pointing away from the signer; the right ƀ hand is held with the palm facing left (if the hand were opened, the fingers would point down).	The hands are held in front of the body; the right hand rests on the left palm.	The right hand moves up and to the right and, at the same time, the thumb rubs across the pads of the fingers.	finance treasurer	1503
The left B hand is held with the palm facing up and the fingers pointing away from the signer; the right ƀ hand is held with the palm facing left (if the hand were opened, the fingers would point down).	The hands are held in front of the body; the right hand rests on the left palm.	The right hand moves away from the signer, brushing the left palm; the movement is repeated.	alimony * maintenance * mortgage * payment * rent *	1504

Notes   * This sign may be produced using a right Â handshape. $\overline{\mathsf{B}\alpha\bot} \quad_\times \hat{\mathsf{A}}<\vee \; {}^{\cdot}_{\overset{\times}{\bot}}$

The left B hand is held with the palm facing up and the fingers pointing away from the signer; the right ƀ hand is held with the palm facing left (if the hand were opened, the fingers would point down).	The hands are held in front of the body; the right hand rests on the left palm.	The right hand makes a short movement up and to the right while opening (forming a 5̇ hand); the fingers then wiggle.	cost * price * how much? *[1]	1505

Notes   * This sign may be produced using one hand only. $\emptyset \quad \hat{\mathsf{B}}\alpha\bot \; {}^{\overset{\circ}{\wedge}}_{\square}{}^{[5]}\, {}_{\wp}$

         1 If non-manual features appropriate for questions are used, the sign produced is **how much?**

The left B hand is held with the palm facing up and the fingers pointing away from the signer; the right ƀ hand is held with the palm facing left (if the hand were opened, the fingers would point down).	The hands are held in front of the body; the right hand rests on the left palm.	The right hand moves away from the signer and, at the same time, opens (forming a 5 hand). The movement is repeated several times.	extravagant spendthrift wasteful spend [1]	1506

Notes   1 If the movement is not repeated, the sign produced is **spend.** $\mathsf{B}\alpha\bot \quad_\times \hat{\mathsf{B}}<\vee \; {}^{\bot}_{\square}{}^{[5]}$

1507 B̄ɑ> B̂⊤∨ ⊤×⊓⊔

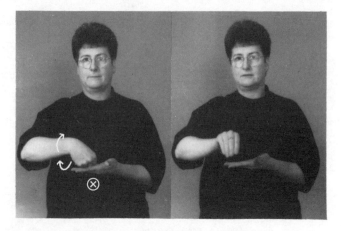

1508 B̄>⊥ ¦ B̂ɑ< ×·

1509 B̄ʊ> × B̂ɑ⊥ (⊓<∨)□ [c]∨[ḇ]#

1510 B̂>⊥ ¦× B̂ʊ⊥∨ (⊓∧∨)

1511 B̿>⊥ B̂ʊ⊥ °

1512 B̤>∧ B̂⊥∨ ⊥×

$\widehat{\mathbf{B}}$

The extended fingers are held together and bent at the palm knuckles with the pad of the extended thumb touching the pads of the index and middle fingers.

Handshape and orientation	Location, hand arrangement and contact	Movement	Glosses	
The left **B** hand is held with the palm facing up and the fingers pointing to the right; the right **B̂** hand is held with the palm facing towards the signer (if the hand were opened, the fingers would point down).	The hands are held in front of the body; the right hand rests on the left palm.	The right hand bends away from the signer from the wrist, so that the right fingers brush across the left palm.	cash deposit donate pay payment alimony [1] maintenance [1]	1507

Notes 1 If the movement is repeated, the sign produced is **alimony, maintenance.** $\overline{\text{Bɑ}>}\ \widehat{\text{B}}\text{т}\vee\ \substack{\text{п}\\\text{ι}\\\text{x}\\\text{п}}\cdot$

The left **B** hand is held with the palm facing right and the fingers pointing away from the signer; the right **B̂** hand is held with the palm facing up (if the hand were opened, the fingers would point to the left).	The hands are held side by side in front of the body.	The backs of the right fingers tap the left palm twice.	cash currency finance funds money treasurer	1508
The left **B̂** hand is held with the palm facing down; the right **B̂** hand is held with the palm facing up (if the hands were opened, the left fingers would point to the right and the right fingers would point away from the signer).	The hands are held in front of the body with the fingertips touching; the left hand is held above the right hand.	The right hand moves down while bending to the left at the wrist and, at the same time, opening (forming a **c** hand); the hand then continues to move down while closing (forming a **B̂** hand).	grapes grapes (bunch of grapes)	1509
The left **B̂** hand is held with the palm facing right; the right **B̂** hand is held with the palm facing down (if the hands were opened, the fingers would all point away from the signer).	The hands are held side by side in front of the body, with thumb and index finger tips touching.	The right hand bends up at the wrist and, at the same time, the hand moves down and towards the signer.	rip * tear * tear off *	1510

Notes * This sign may be produced using two **Â** hands. $\widehat{\text{A}}>\text{ᴛ}\ {}_{\text{ι x}}\ \widehat{\text{A}}\text{ᴐ}\text{ᴛ}\ \substack{(\text{п}\\\text{ʌ})\\\text{ᴛ}\\\vee}$

The left **B̄** hand is held with the palm facing right; the right **B̂** hand is held with the palm facing down (if the hands were opened, the fingers would all point away from the signer).	The hands are held in front of the body; the right hand is held above the left hand.	The right hand moves down, so that the right fingers are held between the left fingers and thumb.	insert put in put into	1511
The left **B̂** hand is held with the palm facing right (if the hand were opened, the fingers would point up). The right **B̂** hand is held with the palm facing away from the signer (if the hand were opened, the fingers would point down).	The hands are held in front of the body; the left hand is held above the right hand.	The right hand moves away from the signer, maintaining contact with the left hand throughout.	backhander bribe *	1512

Notes * Directional verb.

1513 Ø $\overline{Ba}$> x $\hat{B}$<v $\overset{\circ}{\vee}$

1514 Ø $\hat{Ba}$⊥ $\hat{Ba}$⊥ $\overset{\underline{w}}{\perp}$

1515 Ø $\hat{Ba}$⊥ $\hat{Ba}$⊥ $\overset{\circ}{\underset{1}{\vee}}$·

1516 Ø $\hat{Ba}$⊥ ₁ $\hat{Ba}$⊥ $\overset{w}{\cdot}$·

1517 Ø $\hat{Ba}$⊥ ₁ $\hat{Ba}$⊥ $\overset{\perp [55]}{\square}$

1518 Ø $\hat{Ba}$⊥ ₁x $\hat{Ba}$⊥ $\overset{\div [55]}{\square}$

B̂

The extended fingers are held together and bent at the palm knuckles with the pad of the extended thumb touching the pads of the index and middle fingers.

1513-1518

Handshape and orientation	Location, hand arrangement and contact	Movement	Glosses	
The left **B** hand is held with the palm facing up and the fingers pointing to the right; the right **B̂** hand is held with the palm facing left (if the hand were opened, the fingers would point down).	The hands are held in front of the body; the backs of the right fingers are held on the left palm.	The hands remain together and make a short downward movement.	buy * purchase *	1513

Notes   * This sign may also be produced using a right **Â** handshape.   Ø B̄ɑ> ˟ Â<v ˅

| Two **B̂** hands are held with the palms facing up (if the hands were opened, the fingers would all point away from the signer). | The hands are held in front of the body. | The thumbs rub across the pads of the fingers while the hands move away from the signer. | cremate
cremation
smooth * | 1514 |

Notes   * This sign may be produced using one hand only.   Ø B̂ɑ⊥ ⊥

| Two **B̂** hands are held with the palms facing up (if the hands were opened, the fingers would all point away from the signer). | The hands are held in front of the body. | The hands make a short movement down and, at the same time, away from the signer; the movement is repeated. | Greece *
Greek * | 1515 |

Notes   * This sign may be produced using one hand only.   Ø B̂ɑ⊥ ˅⊥ ·

| Two **B̂** hands are held with the palms facing up (if the hands were opened, the fingers would all point away from the signer). | The hands are held side by side in front of the body. | The thumbs rub across the pads of the fingers; the movement is repeated. | ashes *
greasy
cloth †
fabric †
material †
silk † | 1516 |

Notes   * This sign may be produced with a single movement.   Ø B̂ɑ⊥ , B̂ɑ⊥ ᵚ

       † This sign may be produced using one hand only.   Ø B̂ɑ⊥ ᵚ

| Two **B̂** hands are held with the palms facing up (if the hands were opened, the fingers would all point away from the signer). | The hands are held side by side in front of the body. | The hands move away from the signer while opening (forming two **5** hands). | give * †
provide * †
supply * †
spend¹ | 1517 |

Notes   * Directional verb.

       † This sign may be produced using one hand only.   Ø B̂ɑ⊥ ⊥[5]□

       1 If two **O** hands are used, moving away from the signer while opening (forming two **5** hands), the sign produced is **spend**.   Ø Oɑ⊥ Oɑ⊥ ⊥[55]□

| Two **B̂** hands are held with the palms facing up (if the hands were opened, the fingers would all point away from the signer). | The hands are held side by side in front of the body with the fingertips all touching. | The hands move apart and, at the same time, open (forming two **5** hands). | without | 1518 |

1519 Ø $\overline{\hat{B}}a> {}_{|}\hat{B}v\bot$ $^{×ˑˑ×}$

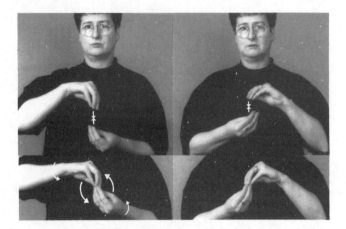

1520 Ø $\hat{B}v\bot$ $\hat{B}v\bot$ ^{ш} ˑ

1521 Ø $\hat{B}v\bot$ $\hat{B}v\bot$ $^{\overset{\dot{\bot}}{(\overset{n}{\wedge})}\overset{\circ}{v}}_{\top}$

1522 Ø $\hat{B}>v$ ${}_{|×}$ $\hat{B}<v$ $^{\overset{n\,[ss]}{\overset{\bot}{\div}}}_{\square}$

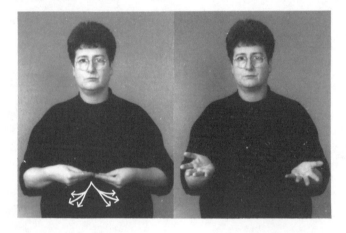

1523 Ø $\hat{B}>\bot$ $\hat{B}<\bot$ $^{\overset{n}{\pi}\wedge}$ ˑ

1524 Ø $\hat{B}>\bot$ ${}_{\pi}$ $\hat{B}<\bot$ $^{\overset{\circ}{v}}$ ˑ

The extended fingers are held together and bent at the palm knuckles with the pad of the extended thumb touching the pads of the index and middle fingers.

Handshape and orientation	Location, hand arrangement and contact	Movement	Glosses	
The left b̂ hand is held with the palm facing up; the right b̂ hand is held with the palm facing down (if the hands were opened, the left fingers would point to the right and the right fingers would point away from the signer).	The hands are held side by side in front of the body; the right hand is held higher than the left hand.	The bunched right fingertips touch the bunched left fingertips; the hands then change places and the fingertips touch again.	create creation fix make mend repair	1519
Two b̂ hands are held with the palms facing down (if the hands were opened, the fingers would all point away from the signer).	The hands are held in front of the body.	The thumbs move from side to side several times, rubbing across the pads of the fingers.	ashes earth flour powder sand soil	1520

Two b̂ hands are held with the palms facing down (if the hands were opened, the fingers would all point away from the signer).	The hands are held in front of the body.	The hands make a short movement away from the signer and then bend up at the wrists while moving towards the signer, before making a short downward movement.	bedspread
			blanket
			sheet*
			spread a bedspread/
			  blanket
			spread a sheet*
			unfold a piece
			  of material*
				1521

Notes   * This sign may also be produced using two Â hands.

$$\varnothing \quad \hat{A}_{\backslash\!o\perp} \quad \hat{A}_{\backslash\!o\perp} \;{}^{\perp}_{(\Lambda)}\!{}^{\lor}$$

The left b̂ hand is held with the palm facing right; the right b̂ hand is held with the palm facing left (if the hands were opened, the fingers would all point down).	The hands are held side by side in front of the body, with the fingertips all touching.	The hands bend away from the signer and apart from the wrists while opening (forming two **5** hands).	distribute give away give out generosity[1] largesse[1]	1522

Notes   1 If the movement is repeated, the sign produced is **generosity, largesse**.

$$\varnothing \quad \hat{B}_{>\lor} \;\;{}_{1}{\times} \quad \hat{B}_{<\lor} \;{}^{\Pi\,[55]}_{\perp}\!\cdot \atop {\div\atop\square}$$

The left b̂ hand is held with the palm facing right; the right b̂ hand is held with the palm facing left (if the hands were opened, the fingers would all point away from the signer).	The hands are held in front of the body.	The hands bend towards and away from the signer from the wrists several times alternately.	cardboard flexible plastic	1523
The left b̂ hand is held with the palm facing right; the right b̂ hand is held with the palm facing left (if the hands were opened, the fingers would all point away from the signer).	The hands are held in front of the body, with the fingertips holding each other.	The hands remain together and make two short movements down and, at the same time, away from the signer.	precious valuable value worth	1524

1525 $\overline{\cap}$ $\hat{B}_{>\wedge}$ $\hat{B}_{<\wedge}$ $\overset{\circ}{\vee}$

1526 $\cup$ $\overset{\bullet}{\int}\hat{B}_{\top\wedge}$ $_{\text{I}}$ $\overset{\bullet}{\int}\hat{B}_{\top\wedge}$ $\overset{\circ}{\underset{H}{\cap}}\sim$ ·

1527 [] $\hat{B}_{\top>}$ $\hat{B}_{\top<}$ $\overset{\times\;\vee\;[55]\;\times}{\underset{\Box}{\circ}}$

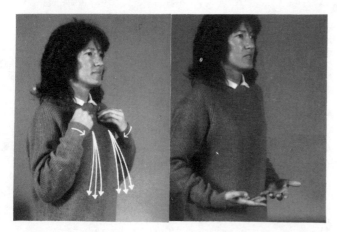

The extended fingers are held together and bent at the palm knuckles with the pad of the extended thumb touching the pads of the index and middle fingers.

Handshape and orientation	Location, hand arrangement and contact	Movement	Glosses	
The left B̂ hand is held with the palm facing right; the right B̂ hand is held with the palm facing left (if the hands were opened, the fingers would all point up).	The hands are held above the head.	The hands make a short, firm downward movement.	hat put on a hat	1525
Two B̂ hands are held with the palms facing towards the signer (if the hands were opened, the fingers would all point up).	The hands are held side by side in front of the chin.	The hands make alternate short bending movements towards and away from the signer, from the elbows.	buffet feast picnic	1526
Two B̂ hands are held with the palms facing down (if the hands were opened, the left fingers would point to the right and the right fingers would point to the left).	The hands are held against the chest.	The hands move down while opening (forming two 5 hands) and, at the same time, twisting at the wrists, so that the palms face up; the movement ends with the sides of the hands touching the waist.	blouse*	1527

Notes * This sign may be produced with the palms touching the lower chest at the end of a downward movement.

$$[] \quad \hat{B}\text{T>} \quad \hat{B}\text{T<}^{\times \underset{\square}{\vee} [55] \times}$$

1528 Ø B̿ʊ⊥ $\overset{\cap\,[\bar{\text{B}}]}{\underset{\#}{\overset{\wedge}{\perp}}}$

1529 Ø B̿⊥∧ $\overset{\circ}{\underset{\#}{\perp}}{}^{[\bar{\text{B}}]}$ ·

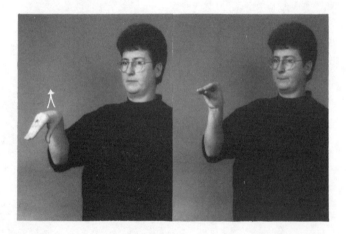

1530 $\overline{\cap}$ B̿ɑ< ${}^{\omega}{}^{\top}$

The extended fingers are held together and bent at the palm knuckles with the extended thumb held parallel to the fingers.

The main *variation* in the production of B̄ concerns the size of the gap between the extended fingers and the thumb: in signs such as **snout** (sign 1533) and **Holland** (sign 1556) the gap is relatively wide; in **cold** (sign 1535) and **Bulgaria** (sign 1540) the gap is relatively narrow.

B̄ has several different *classifier* functions within the productive lexicon and also appears as a classifying element in established signs:

– it is used as a *size and shape* classifier to represent objects with two parallel, flat surfaces such as the beaks of large birds such as swans or emus. The B̄ handshape may be used in contrast with Ḡ or H̄ to indicate different degrees of width;

– it is used as a *tracing size and shape* classifier to trace the shape or outline of narrow objects, as in **radiator** (sign 1551). In conjunction with B̂ it is used to indicate the shape of pointed objects, triangular, or wedge-shaped, as in **snout** (sign 1533), **beard** (sign 1537) and **slice of melon** (sign 1550). It is also used in a comparable way to indicate a layer, rim, strip or chunk of something, as in **layer of custard** (see *Introduction*); it can be used as an alternative to Ḡ or H̄ for this purpose;

– it is used as a *handling* classifier to indicate relatively narrow objects such as a trilby hat, material, cardboard and a wad of money as in the signs **hat** (sign 1530), **handkerchief** (sign 1535), **calendar** (sign 1547) and **salary** (sign 1558);

– it is used as an *instrumental* classifier to represent implements, tools or utensils with parallel extensions such as a large clamp or vice;

– it is used as a *touch* classifier to indicate the touching of soft or springy materials, as in **soft** (sign 1553) and **spongy** (sign 1553);

– the gap between fingers and thumb may be used to indicate *extent*, usually to indicate relative depth or shallowness.

B̄ also has a range of *symbolic* functions within the lexicon. The B̄ handshape forms the first part of a handshape pair in which the open B̄ hand closes to a B̂ handshape. This handshape pair has the generalised meanings of 'copy' or 'absorb'. As such it occurs in a range of signs which are linked with these meanings. Examples include **absorb** (sign 1532), **acquire** (sign 1532), **copy** (sign 1545) and **photocopy** (sign 1545). This meaning can also be expressed by the 5̄ → B̂ handshape pair. The same handshape pairs can also express meanings related to 'disappearance' (see *Introduction*), as in **zoom** (sign 1534), **disappear** (sign 1555) and **vanish** (sign 1555): see the *Introduction* for further discussion of these symbolic functions.

Handshape and orientation	Location, hand arrangement and contact	Movement	Glosses	
The B̄ hand is held with the palm facing down (if the hand were opened, the fingers would point away from the signer).	The hand is held in front of the body.	The hand bends up at the wrist while the fingers and thumb close (forming a B̂ hand).	pick* pick up*	**1528**
Notes * This sign may be produced using an F̄ handshape.		Ø F̄ ᴐ⊥ ⊥/∧/n [B̂] #		
The B̄ hand is held with the palm facing away from the signer (if the hand were opened, the fingers would point up).	The hand is held in front of the body.	The hand makes a short movement away from the signer and, at the same time, the fingers and thumb close (forming a B̂ hand); the movement is repeated several times.	chatter chatterbox moan nag talkative talk on and on	**1529**
The B̄ hand is held with the palm facing up (if the hand were opened, the fingers would point to the left).	The hand is held higher than and in front of the head.	The hand twists towards the signer at the wrist; the movement ends with the palm facing towards the signer.	hat put on a hat	**1530**

1531 ∩ B̿<ʌ #ᵀ [ʙ̌]

1532 ∩ B̿<⊥ #ᵀ [ʙ̌]

1533 ◌ B̿<ʌ #⊥ [ʙ̌]

B

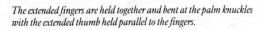*The extended fingers are held together and bent at the palm knuckles with the extended thumb held parallel to the fingers.*

Handshape and orientation	Location, hand arrangement and contact	Movement	Glosses	
The b̄ hand is held with the palm facing left (if the hand were opened, the fingers would point up).	The hand is held in front of the forehead.	The hand bends to the right at the wrist while moving down and, at the same time, closing (forming a b̂ hand).	experience experienced expert skilled	1531
The b̄ hand is held with the palm facing left (if the hand were opened, the fingers would point away from the signer).	The hand is held with the fingers in front of the forehead.	The hand moves towards the signer while closing (forming a b̂ hand).	absorb acquire acquisition learn * pick up * study *	1532

Notes   * This sign may be produced with a repeated movement.   ∩ B̿<⊥ ᵀ [b̂] · ♯

The b̄ hand is held with the palm facing left (if the hand were opened, the fingers would point up).	The hand is held in front of the face.	The hand moves away from the signer and, at the same time, the fingers and thumb close (forming a b̂ hand).	fox snout train	1533

1534 ○ B̄<ʌ ⊥̇[B̄]
                #

1535 ⊔ B̿⊤< ⱽ̊[B̄]·
                   #

1536 ⊔ B̿⊤< ×⊥̊[B̄] ∩[5]
                   ≥   ↓
                   #   ⱽ
                        □

1537 ∪ B̿ɑ< ⱽ[B̄]
                 ×
                 ⱽ
                 #

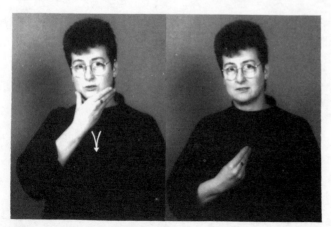

[742]

B̄

The extended fingers are held together and bent at the palm knuckles
with the extended thumb held parallel to the fingers.

1534-1537

Handshape and orientation	Location, hand arrangement and contact	Movement	Glosses	
The b̄ hand is held with the palm facing left (if the hand were opened, the fingers would point up).	The hand is held in front of the face.	The hand moves sharply away from the signer and, at the same time, the fingers and thumb close (forming a b̂ hand).	dash* disappear at speed* rush off* vanish* zoom*	1534

Non-manual features   The lips are rounded, and close at the end of the movement with a sharp intake of breath.

Notes   * This sign can also be produced using a ĉ hand.   ↻   Ḡ<∧   ⊥̇ [ĉ]
    #

The b̄ hand is held with the palm facing towards the signer (if the hand were opened, the fingers would point to the left).	The hand is held in front of the nose.	The hand makes a short downward movement and, at the same time, the fingers and thumb close (forming a b̂ hand); the movement is repeated.	cold* flu* handkerchief* hanky* tissue*	1535

Notes   * This sign may be produced using a ĉ handshape.   ⊔   Ḡ⊤<   v̊ [ĉ] ·
    #

The b̄ hand is held with the palm facing towards the signer (if the hand were opened, the fingers would point to the left).	The hand is held with the fingertips touching the nose.	The hand makes a short movement away from the signer and to the right, while the fingers and thumb close (forming a b̂ hand); the hand then bends sharply down and away from the signer at the wrist, while opening (forming a 5 hand).	could not care less* couldn't care less* do not care* don't care* do not give a damn* don't give a damn*	1536

Non-manual features   The brows are slightly furrowed, the nose is wrinkled and the tongue tip protrudes slightly between the top teeth and the lower lip.

Notes   * Directional verb.

The b̄ hand is held with the palm facing up (if the hand were opened, the fingers would point to the left).	The hand is held with the fingers and thumb at either side of the chin.	The hand moves down while closing (forming a b̂ hand), so that the fingers and thumb brush the sides of the chin.	beard Christmas Father Christmas Santa Claus	1537

1538 ∪ B̿α< ^{v [ɓ]}ˣᵥ# // B̄ɤ> × j̇5<∧ °ₓₒw.

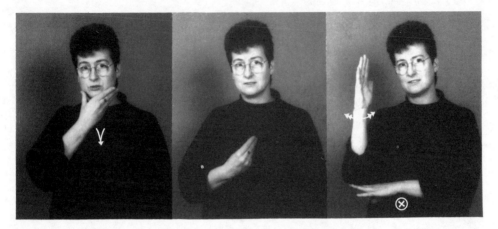

1539 ∪ B̿α< ^{v°v[ɓ]}⊥⊥ˣ#   1540 ⌐ B̿<∧ ^{n[ɓ]}>v#   1541 ⌐ B̿<∧ ^{#[ɓ]}·

1542 ∏ B̿α< ^{×v[ɓ]}⊥#

The extended fingers are held together and bent at the palm knuckles with the extended thumb held parallel to the fingers.

Handshape and orientation	Location, hand arrangement and contact	Movement	Glosses	
The b̄ hand is held with the palm facing up (if the hand were opened, the fingers would point to the left).	The hand is held with the fingers and thumb at either side of the chin.	The hand moves down while closing (forming a b̂ hand), so that the fingers and thumb brush the sides of the chin.	Christmas tree *	1538
The left B hand is held with the palm facing down and the fingers pointing to the right; the right 5 hand is held with the palm facing left and the fingers pointing up.	The left hand is held in front of the body; the right elbow rests on the back of the left hand.	The right hand makes several short twisting movements from side to side at the wrist.		

Notes   * The first part of this sign may be replaced with sign 1304. This is a regional sign.

$$ 5v\!> \;\; Bv\!\perp \;\; {}^{T}_{\times}{}^{\mathring{\Lambda}\,[\Lambda]}_{\#}\;{}^{\mathring{v}}\!\times \quad /\!/ $$
$$ Bv\!> \;_{\times}\; \sqrt{}\,5\!<\!\Lambda \;\; {}^{\mathring{\omega}}_{z}. \quad /\!/ $$

The b̄ hand is held with the palm facing up (if the hand were opened, the fingers would point to the left).	The hand is held with the fingers and thumb touching the sides of the chin.	The hand moves down and, at the same time, away from the signer, maintaining contact with the chin, and then continues to make a short movement down and away from the signer while closing (forming a b̂ hand).	male * man * masculine *	1539

Notes   * This sign may be produced with a repeated movement. $\cup \;\; \bar{\bar{B}}\alpha\!<\!\left({}^{\mathring{v}}_{\times}{}^{\mathring{v}}_{\#}{}^{[\hat{B}]}\right)\cdot$

The b̄ hand is held with the palm facing left (if the hand were opened, the fingers would point up).	The hand is held with the fingers in front of the mouth and chin.	The hand bends to the right at the wrist and, at the same time, moves down while the fingers and thumb come together (forming a b̂ hand).	Bulgaria Bulgarian moustache (handlebar moustache)	1540
The b̄ hand is held with the palm facing left (if the hand were opened, the fingers would point up).	The hand is held beside the mouth.	The thumb and fingers close (forming a b̂ hand); the movement is repeated.	biscuit * lemon *	1541

Notes   * Regional sign.

The b̄ hand is held with the palm facing up (if the hand were opened, the fingers would point to the left).	The hand is held at an angle, so that the thumb and fingers are touching the neck.	The hand moves down and away from the signer while closing (forming a b̂ hand).	dry fancy hunger hungry wish covet [1] craving [1] desire [1] lust [1] thirst *[2] thirsty *[2]	1542

Notes   * This sign may be produced with the lips stretched.

     1 If the tongue protrudes slightly and the mouth is open, the sign produced is **covet, craving, desire, lust.**

     2 If the tongue protrudes between the teeth, the sign produced is **thirst, thirsty.**

1543 ˀ˥ B̄<∧ #T [ʙ̌] x

1544 ŏ̄ B̄ơ⊥ (x ∧° #[ʙ̌]) ·

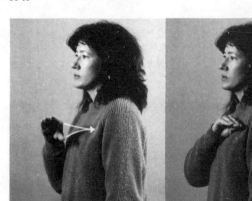

1545 B̲ơ> x ꞊B̄ɑ< #V̇ [ʙ̌] ·

1546 B⊤∧ ⊙ ꞊B̄<⊥ xˇ

1547 B⊤> ꞊B̄⊥∧ᵩ (∩ [ʙ̌] ⊥ # ∧ ⊥3<) ·

The extended fingers are held together and bent at the palm knuckles with the extended thumb held parallel to the fingers.

Handshape and orientation	Location, hand arrangement and contact	Movement	Glosses	
The b̄ hand is held with the palm facing left (if the hand were opened, the fingers would point up).	The hand is held in front of the left side of the upper chest.	The hand moves towards the signer and, at the same time, the fingers and thumb close (forming a b̂ hand); the movement ends with the side of the hand held against the left side of the upper chest.	win*	1543

Notes   * Regional sign.

The b̄ hand is held with the palm facing down (if the hand were opened, the fingers would point away from the signer).	The left arm is positioned across the body; the right hand is held with the fingertips touching the back of the left hand.	The right hand makes a short upward movement and, at the same time, the fingers and thumb come together (forming a b̂ hand); the movement is repeated.	cousin Swede Sweden Swedish	1544
The left B hand is held with the palm facing down and the fingers pointing to the right; the right b̄ hand is held with the palm facing up (if the hand were opened, the fingers would point to the left).	The hands are held in front of the body; the right hand is held below the left hand with the right thumb and fingertips touching the left palm.	The right hand makes a firm downward movement while closing (forming a b̂ hand); the movement is repeated.	copies duplicate* photocopier photocopy Xerox Xeroxes copy*[1]	1545

Notes   * This sign may also be produced with the orientation changed (so that the left hand is held with the palm facing up and the right hand held with the palm facing down): the left hand is held below the right hand and the right hand moves up while closing (forming a b̂ hand). The sign produced is **copy** *(see entries 1 and 2 in the English section)*, **duplicate**.

$$B \perp \wedge_{\varphi} \times \bar{\bar{B}} \top < \overset{\dot{\perp}}{\#} {}^{[\hat{B}]} \cdot$$

1   If the orientation is changed, so that the left hand is held with the palm facing away from the signer and the fingers pointing up, and the right hand is held with the palm facing towards the signer (if the hand were opened, the fingers would point to the left), the sign produced is **copy** *(see entry 3 in the English section).*

$$\overline{} \atop B \alpha > \times \bar{\bar{B}} \sigma \perp \overset{\wedge}{\#} {}^{[\hat{B}]} \cdot$$

The left B hand is held with the palm facing towards the signer and the fingers pointing up; the right b̄ hand is held with the palm facing left (if the hand were opened, the fingers would point away from the signer).	The hands are held in front of the body; the left hand is held between the right thumb and fingers.	The right hand moves down, with the right thumb maintaining contact with the left palm, and the right fingers maintaining contact with the back of the left hand throughout.	glove put on a glove	1546
The left B hand is held with the palm facing towards the signer and the fingers pointing to the right; the right b̄ hand is held with the palm facing away from the signer (if the hand were opened, the fingers would point up).	The hands are held in front of the body; the right hand is held nearer to the signer than the left hand.	The right hand closes (forming a b̂ hand) while bending away from the signer at the wrist; the hand then moves up and away from the signer while twisting at the wrist, so that the palm faces left.	calender notepad turn over a page of a calender/notepad	1547

1548 $\bar{\bar{B}}>\!\perp \odot \bar{\bar{B}}\alpha\!\perp {}^{\vee[\check{\mathtt{B}}]}_{\#}$

1549 $\emptyset \ \bar{\bar{B}}\alpha\!\perp \bar{\bar{B}}\alpha\!\perp {}^{[\check{\mathtt{B}}\check{\mathtt{B}}]}_{\#} \cdot$

1550 $\emptyset \ \bar{\bar{B}}\alpha\!\perp {}_{|\mathsf{x}} \bar{\bar{B}}\alpha\!\perp {}^{\div[\check{\mathtt{B}}\check{\mathtt{B}}]}_{\substack{3\mathsf{x}\\\#}}$

1551 $\emptyset \ \bar{\bar{B}}\mathsf{v}\!\perp {}_{|} \bar{\bar{B}}\mathsf{v}\!\perp {}^{\div3\mathsf{x}}_{\vee}$

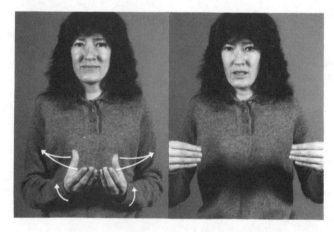

1552 $\emptyset \ \bar{\bar{B}}\!\perp\!\wedge \bar{\bar{B}}\!\perp\!\wedge {}^{[\check{\mathtt{B}}\check{\mathtt{B}}]}_{\#}$

1553 $\emptyset \ \bar{\bar{B}}\!\perp\!\vee \bar{\bar{B}}\!\perp\!\vee {}^{\overset{\circ}{\vee}[\check{\mathtt{B}}\check{\mathtt{B}}]}_{\#} \cdot$

The extended fingers are held together and bent at the palm knuckles with the extended thumb held parallel to the fingers.

Handshape and orientation	Location, hand arrangement and contact	Movement	Glosses	
The left B̄ hand is held with the palm facing left; the right B̄ hand is held with the palm facing up (if the hands were opened, the fingers would all point away from the signer).	The hands are held in front of the body; the right fingers and thumb are held between the left fingers and thumb.	The right hand moves down and, at the same time, the thumb and fingers close (forming a B̂ hand).	**drown** **sink** **solve** **forget** [1] **lost for words** [1] disappear [2] vanish [2]	1548

Notes   1   If the lips are rounded, the sign produced is **forget, lost for words.**

2   This sign may be used as the second part of a compound sign (see the first part of sign 333 for the first part) meaning **disappear, vanish.**

Ц G<∧ ×⊥ⱽ // B̄>⊥ ⊙ B̄ɑ⊥ ⱽ[ɓ] #

| Two B̄ hands are held with the palms facing up (if the hands were opened, the fingers would all point away from the signer). | The hands are held in front of the body. | The hands close (forming two B̂ hands); the movement is repeated. | damp*
 moist*
 wet* | 1549 |

Notes   *   This sign can be produced using one hand only.

∅ B̄ɑ⊥ #[ɓ]·

| Two B̄ hands are held with the palms facing up (if the hands were opened, the fingers would all point away from the signer). | The hands are held side by side in front of the body with the sides of the little fingers touching. | The hands move apart while twisting at the wrists, so that the palms face towards each other; at the same time, the hands close (forming two B̂ hands). | melon <br> slice of melon/ watermelon <br> watermelon | 1550 |

| Two B̄ hands are held with the palms facing down (if the hands were opened, the fingers would all point away from the signer). | The hands are held side by side in front of the body. | The hands move apart, and then twist at the wrists (so that the palms face towards each other) while moving down. | radiator | 1551 |

| Two B̄ hands are held with the palms facing away from the signer (if the hands were opened, the fingers would all point up). | The hands are held in front of the body. | The hands close (forming two B̂ hands). | cease <br> end <br> finish <br> stop <br> conclude*
 conclusion* | 1552 |

Notes   *   This sign may be produced with the hands moving apart, before moving down and towards each other, while closing (forming two B̂ hands).

∅ B̄⊥∧ ǀ B̄⊥∧ ÷×[ɓ] #

| Two B̄ hands are held with the palms facing away from the signer (if the hands were opened, the fingers would all point down). | The hands are held in front of the body. | The fingers and thumb of each hand come together (forming two B̂ hands) and, at the same time, the hands move down; the movement is repeated several times. | soft*†
 spongy*
 springy* | 1553 |

Notes   *   The following notes apply to all glosses:

This sign may be produced using one hand only.

∅ B̄⊥∨ ᵒᵛ[ɓ]·

This sign may be produced with the orientation changed, so that the palms face away from the signer (if the hands were opened, the fingers would all point up).

∅ B̄⊥∧ B̄⊥∧ ᵒᵛ[ɓɓ]· or ∅ B̄⊥∧ ᵒᵛ[ɓ]·

† This sign may be produced without the downward movements of the hands.

∅ B̄⊥∨ B̄⊥∨ #[ɓɓ]· or ∅ B̄⊥∨ #[ɓ]·

∅ B̄⊥∧ B̄⊥∧ #[ɓɓ]· or ∅ B̄⊥∧ #[ɓ]·

1554 $\varnothing$ $\bar{\bar{B}}$>$\vee$ $\bar{\bar{B}}$<$\vee$ $^{\#[\bar{B}\bar{B}]}$

1555 $\varnothing$ $\bar{\bar{B}}$>$\perp$ $_{|\times}$ $\bar{\bar{B}}$<$\perp$ $^{\div\,[\bar{B}\bar{B}]}_{\substack{\circ\\\#}}$

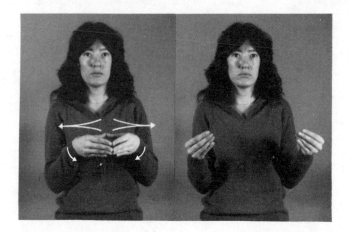

1556 $\circlearrowright$ $\bar{\bar{B}}$v$\wedge$ $\bar{\bar{B}}$v$\wedge$ $^{\div\,[\bar{B}\bar{B}]}_{\#}$

1557 $\ulcorner \urcorner$ $\bar{\bar{B}}$⊤> $\bar{\bar{B}}$⊤< $^{\times\,\overset{\circ}{\underset{\#}{\perp}}\,[\bar{B}\bar{B}]\cdot}$

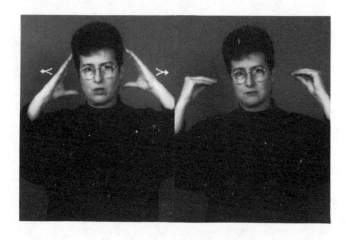

1558 $\varnothing$ $\left(\bar{B}a\perp {}_{\times} \bar{\bar{B}}\perp\wedge {}^{\#[\bar{B}]} \right)^{\top}$

1559 $\varnothing$ $\left(\bar{B}a{>}_{\wp} \bar{\bar{B}}\perp\wedge {}^{\top\,[\bar{B}]\,\times\,\cdot}_{\#} \right)^{<}$

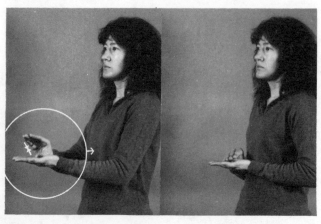

B *The extended fingers are held together and bent at the palm knuckles with the extended thumb held parallel to the fingers.*

Handshape and orientation	Location, hand arrangement and contact	Movement	Glosses	
The left b̄ hand is held with the palm facing right; the right b̄ hand is held with the palm facing left (if the hands were opened, the fingers would all point down).	The hands are held in front of the body.	The fingers and thumbs close (forming two b̂ hands).	flat puncture [1]	1554

Non-manual features The cheeks are slightly puffed out and then the mouth opens a little with a puff of air.

Notes 1 This sign may be produced as the second part of a compound sign meaning **puncture** (see 397 Note 1 for the first part of the sign).

$$^2 5 >\!\perp \text{ , } G \top < \overset{\circ}{} \text{ // } \varnothing \text{ } \bar{\bar{B}} >\!\vee \text{ } \bar{\bar{B}} <\!\vee \text{ }^{\#\,[\hat{b}\,\hat{b}]}$$

The left b̄ hand is held with the palm facing right; the right b̄ hand is held with the palm facing left (if the hands were opened, the fingers would all point away from the signer).	The hands are held in front of the body with the fingertips and the thumbtips touching.	The hands move apart while twisting at the wrists, so that the palms face up and, at the same time, closing (forming two b̂ hands).	disappear * empty * finished * gone * invisible * miss * vanish * worn-out *	1555

Notes * This sign can be produced using one hand only.

$$\varnothing \text{ } \bar{\bar{B}} <\!\perp \text{ } \overset{>\,[\hat{b}]}{\underset{\#}{\scriptstyle\circ}}$$

Two b̄ hands are held with the palms facing down (if the hands were opened, the fingers would all point up).	The hands are held at either side of the head.	The hands move apart and, at the same time, the thumbs and fingers close (forming two b̂ hands).	Dutch Holland Netherlands	1556
Two b̄ hands are held with the palms facing towards the signer (if the hands were opened, the left fingers would point to the right and the right fingers would point to the left).	The hands are held with the fingertips touching the upper chest.	The hands make a short movement down and away from the signer and, at the same time, the fingers and thumbs close (forming two b̂ hands); the movement is repeated.	fur hairy	1557
The left b hand is held with the palm facing up and the fingers pointing away from the signer; the right b hand is held with the palm facing away from the signer (if the hand were opened, the fingers would point up).	The hands are held in front of the body; the back of the right thumb is held on the left palm.	The hands remain together and move towards the signer while the right hand closes (forming a b̂ hand).	pay salary wage withdrawal of money	1558
The left b hand is held with the palm facing up and the fingers pointing to the right; the right b̄ hand is held with the palm facing away from the signer (if the hand were opened, the fingers would point up).	The hands are held in front of the body; the left hand is held lower and nearer to the signer than the right hand.	The right hand moves towards the signer while closing (forming a b̂ hand); the movement ends with the right hand resting on the left palm, and is then repeated several times with both hands moving to the left throughout.	accumulate accumulation collate collation collect collection gather	1559

1560 Ø B̈ↄ> ᵛᵥᵂ꜀

1561 Ø B̈⊥∧ (ᵈ⊥ᵢ)

1562 Ø B̈⊥∧ ꜀ᵢ˙

1563 Ø B̈⊥∧ (ᵈ⊥ᵢ)˙

1564 Ø ↗B̈⊥∧ ꜀ᵢ˙

1565 Ø B̈<⊥ ᵃᵈ˙

The hand is held flat with the fingers held together and bent at the palm knuckles.

B̈ is a relatively frequent handshape within BSL. In some uses, it may be used as a variant of B, although B̈ is normally required in most of the examples cited in this section.

B̈ has several different *classifier* functions in the productive lexicon and is used as a classifying element in established signs:

- it is used as a *size and shape* classifier to represent flat surfaces such as **ceiling** (sign 1567) and **roof** (sign 1567) and relatively narrow, flat objects such as wings in **angel** (sign 1635) and a shelf, as in **ledge** (sign 1637). In these examples the focus is on the flat surface of the fingers. B̈ is typically used rather than B when the surface referred to is regarded as high, from the signer's perspective. In other signs, the focus may be on the bent nature of the hands, as in the bowls of scales in **weigh** (sign 1630) and the curved surfaces of a yacht's sail;
- it is used as a *tracing size and shape* classifier to indicate the outline and/or shape of objects with smooth, but often curved surfaces, as in **sink** (sign 1628) and a globe in **global** (sign 1638)
- it is used as a *handling* classifier to indicate the handling of curved items such as a rugby ball in **rugby** (sign 1589); two-handed forms are used to indicate the handling of something vulnerable or delicate, such as a small animal, or for the action of holding water or snow in

the hands, see **snowball** (sign 1631);
- it is used as an *instrumental* classifier to indicate implements, tools or utensils with a flat surface such as a the blade of a spade in **dig** (sign 1565) or to indicate the curved blades of a plough;
- it is used as a *touch* classifier to indicate the action of tapping either literally or metaphorically, as in **ask** (sign 1562) and **remind** (sign 1562). It is also used for scraping or scratching actions, especially those of animals, as in **ape** (sign 1651);
- it may be used to indicate *extent*, particularly in relation to height, as in **big** (sign 1571), **gigantic** (sign 1573) and **little** (sign 1574). Two-handed forms may indicate the extent of flat surfaces, such as the length of a shelf.

B̈ also has a *deictic* (pointing) function in signs such as **outside** (sign 1563), **abroad** (sign 1564) and **north** (sign 1571).

B̈ occurs in several symbolic functions within the lexicon (see *Introduction*).

B̈ expresses the right hand component of the letter z in the British manual alphabet. As such it occurs in initial letter handshape signs, as in the second part of **New Zealand** (sign 1612).

Handshape and orientation	Location, hand arrangement and contact	Movement	Glosses	
The B̈ hand is held with the palm facing down (if the hand were opened, the fingers would point to the left).	The hand is held in front of the body.	The hand moves down and to the left and, at the same time, the fingers straighten at the palm knuckles; the hand then moves to the left.	chute slide slide down a chute/slide	1560
The B̈ hand is held with the palm facing away from the signer (if the hand were opened, the fingers would point up).	The hand is held in front of the body.	The hand bends away from the signer at the wrist while moving away from the signer.	home	1561
The B̈ hand is held with the palm facing away from the signer (if the hand were opened, the fingers would point up).	The hand is held in front of the body.	The hand makes a short repeated movement away from the signer.	apply* ask* get the attention of * remind* tell*	1562
Notes * Directional verb.				
The B̈ hand is held with the palm facing away from the signer (if the hand were opened, the fingers would point up).	The hand is held in front of the body.	The hand bends away from the signer at the wrist while moving away from the signer; the movement is repeated.	exterior external outdoor outdoors outside	1563
The B̈ hand is held with the palm facing away from the signer (if the hand were opened, the fingers would point up).	The hand is held in front of the body.	The hand makes two short movements away from the signer, bending from the elbow.	abroad exterior external foreign foreigner outdoor outdoors outside overseas pester[1]	1564
Notes 1 If the movement is firm, and the mouth is open with the tongue tip resting on the lower lip, the sign produced is **pester**. This is a directional verb. Ø √B̈⊥∧				
The B̈ hand is held with the palm facing left (if the hand were opened, the fingers would point away from the signer).	The hand is held in front of the body.	The hand moves away from the signer while twisting at the wrist, so that the palm faces up; the movement is repeated.	dig dig a hole garden gardener	1565

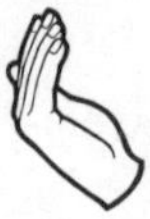

1566 Ø B̈<⊥ ᵅ□ [B]

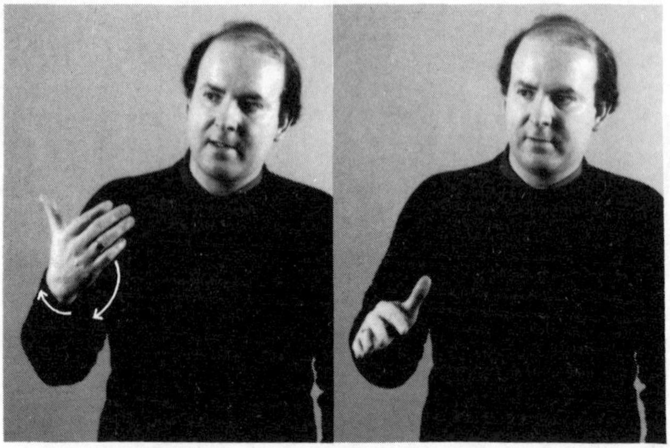

1567 ⁻∩ B̈<∧ ⊥

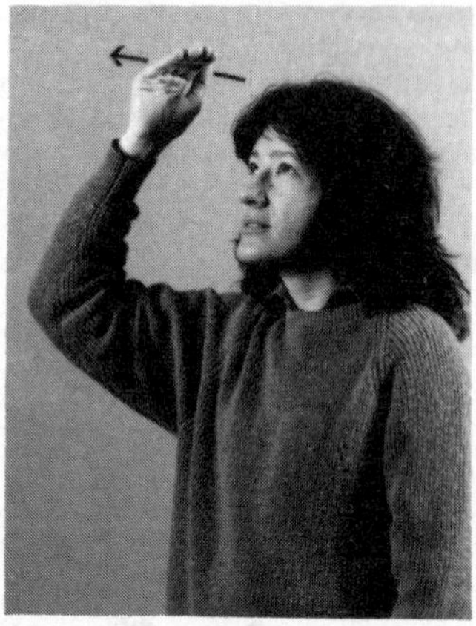

1568 ∩ B̈⊤∧ ×(ᴰ⊥) ˅⊥

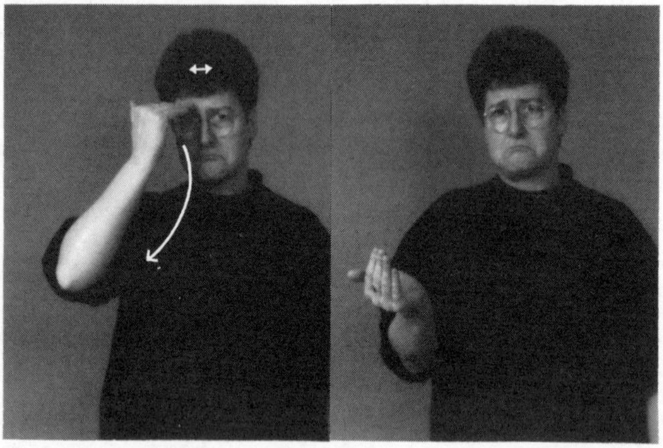

1569 ∩ B̈<∧ ×·

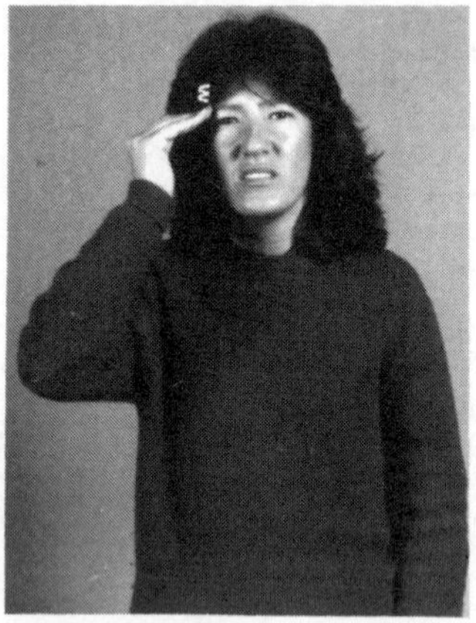

1570 ∩ B̈<∧ °@< ·

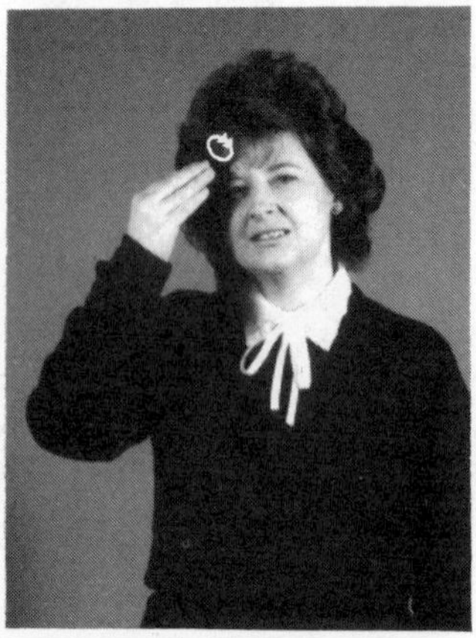

1571 ◌ B̈<∧ ^̇

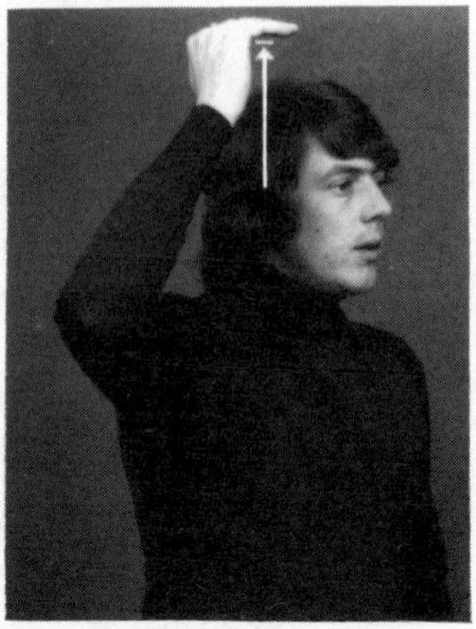

1572 ◌ B̈<∧ °^⊥

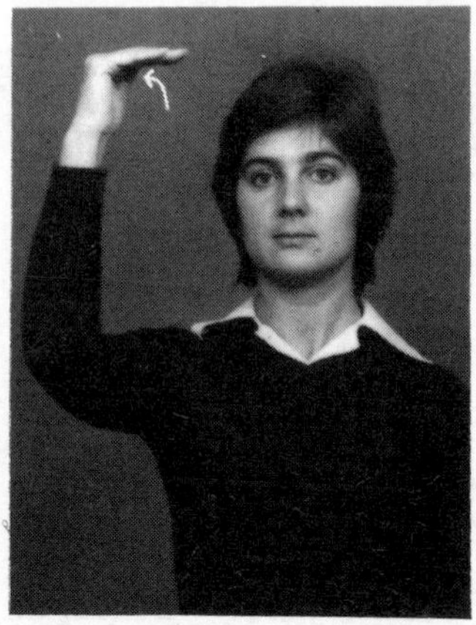

The hand is held flat with the fingers held together and bent at the palm knuckles.

Handshape and orientation	Location, hand arrangement and contact	Movement	Glosses	
The ꞵ̈ hand is held with the palm facing left (if the hand were opened, the fingers would point away from the signer).	The hand is held in front of the body.	The hand twists at the wrist, so that the palm faces down, while opening (forming a ꞵ hand).	depart go away leave been (have been)[1] did[1] done[1] finished[1] have[1]	1566

Notes   1 If the lips are pressed together and the mouth sharply opens, the sign produced is **did, done, finished, have, have been.**

The ꞵ̈ hand is held with the palm facing left (if the hand were opened, the fingers would point up).	The hand is held above the head.	The hand moves away from the signer.	ceiling roof shelter	1567
The ꞵ̈ hand is held with the palm facing towards the signer (if the hand were opened, the fingers would point up).	The hand is held with the fingertips touching the forehead.	The hand bends away from the signer at the wrist while moving down and away from the signer.	do not know don't know	1568

Non-manual features   The corners of the mouth are turned down, and the head shakes slightly.

The ꞵ̈ hand is held with the palm facing left (if the hand were opened, the fingers would point up).	The hand is held with the fingers beside the forehead.	The fingertips tap the side of the forehead twice.	disturbed headache mad mental migraine mind mother* unstable head[1]	1569

Notes   * This sign may also be produced using a ꞶM hand.

    1 If the movement is changed, with the fingers making short bending movements at the palm knuckles, so that the fingertips tap the side of the forehead twice, the sign produced is **head.**

∩   ꞶMᴖᴐʌ   ˣ ·

∩   B<ʌ   (°ₘˣ)·

The ꞵ̈ hand is held with the palm facing left (if the hand were opened, the fingers would point up).	The hand is held with the fingers beside the forehead at an angle, so that the palm is turned towards the signer.	The hand makes small anticlockwise circles in the vertical plane parallel to the signer's body.	fantasise fantasy ignorant imaginary imagination imagine unaware dream[1] day-dream[2] oblivious[3]	1570

Notes   1 If the eyes are closed, the sign produced is **dream.**

    2 If the eyegaze is directed upwards and the mouth is open, the sign produced is **day-dream.**

    3 If the mouth is open and the tongue protrudes slightly, the sign produced is **oblivious.**

The ꞵ̈ hand is held with the palm facing left (if the hand were opened, the fingers would point up).	The hand is held beside the head.	The hand moves firmly upwards.	big huge north tall	1571
The ꞵ̈ hand is held with the palm facing left (if the hand were opened, the fingers would point up).	The hand is held beside the head.	The hand makes a short movement up and, at the same time, away from the signer.	adult big* giant grown-up huge* north tall	1572

Notes   * This sign may be produced with the cheeks puffed out.

1573 ○ B̈<∧ ∧↓°

1574 ○ B̈<∧ ˅·

1575 ○ B̈<∧ ×∧×

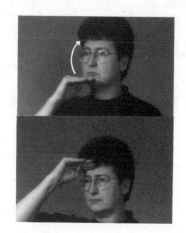

1576 ○ B̈<∧ ×∧×

1577 ○ B̈<∧ ×˅×

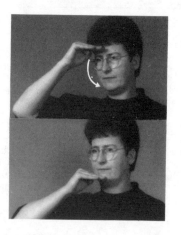

1578 Ӟ B̈<∧ ×·

1579 ○ B̈ɑ> ×

The hand is held flat with the fingers held together and bent at the palm knuckles.

Handshape and orientation	Location, hand arrangement and contact	Movement	Glosses	
The b̈ hand is held with the palm facing left (if the hand were opened, the fingers would point up).	The hand is held beside the head.	The hand moves up and then makes a short, firm movement away from the signer.	giant high (very high) tall (very tall) gigantic[1] towering[1]	1573

Non-manual features   The eyegaze is directed in line with the hand.

    Notes   1 If the cheeks are puffed out, the sign produced is **gigantic, towering.**

The b̈ hand is held with the palm facing left (if the hand were opened, the fingers would point up).	The hand is held beside the head.	The hand moves firmly downwards; the movement is repeated.	little * short * small * wee *	1574

    Notes   * This sign may be produced with a single movement.   Ö B̈<ʌ ˇ

The b̈ hand is held with the palm facing left (if the hand were opened, the fingers would point up).	The hand is held in front of the chin.	The side of the index finger touches the chin and then the hand moves up before the side of the index finger touches the forehead.	stranger summer	1575
The b̈ hand is held with the palm facing left (if the hand were opened, the fingers would point up).	The hand is held with the fingers beside the chin.	The fingertips touch the chin and then the hand moves up before the fingertips touch the right side of the forehead.	hotel	1576
The b̈ hand is held with the palm facing left (if the hand were opened, the fingers would point up).	The hand is held in front of the forehead.	The side of the index finger touches the forehead; the hand moves down and then the side of the index finger touches the chin.	evening * night *	1577

    Notes   * Regional sign.

The b̈ hand is held with the palm facing left (if the hand were opened, the fingers would point up).	The hand is held with the fingers beside the right cheek.	The fingertips tap the cheek twice.	blanket * famous * pretend *	1578

    Notes   * Regional sign.

The b̈ hand is held with the palm facing up (if the hand were opened, the fingers would point to the right).	The hand is held with the side of the index finger against the side of the mouth.	No movement.	whisper	1579

Non-manual features   The lips are rounded.

1580 ⊃ B̈ᴛʌ ×⊥ᵥ // ‾Bɑ⊥ Bʊ< ᵉᐸ⊤ₓ

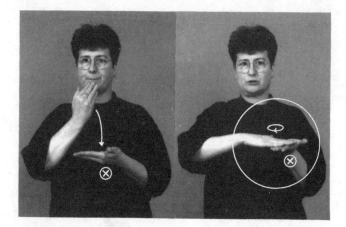

1581 ∪ B̈ᴛʌ ˣ·

1582 ∪ B̈ᴛʌ ᵒₓ³ᵒ

1583 ⊻ B̈ᴛʌ ᵒ⊥ₓ·⊥

1584 ⊻ ꜀̇B̈ᴛʌ ×ᴰ⊥

1585 ⊻ B̈<ʌ ×·

B̈

The hand is held flat with the fingers held together and bent at the palm knuckles.

Handshape and orientation	Location, hand arrangement and contact	Movement	Glosses	
The b̈ hand is held with the palm facing towards the signer (if the hand were opened, the fingers would point up).	The hand is held with the fingertips touching the chin.	The hand moves down and away from the signer while opening (forming a B hand).	absolve apologise apology excuse forgive pardon	1580
The left B hand is held with the palm facing up and the fingers pointing away from the signer; the right B hand is held with the palm facing down and the fingers pointing to the left.	The hands are held in front of the body; the right fingers rest on the left palm.	The right hand makes an anti-clockwise circle in the horizontal plane; the right fingers maintain contact with the left palm throughout.		
The b̈ hand is held with the palm facing towards the signer (if the hand were opened, the fingers would point up).	The hand is held with the fingers in front of the chin.	The fingertips tap the chin several times.	dab hand easy no problem water off a duck's back	1581

Non-manual features   The tongue protrudes between the top teeth and the lower lip and the head is tilted to one side.

The b̈ hand is held with the palm facing towards the signer (if the hand were opened, the fingers would point up).	The hand is held in front of the chin.	The fingers bend at the palm knuckles, so that the fingertips brush the chin; the movement is repeated.	use* useful*	1582

Notes   * Regional sign.

The b̈ hand is held with the palm facing towards the signer (if the hand were opened, the fingers would point up).	The hand is held with the fingertips under the chin.	The hand makes a short movement away from the signer, so that the backs of the fingertips brush the chin; the movement is repeated.	abundance abundant adequate ample enough plenty sufficient	1583

Non-manual features   The mouth is closed and the lips are pushed slightly forward.

The b̈ hand is held with the palm facing towards the signer (if the hand were opened, the fingers would point up).	The hand is held with the backs of the fingertips touching the chin.	The hand moves away from the singer and down, bending from the elbow, so that the palm faces up.	awful fed up sick	1584

Non-manual features   The corners of the mouth are turned down.

The b̈ hand is held with the palm facing left (if the hand were opened, the fingers would point up).	The hand is held beneath the chin.	The backs of the fingers tap the chin twice.	fed up*	1585

Non-manual features   The nose is wrinkled.

Notes   * This sign can also be produced with a single firm upward movement, ending with the backs of the fingers held against the chin.

∪ B̈<∧ ˙∧×

1586 Π B̈⊤∧ ⊸³⊣ˣ³⊣

1587 ⌐Ĭ B̈⊤∧ (°ᵥ⊤ˣ) ·

1588 ⌐Ĭ˂ B̈⊤˂ ᵅ

1589]˂ ᵢ̇B̈α˂ ̂˟ₓ°

1590 Ā⊤>ₚ ˟ B̈α⊥ ˟˂ᵛ@

1591 A>⊥ₚ ₁ B̈˂⊥ ˟·

1592 A>⊥ₚ ˟ B̈˂⊥ ⊥

The hand is held flat with the fingers held together and bent at the palm knuckles.

Handshape and orientation	Location, hand arrangement and contact	Movement	Glosses	
The **B̈** hand is held with the palm facing towards the signer (if the hand were opened, the fingers would point up).	The hand is held beside the neck.	The hand twists firmly away from the signer from the wrist, so that the fingertips brush the side of the neck.	behead decapitate execute	1586
The **B̈** hand is held with the palm facing towards the signer (if the hand were opened, the fingers would point up).	The hand is held above the right shoulder.	The hand makes a short movement down and, at the same time, towards the signer, so that the fingertips touch the shoulder; the movement is repeated.	back	1587
The **B̈** hand is held with the palm facing towards the signer (if the hand were opened, the fingers would point to the left).	The hand is held with the fingertips against the side of the upper chest.	The hand twists at the wrist, so that the palm faces up; the fingers are held against the chest throughout.	exhausted * † tired * † weak * hurt * 1	1588

Non-manual features   The cheeks puff out and the head tilts to one side.

Notes   * Regional sign.

† This sign may be produced using two hands.

1 If the fingers are held against the centre of the chest, the lips are rounded and the brows are slightly furrowed, the sign produced is **hurt**.

$$[] \ddot{B}\top> \ddot{B}\top< \overset{\times}{\alpha}$$

$$[] \ddot{B}\top< \overset{\times}{\alpha}$$

The **B̈** hand is held with the palm facing up (if the hand were opened, the fingers would point to the left).	The hand is held with the fingers resting against the side of the body, and the elbow is held away from the body.	The hand makes a short upward movement, maintaining contact with the side of the body throughout.	rugby rugby player	1589
The left **A** hand is held with the palm facing towards the signer (if the hand were opened, the fingers would point to the right). The right **B̈** hand is held with the palm facing up (if the hand were opened, the fingers would point away from the signer).	The hands are held in front of the body; the left hand is held higher and nearer to the signer than the right hand, with the right fingers resting against the back of the left hand.	The right hand makes an anti-clockwise circle in the vertical plane parallel to the signer's body, maintaining contact with the left hand throughout.	Asian Saturday *	1590

Notes   * Regional sign.

The left **A** hand is held with the palm facing right; the right **B̈** hand is held with the palm facing left (if the hands were opened, the fingers would all point away from the signer).	The hands are held side by side in front of the body; the left hand is held nearer to the signer than the right hand.	The right fingers tap the left knuckles twice.	more	1591
The left **A** hand is held with the palm facing right; the right **B̈** hand is held with the palm facing left (if the hands were opened, the fingers would all point away from the signer).	The hands are held in front of the body; the left hand is held nearer to the signer than the right hand, with the right fingers resting against the backs of the left fingers.	The right hand moves away from the signer.	further * more *	1592

Notes   * This sign may also be produced with a left **B̈** hand.

$$\ddot{B}>\bot_{\varphi} \times \ddot{B}<\bot^{\ \bot}$$

1593 G>∧ × B̈<∧ₒ $^{\overset{N.}{×}}$

1594 B̄a⊥ ¦ B̄a⊥ $^{(\overset{ω}{<})×}$

1595 B̄a⊥ ∫B̈<∧ $^{\overset{n\ ×}{<}}$

1596 B̄a⊥ ¦ B̈<∧ $^{×}$

1597 B̄a> B̈a⊥ₒ $^{\overset{m\ ×}{\underset{⊥}{V}}}$

1598 B̄a> × B̈ɒ⊥ $^{\overset{×\ ·}{\underset{H}{n}}}$

The hand is held flat with the fingers held together and bent at the palm knuckles.

Handshape and orientation	Location, hand arrangement and contact	Movement	Glosses	
The left G hand is held with the palm facing right; the right B̈ hand is held with the palm facing left (if the hands were opened, the fingers would all point up).	The hands are held in front of the body; the side of the right little finger is held against the side of the left index finger.	The right hand moves up and down several times, maintaining contact with the left index finger throughout.	league	1593
The left B hand is held with the palm facing up and the fingers pointing away from the signer; the right B̈ hand is held with the palm facing up (if the hand were opened, the fingers would point away from the signer).	The hands are held side by side in front of the body; the right hand is held higher than the left hand.	The right hand twists to the left from the wrist while moving to the left; the movement ends with the fingertips touching the left palm.	add additional extra increase supplement supplementary	1594
The left B hand is held with the palm facing up and the fingers pointing away from the signer; the right B̈ hand is held with the palm facing left (if the hand were opened, the fingers would point up).	The hands are held in front of the body; the right hand is held higher than the left hand.	The right hand moves down and to the left, bending from the elbow; the movement ends with the right fingertips touching the left palm.	arrival arrive attend get somewhere reach	1595
The left B hand is held with the palm facing up and the fingers pointing away from the signer; the right B̈ hand is held with the palm facing left (if the hand were opened, the fingers would point up).	The hands are held side by side in front of the body; the right hand is held higher than the left hand.	The right fingertips touch the left palm.	touch † note *[1] note (make a note) *[1] paper (put on paper) *[1] record *[1]	1596

Notes   * This sign can be produced using one hand only.

         † The right hand is located as appropriate.

         1 If the right handshape is changed to a ß handshape, the sign produced is **make a note, note, put on paper, record.**

$$\varnothing \quad \hat{B}\perp\wedge \; \overset{\text{n}}{\text{v}}$$

$$\overline{B\alpha\perp} \; , \; \hat{B}<\wedge \; ^{\times}$$

The left B hand is held with the palm facing up and the fingers pointing to the right; the right B̈ hand is held with the palm facing up (if the hand were opened, the fingers would point away from the signer).	The hands are held in front of the body; the right hand is held higher and nearer to the signer than the left hand.	The right hand makes a short movement down and away from the signer, while the fingers straighten at the palm knuckles; the movement ends with the back of the right hand touching the left palm.	bet gamble[1] proposal[2] propose[2]	1597

Notes   1 If the movement is repeated, the sign produced is **gamble.**

$$\overline{B\alpha>} \; \overset{..}{B}\alpha\perp_{\rho} \; \overset{\text{m} \times \cdot}{\underset{\perp}{\text{v}}}$$

         2 If the hands move away from the signer throughout, the sign produced is **proposal, propose.**

$$\varnothing \left(\overline{B\alpha>} \; \overset{..}{B}\alpha\perp_{\rho} \; \overset{\text{m} \times}{\underset{\perp}{\text{v}}} \right)^{\perp}$$

The left B hand is held with the palm facing up and the fingers pointing to the right; the right B̈ hand is held with the palm facing down (if the hand were opened, the fingers would point away from the signer).	The hands are held in front of the body; the right fingertips are held on the left palm.	The right hand bends towards and away from the signer from the wrist several times; the right fingertips are held on the left palm throughout.	cheese *	1598

Notes   * This sign may be produced with the right hand twisting several times from side to side from the wrist.

$$\overline{B\alpha>} \; _{\times} \; \overset{..}{B}\upsilon\perp \; \overset{\times \cdot}{\underset{\text{z}}{\text{w}}}$$

1599 $\overline{B}$ᗩ> $\ddot{B}$<⊥ $\substack{x \circ \circ x \\ x \wedge \vee x \\ m}$

1600 $\overline{B}$ᗩ>₁ $\ddot{B}$<⊥ $\binom{\circ}{v}_{x}^{<}$

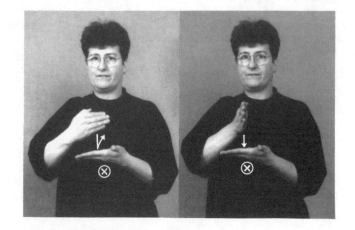

1601 $\overline{B}$ᗝ⊥ x $\ddot{B}$ᗝ⊥ $\substack{m \\ \bot}$

1602 $\overline{B}$ᗝ⊥ x $\ddot{B}$<∧ $\substack{@ \\ <⊥ \\ x}$

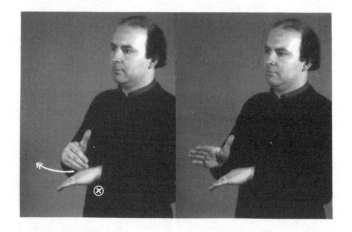

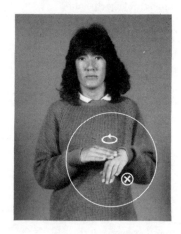

1603 $\overline{B}$ᗝ>₁ $\ddot{B}$ᗝ∧ $\substack{< x}$

B̈ *The hand is held flat with the fingers held together and bent at the palm knuckles.*

Handshape and orientation	Location, hand arrangement and contact	Movement	Glosses	
The left B hand is held with the palm facing up and the fingers pointing to the right; the right B̈ hand is held with the palm facing left (if the hand were opened, the fingers would point away from the signer).	The hands are held in front of the body; the right hand is held above the left hand.	The right hand moves down, so that the side of the hand touches the left palm; the right hand then makes a short upward movement while the fingers straighten at the palm knuckles; the hand finally moves down again to touch the left palm.	aspect divide divide up division features partition partly parts portions sections share share out shares split	1599
The left B hand is held with the palm facing up and the fingers pointing to the right; the right B̈ hand is held with the palm facing left (if the hand were opened, the fingers would point away from the signer).	The hands are held side by side in front of the body; the right hand is held higher than the left hand.	The right hand twists down and, at the same time, to the left from the wrist; the movement is repeated several times, with the hand moving upwards throughout.	exaggerate exaggeration pile it on	1600

Non-manual features   The tongue protrudes between the teeth.

The left B hand is held with the palm facing down and the fingers pointing away from the signer; the right B̈ hand is held with the palm facing down (if the hand were opened, the fingers would point away from the signer).	The hands are held in front of the body; the right fingertips rest on the back of the left hand.	The right hand moves away from the signer while the fingers straighten at the palm knuckles.	does not matter * doesn't matter * do not care * don't care * do not mind * don't mind * ignore * neglect * never mind * not bothered * pay no attention * take no notice *	1601

Notes   * Directional verb.

The left B hand is held with the palm facing down and the fingers pointing away from the signer; the right B̈ hand is held with the palm facing left (if the hand were opened, the fingers would point up).	The hands are held in front of the body; the right fingers rest on the back of the left hand.	The right hand makes an anti-clockwise circle in the horizontal plane, maintaining contact with the back of the left hand throughout.	Asian bald blue * purple ¹ bare ² birthday suit ² naked ² nude ² nudist ²	1602

Notes   * Regional sign.

1 This sign may be used as the second part of a compound sign meaning **purple** (see 348 for the first part of the sign).

2 This sign may be used as the second part of a compound sign meaning **bare, birthday suit, naked, nude, nudist** (see 1081 Note 2 for the first part of the sign).

| The left B hand is held with the palm facing down and the fingers pointing to the right; the right B̈ hand is held with the palm facing down (if the hand were opened, the fingers would point up). | The hands are held side by side in front of the body; the right hand is held higher than the left hand, and at an angle, so that the palm is turned away from the signer. | The right hand moves to the left, moving over the left hand until the heel of the right hand touches the left wrist. | cover
cover up | 1603 |

1604 $\overline{B}$ʊ> $\ddot{B}$ʊ⊥ ×·

1605 $\overline{B}$ʊ> $\ddot{B}$ʊ⊥ ×ᵃ

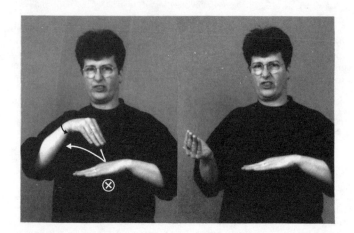

1606 $\underline{B}$ʊ> $\ddot{B}$ʊ⊥ᵩ ⁰⊥·

1607 Bʊ> $\ddot{B}$ʊ⊥ᵩ ᵐ⊥ᵥ

1608 $\overline{B}$ʊ> $\ddot{B}$⊥ʌᵩ ⁽ᵧ̣⁾⊥

1609 $\overline{B}$ʊ> √$\ddot{B}$⊥ʌᵩ ⁰⊥×·

1610 $\underline{B}$⊤> $\ddot{B}$ᵅ⊥ᵩ ^×^

Handshape and orientation	Location, hand arrangement and contact	Movement	Glosses	
The left B hand is held with the palm facing down and the fingers pointing to the right; the right B̈ hand is held with the palm facing down (if the hand were opened, the fingers would point away from the signer).	The hands are held in front of the body; the right hand is held above the left hand.	The right fingertips tap the back of the left hand twice.	bother* naughty* nuisance* pest* pester* trouble* troublesome*	1604

Notes * This sign may be produced with the right fingertips tapping the left forearm.

| The left B hand is held with the palm facing down and the fingers pointing to the right; the right B̈ hand is held with the palm facing down (if the hand were opened, the fingers would point away from the signer). | The hands are held in front of the body; the right hand is held above the left hand. | The right fingertips touch the back of the left hand and then the right hand twists at the wrist, so that the palm faces up. | does not matter doesn't matter do not care don't care do not mind don't mind never mind not bothered | 1605 |

Non-manual features The nose is wrinkled and the tongue tip protrudes between the teeth.

| The left B hand is held with the palm facing down and the fingers pointing to the right; the right B̈ hand is held with the palm facing down (if the hand were opened, the fingers would point away from the signer). | The hands are held in front of the body; the right hand is held lower and nearer to the signer than the left hand. | The right hand makes two short movements away from the signer. | indoor indoors inside internal | 1606 |

| The left B hand is held with the palm facing down and the fingers pointing to the right; the right B̈ hand is held with the palm facing down (if the hand were opened, the fingers would point away from the signer). | The hands are held in front of the body; the right hand is held nearer to the signer than the left hand. | The right hand moves down and away from the signer while straightening at the palm knuckles (forming a B hand). | enter entrance entry go in go into go under internal visit* | 1607 |

Notes * Directional verb.

| The left B hand is held with the palm facing down and the fingers pointing to the right; the right B̈ hand is held with the palm facing away from the signer (if the hand were opened, the fingers would point up). | The hands are held in front of the body; the right hand is held higher and nearer to the signer than the left hand. | The right hand moves away from the signer while bending away from the signer from the wrist. | go over | 1608 |

| The left B hand is held with the palm facing down and the fingers pointing to the right; the right B̈ hand is held with the palm facing away from the signer (if the hand were opened, the fingers would point up). | The hands are held in front of the body; the right hand is held higher and nearer to the signer than the left hand. | The right arm makes a short movement away from the signer, so that the front of the right forearm taps the side of the left hand; the movement is repeated. | abroad exterior external foreign foreigner outdoor outdoors outside   overseas | 1609 |

| The left B hand is held with the palm facing towards the signer and the fingers pointing to the right; the right B̈ hand is held with the palm facing up (if the hand were opened, the fingers would point away from the signer). | The hands are held in front of the body; the right hand is held lower and nearer to the signer than the left hand. | The right hand moves up, so that the backs of the right fingers brush the left palm. | fashion* fashionable* fresh† latest* modern* new | 1610 |

Notes * This sign may be produced with a repeated movement.

B⊤> B̈ɑ⊥ₚ $\overset{\wedge}{\underset{\wedge}{\times}}$ ·

† This sign may be produced with the right hand opening (forming a 5 hand) while moving up.

B⊤> B̈ɑ⊥ₚ $\overset{\wedge [5]}{\underset{\square}{\times}}$

1611 $\overline{B}\top> \times \ddot{B}\perp \wedge_{9} \hat{\perp}$

1612 $\underline{B}>\perp \mid \ddot{B}a< \overset{\wedge}{\overset{\times}{\wedge}} \mathbin{/\!/} B>\perp \mid \ddot{B}<\perp \overset{\circ}{<}^{\times}$

1613 $\overline{\overline{B}}>\perp \mid \ddot{B}a\perp \overset{\circ\circ}{<}$

1614 $\overline{\overline{B}}>\perp \ddot{B}\mho\perp \overset{\circ}{\cdot}$

1615 $\overline{B}a> \ddot{B}\mho\perp \overset{\times}{\cdot}$

1616 $\ddot{B}a> \mid \ddot{B}\mho< {}^{>}$

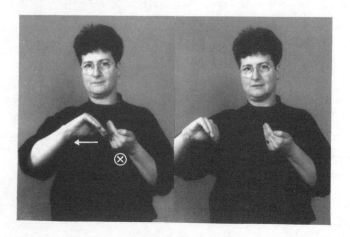

Handshape and orientation	Location, hand arrangement and contact	Movement	Glosses	
The left **в** hand is held with the palm facing towards the signer and the fingers pointing to the right; the right **ʙ̈** hand is held with the palm facing away from the signer (if the hand were opened, the fingers would point up).	The hands are held in front of the body; the right hand is held nearer to the signer than the left hand, with the right palm touching the left index finger.	The right hand moves up and, at the same time, away from the signer.	ahead beyond future prospective	1611
The left **в** hand is held with the palm facing right and the fingers pointing away from the signer; the right **ʙ̈** hand is held with the palm facing up (if the hand were opened, the fingers would point to the left).	The hands are held side by side in front of the body; the left hand is held higher than the right hand.	The right hand moves up, so that the backs of the right fingers brush across the left palm.	New Zealand New Zealander	1612
The left **в** hand is held with the palm facing right and the fingers pointing away from the signer; the right **ʙ̈** hand is held with the palm facing left (if the hand were opened, the fingers would point away from the signer).	The hands are held side by side in front of the body.	The right hand makes a short movement to the left, so that the right fingertips touch the left palm.		
The left **ʙ̄** hand is held with the palm facing right; the right **ʙ̈** hand is held with the palm facing up (if the hands were opened, the fingers would all point away from the signer).	The hands are held side by side in front of the body.	The right hand twists at the wrist, so that the palm faces down, while moving to the left; the movement ends with the right fingers held between the left thumb and fingers.	fit in * include * insert * involve * join * join in * join up * member * participant * participate *	1613

Notes * This sign may also be produced with the right hand held nearer to the signer than the left hand (with the palm facing away from the signer) and bending away from the signer from the wrist; the movement ends with the right fingers held between the left thumb and fingers.

$$\bar{\bar{\text{B}}}{>}{\perp} \quad \ddot{\text{B}}{\perp}{\wedge}_{\varphi} \quad {}^{\cap\,\circ}_{\perp}$$

The left **ʙ̄** hand is held with the palm facing right; the right **ʙ̈** hand is held with the palm facing down (if the hands were opened, the fingers would all point away from the signer).	The hands are held in front of the body; the right hand is held above the left hand.	The right hand moves down, so that the right fingers are held between the left thumb and fingers; the movement is repeated.	contains contents inside internal in [1] include [1] insert [1] into [1]	1614

Notes 1 If the movement is not repeated, the sign produced is **in, include, insert, into.**

$$\bar{\bar{\text{B}}}{>}{\perp} \quad \ddot{\text{B}}{\upsilon}{\perp} \quad {}^{\circ}$$

The left **ʙ̈** hand is held with the palm facing up; the right **ʙ̈** hand is held with the palm facing down (if the hands were opened, the left fingers would point to the right and the right fingers would point away from the signer).	The hands are held in front of the body; the right hand is held above the left hand.	The right hand taps the left hand twice.	keep treasure [1]	1615

Notes 1 If the shoulders are hunched, the sign produced is **treasure.**

The left **ʙ̈** hand is held with the palm facing up; the right **ʙ̈** hand is held with the palm facing down (if the hands were opened, the left fingers would point to the right and the right fingers would point to the left).	The hands are held side by side in front of the body.	The right hand moves to the right.	apart detach exclude isolate separate separation	1616

1617 $\underline{\ddot{B}}{>}\wedge \;|\; \ddot{B}{<}\wedge \;^{\wedge \times}$

1618 $\ddot{B}{>}\wedge_{\varphi} \;\times\; \ddot{B}{<}\wedge \;^{\perp}$

1619 $\ddot{B}{>}\perp_{\varphi} \;|\; \ddot{B}{<}\perp \;^{\overset{\circ}{\top}}$

1620 $\ddot{B}{>}\perp_{\varphi} \;\times\; \ddot{B}{<}\perp \;^{(\overset{\wedge}{\underset{\perp}{\vee}})}$

1621 $\varnothing \;\overline{\ddot{B}a}{>} \;\times\; \ddot{B}{<}\perp \;^{\top}$

1622 $\varnothing \;\underline{B}{<}\vee \;|\; \ddot{B}a{<} \;^{@\mathcal{N}\cdot}_{\overset{\top}{<}}$

1623 $\varnothing \;\ddot{B}a\perp \;\ddot{B}a\perp \;^{m\cdot}$

The hand is held flat with the fingers held together and bent at the palm knuckles.

Handshape and orientation	Location, hand arrangement and contact	Movement	Glosses	
The left B̈ hand is held with the palm facing right; the right B̈ hand is held with the palm facing left (if the hands were opened, the fingers would all point up).	The hands are held side by side in front of the body; the left hand is held higher than the right hand.	The right hand moves up until the back of the right hand touches the left palm.	fill fill up full full up	1617
The left B̈ hand is held with the palm facing right; the right B̈ hand is held with the palm facing left (if the hands were opened, the fingers would all point up).	The hands are held in front of the body with the side of the right index finger touching the side of the left little finger.	The right hand moves away from the signer.	draw equal equality equivalent even fair fairness flat level same	1618
The left B̈ hand is held with the palm facing right; the right B̈ hand is held with the palm facing left (if the hands were opened, the fingers would all point away from the signer).	The hands are held side by side in front of the body; the left hand is held nearer to the signer than the right hand.	The right hand makes a short movement towards the signer.	approach close near short	1619
The left B̈ hand is held with the palm facing right; the right B̈ hand is held with the palm facing left (if the hands were opened, the fingers would all point away from the signer).	The hands are held in front of the body; the right fingers rest against the backs of the left fingers.	The right hand moves away from the signer in an arc.	beyond exceed extend extension extreme further	1620
The left B hand is held with the palm facing up and the fingers pointing to the right; the right B̈ hand is held with the palm facing left (if the hand were opened, the fingers would point away from the signer).	The hands are held in front of the body; the right hand is held on the left palm.	The hands remain together and move towards the signer.	redeemer redemption rescue salvage saviour save up [1] save [2]	1621

Notes 1 If the left hand remains still and the right hand moves towards the signer repeatedly, brushing across the left palm, the sign produced is **save up**.

$$\overline{}\ Ba>_{9}\ \ddot{B}<\perp\ \overset{T\ \cdot}{\underset{T}{\times}}$$

2 If the left hand remains still and the right hand moves sharply towards the signer, brushing across the left palm, the sign produced is **save** (*see entry 1 in the English section*).

$$\overline{}\ Ba>_{9}\ \ddot{B}<\perp\ \overset{\cdot}{\underset{T}{T\!\times}}$$

The left B hand is held with the palm facing left and the fingers pointing down; the right B̈ hand is held with the palm facing up (if the hand were opened, the fingers would point to the left).	The hands are held side by side in front of the body; the left hand is held higher than the right hand.	The hands make alternate anti-clockwise circles in the horizontal plane.	blend blender mingle mix mixed mixed up washing machine (top loading) [1]	1622

Notes 1 If the right B hand is held above the left B̈ hand and the hands make alternate clockwise circles in the horizontal plane, the sign produced is **washing machine (top loading)**.

$$\emptyset\ \ \overline{\ddot{B}}a>_{|}\ B>v\ \overset{@N\cdot}{\underset{>}{\perp}}$$

Two B̈ hands are held with the palms facing up (if the hands were opened, the fingers would all point away from the signer).	The hands are held in front of the body.	The fingers bend towards the signer at the palm knuckles twice.	invitation welcome *	1623

Notes * This sign may be produced using one hand only.

$$\emptyset\ \ \ddot{B}a\perp\ \overset{m\cdot}{}$$

1624 Ø B̈a⊥ B̈a⊥ ^⋅

1625 Ø B̈a⊥ B̈a⊥ ˇ⋅

1626 Ø B̈a⊥ B̈a⊥ ⌃ᵛ
‹

1627 Ø B̈a⊥ ¦ B̈a⊥ ᵐᵖ

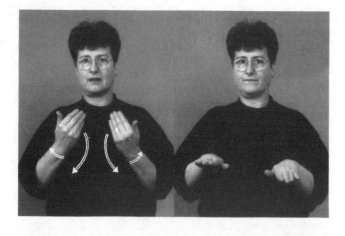

1628 Ø B̈a⊥ ¦ B̈a⊥ ÷ω
x
‹

1629 Ø B̈a⊥ ¦ B̈a⊥ ÷ω // Ø A‹v ᵛ⋅
x
‹ //

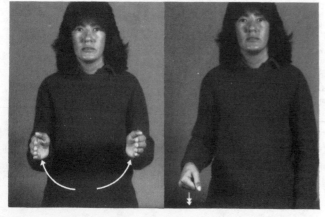

1630 Ø B̈a⊥ ¦ B̈a⊥ ᴧᴧ⋅

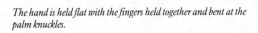

Ё

The hand is held flat with the fingers held together and bent at the palm knuckles.

Handshape and orientation	Location, hand arrangement and contact	Movement	Glosses	
Two Ё hands are held with the palms facing up (if the hands were opened, the fingers would all point away from the signer).	The hands are held in front of the body at an angle, so that the palms are turned away from the signer.	The hands make two short upward movements.	light*	1624

Notes * This sign may be produced using one hand only.

Ø Ёɑ⊥ ^.

Two Ё hands are held with the palms facing up (if the hands were opened, the fingers would all point away from the signer).	The hands are held in front of the body at an angle, so that the palms are turned away from the signer.	The hands make two short downward movements.	now* nowadays* present* today* immediately[1] once (at once)[1] right now[1]	1625

Notes * This sign may be produced using one hand only.

1 If the movement is sharp and not repeated, the sign produced is **at once, immediately, right now**.

Ø Ёɑ⊥ ˇ.

Ø Ёɑ⊥ Ёɑ⊥ ˇ

Two Ё hands are held with the palms facing up (if the hands were opened, the fingers would all point away from the signer).	The hands are held in front of the body at an angle, so that the palms are turned away from the signer.	The hands move to the left in an arc.	deliver*† hand over*† offload*† pass on*† pass to*† carry*[1]	1626

Notes * Directional verb.

†This sign can be produced using one hand only.

1 If the movement is changed, so that the hands make several short up and down movements while moving to the left, the sign produced is **carry**.

Ø Ёɑ⊥ ˇ

Ø Ёɑ⊥ Ёɑ⊥ (ˇ.) or Ø Ёɑ⊥ (ˇ.)

Two Ё hands are held with the palms facing up (if the hands were opened, the fingers would all point away from the signer).	The hands are held side by side in front of the body.	The hands turn over sharply, so that the palms face down and, at the same time, the fingers straighten at the palm knuckles.	leave left	1627
Two Ё hands are held with the palms facing up (if the hands were opened, the fingers would all point away from the signer).	The hands are held in front of the body at an angle, so that the palms are turned away from the signer.	The hands move apart and then up, while twisting at the wrists, so that the palms face towards each other.	basin bowl sink tub washbasin	1628
Two Ё hands are held with the palms facing up (if the hands were opened, the fingers would all point away from the signer).	The hands are held side by side in front of the body.	The hands move apart and then up, while twisting at the wrists, so that the palms face towards each other.	basket carry a basket	1629
The A hand is held with the palm facing left (if the hand were opened, the fingers would point down).	The hand is held at the side of the body.	The hand makes two short downward movements.		
Two Ё hands are held with the palms facing up (if the hands were opened, the fingers would all point away from the signer).	The hands are held in front of the body at an angle, so that the palms are turned away from the signer.	The hands move up and down alternately; the movement is repeated.	balance scales weigh weight weigh up	1630

1631 Ø B̄a> B̈ɒ⊥ ˣˑˣ

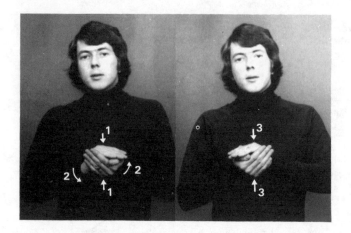

1632 Ø B̈ɒ⊥ B̈ɒ⊥ ⸰⊤

1633 Ø B̈ɒ⊥ B̈ɒ⊥ �ᵛˑ

1634 Ø B̈ɒ> ₁ₓ B̈ɒ< ÷

1635 Ø B̈⊥∧ B̈⊥∧ ᵐˑ

1636 Ø B̄⊥∧ ₁ B̈⊥∧ ⁽∧î⁾∾ˑ

1637 Ø B̈⊥∧ ₁ B̈⊥∧ ÷

The hand is held flat with the fingers held together and bent at the palm knuckles.

Handshape and orientation	Location, hand arrangement and contact	Movement	Glosses	
The left B̈ hand is held with the palm facing up; the right B̈ hand is held with the palm facing down (if the hands were opened, the left fingers would point to the right and the right fingers would point away from the signer).	The hands are held in front of the body; the right hand is held above the left hand.	The hands touch and then change places before touching again.	snow snowball	1631
Two B̈ hands are held with the palms facing down (if the hands were opened, the fingers would all point away from the signer).	The hands are held in front of the body.	The hands make a short movement towards the signer.	abstain keep out reserved stand back stay out timid withdraw withdrawal withhold	1632

Non-manual features   The lips are pressed together and the shoulders move back slightly.

Two B̈ hands are held with the palms facing down (if the hands were opened, the fingers would all point away from the signer).	The hands are held in front of the body.	The hands make two short downward movements.	shop*† shopping*† wait*[1]	1633

Notes   *This sign may be produced using one hand only.

Ø B̈ꝺ⊥ ˇ.

† Regional sign.

1 If the movement is a single, short, firm downward movement, the sign produced is **wait**.

Ø B̈ꝺ⊥ B̈ꝺ⊥ ˇ

Two B̈ hands are held with the palms facing down (if the hands were opened, the left fingers would point to the right and the right fingers would point to the left).	The hands are held side by side in front of the body with the backs of the fingers touching.	The hands move apart.	apart divorce exclude fall out part separate separation split up	1634
Two B̈ hands are held with the palms facing away from the signer (if the hands were opened, the fingers would all point up).	The hands are held at shoulder height in front of the body.	The fingers bend up and down at the palm knuckles several times.	angel fairy wings angel/fairy flying[1] flutter[1] fly[1]	1635

Notes   1 If the movements are short, the sign produced is **angel/fairy flying, flutter, fly**.

Ø B̈⊥ʌ B̈⊥ʌ ᵐ.

Two B̈ hands are held with the palms facing away from the signer (if the hands were opened, the fingers would all point up).	The hands are held side by side in front of the body; the left hand is held higher than the right hand.	The right hand moves up and then makes a short movement away from the signer; the movement is repeated by each hand alternately, with both hands moving up throughout.	climb a stepladder/steps stepladder steps walk up steps	1636
Two B̈ hands are held with the palms facing away from the signer (if the hands were opened, the fingers would all point up).	The hands are held side by side in front of the body.	The hands move apart.	ledge* shelf*	1637

Notes   * This sign may be produced using one hand only.

Ø B̈⊥ʌ >

1638   Ø   B̈⊥ʌ ₁× B̈⊥ʌ $\overset{÷××}{\underset{ą}{∨∨}}$ //   Ø   5ʊ⊥ ₁ 5ʊ⊥ $\overset{÷}{\underset{·}{}}$

1639   Ø   B̈>ʌ₉ $\overset{\^{}}{}$ B̈<ʌ $\overset{∨}{}$ 1640   Ø   B̄>⊥ × B̈ʊ⊥ $\overset{∨}{\underset{·}{⊤}}$ 1641   Ø   B̈>⊥ B̈<⊥ $\overset{\^{}∨}{⊤}$

1642   Ø   B̈>⊥ B̈<⊥ $\overset{°°}{⊤}$ 1643   Ø   B̈>⊥ B̈<⊥ $\overset{°}{m}$[ʙʙ]

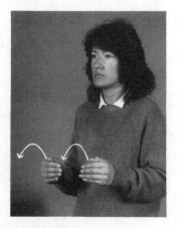 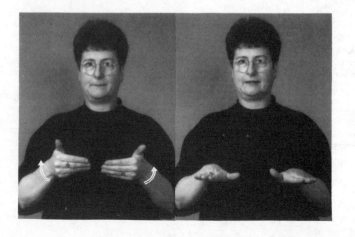

The hand is held flat with the fingers held together and bent at the palm knuckles.

Handshape and orientation	Location, hand arrangement and contact	Movement	Glosses	
Two B̈ hands are held with the palms facing away from the signer (if the hands were opened, the fingers would all point up).	The hands are held in front of the body with the thumbs touching.	The hands move down and apart while twisting at the wrists, so that the palms face up; the hands then continue to move down while moving towards each other, so that the movement ends with the sides of the hands touching.	global* international* world-wide*	1638
Two 5 hands are held with the palms facing down and the fingers pointing away from the signer.	The hands are held side by side in front of the body.	The hands move away from the signer and, at the same time, apart.		

Non-manual features   The cheeks are slightly puffed out.

Notes   * The first part of this sign may be produced using two 5 hands.

$$\emptyset \quad \overset{\frown}{5}\text{ɔ}\bot \;_{|\times}\; \overset{\frown}{5}\text{ɔ}\bot \;\overset{\div\,\times\,\times}{\underset{\text{o}}{\text{v}\,\text{v}}} \;/\!/$$
$$\emptyset \quad \overset{\frown}{5}\text{ɔ}\bot \;_{|}\; \overset{\frown}{5}\text{ɔ}\bot \;^{\div}$$

The left B̈ hand is held with the palm facing right; the right B̈ hand is held with the palm facing left (if the hands were opened, the fingers would all point up).	The hands are held in front of the body; the left hand is held nearer to the signer than the right hand.	The left hand makes a short upward movement and, at the same time, the right hand makes a short downward movement.	inequality unequal inferior [1] inferiority [1] superior [2] superiority [2]	1639

Notes   1 If the movements are firm, the sign produced is **inferior, inferiority**.

$$\emptyset \quad \ddot{B}{>}{\wedge}_{\wp} \;\overset{\text{o·}}{\underset{\wedge}{\vphantom{x}}}\; \ddot{B}{<}{\wedge} \;\overset{\vphantom{x}}{\underset{\vee}{\text{·o}}}$$

Notes   2 If the movements are reversed, so that the right hand moves firmly up and the left hand moves firmly down, the sign produced is **superior, superiority**.

$$\emptyset \quad \ddot{B}{>}{\wedge}_{\wp} \;\overset{\text{o·}}{\underset{\vee}{\vphantom{x}}}\; \ddot{B}{<}{\wedge} \;\overset{\text{·o}}{\underset{\wedge}{\vphantom{x}}}$$

The left B̈ hand is held with the palm facing right; the right B̈ hand is held with the palm facing down (if the hands were opened, the fingers would all point away from the signer).	The hands are held in front of the body; the right hand is held on the the left hand.	The hands remain together and make two short movements down and, at the same time, away from the signer.	friend* friendly* friendship*	1640

Notes   * This sign may also be produced using two B̄ hands, with the left fingers held between the right fingers and thumb.

$$\emptyset \quad \overset{-}{\bar{B}}{>}\bot \;_{\underline{\text{II}}}\; \bar{B}\text{ɔ}\bot \;\overset{\text{o}}{\underset{\text{v}}{\vphantom{x}}}\text{·}$$

The left B̈ hand is held with the palm facing right; the right B̈ hand is held with the palm facing left (if the hands were opened, the fingers would all point away from the signer).	The hands are held in front of the body.	The hands move towards the signer in an arc.	behind move back retreat setback set back	1641
The left B̈ hand is held with the palm facing right; the right B̈ hand is held with the palm facing left (if the hands were opened, the fingers would all point away from the signer).	The hands are held in front of the body.	The hands move away from the signer in an arc.	advance front go ahead move forward proceed progress	1642
The left B̈ hand is held with the palm facing right; the right B̈ hand is held with the palm facing left (if the hands were opened, the fingers would all point away from the signer).	The hands are held in front of the body.	The hands twist sharply at the wrists, so that the palms face down, while the fingers straighten at the palm knuckles (forming two B hands).	been (have been) did done finished late (too late) over	1643

Non-manual features   The lips are pressed together, and then the mouth sharply opens.

1644 ∅ B̈>⊥ ' B̈<⊥ ˣ·

1645 ∅ B̈>⊥ ' B̈<⊥ ᴵ∾·

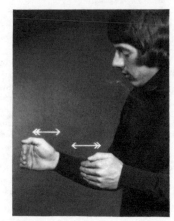

1646 ∅ B̈>⊥ B̈<⊥₉ $\binom{°\,°}{\lambda\,\bot\,\lambda\sim\cdot}$
$_{\bot}$

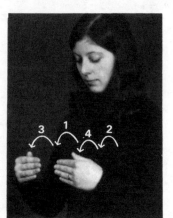

1647 ∩̄ B̈>∧ ₗₓ B̈<∧ $\binom{∩}{÷}$

1648 ◯ B̈⊤∧ B̈⊤∧ $\binom{°_x\cdot}{v}$

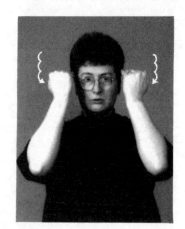

1649 [] B̈ɑ> B̈ɑ< $_x^v$

1650 [] B̈ɑ> B̈ɑ< $_x^{v\,m}_{÷\,x}$

The hand is held flat with the fingers held together and bent at the palm knuckles.

Handshape and orientation	Location, hand arrangement and contact	Movement	Glosses	
The left B̈ hand is held with the palm facing right; the right B̈ hand is held with the palm facing left (if the hands were opened, the fingers would all point away from the signer).	The hands are held side by side in front of the body, at an angle, so that the palms are turned away from the signer.	The fingertips tap together twice.	corner cottage	**1644**
The left B̈ hand is held with the palm facing right; the right B̈ hand is held with the palm facing left (if the hands were opened, the fingers would all point away from the signer).	The hands are held side by side in front of the body.	The hands move towards and away from the signer alternately several times.	budget manage hard up [1]	**1645**

Notes 1 If the lips are stretched and the teeth clenched, the sign produced is **hard up.**

| The left B̈ hand is held with the palm facing right; the right B̈ hand is held with the palm facing left (if the hands were opened, the fingers would all point away from the signer). | The hands are held in front of the body; the right hand is held nearer to the signer than the left hand. | The hands move away from the signer in alternate arcs; the movements are repeated, with the hands moving away from the signer throughout. | logical
procedure
process
get on with [1]
ongoing [1] | **1646** |

Notes 1 If the hands make alternate circles in the vertical plane at right angles to the signer's body, while moving away from the signer throughout, the sign produced is **get on with, ongoing.**

$$Ø \quad B̈_{>⊥} \quad B̈_{<⊥} \begin{pmatrix} e & ∿ & · \\ ⊥ & ∨ & \\ & & ⊥ \end{pmatrix}$$

| The left B̈ hand is held with the palm facing right; the right B̈ hand is held with the palm facing left (if the hands were opened, the fingers would all point up). | The hands are held side by side above the head with the fingertips touching. | The hands move apart while bending apart from the wrists. | heaven | **1647** |

Non-manual features The eyegaze is directed up and forward.

| Two B̈ hands are held with the palms facing towards the signer (if the hands were opened, the fingers would all point up). | The hands are held at either side of the head. | The hands make several short movements towards each other while moving down throughout. | judge | **1648** |
| Two B̈ hands are held with the palms facing up (if the hands were opened, the left fingers would point to the right and the right fingers would point to the left). | The hands are held resting against the chest. | The hands move down, maintaining contact with the chest throughout. | luxurious *
luxury *
rich *
wealth *
wealthy *
well-off *
millionaire [1]
Conservative [2]
Tory [2] | **1649** |

Notes * This sign may be produced using one hand only.

$$[] \quad B̈_{α<} \overset{∨}{\times}$$

1 If the cheeks are puffed out and the eyes are narrowed, the sign produced is **millionaire.**

2 If the palms face towards the signer, and the movement is short and repeated, so that the fingertips brush the chest twice, the sign produced is **Conservative, Tory.**

$$[] \quad B̈_{⊤>} \quad B̈_{⊤<} \overset{\substack{o \\ ∨ \\ \times}}{·}$$

| Two B̈ hands are held with the palms facing up (if the hands were opened, the left fingers would point to the right and the right fingers would point to the left). | The hands are held resting against the upper chest. | The hands, maintaining contact with the chest throughout, move down and then apart while straightening at the palm knuckles (forming two B hands). | blazer
cardigan
jacket
waistcoat | **1650** |

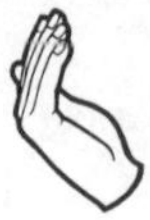

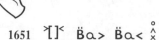

1651 ˃[]˂ B̈a> B̈a< °^× ·

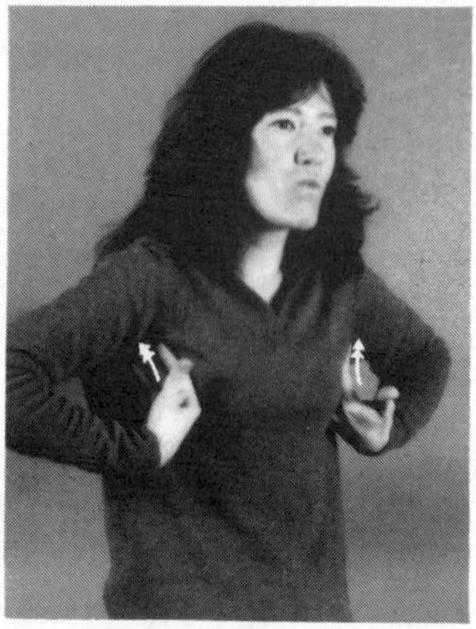

1652 [ˇˇ] B̈ɒ> B̈ɒ< (v×∧) ·

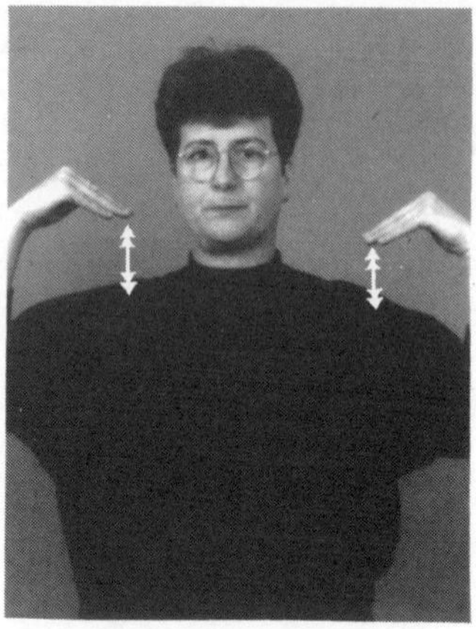

1653 [ˇ] B̈⊤∧ ǀ× B̈⊤∧ °v ×

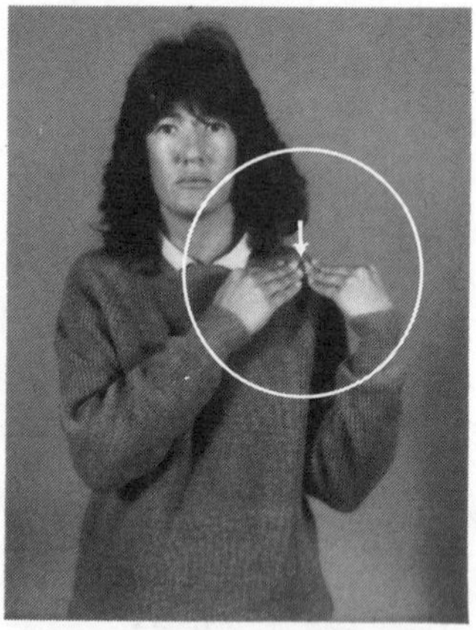

1654 ⌊⌋ B̈⊤v B̈⊤v ^×

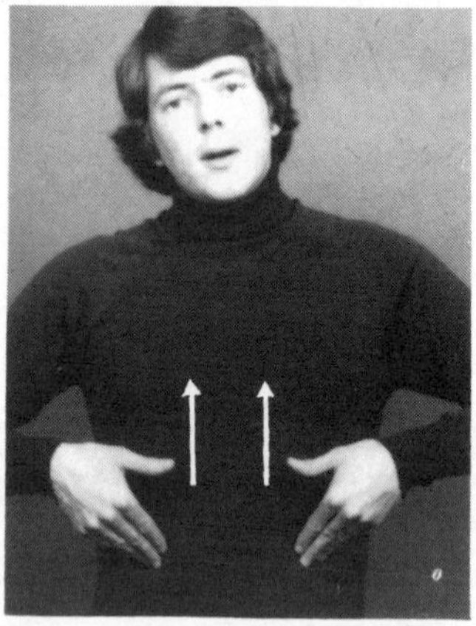

1655 ⌊⌋ B̈⊤v B̈⊤v ×∩v

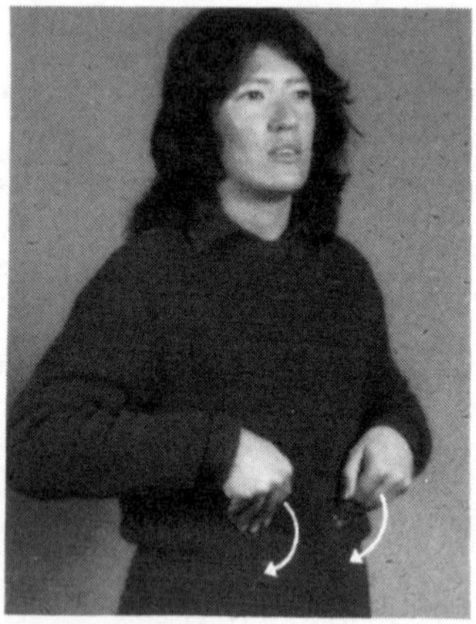

1656 ⌊⌋ B̈⊤v B̈⊤v ×∩v // // Ø 5ɒ⊥ ǀ 5ɒ⊥ ⊥÷

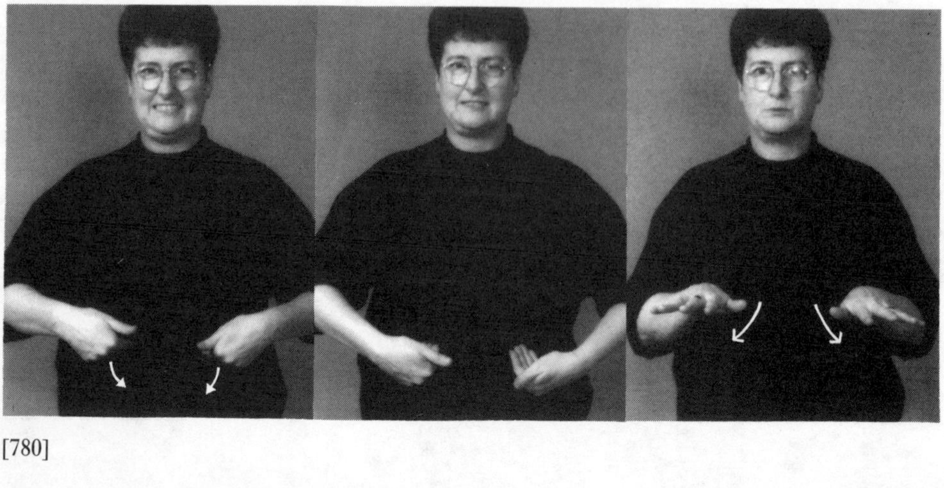

B̈ *The hand is held flat with the fingers held together and bent at the palm knuckles.*

Handshape and orientation	Location, hand arrangement and contact	Movement	Glosses	
Two **b̈** hands are held with the palms facing up (if the hands were opened, the left fingers would point to the right and the right fingers would point to the left).	The hands are held with the backs of the fingers resting against the sides of the body.	The hands make a short upward movement, maintaining contact with the sides of the body; the movement is repeated.	ape* chimpanzee* monkey*	1651

    Notes   * This sign may be produced using one hand only.

$$]^< \quad \ddot{B}a< \quad {}^{\circ}_{\overset{\wedge}{\times}}\cdot$$

Two **b̈** hands are held with the palms facing down (if the hands were opened, the left fingers would point to the right and the right fingers would point to the left).	The hands are held above the shoulders.	The hands move down, so that the fingertips touch the shoulders, and then move up again; the movement is repeated.	gym gymnasium gymnast gymnastics P.E.	1652
Two **b̈** hands are held with the palms facing towards the signer (if the hands were opened, the fingers would all point up).	The hands are held side by side above the left shoulder, angled towards each other, so that the fingertips touch.	The hands make a short downward movement, so that the fingertips touch the left shoulder.	burden* burdened* depend* dependence* dependent* rely* responsibility* responsible*	1653

    Notes   * This sign may be produced using two **Ḧ** hands.

$$\overset{\vee}{[}1 \quad \ddot{H}\tau_\wedge \quad {}_{ix} \quad \ddot{H}\tau_\wedge \quad {}^{\circ}_{\overset{\vee}{\times}}$$

Two **b̈** hands are held with the palms facing towards the signer (if the hands were opened, the fingers would all point down).	The hands are held with the fingertips touching the lower chest.	The hands move up, with the fingertips maintaining contact with the chest throughout.	good morning*†§ morning*†§	1654

    Notes   * Regional sign.

            † This sign may be produced with the hands moving up and away from the signer; the movement ends with the fingertips again touching the chest.

$$LJ \quad \ddot{B}\tau_\vee \quad \ddot{B}\tau_\vee \quad {}^{\times\wedge\times}_{\perp}$$

            § This sign may be produced using one hand only.

$$LJ< \quad \ddot{B}\tau_\vee \quad {}^{\times\wedge\times}_{\perp}$$

Two **b̈** hands are held with the palms facing towards the signer (if the hands were opened, the fingers would all point down).	The hands are held with the fingertips against the lower chest.	The hands bend down from the wrist; the fingertips are held against the lower chest throughout.	Hungarian* Hungary* hunger* hungry* starve[1,2] starving[1,2] famished[2] ravenous[2]	1655

    Notes   * This sign may be produced using one hand only.

$$LJ \quad \ddot{B}\tau_\vee \quad {}^{\times}_{\overset{\cap}{\vee}}$$

           1 If the eyes are narrowed and the lips are stretched, the sign produced is **starve, starving**.

           2 If the eyes are narrowed and the lips are rounded, the sign produced is **famished, ravenous, starve, starving**.

Two **b̈** hands are held with the palms facing towards the signer (if the hands were opened, the fingers would all point down).	The hands are held with the fingertips against the waist.	The hands bend down from the wrists; the fingertips are held against the waist throughout.	famine	1656

Non-manual features   The lips are stretched.

Two **5** hands are held with the palms facing down and the fingers pointing away from the signer.	The hands are held side by side in front of the body.	The hands move apart and, at the same time, away from the signer.	

1657 ⌐⌐ Ḃ⊤< ˣ˃ˣ

1658 B̄˃⊥ ¦ Ḃↄ⊥ ˂ⓞ

1659 ∅ Ḃ⊤˃ ㅍ Ḃ⊤< (ᵒ ṃ .)
        ∧

1660 [] Ḃ⊤˃ Ḃ⊤< ˣ⊥[ʌʌ]ᵒ˅
                  ᵖ̣

The hand is held flat with the fingers held together and bent at the palm knuckles, and the thumb is extended.

Although ፱ is one of the possible *variants* of ፱, it is required in some signs. These are mainly compound signs and signs which involve contact with the extended thumb. In a compound such as **adore** (sign 1660), the extended thumb of ፱ anticipates the extended thumb of the handshape in the second part of the compound, in this case ፱. ፱ is also required in signs where the thumbs contact each other or some other part of the body, as in **butterfly** (sign 1659), or when the thumb needs to be held 'out of the way', as in **fit in** (sign 1658).

Handshape and orientation	Location, hand arrangement and contact	Movement	Glosses	
The ፱ hand is held with the palm facing towards the signer (if the hand were opened, the fingers would point to the left).	The hand is held in front of the upper chest.	The fingertips touch the left side of the upper chest; the hand then moves to the right before the fingertips touch the right side of the upper chest.	**breast** **breast-feed** **good morning** **morning**	1657
The left ፱ hand is held with the palm facing right; the right ፱ hand is held with the palm facing down (if the hands were opened, the fingers would all point away from the signer).	The hands are held side by side in front of the body.	The right hand moves to the left until the right fingers are held between the left thumb and fingers.	**fit in** **include** **insert** **involve** **join** **join in** **join up** **member** **participant** **participate** **context**[1]	1658

Notes 1 If the movement is repeated, the sign produced is **context**. $\bar{\textsf{B}}$>⊥ ⎮ $\dot{\textsf{B}}$ʋ⊥ <⊙·

Two ፱ hands are held with the palms facing towards the signer (if the hands were opened, the left fingers would point to the right and the right fingers would point to the left).	The hands are held crossed over in front of the body with the thumbs linked together.	The hands remain together and move up, while the fingers make several short bending movements from the palm knuckles.	**butterfly** **flutter** **fly** **moth**	1659
Two ፱ hands are held with the palms facing towards the signer (if the hands were opened, the left fingers would point to the right and the right fingers would point to the left).	The hands are held with the fingertips touching the chest.	The hands move away from the signer while closing (forming two ፱ hands) and, at the same time, twisting at the wrists, so that the palms face down; the hands then make a short downward movement.	**adore** *† **fond (be fond of)** *† **love** *† **approve of** *†[1] **favour** *†[1] **favourite**[1] **prefer** *†[1] **preference**[1]	1660

Non-manual features The head nods firmly.

Notes * Directional verb.

>[] $\dot{\textsf{B}}$⟙< $^{×⊥[A]}_{ʋ}$ $^{°}_{ˇ}$
$_{\#}$

† This sign may be produced using one hand only.

1 If the first part of the sign is omitted and the two ፱ hands move away from the signer and then firmly down, the sign produced is **approve of, favour, favourite, prefer, preference**.

Ø ፱ʋ⊥ ፱ʋ⊥ ⊥ˇ

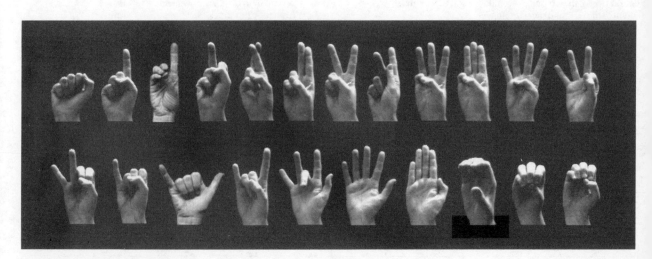

C

Handshape	Handshape description	Type	Sign entries
C	The extended fingers (held together) and the extended thumb are bent to the shape of a "C".	Single dez	1661 – 1676
		Manual tab	1677 – 1683
		Double dez	1684 – 1693
Ċ	The extended fingers (held together) are bent to form a curve and the thumb is extended.	Single dez	1694 – 1695
		Manual tab	1696
		Double dez	1697

1661　Ø Cᴖ⊥ (˚᷅.)

1662　Ø C⊥ʌ ˚᷈.

1663　Ø ˒C⊥< ᴖᴖ ʌ>

1664　Ø C<⊥ <

The main variation in the production of **C** concerns the size of the gap between the bent fingers and thumb.

C has several different *classifier* functions in the productive lexicon and also appears as a classifying element in established signs:

- it is used as a *size and shape* classifier to represent curved or cylindrical objects, as in **glass** (1681), **can** (sign 1681) and **bottle** (sign 1683). It can be used to indicate pieces or chunks, as in chunks of text (e.g. paragraphs) or newspaper columns;
- it can be used as a *tracing size and shape* classifier to indicate the outline or positioning of large, columnar objects such as pillars or blocks of flats. Two-handed forms may indicate long, cylindrical items such as logs or pipes: see also **cable** (sign 1684) and **coach** (sign 1687);
- it can be used as a *handling* classifier to indicate the handling of curved or cylindrical objects such as a glass or a can, or chunks of material, such as a wad of money in **donate** (sign 1679) or blocks in **building blocks** (sign 1688);
- it can be used to express *extent* or *quantity*. One-handed forms can be

used to express thickness as in thick-soled shoes. Two-handed forms can be used to show the extent of curved, oblong or cylindrical objects, for example, high pillars and long logs. Two-handed forms may be used for rows or piles of curved objects, for example, piles of cups and rows of glasses.

C expresses the letter **c** in the American and Irish manual alphabets. As such it is used in initial letter handshape signs borrowed from American Sign Language (ASL) and Irish Sign Language (ISL). Examples include **communication** from ASL and **conscious** from ISL (see *Introduction*). The letter **c** of the British manual alphabet is usually produced in the form of a **c̆** handshape, i.e. index finger and thumb extended and bent. This is used in initial letter handshape signs such as **confidence** (sign 646) and **course** (sign 648). However, with some initial letter **c** signs, **c̆** and **C** are interchangeable, at least for some signers. Examples include **committee** (see *Introduction*) and **coffee** (sign 638). In a few examples, **C** is required rather than **c̆**, as in **curriculum** and **copyright** (see *Introduction*).

Handshape and orientation	Location, hand arrangement and contact	Movement	Glosses	
The **c** hand is held with the palm facing down (if the hand were opened, the fingers would point away from the signer).	The hand is held in front of the body.	The hand makes a short movement to the right; the movement is repeated twice, with the hand moving away from the signer throughout.	**pedestrian crossing*** **zebra crossing***	**1661**
Notes * The following notes apply to all glosses:				
This sign may be produced using a **c̄** hand.		$\varnothing$ Ḡɔ⊥ $\binom{\circ}{\gtrless}.)$		
This sign may be produced using two hands.		$\varnothing$ Cɔ⊥ Cɔ⊥ $\binom{\circ}{\gtrless}.)$ or		
		$\varnothing$ Ḡɔ⊥ Ḡɔ⊥ $\binom{\circ}{\gtrless}.)$		
The **c** hand is held with the palm facing away from the signer (if the hand were opened, the fingers would point up).	The hand is held in front of the body.	The hand makes two short movements downwards and, at the same time, to the left.	**pepper** **salt** **shake pepper/salt/ vinegar** **vinegar** **ketchup**[1] **pour ketchup**[1] **pour sauce**[2] **sauce**[2]	**1662**
Notes 1 If the movements are short and firm, the sign produced is **ketchup, pour ketchup**.		$\varnothing$ C⊥∧ $\overset{\circ}{\underset{\vee}{<}}.$		
2 If the palm faces down and the hand makes an anticlockwise circle in the horizontal plane, the sign produced is **pour sauce, sauce**.		$\varnothing$ Cɔ⊥ $\overset{@}{\underset{\top}{<}}$		
The **c** hand is held with the palm facing away from the signer (if the hand were opened, the fingers would point to the left).	The hand is held in front of the body.	The hand moves to the right in an arc, bending from the elbow, so that the movement ends with the palm facing away from the signer and the fingers pointing to the right.	**arch** **bridge** **rainbow**	**1663**
The **c** hand is held with the palm facing left (if the hand were opened, the fingers would point away from the signer).	The hand is held in front of the body.	The hand moves to the left.	**appoint** **bring in** **employ** **locum** **relief** **reserve** **substitute** **successor**	**1664**

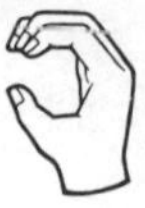

1665 ∩ C<∧ #[A]

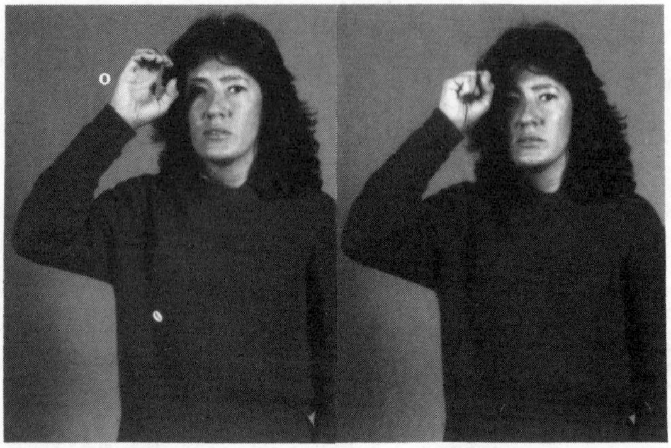

1666 ∩ C<⊥ ×@⊥v

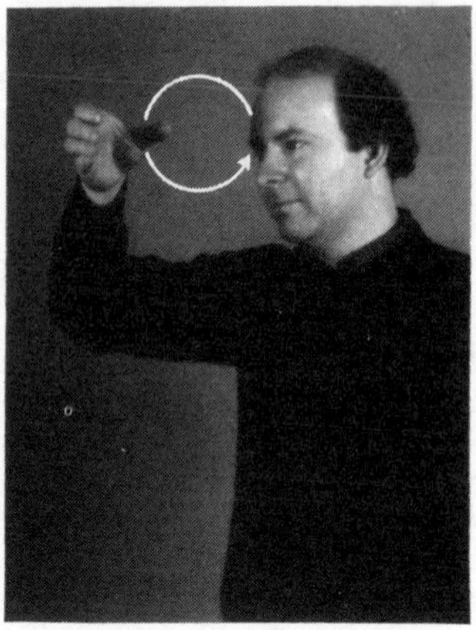

1667 Ͻ C⊤< v

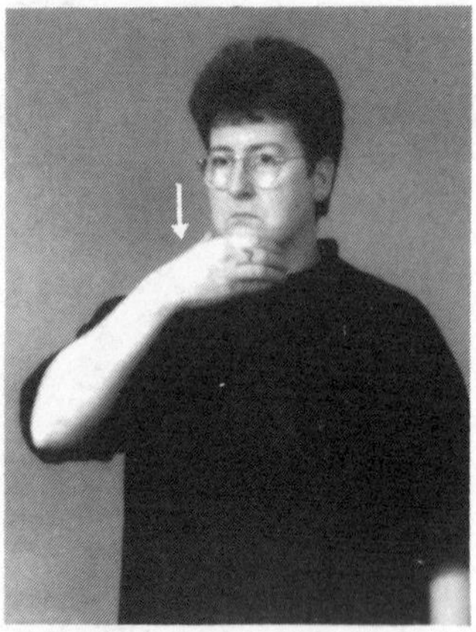

1668 Ͻ C<∧ ⊥v@⊥v

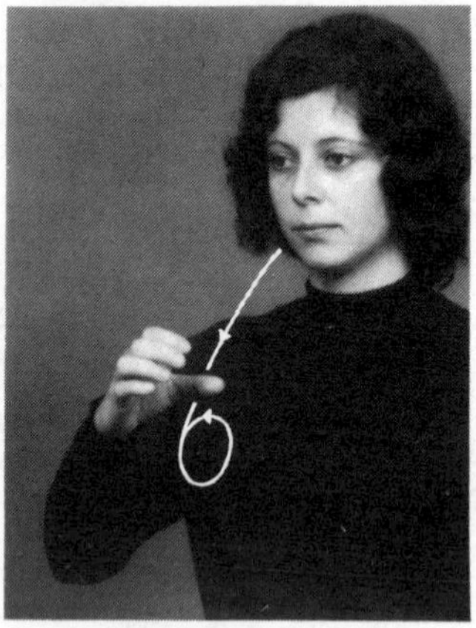

1669 Ͻ J̇C<∧ Ɒ[A]<#

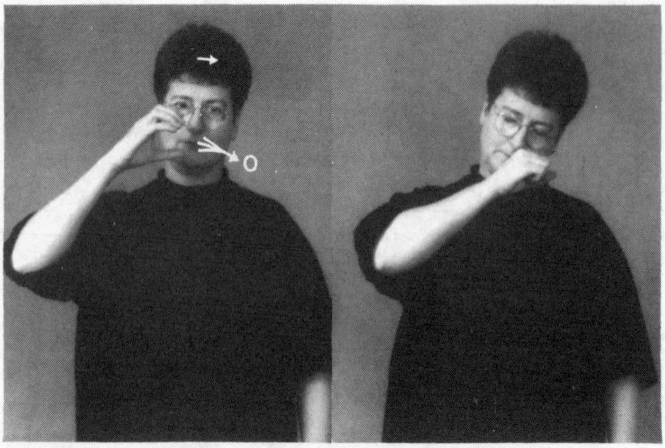

C

The extended fingers (held together) and thumb are bent in the shape of a "C".

Handshape and orientation	Location, hand arrangement and contact	Movement	Glosses	
The c hand is held with the palm facing left (if the hand were opened, the fingers would point up).	The hand is held beside the forehead.	The hand closes (forming an A hand).	memorise memory recall remember concept[1] guess[1]	1665
Notes 1 If the hand moves to the left while closing, the sign produced is **concept, guess**.				
The c hand is held with the palm facing left (if the hand were opened, the fingers would point away from the signer).	The hand is held with the back of the thumb touching the forehead.	The hand makes a clockwise circle in the vertical plane at right angles to the signer's body.	fire brigade fire fighter fireman	1666
The c hand is held with the palm facing towards the signer (if the hand were opened, the fingers would point to the left).	The hand is held in front of the face.	The hand moves down.	melancholy miserable sad sadden pale[1]	1667
Non-manual features The corners of the mouth are turned down.				
Notes 1 If the non-manual feature is not present, the sign produced is **pale**.				
The c hand is held with the palm facing left (if the hand were opened, the fingers would point up).	The hand is held in front of the face.	The hand moves down and, at the same time, away from the signer, and then makes a small clockwise circle in the vertical plane at right angles to the signer's body.	elephant elephant's trunk	1668
The c hand is held with the palm facing left (if the hand were opened, the fingers would point up).	The hand is held in front of the face.	The hand moves down and to the left, bending from the elbow and, at the same time, closes (forming an A hand).	asleep asleep (fall asleep) doze off	1669
Non-manual features The head tilts to the left and, at the same time, the eyes close.				

∩ C<ʌ $_{\#}^{<[A]}$

1670 ⊔ ɿC<ʌ ˣ(ᴒ↓ᵥ)

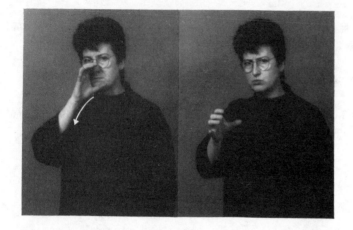

1671 ⌣ C<⊥ ᵒᴒ∧ᴛ

1672 ∪ Cᴕ< ˣ ᵒᵥ[ʌ] ⊥ ≠

1673 π C⊤< ˣᵅ∧

1674]< Cᴕ⊥ >ˆᵅ

1675 ɑ Cᴕ< ᶍ

C

The extended fingers (held together) and thumb are bent in the shape of a "C".

Handshape and orientation	Location, hand arrangement and contact	Movement	Glosses	
The c hand is held with the palm facing left (if the hand were opened, the fingers would point up).	The hand is held in front of the face, with the side of the index finger resting on the nose.	The hand moves down and away from the signer, bending from the elbow.	blast damn	1670
Non-manual features The mouth is closed and then opens as the hand moves, with the lips pushed forward.				
The c hand is held with the palm facing left (if the hand were opened, the fingers would point away from the signer).	The hand is held in front of the chin.	The hand makes a short movement towards the signer and, at the same time, bends up from the wrist.	drink drink from a glass/tumbler drink milk † glass * milk † tumbler * boozing §¹	1671
Notes * This sign may be produced with a repeated movement.				
† Regional sign.				
§ This sign may also be produced with the hand making two anticlockwise circles in the horizontal plane.				
1 If two hands are used, making alternate repeated movements, the sign produced is **boozing**.				
The c hand is held with the palm facing down (if the hand were opened, the fingers would point to the left).	The hand is held resting against the chin.	The hand makes a short movement away from the signer and down, while closing (forming an A hand).	beard Egypt Egyptian goat goatee Jew Jewish man pharaoh	1672
The c hand is held with the palm facing towards the signer (if the hand were opened, the fingers would all point to the left).	The hand is held with the thumb and fingertips touching the neck.	The hand moves up while twisting away from the signer at the wrist, so that the palm faces up.	dinosaur giraffe llama neck of a dinosaur/ giraffe/llama	1673
Non-manual features The eyes are opened wide and the teeth are clenched with the mouth wide open and lips pushed forward.				
The c hand is held with the palm facing down (if the hand were opened, the fingers would point away from the signer).	The hand is held touching the right side of the waist.	The hand moves up and to the right, while twisting at the wrist, so that the palm faces up.	squirrel squirrel's tail tail¹	1674
Notes 1 If an F handshape is used, the sign produced is **tail**.				
The c hand is held with the palm facing down (if the hand were opened, the fingers would point to the left).	The left hand is held in front of the body with the palm facing up; the right hand is held beside the left wrist.	The right hand grasps the left wrist.	pulse pulse (take one's pulse)	1675

1676 ‾℧ C℧⊥ ⌶

1677 A⊤> ⊙ C<⊥ #> [o] ·

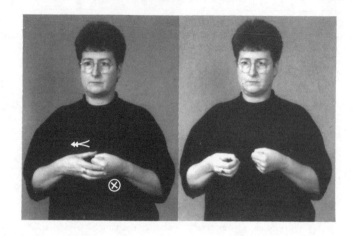

1678 √5⊥∧ ₁ₓ ꜀C⊥< ∧ᵈ

1679 ‾Bɑ> ₓ C⊥∧ ⊥

1680 ‾Bɑ> C<⊥ ⁽ᵛˣ⁾·

1681 ‾Bɑ> ₓ C<⊥ ∧

1682 B̲℧> ₁ Cɑ⊥ <̥

Handshape and orientation	Location, hand arrangement and contact	Movement	Glosses	
The **c** hand is held with the palm facing down (if the hand were opened, the fingers would point away from the signer).	The hand is held above the left wrist which is positioned in front of the body.	The right hand moves down to grasp the left wrist.	**apprentice** * **trainee** *	1676

Notes   * The following notes apply to all glosses:

     This sign may also be produced using an **F̄** handshape.   ŏ F̄ɔ⊥ ᴵ

     This sign may also be produced using an **ŏ** handshape.   ŏ ŏɔ⊥ ᴵ

| The left **A** hand is held with the palm facing towards the signer (if the hand were opened, the fingers would point to the right). The right **c** hand is held with the palm facing left (if the hand were opened, the fingers would point away from the signer). | The hands are held in front of the body; the left hand is held between the right fingers and thumb. | The right hand moves to the right while the fingers and thumb close (forming an **o** hand); the movement is repeated. | **potato** * | 1677 |

Notes   * Regional sign.

| The left **5** hand is held with the palm facing away from the signer and the fingers pointing up; the right **c** hand is held with the palm facing away from the signer (if the hand were opened, the fingers would point to the left). | The hands are held in front of the body; the backs of the right fingers rest against the side of the left forearm. | The right hand moves up and, at the same time, to the right, bending from the elbow. | **branch** | 1678 |

| The left **B** hand is held with the palm facing up and the fingers pointing to the right; the right **c** hand is held with the palm facing away from the signer (if the hand were opened, the fingers would point up). | The hands are held in front of the body; the right hand rests on the left palm. | The right hand moves away from the signer. | **cash**
deposit
donate *
money (wad
  of money)
pay *
payment
sponsor *
alimony [1]
maintenance [1] | 1679 |

Notes   * Directional verb.

     1 If the movement is repeated, the sign produced is **alimony, maintenance**.   B̄ɑ> ₓ C⊥ʌ ⊥ₓ⊥̇

| The left **B** hand is held with the palm facing up and the fingers pointing to the right; the right **c** hand is held with the palm facing left (if the hand were opened, the fingers would point away from the signer). | The hands are held in front of the body; the right hand is held above the left hand. | The right hand moves down to touch the left palm twice. | **Cardiff** | 1680 |

| The left **B** hand is held with the palm facing up and the fingers pointing to the right; the right **c** hand is held with the palm facing left (if the hand were opened, the fingers would point away from the signer). | The hands are held in front of the body; the right hand rests on the left palm. | The right hand moves up. | **can**
glass
jar
tin
tumbler | 1681 |

| The left **B** hand is held with the palm facing down and the fingers pointing to the right; the right **c** hand is held with the palm facing up (if the hand were opened, the fingers would point away from the signer). | The hands are held side by side in front of the body. | The right hand moves to the left, so that the left fingers are held between the right thumb and fingers. | **shoe**
put on a shoe | 1682 |

1683 $\overline{C}{>}{\perp}$ ×C<⊥ ^

1684 Ø C꜀⊥ ǀ C꜀⊥ ÷

1685 Ø C꜀⊥ ₁× C꜀⊥ $_{\wp}^{÷×\,[ẞẞ]\,×}_{\vee\#}$ // Ø G̈>∧ ǀ G̈<∧ ᴵ~˙

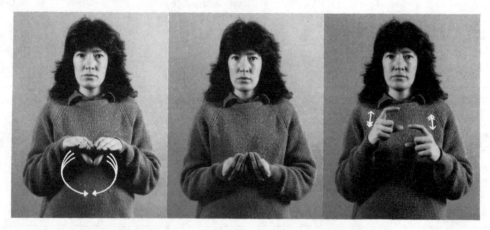

1686 Ø C⊥∧ C⊥∧ $_{\vee}^{\omega~\cdot}_{×}$

1687 Ø C>∧ ⊥× C<∧ᵨ ᵀ

1688 Ø $\overline{C}{>}{\perp}$ ǀ C<⊥ $^{(\,\cdot\cdot)}_{\wedge}$

[794]

Handshape and orientation	Location, hand arrangement and contact	Movement	Glosses	
The left c hand is held with the palm facing right; the right c hand is held with the palm facing left (if the hands were opened, the fingers would all point away from the signer).	The hands are held in front of the body; the right hand rests on the left hand.	The right hand moves up.	bottle can jar tin tumbler	1683
Two c hands are held with the palms facing down (if the hands were opened, the fingers would all point away from the signer).	The hands are held side by side in front of the body.	The hands move apart.	cable * † pipe * † cable T.V. ¹	1684

Notes   * This sign may also be produced using two o hands.

$$\varnothing \quad \text{O}ʊ⊥ \mid \text{O}ʊ⊥ \div$$

† This sign may also be produced using two F̄ hands; the lips are rounded. This sign is typically used to refer to a thin **cable** or **pipe**.

$$\varnothing \quad \bar{\bar{\text{F}}}⊥\wedge \ \bar{\bar{\text{F}}}⊥\wedge \div$$

1 This sign may be used as the first part of a compound sign meaning **cable T.V.** (see 394 for the second part of the sign).

$$\varnothing \quad \text{C}ʊ⊥ \mid \text{C}ʊ⊥ \overset{\div}{/\!/}\,/\!/$$

$$5{>}⊥ \mid \text{G}⊤{<} \overset{\times}{/\!/}\,/\!/ \quad 5{>}⊥ \mid \text{V}{<}\wedge \ ^{\times}$$

Two c hands are held with the palms facing down (if the hands were opened, the fingers would all point away from the signer).	The hands are held side by side in front of the body with the thumbs and index fingers touching.	The hands twist down and apart from the wrists, so that the palms face up; the hands then move towards each other, while closing (forming two ʙ hands); the movement ends with the hands touching.	Total Communication	1685
The left č hand is held with the palm facing right; the right č hand is held with the palm facing left (if the hands were opened, the fingers would all point up).	The hands are held side by side in front of the body.	The hands move towards and away from the signer alternately several times.		
Two c hands are held with the palms facing away from the signer (if the hands were opened, the fingers would all point up).	The hands are held in front of the body.	The hands twist down and towards each other at the wrists alternately; the movements are repeated.	chemist * chemistry * science * scientific * scientist * experiment ¹	1686

Notes   * This sign may be produced using two č hands.

$$\varnothing \quad \bar{\text{G}}⊥\wedge \ \bar{\text{G}}⊥\wedge \ \overset{\omega\sim\,\cdot}{\underset{\vee}{\times}}$$

1 If two F hands are used, the sign produced is **experiment**.

$$\varnothing \quad \text{F}⊥\wedge \ \text{F}⊥\wedge \ \overset{\omega\sim\,\cdot}{\underset{\vee}{\times}}$$

The left c hand is held with the palm facing right; the right c hand is held with the palm facing left (if the hands were opened, the fingers would all point up).	The hands are held in front of the body; the side of the left index finger is held resting against the side of the right little finger.	The right hand moves towards the signer and, at the same time, the left hand moves away from the signer.	bus (single- decker bus) carriage coach	1687
The left c hand is held with the palm facing right; the right c hand is held with the palm facing left (if the hands were opened, the fingers would all point away from the signer).	The hands are held side by side in front of the body.	The hands are placed one above the other alternately, while moving upwards throughout.	blocks (children's building blocks) bricks (children's building bricks) toy blocks toy bricks play with children's building blocks or bricks/toy blocks/ toy bricks	1688

1689 Ø C>⊥ | C<⊥ ÷

1690 Ø C>⊥ | C<⊥ $\overset{\circ}{\underset{x}{\div}}$×

1691 Ỏ C⊥∧ C⊥∧ ÷

1692 ᴝ C>∧ C<∧ ×

1693 π C>∧ C<∧ $\overset{3x}{\underset{v}{}}$

The extended fingers (held together) and thumb are bent in the shape of a "C".

Handshape and orientation	Location, hand arrangement and contact	Movement	Glosses	
The left c hand is held with the palm facing right; the right c hand is held with the palm facing left (if the hands were opened, the fingers would all point away from the signer).	The hands are held side by side in front of the body.	The hands move apart.	brick	1689
The left c hand is held with the palm facing right; the right c hand is held with the palm facing left (if the hands were opened, the fingers would all point away from the signer).	The hands are held side by side in front of the body.	The hands make a short movement away from the signer and, at the same time, towards each other; the movement ends with the backs of the left fingers touching the pads of the right fingers.	category * class * group * module * set *	1690

Notes * This sign may be produced with the hands (held so that the fingers, if straight, would point up) bending firmly away from the signer at the wrists.

$$\emptyset \quad C > \wedge_{\,\shortmid} \quad C < \wedge \; \overset{\cdot}{\underset{\perp}{\shortmid}}$$

Two c hands are held with the palms facing away from the signer (if the hands were opened, the fingers would point up).	The hands are held at either side of the head.	The hands move apart and, at the same time, away from the signer.	pillow *	1691

Notes * This sign may be produced using one hand only.

$$\circ \quad C \perp \wedge \; \overset{\perp}{\underset{>}{}}$$

The left c hand is held with the palm facing right; the right c hand is held with the palm facing left (if the hands were opened, the fingers would all point up).	The hands are held beside the ears.	The fingertips touch the side of the head.	ear muffs headphones personal stereo [1] Walkman [1]	1692

Notes 1 If two V̈ hands are held against the ears, the lips are rounded and the head moves from side to side, the sign produced is **personal stereo, Walkman**.

$$\supset \quad \ddot{V} > \wedge \quad \ddot{V} < \wedge \; ^{\times}$$

The left c hand is held with the palm facing right; the right c hand is held with the palm facing left (if the hands were opened, the fingers would all point up).	The hands are held on either side of the neck.	The hands move down in front of the chest while twisting towards each other from the wrists.	mayor mayoress provost scarf stole	1693

1694 ⊐ Ċᴛʌ °×·̇×̂

1695 ⊔ Ċᴛ< ȧ·

1696 Bʊ> i̇ĊɑᴛႷ ᵑ⊥

1697 ∅ Ċ⊥ᴠႷ ι Ċᴛᴠ (ᵑ<̲)[55] <̲□

The extended fingers (held together) are bent to form a curve and the thumb is extended.

This is a relatively rare handshape. It is used as a *handling* classifier within the productive lexicon and as a classifying element in established signs:
– it is used as a *handling* classifier to indicate the handling of spherical or curved ojects. Examples include **apple** (sign 1695) and **rugby** (sign 1697).

Handshape and orientation	Location, hand arrangement and contact	Movement	Glosses	
The ċ hand is held with the palm facing towards the signer (if the hand were opened, the fingers would point up).	The hand is held in front of the cheek.	The hand makes a short upwards movement, so that the fingertips brush the cheek; the movement is repeated.	water	**1694**
The ċ hand is held with the palm facing towards the signer (if the hand were opened, the fingers would point to the left).	The hand is held below the chin.	The hand twists sharply at the wrist, so that the palm faces up; the movement is repeated.	apple * fruit *†¹	**1695**

Notes   * This sign may also be produced using an Ḧ handshape.   ⌣ Ḧ⊤< ᵅ˙

           † This sign may be produced with a single movement.   ⌣ Ḧ⊤< ᵅ or ⌣ ċ⊤< ᵅ

           1 If the movements are not sharp, the sign produced is **fruit**.   ⌣ Ḧ⊤< ᵅ˙ or ⌣ ċ⊤< ᵅ˙

The left B hand is held with the palm facing down and the fingers pointing to the right; the right ċ hand is held with the palm facing up (if the hand were opened, the fingers would point towards the signer).	The hands are held in front of the body; the right hand is held higher and nearer to the signer than the left hand.	The right hand moves away from the signer, bending from the elbow.	shot put shot putter	**1696**

Non-manual features   The head and the right shoulder are tilted down and to the right and then move up and to the left; the eyegaze is directed in line with the movement of the right hand.

The left ċ hand is held with the palm facing away from the signer; the right ċ hand is held with the palm facing towards the signer (if the hands were opened, the fingers would all point down).	The hands are held side by side in front of the body; the left hand is held nearer to the signer than the right hand.	The hands move to the left while bending to the left at the wrists and, at the same time, opening (forming two 5 hands).	play rugby rugby rugby player	**1697**

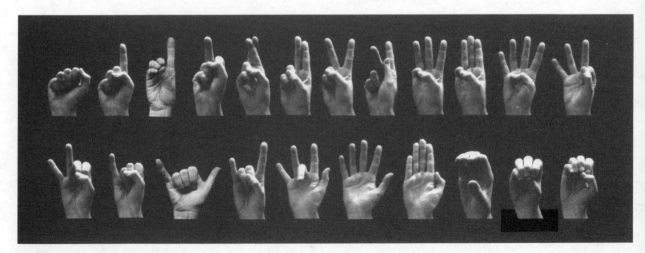

Handshape	Handshape description	Type	Sign entries
o	The extended fingers (held together) and the extended thumb are bent and touch at the tips to form a circle.	Single dez Manual tab Double dez	1698–1713 1714–1719 1720–1733

1698 Ø ⊙ᴖ⊥ □ [ǯ] ·

1699 Ø ⊙ᴖ⊥ ᵛ[ǯ]□

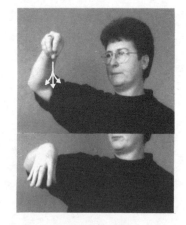

1700 Ø ⊙ᴖ⊥ ᵛ[ǯ]□

1701 Ø ⊙ᴖ⊥ ^ᵛ□[ǯ]>>

1702 Ø ⊙⊥^ (°⊤[ǯ]□ ·)ᵛ

1703 Ø ⊙⊥^ ᴨ[5]⊥□

The extended fingers (held together) and the extended thumb are bent
and touch at the tips to form a circle.

The **O** handshape has no major *variants*. It has several different *classifier* functions within the productive lexicon and is used as a classifying element in established signs:
– it is used as a *size and shape* classifier to represent round or spherical objects or to focus on the circular elements of objects, as in **lens**, **binoculars** and **telescope**. It can be used to indicate small circular containers such as an **egg cup** or **bowl**;
– it is used as a *handling* classifier, especially for long, cylindrical objects where a throwing action is associated with the object, as in **spear** and **javelin**. In many such cases **A** and **O** are interchangeable;
– it can be used to show *extent* such as the length of cylindrical objects, as in a long rod or a short pipe.

The **O** handshape also forms the first part of a handshape pair in which the closed **O** hand opens to a spread **5** handshape. The **A** handshape may occur instead of **O** as the first element in some signs. This handshape pair has several different *symbolic* functions in the language (see *Introduction* for discussion). It is used to express the generalised meaning of 'emit' or 'emanate'. The nature of what is emitted may vary but may include light rays, explosives, water, lava or smoke. See for example, **lamp** (sign 1698), **bomb** (sign 1699), **shower** (sign 1706), **sun** (sign 1707), **volcano** (sign 1715), **chimney** (sign 1719) and **spray** (sign 1725). The same handshape pair is also used to express meanings associated with growth and development, as in **growth** (sign 1718) and to express meanings linked with 'dropping', as in **abandon** (sign 1726).

Handshape and orientation	Location, hand arrangement and contact	Movement	Glosses	
The **o** hand is held with the palm facing down (if the hand were opened, the fingers would point away from the signer).	The hand is held in front of the body.	The hand opens (forming a **5̄** hand); the movement is repeated.	lamp lamp on light light on switch on a lamp/light	**1698**
The **o** hand is held with the palm facing down (if the hand were opened, the fingers would point away from the signer).	The hand is held at head height in front of the body.	The hand moves down while opening (forming a **5̄** hand).	bomb*	**1699**
Notes	* This sign can be produced with two hands.			
The **o** hand is held with the palm facing down (if the hand were opened, the fingers would point away from the signer).	The hand is held in front of the body.	The hand moves down and, at the same time, opens (forming a **5̄** hand).	drop break wind[1] fart[1]	**1700**
Notes	1 If the lips are held tightly together and the closure is released, the sign produced is **break wind, fart**.			
The **o** hand is held with the palm facing down (if the hand were opened, the fingers would point away from the signer).	The hand is held in front of the body.	The hand moves up and then down while moving to the right throughout, before opening (forming a **5̄** hand).	move transfer	**1701**
The **o** hand is held with the palm facing towards the signer (if the hand were opened, the fingers would point up).	The hand is held at head height in front of the body.	The hand makes a short movement towards the signer while opening (forming a **5̄** hand); the movement is repeated twice with the hand moving downwards throughout.	traffic lights	**1702**
The **o** hand is held with the palm facing away from the signer (if the hand were opened, the fingers would point up).	The hand is held in front of the body.	The hand bends away from the signer from the wrist and, at the same time, opens (forming a **5** hand).	mail† mail/post a letter† post† postage return† send† send back† throw† throw away* throw out*	**1703**
Notes	* This sign can be produced using two hands. † Directional verb.			

Ø Oᴐᴛ Oᴐᴛ ^{∨[5̄5̄]∿·}

Ø Oᴛ∧ Oᴛ∧ ^{n[55]}

1704 Ø O<∧ ͦ⊥

1705 Ø O<∧ ⸿⸞⸟

1706 ⎺∩ Oↄ< ⁿ[s]·ⱽ▢

1707 ∩ OT∧ ͦT[s]ⱽ▢

1708 ∩ OT∧ ˣ⊥[s]▢

1709 ∩ O⊥< ˣ͘⊥[s]▢

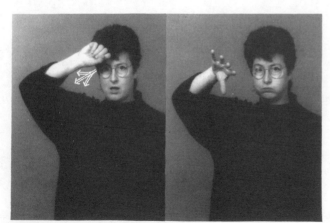

The extended fingers (held together) and the extended thumb are bent and touch at the tips to form a circle.

Handshape and orientation	Location, hand arrangement and contact	Movement	Glosses	
The o hand is held with the palm facing left (if the hand were opened, the fingers would point up).	The hand is held in front of the body.	The hand makes a short firm movement away from the signer.	nil* nothing*† nought* zero*	1704

Notes   * This sign may be produced using an F hand.

Ø F<ʌ

† This sign may be produced with the hand making small clockwise circles in the vertical plane parallel to the signer's body.

Ø O<ʌ   or   Ø F<ʌ

The o hand is held with the palm facing left (if the hand were opened, the fingers would point up).	The hand is held in front of the body.	The hand makes a short movement to the right, and then a short movement down and, at the same time, to the left.	per cent percentage proportion ratio	1705
The o hand is held with the palm facing down (if the hand were opened, the fingers would point to the left).	The hand is held above the head.	The hand bends down from the wrist and, at the same time, opens (forming a 5 hand); the movement is repeated.	shower shower (take a shower)	1706
The o hand is held with the palm facing towards the signer (if the hand were opened, the fingers would point up).	The hand is held at head height in front of the body.	The hand makes a short movement down and towards the signer while opening (forming a 5 hand).	beam* light* ray* sun*¹	1707

Notes   * The hand should be located as appropriate.

1 This sign is typically produced with the palm facing left, and the hand moving down and to the left while opening.

∩ O<ʌ [5]

The o hand is held with the palm facing towards the signer (if the hand were opened, the fingers would point up).	The hand is held with the thumb and fingertips touching the forehead.	The hand moves away from the signer and, at the same time, opens (forming a 5 hand).	forget*	1708

Notes   * This sign may be produced using a 8̂ hand.

∩ 8̂⊤ʌ [5]

The o hand is held with the palm facing away from the signer (if the hand were opened, the fingers would point to the left).	The hand is held with the back of the hand resting against the forehead.	The hand moves sharply away from the signer while opening (forming a 5 hand).	scared stiff* scared to death* terrified*	1709

Non-manual features   The cheeks puff out.

Notes   * The following notes apply to all glosses:

This sign may be produced with the hand held so that the fingers, if straight, would point up.

∩ O⊥ʌ [5]

This sign may be produced with the hand moving away from the signer and down, while opening (forming a 5 hand).

∩ O⊥ʌ [5]   or   ∩ O⊥< [5]

1710 ⊃ OT∧ ˣ⊥[5]ᵥ□

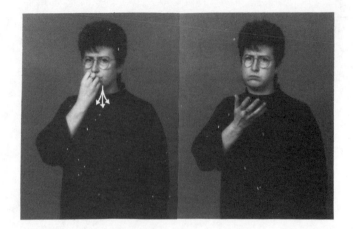

1711 ⊃ O⊥∧ ˣ⊥[5]□

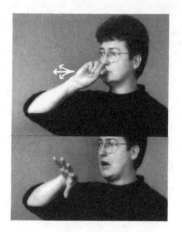

1712 ˃l1 Oɑ⊥ (ṅ)[5̄]ˣ∨⊤∨□

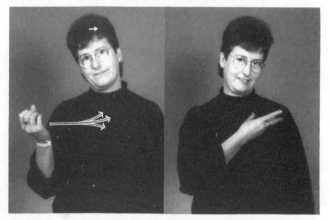

1713 Ħ ˥O⊥∨ ṅ[5]°⊥□

1714 Aʊ˃ ¦ Oʊ˂ <∨[5]<□ ˣ

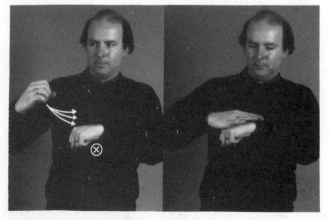

*The extended fingers (held together) and the extended thumb are bent
and touch at the tips to form a circle.*

Handshape and orientation	Location, hand arrangement and contact	Movement	Glosses	
The O hand is held with the palm facing towards the signer (if the hand were opened, the fingers would point up).	The hand is held with the fingertips touching the mouth.	The hand moves down and away from the signer, while opening (forming a 5 hand).	beautiful beauty marvel marvellous superb terrific wonderful	1710
Non-manual features The cheeks puff out.				
The O hand is held with the palm facing away from the signer (if the hand were opened, the fingers would point up).	The hand is held with the back of the hand resting against the mouth and chin.	The hand moves away from the signer and, at the same time, opens (forming a 5 hand).	blow call out cry out scream shout yell	1711
Non-manual features The mouth opens.				
The O hand is held with the palm facing up (if the hand were opened, the fingers would point away from the signer).	The hand is held in front of the chest.	The hand moves sharply to the left and towards the signer, while bending to the left at the wrist and, at the same time, opening (forming a 5̄ hand); the movement ends with the side of the hand touching the left side of the upper chest.	blow me down damn (I'll be damned) fancy fell (I fell for it) fool (you fooled me) have someone on (you were having me on) knock one flat knock one for six knock one sideways	1712
Non-manual features The top teeth are touching the lower lip; as the hand moves, the head tilts to the left and the mouth opens with the lips stretched.				
The O hand is held with the palm facing away from the signer (if the hand were opened, the fingers would point down).	The hand is held beside the hip.	The arm bends at the shoulder, so that the hand makes a short movement away from the signer while opening (forming a 5 hand).	bowls bowls player play bowls	1713
The left A hand is held with the palm facing down (if the hand were opened, the fingers would point to the right). The right O hand is held with the palm facing down (if the hand were opened, the fingers would point to the left).	The hands are held side by side in front of the body.	The right hand moves down and to the left and, at the same time, opens (forming a 5 hand); the hand then moves to the left, maintaining contact with the back of the left hand.	scald* scald on the back of the hand	1714

Notes   * This sign may be located at appropriate parts of the body.

1715 Bʊʌ ₁× Oɑ⊥ $\overset{\wedge[5]}{\underset{\square}{}}$

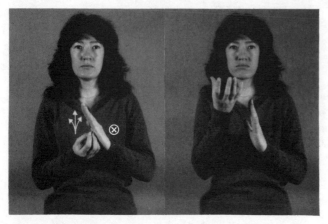

1716 $\overline{\text{B}}$ʊ> × ɟO⊥ʌ $\left(\overset{\cap\,[5]}{\underset{\square}{\underset{\perp}{}}} \; \overset{\omega\cap\,[\text{o}]}{\underset{\#}{<\wedge}} \; \underset{\perp}{\omega} \right)$.

1717 B⊤> × O⊤ᵥ₉ $\overset{\vee[5]}{\underset{\square}{\times}}$

The extended fingers (held together) and the extended thumb are bent and touch at the tips to form a circle.

Handshape and orientation	Location, hand arrangement and contact	Movement	Glosses	
The left B hand is held with the palm facing down and the fingers pointing up; the right O hand is held with the palm facing up (if the hand were opened, the fingers would point away from the signer).	The hands are held in front of the body; the left hand is held at an angle, so that the fingers are turned to the right, and the left palm rests on the right hand.	The right hand moves up and, at the same time, opens (forming a 5 hand).	volcano volcano erupting	1715

Non-manual features   The cheeks puff out.

The left B hand is held with the palm facing down and the fingers pointing to the right; the right O hand is held with the palm facing away from the signer (if the hand were opened, the fingers would point up).	The hands are held in front of the body; the right elbow is held on the back of the left hand.	The right hand bends away from the signer at the wrist while opening (forming a 5 hand); the hand then twists at the wrist, so that the fingers point to the left, before bending up at the wrist while closing (forming an O hand); the hand then twists at the wrist, so that the palm faces away from the signer; the movement is repeated.	lighthouse flashing light [1]	1716

Notes   1 If one hand only is used, the sign produced is **flashing light**.

$$\varnothing \quad O\bot\wedge \left(\begin{smallmatrix} \cap & [5] & \omega & \cap & [O] & \omega \\ \bot & & < & \wedge & & \bot \\ \Box & & & \# & & \end{smallmatrix} \right).$$

The left B hand is held with the palm facing towards the signer and the fingers pointing to the right; the right O hand is held with the palm facing towards the signer (if the hand were opened, the fingers would point down).	The hands are held in front of the body; the right knuckles rest against the left palm.	The right hand moves down, maintaining contact with the left hand, while opening (forming a 5 hand).	roots	1717

1718 C>⊥ ⊙ Oa⊥ $^{\wedge [\frac{5}{5}]}_{\times \square}$ °

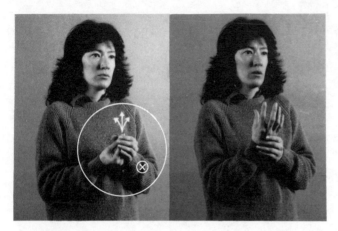

1719 C>⊥ ⊙ √Oa⊥ $^{\square [\frac{5}{5}]}$ ·

1720 Ø Oa⊥ Oa⊥ $^{\wedge [55]}_{\square}$

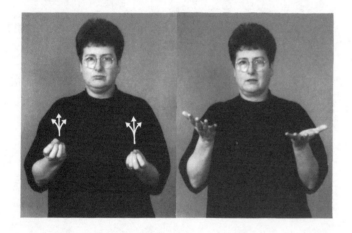

1721 Ø Oa⊥ Oa⊥ $^{\circ [BB]}_{\times \square}$

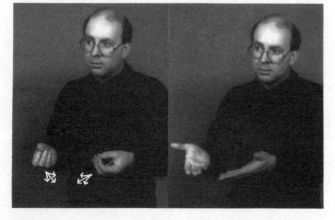

1722 Ø Oa⊥ ¦ Oa⊥ $^{\circ [55]}_{\vee \square}$

The extended fingers (held together) and the extended thumb are bent and touch at the tips to form a circle.

Handshape and orientation	Location, hand arrangement and contact	Movement	Glosses	
The left **c** hand is held with the palm facing right; the right **o** hand is held with the palm facing up (if the hands were opened, the fingers would all point away from the signer).	The hands are held in front of the body; the right fingers are held between the left thumb and fingers.	The right hand makes a short upward movement while opening (forming a **5̄** hand); the back of the right hand maintains contact with the left fingers throughout.	bloom blossom create creation develop development emerge emergence grow growth	1718
The left **c** hand is held with the palm facing right; the right **o** hand is held with the palm facing up (if the hands were opened, the fingers would all point away from the signer).	The hands are held in front of the body with the left hand clasping the right forearm.	The right hand opens (forming a **5̄** hand); the movement is repeated.	chimney smoke smoke/steam coming out of a chimney steam break wind[1] fart[1]	1719

Notes   1 If the left hand holds the right forearm, which is held horizontally in front of the body, and the right hand moves sharply away from the signer while opening, the sign produced is **break wind, fart**. This is a regional sign.   Cɑ> ⊙ √0ɑ⊥ ⁝□ [5̄]

Two **o** hands are held with the palms facing up (if the hands were opened, the fingers would all point away from the signer).	The hands are held in front of the body.	The hands move up while opening (forming two **5** hands).	industrial action strike blow up[1] explode[1] explosion[1] temper (lose one's temper)[1]	1720

Notes   1 If the cheeks are puffed out, the sign produced is **blow up, explode, explosion, lose one's temper.**

Two **o** hands are held with the palms facing up (if the hands were opened, the fingers would all point away from the signer).	The hands are held in front of the body at an angle, so that the fingers are turned towards each other.	The hands move towards each other and away from the signer while opening (forming two **B** hands).	contribute contribution spend	1721
Two **o** hands are held with the palms facing up (if the hands were opened, the fingers would all point away from the signer).	The hands are held side by side in front of the body.	The hands make a short movement down and away from the signer while opening (forming two **5** hands).	ages billions hundreds loads long time lots millions thousands frequent[1] many[1] often[1]	1722

Non-manual features   The cheeks are puffed out.

Notes   1 If the non-manual feature is not present, the sign produced is **frequent, many, often.**

1723 Ø OɑⱢ ₁× OɑⱢ ÷[55]

1724 Ø OᴑⱢ ₁ OᴑⱢ ÷[55]

1725 Ø OᴑⱢ ₁ OᴑⱢ ÷[55]

1726 Ø OⱢᴧ OⱢᴧⱢ ÷[55]

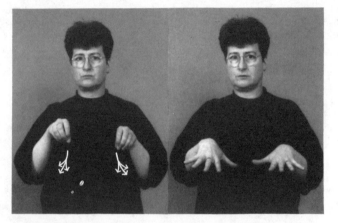

1727 Ø OⱢᴧ OⱢᴧⱢ ÷[55]·

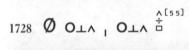

1728 Ø OⱢᴧ ₁ OⱢᴧ ÷[55]

The extended fingers (held together) and the extended thumb are bent and touch at the tips to form a circle.

Handshape and orientation	Location, hand arrangement and contact	Movement	Glosses	
Two o hands are held with the palms facing up (if the hands were opened, the fingers would all point away from the signer).	The hands are held side by side in front of the body with the fingertips bunched together.	The hands move away from the signer and apart while opening (forming two 5 hands).	give away waste wasted	1723
Two o hands are held with the palms facing down (if the hands were opened, the fingers would all point away from the signer).	The hands are held side by side in front of the body.	The hands make a short movement down and apart while opening (forming two 5 hands).	lose lost waste wasted	1724
Two o hands are held with the palms facing down (if the hands were opened, the fingers would all point away from the signer).	The hands are held side by side in in front of the body.	The hands make a short, sharp movement up, apart and, at the same time, away from the signer, while opening (forming two 5 hands).	splash spray break over [1] wash over [1]	1725

Notes 1 If the movement ends with a short downward movement, the sign produced is **break over, wash over**.

$$\emptyset \quad O \cap \top \mid O \cap \top \begin{smallmatrix} \circ \bullet \\ \wedge [55] \, \check{v} \\ \bot \\ \div \\ \Box \end{smallmatrix}$$

Two o hands are held with the palms facing away from the signer (if the hands were opened, the fingers would all point up).	The hands are held in front of the body.	The hands bend away from the signer at the wrists, while opening (forming two 5 hands).	abandon drop*	1726

Notes * This sign can be produced using one hand only.

$$\emptyset \quad O \bot \wedge \begin{smallmatrix} \cap [5] \\ \bot \\ \Box \end{smallmatrix}$$

Two o hands are held with the palms facing away from the signer (if the hands were opened, the fingers would all point up).	The hands are held in front of the body.	The hands bend away from the signer at the wrists while opening (forming two 5̄ hands); the movement is repeated.	magic* magician* stranger†	1727

Notes * This sign may be produced with a single firm movement.

$$\emptyset \quad O \bot \wedge \quad O \bot \wedge \begin{smallmatrix} \bullet \\ \cap [55] \\ \bot \\ \Box \end{smallmatrix}$$

† Regional sign.

Two o hands are held with the palms facing away from the signer (if the hands were opened, the fingers would all point up).	The hands are held side by side in front of the body.	The hands move up and apart while opening (forming two 5 hands).	bloom* bright* clear obvious transparent	1728

Notes * This sign may be produced with the palms facing towards the signer.

$$\emptyset \quad O \top \wedge \mid O \top \wedge \begin{smallmatrix} \wedge [55] \\ \div \\ \Box \end{smallmatrix}$$

1729 Ø O⊥∧ ₁× O⊥∧ $\overset{\wedge}{\underset{\square}{\div}}$ [55]

1730 Ø O>∧ O<∧ $\overset{\circ}{3}$H·

1731 Ø O>∧ O<∧ $\overset{\overset{\circ}{@}}{\underset{\vee}{\times}}$·

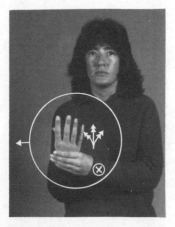

1732 Ø O>⊥ × O<⊥ $\overset{\overset{\circ}{\vee}}{\underset{\perp}{}}$·

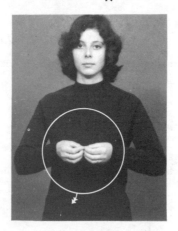

1733 Ø (C>⊥ ⊙ Oα⊥ $\overset{\wedge}{\underset{\square}{\times}}$ [5]·)>

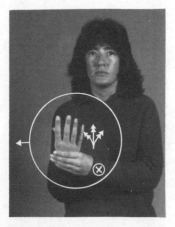

The extended fingers (held together) and the extended thumb are bent and touch at the tips to form a circle.

Handshape and orientation	Location, hand arrangement and contact	Movement	Glosses	
Two **O** hands are held with the palms facing away from the signer (if the hands were opened, the fingers would all point up).	The hands are held together side by side in front of the body.	The hands move up and apart while opening (forming two **5** hands).	burst explode explosion fountain splash spray spread peacock [1]	1729

Non-manual features The cheeks are puffed out and the air is sharply expelled.

Notes 1 If the movement is slow, the sign produced is **peacock**.

The left **O** hand is held with the palm facing right; the right **O** hand is held with the palm facing left (if the hands were opened, the fingers would all point up).	The hands are held in front of the body.	The hands make several very short twisting movements towards and away from the signer at the wrists.	nobody * none * no-one * nothing *	1730

Non-manual features The head shakes.

Notes * The following notes apply to all glosses:

This sign may be produced using two **F** hands. Ø F >∧ F <∧ ‿

This sign may be produced using one hand only. Ø O<∧ ‿ or Ø F<∧ ‿

This sign may be produced with the tongue protruding between the teeth.

The left **O** hand is held with the palm facing right; the right **O** hand is held with the palm facing left (if the hands were opened, the fingers would all point up).	The hands are held in front of the body.	The hands make small circles (the left hand moves clockwise, the right hand moves anticlockwise) in the vertical plane parallel to the signer's body.	nobody * none * no-one * nothing * †	1731

Non-manual features The head shakes.

Notes * This sign may be produced using two **F** hands. Ø F >∧ F <∧ ‿

† This sign may be produced with the hands making a short, firm movement away from the signer. Ø O>∧ O<∧ ⊥ or Ø F >∧ F <∧ ⊥

The left **O** hand is held with the palm facing right; the right **O** hand is held with the palm facing left (if the hands were opened, the fingers would all point away from the signer).	The hands are held in front of the body, with the bunched fingertips held together.	The hands make two short movements down and, at the same time, away from the signer.	learn practice practise student study train trainee training	1732

The left **C** hand is held with the palm facing right; the right **O** hand is held with the palm facing up (if the hands were opened, the fingers would all point away from the signer).	The fingers are held in front of the body; the right fingers are held between the left fingers and thumb.	The right hand moves up while opening (forming a **5** hand), maintaining contact with the left hand; the movement is repeated several times with both hands moving to the right throughout.	grass
			grass/plants/
			  vegetation
			  growing
			grow
			plants
			vegetation
				1733

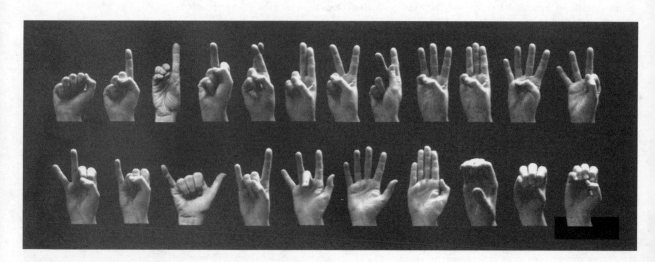

E

Handshape	Handshape description	Type	Sign entries
E	The fingers are held together and tightly bent so that the fingertips touch the thumb which is bent across the palm.	Single dez Manual tab Double dez	1734 – 1735 1736
Ė	The fingers are held together and tightly bent and the thumb is extended.	Single dez Manual tab Double dez	1737 1738 – 1739

1734 Ø E⊥ʌ ^θ_v

1735 ∪ Eɑ> ˣ·

1736 Ø Ēɑ> ⫪ Eʊ< ᶻ·

E

The fingers are held together and tightly bent so that the fingertips touch the thumb which is bent across the palm.

This is an infrequently used handshape in the language. It has some limited use as a *handling* classifier for items with small handles such as a nail brush. It is also used to indicate the two hands grasping each other as in **grapple** (sign 1736).

The **E** handshape expresses the letter **e** in several finger spelling systems, including the Irish and American manual alphabets. As such, it is used in initial letter handshape signs borrowed from Irish Sign Language (ISL) and American Sign Language (ASL). Examples include **Europe** (sign 1734) and **European** (sign 1734) from ISL (and *Gestuno* —see *Introduction*) and **environment** from ASL (see *Introduction*).

Handshape and orientation	Location, hand arrangement and contact	Movement	Glosses	
The **E** hand is held with the palm facing away from the signer (if the hand were opened, the fingers would point up).	The hand is held in front of the body.	The hand makes a small anticlockwise circle in the vertical plane parallel to the signer's body.	**Europe*** **European***	**1734**
Notes * This sign may be produced with the hand making a small anticlockwise circle in the horizontal plane.		Ø E⊥∧		
The **E** hand is held with the palm facing up (if the hand were opened, the fingers would point to the right).	The hand is held beneath the chin.	The heel of the hand taps the chin twice.	**nut*** **peanut***	**1735**
Notes * This sign may be produced with a single movement.		⊻ Eα> ˟		
The left **E** hand is held with the palm facing up; the right **E** hand is held with the palm facing down (if the hands were opened, the left fingers would point to the right and the right fingers would point to the left).	The hands are held in front of the body; the right hand is held above the left hand and the fingers are linked together.	The hands remain linked together and move from side to side several times.	**wrestler** **wrestling**	**1736**
Non-manual features The head moves from side to side.				

1737 ⌣ Ė⊤< ⁰

1738 Ø Ėʊ> (ᑎ⊥)^[ß] ^<□

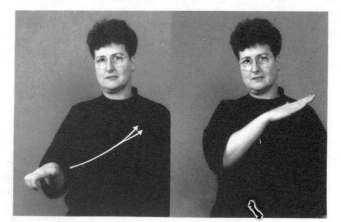

1739 Ø Ėʊ⊥ ¦ Ėʊ⊥ ᵚ˙

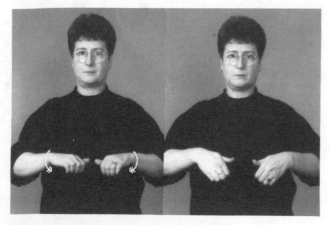

This is a rarely used handshape in the language. It has some limited use as a *handling* classifier for objects which are grasped by the bent fingers, such as **portable phone** (sign 1737), **discus** (sign 1738) and **dominoes** (sign 1739).

Handshape and orientation	Location, hand arrangement and contact	Movement	Glosses	

The Ė hand is held with the palm facing towards the signer (if the hand were opened, the fingers would point to the left).	The hand is held in front of the mouth and chin.	No movement.	dictaphone
			dictate onto a
			  dictaphone
			portable phone/
			  telephone
			speak on a portable
			  phone/telephone
				1737

Non-manual features The lips are tightly rounded.				
The Ė hand is held with the palm facing down (if the hand were opened, the fingers would point to the right).	The hand is held in front of the body.	The hand moves up and to the left while bending away from the signer at the wrist and, at the same time, opening (forming a Ḃ hand).	discus discus thrower throw a discus	1738
Two Ė hands are held with the palms facing down (if the hands were opened, the fingers would all point away from the signer).	The hands are held side by side in front of the body at an angle, so that the knuckles are turned towards each other.	The hands twist towards the signer at the wrists; the movement is repeated.	dominoes * domino player * play dominoes *	1739
Notes * This sign may be produced using two Ğ hands.				

Ø G̈ɔ⊥ ¦ G̈ɔ⊥ ₃⊤ ·

The range of number signs used by different people in Britain provides a particularly interesting example of variation in BSL. Nobody has yet worked out exactly how many ways are used by various groups of signers to express numbers. It would seem, however, that most British signers know each other's number signs well enough to communicate with each other. Most of the systems use lots of one-handed signs. A notable exception is the two-handed number system used by people from the Manchester region.

Some handshapes are used for number signs which don't come up anywhere else in this Dictionary. Another difference is that you don't often see BSL non-manual features used in the production of numbers. One exception is the use of the closed mouth, with the lips pushed forward (sometimes the head makes small movements from side to side, too), to indicate that a given figure is approximate: this might produce glosses such as **25-odd** or **70-ish**. It's also common to see English lip-patterns produced along with number signs.

In this Dictionary, we've decided to show two number systems, which are widely used and understood in the British Deaf community. You can make some predictions about who will use which signs (based on the area a person comes from) although nothing so simple as a 'North/South' divide can be assumed. For the learner, it's enough to be aware that although what you see in the wider community may not be the same as the information presented here, you can be sure that the majority of British Deaf people will understand these signs. Here we give signs corresponding to the basic numbers—sometimes called *cardinal* numbers—up to 30. Above this figure, you just use the same patterns as for 21, 22, and so on, with the appropriately altered digits: so, to produce 37 or 87, just look at 27 and replace the digit '2' with the '3' or '8' from the same system. For three-figure numbers, eg 239, the hand moves to the right between digits: in real life, however, this movement may be so small you can hardly see it.

Basic numbers which tell you about quantities are not the only way that a language gives this kind of information, however. When we want to sign or say something about the order of items, ie 'first' (1st), 'second' (2nd), 'third' (3rd) and so on, we use a different set of items. In BSL, the most general way of expressing these—sometimes called *ordinal* numbers—is like this: the same handshape as for the appropriate basic number is held in front of the body with the palm facing away from the signer and any extended fingers pointing up; the hand twists firmly at the wrist so that the palm faces towards the signer (see signs 301 and 302 in this Dictionary). A second set of signs with the same meanings is produced by holding the appropriate handshape in front of the body with the palm facing down and any extended fingers pointing to the left; the hand makes a short, firm movement away from the signer (see sign 294 in this Dictionary). These two sets of signs are used for ordered numbers up to 10. For 'eleventh' (11th) and above, the basic and ordered number signs are the same. In these and comparable cases, lip-patterns are often used to distinguish between the two signs.

BSL also has signs which might be glossed as **firstly** (or **first thing, first point**) and so on. If you want to express 'secondly', for instance, you can use a two-handed sign—entry 391 in the Dictionary—like this: the basic number handshape is produced with the left hand (palm facing right, extended fingers pointing away from the signer) while the tip of the right index finger, extended from the fist, taps the left middle fingertip. Signers don't use this system for numbers greater than five ('fifthly').

Using the basic numbers in a variety of specific ways, several kinds of information involving numbers can be expressed. Fractions are produced in BSL by giving the two figures—from above and below the line, as they would appear on paper—in succession, located one above

the other (as appropriate) in front of the body. So, for example, the sign glossed as **five sixteenths** could be produced by signing a basic digit '5', moving the hand sharply downwards, and then signing '16'.

It can be helpful to think of decimal figures in BSL as relating to the conventions we use for writing such numbers on paper. Spoken English can express '7.7' with the phrase 'seven point seven', where 'point' stands for the mark appearing like a full-stop in the written number. In BSL, the two digits are produced with 'point' (that is, the hand is held in front of the body with the index finger extended from the fist and the palm facing down; the hand makes a short, firm movement away from the signer) signed between them. Percentages, too, are produced using the basic numbers: the appropriate figure is given, followed by the sign glossed as **per cent** (entry 1705 in this Dictionary).

A sign meaning 'once' can be found in this Dictionary (entry 309). A sign meaning 'twice' can be produced by altering the movement of the basic number sign glossed as **two** to a short downward movement. **Single** is produced in the same way as the sign meaning 'once' referred to above; **double** is commonly produced using the same handshape, location and orientation as the basic number meaning 'two' with the hand making a short, repeated movement from side to side.

So far, these signs are all expressed by units comparable to those which are used in English. However, BSL can also give several kinds of information about numbers using lexical patterns that English doesn't have. There is, for instance, a set of BSL signs which might be glossed as **one-more, two-more** and so on up to **five-more**. These use the handshapes, locations and orientations of the basic numbers, with a repeated flexing movement of the extended fingers.

Information about age can be given by producing figures as for basic numbers, but beginning the movement at the nose. So if you want a sign meaning '35-years-old', for instance, start by holding the handshape of the first digit ('3') touching the tip of the nose (the index fingertip typically contacts the nose); the hand then moves down and away from the signer while opening to form the handshape of the second digit ('5'). BSL has a similar method (not the only means available in the language) for referring to amounts of money. Such numbers are produced with movements rather like those explained above for age; the initial location in this case, however, is the point of the chin. How people use this convention depends on the basic number system they are using. It would seem to be commonly used for figures up to £10.

Time information can also be given by using a modification of the basic numbers. The sign is constructed as the basic number would be, but the orientation and movement are different, which shows that the information is about time. Let's say you want a sign meaning 'four o'clock'; the number '4' handshape is held in neutral space (with the palm facing away from the signer and the extended fingers pointing up) and then twists at the wrist, so that the palm faces towards the signer, before making a short downwards movement. This type of movement is only used for times exactly on the hour. When you are signing about calendar years, BSL often splits the information in two. Suppose you are telling somebody that you were born in 1966; following the patterns for basic numbers, you can sign '19—66'; some signers include a movement to the right between the two elements.

The pattern given above for calendar years is common to other many-digit numbers: that is, these are expressed essentially as groups of single digits, rather than being condensed into their hundreds and thousands. Telephone numbers are another example of the principle. British Deaf people do not sign 'three million, seven hundred and forty-four thousand, seven hundred and fifty-two', but '3-7-4—4-7-5-2': the number of digits in each group may change, pauses may occur between groups, and the hand may move to the right throughout.

Ø O<ʌ ø   1 Ø Gᴛʌ ø   2 Ø Vᴛʌ ø

3 Ø Wᴛʌ ø   4 Ø 4ᴛʌ ø   5 Ø 5ᴛʌ ø

6 Ø Iᴛʌ ø   7 Ø 7ᴛʌ ø   8 Ø Fᴛʌ ø

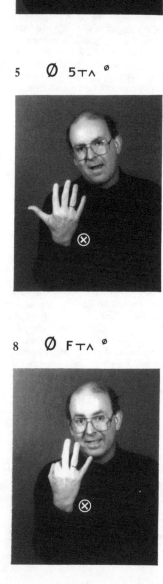

Handshape and orientation	Location, hand arrangement and contact	Movement	Glosses
The o hand is held with the palm facing left (if the hand were opened, the fingers would point up).	The hand is held in front of the body.	No movement.	**0** **nil** **nothing** **nought** **zero**
The G hand is held with the palm facing towards the signer (if the hand were opened, the fingers would point up).	The hand is held in front of the body.	No movement.	**1** **one**
The v hand is held with the palm facing towards the signer (if the hand were opened, the fingers would point up).	The hand is held in front of the body.	No movement.	**2** **two**
The w hand is held with the palm facing towards the signer (if the hand were opened, the fingers would point up).	The hand is held in front of the body.	No movement.	**3** **three**
The 4 hand is held with the palm facing towards the signer and the fingers pointing up.	The hand is held in front of the body.	No movement.	**4** **four**
The 5 hand is held with the palm facing towards the signer and the fingers pointing up.	The hand is held in front of the body.	No movement.	**5** **five**
The I hand is held with the palm facing towards the signer (if the hand were opened, the fingers would point up).	The hand is held in front of the body.	No movement.	**6** **half-a-dozen** **six**
The 7 hand is held with the palm facing towards the signer (if the hand were opened, the fingers would point up).	The hand is held in front of the body.	No movement.	**7** **seven**
The F hand is held with the palm facing towards the signer (if the hand were opened, the fingers would point up).	The hand is held in front of the body.	No movement.	**8** **eight**

9   Ø 4⊤∧ ⌀

10   Ø 5⊤∧ 5⊤∧ ⌀

11   Ø Ȧ<⊥ ω̈z·

12   Ø ᵉG̈⊥∧ ᵐ·

13   Ø ᵉⁱV̈⊥∧ ᵐ·

14   Ø 4̈⊥∧ ᵐ·

15   Ø 5̈⊥∧ ᵐ·

16   Ø I⊥∧ ᵐ·

17   Ø 7̈⊥∧ ᵐ·

Handshape and orientation	Location, hand arrangement and contact	Movement	Glosses
The 4 hand is held with the palm facing towards the signer and the fingers pointing up.	The hand is held in front of the body.	No movement.	9 nine
Two 5 hands are held with the palms facing towards the signer and the fingers pointing up.	The hands are held in front of the body.	No movement.	10 ten
The A̍ hand is held with the palm facing left (if the hand were opened, the fingers would point away from the signer).	The hand is held in front of the body.	The hand makes several short twisting movements from side to side at the wrist.	11 eleven
The Ġ hand is held with the palm facing away from the signer (if the hand were opened, the fingers would point up).	The hand is held in front of the body.	The index finger flexes twice.	12 a dozen twelve
The V̇ hand is held with the palm facing away from the signer (if the hand were opened, the fingers would point up).	The hand is held in front of the body.	The index and middle fingers flex twice.	13 thirteen
The 4̈ hand is held with the palm facing away from the signer (if the hand were opened, the fingers would point up).	The hand is held in front of the body.	The fingers flex twice.	14 fourteen
The 5̈ hand is held with the palm facing away from the signer (if the hand were opened, the fingers would point up).	The hand is held in front of the body.	The fingers and thumb flex twice.	15 fifteen
The ı hand is held with the palm facing away from the signer (if the hand were opened, the fingers would point up).	The hand is held in front of the body.	The little finger flexes twice.	16 sixteen
The 7̈ hand is held with the palm facing away from the signer (if the hand were opened, the fingers would point up).	The hand is held in front of the body.	The little and ring fingers flex twice.	17 seventeen

18 Ø F̈⊥∧ ᵐ·   19 Ø 4̈⊥∧ ᵐ·   20 Ø V⊤∧ $\overset{\omega[A]}{\underset{\#}{\perp}}$

  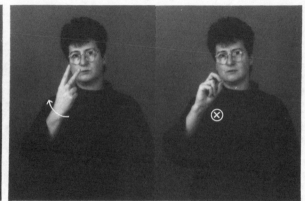

21 Ø V⊤∧ $\overset{\circ}{\underset{\perp}{}}$ // ØG⊤∧ $\overset{\circ}{\underset{\perp}{}}$ 22 Ø V⊤∧ ⁽⊥ˢ⊥⁾

 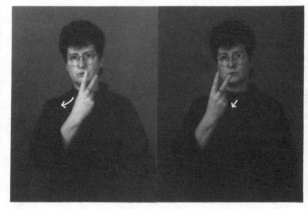

23 Ø V⊤∧ $\overset{\circ}{\underset{\perp}{}}$ // Ø W⊥∧ $\overset{\circ}{\underset{\perp}{}}$ 24 Ø V⊤∧ $\overset{\circ}{\underset{\perp}{}}$ // Ø 4⊤∧ $\overset{\circ}{\underset{\perp}{}}$

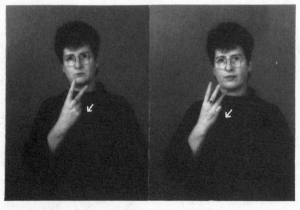 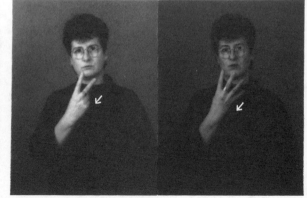

Handshape and orientation	*Location, hand arrangement and contact*	*Movement*	*Glosses*
The F̈ hand is held with the palm facing away from the signer (if the hand were opened, the fingers would point up).	The hand is held in front of the body.	The extended fingers flex twice.	18 **eighteen**
The ä hand is held with the palm facing away from the signer (if the hand were opened, the fingers would point up).	The hand is held in front of the body.	The fingers flex twice.	19 **nineteen**
The v hand is held with the palm facing towards the signer (if the hand were opened, the fingers would point up).	The hand is held in front of the body.	The hand twists at the wrist, so that the palm faces away from the signer and, at the same time, the extended fingers close (forming an Â hand).	20 **a score** **twenty**
The v hand is held with the palm facing towards the signer (if the hand were opened, the fingers would point up).	The hand is held in front of the body.	The hand makes a short movement away from the signer.	21 **twenty-one**
The ɢ hand is held with the palm facing towards the signer (if the hand were opened, the fingers would point up).	The hand is held in front of the body.	The hand makes a short movement away from the signer.	
The v hand is held with the palm facing towards the signer (if the hand were opened, the fingers would point up).	The hand is held in front of the body.	The hand makes a short movement away from the signer and then moves to the right, before making another short movement away from the signer.	22 **twenty-two**
The v hand is held with the palm facing towards the signer (if the hand were opened, the fingers would point up).	The hand is held in front of the body.	The hand makes a short movement away from the signer.	23 **twenty-three**
The w hand is held with the palm facing towards the signer (if the hand were opened, the fingers would point up).	The hand is held in front of the body.	The hand makes a short movement away from the signer.	
The v hand is held with the palm facing towards the signer (if the hand were opened, the fingers would point up).	The hand is held in front of the body.	The hand makes a short movement away from the signer.	24 **twenty-four** **two dozen**
The 4 hand is held with the palm facing towards the signer (if the hand were opened, the fingers would point up).	The hand is held in front of the body.	The hand makes a short movement away from the signer.	

25   Ø VTʌ ^ᶖ // Ø 5Tʌ ^ᶖ

26   Ø VTʌ ^ᶖ // Ø ITʌ ^ᶖ

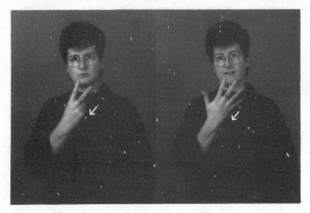

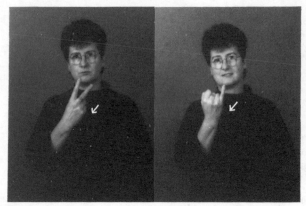

27   Ø VTʌ ^ᶖ // Ø 7Tʌ ^ᶖ

28   Ø VTʌ ^ᶖ // Ø FTʌ ^ᶖ

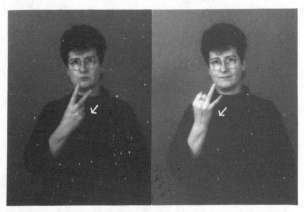

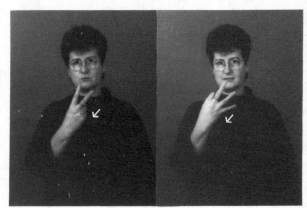

29   Ø VTʌ ^ᶖ // Ø 4T< ^ᶖ

30   Ø WTʌ ^{ɜˇ# [o]}

Handshape and orientation	Location, hand arrangement and contact	Movement	Glosses
The v hand is held with the palm facing towards the signer (if the hand were opened, the fingers would point up).	The hand is held in front of the body.	The hand makes a short movement away from the signer.	**25** **twenty-five**
The 5 hand is held with the palm facing towards the signer and the fingers pointing up.	The hand is held in front of the body.	The hand makes a short movement away from the signer.	
The v hand is held with the palm facing towards the signer (if the hand were opened, the fingers would point up).	The hand is held in front of the body.	The hand makes a short movement away from the signer.	**26** **twenty-six**
The I hand is held with the palm facing towards the signer (if the hand were opened, the fingers would point up).	The hand is held in front of the body.	The hand makes a short movement away from the signer.	
The v hand is held with the palm facing towards the signer (if the hand were opened, the fingers would point up).	The hand is held in front of the body.	The hand makes a short movement away from the signer.	**27** **twenty-seven**
The 7 hand is held with the palm facing towards the signer (if the hand were opened, the fingers would point up).	The hand is held in front of the body.	The hand makes a short movement away from the signer.	
The v hand is held with the palm facing towards the signer (if the hand were opened, the fingers would point up).	The hand is held in front of the body.	The hand makes a short movement away from the signer.	**28** **twenty-eight**
The F hand is held with the palm facing towards the signer (if the hand were opened, the fingers would point up).	The hand is held in front of the body.	The hand makes a short movement away from the signer.	
The v hand is held with the palm facing towards the signer (if the hand were opened, the fingers would point up).	The hand is held in front of the body.	The hand makes a short movement away from the signer.	**29** **twenty-nine**
The 4 hand is held with the palm facing towards the signer (if the hand were opened, the fingers would point up).	The hand is held in front of the body.	The hand makes a short movement away from the signer.	
The W hand is held with the palm facing towards the signer (if the hand were opened, the fingers would point up).	The hand is held in front of the body.	The hand twists at the wrist, so that the palm faces left, while closing (forming an O hand).	**30** **thirty**

40 Ø 4т∧ ³ᵛ# [o]

50 Ø 5т∧ ³ᵛ# [o]

60 Ø lт∧ ³ᵛ# [o]

70 Ø 7т∧ ³ᵛ# [o]

80 Ø Fт∧ ³ᵛ# [o]

90 Ø 4т< ³ᵛ# [o]

Handshape and orientation	Location, hand arrangement and contact	Movement	Glosses
The 4 hand is held with the palm facing towards the signer and the fingers pointing up.	The hand is held in front of the body.	The hand twists at the wrist, so that the palm faces left, while closing (forming an O hand).	**40** **forty**
The 5 hand is held with the palm facing towards the signer and the fingers pointing up.	The hand is held in front of the body.	The hand twists at the wrist, so that the palm faces left, while closing	**50** **fifty**
The I hand is held with the palm facing towards the signer (if the hand were opened, the fingers would point up).	The hand is held in front of the body.	The hand twists at the wrist, so that the palm faces left, while closing (forming an O hand).	**60** **sixty**
The 7 hand is held with the palm facing towards the signer (if the hand were opened, the fingers would point up).	The hand is held in front of the body.	The hand twists at the wrist, so that the palm faces left, while closing (forming an O hand).	**70** **seventy**
The F hand is held with the palm facing towards the signer (if the hand were opened, the fingers would point up).	The hand is held in front of the body.	The hand twists at the wrist, so that the palm faces left, while closing (forming an O hand).	**80** **eighty**
The 4 hand is held with the palm facing towards the signer and the fingers pointing to the left.	The hand is held in front of the body.	The hand twists at the wrist, so that the palm faces left, while closing (forming an O hand).	**90** **ninety**

100 Ø GT∧ $\overset{[o]}{\overset{(\omega)}{\underset{\#}{\vee}}}$

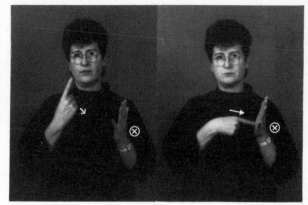

1,000 Ø GT∧ $\overset{\circ}{\bot}$ $/\!/$ 5>⊥ , GT< $^{\times}$

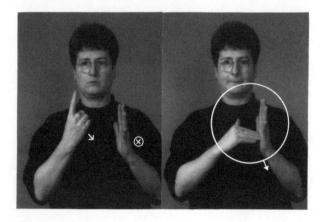

1,000,000 Ø GT∧ $\overset{\circ}{\bot}$ $/\!/$ Ø 5>∧ ₁ₓ B̈<∧ $\overset{\overset{\circ}{\times}}{\underset{\bot}{\vee}}$

Handshape and orientation	Location, hand arrangement and contact	Movement	Glosses
The G hand is held with the palm facing towards the signer (if the hand were opened, the fingers would point up).	The hand is held in front of the body.	The hand moves to the right while twisting at the wrist, so that the palm faces left, and closing (forming an O hand).	**100** **one hundred**
The G hand is held with the palm facing towards the signer (if the hand were opened, the fingers would point up).	The hand is held in front of the body.	The hand makes a short movement away from the signer.	**1,000** **one thousand**
The left 5 hand is held with the palm facing right and the fingers pointing away from the signer; the right G hand is held with the palm facing towards the signer (if the hand were opened, the fingers would point to the left).	The hands are held side by side in front of the body.	The right index fingertip touches the heel of the left hand.	
The G hand is held with the palm facing towards the signer (if the hand were opened, the fingers would point up).	The hand is held in front of the body.	The hand makes a short movement away from the signer.	**1,000,000** **one million**
The left 5 hand is held with the palm facing right and the fingers pointing up; the right B̈ hand is held with the palm facing left (if the hand were opened, the fingers would point up).	The hands are held side by side in front of the body; the right fingertips are held against the heel of the left hand.	The hands remain together and make a short movement down and, at the same time, away from the signer.	

0   Ø O<∧ ø

1   Ø Gт∧ ø

2   Ø Vт∧ ø

3   Ø V̇т∧ ø

4   Ø 4т∧ ø

5   Ø 5т∧ ø

6   Ø Ä т< ø

7   Ø Ġт< ø

8   Ø V̇т< ø

Handshape and orientation	Location, hand arrangement and contact	Movement	Glosses
The o hand is held with the palm facing left (if the hand were opened, the fingers would point up).	The hand is held in front of the body.	No movement.	0 nil nothing nought zero
The G hand is held with the palm facing towards the signer (if the hand were opened, the fingers would point up).	The hand is held in front of the body.	No movement.	1 one
The v hand is held with the palm facing towards the signer (if the hand were opened, the fingers would point up).	The hand is held in front of the body.	No movement.	2 two
The v̇ hand is held with the palm facing towards the signer (if the hand were opened, the fingers would point up).	The hand is held in front of the body.	No movement.	3 three
The 4 hand is held with the palm facing towards the signer and the fingers pointing up.	The hand is held in front of the body.	No movement.	4 four
The 5 hand is held with the palm facing towards the signer and the fingers pointing up.	The hand is held in front of the body.	No movement.	5 five
The Ä hand is held with the palm facing towards the signer (if the hand were opened, the fingers would point to the left).	The hand is held in front of the body.	No movement.	6 half-a-dozen six
The Ġ hand is held with the palm facing towards the signer (if the hand were opened, the fingers would point to the left).	The hand is held in front of the body.	No movement.	7 seven
The v̇ hand is held with the palm facing towards the signer (if the hand were opened, the fingers would point to the left).	The hand is held in front of the body.	No movement.	8 eight

9   Ø   ẇmⲦ< ᵒ

10   Ø   5<∧ ⁰ẇⲍ ·

11   Ø   Ḡ̄⊥∧ # [ĝ] ·

12   Ø   H̄̄⊥∧ # [A] ·

13   Ø   wⲦ∧ ⁰ẓ ·

14   Ø   4Ⲧ∧ ⁰ẓ ·

15   Ø   5Ⲧ∧ ⁰ẓ ·

16   Ø   Ä̇Ⲧ< ⁰ẓ ·

17   Ø   Ġ Ⲧ< ⁰ẓ ·

Handshape and orientation	Location, hand arrangement and contact	Movement	Glosses
The ẅm hand is held with the palm facing towards the signer (if the hand were opened, the fingers would point to the left).	The hand is held in front of the body.	No movement.	9 nine
The 5 hand is held with the palm facing left and the fingers pointing up.	The hand is held in front of the body.	The hand makes several short twisting movements from side to side at the wrist.	10 ten
The Ğ hand is held with the palm facing away from the signer (if the hand were opened, the fingers would point up).	The hand is held in front of the body.	The index finger and thumb tips close (forming a Ğ hand); the movement is repeated.	11 eleven
The Ħ hand is held with the palm facing away from the signer (if the hand were opened, the fingers would point up).	The hand is held in front of the body.	The extended fingers and thumb close (forming an Ħ hand) repeatedly.	12 a dozen twelve
The w hand is held with the palm facing towards the signer (if the hand were opened, the fingers would point up).	The hand is held in front of the body.	The hand makes several short movements from side to side.	13 thirteen
The 4 hand is held with the palm facing towards the signer and the fingers pointing up.	The hand is held in front of the body.	The hand makes several short movements from side to side.	14 fourteen
The 5 hand is held with the palm facing towards the signer and the fingers pointing up.	The hand is held in front of the body.	The hand makes several short movements from side to side.	15 fifteen
The Ä hand is held with the palm facing towards the signer (if the hand were opened, the fingers would point to the left).	The hand is held in front of the body.	The hand makes several short movements from side to side.	16 sixteen
The Ġ hand is held with the palm facing towards the signer (if the hand were opened, the fingers would point to the left).	The hand is held in front of the body at an angle, so that the fingers are turned up.	The hand makes several short movements from side to side.	17 seventeen

18 Ø V̇⊤< $\overset{\circ}{z}$·　　19 Ø Ẇm⊤< $\overset{\circ}{z}$·　　20 Ø V⊤∧ $\overset{\omega\,[A]}{\underset{\#}{\bot}}$

  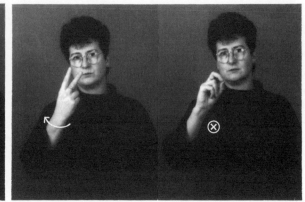

21 Ø V⊥∧ $\overset{\omega\,[G]}{\underset{\#}{\top}}$　　　　22 Ø V⊥∧ $\overset{\bot\omega\bot}{\top}$

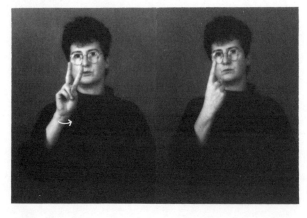 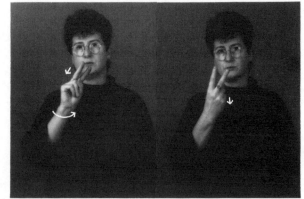

23 Ø V⊥∧ $\overset{\omega\,[V̌]}{\underset{\square}{\top}}$　　　　24 Ø V⊥∧ $\overset{\omega\,[4]}{\underset{\square}{\top}}$

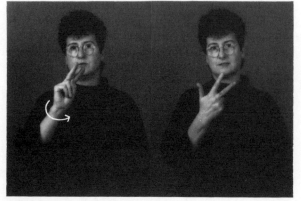 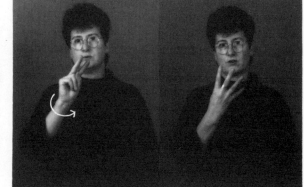

Handshape and orientation	Location, hand arrangement and contact	Movement	Glosses
The v̇ hand is held with the palm facing towards the signer (if the hand were opened, the fingers would point to the left).	The hand is held in front of the body at an angle, so that the fingers are turned up.	The hand makes several short movements from side to side.	18 eighteen
The ẇm hand is held with the palm facing towards the signer (if the hand were opened, the fingers would point to the left).	The hand is held in front of the body at an angle, so that the fingers are turned up.	The hand makes several short movements from side to side.	19 nineteen
The v hand is held with the palm facing towards the signer (if the hand were opened, the fingers would point up).	The hand is held in front of the body.	The hand twists at the wrist, so that the palm faces away from the signer and, at the same time, the extended fingers close (forming an Ậ hand).	20 a score twenty
The v hand is held with the palm facing away from the signer (if the hand were opened, the fingers would point up).	The hand is held in front of the body.	The hand twists at the wrist, so that the palm faces towards the signer, while closing (forming a G hand).	21 twenty-one
The v hand is held with the palm facing away from the signer (if the hand were opened, the fingers would point up).	The hand is held in front of the body.	The hand makes a short movement away from the signer and then twists at the wrist, so that the palm faces towards the signer, before making another short movement away from from the signer.	22 twenty-two
The v hand is held with the palm facing away from the signer (if the hand were opened, the fingers would point up).	The hand is held in front of the body.	The hand twists at the wrist, so that the palm faces towards the signer, while opening (forming a v̇ hand).	23 twenty-three
The v hand is held with the palm facing away from the signer (if the hand were opened, the fingers would point up).	The hand is held in front of the body.	The hand twists at the wrist, so that the palm faces towards the signer, while opening (forming a 4 hand).	24 twenty-four two dozen

25 $\emptyset$ V⊥∧ $\overset{\omega}{\underset{\square}{\top}}$ [s]

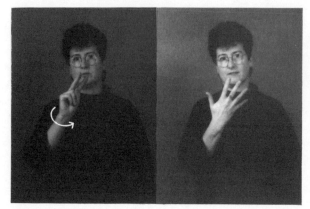

26 $\emptyset$ V⊥∧ $\overset{\omega}{\underset{\#}{\top}}$ [Ä]

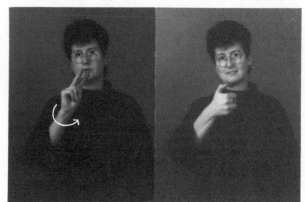

27 $\emptyset$ V⊥∧ $\overset{\omega}{\underset{\#}{\top}}$ [ċ]

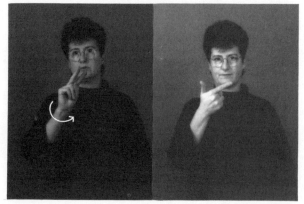

28 $\emptyset$ V⊥∧ $\overset{\omega}{\underset{\square}{\top}}$ [v̇]

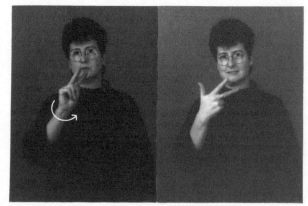

29 $\emptyset$ V⊥∧ $\overset{\omega}{\underset{\square}{\top}}$ [Ẅm]

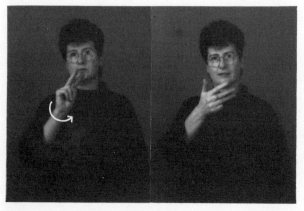

30 $\emptyset$ V̇⊤∧ $\overset{\omega}{\underset{\#}{<}}$ [Ä]

[842]

Handshape and orientation	Location, hand arrangement and contact	Movement	Glosses
The v hand is held with the palm facing away from the signer (if the hand were opened, the fingers would point up).	The hand is held in front of the body.	The hand twists at the wrist, so that the palm faces towards the signer, while opening (forming a 5 hand).	25 **twenty-five**
The v hand is held with the palm facing away from the signer (if the hand were opened, the fingers would point up).	The hand is held in front of the body.	The hand twists at the wrist, so that the palm faces towards the signer, while closing (forming an Ä hand).	26 **twenty-six**
The v hand is held with the palm facing away from the signer (if the hand were opened, the fingers would point up).	The hand is held in front of the body.	The hand twists at the wrist, so that the palm faces towards the signer, while changing (forming a ċ hand).	27 **twenty-seven**
The v hand is held with the palm facing away from the signer (if the hand were opened, the fingers would point up).	The hand is held in front of the body.	The hand twists at the wrist, so that the palm faces towards the signer, while opening (forming a v̇ hand).	28 **twenty-eight**
The v hand is held with the palm facing away from the signer (if the hand were opened, the fingers would point up).	The hand is held in front of the body.	The hand twists at the wrist, so that the palm faces towards the signer, while opening (forming a ẇm hand).	29 **twenty-nine**
The v̇ hand is held with the palm facing towards the signer (if the hand were opened, the fingers would point up).	The hand is held in front of the body.	The hand twists at the wrist, so that the palm faces left, while closing (forming an Ḥ hand).	30 **thirty**

40   Ø 4τ∧ ³˅# [o]

50   Ø 5τ∧ ³˅# [o]

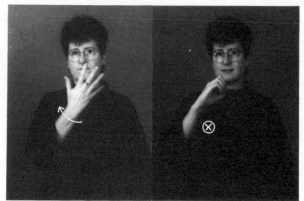

60   Ø Ä̈τ< ³˅□ [o]

70   Ø Ġτ< ³˅# [o]

80   Ø V̇τ< ³˅# [o]

90   Ø Ẇmτ< ³˅# [o]

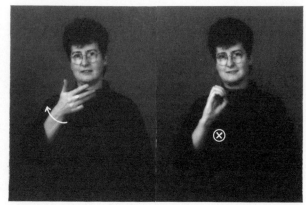

Handshape and orientation	Location, hand arrangement and contact	Movement	Glosses
The 4 hand is held with the palm facing towards the signer and the fingers pointing up.	The hand is held in front of the body.	The hand twists at the wrist, so that the palm faces left, while closing (forming an O hand).	**40** forty
The 5 hand is held with the palm facing towards the signer and the fingers pointing up.	The hand is held in front of the body.	The hand twists at the wrist, so that the palm faces left, while closing (forming an O hand).	**50** fifty
The Ä hand is held with the palm facing towards the signer (if the hand were opened, the fingers would point to the left).	The hand is held in front of the body.	The hand twists at the wrist, so that the palm faces left, while closing (forming an O hand).	**60** sixty
The Ġ hand is held with the palm facing towards the signer (if the hand were opened, the fingers would point to the left).	The hand is held in front of the body.	The hand twists at the wrist, so that the palm faces left, while closing (forming an O hand).	**70** seventy
The v̇ hand is held with the palm facing towards the signer (if the hand were opened, the fingers would point to the left).	The hand is held in front of the body.	The hand twists at the wrist, so that the palm faces left, while closing (forming an O hand).	**80** eighty
The ẇm hand is held with the palm facing towards the signer (if the hand were opened, the fingers would point to the left).	The hand is held in front of the body.	The hand twists at the wrist, so that the palm faces left, while closing (forming an O hand).	**90** ninety

100 ∪ G̈<∧ $\overset{<}{\underset{×}{×}}$

1,000 Ø GT∧ $\overset{○}{⊥}$ $\overset{//}{//}$ Ø Gↄ⊥ $\overset{(∨<)}{\underset{<}{ω}}$

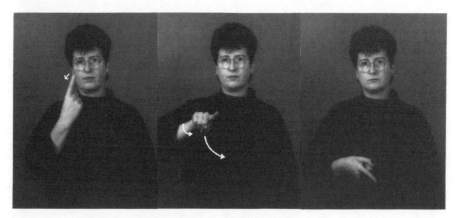

1,000,000 Ø GT∧ $\overset{○}{⊥}$ $\overset{//}{//}$ Ø 5>∧ ₁× B̈<∧ $\overset{×○}{\underset{⊥}{∨}}$

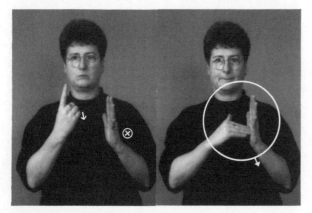

Handshape and orientation	Location, hand arrangement and contact	Movement	Glosses
The Ġ hand is held with the palm facing left (if the hand were opened, the fingers would point up).	The hand is held in front of the chin.	The hand moves to the left, so that the side of the index finger brushes across the chin.	**100** **one hundred**
The G hand is held with the palm facing towards the signer (if the hand were opened, the fingers would point up).	The hand is held in front of the body.	The hand makes a short movement away from the signer.	**1,000** **one thousand**
The G hand is held with the palm facing down (if the hand were opened, the fingers would point away from the signer).	The hand is held in front of the body.	The hand twists at the wrist, so that the palm faces left, while moving down and then to the left.	
The G hand is held with the palm facing towards the signer (if the hand were opened, the fingers would point up).	The hand is held in front of the body.	The hand makes a short movement away from the signer.	**1,000,000** **one million**
The left 5 hand is held with the palm facing right and the fingers pointing up; the right Ḃ hand is held with the palm facing left (if the hand were opened, the fingers would point up).	The hands are held side by side in front of the body; the right fingertips are held against the heel of the left hand.	The hands remain together and make a short movement down and, at the same time, away from the signer.	

It appears to be a widely-held belief amongst the general public in the U.K. that sign language consists entirely of fingerspelling. In fact, fingerspelling accounts for only a small proportion of the lexical content of BSL. Contrary to public perception, fingerspelling can actually be seen as marginal—since it has developed with explicit reference to written English—in comparison with the naturally and independently evolved elements of linguistic behaviour that form the greater part of visual-gestural language interaction.

Fingerspelling is not a modern invention: an early record of the British manual alphabet appears in an anonymous document called "Digiti lingua" from 1698. Nor is there a single universal fingerspelling system—even among countries which share a writing system. The differences can be substantial: the U.S.A. and Ireland (in common with most of the world's Deaf communities) each have their own one-handed systems, whereas a two-handed system is used here in the United Kingdom. It is also incorrect to assume that the individual characters of the fingerspelling alphabet are manual copies of the shapes of written letters. That said, there is indeed a pattern of visual symbolism in the characters—a visible relationship between the written letter-shapes and their manual counterparts—but they are (at most) stylised, partial and rather abstract representations of written characters. Copying writing is simply not necessary.

So fingerspelling in BSL is essentially a means of representing written English using the hands. Each letter of the manual alphabet corresponds to a letter of the written alphabet. However, when it is used fluently, fingerspelling is very quick, and the individual characters form a continuous stream. One of the results of this is that the actual shape a fingerspelt character takes when combined with other characters can vary: the precise point of contact between left and right hands, for instance, is commonly adjusted to take into account the preceding and following movements, smoothing the transitions from each letter to the next and maintaining the rhythm which is a feature of fluent fingerspelling. The non-dominant hand in the vowels **a**, **e**, **i**, **o** and **u** shows this particularly clearly: the point at which the fingers (or finger and thumb) make contact may, depending on the context, be at the very tip of the finger, on the pad of the finger or some way down towards the base of the finger. One result of this is that fingerspelt **e** may at times look much the same as **x**: this is not as confusing as might be feared since the letters involved rarely appear in the same places in words and contextual information solves any problems. Contact between the hands is sometimes reduced to a minimum so that the flow and rhythm of the movement is interrupted as little as possible: when producing a **w**, for instance, the signer may link the hands (as shown) or simply bring the two sets of fingertips into slight contact. Those fingerspelt letters that involve relatively large movements regularly alter the movement to accommodate to the preceding and following letters: the movement involved in **h**, for instance, may be relatively short if a vowel follows, or relatively long if the **h** is the last letter of the word. The left handshape is also subject to quite major variation—see, for example, the two variants of **p**—with extended or closed fingers depending on which fingers have recently been or will soon be contacted. The fingerspelt letter **s** is frequently presented with the right little finger bent quite tightly at the knuckles: in fact, observation of natural signed interaction shows that it is much more usual for the finger to be almost straight (we have illustrated several possible variants).

In all, it has been suggested that almost one hundred distinctive manual letter-shapes are used to represent the twenty-six letters of the English alphabet in fluent signed interaction. This variation in the production of each letter is not a problem for fluent signers—in fact, as a significant part of maximising the efficiency of visual-gestural communication, it makes life easier for them. Signers do not 'read' individual letters when they engage in fluent fingerspelt interaction, so the fingerspeller's task is not to produce a copybook articulation of each element as if the letters were independent of their neighbours. It is the overall shape of the whole fingerspelt word that is crucial, as can be seen in the fact that the viewer's eyegaze does not focus on the hands but remains on the signer's face.

Focusing eyegaze on the face also enables the viewer to take in information from the lip-patterns produced by the signer. It is usually considered improper to mouth individual letters while spelling words. Instead, a lip-pattern corresponding to the whole English word as spoken accompanies the fingerspelling: for example, while fingerspelling **d-i-a-n-a**, the signer mouths 'Diana' rather than 'dee eye ay en ay'. An exception to this pattern is the spelling of abbreviations: when signing a comment about the British Deaf Association, for instance, a person may well fingerspell **b-d-a** accompanied by a lip-pattern representing 'bee dee ay'. With the viewer's eyegaze concentrating on taking in this information, there is no need for the signer to twist his or her hands towards the viewer, even though this means that some features are 'hidden': fluent readers of fingerspelling readily get all the information they need without the signer having to adjust his or her posture.

Certain lexical items of BSL have developed, in various ways, from roots in fingerspelling—entries 370 and 627 in this Dictionary, for instance: these can be said to have become part of the established lexicon (see the *Introduction* to this book for discussion). Fingerspellings other than these are still common in the language, and are patterned in regular ways. Such items constitute a lexical resource that acts as a way of 'borrowing' individual words and phrases from English. Since it is clearly necessary to have an understanding of English in order effectively to borrow items of its vocabulary, the use of fingerspelling tends to vary according to educational experience. It is commonly observed that older signers use more fingerspelling: indeed, having been educated via fingerspelling as a means of instruction at school, they may continue to communicate almost exclusively in fingerspelling into adult life. In contrast, as educational practices have changed over time, it appears that younger Deaf people now make much less use of the manual alphabet to spell out whole words.

As a system complementing the other resources of BSL, fingerspelling has a particular functional role within the signer's repertoire. Growing recognition of BSL in recent times has gone hand in hand with the language being increasingly visible in the public sphere: until the picture began to shift in the last few years, the kind of BSL that was most widely used in these formal and public settings included a relatively large proportion of fingerspelling. The range of vocabulary that is fingerspelt is broad, but has areas of concentration; technical vocabulary (such as occupational jargon) is frequently fingerspelt in the wider community, as is any vocabulary which introduces concepts or objects new to the public (for example, words relating to advances in computer technology). Nevertheless, it would be a mistake to claim that fingerspelling is suitable only for new items of vocabulary: at the opposite extreme, there are a number of 'function words'—the very common words that provide grammatical 'glue' within longer sentences—such as **i-f** and **s-o** which are regularly fingerspelt by many signers. Fingerspelling is also sometimes used as a way of slowing down the flow of a signed utterance so that attention is drawn to the change in pace; the net result is that one part of the sentence is produced with extra emphasis.

On the following pages, we have listed the letters of the British manual alphabet, with some of the most common alternative productions.

Fingerspelling A–D

A

A

B

B

B

C

C

D

D

E

E

E

F

G

H

I

J

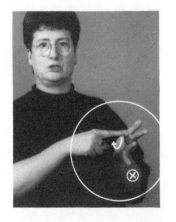

K

Fingerspelling K-P

K

L

M

M

M

N

N

O

P

P

Q

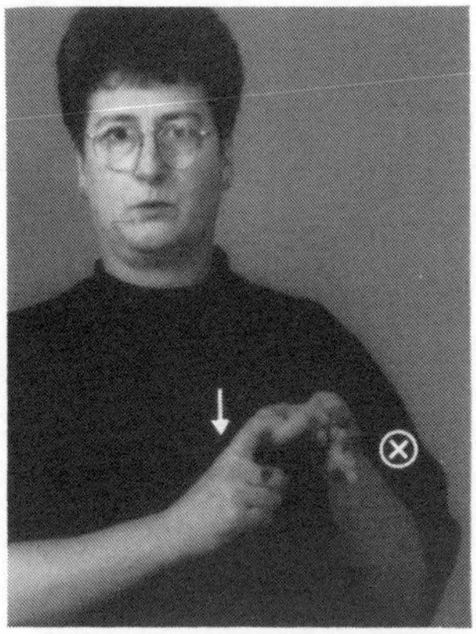

R

S

S

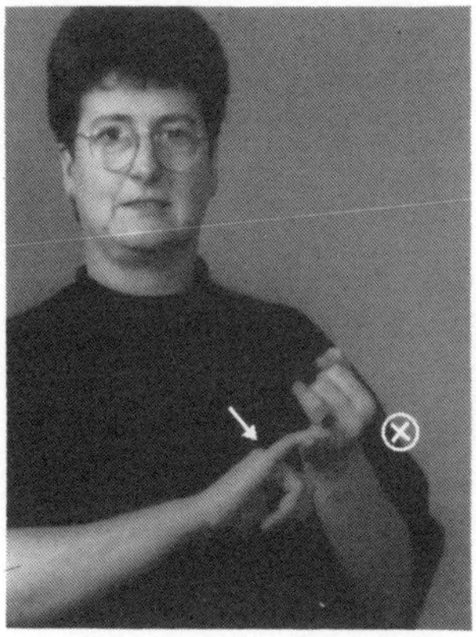

S

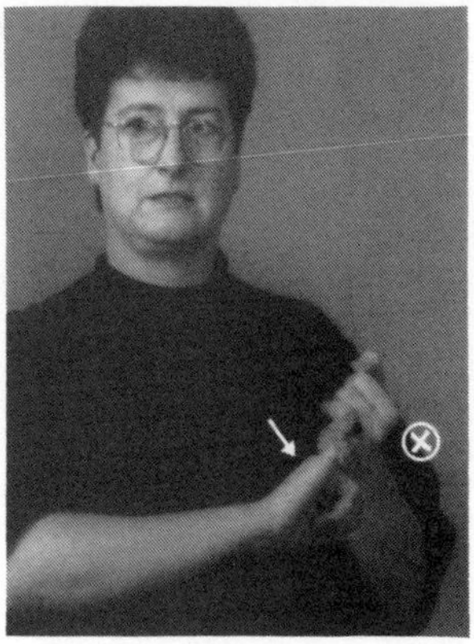

T

U

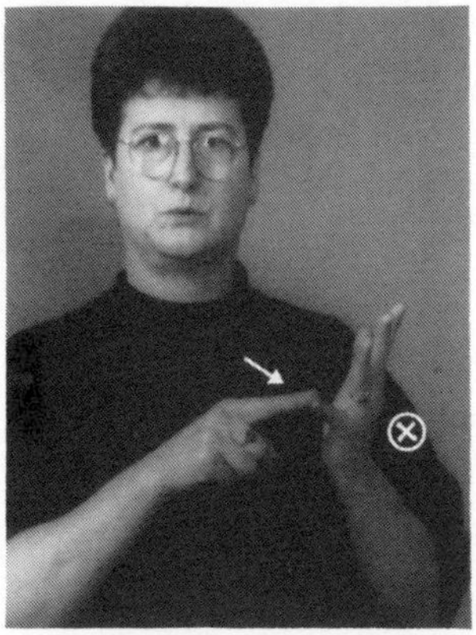

U

Fingerspelling V–Z

V

W

X

X

Y

Z

ENGLISH (GUIDE TO MEANING) SECTION

A, a

A
A is the first letter of the British manual and English alphabets. See page 850.

abandon   1726
1 If you **abandon** a place, thing or person, you leave it permanently or for a long time. *e.g. Some people abandon their pets when they are tired of them.*
2 If you **abandon** a plan, activity or piece of work, you stop doing it. *e.g. I've abandoned my studies until I've earned some money.*

abattoir   184
An **abattoir** is a place where animals are killed for meat. *e.g. These animals will go to the abattoir.*

abbreviate   87
1 If you **abbreviate** something, you make it shorter. *e.g. Don't be afraid to abbreviate your talk if you feel it is too long.*
2 A word or phrase that is **abbreviated** has been made shorter by leaving out some of the letters or by using only the first letter of each word. *e.g. British Deaf Association is often abbreviated to 'BDA'.*

abbreviation   87
An **abbreviation** is a short form of a word or phrase, made by leaving out some of the letters or by using only the first letter of each word. *e.g. British Petroleum is more commonly known by the abbreviation 'BP'.*

ability   335, 477, 572
Your **ability** to do something is the quality or skill that you have which makes it possible for you to do it. *e.g. You have the ability to be a journalist.*

able   335
If someone or something is **able** to do something, they have the physical skill or the knowledge to do it. *e.g. The frog is able to jump three metres.*

able   477, 572
1 If someone or something is **able** to do something, they have the physical skill or the knowledge to do it. *e.g. Linford Christie is able to run faster than any other Briton.*
2 If someone or something is **able** to do something, they have enough freedom, power, time, or money to do it. *e.g. I find I am able to attend the meeting after all.*

abort   1009
If you are a woman and you **abort**, your pregnancy is deliberately ended before the

development of the baby is complete. *e.g. John, if I choose to abort, I want you to stand by me.*

abortion   1009
An **abortion** is the deliberate ending of a pregnancy before the development of the baby is complete. *e.g. She supports the campaign for abortion on demand.*

abortion (have an abortion)   1009
If you **have an abortion**, your pregnancy is deliberately ended before the development of the baby is complete. *e.g. I'm going to have an abortion and that's final.*

about   983, 1224
If you use **about** with a number, you mean that the number is approximate, not exact. *e.g. We went about forty miles.*

about   1360
If you sign, talk, write or think **about** a particular thing, it is the subject of what you are signing, saying, writing or thinking. *e.g. It is a book about India.*

about to   188
If you are **about to** do something, you are going to do it very soon. *e.g. Her father is about to retire.*

above   1342
1 If something is **above** something else, it is in a higher position than the other thing. *e.g. The office is on the floor above.*
2 If an amount or measurement is **above** a particular level, it is greater than that level. *e.g. Children above the age of five are not allowed in.*
3 If someone is **above** you, they are in a position of authority over you. *e.g. He will have an executive above him to whom he reports.*

above all   302
You sign or say **above all** to emphasize that a particular thing is more important than other things. *e.g. I value loyalty above all.*

abroad   1564, 1609
Abroad means to or from another country. *e.g. My friend has gone to live abroad.*

abscond   415
1 If you **abscond** with something, especially something you have stolen, you run away with it. *e.g. He absconded with everyone's wages.*
2 If you **abscond** from somewhere such as a detention centre or a boarding school, you run away from it. *e.g. She absconded from school after being persistently bullied.*

absent   1220
If someone or something is **absent** from a place, they have left and are no longer there. *e.g. You have been absent from the office for twenty minutes.*

absolve   1580
1 If you **absolve** someone from blame or responsibility, you make a formal statement that they are not guilty or are not to blame. *e.g. The captain was absolved from all blame for the shipwreck.*
2 If you **absolve** someone of something wrong that they have done, you forgive them. *e.g. As he was dying the priest absolved him of his sins.*

absorb   1102
1 If something **absorbs** a liquid, gas, light, or heat, it soaks it up or takes it in. *e.g. Frogs absorb water through their skins.*
2 If a larger group **absorbs** a smaller group, the smaller group becomes part of the larger group and loses its individuality. *e.g. Small businesses are absorbed by larger ones: it's the law of the jungle!*

absorb   1532
If you **absorb** information, you learn and understand it. *e.g. I will try and absorb the information to be given in this lecture.*

abstain   1632
1 If you **abstain** from doing something, you deliberately do not do it. *e.g. He agreed to abstain from smoking for six days.*
2 If you **abstain** during a vote, you do not vote. *e.g. The result is fifteen for, three against, with two people deciding to abstain.*

absurd   515
Something that is **absurd** is very foolish or makes very little sense. *e.g. It seemed absurd to carry a twenty-five pound camera about.*

abundance   1583
1 An **abundance** of something is a large quantity of it. *e.g. The police gathered an abundance of evidence.*
2 If something is in **abundance**, there is a lot of it. *e.g. There was grass in abundance.*

abundant   1583
Something that is **abundant** is present in large quantities. *e.g. She always had an abundant supply of food.*

abuse   558
1 **Abuse** of a person or an animal is cruel and

violent treatment of them. *e.g. The boy's stepfather was found guilty of neglect and abuse.*
2 If you **abuse** someone or an animal, you treat them cruelly and violently. *e.g. The geriatric patients were often physically abused.*

academic   166
1 **Academic** is used to describe work done in schools, colleges, and universities, especially work that involves studying and reasoning rather than practical or technical skills. *e.g. Academic standards were high throughout the county.*
2 Children or people who are **academic** are good at studying or are interested in studying. *e.g. It's an exam for academic children.*
3 An **academic** is a member of a university or college who teaches or does research. *e.g. He was rather flattered that an English academic should be planning to write a book about him.*

academic   1500
1 Children or people who are **academic** are good at studying or are interested in studying. *e.g. It's an exam for academic children.*
2 An **academic** is a member of a university or college who teaches or does research. *e.g. He was rather flattered that an English academic should be planning to write a book about him.*

accelerate   1291
1 When moving vehicles **accelerate**, they go faster. *e.g. The car had to accelerate to overtake the tractor.*
2 When you **accelerate** while driving a vehicle, you press down on the pedal which causes the vehicle to go faster. *e.g. I can't accelerate any more, it's no good!*

acceleration   1291
The **acceleration** of a vehicle is the rate at which it gets faster when the driver causes it to do so. *e.g. The acceleration on my little Panda is better than that old thing!*

accept   1012
1 If you **accept** something that you have been offered, you sign or say yes to it. *e.g. I thanked him and accepted the gift.*
2 If you **accept** someone's advice or suggestion, you agree to do what they sign or say. *e.g. I knew they would accept my suggestion.*
3 If you **accept** a story or statement, you sign, say or show that you consider it to be true. *e.g. I accept your explanation of why you are late.*
4 If you **accept** a particular situation that is difficult or unpleasant, you get used to it and recognize that it cannot be changed. *e.g. I know he's dead but I can't accept it.*
5 If you **accept** the blame or responsibility for something, you admit or recognize that you are responsible for it. *e.g. I accept that the breakage was my fault.*
6 If you **accept** something, you take it. *e.g. He held out the gloves and I accepted them gladly.*

acceptable   198, 218
1 If something is **acceptable**, people generally approve of it or allow it to happen. *e.g. The Executive Council considered the working party's recommendations to be acceptable.*
2 If you think something is **acceptable**, you consider it to be good enough. *e.g. He informed me that the article I had written was acceptable.*

access   1305
1 **Access** is the opportunity or right to use or experience something. *e.g. For deaf people, access to using telephones is quite expensive.*
2 **Access** is the opportunity or right to see someone, for example in order to sign or speak to them. *e.g. We all have the right of access to the Prime Minister.*
3 If you **access** something, you get access to it. *e.g. If the student cannot access the lecture, what's the point of being there?*

accident   103
An **accident** happens when two moving vehicles unintentionally hit each other, usually resulting in damage to one or both vehicles and injury or death to their occupants. *e.g. She was killed in a motor accident.*

accident   1136
An **accident** is something unpleasant and unfortunate that happens by mistake. *e.g. She didn't mean to drop the tray, Mum, it was an accident!*

accommodation   1239
Accommodation is a room or building to stay or live in. *e.g. Student accommodation is available.*

accompany someone   712
If you **accompany someone**, you go somewhere with them. *e.g. She asked me to accompany her to church.*

accord   128
1 **Accord** is agreement about what should be done or about the way to do it. *e.g. There are a few issues on which the two are in accord.*
2 An **accord** is a formal agreement or settlement between two or more groups of people. *e.g. The government hopes to reach an accord with its EC partners before the end of the year.*

accountant   727, 1054
An **accountant** is a person whose job it is to inspect or keep detailed records of all the money that a person or business receives and spends. *e.g. You will need the specialist advice of solicitors, an accountant and tax advisers.*

account (on account of)   1492
If something happens **on account of**

something else, it happens because of it. *e.g. The meeting will start earlier on account of the snow.*

accounts   727, 1054
Accounts are a detailed record of all the money that a person or business receives and spends. *e.g. He had to submit accounts of his expenditure.*

accumulate   1322
When you **accumulate** things or when they **accumulate**, they collect or gather over a period of time. *e.g. I don't like to see things accumulate so I'd rather clear up every now and then.*

accumulate   1559
When you **accumulate** things, you collect them over a period of time and from several sources. *e.g. I've managed to accumulate quite a collection lately.*

accumulation   1559
1 An **accumulation** is a large number of things which have been gathered together over a period of time. *e.g. He has an accumulation of facts about steam trains.*
2 **Accumulation** is the collecting together of things over a period of time. *e.g. The accumulation of rare books is where most of his money goes.*

accurate   61, 197
An account or description that is **accurate** gives a true idea of what someone or something is like. *e.g. He gave an accurate account of the meeting.*

accurate   200, 847, 849, 852, 891
1 An account or description that is **accurate** gives a true idea of what a situation, thing or person is like. *e.g. His description of the life of a bee was accurate, but not inspiring.*
2 A person, device, or machine that is **accurate** is able to perform a task precisely and without making a mistake, or to reach a precise target. *e.g. Submarine-launched missiles are becoming more accurate.*

accusation   439
An **accusation** is a statement, which may be either true or false, that someone has done something bad or wrong. *e.g. They faced accusations of cheating.*

accuse   439
1 If you **accuse** someone of something, you sign or say that they have done something bad or wrong. *e.g. He was accused of incompetence and negligence.*
2 If someone is **accused** of a crime, they have been charged with the crime and are on trial for it. *e.g. He is accused of killing ten young women.*

accused 439
The **accused** is the person or group of people being tried in a court for a crime. *e.g. Will the accused please stand?*

accustomed 341, 363
1 If you are **accustomed** to something, you are used to it or familiar with it. *e.g. 'I've grown accustomed to Ian's way of thinking', Kath sighed.*
2 **Accustomed** means usual. *e.g. He drove with his accustomed, casual ease.*

achieve 211, 255, 1130, 1155
If you **achieve** a particular aim or effect, you succeed in doing it or cause it to happen, usually after a lot of effort. *e.g. He hoped to achieve his dream.*

achievement 211, 255, 1130, 1155
An **achievement** is something which someone has succeeded in doing, especially after a lot of effort. *e.g. It was an astonishing achievement to break two world records in a week.*

acoustic modem 936
An **acoustic modem** is a piece of equipment to which the handset of a telephone is connected in order to link a computer to the telephone system so that data can be transferred from one machine to another via the telephone line. *e.g. Clark explained how an acoustic modem works.*

acquire 1532
If you **acquire** a skill or habit you learn it or develop it as you live your daily life or grow up. *e.g. She was lucky enough to acquire sign language naturally from her parents.*

acquisition 1532
The **acquisition** of a skill or habit is the process of learning it or developing it. *e.g. It is a simple matter of the acquisition of knowledge.*

across 385
Something that is situated **across** a street or river is on the other side of it. *e.g. He stared at the man across the street.*

across 1229
1 If you go **across** a room or other place, you go from one side of it to the other. *e.g. We ran across the bridge.*
2 Something that is situated **across** a street or river is on the other side of it. *e.g. There's a little shop across the street.*

act 143
1 If you **act**, or **act a part**, in a play, film or television series, you have a part in it. *e.g. I am acting in a pantomime this Christmas.*
2 An **act** in a show is a short performance which is one of several in the show. *e.g. The Deaf Comedians did a really funny act.*

acting 143
1 **Acting** is the profession of performing in plays, television or films. *e.g. It was not visions of stardom that led McKellen into acting.*
2 **Acting** is the art and skill with which a person plays a part in a play, film or television series. *e.g. I have always been very impressed by his acting.*

actor 143
An **actor** is a man or woman whose occupation is acting in plays, television or films. *e.g. Olivier was a fine actor.*

actress 143
An **actress** is a woman whose occupation is acting in plays, television or films. *e.g. She wants to be an actress and one day win an Oscar like Marlee Matlin.*

actually 195, 323
1 You use **actually** to indicate that a situation exists in real life and not just in theory or in people's imaginations. *e.g. No one actually saw this shark.*
2 You use **actually** to indicate that you are giving correct or true details about a situation. *e.g. He actually died in exile.*

adamant 804
If you are **adamant** about something, you are determined not to change your mind about it. *e.g. He was adamant that we must put less emphasis on nationalism.*

adapt 276
1 If you **adapt** to a new situation or **adapt** yourself to it, you change your ideas or behaviour in order to deal with it successfully. *e.g. He has had to adapt to being free.*
2 If you **adapt** a book or a play, you change it so that it can be made into a film or a television programme. *e.g. Mortimer is adapting the novel for television.*

adaptation 276
1 **Adaptation** is the changing of something to make it suitable for a new purpose or situation. *e.g. Adaptation of the Direct Method approach has proved successful in the teaching of BSL.*
2 An **adaptation** is a film or television programme that was originally written or produced in another form, for example as a novel. *e.g. They are planning to make a television adaptation of 'In This Sign'.*

add 1054, 1162
If you **add** numbers or amounts together, you calculate their total. *e.g. Add all the expenditure for today, and then multiply by seven.*

add 1594
1 If you **add** one thing to another, you put it in the same place as the other thing, usually using

one hand. *e.g. He goes across to add another book to the pile.*
2 If you **add** something when you are signing or speaking, you sign or say something more. *e.g. He wanted to add that the fee would be one hundred pounds.*

addition 1162
Addition is the process of calculating the total of two or more numbers. *e.g. If my addition is right, that makes 3,214 all told.*

additional 1594
Additional things are extra things apart from the ones already present. *e.g. You will be charged an additional cost for a single room.*

address 23, 964
Your **address** is the number of the house, the name of the street, and the town where you live or work. *e.g. Write down your name and address.*

address 1247
An **address** is a formal speech or signed presentation that someone makes to a group of people, often on a special occasion. *e.g. She gave the opening address at the ISLA symposium.*

add up 1054, 1162
If you **add up** several numbers, you calculate their total. *e.g. What's the total when we add all the marks up?*

add up to 1054, 1162
If several amounts **add up to** a particular total, they result in that total when they are put together. *e.g. This adds up to 75,000 miles of new streets.*

adequate 1583
1 If the amount of something is **adequate**, there is just enough of it. *e.g. The pay for the job was adequate.*
2 If something is **adequate**, it is good enough to be used or accepted. *e.g. Her reason for leaving was adequate.*

administer 272
To **administer** a country, company, institution, etc., means to be responsible for managing and supervising it. *e.g. Lilian had to administer a huge office.*

administrate 1433
If you **administrate**, you perform the tasks connected with organising and supervising the way your organisation functions. *e.g. You'll just have to learn to administrate for yourselves.*

administration 272, 1433
1 **Administration** is the range of activities connected with managing and supervising the

way a company, institution, or other organisation functions. *e.g. They need to spend less on administration.*

2 The **administration** of a company, institution, or other organisation is the group of people that manages and supervises it. *e.g. Administration will see to that for you.*

administrator   272, 1433

An **administrator** is a person whose job involves helping to manage and supervise the way that a company, institution, or other organisation functions. *e.g. The post of administrator was advertised on 'No Need to Shout' and 'Earshot'.*

admire   225

If you **admire** someone or something, you like, respect, and approve of them. *e.g. I admire my father for the way he brought us up.*

admit   1204

1 If you **admit** someone or something to a place, they are allowed to enter it. *e.g. They're happy to admit members of staff.*

2 If someone is **admitted** to hospital, they are taken in so that they can be kept there until they are well enough to go home. *e.g. He was admitted to hospital with an ulcerated leg.*

3 If an organisation or group **admits** someone, he or she is allowed to join it. *e.g. He hoped they would admit him as a full member of the academy.*

adopt   212

If you **adopt** a new or different attitude, plan, course of action or way of behaving, you begin to have it or to carry it out. *e.g. The BDA agreed to adopt the new policies.*

adopt   984, 1130

If you **adopt** someone else's child, you take it into your own family and make it legally your son or daughter. *e.g. We want to adopt a deaf child, because we are Deaf ourselves.*

adoption   212

The **adoption** of a particular attitude, plan, course of action or way of behaving is an acceptance that you will begin to have it or carry it out. *e.g. The adoption of a new code of practice was agreed at our last meeting.*

adoption   984, 1130

Adoption is the legal process of taking someone else's child into your own family and making it your son or daughter. *e.g. I'm afraid adoption is out of the question: you are too old.*

adore   235, 1660

1 If you **adore** someone, you feel great admiration and love for them. *e.g. She adored her sister.*

2 If you **adore** something, you like it very

much. *e.g. People will adore this film.*

adult   1572

An **adult** is a mature, fully developed person. *e.g. She behaved like a sensible adult in a difficult situation.*

advance   885

If you **advance** an event in time, you arrange for it to take place at an earlier time than originally planned or agreed. *e.g. We want to advance the date of our departure from the 16th to the 11th of May.*

advance   1642

1 If you **advance** a cause or interest, you support it and help it to be successful. *e.g. The Deaf Broadcasting Campaign has done much to advance deaf people's access to television.*

2 An **advance** is a forward movement of people or vehicles, especially of soldiers. *e.g. The enemy planned an advance.*

3 If a group of people **advance**, they move forward in a united, orderly way. *e.g. OK, it's time for this platoon to advance.*

advancement   885

The **advancement** of an event in time is the act of arranging for it to take place at an earlier time than originally planned. *e.g. The advancement of Jim's talk to two o'clock means that tea is now at four o'clock.*

advantage   861

1 An **advantage** is a benefit or improvement that is likely to result from something. *e.g. One clear advantage of electricity is the lack of fumes.*

2 If something is to your **advantage**, it will be useful for you or will benefit you. *e.g. It is to your advantage to keep him as happy as possible.*

3 If you have the **advantage** of something, you benefit from something unavailable to other people. *e.g. Of course, I have the advantage of having Deaf parents.*

advertise   54

If you **advertise** something such as a product or an event, you inform people about it on television, radio, posters, etc., in order to encourage them to buy the product or take part in the event. *e.g. We need to advertise the garden fête more widely.*

advertise   1309

1 If you **advertise** something such as a product or an event, you inform people about it, especially in newspapers or on posters, in order to encourage them to buy the product or take part in the event. *e.g. We can advertise the sale in the local papers.*

2 If you **advertise** a particular job, or **advertise** for people to do a job, you have an announcement printed, for example in a newspaper, asking anyone interested to apply

for it. *e.g. The council will soon advertise for clerical staff.*

advertisement   1309

An **advertisement** or **advert** is an announcement in a newspaper, on television, or on a poster giving information about, for example a product, event or job vacancy. *e.g. We've received several replies to our advertisement.*

advocacy   229

1 **Advocacy** of a particular action or plan is the act of supporting it in public. *e.g. Her advocacy of unpopular causes was resented by her colleagues.*

2 **Advocacy** is the work of those engaged in creating public support for particular policies or pratices, or advising and supporting individuals or groups seeking to change particular policies or practices. *e.g. The work of the BDA's Advocacy Service has greatly increased over the last five years.*

advocate   229

1 If you **advocate** a particular action or plan you support it in public. *e.g. He advocated the creation of a single European market.*

2 An **advocate** of a particular action or plan is someone who supports it in public. *e.g. My mother was a strong advocate of women's rights.*

aeroplane   932

An **aeroplane** is a vehicle with wings and one or more engines that enables it to fly through the air. *e.g. It's a low-cost aeroplane and it doesn't use much energy.*

aerosol   634

An **aerosol** is a small container in which a liquid such as paint or deodorant is kept under pressure. When you press a button, the liquid is forced out as a fine spray or foam. *e.g. The aerosol contained paint.*

affection   1477

Affection is a feeling of fondness and caring, especially for another person. *e.g. She gazed at him with affection.*

affiliate   898

If an organisation **affiliates** itself or is **affiliated** to another, larger organisation, it forms a close association with it or becomes a branch or member of it. *e.g. If we affiliate to the AUT, we will need to negotiate with them on pension schemes.*

affiliation   898

The **affiliation** of two organisations or of one organisation to another is the formation of an association between the two. *e.g. The affiliation of the two mineworkers' unions is not likely under the present leaders.*

affirmation   1379
An **affirmation** is a solemn promise to tell
the truth, which is made in a court of law by
people who are not Christians and who do not
swear on the Bible. *e.g. He chose to take an
affirmation when he appeared in court.*

afraid   1143, 1180
1 If you are **afraid** to do something, you are
frightened because you think that something
horrible is going to happen. *e.g. She was afraid
to climb the steep cliff above the rocks.*
2 If you are **afraid** that something unpleasant
will happen, you are worried that it may
happen and you want to avoid it. *e.g. Don't be
afraid to ask questions, I won't laugh.*

Africa   18
Africa is the second largest of the continents.
It is almost surrounded by sea, with the
Atlantic on its west side, the Mediterranean to
the north and the Indian Ocean and Red Sea to
the east. *e.g. He lived in Africa for many years.*

African   18
1 Someone or something that is **African**
belongs to or relates to the continent of Africa,
or to its countries or peoples. *e.g. Scientists
from a number of African countries gave papers at
the conference.*
2 **African** means belonging to or relating to
black people who come from Africa. *e.g. I went
to an exhibition of West African sculpture.*
3 An **African** is someone, especially a black
person, who comes from Africa, or whose family
identity relates to Africa. *e.g. The African Said
Aouita is expected to be a strong challenger in the
men's middle-distance track events.*

Afro-   18
Afro- is added to other signs or words which
describe someone or something connected with
both Africa and with another continent or
country. *e.g. Lestor was of Afro-Carribean descent.*

after   21, 154
If something happens **after** a particular date
or event, it happens during the period of time
that follows it. *e.g. She arrived after breakfast.*

afternoon   719
1 The **afternoon** is the part of each day which
begins either at noon or at lunchtime, and
which ends at about six o' clock, or, in winter,
when it gets dark. *e.g. I'll do it this afternoon.*
2 If it is a particular time in the **afternoon**, it is
between noon and the start of the evening. *e.g.
It was four in the afternoon when she arrived.*

afterwards   300
If you do something, or if something happens,
afterwards, you do it, or it happens, during
the period of time that follows a particular
event, date, time, et cetera. *e.g. They moved to*

Hexham in 1912 and she died soon afterwards.

after you   186
If you sign or say **after you**, you mean that
you want to get, do, sign or say something or
be considered immediately after the person
you sign or say it to. *e.g. I would like the book
after you.*

again   751
1 If you do something **again** or if something
happens **again**, you do it or it happens one
more time or on another occasion. *e.g. Try
again in half an hour.*
2 When you are asking someone to repeat
something they have signed or said to you, you
can use **again** in your question. *e.g. What's his
name again?*

against (an upright surface)   1348
If something is positioned **against an upright
surface**, it is touching it and leaning or pressing
on it. *e.g. She placed the card against the wall.*

age   995
Your **age** is the number of years you have
lived. *e.g. Could you tell me your age, please?*

age   1284
You can use an **age** to mean a very long time. *e.g.
It takes her an age to get dressed in the mornings.*

aged   810
Someone or something that is **aged** is very
old. *e.g. He adored his aged aunt.*

ageing   810
1 An **ageing** person, thing, system, etc., is one
that is becoming old, and usually less
attractive or efficient than before. *e.g. It is
sometimes sad to see ageing film stars.*
2 **Ageing** is the process of becoming old. *e.g.
Wrinkles on the skin are a perfectly natural result
of ageing.*

agenda   196
An **agenda** is a list of the items that have to be
discussed at a meeting. *e.g. What is on the
agenda today?*

age old   1480

An **age old** story, tradition, or connection has
existed for longer than people can remember.
e.g. It's an age old custom.

ages   543, 1284, 1480, 1722
If you sign or say **ages**, you mean a very long
time. *e.g. I've known him for ages.*

aggravate   1185
If someone or something **aggravates** you, they
irritate you or make you annoyed. *e.g. Her snoring
will aggravate me if it's like this every night.*

aggravation   1185
1 If something is an **aggravation**, it makes
you annoyed. *e.g. If that yapping dog only knew
what an aggravation it is!*
2 **Aggravation** is the feeling you have when
something irritates or annoys you. *e.g. They
come round here, causing aggravation to all the
pensioners: it's not right.*

aggression   1198
If someone has **aggression** in their character,
they have a quality of anger and determination
that makes them ready to attack people. *e.g. He
can give a good argument when he has his
aggression under control.*

aggressive   1198
A person or animal that is **aggressive** has a
quality of anger and determination in their
character that makes them ready to attack
people. *e.g. The girl was quite aggressive because
she couldn't make people understand her.*

agree   128
1 If one person **agrees** with another, or if two
or more people **agree**, they have the same
opinion as each other. *e.g. I agree with your
proposals.*
2 If you **agree** that something is the case, you
sign or say or believe that it is so. *e.g. I agree
that's what killed her.*
3 If you **agree** to do something or **agree** to
something, you sign or say that you will do it or
you allow someone else to do it. *e.g. She agreed
to let us use her flat while she was away.*
4 If people **agree** on something or **agree**
something, they reach a joint decision on it.
*e.g. The Cabinet agree on the main provisions of
the Bill.*
5 If you **agree** with something such as an
action or a proposal, you approve of it. *e.g. I
agree with what they are doing.*

agree   227
If a group of people **agree** on something or
agree to something, they reach a joint
decision on it. *e.g. After a short discussion, the
group agreed to hold their next conference in
Hartlepool.*

agreement   128
1 An **agreement** means reaching a decision or
conclusion about something that everyone
involved finds acceptable. *e.g. The two leaders
reached an agreement after three hours of
negotiations.*
2 An **agreement** means signing or saying or
showing that you will accept something that
has been proposed. *e.g. We will honour the
ceasefire agreement.*
3 **Agreement** means signing, saying or
showing that you believe that something is
true. *e.g. The two governments declared their
agreement that the imposition of fishing quotas is*

the only way to preserve stocks.
4 If you are in **agreement** with someone, you have the same opinion as they have. *e.g. I find myself in agreement with John.*

agreement   227
Agreement is the act of reaching a decision that is acceptable to the group of people involved. *e.g. There was general agreement on the need for the University Funding Council to provide funding for Deaf Studies and British Sign Language degree courses.*

agreement (in agreement)   227
If a group of people are **in agreement**, they share the same opinion. *e.g. They were in complete agreement.*

ahead   1611
1 **Ahead** means in the future, especially the immediate future. *e.g. There are troubled times ahead.*
2 If you are thinking or planning **ahead**, you are thinking or planning about the future or events in the future. *e.g. I haven't had time to think that far ahead.*

aid   150
1 **Aid** is money, equipment or services that are provided for people in need. *e.g. Financial aid is welcome for the Third World.*
2 If you **aid** a person or an organisation, you help them by providing them with something that they need. *e.g. He crossed the road aided by the young girl.*

AIDS   392
1 **AIDS** is an illness which completely destroys the natural system of protection that the body has against disease; AIDS is an abbreviation for 'acquired immune deficiency syndrome'. *e.g. My cousin died of AIDS last year.*
2 Information on **AIDS** may be obtained from Aids Ahead, BDA Health Promotion Services, 144 London Road, Northwich, Cheshire, CW9 5HH. Telephone: text (0606) 330472, voice (0606) 47047.

aim   1299
1 If you **aim** at or for something or **aim** to do something, you plan or hope to achieve it. *e.g. I will aim for a well paid job and am prepared to quit before I burn out.*
2 If an action or plan is **aimed** at something, it is intended to achieve it. *e.g. Our policies are aimed at securing support from young people.*
3 If you **aim** an action at a particular person or group, you intend they should notice it and be influenced by it. *e.g. We hope to aim the campaign primarily at teenagers.*
4 An **aim** is the thing that an action or plan is intended to achieve. *e.g. It is our aim to set up a workshop.*

air   1463
Air is the mixture of gases, which forms the earth's atmosphere and which we breathe. *e.g. The air was well below freezing.*
2 If you **air** a room or a building, you make it fresh or cool by allowing fresh air to circulate there. *e.g. The big windows had been opened to air the room.*

air force   932
An **air force** or **airforce** is the part of a country's military organisation that is concerned with fighting in the air. *e.g. My father served in the air force during the war.*

air (fresh air)   1463
Fresh air is the air outside, especially when this is considered to be good for you. *e.g. After being in the meeting room all day, we needed some fresh air.*

airline   932
An **airline** is a company which provides aircraft services for passengers and goods. *e.g. No other airlines could offer a direct flight to London.*

airport   950
An **airport** is a place, usually with a lot of buildings and facilities, where aircraft land and take off. *e.g. Crete has a small airport.*

alarm   408
An **alarm** is an automatic device that warns you of danger, for example by ringing a bell. *e.g. The alarm went off, so the building had to be evacuated.*

alarm clock   408
An **alarm clock** is an instrument that shows you what time it is and can be set to make a noise or be connected to an attachment which vibrates, so that it wakes you up at a particular time. *e.g. Remember your alarm clock, please: otherwise I'll never wake up.*

alcoholic   371
Someone who is **alcoholic** is addicted to drinks such as beer, wine and spirits that can make you drunk, and continues drinking even though it makes them ill. *e.g. Her uncle is an alcoholic, so she won't serve drinks tonight.*

alight   818
If you **alight** from a train, bus, or other vehicle, you get out of it. *e.g. Passengers should not alight while the train is in motion.*

alike   424
If two or more things are **alike**, they are very similar or the same in some way. *e.g. They all looked alike to me.*

alimony   1008, 1504, 1507, 1679
Alimony is the money that a court of law orders someone to pay regularly to their former wife or husband after they have been legally separated or divorced. *e.g. I receive my alimony at the end of every month.*

alive   964, 1186
If a person, animal or plant is **alive**, they have life. *e.g. I think his father is still alive.*

all   987, 1234
You use **all** to refer to the whole of a particular group or thing. *e.g. All the girls think it's great.*

all   1104
You use **all** to refer to the whole of a thing or a group of objects. *e.g. Are you sure all the luggage has been brought in?*

alleluia   255
also spelled **halleluia** or **hallelujah**.
Christians sign or say **alleluia** as an exclamation of praise and thanks to God. *e.g. Christ is risen; alleluia!*

alligator   1190
An **alligator** is a large reptile similar to a crocodile with a long body and jaws which lives mostly in the southern United States. *e.g. She was terrified that an alligator might get her.*

all right   165, 215
Also spelled **alright**.
1 If something or someone is **all right**, you mean you find them satisfactory or acceptable. *e.g. His work this term has been all right.*
2 If someone or something is **all right**, they are well or safe. *e.g. Someone should see if she's all right.*

all right   218
Also spelled **alright**.
If something or someone is **all right**, you mean you find them just satisfactory or acceptable. *e.g. 'Do you like this coffee?'—'It's all right.'*

all right?   164
Also spelled **alright?**.
1 If you sign or say **all right?** after you have given an instruction or an explanation to someone, you are checking that they have understood and accepted what you signed or said. *e.g. If you begin to feel dizzy again put your head in your hands, all right?*
2 You may sign or say **all right?** to someone when you are greeting them or when you are meeting them for the first time in the course of a day. *e.g. 'All right?' he signed as I walked towards him.*

all the same   1433
You sign or say **all the same** or **just the same** to indicate that a situation or your opinion has not changed in spite of something

that has happened or been signed or said. *e.g. She knew he wasn't listening but she went on all the same.*

Almighty   1033
The **Almighty** is another name for God. *e.g. They prayed to the Almighty for protection against their enemies.*

Almighty God   1033
Almighty God is an expression used when praying to or addressing God. *e.g. Almighty God, we beseech thee to deliver us from all evil.*

almost   238, 612, 618
Almost means very nearly. *e.g. He almost forgot we were arriving at two o'clock.*

alone   533, 534, 555
1 If you do something **alone**, you do it without help from other people. *e.g. I was left to bring up my two children alone.*
2 If you are **alone**, nobody else is with you. *e.g. I stood alone under the streetlight, praying that the police would arrive soon.*

already   187, 1088
If something has **already** happened, it has happened earlier than you expected. *e.g. By the time he got home, Julie was already in bed.*

also   423
1 You use **also** when you are giving more information about a person or thing, or adding another relevant fact. *e.g. The dress is also available in blue.*
2 You use **also** to sign or say that the same fact applies to someone or something else. *e.g. His first wife was also called Margaret.*

alter   276, 432
If something **alters** or if you **alter** it, it changes. *e.g. America must alter its foreign policy.*

alteration   276, 432
An **alteration** is a change in something. *e.g. Did you see any alteration in his behaviour?*

altogether   1101
1 **Altogether** is used to summarise a situation, opinion or argument. *e.g. Altogether, this has been a successful course.*
2 If several numbers or amounts add up to a particular number or amount **altogether**, that number or amount is the total of them. *e.g. He played in forty-four Test matches altogether.*

always   204, 207, 339, 340
1 If you **always** do a particular thing or if you **always** do things in a particular way, you act in that way all the time or on every possible occasion. *e.g. She always arrives early.*
2 If something is **always** the case, it is the case all

the time. *e.g. It's always frozen in these polar regions.*
3 If you sign or say that someone is **always** doing something or that something is **always** happening, you mean that they do it, or it happens, often and repeatedly. *e.g. He's always looking for faults.*

always   363
1 If you **always** do a particular thing or if you **always** do things in a particular way, you act in that way all the time or on every possible occasion. *e.g. She always arrives early.*
2 If you sign or say that someone is **always** doing something or that something is **always** happening, you mean that they do it, or it happens, often and repeatedly. *e.g. He's always looking for faults.*

amaze   1080
If something **amazes** you, it surprises you so much that you find it almost impossible to believe it. *e.g. And now, a trick that will delight and amaze you.*

amazed   604, 725, 831
If you are **amazed** by something it surprises you so much that you find it almost impossible to believe it. *e.g. I was amazed when I found out the price.*

amazement   1080
Amazement is what you feel when something surprises you so much that you find it almost impossible to believe it. *e.g. Her eyes grew wide with amazement.*

amazing   960, 989, 1472
You sign or say that something is **amazing** when it is very surprising and makes you feel pleasure, approval or admiration. *e.g. New York is an amazing city.*

ambulance   542
An **ambulance** is a special vehicle that is used for taking people to or from hospital. *e.g. She asked someone to ring for an ambulance.*

ambulanceman   542
An **ambulanceman** is a man whose job is to drive an ambulance or take care of sick people in an ambulance until they get to hospital. *e.g. The ambulanceman brought the stretcher to the scene of the accident.*

ambulancewoman   542
An **ambulancewoman** is a woman whose job is to drive an ambulance or take care of sick people in an ambulance until they get to hospital. *e.g. The police took her away, and the ambulancewoman closed the doors.*

amend   276
If you **amend** something that has been

written, signed or said, you change it. *e.g. Last year, the regulations were amended to allow other awards to be made.*

amendment   276
An **amendment** is a passage added to a law or rule in order to change and improve it. *e.g. The committee recommended an amendment to the constitution.*

America   371, 1051
America is the United States of America. *e.g. Many of us went to America for The Deaf Way.*

American   371, 1051
1 Someone or something that is **American** belongs to or relates to the United States of America or its people. *e.g. She had a slight American accent.*
2 An **American** is a person who comes from the United States of America or whose family identity relates to the United States of America. *e.g. We travelled with two terrifically friendly Americans called Elliot and Marina.*
3 The address of the **American** National Association of the Deaf is: 814 Thayer Avenue, Silver Spring, MD 20910, United States of America.

ample   1583
If there is an **ample** amount of something, there is enough of it and probably some extra. *e.g. There is ample time to prepare.*

anaesthetic   1133
An **anaesthetic** is a substance that stops you feeling pain, either in the whole of your body when you are unconscious, or in a part of your body when you are awake. *e.g. He was operated on without an anaesthetic.*

anaesthetise   1133
also spelled **anaesthetize**.
To **anaesthetise** someone means to make them unconscious by giving them an anaesthetic. *e.g. We will have to anaesthetise you one hour before the operation.*

an age   543
An age means a very long time. *e.g. She took an age to put on all her make-up.*

analyse   776
also spelled **analyze**.
If you **analyse** something, you consider it or examine it in order to understand it or to find out what it consists of. *e.g. He analysed the chemical structure of molecules.*

analyst   776
An **analyst** is a person whose job is to analyse a subject and give opinions about it. *e.g. He is employed as a political analyst in the House of Commons.*

and so forth   551
If you sign or say **and so forth**, you mean that there are a number of other items similar to those you have mentioned. *e.g. The bookshop sells notebooks, pens, erasers, typing paper, and so forth.*

and so on   551
If you sign or say **and so on**, you mean that there are a number of other items similar to those you have mentioned. *e.g. The schools need money for books, equipment, building repairs and so on.*

angel   1473, 1635
An **angel** is one of the spiritual beings that some people believe live with God in heaven and act as God's messengers and servants. *e.g. An angel brought a message to Joseph.*

angel/fairy flying   1635
If an **angel** or a **fairy** is **flying**, it moves through the air by flapping its wings. *e.g. Tinkerbell the fairy is flying off to see Peter Pan.*

anger   1195, 1196
Anger is the strong emotion that you feel when you think that someone has behaved in an unfair, cruel or insulting way. *e.g. He felt anger at the sight of so many people injured in such a careless accident.*

angler   279
An **angler** is someone who fishes with a fishing rod, especially as a hobby. *e.g. The old angler told us stories of the ones that got away.*

angling   279
Angling is the activity or sport of fishing with a fishing rod. *e.g. The most popular sport in this country is angling.*

angry   1195, 1196
Someone who is **angry** feels or shows strong emotion about an action or situation which they consider unacceptable, unfair, cruel or insulting, and about the person responsible for it. *e.g. His wife's sarcastic remarks made him angry.*

animal   1168
1 An **animal** is a living creature such as a dog, lion, monkey or rabbit, rather than a bird, fish, reptile, insect, or human being. *e.g. No birds or animals came near.*
2 Any living thing that is not a plant can be referred to as an **animal**. *e.g. What kind of animal shall we pretend to be?*

announce   456
If you **announce** something, you tell people about it in public or officially. *e.g. It was announced that the Prime Minister would speak on television.*

announcement   456
An **announcement** is a public statement which gives information about something that has happened or that will happen. *e.g. The Minister made an announcement today about talks on nuclear disarmament.*

annoy   1185
If someone **annoys** you, or if their behaviour **annoys** you, they make you feel fairly angry. *e.g. He couldn't spell, which used to annoy her.*

annoyance   1185
1 **Annoyance** is the feeling you get when someone or something makes you feel fairly angry. *e.g. The Englishman never lets his annoyance show.*
2 If something is an **annoyance**, it makes you feel fairly angry. *e.g. Well, it's just an annoyance, isn't it—who wants a wheel-clamp fixed to their car?*

annual   547
1 **Annual** means happening or done once every year. *e.g. We always attend the Association's annual meeting.*
2 **Annual** means calculated over a period of one year. *e.g. They have a combined annual income of eighty thousand pounds.*

anorak   287
An **anorak** is a warm, waterproof jacket that has a hood. *e.g. I must buy a new anorak.*

another   391, 767
Another thing or person means an additional thing or person. *e.g. Another point I'd like to make concerns the training of Deaf interpreters.*

answer   371
1 When you **answer** someone who has asked you something, you sign or say something back to them. *e.g. I did my best to answer her.*
2 An **answer** is something that you sign or say when you respond to a question. *e.g. What was your answer when he asked for a loan?*
3 The **answer** to a problem is a solution to it. *e.g. She found the answer to her heating problems.*
4 The **answer** to a question in a test is something that a student writes, signs or says in an attempt to give the facts asked for. *e.g. You have to try to give an answer, even if you aren't sure.*

anticipate   188, 505
If you **anticipate** an event or happening, you realise that it may happen before it actually does happen, so that you are prepared for it. *e.g. They anticipated that a number of staff would be made redundant before the end of the year.*

anticipation   188, 505
Anticipation is the expectation that an event may happen before it actually does happen, which enables you to prepare for it.
e.g. In anticipation of this, we have assumed that student numbers will double before the end of the decade.

antlers   1071
The **antlers** of a male deer or similar animal are a pair of branched horns on its head. *e.g. This was a magnificent creature, with antlers over four feet in width.*

anus   1106
The **anus** of a person or animal is the hole between their buttocks, where faeces leave their body. *e.g. The doctors operated on a little boy who had a growth in his anus.*

anxiety   1144
Anxiety is a feeling of nervousness or worry. *e.g. He showed his anxiety when he realised he had not completed the job satisfactorily.*

anxious   539, 567, 1144
1 If you are **anxious**, you are nervous or worried. *e.g. She was always anxious when meeting new people.*
2 If you are **anxious** about something, thinking about it makes you feel nervous or worried. *e.g. I'm anxious about her disappearing like this.*

any   938
You sign or say **any** in positive statements when you are referring to something or someone without signing or saying exactly what, who, or which kind you mean. *e.g. Any of these big containers will do.*

anybody   297, 938
You use **anybody** to refer to an unknown member or members of a group of people, especially when asking questions. *e.g. Does anybody fancy a trip to Nottingham?*

anyone   297, 938
You use **anyone** to refer to an unknown member or members of a group of people, especially when asking questions. *e.g. Anyone for tennis?*

anyway   1433
You use **anyway** or **anyhow** to change the topic or return to a previous topic. *e.g. Anyway, I'll see you later.*

apart   1616, 1634
1 When something is **apart** from something else, there is a space between them. *e.g. I was sitting apart from the rest.*
2 If two things move **apart** or are pulled **apart**, they move away from each other. *e.g. I tried to pull the dogs apart.*
3 If two people are **apart**, they are no longer living together or spending time together. *e.g. They could not bear to be apart.*

ape 138, 1651
An **ape** is an animal such as a chimpanzee or gorilla. Apes are similar to monkeys, but are larger and have very short tails or no tails at all. *e.g. Her constant companion was an ape called Sarah.*

apologise 34, 921, 1580
also spelled **apologize**.
When you **apologise** to someone, you indicate that you are sorry that you have hurt them or caused trouble for them. *e.g. I apologise for my late arrival.*

apology 34, 921, 1580
An **apology** is something that you sign, say or write in order to tell someone that you are sorry that you have hurt or upset them or caused trouble for them. *e.g. She sent a letter of apology to the Director.*

appalling 904, 911, 914, 918
1 Something that is **appalling** is so bad or unpleasant that it makes you feel disgust or dismay. *e.g. Some of these people live in appalling conditions.*
2 **Appalling** is used to emphasise that something is extremely bad. *e.g. I had the most appalling depression.*

apparent 1243
1 An **apparent** situation, quality or feeling seems to exist, although you cannot be certain that it does exist. *e.g. Their marriage is an apparent success, even though they rarely see each other.*
2 If something is **apparent** to you, you feel that it is clearly the case. *e.g. It's apparent to me that you are madly in love with her.*

appeal 244
1 If you **appeal** to someone in a position of authority against a decision that has been made, you formally ask them to change it. *e.g. McEnroe appealed against the linesman's decision.*
2 If you **appeal** to a court against a legal decision or sentence, you formally ask the court to change the decision or reduce the sentence. *e.g. He appealed against the five-year sentence he had been given.*

appear 553, 630
When something new **appears**, it begins to exist or becomes available. *e.g. The Greens have only recently appeared in British politics.*

appear 1243
If you sign or say that something **appears** to be in the way that you describe it, you mean that the evidence that you have leads you to believe it to be that way. *e.g. He appears confident.*

appendicectomy 190
also spelled **appendectomy**.
An **appendicectomy** is a medical operation to remove a person's appendix (a small tube inside a person's body which is closed at one end and joined to the digestive system at the other end). The operation is usually carried out if the person is suffering from appendicitis (an illness in which the appendix is infected and painful). *e.g. Mr. Speight is scheduled to do an appendicectomy on Monday morning.*

appetising 175, 345, 468
also spelled **appetizing**.
Food that is **appetising** looks and smells nice, and makes you want to eat it. *e.g. The meal looked appetising and the smell was wonderful.*

applaud 1070
If you **applaud**, you raise and shake your hands in the air to show your appreciation for a performance or presentation (particularly when the presenter or audience is Deaf). *e.g. I want to see you all applaud now, Deaf and non-Deaf people alike.*

applaud 1445
When you **applaud**, you clap your hands in order to show your appreciation for a performance or presentation. *e.g. The whole assembly began to applaud.*

applause 1070
Applause is an expression of praise or appreciation for a performance or presentation, shown by raising and shaking your hands (particularly when the presenter or audience is Deaf). *e.g. There was great applause as Princess Diana concluded her signed address to the BDA Congress.*

applause 1445
Applause is an expression of praise or appreciation for a presentation or performance, shown by clapping your hands. *e.g. The delegates burst into loud applause.*

apple 1695
An **apple** is a round fruit which grows on a tree and which has a smooth red, yellow or green skin and firm white flesh inside it. *e.g. We sat under the apple tree.*

apply 1286
If you **apply** something to part of the surface of your body, you rub it onto the surface with your hand or a cloth. *e.g. Apply generously every four hours for as long as symptoms persist.*

apply 1562
If you **apply** to have something or to do something, you fill in a form or write a letter asking formally to be allowed to have it or to do it. *e.g. I'm going to apply for another job.*

apply to one's arm 1286
If you **apply** something **to your arm**, you rub it onto the skin on your arm with your hand or a cloth. *e.g. Just apply this to your arm whenever the burn is inflamed.*

appoint 443, 1664
If you **appoint** someone to a particular post or to do a particular job, you formally choose them for it or ask them to do it. *e.g. She was appointed head teacher in 1957.*

appointee 443
An **appointee** is someone who has been chosen for a particular job or position. *e.g. The new appointee at the State Department will have her work cut out from day one.*

appointment 128
1 If you have an **appointment** with someone, you have arranged to see them at a particular time, usually in connection with their job. *e.g. The appointment with the doctor was for eleven o'clock.*
2 If you do something by **appointment** you arrange in advance to do it at a particular time. *e.g. They allow people to visit at weekends by appointment.*

appointment 443
1 The **appointment** of someone to do a particular job is the choice of that person to do it. *e.g. Her first duty was the appointment of a deputy head.*
2 An **appointment** is a job or position of responsibility. *e.g. She applied for and got the appointment.*

appreciate 1275, 1471
If you sign or say that you **appreciate** something which someone has done for you or that you **appreciate** help or advice which someone has given you, you mean that you are pleased and grateful to them for it. *e.g. I really appreciate what you have done.*

appreciation 1275, 1471
Appreciation of something is gratitude for something which someone has done for you or for the help and advice which they have given you. *e.g. The gift is to show my appreciation.*

apprehension 1144
Apprehension is a feeling of fear that something terrible might happen. *e.g. The boys felt some apprehension at being called before the headteacher.*

apprehensive 539, 1144, 860
1 Someone who is **apprehensive** is afraid that something terrible may happen. *e.g. She felt apprehensive all through the long wait.*
2 If you are **apprehensive** about something, thinking about it makes you feel nervous or worried. *e.g. I felt apprehensive about the operation.*

apprentice   1676
1 An **apprentice** is a young person who works, often for a fixed period of time, with another person whose job involves a particular skill, in order that they can learn the skill. *e.g. He was an apprentice builder.*
2 If you **apprentice** someone to a person whose job involves a particular skill, you arrange for them to work, often for a fixed period of time, with the skilled person so that they can learn how to do the job. *e.g. She was apprenticed to a motor mechanic at the age of 18.*

approach   295, 570, 1619
1 When someone **approaches** you, they come nearer to you. *e.g. He saw her approach and opened the door.*
2 When a future event or date **approaches**, it gradually becomes nearer as time passes. *e.g. The day of the race is approaching rapidly.*

approach   434
1 If you **approach** someone about something, you sign or speak to them for the first time about something. *e.g. I will approach the school on the matter of discipline.*
2 When you **approach** someone, you go towards them. *e.g. Approach this man only with the greatest caution.*

appropriate   128
Something that is **appropriate** is correct, suitable or acceptable. *e.g. We will send an appropriate leaflet.*

approval   212
Approval is agreement which is given to a plan or request. *e.g. He required his father's approval.*

approve   212
1 If you **approve** of an action, event, or situation, you are pleased that it has happened or that it is going to happen. *e.g. My grandfather approved of my marriage.*
2 If someone in a position of authority **approves** something such as a plan or arrangement, they formally or officially agree to it and sign or say that it can happen or be put into effect. *e.g. The directors approved the new plan.*
3 If someone in a position of authority **approves** something such as a product, building or institution, they state formally or officially that it is of an acceptable or suitable standard or that it can be used for a particular purpose. *e.g. The premises were approved by the local authority.*

approve of   1660
If you **approve of** someone or something, you like and admire them. *e.g. She approved of her daughter's husband.*

approximate   983, 1224
1 An **approximate** number, time or position is close to the correct number, time or position, but not exact. *e.g. The approximate value of the property is £200,000.*
2 An idea or description that is **approximate** is not intended to be precisely accurate. *e.g. I realise that's only approximate, but it should help.*

apron   291
An **apron** is a piece of clothing that you put on over the front of your normal clothes and tie round your waist, especially when you are cooking, in order to prevent your clothes from getting dirty. *e.g. Peg put on her apron.*

arch   1663
An **arch** is a structure that has a curved roof or top supported on either side by a pillar or wall. An arch sometimes forms part of a bridge carrying a road or railway or a doorway in a building. *e.g. She grew up in a house beneath the railway arches.*

archer   864
An **archer** is someone who shoots with a bow and arrow. *e.g. Robin Hood was a skilful archer.*

archery   864
Archery is a sport in which people shoot at a target with a bow and arrow. *e.g. We are to learn about archery at summer school.*

area   983, 1018
1 An **area** is a particular part or region of a city, country or the world. *e.g. She comes from the Brighton area.*
2 A particular **area** of a room, building, or other place is a part of it that is used for a particular purpose or activity. *e.g We hope for an outdoor play area for the children.*
3 The **area** of something such as a piece of land is its total extent. *e.g. 'An area large enough for our needs' was how Dad described it.*

argue   437
1 If you **argue** with someone about something, you sign or say things (sometimes angrily) which show that you disagree with them about it. *e.g. They argued about who should sit in front.*
2 If you **argue** that something is the case, you sign or say that you think it is the case and give reasons why. *e.g. M.K. Verma argued the case for the maintenance of 'mother tongue' teaching.*

argue   924
If you **argue** with someone about something, you sign or say things which show that you disagree with them about it, sometimes signing or speaking angrily. *e.g. They argued about who should sit in front.*

argument   437, 924
An **argument** is a disagreement (which may sometimes be carried out in an angry way) between two or more people. *e.g. We accepted the proposal without argument.*

arise   553
When something such as an opportunity, problem, or new state of affairs **arises**, it begins to exist. *e.g. A problem will arise with the marking of exams because the teachers are on strike.*

arise   1201
If you instruct someone to **arise**, you ask them to get up from a kneeling position. *e.g. The Queen said, 'Arise, Sir Francis Drake'.*

arithmetic   1054
1 **Arithmetic** is the part of mathematics that is concerned with the addition, subtraction, multiplication and division of numbers. *e.g. I blame the school for not making him learn arithmetic.*
2 **Arithmetic** is numerical calculations or sums which are worked out from a particular set of figures. *e.g. I was busy correcting Eric's arithmetic at his desk.*

armchair   91
An **armchair** is a comfortable chair which has a support on each side for your arms. *e.g. We bought an armchair and some curtains.*

armed forces   1277
The **armed forces** of a country are its military forces, usually the army, navy, and air force. *e.g. The conference called for the major powers to cut their armed forces by a third.*

army   1277
An **army** is a large organised group of people who are armed and trained to fight on land in a war. *e.g. The army suffered thousands of wounded.*

aroma   994
An **aroma** is a strong, pleasant smell. *e.g. The house was filled with the aroma of coffee.*

around   1018
You can refer to the area **around** a place to mean near it. *e.g. We were the first people around here to have a video recorder.*

arrange   1433
1 If you **arrange** an event or meeting, you make plans for it to happen. *e.g. Progressive Tours arrange holidays in Eastern Europe.*
2 If you **arrange** something for someone, you make it possible for them to have it or to do it. *e.g. We can arrange loans.*

arrangement   1433
1 **Arrangements** are plans and preparations which you make so that something will happen or be possible. *e.g. I've made arrangements for the visit.*

2 An **arrangement** is an agreement that you make with someone to do something. *e.g. He made an arrangement to rent the property.*

3 An **arrangement** is a plan for doing something. *e.g. What are the sleeping and eating arrangements?*

arrest   1171

1 If the police **arrest** someone, they catch them and take them somewhere in order to decide whether they should be charged with an offence. *e.g. They wanted to arrest him for possession of explosives.*

2 If someone is arrested, an **arrest** takes place. *e.g. The arrest was made in the early hours of the morning.*

arrival   1595

1 Your **arrival** at a place is the act of arriving there. *e.g. I apologise for my late arrival.*

2 An **arrival** is someone who has just arrived at a new place. *e.g. One of the new arrivals at college is an old friend.*

arrive   1595

1 When you **arrive** at a place, you reach it at the end of a journey. *e.g. I expect to arrive at the hotel after midnight.*

2 When a letter or piece of news **arrives**, it is brought or delivered to you. *e.g. I hope my letter to you will arrive tomorrow.*

arrogant   1076

Someone who is **arrogant** behaves in a proud, unpleasant way towards other people because they believe that they are more important or clever than others. *e.g. I dislike my bank manager, he is such an arrogant man.*

arse   1106

Your **arse** is your bottom. *e.g. Two-ton Tessie had an arse like the back of a cab, bless her!*

artificial   664

1 An **artificial** state or situation is not natural and exists or happens because people have created it. *e.g. These plant experiments are conducted under artificial conditions.*

2 **Artificial** objects or conditions do not appear naturally and are created by people. *e.g. She loved artificial flowers.*

as…as   423

You use the structure **as…as** when you are comparing things or signing or saying that they are similar. *e.g. She is as skilled as her sister.*

ascend   1209

1 To **ascend** is to move forwards and upwards. *e.g. We must ascend to the next plateau before nightfall.*

2 You sign or say that something such as a flight of steps **ascends** to a higher position when it leads to that position. *e.g. The stairs began to ascend more steeply.*

ascent   1209

1 An **ascent** is an upward slope, especially one you are travelling up. *e.g. John struggled up the rocky ascent.*

2 An **ascent** is a movement or journey upwards and forwards. *e.g. The ascent was hard, but we were fit.*

ashamed   993

1 Someone who is **ashamed** feels embarrassed or guilty because of something that they have done or something that has happened. *e.g. Forgetting people's names is nothing to be ashamed of.*

2 Someone who is **ashamed** to do something does not want to do it because it is something that they feel embarrassed or uncomfortable about. *e.g. I was ashamed to say hello to him after our quarrel.*

3 If you are **ashamed** of someone, you disapprove of something that they have done and feel embarrassed to be connected with them. *e.g. He was bitterly ashamed of her for writing such lies.*

ashes   1516

A dead person's **ashes** are what remains after their body has been burnt in a funeral service. *e.g. She went to collect her mother's ashes from the Crematorium.*

ashes   1520

Ashes are the grey or black powdery substance that is left after something is burnt. *e.g. There was nothing left of the bonfire but ashes.*

Asian   1590, 1602

1 Someone or something that is **Asian** belongs to or relates to the continent of Asia, or to its countries or peoples. *e.g. It was a conference on Asian Linguistics in Bangkok.*

2 An **Asian** is someone who comes from Asia, or whose family identity relates to Asia. *e.g. She is an Asian who moved to London in 1982.*

ask   1562

1 If you **ask** someone something, you sign or say something to them in the form of a question because you want to know the answer. *e.g. I'll go and ask if they're students.*

2 If you **ask** someone to do something, you sign or say to them that you want them to do it. *e.g. They ask me to fetch the bucket, so I fetch it.*

asleep   1669

1 Someone who is **asleep** is sleeping. *e.g. Sleeping Beauty had been asleep for a hundred years.*

2 Someone who is fast **asleep** is sleeping deeply. *e.g. Goldilocks was fast asleep on Baby Bear's bed.*

asleep (fall asleep)   1669

1 When you **fall asleep**, you start sleeping. *e.g. Joan tries to think happy thoughts before she*

falls asleep.

2 If you sign or say that you **fell asleep**, you started sleeping in the past, but you are now awake. *e.g. I fell asleep on the bus and missed my stop!*

asleep (fast asleep)   1138

Someone who is **fast asleep** is completely and thoroughly asleep. *e.g. The girl was lying fast asleep on the sofa.*

asleep (sound asleep)   1138

If you are **sound asleep**, you are sleeping peacefully. *e.g. Chris is still sound asleep.*

aspect   1599

An **aspect** of something is one of the parts or features of its character or nature. *e.g. America has influenced many aspects of British life.*

ass   1462

An **ass** is an animal related to a horse but smaller and with longer ears. *e.g. They kept an ass and sheep on the farm.*

assemble   1119

When a group of people **assemble** or someone **assembles** them, they gather together, usually for a particular purpose. *e.g. The leaders will assemble in Paris.*

assembly   1119

An **assembly** is a gathering of people. *e.g. There was an assembly of ministers for the sake of the press.*

assess   329, 1367, 1413

1 When you **assess** a person, feeling or situation, you consider them and make a judgement about them. *e.g. They meet tomorrow to assess the current financial position.*

2 When you **assess** the amount of money that something is worth or that should be paid for something, you calculate or estimate it. *e.g. She tried to assess the value of the jewellery.*

assessment   329, 1367, 1413

1 An **assessment** of a situation or problem is a consideration of all the facts about it and a judgement or opinion of the position and of what is likely to happen. *e.g. Success in this game depends on making correct assessments of other players' intentions.*

2 An **assessment** of someone or something is an estimate of their quality or worth, especially by using a test or examination. *e.g. New assessment methods will be used with the next group of people.*

3 An **assessment** of the amount of money that something is worth or of how much should be paid for something is a calculation or estimate of the amount. *e.g. Any appeal against your tax assessment should be made within 30 days.*

assessor   1367, 1413

1 An **assessor** is a person who is employed

to calculate the value of something or the amount of money that should be paid, for example in tax. *e.g. He worked as an assessor in the tax office.*
2 An **assessor** is a person who is an expert in a subject and who is asked to pass judgement on that subject. *e.g. She was invited to be an assessor for the communication skills exam.*

assist   150
1 If you **assist** someone, you help them to do something. *e.g. He asked me to assist in keeping the hotel under surveillance.*
2 If you **assist** people, you give them information, advice or money. *e.g. I may be able to assist them with tuition fees.*
3 If someone or something **assists** someone with a task, they make it easier for them. *e.g. With these clues to assist him, he should be able to identify who did it.*

assistance   150
If you are of **assistance** to someone or something, you are helpful or useful to them. *e.g. The information I provided was of great assistance to her.*

assistant   150
An **assistant** is someone whose job it is to help another person in their work. *e.g. I worked as her assistant for two years.*

associate   882, 898
1 If you **associate** one thing or person with another, or one thing or person **associates** with another, the two things are regarded as being connected with each other. *e.g. Deaf people associate speech training with the policy of oralism.*
2 If you **associate** yourself with a particular organisation, cause, point of view, etc., or if you are **associated** with it, you are connected with it in people's minds, especially because you become involved in it or you have signed or said that you agree with it. *e.g. Two of our members became closely associated with the work of the Deaf Women's Health Project.*
3 Your **associates** are the people you are connected with, especially your business colleagues. *e.g. The series is directed by my old associate Jack Good.*
4 **Associate** is used before a rank or title to indicate a slightly different or lower rank or title. *e.g. Non-teachers may become associate members of the British Association of Teachers of the Deaf.*

associates   227
Your **associates** are the people who you are connected with, especially at work. *e.g. My old business associates attended my farewell party.*

association   882, 898
1 An **association** is an official group of people with a common occupation, aim, or interest. *e.g. Sign linguists from all over the world belong to the International Sign Linguistics Association.*
2 Your **association** with a person, group or organisation is the connection that you have with them. *e.g. We shall do what we can while our business association lasts.*

assorted   426, 427, 447
A group of **assorted** things or people is a group of similar items that have different sizes, colours or other qualities. *e.g. There were assorted plastic bags on the floor.*

assortment   426, 427, 447
An **assortment** is a group of similar items that have different sizes, colours or other qualities. *e.g. You will find an assortment of sandwiches on the sideboard.*

assume   510
If you **assume** that something is true, you accept that it is true although you have had no real proof of it. *e.g. When you have a language degree, people assume that you can sign or speak the language fluently.*

assumption   510
If you make an **assumption**, you accept that something is true although you have no real proof of it. *e.g. His suggestions are based on an assumption that the prison system is out of date and worthless.*

astonish   1080
If something or someone **astonishes** you, they surprise you very much. *e.g. I think it will probably astonish you to learn that the jumble sale raised £842!*

astonishment   1080
Astonishment is a feeling of great surprise. *e.g. To the astonishment of his friends, he took off his shoes.*

as well as   423
If you refer to a second thing **as well as** a first thing, you refer to the second thing in addition to the first. *e.g. Women, as well as men, have a fundamental right to work.*

athlete   121
An **athlete** is a person who takes part in athletics competitions. It is used specifically in relation to running events. *e.g. My cousin is an Olympic 800 metres athlete.*

athletics   121, 132
Athletics consists of sports such as running, the high jump, and the javelin, and is used when you do not wish to make reference to any one of these sports in particular. *e.g. She attended the athletics meeting.*

attach   898
1 If someone is **attached** to an organisation or group of people, they are working with them or helping them, often for a short while. *e.g. I was attached to the expedition as medical officer.*
2 If one organisation or institution is **attached** to a larger organisation, it is part of the larger organisation and is controlled and administered by it. *e.g. The Institute is attached to the University of Southern Maine.*

attachment   898
1 If you have an **attachment** to someone or something, you are fond of them. *e.g. They formed a romantic attachment, but it did not last.*
2 The **attachment** of one thing, group or idea to another is the link between them. *e.g. I think the attachment of Stokoe's name to the project was what really created interest.*

attempt   373, 374
1 If you **attempt** something or **attempt** to do something, you try to do it or achieve it, especially when it is something difficult. *e.g. The Great Doctor Merrywomble will attempt to perform this feat without a safety-net.*
2 If you make an **attempt** at something you try to do it. *e.g. They will make an attempt at breaking the record next year.*

attempted   374
An **attempted** crime or other action is an unsuccessful effort to commit the crime. *e.g. He was charged with attempted murder.*

attend   1119, 1595
When a number of people **attend** a meeting or event, they are present at it. *e.g. I expect all of the class to attend the lecture tomorrow.*

attendance   1056, 1119
The **attendance** at a meeting is the number of people who are present at it. *e.g. At Easter, attendances at churches rose.*

attitude   1249
1 Your **attitude** to something is the way that you think and feel about it. *e.g. Their attitude to life is 'easy come, easy go'.*
2 Your **attitude** to someone is the way that you behave when you are dealing with them. *e.g. I resented his attitude.*

attract   774
1 If something **attracts** people or animals, it has features that cause them to come to it. *e.g. The circus attracted large crowds this year.*
2 If something **attracts** support or publicity, it receives support or publicity. *e.g. The women's movement has attracted a lot of support in the last decade.*

attract   845
1 If someone or something **attracts** you, they

have particular qualities which cause you to like or admire them. *e.g. The picture attracted me.*
2 If a particular quality **attracts** you to a person or thing, it is the reason why you like them. *e.g. What attracted me to Britta was her sense of humour.*

attraction   774
Attraction is a quality that something has of being interesting or desirable. *e.g. What was the attraction when you first saw the house?*

auction   242
1 An **auction** is a public sale of goods or property where people offer higher and higher prices until the goods are sold to the person who offers the highest price. *e.g. Dick hoped to buy a table at the auction.*
2 If you **auction** something or **auction** something **off**, you sell it at an auction *e.g. They are going to auction the pictures at the end of the month.*

auctioneer   242
An **auctioneer** is a person in charge of an auction who announces the items for sale, signs or calls out the offers of prices and makes sure that the buyer offering the highest price gets the object for sale. *e.g. The auctioneer did not notice me trying to bid.*

audience   1049
An **audience** is a group of people who are watching or listening to a play, concert, show, film, public speaker or presenter, or attending a special event, and who are usually seated. *e.g. Hearing people are getting used to having groups of deaf persons in the theatre audience.*

audiologist   1178
An **audiologist** is someone who practises audiology. *e.g. Dr. Brown was a skilled audiologist.*

audiology   1178
Audiology is the scientific study of hearing, including the treatment of persons with impaired hearing. *e.g. She is studying audiology as part of her training to become a hearing therapist.*

au fait   341
If you are **au fait** with something, you are familiar with it, and know all about it. *e.g. He thinks he's au fait with the rules of cricket so he can explain them to us.*

aunt   815
Your **aunt**, **auntie** or **aunty** is the sister of your mother or father, or the wife of your uncle. *e.g. Aunt Eileen is coming for the weekend.*

Australia   1241
Australia is the smallest continent and the largest island in the world, situated between the Indian Ocean and the Pacific. It is an independent nation and member of the Commonwealth. *e.g. Clark's lecture tour of Australia seems to have been a success.*

Australian   1241
1 Someone or something that is **Australian** belongs to or relates to Australia or its people. *e.g. We have ordered a copy of the Australian Sign Language Dictionary.*
2 An **Australian** is someone who comes from Australia, or whose family identity relates to Australia. *e.g. Crocodile Dundee is an Australian who finds himself in New York.*

Austria   821
Austria is a republic in Central Europe. *e.g. Romantic Vienna is the capital of Austria.*

Austrian   821
1 Someone or something that is **Austrian** belongs to or relates to Austria or its people. *e.g. The Austrian border can be crossed by travelling up high mountain passes.*
2 **Austrian** is a German dialect which is spoken in Austria. *e.g. He speaks Austrian, actually, but most Germans can understand it easily.*
3 An **Austrian** is someone who comes from Austria, or whose family identity relates to Austria. *e.g. He was, in fact, an Austrian, but he had learned ASL while studying at Gallaudet.*
4 The address of the **Austrian** Deaf Association is: Österreichischer Gehorlosenbund Sekretariat, Herrn Peter Dimmel, Auf der Halde 9, A-4060 Leoding/Linz, Austria.

author   628
1 The **author** of a piece of writing is the person who wrote it. *e.g. Peter Jackson is the author of a book on Britain's Deaf Heritage.*
2 An **author** is a person whose occupation is writing books. *e.g. Simone de Beauvoir, the French author, has written many books.*

authority   170
An **authority** on a particular subject is someone who knows a lot about it. *e.g. She is an authority on health education.*

authority   450
1 The **authorities** are the people who have the power to make decisions, especially the government of a country. *e.g. The union sought talks with the authorities.*
2 An **authority** is an official organisation or government department that has the power to make decisions. *e.g. She works for the Area Health Authority.*
3 **Authority** is the right to command and control other people. *e.g. He was reported to those in authority.*

automatic   371, 383
1 An **automatic** machine is one which can perform a task without needing to be operated by a person. *e.g. She has just bought a new automatic washing machine.*
2 An **automatic** action is one that you do without thinking about it, usually because it has become a habit. *e.g. My automatic response to such questions is to get aggressive.*
3 If something such as an action or a punishment is **automatic**, it always happens as the normal result of something else. *e.g. Speeding offences carry automatic fines.*

automatic doors   1432
Automatic doors open and close by moving from side to side without being touched directly, for example by electronic signals. *e.g. I'm still not used to walking through these automatic doors.*

automatic/sliding doors opening   1432
If **automatic** or **sliding doors** are **opening**, they are moving apart sideways, leaving a space in the middle which you can pass through. *e.g. Are you ready to catch the automatic doors opening and rush out?*

autumn   729
1 **Autumn** is the season between summer and winter. In the autumn, the weather becomes cooler and leaves change colour and fall from many trees and plants. *e.g. He preferred autumn to summer.*
2 **Autumn** means relating to or characteristic of autumn. *e.g. As you can see, autumn colours suit her well.*

avenge   48
If you **avenge** a wrong or harmful act or if you **avenge** someone who has been wronged or harmed, you hurt or punish the person who has done the wrong or harm. *e.g. He was determined to avenge his father's death.*

avenue   702
1 **Avenue** is a name sometimes used for a street in a town. *e.g. Madison Avenue is in New York.*
2 An **avenue** is a wide road with trees on either side, often leading to a large house. *e.g. She lives at the end of a long, open avenue.*
3 An **avenue** is a way of getting something done. *e.g. No sooner was one promising avenue closed than a hundred more opened.*

average   218
Something that is **average** is neither very good nor very bad. *e.g. It is an average piece of work.*

average   982
1 An **average** is the result (or approximate result) you get when you add two or more numbers together and divide the total by the

number of numbers you added together. *e.g. These pupils took a total of 39 examinations, an average of over six examinations for each pupil.*
2 Something that is **average** is neither very good nor very bad. *e.g. It is an average piece of work.*

average   1367, 1413
1 Something that is **average** is neither good nor bad. *e.g. It was an average example of the work of the period.*
2 An **average** is the result you get when you add two or more numbers together and divide the total by the number of numbers you added together. *e.g. So the average life expectancy of the bee is five years.*
3 To **average** a particular amount of things means to do, get or produce that amount as an average over a period of time. *e.g. Their factories average ten times the output of European factories.*
4 On **average** or on an **average** is used to indicate that a number you mention is the average of several numbers. *e.g. On average, they invested £2,000 a year.*

avoid   72
If you **avoid** something, you take action to prevent it happening. *e.g. He gave her a book on how to avoid stress.*

awake   633
1 Someone who is **awake** is not sleeping. *e.g. Do you have dreams when you're awake?*
2 When you **awake**, you wake up. *e.g. I usually awake at six o'clock when I'm working.*

aware   168
If you are **aware** of a fact, you know about it. *e.g. He was aware he'd drunk too much whisky.*

aware   633
1 If you are **aware** of a fact or **aware** that something is the case, you know about it. *e.g. I'm aware now that I have a right to an interpreter.*
2 Someone who is **aware** notices what is happening around them. *e.g. Since the course, he's been more aware about sign language usage.*

awareness   633
Your **awareness** of something is your knowledge about it. *e.g. He showed no awareness of this problem.*

away   1220
1 If you are **away**, you are not in the place such as home or office where people expect you to be. *e.g. He is away in London this week.*
2 If you move **away** from a place, you move

so you are no longer there. *e.g. He rose and walked away.*
3 **Away** can be used as an instruction to someone to leave. *e.g. Away, boy, and stay out of my sight!*

awesome   585
Something that is **awesome** has the power or quality to make people feel fearful because of its size, difficulty, et cetera. *e.g. That's an awesome job to have to tackle.*

awful   585, 1002
If you sign or say that something is **awful**, you mean that it is very unpleasant or shocking. *e.g. That creature in 'Alien' is awful—I would hate to have to act with it.*

awful   904, 911, 914, 918, 1584
1 If you sign or say that something is **awful**, you mean that it is not very good or not very nice. *e.g. Your daughter's behaviour is awful.*
2 If you sign or say that something is **awful** you mean that it is unpleasant or shocking. *e.g. The crossing on the ferry was awful.*
3 If you feel or look **awful**, you feel or look ill. *e.g. My aunt has lost a lot of weight and looks awful.*

B, b

B
B is the second letter of the British manual and English alphabets. See page 850.

baby   1386
A **baby** is a very young child, especially one that cannot yet walk, sign or speak. *e.g. He was a beautiful baby.*

back   1587
Your **back** is the part of your body from your neck to the top of your legs which is behind you and which you cannot easily see. *e.g. He hurt his back.*

backhander   1512
A **backhander** is a small bribe. *e.g. If you give the doorman a backhander, he'll let you into the club.*

back off   112
If you **back off**, you move away in order to avoid problems or a fight. *e.g. I was enthusiastic at first, but his strange behaviour made me back off.*

backpack   234
A **backpack** is a large bag that hikers,

travellers, etc., carry on their backs. *e.g. I need to buy a new backpack before we go on holiday.*

backside   1106
Your **backside** is the part of your body that you sit on. *e.g. I had to follow his backside up the narrow staircase.*

back up   229
1 If you **back up** a statement, you supply evidence to show that it is true. *e.g. This claim is backed up by the fact that every year more and more money is being spent on arms.*
2 If you **back** someone **up**, you help and support them. *e.g. We will back up your efforts to establish a Deaf Club in this area.*
3 If you **back** someone **up**, you confirm that what they are signing or saying is true. *e.g. She backed up his version of what had happened.*

bacon   653, 1312
Bacon is salted or smoked meat which comes from the back or sides of a pig. *e.g. Bacon and eggs, please.*

bad   904, 914
1 Something that is **bad** is unpleasant, harmful,

undesirable, or likely to involve difficulties or problems. *e.g. I have some bad news.*
2 Something that is **bad** is severe or unpleasant to a great degree. *e.g. The weather was bad.*
3 Something that is **bad** is of an unacceptably low standard or quality. *e.g. The meal was bad.*
4 Someone who is **bad** is considered to be evil, wicked or morally unacceptable. *e.g. There are always bad people around who will take advantage of other people's ignorance.*
5 Someone who is **bad** at doing something is not very skilful or successful at it. *e.g. I was bad at sports.*
6 If you have a **bad** leg, heart, eye, etc., it is weak, painful, injured or affected by disease. *e.g. The bed was good for my bad back.*

badge   647, 828
A **badge** is a small piece of plastic, metal or cloth with a design or message on it which you pin or sew onto your clothing to indicate that you have a particular rank, belong to a group or organisation, or support a particular cause. *e.g. He was given a shirt with a company badge.*

badge   781
A **badge** is a small piece of metal or cloth

which you fasten or pin to your clothes. Badges often have messages or designs on them. *e.g. Colin wore a C.N.D. badge.*

badminton 245
Badminton is a game, usually played indoors, in which you use a racket to hit a small feathered object called a shuttlecock over a high net to your opponent. It may be played by two or four players. *e.g. They are members of a local badminton club.*

badminton player 245
A **badminton player** is a person who takes part in a game of badminton. *e.g. The world champion badminton player will present the awards.*

badminton racquet 245
also spelled **badminton racket.**
A **badminton racquet** is a type of very light bat with a long handle to hit the shuttlecock in badminton. The part of the racquet used to hit the shuttlecock has strings stretched across and down on an oval frame. *e.g. I need a new badminton racquet.*

bag 15
A **bag** is a strong container made of cloth, plastic, leather, etc., with a handle, in which you keep personal things that you will need during the day, or put shopping in, or put belongings in when you are travelling somewhere. *e.g. She carried a red bag.*

baggage 15
Your **baggage** consists of the suitcases and bags that you take with you when you travel. *e.g. My baggage is at the check-in counter.*

bake 99
When you **bake** food or when it **bakes**, it is cooked in an oven using dry heat. *e.g. She said she would bake a cake to celebrate.*

baker 99
A **baker** is a person who bakes and sells bread, cakes, et cetera. The **baker** or the **baker's** is used to refer to a shop where bread and cakes are sold. *e.g. Are you going to the baker's?*

bakery 99
A **bakery** is a building where bread, cakes etc., are baked and sometimes sold. *e.g. We loved the smell of fresh bread from the bakery.*

baking 99
Baking is the activity of making bread, cakes, pastry et cetera. *e.g. When I was at catering college baking was one of the subjects we covered in the first year of the course*

balance 1367, 1413, 1630
1 **Balance** is the steadiness that someone or

something has when it is balanced on something. *e.g. She tried to keep her balance as she walked along the narrow plank.*
2 **Balance** is a state or situation in which all the different parts or forces involved have the right amount of importance, influence, or strength, or the same amount of it. *e.g. A balance of power must be found.*
3 A **balance** is a device used for weighing things. It consists of two dishes hanging from the ends of a horizontal bar which is supported at the middle. When items in each dish weigh the same, the bar remains horizontal. *e.g. She weighed the ingredients on the balance.*

balance sheet 1055
A **balance sheet** is a written statement of the amount of money and property a company has, the amount of money it is owed, and the amount of money it owes to other people. *e.g. He asked to see the balance sheet.*

bald 1602
Someone who is **bald** has little or no hair on the top of their head. *e.g. He has been bald since 1975.*

ball 1418
1 A **ball** is a round object that children often play with or that is hit, thrown, or kicked in games such as tennis, cricket and football. *e.g. Can we have our ball back please?*
2 A **ball** is something that has a round shape. *e.g. The cat played on the sofa with a ball of wool.*

ballerina 1405
A **ballerina** is a woman ballet dancer. *e.g. Natalya Bessmertnova is a fine ballerina.*

ballet 1405
1 **Ballet** is a type of dancing in which complicated and carefully planned movements are used to tell a story or to express an idea. *e.g. The ballet was based on the story of Cinderella.*
2 A **ballet** is an artistic work involving ballet dancing, the music written to accompany the dancing, or the performer of the work. *e.g. A ballet by Michael Fokine is on at the Opera House.*
3 A **ballet** is a professional group of ballet dancers. *e.g. The Russian Ballet gave a performance in London.*

ballet dancer 1405
A **ballet dancer** is someone who performs the complicated and carefully planned movements of a ballet. *e.g. He wanted to be a ballet dancer when he grew up.*

balloon 135
A **balloon** is a small thin, rubber bag that you blow air into so that it becomes larger and rounder or longer. Balloons are used as toys or decorations. *e.g. There will be balloons at the party.*

ballot 413, 629
A **ballot** is a secret vote in which people mark a piece of paper to indicate the person they choose in an election, or what they think about some particular subject. *e.g. Committee members were picked by ballot.*

ballpoint pen 614
A **ballpoint pen** or a **ballpoint** is a pen with a small metal ball at the end which transfers the ink onto paper. *e.g. She bought him a ballpoint pen for his birthday.*

ballroom dancer 892
A **ballroom dancer** is somebody who takes part in dances (such as a rhumba or a waltz) in which two people dance together with a fixed sequence of steps and movements. *e.g. He is a natural ballroom dancer.*

ballroom dancing 892
Ballroom dancing is the activity, sometimes competitive, in which two people dance together, using fixed sequences of steps and movements to perform dances such as a rhumba or a waltz. *e.g. Esther used to go ballroom dancing with her brother.*

ban 109, 413, 917
1 To **ban** something means to state officially that it must not be done, shown, used, et cetera. *e.g. 'When did the BBC last ban a play?' he asked, but the Director General could not give a definite answer.*
2 A **ban** is an official statement that something must not be done, shown, used, et cetera. *e.g. We're going to have to propose a ban on alcohol because there have been so many complaints.*

ban 244, 546
If you **ban** a person from doing something, the person cannot do that thing, usually during a specified time. *e.g. He was banned from entering the club for a year.*

banana 713
A **banana** is a long, curved fruit with a yellow skin and cream-coloured flesh. *e.g. She liked to eat a banana for breakfast every day.*

bandage 1350
1 A **bandage** is a long strip of cloth which is wrapped around a wound or a part of your body that you have injured to protect it while it heals. *e.g. Claude will need a bandage for a week.*
2 If you **bandage** a wound or part of someone's body, you tie a bandage around it. *e.g. We will have to bandage his arm.*

bang 124
A **bang** is a loud noise such as the noise of an explosion which may also be felt through vibrations that accompany the noise. *e.g. Walking across the street, we heard a bang.*

bang one's head against a brick wall   506, 928

If you **bang your head against a brick wall**, you try and achieve something difficult or impossible, with little success. *e.g. You're just banging your head against a brick wall trying to get the right sort of information.*

bank   65

A **bank** is an institution where people or businesses can keep their money and which also offers services such as lending, exchanging or transferring money. *e.g. Have you any money in the bank?*

bank   1218

1 A **bank** is the raised ground along the edge of a river or lake. *e.g. He followed the man along the bank.*
2 A **bank** is the sloping side of an area of raised ground. *e.g. We watched her scramble up the bank to the road.*

bankbook   60

A **bankbook** is a booklet showing the money transactions into and out of an account in the bank. *e.g. I'm going to the bank to check the balance in my bankbook.*

bankrupt   544, 1031, 1032

1 A person, business or organisation that is **bankrupt** or goes **bankrupt** does not have enough money to pay their debts. If this is officially declared in a court of law, they have to stop their business activities, their property is sold by an official appointed by the court and the money is used to pay as many of these debts as possible. *e.g. The company has gone bankrupt and ceased trading.*
2 To **bankrupt** a person or organisation means to make them go bankrupt. *e.g. The increase in interest rates has bankrupted many companies.*

baptise   171, 691, 1111

Also spelled **baptize**.
When a member of the clergy **baptises** someone, water is sprinkled on them or they are immersed in water as a sign that they have become a member of a Christian Church and that their sins have been washed away. *e.g. The baby is being baptised tomorrow.*

baptism   171, 691, 1111

A **baptism** is a Christian ceremony in which a person becomes a member of a Christian Church. *e.g. Our local vicar performed the baptism ceremony.*

bar   66

1 A **bar** is a place where you can buy and drink alcoholic drinks. *e.g. Ivor went for a drink in a bar on Second Avenue.*
2 A **bar** is a room in a pub or hotel where alcoholic drinks are served. *e.g. They ordered their meal in the bar while they were finishing their drinks.*
3 A **bar** is a counter at which alcoholic drinks are served. *e.g. Sally serves behind the bar.*

barber   752

A **barber** is a man who cuts men's hair. *e.g. He went to see the barber to please his mother.*

bare   257, 1602

If a part of your body is **bare**, it is not covered by any clothing. *e.g. He was bare from the waist up.*

bargain   1387

When people **bargain** with each other, they discuss what each of them will do, pay or receive. *e.g. Trade unions bargain with employers for better conditions.*

barmaid   66

A **barmaid** is a woman who serves drinks in a bar or pub. *e.g. My daughter works as a barmaid in the Black Bull.*

barman   66

A **barman** is a man who serves drinks in a bar or pub. *e.g. Ask the barman if he has any malt whisky.*

barrier   404

A **barrier** is a fence (with a hinge at one end) that is used to control the movement of people or things from one area to another by blocking the way until it is lifted. *e.g. They were on different sides of the barrier.*

barrier   1227

A **barrier** is an upright fence that is used to divide an area into two parts and prevent movement from one part to the other. *e.g. He's put a barrier up in the lane.*

bars   657

Bars are long, straight, upright pieces of rigid material such as metal. *e.g. The bars were not so strong that a hacksaw couldn't deal with them easily.*

barter   1387

If you **barter** goods, you exchange them for other goods rather than selling them for money. *e.g. They would bring meat or vegetables to barter for grain.*

base   151

1 If something is a **base** for something else, it is the object or surface that is underneath it and supports it. *e.g. I found a cardboard box to use as a base for my tool bag.*
2 If you **base** one thing on another, you develop its general form, subject, or nature from that other thing. *e.g. His films were all based on Britain and British life.*
3 A **base** for something such as a system of ideas or a subject of study is a central and very important part of it from which other ideas or more advanced studies are developed. *e.g. This new discovery formed the base for further teaching and research.*
4 If you have a **base**, you are in a position from which you can achieve power or success, especially in relation to politics or economics. *e.g. The League of Nations had no real power base on which to build.*

basement   1341

The **basement** of a building is the lowest floor, built partly or wholly below ground level. *e.g. He lives in a flat in the basement.*

bashful   364

Someone who is **bashful** is shy and easily embarrassed. *e.g. Most new parents are bashful about asking questions.*

basic   151

You use **basic** to describe things which are the most important or the simplest parts of something. *e.g. The basic theme of his presentation was participation.*

basin   1374, 1628

1 A **basin** is an open, round, bowl-shaped container, used especially for mixing or storing food. *e.g. Cover the basin with a clean cloth.*
2 A **basin** is a washbasin. *e.g. I thought I told you to fill the basin with warm water.*

basis   151

1 The **basis** of something is the central and most important part of it, from which it can be further developed. *e.g. The actors used the script only as a basis for improvisation.*
2 The **basis** for something is the thing that provides a reason for it. *e.g. There is no basis for the belief that deaf children cannot be bilingual.*
3 If you make a decision on the **basis** of something, it provides the reason for making that decision. *e.g. I made my decision on the basis of the information people gave me.*
4 If something is done on a particular **basis**, it is done in that way. *e.g. All new staff are employed on a temporary basis.*

basket   1629

A **basket** is a container that has a fixed shape and is used for carrying things such as shopping or clothes. Baskets are usually made of thin strips of wood or cane woven together and have either one or two handles. *e.g. The prize is a beautiful basket.*

basketball   979

Basketball is a game in which two teams of five players each try to score points by throwing a large ball through a circular net fixed to a metal ring at each end of the court. The winners are the team that score most points. *e.g. They play basketball at school.*

basketball player 979
A **basketball player** is someone who takes part in a game of basketball. *e.g. Michael Jordan is my favourite basketball player. I have all his televised matches on video and a big poster of him in my room.*

bath 137, 149
1 A **bath** is a long, rectangular container which you fill with water and sit or lie in, while you wash your body. *e.g. We have a new bath.*
2 When you have or take a **bath** or when you are in the **bath**, you wash your body while sitting or lying in a bath filled with water. *e.g. I'm going to have a bath.*

bathing costume 1411
A **bathing costume** is a garment that covers your trunk which you wear when you swim, sunbathe or go to the seaside. *e.g. She was wearing a bright blue bathing costume.*

bathrobe 286
A **bathrobe** is a piece of clothing made of towelling, which is like a loose fitting coat which you can wear before or after you have a bath, a shower or a swim. *e.g. He put on his bathrobe and went for a shower.*

bathroom 137, 149
A **bathroom** is a room that contains a bath or shower, a wash-basin, and usually a toilet. *e.g. She went into the bathroom and took a shower.*

bathtowel 143, 149
A **bathtowel** is a very large towel used for drying your body after you have had a bath or shower. *e.g. I brought a bathtowel with me.*

bat (small bat) 249
See **small bat**.

battery 815
A **battery** is a device which produces electricity, used to provide power for something such as a torch or radio. *e.g. The torch battery was dead.*

battle 924
A **battle** is a process in which two people or two groups of people compete for power or try to achieve opposite things. *e.g. The battle to control the administration was getting complicated.*

battle 1120
1 In a war, a **battle** is a fight between armies or between groups of ships or planes. *e.g. He was killed in battle.*
2 To **battle** means to struggle or fight very hard. *e.g. They knew they'd have to battle to reach the final.*

battle 1121
In a war, a **battle** is a fight between armies or

between groups of ships or planes. *e.g. He was killed in battle.*

bay 1226
A **bay** is a part of a coastline where the land curves inwards. *e.g. We built our home overlooking the bay in San Francisco.*

be 161, 977
To **be** means to exist in the world as a real, living or actual thing that can be identified and located. The sign may be translated into English by forms of the verb such as **be, is, am, are**, et cetera. *e.g. Will the sheep be in the fields all night?*

beam 1707
A **beam** of light is a line of light that shines from an object such as the sun. *e.g. A beam of light shone through the window.*

bear 141
A **bear** is an animal that is usually large, strong and wild with thick fur and sharp claws. There are several different kinds of bears, and most of them live in the cooler parts of the world. *e.g. The Koala bear is a cuddly looking animal.*

beard 1537, 1672
A **beard** is the hair that grows on a man's chin and cheeks, or false hair that can be fixed on the face, in particular one that grows down from the lower cheeks and chin. *e.g. When she was dressed in her costume and beard, she was a perfect Santa Claus.*

beat with a cane/strap 269
If someone **beats** another person **with a cane or strap,** they hit them with a cane or a strap so as to hurt or punish them. *e.g. His stepfather beat him with a strap for refusing to work.*

beat with a whisk 262
If you **beat** eggs, cream, butter, etc., **with a whisk,** you mix them thoroughly with a special kitchen tool (a whisk) used for quickly stirring air into them. *e.g. Beat two eggs with a whisk and add them to the butter and sugar.*

beautiful 1487, 1710
1 A **beautiful** woman is considered to be very attractive to look at. *e.g. She is a very beautiful girl.*
2 You sign or say that something is **beautiful** when you find it very attractive or pleasant. *e.g. He has a beautiful house.*

beauty 1487, 1710
1 **Beauty** is the state or quality of being beautiful. *e.g. You can find beauty in anything.*
2 A **beauty** is a beautiful woman. *e.g. Vita had turned into a beauty.*
3 You can sign or say that something is a **beauty** when you think it is very good. *e.g. My bike's a real beauty.*

4 If you sign or say that a particular feature is the **beauty** of something, you mean that this is the attractive quality or feature that makes the thing so good. *e.g. That's the beauty of the plan—it's so simple.*

be awful/bad/dreadful/terrible/wicked 904
See **awful/bad/dreadful/terrible.**

because 368, 1492
You use **because** when stating the reason for something. *e.g. I couldn't see Phyllis' expression because her head was turned.*

become 276
If something **becomes** a particular thing, it starts being that thing. *e.g. The smell is becoming stronger.*

bed 1254
A **bed** is a piece of furniture that you lie on when you sleep. *e.g. His bed is next to the window.*

bedclothes 140
Bedclothes are the sheets and covers which you put over you when you get into bed. *e.g. Jamie pulled back the bedclothes and climbed into bed.*

bedroom 1254
A **bedroom** is a room which is used especially for sleeping in. *e.g. The bedroom was very warm.*

bedspread 1521
A **bedspread** is a decorative cover which is put over a bed, on top of the sheets and blankets. *e.g. She gave her a new lace bedspread.*

beef 257, 530
Beef is the meat of a cow, bull or ox. *e.g. A joint of roast beef was put on the table and broccoli soufflé for the vegetarians.*

been (have been) 1566, 1643
1 If you **have been** to a place, you have gone to it or visited it. *e.g. Have you been to Brighton?*
2 If you **have been** doing something, you have done it for a period of time up until the present. *e.g. I've been teaching for three years.*
3 If someone such as a postman or milkman **has been,** they have called at your house. *e.g. Has the milkman been yet?*

beer (draught beer) 66
Draught beer is a beer served from barrels rather than bottles. Beer is an alcoholic drink made from malted barley and flavoured with hops. There are many different types of beers. *e.g. I prefer draught Guinness to bottled Guinness.*

beer (pull a measure of beer) 66
When someone **pulls a measure of beer** they move a handle which causes beer to flow

from a large container through a pipe and into a glass in order to serve a customer. *e.g. Ask Fred behind the bar to pull a pint for me.*

beetle   1148
A **beetle** is an insect with a hard covering to its body. *e.g. The wall was covered with tiny blue beetles.*

beetle/insect/spider crawling   1148
If a **beetle**, **insect** or **spider** is **crawling**, it is walking on its many tiny legs. *e.g. That spider crawling in the bath gives me the willies.*

before   111
1 If a situation existed, or something happened **before** a particular event or time, this situation existed or the thing happened continuously over a long time previous to this particular event or time. *e.g. Before the first world war, the farmers used to use horses instead of tractors.*
2 If there is a period of time, or if several things are done **before** something happens, it takes that amount of time or effort for this thing to happen. *e.g. It was almost an hour before the ambulance arrived.*

before   434
If someone is **before** something or someone, they are in front of them. *e.g. He will appear before the magistrate.*

before   1242, 1250, 1251
1 If someone has done something **before**, they have done it on a previous occasion. *e.g. Have you been to Greece before?*
2 If something has happened **before**, it has happened in the past. *e.g. Before, I used to go every week, but now I rarely go.*

before   1332
If you sign or say that something happened or was the case **before** another thing to which you refer, then it happened or was the case at a time previous to the other thing taking place or being true. *e.g. So did you open the bottle before you saw the door open?*

beg   1206, 1380
If you **beg**, you ask people, especially people you do not know, to give food or money to you because you are very poor. *e.g. Children beg in the streets: if they can't find food, they eat old newspapers.*

beggar   1206, 1380
A **beggar** is someone who lives by asking people to give him or her money or food. *e.g. In the doorway of the restaurant sat a beggar, his eyes ablaze with reproach.*

begin   209, 1105
1 If you **begin** to do something, you start doing it. *e.g. The actors will begin to rehearse the*

scene as soon as you are ready to watch.
2 When something **begins** or when you **begin** it, it takes place from a particular time onwards. *e.g. The meeting begins at three o'clock.*

beginner   209
A **beginner** is someone who has just started learning to do something and cannot do it very well yet. *e.g. That is the sort of mistake beginners make.*

behave   1475
1 If you **behave** in a particular way, you act in this way, especially because of the situation you are in or the people you are with. *e.g. She wanted to tell him why she was behaving this way.*
2 If you tell someone to **behave** or to **behave** themselves, you are telling them that they should act in a way that people think is correct and proper. *e.g. He's old enough to behave himself.*

behaviour   1475
A person's **behaviour** is the way they act in general, especially in relation to the situation they are in or the people they are with. *e.g. He has studied the behaviour of hundreds of deaf children.*

behead   1586
If you **behead** somone, you cut their head off. *e.g. Queen Mary ordered her executioner to behead Lady Jane Grey in 1554.*

behind   1641
You are **behind** when you have done less work than you should have done or when you have been less successful than anyone else. *e.g. I'm behind with my research paper on classifiers. It's due tomorrow!*

Belfast   1037
1 **Belfast** is the capital city and administrative centre of Northern Ireland. *e.g. I'm away to Belfast this weekend for the festival.*
2 The addresses of Deaf clubs in **Belfast** are: St. Joseph's Centre for the Deaf, 321 Grosvenor Road, Belfast BT12 4LP; and Ulster Institute for the Deaf, 5 College Square North, Belfast BT1 6AR.

Belgian   1264
1 Someone or something that is **Belgian** belongs to or relates to Belgium or its people. *e.g. Belgian cyclists did very well in the Tour of Flanders.*
2 A **Belgian** is a person who comes from Belgium or whose family identity relates to Belgium. *e.g. Her sister is married to a Belgian.*
3 The addresses of the **Belgian** Deaf Associations are: Jules Destreelaan 67, 9050 Gentbrugge, Belgium; and Rue Saxe-Cobourg 28, Brussels, Belgium.

Belgium   1264
Belgium is a kingdom in North West Europe and is a member of the European Community. *e.g. Belgium is noted for its fine lace.*

believe   514
1 If you **believe** something, you think that it is true. *e.g. We believed he was dead.*
2 If you **believe** someone, you accept they are telling the truth. *e.g. I believed him when he gave me an excuse for arriving late.*
3 If you **believe** in things such as God, fairies or miracles you are sure that they exist or happen. *e.g. When I was small, I believed that the tooth fairy left money under my pillow in return for teeth.*

believer   514
1 A **believer** in a particular idea or activity thinks that it is good, right or beneficial. *e.g. Bob is a great believer in jogging.*
2 A **believer** is someone who is sure of the truth of a particular doctrine or religion or the existence of God. *e.g. Some of my friends are Christian believers.*

bellringer   106
A **bellringer** is a person who rings church bells. *e.g. She is a bellringer at St. Cuthbert's.*

bellringing   106
Bellringing is the activity of ringing church bells. *e.g. She went bellringing every Sunday evening.*

belong to her   11, 63
You use **her**, **belong to her** or **hers** to indicate that something is owned by, may be used by or relates to a woman, girl or female animal who has already been mentioned or whose identity is known. *e.g. That car belongs to her.*

belong to him   11, 63
You use **belong to him** or **his** to indicate that something is owned by, may be used by or relates to a man, boy or male animal who has already been mentioned or whose identity is known. *e.g. You see the man in the corner? This is his coat.*

belong to it   11, 63
You use **belong to it** or **its** to indicate that something is owned by, may be used by or relates to a thing or animal that has already been mentioned or of which the identity is known. *e.g. I'm sure this screw belongs to it.*

belong to me   33, 35
You use **belong to me**, **mine** or **my** to indicate that something is owned by, may be used by or relates to you. *e.g. The black Morris Minor is mine.*

belong to them *plural*   13
You use **belong to them**, **their** or **theirs** to

indicate that something is owned by, may be used by or relates to a number of people, things, or animals that have already been mentioned or of which the identity is known. *e.g. The club has two hundred members. It belongs to them, not us, the committee.*

belong to them *singular*   11, 63
1 You can use **belong to them, their** or **theirs** to indicate that something is owned by, may be used by or relates to a single group of people, things, or animals which have already been mentioned or whose identity is known. *e.g. This video camera belongs to them—the group by the blackboard.*
2 You can use **belong to them, their** or **theirs** to indicate that something is owned by, may be used by or relates to a person or a single group of people that has already been mentioned without their identity being specified. *e.g. If the owner of this pen can prove to me that it belongs to them, I will give it back.*

belong to us   32
You use **belong to us, our** or **ours** when you wish to indicate that something is owned by, may be used by or relates to yourself and to one or more other people as a group. *e.g. Our children go to Northern Counties School for the Deaf.*

belong to you *plural*   14
You use **belong to you, your** or **yours** to indicate that something is owned by, may be used by or relates to the people you are singing or speaking to. *e.g. Your votes will decide who is to be the next club secretary.*

belong to you *singular*   9, 63
You use **belong to you, your** or **yours** when you wish to indicate that something is owned by, may be used by or relates to the person you are signing or speaking to. *e.g. This book belongs to you. It has your name in it.*

below   1340, 1341, 1343
1 If something is **below** another thing, it is underneath the other thing. *e.g. It was hidden below the floorboards.*
2 If something is **below** a particular amount, rate, or level, it is less than that amount, rate or level. *e.g. His reading ability is below average.*
3 If someone is **below** you in an organisation, they are lower in rank. *e.g. Below him are fourteen area officers.*

belt   611
A **belt** is a strip of leather, plastic or cloth that you tie or buckle round your waist to keep your clothes in place. *e.g. From his belt dangled a large bunch of keys.*

beneath   1340, 1341
1 Something that is **beneath** another thing is under the other thing. *e.g. If you look beneath*

the back of my car, you'll see the problem.
2 If you refer to what is **beneath** the surface of something, you are referring to aspects of it which are hidden or not obvious. *e.g. It comes across on paper as if his attitude is all sweetness and light, but beneath that I think things may be rather different.*

beneath   1343
1 Something that is **beneath** another thing is in a lower position than the other thing. *e.g. If we look at the part beneath that on the flipchart, we can see the difference.*
2 If you refer to what is **beneath** the surface of something, you are referring to aspects of it or things which are hidden or not obvious. *e.g. Dangerous sharks lurked beneath the glassy surface of the water.*

benefit   861
1 A **benefit** is something that helps you or improves your life. *e.g. The benefits of modern technology cost money.*
2 If something is to your **benefit**, or is of **benefit** to you, it helps you or improves your life. *e.g. This will be of benefit to the country as a whole.*
3 If you have the **benefit** of something, it gives you an advantage. *e.g. I had the benefit of a good education.*

benefit   1008
Benefit is a payment or series of payments, usually made by the government to someone who is entitled to receive it, for example because they are unemployed or ill. *e.g. You are entitled to child benefit for your sons.*

be quiet   352, 354, 1400
See **quiet (be quiet)**.

beside   194
If someone or something is **beside** something, it is at the side of it or next to it. *e.g. The apple pie is beside the roast beef.*

best   192
1 Your **best** is the greatest effort or the highest achievement that you are capable of. *e.g. They tried their best to finish in time.*
2 If you like something **best**, or like it the **best**, you prefer it. *e.g. Which do you like best—tea or coffee?*

be suspicious/wary   934
If you **are suspicious** or **wary** of someone or something, you do not trust them. *e.g. To be honest, I was beginning to be suspicious: why did it take her so long to decide?*

bet   1318, 1597
1 If you **bet** on a future event, such as a horse race, or **bet** someone an amount of money, you agree with someone an amount of money that

they will give to you if the event happens in the way you have predicted. *e.g. I told him which horse and how much to bet.*
2 A **bet** is an agreement that you make with someone when you bet on something. *e.g. I put a bet on the Grand National.*

betray   753
1 If you **betray** someone, you do something which harms them, often by helping their enemies or opponents. *e.g. His best friend betrayed him by taking his girlfriend away.*
2 If you **betray** someone's trust, you behave badly towards them or are disloyal when they trust you. *e.g. Tony's sister had believed all he said, but he betrayed her trust.*

better   193
1 Something that is **better** than something else is of a higher standard or quality. *e.g. The results were better than expected.*
2 Someone who is **better** at something or who does it **better** is more successful or skilful. *e.g. She is a better interpreter than Jack.*
3 If you like one thing **better** than another, you like it more. *e.g. I like this place better than anywhere else.*
4 If you are **better** after an illness or injury, you are feeling less ill. *e.g. I think she's better now, doctor.*

between   1224
1 A relationship, discussion, or difference **between** two people, groups or things is one that involves them both or relates to them both. *e.g. Negotiations between Britain and France are completed.*
2 When something is divided or shared **between** people, they each have a share of it. *e.g. The land was divided equally between them.*
3 If you sign or say that something is **between** or **in between** two amounts or ages, it is greater or older than one and smaller or younger than the other. *e.g. Police are looking for a man aged between twenty and twenty-five.*
4 If something is located **between** or **in between** two objects, it is to the left of one and to the right of the other. *e.g. Can you see it? It's between the clock and the vase of flowers.*

beware   452
If you tell someone to **beware** of a person or thing, you are warning them that the person or thing may harm them. *e.g. Beware of the dog: it bites!*

beyond   1611, 1620
1 If something is **beyond** a place, it is on the other side of it. *e.g. She had been born at a farm out beyond Barnham.*
2 If something extends, continues or progresses **beyond** a particular thing or point, it extends, continues or progresses further than that thing or point. *e.g. My responsibilities go beyond computers.*

bible   203,966
1 The **bible** or **Bible** is the sacred book on which the Christian religion is based, consisting of the Old Testament and the New Testament. *e.g. A translation of the Bible in BSL is being prepared.*
2 The **Bible** is the sacred book on which the Jewish religion is based, consisting of the Old Testament. *e.g. The rabbi read from the Bible.*
3 A **bible** is a copy of the Bible. *e.g. He took a bible from his rucksack and began reading.*

bicycle   92
1 A **bicycle** is a vehicle with two wheels which you ride by sitting on it and pushing two pedals with your feet. You steer it by holding and turning the handlebars which are connected to the front wheel. *e.g. Liam wants a bicycle for his birthday.*
2 When you **bicycle** somewhere, you ride a bicycle there. *e.g. They used to bicycle all over Scotland when they were young.*

bicycle   654
A **bicycle** is a vehicle with two wheels which you ride by sitting on it and pushing two pedals with your feet. You steer it by holding and turning the handlebars which are connected to the front wheel. *e.g. She wanted a bicycle for Christmas.*

bicycle (to bicycle)   654
When you **bicycle** somewhere, you ride a bicycle there. *e.g. They used to bicycle all over Scotland when they were lads.*

big   1064
1 Something that is **big** is large in size. *e.g. She liked big cats.*
2 Something that is **big** is important, significant, serious or complex. *e.g. I have noticed a big change in Sue.*

big   1217,1571,1572
1 Something that is **big** is tall in size. *e.g. My gym teacher was very big.*
2 You can refer to your older brother or sister as your **big** brother or sister. *e.g. He hoped his big brother would take him out again.*

bighead   1076
A **bighead** is a person who thinks that they are very clever and behaves as if they know everything. *e.g. She is just a bighead and thinks she knows best about everything.*

bike   92,654
A **bike** is a bicycle. *e.g. She was given a two-wheeler bike for her birthday.*

bike (on your bike)   160
You sign or say **on your bike** to someone when you want to tell them angrily to go away. *e.g. You're not wanted here. On your bike!*

bikini   472
A **bikini** is a two-piece swimming costume worn by women. *e.g. She wore a red bikini to the beach party.*

bill   607
A **bill** is a written statement of money that you owe for goods or services that you have received. *e.g. The bill came to forty-five pounds.*

billiards   70,79
Billiards is a game played by two people on a large table covered with smooth green cloth in which you use a long stick called a cue to hit small heavy balls against each other or into pockets around the sides of the table in order to score points. The winner is the person who scores the most points. *e.g. A game of billiards was going on in the club.*

billiards player   70
A **billiards player** is a person who takes part in a game of billiards. *e.g. Fred Davies was a champion billiards player.*

billions   1722
You can use **billions** to mean an extremely large amount. *e.g. There are billions of stars in the galaxy.*

bingo   629
1 **Bingo** is a game played for money or prizes, in which numbers are announced to the players who have special cards with numbers printed on them. You win when you can show that all the numbers on your card have been announced. *e.g. We like playing bingo on our holidays.*
2 **Bingo** is a social event, often occurring in clubs and special halls, at which groups of people gather to play bingo. *e.g. Mum has gone to bingo.*

binman   102
A **binman** is a person whose job it is to empty the rubbish from people's dustbins and take it away to be disposed of. *e.g. The binmen start work at seven in the morning.*

bird   479
A **bird** is a creature with feathers, two legs and two wings, which lays eggs. Most birds can fly. *e.g. Of course, there aren't so many birds round here.*

biro   614
A **biro** is a pen with a small metal ball on one end which transfers ink onto paper. *e.g. The biro was invented in 1953.*

birth   1482
1 The **birth** of a baby is the time when it comes out of its mother's body. *e.g. She was told that she had been deaf from birth.*

2 If someone has a particular nationality by **birth**, they have that nationality because their parents have it, or because they were born in the country referred to. *e.g. I think Mr. Ustinov's father was Russian by birth.*

birth control   72
Birth control is the use of contraceptives to prevent a woman from becoming pregnant during sexual intercourse. *e.g. The clinic provides information on birth control.*

birthday   146
Your **birthday** is the anniversary of the date on which you were born. *e.g. I'm planning a birthday party for Wendy.*

birthday suit   1602
If you sign or say that someone is in their **birthday suit**, you mean they are in a state of total nakedness, as at birth. *e.g. She'd just got out of the bath and was in her birthday suit when I walked in.*

birth (give birth)   1482
When a mother **gives birth**, she goes through the natural process of producing a baby from her body. *e.g. Carol gave birth to Liam at five past seven.*

biscuit   1145,1283,1541
A **biscuit** is a small, flat cake that is crisp and usually sweet. *e.g. Do you want a biscuit?*

bit   612
1 A **bit** of something is a small amount or piece of it. *e.g. A bit of cheese won't give you nightmares, silly!*
2 A **bit** means to a small extent or degree. *e.g. Liz is a bit like me.*

bit   637
A **bit** of something is a small amount or piece of it. *e.g. 'Excuse me, is this a bit of your brain?' is my favourite John Cleese line.*

bite   1129
1 When a person or animal **bites** something or takes a **bite** of something, they use their teeth to cut into it or through it. *e.g. If the dog dares to bite anyone, kick it out.*
2 A **bite** is an action of using the jaws and using the teeth to cut into or through something. *e.g. His bark is worse than his bite.*

bitter   525,958
Something that is **bitter** has a sharp, unpleasant taste. *e.g. The medicine was bitter.*

Black   18
1 A **Black** or **black**, or someone who is **Black** or **black**, belongs to a race of people with dark skins, especially a race from Africa. *e.g. We attended an exhibition by the*

Black Deaf artist Trevor Landell.
2 **Black** or **black** may be used to indicate that
something belongs to or relates to Black
people. e.g. *The department is to offer a course
next year entitled 'The Black Experience: the
History of Black People in Britain since 1945'.*

black   22
1 Something that is **black** is of the darkest
colour that there is, the colour of the sky at
night, when there is no light at all. *e.g. She wore
a black leather coat.*
2 **Black** tea or coffee has no milk or cream
added. *e.g. We drank cups of strong black coffee.*

Black person   18
A **Black person** or **black person** is someone
who belongs to a race of people with dark
skins, especially a race from Africa. *e.g. The
BDA is actively seeking to recruit more Black
Deaf people as members.*

Blackpool   22
1 **Blackpool** is a seaside town in Lancashire in
the north-west of England. It is famous for its
tower (158 metres high) and its illuminations.
*e.g. We went to Blackpool last September to see
the illuminations.*
2 The address of **Blackpool** Deaf Club is : 64
Cromwell Avenue, Blackpool, Lancashire,
FY2 9QW.

blame   439, 632, 916, 920
1 If you **blame** a person or thing for
something bad, you think, sign or say that
they are responsible for it. *e.g. She blamed
him for the fight.*
2 If somebody gets, takes, or accepts the
blame for something bad, they are held
responsible for it. *e.g. I will take the blame for
the mix-up in the dates.*

blank   685
Something that is **blank** has nothing written,
recorded or marked on it. *e.g. Give me a blank
tape: this one's been used.*

blanket   140, 1521, 1578
A **blanket** is a large square or rectangle of
warm cloth, especially one which covers you
when you are in bed. *e.g. I was just admiring
your new blanket.*

blank (go blank)   508
If you **go blank** or your mind **goes blank**, you
can't remember or think of something such as
the answer to a question or something you
were about to sign or say. *e.g. I had it a minute
ago, but now I've gone blank.*

blaspheme   905
If you **blaspheme**, you sign or say things that
are considered to be rude or disrespectful
things God, or you use God's name as a swear

word. *e.g. She said he shouldn't blaspheme in
front of the children.*

blast   2, 905, 969, 1670
You sign or say **blast** to express irritation or
annoyance about something or someone; in
English, it is considered to be a mild swear
word by some people. *e.g. Blast! I've stalled the
engine again.*

blast   124
A **blast** is a big explosion, especially one
caused by a bomb. *e.g. Nobody has been burnt
in the blast.*

blast off   405
When a space rocket **blasts off**, it leaves the
ground on its journey into the air. *e.g.
5..4..3..2..1... Blast off! The rocket is on its way
to the moon.*

blaze   1061
1 A **blaze** is an occurrence of uncontrolled
burning which destroys buildings, crops or
trees. *e.g. The forest went up in a big blaze.*
2 Something that is **blazing** is burning and
being damaged or destroyed by an
uncontrolled fire. *e.g. A vehicle that blows up
may blaze for up to three days.*

blazer   1650
A **blazer** is a jacket, often one which is a
special colour and has a badge on it, worn by
members of a particular group or institution
such as a sports team or a school. *e.g. Colin was
dressed in his school blazer.*

bleed   522
When you or a part of your body **bleeds**, you
lose blood from a part of your body as a result
of injury or illness. *e.g. He was bleeding heavily.*

blend   1622
1 When you **blend** two or more substances
together, you mix them together so that they
become one smooth substance. *e.g. Blend the
butter and sugar together.*
2 A **blend** is a mixture of two or more
substances. *e.g. It's a blend of parsnip and apple.*

blender   1622
A **blender** is a machine used in the kitchen for
mixing liquids and soft foods together at high
speed to form a smooth liquid substance. *e.g.
She was given a blender by her mother.*

bless   212, 215, 673
When a priest **blesses** people or things, he
asks for God's favour and protection for them.
*e.g. At harvest, they brought baskets of food to the
church to be blessed.*

blessing   212
If something is done with someone's **blessing**

they approve of it and support it. *e.g. She did it
with the full blessing of her parents.*

blether   603
If you **blether** you talk for a boringly long
time. *e.g. He blethered on for about three hours.*

blind   809
1 Someone who is **blind** is (totally or to a
significant degree) unable to see because their
eyes are very weak or damaged. *e.g. The
accident had left him almost totally blind.*
2 The **blind** are people who are (totally or to a
significant degree) unable to see because their
eyes are very weak or damaged. *e.g. He really
ought to go to a school for the blind.*
3 **Blind** can also mean relating to or
concerned with blind people. *e.g. The
Human Aids to Communication Commission of
Enquiry meeting was held at the Royal
National Institute for the Blind.*
4 Someone who is **blind** to something is
unable to understand it, to make sensible
judgements or to be reasonable about it. *e.g.
They seemed blind to the need for sign language
in education.*
5 If something **blinds** you to the real situation,
it prevents you from noticing or being aware of
its reality. *e.g. I couldn't let affection blind me to
the fact of Jim's drug addiction.*

blind as a bat   787, 808
1 If you sign or say that someone is as **blind as
a bat**, you are teasing them for not being able
to find or see something that is very obvious.
e.g. You're as blind as a bat if you missed that!
2 If you sign or say that someone is as **blind as
a bat**, you mean that they have very poor
eyesight. *e.g. He wants to play with the kids, but
I'm afraid he's as blind as a bat!*

blind person   809
A **blind person** is a person who is identified as
being (totally or to a significant degree) unable
to see because their eyes are very weak or
damaged. *e.g. No blind person would be able to
access this meeting.*

block   72, 80
1 To **block** a road, channel or pipe, means to
put an object across it or in it so that nothing
can get through. *e.g. The road was blocked by
a fallen tree.*
2 If you **block** something that is being
arranged, you prevent it from being done. *e.g.
The council blocked his plans.*

block   1447
1 A **block** of something is a large rectangular
piece. *e.g. I just want a block of stone to use as the
base of a lamp, said Ernst.*
2 A **block** is part or a section of a programme,
schedule or course. *e.g. The second block begins
with a look at teaching methods.*

blocks (children's building blocks)　1688
Children's building blocks or **bricks** are small cubes, usually made of wood or plastic, which children use to play with, for example, by putting one on top of another. *e.g. The building blocks are in the corner.*

blood　522
Blood is the red liquid that flows around inside your body. *e.g. Her hand was covered in blood.*

blood sample　782
A **blood sample** is a small amount of blood drawn from the arm (often from inside the elbow) with a syringe, which is used for testing. *e.g. She had to give a blood sample to see if the infection had cleared.*

bloody　969
You use **bloody** to swear, emphasising how annoyed or angry you are. *e.g. The bloody students are striking for higher grants!*

bloom　1718
When a plant **blooms**, it produces flowers. *e.g. My crocuses are blooming already.*

bloom　1728
When a plant or tree **blooms**, it produces flowers. *e.g. This variety of rose blooms late into the autumn.*

blossom　1718
1 When a plant **blossoms**, the flower buds open. *e.g. She looked closely at the petals of the blossoming flower.*
2 If someone or something **blossoms**, they develop very good, attractive or successful qualities. *e.g. She seemed to blossom after her marriage and became a different person.*

blouse　1527
A **blouse** is a kind of shirt worn by a woman or girl. *e.g. A white blouse is required for her school uniform.*

blow　1711
If you **blow**, you send out a stream of air from your mouth. *e.g. Eric put his lips to the hole and blew gently.*

blow a whistle　641
When you **blow a whistle**, you send out a stream of air through your mouth into a small metal tube and make a loud sound, usually in order to attract someone's attention. *e.g. The railway official blew his whistle and the train began to move.*

blow me down　1712
If you sign or say **'blow me down'** or **'I'll be blowed'** you are expressing surprise at something. *e.g. I'll be blowed! You arrived on time!*

blow up　1720
1 To **blow up** means to destroy something by an explosion. *e.g. They are going to blow up the old building.*
2 If you **blow up**, you lose your temper and become very angry. *e.g. I'd better not be late, my father will blow up.*

blow up a balloon　135
If you **blow up a balloon** you fill it with air by blowing into it. *e.g. I see you've blown up the balloons already.*

blue　1245, 1288, 1602
Something that is **blue** is the colour of the sky on a sunny day. *e.g. Chelsea and Peterborough United both wear blue shirts, so someone has to wear their second strip.*

blush　351
1 When you **blush**, your face becomes redder than usual because you suddenly feel a strong emotion, especially shame or embarrassment. *e.g. I felt myself blushing when the doctor mentioned my weight.*
2 A **blush** is the red colour on your face that results from blushing. *e.g. The freckles on Jack's face disappeared under a blush.*

boast　232, 233
1 If you **boast**, you sign or speak about something that you have done or something that you own in a way that shows you are proud or pleased, usually in order to impress other people. *e.g. 'He chose my painting,' boasted Millie.*
2 A **boast** is a statement that someone makes, usually in order to impress other people, which shows that they are proud of something, usually excessively proud. *e.g. It is his boast that on one such occasion he read Paradise Lost in a single evening.*

boastful　232, 233
Someone who is **boastful** signs or speaks too proudly about something that they possess or have done, usually in order to impress other people. *e.g. She is boastful and selfish. I don't like her.*

boat　1428
A **boat** is a small vehicle which is used for travelling across water. *e.g. John took me down the river in the old boat.*

boat/ferry sailing　1428
When a **boat** or **ferry** is **sailing**, it moves across water. *e.g. The ferry sailing in the distance is called 'The Old Tub' by the locals.*

bob　1381
If something **bobs**, it moves up and down in the water. *e.g. The toy boat began to bob gently in the middle of the lake.*

body　1078
1 A person's or animal's **body** is all their physical parts, including their head, limbs, flesh and organs. *e.g. Her body was covered with spots.*
2 A **body** is the dead body of a person. *e.g. We were unable to find the body of the missing woman.*

body　1176
A **body** is an organised group of people who deal with something officially. *e.g. A local voluntary body is handling community problems.*

bodyguard　442
A **bodyguard** is a person employed to protect someone. *e.g. The film star was accompanied by a bodyguard.*

bold　1200
Someone who is **bold** is not afraid to do things which involve risk or danger. *e.g. It is very bold of you to gamble ten thousand pounds on this race.*

bomb　124
A **bomb** is a device designed to be capable of exploding and damaging or destroying a large area. *e.g. They planted a bomb beneath the house.*

bomb　1699
1 If people **bomb** a place, they attack it by dropping bombs on it from aircraft. *e.g. Coventry Cathedral was bombed during the war.*
2 A **bomb** is a device designed to be capable of exploding and damaging or destroying a large area, when dropped from an aircraft. *e.g. As we ran for the shelter, a bomb fell almost in front of us.*

bone　21, 42, 1175
1 A **bone** is one of the hard parts inside a body which together form a skeleton. *e.g. We found an old bone in the garden.*
2 A **bone** tool or ornament is made of bone. *e.g. Bone knives were found in the ancient cave.*

bones　660
Your **bones** are the hard parts inside your body which together form your skeleton. *e.g. You could see her bones beneath the flesh.*

bonfire　1061
A **bonfire** is a fire that is made outdoors, especially in order to burn rubbish from a garden. *e.g. We baked potatoes in the bonfire.*

book　128, 1318
When you **book** something or someone, such as a hotel room, ticket, guide, etc., you arrange with someone to have or use the thing or the person's services at a particular time. *e.g. I'd like to book an interpreter for the meeting.*

book　1456
A **book** is a number of pieces of paper, usually with words and pictures printed on them, which are fastened together and fixed inside a

cover of stronger paper or cardboard. Books contain such things as information, stories, or poetry. *e.g. He gave her a book on cats.*

bookcase　　　　　　　　　　　　　　1457
A **bookcase** is a piece of furniture with shelves that you keep books on. *e.g. He bought a bookcase made of oak at the auction.*

booked　　　　　　　　　　　　　　244
1 If you are **booked** by a police officer, he or she officially records your name and the offence that you may be charged with. *e.g. I was booked for speeding yesterday.*
2 When a referee **books** a player who has seriously broken the rules of the game, he or she officially records the player's name. In a game such as football, if a player is booked twice, they are sent off the field. *e.g. He was booked for punching another player.*

bookkeeper　　　　　　　　　　　　727
A **bookkeeper** is a person responsible for keeping an accurate record of the sums of money that are spent and received by a business or other organisation. *e.g. I agreed to act as bookkeeper for the gardening club.*

bookkeeping　　　　　　　　　　　727
Bookkeeping is the job or activity of keeping an accurate record of the sums of money that are spent and received by a business or other organisation. *e.g. She went to evening classes in bookkeeping.*

boot　　　　　　　　　　　　　　　1285
A **boot** is a shoe that covers your whole foot and the lower part of your leg. *e.g. He put on his coat and picked up his boots.*

boot out　　　　　　　　　　379, 546
If you **boot** someone **out** of a job, organisation, or place, you force them to leave it. *e.g. We'll just have to boot out anyone who messes about, okay?*

boots　　　　　　　　　　　　　　148
Boots are shoes that cover your whole feet and the lower part of your legs. *e.g. He put on his coat and picked up his boots.*

boozing　　　　　　　　　　　　　1671
If someone is **boozing**, they are drinking a lot of alcoholic drinks. *e.g. They were out boozing until all hours last night.*

border　　　　　　　　　　　　　1432
The **border** between two countries or other political regions is the dividing line between them, and also sometimes the land close to this line. *e.g. He lives in the French Alps near the Swiss border.*

bore　　　　　　　　　　　　　　1255
1 You describe someone as a **bore** when you

think that they sign or talk in a very uninteresting way and often too much. *e.g. Steve is the most frightful bore.*
2 If someone or something **bores** you, they make you tired or impatient because you find them uninteresting and dull. *e.g. Foreign films bore me—all that melodrama and kissing.*

bored　　　　　　　　　　　　　1255
When you are **bored**, you feel tired and often impatient because you have lost interest in something or because you have nothing to do. *e.g. I have nothing to do, I'm bored.*

bored stiff　　　　　　　　　　　1137
If you are **bored stiff** by something, you are not at all interested in it and find it dull and tedious. *e.g. Watch cricket? I'd be bored stiff.*

bored to death　　　　　　　　　1137
If you are **bored to death** by something, you are not at all interested in it and find it dull and tedious. *e.g. I'm bored to death by this lecture.*

bored to tears　　　　　　　　　1137
If you are **bored to tears** by something, you are not at all interested in it and find it dull and tedious. *e.g. You will bore me to tears if you keep going on about the wonders of lap-top computers.*

bore one stiff　　　　　　　759, 779
If something **bores you stiff**, you are not at all interested in it or find it extremely dull and tedious. *e.g. To be perfectly frank, this stuff about taxation bores me stiff.*

bore one to death　　　　　759, 779
If something **bores you to death**, you are not at all interested in it or find it extremely dull and tedious. *e.g. It bores me to death, watching the same old rubbish every Saturday night.*

bore one to tears　　　　　759, 779
If something **bores you to tears**, you are not at all interested in it or find it extremely dull and tedious. *e.g. The reason why I won't watch Arsenal is because football bores me to tears.*

boring　　　　　　　　　　　　　1255
Something that is **boring** is so dull and uninteresting that it makes people feel tired and often impatient. *e.g. Are all your meetings this boring?*

born　　　　　　　　　　　　　　1482
1 When a baby is **born**, it comes out of its mother's body at the beginning of its life. *e.g. Morris had been born and brought up in New York.*
2 If you sign or say that a child is **born** to someone, you are referring to the birth of the child and indicating who its parents are. *e.g. A baby has been born to them.*

borrow　　　　　　　　　　78, 613
If you **borrow** something that belongs to someone else, they allow you to have it or use it for a period of time. *e.g. Could I borrow your car?*

borrower　　　　　　　　　　　　78
A **borrower** is a person or organisation that borrows money. *e.g. They increased the surcharge for big borrowers.*

boss　　　　　　　　　　　　450, 957
1 Your **boss** is the person who is in charge of the organisation or department where you work and who tells you what work to do. *e.g. I met his boss at a dinner party.*
2 If you are the **boss** in a group or relationship, you are the person who makes the decisions and gives orders to the other person or people in the group or relationship. *e.g. She asked her boss if she could attend the conference.*
3 If you are your own **boss**, you work for yourself and do not have to ask other people for permission to do something. *e.g. One of the attractions of being self-employed is that you are your own boss.*

bossy　　　　　　　　　　　450, 957
A **bossy** person enjoys telling other people what to do. *e.g. I remember her as being very bossy.*

bother　　　　　　　　　　　　1604
1 **Bother** is trouble, fuss, or difficulty. *e.g. We found the address without any bother.*
2 If a task or a person is a **bother**, they are boring or irritating. *e.g. Sorry to be a bother, but could you type this for me?*
3 If something **bothers** you, or if you **bother** about it, you are worried, concerned, or upset about it. *e.g. Does it bother you?*

both of us　　　　　　　　　　　760
You use **both of us** when you are referring to two people, including yourself. *e.g. Both of us will have to go.*

both (you both)　　　　　　　　783
You use **you both** or **both of you** when you are referring to two people or things and saying that something is true about each of them. *e.g. I've told you both before, and I'm not going to tell you again!*

bottle　　　　　　　　　　　　1683
A **bottle** is a container for keeping liquids in. Bottles are usually made of glass or plastic and are shaped like a cylinder with a narrow top. *e.g. She brought a bottle of wine to the party.*

bottom　　　　　　　　　　　　1106
Your **bottom** is the part of your body between your back and your legs that you sit on. *e.g. I've got a boil on my bottom.*

bottom   1213, 1341, 1343
1 The **bottom** of something is the lowest
part of it. *e.g. The structure was crumbling at
the bottom.*
2 The **bottom** of an organisation or scale is the
least powerful or important level in it or the
lowest point on it. *e.g. Officials at the top make
the decisions; people at the bottom carry them out.*

bounce a ball/basketball   979
When you **bounce a ball**, or a **basketball**,
you direct it against the ground, so that it
immediately springs upwards again. *e.g.
Don't forget to bounce the basketball while you
are running.*

bounce (of a round object)   62
1 When **a round object** such as a ball
bounces, it moves away from the ground
immediately after hitting it. *e.g. The cabbage
bounced off the ground when it fell from the
back of the lorry.*
2 The **bounce of a round object**, such as a
ball, is the movement away from the ground
which it makes immediately after hitting it.
*e.g. She had not reached the ball before its second
bounce.*

bounce on a trampoline   801
If you **bounce on a trampoline**, you jump
up and down on a piece of apparatus consisting
of a large piece of strong cloth held by springs
in a frame. *e.g. She loved to bounce on the
trampoline when all the children had gone home.*

bouncer   745
A **bouncer** is a person who is employed to stand
at the door of a pub, club, or disco in order to
prevent unwelcome people from coming in and
to remove people if they cause any trouble. *e.g.
He got a job as a bouncer in a nightclub.*

boundary   1432
The **boundary** of an area of land is the line
which marks the outer edge of it and which
separates it from the land adjoining it. *e.g. We
reached the boundary of Snowdonia National
Park before noon.*

bow   864
A **bow** is a weapon for shooting arrows,
consisting of a long piece of wood or similar
material, bent into a curve by a string
attached to both its ends. *e.g. He picked up
the bow: such a weapon could do serious
damage in the wrong hands.*

bow and arrow   864
A **bow and arrow** is a curved weapon with a
string attached to both ends (bow) and a thin
stick with a sharp point (arrow) that can be
fired at a target by being launched from the
string. *e.g. We bought a toy bow and arrow for
his birthday.*

bowl   1374, 1628
A **bowl** is a container that is open at the top,
fairly shallow, and usually circular. Bowls
are used, for example, for serving food,
mixing ingredients when cooking, keeping
fruit in, or washing up. *e.g. A bowl of fruit
stood on the sideboard.*

bowls   1713
Bowls is a game in which the players try to roll
large wooden balls (bowls) as near as possible
to a small ball (jack). A point (or points) is
scored by the player whose ball (or balls)
finishes closest to the jack. It may be played
indoors or outdoors. *e.g. His hobby was indoor
bowls, and he was really good at it.*

bowls player   1713
A **bowls player** is a person who takes part in a
game of bowls. *e.g. The former champion bowls
player David Bryant is famous for not smoking
his pipe during games.*

bow tie   745
A **bow tie** is a piece of cloth, tied in a knot with
two loops and two loose ends under someone's
shirt collar. Bow ties are worn especially by
men for formal occasions. *e.g. I'll buy him a
bow tie for Christmas.*

box   82
To **box** means to fight someone according to
the rules of the sport of boxing. *e.g. He used to
box, run and swim for the school.*

box   1458
A **box** is a square or rectangular container
which sometimes has a lid. *e.g. They took a box
full of old clothes to the jumble sale.*

boxer   82
A **boxer** is someone who takes part in a boxing
match. *e.g. I want to be a boxer when I grow up.*

boxing   82
Boxing is a sport in which two people (usually
boys or men) fight according to special rules,
by punching each other with their fists,
wearing large padded gloves. You win by
scoring more points that your opponent or by
knocking them down for a count of ten or
hurting them to such an extent that the referee
stops the contest. *e.g. Are you going to watch the
boxing match tomorrow?*

boy   483, 529
1 A **boy** is a male child. *e.g. There was a boy
dressed in blue overalls on the lawn.*
2 You can also refer to a young man as a **boy**.
*e.g. That boy you were going to marry was
round here today.*

boyfriend   483
Someone's **boyfriend** is a man or boy with

whom the person is having a relationship
that is romantic, sexual or both. *e.g. This is
my boyfriend, Oliver.*

boyish   529
If you sign or say that someone is **boyish**, you
mean that they are like a boy in appearance or
behaviour. *e.g. You should not be taken in by his
boyish smile.*

brag   232, 233
If you **brag**, you sign or say in a very proud
way that you have done or will do a particular
thing or that you possess a particular thing.
e.g. He bragged about his salary.

braille   1112
Braille is a system of printing for blind people in
which the letters are printed as groups of raised
dots that they can feel with their fingers. *e.g. She
learned braille as her eyesight grew worse.*

brain   511
1 Your **brain** is the organ inside your head
which enables you to think and to feel things
such as heat and pain. *e.g. These drugs can
cause brain damage.*
2 **Brains** refers to the greyish matter which
the brain of a person or animal consists of. *e.g.
The corpse's head was a mess of bone and brains.*

brainwave   213
A **brainwave** is a clever idea that you
suddenly think of. *e.g. His suggestion to send the
information by video letter was a brainwave.*

branch   1678
A **branch** of a tree is the part that grows out
from its trunk and that has leaves, flowers or
fruit growing on it. *e.g. A bird flew across to the
tree and alighted on a branch.*

brass cheek   478
If you sign or say that someone has **brass
cheek**, a **brass cheek** or has the **brass cheek**
to do something, you mean that they dare to do
it, without worry or shame about the results of
their actions. *e.g. What brass cheek! Marching
in like that!*

brass neck   478
If you sign or say that someone has a **brass
neck** or the **brass neck** to do something, you
mean that they dare to do it, without worry or
shame about the results of their actions. *e.g. He
had the brass neck to ask me for more money!*

brass nerve   478
If you sign or say that someone has **brass
nerve**, a **brass nerve** or the **brass nerve** to do
something, you mean that they dare to do it,
without worry or shame about the results of
their actions. *e.g. Do you have the brass nerve to
choose between them?*

brave 1200
Someone who is **brave** is willing to do things which are dangerous and does not show fear in difficult or dangerous situations. *e.g. The soldiers were brave to go into battle with so little ammunition.*

bravery 1200
Bravery is brave behaviour or the quality of being brave. *e.g. Being a nurse requires infinite patience and also bravery.*

bread 1327
Bread is a very common food made from flour, water and often yeast. The mixture is made into a soft dough and baked in an oven. Bread is often cut into slices and eaten with, for example, butter, jam or cheese. *e.g. Take some bread and cheese for lunch.*

break 94
1 When an object **breaks** or when you **break** it, it suddenly separates into two or more pieces, often because it has been hit or dropped. *e.g. My new teapot is broken.*
2 If you **break** a rule, promise, or agreement, you do something to disobey it or you fail to fulfil it. *e.g. We're not breaking the law.*

break 1086, 1495
1 A **break** is a short period of time when you stop what you are doing in order to have a rest before you begin again. *e.g. We all met in the pub during the lunch break.*
2 A **break** is a holiday, or a period of time when you do something different from the job or activity that you are involved with, in order to have a rest from it. *e.g. You need a break. Why don't you take a week off?*

break away 884
If you **break away** from a group of people or a way of doing things, you stop being involved with that group or stop doing things that way. *e.g. The Gang of Four broke away from the Labour party in the early 1980s.*

breakaway 884
A **breakaway** group is a group of people who have separated from a larger group. *e.g. The Fairfield Club was originally a breakaway group from the Liverpool Society for the Deaf.*

breakfast 1501
1 **Breakfast** is the first meal of the day, which most people eat early in the morning. *e.g. What's for breakfast?*
2 If you **breakfast** or **have breakfast**, you eat your first meal of the day, usually early in the morning. *e.g. I've breakfasted already, thanks.*

break over 1725
When a wave **breaks over** something, the water at the top of it falls down, and splashes over the thing. *e.g. The waves were about to break over the boat.*

break wind 1700, 1719
When someone **breaks wind**, they release air from their intestines through their anus. It is considered rude to do so in company. *e.g. Much to my embarrassment, one of the children broke wind as we left.*

breast 1657
A woman's **breast** is one of the two soft, round pieces of flesh on her chest that can produce milk to feed a baby. *e.g. She is to have surgery on her breasts.*

breast-feed 1657
When a woman **breast-feeds** her baby, she feeds it with milk from her breasts rather than a bottle. *e.g. Mothers are encouraged to breast-feed because the milk contains antibiotics against infection and essential vitamins for the baby.*

breast-stroke 1410
Breast-stroke is a particular type of movement you do while swimming in which you lie on your front and move your arms and legs horizontally. *e.g. He preferred to use breast-stroke.*

breathalyse 857
also spelled **breathalyze**.
If the police **breathalyse** you when you have been driving a vehicle, they ask you to breathe into a special bag containing chemicals. The chemicals indicate whether you have drunk more alcohol than you are legally allowed to when you are driving. *e.g. He was breathalysed after the accident.*

breathalyser 857
also spelled **breathalyzer**.
A **breathalyser** is a device consisting of a special bag containing chemicals which the police use to measure the amount of alcohol that someone has drunk. *e.g. He claimed the breathalyser was faulty.*

breath freshener 634
A **breath freshener** is something that can be sprayed into your mouth to make the air expelled smell more pleasant. *e.g. This breath freshener tastes of spearmint.*

breeze 1278, 1463
A **breeze** is a wind that blows very gently. *e.g. There is a refreshing breeze by the door.*

bribe 1512
1 A **bribe** is a sum of money or something valuable that someone gives to an official in order to persuade the official to do something. *e.g. The Vice President admitted accepting the bribe.*
2 If someone **bribes** an official, they give the official a bribe. *e.g. The attempt to bribe the clerk had failed.*

brick 1689
A **brick** is a rectangular block used for building walls, houses, et cetera. Bricks are usually reddish-brown or stone-coloured. *e.g. My house was built of red bricks.*

bricklayer 252
A **bricklayer** is a person whose job it is to build walls using bricks. *e.g. He has a job as a bricklayer.*

bricks (children's building bricks) 1688
Children's building bricks are the same as **children's building blocks**. See under **blocks (children's building blocks)**.

bridge 700, 1663
1 A **bridge** is a structure that is built over a waterway, railway, road, etc., so that people or vehicles can cross from one side to the other. *e.g. We crossed the bridge over the stream.*
2 To **bridge** a river, valley, etc., means to build a bridge across it. *e.g. The problem was how to bridge the river.*

brief 87
A piece of signing, writing or speech that is **brief** does not contain too many signs, words or details. *e.g. They started with a brief description of their work.*

briefcase 15, 247
A **briefcase** is a firm, rectangular case, often made of leather, which has a small handle at the top. You use a briefcase to carry files, papers, books, et cetera. *e.g. Peter gave David a briefcase for his birthday.*

briefs 472
Briefs are a piece of underwear which have two holes to put your legs through and elastic around the third hole which goes round your waist. *e.g. She was wearing white cotton briefs.*

bright 166, 1500
Someone who is **bright** is quick at learning things. *e.g. We have a very bright group of girls in this class.*

bright 1728
1 A **bright** colour is strong and noticeable, and not dark. *e.g. Post-boxes are painted bright scarlet so that you can easily spot them.*
2 A place or day that is **bright** has a lot of light or sunshine. *e.g. We sat in a bright, sunlit room.*

Brighton 989
1 **Brighton** is a town on the south coast of England. It is well-known as a holiday resort. *eg. Martin went to Brighton to visit his father.*
2 The address of **Brighton** Deaf Club is: Carlton Hill, Brighton BN2 2GW.

brilliant 1500
If you describe someone as **brilliant**, you mean that they are extremely clever. *e.g. A brilliant young engineer has been appointed as head of research.*

bring 275
1 If you **bring** someone or something with you when you come to a place, they come with you or you have them with you. *e.g. Please bring your calculator to every lesson.*
2 To **bring** someone or something to a place means to cause them to come to the place. *e.g. Irish monks were responsible for bringing Christianity to Scotland.*

bring forward 885
If you **bring** an event **forward** in time or **bring forward** the time when it is due to take place, you arrange for it to take place at an earlier time than originally planned or agreed. *e.g. If you have to leave by three o'clock, we will have to bring forward the time of your interview.*

bring in 1664
If you **bring in** someone, you get them to take part in an activity. *e.g. It would be better to bring in someone with BSL skills.*

Britain 1037
Britain consists of England, Scotland and Wales. *e.g. Britain is noted for its poor weather in summer.*

British 1037
1 Someone or something that is **British** belongs to or relates to Britain or its people. *e.g. He always buys British cars.*
2 You can refer to people from Britain in general, or a particular group of people from Britain, as the **British**. *e.g. The British, for some unknown reason, always overcook their vegetables.*
3 The address of the **British** Deaf Association is: 38 Victoria Place, Carlisle CA1 1HU.

British manual alphabet 1174
The **British manual alphabet** is a set of conventional arrangements of handshapes, involving both hands, which form the twenty-six letters used in the English writing system. Using such an alphabet, you can spell out words on your hands. *e.g. We are very attached to the British manual alphabet, even though the fact that it uses two hands makes it an oddity like driving on the left side of the road!*

broke 94
Someone who is **broke** has spent or lost all their money. *e.g. At the end of the month, we are all broke.*

brolly 265
A **brolly** is an umbrella. *e.g. Her old brolly would turn inside out if there was a wind.*

brooch 781, 828
A **brooch** is a small piece of jewellery that has a pin on the back of it. Women wear a brooch as a decoration on a dress or blouse. *e.g. Her earrings matched the brooch.*

broom 104
A **broom** is a brush with a long handle. You use a broom for sweeping the floor. *e.g. The broom is in the cupboard.*

brother 133
1 Your **brother** is a boy or a man who has the same parents as you. *e.g. My brother Billy is younger than me.*
2 You might describe as your **brother** a man who belongs to the same race, religion, profession, or trade union as you, or who has ideas that are similar to yours. *e.g. If we all stand together, brothers, we will be successful.*
3 **Brother** is a title given to a man who is a member of a religious order, but who has not taken holy orders. *e.g. Brother Hugh is a Salesian.*

brown 481, 1146, 1287
Something that is **brown** is the colour of earth or wood. *e.g. I like wearing brown jumpers to go with my brown eyes.*

bruise 1147
1 A **bruise** is an injury, usually produced when a part of the body is hit by something and the skin is not broken but is coloured by a purple or brown mark. *e.g. I'm going to have a huge bruise from that fall.*
2 When a part of your body **bruises** or when you **bruise** it, you damage it, especially by hitting it, without breaking the skin but producing a purple or brown mark on the skin. *e.g. I bruise easily.*

bruise on one's arm 1147
When someone has a **bruise on their arm**, this part of their body is usually hit by something and although the skin is not broken, it is coloured by a purple or brown mark. *e.g. The bruise on her arm is turning yellow now.*

brush one's hair 24
If you **brush your hair**, you tidy it using a hairbrush. *e.g. She brushed her hair before going out to work.*

brush one's teeth 258
If you **brush your teeth** you clean them by rubbing toothpaste or some other substance on them with a toothbrush. *e.g. He brushed his teeth after washing his face.*

Brussels 822
Brussels is the capital of Belgium and the major administrative centre of the European Community. *e.g. The European Community*

Regional Secretariat of the World Federation of the Deaf is based in Brussels.

brutal 366
Someone who is **brutal** is cruel and violent. *e.g. The jailer was brutal to the new prisoner.*

brutality 366
Brutality is violent or cruel behaviour which is intended to hurt or kill people. *e.g. Many subjects of torture never rid their dreams of images of brutality.*

bucket 15
1 A **bucket** is a container which is shaped like a cylinder and which has an open top and a handle. Buckets are often used for holding and carrying water. *e.g. The hotel cleaner entered carrying a bucket and a mop.*
2 **Bucket** is used to refer to the amount of liquid which a bucket contains. *e.g. A bucket of warm water should be enough to mix the cement.*

budgerigar 260
A **budgerigar** is the same as a budgie. *e.g. My sister has a blue budgerigar as a pet.*

budget 1645
1 A **budget** is a plan showing how much money a person or organisation has available and how it should be spent. *e.g. We must agree a weekly budget.*
2 If you **budget**, you plan carefully how much you are going to spend on each thing that you want. *e.g. He could count on a regular salary and thus budget for the future.*

budgie 260
A **budgie** is a brightly-coloured bird, like a small parrot. Budgies are often kept as pets. *e.g. She was not allowed to keep budgies.*

buffet 1526
A **buffet** is a meal of cold food, often at a party or public occasion. Guests usually help themselves to the food and eat it standing up. *e.g. The buffet was attended by Sir Peter Ustinov, the new Chancellor of Durham University.*

bugger 50
Bugger may be used as an offensive swear word in English. It is mainly used to express anger, annoyance or contempt, but is sometimes used in a joking way.
1 People call someone a **bugger** or describe them as a **bugger** when they are angry with them. *e.g. You bugger! You had no right to tell him he could come. It's not your party!*
2 People call someone a **bugger** or describe them as a **bugger** when they are pretending to be rude to them, although they are actually fond of them or friendly with them. *e.g. I told the old bugger it was time he retired and gave some thought to looking after himself rather than other people.*

3 People call someone a **bugger** or describe them as a **bugger** in order to show contempt for them when they have done something foolish. *e.g. The stupid bugger walked straight out in front of the car.*

4 People sign or say that a task or a job is a **bugger** when it is very difficult to do. *e.g. This dictionary is a bugger! It will never be finished.*

5 People sign or say **bugger** or **bugger it** when they are angry because something has gone wrong. *e.g. Bugger! I've got a puncture.*

bugger off　　　　　　　　　　160
1 If you tell someone to **bugger off**, you are telling them in an offensive way to go away. *e.g. If he doesn't leave soon, I'll tell him to bugger off.*

2 If someone **buggers off**, they go away quickly or suddenly. *e.g. I got fed up waiting for the lecturer, so I buggered off.*

build　　　　　　　　　　　1423
If you **build** a structure, you make it by joining things together. *e.g. They planned to build a tower.*

builder　　　　　　　　　　1423
A **builder** is a person whose job is to construct houses and other buildings. *e.g. Her father was a builder and a decorator.*

building　　　　　　　　　　1127
A **building** is a structure that has a roof and walls, for example a house or a factory. *e.g. The building stands next to a site of historic interest.*

building　　　　　　　　　　1423
1 A **building** is a structure that has a roof and walls, for example a house or a factory. *e.g. A small farm building was damaged by fire.*

2 **Building** is the activity or process of constructing buildings. *e.g. Building has been the family's trade for decades.*

3 **Building** a feeling or state of mind is the process of helping it to increase or strengthen. *e.g. We are here building understanding between the two parties.*

build up　　　　　　　　　　1423
1 If an amount of something **builds up** or if you **build** it **up**, it gradually gets bigger as more is added to it. *e.g. Mud builds up in the lake after the severe storms.*

2 If you **build up** someone's trust or confidence you gradually make them more trusting or confident. *e.g. I tried to reassure Javed and build up his confidence after he was so badly let down.*

Bulgaria　　　　　　　　　　1540
Bulgaria is a republic in South East Europe on the Balkan Peninsula. *e.g. Bulgaria is becoming more tourist-orientated.*

Bulgarian　　　　　　　　　　1540
1 Someone or something that is **Bulgarian**

belongs to or relates to Bulgaria or its people. *e.g. The Bulgarian Government has issued the following statement.*

2 **Bulgarian** is the main language spoken in Bulgaria. *e.g. The speech was translated from Bulgarian into French and English.*

3 A **Bulgarian** is a person who comes from Bulgaria or whose family identity relates to Bulgaria. *e.g. The Bulgarian, Victor Panev, was awarded the BDA's Medal of Honour.*

4 The address of the **Bulgarian** Union of the Deaf is: 12-14 Denkooglu St., 1000 Sofia, Bulgaria.

bull　　　　　　　　　　893, 956
A **bull** is a male animal of the cow family. *e.g. The farmer always kept the bull in that field.*

bully　　　　　　　　　　527, 584
A **bully** is someone who uses their strength or power to hurt or frighten other people. *e.g. The camp guard was a bully.*

bum　　　　　　　　　　1106
Your **bum** is the part of your body between your back and your legs, which you sit on. *e.g. The doctor said I would have to have an injection in my bum.*

bump into　　　　　　　　　　69
If you **bump into** something while you are driving a vehicle, you have a minor accident in which you hit something. *e.g. He bumped into the car in front of him.*

bumpy　　　　　　　　　　985
1 Something that is **bumpy** has a rough, uneven surface. *e.g. The lawn looked bumpy.*

2 If a journey in a vehicle is **bumpy**, it is uncomfortable, bouncy and rough, usually because you are travelling over an uneven surface. *e.g. The ride may be a bit bumpy but at least you'll get there.*

bun　　　　　　　　　　1154, 1156
A **bun** is a small cake or bread roll sometimes containing currants or spices. *e.g. Would you like a bun with your tea?*

burden　　　　　　　　　　1653
1 Something that is a **burden** causes you a lot of worry or hard work. *e.g. This would relieve the burden on hospital staff.*

2 A **burden** is also a heavy load that is difficult to carry. *e.g. Men and women came with heavy burdens of provisions.*

burdened　　　　　　　　　　1653
If you are **burdened** with something, it causes you a lot of worry or hard work. *e.g. He was burdened with endless paperwork.*

burial　　　　　　　　　　1443
A **burial** is the ceremony that takes place when an object, usually a dead body, is put into

a grave in the ground. *e.g. The bodies are brought home for burial.*

burn　　　　　　　　　　1060
If something **burns,** it is on fire. *e.g. The bonfire will burn for a long time.*

burn　　　　　　　　　　1258
1 If you **burn** a part of your body or if you **burn** yourself, you are injured by fire or by friction. *e.g. I burnt my hand on my cigar.*

2 You sign or say that something **burns** when it gives you a painful hot feeling. *e.g. Skin usually burns in the sun.*

burst　　　　　　　　124, 1729
When something **bursts** or when you **burst** it, it suddenly breaks open or splits open, especially because there is too much pressure inside it, and the air or other substance inside it comes out. *e.g. The water pipe burst causing a great deal of damage.*

Burwood Park School　　　　　1280
1 **Burwood Park School** is a secondary school for deaf children in Surrey. *e.g. I went to Burwood Park School for nine years.*

2 The address of **Burwood Park School** is: Eriswell Road, Burwood Park, Walton on Thames, Surrey KT12 5DQ.

bury　　　　　　　　　　1443
If you **bury** a person or body, they are put into a grave and covered with earth. *e.g. We will bury her body, along with the other cats, in the garden.*

bus　　　　　　　　　　74, 807
A **bus** is a large motor vehicle which carries passengers from one place to another. A bus is usually driven along a particular route and you have to pay to travel on it. *e.g. The introduction of special lanes for buses in the city centre has greatly reduced journey times.*

bushes　　　　　　　　　　1025
Bushes are large plants which are smaller than trees and have a lot of woody branches. *e.g. The house was surrounded by bushes.*

business　　　　　　　　1345, 1354
1 **Business** is work relating to the production, buying and selling of goods or services. *e.g. He had made a lot of money in business.*

2 A **business** is an organisation which produces and sells goods or which provides a service. *e.g. He set up a small travel business.*

3 The particular **business** that you are in is the area of activity in which you work in order to earn your living. *e.g. What business are you in?*

business　　　　　　　　　　1346
1 **Business** is work relating to the production, buying and selling of goods or services. *e.g. He had made a lot of money in business.*

2 The particular **business** that you are in is the area of activity in which you work in order to earn your living. *e.g. What business are you in?*

bus (single-decker bus)   1687
A **single-decker bus** is a large motor vehicle which has one floor (in contrast to a double-decker bus which has two) and which carries passengers from one place to another. A bus is driven along a particular route and you have to pay to travel on it. *e.g. The bus company has introduced a single-decker bus on the Chester-le-Street to Sherburn service.*

busy   1074, 1354, 1356
1 When you are **busy** you are working hard or concentrating on a task, so that you mind is not free to do anything else. *e.g. Don't interrupt me now—I'm busy working this out.*
2 A **busy** time is a period of time during which you have a lot of things to do. *e.g. I've interviewed 20 people—it's been a busy day.*

but   307
1 You use **but** to introduce a statement which contrasts with what you have just signed or said. *e.g. We'll have a meeting, but not today.*
2 You use **but** when you are about to add something further in a discussion or to change the subject. *e.g. Later I'll be discussing this with the club's management committee. But first, let me remind you of some of the issues.*

but   1382
You use **but** when you are about to add something further in a discussion or to change the subject. *e.g. Dr Peter Unsworth will be giving his opinions on the scheme shortly: but now, I think it's time for some music.*

butcher   257, 530
1 A **butcher** is a shopkeeper who prepares and sells meat. *e.g. All of the Calnans became butchers.*
2 You can refer to a shop where meat is sold as a **butcher** or **butcher's**. *e.g. There's a family butcher at the end of our road.*

butter   689
1 **Butter** is a yellowish fat made from cream which you spread on bread or use in cooking. *e.g. There was a shelf where the butter and cheese were kept.*
2 When you **butter** bread, toast, etc., you spread butter on it. *e.g. She buttered a piece of bread.*

butterflies in one's stomach   1144
If you have **butterflies in your stomach** or **butterflies**, you are very nervous about something. *e.g. I always get butterflies in my stomach before an exam.*

butterfly   1659
A **butterfly** is an insect with large colourful wings and a thin body. There are many kinds of butterfly. *e.g. This large blue butterfly became extinct in 1979.*

buy   1318, 1513
If you **buy** something, you obtain it by paying money for it. *e.g. They went to buy a rug in London.*

bye   991
Bye is a way of signing or saying goodbye. *e.g. Well, bye: I hope we'll meet again.*

bygone   1480
Bygone means happening or existing a very long time ago. *e.g. Empires established in bygone centuries are to be the subject of a television series.*

C, c

C
C is the third letter of the British manual and English alphabets. See page 850.

cabbage   1292
A **cabbage** is a vegetable which looks like a large ball of leaves. There are several different kinds of cabbage, with leaves that are mostly various shades of green or purple. *e.g. Let's buy a cabbage today.*

cabinetmaker   134
A **cabinetmaker** is a person who makes high quality wooden furniture. *e.g. My brother is a cabinetmaker.*

cable   1684
1 A **cable** is a very strong thick rope. *e.g. We will need cables to tie between the pillars.*
2 A **cable** is a bundle of wires inside a rubber or plastic covering along which electricity flows. *e.g. There's ten metres of electrical cable.*

cable T.V.   1684
Cable T.V. or **cable television** is a television system in which signals are sent along wires, rather than by radio waves. *e.g. Cable television is the way forward for minority interest programmes.*

CACDP   254
See **Council for the Advancement of Communication with Deaf People**.

café   850
A **café** is a place where you can buy and sit down to consume drinks and light meals or snacks. *e.g. I'll meet you outside the café at quarter past six; please don't be late.*

cage   657
A **cage** is a structure of wire or metal bars in which birds or animals are usually kept. *e.g. The lion glared at us from his cage.*

cake (small cake)   1154, 1156
A **small cake** is a sweet food made by baking a mixture of flour, eggs, sugar, fat, etc., in an oven, in portions that are each intended for one person only. *e.g. Grandma gave me a small cake, and took one for herself.*

calculate   1054
If you **calculate** something, you work out a number or amount from information that you have, usually by doing some arithmetic. *e.g. We will then calculate the number of votes cast in each section.*

calculate using a calculator   1027
If you **calculate** something **using a calculator**, you use such a device to work out a mathematical problem. *e.g. Let me just calculate the volume of cement we'll need on my calculator.*

calculator   1027
A **calculator** is a small electronic device that you use for working out mathematical problems. *e.g. You may take your calculator with you into the exam.*

calendar   1015, 1547
A **calendar** is a chart which shows a particular year divided into months, weeks, and days, and shows what the date of each day is in that year. *e.g. We need a new calendar for 1992.*

call   674
If you **call** someone or something, or they are **called**, by a particular name, that is their name or title. *e.g. Meet us at the restaurant: I think it's called Monet's—anyway, it's in the middle of Helmesley and you'll love it.*

call by phone/telephone   944
If you **call** someone **by phone** or **telephone**, you dial their number on a telephone in order

to contact them for a conversation. *e.g. I will call you tonight from Inverness, darling.*

call for 303, 350

1 If you **call for** something, you demand or strongly claim that it should happen. *e.g. John called for assistance with the chain.*

2 If you **call for** something, you demand that it should be brought to you. *e.g. He called for his pipe and he called for his bowl and he called for his fiddlers three.*

call for 356

If you **call for** something, you demand or strongly claim that it should happen. *e.g. The chairman called for a vote.*

call off 413

If you **call off** an event that has been planned, you officially stop it from happening. *e.g. We had to decide whether we should call off the class because of the lack of students.*

call out 1711

If you **call** something **out**, you shout it in a loud voice because you want someone to hear you. *e.g. Karen called out and told us to be quiet.*

calm 1272, 1476

Someone who is **calm** does not show much worry or excitement. *e.g. Peter is a calm and reasonable man.*

calm down 1037, 1400

If you tell someone to **calm down**, you are telling them to become less upset, excited, or lively. *e.g. 'Please, Mrs Kinter,' said Brody. 'Calm down. Let me explain.'*

camel 1236

A **camel** is a large animal that typically lives in desert areas and is used for carrying goods and people. Camels have long necks and one or two humps on their backs, depending on the species they belong to. *e.g. She loved the camels in the zoo.*

camera 659

A **camera** is a piece of equipment that is used for taking photographs. *e.g. Make sure we take our camera on holiday.*

cameraman 470

A **cameraman** is a man who operates a camera for television or film making. *e.g. He wanted to work as a cameraman.*

camera person 470

A **camera person** is a person who operates a camera for television or film making. *e.g. I don't care who the camera person is, I just want to finish this shot!*

camp 693

1 A **camp** is a place where people live in tents

or stay in tents on holiday. *e.g. The camp had a beautiful view of the mountains.*

2 If you **camp** somewhere, you stay or live there for a short time in a tent or a caravan. *e.g. I camped in the hills.*

can 335, 477, 572

1 If you **can** do something, it is possible for you to do it. *e.g. Anyone can become a teacher, she claims.*

2 If you **can** do something, you have the skill or ability to do it. *e.g. Some people can juggle extremely well.*

3 If you **can** do something, you are allowed to do it. *e.g. My parents said I can go to Switzerland.*

4 You ask someone if they **can** do something as a way of asking them to do it. *e.g. Can you fax that to me next week?*

can 1124

If you **can** sense or feel something, you are experiencing it. *e.g. 'Tell me if you hear anything. Yes or no?'—'Yes, I can.'*

can 1681, 1683

A **can** is a metal container in which something such as food, drink, paint etc., is put. The container is usually sealed so that the contents remain fresh for a long time. *e.g. He bought a can of beans for his supper.*

Canada 37

Canada is a country in North America; it is the second largest country in the world. *e.g. Mary has many relatives in Canada.*

Canadian 37

1 Someone or something that is **Canadian** belongs to or relates to Canada or its people. *e.g. Margaret has a Canadian passport.*

2 A **Canadian** is a person who comes from Canada. *e.g. The Canadian Gary Malkowski is the first Deaf Member of Ontario's Provincial Parliament.*

3 The address of the **Canadian** Association of the Deaf is: Suit 311, 271 Spachina Road, Toronto, Ontario, M5R 2VR, Canada.

canal 703

A **canal** is a long, narrow stretch of water that has been made for boats to travel along or bring water to a particular area. *e.g. The canals of Venice are beautiful.*

cancel 413, 629

1 If you **cancel** something such as a hotel room or a seat at the theatre, you tell the management that you no longer want it. *e.g. If you cancel the booking now, there will be a charge.*

2 If you **cancel** an event that has been arranged, you officially stop it from happening. *e.g. We may have to cancel the performance if this weather doesn't change.*

cancellation 413

1 The **cancellation** of something such as a hotel room or a seat at the theatre is the action of telling the management that you no longer want it. *e.g. That cancellation means we have an empty restaurant tonight.*

2 The **cancellation** of an event that has been arranged is the action of officially stopping it from happening. *e.g. It will be a huge disappointment to the boys if the cancellation of the match is approved by Mr. Barcroft.*

candle 484

A **candle** is a stick or block of hard wax with a piece of string through the middle which you light in order to give a flame that provides light. *e.g. I carried the candle into the kitchen.*

cane 269

1 A **cane** is a long, thin, flexible stick used to hit people as a punishment. *e.g. The teacher's cane was kept in the cupboard.*

2 At school, if a child is given the **cane**, he or she is punished by being hit with a cane. *e.g. I got the cane for smoking.*

3 If you **cane** someone, you hit them with a cane as a punishment. *e.g. When I was at school, you got caned if you were caught signing.*

cannot 421

1 If you **cannot** or **can't** do something, you are not able to do it. *e.g. I can't come to your party next week.*

2 If you sign or say that something **cannot** or **can't** happen, you mean that it is not possible to do. *e.g. A tidal wave cannot be halted.*

3 If you indicate that someone **cannot** or **can't** do something, you mean they should not do it. *e.g. We can't stop here in the dark.*

4 If you sign or say that something **cannot** or **can't** be true or **cannot** or **can't** happen, you mean that you find it hard to believe it is true or that it will happen. *e.g. This cannot be the whole story.*

cannot bear 1007

If you **cannot bear** or **can't bear** something or someone, you dislike them very much. *e.g. I cannot bear the principal of the college.*

cannot be bothered 230, 361, 1132

If you sign or say you **cannot be bothered** or **can't be bothered**, you are emphasising that you are not going to do something because you think that it is unnecessary or that it involves too much effort. *e.g. I can't be bothered to cook for myself.*

cannot believe 315

If you sign or say that you **cannot believe** or **can't believe** something, you mean that you find it difficult to accept or are very surprised to learn that it is true. *e.g. I just cannot believe a pregnant woman would eat charcoal.*

cannot believe one's eyes   831
If you sign or say that you **cannot believe your eyes** or **can't believe your eyes**, you mean that you are very surprised by something you see. *e.g. Peter cannot believe his eyes whenever he sees Jimmy dancing.*

cannot face it   1132
If you sign or say of something that you **cannot face it** or **can't face it**, you mean that you do not feel able to do it or cope with it because it seems so unpleasant. *e.g. I can't face it: he wants us to start all over again!*

cannot stand   1007
If you **cannot stand** or **can't stand** someone or something, you cannot tolerate them or dislike them very strongly. *e.g. I can't stand spiders.*

canoe   90
A **canoe** is a small, narrow, light boat, often pointed at each end which you row using a paddle. *e.g. We will travel up river by canoe.*

canoeing   90
Canoeing is the sport of racing and performing tests of skill in canoes. *e.g. The centre has facilities for rock climbing, sailing and canoeing.*

can't   421
Can't is the usual spoken form of cannot. It appears in writing usually as an informal usage or abbreviation. See **cannot**.

can't bear   1007
See **cannot bear**.

can't be bothered   230, 361, 1132
See **cannot be bothered**.

can't believe   315
See **cannot believe**.

can't believe one's eyes   831
See **cannot believe one's eyes**.

can't face it   1132
See **cannot face it**.

can't stand   1007
See **cannot stand**.

can with a ring-pull   592
A **can with a ring-pull** is a metal container, used especially for soft drinks or beer, which is opened by pulling a circular tab on the top surface. *e.g. Get the cola in cans with a ring-pull, not bottles, because they've got that free offer.*

cap   254
A **cap** is a soft, flat hat which is usually worn by men or boys. *e.g. John couldn't find his school cap.*

capable   335, 477, 572
If a person or thing is **capable** of doing something, they have the quality or ability to do it. *e.g. Was Oswald a man capable of killing the President?*

capitalism   185
Capitalism is an economic and political system in which property, business and industry are owned, or predominantly owned, by private individuals or organisations and not by the state, and in which companies are run in competition with each other in order to make a profit. *e.g. Most of the world's economies are now organised on the basis of capitalism.*

capitalist   185
1 A **capitalist** country or society is one in which the economic and political system is organised or works according to the principles of capitalism. *e.g. The United States is a capitalist society.*
2 A **capitalist** is someone who believes in, and organises their business according to, the principles of capitalism. *e.g. Most of Britain's leading capitalists are members of the Confederation of British Industry.*

capsule   476
A **capsule** is a very small container with powdered medicine in it which you swallow. *e.g. Take two of these capsules to kill the pain.*

captain   617
If you are the **captain** of a group or team of people, you are their leader. *e.g. He was captain of the school cricket team.*

captive   47
1 A **captive** is a prisoner, especially one who is captured in a war. *e.g. The soldiers marched on, driving thousands of captives before them.*
2 A person or animal that is **captive** is being kept imprisoned or enclosed. *e.g. He wrote about the dreadful conditions endured by captive animals.*
3 If you take someone **captive**, or hold them **captive**, you take them or keep them as a prisoner. *e.g. Nine soldiers were taken captive.*

capture   1171
1 If you **capture** someone, you take them prisoner, especially in a war or after a struggle. *e.g. If we can capture them, we will be rewarded.*
2 When military forces **capture** a town or a country, they take control of it by force. *e.g. We aim to capture the capital by winter.*
3 If a person or a place is captured, a **capture** takes place. *e.g. He hadn't eaten anything since the night before his capture.*

car   100
A **car** is a road vehicle that usually has four wheels and is powered by an engine. Cars need

a driver and also have room for a passenger or passengers. *e.g. The first new car came off the production line exactly on schedule.*

caravan   597
A **caravan** is a vehicle without an engine with beds and other equipment inside, which can be towed from place to place and in which people live or spend their holidays. *e.g. The community adviser gave us a caravan to live in.*

card   607, 658
1 A **card** is a piece of stiff paper or thin cardboard that has information written on it. *e.g. The timetable is printed on a card: this is available from reception.*
2 A **card** is a piece of cardboard, paper or plastic with information on it that shows your identity or proves that you have the right to do or have a particular thing. *e.g. The membership secretary asked for his card.*

cardboard   1523
Cardboard is very thick, stiff paper that is used to make boxes and other objects. *e.g. We took old newspaper and cardboard to be recycled.*

Cardiff   1680
1 **Cardiff** is the capital of Wales, situated in the south east of the country. It is the administrative centre for South Glamorgan and is an important port. *e.g. We went to Cardiff last week to see Wales play the All Blacks.*
2 The address of the **Cardiff** Centre for Deaf People is: 163 Newport Road, Cardiff.

cardigan   1650
A **cardigan** is a knitted woollen sweater that you fasten at the front with buttons or a zip. *e.g. She bought a new navy cardigan.*

card player   1099
A **card player** is a person who plays games with playing cards. *e.g. There were four card players seated round the table, plus two observers.*

care   333
If you **care** for someone or something, you look after them and keep them in a good state or condition. *e.g. You must learn how to care for your pet.*

care   452
1 If you do something with **care**, you do it with great attention because you do not want to make any mistakes or cause any damage. *e.g. This is glass—handle with care.*
2 If you take **care** to do something, you make sure that you do it. *e.g. Take care not to spill the mixture.*

career   1345
A **career** is the type of job or profession that someone does for a long period of their life.

e.g. She talked with a counsellor about her choice of career.

careful   452
1 If you instruct someone to be **careful**, you are warning them of a danger or a problem. *e.g. Be careful or you'll fall.*
2 If you are **careful**, you do something with a lot of attention and thought. *e.g. He had to be careful about what he signed.*
3 If you are **careful**, you do something thoroughly and make sure that all the details are correct. *e.g. He made careful preparations, knowing that there would be no second chances.*

careful (be careful)   575
If you tell someone to be **careful**, you are warning them not to be careless or to take any risks. *e.g. Peter's mother told him to be careful when he goes on the road*

careless   1077, 1248
If you are **careless**, you do not pay enough attention to what you are doing and so you make mistakes or produce unsatisfactory results. *e.g. He was careless while cooking and made a mess.*

care (take care)   452
If you **take care** to do something, you do your best to make absolutely certain that you do it or that it happens. *e.g. He was very discreet and took care never to offend visitors.*

care (with care)   452
If you do something **with care**, you do it with great attention because you do not want to make any mistakes or cause any damage. *e.g. Uncle Harry tended the plants with care: but nothing in the world could match the care he showed for Auntie Winnie.*

Carlisle   761
1 **Carlisle** is a city in North West England, the administrative centre of Cumbria. *e.g. The British Deaf Association's Head Office is in Carlisle.*
2 The address of the Cumbria Deaf Association in **Carlisle** is: 3 Compton Street, Carlisle, CA1 1HT.

carol   758
Carols are Christian religious songs that are signed or sung especially at Christmas. *e.g. After the carols, presents were distributed.*

carol singer   758
A **carol singer** is someone who makes musical sounds with their voice, putting together the words and music to produce Christian religious songs sung especially at Christmas. *e.g. A lone carol singer stood at the door, but I couldn't hear him.*

car park   101, 1392
A **car park** or **car-park** is an open area of

ground or a building with several storeys where people can leave their cars, usually if they pay a small amount of money. *e.g. We found the entrance to the car park.*

carpenter   134
A **carpenter** is a person whose job is making and repairing wooden structures. *e.g. I worked as a carpenter in a boat repair yard for many years.*

carpentry   134
Carpentry is the skill and work of a carpenter. *e.g. I enjoyed carpentry at school.*

carpet   1415
1 A **carpet** is a thick, heavy covering, usually made from a material like wool, which is put on floors and stairs so that they are comfortable to walk on. *e.g. There were matching curtains and fitted carpets.*
2 If you **carpet** a room or other area of a building, you lay a carpet on the floor. *e.g. We hadn't got the money to carpet the whole house.*
3 A **carpet** of things is a quantity of them which are so close together that they form a layer which completely covers the ground or some other surface. *e.g. In the wood there was a carpet of bluebells.*

car port   1363
A **car port** is a shelter for vehicles which is attached to a house and consists of a flat roof usually supported on pillars. *e.g. I left the van in the car port.*

carriage   1687
A **carriage** is one of the separate sections of a train that carries passengers. *e.g. All the carriages on the train were full so we had to stand.*

carry   1626
If you **carry** something, you take it with you, holding it so that it does not touch the ground. *e.g. Now you carry the bundle and put it on the bed.*

carry a bag/briefcase/bucket/case/pail/ suitcase   15
If you carry a **bag**, **briefcase**, **bucket**, **case**, **pail** or **suitcase**, you take it with you, holding it by the handle so that it does not touch the ground. *e.g. She carried the bag outside.*

carry a basket   1629
If you **carry a basket** you take it with you, holding it by the handle so it does not touch the ground. *e.g. She carried the basket of shopping home.*

carry a briefcase/handbag   247
If you **carry a briefcase** or a **handbag**, you take it with you, holding it by the handle. *e.g. She carried her briefcase and some papers to the car.*

carry on   652
If you **carry on** doing something, you continue to do it. *e.g. The lecturer was prepared to carry on with his paper despite the interruption.*

carry something over one's shoulder   145
When you **carry something over your shoulder**, you place it on your back and hold one end or part of it with your hands over your shoulder, so that it does not touch the ground and you can take it with you as you go somewhere. *e.g. He carried the sack of potatoes over his shoulders.*

cart   117
A **cart** is a small, wooden vehicle with two or four wheels that is pushed along by hand and used for transporting goods. *e.g. They put the blocks of wood in the cart.*

carton   1458
A **carton** is a large, strong cardboard box in which goods are packed for storage and transport. *e.g. His job was stacking cartons in the warehouse.*

case   15
A **case** is a suitcase. *e.g. Do you have a case? May I help you with it?*

case (in case)   359
You sign or say **in case** or **just in case** to indicate that you have something or are doing something because a particular thing might happen or has happened. *e.g. Do you want me to take my book just in case?*

cash   1318
1 **Cash** is money in the form of notes and coins rather than cheques, credit cards, et cetera. *e.g. He paid the whole amount in cash.*
2 If you **cash** a cheque, you exchange it at a bank for the amount of money that it is worth. *e.g. I must cash a cheque, I need some change.*

cash   1502, 1507, 1508, 1679
Cash is money in the form of notes and coins rather than cheques, credit cards, et cetera. *e.g. We've run out of cash.*

cast a spell   1042
If you **cast a spell** over someone or something, you control this person or object by magical powers. *e.g. The wizard cast a spell on the dog and turned it into a mouse.*

castle   737
A **castle** is a large building or group of buildings with high walls. Most castles were built by royalty or other powerful people in former times for protection and as status symbols. *e.g. We saw Windsor Castle last year.*

cat   899, 1290
A **cat** is a small, furry animal with a tail, whiskers, and sharp claws, which is often kept as a pet. *e.g. Frances' cat was lying on the sofa.*

catalogue   1456
A **catalogue** is a book containing a list of goods that you can buy in a shop or through the post, together with prices and illustrations. *e.g. I got a catalogue from Next.*

catch   1153
1 **Catch** is a game in which two or more people catch a ball which they throw to each other. *e.g. Let's play catch with this old tennis ball.*
2 If you **catch** a small object which is moving through the air, you seize it with your hands. *e.g. The fielder tried to catch the ball from the batsman's firm stroke.*

catch   1171
1 If you **catch** a person, you capture them after pursuing them. *e.g. The police didn't catch the car thieves.*
2 If you **catch** someone doing something wrong or doing something secretly, you notice them when they are doing it. *e.g. If I catch you smoking, you're sacked.*
3 If you **catch** an object which is moving through the air, you seize it by putting both hands around it or part of it. *e.g. Tom tossed his stick in the air and Colin tried to catch it.*

catch someone off guard   1092
If someone or something **catches someone off guard**, they surprise them by doing something or by happening when they are not expecting it. *e.g. If you ask him when other people are here, you may catch him off guard.*

catch someone on the hop   1092
If someone or something **catches someone on the hop**, they surprise the person by doing something or by happening when they are not expecting it. *e.g. He tried to catch the President's representative on the hop by slipping in a question about fiscal policy.*

category   1690
A **category** is a set of people, actions, objects, etc., which all have a particular characteristic or quality in common. *e.g. There are several handshapes that fit into the category of 'classifiers'.*

caterpillar   587
A **caterpillar** is a small, worm-like animal that feeds on plants and develops into a butterfly or moth. *e.g. I found two more caterpillars on the Virginia Creeper today.*

caterpillar crawling up a thin object   587
A **caterpillar crawling up a thin object** is a small, worm-like animal (caterpillar), which feeds on plants and develops into a butterfly or moth, moving away from the ground along something small and narrow by flexing its body in an upward, wave-like motion. *e.g. A caterpillar crawling up a thin object may seem as if it is liable to fall over backwards at any moment: but, in fact, caterpillars have very good grip.*

cathedral   106
A **cathedral** is a very large and important church which has a bishop in charge of it. The area which a bishop administers has one cathedral and many smaller churches. *e.g. Durham Cathedral stands on a hill in the heart of the city.*

Catholic   171
Catholic is short for Roman Catholic. See **Roman Catholic**.

cat's whiskers   899
A **cat's whiskers** are the long, stiff hairs that grow near its mouth. *e.g. The cat's whiskers began to twitch.*

cattle   956
Cattle are cows and bulls that are kept for farming or for carrying loads. *e.g. Cattle were sold for next to nothing.*

cease   1552
1 If something **ceases**, it stops happening or existing. *e.g. The hostilities in the Lebanon must cease soon.*
2 If you **cease** to do something, you stop doing it. *e.g. He knew he should cease speaking in time for the Prime Minister's arrival.*
3 If you **cease** something that you are producing or providing, you stop producing or providing it. *e.g. We are to cease financial support to the University.*

ceiling   152
A **ceiling** is an upper limit on things such as wages that is decided by the government or another organisation, and above which they are not supposed to increase. *e.g. The Minister has imposed a ceiling on price increases.*

ceiling   1567
A **ceiling** is the surface that forms the top part or roof inside a room. *e.g. She likes being in a room with a high ceiling.*

celebrate   954
1 If you **celebrate** or **celebrate** something, you do something enjoyable such as having a party in order to show that an event or occasion is special or to honour someone's success or victory. *e.g. Let's celebrate: it's not every day you finish something as important as this.*
2 If an organisation or country **celebrates**

an anniversary, it has existed for a certain length of time and is doing something special because of it. *e.g. The BDA celebrated its centenary in 1990.*

celebration   954
A **celebration** is a special event that people organise to enjoy themselves because something pleasant has happened, or because it is someone's birthday or anniversary. *e.g. They organised a celebration to welcome the cup winners home.*

cellar   1341
A **cellar** is a room in the ground underneath a building, often used for storing things in. *e.g. We keep our freezer in the cellar.*

cement   252
1 **Cement** is a grey powder of limestone and clay which is mixed with sand and water in order to make concrete. *e.g. You will need a sack of cement.*
2 If you **cement** or **cement over** an area, you cover it with cement. *e.g. Please cement over that broken patch.*

censor   413, 629
If you **censor** a performance, broadcast or publication, you officially examine it and cut out or ban any parts of it that are considered to be immoral, usually according to the instructions of the government. *e.g. I'm afraid we'll have to censor this bad language unless you want it to be shown after midnight.*

central   967
1 Something that is **central** is in the middle of a place or area. *e.g. We saw a film about central Poland.*
2 A place that is **central** is easy to reach because it is in the centre of a city. *e.g. The Club is convenient and central.*
3 A **central** group or organisation makes all the important decisions that are followed throughout a larger organisation or country. *e.g. We rely on support from central government.*
4 The **central** person or thing in a particular situation is the most important one. *e.g. This is really the central point in the debate about future policy.*

centre   967
1 The **centre** of something is the middle of it. *e.g. The club was in the centre of town.*
2 A **centre** is a building where people have meetings, get help of some kind or take part in a particular activity. *e.g. Treatment is available from the new health centre.*

centuries (over the centuries)   1479
When something has existed or happened **over the centuries**, it has existed or happened for a time amounting to several

hundred years. *e.g. British woodlands that have flourished over the centuries are now being destroyed.*

cereal 240,732
Cereal is a food made from grain, usually mixed with milk and eaten for breakfast. *e.g. Carys bought a packet of cereal at the corner shop.*

certificate 562
1 A **certificate** is an official document stating that particular facts are true. *e.g. A medical certificate is required if you are away for more than three days.*
2 A **certificate** is an official document that you receive when you have successfully completed a course of study or training. *e.g. Professor Ebsworth, the Vice-Chancellor, congratulated her on her success and presented her with her BSL Tutor Training Certificate.*

chair 86,97,114
1 A **chair** is a piece of furniture for one person to sit on with a back and four legs. *e.g. I bought a chair at the auction.*
2 If you **chair** a meeting or debate you are the person who is in charge and you decide when each person may contribute to the proceedings. *e.g. The meeting was chaired by Professor Brown.*
3 If you are the **chair** of a meeting, committee or organisation you are in charge and responsible for directing the work of the meeting, committee or organisation. *e.g. Councillor Morrissey should be the next chair of the Council's Education Committee.*

chair 734
A **chair** is a piece of furniture for one person to sit on, with a seat raised above the ground and a support for the back. *e.g. I bought a chair at the auction.*

chairman 86,97,114
1 The **chairman** of a meeting or debate is the person who is in charge and who decides when each person may contribute to the proceedings. Some people object to the use of this English word to refer to a woman. *e.g. The chairman invited members of the audience to put questions to the panel.*
2 If you are the **chairman** of a committee or organisation, you are in charge and responsible for directing the work of the committee or organisaton. Some people object to the use of this English word to refer to a woman. *e.g. Mr. Young was the first Deaf Chairman of the British Deaf Association.*

chairperson 86,97,114
1 The **chairperson** of a meeting or debate is the person who is in charge and who decides when each person may contribute to the proceedings. *e.g. The chairperson called the*

meeting to order.
2 If you are the **chairperson** of a meeting, committee or organisation you are in charge and responsible for directing the work of the meeting, committee or organisation. *e.g. She is the chairperson of the school's governing body.*

chairwoman 86,97,114
1 The **chairwoman** of a meeting or debate is the woman who is in charge and who decides when each person may contribute to the proceedings. *e.g. The chairwoman asked if there were any objections to the proposal.*
2 The **chairwoman** of a meeting, committee or organisation is the woman who is in charge and who is responsible for directing the work of the meeting, committee or organisation. *e.g. She was invited to be the chairwoman of the commission of enquiry.*

chalk 615
1 **Chalk** is a soft, white rock which is made into sticks and used for writing or drawing with. *e.g. He took a piece of chalk from his pocket.*
2 A **chalk** is a small piece of soft, white rock used for writing or drawing with. *e.g. There are coloured chalks in my desk.*
3 If you **chalk** something, you draw or write it using a piece of chalk. *e.g. A young man was chalking on the blackboard.*

chance 630
1 A **chance** is the extent to which something is possible or likely to happen. *e.g. He has a good chance of getting the job.*
2 A **chance** to do something is an opportunity to do it. *e.g. The extra holiday gave us a chance to paint the house.*

change 276
1 When something **changes** or when you **change** it, it becomes different. *e.g. Her disdain changed to respect.*
2 To **change** something also means to replace it with someone new or different. *e.g. I changed my job.*
3 If there is a **change** of something, it is replaced. *e.g. A change of Government is long overdue.*
4 When you **change** your clothes, you take them off and put on different ones. *e.g. She changed her clothes.*
5 If there is a **change** in something, it becomes different. *e.g. I've noticed a change in her attitude lately.*
6 If you sign or say that something is happening for a **change**, you mean that it is different from what usually happens. *e.g. It's nice to go for a walk for a change.*

change 432
1 When something **changes** or when you **change** it, it becomes different. *e.g. Her disdain changed to respect.*

2 To **change** something also means to replace it with someone new or different. *e.g. I changed my job.*
3 If there is a **change** of something, it is replaced. *e.g. A change of Government is long overdue.*
4 When you **change** your clothes, you take them off and put on different ones. *e.g. She changed her clothes.*

changeable 955
Someone or something that is **changeable** is likely to change many times. *e.g. The weather is very changeable.*

change over 446
If you **change over** from one thing to another, you stop being or doing one thing and start being or doing the other. *e.g. He used to be a Liberal then changed over to being a Tory.*

changeover 446
A **changeover** is an alteration or shift from one activity, arrangement or system to another. *e.g. The changeover of computers took place during the holidays.*

change roles 254
If you **change roles**, you set aside the perspective you take in one position that you hold in order to give consideration or make a contribution to a particular issue on the basis of your knowledge, interests or experience which you have obtained as a consequence of, or in relation to, another position that you hold. *e.g. Maybe I could change roles for a moment and give my views as a Deaf consumer rather than a trainer of interpreters.*

chapel 106,1440
1 A **chapel** is part of a church which has its own altar and which is used for private prayer. *e.g. We went to the Chapel together.*
2 A **chapel** is a small church attached to a school, hospital, or prison. *e.g. Our school chapel was built by the teachers and pupils themselves.*
3 A **chapel** is a building used for worship by members of some Protestant churches. *e.g. A Methodist chapel holds services on Sunday evenings.*

character 63
1 When you refer to the English **character**, the Irish **character**, etc., you are referring to the qualities that people from a particular country or race are believed to have. *e.g. English people are considered to be very reserved in character.*
2 Your **character** is all the qualities you have that combine to form your personality, especially in relation to how honest and reliable you are. *e.g. He was asked to write a character reference for Mr. McDonald.*

character 605, 644
Your **character** is all the qualities you have that combine to form your personality, especially in relation to how honest and reliable you are. *e.g. I think you will find his character very suitable for the post.*

characteristic 63
1 A **characteristic** is a quality that is typical of a particular person, place or thing, and that makes them easy to recognise. *e.g. Ambition is a family characteristic of the Smiths.*
2 Something that is **characteristic** of something or someone is typical of that person or thing and makes them easy to recognise. *e.g. Each whale has its own characteristic song.*

charge 274
When you **charge** a battery or **charge** it **up**, you pass an electric current through it in order to make it more powerful or last longer. *e.g. Your car battery is flat—it needs to be charged.*

charge 303, 398
1 If you **charge** someone an amount of money, you ask them to pay that amount for something that they have bought or received. *e.g. The bank charges me 25% interest on the loan.*
2 A **charge** is the price that you have to pay for a service or for something you buy. *e.g. A small charge is made for repairs.*

charge (in charge) 450
If you are **in charge** of something or someone, you have responsibility for them or control over them. *e.g. Lorna is in charge of the project.*

charming 1488
You can sign or say **charming** to indicate that you do not like something or feel disappointed or insulted by something. *e.g. She promised to help today and now she's just rung to say she can't. Charming!*

chart 562
A **chart** is a diagram, illustration, or table which shows information in a visual form. *e.g. Look at the chart to see which benefits you can get if you are unemployed.*

chase 430, 595
1 If you **chase** a person or an animal, you run after them or follow them quickly, usually in order to catch them. *e.g. I tried to chase him.*
2 A **chase** is the activity of running after or following another person or animal, usually in order to catch them. *e.g. She always enjoyed the thrill of the chase.*

chase 442
1 If you **chase** someone, you run after them or follow them quickly, usually in order to

catch them. *e.g. Through the dirty backstreets of Bilbao Fiona chased the thief.*
2 A **chase** is the activity of running after or following someone, usually in order to catch them. *e.g. The chase was exhausting and I had to lie down and rest.*

chat 380
When people **chat** they sign or talk in an informal, friendly way. *e.g. We sat by the fire and chatted all evening.*

chatter 1529
If you **chatter**, you sign or talk quickly and continuously, usually about things which are not important. *e.g. Bill used to chatter about birds and wildflowers.*

chatterbox 603, 1529
A **chatterbox** is a person who talks a great deal, usually about things which are not important. *e.g. Lorna's such a chatterbox, always on about something trivial.*

chauffeur 320
The **chauffeur** of a rich or important person is someone who is employed to look after their car and drive them around in it. *e.g. The chauffeur drives her to work every morning.*

cheap 617
When goods or services are **cheap**, they cost less money than usual or expected. *e.g. I bought my hat from Oxfam; it was really cheap.*

cheat 172
1 When someone **cheats**, they lie or behave dishonestly in order to get what they want. *e.g. He used to cheat in school exams.*
2 If someone **cheats** you of something or **cheats** you out of it, they get it from you by behaving dishonestly or unfairly. *e.g. She cheated her sister out of some money.*
3 A **cheat** is something dishonest or unfair that someone does in order to make people believe that something is true when it is not. *e.g. We will film in England, so it will be a bit of a cheat because it will appear to be Iceland.*
4 A **cheat** is a person who lies or behaves dishonestly in order to get what they want. *e.g. You're a cheat! You're paying me less than you really owe me.*

check 962
1 If you **check** something, you make sure that it is satisfactory, safe or correct. *e.g. He checked that the doors were shut.*
2 A **check** is a process of informal inspection in which you check something. *e.g. Can we have a last check before we call it a day?*

check a document 769, 961
If you **check a document** such as a report or letter, you read through it briefly to make

sure that there are no errors or problems. *e.g. Jane asked me to check her essay and correct any spelling mistakes.*

cheek 257
1 A person who has **cheek** is not afraid or embarrased to do, sign or say things that shock or annoy people. *e.g. I never thought he'd have the cheek to ask to borrow my car again after crashing it last time.*
2 **Cheek** is also signs, words or behaviour that show a lack of respect, for example towards a parent or teacher. *e.g. I've had enough of your cheek—get out of my class!*

cheeky 257
Someone who is **cheeky** is rude or disrespectful. *e.g. That cheeky nephew of yours told me I was a witch!*

cheer 255
When you **cheer**, you show your approval of something or encourage someone who is taking part in a game. *e.g. She cheered on her favourite team.*

cheerio 991
Cheerio is a way of signing or saying goodbye. *e.g. He signed a quick cheerio and left on his own.*

cheer up 1029
When you tell someone to **cheer up**, you are encouraging them to stop feeling depressed and be more happy. *e.g. Come on, cheer up, you'll win next time.*

cheese 1598
1 **Cheese** is a food made from milk. It is usually white or yellow in colour. There are many different kinds of cheese, for example ones that are soft and usually have a mild taste, and ones that are hard and usually have a strong taste. *e.g. You can't live on bread and cheese.*
2 A **cheese** is a solid block of cheese before it has been cut up for selling or eating. *e.g. A big Stilton cheese is what I'd really like for Christmas.*

chef 706
A **chef** is a cook in a restaurant or hotel, especially the head cook. *e.g. He was a chef at the Savoy Hotel.*

chef's hat 706
A **chef's hat** is the tall, white covering made of cotton or a similar fabric that is traditionally worn on his or her head by the cook in a restaurant or hotel. *e.g. She looked really impressive in her chef's hat.*

chemist 912
1 A **chemist** or a **chemist's** is a shop where you can buy medicine, cosmetics and some household goods. *e.g. You need a chemist for vitamins, not a health food shop.*

2 A **chemist** is someone who is qualified to sell medicines prescribed by a doctor. *e.g. She studied for four years to become a chemist.*

chemist   1686
A **chemist** is a person who studies chemistry or who does chemical research or work. *e.g. He is a research chemist at the Ministry of Health.*

chemistry   1686
Chemistry is the scientific study of the characteristics and composition of substances and of the way that they react with other substances. *e.g. She did a degree in chemistry at York University.*

cheque   655,953
A **cheque** is a printed piece of paper that you can use instead of money. You write on it the name of the person you are paying and the amount of money that you are paying them, and then you sign it. *e.g. Her uncle sent a cheque for her birthday.*

chequebook   655,953
A **chequebook** is a book of printed pieces of paper that you can use instead of money (with your bank's name, your name and spaces for details of the payment printed on them) which you are given by your bank to use to pay for things. *e.g. He went to the bank for a new chequebook.*

cherry   790
A **cherry** is a small, round fruit with red or black skin and a small stone at the centre. *e.g. She brought a bowl of cherries.*

chess   826
Chess is a game for two people played on a chess board. Each player has sixteen pieces including a king. The aim is to move your pieces so that your opponent's king cannot escape being taken. *e.g. The World Deaf Chess Individual Championship took place in Edinburgh this year.*

chess player   826
A **chess player** is someone who takes part in a game of chess. *e.g. He's a pretty useful chess player, actually.*

chew   46
1 When you **chew** food you bite it several times with your teeth while it is inside your mouth, so that it becomes softer and easier to swallow. *e.g. He had started to chew a piece of meat.*
2 To **chew** a hole in something means to make the hole by biting it several times with your teeth. *e.g. The dogs must have chewed right through it.*

chew up   46
If you **chew** food **up**, you chew it until it is

completely crushed or softened. *e.g. She put it into her mouth and chewed it up happily.*

chicken   479
1 A **chicken** is a bird which is kept on a farm for its eggs and its meat. Chickens are usually brown, black, white or a mixture of these colours. *e.g. She loved to chase the chickens.*
2 **Chicken** is the meat of a chicken. *e.g. She's a vegetarian who also eats chicken when no-one's looking.*

chicken pox   1177
Chicken pox is a disease caught especially by children in which they have a high temperature and red spots that itch. *e.g. She got chicken pox just before her exam.*

chief   450
The **chief** of an organisation is the person who has responsibility for it or controls it. *e.g. The chief of the company is on his way to Portugal.*

child   1211
A **child** is a young person from the age when he or she is able to stand. *e.g. She has a child of seven.*

children   1216
1 **Children** are sons and daughters. *e.g. I was baby-sitting for my neighbour's children.*
2 You use **children** to refer to a group of boys and girls. *e.g. Children from several schools came to the festival.*

chill   118
1 **Chill** is used to describe the weather when it is cold and unpleasant. *e.g. It was a chill autumn day when I left London.*
2 A **chill** is a unpleasant coldness in the weather or the temperature. *e.g. She turned on the fire to take the chill from the air.*

chilly   118
1 Something that is **chilly** is rather cold and unpleasant or colder than is normal or acceptable. *e.g. It is a bit chilly in the classroom until the heating comes on.*
2 If you feel **chilly**, you do not feel quite warm enough to be comfortable. *e.g. Light the fire if you feel chilly.*

chimney   1719
A **chimney** is a pipe which goes up from a fireplace or factory furnace to above the level of the roof, so that smoke escapes into the air and not into the building. *e.g. Factory chimneys and church spires were silhouetted against the evening sky.*

chimpanzee   1651
A **chimpanzee** or **chimp** is a kind of small African ape. *e.g. She liked the little chimpanzee best in the whole zoo.*

China   451,454
China is a republic in Eastern Asia, the third largest and the most populous country in the world. Some people find these signs offensive. *e.g. China has a fascinating history.*

Chinese   451,454
1 Someone or something that is **Chinese** belongs to or relates to China or its people. Some people find these signs offensive. *e.g. He brought back an expensive Chinese vase.*
2 **Chinese** is the main language spoken in China. Some people find these signs offensive. *e.g. James is studying Chinese as part of his Doctorate.*
3 A **Chinese** is a person who comes from China or whose family identity relates to China. Some people find these signs offensive. *e.g. A young Chinese lent me his bicycle.*
4 The address of the **Chinese** Association of the Deaf is: 44 Biechizi St., Dongcheng District, Beijing, P.R., China 100006.

chips   870
Chips are long thin pieces of potato (or a potato substitute) fried in oil or fat. *e.g. He went to buy a bag of chips.*

chocolate   583
1 **Chocolate** is a sweet, hard, brown food made from cocoa beans, which is eaten as a sweet. *e.g. A bar of chocolate is all I want for Christmas.*
2 **Chocolate** is a hot drink made from a powder containing cocoa. *e.g. Let's have a mug of chocolate before we go to bed.*
3 A **chocolate** is a sweet or nut covered with a layer of chocolate. *e.g. I wanted to say thank you, so I bought a box of chocolates.*

choice   487
1 If there is a **choice** of things or people, there are several of them and you can select the ones that you want. *e.g. There's a choice of eleven sports.*
2 Your **choice** is the people or things that you select from a range of items. *e.g. He congratulated the chef on his choice of dishes.*
3 A **choice** is a decision in which you select some things or people and reject others. *e.g. I'm glad it's not up to me to make the choice.*

choose   487
If you **choose** from several things that are available, you select some of them. *e.g. They went to choose new t-shirts.*

chop   1293
If you **chop** something, you cut it horizontally with a knife or blade. *e.g. Next, chop the pumpkin in two.*

Christ   966
1 **Christ** is Jesus of Nazareth, regarded by Christians as the person who fulfilled Old Testament prophecies of the Messiah. *e.g. There was a painting of Christ on the altar.*

2 Christ is the Messiah or anointed one of God as the subject of Old Testament prophecies. *e.g. We are told that Christ will come again.*

christen 171, 691, 1111
When a baby is **christened**, he or she is given a name during the Christian religious ceremony of baptism, as a sign that the baby is now a member of the Christian Church. *e.g. She was christened Nicola.*

christening 171, 691, 1111
A **christening** is a Christian religious ceremony in which a baby is made a member of a Christian church and is given his or her name. *e.g. We all attended Mathew's christening.*

Christian 171, 966
1 A Christian is a person who believes in Jesus Christ and tries to follow his teachings. *e.g. Is she a Christian?*
2 Christian means relating to religious groups that believe in Jesus Christ and try to follow his teachings. *e.g. There is to be a service for Christian ex-servicemen and women in the Cathedral next Sunday.*

Christmas 1304, 1537
Christmas is the Christian festival on the 25th December when the birth of Jesus Christ is celebrated. *e.g. I'm going home for Christmas.*

Christmas tree 1538
A **Christmas tree** is a fir tree, or an artificial tree that looks like a fir tree, which people put in their houses at Christmas and decorate with coloured lights and balls. *e.g. We decorate the Christmas tree on December 24th.*

chunk 1447
1 A chunk of something is a large, solid piece of it. *e.g. I want a chunk of ice for a table sculpture, please.*
2 A chunk is a large amount or part of something. *e.g. Research now takes up a sizeable chunk of the budget.*

church 106, 1440
1 A church is a building in which Christians worship. *e.g. Father Ryan is the parish priest of St. Godric's church.*
2 A Church is one of the groups of people within the Christian religion, for example Catholics or Methodists, who have their own beliefs and forms of worship. *e.g. Mick was received into the Church last month.*

chute 1560
A **chute** is a steep, narrow slope down which objects such as coal or parcels can slide so that they do not have to be carried. *e.g. The dirty laundry is sent down the chute.*

cigarette 757
A **cigarette** is a small tube of paper containing tobacco which people smoke. *e.g. Boylan lit a cigarette.*

cinema 1014
1 A cinema is a place where people go specifically to watch films. *e.g. I'll meet you outside the cinema.*
2 Cinema is the business and art of making films. *e.g. One of the classic works of Russian cinema is 'Battleship Potemkin'.*

circle 496
1 A circle is a curved line completely surrounding an area. Every part of the line is the same distance from the centre of the area. *e.g. She saw a white circle painted on the floor.*
2 A circle of something is a round, flat piece or area of it. *e.g. Stand the paint tin on a circle of aluminium foil.*

circulate 736
If you **circulate** at a party or other social occasion, you move among the guests and talk to many different people. *e.g. I have to circulate. My mother wants me to meet all her business friends.*

circus 736, 827
A **circus** is a show performed in a large tent, often with animals, clowns, and acrobats. *e.g. We're taking the children to the circus.*

civic 793
Civic is used to describe people or things that are given an official status by the authorities in a particular town or city. *e.g. The winning team was welcomed with a civic reception.*

claim 1219, 1317
1 If you **claim** something, you ask for it because you have a right to it, or think that you have. *e.g. Voluntary workers can claim back travelling expenses.*
2 A claim is a request made in the belief that you have a right to have something. *e.g. Arthur put in a claim for compensation.*

clap 1445
If you **clap**, you hit your hands together several times, usually in order to express appreciation. *e.g. The audience clapped enthusiastically and called for more.*

clapped out 740, 812, 825
Something such as a machine that is **clapped out** is old and no longer working properly. *e.g. My last car was a clapped out old Lada.*

clarify 1314
To **clarify** something means to make it easier to understand. *e.g. If you don't understand, ask the speaker to clarify the point.*

clarity 1314
Clarity is the quality of being explained well and easy to understand. *e.g. I was impressed with the clarity of his lecture.*

clash 563, 915
1 If someone **clashes** with someone else, or if two people **clash**, they fight, argue, or disagree with each other. *e.g. The youths look set to clash with police.*
2 Beliefs, ideas, or qualities that **clash** with each other are very different from each other and therefore are opposed to each other. *e.g. In a situation like this, moral values may clash.*
3 A clash occurs when beliefs, ideas or qualities are opposed to each other. *e.g. It is a personality clash.*

class 840, 1262
A **class** is a group of pupils or students who are taught together. *e.g. There were only six children in the junior class.*

class 1176, 1690
A **class** of things is a group of them with similar characteristics. *e.g. We can identify this class of fern quite easily.*

classroom 1262
A **classroom** is a room in a school where lessons take place. *e.g. There are thirty desks in that classroom.*

clean 4, 88
1 If you **clean** something, you make it free from dirt and unwanted substances or marks, for example by washing or wiping it. *e.g. Clean the bathroom thoroughly.*
2 To clean means to make the inside of a house or other building and the furniture in it free from dirt and dust. *e.g. Jean and Kathleen clean all the offices on this floor.*

clean 1313, 1314
1 Something that is **clean** is free from dirt and unwanted substances or marks. *e.g. Put on clean clothes.*
2 You sign or say that people or animals are **clean** when they keep themselves or their surroundings clean. *e.g. They're very clean and tidy, I must say.*

clean a window 582
If you **clean a window**, you remove dirt from a glass panel in the side of a building or vehicle with paper or a cloth and water. *e.g. I'll clean a window if you hoover one room; is that fair?*

cleaner 4, 88
A **cleaner** is someone who is employed to clean the rooms and furniture inside a building. *e.g. My mother is a cleaner.*

cleaning 4, 88
Cleaning is the activity or work of making the inside of a house or other building and the

furniture in it free from dirt and dust. *e.g. Natasha does the cleaning in our office.*

cleanliness 1314
Cleanliness is the habit of keeping yourself and your surroundings clean. *e.g. Although she lived in a slum, she believed in cleanliness.*

clear 1313, 1314, 1728
1 Something that is **clear** is easy to understand. *e.g. Your explanation was so clear.*
2 Something that is **clear** is obvious and impossible to be mistaken. *e.g. It was clear he wasn't keen.*
3 If you are **clear** about something, you understand it completely. *e.g. Now I'm clear about our plans.*
4 If your mind or your way of thinking is **clear**, you are able to think sensibly, reasonably, and logically. *e.g. Clear thinking will be impossible if we stay up late tonight.*
5 Something that is **clear** is easy to see. *e.g. Every detail in these photographs is clear.*

clear (an obstacle) 742
If you **clear an obstacle** such as a fence, wall or hedge, you jump over it without touching it. *e.g. He was able to clear the hurdle without difficulty and then speed off into the night.*

clear off 160
If you sign or say **clear off** to someone, you are telling them in a rude way to go away. *e.g. Clear off and leave him alone!*

clergy 643
The **clergy** are the officially appointed leaders of the religious activities of a particular church or temple. *e.g. My uncle is a member of the clergy there.*

clergyman 643
A **clergyman** is a male member of the clergy *e.g. The new clergyman arrived last week.*

clerical collar 643
A **clerical collar** is a white band worn around the neck by members of the clergy. *e.g. As he put on his clerical collar, he thought again about his sermon for the day.*

clever 166
1 Someone who is **clever** is intelligent and able to learn and understand things easily or plan or do things well. *e.g. My sister was clever and passed all her exams.*
2 An idea, book, or invention that is **clever** is extremely effective and shows the skill of the people involved. *e.g. It's such a clever gadget.*

clever 1500
Someone who is **clever** is intelligent and able to learn and understand things easily or plan or do things well. *e.g. She was always clever, but we never dared to hope she'd become a lawyer.*

cliff 1339
A **cliff** is a high area of land with a very steep side, especially next to the sea. *e.g. He stood on the cliff.*

cliff edge 1339
A **cliff edge** is the point at which a high area of land drops away forming a very steep side, which often faces the sea. *e.g. We trembled on the cliff edge, looking down at the angry rocks.*

climb up a stepladder/steps 1636
If you **climb up a stepladder** or up **steps**, you move to a higher level by lifting yourself up from each of its steps to the next. *e.g. I can climb up that stepladder in seconds.*

clock 410
A **clock** is an instrument which measures time and shows you what time of day it is. The time may be indicated by the position of two pointers on a circular or rectangular area that has the numbers from one to twelve marked on its edges, or may be shown as a series of digits. Clocks usually stand on a shelf in a room or are fixed to a wall. *e.g. We bought them a new clock for their living room.*

close 385, 434
If something, usually a person, is **close** to something or somebody, it is near to them. *e.g. The vicar stood close to me in church.*

close 1358
1 If you **close** something such as a door, it is moved so that it covers or fills a hole or a gap. *e.g. For heaven's sake, close it quickly or we'll all be done for!*
2 If a shop or a public building **closes** or is **closed**, people cannot use it or do business there. *e.g. We close at half past five every day.*
3 If someone **closes** a business or public building or if it **closes**, all work or activity stops there, usually for ever. *e.g. We had to close the business; we just didn't have enough customers.*

close 1398
1 To **close** something such as a road, a border or an airport means to block it in order to prevent people from using it. *e.g. They decided to close the border with Hong Kong just as my wife and daughters reached it.*
2 When something such as a shop or a public building **closes** or when you **close** it, work or business stops there for a short period, for example at lunchtime, or until the next working day. *e.g. It was Sunday and we were able to close the centre.*

close 1451
If you **close** something, you move two panels or doors so that they block or fill a hole or gap. *e.g. Kindly close the shutters.*

close 1619
1 If something or someone is **close** to you, they are near to you. *e.g. He moved so close I could smell his aftershave.*
2 If you are **close** to something happening or if it is **close**, it is almost certain to happen soon. *e.g. An agreement seems close.*

close down 1359
If someone **closes down** a factory, organisation or business, or if it **closes down**, all work or activity stops there, usually for ever. *e.g. The mines had to close down.*

close/shut a door 1358
If you **close** or **shut a door**, you move it so that it blocks or fills a hole or gap. *e.g. Will you shut that door once and for all?!*

close/shut a small gate 1358
If you **close** or **shut a small gate**, you move it so that it blocks or fills a hole or gap. *e.g. See that little gate in the chicken coop? Will you close it please?*

cloth 4
A **cloth** is a piece of material which you use for cleaning. *e.g. Clean with a soft cloth dipped in warm, soapy water.*

cloth 1516
Cloth is a fabric which is made from cotton, wool, silk, nylon, etc., by weaving, knitting, or a similar process. Cloth is used especially for making clothes. *e.g. I had a new suit made from woollen cloth.*

clothes 1081
Clothes are the things that people wear, such as shirts, coats, trousers, and dresses. *e.g. I buy my clothes from charity shops.*

clothes line 836
A **clothes line** is a rope or wire stretched across a garden or sometimes across a room on which wet washing is hung to dry. *e.g. Can you fix up a temporary clothes line?*

clothing 1081
1 **Clothing** consists of all the things people wear. *e.g. The concern has been with finding food, clothing and shelter for everyone.*
2 **Clothing** is used to describe something which is concerned with the business of designing, manufacturing or selling clothes. *e.g. A clothing factory is to open in the Old Chapel in Dunsmuir Grove.*

cloud 1072
1 If something such as a room **clouds**, or if you **cloud** it, it becomes less easy to see through. *e.g. If you light that cigar, you'll cloud the room with smoke in no time.*
2 If one thing **clouds** another, it confuses

things so that you cannot understand a situation or judge it properly. *e.g. I knew his explanations would cloud the issue.*

cloud 1170
1 A **cloud** is a mass of water vapour that floats in the sky. Clouds are usually white or grey in colour. *e.g. The air was warm and there were little white clouds high in the blue sky.*
2 If one thing **clouds** another, it confuses things so that you cannot understand a situation or judge it properly. *e.g. His explanations served only to cloud the issue.*

cloudy 1170
If it is **cloudy**, there are a lot of clouds in the sky. *e.g. It was a cloudy sky.*

clown 827
A **clown** is a performer in a circus who wears funny clothes and bright make-up, and does silly things in order to make people laugh. *e.g. He is famous as Coco the Clown.*

coach 1687
1 A **coach** is a large motor vehicle which carries passengers on journeys by road. *e.g. They travelled into London on the same coach.*
2 A **coach** is a vehicle carrying passengers that is part of a train. *e.g. Troops piled into the coaches at the front of the train.*

coal 1150
Coal is a hard black substance that is taken from under the earth and burned as a fuel. *e.g. They extract ten million tons of coal a year.*

coalition 1101
1 A **coalition** is a government consisting of people from two or more political parties who have decided to work together in order to govern. *e.g. They remember the fall of Asquith's coalition government.*
2 A **coalition** is a group or organisation consisting of people from different political or social groups who are cooperating to achieve a particular aim. *e.g. Commact is a broad coalition of community groups in the area.*

coat 144
A coat is a piece of clothing with long sleeves that you wear over other clothes, especially in order to keep you warm or to protect you from bad weather. *e.g. She was wearing a heavy tweed coat.*

coat hanger 656
A **coat hanger** or **coathanger** is a curved piece of wood, metal or plastic that you hang clothes on. Coat hangers have a hook in the middle which you can attach to something such as a rail. *e.g. I never seem to have enough coat hangers.*

coat (lightweight coat) 288
A **lightweight coat** is a piece of clothing with

long sleeves that you wear over other clothes (especially in order to keep dry) and which does not weigh very much. *e.g. She was wearing a black lightweight coat and a dark blue scarf.*

coca cola 638
Coca cola is the name of a brown, fizzy, non-alcoholic drink. *e.g. I'll have a coca cola, as I'm so thirsty.*

cock 639, 778
A **cock** is an adult male chicken. *e.g. Somewhere in the distance, a cock began to crow.*

cockscomb 778
A **cockscomb** is the fleshy, red spiked growth on the head of birds such as chickens. *e.g. Percy's cockscomb looked a bit dog-eared after the cat chased him.*

coffee 53, 638, 850
1 **Coffee** is a dark brown drink (usually hot) that you make by pouring hot water onto or forcing steam through a filter holding coffee beans that have been ground up, or by pouring hot water onto a powder or liquid containing extracts from coffee beans. *e.g. She gave him a cup of coffee.*
2 **Coffee** is the roasted seeds of a tropical tree or powder from which the drink coffee is made. *e.g. If you're going out, would you mind buying some coffee?*

coincidence 516
A **coincidence** is what happens when two or more things occur at the same time by chance in a way that is surprising. *e.g. It was a coincidence that my sister was on the same train.*

cold 28, 119
1 **Cold** is used to describe the weather, or the air in a room or building when the temperature is very low or lower than is normal or acceptable. *e.g. The building was cold and draughty.*
2 Something that is **cold** has a very low temperature or a lower temperature than is normal or acceptable. *e.g. Soak the nappies in cold water.*
3 If you are **cold**, your body is at an unpleasantly low temperature or at a lower temperature than is normal or acceptable. *e.g. Can I light the fire? I'm cold.*
4 The **cold** is cold weather. *e.g. Why are you staying out in the cold?*

cold 1535
A **cold** is a mild, very common illness which makes you sneeze a lot and gives you a sore throat or a cough. *e.g. When her cold was better, she came back to work.*

cold (very cold) 118
1 Something that is **very cold** has an extremely low temperature or a very much

lower temperature than is normal or acceptable. *e.g. The sea was very cold when we went swimming on Christmas Day.*
2 **Very cold** is used to describe the weather or the air in a room or building when the temperature is extremely low or very much lower than is normal or acceptable. *e.g. It is always very cold in Alaska.*

collapse 799
If you **collapse**, you suddenly fall down because you are very tired, weak or ill. *e.g. As we walked into the hotel, Jane collapsed.*

collapse 1438
1 If a building or some other structure **collapses**, it suddenly falls down. *e.g. These flimsy houses are liable to collapse in a heavy storm.*
2 The **collapse** of a structure is an occasion on which it collapses. *e.g. The collapse of the shed spurred us into action.*

collar 490
The **collar** of a shirt, blouse or jacket is the part which fits round the neck and is usually folded over making two points at the front. *e.g. He'd forgotten to iron the collar of his shirt.*

collate 1559
When you **collate** pieces of information, you gather them all together. *e.g. We will collate evidence from many sources.*

collation 1559
The **collation** of pieces of information is the act of gathering them all together. *e.g. Collation of the statistics will be Jean's responsibility.*

colleague 224
A **colleague** is a person you work with, especially in a professional job. *e.g. I shall be attending the case conference with a colleague.*

collect 1194
To **collect** is to receive large sums of money which you have not had to work for. *e.g. He had three different insurance policies, so after the accident he knew he would really collect.*

collect 1559
If you **collect** a number of things, you bring them together from several sources. *e.g. We must collect reports from everyone involved.*

collecting tin 1091
A **collecting tin** or **collecting box** is a container that is used to collect donations for a charity or cause. *e.g. She agreed to stand with a collecting tin in the town square.*

collection 1559
1 The **collection** of things is the act of bringing them together from several sources. *e.g. Can you*

take care of the collection of the forms?

2 A **collection** of things is a set of items which have been brought together from several sources. *e.g. This is my week's collection of leaflets.*

collect with a collecting tin   1091

When you **collect with a collecting tin**, you stand, usually in a public place, and encourage people to put donations for a charity or cause into a tin. *e.g. We would like this team to collect with collecting tins, and this team to sell raffle tickets.*

college   448

A **college** is an institution where students study for qualifications or do training courses after they have left school. *e.g. What do you plan to do when you leave college?*

collide   103

If two moving objects **collide**, they hit each other. *e.g. The two vehicles collided.*

collision   103

A **collision** occurs when two moving objects hit each other. *e.g. We were involved in a collision just outside Carlisle.*

colour   990, 1172

1 The **colour** of something is the appearance that it has as a result of reflecting light. Red, blue, and green are colours. *e.g. What colour are your eyes?*

2 A **colour** television, photograph, or picture is one that shows things in all their colours, and not just in black, white and grey. *e.g. Marvellous colour illustrations are one of the impressive features of the book.*

colourful   1172

Something that is **colourful** has bright or impressive colours. *e.g. Colourful posters of Paris and Venice are available.*

comb   253

A **comb** is a flat piece of plastic, metal, or bone with narrow pointed teeth along one edge, which you use to tidy your hair. *e.g. Judith opened her bag and took out her comb.*

combination   1101

A **combination** is the mixture that you get when a number of things are combined together. *e.g. We need a combination of men and women to work on carnival planning.*

combine   1101

1 If you **combine** two or more things or if they **combine**, they exist together. *e.g. We would all prefer to combine liberty with order.*

2 If you **combine** two or more things or if they **combine**, they join together to make a single thing. *e.g. Later the two teams were combined.*

3 If someone or something **combines** two qualities or features, they have both those qualities or features at the same time. *e.g. Carbon fibre combines flexibility with immense strength.*

comb one's hair   253

When you **comb your hair**, you tidy it using a comb. *e.g. He combs his hair in front of the mirror.*

come   295, 570

When a person or thing **comes** somewhere, especially to where you are, they move there. *e.g. I think he will come soon.*

come back   295, 570

1 To **come back** somewhere means to return to that place. *e.g. Please come back to the office before six o'clock.*

2 If a person signs or says that you should **come back**, they mean that you should return to where they are. *e.g. Come back, I want to tell you a secret before you go.*

comedian   663

A **comedian** is a person who makes people laugh (often as a job), especially by telling them jokes or funny stories. *e.g. Morecombe and Wise were my favourite comedians.*

comedy   853

1 **Comedy** is something that makes people laugh or amuses them in literature or in real life. *e.g. The play had plenty of melodrama and excitement as well as comedy.*

2 A **comedy** is a book, play, film or broadcast programme that is intended to make people laugh. *e.g. The latest interpreted play is a comedy by Alan Bennett.*

come here   295

When you sign or say **come here**, you ask or command a person to move near to you. *e.g. Come here and help me with this carton.*

comfort   1401

To **comfort** someone means to make them feel less worried or unhappy. *e.g. Jeannie came to comfort him.*

comfortable   1495

1 Something that is **comfortable** makes you feel physically relaxed and at ease. *e.g. The hotel was large and comfortable.*

2 If you are **comfortable**, or if you make yourself **comfortable**, you are physically relaxed and at ease. *e.g. Sit down and make yourself comfortable.*

comic   283

A **comic** is a magazine, usually for children, that contains stories told in pictures. *e.g. I buy comics like 'The Beano' and 'The Dandy'.*

comic   663, 853

1 A **comic** is a person who tells jokes in order to make people laugh. *e.g. He was a very funny comic.*

2 Something that is **comic** is meant to amuse you and make you laugh. *e.g. And now, a comic sketch filmed by Deaf Owl.*

command   303, 350

1 If you **command** someone to do something, you order them to do it. *e.g. 'I'm commanding you to do it,' signed the General.*

2 If you **command** something, you order it. *e.g. The king had commanded his presence at court.*

command   356

If you **command** someone to do something, you order them to do it. *e.g. The corporal commanded the new recruits to stand by their beds.*

commandment   400

1 A **commandment** is an order or rule. *e.g. He still adhered to the commandment not to eat meat on a Friday.*

2 A **Commandment** is one of the ten rules of behaviour which, according to the Old Testament of the Bible, were given by God to Moses and which we are required to obey. *e.g. His sermon was on the Commandment that we should love our neighbour as ourselves.*

commandments   402

1 **Commandments** are a set of orders or rules. *e.g. After the military takeover the General issued commandments by which the people would be expected to abide.*

2 The Ten **Commandments** are the ten rules of behaviour which, according to the Old Testament of the Bible, were given by God to Moses and which we are required to obey. *e.g. Moses brought down the Commandments inscribed in stone.*

commence   209, 1105

1 When something **commences**, it begins. *e.g. He has been in prison for nine months and his trial commences on Wednesday.*

2 If you **commence** doing something, you begin doing it. *e.g. I commenced a round of visits.*

comment   347, 380

1 A **comment** is something that you sign or say which expresses your opinion about something or which gives an explanation of it. *e.g. Do you have any comment for the press, Minister?*

2 If you **comment** on something, you sign or say something that expresses your opinion of something or which gives an explanation of it. *e.g. He was asked to comment on the rumours.*

commit   594

If you **commit** yourself to a course of action or are **committed** to it you definitely decide you will do it. *e.g. I am committed to completing my Sign Language Studies course.*

commitment 128
1 A **commitment** is something which regularly takes up some of your time. *e.g. She has a family commitment on Wednesday evenings.*
2 If you give a **commitment** to something you promise faithfully that you will do it. *e.g. He gave a clear commitment to an equal opportunities policy within the firm.*

commitment 594
1 **Commitment** is a strong belief in an idea or system. *e.g. He has a strong commitment to world peace.*
2 A **commitment** is something which regularly takes up some of your time. *e.g. She's got family commitments every evening.*
3 If you give a **commitment** to something, you promise faithfully that you will do it. *e.g. He gave a clear commitment to retire in five years.*

comitted (be committed to) 512
If you **are committed to** someone or something, you admire them so much or are so devoted to them that you may be unable to see their faults or weaknesses. *e.g. He was committed to her and the marriage, but she went off with an estate agent.*

committee 828, 853
1 A **committee** is a group of people who represent a larger group or organisation and who make decisions or plans for it. *e.g. A special committee has been set up to deal with noise pollution.*
2 If you are on a **committee**, you are a committee member. *e.g. She's on the committee, but there's no interpreter so she can't access the meeting.*

committee member 647
If you are a **committee member**, you are one of the group of people who represent a larger group or organisation and who make decisions or plans for it. *e.g. She is now a committee member and an example to us all.*

common 1044
1 If something is **common**, it happens often or to a large number of people. *e.g. Underemployment is a common problem for Deaf workers.*
2 If something is **common**, it occurs or is found in large numbers. *e.g. Green is a common name.*

common 1146, 1213
1 Someone who is **common** behaves in a way that shows lack of taste, education and good manners. *e.g. Some common people moved in next door and made a lot of noise.*
2 Behaviour that is **common** shows lack of

taste, education or good manners. *e.g. Would you stop picking your nose: it's so common!*

common 1416, 1417
1 If something is **common**, it happens often or to a large number of people. *e.g. It is a common problem: there are just too few interpreters.*
2 If something is **common** to two or more people, it is possessed, done, or used by them all. *e.g. We share a common language.*
3 If a number of things have a characteristic or feature in **common**, they have the same characteristic or feature. *e.g. In common with many other companies, we like to advertise in the press.*

communism 10
Communism is the political belief in a classless society in which the state should control the means of producing everything and the economy should be centrally planned. *e.g. He has written extensively on communism in Third World countries.*

communist 10
1 A **communist** is someone who believes in communism. *e.g. He remained a communist throughout his life.*
2 **Communist** is used to refer to the political and social system of the former Soviet Union between 1917-1990 and of countries in Eastern Europe such as Poland, Czechoslovakia, Hungary, etc., between 1947-1989. It continues to be used in relation to countries such as the People's Republic of China which organise their social and political systems according to the principles of communism. *e.g. The Communist government in East Germany resigned.*

company 228, 957
A **company** is a business organisation that exists in order to make money by selling goods or services. *e.g. The recession has caused many companies to close.*

compare 1367, 1371
When you **compare** things, you consider them and discover the differences or similarities between them. *e.g. It's interesting to compare the two prospectuses.*

comparison 1367, 1371
1 When you make a **comparison**, you consider two or more things and discover the differences and similarities between them. *e.g. Here, for the sake of a comparison, is the French version.*
2 If something is a particular way in **comparison** or by **comparison**, it is that way when it is compared to something else. *e.g. By comparison with the Japanese, Europeans are lazy people.*

compass 403
A **compass** is an instrument that you use for finding directions. It has a fixed dial and a

movable magnetic needle that always comes to rest pointing to the north. *e.g. I set off on my walk clutching my map and compass.*

compass 773
A **compass** is, or **compasses** are, a hinged V-shaped instrument that you use for drawing circles, measuring distances on maps, et cetera. *e.g. You should use a compass to produce a perfect circle.*

compassion 1401
Compassion is a feeling of pity and sympathy for someone who is suffering. *e.g. The minister showed great compassion for the bereaved relatives.*

compatible 128
If people or things are **compatible**, they can live or exist together happily or safely. *e.g. Janet and John seemed to be a compatible couple despite the difference in their ages.*

compel 1364, 1437
If something or someone **compels** you to do something, they force you to do it. *e.g. Nothing can compel you to intervene.*

competition 565
A **competition** is an event in which many people take part in order to find out who is best at a particular activity. *e.g. The Segovia International Guitar Competition was won by a Yugoslavian band.*

complain 1187, 1199
1 If you **complain**, you tell someone about a situation affecting you that you think is wrong or unsatisfactory and should be changed. *e.g. He decided that he would complain about the awful food.*
2 If you **complain**, you make a formal protest to someone. *e.g. They went to the police station, and I watched them complain bitterly about the noise.*

complete 215, 221, 976
1 If something is **complete**, it has been finished. *e.g. After these questions, your driving test is complete.*
2 If you **complete** something, you finish doing, making or producing it. *e.g. We've completed our preparations for the party.*

complete 1104
1 If something is **complete**, it contains all the parts that it should contain. *e.g. She has a complete set of British Deaf News going back to 1970.*
2 **Complete** is used to emphasise that something is as great in extent, degree, or amount as is possible. *e.g. You need a complete change of diet.*

completion 215, 221, 976
Completion is the finishing of a piece of work.

e.g. The house was due for completion in 1983.

complex   1114, 1172
1 Something that is **complex** has or involves many different parts or things that are connected or related to each other. *e.g. It was a complex lace pattern.*
2 Something that is **complex** is difficult to understand or deal with because it involves so many parts or details. *e.g. Planning the Congress was a complex operation.*

complicate   1114, 1172
To **complicate** a situation or explanation means to make it more difficult to understand or deal with by adding a problem to it or by adding too many details. *e.g. His speech would have been good, but he had to complicate it with all those figures.*

complicated   1114, 1172
Something that is **complicated** has many parts or aspects which are connected to one another in a way that makes it difficult to understand or deal with. *e.g. The British legal system is very complicated.*

compound   1101
1 A **compound** is a combination of two or more features, qualities or parts. *e.g. The new threat was a compound of nationalism and social revolution.*
2 In chemistry, a **compound** is a substance that consists of two or more different substances or chemical elements. *e.g. The bacteria fed initially on various carbon compounds.*
3 In linguistics, a **compound** is a sign, word or expression that has a single meaning but is made up of two or more signs or words. *e.g. BSL makes great use of compounds.*

compress   1378
When you **compress** something, or when it **compresses,** it is pressed or squeezed together so that it takes up less space. *e.g. We had to compress the cardboard boxes to fit them into the dustbin.*

compromise   1388
1 A **compromise** is an agreement between two people or groups in which they both give up something that they originally wanted in order that they should both get an acceptable degree of satisfaction. *e.g. Delegates predict that some compromise will be reached.*
2 If you **compromise** or reach a **compromise,** you reach an agreement with another person or group in which you both give up something that you originally wanted in order that you should both get an acceptable degree of satisfaction. *e.g. The best thing to do is to compromise.*

compulsory   2, 1437
Compulsory is used to describe something

that you have to do or accept because it is a rule or law, or because someone in authority insists on it. *e.g. It is compulsory to wear school uniform at my school.*

computer   1043
A **computer** is an electronic machine that can quickly make calculations, store, rearrange and retrieve information. *e.g. Portable computers can be plugged into T.V. sets.*

conceited   1076
Someone who is **conceited** is excessively proud of their abilities or achievements. *e.g. He is a conceited old fool.*

concept   1665
A **concept** is an idea or abstract principle. *e.g. The concept of subsidiarity is not difficult to understand.*

concern   567, 1134
1 **Concern** is worry that people have about a situation. *e.g. We share your concern at the poor standards of education.*
2 If something **concerns** you, it worries you or makes you upset. *e.g. The rise in vandalism is beginning to concern me.*

conclude   215, 221, 976, 1552
When you **conclude** something, you end it. *e.g. I would like to conclude my speech by thanking all the people who helped me.*

conclusion   215, 1552
The **conclusion** of something that has been taking place is its ending. *e.g. The meeting finally reached its conclusion at five o'clock.*

conclusion   221, 976
1 The **conclusion** of something that has been taking place is its ending. *e.g. At the conclusion of the opening session, cheers were raised for Queen Victoria.*
2 The **conclusion** of a treaty or a business deal is its final settlement. *e.g. The conclusion is a formality—or so we thought.*

conclusion (in conclusion)   1162
In conclusion is used to indicate that you are summing up at the end of what you have signed or said. *e.g. In conclusion, we see that there are many areas in which Deaf people are still denied access.*

conduct a choir/orchestra   878
When someone **conducts an orchestra** or **choir,** they stand in front of the orchestra or choir and direct the performance. *e.g. We saw Roy Whittingham conducting the King's School Chamber Choir.*

conductor   878
A **conductor** is a person who stands in front of

an orchestra or choir and conducts them. *e.g. Brenda used to be the conductor of the British Deaf Choir.*

confectionery   346
You can refer to sweets and chocolates as **confectionery.** *e.g. We are purveyors of high quality confectionery.*

conference   418, 419
1 A **conference** is a meeting at which formal discussions take place. *e.g. The Managing Director has monthly conferences with all staff members.*
2 A **conference** is also a meeting about a particular subject, often lasting a few days. *e.g. Sally Firth's paper at the Amsterdam conference was very well received.*

confess   35, 920, 998
1 If you **confess** to a crime or to having done something wrong, you admit that you were responsible for the crime or wrongdoing. *e.g. He had confessed his guilt.*
2 If you **confess** or you **confess** your sins, you tell God or a priest about your sins so that you can be forgiven. *e.g. He confessed to having committed a number of mortal sins.*

confession   35, 920, 998
1 If you make a **confession,** you admit that you have committed a crime or done something wrong. *e.g. Mary signed that she had a confession to make.*
2 **Confession** is a religious act in which you tell God or a priest about your sins and ask for forgiveness. *e.g. He went to confession on Saturday.*

confidence   646
1 **Confidence** is the belief that you can deal with situations successfully using your own abilities and qualities. *e.g. He is a young man with deserved confidence in his future.*
2 **Confidence** is a feeling of certainty that what you are signing or saying is correct. *e.g. I can say with complete confidence that it would have been desirable not to have informed the public.*

confidence (in confidence)   1470
If you tell someone something **in confidence,** you tell someone a secret or some other information that is not widely known, because you trust them not to tell anyone else. *e.g. I'm telling you this in the strictest confidence.*

confident   646
1 People who are **confident** feel that they are able to deal with a situation successfully and so do not worry about it too much. *e.g. His manner is more confident these days.*
2 If you are **confident** about something, you are certain that it will happen in the way

you want it to. *e.g. I'm quietly confident that we can get a good result.*

confidential   1266, 1470
Something that is **confidential** is meant to be kept secret or private and should not be discussed with other people. *e.g. This information is to be kept strictly confidential.*

confirm   61, 197, 200, 212
1 If something **confirms** what you believe, suspect, or fear, it shows that what you believe, suspect, or fear is definitely true. *e.g. My suspicions were confirmed.*
2 If you **confirm** something, you sign or say that it is true. *e.g. She asked if it was my car and I confirmed that it was.*
3 If you **confirm** an arrangement or appointment you state, usually in a letter or on the telephone, that the suggested arrangement or appointment is now definite. *e.g. I want to confirm my booking on this evening's ferry.*
4 If something **confirms** you in your belief, opinion, intention, etc., it makes your belief, opinion, intention, etc., stronger. *e.g. Everything you have just told me confirms me in my belief that he can't be trusted.*

confirmation   212
1 A **confirmation** of something that was believed, suspected or feared is something that shows that it is definitely true. *e.g. Her findings have provided confirmation of the importance of properly validated interpreter training courses.*
2 A **confirmation** of something that has been stated or suggested is a statement that it is true. *e.g. My employer requires confirmation that I attended the course.*
3 A **confirmation** of an arrangement or appointment is a statement, usually given in writing or by telephone, that the arrangement or appointment is now definite. *e.g. Has Beamish College received confirmation of our booking?*

conflict   924, 1120, 1121
1 A **conflict** is fighting between two or more countries or groups of people. *e.g. Europe has often been the scene of conflict.*
2 A **conflict** is a serious difference between two or more beliefs, ideas, or interests, which seems difficult to reconcile. *e.g. A real conflict is building up over environmental issues.*

confuse   1114
1 To **confuse** someone means to make it difficult for them to know exactly what to do. *e.g. You're trying to confuse me with all this different information.*
2 To **confuse** a situation means to make it complicated or difficult to understand. *e.g. To confuse matters further, her sister is married to her husband's uncle.*

confused   1074, 1114
1 If your thoughts are **confused,** they do not have any order or pattern and are difficult to understand. *e.g. My thoughts were confused and I really needed to lie down and close my eyes.*
2 If you are **confused,** you do not understand what is happening or do not know what to do. *eg. She was bewildered and confused.*

congratulate   225
1 If you **congratulate** someone, you sign or say something to them which indicates that you are pleased that something special and nice has happened to them. *e.g. Friends and relations came to congratulate the parents and see the baby.*
2 If you **congratulate** someone, you praise them for something difficult, skilful or admirable that they have done. *e.g. I congratulate Murray for getting us to work together.*

congratulations   225
1 You sign or say **congratulations** to someone in order to congratulate them on something nice that has happened to them or something admirable they have done. *e.g. Congratulations Chaim on passing the SASLI Stage Three examination.*
2 If you offer someone your **congratulations,** you congratulate them on something nice that has happened to them or on something admirable that they have done. *e.g. She received their congratulations with pleasure.*

congregate   1119
When a number of people **congregate,** they gather together and form a group. *e.g. The crowds began to congregate around the pavillion.*

congress   418, 419, 1119
A **congress** is a large meeting, usually of representatives belonging to a national or international organisation, that is held to discuss issues, ideas and policies. *e.g. Union leaders will meet the week after congress to consider the recommendations.*

connect   883, 898
1 To **connect** one thing to another means to join the two things to each other. *e.g. You must connect the fishing line to the hook.*
2 If you **connect** a piece of equipment, you join it by a wire or cable to an electricity supply or to another piece of equipment. *e.g. The engineer has to connect the telephone line to the terminal.*
3 If you **connect** two rooms of a building, you join them together by some physical construction such as a connecting door or corridor so that it is possible to walk between them. *e.g. John would like to connect these two houses by building a passageway between them.*
4 If you **connect** a person or thing with

something, you realise that there is a relationship or link between them. *e.g. There is no evidence to connect him with the murder.*

connection   883, 898
A **connection** is a link or relationship that exists between two things. *e.g. There's a connection between interest rates and inflation.*

conscientious   1448
Someone who is **conscientious** is very careful to do their work properly. *e.g. He was a very conscientious minister.*

consecrate   201, 673
When a building, place or object is **consecrated,** it is officially declared to be holy and able to be used for religious ceremonies and services. *e.g. We will consecrate the new church next month.*

consensus   227
Consensus is general agreement amongst a group of people about a subject or about how something should be done. *e.g. There was a consensus of opinion that no further disciplinary action should be taken.*

Conservative   1649
Someone who is a **Conservative** is a member of the Conservative Party or has political ideas and attitudes that are traditionally associated with the Conservative Party, in particular a belief in free enterprise and capitalism. *e.g. The industry had been privatised by the Conservative government.*

consider   313
1 If you **consider** something, you think about it carefully. *e.g. He signed that he would consider our proposals.*
2 If you **consider** a person's needs, wishes, or feelings, you pay attention to them. *e.g. I've got a family to consider.*

consideration   313
Consideration is careful thought about something. *e.g. After careful consideration, her parents gave her permission to go.*

consistent   652
1 Someone who is **consistent** never changes their behaviour or attitudes towards people or things. *e.g. John was a consistent supporter of the Labour party.*
2 Something that is **consistent** remains regular and does not fluctuate. *e.g. I think we've seen a consistent lack of awareness on the part of the authorities.*

consistent   1416, 1417
Something that is **consistent** has a regular pattern. *e.g. Figures have been consistent from all areas.*

console 1401
If you **console** someone who is unhappy about something, you try to make them feel more cheerful and hopeful. *e.g. I tried to console her, but the dog's death marked the end of an era for her.*

constable 795
A **constable** is a police officer of the lowest rank in Britain. *e.g. We will send a constable around to take down details of the burglary.*

constant 652
Something that is **constant** happens all the time. *e.g. He was in constant pain.*

constitute 151
To **constitute** something means to form it from a number of parts or elements. *e.g. The recently constituted board may do something to change things.*

constitution 151, 402
The **constitution** of a country or organisation is the system of laws and rules which formally states people's rights and duties. *e.g. The U.S. Constitution was written at the time of the Revolutionary War.*

construct 1423
If you **construct** an object such as a building, vehicle or machine, you build or make it. *e.g. We tried to construct a raft.*

contact 898
1 If you are in **contact** with someone, you meet them, sign or talk to them, or write to them, often as part of your work. *e.g. I'm in contact with a number of schools in Sussex.*
2 If you make **contact** with someone who you have been trying to find, sign or speak to, you manage to sign, speak or write to them. *e.g. I finally made contact with my friend.*
3 If you have **contact** with someone, you are able to send messages to them, especially by radio. *e.g. We made contact with the spacecraft.*
4 If you **contact** someone, you telephone or write to them in order to tell or ask them something. *e.g. As soon as we find out anything, we'll contact you.*

container with a handle 8, 935
A **container with a handle** is any object, such as a jug, used especially for holding liquids. It has an extension on the side (a handle) with which it can be held. *e.g. We need to find a container with a handle.*

contain oneself 531, 816, 1085
If you **contain yourself** or **contain** a laugh or a giggle, you prevent yourself from exclaiming something, laughing or giggling out loud. *e.g. She could hardly contain herself when she saw her boss fall over his feet!*

contains 1614
1 If something **contains** a particular thing, it has that thing inside it. *e.g. The envelope contains money.*
2 If something **contains** something else, it has the other thing among its parts or ingredients. *e.g. Does it contain sugar?*

contempt 970
If you have **contempt** for someone or something, you do not like them and think that they are unimportant or of no value. *e.g. Her contempt for foreigners was obvious.*

content 1271
If you are **content** or **contented**, you are satisfied and quite happy and do not want anything else or any change in your life or situation. *e.g. They smoked for a while, content to watch the world go by.*

contents 1614
1 The **contents** of something are everything that is contained in it. *e.g. He asked what the contents of the package were.*
2 **Content** is used to refer to the part of something which consists of a particular substance or ingredient. *e.g. No other food has so high an iron content.*

context 1658
The **context** of a sign or word, or of a sentence consists of the other signs or words before or after it which help to make the meaning clear. *e.g. What do we mean by 'grow' and 'back' in this context: 'The plant didn't grow so we sent it back'?*

continuation 652
The **continuation** of something is the fact that it keeps happening or existing. *e.g. People take for granted the continuation of economic growth.*

continue 652
1 If you **continue** to do something, you keep doing it and do not stop. *e.g. He continued to talk.*
2 If something **continues** or if you **continue** something, it does not stop happening or existing. *e.g. They want to continue their education.*
3 If you **continue** with something, you keep doing it, using it, or being involved with it. *e.g. The girls should continue with their mathematics.*
4 If you **continue**, you begin signing or speaking again after a pause or interruption. *e.g. 'May I continue?'—'Go on.'*

contract 721
A **contract** is a formal written agreement between two organisations, two people, etc., which states that one of them will supply goods or do work in an agreed way and for an agreed sum of money. *e.g. They were awarded a contract to build 58 planes.*

contract 1395
When something **contracts**, it becomes smaller. *e.g. Metals expand with heat and contract with cold.*

contraction 1395
1 **Contraction** is the activity or process of getting smaller. *e.g. The contraction of the workforce is inevitable in the present economic climate.*
2 A **contraction** is a shortened form of a word or words. *e.g. She used the surname Terson (a contraction of Terry and Nelson).*

contribute 1721
1 If you **contribute** to something, you do things to help to make it successful. *e.g. They all contributed to the party, so they all deserve our thanks.*
2 If you **contribute** to something, you give money to help pay for something. *e.g. She persuaded friends to contribute to the appeal.*
3 If you **contribute** to a magazine or book, you write things that are published in it. *e.g. Distinguished writers have contributed to Signpost.*

contribution 1721
1 If you make a **contribution** to something, you do something to help make it successful. *e.g. The BBC's contribution to the adult literacy campaign has been invaluable.*
2 A **contribution** is a sum of money that you give in order to help pay for something. *e.g. The United Kingdom had to make a contribution of a million pounds to the EC budget.*
3 A **contribution** is something that you write which is published in a book or magazine. *e.g. Several contributions from Deaf people are in this issue.*

control 272
1 **Control** of a country or an organisation is the power to make all the important decisions about the way in which it is run. *e.g. The bank now has control of the company.*
2 If you are in **control** of something, you have the power or ability to make it do what you want it to do. *e.g. He was in control of the class.*
3 If something is under your **control**, you have the power to decide what it will do or what will happen to it. *e.g. The village was under enemy control.*

controller 272
1 A **controller** is someone who has responsibility for everything that happens in a particular section of an organisation. *e.g. He is the Controller of Radio 4.*
2 A **controller** is someone who is in charge of the accounts of a business or government department. *e.g. The financial controller informed staff of the company's difficult financial circumstances.*

controversial 564
Someone or something that is **controversial** causes a lot of discussion and argument, and strong feelings of anger or disapproval. *e.g. Many of the new taxes are controversial.*

controversy 564
Controversy is a lot of discussion and argument about something, often involving strong feelings of anger or disapproval. *e.g. The government tried to avoid controversy.*

convention 418, 419
A **convention** is a large gathering of people who meet to discuss the business of their organisation or political group. *e.g. He's away, attending the annual convention of the Association.*

converge 435
1 When roads, tracks or lines **converge**, they meet or join at a particular place. *e.g. Do the Jubilee and Victoria lines converge at King's Cross?*
2 When different ideas or forces **converge**, they gradually become similar to each other. *e.g. Over the years, the beliefs of father and son began to converge.*

convergence 435
The **convergence** of two societies, beliefs or tendencies is the process by which they stop being separate or different and become similar or the same. *e.g. The banks and building societies have seen a remarkable convergence of the services they offer in recent years.*

conversation 380, 458, 1387
If you have a **conversation** with someone, you sign or speak to each other. *e.g. Roger and I had a conversation about house prices on Sherkin Island.*

converse 380, 458, 1387
If you **converse** with someone, you sign or speak to each other. *e.g. I am pleased to have had the opportunity to converse with you on this topic.*

conversion 432
1 A **conversion** is the act or process of changing something into a new or different form. *e.g. The process involves the conversion of chemical energy into electricity.*
2 A **conversion** is a process in which someone changes their religious or political beliefs. *e.g. His conversion to Buddhism came after living in Tibet for many years.*

convert 432
1 To **convert** something into something else means to change it into a new or different form. *e.g. Prams which convert into pushchairs are popular.*

2 If someone **converts** a building, they alter it in order to use it for a different purpose. *e.g. The house has been converted into two offices.*
3 If you **convert** a vehicle or a system, you change it so that it can use a different fuel. *e.g. They would convert the entire country to gas.*
4 If someone **converts** you, they persuade you to change your religious or political beliefs. *e.g. Birch became converted to communism in the late 1920s.*

convinced 514
If you are **convinced** of something, you are sure that it is true or genuine. *e.g. I was convinced my father was innocent.*

cook 239, 262, 274
1 When you **cook** food, you prepare it for eating by heating it in a particular way, for example by baking, boiling, or frying it. *e.g. I first learned to cook at school.*
2 A **cook** is a person who cooks and prepares food, often as his or her job. *e.g. Are you a good cook?*

cooker 239, 274
A **cooker** is a large metal box-shaped object, usually located in a kitchen that you use for cooking food by gas or electricity. *eg. Our cooker is very efficient because it uses gas.*

cookery 239, 262, 274
Cookery is the activity of cooking and preparing food. *e.g. She had never learned French cookery.*

cooking 239, 262, 274
1 **Cooking** is the activity of preparing and cooking food. *e.g. Boys are just as keen on cooking as girls are in our school.*
2 **Cooking** is food that has been cooked and prepared for eating. *e.g. I like Chinese cooking.*

cool 118
Something that is **cool** has a temperature which is low (but not cold) or lower than is normal or acceptable. *e.g. The evenings are always cool in this part of the country.*

cool 1463
1 Something that is **cool** has a temperature that is low but not cold, or lower than is normal or acceptable. *e.g. Inside the wood, it was cool and dark.*
2 When something **cools** or when you **cool** it, it becomes cooler. *e.g. Put the cake by the window to allow it to cool.*

co-operate 882, 883
1 If people **co-operate**, they work or act together for a purpose. *e.g. If parents, teachers and Deaf people all co-operate, we may be able to improve educational opportunities for deaf children.*

2 If you **co-operate**, you do what someone asks you to do. *e.g. The workers agreed to co-operate with management in rescuing materials from the flooded factory.*

co-operation 882, 883
Co-operation involves people working or acting together for a purpose. *e.g. We want to thank the staff for their co-operation.*

co-ordinate 882, 883
If you **co-ordinate** an activity, you organise the people and things involved in it. *e.g. Peter was asked to co-ordinate the social activities in the local Deaf club.*

co-ordination 882, 883
Co-ordination is the action of organising the people and things involved in a specific activity. *e.g. The co-ordination of the international congresses of the World Federation of the Deaf must be very complex.*

co-ordinator 882
The **co-ordinator** of a project or activity is a person who organises the people taking part in the project or activity and makes sure that they work together properly. *e.g. Peter Jackson is the co-ordinator of the Aids Ahead project.*

copies 1545
1 **Copies** are things that are made to look exactly the same as something else. *e.g. Captain Kirk stared at the pile of copies: how on earth would he find the real one?*
2 **Copies** of a book, newspaper or record are identical ones that have been printed or produced. *e.g. Sixty thousand copies of the record were sold.*

copy 1093
If someone **copies** you, they do what you do or try to be like you, for example by moving, behaving or dressing in the same way. *e.g. She tried to copy my facial movements.*

copy 1545
1 A **copy** is something that is made to look exactly the same as something else. *e.g. I will send you a copy of the letter.*
2 If you **copy** something, you make a copy or copies of it. *e.g. Shall I copy this, then?*
3 If someone **copies** you, they do what you do or try to be like you, for example by moving, behaving or dressing in the same way. *e.g. She tried to copy my facial movements.*

corner 1644
1 A **corner** of something is a point or an area where two or more if its edges, sides or surfaces join. *e.g. Our sandcastle had a tower at each corner.*
2 The **corner** of a room, box, etc., is the area or space inside it near the place where two or

three surfaces or edges meet. *e.g. There was a television set in the corner of the room.*
3 A **corner** is also a place where two streets join, especially one where there is a building. *e.g. There's a telephone box on the corner.*

correct   61, 197, 200
1 Something that is **correct** is accurate and has no mistakes. *e.g. That's the correct answer.*
2 If you are **correct**, what you have signed, said or thought is true. *e.g. Muriel is correct, we will have to change our plans.*
3 The **correct** thing is the thing that is required or is most suitable in a particular situation. *e.g. Make sure you ask for the correct fuse.*
4 **Correct** behaviour is considered to be morally or socially acceptable. *e.g. Your behaviour must be correct in church.*

correct   666
If you **correct** something such as a mistake, you do, sign or say something which puts it right. *e.g. I wish to correct one of the claims made by the young lady.*

correction   666
A **correction** is something which puts right something that has been done, signed, said, written, or believed falsely or in error. *e.g. I have made one correction to your essay.*

correspond   1387
If two people **correspond**, they write letters to each other. *e.g. Elizabeth and I used to correspond regularly.*

correspondence   1387
Correspondence is the act or process of writing letters to someone. *e.g. The judges' decision is final and no correspondence will be entered into.*

corridor   697
A **corridor** is a long passage in a building or train, which has doors and rooms or compartments on one or both sides, or which joins two or more parts of the building. *e.g. I walked down the corridor.*

corrupt   1031, 1032
1 To **corrupt** someone means to cause them to become dishonest, unfair and unable to be trusted. *e.g. Power and wealth corrupted him.*
2 To **corrupt** is to stop someone from believing in or caring about the harmful effects of wrong behaviour. *e.g. It is claimed that television corrupts.*
3 To **corrupt** something means to have a harmful effect on it by making it less pure. *e.g. In the last two hundred years, Europeans have destroyed or corrupted a great number of ancient cultures.*
4 If something **corrupts**, it rots or becomes

damaged or destroyed by decay. *e.g. The body corrupted quite quickly in the heat.*

cost   1505
1 The **cost** of something is the amount of money that is needed in order to buy, do, or make it. *e.g. The total cost of the holiday is three hundred pounds.*
2 If something **costs** a certain figure, that is the amount of money needed to buy, do or make it. *e.g. So this will cost just as much as that one, is that right?*

costly   989
When something is **costly**, you have to pay a lot of money for it, especially over time. *e.g. Commuting to work has been really costly over the years.*

cottage   1644
1 A **cottage** is a public but quite secret place where men meet to arrange or engage in homosexual activities. This sign and word are both used especially within the relevant communities. *e.g. Do you know if they've got the cottage under surveillance?*
2 If you **cottage** or go **cottaging**, you meet men in a particular public but quite secret place in order to arrange or engage in homosexual activities. This sign and word are both used especially within the relevant communities. *e.g. You don't need to go cottaging in Amsterdam because Holland is a much more open society than ours.*

couch   115, 116
A **couch** is a long piece of furniture which more than one person can sit on. *e.g. He put the couch by the window.*

cough   36
1 When you **cough**, you force air out of your throat with a sudden, harsh noise. You cough when your throat is irritated. Some people also cough when they are embarrassed or want to attract someone's attention. *e.g. The cigarette smoke made me cough.*
2 A **cough** is an illness in which you cough often and your chest or throat hurts. *e.g. I get a cough every winter.*

could   335, 477, 572
1 If you **could** do something, you were able to do it. *e.g. I could dance all night when I was younger.*
2 You use **could** to indicate that someone has given permission for something or that something is possible. *e.g. She said that I could go out tonight.*
3 If you sign or say that something **could** happen, you mean that it is possible that it will happen. *e.g. The river could easily overflow.*
4 If you sign or say that something **could** happen, you mean that it is possible to do. *e.g.*

We could do more to improve the school system.
5 If you sign or say that you **could** do something, you mean you would like to do it. *e.g. I could kill you.*
6 If you sign or say that something **could** be the case, you mean that it is possibly the case. *e.g. It could be a blue one, but I'm pretty sure it's green.*

could have happened   1098
If you sign or say that something **could have happened**, you mean that it was possible for it to have taken place although it did not in fact take place. *e.g. We could have crashed into the tree, but Bob swerved just in time.*

could not   421
1 If you **could not** or **couldn't** do something, you were not able to do it. *e.g. We just could not understand why he had failed.*
2 If you sign or say that something **could not** or **couldn't** happen, you mean that it is impossible to do. *e.g. She claimed the present government could not do less for the Health Service.*
3 If you sign or say that you **could not** or **couldn't** do something, you mean that you find it unacceptable or unreasonable. *e.g. I couldn't let you do it on your own.*

could not care less   602, 971, 1536
If you sign or say that you **could not care less** about something, you are indicating in an emphatic way that it does not matter to you at all. *e.g. Well, I'm sorry, but I could not care less about your problems.*

couldn't   421
Couldn't is the usual spoken form of could not. It appears in writing usually as an informal usage or abbreviation. See **could not**.

couldn't care less   602, 971, 1536
See **could not care less**.

council   793, 853
1 A **council** is a group of people who are elected to run a town, borough, city or county. *e.g. We were asked to attend the local council meeting.*
2 A **council** house or flat is owned by the local council. You pay rent to live in it. *e.g. I have lived in my council house for ten years.*

Council for the Advancement of Communication with Deaf People (CACDP)   254
1 The **Council for the Advancement of Communication with Deaf People (CACDP)** is a body which organises examinations in relation to British Sign Language, deaf-blind communication and lip-speaking. It maintains a register of BSL/English interpreters, deaf-blind communicators and lip-speakers. *e.g. Are you going to take the CACDP Stage One assessment?*
2 The address of the **Council for the**

Advancement of Communication with Deaf People is: Pelaw House, School of Education, University of Durham, Durham, DH11TS.

councillor   793
A **councillor** is a member of a local council. *e.g. Councillor Salim Bhutto was elected unopposed and starts work next week.*

count   1054
1 If you **count** or **count up** all the things in a group, you add them up in order to find out how many there are. *e.g. He withdrew to his office to count the money.*
2 A **count** is a number that you get by counting a particular set of things. *e.g. The official government count has now risen to eight million.*
3 If you **count** something when you are making a calculation, you include it in that calculation. *e.g. We must count the infected trees as well as the healthy ones.*

country   1046
The **country** is land which is away from towns and cities. *e.g. We live in the country, fifty miles from London.*

countryside   980, 1046
The **countryside** is land which is away from towns and cities. *e.g. We love to visit the countryside at weekends.*

county council   638
A **county council** is a group of people who are elected to run a self-administrating region or area. *e.g. We are writing to the county council about preserving the countryside.*

couple   783
1 A **couple** is two people who are married, living together, or having a sexual relationship. *e.g. There were mostly married couples on the course.*
2 A **couple** is two people who you see together on a particular occasion. *e.g. He watched a couple on the dance floor.*
3 A **couple** of people means two people. *e.g. A couple of you come with me, the rest go round the back with Ali.*

courage   1200
Courage is the quality shown by someone who decides to do something difficult or dangerous, even though they may be afraid. *e.g. She showed great courage in climbing the mountain as she was scared of heights.*

courageous   1200
Someone who is **courageous** shows courage. *e.g. He was courageous enough to walk into the lion's den.*

course   648
A **course** is a series of lessons or lectures on a particular subject. It usually includes reading and written or recorded work that a student has to do. *e.g. They've developed a computer science course.*

court   242, 1367, 1413
1 A **court** is a place where legal matters are decided by a judge and jury or by a magistrate. *e.g. She was collecting evidence for possible use in court.*
2 If you go to **court** or take someone to **court**, you take legal action against them, with the result that they are tried in a court of law. *e.g. He was forced to take his neighbour to court.*

court case   865
A **court case** or a **case** in law is a trial or other legal inquiry to settle a lawsuit or decide whether a person is guilty or not. *e.g. The court case went on for eleven weeks.*

cousin   1544
Your **cousin** is the child of your uncle or aunt. *e.g. My cousin lives in France, near Toulouse.*

cove   1226
A **cove** is a small bay on the coast. *e.g. We sailed into Fisherman's Cove.*

cover   1293
1 If something **covers** something else, it forms a layer over it. *e.g. Every time you do that, dust will cover my favourite ornament.*
2 An insurance policy that **covers** a person or thing will be paid by the insurance company in relation to that person or thing. *e.g. Private health insurance will cover some members of the family.*
3 If a law **covers** a particular set of people, things or situations, it applies to them. *e.g. The Factories Act already covers workers in factories.*
4 If a sum of money **covers** something, it is enough to pay for it. *e.g. I'll give you a cheque to cover the costs of your journey.*
5 Something that is a **cover** for secret or illegal activities seems respectable and normal but is intended to hide the activities. *e.g. The company was a cover for drug-smuggling.*

cover   1603
1 If you **cover** something, you place something else over it in order to protect it or hide it. *e.g. Please cover the tray with a cloth.*
2 If something **covers** something else, it forms a layer over it. *e.g. Spiders' webs cover the box.*
3 An insurance policy that **covers** a person or thing guarantees that money will be paid by the insurance company in relation to that person or thing. *e.g. Does that cover the contents of the car?*
4 If a sum of money **covers** something, it is enough to pay for it. *e.g. That should cover the taxi fare.*

cover up   1603
If you **cover up** something that you do not want people to know about, you hide it from them. *e.g. She tried to cover up for Willie.*

covet   1542
If you **covet** something, you strongly want to have it for yourself. *e.g. As I covet a Mercedes-Benz, I must work hard until I can buy one.*

cow   956
1 A **cow** is a large female animal that is kept on farms especially for its milk. *e.g. We milk the cows twice a day.*
2 A **cow** is a common farmyard animal, kept as livestock particularly for its meat and the milk produced by females of the species. *e.g. There are cows and sheep in the fields.*

coward   1143, 1180
A **coward** is someone who is easily frightened and who avoids dangerous and unpleasant situations. *e.g. I am a dreadful coward.*

coy   364
If a person or their behaviour is **coy**, they pretend to be shy and modest. *e.g. She gave a coy little smile.*

crabby   1135
If you are **crabby** you are bad tempered and unpleasant to people. *e.g. She was really crabby today.*

cracker   49
A **cracker** is a hollow cardboard tube covered with coloured paper. It can be pulled apart and usually contains a small toy and a paper hat. *e.g. We must have crackers at the birthday party.*

crack the top of a boiled egg   586
When you **crack the top of a boiled egg**, you hit it, usually with a spoon, so that you can move part of the shell and eat the contents. *e.g. In the morning, I always like to crack the top of a boiled egg and eat it in peace before anyone else comes down.*

cradle   1385
1 A **cradle** is a small open-topped, box-shaped bed for a baby. *e.g. The cradle for the new baby was in white and pink.*
2 If you **cradle** something in your arms or hands, you hold it carefully close to your body with your hands beneath it and move it gently from side to side. *e.g. The little girl cradled her new kitten lovingly.*

cradle a baby/doll   1385
If you **cradle a baby** or a **doll**, you hold it carefully close to your body with your hands beneath it and move it gently from side to side. *e.g. Can I cradle Matthew for a while?*

crafty   172
If a person or their behaviour is **crafty**, they obtain or achieve something by deceiving

people in a clever way. *e.g. He's a crafty old thing. He got us all doing his work.*

crash   69
1 A **crash** is an accident in which a moving car or other vehicle hits something and is badly damaged or destroyed. *e.g. Her mother was killed in a car crash.*
2 If a moving car or other vehicle **crashes**, it hits something and is badly damaged or destroyed. *e.g. The lorry crashed within seconds of leaving the yard.*

crash   103
A **crash** is an accident in which two moving cars or other vehicles hit each other and are badly damaged or destroyed. *e.g. Her mother was killed in a car crash.*

craving   1542
A **craving** is a very strong desire for something. *e.g. I get a sudden craving for sweets when I pass a sweetshop.*

crawl   1069
If you **crawl** to someone, you try to please them and to make them like you in order to gain some advantage for yourself. *e.g. I hate the way you crawl to your boss.*

crawl   1168
If you **crawl**, you move forward on your hands and knees, for example in order to get through a small space. *e.g. The cameraman had to crawl to the front.*

crawler   1069
A **crawler** is a person who tries hard to please someone or to make someone like them in order to gain some advantage. *e.g. When my neighbour wants to borrow money, he's a real crawler.*

create   1519
1 To **create** something means to cause it to happen or come into existence. *e.g. Dr. Frankenstein wanted to create a monster.*
2 To **create** something means to invent, design, or manufacture it, especially when it is something new, interesting or useful. *e.g. Can computers create new languages?*

create   1718
To **create** something means to cause it to happen or come into existence. *e.g. He created this programme from nothing.*

creation   1519, 1718
Creation is the act of bringing something new into existence or making something happen. *e.g. Let's hope EC membership will mean the creation of new jobs.*

creep   941
1 If you call someone a **creep**, you mean that

they flatter people in an effort to gain personal advantage. *e.g. She's a cunning little creep.*
2 If you **creep** or **creep** to somebody, you flatter them in an effort to gain personal advantage. *e.g. You always creep to the female teachers, but it won't do any good.*

cremate   1514
When someone is **cremated**, their dead body is burned, usually as part of a funeral service. *e.g. They're planning to cremate him and bring his ashes home.*

cremation   1514
1 A **cremation** is a funeral service during which a dead body is burned. *e.g. I went to my old teacher's cremation.*
2 **Cremation** is the process of burning a dead body at a funeral. *e.g. My father said he would prefer cremation.*

cricket   282, 1295
Cricket is an outdoor game played between two teams of eleven players. A player from one team stands in front of a wicket (three upright sticks called stumps with two small sticks called bails on top of them) and uses a wooden bat to try and hit a hard ball and score points called runs. The players of the other team try to get the batsman out by various methods such as bowling the ball and hitting the wicket or by catching the ball after it has been hit. When the batting team are all out, the team that was bowling start to bat and try to score more runs than their opponents. The team to score the most runs after each team has had the opportunity to bat twice (in professional county championship games and international five-day games) or once (in professional cup competitions, one-day internationals and most amateur games) is the winner. *e.g. Mr. Major spent the afternoon watching cricket.*

cricket bat   282, 1295
A **cricket bat** is a specially shaped, solid piece of wood with a handle, which is used for hitting the ball in cricket. *e.g. Viv Richards uses a very heavy cricket bat.*

cricketer   282, 1295
A **cricketer** is a person who plays cricket. *e.g. Ian Botham is a famous cricketer who now plays for County Durham.*

crimson   348
Something that is **crimson** is of a dark red colour. *e.g. She wore a crimson dress.*

crisps   870
Crisps are potatoes that have been sliced very thin and then fried until they are hard, dry and crunchy. *e.g. We'll have three packets of beef crisps and three pints of Guinness.*

critic   916
Someone who is a **critic** of a person or thing disapproves of them and criticises them publicly. *e.g. He had been a critic of the exclusively oral approach.*

critical   914
A **critical** time or situation is very serious and dangerous. *e.g. He developed a critical illness.*

criticise   666
also spelled **criticize**.
If you **criticise** something such as a piece of work, you indicate the particular fault or faults that are present in it. *e.g. We look at and criticise each other's poems.*

criticise   916
also spelled **criticize**.
If you **criticise** someone or something, you express your disapproval of them. *e.g. He criticised the things she wore.*

criticism   666
A **criticism** is a comment in which you indicate that someone or something, such as a piece of work, has a particular fault. *e.g. I don't mean this as a criticism.*

criticism   916
Criticism is the expression of disapproval of someone or something. *e.g. The Government came in for severe criticism.*

crocodile   1190
A **crocodile** is a large reptile with a long body and jaws. Crocodiles live in rivers and eat meat. *e.g. No-one has ever seen a crocodile in these swamps.*

crop up   553, 630
If something **crops up**, it happens or appears unexpectedly. *e.g. The same point may crop up in the committee meeting.*

cross   636
A **cross** is a shape that consists of a vertical line with a shorter horizontal line across it. It is the most important Christian symbol. *e.g. Above the altar was a cross made from wood: this had escaped the fire.*

cross-examination   848
A **cross-examination** of someone during a trial in a court of law is the process of questioning them about the evidence they have given. *e.g. This witness is too ill to face cross-examination.*

cross-examine   848
If you **cross-examine** someone during a trial in a court of law, you question them about the evidence that they have given. *e.g. The prosecuting counsel will now cross-examine the witness.*

crotchety 1135
A person who is **crotchety** is bad tempered and complains a lot. *e.g. His illness makes him really crotchety.*

crowd 1056
1 A **crowd** is a large number of people who have gathered together. *e.g. A crowd of tourists packed the Barbican today.*
2 When people **crowd** round someone or something, they gather closely together around them. *e.g. We crowded round the ice-cream van.*
3 If a group of people **crowd** a place or **crowd** into it, they fill it completely. *e.g. The T.V. men crowded in, examining our equipment.*

crown 1131
1 A **crown** is a circular ornament for the head, usually made of gold and precious jewels. Kings and Queens wear crowns at official ceremonies. *e.g. We saw the crown of Henry VIII when we visited London.*
2 The **Crown** is the monarchy, regarded as an institution concerned with the government of a country rather than as an individual King or Queen. *e.g. All land in Scotland is ultimately owned by the Crown.*

crucial 1300
Something that is **crucial** is extremely important. *e.g. Free child care is a crucial issue to women.*

cruel 366, 527
1 Someone who is **cruel** deliberately causes pain or hardship to people or animals and shows no pity. *e.g. He was a cruel father: the Social Services did well to act.*
2 Something that is **cruel** is very harsh and causes people pain or hardship. *e.g. It's a cruel world where millions are starving.*

cruelty 366, 527
Cruelty is behaviour that deliberately causes pain or hardship to people or animals and shows no pity. *e.g. Mary and Maria did their best to reverse the effects of years of cruelty to the cats.*

cruise 1425
1 A **cruise** is a holiday during which you travel on a ship and visit one or more places. *e.g. He was on a world cruise.*
2 If a ship **cruises** or you **cruise** on it, it sails at a constant speed that is comfortable and unhurried. *e.g. The plan was to cruise to Miami and then take stock.*

crumble 1497
If you **crumble** something soft or brittle, you break it into a lot of little pieces by rubbing it between your fingers. *e.g. Crumble the biscuit over the pudding.*

crumble a stock cube 1497
When you **crumble a stock cube**, you break it into a lot of little pieces by rubbing it between your fingers. *e.g. She crumbled a stock cube into the soup.*

crummy 825, 1181
If you say that something is **crummy**, you mean that it is in very poor condition or of very bad quality. *e.g. It was a crummy old house.*

crush 1378
If you **crush** something, you squash it or make it into a powder by pressing it or grinding it between two hard surfaces. *e.g. Crush the ice and half fill the glass with it.*

cry 453, 574
1 When you **cry**, you produce tears, usually because you are unhappy, frightened or hurt, but sometimes because you are happy or laughing a lot. *e.g. When they told her the bad news, they knew Helen would cry.*
2 If you have a **cry**, you produce tears, usually releasing your feelings when you are unhappy or relieved. *e.g. You have a good cry, and let it all out.*

cry-baby 453
If you say that someone is a **cry-baby**, especially a young child, you mean that they cry a lot for no good reason. *e.g. You're a lot of cry-babies and sissies.*

crying 453
Crying is the behaviour that happens when someone produces tears because they are unhappy, hungry, tired or hurt. *e.g. They worry about the baby's crying.*

cry out 1711
If you **cry** or **cry out**, you call out loudly because you are frightened, unhappy, or in pain. *e.g. He cried out for help.*

cuddle 139, 141
If you **cuddle** someone, you put your arms round them and hold them close, as a way of showing your affection. *e.g. He cuddled his daughter to stop her crying.*

cuddly 139, 141
People, animals, or toys, that are **cuddly** are soft or furry so that you want to cuddle them. *e.g. The children were given cuddly toys.*

culture 63
1 **Culture** or a **culture** consists of the ideas, customs and art that are produced or shared by a particular society. *e.g. He was an admirer of Roman and Greek culture.*
2 A **culture** is a particular society or civilisation, especially one considered in relation to its customs, ideas, beliefs, institutions, languages, etc., or its distinctive

way of life. *e.g. He recommended that they read Padden and Humphries' book on Deaf culture.*

cup 850
A **cup** is a small round container with a handle from which you drink liquids such as tea and coffee. *e.g. She put the cup on the shelf.*

cup and saucer 872
A **cup** is a small round container with a handle from which you drink liquids such as tea and coffee. A **saucer** is a small curved plate on which you stand a cup. *e.g. She brought me her best cup and saucer.*

cupboard 16
A **cupboard** is a piece of furniture which has one or two doors at the front and usually shelves inside it. It is used for keeping things in, such as crockery, tins of food, or clothes. *e.g. I put the tins in the kitchen cupboard.*

cup of coffee/tea 850
A **cup of coffee** or **tea** is a cup containing a quantity of coffee or tea for drinking. *e.g. Can I get you a cup of coffee or tea while you wait?*

cup of tea 872
A **cup of tea** is a cup containing a quantity of tea for drinking. *e.g. Auntie Winnie enjoys a good cup of tea.*

cuppa 850, 872
A **cuppa** is a cup of tea. *e.g. What about a cuppa, since it's so chilly?*

currency 1502, 1508
1 The **currency** of a country is the system of money that is used in it. *e.g. The world currency markets are in turmoil.*
2 The **currency** of a country is the coins and banknotes that are used in it. *e.g. They will change foreign currency.*

curse 905
1 If you **curse**, you swear or make rude comments because you are angry about something. *e.g. He missed the ball, cursed, and then carried on as if nothing had happened.*
2 If you **curse** someone, you sign or say insulting things to them because you are angry with them. *e.g. I was cursing him under my breath for his carelessness.*
3 If you **curse** something, you complain angrily about it, especially using rude language. *e.g. Cursing my plight, I tried to find shelter for the night.*

curtains 278
Curtains are large pieces of material which hang from the top of a window. You pull them across the window when you want to keep light out or prevent people from seeing in. *e.g. She bought new lace curtains.*

custard   1110
Custard is a sweet, yellow sauce, usually flavoured with vanilla, made from milk and eggs or from milk and a powder. *e.g. The children's tea party ended with jelly and custard.*

custom   363
A **custom** is something that people usually do in a particular situation or at a particular time. *e.g. When you sign 'cheers', the custom is to touch the fingers holding the glass rather than the glass itself.*

custom   1207, 1306
1 A **custom** is a traditional activity or festivity. *e.g. My wife thinks it is a custom worth preserving.*
2 A **custom** is something that the people of a society do in particular circumstances because it is regarded as traditional and the right thing to do. *e.g. The custom in Britain is that brides wear white.*

cut   370
1 If you **cut** some part of your body, a sharp object is pushed into it which marks or damages the body's tissues and usually making you bleed. *e.g. Robert cut his knee quite badly.*
2 A **cut** on your body is the wound (usually quite small) made when a sharp object has been pushed into it marking or damaging the body's tissues and usually making you bleed. *e.g. The cut on her upper arm had stopped bleeding.*

cut   752
1 If you **cut** something, you push the blades of a pair of scissors or a similar tool completely through it by closing the handles in order to mark it, damage it, split it in two or remove a piece of it. *e.g. He cut the ribbon.*
2 If you **cut** something, you push the blades of a pair of scissors or a similar tool into it, and move them forwards, opening and closing the handles as you do so, in order to mark it, damage it, split it in two or remove a piece of it. *e.g. She cut the box along the dotted line.*

cut   1293
If you **cut** something, you push a knife or similar tool completely through it horizontally, in order to remove a piece of it. *e.g. She cut the cabbage by the kitchen sink.*

cut back   752
If you **cut back** something such as expenditure or **cut back on it**, you reduce it. *e.g. Congress cut back the funds.*

cut down to size   57
If you are **cut down to size,** you are shown to be less clever or less important than you think you are. *e.g. My ten year old son finished the crossword before me; I felt really cut down to size.*

cutlery   686
The knives, forks and spoons that you eat your food with are referred to as **cutlery**. *e.g. They provide crockery, cutlery and bed linen.*

cut off   752
1 To **cut** something **off** means to stop providing it to someone. *e.g. Gas supplies had now been cut off.*
2 To **cut** someone **off** means to disconnect them when they are having a telephone conversation. *e.g. Don't complain when they cut you off by mistake.*

cut oneself   370
If you **cut yourself**, you accidentally or deliberately push a sharp object into your body, marking or damaging your body's tissue and usually making you bleed. *e.g. I cut myself shaving my legs again.*

cut one's throat   184
If you **cut your throat**, you push a sharp object, such as a knife, into and then across your throat causing it to bleed, usually with the intention of killing yourself. *e.g. She had cut her throat with a kitchen knife.*

cut one's thumb   370
If you **cut your thumb**, you accidentally or deliberately push a sharp object, such as a knife, into it, marking or damaging it and usually making it bleed. *e.g. He cut his thumb with a scalpel in Miss Goldsmith's biology lesson.*

cut on one's thumb   370
A **cut on your thumb** is the wound (usually quite small) made when a sharp object has been pushed into it, marking or damaging it and usually making it bleed. *e.g. Even a tiny cut on your thumb can go septic.*

cut the top off a boiled egg   682
When you **cut the top off a boiled egg**, you use an instrument (usually a knife) to remove a small part of the shell and egg, usually so that you can eat the insides with a spoon. *e.g. I miss seeing mother cut the top off a boiled egg and settle down with Tiddles every morning.*

cycle   92, 654
1 A **cycle** is a bicycle. *e.g. There is a cycle shop on the corner.*
2 If you **cycle**, you ride a bicycle, turning the pedals around with your feet and steering it by holding and turning the handlebars which are connected to the front wheel. *e.g. I decided to cycle to Union Hall.*

cycle (to cycle)   654
If you **cycle**, you ride a bicycle, turning the pedals around with your feet and steering it by holding and turning the handlebars which are connected to the front wheel. *e.g. I decided to cycle to Union Hall.*

cycling   92, 654
Cycling is the activity or sport of bicycle riding. *e.g. Cycling is very popular during the summer months.*

cyclist   92, 654
A **cyclist** is someone who rides a bicycle. *e.g. The road was crowded with cyclists.*

D, d

D
D is the fourth letter of the British manual and English alphabets. See page 850.

dab hand   1581
If you are a **dab hand** at something, you are very good or skilled at doing it. *e.g. She is a dab hand at finding excuses for their mistakes.*

dad   649, 684
People often call their father **dad**. *e.g. My dad doesn't like her very much.*

daddy   649, 684
People often call their father **daddy**. The English word is usually used by children. *e.g. My daddy works in the car factory.*

daft   316, 511, 663
1 If you sign or say that someone is **daft**, you mean that they are stupid or not sensible. *e.g. Don't be daft.*

2 A **daft** action or way of behaving is one that seems silly or stupid, often in a way that makes other people laugh. *e.g. The comedian got them to do daft things at the first show.*
3 Someone who is **daft** signs, says, or does funny things. *e.g. He was so daft we couldn't stop laughing.*

daily   358
1 If something happens **daily**, it happens every day. *e.g. He wrote to her daily.*

2 **Daily** means relating to a single day or to one day at a time. *e.g. You will be paid a daily wage of fifty pounds.*

dale 1402
A **dale** is a valley. *e.g. Look how the sun moves across the fields in the dale.*

damage 1031, 1032
1 If you **damage** something, you harm or spoil it physically, so that it does not work properly or does not look as good as it did before. *e.g. A fire had severely damaged part of the school.*
2 To **damage** something means to have a harmful effect on it and to make it weaker or less successful. *e.g. He claimed that unofficial strikes damage the British economy.*
3 **Damage** is physical harm that is caused to something, especially harm that stops it working properly or makes it look less good. *e.g. I agreed to help pay for the damage to the floor and the ceiling.*
4 **Damage** is a harmful effect that something has on something else. *e.g. He could not repair the damage done to the party's credibility.*

damn 2, 905, 969, 1670
You sign or say **damn** to express anger or annoyance. The English word is considered to be slightly offensive by some people. *e.g. Damn, I'll be late for my class.*

damn (I'll be damned) 1712
If you sign or say **I'll be damned** or **I'm damned**, you are expressing surprise at something. *e.g. 'Well I'm damned,' he signed, 'I never thought you'd do it.'*

damp 1549
1 Something that is **damp** is slightly wet. *e.g. The building was cold and damp.*
2 **Damp** is slight wetness in the air or on the inside walls of a house. *e.g. The paint had not covered the damp on the walls.*

dance 803, 877
1 A **dance** is a series of steps and rhythmic body movements which you do in time to music. *e.g. Before we knew it, we were doing this dance.*
2 A **dance** is a social event where people can dance with each other. *e.g. I hated the big formal dances at college.*
3 **Dance** is the activity of performing dances, especially as a public entertainment. *e.g. VTOL are supreme artists of dance and physical theatre.*
4 If you **dance**, you make rhythmic movements in time to music. *e.g. Hearing people don't realise that a lot of deaf people like to dance.*

dancer 803, 877
A **dancer** is a person who earns money by

dancing, or a person who is dancing. *e.g. He always wanted to be a dancer.*

dancing 803, 877
Dancing is the activity, sometimes competitive, of performing a series of steps and rhythmic body movements in time to music. *e.g. Dancing is a major leisure activity in Britain.*

Dane 780
A **Dane** is a person who comes from Denmark or whose family identity relates to Denmark. *e.g. We met a Dane called Asgar.*

danger 914, 1240
1 **Danger** is the possibility that someone may be harmed or killed. *e.g. The child is too young to understand danger.*
2 A **danger** is something or someone that can hurt or harm you. *e.g. Cigarette smoking is a danger to health.*

dangerous 914, 1240
Something that is **dangerous** is able or likely to hurt and harm you, directly or indirectly. *e.g. It is dangerous to drive with a dirty windscreen.*

Danish 780
1 Someone or something that is **Danish** belongs to or relates to Denmark or its people. *e.g. We are going to Copenhagen to study Danish Sign Language.*
2 **Danish** is the main language spoken in Denmark. *e.g. He spoke Danish fluently.*
3 You can refer to people from Denmark in general, or to a particular group of people from Denmark, as the **Danish**. *e.g. The Danish set the cat amongst the pigeons with their 'no' vote over closer European union.*
4 The address of the **Danish** Deaf Association is: Danske Doves Landsforbund, P.O.Box 704, Fensmarkgade 1, DK-2200 Copenhagen N, Denmark.

dappled 1157
1 Something, especially an animal, that is **dappled** is marked with spots that are a different and usually darker colour than their background. *e.g. The fawn's back was dappled brown and cream.*
2 **Dappled** is also used to describe a pattern that is made up of patches of light and shadow. *e.g. Under the trees, the sunlight through the leaves dappled the grass.*

daring 584, 1200
Someone who is **daring** does things which might be dangerous or which might shock people. *e.g. She was daring to argue with the boss in that way.*

dark 810, 1072, 1465
1 When it is **dark**, there is not enough light to

see properly. *e.g. The room was dark and empty.*
2 The **dark** is the lack of light in a place. *e.g. He was sitting in the dark at the back of the theatre waiting for his friends.*
3 Something that is **dark** is a colour that is quite near black. *e.g. She had long dark hair.*

darken 1072, 1464
If a place or the sky **darkens**, or is **darkened**, there is less light for example because of shadows, clouds or because it is nearly night. *e.g. The sky darkened as we set out to return home.*

darn 869
When you **darn** something, you mend a hole in it by sewing long stitches across the hole and weaving other long stitches in and out across them, so that the hole is filled in. *e.g. I don't want to darn your socks.*

darts 854
1 **Darts** is any one of various competitive games in which you throw darts at a round board which has numbers in it. *e.g. He is in the local darts team.*
2 **Darts** are the small, narrow objects (with sharp points at one end and small blades at the other end to help guide them through the air) which you throw in a game of darts. *e.g. Can we have the darts, landlord, please?*

darts player 854
A **darts player** is someone who takes part in a game of darts. *e.g. He's a fine darts player, but his wife is better.*

dash 1534
1 If you **dash**, you run or go somewhere quickly and suddenly. *e.g. We'll have to dash, I'm afraid.*
2 A **dash** is a quick or sudden burst of movement in a particular direction. *e.g. He made a dash for the door.*

date 30, 1015
1 A **date** is a particular day, for example 20th January, 1991, or a particular year in which something happened or will happen, for example 1890. *e.g. No date was announced for the talks.*
2 When you **date** something, you give the date when it began or when it was made. *e.g. The letter was dated 18th December, 1955.*

daughter 649
Someone's **daughter** is their female child. *e.g. My daughter is studying to be a biologist.*

dawn 1466, 1467
Dawn is the time of day when light first appears in the sky, before the sun rises. *e.g. We got up at dawn.*

day 358, 1466
1 A **day** is one of the seven twenty-four hour

periods of time in a week. *e.g. Tell me which day you would like to visit.*

2 **Day** is the time when it is light or the time you are awake and doing things. *e.g. The explorers travelled by day and rested at night.*

day after tomorrow 789
The **day after tomorrow** is the period of twenty-four hours from midnight to midnight which follows the one after this one. For example, if today is Monday, the day after tomorrow is Wednesday. *e.g. I have to go to the dentist the day after tomorrow, don't forget.*

day before yesterday 756
The **day before yesterday** is the period of twenty-four hours that occurred before the twenty-four hours that preceded today. For example, if today is Friday, the day before yesterday was Wednesday. *e.g. We've been without gas since the day before yesterday.*

daybreak 1467
Daybreak is the time in the morning when light first appears. *e.g. We will leave the house at daybreak.*

day-dream 1570
1 A **day-dream** or **daydream** is a series of thoughts, usually about things that you would like to happen, that take your concentration away from your present surroundings. *e.g. Winning the pools is a nice day-dream.*
2 When you **day-dream** or **daydream**, you think about pleasant things for a period of time. *e.g. I love to day-dream about becoming a film star.*

day (following day) 519
The **following** day is the day after the one that has just been mentioned. *e.g. I saw him last Wednesday and he died the following day.*

day (next day) 519
The **next day** is the one which happens immediately after the one that has just been mentioned. *e.g. We went to bed on the Sunday full of excitement, but it was still raining next day.*

days (two days ago) 756
If you sign or say that something happened **two days ago**, you mean that it happened approximately forty-eight hours before now, or during the day before yesterday. *e.g. I was stuck here doing this two days ago, so I didn't see it.*

days (two days later) 789
If you sign or say that something happened **two days later**, you mean that it happened approximately forty-eight hours after the time just mentioned. *e.g. Two days later, he died of a heart-attack.*

days (two days' time) 789
If you sign or say that something will happen in **two days' time**, you mean that it will happen approximately forty-eight hours in the future, or during the day after tomorrow. *e.g. It's Thursday today, so the wedding is in two days' time now.*

dead 699
1 A person, animal, or plant that is **dead** is no longer living. *e.g. I thought you were dead.*
2 If a part of your body goes **dead**, you cannot feel any sensation in it for a short time. *e.g. My arm's gone dead.*

deaf 677
1 Someone who is **deaf** is unable to hear, or can do so only to a very limited extent, especially because of illness, injury or a hereditary condition. *e.g. The number of deaf people in Britain is increasing because of industrial noise in the workplace.*
2 The **deaf** are people who are completely or almost completely deaf. *e.g. She goes to a school for the deaf.*

Deaf 677, 678
1 If you are **Deaf**, you are deaf, use a sign language and are identified as a member of a Deaf community. *e.g. All my family are Deaf.*
2 The **Deaf** are people who are deaf, use a sign language and are identified as members of the Deaf community. *e.g. The Deaf tell us that they welcome the new service.*
3 **Deaf** can also mean relating to or concerned with Deaf people. *e.g. The school intends to introduce Deaf history as a curriculum subject from next September.*

deaf and dumb 678
A person who is **deaf and dumb** can neither hear nor speak, or can hear and speak only to a very limited extent. Many people find this English phrase offensive and instead use 'deaf without speech'. See **deaf without speech**. *e.g. People used to call them the deaf and dumb kids, and make fun of their signs.*

deaf-blind 679
1 Someone who is **deaf-blind** can neither hear nor see, or can hear and see only to a very limited extent. *e.g. Representatives of the Deaf-Blind Association attended the meeting.*
2 **Deaf-blind** means of, relating to or concerned with deaf-blind people. *e.g. It's a new braille publication covering deaf-blind issues of all kinds.*

deaf-blind alphabet 1112
The **deaf-blind alphabet** uses a conventional arrrangement of handshapes to create letters and words on the palm and fingers of another person, usually one who is both deaf and blind. *e.g. They learned the deaf-blind alphabet so they could work as home helps with deaf-blind people.*

deaf-blind manual alphabet 1112
The **deaf-blind manual alphabet** uses a conventional arrangement of handshapes to create letters and words on the palm and fingers of another person, usually one who is both deaf and blind. *e.g. Using the deaf-blind manual alphabet, they interpreted the Prime Minister's remarks to the attentive audience.*

deaf-blind person 679
A **deaf-blind person** is someone who can neither hear nor see, or can hear and see only to a very limited extent. *e.g. A deaf-blind person came to the club last night.*

Deaf Communicating Terminal (DCT) 1019
A **Deaf Communicating Terminal** is any device enabling visual messages to be sent as text over the telephone network to individuals who have the same or a similar device. The telephone receiver is fitted on to cups on the device, the number is dialled in the usual way, and communication is achieved by the exchange of electronically transmitted messages, typed on a keyboard on the device and appearing on a narrow screen. *e.g. The arrival of the Deaf Communicating Terminal revolutionised interaction in the Deaf community.*

deaf person 677
A **deaf person** is someone who is unable to hear, or can do so only to a very limited extent. *e.g. There was a deaf person there but he didn't use BSL.*

Deaf person 677, 678
A **Deaf person** is someone who is deaf, uses a sign language, and is identified as a member of the Deaf community. *e.g. When I got on the train, there was a Deaf person there going to Brighton, so we had a chat about this and that.*

deaf without speech 678
Someone who is **deaf without speech** cannot hear, or can do so only to a very limited extent, and cannot or does not choose to communicate by spoken English. *e.g. He makes a point of telling people, on paper, that he's deaf without speech.*

deal 1387, 1388
A **deal** is an agreement or arrangement that is made, especially in business. *e.g. It was probably the best business deal I ever made.*

dealings 1387
Your **dealings** with a person or organisation are the relations that you have with them or the business that you do with them. *e.g. The grocer*

was always honest in his dealings with his customers.

deal with   272
When you **deal with** a situation or problem, you do whatever is necessary to achieve the result you want. *e.g. They learned how to deal with difficult customers.*

dear   989
Something that is **dear** costs a lot of money, more than you expected or more than seems reasonable. *e.g. Oh, that's dear! Let's try the butcher's in the High Street.*

death   699
1 **Death** is the permanent end of the life of a person or animal, when the heart stops beating and all other functions of the body and brain stop too. *e.g. After the death of her parent, she went to live with an aunt.*
2 A **death** is the loss of a person's life. *e.g. The two deaths in the accident could have been prevented.*

debate   437, 564
1 A **debate** is a discussion in which people express opposing opinions about a subject. *e.g. We will hold a debate on current education policy.*
2 When people **debate** something they discuss it fairly formally, putting forward opposing views. *e.g. They debated the notion that the death penalty should be re-introduced.*

debate   1387
When people **debate** something, they discuss it, putting forward various points for consideration. *e.g. Look, I don't want to sit here and debate this for hours.*

debt (in debt)   544
If you are **in debt** or get **into debt**, you owe money. *e.g. Father had been in debt for a long time.*

decapitate   1586
To **decapitate** someone means to cut off their head. *e.g. The French used the guillotine to decapitate their victims.*

deceive   753
If you **deceive** someone, you make them believe something that is not true, usually in order to get some advantage for yourself. *e.g. I deceived her into coming here.*

decide   401, 1329, 1360
1 If you **decide** to do something, you choose to do it, usually after you have thought carefully about the other possibilities. *e.g. She had to decide whether to leave or stay.*
2 When something is **decided**, people choose what something should be like or what should be done. *e.g. The case is to be decided by the International Court.*

3 If an event or fact **decides** something, it makes it certain that there will be a particular result or choice. *e.g. The level of interest rates will decide the future of the company.*
4 If you **decide** that something is the case, you form that opinion after considering the facts. *e.g. I couldn't decide whether she was joking.*

decision   401, 1329, 1360
A **decision** is a choice that you make about what you think should be done or about which is the best of various alternatives. *e.g. The doctor's decision to purchase a text telephone for her practice was widely welcomed by the local Deaf community.*

deckchair   44
A **deckchair** is a light folding chair with a wooden frame and a canvas seat. Deckchairs are used mainly out of doors, for example, in the garden, at the seaside, or on a ship. *e.g. We can hire deck chairs on the beach.*

declaration   456
1 A **declaration** is a firm, emphatic statement which is meant to show that you have no doubts about what you are signing or saying. *e.g. He was embarrassed by her declaration of love, made in the middle of the pub.*
2 A **declaration** is an official announcement or statement. *e.g. It was a formal declaration of war.*

declare   456
1 If you **declare** something, you sign or say it firmly and in a way that is meant to show that you believe it is true. *e.g. He declared he would never steal again.*
2 If you **declare** an attitude or intention, you make it known to other people by expressing it clearly. *e.g. He declared his intention to fight the election.*
3 If you **declare** something, you state it officially. *e.g. At his trial, he was declared innocent.*

decline   1395
1 If something **declines**, it becomes smaller, weaker, or worse than it was. *e.g. Since 1971, the party's influence has declined.*
2 If there is a **decline** in something, it becomes smaller, weaker or worse than it was. *e.g. Britain is experiencing the decline of her motor industry.*

decorate   1347, 1414
If you **decorate** a building or room, you put a new covering such as paint or wallpaper on the walls, ceiling and woodwork. *e.g. We said we would do all the decorating.*

decoration   835
A **decoration** is something, such as a medal, which is given to someone as an official honour or reward. *e.g. He received his decoration for bravery from the Queen.*

decorator   1347, 1414
A **decorator** is a person whose job it is to paint houses or put coverings such as wallpaper on the walls. *e.g. We employed a decorator for the kitchen.*

decrease   728, 1393, 1395
1 When something or the quantity of something **decreases**, it becomes smaller or weaker. *e.g. Our powers of recuperation decrease as we grow older.*
2 A **decrease** is a reduction in the quantity, size, or strength of something. *e.g. There is a decrease in the number of cars on the road.*

decree   401, 456
1 If someone in authority **decrees** that something must happen or is the case, they order or state this officially. *e.g. The chief of police decreed that there would be a full investigation.*
2 A **decree** is an official order, especially one made by the ruler of a country. *e.g. A decree was issued that all firearms were to be banned.*

deduct   1159
When you **deduct** an amount of something from a total, you reduce the total by that amount. *e.g. We will deduct tax automatically from your wages.*

deduction   1159
1 A **deduction** is an amount that has been subtracted from a total. *e.g. This figure indicates the deduction made for National Insurance.*
2 **Deduction** is the subtraction of an amount from a total. *e.g. Deduction of this sum must not occur, except in a Leap Year.*

deep   461
1 If something is **deep**, it extends a long way down from the surface. *e.g. They dug deep into the earth.*
2 If you have a **deep** discussion, you converse seriously and for some time, trying to understand the complexities of a particular subject. *e.g. We had a deep discussion about Le Page's sociolinguistic theories.*

deer   1071
A **deer** is a large, wild animal that eats grass and leaves. Male deer usually have large, branching horns. *e.g. A deer came out of the trees at the roadside.*

defence   72
1 **Defence** is action that is taken to protect someone or something against attack. *e.g. The defence of civil liberties must be continued.*
2 A **defence** is also something that you sign or say in support of ideas or actions that have been criticised. *e.g. His economists have drawn up a defence of his policy.*
3 The **defence** is the case that is presented by a

lawyer for the person in a trial who has been accused of a crime. *e.g. He gave evidence for the defence in the Hennesey case.*

defend   72
1 If you **defend** someone or something, you do something in order to protect them. *e.g. The village had to defend itself against raiders.*
2 In a court of law, when a lawyer **defends** a person who has been accused of a crime, he or she tries to prove that the charges are not true or that there was an excuse for the crime. *e.g. My lawyer will defend me.*
3 If you **defend** yourself, you argue in support of your actions or views when they have been criticised. *e.g. The bank has defended its actions in these cases.*

defend   112
1 If you **defend** someone or something, you do something in order to protect them. *e.g. The village had to defend itself against raiders.*
2 If you **defend** yourself, you argue in support of your actions or views when they have been criticised. *e.g. The bank has defended its actions in these cases.*
3 If a football team, hockey team, etc., **defends**, they are trying to stop the opposing players scoring a goal. *e.g. Middlesbrough defended very well in the first half, but Newcastle United eventually ran out 3—1 winners.*

defender   72
1 A **defender** is a person who does something in order to protect others. *e.g. Robin Hood was a defender of the poor.*
2 A **defender** is a person who actively supports a particular set of beliefs or actions which have been criticised. *e.g. He was known as a defender of monetarist economic theory.*

defensive   112
You use **defensive** to describe things that are intended to protect someone or something. *e.g. Five players formed a defensive wall.*

defer   885
If you **defer** an event or action, you change the time at which it is due to happen and arrange for it to happen at a later date. *e.g. The company will defer payment for whatever length of time you require.*

defer   1461
If you **defer** to someone, you accept their opinion or do what they want you to do, even though you may not agree with it yourself, because you respect them or their authority. *e.g. I defer to you on this matter given your greater experience of teaching BSL.*

deference   1461
Deference is polite and considerate behaviour that you show to someone because

you have a lot of respect from them or for their authority. *e.g. She is treated with deference by her colleagues.*

deferential   1461
Someone who is **deferential** shows respect and regard for someone else's opinions and wishes. *e.g. They were polite and deferential as always.*

deferment   885
Deferment is the changing of the time or date when something is supposed to happen so that it will happen at a later time or date. *e.g. Further deferment of payment will not be allowed.*

definite   401, 1323
If something is **definite**, it is firm and clear, and unlikely to be changed. *e.g. There's a definite date for the wedding.*

degree   875
A **degree** is a qualification which is usually awarded by a university or college to a student who has completed a specified course or as an honorary distinction to a particular individual. It may also refer to the course itself or to the document which records the qualification. *e.g. The then Chairperson of the British Deaf Association, John Young, was awarded an honorary degree by the University of Durham in 1990.*

deity   311
A **deity** is a god or goddess. *e.g. He read about Blake's visions of the deity.*

delay   885, 1003
1 If you **delay** something, you do not do it until a later time. *e.g. She agreed to delay starting divorce proceedings for six months.*
2 If you **delay** doing something, you fail to do it immediately or by a certain time, often because you cannot make your mind up quickly enough. *e.g. Rashid has a tendency to delay making difficult decisions.*
3 If you **delay** doing something, you deliberately take longer than necessary to do it. *e.g. They're delaying in the hope that they won't have to pay.*
4 A **delay** is a period of time during which an action or event is not allowed to happen until a later time. *e.g. They were arguing for a delay in introducing the new law.*
5 A **delay** is a situation in which an action or event cannot happen immediately and which can cause someone or something to be late. *e.g. This interruption is causing delay.*
6 **Delay** is a failure to do something immediately, for example if you cannot make up your mind quickly enough. *e.g. There was no time left for delay or hesitation.*

delegate   647
A **delegate** is a person who is chosen to make

decisions on behalf of a group of other people, especially at a meeting. *e.g. Each delegate was issued with a copy of the Association's annual report as they entered the hall.*

delegate   1205
If you **delegate** duties or responsibilities, you tell someone to do them on your behalf. *e.g. A good manager must learn to delegate and share out the workload.*

deliberate   313
If you **deliberate**, you think about something carefully before making a decision. *e.g. We waited for two days for the jury to deliberate its verdict.*

deliberation   313
Deliberation is careful and often lengthy consideration of an issue. *e.g. After due deliberation, I decided to accept the offer of a place on the course.*

delicious   175, 345, 468
Something that is **delicious** has a very pleasant taste. *e.g. My mother makes delicious apple pie which she always serves on a Sunday.*

delight   1390
1 **Delight** is a feeling of very great pleasure. *e.g. His delight was obvious.*
2 If something **delights** you, it gives you a lot of pleasure. *e.g. It delights me to see her looking so well.*

delighted   1390
If you are **delighted**, you are extremely pleased and excited about something. *e.g. He was delighted to meet them again.*

deliver   1377, 1391
If you **deliver** something stacked up or in a box, you give it to someone. *e.g. He asked me to deliver the papers.*

deliver   1626
If you **deliver** something, you give it to someone. *e.g. Deliver these to Archie with my compliments.*

demand   350
1 If you **demand** something, you ask for it very forcefully. *e.g. The policeman demanded to see their identity cards.*
2 If you **demand**, you ask a question in a forceful way. *e.g. I demanded to know where it was hidden.*
3 A **demand** is a firm request for something. *e.g. Bishop Tutu's demand for sanctions was supported by other church leaders.*

demand   1219, 1317
1 A **demand** is a firm request for something. *e.g. His demand for better working conditions seemed to have helped.*

2 If there is **demand** for something, a lot of people want to buy it or have it. *e.g. The demand for health care is unlimited.*
3 If you **demand** something, you ask for it very forcefully. *e.g. I'm sorry, I have to demand that you hand over the camera.*

demonstrate   1373, 1384
1 If you **demonstrate** something to someone, you show them how it works. *e.g. She will now demonstrate how to make bread.*
2 If someone or something **demonstrates** a fact, theory or principle, they make it clear to people. *e.g. Information like this will clearly demonstrate, to anyone that cares to look, the truth of these statements.*

demonstration   1373, 1384
1 A **demonstration** of something is a talk by someone who shows you how to do it or how it works. *e.g. A demonstration of the new machinery is scheduled for Tuesday.*
2 **Demonstration** is the activity of showing how to do something or how something works. *e.g. Demonstration of the product will probably be more effective than words.*

demonstrator   1373, 1384
A **demonstrator** is a person who shows people how something is done or works, such as an experiment, machine or device, by doing or operating it themself. *e.g. He's a demonstrator of kitchen equipment at Lewis's.*

denial   5, 56
1 A **denial** of something such as an accusation is a statement declaring that it is not true. *e.g. He made a personal denial of all the charges against him.*
2 The **denial** of something that you think people have a right to is a refusal to let them have it, usually by a person or group in authority. *e.g. They protested against the continued denial of civil liberties.*

Denmark   780
Denmark is a kingdom in Northern Europe between the Baltic and the North Sea which is a member of the European Community. *e.g. Britta will be coming over from Denmark for a meeting next week.*

dentist   259
1 A **dentist** is a person who is qualified to examine and treat people's teeth. *e.g. My dentist checks my teeth every six months.*
2 The **dentist's** is used to refer to the surgery or clinic where a dentist works. *e.g. The dentist's is under the viaduct.*

deny   5, 56
1 If you **deny** something, you sign or say that it is not true. *e.g. The minister denied doing anything illegal.*

2 If you **deny** someone something that they want, you do not let them have it. *e.g. He has denied you access to the information you requested.*

deodorant   634
Deodorant or a **deodorant** is a spray that you can use to hide or prevent the smell of perspiration on your body. *e.g. The deodorant's all gone.*

depart   1220, 1566
When someone or something **departs** from a place, they leave it. *e.g. The train was supposed to depart at six o'clock.*

depend   594, 1317, 1380, 1653
1 If you **depend** on someone or something, you need them in order to be able to survive physically, financially, or emotionally. *e.g. The doctors depend on the money paid by patients.*
2 If you can **depend** on someone or something, you know that they will support you or help you when you need them. *e.g. Fortunately, I can depend on Kris to help us out.*
3 If you sign or say that something **depends** on something else, you mean that it will only happen if the circumstances are right. *e.g. The success of the meeting will depend on the chairman being efficient.*

dependence   1380, 1653
Dependence is a constant and regular need that someone has for something in order to be able to live or work properly. *e.g. Laura has developed a dependence on pain-killing drugs.*

dependent   594, 1380, 1653
1 If a country, group or society, etc., is **dependent** on something, it needs that thing in order to be able to survive economically or politically. *e.g. Europe is still dependent on Middle East oil.*
2 If you are **dependent** on someone or something, you need them in order to be able to survive physically, financially, or emotionally. *e.g. I have no pension and therefore am dependent on my daughters.*

depends   450
If you sign or say that something **depends** on something else, you mean that it will only happen if the circumstances are right. *e.g. Will the bid be successful? That all depends on the way we handle the publicity.*

deposit   1318, 1507, 1679
1 When you **deposit** a sum of money, you pay it into a bank account or other savings account, usually with the intention of leaving it there for some time. *e.g. Can you deposit this money in my savings account?*
2 A **deposit** is a sum of money which is in a bank account or other savings account and which will probably be left there for some

time. *e.g. Most banks are paying 11% on deposits of more than £5,000.*
3 A **deposit** is a sum of money which is part of the full price of something such as a car or a house, and which you pay when you agree to buy it. *e.g. We won't be getting married until we've saved enough for the deposit on a house.*
4 A **deposit** is a sum of money which you pay when you start renting something such as a car or a flat. The money is returned to you if you do not damage what you have rented. *e.g. I had to put down one hundred pounds deposit on the flat for breakages.*

depress   1270, 1365
If something **depresses** you, it makes you feel sad and hopeless. *e.g. It depresses me to visit her in hospital.*

depressed   1270, 1365
If you are **depressed**, you are sad and feel hopeless. *e.g. I realised I was becoming depressed and apathetic.*

depressing   1270
If something is **depressing**, it makes you feel sad and hopeless. *e.g. It's just depressing to think how much there is still to do.*

depression   1270, 1365
Depression is a mental state in which you feel extremely unhappy or hopeless and have no enthusiasm for anything. *e.g. He worried himself into a depression.*

depth   461
1 The **depth** of something is the distance between its top and bottom surfaces. *e.g. The lake was 200 metres in depth.*
2 If you deal with a subject in **depth,** you deal with it very thoroughly and consider all the aspects of it. *e.g. We liked to discuss the Sunday sermon in some depth.*

descend   1237
1 To **descend** is to move forwards and downwards. *e.g. The car will descend at an average of twenty-two miles per hour.*
2 You sign or say that something such as a flight of stairs **descends** to a lower position when it leads to that position. *e.g. The valley descends to the banks of the fjord.*

descent   1237
1 A **descent** is a downward slope, especially one you are travelling down. *e.g. We scrambled down the steep descent into the ravine.*
2 A **descent** is an occasion or process of moving downwards and forwards. *e.g. The descent was by far the worst part.*

desert   1046
A **desert** is a large area of land where there is very little water or rain and very few plants.

e.g. He almost died when he was lost in the desert.

design 768
1 When you **design** something, you plan and create a picture of it in your mind and you make a detailed drawing of it from which it can be built or made. *e.g. The house was designed by local builders.*
2 When you **design** something, you plan, prepare and decide on all the details of it. *e.g. Tests have been designed to assess mathematical ability.*
3 A **design** is the detailed plan or scheme for a project or piece of work. *e.g. This is the latest design: as you can see, we've amended it in line with your suggestions.*

designer 768
A **designer** is a person who makes a detailed plan or scheme for a project or piece of work. *e.g. Mr. Fowler was the designer, so perhaps he'll tell us about it.*

desire 1281
1 If you **desire** something, you want it. *e.g. Of course I desire to continue my career in politics.*
2 A **desire** is a strong feeling that you want to do something or to get something. *e.g. My desire now is to see the end of this hardship.*

desire 1490
1 If you **desire** something, you want it very much. *e.g. He passionately desired a career in television.*
2 A **desire** is a strong feeling that you want to do something or to get something. *e.g. They teach BSL because of their desire to see greater communication between Deaf and hearing people.*

desire 1542
1 If you **desire** something, your emotions are aroused because you want it very much indeed. *e.g. I desire an end to this dreadful war.*
2 **Desire** for someone is a strong feeling of sexual attraction towards them. *e.g. Her desire for him disappeared at the very mention of condoms.*
3 If you **desire** someone, you have strong feelings of sexual attraction towards them. *e.g. I desire you: I have always desired you: why do you reject me?*

dessert 240, 732
Dessert is sweet food served usually after the main course or at the end of a meal. *e.g. What would you like for dessert, ice cream or fruit crumble?*

dessert spoon 240
A **dessert spoon** is a spoon, usually used for eating dessert, which is oval in shape and about twice as big as a teaspoon. *e.g. Put the dessert spoons on the table.*

destroy 1031, 1032
1 If you **destroy** something, you cause so much damage to it that it is completely ruined or does not exist any more. *e.g. We will destroy this temple if you do not surrender.*
2 To **destroy** something means to cause it not to exist any more. *e.g. There are some who would like to destroy the state.*
3 If a person or an event **destroys** someone, they ruin their life by making them so depressed that there seems to be no hope for them in the future. *e.g. The loss of his business and of his wife finally destroyed him.*

detach 1616
If you **detach** yourself from something, you feel less involved in it. *e.g. I have decided to detach myself from politics.*

detail 868
1 A **detail** is an individual fact, piece of information, or visual feature which you notice when you look at something carefully or remember when you think about it. *e.g. He described the party down to the last detail.*
2 **Detail** consists of all the small features which are often not noticed when people first look at or think about something. *e.g. Their attention to detail was famous.*
3 If you go into **detail** or **details** about something, you explain it thoroughly, including all the small pieces of information. *e.g. I don't want to go into detail about the assessment procedure used for teachers of British Sign Language.*

detective 261
A **detective** is someone whose job is to discover what has happened in a particular situation and to find the people involved, especially when a crime has been committed. Some detectives work in the police force and others work privately. *e.g. She was interviewed by Detective Inspector Steep.*

deteriorate 926
1 If something **deteriorates**, it becomes worse in condition. *e.g. His eyesight had begun to deteriorate.*
2 If something **deteriorates**, it becomes more difficult or unpleasant. *e.g. By their fifth anniversary, the relationship was starting to deteriorate.*

determined 804
If you are **determined** to do something, you have made a firm decision to do it and will not let anything stop you. *e.g. He is determined to win in the end.*

detest 1007
If you **detest** someone or something, you dislike them very much. *e.g. They detest the thought of living elsewhere.*

devastate 1031, 1032
If something **devastates** a place, it destroys it or damages it very badly. *e.g. The hurricane looks likely to devastate the plantation.*

develop 1063
If something **develops** or you **develop** it, it grows or expands over time into a larger, better or more complete form. *e.g. We'd like to see the Devon tourist industry develop.*

develop 1718
1 When something **develops** or you **develop** it, it grows or changes over a period of time into a larger, better or more complete form. *e.g. The bud develops into a flower.*
2 If a problem **develops**, it starts to exist and gradually becomes more severe. *e.g. A new crisis began to develop.*
3 To **develop** a characteristic, illness, or fault means to begin to have it. *e.g. She developed an enormous appetite.*
4 If someone **develops** something, they produce it by improving the original design. *e.g. Their new engine was developed from a petrol motor.*

development 1718
1 **Development** is the gradual growth or formation of something. *e.g. This can harm a child's psychological development.*
2 A **development** is an event which is likely to have an effect on the situation in a particular place or field of activity. *e.g. Recent developments in Latin America suggest that the situation may be improving.*

device 556
A **device** is an object that has been made or built for a particular purpose, for example for recording or measuring something. *e.g. It's a very handy device, and fits into the smallest pocket.*

devil 939
1 In Christianity, the **devil** or **Devil** is the most powerful evil spirit. *e.g. It is said that some worship the Devil.*
2 You can use **devil** to sign or speak about people. For example, if you call someone a silly **devil**, you are declaring that you think they are silly. *e.g. You lucky devil!*
3 You can lightheartedly call someone a **devil** if they have done something naughty or something likely to make another person angry. *e.g. He spiked my drinks with vodka, the devil.*

devise 768
If you **devise** a plan, system or machine, you have the idea for it and you work out how you could create it and use it. *e.g. It has been necessary to devise new instruments to look at the planets.*

devoted 110
Devoted is used to describe activities which involve great effort, concentration, and dedication. *e.g. She was awarded the BDA's Medal of Honour for her devoted service to the Association over many years.*

devoted (be devoted to) 512
If you **are devoted** to someone or something you admire them so much or are so enthusiastic about them that you may be unable to see their faults or weaknesses. *e.g. I'm afraid she's devoted to her grandchildren: meanwhile, they're out joyriding.*

diagram 562
A **diagram** is a simple drawing that is used to explain how something works. *e.g. This is a simple diagram showing compass directions.*

dialogue 458, 1387
1 **Dialogue** is communcation or discussion between people or groups. *e.g. The unions continued to seek dialogue.*
2 A **dialogue** is a conversation between two people, especially one in a book, film, or play. *e.g. Their dialogue was interrupted by Philip's entrance.*

dictaphone 1737
A **dictaphone** is the name of a particular type of small taperecorder on which you can record letters, etc., so that they can be typed later. *e.g. The dictaphone is on Margaret's desk.*

dictate onto a dictaphone 1737
If you **dictate onto a dictaphone**, you say or read aloud into a dictaphone the letters, etc., you later wish to have typed. *e.g. He dictated onto the dictaphone the letters that were to be sent to the successful applicants.*

dictionary 1456
1 A **dictionary** is a book in which the signs or words of a language are arranged according to linguistic principles, usually by handshape or in alphabetical order, and their meanings are explained. *e.g. He asked if he could borrow her COBUILD English dictionary.*
2 A **dictionary** is a book in which the signs or words of one language are displayed, arranged according to handshape or in alphabetical order, and are followed by signs or words which have the same meaning in another language. *e.g. Maria would like a Welsh-English dictionary for her birthday.*

did 1566, 1643
If you **did** an action, activity or task, you performed it. *e.g. Did you see that excellent interpreting on 'Sign On' last Saturday?*

die 699
When people, animals and plants **die**, they stop living. *e.g. His mother died when he was four.*

differ 429
If two things **differ**, they are unlike each other in some way. *e.g. Modern cars differ from the early ones.*

difference 429
A **difference** is a quality in something which makes it unlike something else. *e.g. Notice the difference in height between John and Julia.*

different 429
1 Someone or something that is **different** is not like someone or something else in one or more ways. *e.g. The meeting was different from previous ones.*
2 Two **different** things are separate and distinct from each other although they are the same kind of thing. *e.g. She has accounts with two different banks.*

difficult 208
1 Something that is **difficult** is not easy to do, understand, or solve. *e.g. That's a difficult question.*
2 Someone who is **difficult** behaves in an unreasonable and unhelpful way. *e.g. She was a difficult child.*

difficulty 208
1 A **difficulty** is something that is a problem for you. *e.g. We will have to overcome many difficulties.*
2 If you have **difficulty** doing something, you are not able to do it easily. *e.g. She could breathe with difficulty.*

dig 153, 1223, 1565
If you **dig**, you break up soil and prepare it for planting by turning it over with a spade or garden fork. *e.g. I was digging the allotment yesterday.*

dig a hole 153, 1223, 1565
If you **dig a hole**, you use a spade or similar tool to remove earth or another substance from a particular place to create an opening in the ground. *e.g. He began to dig a hole by the side of the road.*

digest 536
When you **digest** food, it passes through your stomach and is broken down so that your body can use it. *e.g. I can't digest cheese or eggs.*

digestion 536
1 **Digestion** is the process of passing food through your stomach so that your body can break it down and use it. *e.g. A good walk aids digestion.*
2 Your **digestion** is the system in your body which breaks down food to absorb it. *e.g. The consultant says my digestion is poor.*

dig up 153
If you **dig** something **up**, you remove it from the ground where it has been buried. *e.g. They had to dig up six coffins and move them to the new cemetery.*

dig with a fork 839
If you **dig with a fork**, you turn over or move earth or plant material, using a large garden tool with three or four long prongs attached to a handle. *e.g. Mr. Willett will dig the garden with a fork while you weed the flowerbeds.*

dig with a spade 1223
1 If you **dig with a spade**, you make a hole in the ground using a flat metal blade with a long handle. *e.g. You dig here with a spade, and I'll check the map again.*
2 If you **dig with a spade**, you turn over soil and prepare it for planting. *e.g. I can't dig it with a spade because my back will hurt: I'll have to get down with a trowel.*

diligent 1448
Someone who is **diligent** works hard in a careful and conscientious way. *e.g. He was a diligent man, loved by his constituents.*

dim 1072, 1075
Something that is **dim** is rather dark because there is not much light in it. *e.g. The room was dim.*

din 521
A **din** is a very loud and unpleasant noise that lasts for a long time. *e.g. They were unable to sleep because of the din coming from the bar.*

dinner 583
Dinner is the main meal of the day. *e.g. I haven't had dinner yet.*

dinner 686, 730
1 **Dinner** is the main meal of the day. *e.g. I've made you a lasagne for dinner, all right?*
2 A **dinner** is a social event in the evening at which a meal is served. *e.g. Mrs. Thatcher attended a dinner at the Mansion House last night.*

dinosaur 1673
A **dinosaur** was a large reptile which lived in prehistoric times and which is now extinct. There were many kinds of dinosaur, some of which were very large indeed. *e.g. He collected models of dinosaurs.*

diploma 875
A **diploma** is a qualification which is usually awarded by a university, college or professional organisation to a student who has completed a specified course. It may also refer to the course itself or to the document which records the qualification. A diploma

course is usually at a lower academic level or of shorter duration than a degree. *e.g. Margaret is taking a Diploma in Deaf Studies at the University of Bristol.*

diplomat 1387
1 A **diplomat** is a senior official who negotiates with another country on behalf of his or her own country, usually working as a member of an embassy. *e.g. Nigerian diplomats were saying privately that their confidence in the strategy was ebbing.*
2 A **diplomat** is someone who is skilful at being tactful and signing, saying or doing things in a way that does not offend people. *e.g. William was a good diplomat as well as social worker.*

diplomatic 1387
Someone who is **diplomatic** is able to be tactful and do things without offending people. *e.g. He was very diplomatic when telling the boss he'd made a mistake.*

direct 272
1 The person who **directs** a project or a group of people is responsible for leading and organising it or them. *e.g. She had directed a major mathematics project.*
2 The person who **directs** a film, play, or television programme is in charge of it and organises the way it is made and performed. *e.g. Terry will direct the next 'See Hear' programme.*

direct 1246, 1299
1 **Direct** means going or aimed straight towards a place or object. *e.g. You can get a train direct to London.*
2 A **direct** attack or challenge is one made openly so that there is no doubt about what is being done. *e.g. This policy is a direct challenge to the government.*
3 If you **direct** something at a particular person or thing, you aim it at them or intend it to affect them. *e.g. I'd like to direct my next question at Tariq.*
4 Someone who is **direct** signs, talks or behaves in a very honest, open and perhaps tactless way. *e.g. I warn you, I can be very direct in my manner.*

director 272, 450
1 A **director** is someone who has responsibility for organising and leading a group of people who are working together. *e.g. She is the Director of the University's Business School.*
2 A **director** is someone who is on the board of a company or business organisation or in charge of a government organisation. *e.g. She is to become a director of British Petroleum.*
3 A **director** is someone who decides how a play, film, or television programme will be performed or made. *e.g. He wishes to train as a television director at NEMTC.*

dirt 1020
Dirt is dust, mud or stains on a surface, fabric or person. *e.g. After playing in the fields, my son was covered with dirt.*

dirty 1020
Something that is **dirty** has dust, mud, or stains on it and needs to be cleaned. *e.g. I had never seen a kitchen so dirty.*

disability 561, 1405
1 A **disability** is a physical impairment or mental illness that is considered to severely affect your life. *e.g He was awarded a disability pension after being severely wounded in the war.*
2 **Disability** is the particular disadvantage experienced by people with physical or mental impairments which arises from the present social organisation of society. *e.g. Disability is not something we can walk away from.*
3 You may use **disability** when you are referring to issues, organisations, etc., that belong to or relate to disabled persons. *e.g. Representatives from a number of disability organisations are to attend the meeting.*
4 You may use **disability** in relation to the study, history, etc., of society from the perspective of disabled persons. *e.g. Mike Oliver's lecture was on the politics of disability.*

disabled 561, 1405
1 Someone who is **disabled** is a person with a physical or mental impairment who experiences particular disadvantages as a consequence of the present social organisation of society. *e.g. He suggested they read Vic Finkelstein's article 'We are not disabled, you are'.*
2 Someone who is **disabled** has a physical or mental impairment that is considered to severely affect their life. *e.g. She has to look after a disabled aunt.*
3 You can refer to people who are disabled as the **disabled**. Some people object to this usage. *e.g. It is an organisation for, rather than of, the disabled.*

disabled person 561, 1405
1 A **disabled person** or a **person with a disability** is someone with a physical or mental impairment who experiences particular disadvantages as a consequence of the present social organisation of society. *e.g. A group of disabled persons blocked Oxford Street in protest at their lack of access to public transport.*
2 A **disabled person** or a **person with a disability** is someone with a physical or mental impairment that is considered to severely affect their life. *e.g. As a disabled person, she was entitled to a mobility allowance.*

disagree 130
1 If you **disagree** with someone or **disagree** with what they sign or say, you do not accept

that what they sign or say is true or correct. *e.g. I disagree with John. Why shouldn't hearing parents learn to sign?*
2 If you **disagree** with a particular action or proposal, you disapprove of it and believe that it is wrong. *e.g. Li-Ho disagreed with the abandonment of the project.*

disagreement 130
1 **Disagreement** is the act of signing, saying or showing that you object to something such as a proposal. *e.g. They expressed their disagreement with the proposed policy of integrated education.*
2 **Disagreement** or a **disagreement** is a situation in which people have different opinions and cannot reach a decision. *e.g. There was disagreement as to what should be done.*

disallow 109, 917
If you **disallow** something, you state officially that it is not accepted because it is not permissable or it has not been done correctly. *e.g. The electoral court was always likely to disallow his appeal.*

disappear 1548, 1555
1 If someone or something **disappears**, they go where you can no longer see them. *e.g. I shall disappear in a puff of smoke.*
2 If something **disappears**, it stops existing or happening. *e.g. Some newspapers are going to disappear as a result of this strike.*

disappear at speed 1534
If someone or something **disappears at speed**, they go very quickly some distance away from you, where you can no longer see them. *e.g. He jumped into his car, pressed the accelerator and disappeared at speed down the road.*

disappoint 792
When things or people **disappoint** you, they do not satisfy you because they are not as good or as reliable as you had hoped, or do not do what you want them to do or happen as you had hoped. *e.g. The cancellation of the party will disappoint everyone.*

disappointment 792
A **disappointment** is an event, person or situation that is not as good or successful as you had hoped and which makes you feel disappointed. *e.g. His reply was a disappointment.*

disassociate 884
If you **disassociate** yourself from something or someone, you show that you are not connected with them. *e.g. Some Deaf people wanted to disassociate themselves from the decisions of the committee.*

disc 552
1 A **disc** is a flat, circular shape or object. *e.g. The gold disc commemorated a special occasion.*
2 A **disc** is also a gramophone record. *e.g. She had a large disc collection, plus several shelves of cassettes.*

disconcert 1436
If something **disconcerts** you, it makes you feel uneasy or embarrassed. *e.g. His stare soon began to disconcert me.*

disconnect 752
If a gas, water or electricity company **disconnects** you or **disconnects** your supply of gas, water or electricity, the company stops the supply of gas, water or electricity to your house, usually because you are about to move to another house or because you have not paid your bills. *e.g. The gas company wrote to Mrs. Bullon saying they would disconnect the supply in two days.*

discord 130
Discord is disagreement and unpleasantness between people. *e.g. He's been a source of discord and worry.*

discount 1159
A **discount** is a reduction in the usual price of something. *e.g. There's a 10% discount on all of these.*

discover 328
1 When you **discover** a fact that you did not know, you find out about it. *e.g. I discovered that Greg is a vegetarian.*
2 If you **discover** someone or something, you find them accidentally or by searching for them. *e.g. He was dead before anyone discovered him.*
3 If someone **discovers** something that nobody knew about before, they are the first person to find it, or find out about it. *e.g. Herschel discovered a new planet.*

discovery 328
A **discovery** is the finding of an object or fact that nobody knew about. *e.g. The Chinese discovery of paper-making had a lasting effect on world culture.*

discriminate 909
If you **discriminate** against a person or group, you treat the person or group less well than other people or groups. If you **discriminate** in favour of a person or group, you treat the person or group better than other people or groups. *e.g. The divorce laws discriminated against women and people in paid employment.*

discrimination 909
Discrimination is the practice of treating one person or group of people less fairly or less well than other people or groups. *e.g. He spoke out against racial discrimination.*

discus 1738
1 A **discus** is a heavy, circular object that is thrown as a sport. *e.g. The discus is over by the javelins.*
2 The **discus** is an athletics event in which competitors throw a discus as far as they can. The winner is the person who throws the discus the furthest. *e.g. The discus will take place after the 5000 metres.*

discuss 380, 458, 1387
If you **discuss** something, you consider it throughly and seriously, from different points of view, by signing or talking to someone else about it. *e.g. They said they had an important matter to discuss with you.*

discussion 380, 458, 1387
1 **Discussion** is the act of signing or talking seriously and in detail about something with another person or other people. *e.g. Five hours were spent in discussion of the plans.*
2 A **discussion** is a serious conversation between people. *e.g. We're having a discussion on leisure activities.*

discus thrower 1738
A **discus thrower** is a person who takes part in the discus. *e.g. 'Geoff Capes was Britain's most successful discus thrower.' — 'No, I'm sorry, no points for that answer.'*

disdain 970
1 If you feel **disdain** for someone or something, you think that they have little value or importance. *e.g. He regarded homeless people with disdain.*
2 If you **disdain** to do something, you do not do it, because you feel that it is not important. *e.g. Claire disdained the help of her son.*

disembark 818
If you **disembark** from a ship, aeroplane, or bus, you leave it by getting out of it and going on to the land or on to the ground. *e.g. Half the passengers disembarked at Cherbourg.*

disgust 1007
1 **Disgust** is a feeling of very strong dislike for something or someone, for example because of their appearance or behaviour. *e.g. He couldn't hide his disgust at the sight of so many beggars.*
2 If something or someone **disgusts** you, you dislike them strongly, for example because of their appearance or behaviour. *e.g. To be honest, his attitude to disabled people disgusts me.*

disgusting 1002
Something that is **disgusting** is extremely unpleasant and offends you. *e.g. That's absolutely disgusting couldn't you have wiped your feet?*

dislike 1005
1 If you **dislike** someone or something, you consider them to be unpleasant and do not like them. *e.g. She disliked the theatre.*
2 **Dislike** is the feeling of not liking someone or something. *e.g. I started to dislike the bartender when he ignored me once.*
3 Your **dislikes** are the things that you do not like. *e.g. She has her likes and dislikes, as we all have.*

dismiss 379, 546
If you are **dismissed** from your job, your employer tells you to leave as you are no longer required or they do not wish you to do the job that you have been doing. *e.g. They were dismissed for being drunk on duty.*

dismiss 970
If you **dismiss** something, you decide or declare that it is not important enough for you to think about or consider. *e.g. I dismissed the idea.*

dismissal 379, 546
Dismissal is the act of getting rid of an employee. *e.g. A tribunal will deal with unfair dismissals.*

disorder 1370
Something that is in **disorder** is very untidy. *e.g. The room was in dreadful disorder after the burglary.*

disorient 312
Disorient means the same as disorientate. See **disorientate**.

disorientate 312
If something **disorientates** or **disorients** you, you are confused or lost or not sure where you are. *e.g. Flow diagrams do tend to disorientate people at first.*

disorientation 312
Disorientation is the state of being confused or lost or not sure where you are. *e.g. A feeling of disorientation is often experienced by deep sea divers who resurface too quickly.*

dispatch 1377, 1391
1 If you **dispatch** something, you send it, usually in a container. *e.g. We will dispatch the box to London tomorrow.*
2 The **dispatch** of something is the activity or process of sending it somewhere, usually in a box. *e.g. Yes, we completed the dispatch this morning.*

display 1373, 1384
1 If you **display** something that you want

people to see, you put it in a particular place, for example in a museum or in a shop where it can be seen easily. *e.g. There were cakes displayed in the front window.*

2 A **display** is an arrangement of things, for example in a shop window, that is designed to attract people's attention. *e.g. A display of paperbacks was spread out on the pavement.*

3 A **display** is a public performance or other event which is intended to entertain people. *e.g. We went to watch a firework display.*

dispute 437, 564

1 A **dispute** is a disagreement or quarrel between people or groups. *e.g. There were disputes between unions and employers.*

2 If people are in **dispute**, they disagree with each other. *e.g. We're not really in dispute over this, actually.*

3 If you **dispute** an opinion or action, you sign or say that you think it is untrue or incorrect. *e.g. I'm not about to dispute that point with you.*

dissociate 884

If you **dissociate** yourself from something or someone, you show that you are not connected with them. *e.g. The headmaster dissociated himself from the striking teachers.*

distance 460

1 The **distance** between two points or places is the amount of space between them. *e.g. The town is some distance from the sea.*

2 If you are at a **distance** from something, or if you see it or remember it from a **distance**, you are a long way away from it in space or time. *e.g. From a distance, he saw Jack's tiny figure still waving.*

3 If you can see or hear something in the **distance,** you can see or hear something which is far away. *e.g. The mountain looked miles away in the distance.*

distant 460

1 Something that is **distant** is very far away. *e.g. News arrived of an invasion in a distant part of the country.*

2 An event or time that is **distant** is very far away in the future. *e.g. We'd love to do it, but it won't be until the distant future, I'm afraid.*

distribute 1522

1 If you **distribute** things, you hand them to people. *e.g. Students will distribute the leaflets.*

2 To **distribute** something also means to share it among the members of a group. *e.g. Management should distribute profits to the workforce.*

disturbed 1569

Someone who is **disturbed** is extremely unhappy or mentally ill. *e.g. Emotionally disturbed youngsters can stay here for up to three years.*

dive 722

When you **dive**, you jump head-first from a raised point, usually into water, and often with your arms held straight in line with your body beside your head. *e.g. They used to dive off a rocky ledge into the sea.*

diver 722

1 A person who dives is called a **diver**. *e.g. The divers lined up at the edge of the pool.*

2 A **diver** is a person who works or explores under water or at the bottom of the sea, using special breathing equipment. *e.g. The diver waited on deck in his wetsuit.*

diverge 445

1 If two things **diverge** or one **diverges** from the other, they are different or become different from each other. *e.g. After he married, his interests diverged from those of his old friends.*

2 When two roads or paths **diverge**, they start leading in different directions. *e.g. Here, the two paths will diverge: you need the left fork.*

diverse 426, 427, 447

People or things that are **diverse** are very different from each other. *e.g. There were diverse celebrities such as Bob Dylan, Bob Hope and Ronald Reagan.*

diversion 1296

A **diversion** is a special route arranged for traffic when the normal route cannot be used. *e.g. You cannot use the M1 but there is a diversion onto the A1 to help you reach London.*

divide 502

If you **divide** a larger number by a smaller number, you calculate how many times the smaller number can go exactly into the larger number. *e.g. Divide 35 by 7, and you should get the answer '5'.*

divide 1325, 1599

1 When you **divide** something or it **divides**, it becomes separated into smaller parts. *e.g. Any attempt to divide the population into four social classes is futile.*

2 If something is **divided** into several distinct parts, it consists of these parts. *e.g. The house was divided into offices.*

3 If you **divide** something among a number of people, you give each of them part of it. *e.g. We will have to divide the work fairly.*

divide up 1599

If you **divide** something **up,** you share it out among a number of people. *e.g. We will divide up the proceeds among about four hundred people.*

diving 722

Diving is the sport or activity of jumping into water from a diving board or raised point. *e.g. She only came third overall in the diving contest,*

but she was top in the backward flip section.

diving board 722

A **diving board** is a horizontal board raised above a swimming pool or other area of water from which people can dive into the water. *e.g. She wanted to go on the high diving board!*

division 502

Division is the mathematical process of dividing one number by another by calculating how many times the second number can go into the first number. *e.g. Division sums were very difficult.*

division 1599

The **division** of something is the sharing of it among a number of people. *e.g. The division of responsibility must be fair.*

divorce 438, 696, 1634

1 A **divorce** is the formal ending of a marriage by law. *e.g. I want a divorce.*

2 When someone **divorces** their husband or wife, or when a married couple **divorce,** their marriage is legally ended. *e.g. I want to divorce him, but I don't want to hurt the children.*

divorced 438, 696

A person who is **divorced** has had their marriage legally ended. *e.g. Are you single, married or divorced?*

divorcee 438, 696

A **divorcee** is a person who has had their marriage legally ended. *e.g. She played the part of a divorcee in her last film.*

dizzy 323, 1074

If you feel **dizzy**, you feel that you are losing your balance and are about to fall. *e.g. I can't climb trees; I get dizzy.*

doctor 974

A **doctor** is someone who is qualified in medicine and treats people who are ill. *e.g. She felt so ill we had to call the doctor.*

document 1307

A **document** is an official piece of paper with writing on it. *e.g. This document in fact dates from 1849.*

doddle 362, 520

If you sign or say that something such as a job, task or exam is a **doddle**, you mean that you find it very easy to do. *e.g. Don't worry, the exam will be a doddle.*

does not matter 1601

If something **does not matter** or **doesn't matter**, it is not important because it does not have an effect on the situation. *e.g. It does not matter which method you choose.*

does not matter   1605
If you sign or say to someone that something **does not matter** or **doesn't matter**, you mean that, since they seem so unhelpful or uninterested in their attitude, you will deal with the problem without them or keep your thoughts to yourself. *e.g. Hello, are you paying attention? Oh, what's the point, it doesn't matter.*

doesn't matter   1601
See **does not matter**.

doesn't matter   1605
See **does not matter**.

dog   55, 726, 1289
A **dog** is a very common four-legged animal that is often kept by people as a pet or used to guard or hunt things. There are a lot of different breeds of dog. *e.g. The dog started barking at me.*

dog begging   726
When a **dog** is **begging**, it sits up on its haunches and raises its front paws. *e.g. I can't resist a dog begging for biscuits, but I know I should.*

dog-collar   643
A **dog-collar** is a white collar that fastens at the back of the neck, worn by priests and ministers of the Christian Church. *e.g. The curate took off his dog-collar to join the football game.*

dole   65, 1008
1 **Dole** or the **dole** is money that a person who is unemployed receives as a right from the government, subject to certain conditions. It is paid at regular intervals, during the person's period of unemployment, for up to a maximum of fifty-two weeks at the present time. *e.g. Lengthening dole queues are causing major problems for the government.*
2 If you are **on the dole**, you are unemployed and can receive regular unemployment payments from the government. *e.g. How much do you get on the dole nowadays?*

dole (on the dole)   668
If you are **on the dole**, you are unemployed and can receive regular unemployment payments from the government. *e.g. How much do you get on the dole nowadays?*

doll   1386
A **doll** is a child's toy which looks like a small person or baby. *e.g. She adored her new doll.*

domestic   88
A **domestic** is a person who is paid to come to help with the work that has to be done in a house such as the cleaning, washing and ironing. *e.g. Should the women quit their present jobs and become domestics?*

dominate   1364
1 If someone or something **dominates** a situation or event, they are the most powerful or important thing in it. *e.g. These issues will dominate the election.*
2 If one country **dominates** another, it has power over it. *e.g. Spain used to dominate the Americas in the sixteenth century.*

dominoes   1739
1 **Dominoes** are small rectangular blocks, often made of wood, marked with two groups of spots on one side. Dominoes are used for playing various games. *e.g. He got a set of dominoes for his birthday.*
2 **Dominoes** is one of a number of games in which players put dominoes onto a table in turn, usually by matching the number of spots. *e.g. She turned up an hour late and we'd nearly finished playing dominoes.*

domino player   1739
A **domino player** is a person who takes part in a game of dominoes. *e.g. The domino players are over by the bar.*

donate   862, 871, 1507, 1679
If you **donate** something to a charity or other organisation, you give it to them. *e.g. I want to donate a sum of money to the National Deaf Children's Society.*

donation   862, 871
A **donation** is an amount of money that is given to a charity or other organisation. *e.g. The British Deaf Association received a donation from the Trust.*

done   1566, 1643
1 A task that is **done** has been completed. *e.g. When the washing was done, she left to go shopping.*
2 If you sign or say that a situation or task is **over and done with**, you mean that it is finished and you can forget about it. *e.g. I'm relieved that the housework is over and done with.*

donkey   1462
A **donkey** is an animal which is like a horse but smaller and with longer ears. *e.g. There are donkey rides at Blackpool.*

donor   862, 871
A **donor** is someone (or a group of people) who gives something such as money to a charity or other organisation. *e.g. A significant proportion of the Royal National Institute for Deaf People's income comes from individual donors.*

do not   1221, 1420
Do not or **don't** is used to tell people what action they should not take. *e.g. Andrew, I've told you, do not ask me again.*

do not believe   315
If you sign or say that you **do not believe** or **don't believe** that something is true, you mean that you do not accept, doubt very much or are very surprised to learn that it is true. *e.g. I just do not believe that he is only sixteen years old.*

do not care   1536, 1601, 1605
If you **do not care** or **don't care** about something, it does not matter to you at all or you are not interested in it. *e.g. I do not care about this: you argue about it if you want to.*

do not care a damn   602, 746, 971, 1122
If you sign or say that you **do not care a damn** or **don't care a damn** about someone or something, you mean that you are not at all concerned about them *e.g. She does not care a damn what you think about me.*

do not give a damn   602, 746, 971, 1122, 1536
If you sign or say that you **do not give a damn** or **don't give a damn** about someone or something, you mean that you are not at all concerned about them. *e.g. Monica signed to me that she does not give a damn how much it cost: you should take it back.*

do not know   1568
1 If you **do not know** or **don't know** something, you do not have it correctly in your mind. *e.g. In fact, I have to admit that I do not know Pythagoras' theorem.*
2 If you **do not know** or **don't know** of or about something, you have not been informed about it. *e.g. Many people don't know of the existence of sign language.*
3 If you **do not know** or **don't know** a place or thing, you are not familiar with it. *e.g. We do not know Warrington at all well.*
4 If you **do not know** or **don't know** someone, you have not met or had any conversation with them. *e.g. John, I know; Paul, I know; George, I don't know—is he new?*

do not like   1005
1 If you **do not like** or **don't like** something, you do not find it enjoyable or pleasant. *e.g. I'm a vegetarian, but I don't like parsnips.*
2 If you **do not like** or **don't like** someone, you do not enjoy their company or do not consider their personality or character pleasant. *e.g. I know he's a good teacher, I just don't like him.*

do not mind   1601
If you sign or say that you **do not mind** or **don't mind** about something, you mean that you really do not care about it. *e.g. They don't mind what colour you paint the house.*

do not mind   1605
1 If you sign or say that you **do not mind** or

don't mind something, you mean that you are not annoyed or bothered by it. *e.g. I don't mind personal questions.*
2 If you are offered a choice and you sign or say that you **do not mind** or **don't mind**, you mean that you will be happy with any of the things offered. *e.g. 'Tea or coffee?'—'I don't mind.'*

don't   1221, 1420
Don't is the usual spoken form of do not. It appears in writing usually as an informal usage or abbreviation. See **do not**.

don't believe   315
See **do not believe**.

don't care   1536, 1601, 1605
See **do not care**.

don't care a damn   602, 746, 971, 1122
See **do not care a damn**.

don't give a damn 602, 746, 971, 1122, 1536
See **do not give a damn**.

don't know   1586
See **do not know**.

don't like   1005
See **do not like**.

don't mind   1601
See **do not mind**.

don't mind   1605
See **do not mind**.

door   1353
1 A **door** is a swinging piece of wood, glass or metal, which is used to close the entrance to a building, room, cupboard, etcetera. *e.g. Leave the door alone!*
2 A **door** is the entrance to a room or to a building such as a shop, hotel, theatre, etc.. *e.g. I'll meet you outside the door at ten o'clock.*

doorbell   162
A **doorbell** is a device on the outside of a building which, if pushed, causes a bell inside the building to ring so that the people inside know that you are there and that you want to see them. *e.g. The doorbell is broken.*

doors (double doors)   1431
Double doors are two similar doors which together fill a wide doorway. They may open the same way or be swing doors. *e.g. For your front door, do you want a single or double doors?*

doors (double doors closing)   1451
If **double doors** are **closing**, they move by pivoting at the hinges so that they cover a gap, preventing things or people from passing

through the space. *e.g. And here we see the double doors closing—very smooth.*

doors (double doors opening)   1431
If **double doors** are **opening**, they move by pivoting at the hinges so that they no longer cover a gap, allowing things or people to pass through the space. *e.g. I can't see any problem: the double doors are opening all right, aren't they?*

doubt   1368
1 **Doubt** or a **doubt** about something is a feeling of uncertainty about it, for example not knowing whether it is true or possible. *e.g. One member of the panel expressed a doubt as to his suitability.*
2 If you **doubt** something, you do not think it is the case. *e.g. I doubt we will finish work at five o'clock somehow.*

doubtful   1328, 1368
1 Something that is **doubtful** seems unlikely or uncertain. *e.g. It is doubtful, however, whether the Chairwoman would approve.*
2 If you are **doubtful** about something, you feel unsure or uncertain about it. *e.g. I was a little doubtful about accepting.*

do (will do)   198, 218
If you sign or say or sign that something **will do**, you mean that it is good enough for you. *e.g. This coffee isn't my brand, but it will do.*

down   497
Down means in the direction of the ground or a lower level, or in a lower place. *e.g. The people in the flat down below are very noisy.*

down   1237
1 **Down** means forward towards a lower place. *e.g. We must go down here and through the ford.*
2 If a number or an amount goes **down**, it decreases. *e.g. I've got a feeling that we will see benefits come down again soon.*

down (feel down)   1270, 1365
If you **feel down**, you are unhappy or depressed. *e.g. I feel down when I think about the amount of work still to be done.*

downhill   1237
1 If something is moving **downhill**, it is moving down a slope towards a lower point. *e.g. The children were racing downhill on their sledges.*
2 If someone is going or looking **downhill**, they are going or looking towards the bottom of the hill. *e.g. Looking downhill, we could see the stream through the trees.*
3 If a thing or situation is going **downhill**, it is changing and becoming less pleasant or less acceptable. *e.g. Believe me, after 30 it's all downhill.*

downpour   1165
When there is a **downpour**, a lot of rain falls fast and heavily. *e.g. It was the heaviest downpour ever recorded in the region.*

downstairs   497
1 If something or someone is **downstairs** in a building, they are on the ground floor or on a lower floor than you are. *e.g. My aunt's photograph is on the sideboard in the dining room downstairs.*
2 A **downstairs** room or object is one which is situated on the ground floor or a lower floor of a building. *e.g. Hanif's using the downstairs phone.*
3 If you refer to a person **downstairs**, you are referring to someone who lives in a flat or room on the ground floor or on a lower floor of a building. *e.g. I had to leave the baby with the woman downstairs.*

downward   1237
1 If you move **downward** or **downwards**, you advance towards a lower level. *e.g. We headed downward as night fell.*
2 If an amount or rate moves **downward** or **downwards**, it decreases. *e.g. The trend in the suicide rate is downwards.*

doze off   1669
If you **doze off**, you fall into a light sleep. *e.g. Rob sat in front of the fire and dozed off after another hard day in the studio.*

drag   273
If you **drag** a heavy object somewhere, you pull it along the ground with difficulty, usually because it is too heavy or too big to carry. *e.g. She grasped the bag of soil with both hands and dragged it down the path.*

drama   143, 968
1 A **drama** is a serious play for the theatre, television, or radio. *e.g. I remember her acting in a drama called 'The Garden Party'.*
2 You refer to plays in general and to all work in the theatre as **drama**. *e.g. Dorothy is an expert on modern drama.*

dramatic   960
You can describe something as **dramatic** when it is very exciting or impressive. *e.g. The moon-landing was one of the most dramatic moments of this century.*

draught   1278
A **draught** is a current of air, usually one coming into a room or a vehicle. *e.g. She was sitting in a draught.*

draughts   826
Draughts is a game for two people, played with round pieces on a chequered board. *e.g. Our club lost the draughts tournament.*

draughts player 826
A **draughts player** is someone who takes part in a game of draughts. *e.g. He was a dedicated draughts player who hated losing.*

draw 1409, 1618
1 If two teams, players or people in a game or competition **draw**, their scores or positions are equal at the end of the game. *e.g. I will be happy if we draw.*
2 A **draw** is the result of a game or competition in which two or more people draw. *e.g. The game ended in a 2-2 draw.*

drawer 73
A **drawer** is a part of a desk, chest, or other piece of furniture which is shaped like a box and can be pulled out so that you can put things in it or take things out if it. *e.g. Liam's clothes are in the middle drawer.*

draw near 295, 570
When a person **draws near**, he or she moves close to where you are. *e.g. I watched the man as he drew near.*

dreadful 585
If you sign or say that something is **dreadful**, you mean that it is very bad or terrible. *e.g. The storm was dreadful, and several trees were uprooted.*

dreadful 904, 911, 914, 918
1 If you sign or say that something is **dreadful**, you mean that it is very bad or unpleasant. *e.g. The weather was dreadful.*
2 If you sign or say that something is **dreadful**, you mean that it is of very poor quality. *e.g. His British Sign Language skills were dreadful.*

dreadful 1002
Something that is **dreadful** is disgusting or very unpleasant to experience. *e.g. The mess outside the pub after closing time was dreadful.*

dream 1570
1 A **dream** is an imaginary series of events that you experience in your mind while you are asleep. *e.g. I had a strange dream about you last night.*
2 A **dream** is a situation or event which you often think about because you would very much like it to happen. *e.g. 'I have a dream...,' said Martin Luther King, and America closed its eyes.*
3 If you **dream**, you experience an imaginary series of events in your mind while you are asleep. *e.g. 'Do Deaf people dream in sign language?'—'Of course they do!'*
4 If you **dream**, you often think about a situation or event because you would very much like it to happen. *e.g. Do you dream about zero inflation, Mr. Lamont?*

dress 1081
1 When you **dress** or **dress** yourself, you put on your clothes. *e.g. When he had shaved, he went down to the kitchen and began to dress.*
2 If someone **dresses** in a particular way, they usually wear that style of clothes. *e.g. I must try to change the way he dresses.*
3 You can refer to clothes in general as **dress**. *e.g. She preferred military or naval dress to the women's fashions of the day.*

dress 1083
1 A **dress** is a piece of clothing worn by a woman or girl which covers her body and whose hem reaches to somewhere on her legs. *e.g. She was wearing a short black dress.*
2 You can refer to clothes in general as **dress**. *e.g. More money is spent on dress than on books.*
3 When you **dress** or when you **dress** yourself, you put on your clothes. *e.g. I'll just wash and dress, then we can go shopping.*

dressed 1081
1 If you are **dressed**, you are wearing clothes rather than being naked, or wearing ordinary clothes rather than pyjamas or a nightdress. *e.g. Both men are fully dressed.*
2 If you are **dressed** in a particular way, you are wearing clothes of a particular kind or colour. *e.g. A woman dressed in white came up to me.*

dressing gown 286
A **dressing gown** is a piece of clothing in the form of a loose fitting coat which you wear when you are not dressed in your ordinary clothes (often over pyjamas or a nightdress), for example when you have just got out of bed. *e.g. I bought a new dressing gown in the sale.*

dress up 1081, 1083
1 If you **dress up**, you put on special or different clothes, especially as part of a game played by children in which they pretend to be different people. *e.g. My little boy likes to dress up in his Superman costume.*
2 If you **dress up**, you put on different clothes from the ones you usually wear, in order to look smarter than usual. *e.g. When her mother-in-law comes, Mavis feels she must dress up.*

drink 1671
1 When you **drink** or **drink** something, you take liquid into your mouth and then swallow it. *e.g. She drank her orange juice.*
2 A **drink** is an amount of a liquid which you drink or which is suitable for drinking. *e.g. I asked her for a drink of water.*
3 A **drink** is a small amount of liquid which you swallow in one go. *e.g. She took a drink of her whiskey and smiled at him.*

drink a cup of coffee/tea 850
If you **drink a cup of coffee** or **tea**, you take a

liquid made with coffee or tea into your mouth from a cup and then swallow it. *e.g. I always drink a cup of coffee in the bath.*

drink a cup of tea 872
When you **drink a cup of tea** you do so by holding a cup containing tea by the handle, raising it to your lips, taking some of the tea into your mouth and swallowing it. *e.g. Let's sit down and drink a cup of tea before we get on with the painting.*

drink coffee/tea 850
If you **drink coffee** or **tea**, you take a liquid made with coffee or tea into your mouth and then swallow it. *e.g. If you drink coffee before going to sleep, it gives you nightmares.*

drink from a cup 850, 872
When you **drink from a cup** containing liquid you do so by raising the cup to your mouth, taking some of the liquid into your mouth and swallowing it. *e.g. I much prefer to drink from a cup than from a mug.*

drink from a glass/tumbler 1671
When you **drink from a glass** or **tumbler** containing liquid you do so by lifting the glass or tumbler to your mouth and taking some of the liquid into your mouth and swallowing it. *e.g. I would prefer to drink from a glass rather than a mug.*

drink from a glass with a handle/mug/ tankard 26
When you **drink from a glass with a handle, mug** or **tankard** containing liquid you do so by raising the glass, mug or tankard to your mouth by the handle and taking some of the liquid into your mouth and swallowing it. *e.g. We drank two mugs of tea.*

drink milk 1671
When you **drink milk**, you take milk into your mouth and then swallow it. *e.g. He drank his milk while he watched the television.*

drink tea 872
When you **drink tea** you do so by raising a container, such as a mug or cup, which contains tea, to your lips, taking some of the tea into your mouth and swallowing it. *e.g. I always drink tea first thing in the morning.*

drive a bus/juggernaut/large vehicle/ lorry/truck/van 74
When you **drive a bus, juggernaught, large vehicle, lorry, truck** or **van**, you operate it and control it so that it works and goes where you want to go. *e.g. He drives a lorry for a haulage company.*

drive a car/small vehicle/van 100
When you **drive a car, small vehicle** or **van**,

you operate it and control it so that it works and goes where you want to go. *e.g. It is her turn to drive the car tomorrow.*

drive a tractor 503
When you **drive a tractor**, you operate it and control it so that it works and goes where you want to go. *e.g. If I could, I would drive a tractor about in the fields for my summer holiday.*

drive/go through a tunnel 1363
If you **drive** or **go through a tunnel**, or a vehicle **drives** or **goes through a tunnel**, you travel in a vehicle or it travels into one end of a passage under the ground (a tunnel) and out of the other end. *e.g. I like to drive through the tunnel with my head out of the window.*

drive into a car port/garage 1363
If you **drive**, or a vehicle **drives**, into a car port or garage, you travel in a vehicle or it travels so that the roof of the car port or garage is above it. *e.g. Drive into the garage and we'll take a look.*

driver of a bus/juggernaut/large vehicle/lorry/truck/van 74
The **driver of a bus, juggernaught, large vehicle, lorry, truck** or **van** is the person who drives such a vehicle. *e.g. I got a lift with the driver of a truck.*

driver of a car/small vehicle/van 100
The **driver of a car, small vehicle** or **van** is the person who drives such a vehicle. *e.g. The driver of the van claimed to have been doing twenty-seven miles per hour.*

drizzle 1192
1 **Drizzle** is light rain falling in very small drops. *e.g. He walked home through the mist and drizzle.*
2 If it **drizzles**, light rain falls in very small drops. *e.g. Tonight it may drizzle a little in urban areas, but the temperature will remain good for the time of year.*

drop 786
If something **drops**, it falls straight down. *e.g. The cup dropped from the hook.*

drop 1700, 1726
1 If you **drop** something, you let it fall deliberately or by mistake. *e.g. He dropped his papers.*
2 If you **drop** something that you are doing or dealing with, you stop doing it or dealing with it. *e.g. I've dropped my plan to go to London.*

drown 1548
When someone **drowns**, or when something **drowns** them, they die because they have gone under water or another liquid and cannot breathe. *e.g. People drown with depressing regularity in this river.*

drug 782
A **drug** is a chemical which is given to people in order to treat or prevent an illness or disease. *e.g. The doctor gave her a drug to alleviate her constipation.*

drug abuser 782
A **drug abuser** is a person who uses drugs illegally and excessively, usually because he or she is addicted to their stimulating effect. *e.g. Drug abusers are very often unable to conquer their addiction without support.*

drug addict 782
A **drug addict** is someone who takes harmful drugs and cannot stop taking them. *e.g. My uncle works with drug addicts who are trying to break their habit.*

drugs 782
Drugs are substances that some people inject in their blood because they have stimulating effects. In most countries, this use of drugs is illegal. *e.g. Baudelaire was slowly dying from drugs when he wrote his last book.*

drum 277
A **drum** is a musical instrument consisting of a skin stretched tightly over a round frame. You play a drum by beating it rhythmically with sticks. *e.g. He played the drums.*

drummer 277
A **drummer** is a person who plays a drum or drums in a band or group. *e.g. She is a drummer in a band.*

drumsticks 277
Drumsticks are sticks used for beating a drum. *e.g. He has lost his drumsticks and cannot play in the band!*

drunk 819
1 If someone is **drunk**, they have drunk so much alcohol that they cannot express themself clearly or behave sensibly. *e.g. He was so drunk he couldn't stand.*
2 A **drunk** is someone who is drunk or who often gets drunk. *e.g. We saw a lot of drunks in San Francisco.*

dry 1100
Something that is **dry** has no water or other liquid on it or in it. *e.g. The river bed was dry.*

dry 1542
1 If your throat is **dry**, you are thirsty and need to drink something. *e.g. My throat was so dry I could have drunk a pail of water.*
2 Something that is **dry** has no water or other liquid in it. *e.g. The washing is dry already.*
3 When the weather is **dry**, there is no rain. *e.g. We've had a month of dry weather. Hope it rains soon.*

dry oneself with a towel/bathtowel 149
When you **dry yourself with a towel** or **bathtowel**, you remove all water or moisture from the surface of your body or part of your body, using a towel or bathtowel, usually after washing yourself. *e.g. I dried myself with the tartan towel after I showered.*

dry up 1100
If something **dries up**, it loses all its water or moisture. *e.g. The pool dried up in the late summer.*

duck 711
1 A **duck** is a very common water bird with short legs, webbed feet, a short neck and a large flat beak. There are many kinds of duck, either wild or kept for their eggs, meat or feathers. *e.g. There used to be a duck on the pond in the park.*
2 **Duck** is the meat of a duck. *e.g. We ate duck for dinner, and drank a fine claret.*

due to 1492
If a situation, event, or state of affairs is **due to** something else, it happens or exists as a result of it. *e.g. Over 40% of deaths were due to the spread of this disease.*

duffle bag 234
A **duffle bag** is a bag shaped like a cylinder and made of strong cloth such as canvas. Duffle bags have string at one end which is used to close the bag and to carry it with. *e.g. He threw his stuff in a duffle bag and left.*

dull 1072
1 A **dull** colour or light is not bright. *e.g. The sea was a dull grey.*
2 You sign or say that the weather is **dull** when it is rather cloudy. *e.g. Tomorrow will be dull with rain in most parts by lunchtime. That's all from me: a very good morning to you.*

dull 1255
Someone or something that is **dull** does not seem to have any interesting features. *e.g. I thought the book was dull.*

dumb 316
If you sign or say that an action or statement is **dumb**, you mean it does not show good judgement or intelligence. *e.g. That was a dumb thing to say to her when she's just broken off with her boyfriend.*

duplicate 1545
If you **duplicate** a piece of writing or a drawing, you make exact copies of it using a machine. *e.g. The story was typed and Jane was sent to duplicate it.*

dusk 1072, 1464
Dusk is the time just before night when it is not completely dark. *e.g. Dusk is the best time of the day.*

dustman　　　　　　102
A **dustman** is a person whose job it is to empty the rubbish from people's dustbins and take it away to be disposed of. *e.g. Her father was a dustman.*

dustpan and brush　　　　264
A **dustpan and brush** are pieces of equipment used for collecting dust and dirt. A dustpan is a small, flat container made of metal or plastic, into which you sweep dust and dirt with a brush. *e.g. Look at those crumbs. I'll fetch the dustpan and brush.*

E, e

E
E is the fifth letter of the British manual and English alphabets. See page 851.

each　　　　492
If you refer to **each** thing or **each** person in a group, you are referring to every member of the group and considering them as individuals. *e.g. Each county is divided into several districts.*

eager　　　　1197
1 If you are **eager** for something or to do something, you want to have or do it very much. *e.g. People eager for a quick cure are likely to be disappointed.*
2 If you look or sound **eager**, you look or sound as if you expect something interesting or enjoyable to happen. *e.g. We looked round the circle of eager volunteers.*

earache　　　　343
Earache is a pain in the inside of your ear. *e.g. Paul suffered from terrible earache after years of drilling without ear protection.*

earlier　　　　1250, 1332
Earlier is used to refer to a point or period in time before the present or before the one that you have been referring to. *e.g. I saw Jane earlier this evening.*

early　　　　383, 617
1 **Early** or **early on** means near the beginning of a week, year or other period of time. *e.g. You should have been here early on in the week.*
2 **Early** or **early on** means near the beginning of something such as a piece of work or a process. *e.g. We realised quite early in the race that there were problems.*
3 If someone or something arrives or happens **early**, they arrive or happen before the time that was arranged or expected. *e.g.*

Dutch　　　　1556
1 Someone or something that is **Dutch** belongs to or relates to the Netherlands or its people. *e.g. The Dutch volleyball team came second in the 1992 Olympics.*
2 **Dutch** is the main language spoken in the Netherlands. *e.g. We are learning to speak Dutch and German at school.*
3 You can refer to people from the Netherlands in general, or to a particular group of people from the Netherlands, as the **Dutch**. *e.g. Apparently, the Dutch have the lowest rates of personal income tax in Europe.*

We were all early for the practice and had to wait fifteen minutes.

early　　　　412, 1332
If someone or something arrives or happens **early**, they arrive or happen before the time that was arranged or expected. *e.g. He was three minutes early.*

earmould　　　　623
An **earmould** is usually made of a plastic material and is the part of a hearing aid which fits into the ear. *e.g. Paul had to have a wax impression taken for a new earmould.*

ear muffs　　　　1692
Ear muffs are a pair of ear coverings connected by a band over the top of the head and worn to protect a person's ears from cold or noise. *e.g. He wore ear muffs as protection against the bitter wind.*

earrings　　　　790
Earrings are pieces of jewellery (usually sold as a pair) that people wear fixed to the lobes of their ears. *e.g. Lisa wore a different pair of earrings every day of the week.*

earth　　　　1418
The **earth** is the planet on which we live. *e.g. They say that seeing the earth from space is utterly incredible.*

earth　　　　1520
Earth is the substance on the land surface of this planet in which plants grow. *e.g. The earth seemed hard after the frost.*

earthquake　　　　1039, 1040
An **earthquake** is a shaking of the ground caused by movement of the earth's crust. *e.g. In California, there is an earthquake every year or so.*

4 The address of the **Dutch** Deaf Council is: Stichting Nederlandse Dovenraad, Postbus 19, 3500 AA Utrecht, Netherlands.

dying　　　　699
1 If someone is **dying**, they are so ill or so badly injured that they will not live very much longer. *e.g. An old woman dying of cancer was taken into hospital.*
2 Your **dying** is your death. *e.g. His dying was a shock to his family.*

ease (at ease)　　　　1495
If you are **at ease**, you feel confident and comfortable. *e.g. He was at ease with strangers.*

east　　　　396
1 The **east** is the direction which you look towards in order to see the sun rise. *e.g. We saw dawn break in the east.*
2 The **east** is the part of a place or country which is towards the east. *e.g. He came from the east end of Glasgow.*

Easter　　　　545
Easter is a Christian religious festival when Christians celebrate the death and resurrection of Christ. *e.g. They went to church on Easter Sunday.*

easy　　　　362, 1581
Something that is **easy** can be done without difficulty or effort. *e.g. Everyone else thought making a dictionary would be easy.*

easy　　　　520
1 If you say that something is **easy** or **too easy**, you are criticising someone because you believe that they have simply accepted or done the most obvious or least difficult thing, and have not considered the situation carefully enough. *e.g. It's easy for you to say back out, but I can't.*
2 **Easy** means comfortable and without any troubles or worry. *e.g. I want life to be easy for you when you retire.*
3 Something that is **easy** can be done without difficulty or effort. *e.g. The house is easy to keep clean.*

easychair　　　　91
An **easychair** is a large comfortable chair in which you can relax. *e.g. She made some new covers for the easychair in the front room.*

easy (take it easy)　　　　1495
If you **take it easy** or **take things easy**, you

relax and do not do very much at all. *e.g. Now that I'm sixty-five, I'm going to take things easy.*

eat 1501
1 When you **eat** something or when you **eat**, you put food into your mouth, chew it and swallow it. *e.g. She had never dared to eat Chinese food before.*
2 To **eat** also means to have a meal. *e.g. He said he would eat at his hotel.*

eat an ice cream cone/cornet 27
When you **eat an ice cream cone** or **cornet**, you usually do so by licking the ice cream with your tongue and swallowing it. The cone or cornet is eaten by biting it with your teeth, then chewing and swallowing it. *e.g. We each ate an ice cream cornet on the way home.*

eat cereal/dessert/porridge/pudding/ soup/sweet 732
If you **eat cereal**, **dessert**, **porridge**, **pudding**, **soup** or a **sweet**, you put small quantities of cereal, dessert, porridge, pudding or sweet into your mouth with a spoon. *e.g. You should eat your cereal at the table.*

eat cereal/dessert/porridge/pudding/ sweet with a dessert spoon 240
If you **eat cereal**, **dessert**, **porridge**, **pudding** or a **sweet with a dessert spoon**, you put small quantities of cereal, dessert, porridge, pudding or sweet into your mouth with a special oval-shaped spoon about twice as large as a teaspoon. *e.g. You should eat your pudding with a dessert spoon, not a fork.*

eat chips 870
If you buy chips, they are usually wrapped so that you can **eat chips** by lifting them with your fingers, placing them in your mouth, chewing and swallowing. *e.g. I love to eat chips straight from the packet.*

eat crisps 870
When you **eat crisps**, you lift them with your fingers from a bag and place them in your mouth before chewing and swallowing. *e.g. He always eats crisps with his beer.*

eat ice cream 27
When you **eat ice cream**, you put it into your mouth and swallow it. *e.g. I love eating ice cream.*

eat soup with a soup spoon 240
When you **eat with a soup spoon**, you pick the food up in a tool like a small bowl with a long handle (soup spoon), put it into your mouth, chew it if necessary, and swallow it. *e.g. The old man was eating minestrone soup with one of the club's finest soupspoons.*

eat with a dessert spoon/soup spoon 240, 732
When you **eat with a dessert spoon** or a **soup spoon**, you pick the food up in a tool like a small bowl with a long handle (dessert spoon or soup spoon), put it into your mouth, chew it if necessary, and swallow it. *e.g. Charlotte is a big girl: she's learnt how to eat with a soup spoon like her parents.*

ebb tide 1047
The ebb of the tide is one of the regular periods, about two per day, when it is falling to a lower level; this is called the **ebb tide**. *e.g. The fishermen went out at ebb tide to gather mussels.*

edit 752
If you **edit** a film, video, television or radio programme, you choose some of what has been filmed or recorded and arrange it in a particular order. *e.g. Rachael is editing the film for inclusion in next week's 'Sign On'.*

effort (make an effort) 373, 374, 1354
If you **make an effort** to do something, you try very hard to do it. *e.g. Andrew and Karen made an effort to learn Welsh, but Matthew kept ahead of them.*

egg (boiled egg) 586, 682
A **boiled egg** is the rounded object produced by a hen (which, if it had been fertilised, would have contained a baby bird), cooked in extremely hot water and considered as food for humans. *e.g. I'll have a boiled egg please, Sheila.*

Egypt 1672
Egypt is a country in North East Africa. *e.g. Kathleen has been to Egypt twice.*

Egyptian 1672
1 Someone or something that is **Egyptian** belongs to or relates to Egypt or its people. *e.g. What do you think of the Egyptian government?*
2 **Egyptian** is an Arabic dialect which is spoken in Egypt. *e.g. Can anybody here speak Egyptian? Could you help me out for a minute?*
3 An **Egyptian** is someone who comes from Egypt or whose family identity relates to Egypt. *e.g. He met an Egyptian named Hamid at the party.*

either 933, 948
1 You use **either** when you are stating two or more alternatives (which are the only possibilities or choices that there are). *e.g. You either love him or hate him.*
2 You can use **either** to refer to one of two possible things, people, or situations, when you want to sign or say that it does not matter which one is chosen or considered. *e.g. Either is acceptable.*

elastic 735
1 **Elastic** is a rubber material which stretches

when you pull it and returns to its original size and shape when you let it go. Elastic is often used in clothes to make them fit tightly, for example round the waist. *e.g. The elastic was broken, so I tied them up with string.*
2 Something that is **elastic** is able to stretch easily and then return to its original size and shape. *e.g. This is a softer, more elastic and lighter material.*

elastic band 735
An **elastic band** is a thin circle of a very stretchy rubber material that you can put around bundles of things such as papers in order to hold them together. *e.g. My pencils are tied together by an elastic band.*

elderly 810
1 **Elderly** people are old. *e.g. The coach was full of elderly ladies having a good time.*
2 Something that is **elderly** is rather old or old-fashioned and therefore no longer as good or efficient as when it was new, or not as good or efficient as a modern form of it. *e.g. The ship got under way, her elderly oil-fired steam engines throbbing along.*

elect 413, 443, 629
When people **elect** someone to represent them, they choose him or her to act as their representative by voting. *e.g. They met to elect a new president.*

elect 487
When people **elect** a number of representatives, they choose these representatives to act on their behalf by voting. *e.g. We will just have to elect a new set of committee members.*

election 413, 443, 629
1 An **election** is an organised process in which people vote to choose a person or group of people to represent them in parliament, on a committee or as a governing body, or to hold an official position such as president or chairman of a group. *e.g. I may vote for her at the next election.*
2 The **election** of a particular person or group of people is their success in an organised selection process, as a result of which they gain political power or take up an official position in an organisation. *e.g. His election as chair means that he'll be away even more now.*

election 487
1 An **election** is an organised process in which people vote to choose a group of people to represent them in parliament, on a committee or as a governing body, or to hold official positions within a group. *e.g. The number of people involved in the election was depressingly low.*
2 The **election** of a particular group of people is their success in an organised selection process, as a result of which they take up

official positions within an organisation or governing body. *e.g. I hope that election to the board will not change their attitude.*

electric   304, 815
1 An **electric** device or machine works by using electricity. *e.g. The room was cooled by an electric fan.*
2 An **electric** current, voltage or power supply is one that is produced by electricity. *e.g. There was a powerful electric current running through the wires.*

electric bell   408
An **electric bell** is a device powered by electricity that makes a ringing sound and is used to give a sign or to attract people's attention. *e.g. They installed an electric bell in school, and now nobody is in doubt when play-time finishes.*

electricity   304, 815
Electricity is a form of energy that is used for heating and lighting and to provide power for machines in houses and factories. *e.g. It was an old house; there was no electricity, just gas lamps.*

elephant   1668
An **elephant** is a very large four-legged animal with a long, flexible nose called a trunk, which it uses to pick up things. An adult elephant has tusks of ivory at each side of its mouth. Wild elephants are found in Africa and India. *e.g. She liked to photograph elephants best of all.*

elephant's trunk   1668
An **elephant's trunk** is its long, flexible nose. *e.g. The elephant picked up the box with its trunk.*

elevator   692
An **elevator** is a lift that carries people up and down inside buildings. *e.g. The building has a modern elevator with a glass shaft.*

elicit   774
If you **elicit** a piece of information, you find it out by asking careful questions. *e.g. In five minutes she had elicited the entire Herriard family history.*

else   767
You use **else** having mentioned one thing, person or place to refer in a vague or questioning way to another of the same kind. *e.g. O.K., so John's definitely coming. Someone else replied, too—who was that?*

embankment   1218
An **embankment** is a thick wall or mound of earth that is built to carry a road or railway over an area of low ground, or to prevent water from a river or the sea from flooding the area. *e.g. The car ran up an embankment covered with grass.*

embarrass   351, 993
If something **embarrasses** you, it makes you feel shy, ashamed, or guilty about something. *e.g. It embarrasses me to think about the time I got drunk.*

embarrass   1436
If something that someone does, signs or says **embarrasses** you, it makes you feel uncomfortable because you are worried or not confident. *e.g. The man's attentions began to embarrass her.*

embarrassed   351, 993
A person who is **embarrassed** feels shy, ashamed or guilty about something. *e.g. I was so embarrassed when they told me I'd been walking around with my dress tucked in my knickers!*

embarrassment   351, 993
Embarrassment is a feeling of shyness, shame or guilt. *e.g. There was a moment of embarrassment when no-one knew what to sign.*

embossed   1157
A design or group of letters or words that is **embossed** on something is added to it in such a way that it stands up or sticks out from the surface. *e.g. The bedspread was embossed with roses.*

embrace   139
When you **embrace** someone or something, you put your arms around them and hold them tightly, usually in order to show your love or affection for them. *e.g. They laughed and embraced.*

embroider   869
If you **embroider** something such as a cloth or piece of clothing, you sew a decorative design onto it. *e.g. They want to learn how to embroider like the Russians do.*

embroidery   869
1 **Embroidery** is cloth, clothing or other material on which designs have been sewn. *e.g. Bep began folding up her embroidery.*
2 **Embroidery** is the act or process of sewing designs on cloth or other material. *e.g. Jane's first attempts at embroidery were awful!*

emerge   1718
If a fact or result **emerges** from a period of thought, discussion or investigation, it becomes known as a result of it. *e.g. One really interesting thing emerged from this research.*

emergence   1718
The **emergence** of something is the process or event of its coming into existence. *e.g. Our brainstorming session resulted in the emergence of new ideas.*

emergency   383, 384
1 An **emergency** is an unexpected and dangerous situation which must be dealt with quickly *e.g. This door should only be used in an emergency.*
2 **Emergency** action is taken immediately because an emergency has occurred. *e.g. Sally needed an emergency operation.*

emotion   1082
1 An **emotion** is a feeling such as fear, love, hate, anger or jealousy. *e.g. The meeting raised many emotions.*
2 **Emotion** is feelings such as fear, love, hate, anger or jealousy. *e.g. She looked around her without emotion.*

emotional   1082
1 **Emotional** means concerned with your emotions and the way that you are feeling rather than with your physical health or condition. *e.g. She has emotional problems.*
2 If someone is or becomes **emotional**, they show their feelings very openly, especially because they are upset. *e.g. He became very emotional and started to cry.*

emphasis   1364
Emphasis is special importance that is given to an activity or to a part or aspect of something. *e.g. The army has always laid great emphasis on the use of helicopters.*

emphasise   1364
Also spelled **emphasize**.
To **emphasise** something means to indicate that it is particularly important or true. *e.g. I wish to emphasise the last point.*

employ   1664
If you **employ** someone, you pay them to work for you. *e.g. He was employed as a Research Assistant.*

employer   450, 957
An **employer** is a person who has other people working for him or her, or a company that people work for. *e.g. She has worked for her present employer for two years.*

empty   963, 1555
Something that is **empty** has no people or things in it. *e.g. The biscuit tin was empty again.*

empty   1321
A container that is **empty** no longer has anything in it. *e.g. He noticed that her pint glass was empty.*

empty a dustbin   102
If you **empty a dustbin**, you remove the contents from it by tipping them out. *e.g. He emptied the dustbin into the lorry.*

encourage   229, 560
1 If you **encourage** someone to do something,

you tell them that you think that they should do it, or that they should continue doing it. *e.g. Her husband encouraged her to get a car.*

2 If you **encourage** a particular activity, you support it actively. *e.g. We encourage all of our staff to attend sign language classes.*

encouragement 229, 560
If you give somebody **encouragement**, you support them by telling them that you think they should do something or continue doing it. *e.g. John's encouragement convinced him that he should apply to Durham University to train as an interpreter.*

end 1302, 1303, 1552
1 When a situation or activity **ends**, or when you **end** it, it stops. *e.g. My journey ends in London.*

2 If a piece of writing or a performance **ends** in a particular way, or if the writer or performer **ends** it in that way, its final part consists of the thing mentioned. *e.g. The play will end with all the children playing and reciting.*

3 The **end** of a period of time, an event, or an experience is the last part of it or the final point in it. *e.g. We will leave that till the end.*

endorse 65
If someone's driving licence is **endorsed**, an official record is made on it that they have been found guilty of a driving offence. *e.g. He was ordered to pay a fine of £200 and his licence was endorsed.*

endorsement 65
An **endorsement** is an official record of a driving offence entered on a person's driving licence. *e.g. He had one previous endorsement for speeding.*

endure 179, 181
If you **endure** a painful or difficult situation, you bear it calmly and patiently *e.g. If you want to climb Mount Everest, you must be ready to endure hardships and even death.*

enemy 563, 924
1 You can describe someone who intends to harm you as your **enemy**. *e.g. I have many enemies.*

2 In a war, the **enemy** is the army or country that your country is fighting. *e.g. Enemy aircraft came over nightly.*

energy 6, 75
1 **Energy** is the ability and strength to do active physical things and the feeling that you are full of physical power and life. *e.g. You must eat to give you energy.*

2 **Energy** is the power that is obtained from sources such as electricity, coal, wind or water and that makes machines work and provides heat. *e.g. Coal is an efficient source of energy.*

engaged 47
1 If a telephone or telephone line is **engaged**, it is already being used by someone else so that you are unable to get through. *e.g. The D.S.R.U.'s text telephones are always engaged.*

2 If a toilet is **engaged**, it is already being used by someone else. *e.g. Both toilets were engaged.*

engaged 591
When two people are **engaged** or get **engaged**, they have agreed to marry each other. *e.g. They got engaged two weeks ago.*

engagement 128
1 An **engagement** is an arrangement that you have made to do something at a particular time. *e.g. I phoned my wife to cancel our lunch engagement.*

2 An **engagement** is an arrangement that has been made for a performer to perform somewhere on a particular occasion. *e.g. Dorothy has a T.V. engagement with 'See Hear' next Tuesday.*

engagement 591
An **engagement** is an agreement that two people have made with each other to get married. *e.g. Colin and Therese are having an engagement party.*

engine 608
The **engine** of a car or other vehicle is the part that produces the power which makes the vehicle move. *e.g. The engine in the lorry needed replacing.*

engineer 1193
1 An **engineer** is a skilled person who uses scientific knowledge to design and construct machinery, engines, electrical devices, or roads and bridges. *e.g. Jim Foster, a brilliant young mining engineer, won the contract for the new shafts.*

2 An **engineer** is a person who repairs mechanical or electrical devices such as telephones or central heating systems. *e.g. The telephone engineer can't come until Wednesday.*

engineering 1193
Engineering is the activities and work involved in designing and constructing machinery, engines, electrical devices, or roads and bridges. *e.g. The bridge was a major feat of engineering.*

England 378
England is the largest section of Great Britain bordering on Scotland and Wales. *e.g. The Act of Union of 1707 united England and Scotland.*

English 378
1 Someone or something that is **English** belongs to or relates to England or its people. *e.g. Angela and Mike were among the few English tourists in Patagonia.*

2 **English** is the main language spoken in Great Britain, Ireland, the United States, Canada, Australia, and other countries. *e.g. Half the letter was in Swedish and the rest in English.*

3 You can refer to people from England in general, or a particular group of people from England, as the **English**. *e.g. The English are favourites to win this season's rugby union Five Nations Tournament.*

enjoy 710
If you **enjoy** something or **enjoy** doing it, you find pleasure and satisfaction in doing or experiencing it. *e.g. I really enjoy that programme with Jeremy Beadle.*

enjoy 1390
1 If you **enjoy** something, you find pleasure and satisfaction in doing or experiencing it. *e.g. Painting is something I really enjoy.*

2 If you **enjoy** something, you are lucky enough to have something, for example a right, benefit or privilege. *e.g. They enjoyed exceptional living standards.*

enjoyable 1390
Something that is **enjoyable** gives you pleasure and satisfaction. *e.g. We spent an enjoyable day looking around the museum.*

enjoyment 1390
Enjoyment is the feeling of pleasure and satisfaction that you have when you do or experience something that you enjoy. *e.g. My enjoyment was obvious to everyone.*

enormous 1064
Something that is **enormous** is extremely large in size or amount. *e.g. There was an enormous cat on the counter.*

enough 1267, 1583
1 **Enough** means as much as you need. *e.g. I haven't enough room.*

2 If you sign or say that something is **enough**, you mean that you do not want it to continue any longer or get any worse. *e.g. Two years was enough.*

enquire 848
Also spelled **inquire**.
If you **enquire** about something, you ask for information about it. *e.g. He went to enquire about the times of trains.*

enquiry 865
Also spelled **inquiry**.
1 An **enquiry** is an offical investigation into something. *e.g. There is to be a public enquiry into the food poisoning scandal.*

2 **Enquiries** are questions you ask someone in order to get some information. *e.g. I don't know his name, but I will make some enquiries.*

enter   1607

1 To **enter** means to come into or to go into a particular place. *e.g. He planned to enter the cave at night.*

2 To **enter** an organisation or institution means to become a member of it. *e.g. You could not enter university without Latin when I applied.*

enthusiasm   1197

Enthusiasm is great eagerness to be involved in a particular activity, because it is something you like and enjoy or that you think is important. *e.g. Her enthusiasm for the theatre was boundless.*

enthusiastic   1197

If you are **enthusiastic** about something, you show a lot of excitement, eagerness, or approval of it by the way that you behave, sign or talk. *e.g. Enthusiastic crowds filled the streets.*

entitled   823

If a work of art or piece of literature is **entitled**, for example, 'Sunrise', its proper name is 'Sunrise'. *e.g. A report entitled 'Attitudes Towards Geriatrics' has been released today.*

entrance   1607

1 An **entrance** is a way into a place. *e.g. The tradesmen's entrance is at the side.*

2 Someone's **entrance** is their arrival in a room or building. *e.g. She had only broken off to acknowledge our entrance.*

3 If you gain **entrance** to a particular place, you are able to go in it. *e.g. They must produce identity cards before they can gain entrance.*

4 If you gain **entrance** to a particular profession, society or institution, you are accepted as a member of it. *e.g. She failed her college entrance exams.*

entry   1607

1 If you are allowed **entry** into a country, a building, etc., you are allowed to go into it. *e.g. The gallery will be open on Sunday afternoons; entry will be free.*

2 Someone's **entry** into a particular society or group is their joining of it. *e.g. He succeeded in negotiating British entry to the Common Market.*

envelope   488, 953, 1259

An **envelope** is the rectangular paper cover in which you send a letter or card to someone through the post. *e.g. The envelope had a London postmark.*

envious   1184

If you are **envious** of someone else, you wish that you had things or qualities that they have. *e.g. One envious onlooker actually pinched a bit of the banana.*

environment   1017

1 Someone's **environment** is everything that affects their daily life, including the place in which they live, the people around them, and the things that they experience. *e.g. Could the college provide a smoke-free environment?*

2 The **environment** is the natural world of air, sea, land, plants, animals and so on that exists around us. *e.g. We are fighting pollution to protect the environment.*

envy   580, 583, 1184

1 If you **envy** someone, you wish that you had things or qualities that they have. *e.g. To be honest, I envy him.*

2 **Envy** is the feeling of wishing that you had things or qualities that someone else has. *e.g. Her good looks caused envy and admiration.*

epidemic   319, 1044

An **epidemic** is the occurrence of a disease which affects a very large number of people living in an area and which spreads quickly to other people. *e.g. An influenza epidemic has affected a substantial proportion of the population of Lima.*

equal   1406, 1409, 1618

1 If two things are **equal** or if one thing is **equal** to another, they are the same, usually in size, amount or degree. *e.g. The prevailing belief in a tight monetary policy is held with equal fervour by all political parties.*

2 If you treat people on an **equal** basis or give them **equal** rights, you treat them all in the same way and consider them to have the same rights as each other without considering, for example, their sex, status, disability, religious beliefs, age or race. *e.g. The Association aims to provide equal opportunities for men and women.*

3 If you sign or say that people are or should be **equal**, you mean that everyone has or should have the same rights and opportunities as each other. *e.g. Everyone should be equal before the law.*

4 Someone who is your **equal** has the same ability, status, or rights that you have. *e.g. You learn to treat your opponent as your equal.*

5 If two people do something on **equal** terms, neither person has any advantage over the other. *e.g. This puts us on equal terms for the first time in many years.*

equal   1416, 1417

1 If you treat a number of people on an **equal** basis or give them **equal** rights, you treat them all in the same way and consider them to have the same rights as each other without considering, for example, their sex, status, disability, religious beliefs, age or race. *e.g. We believe in equal pay for equal work.*

2 If you sign or say that a number of people are or should be **equal**, you mean that everyone has or should have the same rights and opportunities as each other. *e.g. Everyone is equal before the law, supposedly.*

3 If a number of things are **equal** to each other, they are the same, usually in size, amount or degree. *e.g. The results were equal for all of the bottles: every single one proved to be too acidic.*

equality   1406, 1409, 1416, 1417, 1618

Equality is the same status, rights and responsibilities for all members of a society, group or family. *e.g. Equality of opportunity between all men and women is our simple goal.*

equipment   1193

Equipment consists of the things which are used for a particular purpose, for example a hobby or job. *e.g. A lot of money was spent on new equipment.*

equivalent   1409, 1618

If things are **equivalent**, they have the same use, function, size or value. *e.g. Women were paid less than men doing equivalent work.*

erase   243

If you **erase** writing, you remove it from somewhere, especially by rubbing it with a rubber. *e.g. I should erase the notes I've written in the margin.*

eraser   243

An **eraser** is a piece of rubber used for rubbing out writing. *e.g. Try to remove dirty marks with an eraser.*

err   436

If you **err**, you make a mistake. *e.g. We have erred in appointing the new committee so soon.*

error   436, 1136

1 An **error** is a mistake. *e.g. He found several grammatical errors in the paper.*

2 If you do something in **error**, it happens because of a mistake. *e.g. Another village had been wiped out in error.*

escalator   692, 805

An **escalator** or **up escalator** is a moving staircase which people can travel from a lower to a higher floor or level on. *e.g. Take the escalator to the third floor for the menswear department.*

escalator   806

An **escalator** or **down escalator** is a moving staircase which people can travel from a higher to a lower floor or level on. *e.g. I fell in love with her on the escalator going down to the bargain basement.*

escape   415

1 If you **escape** from a thing, person, situation or duty that you do not like, you succeed in avoiding them or in getting away from them. *e.g. Ralph escaped when the lion was distracted by a loud explosion.*

2 You can also sign or say that you **escape** when you survive something such as an attack or an accident. *e.g. We escaped from the earthquake without many injuries.*

3 If you **escape** from a place (such as a prison) or situation, you succeed in getting away from there, even though people are trying to capture you and keep you there by force. *e.g. In 1966, the spy George Blake escaped from prison.*

4 An **escape** is an act of escaping from a particular place or situation. *e.g. It was a daring escape.*

escapee   415
An **escapee** is a person who has escaped, especially from prison. *e.g. There has been a steady stream of escapees, none of whom have been recaptured.*

escape one   508
If you sign or say that something **escapes you**, you mean that you can't remember it. *e.g. His name escapes me for the moment, but he had a beard.*

essential   1300
1 The **essential** aspects of something are its most basic or important aspects. *e.g. The essential points of the lecture were translated into English.*
2 Something that is **essential** is fundamental or very important. *e.g. It is essential that we get this right.*

establish   151
If someone **establishes** a system, organisation, or state of affairs, they create it and set it up in a way that is intended to be permanent. *e.g. She set out to establish her own business.*

establishment   151
The **establishment** of an organisation, system or state of affairs is the act of creating it or setting it up for a particular purpose. *e.g. She welcomed the establishment of free trade unions.*

estimate   329
1 If you **estimate** something such as an amount or a quantity, you calculate it approximately. *e.g. She estimated that the chasm was a good eight feet wide.*
2 An **estimate** is an approximate calculation, or the result obtained by such a calculation. *e.g. My estimate would put the value of Bailey-Styles' work in the millions.*

estimation   329
An **estimation** is an approximate calculation, or the result obtained by such a calculation. *e.g. His estimation of the total cost of the project was based on 1992 prices.*

etc   426, 427, 447, 551
You use **etc** at the end of a list to indicate that there are other items which you could mention if you had enough time or space. Etc is a

written abbreviation for 'et cetera'. *e.g. Sign languages share many such features with spoken languages—I'm thinking of pluralisation, negation, aspectual, modulation, etc., all of which you should be familiar with.*

et cetera   426, 427, 447, 551
See **etc**.

eternal   550
1 If something is **eternal**, it lasts for ever. *e.g. The promise of eternal bliss is there in black and white.*
2 You can describe an action as **eternal** when it seems to last for ever. *e.g. He was annoying me with his eternal whining.*

Europe   1734
1 **Europe** is the second smallest of the continents. It has Asia on its eastern side, with the Arctic to the north, the Atlantic to the west, and the Mediterranean and Africa to the south. *e.g. When I was at school in the States, we studied the history of Europe.*
2 In the United Kingdom, people may use **Europe** to refer to all of Europe except the United Kingdom. *e.g. We've just got time to take a quick look at the weather over in Europe.*
3 People may use **Europe** to mean the same as the European Community. *e.g. I gather you are in favour of Britain being in Europe.*

European   1734
1 Someone or something that is **European** belongs to or relates to the continent of Europe. *e.g. European countries were represented at the ecological summit meeting in Brazil.*
2 **European** means belonging to or relating to people who come from Europe. *e.g. She is studying European Literature at university.*
3 A **European** is someone who comes from Europe or whose family identity relates to Europe. *e.g. Kurt Waldheim was the last European to be General Secretary of the United Nations.*
4 **European** may be used to mean belonging to or relating to the European Community. *e.g. She is a Member of the European Parliament.*
5 The address of the **European** Community Regional Secretariat of the World Federation of the Deaf is: ECRS, Rue Franklinstraat 110, B-1040, Brussels, Belgium.

evaluate   329, 1367, 1413
If you **evaluate** something, you decide on its significance, value, or quality after carefully studying its good and bad features. *e.g. He was asked to evaluate the situation.*

evaluation   329, 1367, 1413
An **evaluation** is a decision about the significance, value, or quality of something, based on a careful study of its good and bad features. *e.g. Professor Blume's study will provide an evaluation of the cochlear implant*

programme in Britain and three other European countries.

evasive   1228
If you are being **evasive**, or give an **evasive** answer, you are deliberately trying to avoid signing or speaking about something. *e.g. Victor became evasive, and told us that he had nothing more to say.*

even   1212
A surface that is **even** is smooth and flat. *e.g. The road was even.*

even   1618
1 A surface that is **even** is smooth and flat. *e.g. Look at that shelf now I've planed it: perfectly even.*
2 If a contest or competition is **even**, the people taking part are all as strong, skilful, or successful as each other. *e.g. It is an even battle, with the troops of the two armies equally well equipped.*

evening   718, 810, 811, 1464, 1465, 1577
1 The **evening** is the part of each day between the end of the afternoon and the time when you go to bed. *e.g. He runs five miles each evening.*
2 You can sign or say **evening** to greet somebody when it is between the end of the afternoon and the time you go to bed. *e.g. Evening, all. Dixon of Dock Green here.*

eventually   216
1 **Eventually** means in the end, especially after a lot of delays, problems, or arguments. *e.g. Eventually, in the afternoon, they got through to the hospital.*
2 **Eventually** means at the end of a situation or process or as the final result of it. *e.g. Access to training eventually brought Deaf people to senior posts in business and commerce.*

everlasting   550
Something that is **everlasting** continues to exist or to happen, and never ends, or seems to do so. *e.g. The everlasting snows of the mighty Himalayas were laid out before them like a carpet.*

every   987, 1234
You use **every** to indicate that you are referring to all the members of a group or all the parts of something and not only some of them. *e.g. She spoke to every person at the party.*

everybody   987, 1234
1 You use **everybody** to refer to all the people in a particular group. *e.g. Everybody in the office laughed.*
2 You use **everybody** to refer to all the people in the world. *e.g. Everybody likes to be happy.*

everyday   358
Everyday is used to describe something which happens or is used each day. *e.g. Exercise is part of my everyday routine.*

everyone   987, 1234
1 You use **everyone** to refer to all the people in
a particular group. *e.g. Everyone went home,
except me.*
2 You use **everyone** to refer to all the people in
the world. *e.g. Everyone should have water, food
and shelter.*

everything   987, 1104, 1234
You use **everything** to refer to all the objects,
actions, activities or facts in a particular situation.
e.g. I don't agree with everything he signs.

everywhere   987, 1234
You use **everywhere** to refer to a whole area
or to all the places in a particular area. *e.g.
Everywhere in Asia it is the same.*

evidence   326
1 **Evidence** is anything that you see, experience,
read, or are told that causes you to believe that
something is true or has really happened. *e.g.
Historical evidence suggests that this was the site of
the first school for deaf children in Edinburgh.*
2 **Evidence** is the information which is used in
a court of law to try to prove something. *e.g.
The witnesses' testimony gives us the crucial
evidence that we needed.*

evidence   330
Evidence is anything that you see or read in a
document which causes you to believe that
something is true or has really happened. *e.g.
The solicitor could provide no evidence of quarrels
between them.*
2 **Evidence** is the documentary information
which is used in a court of law to try to prove
something. *e.g. The photograph was part of the
evidence in the divorce case.*

evil   910, 914
1 **Evil** is all the wicked and bad things that
happen in the world. *e.g. The conflict between
good and evil is unending.*
2 The **evils** of a situation or activity are all the
things that are bad or harmful about it. *e.g. His
father gave him a sermon on the evils of drink.*
3 Something that is **evil** causes a great deal of
harm to people. *e.g. Slavery was the most evil
system of labour ever devised.*

evil   939
1 **Evil** is all the wicked and bad things that
happen in the world. *e.g. The conflict between
good and evil is endless.*
2 Something that is **evil** causes a great deal of
harm to people. *e.g. Slavery was the most evil
system of labour ever devised.*
3 Someone or something that is **evil** is
naughty. *e.g. That cat's evil: it's always
scratching my cupboard doors.*

exact   847, 849, 852, 891
1 Something that is **exact** is accurate, correct,

and specific, rather than being based on a guess or
an approximation. *e.g. He noted the exact time.*
2 Something that is **exact** is correct and
complete in every detail. *e.g. It was an exact
replica of Hamburg airport.*
3 Someone who is **exact**, especially in their
work, is very careful and detailed in their
thinking and methods. *e.g. He was a modest
man and an exact and patient scientist.*

exaggerate   1600
If you **exaggerate**, you make the thing that
you are referring to seem bigger, better, worse
or more extreme than it actually is. *e.g. Perhaps
I exaggerate a little.*

exaggeration   1600
1 **Exaggeration** is making the thing that you
are referring to seem bigger, better, worse or
more extreme than it actually is. *e.g.
Exaggeration will get you nowhere.*
2 An **exaggeration** is an attempt to make the
thing that you are referring to seem bigger,
better, worse or more extreme than it actually
is. *e.g. Isn't that a bit of an exaggeration?*

exam   690
An **exam** is a formal test that you take to show
your knowledge or ability in a particular subject.
e.g. They were all nervous before the exam.

examination   690
An **examination** is a formal test that you take
to show your knowledge or ability in a
particular subject. *e.g. We had a three hour
written examination.*

examine   962
If you **examine** something, you look at it
carefully to check that there are no mistakes or
to attempt to understand it or to see something
particular about it. *e.g. Examine the object
thoroughly—do you recognise it?*

examine a document   961
If you **examine a document**, you look at it
carefully to check that there are no mistakes or
to attempt to understand it or see something
particular which is contained in it. *e.g. If you
would examine the document carefully, sir; do
you see the blemish?*

examiner   962
An **examiner** is someone who looks at
something very carefully to check that there
are no mistakes or to attempt to see something
particular about it. *e.g. The examiner checked
the diamonds, and then the cutter got to work.*

exceed   1620
If something **exceeds** a particular amount or
number, it is greater than that amount or
number. *e.g. Numbers attending may exceed
expectations by up to fifty percent.*

excellent   213, 220, 880
Something that is **excellent** is very good
indeed. *e.g. I think the teaching here is excellent.*

exchange   446
1 If you **exchange** one thing for a second
thing, you replace it with the second thing
(which is more satisfactory or more useful).
e.g. The shop refused to exchange the sweater.
2 If you **exchange** your house or job with
someone, you live or work in the place where
they normally live or work, while they live or
work in the place where you normally live or
work. *e.g. The Macardles exchanged houses with
some friends who live in Paris.*
3 If you give something to someone in
exchange for something else, you give it to
them because they are giving the other thing to
you. *e.g. They sold textiles in exchange for
agricultural products.*
4 An **exchange** is the activity of two people
living or working in each other's usual house or
place. *e.g. The exchange was not a great success.*

exchange   1389
1 If two or more people **exchange** things, they
give them to each other. *e.g. The two of us will
exchange addresses.*
2 If you **exchange** one thing for another, you
replace it with the other thing, because the
other thing is more satisfactory or more useful.
e.g. She wanted to exchange the jewels for money.

excite   1197
If someone or something **excites** you, they
make you very interested and enthusiastic. *e.g.
The new plans were bound to excite him.*

excited   1197
If you are **excited**, you are so happy that you are
full of energy and cannot relax, especially
because you are looking forward to an enjoyable
and special event and cannot stop thinking about
it. *e.g. He was so excited he could hardly sleep.*

exclude   1616, 1634
1 If you **exclude** something, you deliberately
do not include it in a piece of work, discussion,
activity, et cetera. *e.g. This Act of Parliament
will exclude cases of death by murder.*
2 If you **exclude** someone, you prevent them
from entering a place or taking part in an
activity. *e.g. We agreed to exclude Miriam from
our trip to Ramsgate.*
3 If you are **excluded** from doing or paying
something, you do not have to do or pay it.
*e.g. Deaf persons are excluded from paying
VAT on Minicoms.*

excuse   1580
1 If you **excuse** someone for something wrong
that they have done, you forgive them for it. *e.g. I
can excuse the delay now that I know the reason.*
2 If you ask someone to **excuse** you, you are

asking them to allow you to leave. *e.g. Will you excuse me just a second?*

3 You sign or say **excuse me** to show politeness when you get someone's attention, especially when you want to ask them a question. *e.g. Excuse me: is this the way to Langwith College?*

4 You sign or say **excuse me** to show politeness when you apologise for disturbing or interrupting someone, or for doing something slightly impolite such as burping or hiccupping. *e.g. Excuse me—green vegetables; you know how it is!*

excuse me   1214

You sign or say **excuse me** to get someone's attention, especially when you want to ask them a question. *e.g. Excuse me, but is there a fairly cheap restaurant near here?*

excuse me   1259

You use **excuse me** to show politeness when you apologise for disturbing or interrupting someone, or doing something slightly impolite such as burping. *e.g. Excuse me butting in.*

execute   1586

To **execute** someone means to kill them as a punishment. *e.g. My aunt was the last woman to be executed.*

Exeter   651

1 **Exeter** is a city in South West England, the administrative centre of Devon. *e.g. Their son went to the Royal School for the Deaf in Exeter.*
2 The address of the **Exeter** Deaf Social Club is: Friendship Centre, Palace Gate, Off South Street, Exeter.

exhausted   930, 1588

If you are **exhausted**, you are very tired, either physically or mentally. *e.g. She was too exhausted to argue.*

exhaust fumes   1109

Exhaust fumes are the gases expelled from motor vehicles when their engines are running. *e.g. On Euston Road, I nearly choked on exhaust fumes.*

exhibit   1373, 1384

1 When something such as a picture or sculpture is **exhibited**, it is put in a public place such as a museum or art gallery, so that people can come to look at it. *e.g. I wanted to exhibit some tapestries I had done in America.*
2 When artists **exhibit**, they show their work in public. *e.g. She was still working last year and hoping to exhibit this summer.*
3 If you **exhibit** something to someone, you show it to them in order to make them believe you or admire you. *e.g. Glenn exhibited the rat's tooth to all his friends.*

exhibition   1373, 1384

1 An **exhibition** is a collection of pictures, sculptures, or other things in a public place where people can come to look at them. *e.g. We wanted to go to the exhibition of Martin Dutton's carvings.*
2 **Exhibition** is the showing of pictures, sculptures, or other things in a public place. *e.g. The film was refused a licence for public exhibition.*

exist   161, 977

Exist means to be present in the world or universe as a real, living or actual thing and not, for example, to be something that people have imagined or made up, or something that has disappeared or been destroyed. *e.g. Tribes who live by hunting and gathering still exist.*

expand   1063

1 If you **expand** something, or it **expands**, it becomes greater in number or amount. *e.g. Between 1960 and 1970, the city's population expanded by 19%.*
2 If a business **expands**, it becomes bigger and more successful. *e.g. Cadburys expanded rapidly between the wars.*

expect   188, 452, 505

1 If you **expect** something to happen, you believe that it will happen. *e.g. He expected the strike to end.*
2 If you **expect** something, you believe that it is going to happen or arrive. *e.g. We are expecting rain.*

expectant   505

If you are **expectant**, you think something interesting is going to happen. *e.g. As the googly was bowled, the slips were alert and expectant.*

expectation   188

An **expectation** is a strong belief of hope that something will happen or should happen. *e.g. My expectation is that we will finish next week.*

expecting   505, 1013

If a woman is **expecting**, she is pregnant. *e.g. Jenny is expecting and everyone is delighted.*

expensive   989

Something that is **expensive** costs a lot of money, more than you expected or more than seems reasonable. *e.g. He liked to buy expensive shoes.*

experience   170, 1531

1 **Experience** is the fact of having worked at a particular kind of job for a period of time. *e.g. She has six months' experience.*
2 **Experience** is the act of seeing, doing, or feeling something or the fact of being affected by it. *e.g. The experience of meeting Deaf adults changed her views on bilingual education.*

3 **Experience** is the things that have happened to you or that you have done. *e.g. I am speaking from personal experience.*

experienced   170, 1531

You describe someone as **experienced** when they are skilled at a particular job because they have done it for a long time. *e.g. She is a very experienced lecturer.*

experiment   962

1 An **experiment** is a scientific test which is done in order to prove or discover something. *e.g. Complete the experiment tomorrow, please.*
2 An **experiment** is the trying out of a new idea or method to see what effect it has. *e.g. The failure of this great experiment in industrial democracy is visible to all.*
3 If you **experiment** with something or experiment on it, you do a scientific test on it in order to prove or discover something. *e.g. He wanted to experiment with some rock samples brought back from the moon.*
4 To **experiment** means to try out a new idea or method to see what effect it has. *e.g. Small businesses anxious to experiment with computers are keen to take part in the scheme.*

experiment   1686

1 An **experiment** is a scientific test which is done in order to prove or discover something. *e.g. Experiments were done to find a cure for the different types of cancer.*
2 If you **experiment** with something or **experiment** on it, you do a scientific test on it in order to prove or discover something. *e.g. He experimented with blood taken from young rats.*

expert   158, 170, 1531

1 An **expert** is a person who is very skilled at doing something. *e.g. An expert was called in to dismantle the bomb.*
2 An **expert** is a person who has studied a particular subject and knows a lot about it. *e.g. I met a financial expert who writes for the Guardian.*
3 Someone who is **expert** at doing something is very skilled at it. *e.g. When you get more expert in these matters, you'll be able to handle it alone.*
4 **Expert** advice, opinion, or help is advice, opinion, or help that is given by someone who has studied a subject thoroughly or is very skilled at a particular job. *e.g. You should get expert treatment from a specialist.*

explain   1311, 1383

1 If you **explain** something, you give details about it so that it can be understood. *e.g. Let me explain the problem.*
2 If you **explain** something, you give people reasons for it. *e.g. He never wrote to me to explain his decision.*

explanation   1311, 1383

1 If you give an **explanation**, you say why

something happened. *e.g. The time for lengthy explanation was over.*

2 If you give an **explanation**, you describe something in detail. *e.g. Scientific explanation of the universe is of growing interest to the general reader.*

explode   124, 1720, 1729
1 When something **explodes**, it bursts loudly and with great force, often causing a lot of damage. *e.g. A bomb exploded in the next street.*
2 You can sign or say that a person **explodes** when they express strong feelings suddenly and violently. *e.g. She exploded with rage when she heard the news.*

exploit   774
If you **exploit** someone, you treat them unfairly by using their work or ideas and giving them very little in return. *e.g. Fagin grew rich by exploiting the little pickpockets.*

explore   776
If you **explore** something, you think about it carefully and discuss it with other people in order to decide whether it is a good thing or idea. *e.g. We will have to explore the possibility of funds from Europe.*

explosion   124, 1720, 1729
An **explosion** is a sudden violent burst of energy, for example one caused by a bomb. *e.g. Twenty men were killed in the explosion.*

expose   1373, 1384
1 To **expose** something means to uncover it and make it visible. *e.g. If we expose this seaweed to the sun, watch how it reacts.*
2 To **expose** a person or situation means to reveal the truth about them, especially when it involves dishonest or shocking behaviour. *e.g. They tried to expose him as a liar.*

express   1084
1 If you **express** an idea or feeling, you tell it to other people through signs, speech or writing. *e.g. Before we start work, I would like to express my thanks to the secretary.*
2 When you **express** yourself, you put ideas into signs or words, especially openly and clearly. *e.g. They could express themselves far better in BSL than in English.*

exquisite   880
You describe something as **exquisite** when it is extremely beautiful in appearance. *e.g. She has the most exquisite jewellery.*

extend   1620
1 If something **extends** for a particular distance, it continues for that distance from a point or central area. *e.g. The road will extend two kilometres more than was planned.*
2 If you **extend** something, you make it bigger or longer. *e.g. Wouldn't you like to extend your house?*
3 If you **extend** something, you cause it to exist or be valid for a longer period of time. *e.g. The authorities agreed to extend her visa.*
4 If you **extend** something, you cause it to include or affect more people or things. *e.g. Congress wants us to agree to extend the law to cover all states.*

extension   1620
1 An **extension** is a new room or building which is added to an existing building. *e.g. An extension to the library was built in 1989.*
2 An **extension** is an extra period of time for which something continues to exist or be valid. *e.g. He asked for an extension of his residence permit.*
3 An **extension** is a development that includes or affects more people, ideas, or activities. *e.g. Nationalist leaders demanded the extension of democratic rights.*

exterior   1563, 1564, 1609
1 The **exterior** of something is its outside surface. *e.g. The exterior of the building needs painting.*
2 You use **exterior** to describe something that is situated or happening outside something. *e.g. Exterior drains must be kept clear.*

external   1563, 1564, 1609
1 **External** means happening, coming from or existing outside a place, person, or area of activity. *e.g. We survive on external funding.*
2 **External** is used to describe people who come into an organisation from outside in order to do a job there. *e.g. The accounts are checked by external auditors.*

extra   1594
An **extra** thing, person, or amount is a thing, person, or amount that is added to others of the same kind. *e.g. You have to pay extra for breakfast.*

extract   774
1 If you **extract** information from someone, you get it from them with difficulty. *e.g. Sir James had extracted from Francis a fairly detailed account.*
2 If someone **extracts** something that gives them an advantage from a situation, they use the situation in order to gain the advantage. *e.g. They will extract the maximum propaganda value from this affair.*

extract a tooth   259
If a dentist **extracts a tooth**, he or she pulls out one of a person's teeth. *e.g. Ouch! I signed, when Mr. Nicol extracted one of my teeth.*

extraction   259
At the dentist's, if you have an **extraction**, the dentist pulls out one of your teeth. *e.g. She had to have an extraction last week and her gum is still very sore.*

extravagant   1506
1 Someone who is **extravagant** spends more money than is reasonable, or than they can afford. *e.g. He was extravagant and lived a life of luxury.*
2 Something that is **extravagant** costs more money than is reasonable or than you can afford. *e.g. Extravagant gifts for all your relatives at Christmas could cause them embarrassment.*

extreme   1620
1 **Extreme** situations and behaviour are much more severe or unusual than you would expect. *e.g. Their methods may seem extreme to many parents.*
2 The **extreme** point, edge, or end of something is its furthest point, edge, or end. *e.g. The extreme tip of the bullet, at this magnification, can clearly be seen to have damaged the bone.*

eye   325
An **eye** is one of the two organs on the face of a person, animal or bird that are used for seeing. *e.g. He went into hospital for an operation on his eye.*

eyesight   755
Your **eyesight** is your ability to see. *e.g. I'm sure my eyesight has improved since I started eating carrots!*

F, f

F
F is the sixth letter of the British manual and English alphabets. See page 851.

fabric   1516
Fabric is cloth or other material produced by weaving cotton, nylon, wool, silk, or other threads together. There are many different kinds of fabrics. They are used for making things such as clothes, curtains and sheets. *e.g. This fabric is specially imported from Italy.*

face   324
Your **face** is the front of your head from your

chin to your forehead. *e.g. You look so sad— your face shows your real feelings.*

facecloth 1244
A **facecloth** is a small cloth made of towelling which you use for washing yourself. *e.g. I bought a new facecloth.*

face (keep a straight face) 531
If you **keep a straight face**, you manage to look serious, although you want to laugh. *e.g. I found it hard to keep a straight face.*

face to face 434
If you come **face to face** with someone, you approach each other until you are in front of each other and can interact directly. *e.g. I came face to face with Karen in the corridor.*

facing 440
1 If something or someone is **facing** a particular thing or person, their front is towards that thing or person. *e.g. The two boys were facing each other.*
2 If you are **facing** something difficult or unpleasant, it is going to affect you or you will have to deal with it. *e.g. She is facing one of the most daunting decisions of her entire political career.*

fact 330
A **fact** is a recorded statement or piece of information that is true. *e.g. This week, 'Sign On' presents the facts as contained in the Institute's own documents.*

fact (in fact) 195
See **in fact.**

factory 228
A **factory** is a large building or group of buildings where goods are made in large quantities, usually with the use of machines. *e.g. My father worked in a car factory.*

factual 1323
Something that is **factual** is concerned with facts or contains facts, rather than giving theories or personal interpretations. *e.g. It is best to be as short, clear, and factual as possible.*

fade away 1100
When something **fades away**, it slowly becomes less intense, strong or important until it ends completely. *e.g. In the direct sunlight, the colours on the eiderdown faded away.*

fag 757
A **fag** is a cigarette. *e.g. He was dying for a fag.*

fail 923, 925
1 If you **fail** to do something that you were trying to do, you do not succeed in doing it. *e.g. Their party failed to win a single seat.*

2 If you **fail** to do something that you should have done, you do not do it. *e.g. He was fined for failing to complete the census form.*
3 If you **fail** a test or examination, you do not reach the standard that is required. *e.g. I passed the video exam but failed my teaching practice.*

failure 925
1 **Failure** is a lack of success in doing or achieving something. *e.g. It was a desperate initiative which ended in failure.*
2 Someone who is a **failure** has not succeeded at something. *e.g. I felt such a failure.*
3 If something is a **failure**, it is unsuccessful. *e.g. The meeting was a failure: none of the objectives were met.*

faint 799
If you **faint**, you lose consciousness for a short time. *e.g. He will faint from the pain if we don't do something quickly.*

faint 1074
Someone who feels **faint** feels dizzy and unsteady. *e.g. She felt faint after the operation.*

fair 108
A **fair** is an event held in a large open area at which people pay to ride on various machines for amusement or try to win prizes in games of skill or luck. Fairs often travel from one town to another. *e.g. I won a doll and a jar of sweets at the fair.*

fair 218, 982
1 **Fair** can mean quite large. *e.g. We have got a fair-sized garden in our new house.*
2 A **fair** guess or idea is one that is likely to be correct. *e.g. She signed that his answer gave her a fair idea of his views.*

fair 1406, 1409, 1618
1 Something that is **fair** is reasonable according to a generally accepted standard or idea about what is right and just. *e.g. She should get a fair trial.*
2 Someone or something that is **fair** gives the same or equal treatment to everyone concerned, especially without allowing personal feelings to influence judgements. *e.g. They are very fair, looking at problems from both sides.*

fairground 108
A **fairground** is a large open area where a fair is being held, where you can ride on various machines for amusement or try to win prizes in games of skill or luck. *e.g. The lane to the fairground was very muddy.*

fairness 1406, 1409, 1618
Fairness is the quality of being reasonable and just and treating all people equally without allowing personal feelings to

influence judgements. *e.g. When will Deaf people be treated with fairness in this country?*

fairy 292, 1635
A **fairy** is a small, imaginary creature with magical powers. Fairies are usually believed to look like tiny girls with wings. *e.g. There is a fairy in my garden.*

faithful 110
You can use **faithful** to describe someone who does something regularly with dedication or determination. *e.g. She was a faithful follower of Coronation Street.*

fake 664
1 A **fake** is something that is made to look like something valuable or real in order to deceive people. *e.g. The experts announced that the paintings were fake.*
2 If you **fake** a feeling or reaction, you pretend that you are experiencing it when you are not. *e.g. Thomas faked a yawn to get his wife to leave the party.*

fall 786
1 If someone or something **falls**, they move quickly downwards onto or towards the ground. *e.g. It fell from the shelf.*
2 A **fall** is a quick downwards movement onto or towards the ground. *e.g. He was rushed to hospital after a forty-foot fall.*

fall for a lie/trick 58, 538, 856
If you **fall for a lie** or a **trick**, you believe something that is not true which was told or done to you in order to obtain something from you or make you do something foolish. *e.g. He told me he had studied for a number of years in the States and obtained a degree from Gallaudet University: how could I fall for a lie like that?*

fall out 915, 1634
If you **fall out** with someone, you have an argument and stop being friendly with them. *e.g. I am going to fall out with certain members of the band if this goes on.*

fall over 799
If someone or something that is standing **falls over**, they accidentally move or are pushed from their upright position so that they end up lying on the ground. *e.g. This ice is dreadful: I keep feeling that I'm about to fall over.*

false 664
1 **False** things are made so that they appear real although they are not. *e.g. She wore false eyelashes.*
2 **False** things are intended to deceive people. *e.g. She travelled under a false name.*
3 Behaviour that is **false** is not sincere and is often intended to deceive people. *e.g. He had a false smile.*

familiar 341
1 If someone or something is **familiar** to you, you recognise them or know them well because you have seen them before or had previous experience of them. *e.g. His face was familiar.*
2 If you are **familiar** with something, you know it well. *e.g. MI5 were familiar with George Marshall's routine: they'd been following his every move for years.*

family 695, 983, 1018
1 A **family** is a group of people who are related to each other, especially parents and their children. *e.g. The Jones family live over the road.*
2 When people talk about their **family**, they can mean their children. *e.g. She has no family of her own.*
3 You can use **family** to describe things that belong to a particular family. *e.g. Ben worked in the family business.*
4 You can use **family** to describe things that are designed to be used or enjoyed by both parents and children. *e.g. The Morris Minor was advertised as the perfect family car.*

famine 1656
Famine or a **famine** is a serious shortage of food in a country which may cause many deaths. *e.g. Many people died during the famine and the drought in Ethiopia last year.*

famished 41, 1655
If you are **famished**, you are extremely hungry. *e.g. He must be famished after three days without food.*

famous 1578
Someone or something that is **famous** is very well known. *e.g. The Mona Lisa is a very famous painting.*

fan 229
If you are a **fan** of someone or something, you admire them and support them. *e.g. My family are all football fans.*

fan 323
A **fan** is an electrical or mechanical device that has several blades which turn round in order to create a current of air. Fans can be used to keep a room cool or to get rid of unpleasant smells. *e.g. If this hot weather continues, I'm going to buy myself a fan.*

fancy 1542
1 If you **fancy** something, you want to have it or do it. *e.g. She used to fancy a flat of her own.*
2 If you **fancy** someone, you feel attracted to them in a sexual way. *e.g. George may fancy Susan, but she's not the least bit interested in him.*

fancy 1712
You sign or say **fancy** when you want to express surprise or disapproval. *e.g. Fancy him remembering.*

fantasise 1570
If you **fantasise**, you think imaginatively about something that you would like to happen but that is unlikely to happen. *e.g. He used to fantasise about leaving prison.*

fantastic 206, 213, 220
If you sign or say that something is **fantastic**, you mean that you think it is very good and you like it very much or are very pleased about it. *e.g. I think it's a fantastic film!*

fantastic 960, 1472
1 If you say that something is **fantastic**, you mean that you think it is very good and you like it very much or are very pleased about it. *e.g. He took a bite of meat, chewed it, savoured it, and signed 'Fantastic!'.*
2 You use **fantastic** to emphasise the size, amount or degree of something. *e.g. The Egyptians believed their gods had fantastic powers.*
3 Something that is **fantastic** or **fantastical** is strange and wonderful. *e.g. He was famous for his sculptures of fantastic beings.*
4 A statement or story that is **fantastic** is very strange and very difficult to believe. *e.g. The truth is scarcely less fantastic than the fable.*

fantasy 1570
A **fantasy** is a situation or event that you think about or imagine, although it is unlikely to happen or be true. *e.g. My fantasy is that the next time Mr. Major is interviewed on 'Panorama' the interview will be conducted in BSL, with a spoken English translation for non-signing viewers.*

far 460
1 If one place, thing or person is **far** away from another, there is a great distance between them. *e.g. The mountains were far from the sea.*
2 If you ask how **far** away a place is, you are asking how great a distance away it is. *e.g. About how far is it to the station?*
3 A time or event that is **far** in the future is a long time from the present. *e.g. Cold winter nights make summer seem so far off.*

faraway 460
A **faraway** place or sound is a long distance from you. *e.g. We received the news from a faraway village.*

farm 185
A **farm** is a large area of land, together with the buildings on it, that is used for growing crops or raising animals, usually in order to sell them. *e.g. They have a farm near Carlisle.*

farmer 185
A **farmer** is a person who owns or manages a farm. *e.g. He wants to be a farmer and raise pigs.*

far-off 460
Something that is **far-off**, or a **far-off** time or place, is a long distance from the present time or place. *e.g. From the train we saw the far-off peaks of Kilimanjaro.*

fart 1700, 1719
To **fart** is to expel wind from the anus. It is considered rude to do so in company. *e.g. He farted as he left the pub.*

fashion 1610
1 **Fashion** is the area of activity that involves styles of clothing and appearance. *e.g. She's working as a fashion designer.*
2 If something is the **fashion** or in **fashion**, it is popular and approved of at a particular time. *e.g. These suits are the fashion now.*

fashionable 1610
Something that is **fashionable** is popular and approved of at a particular time. *e.g. She won't wear anything that's not fashionable.*

fast 187, 382, 383, 384
1 Someone or something **fast**, moves, acts or happens with great speed. *e.g. I bought a fast car last year.*
2 If you ask how **fast** something is moving, you want to know the speed at which it is moving. *e.g. How fast did you run to break the world record?*
3 If something happens **fast**, it happens very soon and without any delay. *e.g. She needed medical help fast.*

fat 214
A **fat** person has a lot of flesh on their body. *e.g. Henry has grown fat.*

father 684
1 Your **father** is the man who is one of your parents. *e.g. My father was born deaf.*
2 In some Christian churches, priests are addressed or referred to as **Father**. *e.g. Father Clarke signed a splendid sermon this week.*
3 Christians often refer to God as 'Our **Father**' or address him as **Father**. *e.g. Heavenly Father, hear our prayers.*

Father Christmas 145, 1537
Father Christmas is an imaginary old man with a long, white beard and a red coat. He is believed to visit children on Christmas Eve and bring them their presents. *e.g. If you are good, Father Christmas will leave you a present.*

fault 910, 998
1 If a bad or undesirable situation is your **fault**, you are the cause of it or are responsible for it. *e.g. It's all the fault of a girl called Sarah.*
2 A **fault** in a person's character or in a system is a weakness or imperfection in it. *e.g. Selfishness is a fault that I recognise in myself.*

3 A **fault** in a machine or structure is a broken part or a mistake in the way it was made. *e.g. A computer fault like this is not easy to fix.*

fault (my fault)　　　　　　　35,920
If you sign or say that a bad or undesirable situation is **your fault**, you mean that you are the cause of it or are responsible for it. *e.g. The mistakes in the manuscript are my fault.*

fault (someone's own fault)　39,176,180
If you sign or say that something is **someone's own fault** you mean that what has happened was caused by them because they behaved badly or stupidly. *e.g. It was his own fault that he was refused entry to the restaurant. He was obviously drunk.*

faulty　　　　　　　　　　　　　998
A machine or piece of equipment that is not working properly is **faulty**. *e.g. It was a faulty light switch.*

favour　　　　　　　229,235,1660
1 If you are in **favour** of something, you support it and think that it is a good thing. *e.g. We favour a policy of disarmament.*
2 If you make a judgement in someone's **favour**, you sign or say that they are right. *e.g. The umpire ruled in her favour.*
3 Something that is in someone's **favour** gives them an advantage. *e.g. In your favour is the fact that this is a first offence.*
4 If you **favour** someone, you treat them better or more kindly than you treat other people. *e.g. Parents may favour the youngest child in the family.*

favour (in favour)　　　　　　227
If people are **in favour** of something, they support it, and think that it is a good thing. *e.g. They are in favour of a bilingual education policy.*

favourite　　　　　　225,235,1660
Your **favourite** thing of a particular type is the one that you like most. *e.g. 'Cheers' is my favourite T.V. programme.*

fear　　　　　　　　　　1143,1180
1 **Fear** or a **fear** is the unpleasant feeling you have when you think that you are in danger. *e.g. She had a great fear of dogs.*
2 If you **fear** someone or something, you are frightened because you think that they will harm you. *e.g. She fears having to walk home at night.*
3 If you **fear** something unpleasant, you think that it might happen, or might have happened, and feel worried about this. *e.g. They fear that they will lose their independence.*

fearful　　　　　　　　1143,1180
Someone who is **fearful** is afraid. *e.g. He was fearful that his mistakes would be found out.*

fearsome　　　　　　　　　585
Something that is **fearsome** is terrible or frightening. *e.g. The dog had a fearsome set of teeth.*

feasible　　　　　　335,477,572
Something that is **feasible** can be done, made or achieved. *e.g. It is feasible for the job to be completed ahead of schedule.*

feast　　　　　　　　　　　1526
1 If you **feast**, you take part in a feast. *e.g. Everyone bring a dish and we can feast all night.*
2 A **feast** is a large and special meal to which several people are invited. *e.g. Jeremy's parents prepared a real feast to celebrate.*

features　　　　　　　　　1599
The **features** of something are the particular parts of it or characteristics that it has. *e.g. Multi-channel signs are one of the interesting features of sign languages.*

fed up　　　　　230,1584,1585
Someone who is **fed up** is unhappy, bored, or tired of something, especially something that they have been doing or experiencing for quite a long time. *e.g. My brother was fed up with cleaning his bicycle.*

feeble　　　　　906,1115,1117
1 Someone or something that is **feeble** has very little power, strength or energy. *e.g. A sheep is a feeble creature most of the time.*
2 You can describe something that someone signs or says as **feeble** when it is not effective, good or convincing. *e.g. They made feeble excuses for not inviting us to the party.*
3 If you are **feeble**, you are easily influenced by other people. *e.g. He's feeble when it comes to serious debate.*

feed　　　　　　　　　239,274
If you **feed** a group of people, you supply or prepare food for them. *e.g. I have to feed twenty people tonight.*

feel　　　　　　　　　965,1082
1 If you **feel** a particular emotion, sensation, physical state, or attitude, you experience it. *e.g. I feel dizzy and sick every morning.*
2 If you **feel** yourself doing something or being in a particular state, you are aware that something is happening to you which you are unable to control. *e.g. I could feel I was blushing.*
3 If you **feel** that something is the case, you have a strong idea in your mind that it is the case, although this idea may be based on intuition rather than on evidence. *e.g. He felt he had made a terrible mistake.*
4 If you **feel** that you should or must do something, you think that you should or must do it. *e.g. I feel I must go back and check on the children.*

feel awful　　　　　　　　965
1 If you **feel awful**, you experience unhappiness or regret. *e.g. She says she feels awful about the accident.*
2 If you **feel awful**, you experience physical pain or discomfort. *e.g. Some mornings I wake up, feel awful, and just stay in bed.*

feel fine　　　　　　　　　965
1 If you **feel fine**, you experience happiness or satisfaction. *e.g. I feel fine now that that's all over.*
2 If you **feel fine**, you have a sensation of well-being and healthiness. *e.g. They will feel fine as soon as the after-effects wear off.*

feel good　　　　　　　　　965
1 If you **feel good**, you experience happiness or satisfaction. *e.g. Nuala says she feels good and has no regrets.*
2 If you **feel good**, you have a sensation of well-being and healthiness. *e.g. If you feel good, why are you sitting in my surgery?*

feel ill　　　　　　　　　　965
If you **feel ill**, you experience physical pain or discomfort. *e.g. You will feel ill for about a week.*

feeling　　　　　　　　　　1082
1 A **feeling** is an emotion, such as anger or happiness. *e.g. There was a strong feeling of jealousy building up inside Norman.*
2 A **feeling** of, for example, hunger or tiredness is a physical sensation that you experience. *e.g. Catherine had a feeling of nausea when she saw the food.*
3 If you have a **feeling** about something, you have an opinion, thought, or idea about it that is based on your intuition rather than on things you know. *e.g. I had a feeling it would work.*

feelings (bottle up one's feelings)　1062
If you **bottle up your feelings**, you do not express them or show them. *e.g. I know he is unhappy, but he bottles up his feelings and I can't get him to tell me about it.*

feel uncomfortable　　　　　1436
If you **feel uncomfortable**, you are worried and embarrassed and not relaxed and confident. *e.g. Her visit made him feel uncomfortable.*

feel well　　　　　　　　　965
If you **feel well**, you have a sensation of well-being and healthiness. *e.g. Now that I've lost all that weight, I really feel well.*

fell　　　　　　　　　　　1394
A **fell** is a mountain, hill or moor. *e.g. We could see sheep on the top of the fell.*

fell (I fell for it)　　　　　1712
You sign or say **I fell for it** when you admit that you were tricked into believing something

that was not true. *e.g. I can't believe it; the foreman signed to me to go and get some tartan paint and I fell for it.*

fellowship   227
1 **Fellowship** is a feeling of friendship that people have when they are doing something together. *e.g. There was an atmosphere of cheerful good fellowship at the meeting.*
2 A **fellowship** is a group of people that join together for a common purpose or interest. *e.g. The Socialist Fellowship meets monthly for discussions.*

female   339
1 A **female** is a person or animal that belongs to the sex that can have babies or young. *e.g. The female of the species may lay thousands of eggs.*
2 Women and girls are sometimes referred to as **females**. *e.g. The advert stated that only ambitious females need apply.*
3 Something that is **female** concerns, relates to, or affects women rather than men. *e.g. Traditionally female areas of work are being replaced by areas such as engineering and medicine.*

feminine   339
Something that is **feminine** relates to or is considered typical of women, in contrast to men. *e.g. Sheila wore feminine clothes: her very favourite item was a beautiful silk scarf.*

feminism   10
Feminism is the belief that women should have the same rights, power, and opportunities as men and that they have a distinctive contribution to make to society. *e.g. She was a strong advocate of feminism and could see no reason why a woman wouldn't be capable of accepting the same responsibilities as a man.*

feminist   10
1 A **feminist** is someone who believes in and supports feminism. *e.g. Sue thought of herself as a feminist and didn't wish to be treated differently from men.*
2 **Feminist** may be used to refer to matters which relate to the study of society, history, etc., from the perspective of women. *e.g. We are doing a course in feminist history this term.*
3 **Feminist** may be used to describe groups, organisations, etc., which seek to promote feminism. *e.g. The Women's Centre has established a feminist publishing company.*

fend off   112
If you **fend off** unwanted questions, enquiries, people, or problems, you deal with them in a defensive way. *e.g. He managed to fend off all the curious questions from reporters.*

ferry   692
1 To **ferry** people or goods somewhere means to transport them there. *e.g. The animals were ferried from one farm to the next.*
2 A **ferry** is a boat that carries passengers or vehicles across a river or a narrow bit of sea. *e.g. We often rode the ferry between Liverpool and Birkenhead.*

ferry   1428
1 A **ferry** is a boat that carries passengers or vehicles across a river or a narrow bit of sea. *e.g. The ferry used to leave at six o'clock every morning.*
2 If you **ferry** something, you transport it by ferry, boat or ship. *e.g. We used to ferry the cargo across every day, but not any more.*

fetch   275
If you **fetch** something or someone, you bring them from a place by going there in order to get them. *e.g. Please fetch the washing.*

few   612, 618, 728, 855, 859, 1393, 1496
1 **Few** or **a few** is used to refer to a small number of things or people. *e.g. There are few seats left for the show.*
2 **Few** is used to indicate that the number of things or people referred to is smaller than is desirable or was expected. *e.g. There are few trains running after ten o'clock.*

fewer   728, 1393
You sign or say that the number of people or things is **fewer** when there are less people or things than before. *e.g. The number of trains to London from Huntingdon got fewer, then they stopped running.*

fiancé   591
A woman's **fiancé** is the man to whom she is engaged to be married. *e.g. Anne introduced her fiancé to her friends.*

fiancée   591
A man's **fiancée** is the woman to whom he is engaged to be married. *e.g. Does your fiancée live in this area?*

fib   528
1 A **fib** is a small lie which is not very important. *e.g. You are not 21 years old! That's a fib.*
2 If you are **fibbing**, you are telling a small lie which is not very important. *e.g. He promised to visit, but I knew he was fibbing.*

fibber   528
A **fibber** is a person who tells a small or unimportant lie. *e.g. You're a fibber. I know you didn't catch a fish that big!*

field   1022, 1285
1 A **field** is an area of land on which a crop is grown, or an area of grass where animals are kept. *e.g. They used to burn off the stubble in the field at about this time of year.*
2 A sports **field** is an area of grass where a sport is played. *e.g. The sports field behind my house has three football pitches and a children's play area.*

fight   437, 924
1 When people **fight** about something, they quarrel. *e.g. They fought about money.*
2 A **fight** is an angry argument or quarrel. *e.g. Let's not have another fight about next door's cat.*

figures   30, 1054
1 **Figures** are particular amounts expressed as numbers, especially those given as statistics in a piece of information. *e.g. Unemployment figures for the last month show a further increase.*
2 Arithmetic can be referred to as **figures**. *e.g. He has a better head for figures than I ever had.*

fill   1617
If you **fill** a container or area, you put a large amount of something into it, with the result that it is full. *e.g. Fill the teapot with boiling water.*

fill in a form   727
When you **fill in a form**, you put down information that is asked of you, usually in several different sections of which the first is typically 'name and address'. *e.g. When you go to the unemployment office on Friday you will have to fill in a form.*

filling station   462
A **filling station** is a place where you can buy petrol and oil for your car. *e.g. I stopped at a B.P. filling station.*

fill up   1617
If you **fill up** a container, you put a large amount of something into it, with the result that it is full. *e.g. Fill up his seed bowl twice a day.*

film   1014
A **film** consists of moving pictures that have been recorded so that they can be shown in a cinema or on television. *e.g. Shall we go and see a film?*

film/television/video camera   470
A **film**, **television** or **video camera** is a piece of equipment that is used for making films or producing television pictures or home movies. *e.g. The television cameras were gathered outside the palace.*

film with a film/television/video camera   470
If you **film** someone or something **with a film, television or video camera**, you use such a piece of equipment to take moving

pictures which can be shown in a cinema or on a television or video monitor. *e.g. If you film with a video camera, he'll be fine: it's just the ones with flashguns he can't stand.*

filth   1020
Filth is a disgusting amount of dirt. *e.g. Filth and deprivation are a way of life here.*

filthy   1020
Something that is **filthy** is very dirty indeed. *e.g. The house had not been lived in for six months; it was really filthy.*

final   1301, 1302, 1303
1 In a series of events, things, or people, the **final** one is the last one. *e.g. It was the final morning of the festival.*
2 **Final** means happening at the end of an event or series of events. *e.g. We did a final summing up.*
3 If a decision is **final**, it cannot be changed or questioned. *e.g. The judge's decision is final.*

finally   216
If someone **finally** does something or if something **finally** happens, it is done or happens after quite a long period of time, sometimes a longer time than it should have done or you would have wished. *e.g. They finally realised the whole thing was a joke.*

finance   1054
1 **Finance** is the management of money, loans, credit and investment, especially on a national level. *e.g. He wants to go into finance, but he isn't qualified for it.*
2 You can refer to the amount of money you have as your **finances**. *e.g. I'll have to check my finances.*

finance   1502, 1503, 1508
1 **Finance** for a project or purchase is the money that is needed to pay for it. *e.g. Obtaining finance may be difficult.*
2 **Finance** is the management of money, loans, credit, and investment, especially on a national level. *e.g. She had a successful job in finance.*
3 You can refer to the amount of money that you have as your **finances**. *e.g. Whether it can be done depends, of course, on your finances.*

find   328, 332, 610
1 If you **find** something, often something that you are looking for, you discover it, see it, or learn where it is. *e.g. Put it in a place where you can find it quickly.*
2 If you **find** something that you need or want, you succeed in getting it. *e.g. He has moved to London to find work.*

find fault   666
If you **find fault** with something or someone,

you look for mistakes and complain about them. *e.g. She was forever finding fault with her husband, no matter what he did.*

find out   328
If you **find out** a fact that you did not already know, you learn it, often by making a deliberate effort. *e.g. I found out the train times.*

fine   165, 1489, 1494
1 If you sign or say that you are **fine**, you mean that you are in good health and reasonably happy; usually signed or said in answer to a question. *e.g. 'How are you feeling?'—'I'm fine.'*
2 If you sign or say that something is **fine**, you mean that it is very satisfactory or acceptable. *e.g. The new timetable looks fine to me.*

fine   213, 220
1 You use **fine** to describe something that is very good or very good quality. *e.g. There is a fine view from the balcony.*
2 You sign or say **fine** to show that you do not object to an arrangement, action or situation that has been suggested. *e.g. If you want to come, that's fine.*

fine   375
1 A **fine** is a punishment, especially one given by law, in which the guilty person is ordered to pay a specific sum of money; also used to refer to the sum of money itself. *e.g. He paid a £10,000 fine for income tax evasion.*
2 If you **fine** someone, you punish them by ordering them to pay a fine. *e.g. He was heavily fined for drunken driving.*

fingerspell   1174
When you **fingerspell**, you use a conventional arrangement of handshapes (in Britain, usually involving both hands) to form the letters of an alphabet with which you can spell out words on your hands. Some of these words are spelled with specific patterns, and become absorbed into the established vocabulary of a sign language. *e.g. Of course, you can fingerspell any word whatsoever.*

fingerspell (using the deaf-blind alphabet)   1112
When you **fingerspell using the deaf-blind alphabet**, you use a conventional arrangement of handshapes to create letters and words on the palm and fingers of another person who is usually both deaf and blind, for the purpose of communication. *e.g. When you fingerspell using the deaf-blind alphabet, is it different from ordinary fingerspelling?*

finish   89, 221, 976, 1552
1 When you **finish** something that you are making or doing, you make or do the last part of it so there is no more for you to do. *e.g. The*

Dictionary should be finished this week.
2 When something **finishes**, it does not continue any longer. *e.g. The course starts in October and will finish in June.*
3 If you **finish** work or school at a particular time, you stop working or studying at that time. *e.g. I shouldn't imagine I'll finish work until about ten tonight.*
4 When you **finish** something that you have been eating, drinking or smoking, you eat, drink or smoke the last part of it. *e.g. We should finish our meal by seven o'clock and we'll meet you then.*

finished   1420
1 Someone who is **finished** with something or someone is no longer doing it or dealing with them or is no longer interested in them. *e.g. I'm finished with Paul.*
2 Something that is **finished** no longer exists or is no longer happening. *e.g. When the divorce papers arrived, he knew that his marriage was completely finished.*

finished   1555
1 When you have **finished** doing, signing or saying something, you have reached the end of whatever you were doing, signing or saying. *e.g. I've almost finished: hang on.*
2 When an item is **finished**, it is all used up. *e.g. That jar of coffee was finished, so I bought another.*

finished   1566, 1643
1 When you have **finished** something that you are making or doing, you make or do the last part of it, so that there is no more for you to do. *e.g. We've finished setting the video cameras up.*
2 If you **finished** work or school at a particular time, you stopped working or studying at that time. *e.g. I finished work at about midnight last night, so I'm pretty exhausted..*

Finland   581
Finland is a republic in North Europe on the Baltic sea. *e.g. We plan to visit Tarja, Antti and the Simons when we go to Finland.*

Finn   581
A **Finn** is a person who comes from Finland or whose family identity relates to Finland. *e.g. Many Finns enjoy taking their holidays by the lakes.*

Finnish   581
1 Someone or something that is **Finnish** belongs to or relates to Finland, or its people. *e.g. The General Secretary of the World Federation of the Deaf, Ms. Liisa Kaupinnen, is Finnish.*
2 **Finnish** is the language which is spoken in Finland. *e.g. He is learning Finnish.*
3 You can refer to people from Finland in

general, or a particular group of people from Finland, as the **Finnish**. *e.g. I find the Finnish very friendly and welcoming people.*
4 The address of the **Finnish** Association of the Deaf is: P.O. Box 57, SF-00401 Helsinki, Finland.

fire 379, 546
If your employer **fires** you, he or she dismisses you from your job. *e.g. Graffman fired him for incompetence.*

fire 1060
1 **Fire** is the hot bright flames produced by things that are burning. *e.g. Fire frightens wild animals.*
2 A **fire** is an occurrence of uncontrolled burning which destroys things. *e.g. A fire had damaged part of the school.*
3 A **fire** is a burning pile of wood or coal that you have set light to, often in order to keep yourself warm. *e.g. He lit a fire and cooked a meal.*
4 Something that is on **fire** is burning and being destroyed. *e.g. Two cars were on fire.*

fire 1396
1 A **fire** is a burning pile of wood, coal or other fuel that you have made and set light to, for example in order to keep yourself warm or to cook food over. *e.g. There were two armchairs near the fire.*
2 A **fire** is an appliance, usually portable or attached to a wall and powered by gas or electricity, which is used to provide heat. *e.g. Switch the fire on, please.*

fire a hand gun/pistol/revolver 463
If you **fire a handgun, a pistol** or a **revolver**, you pull the trigger and cause a bullet to be sent from the gun that you are using. *e.g. Someone could fire a pistol and be lost in the crowd within seconds.*

fire a rifle/shotgun 609
If you **fire a rifle** or a **shotgun**, you cause a bullet to be sent from the rifle or shotgun that you are using. *e.g. The policeman will fire a rifle into the air: this will be your cue to move.*

fire brigade 1666
The **fire brigade** is an organisation which has the job of putting out fires, rescuing people or animals who are trapped and assisting in emergencies. *e.g. Call the fire brigade, there's a shop in flames down there!*

fire fighter 1666
A **fire fighter** is a person whose job it is to put out fires, rescue people or animals that are trapped and assist in emergencies. *e.g. Fire fighters were at the scene within minutes.*

fireman 1666
A **fireman** is a man whose job is to put out fires, rescue people or animals that are trapped

and assist in emergencies. *e.g. Firemen turned their hoses on the flames.*

fireworks 631
Fireworks are small objects with chemicals inside them that burn with coloured sparks or smoke when you light them. Some fireworks shoot into the air or make loud noises. Fireworks are lit to entertain people. *e.g. I'd gone to watch the fireworks.*

firm 68
1 A **firm** decision or opinion is definite and unlikely to change. *e.g. She's a person with firm opinions about interpreter training.*
2 If you stand **firm**, you refuse to change your mind. *e.g. The Government should stand firm in defiance of such threats.*
3 Something that is **firm** does not shake or move when you put pressure on it. *e.g. The ladder seems firm now.*

firm 228, 957
A **firm** is an organisation which sells or produces something or which provides a service which people pay for. *e.g. B.P. is one of Britain's largest firms.*

firm 594, 596
Something that is **firm** does not shake or move when you put pressure on it. *e.g. The ladder seems firm now.*

first 294, 301, 302, 1491
1 The **first** thing, person, event, or period of time is the one that happens or comes before all the others of the same kind. *e.g. The first person in space was a Russian.*
2 When something happens to you or you do something for the **first** time, it has never happened to you or you have never done it before. *e.g. For the first time in our lives, something truly exciting has happened.*
3 You use **first** when you are signing or speaking about what happens in the early part of an event or experience, in contrast to what happens later. *e.g. At first I was reluctant to join the club.*
4 You use **first** to refer to the best or most important thing or person of a particular kind. *e.g. Your family should always come first.*

first aid 542
First aid is simple medical treatment given as soon as possible to a person who is injured or who suddenly becomes ill. *e.g. I packed the first aid kit.*

fish 279
If you **fish**, you try to catch fish with a fishing rod, either for food or as a sport or hobby. *e.g. They went fishing and caught half a dozen trout.*

fish 999
1 A **fish** is a creature that lives in water and

has a tail and fins. *e.g. Emma bought new fish for her fish tank.*
2 **Fish** is the flesh of a fish eaten as food. *e.g. There are different ways of cooking fish.*
3 If you **fish** a particular area of water, you try to catch fish in it. *e.g. It was the first trawler ever to fish those waters.*

fish 1232
1 A **fish** is a creature that lives in water and has a tail and fins. *e.g. As you can see, it's a beautiful fish.*
2 **Fish** is the flesh of a fish eaten as food. *e.g. I'm afraid I never eat eggs or fish.*

fish and chips 1001
Fish and chips (sometimes written **fish 'n' chips**) is a traditional English takeaway meal, in which various types of fish such as cod, haddock or rock salmon are dipped in batter and deep fried, then served with potatoes that have been cut into long thin pieces and also fried. Usually, these are put into paper bags, salt and vinegar is shaken over them and then they are wrapped in sheets of paper. *e.g. We got fish and chips from down the road instead of cooking our own dinner.*

fishcake 1000
A **fishcake** is a savoury food made from pieces of cooked fish mixed together with other ingredients such as flour, potatoes and egg, coated with breadcrumbs and cooked, usually by frying. *e.g. With the left-over cod, he made enough fishcakes for the seven hungry campers.*

fisherman 279
A **fisherman** is a person who catches fish with a fishing rod, usually for sport. *e.g. A fisherman stood under the bridge.*

fisherman 999
A **fisherman** is a person who catches fish, usually as a job. *e.g. Her Uncle John was a fisherman and promised to come to the wedding in a sou'wester and woolly socks.*

fishing 279
Fishing is the sport, hobby, or business of catching fish with fishing rods. *e.g. We did a bit of fishing at the weekend.*

fishing rod 280
A **fishing rod** is a long thin pole with a line and hook attached to it which is used for catching fish. *e.g. He had broken his new fishing rod.*

fishmonger 999
A **fishmonger** is a shopkeeper who sells fish and seafood. *e.g. The fishmonger on the corner sells lobsters.*

fit in 1613
If you **fit in** or **fit into** a particular group,

you seem to belong there because you are similar to the other people in it. *e.g. The Romany children usually fit in very quickly with the other children.*

fit in   1658
If you **fit** something **in** to your schedule, you find time to do it or deal with it. *e.g. How do you manage to fit in so many things each day?*

five-a-side   1058
In a game such as football, a **five-a-side** match involves two teams with five players each, who play and attempt to score against each other, following the amended rules of the game. *e.g. We are playing five-a-side football against the Birmingham Deaf Club team this Saturday.*

fix   47
1 If you are in a **fix**, you are in a difficult situation, especially one that you have caused for yourself. *e.g. I'm in a real fix. I lied and now I've been caught out.*
2 If you **fix** the date or amount of something, you decide exactly what it will be. *e.g. My sister hopes to fix the date of her wedding.*

fix   55, 1519
1 If you **fix** something such as a machine which is damaged or which will not work properly, you repair it. *e.g. He spent the afternoon trying to fix his car.*
2 If you **fix** a meal or a drink, you prepare it for eating or drinking. *e.g. Let me fix lunch: you relax for a while.*

fix   594, 596
If you **fix** the date, time or amount of something, you decide what it will definitely be. *e.g. They wanted to fix the time for the meeting so that they'd be able to get to the pub afterwards.*

fixed   594, 596
1 A **fixed** amount, position, pattern, or method always stays the same. *e.g. A fixed pattern of behaviour is typical of the trauma sufferer.*
2 If you sign or say that someone has **fixed** ideas or opinions, you mean that their ideas or opinions never change. *e.g. Children can be raised without fixed ideas and prejudices.*
3. Something that is **fixed**, such as an arrangement or schedule, has been decided or agreed by those involved. *e.g. O.K., that's fixed: two signed poems, two signed songs, yes?*

fixtures   565
In sport, **fixtures** are matches which have been arranged to take place on a certain date. *e.g. Today's fixtures were cancelled because of the heavy rain.*

fizzle out   1100
If something **fizzles out**, it ends in a weak or

disappointing way. *e.g. The strike fizzled out after three days.*

fizzy drink   969
A **fizzy drink** is full of little bubbles of gas and makes a hissing sound. *e.g. Bring me a fizzy drink with my sandwiches.*

flabbergasted   604, 725, 831
If you are **flabbergasted**, you are extremely surprised. *e.g. I was flabbergasted to learn I'd won the star prize.*

flag   1297
A **flag** is a piece of coloured cloth (or a reproduced image of this) which can be attached to a pole and which is used as a sign, signal or symbol of something, especially of a country. *e.g. We saluted the flag every morning at school assembly.*

flag day   1091
A **flag day** is a day on which people collect money for a charity or cause from people in the street and give them a small badge or paper flag to show that they have given money in support. *e.g. We would like to have a flag day for our Deaf club.*

flag flying   1297
If a **flag** is **flying**, a piece of coloured cloth used as a sign, signal or symbol of something is attached to a pole and can move freely in the breeze. *e.g. Here at Wembley, a flag is flying on one tower but not on the other.*

flames   1060
1 **Flames** are bursts of hot, bright, burning gas that come from something that is burning. *e.g. The flames from the burning house rose hundreds of feet into the air.*
2 If something is in **flames**, it is on fire. *e.g. My shed was in flames.*

flannel   1244
A **flannel** is a special small cloth made from towelling which you use to wash yourself. *e.g. Can I borrow your flannel and soap?*

flashing doorbell   163
A **flashing doorbell** is a device on the outside of a building which, if pushed, causes a light (or lights) inside the building to go on and off so that the people inside know that someone is there and wants to see them. It is a device used especially by deaf people. *e.g. Flashing doorbells are usually installed free of charge.*

flashing light   1716
A **flashing light** is a light that shines with a sudden bright light, at quick, regular intervals. *e.g. The police car's flashing light was really distracting in my mirror.*

flashlight   601
A **flashlight** is a torch, especially a large one. *e.g. I could see the beam of his flashlight waving around in the dark.*

flat   1212, 1415
1 Something that is **flat** is level and horizontal rather than sloping, curved or round. *e.g. The shed needs to stand on a flat surface.*
2 Something that is **flat** has no raised or hollow parts, such as lumps, bumps, or wrinkles. *e.g. Smooth the ironing flat before you start.*

flat   1321
A **flat** battery has lost some or all of its electrical power. *e.g. My battery was flat because I left my car headlights on all night.*

flat   1406
1 A **flat** is a set of rooms for living in, usually on one floor and part of a larger building. *e.g. They rented a furnished flat.*
2 Something that is **flat** is level and horizontal rather than sloping, curved or round. *e.g. He believes that the earth is flat*
3 Something that is **flat** has no raised or hollow parts, such as lumps, bumps or wrinkles. *e.g. You need a flat surface for this game.*

flat   1554
1 A **flat** tyre does not have enough air inside it. *e.g. You've got a flat tyre, son.*
2 A **flat** is a flat tyre. *e.g. I'm late because I got a flat, sir.*

flat   1618
Something that is **flat** is not sloping or curved. *e.g. Right, can you get me a spirit level and check that it's flat?*

flatten   1321
If you **flatten** something, it becomes something which is not sloping or curved and has no raised parts. *e.g. The box had been flattened in the machine.*

flatter   1069
If you **flatter** someone, you declare or imply that they are attractive, important, or clever in order to please them or persuade them to do something. *e.g. Don't try to flatter me; I don't believe you.*

flatterer   1069
A **flatterer** is a person who declares or implies that someone is attractive, important or clever in order to please them or persuade them to do something. *e.g. I never saw a flatterer like him. Every woman gets a compliment.*

flecked   1157
If a surface is **flecked** with small marks, it is covered with them. *e.g. My new sofa is grey flecked with red.*

flee   415
To **flee** from something or someone, or to **flee**
a person or place, means to run quickly away
from the person, place or thing, especially
because of danger or fear. *e.g. He had to flee
Tanzania and hide from his enemies in Kenya.*

flesh   257, 863
1 Your **flesh** is one of the substances your
body is made of, which comes between your
bones and your skin. *e.g. There was a deep gash
in the flesh of her leg.*
2 You can also refer to a person's skin as their
flesh. *e.g. Her flesh is very white.*

flexible   1523
1 A **flexible** object or material can be bent
easily without breaking. *e.g. The tube is flexible
but tough.*
2 Something or someone who is **flexible** is
able to change easily and adapt to different
conditions and circumstances as they occur.
*e.g. My weekend arrangements are flexible—I
can change them to suit you.*

flight   932
1 A **flight** is a journey made by flying,
especially in an aeroplane. *e.g. The flight to
Australia takes over twenty-four hours.*
2 **Flight** is the action of flying. *e.g. Supersonic
flight is very expensive.*
3 A **flight** is an aeroplane that takes you on a
particular journey. *e.g. What time does flight
732 arrive?*

flirt   551
1 If you **flirt**, you encourage sexual advances
from many people without necessarily taking
them further. *e.g. It was not in her nature to flirt.*
2 If you are a **flirt**, you often behave as if you
are sexually attracted to people that you meet.
*e.g. He was always a flirt with the girls when he
was young.*

float   1381
If something **floats** on or in a liquid, it lies or
moves slowly along on the surface. *e.g. There
was seaweed floating on the surface of the water.*

flood   1034
1 If there is a **flood**, **floods** or **flooding**, a
large amount of water covers an area which is
usually dry, for example when a river
overflows. *e.g. In 1975, the flood in India made
233,000 people homeless.*
2 If something **floods** a place which is usually
dry or if the place **floods**, it becomes covered
with water. *e.g. The washing machine will flood
the kitchen if you open the door.*
3 If a river **floods**, it overflows, usually after very
heavy rain. *e.g. The River Ouse floods every year.*

floor   1406, 1415
1 The **floor** of a room is the flat part of it that

you walk on. *e.g. The book fell to the floor.*
2 The **floor** of a valley or forest, or of the sea, is
the ground at the bottom of it. *e.g. Fifty yards
farther out, the ocean floor dropped steeply.*
3 A **floor** of a building is all the rooms that are
on a particular level. *e.g. My office is on the
second floor.*

flop   1438
Something that is a **flop** is a total failure. *e.g.
The party was a flop.*

flour   1520
Flour is a white or brown powder that is made
by grinding grain. It is used to make such
things as bread, cakes and pastry. *e.g. You will
need eight ounces of flour for this recipe*

flow   1021
If a liquid, gas or currrent **flows** somewhere, it
moves there steadily and continuously,
passing over a surface. *e.g. From the bridge, we
watched the river flow over rocks at the
fishermen's feet.*

flower   620, 858
1 A **flower** on a plant is a coloured or white
part that grows on its stems. *e.g. The hawthorn
has white flowers in June.*
2 A **flower** is a small plant that is grown for its
flowers, as opposed to a tree, shrub, or
vegetable. *e.g. He planted flowers on the banks in
the second week of April.*

flu   1535
Flu is an illness which is like a bad cold. When
you have flu, you feel weak and your muscles
ache. *e.g. My uncle was ill with flu.*

fluster   1436
If something or someone **flusters** you, they
make you feel nervous and confused rather
than relaxed and confident. *e.g. The person
doing the driving test may try to fluster you by
asking questions when you least expect them.*

flutter   1635, 1659
1 If wings **flutter**, they wave up and down or
from side to side in small quick movements.
e.g. The baby bird tried to flutter its wings.
2 If something such as small bird or insect
flutters, it moves through the air making
small, fast movements of its wings. *e.g.
Dragonflies fluttered over the flowers.*

fly   1635
When a bird **flies**, it moves through the air.
e.g. My canary tried to fly, but it was too weak.

fly   1659
A **fly** is a small insect with two wings. There
are many kinds of fly, and the most common
are black in colour. *e.g. There were two dead flies
on the window sill.*

fly a kite   126
To **fly a kite** you hold the string attached to
the kite frame, allowing the wind to carry the
kite up into the air. *e.g. Every windy day, he is
out flying his kite.*

fly by aeroplane/plane   949
1 If you **fly by aeroplane** or **plane**, you travel
in an aircraft. *e.g. Go by helicopter to Glasgow?
No thanks, I'd prefer to fly by aeroplane.*
2 If you **fly** someone or something **by aeroplane**
or **plane**, you send them by aircraft. *e.g. We'll
have to fly the supplies out by plane.*

fly in an aeroplane/plane   932
1 If you **fly in an aeroplane** or **plane**, you are
in an aeroplane or plane that is moving
through the air. *e.g. I was so excited the first time
I was able to fly in a plane.*
2 If you **fly** somewhere **in an aeroplane** or
plane, you travel there in an aircraft. *e.g. Next
week I am going to fly to America in a plane.*
3 If you **fly** someone or something somewhere
in an aeroplane or **plane**, you send them
there by aircraft. *e.g. The doctor decided to fly
the injured man to hospital in a plane.*

fog   1072, 1075
When there is **fog**, there are tiny drops of
water in the air which form a thick cloud and
make it difficult to see things. *e.g. I had an
accident driving in fog.*

fold   1438
If a business or organisation **folds** or **folds up**,
it closes or ceases to exist as a result of failure.
*e.g. She had seen too many businesses fold up
through bad management.*

folding chair   44
A **folding chair** is a chair designed so that
you can fold it into a smaller shape for
convenience or storage. *e.g. I've put the
folding chair in the garage.*

folk   482
You can refer to people as **folk**. *e.g. We
arranged a Christmas party for the old folk.*

follow   430
1 If you sign or say that something **follows**,
you mean that it happens as a result of
something else. *e.g. Hunger and poverty
followed the drought.*
2 If you **follow** a path, river, line, or set of
signs, you go along beside it or from one sign to
another, using it or them to show you which
direction to go in. *e.g. We followed a path up
along the creek.*
3 If you **follow** a particular route or course,
you go somewhere by this route or course. *e.g.
Follow the route marked on the map to the church.*
4 If you **follow** a particular course of action,
you do a particular thing in the planned way.

e.g. Inflation forced them to follow a tight fiscal policy.

5 If you **follow** what someone else has done, you do it too because you think it is a good thing or because you want to copy them. *e.g. Other banks tended to follow the trend set by the major ones.*

6 If you **follow** someone in what you do, you do the same thing or job as they did previously. *e.g. Michael Manley followed his father into politics.*

7 If you **follow** a particular religion, belief, or leader, you have the religion or belief or you support the leader mentioned. *e.g. They followed Gandhi because he was a wise man.*

follow   442

If you **follow** someone, you move along behind them. *e.g. Fred followed Sue down the street.*

fond (be fond of)   225, 235, 1660

1 If you are **fond** of someone, you like them and have a feeling of affection for them. *e.g. She said that she was fond of me, but that I shouldn't get too excited.*

2 If you are **fond** of something, you like it. If you are **fond** of doing something, you like doing it. *e.g. I'm fond of salad.*

food   1501

Food is what people and animals eat. *e.g. There was little money left for food and clothing.*

fool   316, 663, 1462

If you call someone a **fool**, you mean that they are silly or have done something silly. *e.g. If you believe all that you read in the papers, you are a fool.*

fool   753

If you **fool** someone, you deceive or trick them. *e.g. She was fooled into believing the story.*

fool   765, 1016

1 If you make a **fool** of someone, you make them appear silly by telling people about something silly that they have done, or by tricking them in some way. *e.g. The teacher had a quick temper and we used to make a fool of him by pretending not to understand the lessons so he would get into a rage.*

2 If you are **fooling**, you are joking or teasing somebody. *e.g. He's only fooling, take no notice of him.*

foolish   663

You can sign or say that people or things are **foolish** when they are so silly that they make you want to laugh. *e.g. They looked foolish in their old clothes.*

fool (you fooled me)   1712

You sign or say **you fooled me** when you

realise that someone has tricked you. *e.g. You fooled me with that story that we would all have to move offices.*

football   1418

1 **Football** is a game played between two teams of eleven players who kick or head a ball around a field in an attempt to score goals. *e.g. The children are playing football.*

2 A **football** is the large ball which is used in the game of football. *e.g. Can you buy me a new football for Christmas, please?*

forbid   109, 917, 1420

If you **forbid** someone to do something, you order them not to do it. *e.g. I forbid you to tell her about it.*

forbidden   1420

If something is **forbidden**, you are not allowed to do it or have it. *e.g. Indoor football is forbidden.*

force   1364

If you **force** someone to do or to have something, you make them do it or have it, although they are very unwilling to. *e.g. They wanted to force him to resign.*

foreign   1564, 1609

Someone or something that is **foreign** belongs to or relates to a country that is not your own. *e.g. Children from foreign countries can play in the Embassy gardens.*

foreigner   1564, 1609

1 A **foreigner** is a person who belongs to a country that is not your own. *e.g. More than a million foreigners visit the United States every year.*

2 A **foreigner** is a person who has come into a community or other group of people from outside it and does not seem to belong there. *e.g. I am still a foreigner in this village.*

foreman   762

A **foreman** is a person, especially a man, in charge of a group of workers. *e.g. The foreman swore at one of the workers.*

forest   1026

A **forest** is a very large area where trees grow close together. *e.g. The deer ran deeper into the forest when they heard the gunfire.*

forever   550, 566

1 Something that will happen or continue **forever** will always happen or continue. *e.g. They thought that their empire would last forever.*

2 People sign or say that something takes **forever** or lasts **forever** when they want to emphasise that it takes or lasts a very long time. *e.g. The next minute seemed to last forever.*

forget   508, 1548, 1708

1 If you **forget** something or **forget** how to do something, you are unable to think of it or think how to do it, even though you have known it, experienced it or been able to do it in the past. *e.g. I always forget names.*

2 If you **forget** something or **forget** to do something, you do not think about it or remember it, for example because you are thinking about other things or because it is unimportant. *e.g. I meant to see her, but I forgot all about it.*

3 If you **forget** something that you had intended to bring or buy, you do not bring or buy it because you did not think about it at the right time. *e.g. I forgot my key.*

forgive   1580

1 If you **forgive** someone who has done something wrong, you stop being angry with them. *e.g. I forgive him everything.*

2 You use **forgive** in polite expressions like 'forgive me' and 'forgive the language' to apologise for signing or saying something that might seem rude, silly, or too complicated. *e.g. Forgive my ignorance, but who is Jane Fonda?*

fork   772

1 A **fork** is a tool with which you eat food. It consists of three or four small prongs on the end of a handle. *e.g. She dropped the fork on the floor.*

2 If you **fork** food into something, you use a fork to pick up food and eat it or put it somewhere. *e.g. She forked up the paella.*

fork   839

1 A **fork** is a large tool that you use for digging in the soil when you are gardening. It consists of three or four long prongs attached to a long handle. *e.g. It will be easier to use the fork to break up the soil.*

2 If you **fork** a garden, you dig in the soil with a fork. *e.g. You fork this part and I'll plant the seedlings.*

form   151

If you **form** an organisation, committee, company, etc., you organise and start it. *e.g. They broke away to form a separate Association.*

former   1242

1 Former is used to describe someone who used to have a particular job, position, or role, but no longer has it. *e.g. He is a former army officer.*

2 **Former** is used to describe something which someone used to have or which used to be a particular thing. *e.g. They have a new house near their former home.*

formerly   1242

You use **formerly** to sign or say that something happened, existed, or was the case at a time before the present time, but it no longer happens, exists, or is the case. *e.g. The salesman formerly worked for a rival organisation.*

fortnight   748, 763
A **fortnight** is a period of approximately fourteen days or two weeks. *e.g. Every year we go to Bridlington for a fortnight.*

fortnight ago   750, 764
If you sign or say that something happened a **fortnight ago**, you mean that it happened approximately fourteen days ago, or during the week before the one that preceded this week. *e.g. A fortnight ago, I was in Trinidad, soaking up the sun.*

fortnight (in a fortnight's time)   763
If you sign or say that something will happen **in a fortnight's time**, you mean that it will happen approximately fourteen days in the future. *e.g. All this will be over in a fortnight's time, thank goodness.*

fortnight later   763
You can sign or say a **fortnight later** to refer to a time approximately fourteen days after the one that has just been mentioned, or some time in the second week after the one that has just been mentioned. *e.g. I swore I'd never go again, but a fortnight later, off I went.*

fortunate   466, 1248
1 Someone who is **fortunate** is lucky. *e.g. I was fortunate enough to find a job.*
2 You refer to an event as **fortunate** if it is lucky for someone. *e.g. It was fortunate for us that Mr. Fox decided to wait, for we were an hour late.*

fortunately   1248
You use **fortunately** with a statement about an event or situation that is good or about which you are relieved. *e.g. Fortunately for us, the damage was only slight.*

fortune   466
Fortune or **good fortune** is good luck. *e.g. He had the good fortune to be promoted.*

forward roll   566
If you do a **forward roll**, you turn upside down on the floor or a mat, and bring your legs over your head. *e.g. We are practising forward rolls in the gym.*

found   151
1 If someone **founds** an institution, company, organisation, etc., they set it up, often by providing the necessary money. *e.g. They founded a new magazine.*
2 If someone **founds** a town, important building, or other place, they begin to build it or cause it to be built. *e.g. Cortes founded Mexico City.*

3 If something is **founded** on a particular thing, such as a source of support or strength, it is based on it. *e.g. The settlement was founded on the new understanding between the two groups.*

foundation   151
1 The **foundation** or **foundations** of something such as a belief or way of life is the basic idea, attitude, or experience on which that belief or way of life is built. *e.g. The rule of law is the foundation of any society.*
2 The **foundations** of a building or other structure are the layer of bricks, concrete, etc., below the ground that it must be built on so that it is solidly supported. *e.g. The house had solid foundations.*
3 The **foundation** of an institution, company, organisation, etc., is the fact or act of setting it up. *e.g. The foundation of a new university used to require an Act of Parliament.*

founder   151
The **founder** of an institution, organisation, etc., is the person who sets it up, or causes it to be built, perhaps by providing the necessary money or leadership. *e.g. John Wesley was the founder of Methodism.*

fountain   1729
A **fountain** is an ornamental feature in a pool which consists of a spray or jet of water that is forced up into the air by a pump. *e.g. We are going to build an ornamental pond with a fountain at the end of the garden.*

fox   1533
A **fox** is a wild animal which looks like a dog and has reddish-brown fur, a pointed face and ears, and a thick tail. *e.g. The fox was chased over the fields by the huntsmen.*

fracture   94
A **fracture** is a crack or break in something, especially a bone. *e.g. They said he had a fracture of the left shoulder blade.*

frame   441
A **frame** is a hollow structure inside which you can fit something such as a window or picture. *e.g. The wooden picture frames were painted gold.*

France   480
France is a republic in Western Europe between the English Channel, the Mediterranean and the Atlantic which is a member of the European Community. *e.g. We are going to France on holiday.*

frank   65
To **frank** a letter or parcel means to put a mark on it that shows that the proper charge has been paid or that no stamp is needed. *e.g. Take the letters to the mail room to be franked.*

freckles   1177
Freckles are small, light brown spots on someone's skin, especially on their face. *e.g. Alice has red hair and freckles.*

free   81
1 If you **free** someone or something, you stop them from being restricted or controlled by others. *e.g. They wanted to see the colonies freed from British rule.*
2 Someone who is **free** is no longer a prisoner or a slave. *e.g. One prisoner in seven was set free.*
3 If you **free** someone or something, you cause them to become available for a task or purpose when they were previously unavailable. *e.g. Take over this job so I can be free to finish my lunch.*

free   685
If something is **free**, you can have it or use it without paying for it. *e.g. My son gets free school meals.*

free   884
1 Someone who is **free** is no longer a prisoner or a slave. *e.g. The prisoner had been set free.*
2 If you **free** someone of something that is unpleasant or restricting, you remove it from them. *e.g. My parents agreed to free me from my household chores so that I could work for my exams.*

free   1087
1 Someone or something that is **free** is not restricted, controlled, or limited, for example by rules, customs, or other people. *e.g. At my college, we are free to attend any class we like.*
2 If you have a **free** period of time or are **free** at a particular time, you are not working or occupied then. *e.g. They have plenty of free time for sports.*
3 If something is **free**, you can have it or use it without paying for it. *e.g. The coffee was free.*

freedom   81, 1087
Freedom is the state of being allowed to do, sign or say what you want to. *e.g. The authorities gave us the freedom to meet wherever we chose.*

freeze   1116
1 When a liquid **freezes** or when something **freezes** it, it becomes solid because it is very cold. *e.g. The water may freeze in the well.*
2 If you **freeze** food, you preserve it by storing it at a temperature below freezing point. *e.g. We can freeze the extra peas from the garden.*
3 If you sign or say that it will **freeze**, you mean that the temperature outside will fall below freezing point. *e.g. It is so cold that I'm sure it will freeze tonight.*
4 If you **freeze**, you become very cold. *e.g. I came out without a coat and I think I'm going to freeze!*
5 You can also state that someone **freezes**

when they suddenly stop moving and become completely still and quiet, for example because they have seen something dangerous. *e.g. She sensed something moving in the forest, and froze at once.*

freezing   118
1 If something is **freezing**, it is very cold indeed. *e.g. The water was black and freezing.*
2 If you sign or say that you are **freezing**, you mean that you feel unpleasantly cold. *e.g. Let's get out of here. I'm freezing.*

French   480
1 Someone or something that is **French** belongs to or relates to France or its people. *e.g. I just adore French bread.*
2 **French** is the main language spoken in France and is an official language of Switzerland, Belgium, Canada, Chad and certain other countries. *e.g. She speaks fluent French.*
3 You can refer to people from France in general, or a particular group of people from France, as the **French**. *e.g. The French are noted for their love of fine food.*
4 The address of the **French** Association of the Deaf is: Présidence de la Fédération Nationale de Sourds de France, 38 Rue de Lavazière, F–81000 Albi, France.

frequent   204, 207, 473, 751, 1722
If something is **frequent**, it often happens or you often see it. *e.g. They made frequent visits to his father's grave.*

fresh   89
1 A **fresh** thing or amount replaces or is added to a previous one. *e.g. Let me make a fresh pot of tea.*
2 Something that is **fresh** has been done or experienced recently. *e.g. We saw fresh footprints in the snow.*
3 If food is **fresh**, it has been made or obtained recently and has not been tinned or frozen. *e.g. This restaurant always serves fresh vegetables.*
4 If you describe something as **fresh**, you mean that it is different in a new and exciting way. *e.g. The new director has a fresh approach to staff management.*
5 If something tastes, smells, or feels **fresh**, it is pleasant and refreshing. *e.g. The mountain resort air is always fresh.*

fresh   1610
1 If food is **fresh**, it has been made or obtained recently, and has not been tinned or frozen. *e.g. They always eat fresh fish.*
2 If you describe something as **fresh**, you mean that it is different in a new and exciting way. *e.g. I find his ideas about teaching fresh and stimulating.*

Friday   685
Friday is the day after Thursday and before Saturday. *e.g. I came here on Friday.*

fridge   28, 29
A **fridge** is a large metal container which is kept cold inside, usually by electricity, so that the food and drink that is in it stays fresh and cold. *e.g. He put the milk back in the fridge.*

friend   224, 1640
1 A **friend** is a person who you know well and like to spend time with. *e.g. He is a friend of the family.*
2 If you are **friends** with someone, you like each other and enjoy spending time together. *e.g. You used to be friends with him, didn't you?*

friendly   1640
1 If you are being **friendly** to someone, you are behaving in a kind and pleasant way to them. *e.g. She's very friendly and very professional.*
2 If you are **friendly** with someone, you like each other and enjoy spending time together. *e.g. I became friendly with a young engineer.*

friendship   1640
1 **Friendship** is the state of being friends with someone. *e.g. He has lost my friendship.*
2 **Friendship** between countries is a relationship in which they help and support each other. *e.g. Our friendship with America is of enormous value to us.*

frighten   1143, 1180
If something or someone **frightens** you, they cause you to feel suddenly afraid, anxious or nervous. *e.g. You frighten me when you shout like that.*

frightening   584
If something is **frightening**, it makes you feel afraid, anxious or nervous. *e.g. It was the most frightening sight she had ever seen.*

frisbee   1498
Frisbee is the name of a particular light plastic disk that one person throws to another as part of a game. *e.g. The frisbee is in the drawer.*

frock   1083
A **frock** is a woman's or girl's dress. *e.g. Put on your party frock and we'll go out.*

frog   820
A **frog** is a small creature with smooth skin, big eyes, and long back legs which it uses for jumping. Many frogs live near water. *e.g. We have a pond full of frogs.*

frog hopping   820
If a **frog** is **hopping**, it is leaping from one place to another by rapidly straightening its long back legs. *e.g. I watched the frog hopping away across the lawn.*

frog jumping   820
If a **frog** is **jumping**, it is leaping from one place to another by rapidly straightening its

long back legs. *e.g. There was a frog jumping around my bed in my dream.*

from   1203, 1360
You use **from** to sign or say what the source of something is, where it began or where somebody grew up. *e.g. She came from Ilford.*

front   1273
1 The **front** of something is the part of it that faces you or faces forwards, or that you normally see or use. *e.g. There was a stain on the front of his shirt.*
2 The **front** door of a building is the main entrance to the building. *e.g. We've just had our front door painted blue.*

front   1642
1 A **front** room, window, garden, etc., is on the side of a building that faces the street. *e.g. Miss Vernon lived in the front room.*
2 Someone or something that is **in front** or **up front** is in the place or position which is nearest to the front of something, for example to the front of a vehicle. *e.g. She got into the bus and sat up front near the driver.*

frontier   1432
A **frontier** is a border between two countries, or between a country and an area of wild, unclaimed land. *e.g. There is a 4,000 mile frontier between the United States and Canada.*

front line   1432
The **front line** is the place where two opposing armies are facing each other and where fighting is going on. *e.g. We came to within a mile and a half of the front line.*

frosty   1116
If it is **frosty**, the temperature outside falls below freezing point, tiny ice crystals form, and the ground becomes white. *e.g. The flowers were killed when the weather got frosty.*

frown   1135
When you **frown**, you wrinkle your forehead and look slightly cross because you are annoyed or worried or concentrating on something. *e.g. I am not allowed to frown while driving—my wife says it's bad for my eyes.*

frozen   1116
1 If a lake, river, etc., is **frozen** or **frozen over**, its surface has turned into ice because the temperature has been below freezing point. *e.g. Part of the Missouri was frozen over.*
2 If the ground is **frozen**, it has become very hard because the temperature has been below freezing point. *e.g. The land is still frozen.*
3 **Frozen** food has been preserved by freezing it. *e.g. She bought a packet of frozen peas.*
4 If you are **frozen**, you are very cold. *e.g. We were frozen—we only had our pyjamas on.*

5 If you are **frozen** with fear, terror, etc., you cannot move because you are so frightened. *e.g. The chained men sat frozen with terror.*

fruit   1695
A **fruit** is something that you can eat which grows on a tree or bush. It has soft flesh, and contains seeds or a stone. Apples and pears are fruit. *e.g. We could see acres of fruit trees.*

frustrate   792
If something **frustrates** you, it makes you feel sad or disappointed because you are dissatisfied by what has happened. *e.g. Working with young offenders frustrates me so much, because we don't have the resources to help them.*

frustrate   1199
If something **frustrates** you, it makes you feel upset and angry because you are unable to do what you would like to do or to do it to your satisfaction. *e.g. It really frustrates me when I can't see things without my glasses.*

frustrated   1195, 1199
If you are **frustrated** by something, it makes you feel upset and angry because it means that you are unable to do what you would like to do or to do something to your satisfaction. *e.g. The bad organisation of the conference made me feel frustrated, as I had no time to give my lecture.*

frustration   792
If you feel **frustration**, you feel sad or disappointed because something unsatisfactory has happened. *e.g. I just feel frustration that there is to be no increase in the grant.*

frustration   1195, 1199
If you feel **frustration**, you feel upset and angry because you are unable to do what you would like to do or to do something to your satisfaction. *e.g. Working on a dictionary leads to a lot of frustration, because there are so many fine details to check.*

fry   239, 1312, 1328
When you **fry** food, you cook it in a pan that contains hot fat or oil. *e.g. Ellen learnt how to fry bacon the Danish way.*

frying pan   239
A **frying pan** is a flat, metal pan with a long handle in which you fry food. *e.g. Julie bought a frying pan for Chris.*

fry up   239
If you **fry up** food, you fry it, especially in order to make a quick, casual meal. *e.g. Make yourself useful and fry up some bacon.*

fuck   969
1 Fuck is an offensive expression used to express shock, disgust or anger. *e.g. The computer's been nicked! Fuck!*
2 You can use **fucking** when you are shocked, disgusted or angry to emphasise your feeling about what you sign or say. This may be considered offensive by some people. *e.g. The fucking car broke down again.*

full   1267, 1293, 1617
Something that is **full** contains as much of a substance or as many objects or people as it is possible for it to hold. *e.g. All the car parks are full.*

full up   1267
1 If you sign or say that something is **full up**, you are emphasising that it contains as much of a substance or as many objects or people as it can. *e.g. My car's full up—can you get any more in yours?*
2 If you sign or say that you are **full up**, you mean that you have had plenty to eat and do not wish to have any more at present. *e.g. No more for me, thanks, I'm full up.*

full up   1617
If you sign or say that something is **full up**, you mean that it contains as much of a substance as it can. *e.g. This box is full up now.*

fumes   1109
Fumes are strong, unpleasant or harmful gases, smells, or smoke. *e.g. I hate tobacco fumes.*

fun   710
1 If you sign or say that an activity is **fun**, you mean that it is enjoyable or amusing. *e.g. Going to see the Deaf Comedians is always fun.*
2 If you have **fun**, you enjoy yourself. *e.g. We had great fun on the beach.*
3 If you sign or say that something is a **fun** thing, you mean that you enjoy it. *e.g. Those were fun times, like being back at school.*

funds   1502, 1508
Funds are amounts of money that are available to be spent, especially money that is given to an organisation or person for a particular purpose. *e.g. Each year they made a public appeal for funds.*

funeral   1443
A **funeral** is the ceremony that is held when the body of someone who has died is buried or cremated. *e.g. A funeral service was held for the victims of the accident.*

funfair   108
A **funfair** is usually an outdoor show offering amusements, sideshows, rides, or games of skill and luck. *e.g. I enjoy going to the funfair in Blackpool.*

funny   626, 630
You sign or say that something is **funny** if it is strange, unexpected or unusual or you cannot make sense of it. *e.g. It's funny that we keep meeting the same people in different places.*

fur   1557
1 Fur is the thick hair that grows on the bodies of many animals. *e.g. Moles have short silky fur.*
2 Fur is the fur-covered skin of an animal that is used to make clothing or rugs. *e.g. When I see a fur coat, I wonder how many animals died to make it.*
3 A **fur** is a coat made from real or synthetic fur, or a piece of fur worn like a shawl or scarf. *e.g. She had been accused of stealing the fur from a department store.*

furious   1196
Someone who is **furious** is extremely angry. *e.g. I was furious and told them to get out of my house.*

furniture   1038
Furniture consists of large moveable objects such as tables, chairs, or beds, that are used in a room. *e.g. Because of the flood, I have to buy new living-room furniture.*

further   1592, 1620
1 Further means more than before or more than something else, or to a greater extent or degree. *e.g. The Chancellor was forced to make further tax cuts.*
2 If something or someone goes **further** or takes a particular thing **further**, they progress to a more advanced stage. *e.g. He hoped that the new offer would develop matters a stage further.*
3 If you sign or say that you will go **further** or take something **further** in a discussion, you mean you will make a more extreme statement or deal with a point more thoroughly. *e.g. We can discuss this further tomorrow.*

fussy   868
Someone who is **fussy** is concerned excessively with details or extremely careful in choosing things. *e.g. I am fussy about my food.*

future   1611
1 The **future** is the period of time that will take place after the present. *e.g. We will have to see what the future holds.*
2 You use **in the future** to refer to a period of time after now. *e.g. I can see nothing in the future but boredom and pain.*
3 Future is used to describe something that relates to the future. *e.g. Let's meet again at a future date.*
4 The **future** is what is going to happen, in contrast to what is now happening or what has already happened. *e.g. We need to face the future. New government legislation will require us to change our working practices.*
5 Your **future** is what will happen to you, especially in your career. *e.g. I decided that my future lay in medicine.*

G, g

G
G is the seventh letter of the British manual and English alphabets. See page 851.

gaffer 762
A **gaffer** is a foreman or overseer who supervises a team of workers. *e.g. The gaffer told me to go home early.*

gain 861, 1155
1 If you **gain** from something, you get some advantage or benefit from it. *e.g. What has Britain gained by being a member of the European Community?*
2 A **gain** is something that has been achieved. *e.g. I think we can consider this a significant gain on the part of the company.*

gain confidence 646
If you **gain confidence**, you feel more sure about your abilities, qualities and ideas. *e.g. After I learned about sign language research, I gained confidence as a Deaf person.*

gale 1439
A **gale** is a very strong wind. *e.g. The garage roof blew off in the gale.*

gamble 1597
If you **gamble**, you bet money in a game such as cards or on the result of a race or competition, especially as a regular activity. *e.g. He gambled heavily on the horses.*

game 1029, 1066
1 A **game** is an activity or sport involving skill, knowledge, or chance, in which you follow rules and try to win against an opponent or try to solve a puzzle. *e.g. You need two to play this game.*
2 A **game** is a particular occasion on which a game is played. *e.g. This had to be our last game before Ben went home.*

game 1120
1 A **game** is an activity or sport involving skill, knowledge or chance, in which your team follows rules and tries to win against an opposing team. *e.g. Rugby is a game I do not understand.*
2 A **game** is a particular occasion on which a team game is played. *e.g. What a game! The finest of the season, without doubt.*

game 1121
A **game** is a particular occasion in which a team game is played. *e.g. What a game! The finest of the season, without doubt.*

gaol 47
1 A **gaol** is the same as a jail or prison. *e.g. He spent two months in gaol.*
2 If you **gaol** someone, you jail them. *e.g. The Judge gaoled her for three months.*

garage 50
1 A **garage** is a building in which you keep a vehicle, such as a car, often built next to or as part of a house. *e.g. I keep the new car in the garage.*
2 A **garage** is a place where you can get your car repaired, buy a car, or buy petrol. *e.g. I would prefer to get petrol at the B.P. garage.*

garage 1363
A **garage** is a building in which you keep a vehicle, such as a car, often built next to or as part of a house. *e.g. I keep the new car in the garage.*

garden 153, 1565
A **garden** is a piece of land next to someone's house where they can grow flowers, vegetables or other plants and which often includes a lawn. *e.g. Martin has lovely flowers in his garden.*

garden 620, 858, 1285
1 A **garden** is a piece of land next to someone's house where they grow flowers, vegetables, or other plants, and which often includes a lawn. *e.g. She looks after the garden.*
2 **Gardens** are a place like a park that has areas of plants, trees, and grass. *e.g. The gardens were created by the famous Capability Brown.*

gardener 153, 1565
1 A **gardener** is a person who is paid to work in someone else's garden. *e.g. The gardener comes to do some work twice a week.*
2 A **gardener** is someone who enjoys working in their garden as a hobby. *e.g. Bridie is a keen gardener.*

gas 1133
1 **Gas** is a substance like air that is neither liquid nor solid and burns easily. It is used as a fuel for fires, cookers, and central heating in people's homes. *e.g. He remembered to turn the gas off before leaving home.*
2 **Gas** fires and gas cookers use gas as a fuel. *e.g. I prefer gas cookers to electric ones.*
3 If you **gas** a person or animal, you kill them by making them breathe poisonous gas. *e.g. She tried to gas herself.*

gas mask 1133
A **gas mask** is a device that you wear over your mouth and nose to protect you from breathing poisonous gases. *e.g. I still have the gas mask that Granny was issued with in the war.*

gate 1352
A **gate** is a door-like structure, used outdoors at the entrance to a field, a garden, or the grounds of a building, which usually consists of connected strips of wood or metal that swing on hinges attached to a frame. *e.g. We reached the gate in the hedge.*

gate (small gate) 1353
A **small gate** is a door-like structure, used outdoors at the entrance to a field, a garden, or the grounds of a building, which usually consists of connected strips of wood or metal that swing on hinges attached to a frame. *e.g. There was a small gate in the wall.*

gather 1559
1 If you **gather** together a number of things that you have spread out, you bring them together again. *e.g. I will gather my maps together and tuck them into the folder.*
2 If you **gather** things, you collect them from a number of different places. *e.g. They began to gather all the papers together.*

gathering 1056
A **gathering** is a crowd of people. *e.g. We had quite a gathering once everybody found the place.*

gauge 403
A **gauge** is a device that measures the amount of something and shows the amount measured. *e.g. The gauge recorded the amount of water lost in the drought.*

gavel 242
A **gavel** is a small hammer used by a chairperson, judge or auctioneer to call for order or attention. *e.g. The gavel was made of teak.*

gaze 788
1 If you **gaze**, you look steadily at someone or something for a long time. *e.g. He gazed at the dead body in the stream.*
2 A **gaze** is a long, steady look at someone or something. *e.g. My gaze seemed to unnerve him and he looked away.*

gem 1149
A **gem** is a jewel that is used in jewellery. *e.g. A bracelet of solid gold, with a gem every few millimetres, was his gift.*

general 978, 1416, 1417
1 **General** is used to summarise a situation or

idea, without considering details or exceptions. *e.g. The general standard of education is high.*

2 General is used to describe something that involves or affects most people, or most people in a particular group. *e.g. It was a topic of general interest.*

3 General is used to describe a statement that involves only the main features of something and not its details. *e.g. The guest speaker gave a general talk about her work for the British Association of the Hard of Hearing, or BAHOH as it is more commonly known.*

generation   1207, 1306

A **generation** is the group of people in your family who share the same position in its history and structure; for example, your parents, aunts, and uncles belong to one generation and you, your brothers and sisters, and your cousins belong to another. *e.g. Property is handed on from generation to generation.*

generosity   1522

Generosity is the quality of being generous, especially in doing or giving more than is usual or expected. *e.g. Philip can afford to go to college because of his uncle's generosity.*

generous   1489, 1494

1 Someone who is **generous** gives more of something, especially money, than is usual or expected. *e.g. Her uncle is very generous. He sends money to Oxfam every month.*

2 Someone who is **generous** is friendly, helpful and willing to see the good qualities in people or things. *e.g. My Aunt Josie is a generous neighbour.*

genius   213

1 Someone who is a **genius** has very great natural ability and talent, usually for a particular subject or activity. *e.g. Einstein was a genius.*

2 Genius is a very great ability or skill in something. *e.g. I admire Dorothy's genius for poetry.*

gentle   520

Movements that are **gentle** do not harm or damage things in any way. *e.g. You must be gentle when you lift the baby.*

gentle   1272

Someone who is **gentle** is kind, mild, and pleasantly calm in character or behaviour. *e.g. He was a gentle, sweet man.*

geography   50

1 Geography is the study of the countries of the world and of such things as land formations, seas, climate, towns and population. *e.g. I did geography at university.*

2 The **geography** of a place is the way that features such as rivers, mountains, towns,

streets, etc., are arranged within it. *e.g. Mr. Lewis described the geography of the valley in terms we all could understand.*

German   317

1 Someone or something that is **German** belongs to or relates to Germany, or its people. *e.g. The Centre for German Sign Language in Hamburg has developed a notation system for recording sign languages.*

2 German is the main language spoken in Germany and Austria, and is an official language of Switzerland. *e.g. Mick is training to be a German interpreter.*

3 A **German** is a person who comes from, or whose family identity relates to, Germany. *e.g. I sat next to a German on the flight to Munich.*

4 The address of the German Deaf Association is: Deutscher Gehörlosen-Bund, E.V., Paradeplatz 3, 2370 Rendsburg, Germany.

Germany   317

Germany is a country in central Europe. It was divided after World War Two into what became known as East and West Germany. The country was reunited in November 1989. Germany is a member of the European Community. *e.g. Germany has the most powerful economy in the European Community.*

get   1012

1 If you **get** a particular sum of money, you receive it as your wages or salary or as an allowance. *e.g. I got £300 last week for working on a building site.*

2 If you **get** a loan or grant, you are given or lent it for a particular purpose. *e.g. The bank manager said we will get a bank loan.*

get   1124

1 If you **get** a letter, telephone call or response from someone, you receive it. *e.g. I get a letter from my son every Monday.*

2 If you **get** a particular sum of money, you receive it as your wages or salary or as an allowance. *e.g. I got £300 last week for working on a building site.*

3 If you **get** a loan or grant, you are given or lent it for a particular purpose. *e.g. The bank manager said we will get a bank loan.*

get   1130

1 If you **get** something, you obtain it. *e.g. He's trying to get a flat.*

2 If you **get** an illness or disease, you become ill with it. *e.g. She will get chicken pox if she doesn't watch out.*

3 If you **get** a joke or **get** the point of something, you understand it. *e.g. Now I get the point of the story.*

get at   444

If you **get at** someone, you criticise or tease

them in an unkind or unsympathetic way. *e.g. You should stop getting at your brother like that.*

get knotted   785

If you sign or say **get knotted**, you strongly reject a comment someone has made or indicate abruptly that you do not want to do something. *e.g. 'Can I borrow your pen?'—'Get knotted! You lost the last one you borrowed.'*

get lost   160, 498

If you tell someone to **get lost**, you are rudely telling them to go away. *e.g. He told me to get lost, so I kicked him in the shins.*

get off   818

If you **get off** a bus, train, etc., you jump or step out of it. *e.g. Get off at Mayfield Church and then wait for the 614 to the Interchange.*

get on   796

If you **get on** a horse, bicycle, or motorbike, you climb on to it so you can ride it. *e.g. The Hell's Angel got on his motorbike and rode away.*

get one's own back   48

If you **get** your **own back** on someone, you have your revenge on them because of something that they have done to you. *e.g. I got my own back on her for getting me into trouble.*

get on with   1646

If you **get on with** something, you continue with something that you have started doing or you start something that you were about to do. *e.g. Perhaps we can get on with the meeting.*

get out   160

You sign or say **get out** to indicate that you no longer want someone or something to participate in a situation. *e.g. I was so angry I told him to get out.*

get out   818

1 If you **get out** of a position or an organisation, you withdraw from it or leave it. *e.g. He was desperate to get out of his boring job.*

2 If you **get out** of a vehicle, you step out of it or leave it. *e.g. Can we stop at the next service area? I want to get out and stretch my legs.*

get someone to do something   526

If you **get someone to do something**, you cause them to do it by asking, persuading or telling them. *e.g. She gets Stuart to help her clean when he visits.*

get somewhere   1595

If you **get somewhere**, you arrive there. *e.g. When we get to Firle Beacon, let's have a rest.*

get stuffed   785

Get stuffed is used to express anger at, and rejection of, what someone has signed, said or done. *e.g. I told him I didn't want to argue any more and he could get stuffed!*

get the attention of   1562
If you try to **get the attention of** someone, you try to get them to notice you so that you can communicate with them. *e.g. He was trying to get the attention of the woman standing by the window.*

get up   1201, 1376
1 When you **get up**, you rise to a standing position after you have been sitting or lying down. *e.g. Please get up when the Head Teacher enters.*
2 When you **get up**, you get out of bed. *e.g. I must get up at eight o'clock.*

giant   1572, 1573
1 A **giant** is an imaginary person who is very big and strong, especially one mentioned in myths and children's stories. *e.g. It was the story of a cruel giant and a wicked witch.*
2 Something that is much larger than usual can be referred to as a **giant**. *e.g. He was a giant of a man.*
3 Something that is much larger than usual can be referred to as a **giant** object. *e.g. It was a giant Christmas tree, much too big for our house.*

gift   1372
A **gift** is something that you give someone as a present. *e.g. Here is a gift from the Russian Ambassador.*

gifted   166
1 Someone who is **gifted** has a natural ability to do something well. *e.g. She was a gifted actress.*
2 A **gifted** child is extremely intelligent. *e.g. She taught in a school for gifted children.*

gigantic   1573
Something that is **gigantic** is very tall. *e.g. The new office block is a gigantic building.*

giraffe   1673
A **giraffe** is a large African animal with a very long neck, long legs and dark patches on its yellowish skin. *e.g. The giraffe nibbled the leaves at the top of the tree.*

girl   339, 360, 509
1 A **girl** is a female child. *e.g. A girl of eleven saved the baby.*
2 Someone's daughter can be referred to as their **girl**. *e.g. She has two girls and a boy.*
3 You can refer to a young woman, usually a teenager, as a **girl**. *e.g. There were over one hundred girls at the school-leavers' dinner.*
4 People sign or say **girls** when they are referring to a group of close friends or women whom they work with. *e.g. The other girls at work go for a drink together every Friday.*

girlfriend   339
1 A person's **girlfriend** is a girl or woman with whom a person is having a relationship that is

romantic, sexual or both. *e.g. His girlfriend walked out on him.*
2 A **girlfriend** is a female friend. *e.g. Mary-Joy went to the movies with some girlfriends.*

give   1205, 1372, 1517
1 If you **give** someone something, or give something to someone, you offer it to them as a present. *e.g. They gave him a silver box.*
2 If you **give** someone something, you hand it over to them. *e.g. Give him that, he needs it more than you.*

give   1391, 1377
1 If you **give** someone something, or **give** something to someone, you offer it to them, usually in a box. *e.g. Give him his present now.*
2 If you **give** someone something, or **give** something to someone, you hand it over to them, usually in a box. *e.g. Give them the box of dynamite and run!*

give a donation/gratuity/tip   862, 871
If you **give a donation**, a **gratuity** or a **tip** to a person or organisation, you give them a sum of money, either to enable them to carry out some service or to thank them for their services. *e.g. The visiting lecturers all received a gratuity for giving a presentation on the Sign Language Studies course.*

give a gift/present   1372
If you **give** someone a **gift** or a **present**, you offer them something which you want them to have, often to mark a special occasion or as a way of thanking them. *e.g. I give him a present every year at Christmas.*

give away   1522, 1723
1 If you **give** something **away**, you give it to someone, usually because you no longer want it. *e.g. I'm not going to give away Great Aunt Edie's picture, no matter what it's worth.*
2 If you **give away** information that should be kept secret, you reveal it to other people. *e.g. Don't give away the results of the examination yet.*

give out   1522
If you **give out** a number of things, you distribute them among a group of people. *e.g. Howard, give out the mystery prizes now, please.*

give up   289
If you **give up** something, you stop doing it. *e.g. I've been on this committee twelve years. It's time for me to give up.*

glad   1275
If you are **glad** about something, you are happy and pleased about it. *e.g. I'm glad your niece enjoyed the film.*

glass   331, 575, 581
Glass is the hard transparent substance that

windows and bottles are made from. *e.g. I want a glass top for this table, please.*

glass   1671, 1681
A **glass** is a container made from glass, which you can drink from and which does not have a handle. *e.g. She bought a glass from a cheap souvenir shop.*

glasses   754
Glasses are two transparent lenses in a metal or plastic frame that someone with poor eyesight wears in front of their eyes in order to help them see better. *e.g. A girl with long hair and glasses went past me.*

glass with a handle   26
A **glass with a handle** is a container made from glass used for drinking. It has an extension on the side (a handle) also made from glass, with which it can be held. *e.g. I prefer to drink beer from a glass with a handle.*

gleam   1057
1 If an object or a surface **gleams**, it shines brightly because it is reflecting light. *e.g. He polished it until it gleamed.*
2 A **gleam** is a bright shine caused by the reflection of light. *e.g. The gleam of a hundred candles flooded the archway.*

glen   1402
A **glen** is a deep, narrow valley. *e.g. My uncle had a croft in a glen in the Highlands.*

glitter   1057
1 If something **glitters**, it shines in a sparkling way. *e.g. Her jewellery glittered under the spotlight.*
2 A **glitter** is a sparkling shine. *e.g. I love the glitter of stars on a sharp, clear night.*

global   1638
Global means concerning or including the whole world. *e.g. We must examine future telecommunications in a global way.*

globe   1418
1 You can refer to the earth as the **globe**. *e.g. These television pictures will be seen all over the globe.*
2 A **globe** is a spherical object, usually fixed on a stand, with a map of the world on it. *e.g. See if you can find Zimbabwe on the globe.*
3 Any object shaped like a ball can be referred to as a **globe**. *e.g. The paperweight is a simple pewter globe on a small plinth.*

glorify   225
If you **glorify** someone or something, you praise them or make them seem important. *e.g. His newspapers glorified his charitable donations.*

glorify   226
If you **glorify** someone or something in

authority over you or whom you look up to, you praise them. *e.g. We glorify God in our prayers.*

gloss   1057
A **gloss** is a bright shine on the surface of something. *e.g. The wood has a high gloss.*

glossy   1057
Something that is **glossy** is smooth and shiny. *e.g. She had glossy brown hair.*

glove   1546
1 A **glove** is a piece of clothing which covers your hand and wrist and has individual sections for each finger. You usually wear gloves to keep your hands warm and dry or to protect them. *e.g. Like Michael Jackson, he wore a single black glove. Weird.*
2 If your hands are **gloved**, you are wearing gloves. *e.g. A gloved hand reached in through the window.*

glue   1324
1 **Glue** is a sticky substance used for joining things together, often for repairing broken things. *e.g. He was mending things with glue.*
2 If you **glue** one object to another, you stick them together using glue. *e.g. Glue the bits together.*

go   498, 1220, 1225
1 When you **go**, you leave the place where you are. *e.g. 'I must go', she signed.*
2 If you **go** and do a particular thing, you move from one place to another in order to do the thing, and you do it. *e.g. I'll go and see him in the morning.*
3 When you **go** somewhere, you move or travel there. *e.g. Go to Moscow then, see if I care!*

go   1229, 1246
1 When you **go** somewhere, you move or travel there. *e.g. I am going to Stockholm on Friday.*
2 If you **go** and do a particular thing, you move from one place to another in order to do the thing, and you do it. *e.g. Can you go and explain our situation?*

goad   444
If you **goad** someone, you make them feel a strong emotion such as anger, often causing them to react by doing something. *e.g. Stop goading Jack about his job—he doesn't want to talk about it.*

go ahead   1642
If an activity **goes ahead** or you **go ahead** with it, it takes place. *e.g. The festival will go ahead according to schedule.*

goal   397
A **goal**, in games such as football or hockey, is an instance in which a player gets the ball into the area marked by posts known as goalposts, or the point (a goal) that is scored by doing

this. *e.g. He scored the winning goal.*

goalkeeper   1474
A **goalkeeper** is the player in a sports team whose job is to guard the goal. *e.g. Pat Jennings was a great goalkeeper.*

go along with   430
1 If you **go along with** a rule, decision or policy, you accept it and obey it. *e.g. You agreed to go along with the decision.*
2 If you **go along with** a person or idea, you agree with the person or idea or accept that what they are saying is true. *e.g. I am willing to go along with Austin.*

goat   1672
A **goat** is an animal with a beard, horns, and a short tail, which is found in mountain areas or on farms. They are reared or kept usually as a source of milk, meat and wool. *e.g. Do Mary and Maria have a goat called Brennan?*

goatee   1672
A **goatee** is a very short, pointed beard that a man wears on his chin. *e.g. He didn't suit the goatee he'd grown.*

go away   498, 1566
1 If you **go away**, you leave your usual place for a period of time. *e.g. I'm going away on holiday tomorrow.*
2 If you tell someone to **go away**, you want them to leave, usually because they are bothering you. *e.g. 'Stop staring at me and go away', signed Lisa.*

gobsmacked   604, 725
If you are **gobsmacked**, you are extremely surprised. *e.g. My niece has grown up so fast. I was gobsmacked when I saw her.*

go by ferry   692
When you **go** somewhere **by ferry**, you ride in a boat that travels across a river or a narrow bit of sea. *e.g. We'll go there and back on the ferry.*

god   311
1 The name **God** is given to the spirit or being who is worshipped as the creator and ruler of the world, especially by Christians, Jews and Muslims. *e.g. We pray to God every day.*
2 People sometimes use **god** in exclamations to emphasise something that they are signing or saying, or to express surprise, fear, shock or excitement. Some people find this offensive. *e.g. My god, Graham, what are you doing here?*
3 A **god** is one of the spirits or beings that are believed in many religions to have power over a particular part of the world or nature. *e.g. Mars was the Roman god of war.*

go down by escalator   806
If you **go down by escalator**, you travel from

one floor or level to a lower one on a moving staircase. *e.g. If I go down by escalator, I'll have to keep an eye out for her in case she's on the stairs.*

go downstairs   806
If you **go downstairs**, you travel from one floor or level to a lower one by walking down a staircase. *e.g. He went downstairs and into the kitchen.*

go home   898
If you **go home**, you travel to the house or place where you live. *e.g. I'm going to go home now: are you coming?*

go in   1607
1 If you **go in** to a place, you enter it. *e.g. Go in and turn left.*
2 If an object **goes in** somewhere, it is or should be placed there. *e.g. This can go in an old shoebox.*

going to   188
If you sign or say that something is **going to** happen, you mean that it will happen in the future, especially soon. *e.g. She told him she was going to leave her job.*

go into   1607
If a person or object **goes into** a room, building, town, country, etc., they move from being outside it to being inside it. *e.g. He should just go into a police station.*

gold   125
1 **Gold** is a valuable, yellow-coloured metal that is used for making jewellery, and as an international currency. *e.g. He gave her a gold bracelet.*
2 **Gold** is used to mean things that are made of gold. *e.g. They stole a million pounds worth of gold from the jewellers.*
3 Something that is **gold** is shiny and yellow-coloured, and looks like gold. *e.g. The sign was written in gold letters.*

golden   125
1 Something that is **golden** is made of gold. *e.g. She wore a tiny golden cross.*
2 Something that is **golden** is bright yellow in colour and looks rather like gold. *e.g. He met a beautiful girl with bright golden hair.*

gondola   127
A **gondola** is a long, narrow boat that is used especially in Venice. It has a flat bottom and curves upwards at both ends. A person (gondolier) stands at one end of the gondola and uses a long pole to move and steer it. *e.g. We travelled part of the way by gondola.*

gondolier   127
A **gondolier** is a person whose job is to take people from one place to another in a gondola. *e.g. The gondolier was a very helpful man.*

gone 1555
Someone or something that is **gone** is no longer present or no longer exists. *e.g. He turned the corner and was gone.*

good 155, 164
1 Something that is **good** is pleasant and enjoyable. *e.g. They had a good time.*
2 Something that is **good** is of a high quality or standard, often in comparison to other similar things. *e.g. It's a good school.*
3 Someone who is **good** is kind to people and always thinks of their feelings and needs. *e.g. Wendy is so good to the old lady next door.*
4 Someone who is in a **good** mood is cheerful and pleasant to be with. *e.g. On pay-days, I'm always in a good mood.*
5 **Good** is what is considered to be right and desirable according to moral standards or religious beliefs, and is often thought of as a force or power. *e.g. He defined politics as the conflict between good and evil.*

goodbye 991
You sign or say **goodbye** to someone when you or they are leaving and you will not see each other for a time. *e.g. We went to say goodbye to my sister when she flew back to Australia.*

good enough 198
If you sign or say that someone or something is **good enough**, you mean that they are acceptable, though not the best. *e.g. A photocopy of the information will be good enough until the new batch of pamphlets arrive from the printers.*

good evening 718
You can sign or say **good evening** when you are greeting someone between the end of the afternoon and the time at which you go to bed. *e.g. Good evening, Mr. Castle. I'm sorry I'm late.*

good looking 1487
Someone who is **good looking** has an attractive face. *e.g. She has two good looking sons.*

good luck 466
1 **Good luck** is success or other desirable consequences that do not come from your own planning, abilities or efforts. *e.g. My good luck lasted right through the season.*
2 If you sign or say **good luck** to someone, you are indicating that you hope they will be successful. *e.g. 'Good luck', signed Judith as we set off.*

good morning 189, 1654, 1657
People may sign or say **good morning** in the morning when they first see each other, or at the beginning of a telephone conversation or a television or radio broadcast in the morning, as a form of greeting. *e.g. Good morning. Lovely day! How do you feel?*

good night 718
You can sign or say **good night** to someone late in the evening, when you or they are going home, going to bed, or going to sleep, or at the end of a telephone conversation or a television or radio broadcast in the evening or at night. *e.g. We all stood up, signed good night, and went to our rooms.*

good (very good) 213
See **very good**.

go (off you go) 498
If you sign or say **off you go**, you are telling someone they should leave. *e.g. Have you got all your things? Fine, off you go now.*

goose 711
1 A **goose** is a large bird that has a long neck and webbed feet and makes a loud noise. Geese exist as wild birds, but are also sometimes kept on farms for their meat, eggs, and feathers. *e.g. Our next door neighbour used to keep a goose in his shed.*
2 **Goose** is the meat from a goose. *e.g. Roast goose with red cabbage and dumplings is a favourite meal of Romanian peasants.*

go over 1608
1 If one thing **goes over** another thing, it is situated directly above it. *e.g. He reached the place where the bridge used to go over the stream.*
2 If you **go over** something such as a river, bridge or boundary, you cross it. *e.g. We went over the Rhine very late that night.*
3 If something **goes over** a particular amount, measurement or age, it becomes more than that amount, measurement or age. *e.g. The figure has now begun to go over £3,000.*

gorilla 138
A **gorilla** is an animal which looks like a very large monkey. It has long arms, a black face, and black fur. Gorillas live on the ground in African forests. *e.g. She took photographs of the gorillas and the lions.*

gosh 989
You sign or say **gosh** to indicate how surprised you are or how strongly you feel about something. *e.g. I met Charles Conquest yesterday. Gosh, he hasn't changed one bit!*

go sightseeing 747
If you **go sightseeing**, you travel around, in order to see the interesting places that tourists usually visit. *e.g. We want to go sightseeing for a day and then get stuck into the museums.*

gossip 355
1 **Gossip** is informal conversation or information about other people, often including comments about their private affairs. *e.g. She is always spreading gossip at the Deaf club.*

2 If you **gossip**, you sign or speak informally with someone, especially about other people or local events. *e.g. I mustn't stay gossiping with you any longer.*

got it 216
Got it may be used to indicate that, after a great deal of effort or time, you have understood, achieved or completed something. *e.g. After reading the chapter three times, she sat back and signed 'Got it. Now I know what she's going on about'.*

go under 1607
1 If you **go under** something, you go from one side of it to the other side and it is above you while you do this. *e.g. The car had to go under a bridge.*
2 If something **goes under** something else, its usual place is below it, either close to it or at some distance from it. *e.g. The booklet can go under the videorecorder.*

go up by elevator/lift 692
If you **go up by elevator** or **lift**, you travel upwards through a vertical shaft inside a special structure like a small room that moves you from one floor of a building to another. *e.g. He loved going up to the top floor in the lift.*

go up by escalator 692, 805
If you **go up by escalator**, you ride to a higher level or floor on a moving staircase. *e.g. I don't want to go up by escalator. It makes me feel queasy.*

go upstairs 805
If you **go upstairs**, you travel from one floor or level to a higher one by walking up a staircase. *e.g. If you would go upstairs and see Mrs. Ashton—she'll be pleased to help.*

govern 272
Someone who **governs** a country or group of people rules the country by making and revising laws, managing the economy, controlling public services, et cetera. *e.g. Many civil servants are sure that they can govern better than the politicians.*

government 50, 1131
1 A **government** is the group of people who are responsible for a country or state by making and revising the laws, managing the economy, controlling public services, et cetera. *e.g. The government has decided to cut back on public expenditure.*
2 **Government** is the departments, ministries and committees that carry out the decisions of the political leaders of a country. *e.g. We must pressurise government to recognise British Sign Language.*

governor 272
1 A **governor** is a person who is responsible

for the political adminstration of a region, for example of a state in the United States of America. *e.g. Mario Cuomo was re-elected as Governor of New York.*
2 A **governor** is the chief political administrator of a colony. *e.g. Chris Patten was appointed Governor of Hong Kong.*
3 A **governor** is a person who is on a committee which controls the conduct and standards of an institution such as a school, hospital, university, et cetera. *e.g. There are training courses for school governors.*
4 A **governor** is the person who is in charge of the administration of a prison. *e.g. That is the view of the governor of Brixton Prison.*

go with someone   712
If you **go with someone** somewhere, you accompany them. *e.g. He will go with Derek to the play.*

grab   984, 1130
If you **grab** something, you take it or pick it up quickly, usually with one hand. *e.g. She fell on her knees and tried to grab the balloon's string.*

grab   1171
If you **grab** something, you take it or pick it up quickly, usually with two hands. *e.g. When the trapeze swings back, grab it.*

graffiti   634
Graffiti is words or pictures that are written or drawn on walls, signs, and posters in public places. Graffiti is usually rude, funny, or contains a personal or political message. *e.g. The tube train was covered with graffiti.*

grant   1008
A **grant** is an amount of money that is given to an individual or to an organisation by a funding body for a particular purpose such as education, welfare or home improvements. *e.g. He gets a student grant.*

grapes   1509
Grapes are small, sweet, round fruits, green or purple in colour, which are usually eaten raw, used for making wine, or dried to make raisins, sultanas or currants. *e.g. Sarah gave her mother grapes when she was in hospital.*

grapes (bunch of grapes)   1509
A **bunch of grapes** is a number of small, sweet, round fruits, green or purple in colour, growing close together on the same stem. They are usually eaten raw, used for making wine, or dried to make raisins, sultanas or currants. *e.g. We picked a bunch of grapes from the supermarket shelf.*

grass   625
1 If you **grass** on someone, you give information to the police or other people in authority about something criminal or wrong which that person has done. *e.g. It was Lucy who grassed on the thieves, not me!*
2 A **grass** is someone who grasses on someone else. *e.g. Don't trust him—he's a grass.*

grass   1285, 1415, 1733
1 **Grass** is a very common green plant with thin leaves that forms a layer covering an area of ground. It is eaten by sheep, cows, etc., and is often planted over large areas in parks, gardens or playing fields. *e.g. The grass withered in the sun.*
2 If you refer to the **grass**, you are referring to an area of ground that is covered with grass, for example in your garden. *e.g. Keep off the grass!*

grass/plants/vegetation growing   1733
When **grass**, **plants** or **vegetation grow**, they increase in size. *e.g. The grass is growing well this year.*

grateful   1261, 1471
If you are **grateful** for something pleasant or useful that someone has done or given you, you have warm, friendly feelings towards them and wish to thank them. *e.g. He was grateful to the surgeon for saving his life.*

gratitude   1261, 1471
Gratitude is the state of feeling grateful. *e.g. I wish to express my gratitude to my family for all their support.*

gratuity   862, 871
A **gratuity** is a gift of money to someone who has done something for you. *e.g. Should I leave a gratuity for the tour guide?*

grave   914
Something that is **grave** is very serious and worrying. *e.g. He made a number of grave mistakes.*

grave   1443
A **grave** is a place where a dead person is buried. *e.g. Flowers had been put on the grave.*

greasy   1516
Something that is **greasy** is covered with oily liquid or contains a lot of fat or oil. *e.g. His tools were worn and greasy.*

great   155, 164, 213, 220, 960
1 Someone or something that is **great** is very good or nice. *e.g. It's a great party.*
2 If you feel **great** you feel very healthy and energetic. *e.g. Now I have recovered from my illness, I feel great.*

great   467
You use **great** ironically to express contempt, scorn, or bitterness. *e.g. If that's what they want to believe in, great.*

great   1064
You use **great** to describe something that is large in size, number or amount. *e.g. This great mound of earth has been here since the Bronze Age.*

Great Britain   1037
Great Britain is the union of England, Scotland, and Wales. Great Britain and Northern Ireland together form the United Kingdom. *e.g. Great Britain are favourites to win the gold medal.*

Greece   1515
Greece is a republic in South East Europe, occupying the southern part of the Balkan Peninsula and many islands in the Ionian and Aegean Seas. Greece is a member of the European Community. *e.g. They went on holiday to Greece.*

greed   20, 31, 40
Greed is a desire for something, for example food, money or power, especially for more than it is necessary or fair for you to have. *e.g. Greed is a particularly unattractive trait.*

greedy   20, 31, 40
Someone who is **greedy** wants more of something such as food, money or power than it is necessary or fair for them to have. *e.g. She was a greedy little girl; she ate all our chocolate biscuits.*

Greek   1515
1 Someone or something that is **Greek** belongs to or relates to Greece, or its people. *e.g. Two students of Greek Sign Language came here last year.*
2 **Greek** is the main language spoken in Greece. *e.g. He found Greek a very difficult language to learn.*
3 A **Greek** is a person who comes from, or whose family identity relates to, Greece. *e.g. Plato was a Greek.*
4 The address of the **Greek** Federation of the Deaf is: 57 Salomou St., Gre 104-32 Athens, Greece.

green   1023
Something that is **green** is the colour of grass or leaves. *e.g. My cat is black and white and has green eyes.*

green   1280
A **green** is a public area of grass in a farm or village. *e.g. They loved to play on the green near Granny's home.*

green   1285
1 Something that is **green** is the colour of grass or new leaves. *e.g. You can't wear red with green because they clash horribly.*
2 A **green** is an area of grass in a town or village. *e.g. The village green was not large, but we managed to play cricket there anyway.*

grey 474, 907
Also spelled **gray**.
Something that is **grey** is the colour mid-way between black and white, like ashes or clouds on a rainy day. *e.g. He wore a new grey suit.*

grill 1202, 1334
1 When you **grill** food, you cook it using strong heat directly above or below it. *e.g. We wanted to grill the chops, but he had other ideas.*
2 A **grill** is part of a cooker that consists of a metal shelf where food is cooked by strong heat from above. *e.g. The grill is faulty on the new cooker.*

grime 1020
Grime is dirt which gathers on the surface of something. *e.g. The windows were thick with grime.*

grimy 1020
Something that is **grimy** is very dirty. *e.g. A grimy office was not the place for a love scene.*

grin and bear it 179, 181, 1182
To **grin and bear it** means to accept a difficult or unpleasant situation without complaining because you know there is nothing you can do to make things better. *e.g. I'll just have to grin and bear it for the next two hours.*

grind 53
If you **grind** something such as corn or pepper, you crush it between two hard surfaces or with a machine until it becomes a fine powder. *e.g. They were grinding peppercorns in the kitchen.*

grinder 53
A **grinder** is a device which crushes something into small pieces or makes it into a powder. *e.g. She bought a coffee grinder for the office.*

grip 1
If you **grip** something, you hold it with your hand and continue to hold it firmly. *e.g. She gripped the stick and would not let it go.*

ground 1415
1 The **ground** is the surface of the earth or the floor of a room. *e.g. He looked carefully at the ground.*
2 The **ground** is the soil and rock on and beneath the earth's surface. *e.g. The ground all round was very wet and marshy.*
3 A **ground** is an area of land which is used for a particular purpose. *e.g. Come to the sports ground tomorrow for a game of tennis.*
4 **Ground** is land. *e.g. A rocky piece of ground lay behind the manor.*
5 A **ground** is an area of land where sport is played. *e.g. Newcastle United's ground at St. James' Park is in superb condition.*
6 The **grounds** of a building are the land which surrounds it and which is owned by the

same people. *e.g. The maintenance of the school grounds is now the responsibility of the governors.*

ground floor 1415
The **ground floor** of a building is the floor that is approximately level with the ground outside. *e.g. There's a bathroom on the ground floor.*

group 840, 1176, 1690
1 A **group** is a number of people or things which are together in one place at one time. *e.g. The group has worked together well.*
2 When you **group** a number of things or people together or when they **group** together, they all come together in one place or within one organisation. *e.g. The students were grouped according to age.*

grovel 824
If you **grovel**, you behave very humbly towards someone, for example if they are very important or because you are frightened of them. *e.g. He had to grovel to his employer to get his job back after he walked out.*

grow 1063
If a place, organisation, or thing **grows**, it increases in size, wealth, or importance. *e.g. One New York investment bank seems to grow faster than all the others.*

grow 1210
When a person, an animal, or their body **grows**, their body increases in size and changes physically over a period of time. *e.g. As my children grew, I passed on their old clothes to my sister's children..*

grow 1718, 1733
1 When plants **grow**, they increase in size. *e.g. Many weeds grow very quickly.*
2 If a plant or plants **grow** in a particular place, they are alive there. *e.g. Dahlias grew in the corner of Bridie's garden.*

grown-up 1217, 1572
1 A **grown-up** is the same as an adult. *e.g. He's a grown-up and knows how to behave.*
2 If you sign or say that someone is **grown-up**, you mean that they are physically and mentally mature. *e.g. Older couples with grown-up children don't come here very often.*
3 If you sign or say that someone is **grown-up**, you mean that they behave in an adult way, especially when they are in fact still a child. *e.g. Your brother's awfully grown-up for his age.*

growth 1718
1 The **growth** of an industry or service is an increase in the demand for and number of goods it produces or services it provides. *e.g. The growth of the company has taken us all by surprise.*
2 **Growth** in a person, animal or plant is the process of increasing in physical size and

development. *e.g. The growth of the plant during the summer was amazing: it was almost four inches taller.*

grow up 1210
When you **grow up**, you gradually change from being a child into being an adult. *e.g. Everyone has to grow up eventually!*

grumble 1187, 1199
If you **grumble**, you complain about something in a bad-tempered way. *e.g. It was just like her to grumble about the arrangements we'd made.*

grumpy 1135
Someone who is **grumpy** is bad tempered, often because they are slightly disappointed, angry or pessimistic. *e.g. My neighbour was grumpy because the ball kept going into his garden.*

guarantee 50
1 If something **guarantees** something else, it is certain to cause that thing to happen. *e.g. This method guarantees success.*
2 If you **guarantee** something, you promise it will definitely happen. *e.g. They guarantee to hold interest rates down next year.*
3 If a company **guarantees** their product or work, they give a written promise that if it has any faults within a particular time, it will be repaired or replaced free of charge. *e.g. They guarantee their roofing work for ten years.*
4 A **guarantee** is a promise made by a company that if their product has any faults within a particular time, it will be repaired or replaced free of charge. *e.g. My watch has a five year guarantee.*

guard 320
A **guard** is a person responsible for watching over a particular person, place, or object carefully in order to protect them. *e.g. Another guard was standing by the fence.*

guard 777
1 If you **guard** a place, person, or object, you watch and protect them. *e.g. Scotland Yard sent an officer to guard the jewels.*
2 If you **guard** someone, you watch them to stop them from escaping. *e.g. She had been locked in her room and was guarded night and day.*
3 If you **guard** something important or secret, you protect or hide it. *e.g. The contents of the lists were a closely guarded secret.*
4 A **guard** is a person responsible for watching over a particular person, place or object carefully in order to protect them. *e.g. I'm here as a guard: she'd go mad if the animals escaped.*

guardian 777
A **guardian** is someone who has been legally appointed to look after a child, usually when

the child's parents have died. *e.g. He became the legal guardian of his brother's daughter.*

guess 1665
If you **guess** something, you give an answer or an opinion about something when you do not know whether it is correct. *e.g. I can only guess at how long it will take to drive there.*

guide 1486
1 A **guide** is someone who shows a place such as a city or museum to tourists. *e.g. He had been appointed as a tourist guide.*
2 A **guide** is something which gives you information or instructions to help you do or understand something. *e.g. This book is meant to be a practical guide to healthy living.*
3 If you **guide** someone round a city, museum or building, you show it to them and explain points of interest. *e.g. OK, so I'll guide you round the market and then we'll stop for a coffee.*

guilt 920
1 **Guilt** is an unhappy feeling that you have because you believe that you have done

something wrong. *e.g. I had agonised feelings of shame and guilt.*
2 **Guilt** is the fact that you have done something wrong or have broken a law. *e.g. He at last made a public admission of his guilt.*

guilty 920
If you feel **guilty**, you feel unhappy because you believe that you have done something wrong. *e.g. They feel guilty about seeing her so little.*

Guinness 50
Guinness is the brand name of an Irish stout. It is a strong, dark beer with a cream-coloured head. Guinness was first brewed in Dublin in 1759. *e.g. The Queen Victoria pub has excellent Guinness.*

gullible 58, 538, 856
Someone who is **gullible** is easily tricked because they are too trusting. *e.g. She is so gullible that she believes everything they tell her.*

gym 1652
1 A **gym** is a building or a large room which is used for physical exercise and usually has

equipment such as bars and ropes in it. *e.g. He was always at the gym.*
2 **Gym** means physical exercises, often using equipment such as bars and ropes, which develop your strength and agility. *e.g. We did an hour of gym.*

gymnasium 1652
A **gymnasium** is a building or a large room which is used for physical exercise and usually has equipment such as bars and ropes in it. *e.g. The school is building a new gymnasium.*

gymnast 1652
A **gymnast** is someone who is trained in gymnastics or takes part in gymnastics. *e.g. She is a keen gymnast.*

gymnastics 1652
Gymnastics are physical exercises, often using equipment such as bars and ropes, which develop your strength and agility. Gymnastic events are sometimes undertaken competitively as a sport. *e.g. They are training for the Olympic gymnastics team.*

H, h

H
H is the eighth letter of the British manual and English alphabets. See page 851.

habit 363
A **habit** is something that you do often or regularly. *e.g. It was his habit to go shopping on Tuesdays.*

habit (be in the habit) 363
If you **are in the habit** of doing something, you do it regularly or often. *e.g. The family were in the habit of eating crumpets for tea on Saturdays.*

habitual 204, 207
A **habitual** action is one that somebody usually does, or often does. *e.g. He is a habitual liar.*

had enough 1420
If you sign or say that you have **had enough**, you mean that you do not want something to continue or get any worse. *e.g. She burst into tears and signed, 'I've had enough of your bullying ways'.*

hail 830
Hail consists of tiny balls of ice that fall like rain from the clouds. *e.g. There will be hail in northern areas before nightfall.*

hailstones 830
Hailstones are tiny balls of ice that fall from the clouds like rain. *e.g. The grass was covered with hailstones.*

hailstorm 830
A **hailstorm** is a storm in which tiny balls of ice fall from the clouds like rain. *e.g. The poor cat got caught in a hailstorm.*

hair 851
1 Your **hair** is the large number of hairs that grow in a mass on your head. *e.g. I went to the 'Upper Room' and Sally cut my hair in her usual dizzy way.*
2 A **hair** is one of the long, fine, thread-like things that grow in large numbers on your head and on other parts of your body. *e.g. The wire that you use must be really thin, like a hair.*

hairbrush 24
A **hairbrush** is an object made of wood, plastic or metal which has a large number of bristles attached to it and is used for brushing your hair. *e.g. I need a new hairbrush.*

hairdresser 752
A **hairdresser** is a person who cuts, washes, and styles people's hair. *e.g. They have a hairdresser's shop in Durham called 'Partners'.*

hairspray 634
Hairspray or a **hairspray** is a fine lacquer kept under pressure in an aerosol can, and sprayed onto hair to hold it in place after it has been arranged by someone, particularly a hairdresser. *e.g. I'm trying this new hairspray.*

hairy 1557
Someone or something that is **hairy** is covered with hair or has a lot of hair growing from it. *e.g. She was terrified of that hairy ape.*

half 387, 1323, 1326
1 **Half** of an amount or object is one of the two equal parts that together make up the amount or object. *e.g. Half the cake will be sufficient*
2 A **half** is half a pint of beer, lager, or cider. *e.g. On second thoughts, make it a half, please.*
3 You can use **half** to describe a half of something. *e.g. The picture won't end for another half hour.*
4 You use **half** to refer to a time that is thirty minutes after a particular hour. For example, if it is half past two, thirty minutes have passed since two o'clock. *e.g. It is half past six.*
5 You can use **half** to sign or say that something is only partly the case or happens to only a limited extent. *e.g. He half expected to see Graham.*

hall 697
A **hall** is the area just inside the front door of a

house, into which some of the other rooms open. *e.g. The hall had just been decorated.*

hallelujah 255
Also spelled **alleluia** or **halleluia**.
Christians sign or say **hallelujah** as an exclamation of praise and thanks to God. *e.g. Christ is risen; hallelujah!*

halt 1392
If someone or something comes to a **halt**, they stop moving. *e.g. The car slowed and came to a halt beside her.*

halt 1435
If someone signs or says **halt**, you are required to stop moving and stand still. *e.g. He tried to push past but the girl told him to halt.*

hammer 251, 267
A **hammer** is a tool that consists of a heavy piece of metal at the end of a handle. It is used for hitting things, for example nails into walls, or for breaking things by force. *e.g. There is a hammer in the garage.*

hammer a nail/tack with a hammer 267
If you **hammer a nail** or **a tack with a hammer**, you hit a nail or tack into something with a hammer. *e.g. He hammered a nail into the bathroom door.*

hand 1205
If you **hand** something to someone, you give it to them directly. *e.g. Hand the plate to Ernst and he can start eating.*

handbag 247
A **handbag** is a small bag used by women to hold items such as money, keys, cheque book, etc., and which they take with them when they go out. *e.g. I left my handbag on the train when I went to London.*

hand bell 241
A **hand bell** is a small hollow, metal object shaped like a cup, which has a loose metal piece inside it and a handle at one end. It is held by hand, and if shaken makes a sound. It is used to give a signal, to attract people's attention or as a musical instrument. *e.g. Tom gave each child a hand bell.*

hand down 1207, 1306
If you **hand** something **down**, you give it or leave it to people who belong to a younger generation. *e.g. Such knowledge was handed down from father to son.*

hand gun 463
A **hand gun** or **handgun** is a weapon consisting mainly of a metal tube from which bullets are fired. *e.g. He pointed the hand gun at them.*

handicap 561, 1405
1 A **handicap** is a physical or mental impairment that you are born with or that is caused by an illness or accident which, it is thought, prevents you from living the life you or others expected you would lead. *e.g. One-third of our employees have a physical handicap.*
2 A **handicap** is a difference in mental or physical functioning from what most people consider to be normal. *e.g. It's a club for children who have any kind of handicap.*

handicapped 561, 1405
1 Someone who is **handicapped** has a physical or mental impairment which, it is thought, prevents them from living the life they or others expected they would lead. *e.g. A journalist friend of his had a handicapped daughter.*
2 Someone who is **handicapped** differs in their mental or physical functioning from what most people consider to be normal. *e.g. She may be handicapped, but she'll go further than you, I'm sure.*
3 People who are handicapped are sometimes referred to as the **handicapped**. Some people find this offensive. *e.g. We are establishing rehabilitation centres for the handicapped.*

handicapped person 1405
1 A **handicapped person** has a physical or mental impairment which, it is thought, prevents them from living the life they or others expected they would lead. *e.g. My friend's daughter is a handicapped person: she's got cerebral palsy.*
2 A **handicapped person** differs in their mental or physical functioning from what most people consider to be normal. *e.g. He did not consider himself to be a handicapped person.*

handkerchief 1535
A **handkerchief** is a small square piece of fabric which you use for blowing your nose or wiping moisture from your face. *e.g. I sneezed into my handkerchief.*

handlebar moustache 715, 1540
See **moustache (handlebar moustache)**.

hand on 1207, 1306
If you **hand** something **on** to someone, you give it or leave it to them. *e.g. They always hand on this jewellery to the eldest son's wife on her wedding day.*

hand over 1205, 1626
1 If you **hand over** to someone, you give them the responsibility of dealing with something which you were previously responsible for. *e.g. I will now hand over the meeting to Mr. Nelson.*
2 If you **hand** something **over** to someone, you pass it to them directly. *e.g. Hand that over to the Head Teacher at once!*

3 A **handover** is a change in the management of an organisation or business. *e.g. Our strike didn't prevent the company's handover to foreign control.*

hand over 1377, 1391
If you **hand** something **over** to someone, you give it to them, usually in a box. *e.g. I will hand over the casket and then we will all bow.*

handsome 1487
A person who is **handsome** has an attractive face. *e.g. He is a tall handsome man.*

hang on 1222, 1435
If you ask or instruct someone to **hang on**, you are asking or instructing them to wait for a short time before taking action. *e.g. I'll come with you if you hang on a minute or two.*

hang on a clothes line/line 836
If you **hang** something **on a clothes line** or a **line**, you fix it there, usually using special pegs, so that it can dry in the breeze. *e.g. I'll just hang these on the line.*

hang onto 1
1 If you **hang onto** something, you hold it very tight. *e.g. The girl's mother told her to hang onto her money.*
2 If you **hang onto** someone or something, you keep them or try to keep them. *e.g. You should hang onto those old coins as they might be valuable one day.*

hang out 836
If you **hang out** clothes that you have washed, you put them on a clothes line to dry. *e.g. Mrs. Connell was hanging out her washing.*

hanky 1535
also spelled **hankie**.
A **hanky** is a small square piece of fabric which you use for blowing your nose or wiping moisture from your face. *e.g. Get me a hanky, these onions have made me cry!*

happen 553, 630
1 When something **happens**, it occurs or is done without being planned. *e.g. A court of enquiry into what happened will not satisfy local residents.*
2 When something **happens** to someone or something, it takes place and affects them, often in an unpleasant way. *e.g. He relived all the ghastly things that had happened to him.*

happy 1271, 1275, 1390
1 Someone who is **happy** has feelings of pleasure, for example because something nice has happened or because they feel satisfied with their life. *e.g. I was happy to learn that you passed your exam.*
2 If you are **happy** about a situation or

arrangement, you are satisfied with it, for example because you think that something is being done in the right way. *e.g. I'm happy with your work so far.*

3 If you sign or say that you are **happy** to do something, you mean that you are very willing to do it. *e.g. He said he would be happy to lend us the money, so long as it was returned by Friday.*

hard   68
1 Something that is **hard** is very firm and stiff rather than soft to touch, and usually not easily bent, cut, or broken. *e.g. The plaster on the wall was hard.*
2 Someone who is **hard** shows no kindness or sympathy towards other people. *e.g. She's very hard. She showed no sympathy for those who are unemployed.*
3 If you are **hard** on someone, you treat them severely or unkindly. *e.g. She's very hard on her staff.*

hard   208
1 If something is **hard** to do or understand, it is difficult. *e.g. He found it hard to make friends.*
2 If your life is **hard**, it is difficult or unpleasant. *e.g. My grandparents' life on the farm was a hard one.*
3 **Hard** work involves a lot of effort. *e.g. It had been a long hard day in the office.*

hardly anyone   855
Hardly anyone means very few people. *e.g. Hardly anyone turned up to the lecture.*

hardly anything   855
Hardly anything means almost nothing. *e.g. There's hardly anything left in this biscuit tin!*

hard up   1645
If you are **hard up**, you have very little money. *e.g. I know we are all hard up, but everybody can afford a drink now and then.*

hard-working   1356
Someone who is **hard-working** does a lot of work. *e.g. Dave the caretaker is the most hard-working person in the building.*

hare   705
1 A **hare** is an animal like a rabbit but larger with long ears, long legs and a small tail. Hares can run very fast and are sometimes hunted for their meat. *e.g. I wonder how fast a hare can run.*
2 **Hare** is the meat of a hare. *e.g. I like jugged hare at Christmas.*

harsh   366
Actions that are **harsh** are unkind and show no understanding or sympathy. *e.g. To the orphans, the matron's orders seemed harsh.*

Hartlepool   1251
1 **Hartlepool** is a port in North East England

in Cleveland on the North Sea. *e.g. My father was born in Hartlepool.*
2 The address of the **Hartlepool** Centre for the Deaf is: 26 Stockton Road, Hartlepool.

haste   383
1 If you do something in **haste**, you do it in a hurry. *e.g. I wrote the letter in haste.*
2 To make **haste** means to act quickly in doing something. *e.g. Make haste, all of you, and get ready.*

hat   1525, 1530
A **hat** is a head covering that often has a brim round it and is usually worn out of doors to give protection from the weather. *e.g. Molly tried on a new hat.*

hate   1007
If you **hate** someone or something, you have an extremely strong feeling of dislike for them or find them very unpleasant. *e.g. You must really hate her.*

haul   273
If you **haul** a heavy object somewhere, you pull it there using a lot of effort. *e.g. My grandfather's job was to haul the carts of coal back to the sorting area.*

have   1124
1 If you **have** something such as a car or a house, it belongs to you. *e.g. I have a new coat.*
2 If you **have** a business or company, you own it and run it. *e.g. She will have her own shop when she is twenty-one.*
3 If you **have** something in a particular place, you keep it there. *e.g. Do you have coal in the outhouse?*
4 If you **have** a relation, he or she is part of your family. *e.g. They have one daughter.*

have   1566
You can use **have** to answer positively to a question asking whether something has been done. *e.g. 'Have you taken that to the bank?'—'Yes, I have.'*

have a look   327, 755
See **look (have a look)**.

have fun   954
If you **have fun**, you enjoy yourself. *e.g. We bought a ball and decided to go down to the park and have fun for a while.*

have got to   1437
1 If you **have got to** do something, you must do it or are forced to do it, without having any choice. *e.g. I'm sorry, I have got to finish this by tomorrow.*
2 If you **have got to** do something, you need to do it. *e.g. I have got to see the dentist soon.*

have not   1263
If you **have not, do not have** or **have not got**

something, you do not possess it or it is absent, even though people might expect otherwise. *e.g. I have not got a single clean pair of socks!*

have no time for   971
If you sign or say that you **have no time for** someone or something, you mean that you do not like them or approve of them. *e.g. I have no time for politicians.*

haven't   1263
If you **haven't, don't have** or **haven't got** something, you do not possess it or it is absent, even though people might expect otherwise. *e.g. 'Have you got a copy of 'Word Formation in BSL'?'—'I haven't, I'm ashamed to say.'*

have someone on   665, 765, 925, 1016
If you **have someone on**, you are teasing them by pretending that something is true when it is not true. *e.g. Joe was always having his teacher on.*

have someone on (you were having me on)   1712
You sign or say **you were having me on** when you realise that someone has been teasing you by pretending that something was true when it was not. *e.g. I've just found out you were having me on about having to work tonight.*

have the nerve   478
When you sign or say that someone **has got** or **has the nerve** or **a nerve** to do something, you mean that they have angered or shocked you by doing something rude, shameless or disrespectful. *e.g. He had the nerve to suggest that I should let him do it.*

have to   1437
1 If you **have to** do something, you must do it or are forced to do it, without having any choice. *e.g. We have to study it in school.*
2 If you **have to** do something, you need to do it. *e.g. I'll have to sit down; I'm feeling really dizzy.*

hazard   1240
A **hazard** is something that could be dangerous to you. *e.g. Drinking alcohol is a health hazard.*

hazardous   1240
Something that is **hazardous** is dangerous to people's health or safety. *e.g. Breathing smoky air may be hazardous to health.*

haze   1075
1 If there is **haze** or a **haze**, you cannot see clearly very far into the distance because of the heat of the air or because of dust or moisture in the air. *e.g. There was a haze over the pond.*
2 If there is a **haze** of something such as smoke or fumes, you cannot see clearly through it. *e.g. The room became cloudy with a haze of blue smoke.*

he   310
You use **he** to refer to or indicate a man or boy who is present or whose identity has been established. *e.g. He's been having meetings this morning: why wasn't I there?*

head   450
1 If you are **head** of something such as a company or organisation, you are in charge of it and in charge of the people in it. *e.g. She was the head of the Policy and Planning Department.*
2 A **head** is a headmaster, headmistress, or head teacher in a school. *e.g. I had coffee with the head after school.*

head   1229
If you **head** in a particular direction, you go in that direction. *e.g. Julie headed for the cupboard.*

head   1569
1 Your **head** is the part of your body which has your eyes, mouth and brain in it. *e.g. It's awfully windy. My hands and feet and head are cold.*
2 When you toss a coin and it comes down **heads,** you can see the side of it which has a head on it. *e.g. Do you want heads or tails?*

headache   568, 1569
A **headache** is a pain that you feel inside your head. *e.g. She took an aspirin to relieve her headache.*

headmaster   450
A **headmaster** is a man who is the head teacher of a school. *e.g. The boy who was late had to see the headmaster.*

headmistress   450
A **headmistress** is a woman who is the head teacher of a school. *e.g. Ms. Smith was the headmistress of the local primary school.*

headphones   1692
Headphones are a pair of speakers inside pads which you wear over your ears in order to listen to a radio, record player, or tape recorder without other people hearing it. *e.g. Graham was listening to the football match through his headphones.*

headteacher   450
A **headteacher** is a teacher who is in charge of a school. *e.g. The governors appointed a new headteacher when Mrs. O'Brien won the pools.*

health   1489, 1494
A person's **health** is the condition of their body and the extent to which it is free from illness or able to resist illness. *e.g. The baby is the picture of health.*

hear   1253
When you **hear** sounds, you are aware of them because they reach your ears. *e.g. I didn't hear anything: which way did the noise come from?*

hearing   342
1 People who are **hearing** possess the sense which makes it possible for them to be aware of sounds and to recognise and understand them. *e.g. If you are hearing, you may well recognise this voice.*
2 A person who is not recognised as a member of the Deaf community may be referred to as **hearing.** *e.g. We know she is hearing, no matter how hard she pretends to be Deaf.*

hearing aid (behind the ear hearing aid)   578
A **behind the ear hearing aid** is an instrument that helps deaf people with some residual hearing to hear better. It is compact and fits on the back of the ear. *e.g. It's surprising how many people wear behind the ear hearing aids.*

hearing aid (body worn hearing aid)   623
A **body worn hearing aid** is an instrument that helps deaf people with some residual hearing to hear better. It has wires which connect that part of the device that fits in the ear to a battery located in a pocket or in a harness worn on the body. *e.g. We had to wait three months before our son was issued with a body worn hearing aid by the clinic.*

hearing person   342
1 You use **hearing person** to refer to an individual who has the sense of hearing. *e.g. The typical hearing person's response to sudden noise is to be shocked.*
2 **Hearing person** may be used to refer to anyone not recognised as a member of the Deaf community. *e.g. I do not think a hearing person should be running a Deaf Awareness course.*

heart   1276
1 Your **heart** is the organ in your chest that pumps the blood around your body. *e.g. It was the first successful heart transplant.*
2 You use **heart** to refer to the part of your chest that is nearest your heart. *e.g. He put his hand to his heart and signed 'I swear'.*
3 You can refer to someone's **heart** when you are referring to their emotions, character or attitudes. *e.g. He has a very soft heart.*

heat   1183
1 **Heat** is the quality of being hot or warm. *e.g. Water retains heat much longer than air.*
2 The **heat** is very hot weather. *e.g. You shouldn't go out in this heat.*

heave   273
1 If you **heave** something, you pull it using a lot of effort. *e.g. I'm sure if we all heave together we'll be able to manage it.*
2 A **heave** is a pull that takes a lot of effort. *e.g. With a great heave, the little man pulled the turnip up.*

heaven   1647
1 In Christianity and some other religions, **Heaven** is a place of eternal happiness where God is believed to live, and where good people are believed to go when they die. *e.g. I believe my father is in Heaven.*
2 The **heavens** are the sky. *e.g. The moon was high in the heavens.*

heavy   1028
1 Something that is **heavy** weighs a lot or weighs more than is usual. *e.g. The boxes were very heavy.*
2 Something that is **heavy** is great in degree, amount, or intensity. *e.g. My course work is really heavy this term.*

Hebraic   1141
Something that is **Hebraic** belongs or relates to the Hebrews and their language or culture. *e.g. They played an ancient Hebraic melody.*

Hebrew   1141
1 **Hebrew** is a language that was spoken by Jews in former times and is now, in a more modern form, the official language of Israel. *e.g. We are studying the Old Testament in Hebrew.*
2 A **Hebrew** was a person in former times who was Jewish and lived in Israel. *e.g. Isaiah was a great Hebrew prophet.*

hedge   1025
A **hedge** is a row of bushes or small trees that form the boundary to a garden, field or road. *e.g. A bird built its nest in our garden hedge.*

helicopter   323
A **helicopter** is an aircraft without wings that has one or two sets of large blades which rotate above it and enable it to take off vertically and to hover in one position. *e.g. A fault developed in the helicopter, so the flying display was postponed.*

hell   939
1 In Christianity and some other religions, **Hell** is the place where wicked and evil people are believed to go after death, and where they will receive eternal punishment. *e.g. They were afraid of going to Hell when they died.*
2 If you sign or say that a situation is **hell,** you mean that it is extremely unpleasant. *e.g. My trip to London was hell.*
3 **Hell** is an expression used to express annoyance or to emphasise what is signed or said. *e.g. Why the hell did you write that card?*

hello   164, 991, 1238
1 You sign or say **hello** to someone when you are greeting them or when you are meeting them for the first time in the course of a day. *e.g. 'Hello', Pat said.*
2 A television or radio presenter often signs or says **hello** at the beginning of a programme, as

part of the introduction. *e.g. Hello, and welcome to 'Sign Extra'.*

help   150
1 If you **help** someone, you make it easier for them to do something. *e.g. I helped him fix his bike.*
2 If something **helps** someone, it makes it easier for them to get something, do something, or bear something. *e.g. An EC grant helped the Unit to establish an advanced sign language training programme.*

helper   150
A **helper** is a person who helps another person or group with a job or activity they are doing. *e.g. We need to recruit a helper.*

hen   639, 778
A **hen** is a female chicken. People often keep hens for their eggs. *e.g. The hen clucked and made a lot of noise.*

her   11, 63
See **belong to her**.

her   310
You use **her** to refer to a woman, girl, or female animal who has already been mentioned, or whose identity is known. *e.g. He caught sight of Galina and followed her.*

here   497
1 You use **here** when you are referring to the room, building or town where you are. *e.g. I live here in Birmingham.*
2 You use **here** to indicate that someone is present in a particular place, often for a particular purpose. *e.g. I am here for the meeting.*

here   1037
You use **here** when you are referring to the room, building, place or town where you are. *e.g. I live here in Birmingham.*

hereditary   1207, 1306
1 A characteristic or illness that is **hereditary** is passed on to a child from its parents before it is born. *e.g. He had a progressive, hereditary disease of certain glands.*
2 A title or position in society that is **hereditary** is passed on as a right from parent to child. *e.g. The man's occupation as gatekeeper was hereditary.*

heredity   1207, 1306
Heredity is the process by which characteristics are passed on from parents to their children before the children are born. *e.g. Some children seem to be thin by heredity.*

heritage   1207, 1306
Heritage is all the qualities, traditions, or features of life that have been continued over many years and passed on from one generation

to another; used especially to refer to things that are of historical importance or that have had a strong influence on society. *e.g. Preserving Deaf history, heritage and culture is very important.*

heroic   1200
Actions that are **heroic** are brave and courageous. *e.g. It was a heroic struggle against great illness.*

her own   11, 63
1 You use **her own** to emphasise that something is owned by or relates to a woman, girl or female animal who has already been mentioned or whose identity is known. *e.g. Morag's own mother won't visit her.*
2 You use **her own** to emphasise that a woman, girl or female animal (who has already been mentioned or whose identity is known) does something without any help from other people. *e.g. Mhairi claimed it was all her own work*

hers   11, 63
See **belong to her**.

herself   493
1 You use **herself** to refer to the same woman, girl or female animal who is mentioned as the one who does something or is affected by another person's action. *e.g. Perhaps Frances will introduce herself.*
2 You also use **herself** to emphasise the woman, girl or female animal you mention and to make it clear who you are referring to. *e.g. Sally herself came back.*
3 If a girl or a woman does something **herself** or by **herself** she does it without any help or interference from anyone else. *e.g. She made the card herself.*

hesitant   1328, 1368
If you are **hesitant** about doing something, you do not do it quickly or directly because you are not certain whether you ought to do it or because you do not know how to do it. *e.g. Some parents are hesitant about usurping the teacher's role.*

hey!   1214
You sign or say **hey!** to attract someone's attention. *e.g. Hey, Dad, what's for dinner?*

hi   1238
You sign or say **hi** to someone when you see them or when you meet them for the first time in the course of a day. *e.g. Hi, Harold: how are you this morning?*

hidden   1266
1 Something that is **hidden** is not easily noticed. *e.g. There are hidden disadvantages to owning a cheque book.*
2 A place that is **hidden** is difficult to find or get

to. *e.g. Her house was hidden amongst the hills.*
3 Something that is **hidden** is in a place where it cannot easily be seen or found. *e.g. All of the children were safely hidden.*

hide   1266, 1470
1 If you **hide** something, you put it in a place where it cannot easily be seen or found. *e.g. The women managed to steal and hide a few knives.*
2 If you **hide**, or if you **hide** yourself, you go somewhere where you cannot easily be seen or found. *e.g. I walked back a few paces to hide myself in the shadows.*
3 If you **hide** something such as your feelings or information, you keep it a secret, so that no-one knows about it. *e.g. She tried to hide her nervousness when she met his mother.*

hide   1469
If you **hide**, or if you **hide** yourself, you go somewhere where you cannot easily be seen or found. *e.g. He hid behind the rose bush.*

hide and seek   1469
Hide and seek is a game in which one player covers his or her eyes until the other players have hidden themselves, and then he or she tries to find them. *e.g. We played hide and seek all over the house.*

high   1210, 1217
1 If something is **high**, it is a long way above the ground, above sea level, or above a person. *e.g. The window was too high for her to see out of.*
2 You use **high** to indicate what size something is when it is measured from the bottom to the top. *e.g. He built a low mud wall a few feet high.*

high flier   553
A **high flier** or **high flyer** is a person who impresses others by being particularly efficient or talented and is soon noticed and promoted for their ability. *e.g. James is a high flier and won't be content with a boring job.*

high-jump   743
The **high-jump** or **high jump** is an athletics event which involves jumping without special equipment over a raised bar after a run-up. *e.g. I was never any good at the high jump at school.*

high-jumper   743
A **high-jumper** or **high jumper** is a person who takes part in the high-jump at sports events. *e.g. Tina was the best high-jumper in our school.*

high tide   1047
High tide is the period when the level of the sea on the shore is at its highest. *e.g. The currents can be dangerous to swim in at high tide.*

high (very high)   1573
If something is **very high**, it is a very long way

above the ground, above sea level, or above a person. *e.g. The shelf was very high and I felt dizzy as I reached up to it.*

hike   123, 234
1 A **hike** is a long walk in the country. *e.g. We're going on a four mile hike tomorrow.*
2 If you **hike**, you go on long country walks for pleasure. *e.g. She went hiking in Switzerland last summer.*

hiker   123, 234
A **hiker** is a person who is walking on a hike. *e.g. My uncle is a keen hiker.*

hiking   123, 234
Hiking is the activity of going for long walks in the country. *e.g. We have maps of the area where we hope to do some hiking.*

hill   1209, 1235, 1237
A **hill** is an area of land that is higher than the land that surrounds it, but not as high as a mountain. *e.g. He walks on Falkland Hill every Sunday afternoon.*

hills   980, 1236
Hills are areas of land that are higher than the land that surrounds them, but not as high as mountains. *e.g. She visited the Malvern Hills.*

hillside   1218
A **hillside** is the sloping side of a hill. *e.g. Any hillside in North Wales is likely to be covered with these pretty pink flowers in August.*

him   310
You use **him** to refer to a man, boy, or male animal who has already been mentioned or whose identity is known. *e.g. She doesn't just like James Joyce, she's fanatical about him.*

himself   493
1 You use **himself** to refer to the same man, boy, or male animal who is mentioned as the one who does something or is affected by another person's action. *e.g. He lacks confidence in himself.*
2 You also use **himself** to emphasise the man, boy or male animal you mention and to make it clear who you are referring to. *e.g. Rupert himself met me at the station.*
3 If a man or boy does something **himself** or by **himself**, he does it without any help or interference from anyone else. *e.g. He made the cakes himself, but the whole family helped him eat them.*

Hindu   321
A **Hindu** is a person who believes in Hinduism, an Indian religion which has many gods and teaches that people live again after they die. *e.g. Arun had been brought up as a Hindu.*

hire   78, 613
1 If you **hire** something, you pay money in order to be allowed to use it for a period of time. *e.g. We hire a car whenever we go to Ireland.*
2 The **hire** of something is the payment of money in order to be allowed to use it for a period of time. *e.g. Hire of a large van costs £300 per week.*

hire out   77
If you **hire out** something such as a car or a person's services, you allow them to be used in return for payment. *e.g. They agreed they would hire out the new Porsche.*

his   11, 63
See **belong to him**.

his own   11, 63
1 You use **his own** to emphasise that something is owned by or relates to a man, boy or male animal who has already been mentioned or whose identity is known. *e.g. Lars asked to borrow my bike—his own is broken.*
2 You use **his own** to emphasise that a man, boy or male animal (who has already been mentioned or whose identity is known) does something without any help from other people. *e.g. Tom is expected to make his own bed.*

historical   1481
1 **Historical** people, things or situations existed in the past and are considered to be a part of history. *e.g. There are manuscripts of historical interest in the local library.*
2 **Historical** books and pictures describe, represent or are based upon real people or things that existed in the past. *e.g. He has written a number of historical novels.*

history   1279, 1479, 1481
1 **History** is the events of the past, especially when they are seen as a long process which leads up to the present. History can refer to the political, social and cultural events of the world in general, or it can be concerned with a particular country, community or area of activity. *e.g. Brian Grant has written about the history of the British Deaf Association.*
2 **History** is also a subject that is studied in schools, colleges, universities, etc., that deals with events that have happened in the past. *e.g. I studied history at university.*
3 If someone has a **history** of something, that thing has happened frequently in their life. *e.g. There is a family history of heart disease.*

hit   69
When something **hits** something else, it touches it with a lot of force. *e.g. The truck had hit a wall.*

hit the bottom/floor/ground   64
If someone or something **hits the bottom** or **floor** of something, or **hits the ground**, they

hit the surface or lowest level having fallen or travelled down to it from above. *e.g. The submarine hit the bottom of the sea.*

hit with a cane/strap   269
If someone **hits** another person **with a cane** or **strap**, they beat them so as to hurt or punish them. *e.g. He hit him with a cane until he cried.*

hit with a rounders bat/small bat   249
If you **hit** a ball **with a rounders bat** or **small bat**, you strike the ball with the rounders bat or small bat causing it to move. *e.g. She hit the ball against the wall with a small bat.*

hit (with one's fist)   69
If you **hit** someone or something **with your fist**, you deliberately touch them with a lot of force using your closed hand. *e.g. He threatened to hit him if he did not leave.*

hockey   282
Hockey or **field hockey** is an outdoor game, played between two teams of eleven players who use long curved sticks to hit a small ball. Each team tries to score goals by hitting the ball into the scoring area marked by posts known as goalposts. The team which has scored the most goals at the end of the game is the winner. *e.g. He played hockey at school.*

hockey player   282
A **hockey player** is a person who plays hockey. *e.g. Jane Sixsmith, the hockey player, was our sports personality of the year.*

hockey stick   282
A **hockey stick** is a long curved stick used to hit the ball in hockey. *e.g. She asked if she could borrow my hockey stick.*

hold   1
When you **hold** something, you have it in your hand and you keep it there by putting your fingers firmly round it. *e.g. She wanted to hold the small, golden cross in her hand when she died.*

hold   1124
1 If people such as an army or a group of fighers **hold** a place, they control it by using force. *e.g. They could only hold the fort for three days.*
2 If you **hold** something such as the departure of a train, you delay it. *e.g. They should hold the train for you if you're late.*
3 If a place such as a hotel or travel agency **holds** something for you, they keep it reserved for you and do not let anyone else have it. *e.g. We can hold the room till half-past six.*

hold against   1124
If someone has done something wrong and you **hold** it **against** them, you treat them more severely because they did it. *e.g. I'll always hold it against him that he stopped my promotion.*

hold on   1124
If you **hold on**, you put your hand over something with your fingers gripping round it in order to prevent yourself from falling over. *e.g. Hold on when the sea gets rough.*

hold on   1222, 1435
If you ask or instruct someone to **hold on**, you are asking or instructing them to wait for a short time before taking action. *e.g. Hold on a second, your paper is right here.*

hold onto   1, 1124
1 If you **hold onto** something, you keep or remember it. *e.g. Hold onto that suggestion Terry, we'll discuss it after lunch.*
2 If you **hold onto** something, you keep your hand grasped firmly round it. *e.g. Hold onto this bar, Jeanne.*

hold tight   1
If you **hold** something **tight**, you keep your hand very firmly round it. *e.g. He held the stick tightly in his hand.*

hold up   152
Something that **holds** something else **up** keeps it fixed or supported in position. *e.g. A block of wood was holding it up.*

hole   496
A **hole** is a hollow space in something solid, with an opening on one side. *e.g. It was a deep hole in the ground.*

holiday   668, 1086, 1460, 1495
1 A **holiday** is a period of time during which you are relaxing and enjoying yourself away from home. *e.g. I went abroad for a holiday.*
2 A **holiday** is a period of time during which you are not working or attending school, college, or university. *e.g. New Year's Day is a national holiday.*

Holland   1556
Holland is a kingdom in North West Europe on the North Sea and is a member of the European Community. Holland is another name for the Netherlands. *e.g. We are going to visit Henk and Bep in Holland.*

holy   201
1 Something that is **holy** refers to God or to a particular religion. *e.g. The chapel had many holy pictures and statues.*
2 Someone who is **holy** leads a pure and good life which is dedicated to God or to a religion. *e.g. Father Kuhn is a holy man.*

holy bible   203
1 The **Holy Bible** is the sacred book on which the Christian religion is based, consisting of the Old Testament and the New Testament. *e.g. He swore on the Holy*

Bible that it was true.
2 The **Holy Bible** is the sacred book on which the Jewish religion is based, consisting of the Old Testament. *e.g. His father presented him with a copy of the Holy Bible.*

holy book   203
1 A **holy book** is a book of writings held to be sacred by a religion. *e.g. The Koran is the holy book of Islam.*
2 The **Holy Book** is sometimes used by people when they are referring to the Christian Bible. *e.g. She read some verses from the Holy Book.*

holy communion   202
Holy Communion is the religious ceremony in the Protestant Churches at which people eat bread and drink wine as a symbol of Christ's body and blood, in remembrance of his death and resurrection. *e.g. He has started to attend Holy Communion.*

Holy Ghost   1095
The **Holy Ghost**, in most Christian religions, is the third member of the Trinity (with God the Father and God the Son), and is believed to bring God's blessings to people. The Holy Ghost is the same as the Holy Spirit. *e.g. God the Father, God the Son, and God the Holy Ghost, be with you all.*

homage   1461
Homage is the way you behave towards someone, usually someone who has done something exceptional or someone in authority, which shows how much you respect or honour them. *e.g. The soldiers gathered in homage to those who had died in battle.*

home   694, 898, 1561
1 **Home** is the place you live and feel you belong, usually because that is where your family is. *e.g. The old man wants to die at home.*
2 **Home** is the area or country where you were born or where your home is. *e.g. Brian and John dreamed of home during their captivity.*
3 **Home** means to or at the place where you live. *e.g. I want to go home.*

honest   357, 1323
1 You sign or say **honest** to emphasise that you are telling the truth. *e.g. Honest, I saw her there.*
2 Someone who is **honest** tells the truth and does not hide anything. *e.g. To be perfectly honest, up until three weeks ago I had never set foot in a nightclub.*

honestly   1323
1 **Honestly** is used to emphasise that you really and truthfully believe or feel what you are saying. *e.g. Do you honestly think this is right?*
2 **Honestly** is used to emphasise that you are

telling the truth and that you want people to believe you. *e.g. I'll go if you like. I don't mind, honestly.*

honour   225, 1461
If you **honour** someone, you give them public praise because they have done something good or brave. *e.g. The students came to honour their teacher on her retirement for her years of dedication.*

honour   226
If you **honour** someone or something in authority over you or whom you look up to, you give them public praise because of what they have done or who they are. *e.g. We have gathered together to honour God.*

honourable   1461
Something or someone that is **honourable** is honest and worthy of respect. *e.g. He was an honourable man.*

hood   287
A **hood** is a part of a coat, cloak, etc., which you can pull up to cover your head. It is usually in the shape of a triangular bag attached to the neck of the coat, cloak, etc., at the back. *e.g. He held the sides of his parka hood closed against the snow.*

hood (put up a hood)   287
If you **put up a hood**, you pull a hood over your head in order to cover it. *e.g. He put up his hood as it started to rain.*

hook   589
A **hook** is a bent piece of metal or plastic that is fixed to an upright surface or ceiling and used for holding things, or for hanging things up. *e.g. Can you put a hook on the bathroom door?*

hook (hang on a hook)   589
If you **hang** something **on a hook**, you place it so that its highest point is supported, using a special handle or loop which fits over a bent piece of metal or plastic fixed to an upright surface or ceiling. *e.g. Hang your coats on those hooks.*

hoops   660
Hoops are strips of a flexible material such as cloth which run around your body, usually as part of an item of clothing. *e.g. Celtic play in shirts with green and white hoops.*

hooray   255
You sign or say **hooray** to show you are very happy and excited. *e.g. Hooray! School ends today!*

hoover   248
1 A **hoover** is a vacuum cleaner. *e.g. We'll have to get a hoover, this carpet sweeper's useless.*

2 If you **hoover** a carpet, you clean it using a vacuum cleaner. *e.g. She began the daily round of washing and hoovering.*

hope   669
1 If you **hope** that something is true or **hope** for something to happen, you want it to be true or to happen and usually believe that it is possible or likely. *e.g. Nothing can be done except to wait and hope that the hostages will be freed.*
2 If you **hope** to do something, you want to do it and intend to do it if you possibly can. *e.g. She hoped to leave that evening for her sister's birthday party.*
3 You sign or say **I hope** when you are being polite and showing your concern that something you are going to sign, say or do, or something you have signed, said or done, either will upset or has upset someone. *e.g. I hope I didn't wake you.*
4 **Hope** is a feeling of desire and expectation that things will go well in the future. *e.g. She never completely gave up hope.*
5 If you have **hopes** of something successful happening in the future, you feel that there is a good chance that it will happen. *e.g. We have great hopes of his doing well in the Air Force.*
6 A **hope** is something that you desire. *e.g. The hopes and dreams of reformers like Martin Luther King live on in us all.*

hope   1281
If you hope that something is true, or will happen, you want it to be true or to happen and usually believe that it is possible. *e.g. He hoped to meet her again.*

horizontal stripes   660
Horizontal stripes are stripes of different colour or texture running across the body, for example from side to side on a shirt or jumper. *e.g. The T-shirt has blue and white horizontal stripes.*

horns   956
Horns are the hard pointed growths that stick out of either side of the heads of some animals. *e.g. The vet cut off the goat's horns.*

horrible   904, 911, 914, 918, 992, 1002
1 Something that is **horrible** is very unpleasant or bad. *e.g. The hotel was horrible.*
2 Something that is **horrible** causes you to feel great shock, fear or disgust. *e.g. It was a horrible form of torture.*

horrid   1002
Something that is **horrid** is very unpleasant indeed. *e.g. The flat was horrid.*

horrify   1080
If someone or something **horrifies** you, you feel dismay or disgust, usually because of something that is signed or said to you or because of some information you receive. *e.g. I*

was horrified at the newspaper story.

horse   107
A **horse** is a large four-legged animal which people ride for enjoyment, hunting or for getting from one place to another, and use for pulling ploughs, carts, et cetera. *e.g. Mandy rewarded her horse with a carrot.*

horse-drawn carriage   281
A **horse-drawn carriage** is an old-fashioned, four-wheeled vehicle used for carrying passengers which is pulled by one or more horses. *e.g. We went for a tour of New York in a horse-drawn carriage.*

hose   601
1 A **hose** is a long, flexible pipe made of rubber or plastic. Water or other liquid is directed through a hose in order to put out fires, clean cars, water gardens and so on. *e.g. The hose soaked him in spray.*
2 If you **hose** something or **hose** something **down**, you spray water or other liquid at it through a long pipe of rubber or plastic. *e.g. You hose the car and I'll wipe the windows.*

hospital   173, 542, 1350, 1452
A **hospital** is a place where people who are ill, injured, require surgery or are about to give birth are treated and cared for by nurses, doctors and other staff. *e.g. I visited him in hospital.*

hot   1183
1 Something that is **hot** has a high temperature. *e.g. The metal of the tank is so hot I can't touch it.*
2 If something is **hot**, it has a particular temperature or degree of heat. *e.g. How hot should the oven be?*

hotel   1239, 1576
A **hotel** is a building where people stay, usually for a few nights, paying for their rooms and meals. *e.g. We ended up at the Hilton Hotel!*

hour   411
An **hour** is a period of sixty minutes. There are twenty-four hours in a day. *e.g. He spent almost an hour carefully cleaning his bike.*

house   694
1 A **house** is a building in which people live, usually the people belonging to one family. *e.g. He has a house in Pimlico.*
2 A **house** is a building which is used for special purposes such as official or business purposes. *e.g. Broadcasting House has been the home of the BBC for decades.*

housework   88
Housework is the work that is done in order to look after a home and the people who live there, for example cooking, cleaning, and

shopping. *e.g. The men shared all the housework, including washing and ironing.*

how?   1191
1 You use **how?** in questions when you are asking someone about the way or manner in which something is done. *e.g. How did you know?*
2 If you sign or speak about **how** something is done, you are referring to the way or manner in which it is done. *e.g. Tell me how to get there.*

how are you?   1494
1 **How are you?** may be used when you are asking about someone's health or feelings. *e.g. How are you after your accident?*
2 **How are you?** may be used as a greeting when meeting people. *e.g. How are you? I've not seen you for a while.*

how dare you?   925
You can sign or say **how dare you?** when you are very shocked and angry about something that someone has done, signed or said. *e.g. How dare you speak to me like that?!*

however   307, 1382
You use **however** when you are adding a comment which is surprising or which contrasts with what has just been signed or said. *e.g. I felt I would not be sufficiently experienced. However, Liz seemed to have confidence in me.*

how many?   988
You use **how many?** to ask how great a quantity is. *e.g. How many are coming to the meeting?*

how much?   988, 1505
If you ask **how much?** something is, you are asking or giving information about the price of something. *e.g. I like that dress—how much is it?*

how old?   995
You ask **how old?** someone is when you want to know their age. *e.g. How old are your children now?*

hug   139
When you **hug** someone, you put your arms around them and hold them tightly because you like them or are pleased to see them. *e.g. He greeted his mother with a hug.*

huge   1571, 1572
Something or someone that is **huge** is extremely large in size. *e.g. He looked huge compared to her.*

human   482
1 **Human** means relating to or concerning people. *e.g. The world could be destroyed through human greed.*
2 You can refer to people as **humans** when you are comparing them with animals or machines. *e.g. I don't think humans will ever be able to run that fast.*

human being 482
A **human being** is a man, woman, or child.
e.g. This is a book on how to get on with your fellow human beings.

hump 1235
1 A **hump** is a small hill or raised piece of ground. *e.g. The humps and hollows of the old golf course provide a safe haven for rabbits.*
2 A **hump** is a large lump on the back of an animal such as a camel, which is used for storing fat and water. *e.g. Thanks to the evolution of its hump, the camel has more stamina in the desert than any other creature.*

hundreds 1722
You can use **hundreds** to mean an extremely large number. *e.g. She handed me hundreds of forms.*

Hungarian 41, 1655
1 Someone or something that is **Hungarian** belongs to or relates to Hungary, or its people. *e.g. It's a Hungarian speciality, he tells me.*
2 **Hungarian** is the main language spoken in Hungary. *e.g. He spoke in his native Hungarian.*
3 A **Hungarian** is a person who comes from, or whose family identity relates to, Hungary. *e.g. Her lover is a Hungarian, and a famous tap dancer.*
4 The address of the **Hungarian** Deaf Association is: Hallasserultek Orzagos Szovetsege VI, Benczuru 21, Postafiok 80, H-1388 Budapest, Hungary.

Hungary 41, 1655
Hungary is a republic in central Europe. *e.g. Budapest is the capital of Hungary.*

hunger 41, 237, 1542, 1655
1 **Hunger** is the feeling of weakness or discomfort that you get when you need something to eat. *e.g. Babies show their hunger by waking up to be fed.*
2 **Hunger** is a serious lack of food which causes suffering or death. *e.g. There were families dying of hunger and disease.*

hungry 41, 237, 1542, 1655
1 When you are **hungry**, you want food. *e.g. I'm hungry and I want supper.*
2 If people go **hungry**, they suffer from hunger. *e.g. There were reports of people going hungry in areas affected by the war.*

hunt 332, 610
1 If you **hunt** for something, you try to find it.
e.g. I'm going to hunt for a really suitable job.
2 If you **hunt** a criminal or an enemy, you search for them in order to catch or defeat them. *e.g. The police were hunting the thieves for three days.*

hunter 332, 610
People who search for things of a particular kind are often referred to as **hunters**. *e.g. Bargain hunters are prepared to queue for hours when the January sales begin.*

hurry 384
1 If you **hurry** somewhere, you go there quickly. *e.g. The rain started so we had to hurry home.*
2 If you **hurry** to do something, you start doing it as soon as you can. *e.g. They had to hurry to finish gardening before it got dark.*
3 If you **hurry** someone or something, you try to make them do something more quickly. *e.g. If you try and hurry them, they will only make more mistakes.*
4 If you are in a **hurry**, you need to do something quickly. *e.g. She was in a hurry to do the shopping as her friend was meeting her at four o'clock.*

hurry up 384
If you sign or say **hurry up**, you mean that they should do more quickly whatever they are doing. *e.g. Hurry up, or we'll never get home in time for 'EastEnders'.*

hurt 989, 1052
1 If you **hurt** yourself, or **hurt** a part of your body, you injure it. *e.g. How did you hurt your finger?*
2 If a part of your body **hurts**, you feel pain there. *e.g. My leg was beginning to hurt.*

hurt 1588
1 If you **hurt** someone or **hurt** their feelings, you make them feel unhappy by being unkind to them. *e.g. Don't criticise her, she's easily hurt.*
2 **Hurt** is the damage to someone's feelings when they think that they have been treated badly. *e.g. The hurt your cruel words have caused him has been sad to witness.*

husband 897
A woman's **husband** is the man she is married to. *e.g. Carol hardly ever sees her husband.*

hush 352, 354
If you sign or say **hush** to someone, you are telling them to be quiet. *e.g. Hush, don't make a noise or the baby will wake up and start to cry.*

hymn 758
A **hymn** is a song that Christians sign or sing in order to praise God. *e.g. She loved the hymns in church.*

hypnosis 1042
1 **Hypnosis** is the practice or skill of hypnotising people. *e.g. Hypnosis is not at all dangerous.*
2 If you are under **hypnosis**, you have been hypnotised. *e.g. Could a person be made to commit a crime while under hypnosis?*

hypnotise 1042
Also spelled **hypnotize**.
If you **hypnotise** someone, you put them into a state in which they seem to be asleep but in which they can see or hear certain things and respond to comments which are made to them. *e.g. I was able to hypnotise him into doing things against his will.*

hypnotist 1042
A **hypnotist** is someone who can hypnotise people, or someone who does this as an entertainer for a living. *e.g. You know him, the hypnotist—he's dead famous—well, he was here this morning!*

hypocrite 675
A **hypocrite** is someone who pretends to have qualities, beliefs, or feelings that they do not really have. *e.g. Those hypocrites said nice things to him but complained about him behind his back.*

hypodermic 782
A **hypodermic**, or a **hypodermic needle** or **hypodermic syringe**, is a medical instrument consisting of a hollow needle attached to a cylinder and plunger. The needle is filled with a drug and used to inject the drug under a person's skin. *e.g. One must be careful how one disposes of hypodermics.*

hysterectomy 1009
A **hysterectomy** is an operation to remove part or all of a woman's womb. *e.g. Your aunt's hysterectomy went well, the doctor said.*

hysterectomy (have an hysterectomy) 1009
If you **have an hysterectomy**, part or all of your womb is removed in an operation. *e.g. She's decided to have an hysterectomy, but she hasn't told him yet.*

I, i

I
I is the ninth letter of the British manual and English alphabets. See page 851.

I 537
A signer, speaker or writer uses **I** to refer to himself or herself. *e.g. Well, I like your dress even if he doesn't.*

ice 1116
Ice is water that has frozen and become solid. *e.g. The water in the pond has turned to ice.*

ice cream 27
1 **Ice cream** is a very cold, sweet-tasting food made from frozen cream or an artificial substitute for cream, with vanilla, chocolate, or other flavouring. *e.g. We had ice cream for dessert.*
2 An **ice cream** is a portion of ice cream that you can buy from a shop, van, et cetera. It is usually sold wrapped in paper or in a container. *e.g. She spent her pocket money buying ice creams.*

ice cream cone 27
An **ice cream cone** is an ice cream cornet. *e.g. Do you want an ice cream cone or a choc ice?*

ice cream cornet 27
An **ice cream cornet** is a thin biscuit shaped like a cone containing ice cream. *e.g. I bought an ice cream cornet for Maria.*

ice-skate 890
An **ice-skate** is a thin, metal strip fastened to a boot and worn for ice-skating. *e.g. Put your ice-skates on in the locker room.*

ice-skater 890
If you are an **ice-skater**, you take part in ice-skating. *e.g. We loved watching the ice-skaters at the rink last week.*

ice-skating 890
Ice-skating is the sport or activity in which you move about on ice wearing ice-skates. *e.g. Ice-skating is very popular in the Netherlands.*

icy 1116
1 **Icy** air or water is extremely cold. *e.g. It is an icy wind.*
2 An **icy** road has ice on it. *e.g. We walked along the icy, muddy lanes.*

idea 314, 619
1 An **idea** is a plan, proposal or suggestion. *e.g. I think that is a good idea: are there any further comments?*

2 An **idea** is an opinion or belief. *e.g. He had his own ideas as to how the film should be made.*
3 If you have an **idea** of something, you know about it to some extent. *e.g. Have you any idea what it will cost?*

identical 424
Things that are **identical** are the same in every detail. *e.g. The two women wore identical hats.*

identical 1416, 1417
A number of things that are **identical** are all the same in every detail. *e.g. Mass-production means that the toys are identical.*

identity 605, 644
Your **identity** is all the qualities, beliefs and characteristics which make you who you are. *e.g. My identity as a Deaf person is central to how I see myself.*

idiot 663, 1462
If you call someone an **idiot**, you mean that you think they have done something very stupid or behaved foolishly. *e.g. John is such an idiot. He's always messing around in class.*

idiotic 663
If you describe someone or something as **idiotic**, you mean that they are extremely stupid. *e.g. It was just an idiotic joke.*

idle 667, 668, 1283
1 Someone who is **idle** is not doing anything, especially when they should be doing something. *e.g. Graham was never idle as a child; he was always doing something all day long.*
2 Someone who is **idle** does not have a job. *e.g. There are 13,000 idle in a workforce of 170,000.*

ignorant 316
Someone who is **ignorant** of something does not know about it, although they should. *e.g. The club secretary is really ignorant about how to keep up a good rapport with the members.*

ignorant 1570
Someone who is **ignorant** of something does not know about it, usually through lack of information or inattention. *e.g. I was largely ignorant of the options open to me.*

ignore 344, 963, 1601
If you **ignore** someone or something that you have seen, heard or experienced, you act as if they are not there or do not exist, or as if the event has not happened. *e.g. Many people ignored him on his first day at work.*

ill 318, 931
Someone who is **ill** is suffering from a disease or health problem which makes them unable to work or to live as they usually do. *e.g. I was ill with flu today and couldn't go to school.*

illness 318
1 **Illness** is the experience of being ill for a period of time. *e.g. During his last illness we only saw him twice.*
2 An **illness** is a particular disease that people can suffer from, such as a cold, measles, or pneumonia. *e.g. She died of a mysterious illness.*

image 324
The **image** of a person or organisation is the way that they appear to other people. *e.g. British Rail is working to improve its image: trains are arriving on time, and the food is fresh.*

imaginary 1570
Something that is **imaginary** exists only in your mind and not in real life. *e.g. Many children develop fears of imaginary dangers.*

imagination 1570
1 Your **imagination** is the part of your mind which you use to form pictures and ideas of things that do not necessarily exist in real life. *e.g. They are creatures of our imagination.*
2 Your **imagination** is that you think that something does not exist in real life or that never happened. *e.g. There's nothing there—it's just your imagination.*

imagine 313, 1570
If you **imagine** something, you think about it and your mind forms a picture or idea of it. *e.g. Can you imagine how it would feel to stand up there and give a lecture?*

imitation 664
Imitation things are not genuine but are made to look as if they are genuine. *e.g. He had a pocket diary bound in black imitation leather.*

immediate 383
Immediate means happening without any delay. *e.g. They called for an immediate meeting with the new Council.*

immediately 1625
If something happens **immediately**, it happens without any delay. *e.g. I have to go to Brighton immediately.*

imminent 188
Something that is **imminent** is almost

certain to happen very soon. *e.g. I believed that war was imminent.*

impolite   1188
1 Someone who is **impolite** is rather rude or disrespectful and offends people. *e.g. It was very impolite of him to ask.*
2 **Impolite** is used to describe expressions or behaviour that are rude or disrespectful and likely to offend people. *e.g. Good food, impolite service—change the staff and we'll come again.*

important   1298, 1300
1 Something that is **important** is very significant, valuable or necessary. *e.g. Cleanliness is the most important aspect of the caterer's job.*
2 Ideas, beliefs, etc., that are **important** to you are ones that have great significance for you and that you consider very seriously. *e.g. My political beliefs are important to me.*
3 Someone who is **important** has influence or power within a society or particular group. *e.g. Judges are important people in our society.*

important   1437
Something that is **important** is very significant or necessary. *e.g. It is important that we get this message across to the government.*

impossible   421
Something that is **impossible** is unable to be done, to happen, or to be believed. *e.g. It was impossible to finish such a huge meal.*

impoverished   544
When someone or something is **impoverished**, they are poor. *e.g. Many countries near the equator are impoverished due to extremes of weather.*

imprison   47
If someone **imprisons** you, they lock you up in prison. *e.g. Cathy is imprisoned at Wormwood Scrubs.*

improve   193, 866
1 If something **improves** or if you **improve** it, it gets better. *e.g. We decided a new bathroom would improve the house.*
2 If you **improve** at a skill or in an area of knowledge, you get better at it by practising or studying. *e.g. His English is improving.*
3 If you **improve** after an illness or an injury, your health gets better. *e.g. She may improve with medical treatment.*

improvement   193, 866
Improvement or an **improvement** is a change made in someone or something which improves its quality or condition. *e.g. Life in East Hedleyhope would be such an improvement on Paris.*

impudent   257, 1188
1 Someone who is **impudent** behaves, signs

or speaks slightly rudely or disrespectfully. *e.g. The impudent child put her feet on the table.*
2 **Impudent** is used to describe expressions or behaviour which are slightly rude or disrespectful and likely to offend a little. *e.g. Her impudent laughter in my classroom is most unwelcome.*

in   1614
If something is **in** another thing, it is closely surrounded or enclosed by the other thing. *e.g. OK, let's see how it looks in the folder.*

in accord   128
If people or organisations are **in accord** about what should be done or about the way to do it, they are in agreement about what or how it should be done. *e.g. The Panel of Four were in accord on the need to establish a commission of enquiry.*

inappropriate   130
Something that is **inappropriate** is not useful or suitable for a particular occasion or purpose. *e.g. These ideas are inappropriate to the Third World.*

incapable   421
Someone who is **incapable** of doing something is unable to do it. *e.g. She is incapable of running a four-minute mile.*

inclination   845
An **inclination** is a feeling that makes you act or want to act in a particular way. *e.g. My inclination is to go to the cinema now, while it's raining.*

incline   845
Something that **inclines** you to act in a certain way, or **inclines** you towards a particular opinion, makes you more likely to act in that way or to accept that opinion. *e.g. What I read in these books inclined me to think again about nationalism.*

include   1613, 1614, 1658
1 If one thing **includes** another, it has the other thing as one of its parts. *e.g. The four-man crew will include one Dane.*
2 If you **include** one thing in another, you make it part of the other thing. *e.g. We will include the curtains in the purchase price.*

income   1008
A person's **income** is the amount of money that they earn from their work or business, or the money that they get from other sources such as pension or investments. *e.g. My monthly income is over £700.*

incompatible   130
Two things that are **incompatible** are unable to exist together because they are completely different. *e.g. Their personalities were so incompatible they divorced.*

inconsistent   955
If something is **inconsistent**, it differs in a particular situation each time it happens. *e.g. The ignition of my car is inconsistent; on cold mornings it tends to let me down*

increase   1063
If something **increases** or, if you **increase** it, it becomes bigger in volume, number, size, importance or amount. *e.g. The membership is increasing slowly.*

increase   1594
If you **increase** something, you add to it so that it becomes larger in amount *e.g. Increase my wages, and I might stay for another year.*

independence   555
If you refer to the **independence** of a person or country, you are referring to the fact that they exist or act separately from other people, countries or groups. *e.g. Every child must struggle for his or her independence.*

independent   533, 534, 804
If you are **independent**, you form your own opinions and arrange your own life, rather than relying on other people or copying them. *e.g. My mother encouraged me to be independent.*

independent   555
1 Something that is **independent** exists, happens or acts separately from other people, groups or things. *e.g. Two independent studies came to the same conclusions.*
2 If someone is **independent**, they form their own opinion and arrange their own life rather than relying on others. *e.g. She was an independent, strong minded woman, and I loved her for it.*

India   321
1 **India** is a republic in South East Asia. It became a republic in 1950 following the division of the Indian sub-continent into India (predominantly Hindu) and Pakistan (predominantly Muslim) in 1947. *e.g. We visited a tea plantation during our visit to India.*
2 The address of the All **India** Federation of the Deaf is: 18 Northend Complex, R.K. Asharm Marg, New Delhi, 110001, India.

Indian   321
1 Someone or something that is **Indian**, belongs to or relates to India or its people. *e.g. There are many people of Indian origin in London.*
2 An **Indian** is a person who comes from, or whose family identity relates to, India. *e.g. The managing director of our company is an Indian.*

indirect   1296
1 Something that is **indirect** is not done or caused directly, but by means of something or

someone else. *e.g. A sudden increase in oil prices would have serious indirect effects.*
2 An **indirect** route or journey does not use the shortest way between two places. *e.g. I arrived in Scunthorpe by an indirect route.*
3 An **indirect** answer or reference does not directly mention the thing that is actually being discussed. *e.g. His reply was indirect.*

individual   492
Individual means relating to each person separately, rather than to a large group. *e.g. The college offers individual tuition.*

individual   533, 534
Individual means relating to yourself alone, rather than to a group. *e.g. It's an individual project, and that's something I find exciting.*

individual   555, 635
1 An **individual** is a person. *e.g. We are dealing with an individual here.*
2 **Individual** means relating to one particular person or to each person separately, rather than to a large group. *e.g. This is an individual event, so you'll have to go one at a time.*

individually   492
If a number of things or people do something **individually**, they do it separately, rather than as a large group. *e.g. The children can work individually or in small groups.*

indoor   1606
You can use **indoor** to describe things which are situated or happen inside a building rather than outside. *e.g. Indoor swimming pools are popular in winter.*

indoors   1606
If something happens **indoors**, it happens inside a building. *e.g. It's cooler indoors when the sun is so hot.*

industrial action   1720
Industrial action consists of strikes and all the other ways in which workers are able to protest about pay, working conditions, et cetera. *e.g. The number of days lost through industrial action is the lowest for many years.*

industrious   1354, 1356
Someone who is **industrious** works very hard. *e.g. Dette was an industrious and brilliant student.*

inebriated   819
Someone who is **inebriated** is drunk. *e.g. I could tell she was becoming inebriated.*

ineffectual   222
Something that is **ineffectual** fails to do what it is supposed to do. *e.g. The policy was ineffectual because it had no funding.*

inequality   1639
Inequality is a difference in social status, wealth, or opportunity between groups in a society. *e.g. In general, Deaf people experience inequality of opportunity with monotonous regularity.*

in fact   195
You sign or say **in fact** to emphasise that something really happened or is true. *e.g. The woman was, in fact, my wife.*

infant   1386
An **infant** is a very young child or baby. *e.g. Mary looked after the infant Jesus.*

infants   1216
Infants are very young children, usually between about two and six years old. *e.g. I taught in an infants school for six years.*

inferior   911, 1340, 1341, 1343, 1639
1 Someone who is **inferior** is less important than other people or has a lower position in society. *e.g. Charlie felt inferior.*
2 Someone or something that is **inferior** to someone or something else is worse than them. *e.g. I know I'm inferior to these impressive athletes.*

inferiority   1340, 1341, 1343, 1639
1 Someone who has feelings of **inferiority** feels less important, or worthy, or lovable than other people. *e.g. In spite of her exam successes, she was torn by feelings of inferiority.*
2 **Inferiority** is the extent or degree to which something is worse, less impressive or less effective than another thing. *e.g. The inferiority of this model was clear to all who used it.*

inflate a balloon   135
When you **inflate a balloon**, you fill it with air by blowing into it. *e.g. We have to inflate hundreds of balloons for the party.*

influence   1021
1 **Influence** is power that you have which makes it likely that other people will agree with you or do what you want. *e.g. She will use her friend's influence to make the event a success.*
2 The **influence** that someone or something has on people or situations is the effect that they have on them. *e.g. 'The influence of religion on society' is the theme for tonight's programme.*
3 Someone or something that is an **influence** on people or things has an effect on them. *e.g. He was a bad influence on the children.*

inform   455
If you **inform** someone of something or **inform** them that something is the case, you tell them about it. *e.g. The principal informed the class of the college rules.*

information   455
If you have **information** about something, you know something about it. *e.g. The Club secretary will give you the information about the coach trip.*

informer   625
An **informer** is someone who gives information about a person to the police or authorities with the result that this person is accused of committing a crime or is shown to be guilty by the informer's evidence. *e.g. Pierre acted as an informer for the secret police.*

inform on   625
If you **inform on** or **against** a person, you give information about them to the police or authorities, with the result that they are accused of committing a crime or shown to be guilty by your evidence. *e.g. It can be difficult for a child to inform on someone he knows.*

infrequent   955
If something is **infrequent**, it does not happen often. *e.g. Mary received infrequent letters from her sister.*

inhale   1109
1 When you **inhale** a gas, you breathe it in. *e.g. I asked him not to smoke as I didn't want my daughter to inhale the fumes.*
2 When you **inhale**, you breathe in through your nose. *e.g. 'Inhale, please,' said the doctor.*

inherit   1194
If you **inherit** money or property, you receive it from someone who has died. *e.g. She was expected to inherit a fortune from an aunt.*

inherit   1207, 1306
1 If you **inherit** something such as a position, situation or attitude, you take it over from someone who came before you and use it or deal with it yourself. *e.g. We often inherit our values from the past.*
2 If you **inherit** something such as money or property, you receive it from someone who has died. *e.g. He inherited his father's horse when he died.*
3 If you **inherit** a characteristic or quality, you are born with it, because your parents or ancestors also had it. *e.g. Some people believe we inherit differences in intelligence.*

inheritance   1194
1 An **inheritance** is money or property which you receive from someone who has died. *e.g. The children decided to split the inheritance equally.*
2 **Inheritance** is an occasion or situation in which you inherit money or property. *e.g. The inheritance of his father's fortune has not changed him.*

inheritance   1207, 1306
1 An **inheritance** is money or property which you receive from someone who has died. *e.g.*

The old family home was his inheritance.
2 Inheritance is also the fact of being born with particular characteristics or qualities which your family or ancestors had. *e.g. To what extent does human nature depend on genetic inheritance as opposed to environment?*
3 An inheritance is a situation or thing which has been taken over from people who came before you. *e.g. Our alphabet is an inheritance from the Greeks.*

initial   209, 302, 1491
You use **initial** to describe something that happens at the beginning of a process, in contrast to what happens later. *e.g. The initial idea was to do it in red, but that was soon overruled.*

initiate   209
If you **initiate** something, you start it or cause it to happen. *e.g. We should initiate talks with the trade unions.*

initiative   619
If you have **initiative**, you are able to see what needs to be done and can then do it in an intelligent and efficient way, without needing other people to give you orders or instructions. *e.g. He showed initiative and was promoted.*

inject   782
If you **inject** someone with a liquid, usually a drug, you use a syringe to get it into their blood. *e.g. The doctor injected a sleeping drug into my arm.*

injection   782
If you have an **injection**, someone puts a liquid, usually a drug, into your blood using a syringe, especially in order to prevent you getting an illness. *e.g. You had a smallpox injection when you were five.*

injure   1052
If you **injure** yourself or a part of your body, or you are **injured**, a part of your body is damaged. *e.g. She was badly injured in the car crash.*

injury   1052
An **injury** is damage done to a person's body. *e.g. I myself suffered a serious injury.*

innoculate   782
If you are **innoculated** against a disease, you are injected with a weak form of the disease as a way of building up your protection against it. *e.g. All babies should be innoculated against German measles.*

innoculation   782
1 An innoculation is an injection with a weak form of a disease which encourages your body to build up protection against the disease. *e.g. Have you had a tetanus innoculation lately?*

2 Innoculation is the injection of a weak form of a disease as a way of building up your protection against it. *e.g. Innoculation of all newborn babies is the only way to ensure they stay healthy.*

inquisitive   334
If you are **inquisitive**, you like finding out about things even if they don't concern you or your curiosity is considered rude. *e.g. He's very inquisitive, he's always reading my letters.*

insect   1148
An **insect** is a small animal that usually has six legs. Most insects have wings. Ants, flies, butterflies and beetles are all insects. *e.g. She studied the behaviour of a small insect from Singapore.*

insert   1511, 1613, 1658
1 If you **insert** an object into something, you put the object inside it. *e.g. I will now insert the mystery message into the box.*
2 An insert is a supplementary or additional pamphlet or sheet of information which can be put into a magazine or journal. *e.g. This week, we include a special insert with details of the GTB diet.*

insert   1614
If you **insert** an object into something, you put the object inside it, usually in a place where it fits tightly. *e.g. She removed the sheet of paper on which she had been typing and inserted a new one.*

inside   1606
1 Someone or something that is **inside** a place, container, or object is surrounded by its sides. *e.g. You left your lighter inside the glove compartment.*
2 The **inside** of something is the part or area that its sides surround or contain. *e.g. The inside of the garage is like Aladdin's cave.*

inside   1614
Inside is used to refer to the part of something which is surrounded and often enclosed or hidden by the main part that you usually see. *e.g. A mango is a fruit with a big seed inside.*

insignificant   612, 618
Something that is **insignificant** is unimportant because it is very small in size, degree, or amount. *e.g. The proportion of Indian capital in the project was relatively insignificant.*

inspect   962
1 If you **inspect** something, you look at every part of it carefully in order to find out about it or check that it is all right. *e.g. She mended the wire, and then held it up to the light to inspect the results.*

2 When an official **inspects** a group of people or a place, they visit it and look at it carefully in order to find out whether regulations are being obeyed. *e.g. The fire prevention branch of the Fire Brigade inspects factories and all sorts of public buildings.*

inspect a document   961
If you **inspect a document**, you look at every part of it carefully in order to find out about it, check that it is all right or find something particular that is contained in it. *e.g. Inspect this document, constable: if you see anything strange, tell me.*

inspector   962
An **inspector** is a person, usually employed by a government agency, who finds out whether individuals or organisations are obeying official regulations, for example health and safety regulations in a work place. *e.g. The inspector's report was released to the public.*

instruct   457
If you **instruct** people in a subject or skill, you teach them about it by giving factual information or by explaining how to do it. *e.g. Terry will instruct you in the finer details of studio techniques.*

instruct   356
If you **instruct** someone to do something, you tell them to do it. *e.g. He instructed her to wait.*

instruction   356
An **instruction** is something that someone tells you to do. *e.g. She was only following the instructions of her supervisor.*

instructor   457
An **instructor** is a person who teaches you, especially in a practical activity such as driving or skiing. *e.g. She was a Swiss ski instructor.*

insult   257
1 If you **insult** someone, you sign or say something rude about them or offend them by doing something that shows you have a low opinion of them. *e.g. You have insulted him by calling him fat.*
2 An insult is a rude remark about someone or an action that offends them. *e.g. I would take it as an insult if you left without saying goodbye.*

insurance   174, 680, 922, 1269
1 Insurance is an agreement in which you pay a fixed sum of money to a special company, usually each month or year. Then, if you become ill or if your property is damaged or stolen, the company pays you a sum of money. *e.g. She took out private health insurance.*
2 Insurance is the amount of money which you pay to a company in order to obtain

insurance, or the amount of money which a company pays to you if you have an accident, become ill, et cetera. *e.g. I paid my car insurance.*

insure   1269
If you **insure** yourself or your property, you pay money to an insurance company so that, if you become ill, or if your property is damaged or stolen, the company will pay you a sum of money. *e.g. Insure your baggage before you leave home.*

intelligence   166
The **intelligence** of a person or animal is their ability to understand and learn things well. *e.g. The first part of the interview involved an intelligence test.*

intelligent   166, 510, 1500
1 A person or animal that is **intelligent** has the ability to understand and learn things well. *e.g. Jamie is really intelligent.*
2 An **intelligent** idea or action is one that is thought to be wise or clever. *e.g. Using a condom is intelligent in this day and age.*

intend   188, 768

1 If you **intend** to do something, you have decided to do it or have planned to do it. *e.g. He had intended staying longer.*
2 If you **intend** something to happen or to have a particular effect or function, you have planned that it should happen or should have this effect or function. *e.g. We intend to run three further courses this academic year.*

intention   188, 768
If you sign or say that something is your **intention** or your **intent**, you mean it is an idea or plan of what you are going to do. *e.g. The intention is to set up a brand new school.*

inter   1443
To **inter** someone means to bury them. *e.g. Thomas was interred next to his mother.*

interact   883
1 When two or more people **interact**, they communicate with each other in a mutually responsive way. They may use sign language, spoken language or communicate through some other type of communicative behaviour. *e.g. Mothers and babies interact with each other in highly complex ways.*
2 When one thing **interacts** with another, the two things react together and affect each other's development or nature. *e.g. The bacteria's genes interact with those of the plant.*

interaction   883
1 **Interaction** occurs when two or more

people communicate with each other in a mutually responsive way. *e.g. There was a great deal of interaction between Deaf and hearing people at the sign language conference.*
2 **Interaction** occurs when two things influence or affect each other: this concept is an important one within the physical sciences. *e.g. The interaction of air and copper resulted in the copper turning green.*

interest   1197
1 If you have an **interest** in something, you are keen to learn more about it. *e.g. She had an interest in old books.*
2 Something that is of **interest** attracts your attention because it is rather exciting or unusual. *e.g. There was an article that might be of interest to you in today's paper.*
3 An **interest** that you have is something you spend time on because you enjoy doing it or learning about it. *e.g. Their shared interest in football brought them closer together.*

interested   1197
1 Someone who is **interested** in something is keen to learn more about it or spend time doing it. *e.g. I'm very interested in birds.*
2 Someone who is **interested** in something thinks that it is important and worth giving attention to. *e.g. We are interested only in the efficiency of the company as a whole.*
3 Someone who is **interested** in doing something is keen to do it. *e.g. My sister is interested in becoming a nurse.*

interesting   1186
If you find something **interesting**, it holds or attracts your attention, for example because you think it is exciting or unusual. *e.g. Collecting match boxes is an interesting hobby.*

interfere   1305
1 If you **interfere** in a relationship or situation between people, you try to influence it, especially when there is a dispute and you aim to solve the problem. *e.g. My mother interferes when I argue with my husband.*
2 If you **interfere** in a conversation between other people, you interrupt them when their conversation does not concern you. *e.g. Please don't interfere, Boris.*
3 Something that **interferes** with a situation or activity has a damaging effect on it, often preventing something from happening or succeeding. *e.g. Child bearing should not interfere with a career.*

interference   1305
Interference is the act of interfering in something. *e.g. He won't accept interference in the way he runs the business.*

interment   1443
The **interment** of a dead person is their

burial. *e.g. They brought back their son's remains for interment in the local village graveyard.*

intermittent   1233
Something that is **intermittent** happens occasionally rather than continuously. *e.g. I became aware of a faint, intermittent noise, somewhere outside.*

internal   1341
1 You use **internal** to describe the political and commercial interests inside a country. *e.g. We should not interfere with the internal problems facing Poland.*
2 You use **internal** to describe something that exists or happens within a particular organisation. *e.g. It was an internal discussion.*

internal   1606, 1607, 1614
1 **Internal** is used to describe things that happen or exist inside a particular place. *e.g. You should lag internal pipes to prevent them freezing.*
2 **Internal** is also used to describe the political and commercial activities that take place inside a country. *e.g. It is difficult to understand the internal politics of China.*
3 **Internal** is used to describe the affairs of a particular organisation that are not intended to be connected with anything outside the organisation. *e.g. The company's internal affairs are a shambles.*

international   1638
International means between or involving different countries. *e.g. He signed an international peace agreement.*

interpret   701
If you **interpret** what someone is signing or saying, you translate it immediately into another language. *e.g. Paul had to interpret for us, and he really did a splendid job.*

interpreter   701
An **interpreter** is a person whose job it is to understand the message being transmitted by a person in one language and translate it into another language. *e.g. We will need an interpreter for this crucial meeting.*

interrupt   1305
1 If you **interrupt** someone, you do something that causes them to pause or stop what they are doing. *e.g. May I interrupt you? I need the stapler from your drawer.*
2 If you **interrupt** an activity, you temporarily prevent it from continuing. *e.g. Fred interrupted the mayor's speech.*

interruption   1305
1 An **interruption** is something which temporarily prevents an activity from continuing. *e.g. There was an interruption while tea was brought in.*

2 Interruption is the act of interrupting something. *e.g. We should be safe from interruption.*

intervene   1305
1 If you **intervene**, you take action in a situation that you were not originally involved in. *e.g. The officer intervened to stop the fight.*
2 If you **intervene**, you interrupt a conversation in order to add something to it. *e.g. Can I just intervene for one moment?*
3 If an event **intervenes**, it happens suddenly in a way that stops, delays, or prevents something. *e.g. Neither bill will become law because the general election will intervene.*

intervention   1305
Intervention is the act of intervening. *e.g. Your intervention saved the meeting from becoming a shambles.*

interview   458, 848, 865
1 An **interview** is a meeting at which someone asks you questions about yourself, your abilities and your experience, especially in order to find out if you are suitable for a particular job. *e.g. I had an interview for a new job yesterday.*
2 An **interview** is a conversation (or the published or broadcast report of that conversation) in which somebody signs or speaks to a reporter about the interesting or important things that they do. *e.g. She is to go for a television interview.*
3 If you **interview** someone, you ask them questions, for example about their suitability for a job or about their interests, ideas or beliefs. *e.g. We interviewed eighty-four people for parts in our film.*

into   1607, 1614
If you put money or information **into** a place, you put it there so that it can be stored. *e.g. The information goes into a computer.*

intoxicated   819
If someone is **intoxicated**, they are drunk. *e.g. Thompson went into town and got intoxicated on cheap whisky.*

introduce   1204
1 If you **introduce** someone to someone else, you formally tell them each other's names, so that they can get to know each other. *e.g. Joan introduced him to Karl.*
2 When someone **introduces** a television or radio programme, they sign or say a few words at the beginning of it to tell you what it will be about. *e.g. Paul Allen will introduce tonight's special edition.*

introduce   1449
1 If you **introduce** someone to someone else, you formally tell them each other's names, so

that they can get to know each other. *e.g. Stuart, let me introduce you to Elisabeth.*
2 If you **introduce** yourself to someone, you formally tell them your name, so that you can get to know them. *e.g. I had better introduce myself. I am Colonel Marc Rodin.*
3 When someone **introduces** a television or radio programme, they sign or say a few words at the beginning of it to tell you what it will be about. *e.g. And here to introduce the programme is Rachell Bastikar.*

introduction   1449
1 The **introduction** of something into a place or system is the act of causing it to exist or be used there for the first time. *e.g. The Government saw the introduction of new technology as vital.*
2 Your **introduction** to something is the occasion when you experience it for the first time. *e.g. China's introduction to modern British ballet was a talking point for months after the event.*
3 An **introduction** is the first part of a book, signed presentation or talk, in which the writer, signer or speaker tells you what the rest of the book, signed presentation or talk is about. *e.g. Brian Johnston contributes a delightful introduction to Anthony Smith's book.*
4 An **introduction** is a book that explains the basic facts about a particular subject. *e.g. This 'Introduction to English Literature' is neither the first of its kind, nor the best.*
5 An **introduction** is the act of formally telling people each other's names so that they can get to know each other. *e.g. He was shaking her hand before I could finish the introduction.*

invalid   318
An **invalid** is someone who is so ill or disabled that they need to be cared for by someone else, either because of their physical condition or because present social provision offers no alternative. *e.g. Her husband is an invalid.*

invent   619
If you **invent** a machine, process or game, you are the first person to think of it. *e.g. He invented a new device to clean fingernails.*

invention   619
1 An **invention** is a machine, device or system that has been invented by someone or that is just being invented. *e.g. He was working on his invention down in the garden shed.*
2 **Invention** is the act of inventing something that has never been made or used before. *e.g. The invention of television changed our lives.*

inverted commas   823
1 **Inverted commas** are the punctuation marks ('and' or "and") that are used in writing to indicate where a quotation begins and ends. Inverted commas are also sometimes used

round the titles of books, songs, etc., or round a word or phrase that is being discussed. *e.g. Did she sign this? Well, then, it should be in inverted commas.*
2 If you sign or say **in inverted commas**, you mean that it is as if something were the case although it is not. *e.g. I suppose you could say he was a professor, in inverted commas, of Royalty Studies.*

invest   1318
1 If you **invest** an amount of money, you pay it into a bank or building society or buy shares with it, so that you will receive a profit. *e.g. We will be able to invest twenty million pounds of public money.*
2 If you **invest** money in something, you use your money in trying to make it a success. *e.g. They were reluctant to invest money in new ideas.*

investigate   776, 848, 1163
If you **investigate** an event, situation, or person, you try to find out all the facts about them. *e.g. I sent my staff to investigate.*

investigation   848
1 **Investigation** is the activity or process of trying to find out all the known facts about an event, situation or person. *e.g. Investigation produced findings that a medium could never have uncovered.*
2 An **investigation** is a procedure of research or questioning in search of evidence. *e.g. The investigation found no new clues.*

investigator   776, 1163
An **investigator** is someone whose job is to investigate events, situations or people. *e.g. The aircraft accident investigator got to the scene quickly.*

invisible   1555
If something is **invisible**, you cannot see it because it has disappeared. *e.g. 'When I put on my magic cloak, I am invisible,' said the fairy.*

invitation   845
An **invitation** is a request to do something or take part in something. *e.g. I received an invitation to attend the meeting.*

invitation   1623
An **invitation** is a request, usually informal, to do something or take part in something. *e.g. Look, I didn't make the invitation, so don't blame me!*

invite   845
1 An **invite** is a request to do something or take part in something. *e.g. I received an invite to attend the meeting.*
2 If someone **invites** you to something such as a party or meal, they ask you to come to it. *e.g. It seems they decided to invite me after all.*

invite 1204
If someone **invites** discussion or criticism, they encourage you to discuss or criticise what they have signed, said or done. *e.g. He promised to stop a little early and invite contributions to the debate.*

involve 1613
1 If you **involve** yourself in something, you take part in it. *e.g. I was reluctant to involve myself in this private fight.*
2 If you **involve** someone else in something, you get them to take part in it. *e.g. I'll try to involve Paul in planning the meeting.*

involve 1658
1 If you **involve** yourself in something, you take part in it. *e.g. It was a private argument which I was not about to involve myself in.*
2 If you **involve** someone else in something, you get them to take part in it. *e.g. If we can just involve him in the musical side, that would be useful.*
3 If a situation or activity **involves** someone or something, it includes them or uses them as a necessary part. *e.g. Tutoring will involve providing new vocabulary in context, testing receptive skills, testing productive skills, and giving dialogue practice.*

Ireland 817, 972
Ireland is an island off North West Europe, divided between the Republic of Ireland (occupying most of the island) and Northern Ireland (occupying the north east of the island). The Republic of Ireland was declared a republic in 1949 and is a member of the European Community. Northern Ireland is a part of the United Kingdom. *e.g. Francis Maginn, the founder of the British Deaf and Dumb Association, was born near Cork in Ireland in 1861.*

Irish 817, 972
1 Someone or something that is **Irish** belongs to or relates to the whole of Ireland, or its people. *e.g. I studied Irish history at Trinity College.*
2 Someone or something that is **Irish** belongs to or relates to the Republic of Ireland, or its people. *e.g. The Irish President, Dr. Robinson, visited Somalia.*
3 **Irish** is the language that some people speak in Ireland and within Irish communities in other parts of the world. *e.g. Irish is one of the ancient Celtic languages.*
4 You can refer to people from Ireland or the Republic of Ireland in general, or a particular group of people from Ireland or the Republic of Ireland, as the **Irish**. *e.g. The Irish were the most popular of the visiting football fans at the last World Cup.*
5 The address of the **Irish** Deaf Society is: Carmichael House, North Brunswick Street, Dublin 7, Ireland.

iron (an iron) 7
An **iron** is a device for removing creases from clothes, sheets, towels, et cetera. An iron has a handle and a flat metal base. You heat it until the base is hot, then rub it over the material. *e.g. If you know it's cotton or linen, use a hot iron.*

ironing 7
1 **Ironing** is the task or activity of ironing clothes in order to get rid of the creases. *e.g. I've got my ironing to do.*
2 **Ironing** is all the things that you have which need ironing. *e.g. She took up the pile of ironing and set it on the dresser.*

iron (to iron) 7
If you **iron** clothes, etc., you remove the creases from them using an iron. *e.g. I iron my clothes at the weekend.*

irregular 955
Irregular actions happen with different periods of time between them. *e.g. The newspaper was printed at irregular intervals.*

irritable 1185
If you are **irritable**, you are in a mood in which you easily become annoyed. *e.g. Judy was feeling hot, tired and irritable.*

irritate 1185
If something **irritates** you, it gradually makes you slightly angry because you do not like it but cannot stop it continuing. *e.g. He knew it would irritate me if he walked slowly because I had told him I had to hurry.*

irritation 1185
1 If something is an **irritation**, it makes you feel slightly angry, because you do not like it but cannot stop it continuing. *e.g. The way he treated his cat was a constant irritation to us.*
2 **Irritation** is the feeling that you get when you feel slightly angry about something, because you do not like it but cannot stop it continuing. *e.g. The irritation and annoyance caused by a single day in London makes me wonder why I ever bother going there.*

island 1127
An **island** is a piece of land that is completely surrounded by water. *e.g. He was born on the island of Cyprus.*

isolate 555, 1616
If something **isolates** you or if you **isolate** yourself, you are physically or socially set apart from other people. *e.g. His wealth seemed to isolate him from his old working class companions.*

isolation 555
1 **Isolation** is a state in which you feel separate from other people, because you live far away from them or you do not have many friends.

e.g. They claim that many Deaf people live in isolation, but I don't know what evidence they have for that statement.
2 If something exists or happens in **isolation**, it exists or happens separately from other things of the same kind. *e.g A single country acting in isolation is vulnerable.*

Israel 1141
Israel is a republic in South West Asia on the Mediterranean sea. It was established in 1948 as a Jewish state. *e.g. We are going to Israel on holiday.*

Israeli 1141
1 Someone or something that is **Israeli** belongs to or relates to Israel, or its people. *e.g. These are Israeli oranges.*
2 An **Israeli** is a person who comes from, or whose family identity relates to, Israel. *e.g. He was an Israeli: it was his daughter who was born in Jordan.*
3 The address of the **Israeli Deaf Association** is: P.O. Box 9001, 61090 Tel Aviv, Israel.

is there 1124
If you state that, or ask if, someone or something **is there**, you are referring to their existence or availability. *e.g. Is there a big towel in the bathroom?*

it 310
You use **it** to refer to a specific object, animal, place, idea, etc., which may not be present but whose identity has been established or recently mentioned. *e.g. It heats up much more quickly than the other one.*

Italian 255
1 Someone or something that is **Italian** belongs to or relates to Italy, or its people. *e.g. I'm looking forward to seeing the new Italian Sign Language dictionary.*
2 **Italian** is the main language spoken in Italy, and one of the official languages of Switzerland. *e.g. Hugh speaks fluent Italian.*
3 An **Italian** is a person who comes from, or whose family identity relates to, Italy. *e.g. There were three Italians in my Advanced English class.*
2 The address of the **Italian** Deaf Association is: Ente Nazionale Sordomuti (E.N.S.), Via Gregorio VII. n. 120, 1-00165 Roma, Italy.

Italy 255
Italy is a republic in Southern Europe. It is located in the Mediterranea m between the Tyrrhenian and the Adriatic Seas. It became a republic in 1946 and is a member of the European Community. *e.g. Italy is a popular holiday destination.*

item 556
An **item** is one of a collection or list of objects. *e.g. The first item he bought was a clock.*

its   11, 63
See **belong to it**.

itself   493
1 You use **itself** to refer to the thing affected by an action when it is the same as the one doing the action. *e.g. Britain must bring itself up to date.*

2 You can use **itself** to emphasise something that you mention and to make it clear what you are referring to. *e.g. The town itself was very small.*

its own   11, 63
1 You use **its own** to emphasise that something is owned by or relates to a thing or animal which has already been mentioned or of which the identity is known. *e.g. Our cat has its own special bowl.*

2 You use **its own** to emphasise that a thing or animal which has already been mentioned, or of which the identity is known, does something without any help. *e.g. We don't need to feed the goat. It finds food on its own.*

J, j

J
J is the tenth letter of the British manual and English alphabets. See page 851.

jab   782
A **jab** is an injection of a substance into your blood to prevent illness. *e.g. Everyone queued up for their flu jabs.*

jacket   288, 1650
A **jacket** is a short coat that has long sleeves and an opening at the front. *e.g. A waiter in a white jacket arrived with drinks.*

jail   47
1 A **jail** is a place where people are kept locked up, either because they have been found guilty of committing a crime or because they are waiting to be tried for a crime. *e.g. This woman has spent years in jail.*

2 If someone is **jailed**, they are put into jail. *e.g. He was jailed for five years.*

jam   80
1 If something such as a part of a machine **jams** or if you **jam** it, it becomes fixed in position and is unable to move freely or work properly. *e.g. The machines jammed and broke down.*

2 If a road is **jammed** with vehicles, it is filled completely with them, so that the traffic cannot move. *e.g. Some side roads soon became jammed.*

3 If there is a **jam** in something such as a part of a machine, it becomes fixed in position and is unable to move freely or work properly. *e.g. There seems to be a jam in the paper tray.*

jam   1324
Jam is a soft, sweet food that is made by cooking fruit with sugar. *e.g. There were pots of raspberry and blackcurrant jam on the kitchen table.*

Japan   451, 454
Japan is a country which lies between the Sea of Japan and the Pacific, consisting of four main islands and over three thousand smaller islands. Some people find these signs offensive. *e.g. The last World Federation of the Deaf Congress was held in Japan.*

Japanese   451, 454
1 Someone or something that is **Japanese** belongs to or relates to Japan, or its people. Some people find these signs offensive. *e.g. A number of linguists are now carrying out research on Japanese Sign Language.*

2 **Japanese** is the main language spoken in Japan. Some people find these signs offensive. *e.g. The Teikyo University students offer classes in Japanese.*

3 You can refer to people from Japan in general, or a particular group of people from Japan, as the **Japanese**. Some people find these signs offensive. *e.g. The Japanese have opened a car factory near Sunderland.*

4 The address of the **Japanese** Federation of the Deaf is: S.K. Building, 130 Yamabuki-cho, Shinjuku-ku, Tokyo 162, Japan.

jar   1681, 1683
1 A **jar** is a container, usually made of glass, that has a wide top and is used for storing food such as jam and preserved fruit. *e.g. Have you any empty fruit jars?*

2 A **jar** is used to refer to the food inside a jar or the amount of food that a jar contains. *e.g. I bought a jar of beetroot.*

javelin   19
1 A **javelin** is a long spear that is used in sports competitions. Competitors try to throw the javelin as far as possible. *e.g. I prefer to train with a heavier javelin.*

2 The **javelin** is the event or sport of throwing the javelin. *e.g. She came first in the javelin.*

javelin thrower   19
A **javelin thrower** is a person who competes in the javelin. *e.g. Tessa Sanderson was a great javelin thrower.*

jealous   580, 583, 1184
If you are **jealous**, you feel anger or bitterness towards someone who has something that you would like to have. *e.g. I am jealous of your success.*

jealousy   580, 583, 1184
1 **Jealousy** is the feeling of resentment and bitterness that you have when you think someone is trying to take away something that you feel belongs to you. *e.g. He was good at talking me out of my suspicion and jealousy.*

2 **Jealousy** is the feeling you have when you wish that you could have the qualities or possessions that someone else has. *e.g. We often feel jealousy of our brothers and sisters.*

jeans   147
Jeans are casual trousers that are usually made of strong denim. Sometimes, trousers made of other cloth such as corduroy or thick cotton are also referred to as jeans. *e.g. He wore jeans and a blue shirt.*

jeer   765, 1016
If you **jeer** at someone, you sign or say rude and insulting things to them. *e.g. All the other boys used to jeer at him whenever he tried to use sign language with them.*

jelly   1040
Jelly is a soft food (usually sweet in flavour) made from gelatine, which wobbles when you move it. *e.g. I will make jelly for the party.*

jersey   136
A **jersey** is a piece of clothing made of knitted wool that covers the upper part of your body and your arms and does not open at the front. *e.g. She bought a striped jersey in the sale.*

Jesus   966
Jesus, also called **Jesus Christ** or **Jesus of Nazareth**, was the founder of Christianity, born in Galilee and brought up as a Jew. He is believed by Christians to be the Son of God. *e.g. We saw Leonardo da Vinci's painting of Jesus and the Apostles at the Last Supper.*

Jew   577
A **Jew** is a person who believes in and practices the religion of Judaism, which is based on the Old Testament of the Bible and the Talmud or book of laws and traditions. Some people find the use of this sign offensive. *e.g. He comes from a family of Jews.*

Jew 1141, 1672
A **Jew** is a person who believes in and practices the religion of Judaism, which is based on the Old Testament of the Bible and the Talmud or book of laws and traditions. *e.g. She married a Jew and moved to Israel.*

jewel 1149
A **jewel** is a precious stone such as a diamond or ruby that is used to decorate valuable things that you wear, such as rings or necklaces. *e.g. It was a jewel of enormous value.*

Jewish 1141, 1672
1 Someone or something that is **Jewish** belongs to or relates to the religion of Judaism or to people who follow this religion. *e.g. The Jewish Deaf Drama Group presented 'The Greatest Story Ever Signed'.*
2 The address of the **Jewish** Deaf Association is : 90 Cazenova Road, London, N16 6AB.

jigsaw 217
A **jigsaw** or **jigsaw puzzle** is a game using a picture on cardboard or wood that has been cut up into odd shapes. You have to make the picture again by putting the pieces together correctly. *e.g. My sister loved jigsaws.*

jigsaw puzzle 217
A **jigsaw puzzle** is the same as a jigsaw. See **jigsaw**.

job 1345
1 A **job** is the work that a person does regularly in order to earn money. *e.g. Jane got a good job as a secretary.*
2 A **job** is a task. *e.g. It may be a fair, but it won't run itself: so what job do you want?*

join 898, 1613, 1658
1 If you **join** a club, society or organisation, you become a member of it or start work as an employee of it. *e.g. We joined the Labour Party.*
2 If you **join** an activity that other people are doing, you take part in it or become involved with it. *e.g. They were invited to join the feasting.*

joiner 134
A **joiner** is a person who makes wooden articles, in particular wooden window frames, door frames, doors and stairs. *e.g. She wanted to be a joiner like her father when she left school.*

joinery 134
Joinery is the skill and work of a joiner. *e.g. My son is doing a part-time joinery course at the local college.*

join in 1613, 1658
If you **join in** an activity, you take part in it or become involved in it. *e.g. Parents should join in these discussions.*

join up 1613, 1658
If someone **joins up**, they become a member of the army, the navy, or the air force. *e.g. He wanted to join up just before the end of the war.*

joke 765, 1016
1 A **joke** is something (such as a funny story) that is signed, said or done to make you laugh. *e.g. Roy told me this joke about a chicken and a steamroller.*
2 If you **joke**, you tell funny stories or say things that are amusing and not serious. *e.g. Don't joke about that, it's no laughing matter.*
3 You can sign or say **you're joking** or **you must be joking** when someone has just signed or said something very surprising. *e.g. You must be joking! She'd kill me if I said that!*

joker 765, 1016
A **joker** is someone who likes making jokes, playing tricks on people or teasing people in order to provide amusement. *e.g. I enjoyed working with Hitchcock. He was a great joker.*

joking (you must be joking) 847
If you sign or say **you must be joking**, you mean that you think the comment someone has just made is ridiculous, or completely untrue. *e.g. 'He's very good at his job, isn't he?'—'You must be joking! He's absolutely useless!'*

journal 283
A **journal** is a magazine for people with a particular interest. *e.g. ADSUP and the BDA produce a regular journal entitled 'Deafness'.*

judge 1367, 1413
1 A **judge** is a person who has been chosen to give his or her opinions in a competition and to decide who or what will be the winner. *e.g. I have been asked to be a judge at the drama competition.*
2 If you **judge** something such as a competition, you decide who or what is the winner. *e.g. The competition was judged by the local mayor.*
3 If you sign or say that someone is a good (or bad) **judge** of something, you mean that they are (or are not) a person whose opinions about that thing are valuable and useful because they are based on a lot of experience or knowledge. *e.g. He knew she would be a good judge of character.*
4 If you **judge** something, you guess the amount or value of it by thinking carefully about it. *e.g. How will they judge which is to be the most reliable?*
5 If you **judge** something, you come to an opinion about how good, useful, or successful it is, after you have carefully examined the evidence. *e.g. You need to be able to judge your own progress.*

judge 1648
A **judge** is the person in a court of law who has

the power to make decisions about how the law should be applied to people, for example how a person who has been found guilty of a crime should be punished. *e.g. Judge Amason set Miss Davis free on bail.*

judgement 1367, 1413
A **judgement** is an opinion that you have or give after thinking carefully about something. *e.g. In our judgement, her plan has definitely succeeded.*

judo 290
Judo is a sport in which two people fight each other, with each trying to throw, hold to the ground or force the other to submit. *e.g. My children go to judo classes every week.*

jug 8
A **jug** is a cylindrical container with a handle and a lip or spout, used for holding and pouring liquids. *e.g. A jug full of fresh milk was placed on the table.*

juggernaut 74
A **juggernaut** is a very large lorry. *e.g. Juggernauts should not be allowed to drive through the village.*

jumble 1114
1 If you **jumble** things, or **jumble** them up, you mix them together so that they are not in the correct order. *e.g. Don't jumble up the disco material with the sports equipment.*
2 A **jumble** is a mixture of things with no ordering or pattern. *e.g. This jumble of shoes will need to be sorted out.*

jumper 136
A **jumper** is a piece of clothing, usually made of wool, that covers the upper part of your body and your arms and that does not open at the front. *e.g. She knitted him a red jumper for his birthday.*

jump over 742
1 If you **jump over** something such as a fence, you move quickly up into the air to get across it. *e.g. I had to jump over the stream.*
2 A **jump over** something is a quick movement into the air to get across it. *e.g. This is followed by a forward roll and a jump over this box and into the sandpit, okay?*

junkie 782
A **junkie** is a drug addict, especially one who injects drugs into himself or herself. *e.g. There were a number of junkies huddled in the doorway.*

just 622, 1250
If you sign or say that something has **just** happened, you mean that it happened a short time ago. *e.g. I just heard the news yesterday.*

just 959
You use **just** to indicate that something is no

more important, impressive, interesting, difficult or greater than you sign or say that it is. *e.g. It's just a story, of course—or is it?!*

just 1409
Someone or something that is **just** is

reasonable and fair. *e.g. Who decides what a just punishment is?*

just now 1250
Just now means a very short time ago. *e.g. She was here just now.*

just so 516
If something is **just so**, it is arranged very neatly so that everything is in its proper place. *e.g. When the Japanese make tea, everything has to be just so.*

K, k

K
K is the eleventh letter of the British manual and English alphabets. See pages 851 and 852.

karate 1434
Karate is a sport in which people fight using their hands, elbows, feet and legs. *e.g. Karate is becoming a popular sport.*

keen 1197
1 Someone who is **keen** wants to do something very much or wants something to happen very much. *e.g. I'm keen to buy the car.*
2 Someone who is **keen** has a great deal of enthusiasm for a particular activity, for example a sport or a hobby, and spends a lot of time doing it. *e.g. He was a keen gardener.*
3 Someone who is **keen** has an enthusiastic nature and is interested in everything they do. *e.g. He seems a keen lad.*

keep 1
If you **keep** something, you have it in your possession. *e.g. Can you keep this banana for me?*

keep 199
If you **keep** something, you have it so that you can use it whenever you need it. *e.g. I'd be ever so grateful if you'd keep the stool for me.*

keep 1615
If you **keep** an object, you continue to possess it. *e.g. Dad said that I could keep the change.*

keep a straight face 816, 1085
If you **keep a straight face**, you manage to look serious, although you want to laugh. *e.g. She couldn't keep a straight face any longer and gave the game away.*

keeper 320
A **keeper** is a person who takes care of the animals in a place such as a game reserve or a zoo. *e.g. I interviewed a number of retired zoo keepers.*

keep out 1632
If you **keep out** of a situation, you do not want to get involved in it. *e.g. I have decided to keep out of the elections this year.*

kerb 1339
A **kerb** is the raised edge between a pavement and a road. *e.g. She stepped off the kerb.*

ketchup 1662
Ketchup is a thick, cold sauce made from tomatoes. *e.g. Do you have any ketchup?*

kettle 935, 936
A **kettle** is a covered ontainer that you use for boiling water. It has a handle to lift it with and a spout to pour the water out. *e.g. What about buying a new kettle while we're here?*

key 250
1 A **key** is a specially shaped piece of metal which you place in a lock and turn, in order to open a door, a suitcase, a cupboard, etc., or to close it so that it stays closed. *e.g. Keep a list of anyone who has a front door key.*
2 A **key** is a specially shaped piece of metal or plastic that you use to wind up clocks, clockwork toys, et cetera. *e.g. Where is the key for the clock on the mantelpiece?*

keyboard 1043
1 The **keyboard** of a piano or organ is the set of black and white keys that you press in order to play it. *e.g. He lifted the lid and gazed at the keyboard.*
2 The **keyboard** of a typewriter or a computer terminal is the set of keys that you press in order to operate it. *e.g. She looks the part as soon as she sits down at the keyboard.*

keyboard operator 1043
A **keyboard operator** is a person who works on a keyboard. *e.g. Give those accounts to the keyboard operator.*

kick 546
If you **kick** someone or something, you hit them with your foot. *e.g. The man kicked the door.*

kick out 379, 546
If you are **kicked out** of a place or a group of people, you are forced to leave. *e.g. I was kicked out for anti-social behaviour.*

kid 765, 1016
1 If you **kid** someone, you tease them. *e.g. Tim's*

friends used to kid him about his odd clothes.
2 If you are **kidding**, you are signing or saying something that is not really true, as a joke. *e.g. I'm not really twenty-one; I was only kidding.*

kid 1211
You can refer to a child as a **kid**. *e.g. My kid only eats junk food.*

kidding (you're kidding) 847
If you sign or say **you're kidding**, you mean that you do not believe the comment someone has just made. *e.g. 'I passed the exam.'—'You're kidding!'*

kids 1216
You can refer to children as **kids** *e.g. These two kids are mine.*

kill 366, 532
When someone or something **kills** a person, animal or plant, they cause the person, animal or plant to die. *e.g. He killed his wife by putting arsenic in her coffee.*

kill oneself to do something 367
If you **kill yourself to do something**, you make a great effort to do it, even though it causes you a lot of trouble or suffering. *e.g. I'm killing myself to get this finished before the deadline.*

kilt 1089
A **kilt** is a short, full, pleated tartan skirt that is traditionally worn by Scotsmen and can also be worn by other people. *e.g. Mr. Smith was fitted for a new kilt.*

kind 1489, 1494
1 Someone who is **kind** behaves in a gentle, caring and helpful way towards other people. *e.g. The staff were kind towards my mother.*
2 You tell someone that they have been **kind** when you are thanking them for something that they have done for you. *e.g. It was kind of you to come.*

kind-hearted 1489, 1494
Someone who is **kind-hearted** is kind, loving and gentle. *e.g. He was one of the most kind-hearted men that she had ever met.*

kinds (all kinds of)   426, 427, 447
You use **all kinds of** things or people to refer to a variety of different things or people. *e.g. There were all kinds of people from different countries there.*

king   1131
A **king** is a man who rules a country as its monarch. Kings are not elected, but are born into a royal family. *e.g. The legend of King Arthur was my favourite story.*

kirk   106, 1440
1 A **kirk** is a church belonging to the National Church of Scotland or the Episcopal Church of Scotland. *e.g. I go to the kirk every Sunday.*
2 A **kirk** is a church. *e.g. Look at that lovely kirk on the hillside.*

kiss   681
1 If you **kiss** someone, you touch them with your lips to show affection or to greet them. *e.g. If I give you this, will you kiss Veronica Dribblethwaite?*
2 A **kiss** is the action of touching someone with your lips to show affection or to greet them. *e.g. When Gran comes, I always give her a kiss.*

kitchen   588
A **kitchen** is a room that is used for cooking and for household jobs such as washing dishes. *e.g. Sarah went into the kitchen to wash the dishes.*

kite   126
A **kite** is an object consisting of a light frame covered with paper, plastic or cloth which you fly in the air. It has a long string attached to it which is used to control the kite when it is in flight. *e.g. She was given a new Japanese kite.*

knead   99
When you **knead** clay, dough or other food, you press and squeeze it with your hands so that it becomes smooth and ready to use. *e.g. Knead the dough on a well-floured surface.*

kneel   824
If you **kneel** or **kneel** down, you bend your legs and your knees are touching the ground. *e.g. He was told to kneel before the priest.*

knees up   954
A **knees up** or **knees-up** is a lively, noisy celebration, especially one with dancing. *e.g. Why don't we go to the Co-op hall and have a knees up?*

knickers   472
Knickers are a piece of women's underwear which have two holes to put your legs through and elastic around the third hole which goes round your waist. *e.g. She bought some knickers in Marks and Spencers.*

knife   686
A **knife** is an object that you hold in your hand and use to cut things or as a weapon. It usually consists of a sharp, flat piece of metal attached to a handle. *e.g. I need a knife as well as a fork.*

knitting   376
1 **Knitting** is something such as a garment that is being knitted. *e.g. The knitting lay on the chair.*
2 **Knitting** is the action or process of making things such as clothes from wool or a similar thread using knitting needles. *e.g. I hate knitting: it's so monotonous.*

knitting machine   3
A **knitting machine** is a machine that you can use for knitting things. It enables you to make things from wool (or a similar thread) by making loops of wool and joining them togther. *e.g. I made this jumper on my knitting machine.*

knit with a knitting machine   3
If you **knit with a knitting machine** you make something from wool (or a similar thread) by using a machine to make loops of wool and joining them together. *e.g. If I knit the scarf with my knitting machine it will take only a few hours.*

knit with knitting needles   376
If you **knit with knitting needles,** you make something from wool or a similar thread by using two long, thin pieces of metal with sharp points at one end (knitting needles) to make loops of wool and join the loops together. *e.g. I'm knitting myself a jumper.*

knock one flat/knock one for six/knock one sideways   1712
If something **knocks you flat, for six** or **sideways**, it surprises you so much you do not know how to react. *e.g. I was knocked for six when I learned he'd got the job.*

knot   887
1 If you **knot** a piece of string, cord or ribbon, you pass one end of it through a loop and pull it tight. *e.g. Knot the string around this parcel to make it secure.*
2 A **knot** is a place in a piece of string, cord or ribbon where one end has been passed through a loop and pulled tight. You tie a knot in order to join two things together or to keep something firmly in place. *e.g. I've joined these two pieces of string with a knot. Now watch carefully!*

know   168
1 If you **know** a fact, a piece of information, or an answer, you have it in your mind and are certain that it is correct. *e.g. I know her new address.*
2 If you **know** of something, you are aware of it but you do not necessarily have a lot of information about it. *e.g. I know of one girl who moved into a local flat.*
3 If you **know** someone, you are familiar with them because you have met them and signed or spoken to them before. *e.g. She knew Judith very well.*
4 If you **know** how to do something, you have the necessary skills and knowledge to do it. *e.g. Do you know how to drive?.*

know-all   1076
A **know-all** is someone who thinks that they are clever and behave as if they know a lot more than other people. *e.g. My sister is a know-all. You can't tell her anything.*

knowledge   168
Knowledge is information and understanding about a subject which someone has in their mind. *e.g. He has a lot of knowledge about the organisation's history.*

knowledgeable   170
Someone who is **knowledgeable** has or shows a clear understanding of many different facts about the world or about a particular subject. *e.g. He was very knowledgeable about her work on classifiers.*

know someone/something   169
If you **know someone** or **something**, you can recognise who or what they are. *e.g. I know that woman over there.*

know what someone means   167
If you **know what someone means**, you know or understand what they are referring to. *e.g. I know what you mean when you describe her as stuck-up.*

Korea   451, 454
1 **Korea** is a former country in East Asia divided since 1948 into the Democratic People's Republic of Korea (North Korea) and the Republic of Korea (South Korea). Some people find these signs offensive. *e.g. We went to Korea for the Olympic Games.*
2 The address of the Deaf Association of the Republic of **Korea** is: Korea Welfare Association of the Deaf, 681-50 Yeok Sam-Dong, Kang Nam-ku, Seoul, Republic of Korea.

Korean   451, 454
1 Someone or something that is **Korean** belongs to or relates to either North Korea or South Korea, or their people. Some people find these signs offensive. *e.g. I love Korean food.*
2 **Korean** is the main language spoken in North Korea and South Korea. *e.g. The article I received was written in Korean.*
3 A **Korean** is a person who comes from, or whose family identity relates to, North Korea or South Korea. *e.g. A Korean asked me for directions to the university.*

kung-fu   1434
Kung-fu is a Chinese style of fighting which involves using only your hands and feet. *e.g. Kung-fu has received much television publicity.*

L, l

L

L is the twelfth letter of the British manual and English alphabets. See page 852.

laborious 1356
Something that is **laborious** takes a lot of effort. *e.g. Compiling a dictionary is terribly laborious.*

labour 1345, 1354
1 **Labour** is very hard work, often work that does not need a lot of skill. *e.g. I really enjoy manual labour.*
2 If you **labour** at something, you work very hard, for example doing physical work such as digging. *e.g. They laboured every weekend for a month to prepare the foundations for the house.*

labourer 104, 1345
A **labourer** is a person who does a job which involves a lot of hard physical work. *e.g. He eventually found work as a labourer.*

Labour Party 1345
The **Labour Party** in Great Britain is the main organised political group with a tradition of beliefs in socialism and social reform rather than capitalism. It was founded in 1900 by trade unions and a number of socialist organisations to represent their interests and those of their members. *e.g. A number of Deaf people are attending the Labour Party Conference as observers.*

lace 887
1 If you **lace** something or **lace** it up, you fasten it by pulling the two ends of a piece of cord or string tight and then tying them together. *e.g. He laced up his running shoes.*
2 **Laces** are pieces of cord or string that are put through holes along the two edges of something and tied in order to fasten the two edges together. *e.g. I need new laces for my skates.*

lad 483
A **lad** is a boy or young man. *e.g. He used to collect stamps when he was a lad.*

lady 339
1 You can use **lady** as a way of referring to a woman. *e.g. A rich American lady got into the lift.*
2 You can sign or say **ladies** when you are addressing a group of women or a group that includes women. *e.g. Welcome, ladies and gentlemen, to this important Charter 88 meeting.*
3 **Lady** is a title used in front of the names of some female members of the nobility. *e.g. Lady Suzanne Walker has agreed to open the Dance Festival.*

lake 986
A **lake** is a large area of fresh water, surrounded by land. *e.g. The calm waters of Lake Michigan are good for fishing.*

lamp 1698
A **lamp** is a device which, when turned on, produces light. *e.g. I like a lamp near the bed so I can read.*

lamp on 1698
When a **lamp** is **on**, it produces light. *e.g. Leave the lamp on when you go to bed.*

landed with 361
If someone is **landed with** a difficult situation or person, they have to deal with the difficulties involved in making the necessary arrangements. *e.g. Her car broke down so I was landed with having to take them to Newcastle.*

land in an aeroplane/plane 950
When you **land in an aeroplane** or **plane**, the aircraft you are travelling in comes down to the ground after flying through the air. *e.g. We will land in a plane at six o'clock and Prince Charles arrives by helicopter at seven.*

landing of an aeroplane/plane 950
The **landing of an aeroplane** or **plane** is the activity or event in which it comes to the ground after flying through the air. *e.g. The landing may be a little bumpy, because the plane is damaged.*

language 1308
1 A **language** is a system of communication which consists of a set of signs or sounds and written symbols which are used by the people of a particular country or community for signing, speaking or writing. *e.g. I can use three languages fluently.*
2 **Language** is the ability to use signs or words to communicate. Human beings have this ability but animals do not. *e.g. This research helps us to understand how children acquire language.*
3 When you refer to the **language** of a piece of writing or a presentation, you are referring to the style in which it is written or presented. *e.g. I admire the directness of the language.*

large 1064
1 Something that is **large** is greater in size or amount than usual or average. *e.g. He's a large cat with ginger fur: have you seen him?*
2 A **large** organisation or business does a lot of work or commercial activity and employs

a lot of people. *e.g. They work in a large advertising company.*
3 **Large** is used to describe a particular size of a product, such as an item of food or clothing, which is sold in several sizes. *e.g. Do you want large or extra-large?*

large fire 1061
1 A **large fire** is a major occurrence of uncontrolled burning which destroys things. *e.g. Neighbours said a large fire had engulfed the house.*
2 A **large fire** is a big pile of burning wood or coal that you have set light to. *e.g. The scouts made a big fire and were soon singing merrily.*

largesse 1522
Largesse is the quality of giving much more than is usual or expected as gifts. *e.g. The largesse of the staff has made it possible to send the sick children on holiday.*

large vehicle 74
A **large vehicle** is a machine such as a bus, juggernaut, lorry, truck or van that carries people or things from place to place. *e.g. He could see a large vehicle parked in the field.*

lass 339, 360, 509
A **lass** is a young woman or girl. *e.g. She'd worked on the farm when she was a lass.*

last 923, 1301, 1302, 1303
1 The **last** thing or part is the one that comes at the end. *e.g. He missed the last bus.*
2 The **last** thing or part is the one at the end of a row of things. *e.g. I'm in the last classroom along the corridor.*
3 The **last** thing or part is the only one that remains. *e.g. He drank the last of the brandy.*

last (at last) 216
1 If you sign or say that something has happened **at last** or **at long last**, you mean it has happened after you have been waiting for it for a long time. *e.g. I'm free at last.*
2 If something happened **at last**, it happened at the end of a long period of time. *e.g. At last Graham stopped work and stood up.*

late 409
1 If you sign or say that something happened **late**, you mean that it happened near the end of a particular evening, day, year, et cetera. *e.g. He did call yesterday evening, but it was pretty late.*
2 If you are **late** for something, arrive **late**, get up **late**, etc., you arrive, get up, etc., after the time that was arranged or expected. *e.g. If I'm late, I'll wait in the lobby, okay?*

3 If an action or event is too **late** or happens too **late**, it is useless or ineffective because it occurs at a time after the proper or best time for it. *e.g. It's too late to change now: you've used up all the time we had.*

later   300
1 You use **later** in relation to a time or situation that is after the one that you have been referring to, or after the present one. *e.g. I returned three weeks later.*
2 You use **later** to refer to a time or situation that is after the present one. *e.g. I have to go now, but I'll see you later.*

latest   1610
Latest is used to describe something that is the most recent thing of its kind or in a series of similar things. *e.g. Her latest book is called 'Second Class Citizen'.*

late (too late)   1643
If it is **too late** for something, that thing is no longer possible or useful. If something happens **too late**, the right time for it has passed. *e.g. I realised my mistake too late.*

laughter (suppress one's laughter)   531
If you **suppress your laughter**, you stop yourself laughing, even though you want to do so. *e.g. We just couldn't suppress our laughter any longer.*

launch   151, 209
To **launch** an activity, for example a political movement, means to start it. *e.g. The government has launched a massive literacy campaign.*

launch   405
To **launch** a rocket, missile or satellite means to send it into the air or space. *e.g. Russia was the first country to launch a spacecraft into space.*

launch   1426
A **launch** is a motorboat that is used for carrying people on rivers and lakes and in harbours. *e.g. He led me out to his launch.*

launch   1430
1 To **launch** an activity, for example a political movement, means to start it. *e.g. The organisation will launch its new anti-smoking campaign next week.*
2 If a company **launches** a new product, it starts to make it available to the public. *e.g. The BDA will launch the Dictionary in December.*
3 The **launch** of something is the beginning of use of it or the start of its activities. *e.g. Sales were good immediately after the launch, but then fell sharply.*

launch pad   405
A **launch pad** is a platform from which rockets,

missiles or satellites begin their journey. *e.g. There was a problem with the launch pad, so the take-off of the rocket was delayed.*

law   401
1 The **law** is a system of rules that a society or government develops over time in order to deal with business agreements, social relationships and crimes. *e.g. Every company must by law submit accounts annually.*
2 A **law** is one of the rules in a system of law which deals with a particular type of agreement, relationship, or crime. *e.g. This newly-passed law is very clear on the subject of control of domestic animals.*

lawnmower
(manually operated lawnmower)   85
A **manually operated lawnmower** is a machine used for cutting grass which cuts the grass as it is pushed backwards and forwards over it. *e.g. He cursed when his 1950s handpowered lawnmower broke down for the second time that weekend.*

lawnmower
(mechanically operated lawnmower)   85
A **mechanically operated lawnmower** is a power-driven machine used for cutting grass. Such machines are powered by petrol or electricity *e.g. We need a petrol driven lawnmower to cut the grass.*

lay off   244
If someone is **laid off** by their employers, they have been told to leave their job, usually because there is no more work for them to do. *e.g. The directors made plans to lay off 3,000 workers.*

lay on   1317, 1333
If you **lay** something **on** another thing, you put or place it there in a careful, gentle, or neat way. *e.g. Would you lay the wreath on the coffin, please?*

lazy   667, 668, 1283
1 Someone who is **lazy** does not want to work or make any effort to do anything. *e.g. He became remarkably lazy.*
2 When you are being **lazy**, you are resting or taking things easy. *e.g. I feel really lazy in the sun.*

lead   1486
1 If you **lead** a group of moving people, you walk or ride in front of them. *e.g. He led a group of tourists through the House of Commons.*
2 If you **lead** a group of people or an organisation, you are officially in charge of them or it. *e.g. The Labour Party was led by Michael Foot.*

leader   1486
The **leader** of an organisation or a group of people is the person who is in charge of it. *e.g. He was a Deaf leader who clearly articulated the views of Deaf people in this country.*

leaf   471
The **leaf** of a tree or plant is one of the parts that are flat, thin and usually green. Many plants and trees lose their leaves in the autumn and grow new leaves in the spring. *e.g. I swept the yard until not a single leaf was left.*

league   219, 1593
A **league** is a group of people, clubs, or countries that have joined together for a particular purpose or because they share a common interest, and are ranked according to their achievements or results. *e.g. Celtic are top of the league.*

lean (against an upright surface)   1348
If you **lean** an object **against an upright surface**, you place the object so that its weight is partly supported by the thing it is resting against. *e.g. I'll lean the ladder against the wall.*

leap over   742
1 If you **leap over** something, you move quickly up into the air to get across it. *e.g. The boy managed to leap over the fence.*
2 A **leap over** something is a quick movement up into the air to get across it. *e.g. One more leap over this bar and I'll be exhausted.*

learn   1330, 1532, 1732
1 If you **learn** facts or **learn** a skill, you obtain knowledge of the facts or gain the skill as a result of studying or training. *e.g. Children are often keen to learn new languages.*
2 If you **learn** something such as a poem or the script of a play, you study or repeat the signs or words so much that you can remember them without seeing them. *e.g. We have to learn the whole poem.*
3 You sign or say that people **learn** to behave in a particular way when they gradually start behaving that way as a result of a change in their attitudes. *e.g. These people should learn to live together.*

learned   1500
1 Someone who is **learned** has gained a lot of knowledge by studying. *e.g. She is learned in the legal field.*
2 Learned books or papers have been written by someone with a lot of academic knowledge. *e.g. He is the editor of a learned journal.*

learner   1330
A **learner** is someone who is learning about a particular subject or how to do something. *e.g. She is a learner driver.*

leave   1220, 1566, 1627
1 When you **leave** a place, you go away from it. *e.g. They will leave my house at four o'clock.*
2 If you **leave** a place or institution, you go away permanently from it. *e.g. When will you leave school?*

leave out 963
If you **leave** someone **out**, they are not included in a group or activity that they want to be a part of. *e.g. She was always complaining, so they decided they would leave her out.*

leaves (falling leaves) 729
Falling leaves are the parts of a plant that are flat, thin and usually green (the leaves) when they change colour, become detached from the plant and drop onto or towards the ground. *e.g. In the late October sun, he watched the last falling leaves drifting from the beech trees.*

lecture 1247
1 A **lecture** is a presentation on a particular subject that is given in order to teach people about that subject, for example, by a university or college teacher. *e.g. I attended the lecture on psychology.*
2 If you **lecture**, you give a lecture or a series of lectures. *e.g. I don't usually lecture on this subject, so you will have to forgive my rustiness.*

lecturer 1247
A **lecturer** is a person who teaches at a university or college. *e.g. She is a lecturer in sociology.*

ledge 1339, 1637
A **ledge** is a piece of rock on the side of a cliff or mountain, which is in the shape of a narrow shelf. *e.g. He fell onto the ledge.*

Leeds 651
1 **Leeds** is a city in northern England, in West Yorkshire on the River Aire. *e.g. The Centre for the Deaf in Leeds is one of the biggest in Britain.*
2 The address of the **Leeds** Centre for the Deaf is: Centenary House, North Street, Leeds LS2 8AY.

left 1331
1 **Left** means on or towards the side which, in English writing, has the first letter of a word. For example, when you look at the word 'me', the 'm' is to the left of the 'e'. *e.g. He turned left and began strolling slowly down the street.*
2 The **left** is the left side, direction, or position. *e.g. There was a gate on the left leading into a field.*
3 The **left** one of a pair of items, such as shoes, is the one that is intended to be used on the left side of the user. *e.g. Look, it's got an 'L' on the left shoe to help you.*

left 1627
If something is **left**, it is still there after the rest has been taken away or used. *e.g. I only have two pounds left.*

left-hand 1331
Left-hand is used to describe something which is on the left side. *e.g. She made a note in the left-hand margin.*

left-handed 1331
1 Someone who is **left-handed** uses their left hand rather than their right hand for activities such as writing or throwing a ball. *e.g. They both play golf left-handed.*
2 If you do something **left-handed**, you do it with your left hand. *e.g. Let me try painting left-handed.*
3 A **left-handed** object is made for use by people who are left-handed. *e.g. I've found a left-handed pair of scissors at last!*

legislate 402
When a government or state **legislates**, it officially passes a new law. *e.g. Parliament must legislate against fox hunting.*

legislation 402
1 **Legislation** consists of the law or laws that are passed by a government or state concerning a particular situation or thing. *e.g. Current tax legislation favours the rich.*
2 **Legislation** refers to the act or process of passing a law. *e.g. The Government rejected any idea of major legislation with regard to the rights of disabled people.*

legless 819
If someone is **legless**, they are extremely drunk. *e.g. He was legless by the end of the evening and couldn't string two signs together.*

leisure 954, 1086, 1495
Leisure is time when you are not working and can do things that you enjoy doing. *e.g. We would prefer more leisure time during the week.*

lemon 1541
1 A **lemon** is a bright yellow fruit with sour juice. *e.g. Do you want a slice of lemon?*
2 **Lemon** is a drink that tastes of lemons. *e.g. A glass of lemon for me please.*

lemonade 969
Lemonade is a sweet fizzy drink that tastes of lemon. *e.g. Would you prefer orange juice or lemonade with your dinner?*

lend 77
If you **lend** someone money, or something that you own, you allow them to have it or use it for a period of time. *e.g. I had to lend him a pound to pay for the tea.*

lender 77
A **lender** is a person or an institution that lends money, etc., to people. *e.g. They were considered a good risk by lenders.*

length 1454
1 The **length** of something is the amount it measures from one end to the other. *e.g. The snake was one metre in length.*
2 A **length** of wood or other material is a

piece of it. *e.g. We found a length of wood that we can use.*

lesbian 464
1 A **lesbian** is a homosexual woman. *e.g. A number of lesbians have challenged the church's position on same sex relationships.*
2 **Lesbian** also means relating to or characteristic of lesbians, their activities, organisations and publications. *e.g. 'Out' was an excellent programme which focused on lesbian and gay issues.*

less 87, 728
1 **Less** means not as much as before or not as much as something else. *e.g. A shower uses less water than a bath.*
2 **Less** means to a smaller extent than before or than is usual. *e.g. I go to the club less than I used to.*

lessen 728
If something **lessens** or is **lessened**, it becomes smaller in size, amount, degree or importance. *e.g. Separating the sick from the healthy lessens the chance of infection.*

lesser 728
Lesser is used to indicate that something is smaller in degree, importance or amount than something else. *e.g. These customs are common in Czechoslovakia and to a lesser extent in Hungary and Romania.*

letter 174
A **letter** is a message which is written down on paper and which you send to someone in an envelope by post. *e.g. Anne received a letter from Ernst.*

level 1212, 1406, 1415
The **level** of a liquid in a container or of the water in a lake, river, or sea is the height of its surface. *e.g. The level of the lake continues to rise.*

level 1212, 1406, 1415, 1618
Something that is **level** is completely flat and with no part higher than any other. *e.g. It was a good, level field for playing cricket on.*

level 1406, 1415
1 If two things are on a **level**, they are both the same height. *e.g. The tables were on a level with each other.*
2 **Level** is used to describe the standard of something. *e.g. The level of political debate was poor.*
3 A **level** is a stage or part of a process. *e.g. I've reached level two in my course.*

level crossing 1431
A **level crossing** is a place where a railway line crosses a road at the same level (instead of using a bridge or tunnel) and the road can be blocked temporarily with special gates. *e.g. We lived in a caravan near the Wolvercote level crossing.*

level crossing closing   1451
If a **level crossing** is **closing**, special gates move so that road traffic cannot cross a railway while the stretch of railway line is in use. *e.g. Watch the level crossing closing, Mandy.*

level crossing opening   1431
If a **level crossing** is **opening**, special gates move so that road traffic can cross a railway after being prevented from doing so for safety when the stretch of railway line is in use. *e.g. Dad, Dad, the level crossing's opening, we can go now!*

liaise   883
When organisations or people **liaise** with each other, they work together and keep each other fully informed. *e.g. All staff members can help to liaise with the press for improved publicity.*

liaison   883
Liaison is the co-operation and the exchange of information between different organisations or between different sections of an organisation. *e.g. There must be good liaison between students and tutors.*

liar   528
A **liar** is someone who tells lies. *e.g. Your story isn't true—you're a liar!*

liberate   81
If someone or something **liberates** a place or a person, they set that place or person free after they had been captured or imprisoned. *e.g. The American forces liberated Paris.*

liberation   81
Liberation is the state of being freed after capture or imprisonment or political or military control by another country, area or group of people. *e.g. Their aim was the liberation of all South Africans from the yoke of apartheid.*

library   1457
A **library** is an institution or a part of an institution that keeps books, newspapers, videos (including subtitled videos), compact discs, etc., for people to read, study, or use. Most libraries allow their members to borrow items for certain periods of time. *e.g. The library has a number of subtitled videos.*

lie   528
1 A **lie** is something that someone signs or says which they know is untrue. *e.g. I hope you aren't going to fall for a lie like that.*
2 If you **lie** or **tell lies**, you sign or say something which you know is untrue. *e.g. I promise I will never lie to you again.*

lie   802
If you **lie**, you are in a horizontal position, not standing or sitting. *e.g. I like to lie in my bed thinking about getting up.*

lie   1380
If an object **lies** in a particular place, it is in that place, often for some time. *e.g. The sheets of metal lie rusting on the ground.*

lie down   802
1 If you **lie down**, you move into a horizontal position, usually in order to rest or sleep. *e.g. I have to lie down for a while, then I'll be fine.*
2 A **lie-down** is a short rest, usually in bed. *e.g. He went for a lie-down.*

lie in   1138
1 If you **lie in**, you stay in bed later than usual in the morning. *e.g. I think I'll lie in tomorrow.*
2 A **lie-in** is an occasion when you stay in bed later than usual in the morning. *e.g. A good lie-in is what you need.*

life   964, 1186
1 **Life** is the quality which people, animals and plants have when they are not dead and which objects and substances do not have. *e.g. Her last hours of life were peaceful.*
2 Someone's **life** is their state of being alive. *e.g. He nearly lost his life.*
3 **Life** is the events and experiences that happen to people, either generally or in a particular place. *e.g. Life is harder for women.*

lifeboat   1427
1 A **lifeboat** is a boat which is sent out from a port or harbour in order to rescue people who are in danger at sea. *e.g. The lifeboat was called out again during the night.*
2 A **lifeboat** is a small boat which is carried on a ship and which people on the ship use to escape when the ship is in danger of sinking. *e.g. The ship's cargo was intact and the lifeboat was in place.*

lift   692
A **lift** is a device like a small room that moves up and down inside a vertical shaft in a building. You can travel in it or take goods from one floor to another in it. *e.g. They've put in a lift for disabled persons.*

lift   1201
1 If you **lift** something, you raise it up. *e.g. 'Lift!' he signed to the fork-lift truck driver.*
2 A **lift** is a device like a small room that moves up and down inside a vertical shaft in a building. You can travel in it or take goods from one floor to another in it. *e.g. Take the lift if you like, but I'll beat you on foot.*

lift   1453
If you **lift** something, you pick it up, holding it with a hand at each end, ready to move it out of the way or to another place. *e.g. Lift that box off the coffee table for a second, please.*

lift off   405
1 When an aircraft or rocket **lifts off**, it leaves the ground and rises into the air. *e.g. As the rocket began to lift off, the ground seemed to open beneath them.*
2 **Lift-off** or a **lift-off** is the act of launching a rocket into space, when it leaves the ground and rises into the air. *e.g. 'We have lift-off!' exclaimed the controller, as the rocket struggled upwards in defiance of gravity.*

light   1376, 1624
1 Something that is **light** does not weigh very much or weighs less than you would expect it to. *e.g. We need a light metal like aluminium.*
2 A **light** meal is small in quantity. *e.g. We had a light lunch, and then went shopping.*

light   1466
1 **Light** is the brightness that lets you see things that comes from the sun, moon, light or lamps. *e.g. Heat and light are essential to our comfort.*
2 **Light** is the natural light that occurs during the daytime and that is produced by the sun. *e.g. We wanted to get home during the light.*
3 Something that is **light** in colour is pale and not strong or bright in colour. *e.g. She was wearing a light blue blouse.*

light   1698
A **light** is a device usually powered by electricity, which when turned on, produces light in a house or other building, or in a street. *e.g. We need a light in this hallway. It's dark.*

light   1707
Light is the brightness which comes from the sun, moon, light or lamps that lets you see things. *e.g. Heat and light are essential to our comfort.*

light a match   873
If you **light a match** you make a small, thin bit of wood with a chemical substance on the end (a match) start burning, for example by brushing it hard against the side of a matchbox or some other rough surface. *e.g. Please light a match so that I can see where I've dropped my keys.*

lighten   1467
When something **lightens** or when you **lighten** it, it becomes less dark in colour. *e.g. After the rain stops, the sky will lighten.*

lighter   159
A **lighter** or **cigarette lighter** is a small device which produces a flame which you can use to light cigarettes, pipes, et cetera. *Can I borrow your lighter? I've run out of matches.*

lighthouse   1716
A **lighthouse** is a tower containing a powerful flashing lamp that is built on the coast or on a small island or rock in the sea. Lighthouses are used to guide ships or to warn them of danger. *e.g. She walked down the quay towards the lighthouse.*

lightning 304
Lightning is the very bright flashes of light in the sky that can be seen during a thunderstorm. *e.g. He was struck by lightning and nearly died.*

light on 1698
If a **light** is **on**, it produces light. *e.g. The light was on in the front room.*

light rain 1192
You sign or say that there is **light rain**, or a **light rain**, when a little water falls gently from the clouds in small drops. *e.g. When we arrived in Wales, a light rain was falling.*

like 423, 424
1 If you sign or say that one person or thing is **like** another, you mean that they have similar characteristics. *e.g. She's nothing like I imagined.*
2 If you ask someone what something is **like**, you are asking them to indicate what it is similar to. *e.g. What did they taste like?*
3 You can use **like** to introduce an example of the thing that you have just mentioned. *e.g. You only get them in big countries, like Brazil or India.*
4 You can use **like** to sign or say that someone or something is in the same situation as another person or thing. *e.g. She died in childbirth, like Sir Thomas More's wife Jane.*
5 If you indicate that something is **like** you remembered or imagined it, you mean that it is the way you remembered or imagined it. *e.g. This is just like I thought it would be: it's uncanny!*

like 710
If you **like** something, you enjoy it. *e.g. I like going to the pictures so much I bought a season ticket.*

like 1273
1 If you **like** something, you enjoy it or find it pleasant or atttractive. *e.g. I like reading.*
2 If you **like** someone, you enjoy being with them because they are interesting and pleasant. *e.g. She's a nice girl, I like her.*
3 If you ask someone how they **like** something, you are asking them for their opinion or judgement about it and whether they enjoy it. *e.g. Do you like it here?*
4 If you **like** something such as a particular course of action or way of behaving, you approve of it. *e.g. He liked the examination procedure.*
5 If you sign or say that you would **like** something, or would **like** to do something, you are indicating a wish or desire that you have. *e.g. He would have liked a drink before he started.*
6 Someone's **likes** are the things that they enjoy or find pleasant. *e.g. Try to discover your guest's various likes and dislikes.*

like (if you like) 1004
You use **if you like** to indicate that someone can decide for themself whether or not they wish to do something. *e.g. You can do more puzzles if you like, or come with us.*

limit 152
A **limit** is the greatest amount, extent or degree of something that is possible or allowed. *e.g. Ten students per class is our limit.*

limited 1446
Something that is **limited** is not very large in amount or degree. *e.g. The choice was limited.*

line 836
A **line** is a narrow piece of rope or wire on which you hang clothes or other objects so that they will become dry. *e.g. There is a line for hanging clothes in the basement.*

line 1024
A **line** of people or things is a number of them positioned one behind the other. *e.g. On each side of the road was a line of poplar trees.*

liner 1425
A **liner** is a large ship in which people travel long distances or go on holiday cruises. *e.g. She stood on the deck of a liner bound from Southampton to New York.*

liner/ship sailing 1425
If a **liner** or **ship** is **sailing**, it is moving across water. *e.g. There was a small passenger ship sailing up the Hudson River.*

line up 1024
If people **line up** or if you **line** them **up**, they form a queue. *e.g. I will ask the team to line up to receive their medals.*

link 898
1 You sign or say that two things are **linked** when there is a relationship between them, for example because one causes the other. *e.g. Evidence has been offered linking the group to a series of bomb attacks.*
2 You sign or say that two places or objects are **linked** when there is a physical connection between them so that you can travel or communicate between them. *e.g. The canal linking the Pacific and Atlantic oceans was completed in 1914.*
3 A **link** between two things is a relationship between them. *e.g. There is a clear link between rates of unemployment and criminal activity.*
4 A **link** is a physical connection allowing travel or communication between two places or objects. *e.g. A telephone link between Washington and Moscow was established.*

linoleum 1415
Linoleum, often called **lino**, is a floor covering which is made of cloth covered with a hard shiny substance. *e.g. Shiny linoleum floors were common in the fifties.*

lion 1168
A **lion** is an animal with brownish-yellow fur

which looks like a big cat and kills and eats other animals. A female lion is often called a lioness. *e.g. The lion is a supreme hunter.*

lipread 814
If someone can **lipread**, they can understand what you are saying by watching the way your mouth and lips move. *e.g. She will try to lipread the teacher.*

lipreader 814
A **lipreader** is someone who tries to understand what you are saying by watching the way your mouth and lips move. *e.g. She was a very good lipreader at school.*

lipspeak 814
If you **lipspeak**, you move your mouth and lips to form words in such a way that people who cannot hear will be able to watch you and try to understand what is being said. *e.g. I know you are a qualified interpreter, but can you lipspeak for our client?*

lipspeaker 814
A **lipspeaker** is someone who, often as a job, moves their mouth and lips to form words in such a way that people who cannot hear will be able to watch him or her and try to understand what is being said. *e.g. He is listed as a lipspeaker in the directory.*

liquidate 544
When someone **liquidates** a company, they close it down, usually because it has large debts that it cannot pay. *e.g. The official receiver decided to liquidate the company.*

list 196, 720
1 A **list** is a set of things which are written down one below the other. *e.g. Look at the list of things to be mended.*
2 To **list** a set of things means to mention them all one after the other. *e.g. There was a label on each case listing its contents.*

list 607
A **list** is a set of things which are written down one below the other. *e.g. Look at your list of things to be mended.*

listen 1253
1 If you **listen** to someone who is talking or **listen** to a sound, you give your attention to the person or the sound. *e.g. Listen carefully to what he says.*
2 If you **listen** for a sound, you keep alert or are ready to hear it if it occurs. *e.g. She sat quite still, listening for her baby's cry.*

little 612, 618
1 **Little** is used to indicate that there is only a small amount of something or almost none at all, often when this is not enough. *e.g. Bill and*

I had little money left.
2 **Little** may mean not very often or to only a small extent. *e.g. Richardson interrupted little and was a model of concentration.*
3 A **little** of something is a small amount of it, but not very much. *e.g. He knew a little French.*

little 637
A **little** of something is a small amount or piece of it. *e.g. Just a little of the cheddar for me, please.*

little 1213, 1574
1 A **little** child is young and therefore quite small in size. *e.g. The little girl played in the sand.*
2 Your **little** sister or brother is younger than you are. *e.g. She was bringing her little brother Kevin with her.*
3 You use **little** to describe something that is short from bottom to top. *e.g. It's just a little evergreen tree for the patio.*

little 1450
You use **little** to describe something that is small in physical size. *e.g. We gave her a little pot with a message inside it.*

live 23
If someone **lives** in a particular place, their home is there. *e.g. Where do you live?*

live 964, 1186
1 If you **live** in a particular place, your home is there. *e.g. I live quite near to the motorway.*
2 If you **live** in particular circumstances or **live** a particular kind of life, you are in those circumstances or your life is of that kind. *e.g. We had to live simply.*
3 To **live** means to be alive . *e.g. Women live longer than men.*
4 A **live** television or radio programme is one that is broadcast at the same time as it happens, rather than being recorded first. *e.g. The Olympics will be shown live.*
5 A **live** performance is done before an audience rather than being recorded and then broadcasted or shown on film. *e.g. My parents prefer to see plays live on stage rather than on television.*

Liverpool 464
1 **Liverpool** is a city in North West England on the River Mersey and is the administrative centre of Merseyside. *e.g. She was born in Liverpool in a terraced house overlooking the Mersey.*
2 The address of the Merseyside Society for the Deaf in **Liverpool** is: Queens Drive, Liverpool L13 0DJ, West Derby.

Liverpudlian 464
To be **Liverpudlian** is to be from or characteristic of Liverpool. *e.g. The person sat next to me was a Liverpudlian.*

livid 1196
Someone who is **livid** is extremely angry. *e.g. He wouldn't let me into the disco! I was livid.*

llama 1673
A **llama** is a South American animal that is like a small camel without a hump. Llamas have thick hair on their bodies. *e.g. We saw llamas during our travels in Peru.*

loads 473, 1053, 1722
If you refer to **loads** of something, or a **load** of something, you mean a lot of it. *e.g. They had loads of money thirty years ago.*

loads 813, 1010
If you refer to **loads** of something or a **load** of something, you are referring emphatically to a very large amount of it. *e.g. There are loads of books in his study.*

loaf 1327
A **loaf** is bread that has been shaped and baked as a large lump which you can slice. *e.g. The price of a loaf has gone up again.*

loan 78
1 A **loan** is a sum of money that you borrow. *e.g. It was impossible to get a bank loan.*
2 If someone gives you a **loan** of something or if you have the **loan** of it, you borrow it from them. *e.g. He asked for the loan of twelve dozen glasses.*
3 If something is on **loan**, it has been borrowed. *e.g. Most of his books are on loan from the library.*

loathe 1007
If you **loathe** something or someone, you dislike them very much or find them very unpleasant. *e.g. I loathe him because he is so big-headed.*

local 983, 1018
1 **Local** means responsible for or concerned with a small area of a country, for example a county or city. *e.g. Local government expenditure is down by 10%.*
2 **Local** means existing in or belonging to the area in which you live or work or the area to which you are referring. *e.g. Members are drawn from sections of the local community.*

locality 983, 1018
A **locality** is a small area of a country or city. *e.g. People living in the locality of Marshall Street are advised not to drink tap water.*

locate 328
If you **locate** something or someone, you find them. *e.g. If you do locate him, call me.*

location 983, 1018
A **location** is a place, especially the place where something happens or where

something is situated. *e.g. The new job involves a new employer, new location and new colleagues.*

loch 986
A **loch** is a lake. *e.g. Loch Lomond is famous but not for monsters.*

lock 67
1 When you **lock** something such as a door, drawer or case, you fasten it by means of a key, so that other people cannot open it. *e.g. I tried the front door and found that it was locked.*
2 A **lock** is a device which is used to keep shut a door, drawer, case, etc., by means of a key, so that other people cannot open it. *e.g. The lock was made of steel.*

lock and key (under lock and key) 67
If something is **under lock and key**, it is in a room or container which has been locked. *e.g. She kept her private papers under lock and key in her bedroom.*

lock in 67
If you **lock** someone **in**, you put them in a room, prison cell, or other place and lock the door so that they cannot get out. *e.g. The prisoners were locked in their cells at nine o'clock every night.*

lock out 67
If you **lock** someone **out** of a place, you prevent them from entering it by locking the doors. *e.g. She had been locked out of the house in her nightdress.*

lock up 67
When you **lock up**, you make sure that all the doors and windows of a building are properly closed or locked so that burglars cannot get in. *e.g. Don't forget to lock up when you leave.*

lock with a key 250
When you **lock** something **with a key**, such as a door or a container that has a lock, you fasten it by placing the key in the lock and turning it, so that other people cannot open it. *e.g. He locked his room with a key.*

locum 1664
A **locum** fills an office for a time or temporarily takes the place of another person; the English word is used especially with reference to a doctor or clergyman. *e.g. My doctor was on holiday so we went to see the locum.*

lodge 1239
If you **lodge** in someone else's house, or you are **lodged** there, you pay to live there, often for only a short period of time. *e.g. I hoped I'd be able to lodge with his aunt.*

logical 1646
A **logical** argument or analysis is one in which

each step or point must be true if the step that came before it is true. *e.g. His paper presents a logical analysis of the issue.*

London   521
1 **London** is a city in South East England on the River Thames, and is the capital of the United Kingdom. *e.g. David Buxton is a Deaf Liberal Democrat councillor for the Borough of Southwark in London.*
2 The address of the British Deaf Association's **London** Office is: 25, Cockspur Street, London SW1Y 5PN.

lone   533, 534, 555
A **lone** person or thing is alone or is the only one in a particular place or group. *e.g. I was left, a lone figure on an empty platform.*

lonely   1138
Someone who is **lonely** is unhappy because they do not have any friends or do not have anyone to enjoy conversation with. *e.g. Everyone is on holiday this week; I feel lonely.*

loner   533, 534, 555
A **loner** is a person who prefers to be alone rather than with a group of people, and who perhaps has opinions which are different from other people's. *e.g. He was aloof, a loner. He kept his distance.*

long   460
A **long** distance or journey is a great distance or covers a great distance. *e.g. It may look a long way on the map, but it isn't.*

long   543, 1284
1 You use **long** to indicate that a great amount of time passes while something is happening or is in existence. *e.g. I won't be long finishing this video.*
2 A **long** period of time, event or task lasts for a great amount of time or takes a great amount of time. *e.g. After his lecture, there was a long pause.*
3 **Long** is used to ask questions about amounts of time, or to give information about amounts of time. *e.g. How long have you been married?*

long   1454
You use **long** when giving information or asking questions about how much something measures from one end to the other. *e.g. The box is four feet long.*

long ago   1480
You use **long ago** to refer to past time. If something happened a long time ago, a great deal of time has passed since it happened. *e.g. It happened in schools long ago.*

long-handled brush   104
A **long-handled brush** is a broom. It is

made of wood, plastic or metal with a large number of bristles at one end to which a long handle is attached. It is used for sweeping the floor or outside areas such as paths, et cetera. *e.g. He bought a long-handled brush from the hardware store.*

long jump   733
The **long jump** or **long-jump** is a sports event where competitors try to leap as far as possible, usually into a sandpit, after a run-up. The length of each jump is measured and the winner is the person who has achieved the largest jump. *e.g. She won the long jump, to her own surprise.*

long jumper   733
A **long jumper** or **long-jumper** is someone who takes part in the long jump at sports events. *e.g. He's one of our best long jumpers.*

long time   1722
You can use a **long time** to mean for a great amount of days, months or years. *e.g. He has been a member of the BDA a long time.*

look   327
1 If you sign or say that someone should **look** at something or in some direction, you suggest that they turn their eyes to see what it is like or what is there. *e.g. You look in the furniture department and I'll check the bargain basement.*
2 To **look** at something also means to read or examine it, usually not thoroughly. *e.g. Are they your answers? Can I look?*
3 A **look** somewhere or at something is the act of ensuring a clear line of vision and turning your eyes to see what is happening there. *e.g. One look at a souffle during cooking and you will completely ruin it.*

look   755, 788
1 If you **look** in a particular direction, you direct your eyes in that direction, especially so that you can see what is there or see what something is like. *e.g. Look at that dog outside.*
2 If you **look** at something that is moving or happening, or at the television, you watch it. *e.g. Can I just look at this for five minutes, then I'll come.*

look after   333, 777
1 If you **look after** someone or something, you do what is necessary in order to keep them safe, well, or in good condition. *e.g. Your husband ought to be looking after that; it'll be valuable one day.*
2 If you **look after** something, you are responsible for it and deal with it. *e.g. The duty of the local authority is to look after the interests of local people.*

look around   747
If you **look around** a building or place, or have a **look around** it, you walk round it and look at all the different parts of it. *e.g. We enjoyed having a look around the University.*

look as if   1243
If it **looks as if** something is the case, it seems to be true. *e.g. It looks as if the shop has closed down.*

look for   332, 610
If you **look for** someone or something, you try to find them. *e.g. June was looking for you everywhere.*

look (have a look)   327, 755
If you **have a look** at an object, problem, or situation, you study it with your eyes. *e.g. Let's have a look at what's happening through the square window, shall we?*

look like   1243
If it **looks like** something is the case, it seems to be true. *e.g. It looks like you are in luck! Here she is.*

look out   327
If you **look out** for something, you make sure you notice it when it is there. *e.g. Look out for an announcement in the British Deaf News.*

lord   450
1 **Lord** is the title used in front of the name of British earls, viscounts, marquesses, et cetera. *e.g. Lord Salisbury is President of the British Deaf Association.*
2 **Lord** is also used as part of the title of certain officials of very high rank in Britain. *e.g. We saw the procession of the Lord Mayor of London.*
3 In former times, especially in medieval times, a **lord** was a man who owned land or property and who had power and authority over other people. *e.g. Serfs would provide their lord with labour and produce, and in exchange he would protect them.*
4 A **lord** is a man who has a high rank in the British nobility. *e.g. Lords and Ladies are present at Royal ceremonies.*
5 In the Christian church, people refer to God and to Jesus Christ as **Lord**. *e.g. Let us praise the Lord.*

lorry   74
A **lorry** is a large vehicle that is used to transport goods by road. *e.g. He ran across the road and the lorry couldn't possibly stop.*

lose   1724
1 If you **lose** something, you do not know where it is, for example because you forgot where you put it. *e.g. If you lose your ticket, you'll be in trouble.*
2 If you **lose** a competition or argument, someone does better than you and defeats you. *e.g. I hope we won't lose any more football matches this season.*

3 If you **lose** something such as a job, you no longer have it. *e.g. When the women lost their jobs at the factory, they staged a protest.*

lose confidence　　　　　　　　　　646
If you **lose confidence**, you feel less sure about your abilities, qualities and ideas. *e.g. At the meetings, people ignore me, and I lose confidence very easily.*

lost　　　　　　　　　　　　　　　　1724
If you are **lost**, you don't know where you are or you can't find your way. *e.g. Sean got lost trying to find the studio.*

lost for words　　　　　　　　　　1548
If you are **lost for words**, you are temporarily uncertain what to sign or say, usually because you are surprised or cannot think of a good way to express your thoughts. *e.g. I was lost for words when asked to describe the person I had just met.*

lot　　　　　　　　　　　473, 1010, 1053
A **lot** of something, or **lots** of something, is a large amount of it. *e.g. A big house with a lot of windows is what I want.*

lots　　　　　　473, 813, 1010, 1053, 1722
Lots of something, or a **lot** of something, is a large amount of it. *e.g. There were lots of broken windows.*

loud　　　　　　　　　　　　　　　　521
1 A **loud** sound or producer of sound consists of or produces a large amount of noise. *e.g. Your hearing aid has a loud whistle.*
2 If you sign or say that something is **loud**, you mean that it makes a lot of noise. *e.g. Can you turn it down: it's rather loud.*

lousy　　　　　　　　　　　　　740, 812
If you describe something as **lousy**, you mean that it is of very bad quality or that you do not like it at all. *e.g. I thought that game show on television last night was lousy.*

lousy　　　　　　　　　　　　　　　825
If something is extremely dirty and unpleasant, you can describe it as **lousy**. *e.g. I couldn't believe it. The hotel room was lousy. It looked as if it had never been cleaned.*

love　　　　　　　　　　　　　235, 1660
1 If you **love** someone, you have very strong feelings of affection towards them and feel romantically or sexually attracted to them, and they are very important to you. *e.g. Trevor told me he loved Jane.*
2 If you **love** someone, you feel that their happiness is very important to you, and usually show this feeling in the way you behave towards them. *e.g. He loved his son.*
3 If you **love** something, you feel that it is

important and want to protect it or help it. *e.g. People who love freedom will die for it if necessary.*
4 If you **love** something, you like it very much. *e.g. My wife and I love going to the pictures on Saturday mornings.*
5 **Love** is a deep liking for something or enjoyment of it, or a belief that it is important. *e.g. Her love of the countryside was reflected in her work for the National Trust.*

love　　　　　　　　　　　　　　1477
1 If you **love** someone, you have very strong feelings of affection towards them and feel romantically or sexually attracted to them, and they are very important to you. *e.g. I love you, Carol.*
2 **Love** is very strong feelings of affection towards someone who you are romantically or sexually attracted to. *e.g. It was obvious they had married for love.*
3 If you **love** someone, you feel that their happiness is very important to you, and usually show this feeling in the way you behave towards them. *e.g. 'I love my grandchildren,' signed Ruby.*
4 **Love** is the feeling that a person's happiness is very important to you, and the way you show this feeling in your behaviour towards them. *e.g. Children need love and understanding.*
5 If you **love** something, you feel that it is important and want to protect it or help it. *e.g. I teach BSL because of my love for the language.*
6 If you **love** something, you like it very much. *e.g. We love dancing.*
7 **Love** is a deep liking for something or enjoyment of it, or a belief that it is important. *e.g. His love of sport took him all over the world.*

lovely　　　　　　　　　　　　175, 465
1 Someone or something that is **lovely** is very beautiful and therefore pleasing to look at, watch, or listen to. *e.g. I think Wales is a lovely country.*
2 A **lovely** person is one that you like very much because they are friendly, kind or generous. *e.g. We live next door to a lovely retired couple.*
3 If you describe something as **lovely**, you are signing or saying how much you like it. *e.g. It was a lovely wedding.*

lovely　　　　　　　　　　　　345, 468
If you sign or say that something tastes **lovely**, you are indicating that you like the flavour of it. *e.g. My husband cooks a lovely jugged hare.*

low　　　　　　　　　　　　1211, 1213
1 Something that is **low** measures a short distance from the bottom to the top, or from the ground to the top. *e.g. I've got a low table that your daughter can put her book on.*
2 **Low** means small in amount, value or degree. *e.g. Temperatures are low on the Continent at present.*

3 If the quality or standard of something is **low**, it is bad. *e.g. This is a low-grade material, but cheap.*
4 **Low** is used to describe people who are near the bottom of a particular scale of system. *e.g. She started low, but she's worked her way up to Personal Assistant.*
5 If a sound is **low**, it is not loud or high-pitched. *e.g. It's like a low vibratring noise in my left ear.*

low　　　　　　　　　　　　　　1343
1 If the quality or standard of something is **low**, it is bad. *e.g. It was dreadful that they had to put up with such a low standard of living.*
2 **Low** is used to describe people who are near the bottom of a particular scale or system. *e.g. He is a junior executive of low grade.*
3 You also use **low** to describe people and actions which are not respectable and which you disapprove of. *e.g. Mixing with low company will get you nowhere.*

low tide　　　　　　　　　　　　1047
Low tide is the period when the level of the sea on the shore is at its lowest. *e.g. The rocks were exposed at low tide.*

luck　　　　　　　　　　　　466, 1248
Luck is success or good fortune that does not come from your own planning, abilities or efforts. *e.g. He wished me luck.*

luckily　　　　　　　　　　　　1248
You may add **luckily** to a comment to indicate you are glad something happened. *e.g. Luckily, the weather was good for our garden fete.*

lucky　　　　　　　　466, 1077, 1248
1 Someone is **lucky** when they have something which is very desirable or when they are in a desirable situation. *e.g. She was a lucky girl, your sister, to have such a good teacher.*
2 You sign or say that someone is **lucky** when they always seem to have good luck. *e.g. I am always lucky at cards.*
3 When you describe an event or situation as **lucky**, you mean that it had good effects or consequences although it happened by chance and not as a result of planning or preparation. *e.g. It was lucky I had cooked plenty of food, for unexpected visitors arrived.*
4 People describe something they wear or have with them as **lucky** when they believe it helps them to be successful. *e.g. He wore his lucky sweater whenever he played tennis.*

ludicrous　　　　　　　　　　　515
If you describe something as **ludicrous**, you mean that it is extremely foolish, unreasonable or unsuitable. *e.g. One teacher for every 100 pupils was ludicrous.*

luggage　　　　　　　　　　　　　15
Luggage consists of the suitcases, bags, etc., that

you have with you when you are travelling. *e.g. I left my luggage in the hotel foyer.*

lunch   730, 1501
1 **Lunch** is a meal that you have in the middle of the day. *e.g. What did you have for lunch?*
2 **Lunch** is the time around midday when you have a meal. *e.g. Next day, after lunch, I visited the doctor.*
3 When you **lunch**, you eat a meal in the middle of the day, especially at a restaurant. *e.g. Why don't you two lunch with me tomorrow?*

lunch (packed lunch)   1310
A **packed lunch** is a cold midday meal which is wrapped up or kept in a container so that it is portable and ready to eat at once. *e.g. You may*

be able to get a packed lunch from the Youth Hostel before you leave.

lure   845
1 To **lure** someone means to attract them and tempt them to do something or go somewhere. *e.g. Jeff lured me away.*
2 A **lure** is an attractive quality that something has. *e.g. The lure of being able to work full-time with other Deaf researchers was sufficient reason to give the offer serious consideration.*

lust   1542
1 **Lust** is a feeling of strong sexual desire for someone. *e.g. He caught himself gazing with idle lust at one of the girls who served behind the bar.*
2 A **lust** for something is a very strong and

eager desire to possess or gain it. *e.g. The lust for power led him to kill.*
3 If you **lust** for or after someone or something, you desire them passionately. *e.g. I have to admit that I lusted after him for weeks.*

luxurious   1649
Something that is **luxurious** is not necessary, but is very comfortable or pleasurable, and often expensive. *e.g. Their new car is really luxurious—soft leather cushions and everything.*

luxury   1649
Luxury is very great comfort, especially among beautiful and expensive surroundings and possessions. *e.g. At our holiday hotel, we lived in luxury.*

M, m

M
M is the thirteenth letter of the British manual and English alphabets. See page 852.

mac   288
A **mac** is the same as a mackintosh. *e.g. I'll take my plastic mac in case I get caught in a shower.*

machine   608, 1193
A **machine** is a piece of equipment which does a particular type of work and which usually uses power from an engine or electricity. *e.g. The machine is being repaired.*

machinery   608
Machinery means equipment in general which uses electricity or power from an engine. *e.g. We export textile machinery to the Far East.*

mackintosh   288
Also spelled **macintosh**.
A **mackintosh** is a raincoat, especially one made from a particular kind of waterproof cloth. *e.g. Have you got your mackintosh; it looks like rain.*

mad   1196
You sign or say that someone is **mad** when they are very angry. *e.g. Jeanny gets mad when you talk like that.*

mad   1569
1 Someone who is **mad** has a mind that is considered not to work in a normal way, so that their behaviour is very strange and sometimes frightening. *e.g. She was married to a man who had gone mad.*
2 You can say that someone is **mad** when they do, sign or say things that you think are very

foolish. *e.g. You must be mad.*
3 You use **mad** to describe behaviour that is wild and uncontrolled. *e.g. I was dashing around in a mad panic.*

magazine   283
A **magazine** is a publication with a paper cover which is issued regularly, usually weekly or monthly and which contains articles, stories, photographs and advertisements. *e.g. I found the recipe in a woman's magazine.*

maggot   593
A **maggot** is a tiny, roughly tube-shaped creature that looks like a very small worm. Maggots turn into flies. *e.g. If I were a maggot, I don't think I'd like to go fishing.*

maggot / worm crawling   593
A **maggot** or **worm crawling** is a small, roughly tube shaped creature (maggot or worm) which is moving by flexing its body in a wave-like motion. *e.g. There is a maggot crawling along in there, and I wish you would kill it!*

magic   1727
1 In fairy stories, **magic** is a special power that can make apparently impossible things happen. For example, it can control events in nature or make people disappear. *e.g. There was magic in the wood. All the animals could sign.*
2 **Magic** is the art and skill of performing tricks to entertain people, for example by seeming to make things appear and disappear. *e.g. He was in the bedroom practising magic tricks.*

magician   1727
A **magician** is a person who performs tricks as a form of entertainment. *e.g. They had booked Doug*

as a magician for the children's party.

maid   1011
A **maid** is a woman who works as a servant in a hotel or private house. *e.g. The maid will bring you your wine in a moment.*

mail   174
1 **Mail** is the letters and parcels that the post office delivers to you. *e.g. Margaret's job is to sort the mail.*
2 The **mail** is the system used by the post office for collecting and delivering letters and parcels. *e.g. Send the information to me by mail.*

mail   1499, 1703
1 **Mail** is the letters and parcels that the post office delivers for you. *e.g. Take the mail when you leave.*
2 If you **mail** something, you post it. *e.g. The exam results were mailed on Friday.*

mail / post a letter   1499, 1703
If you **mail** or **post a letter**, you send a letter to someone by putting the correct postage on it and placing it in a postbox for collection by the Royal Mail, which delivers it. *e.g. I posted the letter to you on Thursday.*

mainframe computer   420
A **mainframe computer** or **mainframe** is a large, powerful computer which can be used by many people at the same time, and which can do complicated tasks. *e.g. The information will be transferred to the mainframe computer.*

maintenance   1008, 1504, 1507, 1679
Maintenance is money that someone gives to a person who they are legally responsible for,

but are not living with, in order to pay for necessary things such as food and clothes. For example, a man may have to pay maintenance to his ex-wife after a divorce. *e.g. The solicitor has told me what my maintenance will be.*

major   1064
1 You use **major** when you want to describe something which is more important, serious or significant than other things. *e.g. There have been many problems; finding a solicitor was the major one.*
2 You use **major** to describe something important, serious or significant. *e.g. There will be major changes.*

majority   373, 1017, 1064
The **majority** of people or things in a group is a number of them that form more than half of the group. *e.g. A majority of Deaf people over the age of 40 went to residential school.*

make   1519
1 If you **make** something, you create or produce it by putting different things together or by some kind of effort; used especially when you are signing or speaking about activities such as cooking, sewing or handicrafts. *e.g. Shelly likes to make all her own clothes.*
2 If you **make** a meal or a drink, you prepare it so that it is ready for eating or drinking. *e.g. I'll go and make some dinner.*

make a note of   721
When you **make a note of** something, you write it down to help you remember it. *e.g. Make a note of Jerry's address please, Joyce.*

make-believe   54
You refer to someone's behaviour as **make-believe** when they pretend that things are better or more exciting than they really are. *e.g. His whole life these days was a game of make-believe.*

make notes   720
If you **make notes**, you write down things that you want to remember later, for example what someone signed or said, or what you plan to sign or say. *e.g. I must make notes of the lecture on grammar.*

make porridge   723
When you **make porridge** for breakfast, you cook oats by sprinkling them into water or milk and stirring. *e.g. Murray makes perfect porridge.*

male   1539
1 A **male** is an animal that belongs to the sex that cannot have babies or lay eggs. *e.g. Male hamsters do not like courgettes, for some unknown reason.*
2 You can refer to a **man** or a boy as a **male**. *e.g. He claimed that the typical American male*

loves baseball and peanut butter.
3 If somebody is **male**, they are a man. *e.g. Your boss was promoted because he is male.*

mam   838
Your **mam** is your mother. *e.g. My mam has gone to the shops.*

mammy   838
People often call their mother **mammy**. The English word is usually used by children. *e.g. What did your mammy sign?*

man   178, 1539, 1673
A **man** is an adult male human being. *e.g. He was a man in his fifties.*

manage   216
If you **manage** to do something, you succeed in doing it, even though it may have taken a long period of time, sometimes a longer time than it should have done or you would have wished. *e.g. I've managed to mark all the homework, but it has taken me three weeks to do so.*

manage   272
If you **manage** an organisation, business, or system, you are responsible for controlling it. *e.g. It seems to be better managed than the other car companies.*

manage   1433
1 If you **manage** an organisation, business, or system, you are responsible for controlling it. *e.g. I know you can manage this company, Geoff.*
2 When people **manage**, they are able to continue with an acceptable way of life, although they do not have much money. *e.g. I always manage, but it is never easy.*

manage   1645
When people **manage**, they are able to continue with an acceptable way of life, although they do not have much money. *e.g. She signed that she found it hard to manage on state benefits.*

management   272, 1433
Management is the control and organising of a business or other organisation. *e.g. He was sacked for poor management.*

manager   272, 450, 957, 1433
1 A **manager** is a person who is responsible for running a business, department or other organisation. *e.g. What you need is advice from your bank manager.*
2 A **manager** is a person who is responsible for the business interests of a singer, pop group, actor or entertainer. *e.g. He is the manager of U2.*
3 A **manager** is a person who is responsible for organising and training a sports team. *e.g. The Manchester United manager refused to comment after the match.*

manageress   450, 957
1 A **manageress** is a woman who is responsible for running a business, department or other organisation. *e.g. The manageress is not here today, I'm afraid.*
2 A **manageress** is a woman who is responsible for the business interests of a singer, pop group, actor or entertainer. *e.g. She doesn't need a manageress—she needs talent!*
3 A **manageress** is a woman who is responsible for organising and training a sports team. *e.g. If I were the manageress, I'd put her on the right wing straightaway.*

mandatory   2
If something is **mandatory**, there is a law or rule stating that it must be done. *e.g. It is mandatory to wear seat-belts in a car.*

manipulate   272
1 If you **manipulate** people, you skillfully cause them to behave in a way that you want them to. *e.g. Small children are sometimes able to manipulate grown ups.*
2 If you **manipulate** a situation or system, you cause it to develop or operate in the way that you want it to. *e.g. She manipulated the situation for her own benefit.*

manipulator   272
A **manipulator** is a person who skilfully controls events, systems, or people. *e.g. He has a reputation as a financial manipulator.*

manner   1475
Your **manner** is the way in which you sign or speak and behave on a particular occasion. *e.g. The judge was impressed by his manner.*

manners   1475
Manners are ways of behaving, signing or speaking, particularly when they are considered to be good or polite. *e.g. She had beautiful manners.*

many   473, 1053, 1722
You use **many** to refer to a large number of things or people. *e.g. Many people have been killed.*

many   1010
You use **many** to refer to a large number of things or people when you are emphasising how large the number is. *e.g. Many people were killed in the plane crash.*

marble   246
A **marble** is one of the small balls used in the game of marbles. *e.g. He swopped his best marble.*

marbles   246
Marbles is a children's game played with small balls made of coloured glass known as marbles. You roll your marble along the

ground and try to hit an opponent's marble with it. *e.g. He loves marbles.*

margarine 689
Margarine is a yellow substance that looks like butter and is made from vegetable oil and animal fats. You can spread it on bread or use it for cooking. *e.g. Melt the margarine in a frying pan.*

marge 689
Marge is the same as margarine. *e.g. Do you mind marge on your toast?*

market 268
1 To **market** a product means to sell it in an organised way and on a large scale. *e.g. The felt-tip pen was first marketed by the Japanese.*
2 The **market** for a product is the number of people who want to buy it. *e.g. There is a large market for this item.*
3 If something is on the **market**, it is available for people to buy. *e.g. That style has been on the market for three years.*

marketing 268
Marketing is that part of business which is concerned with the way a product is sold, for example its price and the way it is advertised. *e.g. Steve is in charge of marketing.*

marmalade 1324
Marmalade is a jam-like food made from oranges, lemons, or other fruit and usually eaten on bread or toast at breakfast. *e.g. Toast and marmalade is the best way to start the day.*

marriage 896, 1337
A **marriage** is the relationship between a husband and wife. *e.g. Their marriage lasted 43 years.*

married 896, 1337
1 If you are **married**, you have a husband or a wife. *e.g. She is a young married woman.*
2 If you get **married**, you become someone's husband or wife. *e.g. We decided to get married.*
3 You use **married** to describe things that involve marriage. *e.g. Their early married life was, of course, utterly blissful.*

marry 895
When a man and woman **marry**, they become each other's husband and wife at a special ceremony. *e.g. They are planning to marry soon.*

martial arts 1434
Martial arts are the techniques of self-defence that come from the Far East, for example karate and kung-fu. *e.g. He is an expert in martial arts.*

marvel 1472, 1710
1 If you **marvel** at something, it fills you with surprise or admiration. *e.g. The travellers marvelled at the relics in Greece.*

2 A **marvel** is something that makes you feel great surprise or admiration. *e.g. Durham Cathedral is one of the marvels of English architecture.*

marvellous 213, 220, 960, 1472, 1710
If you sign or say that people or things are **marvellous**, you mean that they are wonderful and that you are very pleased indeed with them. *e.g. It was a marvellous theatrical performance.*

masculine 1539
Something that is **masculine** relates to or is considered typical of men, in contrast to women. *e.g. I think it must have something to do with masculine pride.*

master 450
1 A **master** is a person, usually a man, who has authority over a servant. *e.g. He has written on the relationships that existed between masters and their slaves.*
2 If you are **master** of a situation, you have complete control over it. *e.g. Man will never be total master of his environment.*
3 A **master** is a male teacher at a school. *e.g. The new science master is ever so good-looking.*

match 873
A **match** is a small thin stick of wood, or sometimes cardboard, which is covered at one end with a chemical substance. This end of the match produces a flame when you brush it hard against the side of a matchbox or some other rough surface. *e.g. Have you got a match?*

match 1120, 1121
A **match** is an organised game of football, cricket or other team sport. *e.g. The football match began a little late due to crowd problems.*

mate 224
Your **mate** is your friend. *e.g. He went off with his mate.*

material 1516
A **material** is cloth, such as cotton or wool that you can use to make clothes and other things. *e.g. The sleeping bags are made of quilted material.*

mathematician 1054
1 A **mathematician** is a person who is trained in the study of numbers and calculations. *e.g. For decades, mathematicians have wrestled with this complex problem.*
2 A **mathematician** is a person who is good at doing calculations and using numbers. *e.g. They only took me on because I was a good mathematician.*

mathematics 30, 1054
Mathematics is a subject which involves

the study of numbers, quantities, shapes, et cetera; used especially of the academic subject which is studied at schools and universities. *e.g. She studied mathematics at Bristol University.*

maths 30, 1054
Maths is the same as mathematics. *e.g. I know nothing about modern maths.*

mauve 173, 1257
Something that is **mauve** is of a pale purple colour. *e.g. She used mauve ink which she thought looked very feminine.*

maximum 152
The **maximum** amount of something is the largest amount that is possible or allowed. *e.g. The maximum daily dosage is 150 milligrams.*

maybe 937, 1264, 1368
You use **maybe** to make what you sign or say less definite or to indicate that something is possibly true, but you are not certain or confident about it. *e.g. Maybe he'll be Prime Minister one day.*

mayor 793, 1142, 1693
1 The **mayor** of a town or city council is the man who has been elected to be its head for one year and to represent it at certain official occasions. *e.g. He was elected mayor in 1990.*
2 A **mayor** is a man who has been elected mayor. *e.g. Councillor Morrissey is to be the next mayor.*

mayoress 793, 1142, 1693
1 The **mayoress** of a town or city council is the woman who has been elected to be its head for one year and to represent it at certain official occasions. *e.g. The mayoress will open the new shopping centre on Saturday.*
2 The **mayoress** is the wife of the man who is the mayor, or a female relative or friend, who is nominated by the mayor to accompany him on official functions as mayor. *e.g. The mayoress will arrive at the town hall at nine o'clock.*

me 537
A signer, speaker or writer uses **me** to refer to himself or herself. *e.g. 'Who wants to go swimming?'—'Me!'*

meadow 1022
A **meadow** is a field which has grass and flowers growing in it. *e.g. We had a picnic in the meadow near the river.*

meal 686, 730, 1501
1 A **meal** is an occasion when people eat part of their main nourishment for the day or the quantity of food that they eat on that occasion. *e.g. When the meal was over, Thomas went out.*
2 If you have a **meal**, you eat a quantity of food which is part of your main

nourishment for the day. *e.g. Let's have a meal together in the cafeteria.*

mean   1077, 1116
Someone who is **mean** is unwilling to spend much money or to use very much of a particular thing. *e.g. He was a mean boss.*

mean   1311
1 If you ask what a word, sign, symbol, expression, or gesture **means**, you want it to be explained to you. *e.g. What does 'imperialism' mean?*
2 If you ask someone what they **mean**, you are asking them to explain exactly what they are referring to or intending to sign or say. *e.g. You mean she disliked Lucy?*
3 If one thing **means** another, it shows that the second thing exists, is true, or will happen. *e.g. A cut in taxes will mean a cut in government spending.*

meaning   1311
1 The **meaning** of a word, sign, symbol, expression or gesture is the thing that it refers to or expresses. *e.g. Do you know the meaning of the phrase 'cock and bull story'?*
2 The **meaning** of what someone signs or says, or of something such as a poem or story, is the thought or idea that it is intended to express. *e.g. The meaning of the remark was clear.*

meanwhile   1453
Meanwhile means while something else is happening. *e.g. So Snow White was happy in the little cottage. Meanwhile, the Wicked Queen was making plans.*

measles   1177
Measles is an infectious illness that gives you a high temperature and red spots on your skin. *e.g. Sam's got measles.*

measure   888
1 When you **measure** something, you find out how big or great it is by using an instrument or device. You can measure the length of something by using a ruler, for example. *e.g. She measured the material and marked where to cut it.*
2 If something **measures** a particular distance, its length, width or depth is that distance. *e.g. The shelf measures two feet across.*

meat   257, 530, 532
Meat is the flesh of a dead animal that people cook and eat. *e.g. He no longer eats meat.*

mechanic   1193
A **mechanic** is someone whose job is to repair and maintain engines. *e.g. The mechanic will have a look at your car.*

medal   835
A **medal** is a small piece of metal often in the shape of a rectangle, circle or cross. It is given as an award for bravery or as a prize in a sporting event. *e.g. He was wearing full army uniform complete with badges and his medal from Vietnam.*

medical   974
Medical means relating to medicine or to the care of people's health. *e.g. She had to undergo medical treatment.*

medicine   912
Medicine is a substance that you drink or swallow in order to cure an illness. *e.g. I'm going to get some medicine for my cold.*

meek   1476
Someone who is **meek** is gentle and quiet, and likely to do what other people sign or say. *e.g. She seemed such a meek person.*

meet   434
1 If you **meet** someone, you happen to be in the same place as them and can converse with them directly. *e.g. I met her when she came for an interview in Durham, and now she's going to be my wife!*
2 If you **meet** somebody, you both go to the same place at the same time, so that you can talk or do something together. *e.g. Meet me under the clock.*
3 If you **meet** somebody, you are introduced to them. *e.g. Come and meet Chris, the century-making opening batsman from Stoke-on-Trent.*
4 If you **meet** someone who is coming to see you or if you meet their train, boat, plane or bus, you go to the station, harbour, airport or bus-stop in order to be with them when they arrive there. *e.g. I'm going to meet Brita and Inger at the airport.*

meet   1119
When a group of people **meet**, they gather together for a purpose. *e.g. Teachers in Tokyo are to meet to discuss methods of teaching sign language.*

meeting   418, 419
1 A **meeting** is an event in which a group of people meet, usually inside a building, in order to discuss proposals and make decisions together *e.g. Mr. Elliott was, as usual, in full control of the meeting with the school's governors.*
2 You can refer to the people attending a meeting as the **meeting**. *e.g. The meeting accepted his proposal.*

melancholy   1667
If you feel **melancholy**, you feel sad. *e.g. When she left, he sank into melancholy.*

melon   1550
A **melon** is a large fruit which is sweet and juicy inside and has a hard green or yellow skin. *e.g. They had melon and roast chicken for dinner.*

member   898, 1613
1 A **member** of an organisation such as a club or a political party is a person who has joined the organisation in order to take part in its activities. *e.g. He is a member of the Deaf Caravan and Camping Club.*
2 A **member** country, **member** state, etc., is one of the countries that has joined an international organisation or alliance. *e.g. All the member countries are under pressure to conform.*

member   1658
1 A **member** of a group is one of the people, animals, or things belonging to the group. *e.g. The weaver bird is a member of the sparrow family.*
2 A **member** of an organisation such as a club or a political party is a person who has joined the organisation in order to take part in its activities. *e.g. He is a member of Greenpeace.*
3 A **member** country, **member** state, etc., is one of the countries that has joined an international organization or alliance. *e.g. All the member countries are under pressure to conform.*

memorise   513, 1665
If you **memorise** something, you learn it thoroughly so that you can remember it exactly. *e.g. I was able to read a whole page and memorise it in under three minutes.*

memory   513, 1665
1 Your **memory** is your ability to remember things. *e.g. If you have a good memory, you won't need a diary.*
2 A **memory** is something that you remember about the past. *e.g. My memories of a London childhood are happy ones.*

mend   55, 1519
If you **mend** something that is broken or not working, you repair it, so that it can be used again. *e.g. I tried to mend some toys for her.*

menial   1213
Menial work is very boring and tiring and has low status. *e.g. I was made to do a good deal of menial work.*

mental   1569
1 **Mental** means relating to the health of a person's mind. *e.g. Mental illness is more widespread than most people realise.*
2 You can refer to someone whose behaviour is considered shocking, foolish or frightening, or to such behaviour, as **mental**; some people find this offensive. *e.g. The England fans were absolutely mental; it was terrifying.*

mention   347, 380
1 If you **mention** something, you sign or say it, but do not spend very long discussing it. *e.g. Why don't you just mention that in passing?*
2 If you **mention** something, you sign or say something with reference to it, usually

briefly. *e.g. She mentioned she would be away at the weekend.*

merciful 1215
Someone who is **merciful** shows kindness and forgiveness to people who are in their power. *e.g. I begged him to be merciful.*

mercy 1215
Mercy is kind and considerate treatment that you show to someone, especially when you forgive them or do not punish them. *e.g. The priest showed mercy to the thief.*

mesh 1193
If things **mesh** together, they fit together very closely. *e.g. The group seemed to mesh very quickly.*

mess 1370
If you sign or say that something is a **mess**, you mean that it is in a very untidy state. *e.g. I'm sorry the house is in such a mess.*

messy 1370
1 Someone who is **messy** leaves things in a dirty or untidy state. *e.g. Sometimes I'm neat, sometimes I'm messy.*
2 Something that is **messy** looks unpleasant because it is dirty or untidy. *e.g. My daughter's bedroom is always messy.*

metal 581
Metal or a **metal** is a hard substance such as iron, steel, copper or lead. Metals are used for making tools, coins, machinery, wire, et cetera. *e.g. This tool will cut metal.*

meter 403
A **meter** is a device that measures and records something, such as the amount of gas you have used. *e.g. The man who came to read the meter said we should get it fixed.*

method 702, 1444
A **method** is a particular way of doing something. *e.g. Berlitz has a special method for teaching languages.*

meticulous 847, 849, 852, 868, 891
A **meticulous** person does things very carefully and with great attention to detail. *e.g. He was meticulous when it came to setting the table.*

metro 414, 807
The **metro** is the underground railway system in some cities, for example in Paris. *e.g. The Moscow metro system was bigger than she expected.*

Mexican 448, 1468
1 Someone or something that is **Mexican** belongs to or relates to Mexico or its people. *e.g. They intend to open a Mexican restaurant in Newcastle.*

2 A **Mexican** is a person who comes from, or whose family identity relates to Mexico. *e.g. Pancho Villa was a Mexican.*

Mexico 448, 1468
Mexico is a republic in North America, on the Gulf of Mexico and the Pacific. *e.g. We went to Mexico to do courses on Mayan and Aztec history.*

midday 738
Midday is the time around twelve noon, the middle of the day. *e.g. We arranged to meet at midday for lunch.*

middle 967
The **middle** of something is the part of it that is furthest from its edges, ends, or outside surface. *e.g. In the middle of the lawn was an oak tree.*

Midlands 967
The **Midlands** are the central counties of England. *e.g. Birmingham is a city in the west Midlands.*

midnight 738
Midnight is twelve o'clock at night. *e.g. We didn't get to bed until midnight.*

might 6, 75
Might is the power or strength that someone or something has. *e.g. We were crushed by the might of the army.*

might have happened 1098
If you sign or say that something **might have happened**, you mean that it was possible for it to have taken place although it did not in fact take place. *e.g. They always go on about chip pans going up in flames, and it might have happened to us if it hadn't been for Jane's quick thinking.*

migraine 568, 1569
Migraine or a **migraine** is an extremely painful headache that makes you feel very ill indeed. *e.g. I can't go to work today, I've got a migraine.*

mild 1272
If someone or their behaviour is **mild**, they are gentle, kind and warm-hearted. *e.g. My wife is a mild woman.*

miles 143
Miles is the plural of mile. A mile is a unit of distance that is 1760 yards. It is equal to 1.6 kilometres. *e.g. My home is thirty miles from here.*

militant 10
Someone who is **militant** is very active in trying to bring about radical political or social change. *e.g. Militant students questioned the M.P. at the meeting.*

military 1277
1 **Military** means relating to the armed forces

of a country. *e.g. The President threatened the students with military action.*
2 The **military** are the armed forces of a country. *e.g. The military are going to support the new President.*

milk 129, 133
1 **Milk** is the white liquid produced by cows, goats, etc., which people drink and from which you can make cheese, butter, and yoghurt. *e.g. I take milk in coffee.*
2 When someone **milks** a cow, goat, etc., they get milk from it by pulling and squeezing its teats. *e.g. Noel has to be home in time to milk the cows.*

milk 1671
Milk is the white liquid produced by cows, goats, etc., which people drink and from which you can make cheese, butter, and yoghurt. *e.g. I would like some milk.*

millionaire 1649
A **millionaire** is a very rich person who has money or property worth at least a million pounds, dollars, et cetera. *e.g. She said her father was a millionaire.*

millions 1722
Millions is often used to mean an extremely large number. *e.g. There are millions of mosquitoes in the jungle.*

mind 511, 1569
1 Your **mind** is your ability to think, including all the thoughts that you have. *e.g. You can improve your mind by reading good books.*
2 If you have a particular type of **mind**, you have a particular way of thinking which is part of your character or a result of your education or professional training. *e.g. You have the mind of a child.*
3 You can refer to someone as a particular kind of **mind** as a way of saying that they are clever, intelligent or imaginative. *e.g. Great minds think alike.*

mind (bear in mind) 513
If you tell someone to **bear in mind** that something is the case or to **bear** something **in mind**, you are reminding or warning them about something important which they should remember. *e.g. It shouldn't be difficult for you. Bear in mind that these are sixty-five-year-old men.*

minder 442
A **minder** is a person whose job it is to look after someone or protect them. *e.g. The businessman always travelled with a minder.*

mind (go from one's mind) 508
If something **goes from your mind**, you can't remember it. *e.g. Every time I sit in front of a video camera, my ideas just go from my mind.*

mind (keep in mind)   513
If you tell someone to **keep in mind** that something is the case or to **keep** something **in mind,** you are reminding or warning them about something important which they should remember. *e.g. If you just keep in mind that the brake is in the middle, you will be quite safe.*

mind (slip one's mind)   508
If something **slips your mind**, you forget about it or forget to do it. *e.g. I'm sorry I didn't go to the meeting; it just slipped my mind.*

mine   33, 35
See **belong to me.**

mingle   1622
1 If things such as sounds, feelings, or smells **mingle** or are **mingled**, they become mixed together but are usually each recognisable. *e.g. It was a cry which mingled fright with surprise.*
2 If you **mingle**, you move around in a group of people, especially at a party when you chat to people you do not know. *e.g. Get out and mingle a bit.*

Minicom   1019
1 **Minicom** is the name of a particular text telephone now in widespread use in Britain. *e.g. I wouldn't be without my Minicom, now that the AA and even some police stations have them.*
2 If you **minicom** somebody, you make a text telephone call to contact them. *e.g. Why don't you minicom him this evening?*

minimise   728, 1393
Also spelled **minimize.**
1 If you **minimise** something, you reduce it to the smallest amount or degree possible. *e.g. Crop rotation will help to minimise disease.*
2 If you **minimise** something, you make it seem smaller or less important. *e.g. He plays up his strong points and minimises his weaknesses.*

minimum   87, 728, 1393
1 The **minimum** amount of something is the smallest that is possible, allowed, or required. *e.g. You'll need a minimum deposit of five hundred pounds.*
2 The **minimum** is the smallest amount of something that is possible, allowed, or required. *e.g. An interpreter must have a minimum of three years' training.*

minister of religion   643
A **minister of religion** is a member of the clergy in a church, especially a Protestant church. *e.g. She never thought it would be possible for a woman to become a minister of religion in her lifetime.*

minor   612
Something that is **minor** has very little importance, or significance, especially in

relation to other things of the same sort. *e.g. The differences were minor: the fake would easily pass as the real thing.*

minutes   720
1 **Minutes** are written records of the things that are signed, said or decided at a meeting. *e.g. The need for a minibus was noted in the minutes of the meeting.*
2 If you take the **minutes** at a meeting, you make a written record of the things that are signed, said or decided at it. *e.g. Hilary will take the minutes for today.*

minutes ago   1250
Minutes ago refers to a very recent period of time, usually within the last fifteen minutes. *e.g. The taxis arrived and they took off minutes ago.*

minutiae   868
Minutiae are small details. *e.g. He was confused by the minutiae in his contract of employment.*

mirror   1245
A **mirror** is a flat piece of glass which reflects light, so that when you look at it you can see yourself reflected in it. *e.g. She stared at herself in the mirror.*

miser   1077, 1116
A **miser** is a person who is very mean and enjoys saving money rather than spending it. *e.g. Soon she discovered she had married a miser.*

miserable   1135
If you are **miserable**, you are very gloomy and unfriendly. *e.g. I'm always miserable first thing in the morning.*

miserable   1667
If you are **miserable**, you are very unhappy. *e.g. They all looked miserable.*

miserly   1077, 1116
Someone who is **miserly** is very mean and enjoys saving money rather than spending it. *e.g. A miserly woman lived across the road.*

miss   436
1 If you **miss** something, you do not notice it. *e.g. It's on the first floor—you can't miss it.*
2 If you **miss** something, you fail to hit it when you have aimed something at it. *e.g. She threw the cup at his head but knew she would miss.*
3 If you **miss** a chance or opportunity, you fail to take advantage of it. *e.g. I'm going to miss my chance to take over from the leading actress.*

miss   787, 808
If you sign or say that someone **misses** something, you are gently critical of the fact that they fail to notice it. *e.g. A small detail,*

which many missed, was in this section in the bottom corner.

miss   792
If you **miss** someone, you feel sad that they are no longer with you. If you **miss** something, you regret that you no longer have it or experience it. *e.g. I miss living in London.*

miss   1555
1 If you **miss** something, you fail to notice it. *e.g. You might miss the posters, but you'll see the main door.*
2 If someone or something is **missing**, they are not in the place where you expect them to be, and you cannot find them. *e.g. The book about Deaf culture is missing from my desk.*

missile   405
A **missile** is a weapon like a rocket that moves long distances through the air and explodes when it reaches its target. *e.g. The missile carries a warhead four times more powerful than the bomb which devastated Hiroshima.*

missioner to the deaf   661
A **missioner to the deaf** was a person who was responsible for administering a particular mission to the deaf. Missions were established in cities and towns to bring the gospel to those who could not hear. Missions provided social centres where deaf people could meet and interact using sign language. In addition to conducting religious services, missioners were particularly associated with finding employment for deaf people and interpreting. *e.g. Francis Maginn was a Deaf missioner to the deaf.*

mist   1072, 1075
Mist consists of a large number of tiny drops of water in the air which form a thin cloud and make it a little difficult to see things. *e.g. Everything was covered in mist.*

mistake   436, 1136
1 A **mistake** is an action or opinion that is wrong, or that is not what you intended to do. *e.g. Her letter contained not one spelling mistake.*
2 If you **mistake** something, you are wrong about it. *e.g. He thought he had mistaken the address.*

mistress   450
1 A servant's **mistress** is the woman who employs him or her. *e.g. The housekeeper said that her mistress had been rather odd in her manner.*
2 A **mistress** is a female teacher. *e.g. The games mistress had absolutely no sense of humour.*

misunderstand   436
If you **misunderstand** someone, you do not comprehend properly what they sign, say or write. *e.g. She misunderstood my question.*

misunderstanding   436
A **misunderstanding** is a failure to comprehend something such as a situation or a person's remarks. *e.g. This whole criticism seems to rest on a misunderstanding.*

mix   1622
1 If you **mix** two substances, or **mix** one substance with the other, you combine them in some way so that they become a single substance. *e.g. You mix whisky and ginger and that's it.*
2 A **mix** is a powder containing the correct amounts of all the substances that you need in order to make something such as a cake, cement, et cetera. You buy the mix in a packet and add water or another liquid to the powder. *e.g. The sponge came from a cake mix.*
3 If you **mix** two activities, or **mix** one activity with another, you do them both at the same time. *e.g. I see no harm in allowing oneself to mix business with pleasure.*
4 If you **mix** with other people, you meet them and sign or speak to them at a social event such as a party. *e.g. He mixes easily with people.*

mixed   1622
1 **Mixed** is used to describe something which includes or consists of different things of the same general kind. *e.g. It's mixed salad, nothing fancy.*
2 **Mixed** is used to describe something which involves people from two or more different races. *e.g. If they're happy with a mixed marriage, what's the problem?*
3 **Mixed** is used to describe feelings, reactions, reviews, etc., which consist of both some good and some bad things. *e.g. He has mixed feelings about having a stepdaughter.*

mixed up   1622
If you **mix up** a number of things that are in a special order or arrangement, you change the order or arrangement. *e.g. If I mix up these cards, he'll never know.*

mix-up   1114
A **mix-up** is a disorganised or confused state of affairs or group of objects without order or pattern. *e.g. What a mix-up! This will take all night to deal with!*

mix with a whisk   262
If you **mix** two or more substances **with a whisk**, you stir them together with a special kitchen tool (a whisk) used for quickly stirring air into them, so that they become a single substance. *e.g. She mixed the flour and water with the whisk.*

moan   1187, 1199
If you **moan** about something, you are very cross or extremely angry and show this in the way you behave and express yourself. *e.g I will moan about it if I want to!*

moan   1529
1 If you **moan** about something, you complain about it at length and in person. *e.g. You always moan about your colleagues.*
2 A **moan** is an occasion when you complain about something at length and in person. *e.g. He had a moan about it at lunchtime. He just went on and on.*

mock   664
1 You use **mock** to describe something which is deliberately not genuine. *e.g. She lived in a mock Tudor house.*
2 A **mock** examination or battle is not real but is intended to be like the real event so that people can practise and prepare for the real event. *e.g. We have a mock exam on Friday.*

mock   765, 1016
If you **mock** someone, you make them appear foolish, for example, by saying something funny about them, or by imitating their behaviour. *e.g. They could mock her all they liked: she knew it was right and good to sign.*

modern   1610
1 **Modern** means relating to the present time. *e.g. The social problems in modern society are mounting.*
2 Something that is **modern** is new and involves the latest ideas and latest equipment. *e.g. This modern kitchen is a homeowner's dream.*

modest   1476
A **modest** person avoids signing or speaking about their abilities, qualities, or possessions. *e.g. He is very modest about his achievements.*

module   1690
In education, a **module** is one unit in a course taught in units at a college or university. *e.g. In the next module, we will concentrate on Deaf culture.*

moist   1549
Something that is **moist** is slightly wet. *e.g. The earth was black and moist.*

money   1502, 1508
Money is the coins or bank notes that you use when you buy something, or when you pay for a service. The money that a person has includes their savings in a bank, building society, etc., but does not include their other possessions. *e.g. Do you have any money on you?*

money (wad of money)   1679
A **wad of money** is a tight bundle of banknotes. *e.g. He gave the cashier a wad of money.*

monitor   777
If you **monitor** something, you check regularly how it is changing or developing over a period of time. *e.g. We will have to monitor the child's progress.*

monk   287
A **monk** is a man who has made a special set of solemn religious promises to dedicate his life to God through prayer, service and obedience. He does not marry or possess any wealth, and usually lives in a religious community of men that is separated from the rest of society. *e.g. This monastery was founded by a monk from Northumbria.*

monkey   1651
A **monkey** is an animal which has a long tail and skilful hands which it uses for climbing trees and moving from branch to branch. Wild monkeys usually live in hot countries. *e.g. The monkey stole the bananas.*

moody   1135
Someone who is **moody** is depressed or unhappy, so that they do not sign or speak very much or are impatient with other people. *e.g. He's only moody because things aren't working out for him.*

moon   616
1 The **moon** is the distant, white or yellowish object in the sky that goes round the Earth once every four weeks and that you can often see at night. *e.g. It's amazing to think men have been to the moon.*
2 A **moon** is an object like a small planet that travels round a planet. *e.g. Jupiter has four moons.*

more   1591
1 If something happens **more**, it happens to a greater extent. *e.g. Plays that are relevant to today will attract them more.*
2 **More** is used to refer to an additional thing or amount of something. *e.g. Do you want more coffee?*

more   1592
1 You can use **more** to indicate that there is a greater number of things or a greater amount of something than before or than is involved in something else. *e.g. Do you spend more time teaching or doing research?*
2 **More** may mean to a greater extent or degree. *e.g. I'm more interested in books that are true to life.*
3 You can use **more** to indicate that something continues to happen for a further period of time. *e.g. They worked some more before going home.*

morning   189, 1654, 1657
1 The **morning** is the part of each day between the time that people usually wake up and noon or lunchtime. *e.g. I read the paper this morning.*
2 The **morning** is the part of the day between midnight and noon. *e.g. She died in the early hours of the morning.*

3 If you sign or say that something will happen in the **morning**, you mean that it will happen during the morning of the following day. *e.g. You'll feel awful in the morning if you drink so much.*

mortgage   1504

1 A **mortgage** is a loan of money which you get from a bank, building society, or other financial institution in order to buy a house or property. *e.g. We can't get a mortgage to buy a new house.*

2 You can refer to one of the repayments of a mortgage as the **mortgage**. *e.g. Have you paid this month's mortgage yet?*

most   373

1 You can use **most** to refer to the majority of a group of things or people or the largest part of some thing. *e.g. Most Flemish people understand Dutch.*

2 You can use the **most** to refer to an amount that is greater than the amount that anyone or anything else has, or that is more than has ever existed before. *e.g. Don took the most photographs at the BDA Congress.*

mostly   373

Mostly is used to indicate that a statement is generally true, for example true about the majority of a group of things or people, true for the majority of the time, or true in the majority of features. *e.g. The men at the party were mostly very young.*

moth   1659

A **moth** is an insect with large wings, which usually flies about at night and is attracted to bright lights. *e.g. Annabel hates moths.*

mother   838

Your **mother** is the woman who gave birth to you. *e.g. I always did what mother told me.*

mother   1569

1 Your **mother** is the woman who gave birth to you. *e.g. I have an enormous amount of respect for my mother and father.*

2 If you **mother** someone, you look after them and bring them up, usually when you are their mother. *e.g. Female monkeys who were badly mothered became bad mothers themselves.*

mottled   1157

Something that is **mottled** is covered with patches of different colours which do not form a regular pattern. *e.g. Her old sleeping bag was mottled with damp patches.*

motor   608

A **motor** is part of a machine or vehicle that uses electricity or fuel to produce movement so that the machine or vehicle can work. *e.g. The lawnmower is driven by a petrol motor.*

motorboat   1426

A **motorboat** is a boat that is driven by a small engine. *e.g. She bought a motorboat with the prize money.*

motorway   707, 1059

A **motorway** is a road with at least two lanes in each direction that has been specially built for fast travel by vehicles over long distances. *e.g. We ate in a cafe by the motorway.*

mound   1235

1 A **mound** is a pile of earth, stones, etc., like a very small hill. *e.g. Each house was separated from the next by a mound of earth.*

2 A **mound** is a large and rather untidy pile of things. *e.g. He threw his clothes into a growing mound in the corner.*

mount   796

When someone **mounts** something such as a horse or a bicycle, they climb on to the saddle so that they can ride it. *e.g. The brothers watched as she mounted the mare.*

mount   1394

Mount is used as part of the name of a mountain. *e.g. His ambition is to climb Mount Everest.*

mountain   1394

A **mountain** is a very large raised part of the earth's surface with steep sides which are usually difficult to climb. *e.g. We want a pleasant hotel at the foot of a mountain.*

mountain range   1236

A **mountain range** or **range of mountains** is a row of mountains. *e.g. We could just see beyond the next mountain range.*

mountains   1236

Mountains are very large raised parts of the earth's surface with steep sides which are usually difficult to climb. *e.g. The mountains have been my life: I've never wanted to do anything but climb.*

mouse   518, 571

A **mouse** is a very small, furry animal with a long tail. There are many kinds of mouse; some live in people's houses and some live in the countryside. *e.g. There's a mouse in my room, right next to the cupboard!*

moustache   480 899

A **moustache** is the hair that grows on a person's (usually a man's) upper lip. *e.g. He was a tall man with a moustache.*

moustache (handlebar moustache)
                                                          715, 1540

A **handlebar moustache** is the hair that grows on a man's upper lip (a moustache) shaped in the form of handlebars. It curves down and out on

both sides and is usually narrow at both ends. *e.g. I remember him standing there, twirling the ends of his handlebar moustache.*

move   1040

If a person or thing **moves** as a consequence of shaking, their position changes and they do not remain still. *e.g. Anyone can see that that washing machine moves when it's on the spin cycle.*

move   1453

1 When you **move**, you change your position to a different place. *e.g. He had to move away from the door.*

2 If you **move** something, its position changes. *e.g. The men agreed to move the desk away from the window for me.*

move   1701

If you **move** or are **moved** from one place or job to another, you go from one place or job to another. *e.g. He moved to the BBC from Yorkshire Television.*

move back   1641

If you **move back**, you change your position by going away from the space in front of you. *e.g. I tried to move back to let the old lady pass me.*

move forward   1642

1 If someone **moves forward**, they move in a direction in front of them. *e.g. When I turn my back, you should move forward, but don't let me catch you!*

2 If something **moves forward**, progress is made or it becomes more modern. *e.g. OK, now we're beginning to move forward.*

move towards   295, 570

If someone **moves towards** you, they come closer to where you are. *e.g. The policeman moved towards me and I froze.*

movie   1014

1 A **movie** is a cinema film. *e.g. I went to a movie.*

2 The cinema is sometimes called the **movies**. *e.g. We're going to the movies.*

3 The film and cinema industry is sometimes referred to as the **movies**. *e.g. I had a great life working in the movies, you know.*

**mow with a manually operated
lawnmower**   85

If you **mow** an area of grass **with a manually operated lawnmower**, you cut it using a machine which cuts the grass as it is pushed backwards and forwards over it. *e.g. Mowing the grass with a manually operated lawnmower is good exercise.*

**mow with a mechanically operated
lawnmower**   85

If you **mow** an area of grass with a **mechanically operated lawnmower**, you cut it using a machine which is powered by electricity or petrol. *e.g. Using a mechanically operated lawnmower makes mowing the grass very easy.*

much   473, 1010, 1053
You use **much** to refer to a large amount or proportion of something. *e.g. We never had much money.*

mug   26
A **mug** is a large, deep cup, usually one which has straight sides and a handle on one side. *e.g. I won a mug with Postman Pat on it.*

mule   1462
A **mule** is an animal whose parents are a horse and a donkey. Mules are often used to carry people or goods in mountainous areas. *e.g. He journeyed into the Andes on a mule.*

mull over   313
If you **mull** something **over**, you think about it for a long time, often before deciding what to do. *e.g. I need to mull things over before I accept the job.*

multiplication   372
Multiplication is the process of calculating the total when you multiply one number by another number. *e.g. I'm always glad I learned the multiplication tables.*

multiply   372
If you **multiply** one number by another, you calculate the total which you get when

you add the number to itself a particular number of times. For example, 2 multiplied by 3 is equal to 2 plus 2 plus 2, which equals 6. *e.g. Multiply this figure by the number of years you have worked.*

mum   838
Your **mum** is your mother. *e.g. We are going to see my mum on Friday.*

mummy   838
People often call their mother **mummy**. The English word is usually used by children. *e.g. I went to a pantomime with my mummy.*

mumps   1179
Mumps is a disease usually caught by children. It causes a mild fever and painful swelling of the glands in the neck. *e.g. Jenny's just had mumps.*

murder   184
1 **Murder** or a **murder** is the deliberate and unlawful killing of a person. *e.g. He pleaded guilty to seven counts of murder.*
2 If you **murder** someone, you kill them deliberately and in an unlawful way. *e.g. His father, mother, and sister were all murdered by the terrorists.*

music   878, 1118
Music is a combination of sounds that are put together in a pattern and performed by people who are singing or playing instruments. *e.g. She loved the beat of rave music and played it frequently.*

Muslim   1399
A **Muslim** is a person who believes in Islam and lives according to its rules. *e.g. When he prays, a Muslim faces towards Mecca.*

must   2, 1437
If you sign or say that something **must** happen, you mean that it is very important or necessary that it happens. *e.g. There must be an end to apartheid in South Africa.*

my   33
See **belong to me.**

my own   33, 35
1 A signer or speaker uses **my own** to emphasise that something belongs to, may be used by or relates to himself or herself. *e.g. My own daughter told me about the rumours.*
2 A signer or speaker may use **my own** to emphasise that he or she can do something without any help from other people. *e.g. I make my breakfast on my own every morning.*

myself   534
1 You use **myself** to refer to yourself when you mention that you alone did something or were affected by another person's action. *e.g. I shot myself in the foot to escape the trenches.*
2 You use **myself** to emphasise that you are referring to yourself. *e.g. I myself find it a bit odd, too.*
3 You use **myself** in order to sign or say that you did something without any help or interference from anyone else. *e.g. I dealt with it myself.*

N, n

N
N is the fourteenth letter of the British manual and English alphabets. See page 852.

nag   1529
If you **nag** someone, you keep complaining to them in an irritating way about something you want them to do which they are not doing to your satisfaction. *e.g. I saw her nag her husband about it.*

naked   257, 1602
Someone who is **naked** is not wearing any clothes. *e.g. The men's naked bodies steamed as they emerged from the shower.*

name   674
1 The **name** of a person, thing or place is the word or group of words that you use to identify them. *e.g. His name is Richard Arnasson.*

2 If you **name** someone or something, you give them a name. *e.g. She plans to name the baby after her mother.*

narrow   1450
Something that is **narrow** has a very small distance from one side to the other, especially in comparison to its length or height. *e.g. We turned left off the main road into a narrow lane.*

nasty   992
Something that is **nasty** is very unpleasant to see, experience or feel. *e.g. This medicine is really nasty.*

national   1017, 1044
National means relating to the whole of a country (rather than to part of it or to several countries). *e.g. It was printed in the national newspapers.*

natural   688
1 If you sign or say that someone's behaviour is **natural** in particular circumstances, you mean that it is the way people usually behave in those circumstances. *e.g. It's natural that she's upset when her mother's ill.*
2 You also sign or say that someone's behaviour is **natural** when they are not trying to hide anything or pretend in any way. *e.g. When we were talking, he was relaxed and natural.*
3 A **natural** ability or way of behaving is one that you were born with and have not learned. *e.g. They are both natural leaders.*
4 **Natural** is used to describe things that exist in nature and that were not made or caused by people. *e.g. There were not buildings or roads, just a natural landscape.*

naughty   1604
1 A child who is **naughty** behaves badly or is

disobedient. *e.g. Don't be a naughty boy.*
2 Something that is **naughty** is slightly rude or indecent. *e.g. He told a naughty joke.*

nausea 1144
If you have a feeling of **nausea**, you feel sick and as if you are going to vomit. *e.g. She experienced a wave of nausea as she looked at the injured man.*

nauseous 1144
If you feel **nauseous**, you feel sick and as if you are going to vomit. *e.g. I felt dizzy and nauseous when I got off the helter skelter.*

naval 1483, 1484
Naval is used to describe people or things that belong to, relate to, or involve a country's navy. *e.g. British naval forces were anchored off the Isle of Wight.*

navigate 403
If you **navigate**, you work out the direction to go while you are travelling by using a compass. *e.g. Andy had to navigate our way.*

navigator 403
A **navigator** is someone who works out the direction in which a ship or aeroplane is travelling. *e.g. He had many years experience as a sea captain and navigator.*

navy 1483, 1484
A country's **navy** is the part of its armed forces that fights at sea. *e.g. My father is in the navy.*

near 385, 434
If you **near** a place or person, you approach them. *e.g. As he neared the guard, Davis felt his fear increase.*

near 385, 434, 1619
1 If something is **near** a place or thing or **near to** it, it is only a short distance from it. *e.g. I wish I lived near London.*
2 If something is similar to something else, you can sign or say that it is **near** it or **near to** it. *e.g. Most views were near to the truth.*
3 If a time or event is **near**, it will happen very soon. *e.g. As her wedding day grew near, she thought back to that evening at Beamish.*

nearly 238, 612, 618
Nearly means not completely or exactly, but almost so. *e.g. Howard had waited for nearly one hour.*

necessary 1490
Something that is **necessary** is needed in order to obtain the result or effect you want. *e.g. A map of Liverpool is necessary if you want to be sure of arriving at the Deaf club on time.*

neck of a dinosaur/giraffe/llama 1673
The **neck of a dinosaur, giraffe** or **llama** is

the long part of such a creature's body which joins their head to the rest of their body. *e.g. The small boy gazed up at the giraffe's neck.*

neck of an ostrich/swan 642
The **neck of an ostrich** or a **swan** is the part of such a bird that joins its head to the rest of its body. *e.g. The neck of an ostrich can be several feet long.*

need 1281, 1490
1 If you **need** something, you must have it because you depend on it in order to live and be healthy. *e.g. These animals need food throughout the winter.*
2 If you **need** something, you must have it if you are going to do a job, solve a problem, or achieve a particular result successfully. *e.g. I need a BSL dictionary to check this sign.*
3 If you **need** something, you want it very much because you think you would benefit from it. *e.g. I need to learn how to use the computer.*
4 If you **need** something, you want it because you do not already own one or because the one you have is broken; used especially of things which are useful, and not just luxuries. *e.g. We need a washing machine now that both of us are working.*
5 If you **need** to do something, it is necessary for you to do it. *e.g. You will need to see a specialist.*
6 If you sign or say that something **needs** a particular action or that an action **needs** doing, you mean that this action will benefit or improve a situation. *e.g. The shed needs a good clean out.*
7 If you sign or say that we **need** something, or that something is **needed**, you mean that a particular action would serve a useful purpose, although you may not intend to do that action yourself. *e.g. We need firmer rules about exact working hours.*

needle 841
A **needle** is a small, very thin piece of polished metal which is used for sewing. It has a sharp point at one end and a hole in the other end for a thread to go through. *e.g. I found the needle.*

negative 407
1 If you sign or say that someone is **negative** or that they have a **negative** attitude, you mean that they consider only the disadvantages and bad aspects of a situation, rather than the advantages and good aspects. *e.g. He had a negative attitude towards our plans.*
2 If a medical or other scientific test is **negative**, it shows that something has not happened or is not present. *e.g. A negative pregnancy test can be a matter of enormous relief or sorrow.*

neglect 1601
Neglect is a failure to look after someone or

something properly. *e.g. It was obvious that the property had suffered from neglect.*

negotiate 1387
1 If you **negotiate** an agreement or a deal, you obtain it by having discussions with other people. *e.g. He tried to negotiate a trade agreement with Brazil.*
2 If you **negotiate** for something, you try to obtain it by having discussions with other people. *e.g. Paul is preparing to negotiate for a share in the profits.*

negotiations 1387
Negotiations are discussions that take place between people who have different interests, especially in business, politics, or international affairs, in order for them to be able to come to an agreement about something, solve a problem, or make arrangements. *e.g. The early stages of their negotiations with the Government were unsuccessful.*

neighbour 154, 194
1 Your **neighbour** is a person who lives near you, especially a person who lives next door to you. *e.g. She was afraid of what her neighbour would think.*
2 Your **neighbour** is the person who is standing or sitting next to you. *e.g. Jenny turned her head towards her neighbour.*

neighbourhood 1018
1 A **neighbourhood** is part of a town where people live. *e.g. I prefer my neighbourhood grocery shop.*
2 If something is in the **neighbourhood** of a place, it is near to it. *e.g. It's in the neighbourhood of the Avenues, near the park.*

neighbours 157
1 Your **neighbours** are the people who live near you, especially the people who live next door to you. *e.g. Don't be afraid of what the neighbours will think.*
2 Your **neighbours** are people who are standing or sitting next to you. *e.g. Her neighbours in the queue agreed to keep her place while she went to the toilet.*

nervous 539, 1117
1 Someone who is **nervous** is worried and frightened and shows this in their behaviour. *e.g. He was so nervous, he even began to bite his nails.*
2 If you are **nervous** about something, you feel slightly afraid of it and worried about it. *e.g. He was nervous about taking his driving test.*

netball 1108
Netball is a game played by two teams of seven players, usually women. Each team tries to score points by throwing a ball through one of the two nets which are at the top of two poles

at the ends of the court. The team to score the most points are the winners. *e.g. She was captain of the netball team.*

netball player   1108
A **netball player** is a person, usually a woman, who plays netball. *e.g. Anne is the best netball player in this league.*

Netherlands   1556
Also called **Holland**.
The Netherlands is a kingdom in North West Europe on the North Sea. It is a member of the European Community. *e.g. Jan and Anneke used to live in the Netherlands.*

never   1294
1 **Never** means at no time in the past or at no time in the future. *e.g. I've never been to Europe and what's more, I never want to go!*
2 **Never** means not in any circumstances at all. *e.g. Bringing up children in an inner city is never easy.*

never mind   1433
1 You sign or say **never mind** to try and make someone feel better when they have failed to do something or when something unpleasant has happened to them. *e.g. You didn't copy the tape? Never mind, I will do it.*
2 You sign or say **never mind** to indicate that something is not important, especially when someone is apologising to you. *e.g. 'Some of the towels are soaking wet, I'm afraid.'—'Never mind.'*
3 You sign or say **never mind** to tell someone that they need not do something, because it is not important or because you will do it yourself. *e.g. Never mind about those, Sam!*

never mind   1601
You use **never mind** to indicate that something is not important. *e.g. 'I'm sorry I broke your cup.'—'Never mind, I'll buy another tomorrow.'*

never mind   1605
You use **never mind** when someone seems so unhelpful or uninterested in their attitude that you decide not to tell them something or discuss something with them. *e.g. Are you listening to me? Oh, never mind, I give up, honestly!*

nevertheless   1382, 1433
Nevertheless means in spite of what has just been done, signed or said. *e.g. She saw Clarissa immediately, but nevertheless pretended to look around for her.*

new   1610
Something that is **new** has been recently made or created. *e.g. Smart new houses are to be built there.*

2 Something that is **new** has not been used or owned by anyone else. *e.g. Her father gave her a new car.*
3 Something that is **new** is different from what you had, used or experienced before. *e.g. The villagers were suspicious of anything new.*
4 Something that is **new** has only recently been discovered. *e.g. Herschel discovered a new planet.*
5 When you refer to the beginning of a **new** day or period of time, you are referring to the beginning of the next day or period of time. *e.g. It was the beginning of a new era.*
6 **New** is also used to show that something has only just happened. For example, a **new** parent has only recently become a parent. *e.g. From a new mother's point of view, it's a disgrace.*
7 If you are **new** to a situation or place or if the situation or place is **new** to you, you have not experienced it or seen it before. *e.g. I'm new here.*

Newcastle   737
1 **Newcastle** is a city in North East England on the river Tyne. It is the administrative centre of Tyne and Wear. *e.g. I got the train from Edinburgh to Newcastle.*
2 The addresses of Deaf clubs in **Newcastle** are: Our Lady of Lourdes Deaf Centre, 2 Summerhill Grove, Newcastle upon Tyne; and The Northumbria Social Club for the Deaf which meets above Heroes, Clayton Street West, Newcastle upon Tyne.

news   724
1 **News** is information about a recent event or a recently changed situation. *e.g. I've got some news for you.*
2 **News** is information that is given in newspapers, and through broadcast media, about recent events in the world. *e.g. He's been in the news again.*

newspaper   284
1 A **newspaper** is a number of large sheets of folded paper on which news, advertisements and other information is printed. Some newspapers are produced every day from Monday to Saturday, and others once a week. *e.g. I went into the shop and bought a newspaper.*
2 A **newspaper** is an organisation that produces a newspaper. *e.g. I work for a newspaper.*

newspaper article   285
A **newspaper article** is a piece of writing that has been written for publication in a newspaper. *e.g. I read a newspaper article by Sir Jack Ashley—it was in the Guardian, I think.*

newspaper column   285
A **newspaper column** is a regular piece of writing in a newspaper which is always written by the same person or is always about the same topic. *e.g. She writes a sports column for the local newspaper.*

New York   952
New York is a city in the south east of New York State at the mouth of the Hudson River. It is the largest city and chief port of the United States. *e.g. My aunt lives in New York.*

New Zealand   1612
1 **New Zealand** is a country that is an independent dominion within the Commonwealth, occupying two main islands (North Island and South Island) and a number of smaller islands in the South Pacific. *e.g. Apparently, people in New Zealand sign rather like people in Britain.*
2 **New Zealand** is used to refer to someone or something that belongs to or relates to New Zealand, or its people. *e.g. New Zealand lamb is the finest in the world.*
3 The address of the **New Zealand** Association for the Deaf is: P.O. Box 20051, Glen Eden, Auckland, New Zealand.

New Zealander   1612
A **New Zealander** is a person who comes from, or whose family identity relates to, New Zealand. *e.g. My sister married a New Zealander.*

next   154, 194
1 The **next** period of time, event, person, or thing is the one that happens or comes immediately after the present one or after the previous one. *e.g. I'm getting married next month.*
2 The **next** place or person is the one that is nearest to you or the first one that you come to. *e.g. Pull into the next lay-by.*
3 The thing that happens **next** is the thing that happens immediately after something else. *e.g. It's your turn next.*
4 If one thing is **next** to another thing, it is at the side of it. *e.g. There was a goldfish bowl next to the television.*

next door   154, 194
A house or flat that is **next door** to your house or flat is on one side of it. *e.g. She lived next door to the Turners.*

next (my go next)   186
If you sign or say **my go next** or **my turn next**, you mean you want to do, sign or say something, or be considered, immediately after the person you sign or say it to, or the person who is presently doing it or who is presently signing or speaking. *e.g. It's my go next on the bike.*

next (my turn next)   186
See **next (my go next)**.

nice   175, 465
1 You can use **nice** in expressions such as 'nice to meet you' when you meet someone

for the first time or 'nice to have met you' when you are signing or saying goodbye to someone you have met for the first time. *e.g. Nice to meet you, John. My daughter has told me a lot about you.*

2 If you sign or say that something is **nice**, you mean that you find it attractive or pleasant. *e.g. That's a nice pullover.*

3 If you sign or say that someone is **nice**, you mean that they are friendly and pleasant and that you like them. *e.g. He was a nice man. He used to send me flowers every week.*

4 If the weather is **nice**, it is warm and pleasant. *e.g. It is a very nice day.*

nice   345, 468
If you sign or say that something tastes **nice**, you mean that it has a pleasant flavour. *e.g. I know it's nice with cream, but custard would probably be good too.*

nice (very nice too)   467, 1488
You sign or say **very nice too** to indicate that you do not like something or are not happy about it. *e.g. I was left behind to clear up—very nice too!*

nick   1126, 1151
If you **nick** something, you steal it. *e.g. I saw you nick that pen.*

niece   815
Someone's **niece** is the daughter of their sister or brother. *e.g. My niece loves horse riding.*

night   718, 810, 811, 1290, 1465, 1577
1 The **night** is the part of each period of twenty-four hours when it is dark outside, especially the time when most people are sleeping. *e.g. He went out late at night.*

2 The **night** is the period of time between the end of the afternoon and the time when you go to bed. *e.g. I went on Friday night.*

3 If it is a particular time at **night**, it is between the time when it gets dark and midnight. *e.g. Eleven o'clock at night is not a good time to start work.*

nightdress   1252
A **nightdress** is a type of dress that women or girls wear in bed. *e.g. Look at that pretty nightdress, Gladys.*

nightgown   1252
A **nightgown** is the same as a nightdress. *e.g. Wee Willie Winkle ran upstairs and downstairs in his nightgown.*

nightie   1252
A **nightie** is a nightdress. *e.g. Put on your nightie, then I will tell you a story.*

nil   1704
Nil means the same as nought; often used in

scores of sports games. *e.g. Wales beat England three-nil.*

nitpicking   868
If you sign or say that someone is **nitpicking**, you mean that they concentrate on small and unimportant details, especially so they can find fault with something. *e.g. My mother is always nitpicking about what I wear.*

no   5
If someone signs or says **no**, they are indicating that you cannot have or do something you want or wish to do. *e.g. The headteacher signed: 'No, you can't go!'*

no   1221, 1420
1 You use **no** to indicate that you do not want someone to do something. *e.g. 'Marry you?' she shrieked. 'No, never!'*

2 You use **no** to emphasise that someone or something is not a particular kind of person or thing. For example, if you sign or say that someone is **no** fool, you mean that they are definitely not a fool. *e.g. She is no friend of mine.*

3 **No** is used to sign or say that a particular thing is forbidden. *e.g. No smoking please.*

nobody   1730, 1731
Nobody means not a single person. *e.g. Nobody noticed me sitting there.*

no good   222
1 When someone or something is **no good**, they are useless. *e.g. I was no good at French.*

2 If you sign or say something is **no good**, you mean there is no point in doing it as it will have no effect or will not achieve the result you wish. *e.g. It is no good arguing with Peter, he thinks he has all the answers.*

noise   521
1 A **noise** is a sound that someone or something makes. *e.g. Dolphins make many different noises.*

2 **Noise** is a loud or unpleasant sound. *e.g. The noise from the road drill got on her nerves.*

noisy   521
1 Someone or something that is **noisy** makes a lot of noise, especially loud or unpleasant noise. *e.g. The room was full of noisy children.*

2 A place that is **noisy** is full of a lot of noise, especially loud or unpleasant noise. *e.g. The bar was crowded and noisy.*

nominate   443
If you **nominate** someone, you formally suggest them as a candidate in an election or competition or for a job. *e.g. Governor Clinton was nominated by the Democrats.*

nomination   443
A **nomination** is an official suggestion of

someone as a candidate in an election or competition or for a job. *e.g. Check the list of nominations, please.*

nominee   443
A **nominee** is someone who is nominated for, or to, something. *e.g. Bob is this year's nominee for the exchange scheme.*

none   1730, 1731
None means not a single thing or person, or not even a small amount of a particular thing. *e.g. None of us were allowed to go.*

nonsense   515
1 You use **nonsense** to refer to things that are meaningless or not reasonable. *e.g. You can confuse the computer programme by typing in nonsense.*

2 You use **nonsense** to refer to something signed, spoken or written that you think is untrue or stupid. *e.g. 'Nonsense,' he signed, 'You're not my daughter'.*

noon   738
Noon is twelve o'clock during the day. *e.g. We will stop for lunch at noon.*

no-one   1730, 1731
No-one means not a single person. *e.g. Sorry, there's no-one here called Nikki.*

no problem   362, 520, 1581
You can sign or say **no problem** to tell someone that you think you can easily do something. *e.g. Ian said it would be no problem to send us a price list by tomorrow morning.*

normal   204, 207, 688
Something that is **normal** is usual or ordinary and what people expect. *e.g. On normal Fridays we finish at five, but if there's extra work we stay till six o'clock.*

north   296
The **north** is the direction which is on your left when you are looking towards the direction where the sun rises. *e.g. Can you tell me which trains go to the north?*

north   687, 1571, 1572
1 The **north** is the part of a place or country which is towards the north. *e.g. I met a man from the north of England.*

2 **North** means towards the north or to the north of a place or thing. *e.g. It is one hundred and fifty miles north of Salisbury.*

3 The **north** part of a place or country is the part which is towards the north. *e.g. She has a flat in north London.*

4 The **north** is the direction which is on your left when you are looking towards the direction where the sun rises. *e.g. The land to the north was low-lying*

Norway   717
Norway is a kingdom in North West Europe occupying the Western part of Scandinavia. *e.g. He worked in Norway for many years.*

Norwegian   717
1 Someone or something that is **Norwegian** belongs to or relates to Norway or its people. *e.g. They described their work on the grammar of Norwegian Sign Language.*
2 **Norwegian** is the main language spoken in Norway. *e.g. She translated his speech into Norwegian.*
3 A **Norwegian** is a person who comes from, or whose family identity relates to Norway. *e.g. My ski-instructor is a Norwegian.*
4 The address of the **Norwegian** Deaf Association is: Norges Doveforbund, Box 6850, N-0130 Oslo 1, Norway.

nose (hooked nose)   577
A **hooked nose** is the part of a person's face which sticks out above their mouth and which is considered to be large and curved. *e.g. The witch had green eyes and a hooked nose.*

nosey   334
Someone who is **nosey** or **nosy** tries to find out about things which do not concern them. *e.g. 'Who's at the door?'—'Don't be nosy!'*

nosey-parker   334
A **nosey-parker** or **nosy-parker** is someone who is always asking questions about other people's affairs. *e.g. 'He's a right nosy-parker, that man,' signed Judith indignantly.*

not   1420
1 You use **not** to make clauses or sentences negative. *e.g. I'm going to Birmingham tomorrow but I'm not going to Coventry afterwards.*
2 You use **not** with expressions meaning 'all', 'every' and so on, when you are referring to only some members of a group or some occasions. *e.g. Not everyone agrees with me.*
3 You can use **not** in a question after a positive statement to offer the opposite choice. *e.g. Do you want to go or not?*
4 You use **not** to represent the negative of a sign, word, group or clause that has just been used. *e.g. They'd know if it was all right or not.*
5 You can use **not** or **not even** as an emphatic way of saying that there is none at all of what is being mentioned. *e.g. Not one part was missing.*

not allow   109, 917
If you do **not allow** something, you do not permit it to happen or you try to stop it happening. *e.g. Smoking is not allowed in my office.*

not allowed   1420
When someone or something is **not allowed**, they are forbidden. *e.g. People under eighteen are not allowed in here.*

not bad   903
1 If you refer to something as **not bad**, you mean it is quite good or acceptable. *e.g. It was an awful job, but the money was not bad.*
2 If someone asks how you are or how things are going, you can answer **not bad** if you mean that matters are satisfactory but not perfect. *e.g. 'How's things?'—'Not bad, thanks. And you?'*

not bothered   1601
If you sign or say that you are **not bothered** about something, you mean that you do not mind what someone else does in a particular situation. *e.g. 'Shall I open the window?'—'I'm not bothered.'*

not bothered   1605
If you sign or say that you are **not bothered** about something, you mean that you really do not have the slightest interest in what someone else does in a particular situation. *e.g. Look, I've told you, I'm not bothered— just leave me alone!*

note   1596
A **note** is something that you write down to remind you about something, for example what someone signed or said or what you intend to do. *e.g. I have a note here about the awards ceremony.*

note down   720
If you **note down** something, you write down the important points of some information that is presented so that you will be able to refer to them later. *e.g. I'd better note down everyone's addresses.*

note (make a note)   1596
If you **make a note** of something, you write it down to help you remember it. *e.g. Please make a note of your complaints and we'll deal with them later.*

notepad   1547
A **notepad** is a pad of paper that you use for writing notes or letters on. *e.g. The information is on the notepad.*

notes   628, 720
You write, make, or take **notes** by recording ideas or comments on paper so that you can refer to them again and remember things (for example, what someone signed or said or what you intended to sign or say). *e.g. People took notes of their industrial figures.*

notetaker   628
A **notetaker** is someone who makes notes for other people. *e.g. I got a grant to pay for a notetaker for my college course.*

notetaking   628
Notetaking is the act of recording important points, ideas or comments on paper for reference. *e.g. Your writing must be neat to do the notetaking.*

nothing   963, 1263
1 You use **nothing** to sign or say that no objects, events, or ideas are present, even though people might expect that some would be present. *e.g. After all the excitement, there was nothing in the box.*
2 If you have got **nothing** or **nothing at all**, you have no objects or notions, even though people might expect that some would be present. *e.g. What do you have for the party?— Me? Nothing.*

nothing   1704, 1730, 1731
1 You use **nothing** when you are referring to no things, for example no objects, events, or no ideas. *e.g. She's had nothing to eat.*
2 If you sign or say that someone or something is **nothing** you mean that they are very unimportant. *e.g. What does he know? He's nothing.*
3 If you sign or say **nothing** or **it's nothing**, you are signing or saying that something is not as important, serious or significant as people think. *e.g. 'Is there anything wrong?'—'Oh, it's nothing.'*

nothing (for nothing)   1355
If you sign or say that an action was done **for nothing**, you mean that it was done either without a good reason or without achieving any worthwhile results. *e.g. I made an effort to get here on time for nothing.*

nothing special   590
If you sign or say that something is **nothing special**, you mean it is quite ordinary and unexciting. *e.g. My trip to Bournemouth was nothing special.*

nothing to write home about   590
If you sign or say that something is **nothing to write home about**, you mean that it is not very interesting or exciting. *e.g. The party was nothing to write home about.*

notice   223
A **notice** is a written announcement which is put in a place where it can be read by everyone. *e.g. We must prepare some notices advertising the time and place of the AGM.*

notice   755
If you **notice** something, you become aware of it by looking. *e.g. I began to notice the change in the weather today.*

notice board   223
A **notice board** or **noticeboard** is a board which people pin notices to. *e.g. The train timetable is on the notice board.*

notion   314, 619
A **notion** is a belief or idea. *e.g. This notion that devaluation of the pound is the only option is clearly nonsense.*

not on your life   971
If someone signs or says **not on your life**, they are totally rejecting a suggestion that has been made. *e.g. What? And leave you here? Not on your life!*

not so bad   903
1 If you refer to something as **not so bad**, you mean it is quite good or acceptable. *e.g. That's not so bad, either! You've been practising!*
2 If someone asks how you are or how things are going, you can answer **not so bad** if you mean that matters are satisfactory but not perfect. *e.g. 'How was your holiday?'—'Not so bad.'*

not sure   183, 982
1 If you are **not sure** that something is true, you are not certain that it is true. *e.g. I'm not sure, but I think the train leaves at half past five.*
2 If you are **not sure** about your feelings, wishes or intentions, you do not know exactly what you feel, want or intend to do. *e.g. Jane wasn't sure she wanted to get married.*
3 If you are **not sure** about a person, you do not know whether you can trust or rely on them. *e.g. John's fine, but I'm not sure about Burt.*

not too bad   903
1 If you refer to something as **not too bad**, you mean it is quite good or acceptable. *e.g. The goalkeeper's not too bad, but the defenders are lousy.*
2 If someone asks how you are or how things are going, you can answer **not too bad** if you mean that matters are satisfactory but not perfect. *e.g. She's not too bad today.*

not true   183
A story or account that is **not true** is not based on things which actually happened

and may be imagined or invented. *e.g. The murder story wasn't true.*

not trust   183
If you do **not trust** someone or something, you feel that they are not reliable or safe. *e.g. I do not trust him to honour his commitments.*

not yet   111, 1113
If you sign or say that an event is **not yet** happening or has **not yet** happened, you mean that it has not occurred before the present time, although it is expected to happen at some time in the future. *e.g. 'Has he arrived?'—'Not yet.'*

nought   1704
Nought is the number 0. *e.g. Write 'nought point seven five' in figures.*

now   1625
You use **now** to refer to the present time, often in contrast to a time in the past or the future. You may be referring to what is actually happening at the moment or to the present stage of history. *e.g. I'm going home now.*

nowadays   1625
Nowadays means at the present time in general, in contrast with the past. *e.g. Secure employment is difficult to find nowadays.*

now and then   299
If you sign or say that something happens **now and then**, you mean that it happens sometimes but not very often. *e.g. Every now and then there is a confrontation, but mostly all is quiet.*

nude   257, 1602
Someone who is **nude** or in the **nude** is not wearing any clothes. *e.g. I sunbathed in the nude.*

nudist   1602
A **nudist** is a person who believes in spending periods of time naked, occasionally or regularly, for reasons of health, religion or

freedom of spirit. *e.g. She has been a nudist for the past seven years.*

nuisance   1604
If you sign or say that someone or something is a **nuisance**, you mean that they annoy you or cause you problems. *e.g. I'm sorry to be a nuisance.*

number   30
1 A **number** is any of the signs or words such as 'two', 'nine', or 'eleven', or the symbols such as 1, 3, or 47. You use numbers to sign or say how many things you are referring to or where something comes in a series. *e.g. He lives at number 19 King Street.*
2 Someone's **number** is the series of digits that you dial when you telephone them. *e.g. What is the telephone number?*
3 If you **number** something, you give it a number in a series and write that number on it. *e.g. I haven't numbered the pages yet.*

numerous   473, 1010, 1053
1 If you refer to **numerous** things or people, you mean a lot of things or people. *e.g. George was the only survivor of her numerous children.*
2 If people or things are **numerous**, there are a lot of them. *e.g. Small enterprises have become more numerous.*

nurse   542, 731
A **nurse** is a person whose job it is to care for sick people, especially in hospital. *e.g. She's a trained nurse.*

nut   1735
A **nut** is a fruit that grows on certain trees. It has a hard shell and a firm part inside that can be eaten. *e.g. The cake has chopped nuts in it.*

nylons   876
Nylons are stockings made of nylon, or some other synthetic material. *e.g. During the second world war, it was very fashionable to wear nylons with seams.*

O, o

O
O is the fifteenth letter of the British manual and English alphabets. See page 852.

oars   95
Oars are long poles with blades at one end that are used for rowing a boat. The oars are fixed on each side of the boat, and when you pull the top ends of the poles, the blade ends move in the opposite direction through the water, causing the boat to move. *e.g. Take a*

firm grip of the oars.

oath   1379
An **oath** is a promise, especially the promise that you make to tell the truth in a court of law. *e.g. A man took the oath in court.*

obedience   1461
Obedience is your behaviour when you do what is required of you, or what someone asks or tells you to do, especially when you do it out

of respect for the rules that guide your behaviour or for the person who asked or told you to do it. *e.g. She has always shown proper obedience to the Mother Superior.*

obeisance   1399, 1461
1 **Obeisance** is an attitude of deference or homage. *e.g. Let us pay obeisance to our Queen.*
2 An **obeisance** is a bow that you make in order to show your respect for someone or something. *e.g. The emperor entered the temple*

and made a low obeisance before the statue.

obese 214
Someone who is **obese** is very fat. *e.g. If you overeat, you are likely to become obese.*

obesity 214
Obesity is the condition of being very fat. *e.g. Obesity is a real health hazard.*

obey 1461
If you **obey** a person, a command or an instruction, you do what you are required, told or advised to do, especially because you respect the person who gave the command or instruction or the rules on which it is based. *e.g. He obeyed without question.*

object 556
An **object** is anything that has a fixed shape or form, that you can touch or see, and that is not alive. *e.g. The table was strewn with mats, bowls and other objects.*

object 909
If you **object** to something, you express your opposition, dislike or disapproval of it. *e.g. I object to the way you are behaving.*

objection 909
An **objection** is something that you sign or say in which you express your opposition to something or your disapproval of it. *e.g. They raised one objection to the Chairman's decision.*

obligatory 2, 1437
If something is **obligatory**, you must do it, because of a custom, a rule, or a law. *e.g. English is an obligatory subject under the National Curriculum.*

obliging 1489, 1494
Someone who is **obliging** is willing and eager to be helpful. *e.g. She was really obliging in allowing us to use her minicom.*

oblivious 1570
If you are **oblivious** to something, you are not aware of it. *e.g. She was oblivious to the fact that everyone was staring at her.*

observation 755, 788
Observation is the activity of watching people, things or events carefully in order to learn or understand something about them. *e.g. Careful observation should confirm this hunch.*

observe 755, 788
If you **observe** someone or something, you watch them carefully, especially in order to learn or understand something about them. *e.g. The team observe mothers looking after their babies.*

observer 755, 788
An **observer** is someone who spends time watching an activity or event in order to see what happens, but without actually taking part. *e.g. Both political observers and media commentators criticised the showpiece rally in Sheffield.*

obtain 1130
If you **obtain** something, you get it or achieve it. *e.g. She obtained her degree in 1951.*

obvious 1728
1 Something that is **obvious** is easily seen or understood and cannot be doubted. *e.g. It was obvious that he knew very little about children.*
2 If you describe something that someone signs or says as **obvious**, you mean that it is unnecessary or shows a lack of imagination. *e.g. You shouldn't tell such obvious lies.*

occasional 299, 1233
Occasional means happening or being present sometimes, but not often. *e.g. We made an occasional trip to Aberdeen.*

occasion (on occasion) 299
If something happens **on occasion** or **on occasions**, it happens sometimes but not very often. *e.g. You have on occasions surprised people.*

occur 553, 630
1 When something **occurs**, it happens. *e.g. The attack occurred six hours ago.*
2 When something **occurs**, it exists or is present in a particular place. *e.g. The phrase occurs in the Koran.*

ocean 981, 1045
1 The **ocean** is the sea. *e.g. We could see the ocean from our hotel.*
2 An **ocean** is one of the five very large areas of sea on the earth's surface. *e.g. He claimed that St. Brendan was the first person to sail across the Atlantic Ocean.*

odd 626, 630
If someone or something is **odd**, you mean that it is strange or unusual. *e.g. It was odd that she still lived with her parents at her age.*

odour 1109
An **odour** is a smell, especially a strong one. *e.g. It was an unpleasant odour.*

offer 1372
1 If you **offer** something to someone, you ask them if they would like to have it or to use it. *e.g. He was offered a place at Gallaudet University.*
2 An **offer** in a shop is a specially low price for a product, or something extra that you get by buying the product. *e.g. Special offers this week include twenty per cent off all linguistics books.*

3 An **offer** is something that someone indicates they will give you or do for you if you want them to. *e.g. He said he would offer to negotiate if we thought it would help.*

office 614, 1043
1 An **office** is a room, usually not in your home, where you do your job, especially when it involves work of a clerical, administrative, or professional kind. *e.g. I had to go and see Maureen in her office.*
2 An **office** is a building or set of rooms where people do clerical, administrative or professional work. *e.g. Did you go to the office today?*
3 **Office** work is clerical, administrative or secretarial work. *e.g. I just got on with some office work by myself.*

officer 794
An **officer** is a person who has a position of authority in a security force or the armed forces. *e.g. They are retired army officers.*

official 647
An **official** is a person who holds a position of authority in an organisation. *e.g. Trade union officials will discuss pay claims.*

offload 1626
If you **offload** something that you do not want, you get rid of it, especially by giving it to someone else. *e.g. He tried to offload the responsibility onto his colleagues.*

often 473, 751, 1722
If something happens **often**, it happens many times or much of the time. *e.g. We often get cold winters here.*

oil 205
Oil is a smooth, thick sticky liquid that is made from plants or animals and is used for cooking or putting on food. *e.g. We will need an oil dressing.*

oil 462
1 **Oil** is a smooth, thick, sticky liquid that is used as a fuel and for lubricating machines. *e.g. Need an oil change, sir?*
2 If you **oil** something, you lubricate it using a liquid such as oil. *e.g. You'll have to oil the hinges.*

OK 165, 215
OK is the same as okay. See **okay**.

okay 165, 215
also spelled **OK**.
1 If something is **okay**, it is acceptable. *e.g. Is the trip to Glasgow okay with you, Granville?*
2 If you sign or say that someone is **okay**, you mean that they are safe and well. *e.g. Jane's okay—just dazed.*

old 810
1 Someone who is **old** has lived for many years and is no longer young. *e.g. It belongs to the old lady.*
2 Something that is **old** has existed for a long time and is no longer new. *e.g. The house was old and needed a great deal of attention.*
3 Something that is **old** is no longer in a good or new condition because of its age or because it has been used a lot. *e.g. The wardrobe was full of old clothes.*
4 If you sign or say that someone or something is a particular number of years and months **old**, you mean that they have lived or existed for that length of time. *e.g. The Association was a hundred years old.*

Olympic Games 881
The **Olympic Games** are a set of international sports competitions which take place every four years, each time in a different country, modelled on the ancient Greek games held at Olympia. *e.g. My wife competed in last year's Olympic Games.*

Olympics 881
The **Olympics** is another name for the Olympic Games. *e.g. Didn't she win a gold medal at the Olympics?*

on 1333
1 If you sign or say something is **on** a surface, it is supported by that surface. *e.g. The book is on the desk.*
2 If there is something **on** a piece of paper, it has been written or printed there. *e.g. I want that information on paper.*
3 If you are **on** a bus, train, or plane, you ride in it in order to travel somewhere. *e.g. On the plane, we watched a film.*
4 If you put or drop something **on** a surface, you move it or drop it so that it is supported by the surface. *e.g. Put the tray on the table, please.*
5 If something or someone is **on** television, they appear as part of a television programme. *e.g. Look, that's my son on television!*
6 If you are **on** an organisation such as a committee, you are a member of it. *e.g. She will be on the committee for a year.*

on account of 1492
See **account (on account of)**.

on (an upright surface) 1348
You use **on** to indicate that something is touching, attached to, or visible when you look at an upright surface. *e.g. The posters on the walls will have to be removed.*

once 309
If something happens **once**, it happens on one occasion only, or on one occasion within a particular period of time. *e.g. I went out with him once, but never again.*

once (at once) 1625
At once means immediately and without delay. *e.g. Go to bed at once!*

once in a while 299
See **while (once in a while)**.

once upon a time 1480, 1481
See **time (once upon a time)**.

one o'clock 301
You use **o'clock** after numbers from one to twelve to state a time which is that number past noon or midnight. **One o'clock** is the time one hour after noon or midnight. *e.g. I didn't go to bed until one o'clock, so I slept through breakfast*

ongoing 1646
An **ongoing** event or situation has been happening for quite a long time and is continuing to happen. *e.g. There is an ongoing discussion within the party about this.*

onion 574
An **onion** is a small, round, white vegetable with a brown, papery skin that grows underground and has a strong, sharp smell and taste. *e.g. She made wonderful onion soup.*

only 309
1 You use **only** to indicate the one thing or person that is involved or that happens in a particular situation. *e.g. Only mother knows.*
2 If you sign or speak about the **only** thing or person involved in a particular situation, you mean that there are no others. *e.g. I was the only one smoking.*

on occasion 299
See **occasion (on occasion)**.

oops 1096
You sign or say **oops** or **whoops** to indicate that there has been a slight accident or mistake. *e.g. Oops, I've just poured coffee all over the floor.*

oops sorry 1096
You sign or say **oops sorry** or **whoops sorry** to indicate that there has been a slight accident or mistake, or to apologise to someone because a slight accident or mistake has been made. *e.g. Oops! Sorry, I didn't know you were busy, or I wouldn't have come in.*

open 1373
1 If you describe someone or their character as **open**, you mean that they are honest and do not want or try to hide anything or to deceive anyone. *e.g. Arthur was an open person and gave freely of himself.*
2 If you are **open** to ideas or suggestions, you are ready and willing to accept them and to try

to understand their good qualities and possible benefits. *e.g. We are open to suggestions for improvements.*
3 If a meeting, invitation or organisation is **open**, anyone is allowed to join in, accept or compete in it. *e.g. The club is open to anyone on Friday nights.*

open 1384
1 If you describe someone or their character as **open**, you mean that they are honest and do not want or try to hide anything or to deceive anyone. *e.g. Arthur was an open person and gave freely of himself.*
2 If you are **open** to ideas or suggestions, you are ready and willing to accept them and to try to understand their good qualities and possible benefits. *e.g. We are open to suggestions for improvements.*
3 When a public event such as a conference or an artistic event such as a play or film **opens**, it begins to take place, be shown, or be performed. *e.g. The film opened with a charity premiere.*
4 If a meeting, invitation or organisation is **open**, anyone is allowed to join in, accept or compete in it. *e.g. The club is open to anyone on Friday nights.*

open 1430
1 If you are **open** to ideas or suggestions, you are ready and willing to accept them and to try to understand their good qualities and possible benefits. *e.g. We are open to suggestions for improvements.*
2 When a shop, office, facility or public building **opens** or you **open** it, access is allowed to it, the people in it start working and customers or clients can use it. *e.g. He waited for the bar to open.*
3 If you **open** a building, public area or institution, you declare officially, usually at a public ceremony, that is is now ready to be used or to start operating. *e.g. The Prince of Wales will open the new hospital.*
4 When a public event such as a conference or an artistic event such as a play or film **opens**, it begins to take place, be shown, or be performed. *e.g. The film opened with a charity premiere.*
5 If you **open** something that is blocked or it **opens**, the obstruction is removed and you can pass through. *e.g. The road was cleared because we must open it to traffic at once.*
6 If a meeting, invitation or organisation is **open**, anyone is allowed to join in, accept or compete in it. *e.g. The club is open to anyone on Friday nights.*

open a brolly/parasol/umbrella 265
If you **open a brolly**, **parasol** or **umbrella**, you release and spread the folding frame of the brolly, parasol or umbrella which is covered in cloth or plastic. *e.g. She opened her umbrella when it began to rain.*

open a can with a ring-pull   592
When you **open a can with a ring-pull**, you insert your index finger in the circular tab and pull it, so that part of the surface moves to make an opening. *e.g. Tommy loves to open a can with a ring-pull. I have to hide them from him.*

open a cupboard   16
If you **open a cupboard**, you move the door of the cupboard so that you can see inside it, usually in order to put things in or take things out. *e.g. Open the cupboard and put these clothes away.*

open a drawer   73
If you **open a drawer**, you pull it towards you so that you can see inside it, usually to put things into it or to take things out of it. *e.g. He opened the drawer and took out his passport.*

open a fridge/refrigerator   29
If you **open a fridge** or **refrigerator**, you move the door of the fridge or refrigerator so that you can see inside it, usually in order to put things into it or to take things out of it. *e.g. Open the fridge and see if there is any orange juice left.*

open a gate   1352
When you **open** a gate, you move it so that it no longer covers a gap, allowing vehicles, animals or people to pass through the space. *e.g. I opened the gate at the bottom of the field.*

operate   190
When doctors **operate**, they cut open a person's body in order to remove, replace or repair a diseased or damaged part of it. *e.g. They operated to save his life.*

operate on the face   173
When doctors **operate on your face**, they cut open your face in order to remove, replace or repair a diseased or damaged part of it. *e.g. The doctor said he would have to operate on my face when I broke my cheekbone.*

operating button   162
An **operating button** or a **button** is a small object that you press in order to operate a machine or an electrical device. *e.g. I couldn't remember which button turns the washing machine off.*

operation   190
A medical **operation** is a form of treatment in which a doctor cuts open a patient's body in order to remove, replace or repair a diseased or damaged part of it. *e.g. His mother had a major operation.*

operation on the face   173
An **operation on the face** is a form of medical treatment in which a doctor cuts open a patient's face in order to remove, replace or repair a diseased or damaged part of it. *e.g. She had an operation on her nose.*

opponent   459
1 A politician's **opponents** are other politicians who belong to a different party or have different aims and policies. *e.g. She may be a political opponent, but she's still a great personal friend.*
2 In a game, your **opponent** is the person who is playing against you. *e.g. He beat his opponent with ease.*
3 The **opponents** of an idea or policy do not agree with it, and do not want it to be carried out. *e.g. Mr. Smith was a leading opponent of the Poll Tax.*

opportunity   630
An **opportunity** is a situation that makes it possible for you to do something that you want to do. *e.g. Now's my opportunity to show these people what I'm capable of.*

oppose   459
If you **oppose** something, you take a different view of it to that of other people. *e.g. This group will oppose the motion that Sign Supported English should be used in the education of deaf children.*

oppose   909
1 If you **oppose** someone or something, you express your strong disagreement with them or disapproval of them, often in a formal way by making speeches or writing letters. *e.g. Your father opposed your wish to become a sculptor.*
2 If you are **opposed** to something, you strongly disapprove of it because you think it is wrong, evil, or stupid. *e.g. He was opposed to the development of nuclear weapons.*

opposite   385, 440
1 If one person or thing is **opposite** another, they are on the other side of a space from the other person or thing. *e.g. Theresa sat opposite him.*
2 The **opposite** side or part of something is the side or part that is farthest away from you. *e.g. We live on the opposite side of the street.*

opposite   459
1 **Opposite** is used to describe things of the same kind which are as different as possible in a particular way. For example, north and south are opposite directions. *e.g. I wanted to impress them, but it probably had the opposite effect.*
2 If two things of the same kind are completely different in a particular way, you can sign or say that one is the **opposite** of the other. *e.g. My interpretation was the opposite of Lorna's.*

opposition   459
The **opposition** is used to refer to the politicians, political party, or group of parties that form part of a country's parliament but are not in the government. *e.g. She became the leader of the opposition.*

opposition   909
Opposition is strong, angry, or violent disagreement and disapproval. *e.g. It was only built after much opposition from the planners.*

oppress   1364
To **oppress** someone means to treat them cruelly or unfairly. *e.g. Institutions that oppress women must be exposed.*

oppression   1364
Oppression is the cruel or unfair treatment of a person or a group of people. *e.g. This organisation was known for its oppression of the weak and defenceless.*

optician   754
An **optician** is someone whose job involves testing people's eyesight or providing glasses and contact lenses. *e.g. I went to see the optician on Tuesday to see about bi-focals.*

oral   814
1 **Oral** means relating to or concerned with speech, lipspeaking and lipreading. *e.g. Oral methods will never be used in this school.*
2 Someone who is **oral** is deaf and prefers to use speech rather than visual-gestural communication. *e.g. He is oral himself, but his wife uses BSL.*

oralism   814
Oralism is the communication strategy or perspective which stresses the value to deaf people (particularly in the education of deaf children) of using speech, lipspeaking, lipreading and whatever residual hearing they may have, through the use of the most advanced hearing aid technology. *e.g. The supposed strengths of oralism have not, it would seem, impressed most Deaf people.*

oralist   814
1 An **oralist** is someone who supports the communication strategy or perspective which stresses the value to deaf people (particularly in the education of deaf children) of using speech, lipspeaking, lipreading, and whatever residual hearing they may have, through the use of the most advanced hearing aid technology. *e.g. Yes, I am an oralist who believes strongly in the child's right to use spoken language.*
2 **Oralist** means relating to or concerned with the movement which supports the communication strategy or perspective that stresses the value to deaf people (particularly

in the education of deaf children) of using speech, lipspeaking, lipreading and whatever residual hearing they may have, through the use of the most advanced hearing aid technology. *e.g. There is a great deal of oralist literature arguing the case for English as the native language of deaf children.*

orange 1140
1 Something that is **orange** is a colour between red and yellow. *e.g. She wore an orange silk scarf.*
2 An **orange** is a round fruit that is juicy and sweet. It has a thick orange skin and is divided into sections inside. *e.g. Billy likes to have an orange and a banana for breakfast.*
3 **Orange** is a drink made from oranges. *e.g. He ordered a glass of orange, which he said was the most refreshing thing he could wish for.*

orchestra 878
An **orchestra** is a large group of musicians who play a variety of different instruments together. An orchestra usually plays classical music. *e.g. The orchestra played Beethoven's Ninth Symphony to celebrate the dismantling of the Berlin Wall.*

order 156, 157, 196
If a set of things are arranged or done in a particular **order**, one thing is put first or done first, another thing second, another thing third, and so on. *e.g. The names are in alphabetical order.*

order 303, 350, 356, 456
1 If someone in authority **orders** you to do something, they tell you to do it. *e.g. The Minister ordered them to set up an official enquiry.*
2 If someone in authority gives you an **order**, they tell you to do something. *e.g. He received an order to report to the barracks by ten o'clock.*

ordinary 204, 207, 590
Something that is **ordinary** is not special or different in any way and may, for example, be rather dull. *e.g. The meeting was pretty ordinary.*

organisation 768, 1433
Also spelled **organization**.
Organisation or the **organisation** of an activity or public event involves making all the arrangements for it. *e.g. The street party celebrations require a lot of organisation.*

organise 768, 1433
Also spelled **organize**.
1 If you **organise** an activity or public event, you make all the arrangements for it. *e.g. Let's organise a jumble sale at the village hall.*
2 If you **organise** things, you arrange them so that they are in a sensible order or in sensible

places. *e.g. Once a month, I organise my working area so I know where everything is.*

organiser 768, 1433
Also spelled **organizer**.
The **organiser** of an activity or public event is the person who makes all the arrangements for it. *e.g. I think we owe a round of applause to the organiser of the raffle, Miss Jenkins.*

orienteering 403
Orienteering is a sport in which people run from one place to another, using a compass and a map to guide them between points that are marked along the route. *e.g. Colin enjoys orienteering, but isn't keen on the idea of taking it up competitively.*

original 209, 302, 1491
You use **original** to describe the form or use that something had wh. n it first existed, or something that existed at the beginning of a process. *e.g. The original idea was mine, but the whole team was involved in the development work.*

originate 209
If something **originated** at a particular time or in a particular place, it began to happen or exist at that time or in that place. *e.g. These beliefs originated in the sixteenth century.*

ostrich 642
An **ostrich** is a large African bird that cannot fly. It has long legs, a long neck, a small head, and large soft feathers. *e.g. The ostrich is said to run very fast.*

other 391, 767
When you have mentioned the first of two things, you can refer to the second one as the **other** one. *e.g. Now what was the other thing?*

others 551
You use **others** or the **others** to refer, without being specific, to people or things in addition to those you have just mentioned. *e.g. Arsenal, Liverpool, Everton and others are opposed to the deal.*

ought 2
1 If you sign or say that someone **ought** to do something, you mean that it would be a good idea or the right thing to do. *e.g. She ought to see the doctor.*
2 If you sign or say that something **ought** to happen, you mean that you think it will probably happen. *e.g. Nigel Mansell ought to win the British Grand Prix.*

ought not 1420
When you sign or say that someone **ought not** to do something or to have done something, you mean you think they are or were doing

something wrong. *e.g. You ought not to leave a small child near an open fire.*

our 32
See **belong to us**.

our own 32
1 You use **our own** when you wish to emphasise that something belongs or relates to yourself and to one or more other people as a group. *e.g. Our own children deserve a better standard of education.*
2 Your use **our own** when you wish to emphasise that yourself and one or more other people as a group do something without help. *e.g. This work is all our own: we hope you like it.*

ours 32
See **belong to us**.

ourselves 569
1 You use **ourselves** to refer to yourself and one or more other people who all do something or are affected by what someone does. *e.g. We almost made ourselves ill.*
2 **Ourselves** is also used to refer with emphasis to the signer or speaker and the people they are addressing. *e.g. In teaching, we ourselves have to do a lot of learning.*
3 You can also use **ourselves** or **by ourselves** in order to sign or say that you, together with one or more other people, do something without any help or interference from anyone else. *e.g. We were such a great team, we made the thing all by ourselves!*

outdoor 1563, 1564, 1609
Outdoor activities or clothes take place or are used in the open air rather than in a building. *e.g. He loved outdoor work.*

outdoors 1563, 1564, 1609
1 **Outdoors** means in the open air rather than in a building. *e.g. Children of all ages should be outdoors several hours a day.*
2 The **outdoors** refers to a way of life or activities in which you spend a lot of time in the open air, especially in the countryside. *e.g. Yes, city life is all very well, but there's nothing to beat the great outdoors.*

out of work 1424
People who are **out of work** do not have a paid job. *e.g. My uncle was out of work for ten years after the shipyard closed down.*

outside 1463
You use **outside** to refer to something that is situated or happening in the open air rather than in a building. *e.g. Let's go for a walk outside.*

outside 1563, 1564, 1609
1 If you are **outside**, you are not in a building

but are quite close to it. *e.g. There was a fight outside the pub.*

2 If you are **outside** a room, you are not in it but are in the hall or corridor next to it. *e.g. He's on the landing outside.*

3 When you refer to the **outside** world, you are referring to things that happen or exist in places other than your home or community. *e.g. They don't want to leave school and go into the outside world.*

oven   1202, 1334
An **oven** is a cooker or part of a cooker that is like a box with a door. You put food inside the oven to cook it. *e.g. The cat keeps scratching the oven door.*

over   1342
1 If something is **over** a particular amount, measurement or age, it is more than that amount, measurement or age. *e.g. They paid out over three million pounds.*

2 Something that is **over** another thing is positioned above, but not touching, the other thing. *e.g. You need to fix this one over the door frame, and let that one hang down.*

over   1643
If you sign or say that an activity is **over** or all **over**, you mean that it is completely finished. *e.g. Bob's search for an aardvark is now over.*

overall   978
Overall is used to describe a situation in general, including everything but not considering the details. *e.g. The overall weather forecast is fair.*

overcast   1072
If it is **overcast**, there are a lot of clouds in the sky and the sunlight is not bright. *e.g. It was a warm day but overcast.*

overcoat   144
An **overcoat** is a thick, warm coat. *e.g. He bought a woollen overcoat for the winter.*

overcome   1364
1 If you **overcome** a problem or a feeling, you successfully deal with it or control it. *e.g. I was still trying to overcome my fear of the dark.*

2 If you **overcome** an enemy, you defeat them. *e.g. Next week, can Robin Hood overcome the Sheriff of Nottingham once and for all?*

overdue   409
1 If a person, bus, or train is **overdue**, they have not arrived and it is after the time when they were expected to arrive. *e.g. My parents are an hour overdue and the dinner is ruined.*

2 If something borrowed or due to be paid or handed over is **overdue**, it is now later than the date when it should have been returned, paid or handed over. *e.g. My library books are overdue: I'll have to pay a fine.*

overflow   1034
If a liquid or a river or the place it is in **overflows**, it flows over the edge of the container it is in or the place where it usually is. *e.g. Watch that the bath does not overflow.*

overseas   1564, 1609
Overseas means relating to or belonging to

other countries that are on the other side of a sea or ocean. *e.g. There is a vast overseas market for our goods.*

oversleep   1138
If you **oversleep**, you sleep longer than you intended to and wake up late. *e.g. Sorry I'm late—I managed to oversleep again.*

overtake   431
If you **overtake** a moving vehicle, person or animal on a road or path, you pass them because you are moving faster than they are. *e.g. I overtook the motor bike.*

overturn   1231
If an object like a car **overturns** or you **overturn** it, it falls on its side. *e.g. If you watch, you'll see Senna's car overturn.*

overworked   1356
If you are **overworked**, you have been working too hard. *e.g. We are overworked this month. I'm exhausted.*

owl   832
An **owl** is a bird with a flat face, large eyes, and a small sharp beak. Owls obtain their food by hunting small animals at night. *e.g. The owl swooped down on the frightened mouse.*

owner   957
The **owner** of something is the person to whom it belongs. *e.g. Nan, owner of the bookstore, was sitting at her desk.*

P, p

P
P is the sixteenth letter of the British manual and English alphabets. See pages 852 and 853.

package   1458
A **package** is a small parcel. *e.g. The postman delivered a package for you today; it's on your desk.*

packed lunch   1310
See **lunch (packed lunch)**.

pact   128
A **pact** is a formal agreement between two or more people, groups or governments to do a particular thing or to help each other. *e.g. A similar pact was signed in 1967 banning all military activity.*

paddle a canoe   90
If you **paddle a canoe**, you move it through

water using a paddle. *e.g. The people paddle canoes from village to village.*

pail   15
1 A **pail** is a bucket, especially one made of metal or wood. *e.g. He left a large metal pail for bringing water from the well.*

2 **Pail** is also used to refer to the contents of a pail or the amount it contains. *e.g. They boiled five or six pails of water.*

pain   989, 1052
1 **Pain** or a **pain** is an unpleasant feeling which you have in a part of your body because you have been hurt or are ill. *e.g. He was in pain.*

2 If a part of your body **pains** you, it hurts. *e.g. On nights like this, his wounded foot pained him.*

painful   989, 1052
1 If a part of your body is **painful**, it hurts

because it is injured or because there is something wrong with it. *e.g. My back is so painful that I cannot stand upright any more.*

2 Something that is **painful** causes someone physical pain. *e.g. My Dad had a long painful illness.*

paint   716
1 **Paint** is a coloured liquid that you put onto a surface (sometimes after diluting it) using a brush in order to protect the surface, make it look nice or make a design or picture. *e.g. She bought a small tin of enamel paint for the cot.*

2 A covering of dried paint on an object is referred to as the **paint**. *e.g. That paint needs to be scraped off.*

3 When you **paint** walls, woodwork or objects, you cover them with paint. *e.g. I'll finish painting the window frames then have coffee.*

4 If you **paint** something or **paint** a picture of

it, you make a picture of it on paper or canvas using paint. *e.g. She painted a pot of geraniums for her parents.*

5 When you **paint** a design or message on an upright surface, you put it on the surface using paint. *e.g. Whoever painted this graffiti should be shot.*

paint   1347
1 **Paint** is a coloured liquid that you put onto a surface (sometimes after diluting it) using a brush in order to protect the surface, make it look nice or make a design or picture. *e.g. We'll need lots of paint for this mural.*
2 A covering of dried paint on an object is referred to as the **paint**. *e.g. The paint was flaking off the wall.*
3 When you **paint** walls, woodwork or objects, you cover them with paint. *e.g. We want to paint the room green.*

painter   1347
A **painter** is someone whose job is painting the walls, doors, and other parts of buildings. *e.g. Her brother is a painter.*

paint the town red   954
If you **paint the town red**, you celebrate freely, energetically and joyfully. *e.g. When I get my diploma, watch out, because I'm going to paint the town red!*

pair   783
You can refer to two people as a **pair** when they are standing, sitting, or walking together, or when they have some kind of relationship with each other. *e.g. They are a devoted pair.*

pair of us   760
You use **pair of us** to refer to another person and yourself (when some kind of relationship exists). *e.g. The pair of us will be bridesmaids at Shona's wedding.*

Pakistan   321
1 **Pakistan** is a republic in Southern Asia on the Arabian sea. It was established following the division of the Indian sub-continent into Pakistan (predominantly Muslim) and India (predominantly Hindu) in 1947. Some people find this sign offensive. *e.g. Hanif was brought up in Pakistan and then moved to England.*
2 The address of the All-**Pakistan** Deaf and Dumb Welfare Society is: 47 Ahmed Block, New Garden Town, Lahore, Pakistan.

Pakistan   616
1 **Pakistan** is a republic in Southern Asia on the Arabian sea. It was established following the division of the Indian sub-continent into Pakistan (predominantly Muslim) and India (predominantly Hindu) in 1947. *e.g. Hanif was brought up in Pakistan and then moved to England.*

2 The address of the All-**Pakistan** Deaf and Dumb Welfare Society is: 47 Ahmed Block, New Garden Town, Lahore, Pakistan.

Pakistani   321
1 Someone or something that is **Pakistani** belongs to or relates to Pakistan, or its people. Some people find this sign offensive. *e.g. I hope to visit a Pakistani Deaf club when I go to Islamabad.*
2 A **Pakistani** is a person who comes from, or whose family identity relates to, Pakistan. Some people find this sign offensive. *e.g. Imran Khan, the world's greatest all-round cricketer, is a Pakistani.*

Pakistani   616
1 Someone or something that is **Pakistani** belongs to or relates to Pakistan, or its people. *e.g. I hope to visit a Pakistani Deaf club when I go to Islamabad.*
2 A **Pakistani** is a person who comes from, or whose family identity relates to, Pakistan. *e.g. Imran Khan, the world's greatest all-round cricketer, is a Pakistani.*

pal   224
Your **pal** is your friend. *e.g. Where is your pal tonight?*

pale   1667
If someone looks **pale**, the skin of their face looks whiter than usual, usually because they are ill, frightened or shocked. *e.g. You look very pale. Do you feel ill?*

pantomime   1351
1 A **pantomime** or **panto** is a funny musical play for children, that is based on a fairy story and usually performed at Christmas time. *e.g. 'Dick Whittington' is the pantomime this year.*
2 **Pantomime** is the theatrical tradition of performing pantomimes. *e.g. Where would school holidays be without pantomime?!*

pants   472
Pants are a piece of clothing worn under your other clothes, which have two holes to put your legs through and elastic around the hips or waist to keep them up. *e.g. He took off his trousers and pants and got into bed.*

paper   224, 417, 627
1 **Paper** is a material that you write on or wrap things with. The pages of this book are made of paper. *e.g. We visited a paper factory.*
2 A **paper** is a sheet of paper with information on it, such as an exam paper. *e.g. Where is the paper with the information about the meeting?*

paper   349
1 A **paper** is an essay written as an academic text, which may be published in a book or journal or used as the basis of a presentation to

an audience. *e.g. They worked hard on their paper for the book of the Salamanca symposium.*
2 A **paper** is a written document, usually circulated prior to a meeting, providing background information or proposals on a subject to be discussed by those attending the meeting. *e.g. The Treasurer will prepare a paper on the Association's financial situation for the next Executive Council meeting.*

paper   562
A **paper** is a sheet of paper with information on it, such as an exam paper. *e.g. Where is the paper with the information about the meeting?*

paper   1247
A **paper** is a presentation on an academic subject. *e.g. I gave a paper at the Deaf Way Conference on training teachers of BSL.*

paper   1347, 1414
If you **paper** a wall, you put wallpaper on it. *e.g. We will have to paper the lounge first.*

paper (put on paper)   1596
If you **put** something **on paper**, you write it down, so that it is available as a formal record if necessary. *e.g. Put that on paper, then we will discuss the matter again.*

parallel   422
1 If something **parallels** something else, it is as good as that thing or similar to it. *e.g. His career almost exactly paralleled that of Hopper.*
2 A **parallel** event or situation takes place at the same time as another one that is mentioned, or is similar to it. *e.g. Running parallel with this was an increase in her blood pressure.*
3 Two lines or two long things that are **parallel** are the same distance apart all along their length. *e.g. Vanderhoff Street ran parallel to Broadway.*

parasol   265
A **parasol** is an object like an umbrella that provides shade from the sun. Large parasols are often placed over tables out of doors. *e.g. She walked out in the sun with her parasol.*

parcel   1458
A **parcel** is something wrapped in paper, especially so that it can be sent by post. *e.g. The Red Cross have sent parcels of food and blankets to the disaster area.*

pardon   1580
1 You sign or say 'I beg your **pardon**' or 'I do beg your **pardon**' as a way of apologising for accidentally doing something wrong, for example, disturbing someone or making a mistake. *e.g. It is treated in the sentence as a noun—I beg your pardon—as an adjective.*
2 You sign or say **pardon me** to apologise for interrupting someone or asking for their

attention. *e.g. Pardon me, Sergeant, I wonder if you'd do me a favour?*
3 If you **pardon** someone, you forgive them or do not punish them for doing something bad or wrong. *e.g. I hope they pardon him for whatever crime he has committed.*

pardon me   1259
You use **pardon me** to show politeness when you apologise for disturbing or interrupting someone, or doing something slightly impolite such as burping. *e.g. Pardon me, Sarah, may I come in?*

parent(s)   838
1 Your **parents** are your father and mother. *e.g. Her parents are well-off.*
2 **Parent** may be used to refer to or indicate a mother or father who is mentioned without their identity being specified. *e.g. If any parent would like to come to the Nativity play, could they please let us know by Friday.*

Paris   704
Paris is a city in the north of France on the River Seine and is the capital of France. *e.g. Paris is a beautiful city to visit.*

park   1280
A **park** is a public area of land with grass and trees, usually in a town, where people go in order to relax and enjoy themselves. *e.g. She took her children for a walk in the park.*

park   1392
When you **park** a vehicle, such as a car, you drive it into the position where it can stay for a period of time or leave it there. *e.g. You can park in front of the doorway.*

park with swings   122
A **park with swings** or a **playground with swings** is an area of land on which there are swings for children to play on. *e.g. We spent most of the morning in a park with swings.*

parrot   639
A **parrot** is a tropical bird with a curved beak and grey or brightly-coloured feathers. Parrots are sometimes kept as pets and may sometimes copy what people say. *e.g. He brought the parrot back from overseas.*

part   1326
1 Something or someone that is **part** of a particular thing or group is one of the pieces, areas, things or people of which it is made up. *e.g. That part of town has plenty of restaurants.*
2 When you refer to **part** of something or a **part** of it, you are referring to some of it or to a section of it. *e.g. My job is part of the whole project.*

part   1634
When two people **part**, they leave each other.

e.g. A year ago, they agreed to part.

participant   1613, 1658
Someone who is a **participant** in a particular activity, action, or system takes part in it. *e.g. She was an active participant in these campaigns.*

participate   1613, 1658
If you **participate** in a particular activity, action or system, you take part in it. *e.g. We asked secondary school students to participate in an anti-drugs campaign.*

partition   1227
1 A **partition** is an upright wall or screen that separates one part of a room or vehicle from another. *e.g. Keith tapped on the glass partition to get their attention.*
2 If you **partition** a room, you separate one part of it from another by means of a partition. *e.g. They had partitioned the inside into offices.*

partition   1599
1 **Partition** is the dividing of a country into parts so that each part becomes an independent country. *e.g. Partition was, in this case, not a good idea.*
2 If a country is **partitioned** into parts, each part becomes an independent country. *e.g. The peace conference is to discuss how the old Yugoslavia should be partitioned.*

partly   1326, 1599
Partly means to some extent, but not completely. *e.g. I came to Durham partly because of the special services offered here to deaf students.*

partner   712
1 Your **partner** is the person you are married to, or with whom you are having a relationship (romantic, sexual, or both). *e.g. Sarah and her partner are coming to stay.*
2 Your **partner** is the person you are doing something with. *e.g. Find a partner to work with you on this.*

partner someone   712
If you **partner someone**, you act as a team with them in a game or share an activity (such as attending a social occasion) with them. *e.g. Will George partner you to the banquet?*

parts   1599
The **parts** of a particular thing are the pieces, sections, areas or things of which it is made up. *e.g. The course has three parts.*

party   840, 1176
1 A **party** is a political organisation whose members have similar aims and beliefs, usually an organisation that tries to get its members elected to the government of a country. *e.g. The Tory party did well in the local elections in the south of England.*

2 A **party** is a group of people. *e.g. Can my party come this way, and Mrs. Hartley's lot go over there?*

party   877, 954
A **party** is a social event, often in someone's home, at which people enjoy themselves doing things such as eating, drinking, dancing, signing, talking, or playing games. *e.g. We always have a big family party to celebrate New Year.*

pass   607, 658
A **pass** is a document that allows you to do something such as visit a particular place or travel on a train or bus without paying. *e.g. Each journalist will be issued with a pass.*

pass   1205
If you **pass** something to somebody, you give it to them. *e.g. Pass the cakes to Mrs. Lewis, Harry.*

pass   1329
1 If someone or something **passes** a test, or is **passed** by someone, they are assessed and considered to be of an acceptable standard. *e.g. Did you pass your driving test?*
2 When people in authority **pass** a new law or proposal, they formally agree to it or approve it. *e.g. Many of the laws they pass in Parliament are never enforced.*
3 A **pass** in an examination or test is a successful result in it. *e.g. I got a pass in physics, but I failed chemistry.*

passable   218
If you sign or say that something is **passable**, you mean that its quality is of an acceptable standard. *e.g. There are some passable small restaurants in the city centre.*

pass down   1207, 1306
If you **pass** something **down** to someone, you give it or leave it to them. *e.g. It is my intention that this work of art should pass down through the family.*

pass on   1205, 1306, 1626
If you **pass** something **on** to someone, you give it to them after you have used it or been given it. *e.g. He agreed to pass on the information.*

passport   60, 65, 1456
A **passport** is an official document containing your name, photograph, and personal details, which you may need to show at the border in order to be allowed to go into a foreign country. *e.g. He travelled to Greece without his passport.*

pass to   1626
If you **pass** something **to** someone, you give it to them. *e.g. Please pass the dish to Brian.*

past   1242, 1279, 1480, 1481
1 The **past** is the period of time before the present, and the things that happened in that period. *e.g. She was highly praised in the past.*
2 Someone's or something's **past** is all the things which have happened to them in the time before the present. *e.g. He never discussed his past.*
3 **Past** things are things that happened or existed before the present time. *e.g. She refused to answer questions about her past business dealings.*
4 You can use **past** to describe a period of time which happened a long time ago. *e.g. Our beliefs were developed in centuries past.*

paste   689
A **paste** is a soft, smooth, sticky mixture of food that you spread onto bread or toast. *e.g. We took sandwiches filled with salmon paste.*

paste   1324
1 A **paste** is a soft, smooth, sticky mixture which consists of a solid substance and a liquid, and which can be spread easily. *e.g. Mix the melted butter and flour into a paste.*
2 **Paste** is a mixture of water and flour or starch that is used for sticking paper to things. *e.g. Wallpaper paste is notoriously difficult to use.*

pasture   1022
Pasture is land that has grass growing on it and that is used for farm animals to graze on. *e.g. The cows were taken to the lower pasture every morning.*

pâté   689
Pâté is a mixture of meat, fish, nuts or vegetables with various flavourings. The ingredients are blended together into a paste and eaten. *e.g. I found a delicious chicken liver pâté.*

paternalist   1215
Paternalist behaviour or attitudes involve treating other people as if you are superior to them or in a better position than them and can therefore afford to pity and help them with what you consider to be their problems. *e.g. We don't need this kind of paternalist attitude. We're not here to be the objects of your pity.*

path   702, 1444
1 A **path** is a long, thin line of ground that has been marked by people walking, for example through a forest or up a mountain. *e.g. The path was easy to follow.*
2 A **path** is a strip of ground, often covered with concrete or gravel, intended for people to walk on. Paths are often made in gardens, parks, or along the sides of roads. *e.g. The path to the front door was overgrown with weeds.*
3 Your **path** is the space ahead of you which you are moving towards. *e.g. He found his path*

barred and stopped to think what he should do.
4 A **path** that you take is a particular course of action or way of doing something. *e.g. Public ownership is one of the paths to achieving a socialist society.*

pathetic   740, 812
If you describe someone or something as **pathetic**, you mean that they are so bad or weak that they make you feel impatient or angry. *e.g. Our efforts so far have been really rather pathetic.*

patience   179, 181
Patience is the quality or characteristic that enables you to stay calm and not get annoyed, for example when you are waiting for something. *e.g. Paul waited his turn with patience.*

patient   179, 181, 476
1 If you are **patient**, you are able to control your feelings so that you do not get annoyed, even in situations which other people would find annoying or frustrating. *e.g. He was very patient and explained the problem to me in detail.*
2 If you are **patient**, you are able to wait calmly for something or to do something very difficult or uninteresting without complaining or giving up. *e.g. He waited patiently, and was rewarded with a marvellous close-up of the badger.*

patronise   1215
If you **patronise** someone, you sign, speak or behave towards them in a way that seems friendly but which shows that you think you are superior to them in some way. *e.g. I do not wish to patronise you because you are poor.*

pattern   428
A **pattern** is a particular way in which something is usually done or organised. *e.g. Morse began to see a pattern in the villain's movements.*

pattern   1173
1 A **pattern** is a design made up of an arrangement of lines or shapes, especially one in which the same shape is repeated at regular intervals over a surface. *e.g. She wore a dress with a pattern of little red apples.*
2 If you **pattern** something or it is **patterned**, it is covered with a pattern or design. *e.g. I think we should pattern the ties more boldly.*

paunch   185
If a man has a **paunch**, he has a rather fat stomach. *e.g. John has acquired a middle-age paunch!*

pause   1435
1 If you **pause** while doing something, you stop doing it for a short time. *e.g. He paused*

and then went on in a low voice.
2 A **pause** is a moment of stillness or silence when an action or sound stops before beginning again. *e.g. She continued signing after a pause.*

pay   1507, 1679
When you **pay** an amount of money to someone, you give them the money because you are buying something from them or because you owe it to them. When you pay a bill, debt, fare, etc., you pay the amount that is owed or required. *e.g. George had to pay for the minicom.*

pay   1558
Your **pay** is the amount of money you get from your employers. *e.g. He got good pay for his age.*

payment   1504, 1507, 1679
1 **Payment** is the act of paying money to somebody. *e.g. Once the payment has been completed, we can relax.*
2 A **payment** is an amount of money that is paid to someone. *e.g. When will I make the first payment?*

pay no attention   344, 1601
If you **pay no attention** to someone or something, you behave as if you are not aware of them or as if they do not matter. *e.g. We were advised to pay no attention to him.*

pay off   244
If you **pay** someone **off**, you give them their final payment and dismiss them from their work, usually because there is no more work for them to do. *e.g. Forty workers were paid off last week.*

pay phone   942
A **pay phone** or **payphone** is a coin-operated telephone (in Britain, with facilities for voice calls only), usually in a public place such as a restaurant or theatre. *e.g. We can ring home from the pay phone at the theatre during the interval.*

P.E.   1652
P.E. is physical exercise and the playing of physical games and sports, particularly by school children. P.E. is an abbreviation for 'Physical Education'. *e.g. My niece is a P.E. teacher in a secondary school.*

peace   879
1 If you have **peace**, you are not being disturbed, and you are in calm, quiet surroundings. *e.g. Go away and leave us in peace.*
2 When a country has **peace** or is at **peace**, it is not in a state of war. *e.g. Since 1776, Britain has been at peace with the United States.*

3 If there is **peace** among a group of people, or if they live at **peace** with each other, they live or work together in a friendly way and do not quarrel or fight. *e.g. She did it to keep the peace in the family.*

peaceful   879
1 A **peaceful** place or time is quiet and calm and free from disturbance. *e.g. We hope for a peaceful Christmas.*
2 Someone who feels **peaceful** is free from worry or anxiety. *e.g. After the examinations, he felt peaceful and relaxed at last.*
3 **Peaceful** people try to avoid quarrelling or fighting with other people. *e.g. South American tribes are among the most peaceful people on earth.*

peacock   1729
A **peacock** is a large bird. The male has a very long tail which it can spread out like a fan and which is marked with beautiful blue and green spots. *e.g. Peacocks strutted around the courtyards of the King's Manor.*

peak   1298
1 The **peak** of a process or an activity is the point at which it is at its strongest, most successful, or most fully developed. *e.g. Computer technology has not yet reached the peak of its development.*
2 The **peak** of a mountain is the pointed top of it. *e.g. There was snow on the peak of the mountain.*

peanut   1735
Peanuts are small, oval-shaped nuts that grow under the ground. Peanuts are often eaten as a snack, especially roasted and salted. *e.g. We ate peanuts while we waited.*

pear   791
A **pear** is a sweet, juicy fruit which is narrow near its stalk and wider and rounded at the bottom. Pears have white flesh and thin green or yellow skin, and grow on trees. *e.g. A long garden full of pear and apple trees would be ideal for him.*

peck   639
When a bird **pecks** something, it bites at something with a sudden forward movement of its beak. *e.g. A pigeon began to peck at the putty.*

peck   681
If you **peck** someone, or give them a **peck** on the cheek or elsewhere on their face, you give them a quick, light kiss. *e.g. He gave her a peck on the forehead.*

peculiar   626
If you describe someone or something as **peculiar**, you mean that they are unusual or unexpected, for example in behaviour or appearance. *e.g. He was wearing a peculiar suit.*

peculiar   630
If you describe an event or situation as **peculiar**, you mean that something about it seems unusual or out of place. *e.g. 'How peculiar,' she signed, 'what's that doing there?'*

pedal   92, 654
1 When you **pedal** a bicycle, you push the two levers connected to the chain around with your feet to make it move. *e.g. His legs were aching from pedalling too fast.*
2 When you **pedal** somewhere, you go there on a vehicle such as a bicycle. *e.g. I pedalled in to work that night.*

pedantic   868
If you describe someone as **pedantic**, you mean that they are too concerned with unimportant details or traditional rules, especially in connection with academic subjects. *e.g. The Chairwoman was pedantic about the English used in the reports.*

pedestrian crossing   1661
A **pedestrian crossing** is a place with special road-markings where pedestrians can cross a road, and where motorists must stop to let them cross. *e.g. All the neighbours agreed to campaign for a pedestrian crossing near to the school.*

peek   1469
If you **peek** at someone or something, you have a quick look at them, especially secretly or quietly. *e.g. He peeked out from behind the curtain.*

peel a banana   263
If you **peel a banana**, you take its skin off. *e.g. She peeled the banana and gave it to her son.*

peel a round vegetable/fruit with a peeler   210
When you **peel a round vegetable** or **fruit with a peeler**, you use a special knife (peeler) to remove its skin. *e.g. She told him to peel the apple with the peeler that was in the drawer.*

peeler   210
A **peeler** is a special knife used for removing the skin from fruit and vegetables. *e.g. He's still got my potato peeler.*

peel potatoes/spuds   210
If you **peel potatoes** or **spuds**, you remove their skins with a knife. *e.g. I peeled the potatoes this morning.*

peep   1469
If you **peep** at something, you look at it very quickly, especially secretly or quietly. *e.g. They crept up to the door and peeped inside.*

Peeping Tom   1469
Someone who is referred to as a **Peeping Tom** secretly looks at other people when they believe they are not being watched, especially when they are undressing. *e.g. The papers say that he was a Peeping Tom.*

peg out on a clothes line/line   836
If you **peg out** clothes, sheets, etc., on a **clothes line** or a **line**, you fasten them to a washing line with special pegs. *e.g. She trudged up the garden and began to peg out the clothes on the line.*

pen   614
A **pen** is a long, thin object with which you write in ink. *e.g. Can I borrow a pen to write a cheque?*

penalty   269, 375
1 A **penalty** is a legal punishment or a fine. *e.g. The court considers a financial penalty to be appropriate.*
2 A **penalty** is a punishment in the form of a disadvantage for breaking the rules or for not fulfilling the terms of an agreement or contract. *e.g. There is a penalty clause written into the contract in relation to late completion of the work.*

pencil   614
A **pencil** is an object that you write or draw with. It consists of a thin piece of wood with a rod of graphite in the middle. *e.g. I can't find a pencil in this drawer.*

penguin   1421
A **penguin** is a large black and white bird found especially in the Antarctic. Penguins cannot fly, but use their wings for swimming in water. *e.g. They made a television programme about a penguin in the far north.*

penguin waddling   1421
If a **penguin** is **waddling**, it is moving with short, quick steps, swaying slightly from side to side. *e.g. There was a lone penguin waddling along the shoreline.*

pension   1008
Someone who has a **pension** regularly receives a sum of money from the state, or from a former employer because they have retired or because they are widowed or disabled. *e.g. I receive a pension, but what does that pay for these days?*

people   304, 482
1 **People** are men, women and children. *e.g. There were 120 people at the lecture.*
2 When you refer to the **people**, you are referring to ordinary men and women in contrast to the upper classes or the government. *e.g. 'Power to the people' is a famous democratic slogan.*
3 You sometimes use **people** to refer to the

members of a particular group of individuals. *e.g. He spoke at length and I think people got rather bored.*

pepper   1662
Pepper is a spicy-tasting, black or cream-coloured powder which is used to flavour food. *e.g. Add pepper to the stew.*

per cent   1705
If you express an amount as being, for example, 28 **per cent** of a total, you are signing or saying that if the total were divided into 100 parts, the amount that you are referring to would represent 28 of these 100 parts. *e.g. The interest is three per cent (3%) a month.*

percentage   1705
A **percentage** is a fraction of something which, if the whole thing were divided into 100 parts, would be equal to a particular number of these parts. *e.g. According to a recent opinion poll, the percentage of British people in favour of the establishment of a Scottish Parliament has now risen to 23%.*

perfect   847, 849, 852, 880, 891
Something that is **perfect** is as good as it can possibly be. *e.g. I've found the perfect house to live in.*

performance   143
A **performance** is the presentation of a piece of music, a dance, a play, etc., in front of an audience. *e.g. I saw a performance of 'Signs of the Tyne' by Our Lady of Lourdes Deaf Club.*

perfume   634
A **perfume** is a liquid that smells pleasant, and that you spray on your skin or clothing to make it smell nice. *e.g. Mother gave me perfume for Christmas.*

perhaps   937
You use **perhaps** to indicate that you are not sure whether something is true, correct, possible or likely to happen. *e.g. Perhaps Wendy made the correct decision after all.*

period   1265
A woman's **period** is the bleeding from her womb that happens each month. *e.g. I don't feel like going out; I have my period.*

periodical   283
A **periodical** is a magazine, especially a serious or academic one. *e.g. We intend to publish a new history periodical.*

permanent   652
1 Something that is **permanent** lasts forever or for a very long time. *e.g. Some drugs may cause permanent brain damage.*
2 Something that is **permanent** is present all

the time or happens all the time. *e.g. The only permanent water supply in this region comes from underground.*

pernickety   868
Someone who is **pernickety** worries too much about small, unimportant details. *e.g. My father was pernickety about his carpentry tools, and wouldn't let anyone touch them.*

Pernod   6
Pernod is an aniseed-flavoured alcoholic drink. *e.g. Frances ordered a Pernod and a pint of Guinness.*

perseverance   179, 181
If you do something with **perseverance** or if you have **perseverance**, you keep trying to do it and you do not give up, even though it is very difficult. *e.g. He finally benefited from his perseverance and hard work, when he got his degree.*

persevere   179, 181
If you **persevere** with something, you keep trying to do it and you do not give up, even though it is very difficult. *e.g. Everyone had to persevere and face up to innumerable setbacks.*

person   635
A **person** is a man, a woman or a child. *e.g. One person asked me for a copy of my lecture. Who was it?*

personal   493
1 **Personal** matters relate to someone's feelings, relationships or health, which they may find embarrassing. *e.g. I don't want to pry into your personal affairs.*
2 A **personal** thing belongs or relates to a particular person rather than to other people. *e.g. She asked her father to give her a personal allowance.*

personal   533, 534
1 **Personal** matters relate to your feelings, relationships or health, which you may find embarrassing. *e.g. They asked a lot of questions about my personal problems.*
2 A **personal** thing belongs or relates to yourself rather than to other people. *e.g. It was a matter of personal honour to me.*

personality   605, 644
Your **personality** is your whole character and nature. *e.g. He had a very amusing and original personality.*

personally   493
1 You use **personally** to emphasise that someone is giving their own opinion about something. *e.g. She signed that she couldn't personally see any reason to go.*
2 If someone does something **personally**,

they do it themself rather than letting someone else do it. *e.g. She will personally supervise the group.*

personally   534
1 You use **personally** to emphasise that you are giving your own opinion about something. *e.g. Personally, I feel we shouldn't accept him on the course.*
2 If you do something **personally**, you do it yourself rather than letting someone else do it. *e.g. I'd rather go to the shop and see the suit personally.*

personal stereo   1692
A **personal stereo** is a radio, compact disc player or tape recorder with headphones which people carry around so that they can move from place to place while listening to music, etc., without other people hearing it. *e.g. Her parents bought her a personal stereo for Christmas.*

person with a disability   561
1 A **person with a disability** is a person with a physical or mental impairment who experiences particular disadvantages as a consequence of the present social organisation of society. *e.g. Any person with a disability would agree that this policy is fundamentally flawed.*
2 A **person with a disability** is a person with a physical or mental impairment that is considered to severely affect their life. *e.g. Their policy was to interview all persons with disabilities who applied.*

person with AIDS   392
A **person with AIDS** is somebody who is identified as having an illness which completely destroys the natural system of protection that the body has against disease. AIDS is an abbreviation for 'acquired immune deficiency syndrome'. *e.g. Aids Ahead provides a range of services for persons living with AIDS.*

persuade   560, 1021
If you **persuade** someone to do something, you cause them to do it by signing, saying or doing things which influence their thoughts and behaviour. *e.g. I will persuade him to leave the car at home, so we can both have a drink.*

persuasion   560, 1021
Persuasion is the act of causing someone to do something by signing, saying or doing things which influence their thoughts and behaviour. *e.g. A little gentle persuasion is what's required.*

pest   1604
You describe someone, especially a child, as a **pest** when they keep bothering you or doing annoying things. *e.g. He threatened to send him to his room if he was too much of a pest.*

pester 1564, 1604
If you **pester** someone, you keep asking or telling them to do something, or keep bothering them. *e.g. Don't pester me to stop smoking.*

Peterborough 524
Peterborough is a city in the East Midlands on the River Nene. *e.g. The Queensgate shopping centre in Peterborough is a work of genius.*

petrol 462
Petrol is a liquid which is obtained from petroleum and which is used as a fuel to drive motor vehicles. *e.g. Petrol used to cost one pound fifty pence a gallon then.*

petrol fumes 1109
1 **Petrol fumes** are the gases given off by petrol. *e.g. While filling his tank, he felt giddy from the petrol fumes.*
2 You can refer to the gases expelled by motor vehicles when their engines are running as **petrol fumes**. *e.g. It has been shown that petrol fumes can harm children.*

petrol (put petrol in a petrol tank/ container) 462
If you **put petrol in a petrol tank** or a **container**, you operate the nozzle of a petrol pump, so that petrol is collected in it which you can then use as fuel. *e.g. Every time I put petrol in my petrol tank, the smell almost makes me sick.*

petrol station 462
A **petrol station** is a garage by the side of the road where petrol is sold and put into vehicles. *e.g. He opened a self-service petrol station.*

pharaoh 1672
A **pharaoh** was a king of ancient Egypt. *e.g. Thutmose the third was a pharaoh of the eighteenth dynasty.*

pharmacist 912
A **pharmacist** is a person who is qualified to prepare and sell medicines. *e.g. My uncle is a well-known pharmacist in Ayr.*

pharmacy 912
A **pharmacy** is a shop where medicines are sold. *e.g. If you take the doctor's prescription to the pharmacy, you will be given the antibiotics.*

philosopher 313
A **philosopher** is a person who creates or studies theories about the nature of existence, knowledge, etc., or about how people should live and behave. *e.g. Thales was a Greek philosopher, and a very wise one, too.*

philosophy 313
1 **Philosophy** is the study or creation of theories about the nature of existence, knowledge, etc., or about how people should live and behave. *e.g. She is an expert on Middle Eastern philosophy.*
2 A **philosophy** is a particular set of ideas that a philosopher has. *e.g. Socratic philosophy is based on the value of logic.*
3 A **philosophy** is a particular theory that a person or organisation has about how to live or how to deal with a particular situation. *e.g. The new policy is based on a bi-lingual philosophy.*

phone 944
1 The **phone** is an electrical system that you use to converse with someone else in another place by dialling a number on a piece of equipment and typing or speaking into it. *e.g. She has contacted us by phone a couple of times.*
2 A **phone** is the piece of equipment that you use when you converse with someone by phone. *e.g. The phone seems to have developed a fault.*
3 When you **phone** someone, you dial their phone number and converse with them by phone. *e.g. I went back to the office to phone Carol.*
4 If you are on the **phone**, you are conversing with someone by phone. *e.g. I spent an hour on the phone trying to sort things out.*
5 If you are on the **phone**, you have a phone in your home or place of work so that you can be contacted by phone. *e.g. Are you on the phone?*

phone call 944
When you make a **phone call**, or a **phone-call**, or a **call**, you phone someone. *e.g. I made a phone call: I hope that's okay.*

photo 1093
A **photo** is a photograph. See **photograph**.

photocopier 1545
A **photocopier** is a machine which quickly copies documents onto paper by photographing them. *e.g. We ordered a new photocopier for the office.*

photocopies 1545
Photocopies are copies of a document made using a photocopier. *e.g. I'd like twenty photocopies of each, if that's allowed.*

photocopy 1545
1 A **photocopy** is a copy of a document made using a photocopier. *e.g. We need to make a photocopy to send to staff members.*
2 If you **photocopy**, you make copies of a document using a photocopier. *e.g. I'm going to photocopy this, okay?*

photograph 659
1 A **photograph** is a picture that is made using a camera containing film which changes when light falls on it and which is then printed on special paper. *e.g. I take photographs of things which interest me.*
2 When you **photograph** someone or something, you use a camera to obtain a photograph of them. *e.g. I'd like to photograph the old cottage.*

photograph 1093
A **photograph** is a picture that is made using a camera containing film which changes when light falls on it and which is then printed on special paper. *e.g. The finest photograph in the exhibition is a study of Ukranian children in a dancing class by Andrew Lang.*

photographer 659
A **photographer** is a person who takes photographs, especially as a job. *e.g. Robert Beck was a photographer for Life magazine.*

pianist 1118
A **pianist** is a person who plays the piano, especially as their profession. *e.g. The great Brazilian pianist, Guiomar Novaes, is to play with the Birmingham Symphony Orchestra.*

piano 1118
A **piano** is a large musical instrument with a row of black and white keys. When these keys are pressed down by the player's fingers, little hammers hit wire strings and different notes are played, or synthesized versions of these sounds are emitted. *e.g. Her house had a piano in every room.*

pick 487
1 If you **pick**, you choose certain items from a range. *e.g. Pick the ones you like best.*
2 If you are told to take your **pick**, you can choose any that you like from a group of things. *e.g. You can have any you like—take your pick!*

pick 1528
1 If you **pick** something from a place, you remove it from there with your hand. *e.g. He went to pick his blazer off the chair.*
2 If you **pick** a particular thing, you choose that one. *e.g. Come on, son, pick a prize from the barrel.*
3 If you are told to take your **pick**, you can choose any one that you like from a group of things. *e.g. Take your pick, ladies and gentlemen, they're all free!*

pick up 1453
If you **pick** something **up**, you lift it, holding it with one hand at each end. *e.g. You see if you can pick it up, then.*

pick up 1528
1 When you **pick up** something or someone that is waiting to be collected, you go to the place where they are and take them away, often in a car. *e.g. I might get my brother to come and pick up this parcel.*

2 If someone is **picked up** by the police, they are arrested and taken to a police station. *e.g. I don't want them to pick you up for being drunk and disorderly.*
3 If you **pick** something **up**, you lift it up. *e.g. Pick that coat up off the table this minute!*

pick up   1532
If you **pick up** something such as a skill or an idea, you acquire it without great effort. *e.g. I thought I would pick up some Italian Sign Language when I lived there, but you have to study these things.*

picnic   1526
1 When people have a **picnic**, they eat a meal out of doors, usually in a field or wood or at the beach. *e.g. They often went for a picnic.*
2 If you **picnic**, you eat a meal out of doors, usually in a field or wood or at the beach. *e.g. We can picnic on cold pizza in the sand dunes.*

picture   441, 562
A **picture** consists of lines and shapes that are drawn, painted, or printed on a surface and that show a person, thing, or scene. *e.g. It is the most important picture Picasso ever painted.*

picture   659
1 A **picture** is a photograph. *e.g. We had our picture framed for the mantelpiece.*
2 When you take a **picture**, you use a camera to obtain a photograph. *e.g. Dad, take a picture of me in the paddling pool!*

picture   1014
You can refer to a film made for the cinema as a **picture**. *e.g. We worked together in the last picture I made.*

pictures   1014
1 **Pictures** are films made for the cinema. *e.g. I just love those old pictures, especially the silent ones.*
2 If you go to the **pictures**, you go to see a film at the cinema. *e.g. When was the last time we went to the pictures?*

pie (small pie)   1154, 1156
A **small pie**, which consists of meat, vegetables or fruit baked in pastry, is usually intended for one person only. *e.g. She hates to eat a small pie with a knife and fork.*

pig   20, 518
1 A **pig** is a fat animal with short legs, floppy ears, a snout and not much hair on its skin. Pigs are often kept on farms for their meat. *e.g. He sold his pigs at the market in Skibbereen.*
2 If you call someone a **pig**, you mean that they are unpleasant in some way, especially that they are greedy, untidy or unkind. *e.g. Her husband was a real pig; he never lifted a finger to help around the house.*

pile it on   1600
To **pile it on** is to exaggerate, or to sign or say too much. *e.g. She was trying to impress the interviewer so she really piled it on.*

pile up   1322
If you **pile up** a quantity of things, or if they **pile up**, you put them somewhere or they collect somewhere, forming a stack. *e.g. She just lets the newspapers pile up for months at a time.*

pill   476
1 A **pill** is a small, round mass of medicine that you swallow. *e.g. I took a sleeping pill.*
2 The **pill** is a type of pill containing chemicals that some women take regularly to reduce their chances of becoming pregnant. *e.g. She wanted to have a baby and so stopped taking the pill.*

pillow   1691
A **pillow** is a rectangular cushion which you rest your head on, especially when you are in bed. *e.g. My pillow was lumpy.*

pin   841
1 A **pin** is a very small, thin, metal rod with a point at one end. Pins can be stuck through things to hold them together, for example two pieces of cloth. *e.g. There is a pin in the sleeve: be careful.*
2 If you **pin** something somewhere, you fasten it there with a pin. *e.g. You can pin the hem of your trousers up.*

pinch   984, 1126, 1151
If you **pinch** something, you steal it. *e.g. I wanted to pinch the book, but they were watching me.*

pinch   1497
A **pinch** of a powder or a substance made up of small pieces is the amount of it that you can hold between your thumb and your first finger. *e.g. Add a pinch of cinnamon and stir well.*

ping pong   1316
Ping pong means the same as table tennis. See **table tennis**.

pink   662
Something that is **pink** is of a colour between red and white. *e.g. The cherry blossom was a beautiful pink.*

pipe   946
1 A **pipe** is an object which is used for smoking tobacco or other substances. You put the tobacco into a small container at one end of the pipe, light it, and inhale the smoke through a narrow tube. *e.g. Beth bought Bob a pipe for Christmas.*
2 A **pipe** is a long, round, hollow object, usually made of metal or plastic, through which a liquid or gas can flow. *e.g. We live in the country and there are no gas pipes to our home.*

pipe   1684
A **pipe** is a long, round, hollow object, usually made of metal or plastic, through which a liquid or gas can flow. *e.g. We live in the country and there are no gas pipes to our home.*

pipe tobacco   946
Pipe tobacco is a substance that people smoke in pipes which is made from the dried leaves of tobacco plants. *e.g. I need some more pipe tobacco.*

piss off   160
If you tell someone to **piss off**, you are telling them in a rude way to go away. *e.g. She was shocked to be told to piss off.*

pistol   463
A **pistol** is a small gun that you hold in your hand. *e.g. The pistol felt light and comfortable in his hand.*

pity   2, 904
1 If you sign or say that something is a **pity**, you mean that it is a circumstance or state of affairs that causes disappointment or regret. *e.g You have to leave tomorrow? What a pity!*
2 If you sign or say **pity**, you are confirming that you are disappointed at something you have just been told. *e.g. 'Someone told me she is leaving.'—'Pity! She was a lovely tea-lady.'*

pity   1215
1 If you feel **pity** for someone, you feel very sorry for them because they are experiencing great misfortune, unhappiness or sorrow. *e.g. She felt pity for the child.*
2 If you **pity** someone, you feel pity for them. *e.g. I pity anyone sleeping rough in this weather.*

place   983, 1018
1 A **place** is a location, for example an area, a point, or a building. *e.g. We were looking for a good place to camp.*
2 A **place** is a town, country, island, or other area that usually has a name. *e.g. The bungalow is at a place called Currabeg.*
3 A **place** is an area, town, building, or institution that has been mentioned or of which the identity is understood. *e.g. Mr. Evans seemed to know the place well.*
4 Someone's **place** of work, **place** of birth, etc., is the address or town where they work, were born, et cetera. *e.g. Please give your name, address, age, place of birth, and religion.*

place   1125, 1127
1 A **place** is a location, for example an area, a point, or a building. *e.g. Is this the place Maureen was on about?*
2 A **place** is a town, country, island, or other area that usually has a name. *e.g. And this is Beamish, the place where your mother and I met.*
3 A **place** is an area, town, building, or

institution that has been mentioned or of which the identity is understood. *e.g. He recognised the place she was talking about.*
4 Someone's **place** of work, **place** of birth, etc., is the address or town where they work, were born, et cetera. *e.g. And what is your place of work, Mr. Askew?*
5 If you **place** something somewhere, you hold it in one hand with your fingers over it and put it in a particular place or position, especially in a careful, firm or deliberate way. *e.g. Watch what happens if I place the stone here.*

place   1317
If you **place** something somewhere, you put it in a particular place or position, especially in a careful, firm or deliberate way. *e.g. She went to place the book on the table.*

place on   1333
If you **place** something **on** another thing, you put it there, especially in a careful, firm or deliberate way. *e.g. If you place the mat on the table, you will see that it doesn't slip.*

plain   959
1 **Plain** things are very simple in style. *e.g. She wore a very plain dress.*
2 A woman or girl who is **plain** is not considered beautiful. *e.g. A plain, plump girl with pigtails skipped round the corner.*

plan   768
1 A **plan** is a method of achieving something that you have worked out in detail beforehand. *e.g. They have a plan to give women more power.*
2 If you **plan** what you are going to do, you decide it in detail. *e.g. We must plan our future courses carefully.*

plane   134
1 A **plane** is a tool that has a flat bottom with a sharp blade in it. You move the plane over a flat piece of wood in order to remove thin pieces of its surface. *e.g. He gave her a plane for her birthday.*
2 If you **plane** a piece of wood, you make it smaller or make it level or smooth by using a plane. *e.g. I will have to plane the bottom of the door.*

plane   932
A **plane** is a vehicle with wings and one or more engines that enable it to fly through the air. *e.g. Liz went to London by plane.*

planner   768
A **planner** is a person who makes detailed arrangements for achieving particular goals in the future. *e.g. We seem to have convinced the planners to give the programme for Deaf viewers a peak-time slot.*

plant   843
When you **plant** a seed, you put it into the

ground so that it will grow there. *e.g. I'll see if my husband can plant the cabbages.*

plants   1733
Plants are living things that grow in the earth and have stems, leaves and roots. *e.g. Rabbits have eaten all my plants.*

plaster   191
A **plaster** is a strip of sticky material with a small pad used for covering small cuts, blisters, etc., on your body. *e.g. I bought some plasters in the chemist's.*

plastic   1523
1 **Plastic** is a material which is produced by a chemical process and which is used to make many objects and coverings. It is light in weight, can be formed easily into shape when heated, and does not break easily. *e.g. We decided that plastic would be cheaper.*
2 Something that is **plastic** is made of plastic. *e.g. The seats were plastic.*
3 You can use **plastic** to describe something that can be bent easily without breaking. *e.g. As you can see, it is quite plastic and supple.*

plasticene   1020
Plasticene is a soft substance like clay used by children for making little models. *e.g. With plasticene she made animals for her toy farm.*

plate   552
A **plate** is a round or oval flat dish that is used to hold food. Plates are sometimes used to hold other things, such as money that is being collected. *e.g. Can you tell me more about that plate in the window?*

platform   1406, 1415
1 A **platform** is a flat structure, usually made of wood, which people stand on when they make a presentation or give a performance. *e.g. He stood in the middle of the platform and began his lecture.*
2 A **platform** in a railway station is the area beside the rails where you wait for or get off a train. *e.g. The London train goes from platform one.*

play   143, 968
1 A **play** is a literary work which is intended to be performed in a theatre, on the radio, or on television, and which consists of the signs or words that a set of characters sign or say, and instructions relating to the setting and their actions. *e.g. Ian Townley's play 'The Last Flickering Light of Hope' is a work of great power.*
2 A **play** is a performance of a play. *e.g. I went to see an excellent play at the Gulbenkian.*

play   1029, 1066
1 When people (especially children) **play**, they spend time using their toys or taking part in games. *e.g. We played with the old toys all day.*

2 When you **play** a sport, game, or match, you take part in it. *e.g. Who wants to play French cricket?*

play a joke on   765, 1016
If you **play a joke on** someone, you do something intended to deceive them or make them look foolish. *e.g. Let's play a joke on Sally by giving her an apple-pie bed.*

play badminton   245
If you **play badminton**, you take part in a game of badminton. *e.g. They play badminton in the church hall every Tuesday.*

play basketball   979
If you **play basketball**, you take part in a game of basketball. *e.g. My dream was to play basketball with Larry Bird.*

play billiards   70
If you **play billiards**, you take part in a game of billiards. *e.g. He asked if I would like to play billards.*

play bowls   1713
If you **play bowls**, you take part in a game of bowls. *e.g. We will be playing bowls at the Polmont club next Saturday.*

play cards   1099
If you **play cards**, or **play** a game of **cards**, you play a game using playing cards. *e.g. We went to the club to play cards.*

play chess   826
If you **play chess**, you take part in a game of chess. *e.g. I like to play chess at least once a week.*

play cricket   282, 1295
If you **play cricket**, you take part in a game of cricket. *e.g. We play cricket every Sunday.*

play darts   854
If you **play darts**, you take part in a game of darts. *e.g. The men's team play darts on Tuesday, and the women play on Thursday.*

play dominoes   1739
If you **play dominoes**, you take part in a game of dominoes. *e.g. They play dominoes in the Deaf club every night.*

play draughts   826
If you **play draughts**, you take part in a game of draughts. *e.g. That's the last time I play draughts with you, you cheat!*

playground   1065
A **playground** is a piece of land, such as part of a school, or a public area where children can play. Playgrounds often have equipment such as swings and slides. *e.g. He saw the children in the school playground.*

play hockey 282
If you **play hockey**, you take part in a game of hockey. *e.g. He played hockey for Great Britain at the Seoul Olympic Games.*

playing cards 1099
Playing cards are rectangular pieces of thin cardboard with numbers or pictures printed on them, which together form a set of fifty-two (in four groups called clubs, diamonds, hearts and spades), that you use to play games like bridge and pontoon. *e.g. I had a pack of playing cards with me.*

play marbles 246
If you **play marbles**, you take part in a game of marbles. *e.g. Killian asked Anna if she wanted to play marbles.*

play netball 1108
If you **play netball**, you take part in a game of netball. *e.g. The boys signed that they wanted to play netball against the girls.*

play ping pong/table tennis 1316
If you **play ping pong** or **table tennis**, you take part in a game of table tennis. *e.g. Let's play table tennis in the garage.*

play pool 70
If you **play pool**, you take part in a game of pool. *e.g. You can play pool at the Conservative Association's Social Club.*

play rounders 249
If you **play rounders**, you take part in a game of rounders. *e.g. She plays rounders with the West Rainton school team.*

play rugby 1697
If you **play rugby**, you take part in a game of rugby. *e.g. At school, I played rugby every Saturday afternoon.*

play snooker 70
If you **play snooker**, you take part in a game of snooker. *e.g. They play snooker at the Deaf Club.*

play squash 12
If you **play squash**, you take part in a game of squash. *e.g. I wish someone would teach me how to play squash properly.*

play the piano 1118
If you **play the piano**, you make music by pressing on the row of black and white keys at the front of the instrument, so that little hammers hit on wire strings and different notes are played or synthesized versions of these sounds are emitted. *e.g. She used to play the piano in the pub.*

play volleyball 76
If you **play volleyball**, you take part in a

game of volleyball. *e.g. They play volleyball at the sports centre.*

play waterpolo 1407
If you **play waterpolo**, you take part in a game of waterpolo. *e.g. Do you want to play waterpolo at Durham baths?*

play with children's building blocks/ building bricks/toy blocks/toy bricks 1688
When children **play with children's building blocks, building bricks, toy blocks** or **toy bricks**, they spend time doing enjoyable things with the blocks or bricks, such as piling them on top of each other. *e.g. Liam loves playing with his building blocks.*

please 1261
1 You sign or say **please** when you are politely asking someone to do something. *e.g. Follow me, please.*
2 You sign or say **please** when you are politely asking for something. *e.g. Could I speak to Sue, please?*
3 You sign or say **please** when you are accepting something politely. *e.g. 'Do you want some milk?'—'Yes, please.'*

please 1275
If someone or something **pleases** you, they make you feel happy and satisfied, or give you enjoyment and pleasure. *e.g. The idea pleases me.*

pleased 1390
If you are **pleased**, you are happy about something or satisfied with something. *e.g. I am pleased to see you.*

please yourself 1004
You use **please yourself** to indicate that you do not mind or care whether the person you are with does a particular thing or not and they should decide for themself. *e.g. 'Do you mind if I wait?' I asked. Melanie shrugged and signed, 'Please yourself'.*

pleasure 1390
1 **Pleasure** is the activity of enjoying yourself, especially rather than working or doing what you have a duty to do. *e.g. He was a man who lived for pleasure.*
2 **Pleasure** is a feeling of happiness or enjoyment. *e.g. Bridie said she felt nothing but pleasure when she saw her grandchildren.*

pleasure 1612
Pleasure is a feeling of happiness, satisfaction, or enjoyment. *e.g. My boss showed his pleasure at my resignation.*

pledge 1379
1 If you **pledge** something, you promise solemnly that you will do it. *e.g. I had to pledge

to repay the stolen money.*
2 A **pledge** is a solemn promise to do something. *e.g. He gave the jury a pledge that he would mend his ways.*

plenty 1583
If there is **plenty** of something, there is a large amount of it. If there are **plenty** of things, there is a large number of them. *e.g. There is plenty of work to do.*

plumber 946
A **plumber** is a person whose job is to connect and repair things such as water and drainage pipes, baths and toilets. *e.g. The hotel had to wait for the plumber to arrive to mend the dripping taps.*

plus 389
1 You sign or say **plus** or write a **plus** sign (+) to show that one number or quantity is being added to another. *e.g. That's seventy-two plus ninety-six, which equals one hundred and sixty-eight.*
2 Teachers use **plus** in grading work in schools and colleges. 'B plus' is better than grade 'B', but it is not as good as 'A'. *e.g. I was a bit disappointed to get a 'D plus' in History after my 'C' last week.*

pocket 1282
1 A **pocket** in a piece of clothing is a small bag that is sewn into the garment or onto the outside of it, and that is used for carrying small things such as money or a handkerchief, or for putting your hands in. *e.g. She put her hand in her coat pocket.*
2 If someone **pockets** something, they put it in their pocket. *e.g. I locked the door and pocketed the key.*

pocket diary 607
A **pocket diary** is a book, small enough to carry in your pocket, which has a separate space for each day of the year, and can be used to write down your appointments and plans. *e.g. The meeting was finally fixed, so Magnus made a note of the date in his pocket diary.*

pocket money 1282
Pocket money is money which a child is given regularly by his or her parents to spend or save. *e.g. When he was ten, his pocket money was fifty pence a week.*

point 627, 867
1 A **point** is something that you sign or say which expresses a particular fact, idea, or opinion. *e.g. That's a good point.*
2 The **point** is the conclusion or the most important part of what you are signing, saying or discussing. *e.g. You've missed the point.*
3 In some sports, competitions, and games, a **point** is one of the single marks that are added

together to give the total score. *e.g. The panel of judges gave him seventeen points out of twenty.*

point (to the point)   1299
If something is **to the point**, it is relevant and direct. *e.g. Is that question really to the point just now?*

poison   912
1 **Poison** is a substance that harms or kills people or animals if it is swallowed or absorbed by them. *e.g. He put down rat poison.*
2 If you **poison** a person or animal, you deliberately kill them or make them very ill by means of poison. *e.g. He had been poisoned with strychnine.*

poke   248
If you **poke** a fire, you move the burning coal or wood with a poker so that it burns better. *e.g. She was on her knees, poking the fire.*

poker   248
A **poker** is a metal bar which you use to move the burning coal or wood in a fire so that it burns better. *e.g. She stirred the fire with the poker.*

pole vault   105
1 A **pole vault** is a very high jump which athletes make over a high bar, using a long flexible pole to lift themselves up. *e.g. His best pole vault this season was over 15 metres.*
2 The **pole vault** is the athletic field event in which athletes compete to see who can do the highest pole vault. *e.g. The pole vault will commence at three o'clock.*

pole vaulter   105
A **pole vaulter** is a person who takes part in a pole vault competition. *e.g. Bubka is without doubt the world's best pole vaulter.*

police   795
1 The **police** are the official, national organisation responsible for making sure that people obey the law, for protecting people and property, and for arresting criminals. *e.g. The police were called after the burglary.*
2 The **police** are the men and women who are members of this organisation. *e.g. One hundred and twenty police and demonstrators were injured.*

policeman   795
A **policeman** is a man who is a member of the official, national organisation responsible for making sure that people obey the law, for protecting people and property, and for arresting criminals. *e.g. My brother was a policeman for twenty years.*

police officer   795
A **police officer** is a person who is a member of the official, national organisation responsible for making sure that people obey the law, for protecting people and property, and for arresting criminals. *e.g. We need to send extra police officers to control the crowds at the football match.*

policewoman   795
A **policewoman** is a woman who is a member of the official, national organisation responsible for making sure that people obey the law, for protecting people and property, and for arresting criminals. *e.g. My niece is very keen to be a policewoman when she leaves school.*

policy   402
A **policy** is a general set of ideas or plans that has been officially agreed on by people in authority and which is used as a basis for making decisions. *e.g. Two television debates on economic and foreign policy have been planned.*

polish   4
1 **Polish** is a substance that you put on the surface of an object in order to clean it, protect it, and make it shine. *e.g. You should use wax polish on wooden furniture.*
2 If you **polish** something, you put polish on it. *e.g. Leather needs polishing with a good quality cream.*

politician   886
A **politician** is someone whose job is in politics, especially one who is a member of parliament or who is involved in some way in governing a country at national or local level. *e.g. Haldane was a Scottish lawyer, philosopher and politician.*

politics   886
1 **Politics** refers to the actions or activities which people use to achieve power in a country, society, or organisation, or which ensure that power is used in a particular way. *e.g. Emily has always been interested in politics.*
2 Someone's **politics** are their beliefs about how a country ought to be governed. *e.g. Her politics at this time could be described as radical.*
3 **Politics** also refers to the study of the ways in which a country is governed and power is acquired and used in that country. *e.g. She went up to Cambridge at the age of seventeen to read Politics, Philosophy and Economics.*

pond   986
A **pond** is a small area of water, often created by people rather than naturally occurring, that is smaller than a lake. *e.g. We built an ornamental pond in the garden.*

ponder   313
If you **ponder**, you think about something carefully. *e.g. I pondered the ethics of the situation for several days.*

pong   893
1 A **pong** is an unpleasant smell. *e.g. The house had been empty for years and there was a dreadful pong.*
2 If you sign or say that something **pongs**, you mean that it has an unpleasant smell. *e.g. Take that old dishcloth out of the room—it pongs!*

pool   70
Pool is a game played by two people using a table with six holes around the edge. Players use long, thin sticks (called cues) to hit a white ball (the cue ball) against balls of other colours which are usually numbered. The coloured balls form two sets of equal numbers. The winner is the first person to knock their set of numbered or coloured balls, and a final black ball, into the holes. *e.g. The women's pool team were very successful last year.*

pool player   70
A **pool player** is a person who takes part in a game of pool. *e.g. Paul Newman played the part of an ageing pool player in the film 'The Color of Money'.*

poor   911
1 If you describe something as **poor**, you mean that it is of a low quality or standard or that it is in bad condition. *e.g. The workmanship was poor.*
2 You also use **poor** to describe someone who is not very skilful in a particular activity. For example, a poor cook cooks badly. *e.g. She was a poor swimmer.*

poor   1146
1 Someone who is **poor** has very little money and few possessions. *e.g. He came from a poor family.*
2 A **poor** place is inhabited mainly by people with very little money and few possessions. *e.g. Aid is to go to the poor countries in the east of the region.*

poor   1215
You can use **poor** to describe someone who you are expressing sympathy for. *e.g. Poor old Dennis, he can't do a thing right.*

poorly   318, 931
If someone is **poorly**, they are ill. *e.g. Your sister's had an operation and she's quite poorly.*

pop   969
You can refer to fizzy drinks such as lemonade as **pop**. *e.g. She loves ginger pop.*

popular   225
1 Something that is **popular** is enjoyed or liked by a lot of people. *e.g. Swimming is a popular sport.*
2 Someone who is **popular** is liked by most people. *e.g. He became a popular president.*

population 482
1 The **population** of a country or area is all the people who live in it. *e.g. The country is unable to feed its population.*
2 The **population** of a country or area is all the people of a particular type in it. *e.g. A prison population of 44,000 is only possible with overcrowding in many prisons.*

pork 20
Pork is meat from a pig. *e.g. We will have pork chops for dinner.*

porridge 240, 723, 732
Porridge is a thick, wet food made from oats cooked in water or milk, usually eaten for breakfast. *e.g. Porridge is better eaten with salt.*

portable phone/telephone 1737
A **portable phone** or **portable telephone** is one which transmits telephone conversations by radio waves and which can be easily carried, enabling you (if you are a hearing person) to make and receive calls wherever you may be. *e.g. Elizabeth rang him by portable phone as she was travelling to The Lake District.*

portion out 1325
1 If you **portion out** something, you share it out among a group of people or organisations. *e.g. It fell to Tim to portion out the food under Jill's watchful eye.*

portions 1599
The **portions** of something are the parts into which it is divided or the parts of which it consists. *e.g. They cut the cake into equal portions.*

Portugal 573
Portugal is a republic in South West Europe beside the Atlantic Ocean and is a member of the European Community. *e.g. Portugal has many beautiful walled cities.*

Portuguese 573
1 Someone or something that is **Portuguese** belongs to or relates to Portugal, or its people. *e.g. Well, I've never seen a Portuguese car before.*
2 **Portuguese** is the main language spoken in Portugal and Brazil. *e.g. Did you know that Portuguese is the native language of about 110 million people?*
3 You can refer to people from Portugal in general, or a particular group of people from Portugal, as the **Portuguese**. *e.g. They really know how to make port, these Portuguese.*
4 A **Portuguese** is a person who comes from, or whose family identity relates to, Portugal. *e.g. My aunt married a Portuguese who lived in Liverpool.*
5 The address of the **Portuguese** Deaf Association is: Asociacao de Surdos, Avenida de Libertad 157, 2D, Lisboa, 1200 Portugal.

poser 232, 233
A **poser** is a poseur. See **poseur**.

poseur 232, 233
If you call someone a **poseur** or a **poser**, you mean that they are behaving in a particular way in order to impress people. *e.g. Nobody likes him—he's such a poseur.*

posh 524, 676
1 If you describe something as **posh**, you mean that it is smart, fashionable or expensive. *e.g. She had stayed in posh hotels.*
2 If you describe a person as **posh**, you mean that they belong to the wealthiest group in society, or act in a way which you consider typical of members of this group of people. *e.g. Your posh friends think they have a monopoly on good taste.*

positive 389
1 If you have a **positive** attitude to things, you are hopeful and confident. *e.g. I began to feel more positive.*
2 If the response to something is **positive**, it shows agreement, approval, or encouragement. *e.g. Thomson's reply—'There will be no change in policy'—was certainly positive.*

positive 1323
1 If you are **positive** about something, you are completely sure about it. *e.g. He was positive he'd seen it in the newspaper.*
2 **Positive** evidence gives definite proof of the truth or identity of something. *e.g. I think this is the positive identification we've been waiting for.*

positively 1323
You use **positively** to emphasise that you really mean what you are signing or saying. *e.g. This is positively the last time that you'll see me.*

possess 1124
If you **possess** something, you own or have it. *e.g. He was desperate to possess a driving licence.*

possible 335, 477, 572
1 If it is **possible** to do something, it can be done, or it is permissable that it may be done. *e.g. I wish to leave this weekend; is this possible?*
2 A **possible** event is one that might happen. *e.g. His boss warned him he faced possible dismissal.*
3 If you sign or say that it is **possible** that something is true or correct, you mean that although you do not know whether it is true or correct, you accept that it might be. *e.g. It's possible your father won't come until after tea.*
4 If you describe someone or something as a **possible** you mean that they are one of several people or things that could be chosen for a particular job or purpose. *e.g. This house is a possible, but I'd like to see it in daylight.*

possible 937
Something that is **possible** may happen or be done by someone in the future, but is not certain to happen or to be done by them. *e.g. She says it's possible that there'll be an election in November.*

possibly 335, 477, 572, 937
You use **possibly** to indicate that you are not sure whether something is true or will happen. *e.g. Television is possibly to blame for the increase in violence.*

post 1499, 1703
1 The **post** is the public service or system by which letters and parcels are collected and delivered. *e.g. Winners will be notified by post.*
2 If you **post** a letter or parcel, you send it to someone by putting the correct postage on it and placing it in a post-box or by taking it to a post office, which delivers it. *e.g. I'm going to post her a birthday card.*

postage 1499, 1703
Postage is the money that you pay for sending letters and parcels by post. *e.g. Send 25p extra for postage and packing.*

postcard 488
A **postcard** is a piece of thin card, often with a picture on one side, which you can write on and send to people without using an envelope. *e.g. Muriel sent us a postcard from Malta.*

poster 223, 562
A **poster** is a large notice or picture that you stick on a wall or notice board, often in order to advertise something. *e.g. My daughter's bedroom is covered in posters of horses.*

postman 145
A **postman** is a man whose job is to collect and deliver letters and parcels that are sent by post. *e.g. The postman delivers the mail around eight o'clock.*

postpone 885
If you **postpone** an event, you delay it happening or arrange for it to take place at a later time than was originally planned or agreed. *e.g. We cannot postpone the meeting again.*

postponement 885
A **postponement** is the act of delaying something or arranging for it to take place at a later time than originally planned or agreed. *e.g. I'd like to apply for a postponement of my return to work.*

posts 657
Posts are strong, upright poles made of wood or metal that are fixed into a surface or into the ground. *e.g. The garden was surrounded by wooden posts.*

postwoman 145
A **postwoman** is a woman whose job is to collect and deliver letters and parcels that are sent by post. *e.g. The postwoman delivered all the parcels.*

potato 210, 817, 1677
A **potato** is a roundish, white vegetable with a brown, red or yellowish skin. Potatoes grow underground. *e.g. He has gone to dig up some potatoes.*

pot belly 185
Someone who has a **pot belly** has a round, fat stomach which sticks out, caused either by eating or drinking too much or else by bad quality food and starvation. *e.g. The news showed film of starving children with pot bellies and extremely thin arms and legs.*

potential 335, 477, 572
1 You use **potential** to describe something as capable of becoming a particular kind of thing. *e.g. Everyone who came to the meeting is a potential member.*
2 Your **potential** is the range of abilities and talents that you have although these abilities and talents may not be in full use yet. *e.g. He has the potential to be a good manager.*

pound 399
A **pound** is a unit of money. In Britain, one pound is divided into one hundred pence. The British pound, or pound sterling, can be referred to in writing by the symbol '£'. *e.g. She was given twenty-five pounds for her birthday.*

pour from a container with a handle 8
If you **pour from a container with a handle**, you make the liquid or other substance in the container flow steadily out by holding the handle so that the container is at an angle. *e.g. He poured beer from the landlord's special container with the brass handle.*

pour from a container with a handle/ kettle/teapot 935
If you **pour from a container with a handle**, a **kettle** or a **teapot**, you make the liquid or other substance in the container flow steadily out by holding the handle so that the container is at an angle. *e.g. When you pour boiling water from a kettle, you must be very, very careful.*

pour from a jug 8
If you **pour from a jug**, you make the liquid in the jug flow steadily out by holding the handle so that the jug is at an angle. *e.g. He poured milk from the jug.*

pour from a teapot 8
If you **pour from a teapot**, you make the tea in the teapot flow steadily out by holding the handle so that the teapot is at an angle. *e.g. He poured the tea for his uncle from the brown teapot.*

pour ketchup 1662
If you **pour ketchup**, you add it to food by holding the bottle of ketchup over the food and shaking it so that the ketchup comes out. *e.g. He poured some ketchup on his bacon.*

pour oil 205
If you **pour oil** out of a container, you add it to food by holding the container at an angle and moving it over the food so that the oil flows out. *e.g. He poured oil over his salad.*

pour sauce 1662
If you **pour sauce** from a bottle, you add it to food by holding the bottle at an angle and moving it over the food so that the sauce flows out. *e.g. She poured some brown sauce on her chips.*

poverty 544, 1146
Poverty is the state of being extremely poor. *e.g. Thousands live in poverty.*

powder 1520
1 **Powder** or a **powder** consists of many tiny particles of a solid substance. *e.g. Over the years, their bones turned to powder.*
2 A **powdered** substance is one which is in the form of a powder. *e.g. We bought a tin of powdered milk.*

power 6, 75
1 If someone has **power**, they have a lot of control over people and activities. *e.g. The chairperson exerts a tremendous amount of power over the committee.*
2 If someone in authority has the **power** to do something, they have the legal right to do it. *e.g. The court has the power to imprison him for his crime.*
3 **Power** is the energy that is obtained by burning fuel or using the wind or sun. *e.g. The house was heated by a solar powered system.*
4 Electricity is often referred to as **power**. *e.g. The house was in darkness for two hours due to a power failure.*

powerful 6, 75
1 A person, government, or organisation that is **powerful** is able to control or influence events or other people's behaviour. *e.g. The Treasury is the most powerful government department.*
2 A **powerful** machine, device, substance, etc., is one that is very effective, for example because it is strong and efficient or because it can be used with great force. *e.g. It was a powerful engine.*

practice 1330, 1732
Practice is regular training or exercise in something, or a lot of experience in it. *e.g. With practice, it becomes less of an effort.*

practise 1330, 1732
If you **practise** something, you keep doing it regularly in order to be able to do it better. *e.g. It's hard to do until you've had time to practise a bit.*

praise 225
1 If you **praise** someone or something, you express approval for their achievements or qualities. *e.g. They praised his performance.*
2 **Praise** is what you sign, say or write about someone when you are praising them. *e.g. Austin was singled out for special praise.*

praise 226
1 If you **praise** someone or something in authority over you, or whom you look up to, you honour or express approval for their achievements or qualities. *e.g. They praised the achievements of the Executive Council.*
2 **Praise** is what you sign, say or write about someone in authority over you, or whom you look up to, when you are praising or honouring them. *e.g. 'Praise be to God,' he signed.*

pram 84
A **pram** is a four-wheeled carriage which is pushed by hand and in which a baby can sleep or be conveyed. *e.g. Siobhan's pram is in the kitchen.*

pray 669
When someone wants something very much, you can sign or say that they **pray** for it. *e.g. I prayed he would arrive in time to catch the plane.*

pray 1440, 1441, 1442
1 When people **pray**, they express their thanks to God or ask for his help. *e.g. I will pray for forgiveness.*
2 When someone wants something very much, you can sign or say that they **pray** for it. *e.g. I think we should pray for a mild winter.*

prayer 1440, 1441, 1442
1 **Prayer** is the activity of praying to God. *e.g. Her eyes were closed and her lips moved in prayer.*
2 A **prayer** is the signs or words that you sign or say when you pray on a particular occasion. *e.g. I said a prayer for her quick recovery.*

preach 1247
When a person (usually a member of the clergy) **preaches** a sermon or **preaches**, he or she gives a talk on a religious or moral subject, especially during a church service. *e.g. The chaplain used to preach to a packed church every Sunday.*

preacher 1247
A **preacher** is a person who preaches sermons as part of a church service. Preachers are often members of the clergy. *e.g. Tony inherited his eloquence from his father, a Christian preacher.*

precede   442
If someone or something **precedes** you somewhere, they go there in front of you. *e.g. She slung her bag over her shoulder and preceded him across the vast hallway.*

precede   1332
If one event or period of time **precedes** another, it happens before the second event or period of time. *e.g. The children's dinner will precede the party games.*

precious   131, 1524
1 Something that is **precious** is considered to be important, valuable, and useful, and therefore should not be wasted or used badly. *e.g. They have lost precious working time.*
2 Something that is **precious** is worth a lot of money because it is rare. *e.g. Salt is nearly as precious as gold in many places.*
3 **Precious** possessions or memories are very important to you because they are concerned with people or events in your life which you remember with pleasure. *e.g. To me, our friendship is a very precious thing.*

precise   847, 849, 852, 891
1 Something that is **precise** is accurate and complete in all its details. *e.g. The timing had to be precise.*
2 Someone who is **precise** is extremely careful and particular about details. *e.g. He was very precise in his way of giving instructions.*

prefer   177, 198, 1660
If you **prefer** someone or something, you like that person or thing better than another, and so are more likely to choose them if there is a choice. *e.g. I would prefer a glass of whiskey, if you have any.*

preference   177, 198, 1660
1 **Preference** is the desire to have, do, or choose one thing rather than another if there is a choice, because you like it better, or because it is more convenient for you. *e.g. Do you have a preference for Italian or Spanish food?*
2 A **preference** is the thing in a group that you like better than other things in the group. *e.g. My own preference is traditional jazz.*

pregnant   1013
If a woman or female animal is **pregnant**, she has a developing baby or babies in her body. *e.g. My sister and her dog Silky were pregnant at the same time.*

prehistoric   1480
Prehistoric people and things existed at a time before information was written down. *e.g. Prehistoric cooking pots were found during the excavation.*

prehistory   1480
Prehistory is the time in history before any information was written down. *e.g. What do we know about the prehistory of our country?*

premiere   1351
A **premiere** is the first public performance of a new play or film. *e.g. The charity benefited from the proceeds of the premiere.*

preparation   1088
1 **Preparation** is the activity of getting something ready for use or for a particular purpose. *e.g. Smith was involved in the preparation of the manifesto.*
2 **Preparations** are all the things that are done and the arrangements that are made before an event that will happen in the future. *e.g. He made preparations for the Congress.*

prepare   1088
1 If you **prepare** someone or something, you make them ready for an event or action that will happen in the future. *e.g. She was expecting me and prepared a room.*
2 If you **prepare** for an event or action that will happen soon, you get yourself ready for it. *e.g. Guests prepared to leave, collecting their coats and signing farewells.*
3 If you **prepare** food, you clean it, cook it, etc., so that it is ready to be eaten. *e.g. He spent all morning preparing the meal.*

prescription   607
A **prescription** is a piece of paper on which a doctor has written the name of a medicine you need. You give it to the chemist in exchange for the medicine. *e.g. My doctor gave me a prescription for sleeping tablets.*

present   1372
1 A **present** is a gift that you give to someone, for example, at Christmas or when you visit them. *e.g. Liz brought home a present for Rob.*
2 If you **present** someone with something, such as a prize, or if you **present** it to them, you formally give it to them. *e.g. He will present her with a copy of his book.*
3 When you **present** information, you give it to people in a formal way. *e.g. We need to find a way of presenting this information.*
4 If someone **presents** a programme on television or radio, they introduce each part of it or each person on it. *e.g. 'See Hear' was presented by Clive Mason and Maureen Denmark.*

present   1625
1 You use **present** to describe people, situations or things that exist now, especially when you want to distinguish them from others that they have replaced or that will replace them in the future. *e.g. Economic planning cannot succeed in present conditions.*

2 The **present** is the period of time or the part of your life that is taking place now. *e.g. We have to come to terms with the present.*
3 If you sign or say that something exists, is the case, or is happening at **present**, or at the **present** time, you mean that it exists, is the case or is happening at the time when you are writing, signing or speaking, rather than in the future. *e.g. I don't want to get married at present.*

preserve   199
If you **preserve** a situation or condition, you make sure that it remains as it is, and is not changed or ended. *e.g. I was determined to preserve my dignity.*

preside   86, 97
If you **preside** over a formal gathering such as a meeting, you act as the chair or chairperson. *e.g. Feynman had offered to preside over the seminar for theoretical physicists.*

president   86, 97, 241, 1142
1 The **president** of a republic is the person who has the highest political position, and who is also the Head of State. *e.g. We received a letter from the President of the United States.*
2 The **president** of an organisation or society is the person who has the highest position in it. *e.g. He was welcomed by the president of the Rotary Club.*

press   7
If you **press** clothes, you iron them in order to get rid of the creases. *e.g. Ivor learned how to press his uniform.*

press   1378
1 If you **press** on something, you push down hard against it. *e.g. She tried to press the pages together.*
2 If you **press** plants, you keep them squeezed between two flat surfaces until they become dry so that you can preserve them or use them for making a picture. *e.g. She's going to press the rose he gave her.*
3 A **press** is a piece of equipment used for squeezing things between two flat surfaces. *e.g. Could you pass me the press, please?*

press a doorbell   162
When you **press a doorbell**, you push a small device, usually positioned on or by the side of a door, which causes a bell to ring inside the building. The sound of the bell informs people inside the building that you are there and that you want to see them. *e.g. She pressed the doorbell and waited.*

press a flashing doorbell   163
When you **press a flashing doorbell**, you push a small device usually positioned on, or by the side of the door, which causes a light (or

lights) inside the building to go on and off. The flashing light (or lights) informs people inside the building that you are there and that you want to see them. Flashing doorbells are used especially by Deaf and deaf people. *e.g. She pressed the flashing doorbell but nobody came to the door.*

press an operating button 162
When you **press an operating button** or **press a button**, you push a small device (button) in order to operate a machine or electrical device. *e.g. She pressed the operating button and the escalator started to move.*

Preston 754
1 **Preston** is a town in North West England, which is the administrative centre of Lancashire. *e.g. Mark comes from Preston.*
2 The address of **Preston** Deaf Club is: Mary Cross Trust, Brockholes Brow, Preston.

presume 510
1 If you **presume** that something is the case, you decide that it is very likely to be the case, although you cannot be certain. *e.g. I presume that they just send out a folder.*
2 If something is **presumed** to be the case, people believe that it is the case, although they cannot be certain. *e.g. He got away and is presumed to be living in Spain.*

presumption 510
A **presumption** is something that is believed to be true, even though it is impossible to be certain. *e.g. I don't agree that that's a false presumption.*

pretend 664, 1578
1 If you **pretend** that something is the case, you act in a way that is intended to make people believe that it is the case, although in fact it is not. *e.g. I am going to pretend that I cannot see him waving.*
2 Something that is **pretend** is not real or genuine. *e.g. I'm going to put this pretend slug on the teacher's chair!*

pretty 465
1 If you describe someone as **pretty**, you mean that they are nice to look at and attractive. *e.g. Who are those pretty children?*
2 A place or thing that is **pretty** is nice to look at. *e.g. It was a very pretty garden.*

prevent 72
1 If you **prevent** someone from doing something, you do not allow them to do it. *e.g. The idea was to prevent him from interrupting the meeting.*
2 If people or things **prevent** something from happening, they ensure that it does not happen. *e.g. They did everything they could to prevent the accident.*

prevention 72
Prevention is action that does not allow something to happen. *e.g. We had an interpreted talk about fire prevention.*

previous 1250, 1332
A **previous** event or thing is one that happened or came before the one that you are talking about. *e.g. He had two children from a previous marriage.*

previously 1250, 1332
Previously means at some time before the period you are referring to. *e.g. Previously, he had lived the life of a beggar, but he is now a wealthy man.*

price 1505
1 The **price** of something is the amount of money that you must pay in order to buy it. *e.g. The price of petrol is too high.*
2 If something is **priced** at a particular amount, it costs that amount to buy. *e.g. Apparently, they price things cheap in Blackpool.*

pride 232
1 **Pride** is a good feeling of happiness and eagerness for praise, which you have when you or people that you like have done something good, or when you own something that you think is good. *e.g. She pointed with pride to the fine horses she had trained.*
2 If you have or take **pride** in something that you have or do, you feel pleased and happy because of it. *e.g. I take pride in the success of my students.*

priest 643
A **priest** is a member of the Christian clergy in the Catholic, Anglican or Orthodox church. *e.g. My son has recently become a priest.*

primary 302
You use **primary** to refer to something that is considered to be the main or most significant one of its kind. *e.g. The primary concern in such cases is always to make sure that humanitarian aid gets through.*

prince 1131
A **prince** is a male member of the royal family, especially the son of the king or queen of a country or the husband of a reigning queen. *e.g. Prince Charles has strong ideas about architecture.*

princess 1131
A **princess** is a female member of a royal family, usually the daughter of a king or queen or the wife of a prince. *e.g. The Princess of Wales is the Patron of the British Deaf Association.*

principal 450
A **principal** is the person in charge of a school, college or institution. *e.g. Complaints began arriving at the principal's office.*

principle 401
1 A **principle** is a general belief that you have about the way you should behave which influences your behaviour. *e.g. Every effort is made to uphold the principle that human life is sacred.*
2 If you do something on **principle**, you do it because of a particular belief that you have. *e.g. On principle, I felt that I had to vote for that motion.*

principles 402
Principles are the general beliefs that you have about the way you should behave which influence your behaviour. *e.g. He never goes to parties because of his anti-drinking principles.*

print 1309
1 If you **print** a book, a newspaper, or a leaflet, you produce quantities of it by means of a mechanical process. *e.g. They wanted to print a thousand posters.*
2 If you **print** a piece of a signed presentation, speech or writing, you include a written version of it in a newspaper, magazine, or book. *e.g. We can't print this interview in a family magazine!*

printer 1309
1 A **printer** is someone who prints books, newspapers, leaflets, etc., usually as an employee of a printing firm. *e.g. The printers tried to dictate how he should run his business.*
2 A **printer** is a machine that is connected to a computer or word-processor and that prints out information or calculations from the computer or word-processor onto paper. *e.g. Let me show you our new dot-matrix printer.*

priority 302
1 Something that is a **priority** must be done or dealt with as soon as possible. *e.g. Getting food into Somalia is the main priority.*
2 If someone or something has **priority** or is given **priority** over other people or things, they are considered more important than other people or things and are therefore dealt with first. *e.g. Older children are given priority when day nursery places are allocated.*

prison 47
A **prison** is a building where criminals are kept in order to punish them and to protect other people from them or where people waiting to be tried for a crime are kept before their trial. *e.g. He was sent to prison for two years for stealing the car.*

prisoner 47
1 A **prisoner** is someone who is kept in a prison as a punishment. *e.g. The two policemen took the new prisoner to his cell.*

2 A **prisoner** is someone who has been captured by an enemy, for example in a war. *e.g. The Russian prisoners were escorted to the train.*

private   1265, 1266, 1470
1 Something that is **private** is for the use of one person or group only, rather than for the general public. *e.g. All rooms have got a private bath, shower and W.C.*
2 **Private** discussions or interviews take place between a small group of people and are kept secret from other people. *e.g. I have asked the editors to apply to the Prime Minister for a private interview.*
3 If you do something in **private**, you do it without other people being present, usually because it is something that you want to keep secret. *e.g. Could we talk to you in private?*
4 **Private** activities and belongings are connected with your personal life rather than with your work or business. *e.g. She never spoke about her private life.*
5 Your **private** thoughts or plans are thoughts and plans which are personal to you and which you do not sign or speak about to other people. *e.g. He has his own private plans for the future.*
6 If you describe a place as **private**, you mean that it is quiet and you can be alone there without being interrupted or disturbed. *e.g. This office is nice and private.*
7 A **private** person is very quiet by nature and does not share his or her thoughts and feelings with other people. *e.g. Away from the glare of publicity, he is an intensely private man.*
8 **Private** is also used to describe services that you pay for or industries that are owned by an individual person or group, rather than services and industries that are controlled by local or national government. *e.g. She had gone to a private school in Oxford.*

problem   208
A **problem** is a situation that is unsatisfactory and causes difficulties for people. *e.g. The family next door have financial problems.*

procedure   156, 157, 196, 1646
A **procedure** is a way of doing something, especially the usual or correct way. *e.g. She explained the procedure for recording the administration of drugs.*

proceed   1642
If someone **proceeds** with something, they continue to follow a course of action that they have already started. *e.g. It is necessary to examine this claim before we proceed further.*

process   1646
A **process** is a series of actions which are carried out in order to achieve a particular result. *e.g. It has been a long process getting this information.*

proclaim   456
If you **proclaim** something, you make a public announcement about it. *e.g. America proclaimed its independence in 1776.*

proclamation   456
A **proclamation** is a public announcement about something important. *e.g. Bentley proclaimed his innocence, but they hanged him anyway.*

produce   272
A person who **produces** a play, film, television programme, etc., organises its preparation and gets it ready to present to the public. *e.g. The film was produced by Mel Brooks.*

producer   272
A **producer** is a person whose job is organising the preparation of a play, film, television programme, etc., and getting it ready to present to the public. *e.g. The producer of 'Sign On' was the guest of honour.*

professional   975
1 **Professional** means relating to the work that a person does for an occupation, especially work that requires special training. *e.g. He started his professional life as a comedian.*
2 **Professional** means having a job in which you receive money for doing something that many people do as a hobby or do for themselves, for example sport, music, or cooking. *e.g. She left the shop in which she had been working and became a professional actress.*
3 A **professional** is a person with a job in which they receive money for doing something that many people do as a hobby or do for themselves. *e.g. He has seventeen major championship victories as a professional plus two amateur titles.*
4 A **professional** is a person who has a job that requires special training and brings a fairly high status. *e.g. Nurses, doctors, social workers, and other professionals will be at the meeting.*
5 If something that someone does or produces is **professional**, it is very skilful and of a very high standard. *e.g. He had typed the whole scheme out and it looked very professional.*
6 A **professional** is a person who shows great skill and high standards in the work that they do. *e.g. We are all professionals: let's keep our standards up.*

profile   324
Your **profile** is the outline of your face as it is seen when someone is looking at you from the side. *e.g. Your profile is just like your father's.*

profit   861
1 A **profit** is an amount of money that you gain when you are paid more for something than it cost you to make it, get it, or do it. *e.g. Make as much profit as you can: the*

association needs the money.
2 If you **profit** from something, you gain benefit or advantage from it. *e.g. The entire Deaf community will profit from this major step forward.*

programme   196
A **programme** of actions or events is a series of actions or events that are planned to take place. *e.g. The programme of meetings will last for two days.*

programme   1014
A television or radio **programme** is something that is broadcast on television or radio. *e.g. Gardening programmes are my favourite.*

progress   1642
1 **Progress** is the change or advance in a society that makes life better or more civilised. *e.g. There has been great technological progress.*
2 To **progress** means to become more advanced or skilful over a period of time. *e.g. Technology will progress rapidly in the twenty-first century.*

prohibit   109, 917
If you **prohibit** something, you forbid it by means of a law, rule, or official agreement. *e.g. The new law will prohibit members of the armed forces from striking.*

promiscuous   551
Someone who is **promiscuous** has sex with many different people. *e.g. Since her marriage broke up she's been really promiscuous.*

promise   357
If you **promise** that you will do something, you sign or say to someone that you will definitely do it. *e.g. 'I'll be back at twelve o'clock, I promise,' signed Liz.*

promote   54
1 If you **promote** something, you help it to happen, increase or spread. *e.g. The government could do more to promote the anti-smoking campaign.*
2 If you **promote** something, you try to make it more popular or successful. *e.g. The new town was promoted as an ideal place to live.*

promote   866
If someone is **promoted**, they are given a more important job in the organisation they work for. *e.g. He had recently been promoted to assistant manager.*

promotion   866
If you are given **promotion** or a **promotion**, you are given a more important job in the organisation you work for. *e.g. What, if any, are the chances of promotion?*

pronounce   456
If someone **pronounces** a verdict or opinion on something, they formally give their verdict or opinion. *e.g. Are the people ready to pronounce their verdict?*

pronounce   524
If you **pronounce** a word, you say it in the way it is usually said or in a particular way. *e.g. I can't pronounce his name.*

pronouncement   456
A **pronouncement** is a formal or official statement. *e.g. There hasn't yet been any pronouncement from the back benches which would dampen enthusiasm for the deal.*

pronunciation   524
1 The **pronunciation** of a word or spoken language is the way in which it is usually said. *e.g. A typical New York pronunciation would be more like this.*
2 Someone's **pronunciation** of a spoken word is the way in which they pronounce it. *e.g. He tried to correct Franco's pronunciation.*

proof   326, 1344
Proof of something is evidence or facts that show that it is true or that it exists. *e.g. What proof have you got that this is your briefcase?*

proof   330, 848
Proof is a documented fact or facts or piece of evidence which shows that something is true or exists. *e.g. He presented a receipt as proof that he had paid his bill.*

prop   152
1 A **prop** is a piece of wood or other object that you use to put under something to support it. *e.g. They still use wooden props in coal mines today.*
2 If you **prop** an object **up**, you support it by putting something underneath it. *e.g. We will have to prop up the ceiling.*

propaganda   54
Propaganda is information, often exaggerated or false information, which an organisation publishes or broadcasts in order to influence people. *e.g. She did not like the propaganda campaigns of the main political parties.*

propeller (of a boat)   406
A **propeller** is a device with blades which is attached to a boat. The engine makes the propeller spin round and causes the boat to move. *e.g. This is the propeller from a 1938 Cornish trawler.*

proper   61, 197, 200, 847, 849, 852, 891
1 You use **proper** to describe things that you consider to be real and satisfactory rather than inadequate in some way. *e.g. He wants to get a proper job.*

2 The **proper** thing is the one that is correct or most suitable. *e.g. What is your proper address?*
3 If you refer to a way of behaving as **proper**, you mean that it is considered socially acceptable and right by a particular group or society. *e.g. She told the small boy that the proper way to eat a yoghurt was with a spoon, not his fingers.*

proportion   1705
1 A **proportion** of a whole thing or group is a part of it; used when you are thinking about the relative sizes of the part and the whole. *e.g. Courts are now sending a smaller proportion of offenders to prison.*
2 The **proportion** of one kind of thing in a group is the amount or number of that kind of thing that is included in the group. *e.g. The proportion of women in the total workforce has risen.*

proposal   1597
A **proposal** is a suggested plan which is put forward for people to think about and decide upon. *e.g. My proposal is that the shelter be built as soon as possible.*

propose   443
When you **propose** someone for an office, you nominate them for that position. *e.g. I propose Jeff for treasurer.*

propose   1597
If you **propose** a plan or idea, you suggest it for people to think about and decide upon. *e.g. I propose that the culprits be tried.*

prosecute   244
If someone is **prosecuted**, they are charged with a crime and put on trial. *e.g. The police decided to prosecute the drunken driver.*

prosecution   244
Prosecution is the bringing of criminal charges against someone. *e.g. We could still face prosecution.*

prospective   1611
Prospective is used of someone who intends to do a particular thing, for example to have a particular profession. *e.g. She is married to a prospective Member of Parliament.*

prostitute   22, 261
A **prostitute** is a person who has sex with another person in exchange for money. *e.g. The police claimed she was a prostitute.*

prostitution   22
Prostitution is the work of people who have sex with other people in exchange for money. *e.g. Prostitution is not illegal in Holland.*

protect   72
To **protect** someone or something means to prevent them from being harmed or damaged.

e.g. The Common Law has always protected individuals' rights.

protect   777
To **protect** someone or something means to watch over them and prevent them from being harmed or damaged. *e.g. I will have to protect that vase and make sure the customs people don't damage it.*

protection   72
If something gives **protection** against something unpleasant, it prevents people or things from being harmed or damaged by it. *e.g. We need protection from the sun's rays.*

protector   72
A **protector** is someone who prevents other people, animals or objects being harmed or damaged. *e.g. We are an informal group of ecologists and protectors of wildlife.*

protest   909
If you **protest** about something or against something, you declare or show in public that you object to something that someone, especially someone in authority, is doing or is intending to do. *e.g. Ministers felt bound to protest against the change in Government policy.*

Protestant   1269
1 Someone or something that is **Protestant** belongs to or relates to the branches of the Christian church which separated from the Catholic church in the sixteenth century. *e.g. Protestant services are held in the hospital chapel at nine and eleven o'clock every Sunday.*
2 A **Protestant** is a person who belongs to the Protestant church. *e.g. The vast majority of the workers here are Protestants.*

proud   232
If you feel **proud**, you feel glad about something that someone has done or possesses, and think it is a good thing to have done or to possess. *e.g. I'm working class and proud of it.*

prove   1344, 1373, 1384
1 To **prove** that something is true or correct means to show definitely that it is true or correct. *e.g. The autopsy will prove that she drowned.*
2 If you **prove** someone or something to have a particular quality or capability, you show that they have that quality or capability. *e.g. I think he will prove to be extremely reliable.*

provide   1517
If you **provide** something that someone needs or wants, you give it to them or make it available. *e.g. Parents are expected to provide a home for their children.*

provoke 444, 558
If you **provoke** someone, you deliberately annoy them and try to make them behave aggressively. *e.g. Ray was trying to provoke them into a fight.*

provost 1142, 1693
A **provost** of a town or city in Scotland is the person who has been elected to be the head of the town or city for one year, and to represent it at certain formal occasions. *e.g. Mr. Bill Smith was elected Provost of Edinburgh.*

prowl 736
1 When an animal or person **prowls**, they move around quietly and carefully, trying not to be noticed, for example when they are hunting another animal or person. *e.g. Tigers prowl through the forest in search of their prey.*
2 If an animal is on the **prowl**, they are moving around quietly and carefully, and trying not to be noticed. *e.g. We heard the bark of a jackal setting out on the prowl for food.*
3 A **prowl** is a quiet, careful walk around an area which a person or animal takes in order to observe what is happening there (for example, when hunting). *e.g. He's going for a prowl around his den.*

pry 334
If you **pry**, you try to find out about someone else's private affairs, often secretly. *e.g. I caught her prying in my desk.*

pseudo 664
Pseudo is used to describe something as not being the thing that it is claimed to be. For example, if you describe a country as a pseudo-democracy, you mean that it is not really a democracy, although it is claimed to be one. *e.g. He is a pseudo-intellectual.*

psychiatrist 507
A **psychiatrist** is a doctor who treats people suffering from mental illnesses. *e.g. It was arranged that I should see a psychiatrist.*

psychiatry 507
Psychiatry is the branch of medicine concerned with the treatment of mental illnesses. *e.g. Whittingham Hospital, near Preston, has a department of psychiatry for Deaf people.*

psychological 1361
1 **Psychological** means concerned with a person's mind and thoughts. *e.g. Are there important psychological differences between the two sexes?*
2 **Psychological** also means relating to psychology. *e.g. Psychological tests have been criticised many times in the past.*

psychologist 1361
A **psychologist** is a person who studies the

human mind and tries to explain why people behave in the way that they do. *e.g. He's really a psychologist, but he got interested in sign language.*

psychology 1361
1 **Psychology** is the scientific study of the human mind and the reasons for people's behaviour. *e.g. He has a psychology degree.*
2 The **psychology** of a person is the kind of mind that they have which makes them think or behave in the way that they do. *e.g. The psychology of the terrorist is incomprehensible to most people.*

pub 66
A **pub** is a building where people can purchase and consume drinks, especially alcoholic drinks, and meet their friends. *e.g. I used to meet Fred in a pub called The Bridge.*

public 456
If a fact is made **public**, it becomes known to everyone rather than kept secret. *e.g. When the names of the new Cabinet Ministers were made public, there was much disappointment.*

public 482
1 You can refer to people in general, or to all the people in a particular country or community, as the **public**. *e.g. All members of the public are welcome.*
2 You can refer to a set of people in a country who share a common interest, activity, or characteristic as a particular kind of **public**. *e.g. Literature available to the general reading public does not explain this clearly.*
3 **Public** means relating to all the people in a country or community. *e.g. The campaigners have attracted significant public support.*

public 1373, 1384
1 A **public** statement, action, or event is made or done with members of the public present or able to know about it. *e.g. Her very last public appearance was at the Old Vic in 'Romeo and Juliet'.*
2 If a fact is made **public**, it becomes known to everyone rather than being kept secret. *e.g. The job vacancy was made public last week.*

public house 66
A **public house** is a pub. See **pub**.

publicize 54, 456
also spelled **publicise**.
If you **publicize** a fact or event, you make it widely known to the public. *e.g. We will publicize Deaf Awareness week with support from Barclays Bank.*

publicity 54
Publicity is information or actions intended to attract the public's attention to someone or

something. *e.g. There was some advance publicity for the book on television.*

publish 1309
1 When a company **publishes** a book, magazine, etc., it has copies of it printed, which are then sent to shops and sold. *e.g. We publish very few scientific works, actually.*
2 When the people in charge of a newspaper or magazine **publish** a piece of writing, they print it in their newspaper or magazine. *e.g. They plan to publish my article in January.*

publisher 1309
A **publisher** is a person or a company that publishes books. *e.g. The publisher of this Dictionary is Faber and Faber.*

pudding 240, 732
1 A **pudding** is a cooked, sweet food made with suet, rice, or flour, fat and eggs. It is usually served hot and has the shape of the bowl that it was cooked in. *e.g. She loved treacle pudding.*
2 A **pudding** is the sweet course of a meal which is usually served after the main course or at the end of a meal. *e.g. What are we having for pudding?*

puddle 496
A **puddle** is a small, shallow pool of liquid that has spread on the ground. *e.g. The road was filled with puddles from the rain.*

pull 273
When you **pull** something, you hold it firmly, usually with both hands, and use force to move it towards you. *e.g. He tied the rope to the car bumper and then pulled with all his might.*

pull a cracker 49
When a **cracker** is **pulled**, usually by two people, it comes apart. People often pull crackers at parties. *e.g. Who will pull my cracker with me?*

pullover 136
A **pullover** is a woollen piece of clothing, which may be sleeveless, that covers the upper part of your body and does not open at the front. *e.g. He wore a new blue pullover.*

pull someone's leg 52, 665, 765, 1016
If you **pull someone's leg**, you try to make them believe something that is not true, for a joke. *e.g. He pulled his girlfriend's leg about how much he paid for the ring, but finally told her that he had bought it in the sale.*

pulse 1675
Your **pulse** is the regular beating of blood through your body, which you can feel when you touch particular parts of your body (usually your wrist). *e.g. Your pulse is normal—that's a good sign.*

pulse (take one's pulse) 1675
When someone **takes** or **checks your pulse**, they find out the speed of your heartbeat by feeling the pulse in your wrist with their fingers and calculating the number of beats in one minute. *e.g. The G.P. took my pulse when I went for my medical examination on Friday.*

puncture 397
1 A **puncture** is a small hole in a tyre, that has been made by a sharp object, which allows the air inside the tyre to escape. *e.g. I must minicom the AA. I've got a puncture.*
2 To **puncture** a tyre, or something else that is inflated with gas or liquid, means to make a small hole in it so that the gas or liquid escapes. *e.g. Nothing could puncture such strong material.*

puncture 1554
A **puncture** is a flat tyre. *e.g. The neighbours' car has got a puncture.*

punish 269
If you **punish** someone, you make them suffer in some way because they have done something wrong. *e.g. They discovered he did it and punished him for it.*

punishment 269
Punishment is the act of punishing someone. *e.g. Punishment will not reform the hardened criminal.*

punt 127
1 A **punt** is a long boat with a flat bottom. You move the punt along by standing at one end and pushing a long pole down against the bottom of the river. *e.g. We decided to use the punt, not the rowing boat.*
2 When you **punt**, you travel along a river in a punt. *e.g. I punted slowly down the river.*

purchase 1513
1 When you **purchase** something, you buy it. *e.g. He finally got the house he had tried to purchase only two years before.*
2 **Purchase** is the act of buying something. *e.g. He advised them on the purchase of their new car.*
3 A **purchase** is something you have bought. *e.g. Do you want to see my purchase from Harrod's?*

pure 1314
1 **Pure** means not mixed with anything else. *e.g. She wore a dress of pure silk.*
2 Something that is **pure** is clean, healthy and does not contain any harmful substances. *e.g. The water supply is completely pure.*

purity 1314
1 The **purity** of something is the degree or extent to which it is not mixed with anything else. *e.g. Her lecture was entitled 'The Purity of the French Language—Myth or Reality?'.*

2 Something that is in a state of **purity** is clean, healthy and does not contain any harmful substances. *e.g. I could not vouch for the purity of their drinking water.*

purple 173, 1245, 1257, 1602
Something that is **purple** is of a reddish-blue colour. *e.g. Kris changed, putting on clean jeans and a purple shirt.*

purpose (on purpose) 182
If you do something **on purpose**, you do it deliberately and not by accident or chance. *e.g. He had gone there on purpose to see what happened.*

pursue 595
If you **pursue** someone or something, you follow them, usually in order to catch them. *e.g. The stewards pursued the wrong man.*

pursuit 595
The **pursuit** of someone or something is the act of chasing them. *e.g. The gamekeeper was in pursuit of a poacher and did not notice the booby-trap.*

push 1397
1 When you **push** something, you press it using force, usually with your hands, in order to move it. *e.g. I pushed open the heavy door.*
2 When you **push** someone, you try to move them or get past them. *e.g. Don't push, get in the line.*
3 If you **push** someone into doing something, you urge or force them to do it. *e.g. My parents had to push me into trying for university—I'm grateful now.*
4 If you **push** people to complete something, you get them to hurry with it. *e.g. The boss had to push them to get the order out.*

push a cart/wheelbarrow 117
When you **push a cart** or a **wheelbarrow**, you cause it to move along in front of you by lifting up the two handles and walking behind it. *e.g. She pushed the wheelbarrow out of the way.*

push a pram/pushchair/trolley 84
When you **push a pram**, **pushchair** or **trolley**, you cause it to move along in front of you by walking behind it and pressing against it continuously with your hands. *e.g. He pushed the pram up the hill.*

pushchair 84
A **pushchair** is a small folding chair on wheels, in which a baby or small child can sit and be wheeled around. *e.g. We bought a new pushchair for Maria.*

put a jigsaw/jigsaw puzzle together 217
If you **put a jigsaw** or **jigsaw puzzle together**, you fit the individual pieces of the

jigsaw together so that they form a picture (the same as that shown on the cover of the box in which the pieces were packaged). *e.g. Would you like to help me put this jigsaw together?*

put a plaster/sticking plaster on the back of the hand 191
If you **put a plaster** or **sticking plaster on the back of your hand**, you cover a small cut, blister, etc., on the back of your hand with a plaster or sticking plaster. *e.g. She put a plaster on the back of his hand where the bee had stung him.*

put back 885
If you **put** something **back** to a later time, you postpone it. *e.g. We've had to put back the seminar again.*

put down 1317, 1333
If you **put down** something that you are holding or carrying, you place it onto a surface, for example onto the floor or a table. *e.g. She put the paper down on the desk.*

put forward an idea/recommendation/suggestion 504
If you **put forward an idea**, a **recommendation** or a **suggestion**, you present it as a potentially useful course of action in order for people to consider and discuss it. *e.g. Carson put forward a suggestion that we postpone the decision until later.*

put in 1334, 1511
If you **put** one thing **in** another thing, you place it inside the other thing so that it is enclosed or surrounded by the other thing. *e.g. She put the note in her purse.*

put in one's place 1272
If you are **put in your place** or something **puts you in your place**, you are shown to be less important or clever than you think. *e.g. I gave a totally incorrect answer to the question, which put me in my place.*

put into 1511
If you **put** one thing **into** another thing, you place it inside the other thing so that it is enclosed or surrounded by the other thing. *e.g. Put that into the envelope, too.*

put into an oven 1202, 1334
If you **put** something **into an oven**, you lift it into a cooker or part of a cooker that is like a box with a door. *e.g. She put the pie into the oven.*

put off 885, 1003
If you **put** something **off**, you delay doing it. *e.g. I wanted to put off doing the washing, so I lounged around the house for a while.*

put on 1317, 1333
If you **put** something **on** or **onto** another

thing, you move it so that it is resting on the surface of that thing. *e.g. Put the newspaper on the television.*

put on a bathrobe/dressing gown   286
When you **put on a bathrobe** or **dressing gown**, you place your arms in the sleeves and position it on your body so that you can wear it. It is kept in position by a belt which is usually fastened in a knot. *e.g. He put on his dressing gown and answered the door.*

put on a coat/an overcoat   144
When you **put on a coat** or **an overcoat**, you place your arms in the sleeves and position it on your body so that you can wear it. *e.g. He put on his coat and waved goodbye.*

put on a coat (lightweight coat)/jacket/mac/mackintosh   288
When you **put on a lightweight coat**, **jacket**, **mac** or **mackintosh**, you place your arms in the sleeves and position it on your body so that you can wear it. *e.g. He put on his jacket and signed goodbye.*

put on a glove   1546
When you **put on a glove**, you pull it over your hand so that you can wear it. *e.g. Put on your glove or you'll lose it.*

put on a hat   1525
You **put on a hat** when you fit it on your head, usually holding it by the brim, so that you can wear it. *e.g. Put on a hat. It's really cold outside.*

put on a hat   1530
You **put on a hat** when you fit it on your head, usually holding the front of it in one hand, so that you can wear it. *e.g. What would it look like if I put on a hat?*

put on a jersey/jumper/pullover/sweater   136
You **put on a jersey**, **jumper**, **pullover** or **sweater** by pulling it over your head and down onto the upper part of your body in order to wear it. *e.g. It was cold, so he put on a jumper.*

put on (an upright surface)   1348
If you **put** something **on an upright surface**, such as a wall, you attach it to that surface so that it is positioned parallel to the surface. *e.g. Well, put it on the wall and we can have a look.*

put on a plaster/sticking plaster   191
If you **put on a plaster** or **sticking plaster**, you place a plaster or sticking plaster over a small cut,

blister, etc., on your body in order to protect it. *e.g. I dabbed the cut and put a plaster on it.*

put on a shoe   1682
When you **put on a shoe**, you place your foot in it and, if necessary, fasten it in order to wear it. *e.g. She put on one shoe but couldn't find the other.*

put on boots/wellingtons   148
When you **put on boots** or **wellingtons**, you place your right foot into the right boot or wellington and pull it over your foot and up the lower part of your leg. The action is repeated for the left boot or wellington. *e.g. She sat in an armchair and put on her boots.*

put one's foot down   1291
If you **put your foot down** when you are driving a vehicle, you cause it to travel faster by pressing down on the accelerator pedal. *e.g. Come on, put your foot down, he's getting away!*

put on jeans/tights/trousers   147
When you **put on jeans**, **tights** or **trousers**, you place your legs into them and pull them up to your waist in order to wear them. Jeans and trousers have a front or side opening which you close, usually by buttons or a zip, after you have pulled them up to your waist. *e.g. She put on her jeans and an old sweater after her bath.*

put on nylons/stockings   876
If you **put on nylons** or **stockings**, you pull one nylon or stocking over one of your feet and then, holding the top of the nylon or stocking carefully with two hands, you pull it up to the top part of your thigh. You repeat this process with the other nylon or stocking on your other foot and leg. *e.g. My grandmother always wore gloves to put on stockings so that she would not damage them with her nails.*

put on paper   1596
See **paper (put on paper)**.

put right   61, 197, 200
If you **put right** a mistake or unsatisfactory situation, you do something to make things satisfactory. *e.g. See that this mess is put right before you leave.*

putt   266, 282
1 A **putt** is a stroke in golf that you make with a special club (a putter) when the ball has reached the green. *e.g. Roy sunk a twenty-foot putt on the last green.*
2 When you **putt**, you strike a golf ball on the

green with a putter in order to roll the ball into or near the hole. *e.g. She putted very well during the first round.*

putter   266, 282
A **putter** is a golf club with a short shaft for putting, usually having a solid metal head. *e.g. Nick Faldo gave Mr. Benzie one of his old putters.*

put under a grill   1202, 1334
If you **put** something (usually food) **under a grill**, you lift it into the part of the oven where you can cook it with strong direct heat from above or below. *e.g. Put it under the grill for twenty minutes.*

put up a hood   287
See **hood (put up a hood)**.

put up a poster/notice   223
If you **put up a poster** or a **notice**, you fix it to a notice board or wall so that it can be seen. *e.g. She put up a poster advertising the British Deaf Chess Championship.*

put up with   179, 181, 1182
If you **put up with** something or someone, you tolerate or accept them, even though you find them unpleasant or unsatisfactory. *e.g. I'm prepared to put up with the job for the next six months.*

puzzle   313
1 If you **puzzle** over something, you try hard to think of the answer to it or the explanation for it. *e.g. Astronomers had puzzled over the strange lights in the sky for some time.*
2 You can describe anything hard to understand as a **puzzle**. *e.g. His lecture was a complete puzzle to me.*

pyjamas   1079
also spelled **pajamas**.
A pair of **pyjamas** consists of loose trousers and a loose jacket or top that people, especially men and children, wear in bed. *e.g. He was sitting there in striped pyjamas.*

pyramid   1394
1 A **pyramid** is a shape, object or pile of things with a flat base and flat triangular sides that slope upwards and inwards to a single point. *e.g. She made a pyramid of stones.*
2 The **Pyramids** are ancient stone buildings built over the tombs of dead kings and queens in Egypt. They have triangular walls that slope upwards and inwards to a single point. *e.g. Kathleen enjoyed her visit to the pyramids on her Egyptian holiday.*

Q, q

Q
Q is the seventeenth letter of the British manual and English alphabets. See page 853.

qualification   598
1 A **qualification** is an official record of achievement that you get when you have successfully completed a course of training or passed an exam. *e.g. I haven't got any qualifications at all in English Literature.*
2 **Qualification** is the act of successfully completing a course of training or passing the exams that you need to pass in order to work in a particular profession. *e.g. Even after qualification, jobs were hard to find.*

qualified   975
Someone who is **qualified** has successfully completed a course of training or passed the exams that they need to pass in order to work in a particular profession. *e.g. Don't you have to be qualified to interpret in a court of law?*

qualify   598
1 If you **qualify** as something, you successfully complete a course of training or pass the exams necessary in order to be entitled to work in a particular profession. *e.g. I was thirty-three before I qualified as a doctor.*
2 If you **qualify** in a competition, you are successful in one part of it and go on to the next stage. *e.g. I just wanted to qualify for the final.*

quarrel   915, 924
A **quarrel** is an angry argument between two or more people. *e.g. It was a family quarrel.*

quasi   823
1 **Quasi** is added to other signs or words to indicate that someone or something does not have the qualities mentioned. *e.g. The quasi-academic world of research institutes is under scrutiny.*
2 **Quasi** is added to other signs or words to indicate that someone or something is not or is only pretending to be what is mentioned. *e.g. They have turned their countries into quasi-republics.*

queasy   1144
If you feel **queasy**, you feel rather ill, as if you are going to be sick. *e.g. She felt a little queasy on the boat.*

queen   1131
1 A **queen** is a woman who rules a country as its monarch. Queens are not elected, but are born into a royal family. *e.g. Queen Victoria*

reigned for many years.
2 A **queen** is a woman who is married to a king. *e.g. Henry the Eighth married his first queen in the Tower of London.*

query   848, 865
1 A **query** is a question. *e.g. If you have a query, don't hesitate to write.*
2 If you **query** something, you check it by asking about it because you are not sure if it is correct. *e.g. I wish to query your expenses claim.*

question   848
1 A **question** is something which you sign, say or write in order to ask someone about something. *e.g. Jill asked Jack a question about his childhood: this seemed to wake him up a bit.*
2 If you **question** someone, you ask them a lot of questions about something. *e.g. I started to question her about international signing.*

question   865
If you **question** someone, you ask them a lot of questions about something. *e.g. It was her turn to question the witness.*

queue   1024
1 A **queue** is a number of people who are standing in a line waiting for something. *e.g. She is in the queue for coffee.*
2 When people **queue** or **queue up**, they stand in a line waiting for something. *e.g. You will have to queue for hours to get tickets.*

quick   187, 382
Someone or something that is **quick** moves or performs actions with great speed. *e.g. Crikey, you were quick!*

quick   383
1 Something that is **quick** happens without any delay or with very little delay. *e.g. You're more likely to get a quick reply if you telephone.*
2 Something that is **quick** takes or lasts only a short time. *e.g. Let's have a quick look at that.*

quick (be quick)   384
If you tell someone to **be quick**, you mean that they should do something without delay. *e.g. Well, all right then, but be quick!*

quiet   354
If you are **quiet**, you do not make any noise. *e.g. They are never quiet at play time.*

quiet   879
1 Someone or something that is **quiet** makes only a small amount of noise or is making

much less noise than usual. *e.g. My new car is very quiet compared to my old one.*
2 If a place is **quiet**, there is very little noise there. *e.g. The front bedroom is very noisy because of the traffic, but the back bedroom is very quiet.*
3 If you are **quiet**, you do not sign or say anything at all. *e.g. When the Princess comes, be quiet.*
4 Persons who are **quiet** do not make themselves noticed by signing or speaking, or by their actions. *e.g. She is a quiet woman. She never joins in the Club activities.*

quiet   1272
A **quiet** person behaves in a calm way and is not easily made angry or upset. *e.g. She is a thoughtful, quiet person.*

quiet (be quiet)   352, 354
If you tell someone to **be quiet**, you tell them not to make any noise. *e.g. Be quiet and pay attention.*

quiet (be quiet)   1400
If you tell someone to **be quiet**, you tell them to behave calmly. *e.g. Children! Be quiet, please, and let the nurse finish.*

quit   289
If you **quit**, or **quit** a job, you resign from it. *e.g. A week later she quit, and went home to America.*

quiver   1040
If a person, animal or thing **quivers**, it shakes or trembles. *e.g. The bridge quivered beneath my feet.*

quote   823
1 If you **quote** someone or something, you repeat the exact signs or words that they have signed, said, or written. *e.g. She quoted a Chinese proverb.*
2 A **quote** is a phrase or passage that someone has signed, said, or written which you repeat. *e.g. Let me offer you a short quote from the Bible.*
3 **Quotes** are the punctuation marks ('and' or "and") that are used in writing to indicate where a quotation begins and ends. *e.g. If it's what she signed, put it in quotes.*
4 You can sign or say **quote** or **quotes** in front of a sign, word or phrase when you want to indicate that (even though you may be repeating what someone else signed, said, or wrote) you do not think it is the appropriate or right sign, word or phrase to use. *e.g. A group of, quote, neo-disabled activists caused uproar in Westminster today.*

R, r

R

R is the eighteenth letter of the British manual and English alphabets. See page 853.

rabbit	705

1 A **rabbit** is a small, furry animal with long ears, often kept as a pet. In the wild, rabbits live in holes in the ground. *e.g. Rabbits ate all the lettuce in the garden.*
2 **Rabbit** is meat or fur obtained from rabbits. *e.g. The hat was rabbit and cost over £40.*

radiator	946, 1551

A **radiator** is a hollow, metal device, usually connected by pipes to a central heating system, that is used to heat a room. *e.g. The radiator has been switched off for the summer.*

radical	10

A **radical** is someone who believes that there should be very great or extreme changes in society. *e.g. Archbishop Romero was considered to be a radical by the government.*

radio	1178

1 **Radio** is a system of sending sound over a distance by transmitting electrical signals. *e.g. We established radio communication.*
2 A **radio** or a **radio set** is the piece of equipment that you use when you listen to radio programmes. *e.g. She switched on the radio.*
3 **Radio** refers to all the programmes such as plays, films and news that are broadcast and that the public can listen to using a radio. *e.g. Radio in Britain has gone downhill since all the independent stations were legalised.*
4 **Radio** is the business or industry concerned with making programmes and broadcasting them on radio. *e.g. Tamsin studied music, drama and dance, but never thought she'd end up in radio.*

rage	196

1 **Rage** is a feeling of extremely strong anger that is very difficult to control. *e.g. She was trembling with rage and frustration.*
2 A **rage** is a feeling of extremely strong anger that is very difficult to control. *e.g. She flew into a rage when I told her what had happened.*

railings	657

Railings are a fence made from upright metal bars. *e.g. I peered through the railings into the courtyard.*

railway	17

1 A **railway** is a route between two places along which trains travel on steel rails. *e.g. The railway will stay open as long as there is sufficient public demand.*
2 A **railway** is a company or organisation that operates railway routes. *e.g. Years ago, this line was run by the London, Midland and Scottish Railway Company.*

railway station	17

A **railway station** is a building by a railway line where a train stops to allow passengers to get on or off, and goods to be put on or taken off the train. *e.g. Newcastle railway station has an open-platform policy.*

rain	1041

1 **Rain** is water that falls from the clouds in small drops. *e.g. You can't go out in this rain.*
2 If it **rains**, rain falls. *e.g. Just then, it began to rain.*
3 If something **rains** from above, it falls rapidly and in large quantities. *e.g. Ash rained from the sky.*

rainbow	1663

A **rainbow** is an arch of different colours that you can sometimes see in the sky when it is raining. *e.g. The sun shone through the rain and we could see a rainbow.*

rain (heavy rain)	1165

You sign or say that there is **heavy rain** when a large amount of water falls steadily from the clouds in large drops. *e.g. The heavy rain has left puddles on the lawn.*

raining cats and dogs	1165

If you sign or say that it is **raining cats and dogs**, you mean that it is raining very heavily. *e.g. It could be raining cats and dogs on Monday, but she'll still do the washing.*

rainstorm	1165

A **rainstorm** is a fall of very heavy rain. *e.g. After the rainstorm, the air smelled sweet and clean.*

raise	1201, 1376

1 To **raise** the standard of something means to improve it. *e.g. We hope to raise education standards.*
2 If you **raise** something, you increase the distance between it and the floor. *e.g. The Deaf high jump champion asked them to raise the bar again.*

raise	1210

1 If you **raise** a child, you are responsible for it until it is grown up. *e.g. He decided to raise his children in the Catholic faith.*
2 If you **raise** something, you increase the distance between it and the floor. *e.g. Could you raise the curtain about a foot, please?*

rake	1126, 1151

1 A **rake** is a garden tool consisting of a row of metal teeth attached to a long handle. You can use a rake, for example, to loosen the earth and make it level before putting in plants, or to gather dead leaves. *e.g. I must buy a rake.*
2 If you **rake** a surface, you move a rake across it in order to make it smooth and level. *e.g. Always rake the sand in the long-jump pit after each jump.*
3 If you **rake** things such as leaves or weeds together, you move them together using a rake. *e.g. Rake the dead leaves into a pile.*

rake	1163

If you **rake** through something, you look through it closely, searching for an object which you suspect may be hidden there. *e.g. She started to rake through the drawers to find her passport.*

ramble	123, 234

1 A **ramble** is a long walk in the countryside. *e.g. We were out on a country ramble.*
2 If you **ramble**, you go on a long walk in the countryside. *e.g. We ramble in the Lake District every year.*

rambler	123, 234

A **rambler** is a person who goes on rambles in the countryside, usually as part of an organised group. *e.g. The group of ramblers met at the foot of the Mendips.*

rambling	123, 234

Rambling is the activity of going for long walks in the countryside. *e.g. Norah and Margaret enjoy rambling.*

range	426, 427, 447

A **range** of things is a number of different things of the same general kind. *e.g. M&S have a range of clothes second to none in the High Street.*

rare	618

Something that is **rare** is not done or does not happen very often. *e.g. Cases of smallpox are extremely rare.*

rasher of bacon	653

A **rasher of bacon** is a thin slice of salted or smoked meat from the back or side of a pig. *e.g. How many rashers would you like?*

raspberry	579

A **raspberry** is a small, red fruit which is soft

and sweet and which you can eat. *e.g. I love home-made raspberry jam.*

rat 571
A **rat** is a small animal which has a long tail and looks rather like a large mouse. *e.g. Rats carry nasty diseases.*

rather 618
If you sign or say that you would **rather** do a particular thing, you mean you would prefer to do that thing. If you indicate that you would **rather** someone did a particular thing, you mean you would prefer them to do that thing. *e.g. I would rather play golf than squash.*

ratio 1705
A **ratio** is a relationship between two amounts or measurements, which shows how much greater one is than the other when they are compared. *e.g. We advise you to aim for a ratio of one tutor to ten BSL students.*

ravenous 41, 1655
If you are **ravenous**, you are very hungry indeed. *e.g. By six o'clock, I was ravenous.*

rave up 954
A **rave up** is a lively party. *e.g. They had a rave up in Trafalgar Square on New Year's Eve.*

ray 1707
A **ray** is a beam of heat or light. *e.g. Her skin condition was treated with ultra-violet rays.*

razor 256
A **razor** is a tool that you use for removing hair from your skin. It cuts the hair close to the skin with a sharp blade. *e.g. Who's been using my razor to shave their legs?*

razor blade 256
A **razor blade** is a small, thin, flat piece of metal with a very sharp edge that you fasten to a razor and use for shaving. *e.g. Remember to buy some razor blades when you go shopping.*

reach 1595
When you **reach** a place, you arrive there. *e.g. It will be dark by the time I reach your house.*

read 771
When you **read** something written, you look at written words or symbols on a page and understand them. *e.g. Have you read the article?*

read a document 769, 771
When you **read a document**, such as a report or a piece of writing, you look at the written words or symbols contained in it and understand them. *e.g. How am I supposed to read a document like this: don't they know that English is my second language?*

ready 1088, 1490
1 If someone or something is **ready**, they have prepared themself or have been prepared for something, or they have the right qualities for something. *e.g. She was ready to leave at eight o'clock.*
2 If you are **ready** for something, you need it or want it. *e.g. I'm ready to eat. I'm starving.*
3 If something is **ready**, it is able to be used, taken, or bought after a period of preparation. *e.g. Your tablets will be ready tomorrow.*

real 1323
1 Something that is **real** actually exists and is not imagined, invented, or theoretical. *e.g. You must know the difference between what's real and what's make-believe.*
2 Something that is **real** is natural or traditional, and not artificial or an imitation. *e.g. She signed she wanted a real leather jacket.*
3 You also use **real** to say that something is the true or original thing of its kind, in contrast to one that people may wrongly believe to be true. *e.g. My real home is in London.*

realise 619
Also spelled **realize**.
If you **realise** something, you understand or become aware of it, either by thinking about it and connecting together the information you have, or as a result of discovering new information. *e.g. I realised in the end that I should resign.*

really 1323
1 You can use **really** to emphasise a statement that you are making or an opinion that you are giving. *e.g. It really is beautiful, isn't it?*
2 You can use **really** to emphasise the exact truth or facts about a situation. *e.g. This year the grant was £380 with fees, so that was really £440.*
3 You can use **really** to emphasise that something happens to a much greater extent and more seriously than before. *e.g. It is at the postgraduate level that the pressure really begins.*

really? 1143
When you use **really?** as a question, you are expressing surprise about something. *e.g. Really, you have four grown children?*

reason 368
1 The **reason** for something is the fact or situation which explains why it happens or exists. *e.g. I asked the reason for the decision.*
2 If you indicate that you have **reason** to believe something or to feel something, you mean that there is a valid explanation as to why you believe it or feel it. *e.g. You had good reason to feel so upset.*

rebel 5, 56, 89
1 A **rebel** is someone who is actively involved in fighting against the army of the

government of their own country because they want to bring about a new political system. *e.g. Sources said that rebels had made regular attacks on the railways.*
2 If you **rebel**, you act with other people against the rulers of your country, often using violent methods, in order to force a change in the system of government. *e.g. The Duke of Monmouth rebelled against his uncle James the Second in 1685.*
3 If you **rebel**, you behave in a way that is not usual or expected because you have rejected the values of your parents, society, or culture. *e.g. Rosa Parkes rebelled against segregated seating on public transport by sitting at the front of the bus.*

rebellion 5, 56, 89
A **rebellion** is an organised action, often violent, taken by a large group of people against the rulers of their country, usually in order to force a change in the system of government. *e.g. A rebellion led by army officers overthrew the government.*

rebuff 1397
If you **rebuff** someone, you refuse to cooperate with them or to agree to what they suggest. *e.g. He flirts with them all, but Ruth always rebuffs him.*

rebuke 308
If you **rebuke** someone, you sign or speak severely to them because they have signed, said or done something that you do not approve of. *e.g. She often rebuked him for his authoritarian attitude.*

recall 1665
When you **recall** something, you remember it. *e.g. I recalled seeing a poster on the wall.*

receipt 607, 658
A **receipt** is a piece of paper that you give or send to someone to confirm that you have received money or goods from them. *e.g. Ask for a receipt and make sure you get it.*

receive 1012
When you **receive** something, you get it after it has been given to you or sent to you. *e.g. Northcliffe received a letter from his brother.*

recent 1250
1 Something that is **recent** happened or appeared only a short time ago. *e.g. They talked about Judith's recent trip to Africa.*
2 Something that is **recent** happened or appeared during a short period of time before the present. *e.g. Tonight we will look at recent research developments.*

recently 1250
If something happened **recently**, it happened

only a short time ago. *e.g. Frances recently attended a conference in Stockholm.*

recognise someone/something 169
If you **recognise someone** or **something**, you know who or what they are. *e.g. Yvonne hasn't changed. I recognised her as soon as she came in.*

recommend 504
If you **recommend** an action, or **recommend** that somebody should do something, you suggest that it should be done. *e.g. They recommended a merger of the two supermarket groups.*

recommend 599
1 If you **recommend** an action, or **recommend** that somebody should do something, you suggest that it should be done. *e.g. They recommended a merger of the two supermarket groups.*
2 If you **recommend** someone or something, you suggest that they are suitable for a particular job or purpose. *e.g. She asked me to recommend a good doctor.*

recommendation 599
1 If you make a **recommendation**, you suggest that someone should have something or use something, because it is good or useful. *e.g. The best way to find a gardener is through personal recommendation.*
2 If you make a **recommendation**, you advise someone on the best thing to do. *e.g. He asked for my recommendation, and I told him I thought it best to go immediately.*

record 552
A **record** is a round, flat piece of black plastic on which sound, especially music, is stored. You listen to the sound by playing the record on a record player. *e.g. She had many jazz records and couldn't wait to buy Pete Wilson's critically acclaimed solo album.*

record 1596
If you **record** something, you write it down so that it can be referred to later. *e.g. Hold on! Let me record that sign you just made.*

recreation 954
Recreation is enjoyable activity in which you exercise your body or use your mind when you are not working. *e.g. Sport and recreation has always been a part of university life.*

recreation ground 1280
A **recreation ground** is a piece of public land, usually in a town, where people can go to play sport and games. *e.g. There are swings at the recreation ground.*

red 348, 529
Something that is **red** is the colour of blood

or of a ripe tomato. *e.g. He gave her a bunch of red roses.*

Red Cross 542
The **Red Cross** is an international humanitarian organisation (officially called the Red Cross Society) formally established by the Geneva Convention of 1864. Its services include liaison between prisoners of war and their families, relief to victims of natural disasters and famine, et cetera. *e.g. The Red Cross tried to open negotiations, but access was denied.*

redeemer 1621
In the Christian Church, Jesus Christ can be referred to as the **Redeemer** to stress the belief that his crucifixion made possible human freedom from the consequences of sin and evil. *e.g. Let us worship the Redeemer.*

redemption 1621
In the Christian church, **redemption** is freedom from the consequences of sin and evil, which Christians believe was made possible by Jesus Christ's death on the cross. *e.g. They prayed at Thomas à Becket's shrine for redemption.*

red-faced 351
If you are **red-faced**, your face turns much redder than it normally is, usually because you are embarrassed or very angry. *e.g. Ralph clenched his fist and became red-faced as he watched the thieves run off laughing.*

reduce 728, 1393, 1395
To **reduce** something means to make it smaller in size or amount, or less in degree. *e.g. They have promised to reduce public expenditure.*

reduction 728, 1393, 1395
When there is a **reduction** in something, it is made smaller in size or amount or less in degree. *e.g. There has been a 6% reduction in investment.*

redundant (make redundant) 244
If you are **made redundant**, you are dismissed by your employer because your job is no longer necessary or because your employer cannot afford to keep paying you. *e.g. The company will be making 250 workers redundant next month.*

refer 353
1 If you **refer** to a particular subject or person, you mention or comment on them. *e.g. I am not allowed to refer to the officers by name.*
2 To **refer** someone who is ill to a doctor or hospital means to make official arrangements for them to be received so that they can be treated. *e.g. He would have to refer her to a specialist.*
3 If you **refer** a task or problem to a

particular person or organisation, you formally let them know about it so that they can deal with it. *e.g. She referred the matter to the European Court of Justice.*

referee 641
The **referee** is the official who controls a sports match such as a football or hockey game. *e.g. He is a qualified football referee.*

referent 353
The **referent** of a comment or utterance is the subject, person or thing that is being signed or talked about. *e.g. That boy in particular was the referent of many impolite remarks.*

reflect 313
When you **reflect** on something, or **reflect** over it, you think deeply about it. *e.g. Hutchinson reflected long over Casson's argument.*

reflection 313
Reflection is thought. You can refer to your thoughts about something as your **reflections**. *e.g. 'You ought to take it,' she signed, after a moment's reflection.*

reflection 1245
A **reflection** is an image of someone or something that can be seen in a mirror or on a shiny surface. *e.g. She stood looking at the reflection in the window.*

refrigerator 28, 29
A **refrigerator** is a large, metal container which is kept cold inside, usually by electricity, so that the food and drink in it stays fresh and cold. A refrigerator is another name for a fridge. *e.g. Put the butter in the refrigerator.*

refusal 5, 25, 56
1 You describe someone's behaviour as a **refusal** to do something when they sign or say firmly that they will not do it. *e.g. All appeals met with bureaucratic refusal.*
2 You refer to someone's behaviour as a **refusal** when they do not accept something that has been offered to them. *e.g. His refusal of the gift will cause offence.*

refuse 5, 25, 56, 1221
1 If you **refuse** to do something, you deliberately do not do it. *e.g. I know he will refuse to accept their advice.*
2 If you **refuse** to do something, you sign or say firmly that you will not do it. *e.g. I refuse to accept that it can't be done.*
3 If you **refuse** something that is offered to you, you do not accept it. *e.g. I offer him wine but he refuses it.*

refuse collector 102
A **refuse collector** is a person whose job it is

to empty the rubbish from people's dustbins and take it to be thrown away. *e.g. He works as a refuse collector for the council.*

region 983, 1018
A **region** is a large area of land that can be identified as distinct from other areas of land, for example because it is one of the different parts of the country, or because it has a particular geographical feature. *e.g. We travelled through the Loire region for six days when we were on holiday.*

regional 983, 1018
Regional organisations and activities relate to a particular area of the country. *e.g. It's the North East regional final this weekend.*

regret 2, 34, 921
1 If you **regret** something that you have done, you wish that you had not done it. *e.g. I regret that I was rude.*
2 A **regret** is a wish that something which did happen had not happened. *e.g. My regret concerns your son: since I cannot accept his behaviour, I am afraid he will be required to leave the school.*

regret something 1036
If you **regret something**, you wish that you had not done it or it had not happened. *e.g. She signed that she had begun to regret her action and apologised.*

regular 204, 207
1 **Regular** events or activities continue to happen according to a definite arrangement or plan so that they happen, for example, at the same time each day or each week. *e.g. You need to take regular exercise.*
2 A **regular** event is one which happens often. *e.g. She made regular trips to town to shop.*
3 If you are a **regular** customer at a shop or visitor to a place, you go there often. *e.g. We are regular church goers.*

regulations 402
Regulations are written rules made by a government or another authority which are intended to control the way something is made or done, or the way people are allowed to behave. *e.g. You can't do that—it's against the regulations.*

rehearse 1330
If people **rehearse** a play, dance, or piece of music, they practise it. *e.g. The drama group had to rehearse in the school gym.*

reindeer 1071
A **reindeer** is a particular type of deer with large antlers that lives in northern areas of Europe, Asia and America. *e.g. Herds of reindeer are found in Lapland.*

reinforce 1364
If something **reinforces** an idea or point of view, it provides more evidence or support for it. *e.g. This report reinforces practically everything that has been said.*

reiterate 1383
If you **reiterate** something, you sign or say it again. *e.g. He reiterated his advice several times during the meeting.*

reject 909
1 If you **reject** a proposal or request, you declare that you have definitely or officially decided not to agree to it. *e.g. If you reject this amendment, there will be trouble ahead.*
2 If you **reject** something such as a belief or a political system, you decide that you do not believe in it and do not want to live by its rules. *e.g. She rejected her family's strong religious beliefs.*

reject 970
1 If you **reject** something such as a belief or a political system, you decide that you do not believe in it and do not want to live by its rules. *e.g. She rejected her family's strong religious beliefs.*
2 If you **reject** someone who expects love, affection or kindness from you, such as a member of your family, your lover or a friend, you behave towards them in a very cruel or hostile way, sometimes even refusing to accept them any longer as part of your family or as your lover or friend. *e.g. His natural parents chose to reject him.*

rejection 909
1 **Rejection** of something such as a belief or a political system is deciding that you do not believe in it and do not want to live by its rules. *e.g. There had been widespread rejection of this view.*
2 **Rejection** of a proposal or request is declaring that you have definitely or officially decided not to agree to it. *e.g. Ministers were angered by his rejection of calls for military action.*

relate 883, 898
1 If you **relate** one thing to another, you make a connection between the two things. *e.g. Let us examine how words in a sentence relate to each other.*
2 If you can **relate** to someone, you can understand how they feel or behave and so are able to communicate with them or deal with them easily. *e.g. Children need to learn to relate to other children.*

relate an event/a story 455, 1383
If you **relate an event** or **a story**, you describe what happened or is imagined to have happened. *e.g. Dorothy related her experiences of staying in Hawaii.*

related 883, 898
1 People who are **related** belong to the same family. *e.g. People closely related to each other often look alike.*
2 If you sign or say that different types of animal or different languages are **related**, you mean that they have developed from the same type of animal or language. *e.g. French and Spanish are related languages.*

relation 883, 898
If you refer to the **relation** of one thing to another, you are referring to the connection or similarity between them *e.g. She argued that literature often has some relation to reality.*

relationship 883, 898
1 The **relationship** between two people or groups is the way in which they feel and behave towards each other. *e.g. Pakistan's relationship with India has changed.*
2 A **relationship** is a close friendship between two people, especially one involving romantic or sexual feelings, or both. *e.g. I was hurt when our relationship ended.*
3 The **relationship** between two things is the way in which they are connected. *e.g. Some people claim that there is a relationship between language and thought.*

relax 236, 1086, 1493, 1495
If you **relax**, or if something **relaxes** you, you feel more calm and less worried or tense. *e.g. Just sit back and relax.*

relaxation 236, 1086, 1493, 1495
Relaxation is a way of spending time that is restful. *e.g. It is necessary to have some time for relaxation.*

release 81
1 If you **release** a person or animal that has been in captivity, you set the person or animal free. *e.g. They had just been released from prison.*
2 If you **release** someone from their work, you allow them to spend a period of time away from their work. *e.g. The release of staff for training purposes is actively encouraged.*
3 If you **release** someone from a particular demand or restriction, you free them from it. *e.g. We will release you from your responsibilities as cricket captain at the end of term.*

release 884
If you **release** a device, you make it able to move freely again, for example by moving something that is blocking it.
e.g If you give it a good firm wallop, that'll release the catch.

reliable 594
If something or someone is **reliable**, you can trust them to work hard or well, or always to act, behave, or happen in the way

that you want them to. *e.g. Gill is a reliable secretary.*

relief 1271
If you feel **relief**, you feel glad because something unpleasant has not happened or is no longer happening. *e.g. To my relief, my headache disappeared after I had taken an aspirin.*

relief 1664
A **relief** is a person who takes your place and continues to do the job or duty that you have been doing, when it is time for you to go home. Sometimes, this is a person who has been specially asked to come and do the work instead of a regular employee who is ill. *e.g. When does your relief come on duty?*

religion 1442
1 **Religion** is belief in a god or gods and the activities that are connected with this belief, such as prayer or worship in a church or temple. *e.g. Religion was a daily topic of conversation.*
2 A **religion** is a particular system of belief in a god or gods and the activities that are connected with this system. *e.g. What is your religion?*

religious 1442
1 You use **religious** to describe things connected with religion or with one particular religion. *e.g. A religious discussion group meets in the Chaplaincy every Friday lunchtime.*
2 Someone who is **religious** has a strong belief in a god or gods. *e.g. My parents were extremely religious people.*

rely 594, 1653
1 To **rely** on something or someone means to need them and depend on them in order to survive or work properly. *e.g. She is forced to rely on social security benefits.*
2 If you **rely** on someone or something, you trust them to work hard or well, or always to act, behave or happen in the way that you want them to. *e.g. You can always rely on her to arrive on time.*

remain 594, 651
If you **remain** in a place, you stay there and do not move away. *e.g. I was allowed to remain at home.*

remain 652
To **remain** in a particular situation, state or condition means to stay in that situation, state or condition and not change. *e.g. She remained single all her life.*

remember 513, 1665
1 If you **remember** people or events from the past, your mind still has an impression of them

and you are able to think about them. *e.g. He remembered the man well.*
2 If you can **remember** something, you are able to bring it back into your mind by making an effort to do so. *e.g. I'm trying to remember what I should do.*
3 If you **remember** to do something, you do it when you intend to. *e.g. I must remember to go to the bank before it closes.*
4 You sign or say **remember** when you are reminding someone of something. *e.g. Remember that women didn't get the vote until 1918.*

remembrance (in remembrance) 513
If you do something **in remembrance** of someone who has died, you do it so people will not forget that person. *e.g. A fund was set up in remembrance of Professor Philip Abrams.*

remind 1562
1 If you **remind** someone of a fact or event that they are already aware of, you sign or say something which makes them think about that fact or event. *e.g. You do not need to remind people of their mistakes all the time.*
2 When someone **reminds** you to do something, they sign or say something to you to make you remember a particular task or activity that you know you ought to deal with. *e.g. Don't forget to remind her about the party.*

remote 460
1 **Remote** areas are far away from places where people live and are therefore difficult to get to. *e.g. Most children living in remote places cannot get to the playgroup.*
2 The **remote** future is a time long after now. *e.g. We may get round to it at some time in the remote future.*

rent 1504
1 If you **rent** something, you pay its owner a certain amount of money every week or every month in order to be able to have it and use it yourself. *e.g. He wanted to rent a colour television.*
2 **Rent** is the amount of money that you pay regularly to rent something such as a house, flat, or piece of land. *e.g. Forty per cent of his income goes on rent.*

repair 55, 1519
1 A **repair** is something that you do to mend a machine, piece of clothing, or other thing that has been damaged or is not working properly. *e.g. He asked the landlord to see that the repair was done as soon as possible.*
2 If you **repair** something that has been damaged or is not working properly, you mend it so that it works properly again. *e.g. No-one knew how to repair the engine.*

repeat 751
1 If you **repeat** something, you sign, say or

write it again. *e.g. I don't want to repeat this story twenty times.*
2 If a television or radio programme is **repeated**, it is broadcast again. *e.g. The series is being repeated on Channel 4 starting next Saturday.*
3 A **repeat** is something which is done again or which happens again. *e.g. A repeat performance of the play, with an interpreter, would be very popular.*

repent 35
If you **repent**, you feel sorry for something bad that you have done in the past. *e.g. He should repent his sins.*

repentance 35
Repentance is sorrow and regret that you feel for something bad that you have done in the past. *e.g. She is offering daily prayers of repentance.*

repetition 751
When there is a **repetition** of something that has happened before, it happens again. *e.g. He didn't want a repetition of the scene with his mother.*

replace 889, 1164, 1389
1 When one thing **replaces** another, the first thing takes the place of the second thing. *e.g. The new model replaces the 1979 model.*
2 If you **replace** something, you get something new or different instead of it. *e.g. I will have to replace this kettle: it's leaking.*
3 If you **replace** one thing with another, you use or have the second thing in place of the first one. *e.g. I replace this one with this one and suddenly the puzzle is easy to solve!*

replacement 889, 1164, 1389
1 A **replacement** is a substitute. *e.g. You can use this as a replacement for the Italian one which is made with olive oil.*
2 **Replacement** is the activity of substituting one thing for another. *e.g. I'm afraid a replacement is all we can offer, a refund is not possible.*

reply 371
A **reply** is something you sign or say when you respond to something that has been signed or said to you. *e.g. His reply to my question was unrepeatable.*

reply 433
1 When you **reply** to something that someone has signed or said to you, you sign or say something as an answer. *e.g. He gave me no chance to reply to his question.*
2 If you sign, say or do something in **reply** to something that someone else has signed, said or done, you sign or say or do it as an answer to them. *e.g. I have nothing to say in

reply to your question.

3 A **reply** is something you sign or say when you respond to something that has been signed or said to you. *e.g. His reply to my question was unrepeatable.*

repress   1364
1 If you **repress** a feeling, you succeed in not showing it, or not feeling it. *e.g. I couldn't repress my joy.*
2 If a group of people **repress** those they have authority over, they restrict their freedom and control them by force. *e.g. The military helped the dictator to repress his own people.*

repression   1364
Repression is the use of force to control the way of life of a group of people, especially the inhabitants of a country. *e.g. They wanted to fight all forms of injustice and repression.*

rescue   1621
If you **rescue** someone, you get them out of a dangerous or unpleasant situation. *e.g. We can rescue her from the sinking boat by helicopter.*

rescue boat   1427
A **rescue boat** is a boat which is sent out from a port or harbour in order to help people who are in danger at sea. *e.g. The rescue boat carried a crew of eight.*

research   776
1 **Research** is work that involves studying something and trying to discover facts about it. *e.g. We have funding for further scientific research.*
2 If you **research** something, you try to discover facts about it. *e.g. I spent time researching abroad.*

researcher   776
A **researcher** is somebody who studies something and tries to discover facts about it. *e.g. Forty years ago, nobody could imagine what a sign language researcher might do.*

reserve   199
If something is **reserved** for a particular person or purpose, it is kept specially for that person or purpose. *e.g. I had a place reserved at the Youth Hostel.*

reserve   1664
A **reserve** is someone who has not been chosen for a sports team, but who will be asked to play in it if one of its members cannot play. *e.g. He was surprised to learn he had only been chosen as a reserve.*

reserved   1632
Someone who is **reserved** keeps their feelings hidden. *e.g. He is reserved and cautious, never making a swift decision.*

reside   1239
If you **reside** somewhere, you live there for a time and it is your home. *e.g. A famous poet wanted to reside here.*

resign   289
If you **resign** from a job or position, you formally announce that you are leaving it, usually because of something that has happened. *e.g. She resigned from the Government over the poll tax.*

resignation   289
A **resignation** is a formal statement of your intention to leave a job, position, or organisation. *e.g. His resignation from the company was widely reported in the newspapers.*

resist   72, 112
1 If you **resist** something, such as a change, you refuse to accept it or try to prevent it. *e.g. He resisted requests for a meeting.*
2 If you **resist** someone, or **resist** an attack by them, you fight back against them. *e.g. We will resist any attack with force if necessary.*

resist   1397
1 If you **resist** something such as a change, you refuse to accept it or try to prevent it. *e.g. Many people still resist the idea that BSL is a language.*
2 If you **resist** the temptation to do something, you stop yourself from doing it, though you would like to do it. *e.g. Should I? No, I've got to resist that second piece of cake!*

resistance   72
1 **Resistance** to something, such as a change or a new idea, is a refusal to accept it. *e.g. There was a lot of resistance to the plan.*
2 The **resistance** of your body to germs or diseases is its power to remain unharmed or unaffected by them. *e.g. My resistance to infection is very low.*
3 **Resistance** to an enemy or attacker is fighting or other action that people take in order to keep their freedom or avoid being defeated or forced to do something. *e.g. The army encountered resistance in the mountain villages.*

resistance   112
1 **Resistance** to an enemy or attacker is fighting or other action that people take in order to keep their freedom or avoid being defeated or forced to do something. *e.g. The army encountered resistance in the mountain villages.*
2 **Resistance** to something, such as a change or a new idea, is a refusal to accept it. *e.g. We could not understand his resistance to the proposed change.*

respect   1461
1 If you have **respect** for someone, you believe that their opinions and feelings are important. *e.g. I had great respect and admiration for him.*
2 If you **respect** someone, you have a good

opinion of their character or of their ideas, judgements, et cetera. *e.g. I respect and support his views on the need to increase the number of deaf-blind people employed in schools.*
3 If you **respect** someone's wishes, you do something in the way that they want or need it to be done. *e.g. It is necessary to respect their wishes.*
4 If you **respect** someone's opinion, judgement, etc., you consider that it is interesting or important, although you may not agree with it. *e.g. I respect the other point of view.*
5 If you **respect** something such as a custom or tradition, you do not interfere with it because you do not want to offend anyone. *e.g. They were asked to respect the Maya's customs and traditions during their stay in the village.*

respond   433
When you **respond** to something that is done, signed or said, you react to it by doing, signing or saying something yourself. *e.g. You must respond to the welcoming speech.*

response   433
Your **response** to an event or to something that is signed or said is what you do, sign or say as a reaction or reply to it. *e.g. The Minister's response to this bit of investigative journalism was brief and dismissive.*

responsibility   1653
1 If you have **responsibility** for something, or if something is your **responsibility**, it is your duty to deal with it and make decisions relating to it. *e.g. She took over responsibility for the project.*
2 If you accept **responsibility** for something that has happened, you agree that you were to blame for it or caused it. *e.g. I made a mistake and I will accept responsibility for it.*
3 If you have a **responsibility** to someone, you have a duty to help them or to look after them. *e.g. I presume you take your responsibility to your students seriously.*

responsible   1653
1 If you are **responsible** for something, it is your job or duty to deal with it and make decisions relating to it. *e.g. The children were responsible for cleaning their own rooms.*
2 If you are **responsible** for something bad that has happened, you caused it or allowed it to happen. *e.g. I hold you personally responsible for all this.*
3 If you are **responsible** to a person or group, you are controlled by them and have to report to them about what you have done. *e.g. We're responsible to a development committee.*
4 You describe someone as **responsible** when they behave properly without needing to be directed by anyone else. *e.g. She's a responsible member of the local community.*

rest 1495

1 If you rest, or if you **rest** your body, you do not do anything active for a period of time. *e.g. Go back to bed and rest.*

2 If you get some **rest**, or have a **rest**, you sit or lie quietly, not doing anything active, and relax. *e.g. They wanted a rest.*

restaurant 686, 730

A **restaurant** is a place where you can buy and eat a meal. *e.g. A splendid restaurant called Café Procope was the venue for our first meeting.*

restrain oneself 1062

If you **restrain yourself**, you do not sign or say what you were going to sign or say. *e.g. It was all I could do to restrain myself from shouting abuse at the referee.*

results 219

1 The **results** are the final situations that exist at the end of a number of contests. *e.g. The football results are on television now.*

2 Your **results** are the marks or grades that you get for examinations you have taken. *e.g. You need good GCSE results to get a place on the course.*

3 **Results** are the numbers that you get when you do a series of calculations. *e.g. When you have worked out the results, write them on the board.*

results 1054

Results are the numbers that you get when you do a series of calculations. *e.g. When you have worked out the results, write them on the board.*

retire 236

When someone **retires**, they leave their job, usually because they have reached the age when they can get a pension. In Britain, women usually retire at the age of 60, and men at the age of 65. *e.g. He retired from his business six years ago.*

retired 236

Someone who is **retired** has left their job, usually because they have reached the age when they get a pension. *e.g. She is the daughter of a retired teacher.*

retirement 236

Retirement is the period in a person's life during which they are no longer employed because they have retired. *e.g. You should get a full retirement pension.*

retreat 112

When you **retreat**, you move away, for example because you are afraid or embarassed. *e.g. As I started to retreat, I tripped and fell.*

retreat 1641

1 When an army **retreats**, it moves away from opposing forces in order to avoid fighting them. *e.g. They had to retreat a few kilometres,*

then sent in aircraft.

2 A **retreat** is a withdrawal by an army when it is faced with a stronger force which it does not want to fight. *e.g. The winter retreat of Napoleon's army from Moscow was an historic event.*

return 295, 570

When you **return** somewhere, you come back there after you have been away. *e.g. My husband will return at three o'clock.*

return 1703

If you **return** something that you have borrowed or taken from someone else, or **return** something you have been asked to complete and return, you give or send it back to them, for example by post. *e.g. Please fill in your postgraduate registration form and return it to us at once.*

revenge 48, 432

1 **Revenge** involves hurting someone who has hurt you. You hurt them in return for having hurt you. *e.g. They were eager for revenge.*

2 If you **revenge** yourself on someone who has hurt you, you hurt them in return. *e.g. She will revenge herself on those who helped him to escape.*

review a document 961

1 If you **review a document**, you read it or look at it to check that you are satisfied with the contents. *e.g. I'll review the introduction: you check the bibliography.*

2 If you **review a document** such as a book, you write an article or give a presentation in which you express your view of it. *e.g. He is going to review the document for 'Signpost'.*

revise 270

When you **revise**, you read or look at something again in order to learn or remember it so that you can answer questions about it in an examination. *e.g. I've been revising for the last three days.*

revision 270

Revision is the activity of reading or looking at something again in order to learn or remember it before you take an examination. *e.g. I must do some revision for my history exam.*

revolt 89, 1237

1 **Revolt** is violent action taken by a large group of people against the rulers of their country because they want a different system of government. *e.g. The settlers rose in revolt in 1960.*

2 A **revolt** is a series of actions taken by a group of people within an organisation in order to try and change its aims or policies. *e.g. Morale was low and several back-bench revolts had occurred.*

revolting 1002

Something that is **revolting** is so unpleasant to see or smell that you feel disgusted by it. *e.g. He thinks he can cook, but the food is revolting.*

revolution 89

A **revolution** is a successful attempt by a large group of people, often using violent methods, to change the political system of their country. *e.g. He fled from Russia during the revolution.*

revolver 463

A **revolver** is a kind of gun that you hold in your hand and that can fire several bullets quickly. *e.g. He had a revolver in his coat pocket.*

rhubarb 1315

Rhubarb is a plant with long, reddish stems which are cooked in puddings and can be used to make jam or wine. *e.g. I had rhubarb tart with a lot of cream.*

ribcage 660

Your **ribcage** is the structure of ribs in your chest. *e.g. On the X-ray, his ribcage was clear.*

ribs 660

Ribs are the bones that go from the backbone to the chest of mammals. *e.g. Several ribs were broken.*

rich 1649

1 Someone who is **rich** has a lot of money or valuable possessions. *e.g. Her father was a rich man.*

2 If something is **rich** in a desirable substance or quality, it contains a lot of that substance or quality. *e.g. The land is rich with oil.*

3 Food that is **rich** contains a lot of fat, eggs, sugar, etc., and is therefore unhealthy if eaten in large quantities. *e.g. The restaurant food was very rich.*

ride 692

1 A **ride** is a journey in a car or other vehicle. *e.g. They have these electric cars to give you a ride around the museum.*

2 A **ride** is a free trip in a vehicle that someone else is driving, especially a car. *e.g. Could you give me a ride to the station?*

3 If you **ride** in a car or other vehicle, you are transported from one place to another in it. *e.g. That afternoon he would get to ride to town in the new jeep.*

ride a bicycle/bike 92, 654

If you **ride a bicycle** or a **bike**, you cycle. *e.g. Rosie is learning how to ride a bicycle.*

ride a horse 107

When you **ride a horse**, you sit on it and control its movements as it moves along. *e.g. Every morning she would ride her horse across the fields.*

ridicule 765, 1016
1 If you **ridicule** someone or **ridicule** what they sign or say or do, you make fun of them in an unkind way. *e.g. Of course, the Pharisees would ridicule his prophecy.*
2 **Ridicule** is the activity of making fun of someone or their behaviour in an unkind way. *e.g. Ridicule is easy: solutions are much more difficult.*

ridiculous 515
If you sign or say that something is **ridiculous**, you mean that it is very foolish. *e.g. It would be ridiculous to pretend there are no difficulties.*

rifle 609
A **rifle** is a gun with a long barrel that you can use for shooting things that are a long way away. You fire it with the handle pressed against your shoulder. *e.g. He pointed the rifle at her head.*

right 61, 197, 200
1 If something is **right**, it is correct and in accordance with the facts. *e.g. That's the right answer.*
2 If someone is **right** about something, they are correct in what they think or state about it. *e.g. The builder was right about the cost of the repairs.*
3 If something such as a choice, action, or decision is the **right** one, it is the best or most suitable one. *e.g. To resign is the right thing to do in the circumstances.*
4 **Right** is used to refer to actions that are considered morally good and acceptable. *e.g. He is able to distinguish between right and wrong.*

right 1338
1 **Right** means on or towards the side which, in English writing, has the last letter of a word. For example, when you look at the word 'me', the 'e' is to the right of the 'm'. *e.g. Turn right off Broadway into Caxton Street.*
2 The **right** is the right side, direction or position. *e.g. It's the fourth door down on the right.*
3 The **right** one of a pair of items, such as shoes, is the one that is intended to be used on the right side of the user. *e.g. So what have you done with the right glove?*

right-hand 1338
Right-hand is used to describe something which is on the right side. *e.g. We lived in a biggish house on the right-hand side of the road.*

right-handed 1338
1 Someone who is **right-handed** uses their right hand rather than their left hand for activities such as writing or throwing a ball. *e.g. He is a right-handed batsman.*
2 If you do something **right-handed**, you do

it with your right hand. *e.g. He wants to try it right-handed, just to see.*
3 A **right-handed** object is made for use by people who are right-handed. *e.g. Do you not have an ordinary right-handed pair of scissors?*

right now 1625
Right now means immediately and without any delay. *e.g. Take that ridiculous hat off right now!*

ring 895
A **ring** is a small circle, usually made of gold, silver, or another metal, that you wear on your finger as an ornament or to show that you are engaged or married. *e.g. She wore an emerald ring.*

ring a bell with a rope 106
When someone **rings a bell with a rope**, they ring it repeatedly by pulling a rope attached to the bell. When the bell rings, it makes a clear, loud sound. *e.g. They ring the bells every Sunday evening.*

ring a doorbell 162
When you **ring a doorbell**, you push a small device, usually positioned on or by the side of a door, which causes a bell to ring inside the building. The sound of the bell informs people inside the building that you are there and that you want to see them. *e.g. She rang the doorbell and a child came to the door.*

ring a flashing doorbell 163
When you **ring a flashing doorbell**, you push a small device, usually positioned on or by the side of the door, which causes a light (or lights) inside the building to go on and off. The flashing light (or lights) informs people inside the building that you are there and that you want to see them. Flashing doorbells are used especially by Deaf and deaf people. *e.g. She rang the flashing doorbell and the receptionist came to the door.*

ring a hand bell 241
If you **ring a hand bell**, you shake it so it makes a sound. *e.g. Linda rang the bell at the end of playtime.*

ring of an electric bell 408
The **ring of an electric bell** is the sound it makes which is used as a signal or to attract people's attention. *e.g. Every time I hear the ring of an electric bell I long to hear real bells, ringing out over the Fens from Ely Cathedral.*

ring-pull 592
A **ring-pull** is a device like a circular tab found on the top of some cans that is used to open them. *e.g. The ring-pull has broken off this can.*

riot 89
A **riot** is a crowd of people shouting, fighting, throwing stones, etc., and so causing injury to

people and damage to buildings and vehicles. *e.g. There were a number of student riots in Korea last year.*

rip 1510
1 If you **rip** something, or it **rips**, it is torn violently, usually by hand. *e.g. If you rip that, I'll be furious.*
2 A **rip** in something is a tear that has been, or appears to have been, made by hand. *e.g. There was a small rip in the cover of the book.*

ripple 985
A **ripple** is a wavy movement on the surface of an expanse of liquid. *e.g. The wind caused ripples on the pond.*

rise 553
Someone's **rise** is the process by which they become more important, successful or powerful. *e.g. We envied her rise to fame.*

rise 1201, 1376
1 When you **rise**, you stand up. *e.g. Please rise when the Mayor enters the room.*
2 When you **rise**, you get out of bed. *e.g. I would like you all to rise at five o'clock so we can catch the early train.*

risk 860, 1240
1 If there is a **risk** of something unpleasant, there is a possibility that it will happen. *e.g. There is a risk of infection if you drink the local water.*
2 If something you do is a **risk**, it might have unpleasant or undesirable results. *e.g. To make such a speech would be taking a risk.*
3 You can refer to an object as a **risk** when it is likely to cause danger. *e.g. Your television is a fire risk if left plugged in overnight.*
4 If you **risk** something, you take a chance on it. *e.g. You mean you are prepared to risk getting swept away by the current?*

risky 860, 1240
If you refer to an activity or action as **risky**, you mean that it is dangerous or likely to fail. *e.g. It is risky to go climbing alone.*

river 703
A **river** is a large amount of fresh water, flowing continuously in a long line across land. *e.g. We fished in the river after lunch.*

road 702, 1444
1 A **road** is a long, smooth, hard piece of ground which is built between two places, for example between two towns, on which you can travel easily from one place to the other. *e.g. We took the road from Belfast to Ballycastle.*
2 A **road** is a street in a town or city, which is built for people or cars to use, but which also has houses along it. *e.g. We travelled to school every day along Crescent Road.*

roam 736
If you **roam** an area, or **roam** around it, you wander or travel around it without having a particular purpose. *e.g. He roamed the streets at night.*

roast 1334
1 When you **roast** food (usually meat), or when it **roasts**, you cook it by dry heat in an oven. *e.g. We will roast a joint of beef for Sunday dinner.*
2 **Roast** food is food that has been cooked by roasting. *e.g. I ordered roast pork.*
3 A **roast** is a piece of food (usually meat) that has been cooked by roasting. *e.g. The roast was enough for five people.*

rob 1126, 1151
If you **rob** someone, or **rob** a shop or office, you steal money or property from them. *e.g. I shall have to rob a bank to get the money.*

robber 1126, 1151
A **robber** is a person who steals money or property from a bank, shop, train, etc., often using force or threats. *e.g. The robbers escaped with the jewels.*

robbery 1126, 1151
1 **Robbery** is the crime of stealing money or property from a bank, shop, office or vehicle, often using force or threats. *e.g. He was arrested on charges of armed robbery.*
2 When there is a **robbery**, someone steals money or property from a bank, shop, office or vehicle. *e.g. If he had committed the robbery, he would have admitted it.*

rock 21, 1150
1 **Rock** is the hard substance which the earth is made of. *e.g. The geologist examined the rock formation in the valley.*
2 A **rock** is a stone that you can pick up. *e.g. She started to put the rock into her pocket.*

rock 1385
When you **rock** someone or something, you hold them close to your body with your hands beneath them and move them slowly from side to side. *e.g. Rita and Luke take it in turns to rock Zoe to sleep—they're so patient!*

rock a baby/doll 1385
If you **rock a baby** or a **doll**, you hold it close to your body with your hands beneath it and move it slowly from side to side. *e.g. She likes to rock her doll and play at making faces at it, like a Deaf mother would.*

rockery 1167
A **rockery** is a raised part of a garden which is built of stones and soil and on which small plants are grown. *e.g. Outside there was a little front garden with a rockery.*

rocket 405
1 A **rocket** is a space vehicle that is shaped like a long tube. *e.g. A space rocket such as this could help us a great deal in our exploration of the moon.*
2 A **rocket** is a missile containing explosive that drives itself through the air by sending out burning gas. *e.g. Rebels fired anti-tank rockets for three consecutive nights.*

rocks 1167
Rocks are stones that lie on the ground or floor. *e.g. These rocks aren't sculpture—be serious!*

rodent 571
A **rodent** is a small mammal which has sharp front teeth. *e.g. Some of the crops were eaten by rodents.*

rodeo 107
A **rodeo** is a public entertainment, especially in North America, in which cowboys show different skills, including riding wild horses and catching calves with ropes. *e.g. He worked with the rodeo in Iowa.*

roll 566
1 When a round object **rolls** or when you **roll** it, it moves along a surface, turning over and over many times. *e.g. The tin rolled down the path.*
2 If a machine **rolls**, it is operating. *e.g. The printing machines rolled twenty-four hours a day.*
3 A **roll** of paper or cloth is a long piece of it, wrapped several times around itself or around something else. *e.g. I'm looking for a small roll of bandage.*

roll 1154, 1156
A **roll** is a small loaf of bread that is usually eaten by one person. *e.g. They offered to make us a ham roll each.*

rolling pin 1408
A **rolling pin** is a cylinder that you usually use to roll several times over uncooked pastry to spread it. *e.g. My rolling pin is made of Swedish wood.*

roll out 1408
You **roll out** pastry by using a rolling pin to spread it. *e.g. Roll out the pastry until it is an eighth of an inch thick.*

Roman Catholic 171
A **Roman Catholic** or **Catholic** is someone who is a Christian and is a member of that Christian church which has the Mass as its main religious service and has a body of religious beliefs based on Christ's teachings which have been formulated by the Roman Catholic Church. The Pope is the leader of the Catholic Church and lives in the Vatican in Rome, which is the administrative centre of the Roman Catholic Church. *e.g. Father Peter McDonough is a Deaf Roman Catholic priest.*

roof 1567
A **roof** is the covering on top of a building which protects people and their possessions from the weather. *e.g. The roof of the garage needs to be repaired.*

room 559, 1458
1 A **room** is one of the separate sections in a house or other building, which has its own walls, ceiling, floor and door, and is used for a particular kind of activity. *e.g. You can go straight up to room sixty-four.*
2 A **room** is someone's private room, especially their bedroom at home or their office at work. *e.g. He wants you to go to his room.*

roots 1717
1 The **roots** of a plant are the parts that grow under the ground. *e.g. The roots of the old oak tree were beginning to make the pavement crack.*
2 If something **roots** or **takes root**, it starts to grow or develop. *e.g. The seedlings of bushes will root well in this part of the park.*

rotate 503, 566
When something **rotates**, or you **rotate** it, it turns end over end with a circular movement. *e.g. Rotate the drum to face this way.*

rotten 740, 812, 911
1 If you describe something as **rotten**, you mean that it is of very poor quality. *e.g. It was a rotten school.*
2 If you describe something as **rotten**, you mean that it is in very poor condition. *e.g. The mechanic at the garage advised Frances to get a new car becuase hers was old and rotten.*

rotten 825, 1181
If you describe something as **rotten**, you mean that it is in very poor condition. *e.g. The mechanic at the garage advised Frances to get a new car becuase hers was old and rotten.*

rough 1224
A **rough** calculation or guess is approximately correct. *e.g. Multiply the weekly amount by fifty-two to get the rough annual cost.*

round 496
1 Something that is **round** is shaped like a circle. *e.g. It was a small, round plate set into the ground.*
2 The distance **round** something is the length of its boundary or circumference. *e.g. It measures fifteen feet round the trunk.*
3 Something that is **round** another thing is in a circle at the edges of it or surrounding it. *e.g. We want it in a circle round that heap.*

round   1418
1 Something that is **round** is shaped like a ball.
e.g. Heavy round stones were placed at the edges of the driveway.
2 Something that goes **round** an object is placed at, or near to, the surface of the object, roughly in the shape of a ball. *e.g. Wrap the cloth round the pumpkin while your partner holds it.*

roundabout   496
A **roundabout** is a circle at a place where several roads meet. You drive round it until you come to the road that you want. *e.g. He got stuck in a traffic jam at the roundabout.*

roundabout   736
1 At a funfair, a **roundabout** is a large, circular, mechanical device with seats, often in the shape of animals or cars, on which children sit and go round and round. *e.g. She was afraid to go on the roundabout.*
2 In a playground, a **roundabout** is a circular platform that children sit or stand on. The platform is made to rotate by being pushed. *e.g. When I was seven, I fell off the roundabout and broke my arm.*

roundabout   1228, 1296
If you do, sign or say something in a **roundabout** way, you do not do, sign or say it simply, directly or openly. *e.g. He told me I was sacked in a rambling, roundabout way, taking twenty minutes.*

rounders   249
Rounders is a game played by two teams in which a player scores a point (a rounder) by hitting a ball thrown by a member of the other team and running round all four sides of a square before members of the other team can get the ball back. The team scoring the most rounders wins the game. *e.g. At school, I was very good at rounders.*

rounders bat   249
A **rounders bat** is a short, wooden bat with circular ends and straight sides used for hitting the ball in rounders. *e.g. She collected the rounders bat from the P.E. teacher.*

row   95
1 When you **row**, you sit on a boat and make it move through the water by using oars. *e.g. We rowed slowly towards the centre of the river.*
2 If you **row** people or goods somewhere, you take them there in a boat, using oars. *e.g. I rowed them there and set them ashore.*

row   915
1 A **row** is a serious disagreement between politicians or public institutions. *e.g. The row broke out on the eve of the Congress.*
2 If people **row** or have a **row**, they have a noisy argument or quarrel. *e.g. He never liked to row with her mother.*

rowing   95
Rowing is a sport in which individuals or teams race against each other in specially built rowing boats. *e.g. They belong to a rowing club.*

rowing boat   95
A **rowing boat** or **rowing-boat** is a small boat that you sit in and move through the water by using oars. *e.g. He set off down the river in an old rowing boat.*

royal   1131
1 Someone or something that is **royal** belongs to or relates to a king, a queen, or a member of their family. *e.g. He's going to Gibraltar on the royal yacht.*
2 **Royal** is used in the titles of organisations, regiments, societies, etc., that are supported by or appointed by the king or queen of a country or by a member of their family. *e.g. The Royal National Institute for Deaf People has Prince Philip as its Patron.*

rub   1286
If you **rub** a substance into or over your skin, you press the substance into it by continuously moving something such as your hand or a cloth over it. *e.g. The soothing paste his father used to rub into his wounds always made them feel better.*

rubber   243
A **rubber** is a small piece of rubber that you use to rub out mistakes which you have made while writing, drawing or typing. *e.g. Our new office will need pencils, rubbers and paper clips.*

rubbish   51
1 **Rubbish** consists of unwanted things or waste material. *e.g. That old shed is full of rubbish.*
2 You can refer to something as **rubbish** when you think that it is foolish or wrong. *e.g. How can you believe such rubbish?*

rubbish   515
You can refer to something as **rubbish** when you think that it is foolish or wrong. *e.g. How can you believe such rubbish?*

rubbish   740, 812
1 **Rubbish** consists of unwanted things or waste material. *e.g. That old shed is full of rubbish.*
2 You can refer to something as **rubbish** when you think that it is foolish or wrong. *e.g. How can you believe such rubbish?*
3 You can refer to something as **rubbish** when you think that it is of very poor quality. *e.g. There is so much rubbish on television these days.*

rubbish   825
Something that is **rubbish** is very poorly made or in very poor condition. *e.g. Everyone says these cars are rubbish.*

rubbish   911
You can refer to something as **rubbish** when you think that it is of very poor quality. *e.g. There is so much rubbish on television these days.*

rub in   1286
If you **rub** something **in** to your skin, you press it into your skin by making continuous, smooth, to-and-fro movements with your hand or a cloth. *e.g. Now you rub that in, Johnny, and you'll be as right as rain by bedtime.*

rub into one's arm   1286
If you **rub** something **into your arm**, you press it into the skin of your arm by making continuous, smooth, to-and-fro movements with your hand or a cloth over the skin of your arm. *e.g. Rub the ointment into your arm.*

rub off   1286
If you **rub off** something that has marked your skin or clothes, you remove it by cleaning it off, using your hand or a cloth which you move firmly to-and-fro across the marked area. *e.g. You can just rub off that fake tattoo this instant, young lady.*

rub off one's arm   1286
If you **rub** something **off your arm** that has marked it, you remove it by making continuous, firm, smooth to-and-fro movements with your hand or a cloth over the skin of your arm. *e.g. She rubbed the cream off her arm.*

rub on   1286
If you **rub** something **on** your skin or clothes, you smooth it firmly over your skin by making continuous, smooth to-and-fro movements with your hand or a cloth. *e.g. You rub that lotion on there, and I'll do your back.*

rub one's arm   1286
If you **rub your arm**, you make continuous, firm, smooth, to-and-fro movements with your hand over the skin of your arm. *e.g. Rub your arm and get your circulation going again.*

rub on one's arm   1286
If you **rub** something **on your arm**, you make continuous, smooth, to-and-fro movements with your hand or a cloth over the skin of your arm. *e.g. He rubbed the sore patch on his arm.*

rub out   243
If you **rub out** something that someone has written on paper, you remove it by making to-and-fro movements across it, pressing with a rubber. *e.g. Please rub out that old diagram.*

rucksack   234
A **rucksack** is a bag with shoulder straps for carrying things on your back, for example when you are walking or climbing. *e.g. Barry had to have a new rucksack for Scouts camp.*

rude   1188
1 When people are **rude**, they behave in a way that is not polite. *e.g. It's rude to stare.*
2 **Rude** is used to describe signs, words and behaviour that are likely to embarrass or offend people, often because they relate to sex or other bodily functions. *e.g. Rude jokes and stories are very popular in some rugby clubs.*

rugby   1589, 1697
Rugby is a game played by two teams who try to score points by carrying an oval ball to their opponents' end of the pitch, or by kicking the ball over a bar fixed between two goalposts. There are two forms of rugby, called rugby league and rugby union. In rugby league (played by both professional and amateur players), each team has thirteen players. In rugby union (played only by amateurs), each team has fifteen players. *e.g. He is a keen rugby fan.*

rugby player   1589, 1697
A **rugby player** is a person who is a member of either a rugby league or rugby union team and who takes part in games of either rugby league or rugby union. *e.g. John signed that Will Carling was his favourite rugby player.*

ruin   1031, 1032
1 To **ruin** something means to severely harm, damage or spoil it. *e.g. You will ruin your health by drinking so much.*
2 **Ruin** is the state of being severely damaged or spoiled, or the process of reaching this state. *e.g. The house is crumbling into ruin.*
3 **Ruin** is the state of no longer having any power or money. *e.g. His arrogance and greed led to his ruin.*
4 If something is **in ruins**, it is severely damaged, with very little of what previously existed remaining. *e.g. My professional reputation is now in ruins.*
5 To **ruin** someone means to cause them to no longer have any money. *e.g. The contract will ruin him.*

rule   401
1 A **rule** is an official instruction, often written down, which tells you what you are allowed to do and what you are not allowed to do in a game or in a particular place or situation. *e.g. If you break the rules, you will be punished.*
2 A **rule** is the way of behaving or taking part in something that most people agree is right and acceptable. *e.g. We accepted the rule that contributions to the debate should only be made in sign language.*

ruler   486
A **ruler** is a long, narrow, flat piece of wood, metal or plastic with straight edges marked in inches or centimetres, which you use to measure things or to guide you when you draw

straight lines. *e.g. It would be more accurate to use a ruler to measure the distance.*

rules   402
1 **Rules** are official instructions, often written down, which tell you what you are allowed to do and what you are not allowed to do in a game or in a particular place or situation. *e.g. You can't start changing the rules just because too few goals are being scored.*
2 **Rules** are the ways of behaving or taking part in something that most people agree are right and acceptable. *e.g. He stated that these are the fundamental rules of an Islamic society.*

ruling   401
A **ruling** is an official decision by a judge or court. *e.g. The court ruling is still effective.*

rummage   1163
If you **rummage** somewhere, you search for something there by moving things in a careless way. *e.g. He began to rummage around in the drawer.*

rumour   355
1 A **rumour** is a story or piece of information that may or may not be true, but that people are signing or speaking about. *e.g. The rumour is that she's pregnant.*
2 If something is **rumoured**, people are suggesting that it is true, but they do not know for certain. *e.g. He was rumoured to be living in Glasgow.*

run   121
When you **run**, you move quickly by putting one foot in front of the other, leaving the ground during each stride, because you are in a hurry to get somewhere or because you are taking part in a race. *e.g. I ran a mile today.*

run after   595
If you **run after** someone or something, you chase them in order to catch them or stop them. *e.g. The group walked towards the pub, and he began to run after them.*

run away   415
1 If you **run away** from a place, you leave it because you are unhappy there. *e.g. I ran away and never looked back.*
2 If you **run away** from something unpleasant or worrying, you try to avoid dealing with it or thinking about it. *e.g. I often run away from the housework.*

run into   69
If a vehicle **runs into** an object, it accidently hits the object. *e.g. Her car ran into the back of the bus.*

runner   121
A **runner** is a person who runs, especially for

sport or pleasure. *e.g. A long-distance runner needs stamina and determination.*

running   121
Running is the activity undertaken by those who run. *e.g. I keep fit by running in the park every morning.*

runway   951
A **runway** is a long, narrow strip of ground with a hard, level surface which is used by aeroplanes when they are taking off or landing. *e.g. The runway was closed because of the heavy snowfall.*

rush off   1534
If you **rush off**, you go away from somewhere in a hurry. *e.g. I have to rush off to catch my train.*

Russia   10
1 **Russia** is an independent republic in Eastern Europe and Asia. It was formerly the largest of the Soviet Republics that, until 1990, formed the Soviet Union. It is now the largest member of the Commonwealth of Independent States (CIS). This sign is associated with the period of Communist government, and is now less frequently used. *e.g. Decisions made in Russia in 1968 sparked off tremendous demonstrations in Prague.*
2 **Russia** is another name for the Soviet Union. *e.g. We visited Russia in 1974.*
3 The address of the All **Russia** Federation of the Deaf is : 1905 Goda Street 10-a 123022 Moscow, Russia.

Russia   528, 529
1 **Russia** is an independent republic in Eastern Europe and Asia. It was formerly the largest of the Soviet Republics that, until 1990, formed the Soviet Union. It is the largest member of the Commonwealth of Independent States (CIS). *e.g. We hope to visit a number of Deaf Clubs when we go to Russia.*
2 The address of the All **Russia** Federation of the Deaf is : 1905 Goda Street 10-a 123022 Moscow, Russia.

Russian   10
1 Someone or something that is **Russian** belongs to or relates to Russia or the Soviet Union, or its people. This sign is associated with the period of Communist government, and is now less frequently used. *e.g. He claimed that Russian living standards had failed to rise in the 1970s.*
2 **Russian** is the main language spoken in Russia and was the official language of the Soviet Union. This sign is associated with the period of Communist government, and is now less frequently used. *e.g. Speakers of Russian were in great demand.*
3 A **Russian** is a person who comes from, or

whose family identity relates to, Russia or the Soviet Union. *e.g. Yuri Gagarin, a Russian, was the first person in space.*

Russian   528, 529
1 Someone or something that is **Russian**

S, s

S
S is the nineteenth letter of the British manual and English alphabets. See page 853.

sabotage   1031, 1032
1 If a machine, railway line or bridge is **sabotaged**, it is deliberately damaged or destroyed, for example in a war or as a protest. *e.g. The railway lines were sabotaged by enemy troops.*
2 If someone **sabotages** a plan or a meeting, they deliberately prevent it from being successful. *e.g. Troublemakers were planning to sabotage the meeting.*

sack   379, 546
1 If your employers **sack** you, they sign or say that you can no longer work for them, often because your work is not good enough. *e.g. He was sacked for poor timekeeping.*
2 If you **get the sack**, or you are **given the sack**, your employer dismisses you from your job. *e.g. He was given the sack because he was caught stealing.*

sad   1256, 1270, 1365, 1667
1 If you are **sad**, you are not happy, usually because something has happened that you do not like. *e.g. She looked sad when she saw how the garden had been spoiled.*
2 **Sad** news and **sad** stories make you feel sad. *e.g. It seems rather sad that this should happen to you.*

sadden   1667
If something **saddens** you, it makes you feel sad. *e.g. I'm saddened that so many died for nothing.*

safe   215
1 You are **safe** from something when you cannot be harmed by it. *e.g. We're safe now, they've gone.*
2 A **safe** journey or arrival is one in which people or things reach their destination without being harmed. *e.g. Have a safe trip home.*

sail   1425, 1428
1 When a ship moves over water, it **sails**. *e.g. The QE2 can sail for weeks without refuelling.*
2 When you move over water in a ship, you **sail**. *e.g. We were shortly to sail to New York.*

sail   1459
1 A **sail** is a large piece of material attached to the mast of a boat. The wind blows against the sail and pushes the boat along. *e.g. The white sails of the yacht could be seen in the distance.*
2 To **sail** a boat means to make it move across water using its sails. *e.g. I spent two weeks swimming and sailing in the Lake District.*

sailing   1425, 1428
A **sailing** is a voyage made by a ship when it takes passengers from one place to another. *e.g. There are regular sailings from Portsmouth.*

sailing   1459
Sailing is the activity or sport of sailing boats. *e.g. They go sailing every weekend.*

sailor   1483, 1484
A **sailor** is a person who works on a ship as a member of its crew. *e.g. He is a sailor in the navy.*

salary   1008, 1558
A **salary** is the money that someone is paid for their job each month, especially when they have a professional job. *e.g. She earns a high salary as an accountant.*

sale   268
1 The **sale** of goods is the selling of them for money. *e.g. We've just made our first sale.*
2 A **sale** is a time when a shop sells things at less than their normal price. *e.g. There is a sale at Smith's this week.*

salt   1497, 1662
1 **Salt** is a strong tasting substance, in the form of white powder or crystals, which is used to improve the flavour of food or to preserve it. Salt occurs naturally in sea water. *e.g. There's too much salt in the potatoes.*
2 When you **salt** food, you add salt to it. *e.g. The potatoes should be lightly salted.*
3 When you sign or say **the salt**, you may mean a salt cellar or other container with salt inside and a hole at the top to shake it out of. *e.g. Pass the salt, please.*

salvage   1621
When you **salvage** things, you manage to save

belongs to or relates to Russia or its people. *e.g. Galina Zaitseva, the Russian sign linguist, is to visit Britain.*
2 **Russian** is the main language spoken in Russia, and is widely spoken in certain member states of the Commonwealth of Independent States. *e.g. I'm going to Moscow for six months to study Russian.*
3 A **Russian** is a person who comes from, or whose family identity relates to, Russia. *e.g. Aleksandr Blok was a Russian who wrote romantic and tragic poetry.*

them, for example from a ship that has sunk or a building that has been destroyed. *e.g. We can salvage the finely decorated window from that old chemist's shop.*

Salvation Army   731
The **Salvation Army** is a Christian organisation that has military-style uniforms and ranks, holds simple religious services with music, and is well known for its help for poor people. *e.g. My neighbour is a member of the Salvation Army and attends services every Sunday.*

same   423, 424
1 If two things are the **same**, or if one thing is the **same** as another, the two are exactly like each other in some way. *e.g. They both wore the same raincoats.*
2 If two things have the **same** quality, or if one thing has the **same** quality as another, they both have that quality. *e.g. He and Tom were the same age.*
3 Something that is still the **same** has not changed in any way. *e.g. The village stayed the same.*
4 You use **same** to indicate that you are referring to only one thing, and not to different ones. *e.g. We come from the same place.*

same   1409, 1618
1 If two things are the **same**, or if one thing is the **same** as another, the two are exactly like each other in some way. *e.g. It was the same as the old one.*
2 If two things have the **same** quality, or if one thing has the **same** quality as another, they both have that quality. *e.g. They have the same charm, the same charisma.*

same   1416, 1417
1 If a number of things are the **same** as each other, they are all alike. *e.g. Look! They're all exactly the same!*
2 If a number of things have the **same** quality, they all have that quality. *e.g. As you can see, they've all got the same strong character.*
3 A number of things that are still the **same** have not changed in any way. *e.g. The flowerbeds are the same as they were in Ruskin's day.*

4 If you sign or say that something is happening the **same** as in other places, you mean that it is happening in a similar or identical way there. *e.g. The tradition is dying out in Scotland the same as everywhere else.*

sanctify   201,673
If a priest or other holy person **sanctifies** something, they bless or approve it and declare it holy. *e.g. The new cemetery was sanctified by the Bishop.*

sand   1520
Sand is a powdery substance that consists of extremely small pieces of stone. Most deserts and beaches are made of sand. *e.g. The children played in the sand.*

sandwich   1310
A **sandwich** is two or more slices of bread with a layer of food, such as meat, cheese or jam, between them. *e.g. I had a bacon sandwich for lunch.*

Santa Claus   145,1537
Santa Claus is an imaginary old man with a long white beard and a red coat. Many young children believe that he brings them their presents at Christmas. *e.g. Santa Claus will be at the Christmas party.*

Satan   939
Usually spelled **Shaitan** by Muslims.
Satan is the Devil, considered by Christians, Jews and Muslims to be the chief opponent of God. *e.g. He believes that Satan is ready to tempt him as soon as he stops being wary.*

satchel   234
A **satchel** is a bag with a shoulder strap in which schoolchildren carry their books, packed lunch, et cetera. *e.g. He went off to school with a satchel over his shoulder.*

satellite (beam by satellite)   386
Information or a signal that technicians **beam by satellite** is sent out to part of a communications system set up in space, and back to Earth, using radio waves. *e.g. The Olympic Games are instantly beamed by satellite to the other side of the globe.*

satellite (communication satellite)   386
A **communication satellite** is part of a technical system put into space to relay or transmit information at great speed by means of radio waves. *e.g. The latest French communication satellite goes into orbit next week.*

satellite television   394
1 Satellite television is the equipment, including a reception dish, which is needed to receive programmes broadcast for television by companies using satellite transmitters instead of the more usual radio transmitters. *e.g. Our neighbours have now got satellite television.*
2 Satellite television is the system of sending pictures and sounds by electrical signals using satellites, so that people with suitable conversion equipment can receive television pictures. *e.g. We would like to thank CNN for the use of their satellite television pictures during this report.*
3 Satellite television refers to all the programmes that can be watched with satellite television receiving equipment. *e.g. We watched satellite television right through the night.*
4 Satellite television is the business or industry concerned with making programmes and broadcasting them on satellite television. *e.g. Satellite television is providing a second career for many former BBC and ITV presenters.*

satellite (transmit by satellite)   386
A signal or information that technicians **transmit by satellite** is beamed out to part of a communication system in space, and back to Earth, using radio waves. *e.g. They will soon be able to transmit my lectures to Zanzibar by satellite.*

satellite T.V.   394
Satellite T.V. means the same as satellite television. See **satellite television**.

satisfaction   1271
1 Satisfaction is the pleasure that you feel when you are doing or have done something that you wanted or needed to do. *e.g. To see the task finished gave them a sense of satisfaction.*
2 If you do something to someone's **satisfaction**, they are happy with it. *e.g. Every detail was worked out to everyone's satisfaction.*
3 Satisfaction is something such as money or apology which you get from someone because of some harm or injustice which has been done to you. *e.g. In normal circumstances, you should be able to get satisfaction from your local branch.*

satisfactory   1271
Something that is **satisfactory** is good enough to be acceptable or to fulfil a particular need or purpose. *e.g. He considered the answers to the questions and found them satisfactory.*

satisfy   1271
1 Someone or something that **satisfies** you gives you enough of what you want to make you pleased or contented. *e.g. It satisfies us to know that our daughter's progress is steady.*
2 Someone or something that **satisfies** you convinces you of the truth of something, especially of something that you had doubted. *e.g. One more eyewitness statement will satisfy me that her death was accidental.*

Saturday   4,1590
Saturday is one of the seven days of the week. It is the day after Friday and before Sunday. *e.g. What did you do on Saturday?*

sauce   1662
A **sauce** is a thick liquid, often made from vegetables or fruit, which is added to other food to improve the flavour, and is sold in bottles. *e.g. The bottle of tomato sauce is on the bottom shelf.*

saucepan   239
A **saucepan** is a deep, metal cooking pot, often with a long handle and usually with a lid. *e.g. There is a saucepan on the top shelf.*

saucer   554
A **saucer** is a small, curved plate on which you stand a cup. *e.g. Could you pass me a saucer to stand this mug on?*

sausages   714
Sausages are portions of meat, especially pork or beef, or a meat substitute, which are mixed with other ingredients such as herbs and fat and then put into a thin casing like a tube. There are different kinds of sausage: some are sliced and eaten cold, and some are cooked and eaten hot. *e.g. We ate bread and sausages.*

save   1621
1 If you **save** someone or something, you help them to avoid harm or to escape from a dangerous or unpleasant situation. *e.g. An artificial heart could save his life.*
2 If you **save** time or money, you prevent the loss or waste of it. *e.g. An attempt to save costs may misfire.*
3 If someone or something **saves** you from doing something, or **saves** you the trouble of doing it, they do it for you or change the situation so that you do not have to do it. *e.g. A vote would save a lot of trouble.*

save up   1621
If you **save up** money, you collect it by not spending it, usually so that you can buy something that you want. *e.g. It took me a year to save up for a new coat.*

saviour   1621
1 A **saviour** is a person who saves people from danger. *e.g. Many people regarded Churchill as the saviour of the country.*
2 In Christianity, the **Saviour** is Jesus Christ. *e.g. I know that my Saviour lives.*

saw   71
1 A **saw** is a tool for cutting wood and other materials, which has a blade with sharp teeth along one edge. You use it by pushing it by hand backwards and forwards across a piece of wood or other material. *e.g. The saw is in the garage.*

2 To **saw** something means to cut it with a saw. *e.g. He sawed the branch in half.*

saw a piece of wood   71
If you **saw a piece of wood**, you cut it up into two or more smaller pieces using a saw. *e.g. He spent the morning sawing wood for his mother.*

say   347
1 When you **say** something, you speak words or sign signs. *e.g. Did I hear you say you think linguistics is boring?*
2 You use **say** when you report the actual words or signs that someone has uttered. *e.g. British Deaf News reported that Clark Denmark had said 'More attended than at the old Delegates' Conferences'.*
3 You use **say** when you give an approximate report of the words or signs that someone has uttered. *e.g. He said it was an accident.*
4 To **say** something means to express an idea, fact or opinion using words or signs. *e.g. I said she should resign.*
5 If you have a **say** in something, you have the right or the opportunity to give your opinion, especially when there is a decision to be taken. *e.g. Teachers should have a say in the new curriculum.*

scald   1714
1 If you **scald** yourself, or **scald** a part of your body, you burn yourself with very hot liquid or steam. *e.g. You'll scald yourself if you play with that kettle.*
2 A **scald** is a burn that has been caused by very hot liquid or steam. *e.g. This ointment is excellent for cuts and scalds.*

scald on the back of the hand   1714
1 If you **scald** yourself **on the back of the hand**, you burn yourself on the back of your hand with very hot liquid or steam. *e.g. I scalded myself on the back of the hand when I was pouring hot water into the teapot.*
2 A **scald on the back of the hand** is a burn on the back of the hand caused by very hot liquid or steam. *e.g. You will need some ointment for the scald on the back of your hand.*

scales   1367, 1413, 1630
Scales are a device or machine used to weigh things or people. *e.g. The kitchen scales were damaged when we moved house.*

scan a document   769
If you **scan a document**, such as a report or a piece of writing, you look at it carefully usually because you are looking for something in particular. *e.g. He scanned the list for his name.*

scare   1143, 1180
1 Something or someone that **scares** you makes you feel frightened or alarmed. *e.g. I didn't mean to scare you.*

2 If you have a **scare**, you have a sudden unpleasant experience that makes you frightened or alarmed. *e.g. I had a scare when I saw the door swing open.*

scared   539
1 If you are **scared** of someone or something, you are frightened of them. *e.g. He's scared of his new boss.*
2 If you are **scared** that something unpleasant might happen, you are nervous or worried because you think that it might happen. *e.g. I'm scared to make a fool of myself.*

scared stiff   947, 1006, 1709
If you are **scared stiff**, you are extremely afraid or frightened. *e.g. I am scared stiff of spiders.*

scared to death   947, 1006, 1709
If you are **scared to death**, you are extremely frightened. *e.g. I am scared to death of snakes.*

scarf   731, 1693
A **scarf** is a piece of cloth that you wear round your neck, shoulders, or head to keep yourself warm, or to make yourself look attractive. Scarves are usually long and narrow, but sometimes they are square or triangular in shape. *e.g. Her husband bought her a silk scarf for her birthday.*

scarlet   348
Something that is **scarlet** is bright red. *e.g. I lost my scarlet handkerchief.*

scar on the face   173
A **scar on the face** is a line or mark on the skin of someone's face which is left after a wound has healed. *e.g. He had a scar on his right cheek.*

scar on the side of the stomach   190
A **scar on the side of the stomach** is a line or mark on the skin on the side of someone's stomach which is left after a wound has healed. *e.g. She had a scar on the right side of her stomach.*

scatter   1498
If you **scatter** things over an area of ground, you throw or drop a lot of them so that they are spread all over the area. *e.g. The gardener scattered grass seeds for his new lawn.*

scent   994
A **scent** is a pleasant smell. *e.g. The magnificent scent of English flowers will fill your garden.*

school   671, 672, 1262, 1280
1 **School** or a **school** is a place where children are educated. *e.g. I went to Beverley School for the Deaf and Partially Hearing.*
2 University departments and colleges are sometimes called **schools**. *e.g. Roy went to art school in Edinburgh.*

3 If you sign or say that someone was at your **school**, or at **school** with you, you mean that you were educated at the same time in the same establishment. *e.g. There's Tracy; she was at my school.*

science   1686
1 **Science** is the study of nature and the behaviour of natural things, and the knowledge that we obtain about them. *e.g. Why don't many girls go into science?*
2 A **science** is a particular branch of science, for example physics or biology. *e.g. She would like to do a science subject at 'A' Level.*

scientific   1686
Scientific is used to describe things that relate to science or to a particular science. *e.g. We hope scientific research will provide a cure for AIDS in the near future.*

scientist   1686
A **scientist** is an expert who does work especially research work, in one of the sciences. *e.g. Dr. Burton, a distinguished medical scientist, is to visit the department next week.*

scissors   752
A pair of **scissors** is a small tool that you use for cutting paper or cloth. It consists of two sharp blades, and two rings in which you put your thumb and two or three of your fingers. You move your thumb and fingers so that the blades move together and cut something. *e.g. I wish I'd brought some scissors.*

scold   308
If you **scold** someone, you sign or speak angrily to them because they have done something wrong. *e.g. He scolded his daughter for keeping them waiting.*

scone   1154, 1156
A **scone** is a small cake made from flour and fat and usually eaten with butter. *e.g. There's one scone left for you.*

scores   1054
Scores are the numbers of goals, runs or points obtained by the teams or competitors in matches or competitions. *e.g. What are the latest football scores?*

Scot   38
1 A **Scot** is a person who comes from, or whose family identity relates to, Scotland. *e.g. My father-in-law is a Scot.*
2 **Scots** is a dialect of the English language that is spoken in Scotland. *e.g. He speaks broad Scots.*
3 Someone or something that is **Scots** belongs to or relates to Scotland or its people. *e.g. He has a strong Scots accent.*

Scotland 38
Scotland is a country that is part of the United Kingdom, occupying the north of Great Britain. *e.g. She grew up in Scotland.*

Scottish 38
1 Someone or something that is **Scottish** belongs to or relates to Scotland or its people. *e.g. The Scottish Regional Council is one of the regional councils of the BDA.*
2 **Scottish** is a dialect of the English language that is spoken in Scotland. *e.g. Tom Leonard writes wonderful poetry in Scottish.*
3 You can refer to people from Scotland in general, or a particular group of people from Scotland, as the **Scottish**. *e.g. The Scottish gave great support to their team in Sweden.*

scowl 1135
If you **scowl**, you frown to show that you are angry or displeased. *e.g. He scowls at the dog, the dog bites the postman.*

scram 160
If you **scram**, you leave a place quickly. *e.g. Maybe we both should scram.*

scrape 1189
1 If something **scrapes** an object, or **scrapes** against it, it rubs against the object and damages it slightly or makes a harsh noise. *e.g. The branches scrape the window at night.*
2 A **scrape** is the injury or damage left when one thing scrapes another. *e.g. Ah, it's just a scrape—nothing broken.*

scratch 1189
1 A **scratch** is a small cut on your body. *e.g. Don't make such a fuss, it's only a scratch.*
2 A **scratch** is a mark where something has been scratched. *e.g. White shoe polish can hide a scratch like that on white woodwork.*
3 If you **scratch** something, you make shallow cuts on it by rubbing a sharp object over or against it. *e.g. He scratched the dining room table with his toy motor car.*
4 If you do something from **scratch**, you do it without making use of anything that has been done before. *e.g. Now we have to start again from scratch.*

scream 1711
1 When someone **screams**, they make a very loud, high-pitched cry, usually because they are in pain or very frightened. *e.g. The children screamed when the soldiers began to shoot.*
2 If someone **screams** something, they shout it in a very loud, high-pitched voice. *e.g. Our teacher used to scream at us, but we couldn't understand her.*

screen 1227
A **screen** is a vertical panel which can be moved around. It is used to keep cold air away

from part of a room, or the boundary of a smaller area within the room. *e.g. We can erect a screen here to form your office space.*

screw up 312
If something **screws** you **up**, it makes you feel very confused or worried or disorganises your thoughts. *e.g. If I drink too much, it'll screw up my reasoning.*

scribble 628
1 If you **scribble** something, or if you **scribble**, you write quickly and roughly, often with the result that what you have written is hard to read. *e.g. She was scribbling a letter to her mother.*
2 A **scribble** is something that you have written or drawn quickly, roughly, or untidily. *e.g. She was looking at my scribble, trying to work out what it said.*

scribe 628
1 A **scribe** is a person who writes copies of things such as letters or documents. *e.g. My mother asked the village scribe to write a letter for her.*
2 In a primary school, an adult or child who is able to write may **scribe** for a child who has not yet learned how to do so, for example when the child tells a story which she or he or the teacher wishes to have written down. *e.g. The teacher sat in the writing corner and scribed for Ben as he signed his story about going to the Houghton Feast.*

scripture 203
You use **scripture** or **scriptures** to refer to writings that are regarded as sacred in a particular religion, for example the Bible in Christianity. *e.g. The Scriptures state 'You should love your neighbour as yourself.'*

scruffy 1146
Someone or something that is **scruffy** is dirty and untidy. *e.g. His clothes were scruffy and torn.*

scull 95
1 To **scull** means to move a boat through water using sculls. *e.g. I go sculling every morning on the River Wear.*
2 **Sculls** are small oars which are held and operated by one person to move a racing boat through the water. *e.g. He has a pair of the new lightweight sculls.*

sea 981, 1045
1 The **sea** is the salty water that covers about three quarters of the earth's surface. *e.g. The sea was calm.*
2 The **sea** is the area on or close to the edge of the sea, especially as a place where people go on holiday. *e.g. A nice weekend break at the sea is what you need.*
3 A **sea** is a particular area of the salty water that covers about three quarters of the earth's

surface. *e.g. The North Sea is absolutely freezing at this time of year—and most other times of year, too, come to think of it.*

seal 1404
A **seal** is a large mammal that eats mostly fish and lives in the wild partly on land and partly in the sea, usually in cold parts of the world. *e.g. A seal was glimpsed off the shore.*

seal an envelope 1259
If you **seal an envelope**, you stick down the flap so that the envelope cannot be opened without being torn. *e.g. He sealed the envelope and wrote 'S.W.A.L.K.' on the back.*

search 332
1 If you **search** for something, you look carefully for it. If you **search** a place, you look carefully for something there. *e.g. He searched the city for digs.*
2 A **search** is an attempt to find something by looking for it. *e.g. My search for the mysterious Maltese falcon was over.*

search 610, 1163
1 If you **search** for something, you look around you for it, often moving things in a careless way. If you **search** a place, you look around you for something there, often moving things in a careless way. *e.g. He would have to search to find the photo.*
2 A **search** is an attempt to find something by looking around you for it, often moving things in a careless way. *e.g. I found the keys after a long search.*

seat 86, 97, 114, 698, 734
1 A **seat** is an object that you can sit on, for example a chair. *e.g. Can someone find a seat for Arthur, please?*
2 If you **seat** yourself somewhere, or take a **seat**, you sit down. *e.g. Bernard was seated behind the desk.*

second 391
1 The **second** item in a series is the one that you count as number two. *e.g. In the second week of August, I'll be in Edinburgh.*
2 You sign or say **second** when you want to make a second point, or give a second reason for something. *e.g. And second, this kind of policy doesn't help to create jobs.*

second 748, 749
The **second** item in a series is the one that you count as number two. *e.g. His father's second marriage was to a German woman.*

secondly 391
You sign or say **secondly** when you want to make a second point or give a second reason for something. *e.g. I prefer the red suit. Firstly, it is cheaper, and secondly, it would go with my red car.*

seconds ago　　　　　　　　　1250
Seconds ago refers to a very recent period of time, usually within the last minute. *e.g. You've just missed him. He left seconds ago.*

secret　　　　　　1265, 1266, 1470
1 Something that is **secret** is known about by only a small number of people, and is not told or shown to anyone else. *e.g. The position of the safe was secret.*
2 If you do something in **secret**, you do it without anyone else knowing. *e.g. I met him in secret in a hotel in Paris.*
3 You use **secret** to describe someone who does something that they do not tell other people about. For example, if someone is your **secret** admirer, they admire you secretly. *e.g. She had become a secret drinker.*
4 A **secret** is a fact or piece of information that is known by only a small number of people, and is not told to anyone else. *e.g. I'll tell you a secret.*
5 If you sign or say that a particular way of doing things is the **secret** of achieving something, you mean that it is the best or only way to achieve it. *e.g. If you want to get the job done quickly, the secret is not to involve too many people.*

secretary　　　　　　　628, 1043
A **secretary** is a person who is employed to do office work, such as typing letters, answering phone calls, and arranging meetings. *e.g. Margaret and Sarah are the Departmental secretaries.*

section　　　　　　　　　　1447
A **section** of something is one of the separate parts into which it is divided or from which it is formed. *e.g. I passed the written part easily but failed the oral section.*

sections　　　　　　　　　　1599
The **sections** of something are the separate parts into which it is divided or from which it is formed. *e.g. Let's look at these sections one by one.*

see　　　　　　　　327, 755, 788
1 When you **see**, you use your eyes in order to recognise things or look at them. *e.g. Some animals can see in dim light.*
2 When you **see** something, you become aware of it or recognise it, using your eyes. *e.g. I could see Peg in the kitchen.*
3 When you **see** a performance of a play, a television programme, etc., you watch it. *e.g. We went to Blackpool to see the three plays in the final of the BDA's National Drama Competition.*

see　　　　　　　　　　　　1130
If you **see** what someone means, or **see** why something happened, you understand what they mean or understand why it happened. *e.g. Now I see your point.*

seed　　　　　　　　　　　　843
1 If you **seed** a piece of land, you plant seeds in it. *e.g. One rancher has seeded his land with maize.*
2 You can refer to a quantity of seeds as the **seed**. *e.g. Some of the seed will fall on stony ground.*

seeds　　　　　　　　　　　843
Seeds are the small, hard parts of a plant from which new plants grow. *e.g. I was given a packet of sunflower seeds.*

seek　　　　　　　　　　332, 610
If you **seek** something such as a job or a place to live, you are trying to find one. *e.g. Thousands seek food here: Somalia in 1992 is like Bangladesh in 1971.*

see (let's see)　　　　　　　327
1 You sign or say **let's see** or **let us see** to request or demand that you, or you and others, be allowed to look at something. *e.g. Come on, let's see, don't be so selfish!*
2 You sign or say **let's see** or **let us see** to suggest that you, or you and others, look at something. *e.g. Let's see what Anji's painting is like.*
3 People sign or say **let's see** or **let us see** to indicate that they do not intend to make a decision or do something immediately, and will wait and find out what is about to happen before acting. *e.g. Let's see how the meeting goes and then decide what to do.*

see (let us see)　　　　　　　327
See **see (let's see)**.

seem　　　　　　　　　　　1243
1 If someone or something **seems** to you to have a particular quality or attitude, they give you the impression of having that quality or attitude. *e.g. He seems confident.*
2 If something **seems** to be the case, you get the impression that it is the case. *e.g. It seems that everyone smokes.*
3 You use **seem** to indicate that you are not completely certain that what you are signing or saying is correct, but that the evidence you have tends to suggest that it is. *e.g. Experiments seem to prove that sugar is bad for you.*

seesaw　　　　　　　　　　1403
A **seesaw** is a long board which is balanced on a fixed pivot in the middle. If you sit on one end of the board, the other end goes up in the air. Children play on seesaws by making the board tilt up and down when one child sits on each end. *e.g. There is a padding pool, a sand pit, a seesaw, and swings.*

see through　　　　　　　　331
1 If you **see through** something, it does not stop you seeing what is behind it, even though it stands between you and the object. *e.g. If I had x-ray vision, I'd see through the front door.*

2 Something that is **see through** is made of thin material which does not stop you seeing what is behind it. *e.g. She realised when she got home that she had bought a see-through blouse by mistake.*

see through　　　　　　　　621
If you **see through** someone, or **see through** what they are doing, you realise what their intentions are, even though they are trying to hide them. *e.g. You think I don't know, but I can see through you.*

seize　　　　　　　　　984, 1171
1 When a group of people **seize** a place, or **seize** control of it, they take control of it quickly and suddenly, using force. *e.g. The airfield had been seized by US troops.*
2 If you **seize** someone, you arrest or capture them. *e.g. A double-glazing salesman was seized on Wednesday by three armed men.*
3 If you **seize** something, you take hold of it quickly and firmly. *e.g. 'Seize the control device,' shouted Doctor Spock, 'and do not let go!'*

seldom　　　　　　　　　　618
If something **seldom** happens, it happens only occasionally. *e.g. He seldom bathed because the shower was much quicker.*

select　　　　　　　　　　487
When you **select** from a range of things or people, you choose certain ones in preference to others. *e.g. The delegates voted to select a new committee.*

select　　　　　　　　　　845
If someone **selects** you, you are chosen in preference to other people. *e.g. Why they decided to select me, I'll probably never know.*

selection　　　　　426, 427, 447
A **selection** of items, such as goods in a shop, is the range of items that is available and from which you can choose what you want. *e.g. The delicatessen counter offers a selection of fine cheeses.*

selection　　　　　　　　　487
1 **Selection** is the activity of choosing one or more people or things from a group. *e.g. The judges may revise their selection process.*
2 A **selection** is a set of people or things that have been chosen from a group. *e.g. The orchestra was playing a selection of tunes from their wide repertoire.*

selection　　　　　　　　　845
The **selection** of a person is the activity of choosing them in preference to other people. *e.g. My selection for the post of manager came out of the blue.*

selective　　　　　　　　　487
When someone is **selective**, they choose a limited number of items from a range. *e.g.*

Our tight budget forced us to be extremely selective.

selfish   20, 31, 40, 1077, 1116
If you are **selfish**, you care only about yourself and tend to avoid sharing with other people. *e.g. It is selfish of you to keep all those sweets to yourself.*

sell   268
1 If you **sell** something, you let someone have it in return for an agreed sum of money. *e.g. I hope to sell the house this week.*
2 If a shop **sells** a particular thing, it has it in the shop for people to buy. *e.g. We sell a range of fruit from the West Indies.*

send   498
If you **send** someone somewhere, you tell them to go there. *e.g. She sent me to a specialist for a second opinion.*

send   1703
When you **send** something to someone, you arrange for it to be taken and delivered to them, for example by post. *e.g. You will be sent a timetable.*

send back   1703
When you **send** something **back** to someone, you return it. *e.g. Let me borrow that book and I'll send it back next week.*

send for   498
If you **send** someone **for** something or someone, you tell them to go and fetch that thing or person. *e.g. She had to send her daughter for the doctor.*

sensation   1082
1 **Sensation** is your ability to feel things physically, especially through your sense of touch. *e.g. He had no sensation in his right arm.*
2 A **sensation** is a general feeling or impression caused by a particular experience. *e.g. It was a strange sensation to return to school.*

sense   1082
If you **sense** something, you become aware of it, or realise that it is going to happen, often in an unconscious way and without receiving any direct information. *e.g. The doctor seemed to sense that she was unhappy.*

sensible   511
1 A **sensible** person is able to make good decisions and judgements based on reasons rather than emotions. *e.g. It seemed sensible to move to a smaller house.*
2 A **sensible** idea or action is one which is wise or reasonable. *e.g. Now that's a sensible idea: thank you, Haley.*

sensitive   965
1 If you are **sensitive** to other people's feelings and problems, you show understanding and awareness of them. *e.g. My boss is very sensitive to the difficulties faced by working mothers.*
2 If you are **sensitive** about something, it worries you or makes you upset or angry. *e.g. He is very sensitive to criticism.*
3 A **sensitive** subject or issue needs to be dealt with carefully because it is likely to cause disagreement or make people angry or upset. *e.g. Education cutbacks are a sensitive issue.*
4 Something that is **sensitive** to a physical force, substance or condition is easily affected by it, and often harmed by it. *e.g. Children's bones are very sensitive to radiation.*

sentence   390
1 A **sentence** is a structure of syntax that contains one or more complete clauses. *e.g. O.K., now we're going to look at the notion of 'sentence' in BSL.*
2 A **sentence** is a group of words which, when it is written down, begins with a capital letter and ends with a full stop. *e.g. Most of them could read a simple sentence in English.*

separate   1616, 1634
1 If one thing is **separate** from another, the two things are apart from each other and are not connected. *e.g. The two items can be kept separate inside the bomb casing.*
2 If you **separate** people or things, you move them or keep them apart so that they are not connected or cannot communicate. *e.g. Even at dinner time, we had to separate them.*
3 If you **separate** ideas from each other, you consider them individually and show the distinction between them. *e.g. Faith and God are to me the same thing. I can't separate them.*
4 If a couple who are married or living together **separate**, they decide to live apart. *e.g. Her parents decided to separate when she was eleven.*

separation   1616, 1634
1 The **separation** of two or more people, things, or groups is their movement away from each other, or their state of being kept apart from each other. *e.g. The separation of an infant from its mother is most damaging.*
2 A **separation** between two or more people is a period of time that they spend apart from each other. *e.g. Children recover remarkably quickly from a brief separation from their parents.*
3 If a couple who are married or living together have a **separation**, they decide to live apart. *e.g. Last night we talked about a separation.*

sequence   156, 157, 196
1 A **sequence** of events or things is a number of events or things that come one after another in a particular order. *e.g. He described the strange sequence of events that led up to the murder.*
2 A **sequence** is a particular order in which things happen or are arranged. *e.g. The paintings are exhibited in sequence according to when they were painted.*

series   156, 157, 196
1 A **series** of things or events is a number of them that come one after the other. *e.g. I am to give a series of lectures on European politics.*
2 A radio or television **series** is a set of programmes of a particular kind which have the same title. *e.g. The new series of 'A Question of Sport' starts later this year.*

serious   914
Problems or situations that are **serious** are very bad and cause people to be worried. *e.g. He suffered from a serious illness.*

serious   1256
1 Problems or situations that are **serious** are very bad and cause people to be worried. *e.g. He suffered from a serious illness.*
2 **Serious** work or consideration of something involves thinking about things deeply and carefully because they are important. *e.g. The programme aims for a serious political discussion.*

serious (you can't be serious)   847
If you sign or say **you can't be serious**, you mean that you are amazed by the comment that someone has just made, or you find it hard to believe. *e.g. She's going to get a job in Switzerland? You can't be serious!*

sermon   1247
A **sermon** is a signed presentation or talk on a religious or moral subject that is given by a member of the clergy as part of a church service. *e.g. Father Foley's sermon was on the importance of humility.*

servant   1011
A **servant** is someone who works completely under another person's control, often in that person's house, for example as a cleaner or gardener. *e.g. What did your last servant die of?*

serve   1369
Someone who **serves** customers in a shop or a bar helps them and provides them with what they want to buy. *e.g. The bar tender refused to serve us.*

serves someone right   39, 176, 180
If you sign or say that something **serves someone right**, you mean that what has happened is their own fault because they have behaved badly or stupidly. *e.g. You feel terrible? It serves you right for drinking too much last night.*

serve with a tennis racquet   59
When you **serve with a tennis racquet** in a game of tennis, you throw the ball up and hit it

with your tennis racquet to put the ball in play. *e.g. She served an ace.*

services   1369
Services are jobs that an organisation can do for you. *e.g. The organisation has improved its services to customers.*

service station   462
A **service station** is a roadside garage that sells petrol, oil, and often has a restaurant, toilets and other facilities. *e.g. There's a service station eleven miles ahead.*

set   1116
When something such as glue, jelly or cement **sets**, it becomes firm or hard. *e.g. Leave the jelly in the fridge to set.*

set   1690
A **set** is a number of things of the same kind that belong together, or that are thought of as a group. *e.g. The teacher divided the children into sets according to their hair colour.*

set back   1641
1 If something **sets** you **back**, or **sets back** a project or scheme, it causes a delay. *e.g. Bad weather set us back three weeks.*
2 If something is **set back** from a place, there is a space or an area of open ground between them. *e.g. The house is set back from the road.*

setback   1641
A **setback** is an event that delays your progress or makes your position less favourable than it was before. *e.g. This change of funding policy is the worst setback for sign language studies in the last decade.*

settee   115, 116
A **settee** is a long seat with a back and usually with arms, which is covered in soft material and which two or more people can sit on. *e.g. The settee matched the two chairs.*

settle   1037
1 If you **settle** somewhere, you become used to living in a particular house, town or area. *e.g. We hope to settle here and start a family.*
2 If you **settle** or **settle** yourself, you sit and make yourself comfortable. *e.g. I'll just let him settle while I make a cup of tea.*

settle down   1037
If you **settle down**, you stop behaving energetically, or being worried, and become calm. *e.g. When you have settled down, we can discuss the problem.*

set up   151
If you **set** something **up**, you make the preparations that are necessary to start it. *e.g. It took a long time to set up the course.*

several   551, 1496
Several people or things means a fairly small number of people or things. *e.g. Several members of staff are single.*

severe   914
You use **severe** to describe something that is very bad or undesirable. *e.g. There was a severe shortage of food after the draught.*

sew   844, 869
1 If you **sew**, you join pieces of cloth together, or attach things such as buttons to cloth, by passing thread through them with a needle. *e.g. Sew the edges together to finish the dress.*
2 When someone **sews** something such as a piece of clothing, they make it by sewing cloth together using a needle and thread. *e.g. Would you sew a little hat for Daniel's third birthday?*

sew   1419
1 If you **sew**, you use a machine to join pieces of cloth together, or attach things to cloth, by passing thread through them with a needle. *e.g. You can sew much faster than me.*
2 If you **sew** something, you make it by sewing cloth together on a machine. *e.g. I once saw a boy damage his finger trying to sew a wall-hanging.*

sewing   869
Sewing is the skill of making or mending clothes or other things using a needle and thread. *e.g. She went to Roba's sewing class at the City Lit.*

sewing machine   1419
A **sewing machine** is a machine that you use for sewing, with a needle that is driven by an electric motor or by movements of your hand or foot. *e.g. It's just a cheap sewing machine but it serves its purpose.*

sewing machinist   1419
A **sewing machinist** is a person who uses a sewing machine, usually as a job. *e.g. She found work as a sewing machinist.*

sex   43
1 **Sex** is the activity by which people and animals can produce young, involving the interaction of the male and female sex organs. *e.g. We weren't taught anything about sex when I was at school.*
2 **Sex** is the physical activities by which people satisfy their sexual desires with another person, and through which they may express their love for each other. *e.g. She did not agree with her mother's views on sex before marriage.*
3 **Sex** is also used to refer to the feelings and activities that are connected with having sex or with the desire to have sex. *e.g. He talked non-stop about sex.*

sex (have sex)   43
If two people **have sex**, they perform an act of sex. *e.g. She said she'd never had sex with a man.*

sexual intercourse   43
Sexual intercourse is the physical act of sex between a man and a woman. *e.g. Sexual intercourse is illegal with a girl under the age of sixteen.*

sexual intercourse (have sexual intercourse)   43
If you **have sexual intercourse**, you engage in the physical act of sex with a person of the opposite sex. *e.g. The leaflet explained the precautions you should take if you have sexual intercourse.*

sh   352, 354
Sh is what you sign or say in order to tell someone to be quiet. *e.g. Sh! The boys are in bed.*

shadow   442
1 A **shadow** is someone, for example a child, who does not like being separated from someone else and follows them about. *e.g. Peter had become Nina's adoring shadow.*
2 A **shadow** is someone, for example a detective, who follows someone secretly in order to find out what they are doing or where they are going. *e.g. Burke had to be watched, and it was my job to be the shadow reporting on his movements.*
3 If someone **shadows** you, they follow you very closely wherever you go. *e.g. They were already having him shadowed by a plain-clothes detective.*

shake   1040
If a person, animal, or thing **shakes**, they make small quick trembling movements. *e.g. The vet said I should hold the cat, because the injection might slip if he started to shake.*

shake   1091
If you **shake** someone or something, you hold them with one hand and move them quickly backwards and forwards. *e.g. She shook the boy's arm.*

shake pepper/salt/vinegar   1662
When you **shake pepper**, **salt** or **vinegar**, you scatter pepper, salt or vinegar usually over food, by holding the pepper, salt or vinegar container over the food and moving it from side to side so that the pepper, salt or vinegar comes out. *e.g. Do you want me to shake some vinegar on your chips?*

shall   21
1 If you sign or say that something **shall** happen, you are emphasising that it will definitely happen. *e.g. It must be done and therefore it shall be done.*

2 You use **shall** in questions when you are asking someone if they would like you to do something. *e.g. Shall I shut the door?*

shallow   1391
A **shallow** hole, container or layer of something measures only a short distance from the top to the bottom. *e.g. You can see the fish in the shallow water.*

shame   2, 1215
If you sign or say that it is a **shame** that something happened, you are expressing your regret about it, and indicating that you are sorry that it happened. *e.g. It's a shame he didn't come too.*

shame   904
1 If you sign or say that something is a **shame**, you are expressing your regret about it and indicating that you think it ought not to be as it is. *e.g. Shame! And I thought things were looking so good for the two of them.*
2 If you sign or say **shame**, you are confirming that you think something you have been told is bad news. *e.g. It's a shame he lost his job after ten years.*

shame   993
1 **Shame** is an uncomfortable feeling of guilt and failure that you have because you have not behaved in an acceptable way, or because someone close to you has not behaved in an acceptable way. *e.g. The memory of our fight fills me with shame.*
2 **Shame** is the loss of the good opinion and respect that other people have for you and the uncomfortable feeling that this loss causes you. *e.g. He feels that bankruptcy means lasting shame.*
3 If you sign or say that you have done something to your **shame**, you mean that you feel guilty about it because you know that it is wrong. *e.g. I admit, much to my shame, that I fiddled the bill.*

share   1325, 1599
If you **share** something with a number of people, organisations or groups, you each have, use or do an equal or fair part of it. *e.g. Okay, if we share it we'll all be happy.*

share out   1325, 1599
If you **share out** an amount of something, you give each person or organisation in a group an equal or fair part of it. *e.g. Let's share out the work.*

shares   1318, 1325, 1599
Shares in a company are the many equal parts into which the ownership of the company can be divided. Shares can be bought by people as an investment. *e.g. I wonder how many companies he has shares in.*

sharp   382
1 A **sharp** object has a very thin edge that is good for cutting things. *e.g. He carried a sharp knife.*
2 Someone who is **sharp** is quick to notice, hear, or understand things. *e.g. His sharp eyes would never miss it.*

shave with a razor   256
When someone **shaves with a razor**, they cut the hair from their face, very close to the skin, with a razor. *e.g. Whenever I shave with a razor, I cut myself.*

she   310
You use **she** to refer to or indicate a woman or girl who is present or whose identity has been established. *e.g. If she'd done this properly, I wouldn't have to do it again.*

sheep   929
A **sheep** is a farm animal with a thick woolly coat. Sheep are usually kept for their wool or for their meat. *e.g. No, the sheep is called Brennan, and it's just had several lambs.*

sheet   874, 1521
A **sheet** is a large, rectangular piece of cloth, usually made of cotton or some similar fine material. Sheets are used with blankets or a duvet to make a bed. *e.g. Clean sheets are put on the bed every Friday.*

Sheffield   686
1 **Sheffield** is the name of a city in South Yorkshire on the River Don. It is an important centre of steel manufacture and of the cutlery industry. *e.g. I was born in Sheffield, but I never appreciated what a great city it is until I'd lived down south for a while.*
2 The addresses of Deaf clubs in **Sheffield** are: Sheffield Deaf Club, 57 Psalter Lane, Sheffield 611 8YP; and Sheffield Central Deaf Club, 2 Surrey Place, Sheffield S1 2LOP.

shelf   1406, 1637
A **shelf** is a flat piece of hard material, for example wood, metal, or glass, which is attached to a wall or to the sides of a cupboard. Shelves are used for keeping things on. *e.g. There were a lot of books on the shelf.*

shelter   1567
1 A **shelter** is a small building or covered place which is made to protect people from bad weather or danger. *e.g. The shelter didn't give us much protection against the wind.*
2 If a place provides **shelter**, it provides protection from bad weather or danger. *e.g. He found shelter in the caves.*

shift   1453
1 If you **shift** something, it moves. *e.g. We tried to shift the chair closer to the bed.*
2 A **shift** in opinion or in a situation is a slight change in it. *e.g. It seems there is now a shift of attitudes within group.*
3 If you **shift** your opinion, perspective, etc., you change it slightly. *e.g. I must admit my view may shift if this continues.*

shimmer   1057, 1245
If something **shimmers**, it shines with a shifting, unsteady light, for example as shiny material does under a spotlight. *e.g. The velvet curtains shimmer with gold embroidery.*

shindig   954
A **shindig** is a noisy party or dance. *e.g. We had a glorious shindig at the Drury's last Saturday.*

shine   1057
1 Something that has a **shine** is bright because it reflects light. *e.g. The shine of the brass handle catches the cat's eye.*
2 If something **shines**, it is bright because it reflects light. *e.g. The windows, newly polished, shine as the sun rises.*

shiny   1057
Something that is **shiny** is bright because it reflects light. *e.g. He has a shiny new car.*

ship   1425
1 A **ship** is a large boat which carries passengers or cargo on sea journeys. *e.g. The ship was due to dock the following morning.*
2 If you **ship** something, you send it by ship. *e.g. We ship the oil to North Africa.*

shirt   490
A **shirt** is a piece of clothing worn on the upper part of your body which is made of a lightweight material and often has a collar, sleeves and buttons down the front. *e.g. He wore a suit, shirt and tie.*

shit   622
1 **Shit** is waste matter from the body of a human being or an animal. *e.g. The dog came home from the farm covered in shit.*
2 **Shit** is used to express anger, impatience or disgust. Some people find this offensive. *e.g. Oh, shit, I've dropped my shoe in the canal.*
3 People sometimes refer to things they do not like as **shit**. Some people find this offensive. *e.g. Don't give me that shit about pay cuts.*

shiver   118
When you **shiver**, your body shakes slightly because you are cold. *e.g. I stood shivering on the doorstep waiting for the shop to open.*

shock   1080
1 A **shock** is a strong feeling of fear or distress that you get when something unpleasant suddenly happens to you. *e.g. Her death was a shock to me.*

2 **Shock** is a person's emotional and physical condition when something very frightening or distressing has happened to them. *e.g. Numb with shock, she stood watching as they took his body away.*

3 **Shock** is a serious physical condition in which your blood cannot circulate properly, for example because you have a bad injury. *e.g. She was taken to hospital suffering from shock.*

4 A **shock** is something sudden and unexpected that threatens the beliefs, traditions, or way of life of a group of people. *e.g. The abdication of the King was a great shock.*

5 If something **shocks** you, it makes you feel very upset because it involves death or suffering and because you had not expected it. *e.g. I think her husband's death will shock the whole family.*

6 If something **shocks** you, it makes you feel upset or angry because you feel it is morally wrong. *e.g. Do scenes like this shock you?*

shoddy 911
Something that is **shoddy** has been done or made carelessly or badly. *e.g. That's an example of shoddy workmanship, if I ever saw it.*

shoe 1682
A **shoe** is one of a pair of objects which you wear on your feet. It covers all of your foot and is usually worn over your sock or stocking. Shoes are usually made of leather or a similar strong, flexible material. *e.g. Where is my other shoe?*

shoot an arrow with a bow 864
If you **shoot an arrow with a bow**, you place the arrow against the bowstring and then fire the arrow by releasing the string. *e.g. If you shoot a single arrow at my door with that bow, I shall take it from you!*

shooting 463
1 If a **shooting** occurs, somebody is injured by a bullet fired from a gun. *e.g. News of the shooting spread throughout the community.*

2 **Shooting** is the firing of bullets from a gun or guns. *e.g. The shooting continued through the afternoon.*

shooting with a hand gun/pistol/ revolver 463
A **shooting with a hand gun**, a **pistol** or a **revolver** is an occasion when someone is killed or injured by the firing of a bullet or bullets from such a gun. *e.g. Tonight's headlines: yesterday's shooting with a police revolver was not the work of police marksmen, says Superintendent.*

shooting with a rifle/shotgun 609
A **shooting with a rifle** or a **shotgun** is an occasion when someone is killed or injured by the firing of a bullet or bullets from such a gun. *e.g. The shooting of ten sheep, with a rifle found at*

the scene of the crime, is being investigated by the local constabulary.

shoot with a film/television/video camera 470
If you **shoot with a film camera**, a **television camera** or a **video camera**, you take moving pictures of a scene or event using such a piece of equipment. *e.g. Shoot this with a video camera, and then take some stills of the players.*

shoot with a hand gun/pistol/revolver 463
1 If you **shoot with a hand gun**, a **pistol** or a **revolver**, you fire a bullet from such a gun. *e.g. The soldiers were taught to shoot with a pistol without giving away their position.*

2 If you **shoot** a person or animal **with a hand gun**, a **pistol** or a **revolver**, you kill them or injure them by firing such a gun at them. *e.g. I saw him shoot eighteen pheasants that morning with a revolver.*

shoot with a rifle/shotgun 609
1 If you **shoot with a rifle** or a **shotgun**, you fire a bullet from such a gun. *e.g. Nobody is allowed to shoot with a shotgun within this designated woodland area.*

2 If you **shoot** a person or animal **with a rifle** or a **shotgun**, you kill them or injure them by firing such a gun at them. *e.g. My Uncle Pat used to shoot crows with a shotgun in the summer to protect the corn.*

shop 952, 1633
1 A **shop** is a building or part of a building where things are sold. *e.g. A shoe shop in the arcade was broken into last week.*

2 When you **shop**, you go to shops and buy things. *e.g. At weekends, I like to shop and sleep.*

shoplifter 1126, 1151
A **shoplifter** is a person who steals from a shop by removing items from display and hiding them in a bag, or in their clothes, before trying to escape. *e.g. Shoplifters will be prosecuted.*

shoplifting 1126, 1151
Shoplifting is stealing from a shop by removing items from display and hiding them in a bag, or in your clothes, before trying to escape. *e.g. She was caught shoplifting in the chemist's.*

shopping 15, 952, 1633
Shopping is the activity of going to shops and buying things. *e.g. Who's going to do the shopping?*

shop steward 828
A **shop steward** is a trade union member who is elected by members of the union in

their place of work to express their views at meetings, and to deal with other union business. *e.g. He became a prominent shop steward in the Transport and General Workers' Union.*

short 87
1 If a name is **short** for another name, it is the short version of that name. *e.g. Fred is short for Frederick.*

2 If something is cut **short**, it is forced to stop before it has finished. *e.g. We'll have to cut short this discussion.*

3 If you sign or say that you would like a **short** word, or a few **short** words, with someone, you mean that you would like a brief conversation with them. *e.g. There was only time for a few short words before the meeting.*

short 650
A **short** is a small amount of strong alcoholic drink, especially spirits such as whiskey or brandy. *e.g. I'll have a beer and a short.*

short 1446
1 If something lasts for a **short** time, it does not last very long. *e.g. They had a short break before this lecture.*

2 Something that is **short** measures only a small amount from one end to the other. *e.g. I'm looking for a short piece of wood.*

3 If you are **short** of something, or if it is **short**, you do not have enough of it. *e.g. We are really short of typing paper.*

short 1574
Someone who is **short** is not as tall as most people are. *e.g. His grandfather was a short, fat man.*

short 1619
1 A **short** hour, day, etc., is one that seems to pass very quickly. *e.g. Crikey, that was a short half-hour!*

2 If you have to do something at **short** notice, you do not have as much time as usual, or as you wish, in which to prepare yourself or to make the necessary arrangements. *e.g. My visit was arranged at short notice.*

shortage 87
If there is a **shortage** of something, there is not enough of it. *e.g. There's a world shortage of fuel.*

shotgun 609
A **shotgun** is a gun used for shooting birds and animals which fires a lot of metal balls at one time. *e.g. He was quite good at using a shotgun.*

shot of a hand gun/pistol/revolver 463
The **shot of a hand gun**, a **pistol** or a **revolver** is the act of such a gun being fired. *e.g. The shot of a pistol echoed around the hall.*

shot of a rifle/shotgun   609
The **shot of a rifle** or a **shotgun** is the act of such a gun being fired. *e.g. On average, the shot of a rifle can be heard over a mile away.*

shot put   1696
The **shot put** is an athletic competition in which the contestants throw a heavy metal ball, called a shot, as far as possible. *e.g. He won a bronze medal in the shot put.*

shot putter   1696
A **shot putter** is a person who takes part in the shot put. *e.g. She was the school's champion shot putter last year.*

should   2
1 If you sign or say that something **should** happen, or **should** be true, you mean that you think it will probably happen or is probably true. *e.g. She should win a medal at the Olympic Games.*
2 If you sign or say that something **should** happen, you mean that you think it is right or a good idea. *e.g. The government should recognise BSL.*

should   1437
If you sign or say that something **should** happen, you mean that you think it is right or necessary for it to happen. *e.g. The authorities should stop these massacres.*

shoulder-bag   234
A **shoulder-bag** is a bag that has a long strap so that it can be carried on a person's shoulder. *e.g. I use a shoulder-bag to keep my hands free to sign.*

should have   2
Should have is used to indicate that something was expected or intended to happen but did not happen. *e.g. Betty should have won.*

should not   1420
If you sign or say that someone **should not** do something, or something **should not** happen, you mean that you think what they are doing, or what is happening, is wrong. *e.g. I think animals should not be shut up in cages in a zoo.*

shout   1711
1 A **shout** is a loud call or cry, for example made by children when they are playing or by a person who is ordering someone to do something. *e.g. We heard excited shouts from the playground.*
2 If you **shout**, you say words as loudly as you can, so that you can be heard from a long distance away. *e.g. She was ready to shout for help.*
3 If you **shout** at someone, you talk angrily to them in a loud voice. *e.g. She shouted at us for spoiling her evening.*
4 If you **shout** something, you say it in a very loud voice. *e.g. 'Stop it!' he shouted.*

shove   1397
1 If someone **shoves** something or someone, they push them with a quick, violent movement. *e.g. The police closed in and started to shove us towards the gates.*
2 A **shove** is a quick, violent push. *e.g. One shove and it'll move easily.*

shovel   153
1 A **shovel** is a tool like a spade, used for lifting and moving earth, coal, snow, et cetera. *e.g. The coal shovel was missing from the coal house.*
2 If you **shovel** earth, coal, snow, etc., you lift and move it with a shovel. *e.g. She helped us shovel the snow off the front path.*

show   968
A **show** is a form of entertainment at the theatre or on television that usually consists of several items. *e.g. We are going to put on a Christmas show at the Deaf club.*

show   1373, 1384
1 If you **show** someone something, or **show** something to someone, you allow them to see it. *e.g. I'll show you where the restaurant is.*
2 A **show** is a display of objects for people to look at. *e.g. The vegetable show was a bigger success than ever.*

show contempt/disdain   970
If you **show contempt** or **disdain** of, or for, someone or something, you behave or express yourself in a way that can be seen by others to demonstrate that you do not accept, or are not impressed by, the person or thing. *e.g. The minister may show contempt for the tabloids in public, but he has been badly wounded by the scandal.*

shower   1192
A **shower** is a short period of light rain. *e.g. There was a shower this morning, but it's been mostly dry since.*

shower   1706
1 A **shower** is a device used for washing yourself. It consists of a pipe or hose which ends in a flat piece with a lot of holes in it that direct the water out in a spray. *e.g. All rooms have got a bath, shower, and toilet.*
2 If you have a **shower**, you wash yourself by standing under a spray of water from a shower. *e.g. A hot shower and a change of clothes would be wonderful.*

shower (take a shower)   1706
If you **take a shower**, you wash yourself by standing under a spray of water from a shower. *e.g. Eamon is taking a shower.*

show off   232, 233
If you **show off**, you behave in a way that makes your skills, abilities, or good qualities

very obvious, in order to impress people. *e.g. She accused him of showing off.*

show-off   232, 233
If you refer to someone as a **show-off**, you mean that they behave in a way that makes their skills, abilities, or good qualities very obvious, in order to impress people. *e.g. He is a show-off.*

show of presents   1373, 1384
A **show of presents**, especially in Scotland, is the occasion prior to a wedding, when people who have given a gift to the bride and groom are invited by the bride's family to view all the wedding gifts. *e.g. The show of presents will take place in the community centre.*

show up   553, 630
If you **show up**, you appear at a place where you are expected by someone. *e.g. He showed up at ten o'clock the next morning.*

shrink   1393, 1395
If something **shrinks**, or you **shrink** it, it becomes smaller in size or area. *e.g. If you wash your woollens in hot water, they may shrink.*

shrinkage   1395
Shrinkage is a decrease in the size or amount of something. *e.g. The factory closed due to the shrinkage of export orders.*

shuffle playing cards   1099
If you **shuffle playing cards** or **shuffle a pack of cards**, you mix them up before you begin a game. *e.g. He shuffled the playing cards before putting them down on the table.*

shut   1358, 1398
1 When an establishment such as a shop or pub **shuts**, or when someone **shuts** it, it is closed and you cannot go into it until the next time that it is open. *e.g. What time do the shops shut?*
2 If you **shut** something, or it **shuts**, its position is changed so that it fills or blocks a hole or gap. *e.g. Shut everything, the sandstorm will strike any minute.*
3 If something is **shut**, it has been shut. *e.g. Aye, aye, skipper: everything's shut.*

shut   1451
1 If you **shut** something, you move two panels or doors, pivoting on their hinges, to block or fill a hole or gap. *e.g. Shut the doors, here comes trouble!*
2 If two panels or doors are **shut**, they have been shut. *e.g. Yes, they're well and truly shut.*

shut down   1359
If a factory, organisation or business **shuts down**, or if someone **shuts** it **down**, it closes and stops its work, usually for ever. *e.g. The factory had to shut down after a series of terrorist attacks.*

shut one up 1260
If you **shut someone up**, you do, sign or say something which makes them stop complaining, or trying to impress people, by showing that you are better, wiser or more deserving than they are. *e.g. I was moaning about my pay, till he signed he lived on £40 a week: that shut me up.*

shy 364
1 A **shy** person is nervous and uncomfortable in the company of other people, especially people that he or she does not know. *e.g. He was too shy to talk.*
2 If you are **shy** of doing something, you are unwilling to do it because you are afraid of what might happen. *e.g. Don't be shy of telling them what you think.*

sick 318, 931
If you are **sick**, you are ill. Sick usually means physically ill, but it can sometimes mean mentally ill. *e.g. Your uncle is sick and needs medical care.*

sick 1584
1 If you sign or say that something makes you **sick**, you mean you feel angry or disgusted about it. *e.g. It makes me sick the way they waste our money.*
2 If you are **sick** of something, you are very annoyed by it and want it to stop. *e.g. He was sick of war.*
3 You describe acts, stories, or jokes as **sick** when they deal with matters like death, cruelty or suffering in a way that is considered unacceptable. *e.g. She told a rather sick joke.*

side 1227
The **sides** of something such as a building or a vehicle are the vertical outer parts which are not its front or its back. *e.g. He leaned his bike on the side of the garage.*

side by side 422
If two things develop **side by side**, they do it together or at the same place and time. *e.g. Two interdependent communities evolved side by side.*

sight 327, 755
Sight is the ability to see. *e.g. I had my sight tested at the optician's.*

sightseeing 747
Sightseeing is travelling around, seeing the interesting places that tourists usually visit. *e.g. Allow some time in the major cities for sightseeing.*

sign 1067
If you **sign**, you communicate by using sign language. *e.g. All my family can sign, I'm lucky.*

signature 721
Your **signature** is your name written in your own characteristic way, often at the end of a piece of writing as a way of officially identifying the writing as yours, or of showing that you agree with what it says. *e.g. He underlined his signature with a little flourish.*

sign for 721
1 If you **sign for** an item, you put your signature on an official form or book, as proof that you have received the item. *e.g. When signing for any parcel, always add 'not inspected'.*
2 If you **sign for** something, you put your signature on a form, list or contract, by which you agree to do something. *e.g. It was in the same week that he signed for his second film.*

sign in 721
1 If you **sign in**, you sign your name in a book, or on a special form, when you arrive at a hotel or club. *e.g. They signed in at the reception desk.*
2 If you **sign** someone **in** at a club, institution, etc., of which you are a member, you sign your name in a special book in order to allow them to be there as your visitor since they are not a member. *e.g. Just get someone who's on the committee to sign you in.*

sign language 1067, 1068
1 A **sign language** is a visual-gestural language used especially within the Deaf community in a particular country. *e.g. The students studied the structure of British Sign Language.*
2 **Sign language** is linguistic behaviour produced using a visual-gestural system. *e.g. Sign language tells us things about the human capacity for communication which could never otherwise have been known.*

sign on 721
1 If you **sign on**, you put your signature on a contract, form, or other document, which states that you will work for a particular organisation, study on a particular course, et cetera. *e.g. He signed on the next morning with the Royal Air Force.*
2 If you **sign on**, you go to your local social security office and put your signature on a statement declaring that you are unemployed, so that you can get social security benefits, especially unemployment benefit. *e.g. You have to sign on every fortnight, so don't lose this card.*

sign one's name 614, 721
If you **sign your name** on something, or **sign** something, you write your name on it in your own characteristic way, usually either at the end or in a special space. You do this to show, for example, that you have written the document, that you agree with what is written, or that you have been present on a particular occasion. *e.g. Sign your name on MJ and Betty's card.*

silence 354, 879
If there is **silence**, there is no noise of any kind. Within the Deaf community, silence may also refer to a lack of signing or other movement. *e.g. When Gloria delivered her lecture, there was absolute silence in the hall.*

silence one 1260
If you **silence someone**, you do, sign or say something which makes them stop complaining, or trying to impress people, by showing that you are better, wiser or more deserving than they are. *e.g. One day I'll beat him in the maths test and that'll silence him!*

silent 354
Someone who is **silent** is not making any noise. *e.g. Let's practice being silent, shall we, children?*

silent 879
1 Someone who is **silent** does not sign or speak to people very much and may therefore give an impression of being unfriendly. *e.g. She was a silent girl.*
2 Something that is **silent** makes no sound at all. *e.g. He invented a flashing light alarm that was silent.*
3 A **silent** film has no sound or speech. Such films were common in the early part of the twentieth century, before the widespread use of soundtrack facilities. *e.g. There were several deaf actors in silent films.*

silent (be silent) 352, 354
If you tell someone to **be silent**, you are telling them not to make any noise. *e.g. Be silent this instant, boy.*

silk 1516
Silk is a kind of smooth, fine cloth which is made from a substance produced by silk worms. *e.g. Give him a white silk scarf for Christmas.*

silly 663
If you sign or say that someone or something is **silly**, you mean that they are foolish or childish. *e.g. You're a silly boy.*

silver 913
1 **Silver** is a valuable, greyish-white metal that is used especially for making jewellery and ornaments. *e.g. A little metal box made of solid silver stood on the shelf.*
2 In a house, **silver**, or **the silver**, is the things there that are made from silver, especially cutlery and dishes. *e.g. The silver and glasses sparkled in the candlelight.*
3 You describe something as **silver** when it is greyish-white in colour. *e.g. She used silver paint.*

similar 423
If something is **similar** to other things, or a

number of things are **similar**, they are almost alike. *e.g. The four restaurants were all selling similar food at similar prices.*

simple   362, 520
1 If something is **simple**, it is not complicated, and is therefore easy to understand. *e.g. It involves a very simple calculation.*
2 If a problem is **simple**, or if its solution is **simple**, the problem can be solved easily. *e.g. The solution is very simple.*
3 A **simple** task is easy to do. *e.g. It's a simple operation, you can do it in a lunch hour.*

simple   959
If something is **simple**, it consists only of things that are functional or necessary, without any extra or decorative features. *e.g. A tall woman in a simple brown dress stood beside the fire.*

simultaneous   425
Things which are **simultaneous** happen or exist at the same time. *e.g. We couldn't believe that there was a simultaneous failure of all the lifts in the building.*

sin   910, 911
1 **Sin**, or a **sin**, is behaviour which is considered to be very bad and immoral. *e.g. Saint Ignatius taught that lack of gratitude was the root of all sin.*
2 If you **sin**, you do something that is believed to be very bad and immoral. *e.g. I think we sin whenever we are selfish.*

since   1491
If something has happened **since** a particular time or event, it has happened from that time or event until now. *e.g. She's been a bus driver since April last year.*

sing   758
1 If you **sing**, or if you **sing** a song, you make musical sounds with your voice, usually producing words that fit a tune. *e.g. I started to sing as she came into the room.*
2 If someone **sings** a particular type of music, or a particular musical role, they perform it as a singer, especially as a professional. *e.g. She has been singing opera for five years.*

singer   758
A **singer** is a person who sings, especially one who earns a living by singing. *e.g. His mother was an actress and a singer.*

single   555
1 If you refer to a **single** thing, you mean only one and not more. *e.g. A single plate would sell, but not a set of six.*
2 If you are **single**, you are not married. *e.g. A single woman and her daughter have moved in next door.*

sink   1548
If something **sinks**, it moves slowly downwards and disappears from sight, especially below the surface of water. *e.g. The aircraft carrier blew up and we watched it sink without a trace.*

sink   1374, 1628
1 A **sink** is a large basin in a kitchen with taps that supply water, used especially for washing pans, crockery and cutlery. *e.g. The kitchen sink was pink!*
2 A **sink** is the same as a washbasin. *e.g. He has gold taps on his sink and bathtub.*

sister   576
1 Your **sister** is a girl or woman who has the same parents as you. *e.g. My sister Jane married a farmer.*
2 A **sister** is a senior female nurse who is in charge of a hospital ward. *e.g. Sister Janis is in charge of the ante-natal ward.*
3 A woman sometimes refers to other women as her **sisters** when she feels very close to them because they work for the same organisation, or have the same aims or beliefs. *e.g. We support our sisters in Bradford in their new publishing venture.*

sit   86, 97, 114, 698, 734
1 If you are **sitting** somewhere, for example in a chair, your weight is supported in it by your buttocks rather than your feet, and the upper part of your body is upright. *e.g. I was sitting at my desk reading.*
2 If you **sit** somewhere, you lower your body until you are sitting on something, usually a chair. *e.g. He came into the room and sat in his usual chair.*

sit   1380
If you sign or say that an object **sits** in a particular place, you mean that it is in that place, usually for some time. *e.g. These papers just sit on his shelves, unread.*

sit in an armchair/easychair   91
1 If you are **sitting in an armchair** or an **easychair**, your weight is supported in it by your buttocks rather than your feet, and the upper part of your body is upright. *e.g. Sitting in the armchair, I felt all the tension of the last few days melt away.*
2 If you **sit in an armchair** or an **easychair**, you lower your body until you are sitting on it. *e.g. She sat in the armchair by the window.*

sit on a couch/settee/sofa   115, 116
1 If you are **sitting on a couch**, a **settee** or a **sofa**, your weight is supported in it by your buttocks rather than your feet, and the upper part of your body is upright. *e.g. The children were sitting on the sofa watching the television.*
2 If you **sit on a couch**, a **settee** or a **sofa**, you

lower your body until you are sitting on it. *e.g. She took one look at the soggy dog and got up and sat on the sofa.*

situation   983, 1018
1 You use **situation** to refer generally to what is happening in a particular place at a particular time. *e.g. The present situation is impossible: too many people, too little food.*
2 You use **situation** to refer to a particular aspect of what is happening in a place. *e.g. They were angry about the housing situation.*
3 The **situation** of a building or town is the kind of place where it is, for example the kind of surroundings that it has, or its distance from other buildings or towns. *e.g. The city is in a beautiful situation.*

skeleton   660
Your **skeleton** is the framework of bones which supports and protects your organs and muscles. *e.g. They found the skeleton of a gigantic whale.*

ski   120
1 **Skis** are long, flat, narrow pieces of wood, metal, or plastic that are fastened to boots, which you wear in order to move easily on snow. *e.g. He bought her a pair of skis.*
2 When people **ski**, or **go skiing**, they move on snow wearing skis, especially as a sport or a holiday activity. *e.g. They ski every winter.*

skid   1320
1 If a person or vehicle **skids**, they slide sideways or forwards while moving, for example when they are trying to stop their car suddenly on a wet road. *e.g. He slammed on his brakes but the car began to skid.*
2 A **skid** is the movement that occurs when you skid. *e.g. It must have been quite a skid, judging by the marks on the road.*

skier   120
A **skier** is a person who skis. *e.g. The British Olympic skiers train in Austria.*

skiing   120
Skiing is the sport or activity in which people ski. *e.g. There are skiing championships every year.*

skill   158
Skill is the knowledge and ability that enables you to do something such as a job, game, or sport, very well. *e.g. Martin Dutton's carvings show remarkable skill.*

skilled   975
1 Someone who is **skilled** has the knowledge and ability needed to do something well. *e.g. A skilled engineer takes at least four years to train.*
2 **Skilled** work involves or requires a certain level of trained ability; used especially of

manual and industrial work. *e.g. There is still a shortage of labour in some industries with respect to skilled work.*

skilled 1531
Someone who is **skilled** has the knowledge and ability needed to do something well. *e.g. She is very skilled in her field.*

skim a document 769
If you **skim a document** such as a report or a piece of writing, you read through it quickly. *e.g. I thought I would skim through a few of the letters.*

skin 863
Your **skin** is the natural covering of your body. *e.g. Poison may be absorbed through the skin.*

skipping rope 271
A **skipping rope** is a rope, usually with a handle at both ends, used for skipping. *e.g. Ruth got a new skipping rope for Christmas.*

skip with a skipping rope 271
When someone **skips with a skipping rope**, they jump up and down over a rope, usually with a handle at both ends (skipping rope), which they are holding at each end and turning round and round. *e.g. Colleen was skipping in the playground when Wendy arrived.*

skirt 1485
1 A **skirt** is a piece of clothing worn by women and girls, which fastens at the waist and hangs down from the waist. *e.g. She was dressed in a very short skirt.*
2 The **skirt** of a dress or coat is the part which hangs below the waist. *e.g. She danced about, making the skirt of her dress flare out.*

slacks 709
Slacks are casual trousers. *e.g. I put on a pair of golfing slacks and a blazer.*

slaughter 184
1 To **slaughter** a large number of people means to kill them in a way that is cruel, unjust, or unnecessary. *e.g. On the Western Front, men were being slaughtered to no purpose.*
2 To **slaughter** animals such as cows and sheep means to kill them for their meat. *e.g. A freshly slaughtered bullock was delivered to the butcher.*

slaughterhouse 184
A **slaughterhouse** is a place where animals are killed for their meat. *e.g. The sheep are on their way to the slaughterhouse.*

slave 47
A **slave** is a person who belongs to someone else as their property and has to work for them. *e.g. His father had been a slave in Alabama.*

slavery 47
1 **Slavery** is the system by which people can be owned by other people as slaves. *e.g. He campaigned for the abolition of slavery.*
2 **Slavery** is the state of not being free because you have to work very hard or because you are strongly influenced by something. *e.g. I had at last been freed from the slavery of factory work.*

sled 1349
A **sled** is a vehicle which can travel over snow. It consists of a framework which is fixed onto two long, narrow pieces of wood or metal which slide over the snow. *e.g. A sled was descending the snowy hill.*

sledge 1349
A **sledge** is a vehicle which can travel over snow. It consists of a framework which is fixed onto two long narrow pieces of wood or metal which slide over the snow. *e.g. She has a brand new sledge.*

sledge pulled by animals 281
A **sledge pulled by animals** is a vehicle which can slide over snow, having a framework fixed onto two long, narrow pieces of wood or metal. It is attached to one or more animals, such as a horse or pack of dogs, which pull it across the snow. *e.g. We were taken for a ride around Central Park in a sledge pulled by two horses.*

sleep 1254
1 **Sleep** is the natural state of rest in which your eyes are closed and your mind and body are inactive and unconscious, usually for several hours every night. *e.g. Now go to sleep and stop worrying about it.*
2 A **sleep** is a period of sleeping. *e.g. You'll feel better if you have a little sleep.*
3 When you **sleep**, you rest in a state of sleep. *e.g. Jaime couldn't sleep at all because she was so excited about flying to China.*

sleep (deep sleep) 1138
If you are in a **deep sleep**, you are sleeping peacefully and it is difficult to wake you. *e.g. About three in the morning, I awoke from a deep sleep.*

sleep like a log 1138
If you **sleep like a log**, you are deep asleep. *e.g. I was able to sleep like a log because the baby didn't cry.*

sleigh pulled by animals 281
A **sleigh pulled by animals** is a vehicle which can slide over snow, having a framework that is fixed onto two long, narrow pieces of wood or metal. It is attached to one or more animals, such as a horse or horses, which pull it across the snow. *e.g. Santa drives a big, red sleigh pulled by reindeers.*

slender 1478
A **slender** person is thin and graceful. *e.g. My cousin was tall and slender.*

slice 1293
If you **slice** something, you cut through it horizontally with a knife or blade. *e.g. I like to slice the carrots in two and then steam them.*

slice of melon/watermelon 1550
A **slice of melon** or **watermelon** is a section cut out of such a fruit. *e.g. Would you care for a slice of watermelon, Katherine?*

slide 1237, 1560
1 A **slide** is a structure, often found in playgrounds, that has a steep slope for children to slide down. *e.g. There were a few slides and climbing frames.*
2 If you **slide**, you move smoothly down a slope. *e.g. I'm going to slide on this one.*
3 If you sign or say that currencies or prices **slide**, you mean that they gradually change to a worse state or condition. *e.g. The pound will slide, say dealers.*

slide down a chute/slide 1237, 1560
If a person or object **slides down a chute** or a **slide**, they move smoothly down and towards the ground across it. *e.g. Now you slide down the chute, Danny.*

sliding doors 1432
Sliding doors are panels made out of wood, glass, or metal, which are used to open and close the entrance to a building, room, etc., and which move smoothly from side to side. *e.g. The sliding doors leading to the patio were locked.*

slim 1478
Someone who is **slim** is usually considered to have an attractively thin and well-shaped body. *e.g. A tall, slim girl with long, straight hair was standing by the door.*

slip 607, 658
A **slip** is a small piece of paper or card, sometimes with information written or printed on it. *e.g. The slip showed the date, time and amount of the withdrawal.*

slip 1320
If you **slip**, you accidentally slide and lose your balance. *e.g. I slipped on the snow and sprained my ankle.*

slipper 1336
A **slipper** is a loose, soft shoe made to be worn especially in the house. *e.g. The dog had taken one of his slippers.*

slippery 1320
Something that is **slippery** is smooth, wet, or

greasy, and is therefore difficult to get a grip on. *e.g. The frost had made the pavement slippery.*

slipshod 1370
Something that is **slipshod** is done without care or thoroughness. *e.g. It was a slipshod piece of work, and she knew it.*

slope 1209, 1237
1 A **slope** is the side of a mountain, hill, or valley. *e.g. He owned a tiny cottage high up on the slopes of the Blue Ridge Mountains.*
2 A **slope** is a surface that is flat and at an angle, so that one end is higher than the other. *e.g. All heads turned to look up the slope.*
3 If a surface **slopes**, it is at an angle, so that one end is higher than the other. *e.g. My garden slopes down to this beach.*
4 The **slope** of something is the angle at which it slopes. *e.g. A slope of seventy degrees would be normal.*

sloppy 1370
Something that is **sloppy** is messy, careless or muddled. *e.g. I complained about his sloppy workmanship.*

slow 543, 1284
1 Something or someone that is **slow** moves along, does something or happens without very much speed. *e.g. The work was hard and progress was slow.*
2 Something that is **slow** takes a long time, especially more time than is usual or expected, or is done after a delay. *e.g. Don't worry if your child is slow to learn to walk.*
3 If a clock or watch is **slow**, it shows a time that is earlier than the correct time. *e.g. The clock's half an hour slow.*

slug 571
A **slug** is a small, slow-moving creature with a long, slimy body like a snail without a shell. *e.g. Slugs ate the cabbages I'd planted.*

sly 172
1 If you give a **sly** look, gesture, or remark, you show that you know something that other people present might not know. *e.g. He gave a sly smile as he opened his door.*
2 If someone does something **on the sly**, they do it in a secretive way, often because it is something that they should not be doing. *e.g. They were sitting in the toilets smoking on the sly.*

small 637
Something that is **small** is not large in physical size, and usually of a size that you could hold between your finger and thumb. *e.g. He had several small tropical fish.*

small 728
A **small** group or amount consists of fewer things or less of something than is usual or

expected. *e.g. Last Friday's turnout at the Deaf club was rather small.*

small 1213
1 Something or someone that is **small** is not large in height compared with other things of the same kind, or with other people. *e.g. She was rather small and wore glasses.*
2 A **small** child is a young child. *e.g. She was only small then, of course, but she seemed to get used to the new house easily.*

small 1450
1 Something that is **small** is not large in physical size, and usually of a size that you could fit between your hands if you held them close together. *e.g. It's just a small pot; I thought it would look nice on top of the television.*
2 Something that is **small** does not contain or occupy a lot of space compared with other things of the same kind. *e.g. The Peugot 205 is one of the most popular small cars.*

small 1574
Something or someone that is **small** is not large in height compared with other things of the same kind, or with other people. *e.g. She was rather small and wore glasses.*

small bat 249
A **small bat** is an object used for hitting a ball in games. The part used for hitting the ball is not large and the bat is held by the handle with one hand. *e.g. He could only hold a small bat.*

smaller 728
You can sign or say that a number, or amount of something, is **smaller** when it is not as big as it used to be, or when it is not as big as some other number or amount. *e.g. Five-eighths or six-sevenths; which is smaller?*

small (feel small) 57
If something makes you **feel small**, or **look small**, it makes you feel or look ridiculous so that you are ashamed and humiliated. *e.g. When I stood up to recite my poem, I could not remember the first line. I felt so small and stupid.*

small part 637
A **small part** of something is a bit or section of it that is not large. *e.g. Where is the small part that fits in here?*

small piece 637
A **small piece** of something is a bit or section of it that is not large. *e.g. Here's a small piece from the broken vase.*

small vehicle 100
A **small vehicle** is a car or van that takes a limited number of passengers or objects. *e.g. After driving the big lorry, it was strange to be in a small vehicle again.*

smart 230, 676
Someone who is **smart** is clean and neatly dressed. *e.g. The boys looked smart in their school uniforms.*

smart 1500
You can describe someone as **smart** when they are clever. *e.g. She's a smart student, and the school is very proud of her.*

smashing 213, 220
If you describe something as **smashing**, you mean that you like it very much. *e.g. We had a smashing time.*

smell 994, 1109
1 The **smell** of something is the effect that it has on your nose, especially when the effect is unpleasant. *e.g. What's that smell?*
2 If something **smells**, it has an effect on your nose. *e.g. The papers smell musty and stale.*
3 If you **smell** something, you breathe the odour of it into your nose. *e.g. Smell that sugarbeet, will you? That really reminds me of home.*

smelly 1109
Something that is **smelly** has an unpleasant smell. *e.g. A rather smelly cheese was placed in the middle of the table.*

smoke 757
1 When someone **smokes** a cigarette or a cigar, they have the end of it that is not lit in their mouth, sucking the smoke into their mouth and lungs, and blowing it out again. *e.g. He smoked only at work.*
2 If you **smoke**, you have the habit of smoking cigarettes or cigars. *e.g. Do you smoke?*

smoke 1061
1 **Smoke** consists of gas and small bits of solid material that are sent into the air when something burns. *e.g. The room was full of smoke from the log fire.*
2 If something **smokes**, it sends out smoke. *e.g. This material will smoke and smoulder for some time.*

smoke 1719
Smoke consists of gas and small bits of solid material that are sent into the air from a chimney when something burns. *e.g. The white smoke informed the watching crowd that a new Pope had been elected.*

smoke a cigarette/fag 757
If you **smoke a cigarette** or a **fag**, you have the end (that is not lit) of a tube of paper containing tobacco in your mouth, sucking the smoke into your mouth and lungs, and blowing it out again. *e.g. I could never smoke a cigarette again after that day.*

smoke a pipe 946
If you **smoke a pipe**, you have the thin end of

a pipe in your mouth, sucking the smoke from a small pot of burning tobacco at the other end into your mouth and lungs, and then blowing it out again. *e.g. Please do not smoke your pipe on the plane.*

smoke/steam coming out of a chimney   1719
If **smoke** or **steam is coming out of a chimney**, it is being allowed to escape into the air through a chimney from a fireplace, furnace, machine, et cetera. *e.g. The smoke coming out of the factory chimney was very black.*

smoking   757
1 **Smoking** is the act or habit of smoking cigarettes or other forms of tobacco. *e.g. Does smoking cause cancer?*
2 A **smoking** section or compartment is intended for people who want to smoke. *e.g. Do you want to go in the smoking section or the non-smoking section?*

smooth   1212
A **smooth** surface or object has no roughness, lumps or holes. *e.g. Is that piece of wood smooth?*

smooth   1335
1 A **smooth** surface or object has no roughness, lumps, or holes. *e.g. Feel this marble—so smooth.*
2 If you **smooth** something, such as a lotion, onto a surface, you apply it carefully so that it forms an even layer without lumps or gaps. *e.g. Smooth the ointment onto the burn every day.*

smooth   1514
A liquid or mixture is **smooth** if it is mixed well and has no lumps. *e.g. Beat the mixture till it is smooth.*

snail   600
A **snail** is a small, slow-moving creature with a long, slimy body and a spiral-shaped shell on its back. *e.g. Snails had invaded the garden.*

snail crawling   600
A **snail crawling** is a small creature with a long, slimy body and a spiral-shaped shell on its back (snail) moving slowly by flexing its body in a rippling motion. *e.g. The cat seemed to fall asleep watching the snail crawling across the yard.*

snake   1090
A **snake** is a long, thin reptile with no legs. *e.g. He was bitten by a poisonous snake.*

snap   94
If something **snaps**, or if you **snap** it, it breaks suddenly, usually with a sharp, cracking noise. *e.g. As I walked through the woods, I felt the twigs snap under my feet.*

snap   659
A **snap** is a photograph that is taken quickly and casually. *e.g. I had many snaps of Peter.*

snap   1129
1 If a dog or other animal **snaps**, it shuts its jaw quickly. *e.g. The dog loves to snap at the postman.*
2 If you **snap** at someone, you sign or speak to them in a sharp, unfriendly way. *e.g. He was foolish to snap at his secretary.*

snapshot   659
A **snapshot** is a photograph that is taken quickly and casually. *e.g. It's like a snapshot: just one image captured at one moment in one place.*

snatch   984, 1130
If you **snatch** something, you take it or pull it away quickly. *e.g. He snatched the letter and began to read it.*

sneak   625
1 A **sneak** is someone who tells people in authority that someone else has done something naughty or wrong. *e.g. He has a reputation as a sneak.*
2 If you **sneak** on someone, you tell the authorities that he or she has done something naughty or wrong. *e.g. If you sneak on me, I'll bash your head in.*

sneeze   517
When you **sneeze**, you suddenly take in your breath and then blow it down your nose noisily. You cannot help sneezing when there is a tickling feeling in your nose or when you have a cold. *e.g. We sneezed a lot with hay fever.*

snob   524
1 A **snob** is someone who belongs to or admires those who are of the wealthiest and most powerful class in society, and looks down on those who are not of this group. *e.g. Like both her parents she was a snob.*
2 A **snob** is someone who believes that their own special tastes, interests and abilities are superior to those of other people. *e.g. He is a dreadful intellectual snob.*

snobbish   524
Someone who is **snobbish** is too proud of their social status, intelligence or taste. *e.g. Because she was too snobbish to mix with her neighbours, she had few friends.*

snooker   70, 1429
Snooker is a game played on a large table covered with smooth, green cloth. The players use a long stick (called a cue) to hit a white ball (the cue ball) against balls of other colours. Points are scored by knocking the coloured balls into the pockets at the sides of the table. The winner is the person who scores the most points. *e.g. He watched the snooker on television.*

snooker player   70
A **snooker player** is a person who plays snooker. *e.g. Professional snooker players can earn large sums of money.*

snooze   1138
1 A **snooze** is a short, light sleep, especially during the day. *e.g. I've just had a nice snooze.*
2 If you **snooze**, you sleep briefly and not very deeply, especially during the day. *e.g. Let me snooze for a while.*

snore   1138
If you **snore**, you breathe very noisily when you are sleeping, usually because you have got your mouth open. *e.g. He's fast asleep: listen to him snore!*

snout   1533
The **snout** of an animal is its long nose. *e.g. The animal's snout seemed cold.*

snow   1035
1 **Snow** consists of a lot of soft, white bits of frozen water that fall from the sky in cold weather. *e.g. The snow made it hard for drivers.*
2 When it **snows**, snow falls from the sky. *e.g. I think it may well snow tonight.*

snow   1631
Snow consists of a lot of soft, white bits of frozen water that fall from the sky in cold weather. *e.g. Let's go out and play in the snow.*

snowball   1631
A **snowball** is a ball of snow. Children sometimes play at throwing snowballs at each other. *e.g. They had a snowball fight after tea.*

snowfall   1035
A **snowfall** is a quantity of falling or fallen snow. *e.g. A heavy snowfall is forecast for the weekend.*

snuff   620
Snuff is powdered tobacco which is taken by sniffing it up your nose. *e.g. My father takes snuff, but he wishes he'd never started.*

snuggle up under a blanket/the bedclothes   140
If you **snuggle up under a blanket**, or **under the bedclothes**, you put the blanket or bedclothes tightly round you and settle yourself in a warm comfortable position. *e.g. He snuggled up under the bedclothes and asked her to read him a story.*

soak up   1102
When a soft or dry substance **soaks up** a liquid, the liquid goes into the substance. *e.g. The soil will soak up a huge volume of water.*

soap   1362
Soap is a substance that you use with water for

washing yourself. It is made from oil or fats and alkali and is sold in small, hard pieces, or as a liquid. *e.g. She bought a bar of yellow soap.*

sober 395
When you are **sober**, you are not drunk. *e.g. Rudolph knew he had to stay sober to drive home.*

so-called 823
You can sign or say that someone or something is **so-called** to indicate that they are thought to be, or pretend to be, what they are not. *e.g. She is living with her so-called friends.*

social 954
A **social** is a leisure activity involving meeting other people. *e.g. When is the next social at the Deaf club?*

socialism 10
Socialism is a set of left-wing political principles based on the belief that the major means of production, distribution and exchange should be under collective ownership, and controlled and operated in the public interest. It advocates that the economic organisation of society should be based on production for use, rather than profits. *e.g. He voted Labour and firmly believed in socialism.*

socialist 10
1 **Socialist** means based on socialism or relating to socialism. *e.g We need a Labour government with socialist policies.*
2 A **socialist** is a person who believes in socialism, or who is a member of a socialist party. *e.g. Bill is a committed socialist and believes in equality of opportunity.*

social worker 661
A **social worker** is a person who works for an organisation, such as a local authority social services department or related voluntary agency, whose job it is to do social work. This includes giving advice to people about their rights and responsibilities, and supporting them with family, personal or financial problems. *e.g. The panel were absolutely unanimous in their view that Fiona would make an excellent social worker.*

socks 876
Socks are pieces of clothing which cover your foot and ankle and are worn inside shoes. *e.g. He wore a pair of dark blue woollen socks.*

sod off 160
Sod off is an insulting and offensive way of telling someone to go away. *e.g. I wish you would sod off and leave me alone.*

sofa 115, 116
A **sofa** is a long, comfortable seat with a back, and usually with arms, which more than one

person can sit on. *e.g. We need a new sofa.*

soft 1553
1 Something that is **soft** changes shape or bends easily when you press it. *e.g. His feet left prints in the soft soil.*
2 Something that is **soft** is pleasant to touch and not rough or hard. *e.g. The woollen jumper felt very soft.*

soft 520
1 Something that is **soft** changes shape easily, or bends easily when you press it. *e.g. The pillow was really soft.*
2 Someone who is **soft** is not strict enough or severe enough. *e.g. That young teacher is too soft with those children.*

soil 1520
Soil is the substance on the land surface of the earth in which plants grow. *e.g. The soil here is very fertile.*

soldier 1277
A **soldier** is a person in an army. *e.g. These buildings are guarded by soldiers.*

sole 533, 534, 555
1 The **sole** thing or person of a particular type is the only one of that type. *e.g. I was the sole man in the room.*
2 If you have **sole** charge or ownership of something, you are the only person in charge of it or who owns it. *e.g. At twenty-five, I had sole responsibility for the firm.*

solemn 1256
1 Someone or something that is **solemn** is very serious rather than cheerful or humorous. *e.g. The funeral service was accompanied by solemn music.*
2 A **solemn** promise or agreement is one that you make in a very formal, sincere way. *e.g. The government has made solemn commitments and must honour them.*

solve 1548
If you **solve** a question or a problem, you find an answer to the question or a satisfactory solution to the problem. *e.g. How do we solve the problems caused by the shortage of interpreters?*

sombrero 448
A **sombrero** is a hat with a very wide brim, which is traditionally worn by Mexican men. *e.g. On holiday in Acapulco, he bought a sombrero to wear with his bermuda shorts in the sun.*

some 612, 1496
1 You use **some** to refer to a quantity of something or to a number of people or things, when you are not stating the

quantity or number precisely. *e.g. Some of my friends will be here.*
2 If you refer to **some** of the people or things in a group, you mean a few of them but not all of them. If you refer to **some** of a particular thing, you mean a part of it but not all of it. *e.g. Some sports are very dangerous.*

somebody 297
You use **somebody** to refer to a person without signing, saying or writing exactly who you mean. *e.g. I think somebody took my pencil sharpener.*

someone 297
You use **someone** to refer to a person without signing or saying exactly who you mean. *e.g. Someone wants to see you in the lobby.*

somersault 566
1 If you **somersault**, you make a rolling or turning movement by turning upside down and bringing your legs over your head. *e.g. I bet you can't somersault like me.*
2 A **somersault** is a rolling or turning movement which you make by turning upside down and bringing your legs over your head. *e.g. The teacher asked the children to somersault from a stationary position.*

something 556
You use **something** to refer in a vague way to anything that is not a person, for example an object, action or quality. *e.g. Liz saw something ahead of her.*

sometimes 955
You use **sometimes** to sign or say that something happens on some occasions. *e.g. I go back to my old home sometimes.*

somewhere 983
1 You use **somewhere** to refer to a place without signing or saying exactly where you mean. *e.g. They lived somewhere near Wolverhampton.*
2 You sign or say **somewhere** to indicate that an amount, number, time, etc., that you are mentioning is approximate. *e.g. Somewhere between 55,000 and 60,000 men were recruited.*

somewhere 1018
You use **somewhere** to refer to a place without signing or saying exactly where you mean. *e.g. I know it is somewhere close to the park.*

song 758
1 A **song** is a combination of words and music that are produced as sounds with the voice. *e.g. We all burst into song.*
2 A **song** is a set of carefully arranged signs which are chosen for their beauty or imagery, or such signs in combination with music and sometimes words. *e.g. Colin Thompson*

explained that he likes to perform this song because it can be interpreted in relation to the Deaf experience.

soon (as soon as possible) 384
If you ask someone to do something as **soon as possible**, you ask them to do it quickly and with the smallest amount of delay they can manage. *e.g. Let us know as soon as possible.*

sore 989, 1052
If a part of your body is **sore**, it causes you pain and discomfort, for example because of a wound or infection, or because your muscles have been used too much. *e.g. He was sore all over.*

sorrow 34, 921
Sorrow is a feeling of deep sadness or regret. *e.g. She wrote to express her sorrow at the tragic death of their son.*

sorry 34, 921, 1136
1 You sign or say **sorry**, or **I'm sorry**, as a way of apologising to someone for something that you have done which has upset them or caused them difficulties. *e.g. Sorry I'm late.*
2 If you are **sorry** about a situation, you feel sadness, regret, or disappointment about it. *e.g. He was sorry to see me go.*
3 You sign or say **I'm sorry** to express your regret and sadness when you learn of sad or unpleasant news. *e.g. 'Jerry's dead,' I told him. 'I'm sorry,' he said.*

sorry 920
You sign or say **sorry**, or **I'm sorry**, as a way of apologising to someone for something that you have done which has upset them or caused them difficulties. *e.g. I'm sorry if I worried you.*

sorry something has happened 1036
If you are **sorry** that **something has happened**, you wish it had not happened. *e.g. She was sorry that the dog died, but signed that she could do nothing about it.*

sort out 1433
1 If you **sort out** a group of things, you organise or tidy them. *e.g. It took a while to sort out our luggage.*
2 If you **sort out** a problem, you deal with it and find a solution to it. *e.g. We can sort things out in the morning.*
3 A **sort out** is a process of organising or tidying things up. *e.g. This shed needs a good sort out.*

sorts (all sorts of) 426, 427, 447
If you refer to **all sorts of** something, you mean a wide range of the different types of that thing. *e.g. This band play all sorts of music with flair and boundless energy.*

so-so 982
If you sign or say that something is **so-so**, you

mean that it is average in quality rather than being very good, or very bad. *e.g. Sometimes the food is great, sometimes it's just so-so.*

soul 1095
A person's **soul** is the spiritual part of them which is believed to continue existing after the body is dead. *e.g. They prayed for the soul of the dead man.*

sound 521
1 A **sound** is something that can be heard. *e.g. He heard the sound of footsteps.*
2 **Sound** is what can be heard. *e.g. Under water, sound is distorted.*
3 The **sound** is what can be heard on a television, video monitor or at the cinema. *e.g. When the news had finished, Brenda would turn down the sound and get out a book.*

soup 240, 732
Soup is liquid food made by boiling meat, fish, or vegetables in water. *e.g. He likes chicken soup.*

soup spoon 240
A **soup spoon** is an object used especially for eating soup. It is shaped like a small, shallow bowl at one end and has a long, thin handle. *e.g. Please put the soup spoons on the table.*

sour 525, 958
1 Something that is **sour** has a sharp taste, like the taste of a lemon or of an apple that is not yet ripe. *e.g. These plums are sour.*
2 **Sour** milk has an unpleasant taste because it is no longer fresh. *e.g. It's so hot, this milk's gone sour already.*

south 497
South is the direction which is on your right when you are looking towards the direction in which the sun rises. *e.g. The island is a mile in length from north to south.*

south 908, 1211, 1213
1 The **south** is the part of a place or country which is towards the south. *e.g. I met a woman from the south of France.*
2 **South** means towards the south or to the south of a place or thing. *e.g. Durham is about fifteen miles south of Gateshead.*
3 The **south** part of a place or country is the part which is towards the south. *e.g. He lives in South Wales.*
4 **South** is the direction which is on your right when you are looking towards the direction in which the sun rises. *e.g. The wetlands to the south are a conservation area.*

Soviet 10
1 **Soviet** is used to describe someone or something that belonged to or related to the former Soviet Union or its people. *e.g. Latvia was part of the Soviet bloc countries.*

2 A **Soviet** was a person who came from, or whose family identity related to, the Soviet Union. *e.g. In a poem, the Soviet Yevgeny Yevtushenko said that you should 'forgive no error you recognise'.*
3 You can refer to people who came from the Soviet Union in general, or a particular group of people who came from the Soviet Union, as the **Soviets**. *e.g. In 1957, the Soviets put an astronaut into space.*

Soviet Union 10
The **Soviet Union** was a federal republic in Eastern Europe and Central and Northern Asia. It was established in 1922, and was the largest country in the world. In 1990, the union of republics was dissolved and the individual republics were recognised as independent states. A number of these independent states have formed an association known as the Commonwealth of Independent States (CIS). *e.g. We visited the southern regions of the Soviet Union in 1984.*

sow 843
If you **sow** seeds, you plant them in the ground in order to grow something. *e.g. It's time to sow the winter wheat.*

space 405
Space is the work of research, scientific engineering and exploration that has developed as human beings attempt to understand the vast area that is beyond the Earth's atmosphere. *e.g. He always dreamed about getting involved in the space programme.*

spacecraft 405
A **spacecraft** is a rocket or other vehicle that can travel in the area beyond the Earth's atmosphere. *e.g. The new spacecraft was built using French and British technology.*

spaceship 405
A **spaceship** is a rocket or other vehicle that can travel in the area beyond the Earth's atmosphere. *e.g. This spaceship is one of mankind's greatest feats of engineering.*

spade 153, 1223
A **spade** is a tool used for digging, with a flat, metal blade and a long handle. *e.g. They bought a spade and some plants at the garden centre.*

sparkle 1057
If something **sparkles**, it is clear and bright, and often shines with a lot of very small points of light, that look like flashes of silver or gold, being reflected all over the surface. *e.g. The lawn outside sparkled with frost in the wintry sunshine.*

speak 380
1 When you **speak** to someone, you have a

conversation with them. *e.g. I'd like to speak to you in my office.*

2 When you **speak**, you express yourself using words or signs. *e.g. I could tell from the way he spoke that he was making it all up.*

speaker 1247

A **speaker** is a person who is making a presentation to a group of people. *e.g. The chairman got up to introduce the speaker.*

speak on a portable phone/telephone 1737

If you **speak on a portable phone** or a **telephone**, you have a spoken conversation with another person, using a portable phone or a telephone. *e.g. He was speaking on his portable phone when the car in front of him suddenly braked.*

spear 19

A **spear** is a weapon consisting of a long pole with a sharp point. *e.g. Spears are used for hunting in New Guinea.*

specs 754

Specs are two transparent lenses in a metal or plastic frame that someone with bad eyesight wears in front of their eyes in order to help them see better. Specs is short for spectacles. *e.g. I need a new pair of specs: these are no use.*

spectacles 754

Spectacles are two transparent lenses in a metal or plastic frame that someone with bad eyesight wears in front of their eyes in order to help them see better. *e.g. The teacher with the horn-rimmed spectacles told me where to find the headmaster.*

spectator 788

A **spectator** is a person who watches something, especially a sporting event. *e.g. I was a spectator, not a player, at the tennis tournament.*

speech 524

1 Speech is the ability to speak or the act of speaking. *e.g. She was so shocked that she lost her powers of speech.*

2 Speech is spoken language. *e.g. In ordinary speech, we often shorten the word 'cannot' to 'can't'.*

3 Your **speech** is the way in which you speak. *e.g. I detected a slight Brooklyn accent in her speech.*

4 The **speech** of a particular country or region is the language or dialect spoken in that country or region. *e.g. He can mimic Cockney speech quite well.*

speech 1247

1 A **speech** is a formal presentation which someone gives to an audience. *e.g. Mr.*

Macmillan presented the prizes and made a speech on the importance of education.

2 A **speech** is a long passage to be signed or spoken by a character in a play. *e.g. She recited Shylock's speech from 'The Merchant of Venice'.*

speed 382

1 Speed is very fast movement or travel. *e.g. The car is travelling at speed.*

2 Speed is a very fast rate at which something happens or is done. *e.g. We can't add up with the speed and accuracy of a computer.*

speedboat 1426

A **speedboat** is a boat that is propelled by an engine and can travel at high speeds. *e.g. Donald Campbell broke the world speed record on water in his speedboat, Bluebird.*

speed up 384

1 When you **speed up** in a vehicle, or a vehicle **speeds up**, the rate at which it moves is caused to increase, so that it travels faster. *e.g. We will have to speed up to overtake that blue car.*

2 When a process or activity **speeds up** or when something **speeds** it **up**, it happens at a faster rate. *e.g. The really hot weather has speeded up the growth of my tomatoes.*

speed up 1291

When you **speed up** in a vehicle, you cause the rate at which it moves to increase, so that it travels faster. *e.g. Tom likes to speed up and chase anyone who overtakes him.*

spell 1042

A **spell** is a situation in which events are supposedly controlled by a magical power. *e.g. The spell of the wicked fairy was broken.*

spell 1174

When you **spell** a word, you fingerspell, write or speak the individual letters of the word in the correct order. *e.g. How do you spell your last name?*

spend 1506, 1517, 1721

When you **spend** money, you pay money for something that you want. *e.g. We will have to spend a lot of money on getting this fixed.*

spendthrift 1506

A **spendthrift** is a person who spends money in a wasteful or extravagant way. *e.g. What a spendthrift! All the money he makes goes on new cars.*

sphere 1418

A **sphere** is an object or figure that has the shape of a perfectly round ball. *e.g. It's impossible to make a sphere out of those bricks, silly!*

spherical 1418

Something that is **spherical** has the shape of a sphere. *e.g. The earth is spherical and moves around the sun.*

spider 1148

A **spider** is a small creature with eight legs that looks like an insect. Most types of spider make webs in which they catch insects for food. *e.g. There is a spider on the table.*

spin 298, 503

If something **spins**, or if you **spin** it, it turns quickly around a central point. *e.g. The cowboy could make his lasso spin in both tiny and wide circles.*

spin 323

If your head **spins**, you feel as if you are dizzy because you are excited or slightly drunk. *e.g. His head was spinning from drinking wine and liqueurs.*

spin dryer (front loading) 1230

A **front loading spin dryer** is a machine that gets water out of clothes, sheets, etc., after you have washed them. You put things into the machine through a door at the front and it spins them round very rapidly. *e.g. Put the sheets in the spin dryer.*

spinning top 298

A **spinning top** is a cone-shaped toy that can spin on its pointed end. *e.g. Marie was given a spinning top for Christmas.*

spirit 1095

1 Your **spirit** is the part of you that is not physical and that is connected with your deepest thoughts and feelings. *e.g. Fulfilment is sought through the spirit, not the body or mind.*

2 The **spirit** of a dead person is a non-physical part of them that is believed to remain alive after their death. *e.g. We prayed to our dead ancestor's spirit.*

splash 1725, 1729

1 If someone or something **splashes**, they cause an amount of water to fly up into the air with a loud noise, by hitting or disturbing the water. *e.g. How many times must I tell you not to splash in the bath?*

2 A **splash** is an amount of water flying up into the air with a loud noise, caused by someone or something hitting or disturbing the water. *e.g. The little girl was crying because she had been soaked by a big splash from her brother.*

split 1325, 1599

If something is **split**, or you **split** it, it divides into two or more parts. *e.g. We decided to split the group into smaller numbers.*

split up 1634

If two people **split up**, they end their relationship or marriage. *e.g. He went to Arizona after he'd split up with his wife.*

spoil 1031, 1032

1 If you **spoil** something, you make it less

enjoyable, attractive, or interesting than it would otherwise have been. *e.g. The presence of the slag heap spoiled his enjoyment of the view somewhat.*
2 If you **spoil** something, you damage it so that it loses part of its value, beauty or usefulness. *e.g. I spoiled my new evening gown by spilling red wine on it.*

spoil   925
If you **spoil** something, you prevent it from being successful or satisfactory. *e.g. You will spoil our evening if you behave like that.*

spongy   1553
Something that is **spongy** is soft and squashy. *e.g. The mat at the judo centre was made of a spongy material.*

sponsor   1679
1 If people or organisations **sponsor** something such as an event or someone's training, they pay some or all of the expenses connected with it, often in order to get publicity for themselves. *e.g. Reebok sponsored the BDA's 1992 Congress in Blackpool.*
2 A **sponsor** is a person or organisation that pays some or all of the expenses connected with something such as an event or an athletics meeting. *e.g. We hope that Cornhill will continue to be a major sponsor of international cricket.*

sporadic   1233
Sporadic occurrences of something happen at irregular intervals. *e.g. The fault was a sporadic one, but it needed fixing all the same.*

sport   132
1 A **sport** is a game, such as football or cricket, or enjoyable activity, for which you need physical or mental skill. It is often organised competitively or as a form of entertainment for people to watch or to take part in. *e.g. At school, my favourite sport was netball.*
2 If you sign or say that someone is a **sport**, you mean that they accept defeat or teasing in a cheerful way. *e.g. He lost every game, but was a good sport.*

sports   132
Sports are games, such as football and cricket, and other activities, which need physical effort and skill. Such activities are often organised competitively and as entertainment for people to watch or take part in. *e.g. My favourite sports are football and volleyball.*

spot on   516
1 If you sign or say that someone is **spot on** or **spot-on** you mean that they are exactly right. *e.g. John was, in fact, spot on: there were 2,317 sweets in the jar.*
2 If you sign or say that something is **spot on** or **spot-on**, you mean that it is exactly

accurate. *e.g. Angela Tierney's copy of Van Gogh's 'Sunflowers' was spot on.*

spouse   897
Somebody's **spouse** is the person they are married to. *e.g. You and your spouse can renew your marriage vows at a special service.*

spray   1725, 1729
1 A **spray** is a lot of small drops of water which are being splashed or forced into the air. *e.g. She got caught in the spray from the hose pipe.*
2 If a liquid is **sprayed** over someone or something, they are covered with small drops of the liquid. *e.g. As a car went through the puddle, dirty water was sprayed over the dogs.*

spray breath freshener   634
When you **spray breath freshener** into your mouth, you spray drops of a fresh-tasting liquid into your mouth using a small aerosol container. *e.g. My dentist told me that if you spray breath freshener in your mouth, it can rot your teeth.*

spray deodorant   634
If you **spray deodorant** on a part of your body, you cover it with a fine mist of liquid from an aerosol can which makes it smell nice or prevents perspiration. *e.g. You're meant to spray deodorant under your arms, not all around the bathroom!*

spray hairspray   634
If you **spray hairspray** on your hair, the hair is covered with drops of lacquer forced out in a fine mist from an aerosol can; the lacquer helps to keep your hair in place. *e.g. Don't spray hairspray like that on me, thank you.*

spray perfume   634
If you **spray perfume** on a part of your body, you cover it with drops of pleasant-smelling liquid from an aerosol container to make yourself smell attractive. *e.g. Have you been spraying perfume on?*

spray with an aerosol   634
If you **spray** something **with an aerosol**, you cover it with drops of liquid that have been kept under pressure in a cannister and are forced out when you press a button. *e.g. The nurses spray the rooms with an aerosol that contains disinfectant.*

spread   1044, 1729
1 If something **spreads**, such as a fire or disease, it gradually reaches or affects a larger and larger area, or more and more people. *e.g. These viruses can spread at an alarming rate.*
2 The **spread** of something is the process by which it gradually reaches or affects a larger and larger area or more and more people. *e.g. The spread of higher education has not resulted in

a larger percentage of working class children going on to university.*

spread   1324
1 A **spread** is a soft food made from something such as meat or cheese, which is usually put on bread. *e.g. Cheese spread now comes in pots and in tubes.*
2 If you **spread** a substance on a surface, or if you **spread** the surface with the substance, you smooth a thin layer of the substance over the surface with a flat tool or brush. *e.g. I spread treacle on the windowsill to keep the wasps out.*

spread a bedspread/blanket   1521
When you **spread a bedspread** or a **blanket**, you hold it at one end, shake it so that it unfolds to its full extent, and lay it over a surface such as a bed or table, or on the ground. *e.g. Every time I spread a blanket on here, one of the kids jumps all over it.*

spread a sheet   1521
When you **spread a sheet**, you hold it at one end, shake it so that it unfolds to its full extent, and lay it over a surface such as a bed or table, or on the ground. *e.g. You spread a sheet on the bed and I'll show you how to do a hospital corner.*

**spread butter/margarine/marge/paste/
pâté with a knife**   689
When you **spread butter**, **margarine**, **paste** or **pâté with a knife** onto a surface, you put a thin layer of the substance over the surface using a tool with a flat blade and a long handle (knife). *e.g. We each spread butter with a knife onto our bread and then dipped it into the pan of jam Ma had made.*

spread glue/jam/marmalade/paste 1324
If you **spread glue**, **jam**, **marmalade** or **paste** on a surface, or if you **spread** the surface with the substance, you smooth a thin layer of the substance over the surface with a flat tool or brush. *e.g. I spread marmalade thickly on my toast every morning.*

spread out a sheet/tablecloth   874
When you **spread out a sheet** or **tablecloth**, you hold it at one end, shake it so that it unfolds to its full extent, and lay it over a surface such as a bed or table, or on the ground. *e.g. She spread out the tablecloth on the ground for the picnic.*

spread with a knife   689
When you **spread** a substance **with a knife**, you use a tool with a flat blade and a long handle (knife) to put a thin layer of the substance over a surface. *e.g. Spoon a little of the mixture onto the bread and spread with a knife until the layer is nice and even.*

spring-clean 88
When you **spring-clean** a house, you thoroughly clean everything in it, including things that you do not clean very often. *e.g. We will spring-clean the house before we go on our summer holiday.*

spring-cleaning 88
Spring-cleaning is the activity of thoroughly cleaning everything in a house, including things that are not cleaned very often. *e.g. Kathleen and Jean came to give me a hand with the spring-cleaning.*

springy 1553
If something is **springy**, it returns quickly to its original shape after you press it. *e.g. We bought a springy new mattress.*

sprinkle 1497
If you **sprinkle** something such as powder over an object or surface, you scatter it over the object or surface. *e.g. She sprinkled oregano on the pizza.*

sprinkle from a spoon 670
If you **sprinkle** something **from a spoon** over something, you scatter it there from a small bowl with a long handle (spoon). *e.g. She sprinkled hundreds-and-thousands from a spoon over the cakes.*

sprinkle salt 1497
If you **sprinkle salt** over an object or surface, you scatter it over the object or surface. *e.g. He sprinkled salt on the potatoes.*

sprinkle sugar 1497
If you **sprinkle sugar** over an object or surface, you scatter it over the object or surface. *e.g. He sprinkled sugar on the cake.*

sprinkle sugar from a spoon 670
If you **sprinkle sugar from a spoon**, you scatter sweet-tasting crystals (sugar) from a small bowl with a long handle (spoon). *e.g. You can either sprinkle sugar from a spoon or pour it straight out of the packet.*

sprinkle vinegar 205
If you **sprinkle vinegar** over something, such as food, you shake the vinegar over it so that small drops of vinegar fall on it. *e.g. She sprinkled vinegar on the chips before wrapping them.*

spud 210
A **spud** is a potato. *e.g. Are the spuds cooked yet?*

spy 1469
1 A **spy** is a person whose job it is to find out secret information about another country, business or organisation, by becoming involved in their work without them realising. *e.g. A member of his staff was discovered to be a foreign spy.*

2 Someone who **spies** tries to find out secret information about another country, business or organisation. *e.g. Three of the embassy officials have been expelled for spying.*
3 If you **spy** on someone, you watch them secretly. *e.g. She did not like the idea of spying on her husband, but she had to find out if he was telling the truth.*

squabble 924
When people **squabble**, they quarrel noisily, usually about something which is not really important. *e.g. The children are always squabbling over their toys.*

square 562
A **square** is a shape with four sides of the same length and four corners that are all right angles. *e.g. The courtyard was paved in black and white marble squares.*

squash 12
Squash is a game for two or four players in which a small rubber ball is hit against the walls of a court using light, long-handed racquets. *e.g. I spent the afternoon watching a game of squash.*

squash 1378
If you **squash** something, you press it or crush it, often with great force, so that it becomes flat or loses its shape. *e.g. I sat on my bag, unfortunately, and managed to squash the tomatoes!*

squash racquet 12
also spelled **squash racket.**
A **squash racquet** is a type of light bat with a long handle used to hit the ball in squash. The part of the racquet used to hit the ball has strings stretched across and down in an oval frame. *e.g. I bought a squash racquet when I was in Pakistan.*

squash player 12
A **squash player** is a person who plays squash. *e.g. Jonah Barrington, the squash player, opened the sports centre.*

squeeze 1160
When you **squeeze** a fruit such as a lemon or an orange on a squeezer, you get juice out of it by cutting it in half and pressing each half against the squeezer. *e.g. I watched Bernard squeeze the limes.*

squeezer 1160
A **squeezer** is a special object used in squeezing juice from fruit such as lemons or oranges. *e.g. Give me the squeezer and we'll have fresh orange juice.*

squeeze something from a tube onto a small implement 606
When you **squeeze something from a tube**

onto a small implement, you force some of the contents out of a thin, flexible container with a hole at one end (tube) onto a tool that is not large, which you hold with one hand. *e.g. Squeeze the glue from the tube onto a small implement, such as a spatula.*

squeeze toothpaste from a tube onto a toothbrush 606
When you **squeeze toothpaste from a tube onto a toothbrush**, you force some of the soft mixture for cleaning teeth and gums (toothpaste) out of a thin, flexible container with a hole at one end (tube) onto a tool with a handle and bristles which is used for cleaning teeth and gums (toothbrush). *e.g. Each child had to squeeze toothpaste from a tube onto their toothbrush before going to the bathroom to brush their teeth.*

squirrel 1674
A **squirrel** is a small furry animal with a long bushy tail. It eats nuts and usually lives in trees. There are many kinds of squirrel. *e.g. She was staring out of the window at a red squirrel in the elm tree.*

squirrel's tail 1674
A **squirrel's tail** is the part of the squirrel that grows out and up from the end of its body furthest from its head. *e.g. All she could see was the squirrel's tail.*

stage 1406
1 A **stage** is a raised platform in a theatre on which actors or other entertainers perform. *e.g. He walked onto the stage to great applause.*
2 A **stage** is a part of a process. *e.g. I've successfully completed the first stage of my training.*

staggered 604, 725, 831
If you are **staggered** by something, it makes you feel surprised and shocked, usually because it is so unexpected that you can hardly believe it. *e.g. We were staggered to learn about your marriage.*

stairs 805, 806
Stairs are a set of steps, usually inside a building, which go from one level to another. *e.g. The stairs are on the right.*

stamp 65
1 A **stamp** is a small block of wood or metal which has a pattern or a group of letters on one side. You press it onto a pad of ink, and then onto a piece of paper in order to produce a mark on the paper. *e.g. From the printing set he made up a stamp reading 'St. Godric's Parish Church'.'*
2 If you **stamp** a mark, word, etc., on an object, you put the mark, word, etc., on it using a special tool or machine, usually in

order to identify it, to make it valid, or to inform people how to use it. *e.g. They stamp the card and send it back to you.*

stamp　　　　　　　　　　　　　　174, 680
A **stamp** or a **postage stamp** is a small piece of gummed paper which you stick on an envelope or parcel before you post it to show you have paid for the delivery. *e.g. His hobby was collecting stamps.*

stand　　　　　　　　　　　　　　　　800
When you **stand**, your body is upright, your legs are straight, and your weight is supported by your feet, which do not move. *e.g. She had to stand at the bus stop for an hour.*

standard　　　　　　　　　　　1416, 1417
Standard is used to describe something which is usual and normal, rather than being special or extra. *e.g. There is a standard procedure for recording drugs given to patients.*

stand back　　　　　　　　　　　　1632
1 If you **stand back**, you move a short distance backwards so that you are standing in a different place. *e.g. Please stand back, and let the Princess pass.*
2 If you **stand back**, you do not get involved in a situation. *e.g. I'm just going to stand back and see how it develops.*

stand firm　　　　　　　　　　　　804
If you **stand firm** about something, you will not let anyone influence your behaviour or change your mind about it. *e.g. Bill Heine is standing firm against the council's demands to remove the fibreglass shark from his roof.*

stand up　　　　　　　　　　　　1201
If someone indicates to you that you should **stand up**, they ask you or instruct you to change your position so that your body is upright with your weight on your feet, rather than sitting or kneeling. *e.g. The priest told the couple to stand up.*

stare　　　　　　　　　　　　　　788
1 If you **stare** at something, you look at it intently for a long time. *e.g. He stared at the photograph—it reminded him of his mother.*
2 A **stare** is a long, intense look at something. *e.g. Paddington Bear gave the postman one of his best hard stares.*

stars　　　　　　　　　　　　　　449
Stars are large balls of burning gas in space which appear to us as small points of light in the sky on clear nights. *e.g. She watched the stars at night.*

stars　　　　　　　　　　　　　　744
1 **Stars** are large balls of burning gas in space which appear to us as small points of light in

the sky on clear nights. *e.g. She watched the stars at night.*
2 A two-**star**, three-**star**, etc., establishment, such as a hotel or restaurant, has been awarded a particular number of stars to indicate that it is has achieved a certain standard of excellence. *e.g. A four-star hotel: this will do nicely.*

start　　　　　　　　　　　　209, 1105
1 If you **start** to do something, you do something that you were not doing before. *e.g. He started work at the age of sixteen.*
2 When something **starts**, or when you **start** it, it takes place from a particular time. *e.g. Planning for the Congress will start next week.*
3 The **start** of something is the beginning of it. *e.g. The start of the project was delayed by bad weather.*

startle　　　　　　　　　　　　　1080
If you **startle** someone, or they are **startled** by something you do, you surprise and often slightly frighten or worry them by doing something that they do not expect you to do, for example by making a sudden movement or loud noise. *e.g. You startled me—I didn't see you in the dark.*

startling　　　　　　　　　　　　1080
Something that is **startling** is so different, unexpected, or remarkable that people react with surprise. *e.g. The exam results were startling.*

starve　　　　　　　　　　　　41, 1655
1 When people **starve**, they suffer greatly from lack of food and sometimes die. *e.g. People may starve because of the drought.*
2 To **starve** someone means to give them no food. *e.g. It was discovered that the prison guards had starved their prisoners.*

starving　　　　　　　　　　　41, 1655
If you sign or say that you are **starving**, you mean that you are very hungry. *e.g. I've got to have something to eat. I'm starving.*

state　　　　　　　　　　　　　　347
If you **state** something, you sign or say it in a formal and definite way, for instance to give information, a conclusion, or an opinion. *e.g. The minister has stated that the unions and employers should be free to negotiate pay without government interference.*

statement　　　　　　　　　　　　347
1 A **statement** is something which is signed or said, especially when facts or information are given in a formal way. *e.g. The statement made by the Minister of Health was confirmed by the Prime Minister.*
2 The **statement** of a policy or theory is the expression of it in a fairly formal and

definite way. *e.g. This is a statement of fact, not a list of complaints.*

station　　　　　　　　　　　　　143
1 A **station** is a building by a railway line where a train stops to allow passengers to get on or off and goods to be put on or taken off the train. *e.g. We waited at Oxford station.*
2 A bus **station** or a coach **station** is a place where buses or coaches stop in order to collect passengers or allow them to get off. *e.g. I will meet you at the bus station at eight o'clock.*

stationary　　　　　　　　　　　1392
If you sign or say that a vehicle, such as a car, is **stationary**, you mean that it is not moving. *e.g. The vehicle remained stationary.*

statistician　　　　　　　　　　　1054
A **statistician** is a person who studies statistics or who works using statistics. *e.g. He's a statistician in the Civil Service.*

statistics　　　　　　　　　　　　1054
1 **Statistics** are facts which are obtained by analysing information expressed in numbers, for example information about the number of times that something happens. *e.g. The Department of Education can provide statistics on the number of deaf children attending residential schools.*
2 **Statistics** is a branch of mathematics concerned with the study of facts obtained by analysing information expressed in numbers. *e.g. A professor of statistics explained the figures to him.*

stay　　　　　　　　　　　　594, 651
1 If you **stay** in a place, you continue to be there and do not move away. *e.g. I will stay at home and babysit.*
2 If you **stay**, you remain in a role or job and do not try to change or move from it. *e.g. She stayed in the one job all her life.*

stay　　　　　　　　　　　　　　652
If you **stay** in a role or job, you remain in it and do not try to change or move from it. *e.g. I stayed in quality control until 1975 and then joined the management team.*

stay　　　　　　　　　　　　　　1239
If you **stay** in a place, you live there for a short time as a guest or a visitor. *e.g. She stayed with me for a week in the summer.*

stay on　　　　　　　　　　　　　652
If you **stay on** in a place or position, you remain in that place or position. *e.g. Will you agree to stay on as assistant manager?*

stay out　　　　　　　　　　　　1632
If you **stay out** of a situation, you do not get involved in the situation. *e.g. This is a*

quarrel between you and your husband; I shall stay out of it.

steadfast   110
If you are **steadfast** in something that you do, you are determined that what you are doing is right and you refuse to change or to give up. *e.g. The Member of Parliament was steadfast in his support for government recognition of BSL.*

steal   1126, 1151
If you **steal** something from someone, you take it away from them without their permission and without intending to return it. *e.g. He tried to steal a video.*

steam   1719
1 **Steam** vehicles and machines are operated using steam as a means of power. *e.g. The first steam locomotive was introduced in 1825.*
2 If something **steams**, it gives off steam. *e.g. The old train creaked and steamed as it started up.*

steel   581
Steel is a very strong metal which is made mainly from iron but also contains carbon and other elements. Steel is used for making many things, for example bridges, vehicles and household things such as cutlery. *e.g. A modern tower of concrete and steel is being built in the city centre.*

steep   1209, 1237
1 A **steep** slope rises and falls sharply, forming a large angle with the horizontal, and is difficult to go up. *e.g. The house is at the top of a steep road.*
2 A **steep** increase or decrease in something is a very big increase or decrease. *e.g. There's likely to be a steep increase in unemployment.*

stench   893, 1109
A **stench** is a strong and very unpleasant smell. *e.g. The stench of rotten eggs made me feel sick.*

step   1339
A **step** is a raised, flat surface, often one of a series of surfaces at different heights, on which you put your feet in order to walk up or down to a different level. *e.g. There is a step outside the door.*

stepladder   1636
A **stepladder** is a ladder that can be folded for carrying and consists of two sloping parts, hinged together at the top so that it will stand up on its own. *e.g. Use the stepladder to reach the cupboard.*

steps   1636
Steps are a series of raised, flat surfaces at different heights on which you put your feet in order to walk up or down to a different level. *e.g. On the right, you will find steps to the attic.*

steward   647, 828
A **steward** is someone who helps to organise a race, march, or some other public event. *e.g. Stewards must be selected for the rally.*

stick   80
If you **stick**, you stop what you are doing and do not go any further; often used in card games when you decide not to play any more cards. *e.g. 'Do you want to twist or stick?'—'I'll stick.'*

sticking plaster   191
Sticking plaster is material that you can stick over a cut, blister, etc., in order to protect it. *e.g. There is a sticking plaster in the drawer.*

stickler   847, 849, 852, 868, 891
If you are a **stickler** for something, you always insist on it. *e.g. He was a stickler for routine.*

stick to   430
1 If you **stick to** a promise, decision, or agreement, you do what you have promised, decided, or agreed to do, and do not change your mind. *e.g. Make sure everyone sticks to the agreement.*
2 If you **stick to** an activity or subject, you keep doing the same activity or discussing the same subject, and do not change to something else. *e.g. Will you please stick to the topics on the agenda?*
3 If you **stick to** a law, instruction, or rule, you behave in the way that it tells you to. *e.g. We'd better stick to the rules.*

stick to   442
If you **stick to** someone, you follow them closely and watch them carefully, not losing track of where they are. *e.g. Look, just stick to him and don't let him out of your sight.*

stick with   430
If you **stick with** an activity or subject, you keep doing the same activity or discussing the same subject, and do not change to something else. *e.g. I stuck with the job of stapling the folders, even though it was incredibly boring.*

stick with   442
If you **stick with** somebody, you follow them closely and watch them carefully, not losing track of where they are. *e.g. I'll stick with the centre forward: you mark the winger.*

sticky   973
1 Something that is **sticky** is covered with a substance that can attach it to other things and leave unpleasant marks. *e.g. Her hands were sticky from the ice cream.*
2 **Sticky** paper has glue on one side so that you can attach it to surfaces. *e.g. We need more sticky labels for the addresses.*

still   161, 977
If someone or something is **still** in a place,

they remain there and have not gone away or been removed. *e.g. 'Has the old Town Gate gone?'—'No, it's still there, next to the Guildhall.'*

still   651
When someone or something is **still**, they are not moving. *e.g. That child can't keep still, she's into everything.*

still   652
If a situation that used to exist **still** exists, it has continued and exists now. *e.g. Ann still lives in London.*

still   879
1 If a place is **still**, it is quiet and shows no sign of activity. *e.g. Around them, the forest was still.*
2 When someone or something is **still**, they are not moving. *e.g. The whole congregation remained completely still.*

still not   111
You use **still not** when you are referring to something that has not occurred up to a certain time. *e.g. He's still not told me his name.*

stimulate   1197
If something **stimulates** you, it makes you feel full of ideas and enthusiasm. *e.g. The art course began to stimulate me as soon as we moved beyond the use of black and white.*

stink   893
1 Something that **stinks** smells extremely unpleasant. *e.g. The butcher's shop stinks in hot weather.*
2 If you sign or say that an activity or a situation **stinks**, you mean it is extremely bad. *e.g. 'What do you think of the new course?' he asked. 'It stinks!' she replied.*
3 A **stink** is an extremely unpleasant smell. *e.g. Where is that stink coming from?*

stir   108
1 When you **stir** a liquid, you mix it inside a container by moving something such as a spoon around in it with a circular motion. *e.g. The sauce should be stirred constantly with a wooden spoon.*
2 If you sign or say that someone is **stirring**, you mean that they are deliberately trying to cause trouble in an unpleasant way. *e.g. Just ignore George, he's only stirring!*

stir and sprinkle   723
When you **stir** a liquid, you mix it inside a container by moving something such as a spoon around in it with a circular motion. If you **sprinkle** something into a container, you scatter it with your fingers. While cooking, you may **stir and sprinkle** ingredients for making sauce, gravy, custard, porridge, et cetera. *e.g. Stir the stock*

and sprinkle the powder into the mixture, making sure you get rid of any lumps.

stirrer 108
If you refer to someone as a **stirrer**, you mean that they deliberately cause trouble whenever they can. *e.g. Anita had a reputation as a stirrer; she was always arguing.*

stir with a teaspoon 842
When you **stir** a liquid **with a teaspoon**, you mix the ingredients of the liquid together by moving it around with a teaspoon. *e.g. He put sugar into his coffee and stirred it with a teaspoon.*

stitch 869
1 When people **stitch** material, they use a needle and thread to join two pieces together. *e.g. She admired the finely stitched collars.*
2 A **stitch** is one of the short pieces of thread that can be seen on a piece of material when it has been stitched. *e.g. She used little stitches in the canvas she was making.*
3 When doctors **stitch** a wound, or **stitch** it up, they use a special needle and thread to tie the skin together. *e.g. They stitched up the gash in her head.*

stock cube 1497
A **stock cube** is a solid cube made from dried meat, vegetable juices and other flavourings. Stock cubes are used for adding flavour to stews, soups, et cetera. *e.g. I need a stock cube.*

stockings 876
Stockings are pieces of clothing, usually worn by women, and made of a thin, stretchy material such as nylon, which fit closely round each foot and leg up to the top part of the thigh. They are usually held in place by suspenders. *e.g. A woman in a flowered skirt and black stockings and shoes walked by.*

stoke 248
If you **stoke** a fire, you make it burn faster and hotter by moving the coal or wood with a stick or poker. *e.g. He told me what had happened as he stoked the fire.*

stole 1693
A **stole** is a long scarf or shawl worn around the shoulders by women. *e.g. She wore her silver evening dress and stole.*

stone 581, 1150
1 **Stone** is a hard, dry substance which is dug out of the ground, and which is often used for building houses and walls. *e.g. Many houses in this area are built of grey stone.*
2 A **stone** is a small piece of rock which you find on the surface of the ground. *e.g. She tripped over a stone.*

stone 1149
You can refer to a jewel as a **stone**. *e.g. He gave her a ring with a white stone in it.*

stop 1392
A **stop** is a break in a journey by vehicle. *e.g. The first stop was a hotel outside Paris.*

stop 1435, 1552
1 When people or things **stop**, they no longer do what they were doing. *e.g. Just stop for a moment and look at where you are.*
2 When people or things that are moving **stop**, they no longer move. *e.g. Stop! Now put it into first gear.*

storm 1439
A **storm** is very bad weather with heavy rain, strong winds, and often thunder and lightning. *e.g. Don't go out until the storm ends.*

stormy 1439
If the weather is **stormy**, there are strong winds and heavy rain. *e.g. It was a stormy winter's evening.*

story 455, 1311, 1383
1 A **story** is a description of imaginary people or events, which is written, signed or spoken in order to inform or entertain people. *e.g. I love reading ghost stories.*
2 The **story** of something is a description of all the important things that have happened to it since it began. *e.g. Her life story was an exciting one.*
3 A **story** is a report or an account of an event, or series of events, which is claimed or believed to be true. *e.g. The true story of what happened that night may never be told.*

stout 214
Someone who is **stout** is rather fat. *e.g. He was accompanied by a short, stout man.*

straight 1246
1 If you go **straight** to a place, you go there directly and without delay. *e.g. I must go straight home.*
2 You use **straight** to describe an action that you do, or that happens, without any break or interruption. *e.g. Youngsters go straight from school onto the dole queue.*
3 If you describe someone as **straight**, you mean that they are attracted romantically, sexually, or both romantically and sexually, to people of the opposite sex. *e.g. The club accepts both gay and straight members.*
4 If someone signs or talks **straight**, they keep to the point and do not try to change the impact of their words to deceive people. *e.g. OK, I'll tell you straight; I'm firing you.*

straight 1406
1 A **straight** choice, a **straight** fight, etc., involves only two people or things. *e.g. The voters have a straight choice between two candidates.*

2 Something that is **straight** is level in the horizontal plane. *e.g. Can someone tell me if this is straight?*

straight ahead 1246
If someone or something goes **straight ahead**, they continue in the same direction and do not bend or turn away. *e.g. We could see the road rolling straight ahead for miles.*

straightforward 362, 520
Something that is **straightforward** is clear and simple, without any special difficulties or complications. *e.g. The instructions he gave were straightforward.*

straight on 1246
If you indicate the direction of something as **straight on**, especially when giving directions, you mean that no turns are necessary. *e.g. Go straight on to the second traffic lights, then turn left.*

strange 626, 630
Something that is **strange** is unusual or unexpected. *e.g. Liz said she had a strange dream last night.*

stranger 1575, 1727
1 A **stranger** is a person you do not know, or have never met before. *e.g. Her mother didn't trust him, because he was a stranger.*
2 A **stranger** is a person who does not know a place very well, for example because they have only just arrived there or because they do not live there. *e.g. She is a stranger in the village and has lost her way in the fog.*

strap 269
A **strap** is a strong narrow piece of leather which is used for hitting people as a punishment, especially in former times. *e.g. My class teacher was always using the strap.*

strategy 768
1 A **strategy** is a plan you use to achieve something. *e.g. He adopted a strategy of massive deflation.*
2 **Strategy** is the art of planning the best way to achieve a particular aim. *e.g. The American generals won the debate over strategy in the Gulf.*

strawberry 579
A **strawberry** is a small, red fruit which is soft and juicy, and has tiny yellow seeds on its skin. *e.g. They had tea with strawberry tarts.*

stream 703
A **stream** is a small, narrow river. *e.g. There is a stream at the bottom of my garden.*

street 702, 1444
1 A **street** is a road in a town or village which has houses or other buildings along it, and

which usually has a pavement on each side of it. *e.g. The street was narrow and packed with parked cars.*

2 You can also use **street** to refer to something that happens outdoors in a town, or to someone who is outdoors rather than inside a building. *e.g. There were riots in the streets.*

strength   6, 75

1 Your **strength** is the physical energy that you have which gives you the ability to perform various actions, such as lifting or moving things. *e.g. I needed all my strength to lift the chair.*

2 You can use **strength** to refer to someone's confidence or courage in a difficult situation. *e.g. I don't know how I had the strength to go on after my wife died.*

3 Your **strengths** are the qualities and abilities that you have which are an advantage to you. *e.g. Her particular strength is interpreting from BSL into English.*

stress   1364

If you **stress** a point in a discussion, you put extra emphasis on it because you think it is important. *e.g. He tried to stress the importance of better public relations.*

strict   847, 849, 852, 868, 891

Someone who is **strict** does not tolerate impolite or disobedient behaviour, especially from children. *e.g. He was strict with his own children.*

strike   1720

A **strike** is a refusal by workers to continue working, usually because they are demanding more pay or better conditions, or because they are protesting about some other matter relating to their employment working conditions. *e.g. The workers went on strike for better pay.*

strike a match   873

If you **strike a match**, you make a small, thin stick of wood with a chemical substance on the tip (a match) start burning, by brushing it hard against the side of a matchbox or some other rough surface. *e.g. You will have to strike a match to light the gas fire, because the ignition device is broken.*

string   888

String is thin cord made of twisted threads. It is used, for example, for tying things together or for tying up parcels. *e.g. She took the parcel and started to undo the string.*

string someone along   665

If you **string someone along**, you pretend to be fonder of, or more friendly towards, that person than you really are, in order to obtain some advantage for yourself. *e.g. I realised he was stringing me along for my money.*

stroke   1290

If you **stroke** someone or something such as a small animal, you move your hand smoothly over them, touching them gently. *e.g. She put out a hand and stroked the dog.*

strong   6, 75

1 People or animals that are **strong** have well-developed muscles and great physical ability so that, for example, they can work hard, carry heavy objects, or hold things very tightly. *e.g. I need a strong person to help me move these boxes.*

2 People who are **strong** have the confidence or courage to deal with a difficult situation. *e.g. I will have to be strong for the sake of the children.*

3 Your **strong** points, or your **strong** subjects, are things which you are good at or which are likely to make you popular or successful. *e.g. Sociology was his strong subject.*

4 Alcoholic drinks that are **strong** contain a lot of alcohol. *e.g. Poitín is a strong, illegal Irish drink.*

structure   83

1 The **structure** of something is the way in which it is made, built, or organised, with all its different parts or aspects forming a particular shape, pattern, or system. *e.g. Linguistics is the study of the structure of language.*

2 The **structure** of a group of people such as a family, an organisation, or a society, is the pattern of their relationships with each other and the way their various roles, powers, laws, etc., are arranged. *e.g. The company developed a career structure that would attract able engineers.*

struggle   112

1 If you **struggle** to do something, you try very hard to do it, although it is difficult for you. *e.g. It was a struggle to survive.*

2 If you **struggle** when you are being held, you twist, kick and move violently in order to get free. *e.g. She struggled in his embrace.*

stubborn   68, 804

Someone who is **stubborn** is determined to do what they want and is very unwilling to change their mind. *e.g. Our daughter is stubborn and rebellious.*

stuck   80

1 If something is **stuck** in a particular position, for example in a gap between two things, it is fixed tightly in this position and unable to move. *e.g. The lift was stuck between the second and third floors.*

2 If you are **stuck** when you are trying to do something, you are unable to continue doing it, because it is too difficult or because there is something you do not understand. *e.g. I was stuck for an answer to the second question.*

3 If you are **stuck** in an unpleasant situation, you are in this situation and unable to change

it. *e.g. They are stuck in boring jobs.*

4 If you are **stuck** in a place, you are unable to get away from it. *e.g. She called to say she was stuck in Carlisle.*

stuck with   361

If you are **stuck with** something that you do not want, you are burdened with it and cannot get rid of it. *e.g. I'm stuck with looking after her parrot until she returns.*

student   635, 1330, 1732

A **student** is a person who is studying at a university or college or attending a particular course. *e.g. She is a student in my BSL class.*

studio   559

1 A **studio** is a room where an artist such as a painter or a photographer works. *e.g. Upstairs he had a studio where he painted.*

2 A **studio** is a room where radio or television programmes are recorded, records are produced, or films are made. *e.g. In the studio with me today is Richard Williams, the first Deaf person to be elected to a community council in Wales.*

study   270, 1732

1 If you **study** a particular subject, you spend time learning about it, especially by reading books and doing a course at a university or college. *e.g. He studied Chemistry at university.*

2 **Study** is the activity of studying a subject. *e.g. There are no rooms specifically set aside for quiet study.*

3 **Studies** are subjects which are studied, especially ones which deal with different aspects of one particular area of interest or one particular theme. *e.g. I work at the Centre for Deaf Studies at Bristol University.*

study   1330, 1532

1 If you **study** a particular subject, you spend time learning about it, especially by reading books and doing a course at a university or college. *e.g. He wanted to study Sociology at university.*

2 **Study** is the activity of studying a subject. *e.g. There are no rooms specifically set aside for quiet study.*

stunning   989

Something that is **stunning** is really beautiful and impressive. *e.g. The first BSLTTC certificate awards ceremony at Durham was so stunning, I cried.*

stupid   51, 316

1 Something or someone that is **stupid** shows a lack of good judgement or intelligence, and is not at all sensible. *e.g. I turned the job down, which was stupid of me.*

2 You sign or say that something is **stupid** to indicate that you think it is very silly or childish. *e.g. I think it's a stupid game.*

style   702, 1444

1 The **style** of something is the general way in which it is done or presented which often shows the attitudes of the people involved. *e.g. Some people find our style of decision-making rather frustrating.*

2 Someone's **style** is all their general attitudes and usual ways of behaving. *e.g. In characteristic style, he peered over his glasses.*

subdued   1256

Someone who is **subdued** is very quiet, often because they are sad. *e.g. They were subdued and silent.*

substitute   446, 766

1 If one thing **substitutes** for another, it takes the place or performs the function of the other thing. *e.g. In the past, oil has substituted for certain natural materials.*

2 If you **substitute** one thing for another, you use it instead of the other thing. *e.g. O.K. if I substitute this blue one for the grey?*

3 If someone is a **substitute** for someone else, they are ready to take the place or perform the function of that person. *e.g. Lucy was a poor substitute for Mick.*

substitute   889, 1164, 1389

1 If you **substitute** one thing for another, you use it instead of the other thing. *e.g. Vegans may wish to substitute another item for this, which of course contains animal fats.*

2 If one thing **substitutes** for another, it takes the place or performs the function of the other thing. *e.g. If you can't find a Polish one, a Hungarian item will substitute perfectly adequately.*

substitute   1664

If someone is a **substitute** for someone else, they are ready to take the place or perform the function of the other person. *e.g. Lucy was a poor substitute for Mick.*

substitution   446, 766

1 The **substitution** of one thing for a second thing is the replacement of the second thing by the first thing. *e.g. The substitution of bone meal for the fertiliser will not affect the soil unduly.*

2 A **substitution** in sport is the replacement of one player by another. *e.g. And the substitution has paid immediate dividends for Kenny Dalglish.*

substitution   889, 1164, 1389

The **substitution** of one thing for a second thing is the replacement of the second thing by the first thing. *e.g. If such a thing is available, the substitution of a harmless drug for the morphine would, of course, be vastly preferable.*

subtitles   489

Subtitles are the printed text which you can sometimes see at the bottom of a cinema or television screen when the soundtrack is not in a language that all the viewers can be expected to understand. *e.g. Why don't they get rid of the subtitles and make the interpreter bigger?*

subtract   1159

If you **subtract** one number from another, you do a calculation in which you take it away from the other number. For example, if you subtract 3 from 5, you get 2. *e.g. Teaching children to subtract and multiply is not at all easy.*

subtraction   1159

Subtraction is the act or skill of subtracting numbers from each other. *e.g. I'm better at addition than subtraction.*

suburbs   1152

The **suburbs** of a town or city is the area or areas of it which are not close to the centre. People who work in the town or city often live in the suburbs. *e.g. We're going to move to the suburbs; the city's just too crowded.*

subway   414

1 A **subway** is a passage for pedestrians underneath a busy road. *e.g. Cross by the subway and then you'll walk straight into Monument Mall.*

2 A **subway** is an underground railway. This word is used particularly in American English. *e.g. I walked to the subway station at 72nd and Broadway.*

subway   807

A **subway** is an underground railway. This word is used particularly in American English. *e.g. The subway was closed due to a bomb-scare.*

succeed   211, 255

1 If you **succeed** in doing something, you manage to do it. *e.g. I succeeded in getting the job.*

2 If something **succeeds**, it has the result that is intended. *e.g. The appeal succeeded in raising the money required to build a new daycare centre.*

success   211, 255

1 **Success** is the achievement of something that you have been trying to do. *e.g. They went out for a meal to celebrate his success in being offered a place on the interpreting course.*

2 **Success** is the achievement of a high position in a particular field, for example in business or politics. *e.g. Dr. O'Reilly's success on becoming the President of the Heinz Corporation was widely reported in the newspapers.*

3 Someone or something that is a **success** achieves a high position, makes a lot of money, or becomes very popular. *e.g. The play was a huge success.*

successful   211, 255

1 Something that is **successful** achieves what it was intended to achieve. *e.g. The United States was successful in landing a man on the moon.*

2 Someone who is **successful** achieves a high position in what they do, for example in business or politics. *e.g. Anita Roddick of the Body Shop is a very successful business woman.*

successor   1664

A **successor** is someone or something that comes directly after, and takes the place of, another person or thing, especially in an important job or position. *e.g. Who will be Gooch's successor?*

suck   1102

If something **sucks** an object, gas or liquid in a particular direction, it draws it there with a powerful force. *e.g. The roots suck the water in from the soil.*

sucker   58, 538, 856

If you call someone a **sucker**, you mean that it is very easy to cheat them, because they believe anything they are told. *e.g. He'd believe anything, he's such a sucker.*

suck up to   1069

If you **suck up to** someone in a position of authority, you try to please them by flattering them or by doing things to help them. *e.g. He's been sucking up to his boss, but it won't get him anywhere.*

sudden   383, 553, 630

Something that is **sudden** happens quickly and unexpectedly. *e.g. My uncle's sudden death upset us all.*

suddenly   553, 630

Something that happens **suddenly** happens quickly and unexpectedly. *e.g. Suddenly, the door opened and in walked the boss.*

sue   244

If you **sue** someone, you start a legal case against them, usually in order to claim money from them because they have harmed you in some way. *e.g. The machine was faulty and I lost a finger, so I am going to sue them.*

suffer   1052

1 If you **suffer** pain, you feel it in your body or mind, either because of an illness or injury, or because something has made you unhappy. *e.g. She was admitted to hospital: they said it was natural to suffer from shock after such an accident.*

2 If you **suffer**, you are badly affected by an unfavourable event or situation. *e.g. If the school closed, the children would suffer.*

sufficient   1267, 1583

If something is **sufficient** for a particular purpose, there is as much of it as is necessary. *e.g. There will be sufficient food for everyone.*

sugar　　　　　　　　　　670, 1097, 1497
Sugar is a sweet substance, often in the form of white or brown crystals, which is used to sweeten food and drink. *e.g. I like coffee with sugar.*

suggest　　　　　　　　　　314, 504
1 If you **suggest** something, or **suggest** that someone should do something, you put forward a plan or an idea for them to think about. *e.g. We have to suggest a theme for next year's conference.*
2 If you **suggest** something to someone, you sign or say something to them which puts an idea into their mind. *e.g. Someone should suggest he retires.*

suggestion　　　　　　　　　314, 504
A **suggestion** is an idea or a plan which is put forward for people to think about. *e.g. I made a suggestion about how we could spend the afternoon.*

suicide　　　　　　　　　　　184
Suicide is the act of deliberately killing yourself because you do not want to continue living. *e.g. There has been an increase in the number of suicides in recent years.*

suicide (commit suicide)　　　　184
People who **commit suicide** deliberately kill themselves because they do not want to continue living. *e.g. He could not believe she had committed suicide.*

suit　　　　　　　　　　　　　128
1 If something **suits** you it is the best thing for you in the circumstances. *e.g. The doctor says you should do what suits you and the baby best.*
2 If something **suits** you, it makes you look attractive. *e.g. The colour suits you.*
3 If something **suits** you, it is convenient for you. *e.g. Would Monday suit you?*
4 If something **suits** you, you like it. *e.g. An indoor job suits me.*

suit　　　　　　　　　　　　　230
1 A **suit** is an outfit, usually worn by a man, consisting of a jacket, trousers, and sometimes a waistcoat, all made from the same fabric. *e.g. He always wore an expensive grey suit and a dark tie.*
2 A women's **suit** is an outfit consisting of a jacket and skirt, or sometimes trousers, all made from the same fabric. *e.g. She wore a blue suit for the wedding.*

suitable　　　　　　　　　　　128
Someone or something that is **suitable** for a particular purpose or occasion has qualities that are right or appropriate for that purpose or occasion. *e.g. Only two of the candidates were suitable for the job.*

suitcase　　　　　　　　　　　15
A **suitcase** is a case, with a handle, in which you can carry your clothes when you are travelling. *e.g. I left my suitcase on the train.*

suit yourself　　　　　　　　1004
If you sign or say **suit yourself**, you indicate that someone should decide something for themself and that other opinions should not affect them. *e.g. You can suit yourself, whether you go or not.*

sulk　　　　　　　　　　　　1135
If you **sulk**, you are inexpressive and bad tempered for a while because you are annoyed about something. *e.g. He went off to sulk and continued to behave badly for weeks after I refused.*

summary (in summary)　　　　1162
You use **in summary** to indicate that what you are going to sign or say next is a short account of the main points of what has just been presented. *e.g. In summary, the changes will mean that every member of staff will work shorter hours and have a reduced work load.*

summer　　　　　　　　1183, 1575
1 **Summer** is the season between spring and autumn. In the summer, the weather is usually warm or hot. *e.g. I am going to Greece in the summer.*
2 **Summer** means relating to or characteristic of summer. *e.g. It is a summer fragrance, with hints of sea air and roses in bloom.*

summit　　　　　　　　　　1298
The **summit** of a mountain is the top of it. *e.g. It took the climbers two days to reach the mountain summit.*

summon　　　　　　　　　303, 350
If you **summon** someone, you order them to come to you. *e.g. She summoned her secretary.*

sums　　　　　　　　　　　1054
Sums are simple calculations in arithmetic. *e.g. Gabriel couldn't do his sums, so his father helped him.*

sum up　　　　　　　　　　1162
If you **sum up** after signing or saying something, or **sum up** what has been signed or said, you briefly state the main points again. *e.g. To sum up: within our society there still exist great inequalities which we must seek to reduce.*

sun　　　　　　　　　　　　1707
1 The **sun** is the star in the sky that the earth goes round, and that gives us heat and light. *e.g. The sun sets in the west.*
2 You also refer to the **sun** to mean the light and heat that reach us from the sun. *e.g. You need plenty of sun and fresh air.*

Sunday　　　　　　　　　　1440
Sunday is one of the seven days of the week. It is the day after Saturday and before Monday. In many Western and Christian countries, Sunday is a special day when shops are closed and some people go to church. *e.g. I never eat breakfast on Sunday.*

sunset　　　　　　　　　　1158
1 **Sunset** is the time in the evening when the sun disappears out of sight below the horizon. *e.g. We'll leave just before sunset.*
2 A **sunset** is the colours and light that you see in the western part of the sky when the sun disappears in the evening. *e.g. I saw a beautiful sunset when I was staying at Bieng.*

sun sets　　　　　　　　　1158
If the **sun sets**, it disappears out of sight below the horizon at the end of the day. *e.g. The sun rises in the east and sets in the west.*

sun sinks　　　　　　　　1158
If the **sun sinks**, it disappears out of sight below the horizon at the end of the day. *e.g. As the sun sinks in the west, the creatures of the night begin to stir.*

superb　　　　　213, 220, 880, 1710
If something is **superb**, its quality is very good indeed. *e.g. The children's library is superb.*

superior　　　　　　　　　1298
1 Someone who is **superior** to another person is more important or has more authority than that person. *e.g. These matters are best left to someone superior to you.*
2 Your **superior** is a person who has a higher rank in an organisation, or a higher social position, than you. *e.g. My superior told me she will recommend me for promotion!*

superior　　　　　　　　1342, 1639
1 Someone who is **superior** to another person is more important or has more authority than that person. *e.g. These matters are best left to someone superior to you.*
2 Something or someone that is **superior** to something or someone else is better than them. *e.g. These boots are superior to those cheap things!*

superiority　　　　　　　1342, 1639
1 If you have feelings of **superiority** over other people, you believe you are better than they are. *e.g. His feelings of superiority, sadly, set him apart from his peers.*
2 The **superiority** of something is the extent or degree to which it is better, more impressive or more effective than another thing. *e.g. We all felt it was the superiority of the brake system which won us over.*

supervise　　　　　　　　　777
If you **supervise** an activity or a person, you make sure that the activity is done correctly, or that the person is behaving properly. *e.g. She had to supervise meal times.*

supervisor   647, 762, 777
A **supervisor** is a person who makes sure that activities are done correctly or that people (especially workers or students) behave properly. *e.g. My supervisor recommended me for the course.*

supper   1501
1 **Supper** or a **supper** is a meal eaten in the early part of the evening, especially by members of a family eating together. *e.g. I'm tired and hungry and I want some supper.*
2 **Supper** is a small meal eaten just before you go to bed at night. *e.g. Do you want some supper?*
3 If you have **supper**, you eat a meal in the early evening or just before you go to bed. *e.g. Shall we have supper?*

supplement   1594
1 If you **supplement** something, you add something to it, especially in order to make it more adequate. *e.g. I tried to supplement my diet with vitamin pills.*
2 A **supplement** is something that is added to something else, especially in order to make it more adequate. *e.g. They will sometimes eat fish as a supplement to their natural diet.*

supplementary   1594
Supplementary is used to describe something that is added to another thing in order to make it more adequate. *e.g. You can claim a supplementary pension.*

supply   1517
If you **supply** someone with something, you provide them with it. *e.g. I can supply the food and drink.*

support   150, 229
1 If you **support** someone, or their ideas or aims, you agree with them, want them to succeed, and perhaps help them. *e.g. A lot of building workers supported the campaign.*
2 If you **support** a sports team, a football team, you want them to win and perhaps go regularly to watch their games. *e.g. Terry supports Oxford United.*

support   152
If something **supports** an object, it is underneath the object and holding it up. *e.g. The steel girders supported the walkway.*

supporter   150, 229
A **supporter** is someone who supports someone or something, for example a political leader, a political party, or a sports team. *e.g. He is a Celtic supporter.*

suppose   510
1 If you **suppose** that something is true, you think it is likely to be true. *e.g. I suppose England lost the Test Match again.*

2 You use **suppose** or **supposing** when you are considering a possible situation or action and trying to think what effects it would have. *e.g. Suppose something should go wrong, what would you do?*

supposed to happen   852
If you sign or say that something was **supposed to happen**, you mean that it was planned or intended that it should happen; used especially when the particular thing does not happen. *e.g. I was supposed to go last summer, but the neighbours changed their minds at the last minute.*

supposition   510
A **supposition** is an idea or statement which is thought to be true or correct, or one which people assume to be true or correct in order to discuss what its consequences would be. *e.g. Do you agree with his supposition that it was an accident?*

suppress   1364
1 If an army or government **suppresses** an activity, they prevent it from continuing. *e.g. The army aimed to suppress the revolt.*
2 If someone **suppresses** information, they prevent it from becoming known to the general public. *e.g. The committee will make every effort to suppress the report.*
3 If you **suppress** your feelings, you prevent yourself from expressing them. *e.g. Suppress your anger, she told herself. Smile at him.*

suppress one's laughter   816, 1085
If you **suppress your laughter**, you prevent yourself from laughing although you want to do so. *e.g. We managed to suppress our laughter, but he saw us anyway.*

sure   1323
1 If you are **sure** that something is true, you are certain that it is true. *e.g. I'm sure he said five o'clock.*
2 If you are **sure** about your feelings or wishes, you know exactly what you feel or what you want to do. *e.g. Are you sure you don't want another drink?*
3 If you sign or say that something is **sure** to happen, you mean that it will certainly happen. *e.g. You are sure to win.*

surely   1323
1 You use **surely** in order to emphasise that you think something is true, or to express surprise that other people do not necessarily agree with you. *e.g. She was surely one of the rarest women of our time.*
2 You use **surely** in order to express surprise in response to something that seems to contradict what you are signing or saying. *e.g. Ivan didn't know? But he must have done, surely.*
3 If someone signs or says that something will

surely happen, they mean that it will definitely happen. *e.g. Please send them money or they will surely die.*

sure (make sure)   182
If you **make sure** that something is the way you want it to be or expect it to be, you confirm that it is that way, especially by looking. *e.g. She watched the baby to make sure she was asleep.*

surf   113
Surf is the mass of white foam that is formed by waves as they fall upon the shore or crash against rocks. *e.g. We watched the children play in the surf.*

surface   1335
The **surface** of something is the top part of it, or the outside of it. *e.g. The surface of the lake looked like glass in the still, midday heat.*

surgery   190
Surgery is medical treatment in which the body of a person or animal is cut open so that a surgeon (a doctor who performs operations) can repair, remove or replace the part which is causing the problem. *e.g. You will be given an anaesthetic before undergoing surgery.*

surgery (facial surgery)   173
Facial surgery is medical treatment in which the face of a person or animal is cut open so that a surgeon (a doctor who performs operations) can repair, remove or replace the part which is causing the problem. *e.g. Three of the injured required facial surgery.*

surprise   1080
1 A **surprise** is an unexpected event. *e.g. The party was a surprise to me.*
2 A **surprise** is a gift or some other pleasant experience which is unexpected. *e.g. What a lovely surprise!*
3 **Surprise** is the feeling you have when something unexpected happens. *e.g. He looked at her in surprise when she returned.*
4 If you **surprise** someone, you startle them by doing something unexpected. *e.g. I'll try not to surprise you in the middle of the night.*

surprised   1143
When you are **surprised**, something has happened that you didn't expect. *e.g. I'm surprised that Robert got that new job.*

surrounding   1018
You use **surrounding** to describe the area which is all around a particular place. *e.g. Foxes started coming in from the surrounding countryside.*

surveillance   777
Surveillance means the careful watching of someone, especially by an organisation such as

the police or army. *e.g. The house was under surveillance by the police.*

survey   776

A **survey** is a detailed investigation of something, for example people's behaviour or opinions. *e.g. A national survey of eye diseases amongst children has shown that garden pesticides may be a major hazard.*

survey   962

1 If you **survey** something, you look carefully at the whole of it. *e.g. Survey the bookshelves for suspicious packages.*

2 If you **survey** a group of people, you find out about their opinions or behaviour, usually by asking them detailed questions. *e.g. In forty-five of the families that were surveyed, non-farm work provided most of the income.*

3 To **survey** an area of land means to make an examination of it in order to measure it and make a map of it. *e.g. He had had to survey the land from a helicopter.*

4 To **survey** a house means to examine it carefully and report on any problems with its structure, often in order to give advice to someone who is considering buying it. *e.g. I'll have to get them to survey the house first, before I can make you an offer.*

5 A **survey** is a detailed investigation of something, for example people's behaviour or their opinions. *e.g. This chapter includes a brief survey of the more commonly used drugs.*

6 A **survey** is an examination of an area of land, which is made in order to measure it and to make a map of it. *e.g. They did a preliminary survey and then started drilling.*

7 A **survey** is a careful examination of the condition of a house in order to say what the price of the house should be. *e.g. After I saw the results of the survey, I decided not to buy it.*

surveyor   962

A **surveyor** is a person whose job is to survey houses or land. *e.g. He works as a surveyor for a building society.*

suspect   919

1 If you **suspect** something, you doubt that it can be trusted or that it is reliable. *e.g. I had many good reasons to suspect this approach.*

2 If you **suspect** something bad or unpleasant has occurred or is the case, you think that it may have occurred or it is possibly the case. *e.g. I suspect that a murder has been committed.*

suspect   934

1 If you **suspect** something, you doubt that it can be trusted or that it is reliable. *e.g. I had my reasons for beginning to suspect his declarations of innocence.*

2 If you **suspect** someone of doing something, you think it is likely that they were responsible for it happening. *e.g. I suspect him: he was the*

only one there at the time.

3 If something is **suspect**, it cannot be trusted or regarded as genuine. *e.g. Her qualifications were thought to be suspect.*

4 Someone who is a **suspect** is thought likely to be responsible for something which has happened. *e.g. She is an obvious suspect, given her history of crime.*

suspend   244, 379, 546

If someone is **suspended**, they are prevented from holding a particular job or position for a fixed length of time, usually as a punishment. *e.g. The Committee decided to suspend him from the club for three months for inappropriate conduct.*

suspension   244, 379, 546

Someone's **suspension** is their removal from a job or position or ban from a particular place for a specific period of time, usually as a punishment. *e.g. The Arsenal centre-half was given a three week suspension.*

suspicious   919, 934

If you are **suspicious** of someone, or **suspicious** about someone's actions, you do not trust them. *e.g. The policeman became suspicious of the men standing in the doorway of the shop.*

suss   621

1 If you **suss** something, or **suss** something out, you discover what it is, how it works, how to do it, or what is happening in a certain situation. *e.g. It was easy to suss their plan, because it was written all over their faces.*

2 If you **suss** someone out, you discover what their true character is. *e.g. She had me sussed out in ten minutes.*

swallow   535

If you **swallow** something, you cause it to go from your mouth down into your stomach. *e.g. He swallowed the pill and picked up another bottle.*

swallow a statement/story   58, 538, 856

If someone **swallows a statement** or **story**, they believe it completely, without thinking that it might not be true. *e.g. Do you think he is going to swallow that story—it didn't fool me!*

swan   642, 711

A **swan** is a large bird, with a long neck, which often lives on rivers and lakes on which it swims. *e.g. Several kinds of swan are protected by law.*

Swansea   711

1 **Swansea** is a city and port in West Glamorgan in South Wales. *e.g. Dylan Thomas, the poet, grew up in Swansea.*

2 The address of the Deaf club in **Swansea** is:

Church of the Holy Name Mission to the Deaf, St. James' Gardens, Swansea SA1 6DY.

swap   446, 766, 889, 1164, 1389

If you **swap** one thing for another, or do a **swap**, you give the first thing to someone and receive the other thing in exchange. *e.g. If we swap, you can keep this one until next week.*

swear   357

1 If you **swear** to do something, you solemnly promise that you will do it. *e.g. I swear I will never tell anyone.*

2 If you sign or say that you **swear** that something is true, or that you can **swear** to it, you are declaring very firmly that it is true. *e.g. I swear that he never consulted me.*

swear   905

If you **swear**, you use language that is considered to be rude or blasphemous. Some people often swear when they are angry. *e.g. Glenys leant out of the car window and began to swear at the other driver.*

swear   1379

If you **swear** in an official setting such as a court of law, you solemnly promise that everything you say to the officials will be true. *e.g. They were asked to swear on the Bible.*

swear in   1379

When someone is **sworn in**, they make a solemn promise or promises, either at the beginning of a trial in a court of law, or when they are starting a new official appointment. *e.g. We have to swear in the jury first and then we're down to business.*

sweater   136

A **sweater** is a warm, knitted piece of clothing which covers the upper part of your body and your arms and does not open at the front. *e.g. The girl came out wearing jeans and a sweater.*

Swede   1544

A **Swede** is a person who comes from, or whose family identity relates to, Sweden. *e.g. For a Swede, owning a vacation cottage in the country is not so unusual.*

Sweden   1544

Sweden is a kingdom in North West Europe occupying the eastern part of Scandinavia. *e.g. They went to Sweden on holiday.*

Swedish   1544

1 Someone or something that is **Swedish** belongs to or relates to Sweden or its people. *e.g. We bought Swedish glass.*

2 **Swedish** is the main language spoken in Sweden, and is an official language of Finland. *e.g. He passed his Swedish exam.*

3 You can refer to people from Sweden in

general, or a particular group of people from Sweden, as the **Swedish**. *e.g. The Swedish remained neutral during the Second World War.*
4 The address of the **Swedish** Deaf Association is: Sveriges Dovas Riksforbund, Box 200, S-793 01 Leksand, Sweden.

sweep　　　　　　　　　　　　104
If you **sweep** a floor or other surface, you clean it by pushing a broom over it in order to collect the dirt in one place. *e.g. He started sweeping out the hut.*

sweeper　　　　　　　　　　　　104
A **sweeper** is a person who keeps an area clean by sweeping up the dirt and rubbish in that area. *e.g. He was employed as a council roadsweeper for twenty years.*

sweep up with a dustpan and brush　264
If you **sweep up with a dustpan and brush**, you push dust and dirt onto a dustpan using a small brush. *e.g. He swept up the crumbs with a dustpan and brush.*

sweet　　　　　　　　　　　　175
1 Food or drink that is **sweet** tastes as if it contains a large proportion of sugar. *e.g. The tea is very sweet.*
2 A **sweet** is the course such as fruit or pudding that you eat at the end of a meal. *e.g. The sweet today is apple pie.*
3 If you describe a feeling as **sweet**, you mean that it gives you great pleasure and satisfaction. *e.g. However sweet love is, there is always bitterness when it ends.*
4 A **sweet** smell is pleasant and fragrant. *e.g. She loved the sweet smell of ripe blackberry bushes.*
5 A **sweet** sound is pleasant, smooth, and gentle. *e.g. He stood by the open window listening to the sweet song of the skylark.*
6 If you describe someone as **sweet**, you mean that they are pleasant, kind, and gentle towards other people. *e.g. She's a sweet person.*

sweet　　　　　　　　　　　240, 732
A **sweet** is the course such as fruit or pudding that you eat at the end of a meal. *e.g. In our canteen, we can get a main meal and a sweet for £2.50.*

sweet　　　　　　　　　　　　346
1 Food or drink that is **sweet** tastes as if it contains a large proportion of sugar. *e.g. A cup of sweet tea is good for shock.*
2 A **sweet** is a small, sugary item of food such as a toffee, chocolate or mint. *e.g. Sweets are bad for your teeth.*
3 A **sweet** is the course such as fruit or pudding that you eat at the end of a meal. *e.g. I only have soup and a sweet at lunchtime.*

sweet　　　　　　　　　　　　465
1 If you describe someone as **sweet**, you mean that they are pleasant, kind, and gentle

towards other people. *e.g. She's a sweet person, never complains.*
2 If you describe someone or something that is small as **sweet**, you mean that they are pretty, attractive, and delightful. *e.g. The kittens are so sweet.*

sweet　　　　　　　　　　　　468
Food and drink that is **sweet** tastes as if it contains a large proportion of sugar. *e.g. That is a bit too sweet for me.*

swim　　　　　　　　　　　　323
If your head **swims**, you feel dizzy. *e.g. All that dancing has made my head swim.*

swim　　　　　　　　　　　　1232
When a fish **swims**, it moves through water by making movements with its tail and fins. *e.g. At this time of year, the salmon swim upstream.*

swim　　　　　　　　　　　　1410
1 When you **swim**, you move through water by making movements with your arms and legs. *e.g. I learned to swim at school.*
2 A **swim** is an occasion when you swim. *e.g. I'm going for a swim before breakfast.*

swimmer　　　　　　　　　　　1410
A **swimmer** is a person who is swimming, or who knows how to swim. *e.g. Are they all good swimmers?*

swimming　　　　　　　　　　1410
Swimming is the activity of swimming, especially as sport or recreation. *e.g. My favourite sports are netball and swimming.*

swimming costume　　　　　　1411
A **swimming costume** is a garment that covers your trunk and which you wear for swimming, sunbathing or relaxing on a beach. *e.g. You can even hire a swimming costume and a towel!*

swimming trunks　　　　　　　1412
Swimming trunks are a piece of clothing worn by men and boys for swimming, sunbathing, or relaxing on a beach. Swimming trunks are similar to a pair of shorts or underpants. *e.g. He bought a pair of swimming trunks.*

swimsuit　　　　　　　　　　1411
A **swimsuit** is a piece of clothing that covers your trunk and which you wear for swimming, sunbathing or relaxing on a beach. *e.g. Did you see that red swimsuit in the new catalogue?*

swing　　　　　　　　　　　　122
1 A **swing** is a seat hanging by two ropes or chains from a metal frame, or from the branch of a tree. You can sit on the seat and move forwards and backwards through the air. *e.g.*

We have a swing in the garden.
2 If you **swing** or **go for a swing**, you sit on a swing and make it move or have someone push it backwards and forwards. *e.g. Would you like to go for a swing?*

Swiss　　　　　　　　　　　　645
1 Someone or something that is **Swiss**, belongs to or relates to Switzerland, or its people. *e.g. We are going skiing in the Swiss Alps.*
2 A **Swiss** is a person who comes from, or whose family identity relates to, Switzerland. *e.g. Muriel visits her aunt, a Swiss, from time to time.*
3 You can refer to people from Switzerland in general, or a particular group of people from Switzerland, as the **Swiss**. *e.g. The Swiss joined the European Free Trade Association in 1960.*
4 The address of the **Swiss** Federation of the Deaf is: Federation Suisse des Sourds, Secretariat General, C.P. 84, CH—1663, Grandvaux, Switzerland.

switch　　　　　　　　　　　446
If you **switch** with someone else, you change places with them. *e.g. Let's switch: you wash, I'll dry.*

switch　　　　　　　766, 889, 1389
1 If you **switch** something with someone else, you exchange it with them for something different. *e.g. Shelly and I switched, and now she's got the green one and I've got the orange one.*
2 If you **switch** something, you remove it and replace it with something else. *e.g. Somebody switched these: this one's not mine!*

switch　　　　　　　　　　　846
A **switch** is a small control for an electrical device such as a light; you move the switch up or down to turn the device on or off. *e.g. That is the wrong switch.*

switch hats　　　　　　　　　254
If you **switch hats**, you set aside the perspective you take in one position that you hold in order to give consideration to, or make a contribution to, a particular issue on the basis of your knowledge, interests or experience which you have obtained in relation to another position that you hold. *e.g. Perhaps I could switch hats at this point and inform you of my concerns as a Deaf teacher, rather than as a member of this committee.*

switch off　　　　　　　　　846
If you **switch off** an electrical device, you make it stop working by moving a switch. *e.g. Please switch off the light.*

switch off a lamp/light　　　1090
If you **switch off a lamp** or a **light**, you cause it to stop working by pressing a switch. *e.g. You can switch off the garage light from inside the house, if you like.*

switch on   846
If you **switch on** an electrical device, you make it begin working by moving a switch. *e.g. Switch on the video recorder on this shelf and wait for the red light to come on.*

switch on a lamp/light   1698
If you **switch on a lamp** or a **light**, you cause it to start working by pressing a device called a switch. *e.g. Please switch on that light as you go out.*

Switzerland   645
Switzerland is a federal republic in North Central Europe. *e.g. Switzerland is known to be a neutral country.*

swollen glands   1179
If you have **swollen glands**, organs in your neck (glands), which are responsible for the presence of certain substances in your body, bulge outwards because of infection. *e.g. The poor chap has swollen glands, so he's staying in bed.*

swot   270
If you **swot**, you study very hard, especially when you are preparing for an examination. *e.g. How do you find time to swot for exams?*

sympathise   1215
If you **sympathise** with someone when something bad or unpleasant has happened to them, you are sorry for them, and show this in the way you behave towards them. *e.g. I did my best to sympathise with her and tried to help.*

sympathy   1215
If you have **sympathy** for someone when something bad or unpleasant has happened to them, you are sorry for them, and show this in the way you behave towards them. *e.g. People felt immediate sympathy for this man, left alone with his children.*

syringe   782
A **syringe** is a small tube with a suction device, such as a plunger, at one end and a fine hollow needle with a tiny hole in it at the other. Syringes are used for putting liquids into something and for taking liquids out, for example for injecting drugs into a person's body or for taking blood samples from them. *e.g. I attached the syringe and injected 10cc of the drug.*

system   702, 1444
1 A **system** is a way of working, organising or doing something in which you follow a set plan or set of rules. *e.g. The new system for gathering information is remarkably efficient.*
2 A **system** is also the way that a whole institution or aspect of society has been organised and arranged. *e.g. There is a difference between the Scottish legal system and the English one.*

T, t

T
T is the twentieth letter of the British manual and English alphabets. See page 853.

table   1415
A **table** is a piece of furniture with a flat top, usually supported by legs, that you put things on. *e.g. She bought a new pine table.*

tablecloth   874
A **tablecloth** is a cloth used to cover a table and keep it clean, for example while you are eating a meal. *e.g. I inherited a lace table cloth.*

tablet   476
A **tablet** is a small, hard piece of medicine which you swallow. *e.g. Take three tablets after each meal.*

table tennis   1316
Table tennis is a game played indoors by two or four people. They stand at each end of a long table which has a low net across the middle and hit a small, light ball to each other, using small bats. *e.g. My friend is a table tennis champion.*

table tennis player   1316
Someone who is a **table tennis player** takes part in a game of table tennis. *e.g. Would someone like to be our fourth table tennis player?*

taboo   109, 917
1 A **taboo** is a religious custom that forbids people to sign, say or do something because they believe they will be punished by God or the gods. *e.g. It is taboo to kill animals which are considered sacred.*
2 A **taboo** is a social custom that certain words, subjects or actions must be avoided because people think they are embarrassing or offensive. *e.g. There used to be a taboo on kissing in public.*
3 Something that is **taboo** is considered socially unacceptable. *e.g. Birth control is no longer a taboo subject.*

tack   844
If you **tack** something, or **tack** something up, you use a needle and thread to make a series of long, loose, temporary stitches when you are sewing or dressmaking. *e.g. Just tack the hem for now.*

tacky   812, 825, 1181
Something that is **tacky** is badly made and unpleasant to look at. *e.g. The shop only had tacky souvenirs for sale.*

tacky   973
Something that is **tacky** is slightly sticky and not yet dry. *e.g. Press the two parts together while the glue is still tacky.*

tail   1674
A **tail** is the part of an animal that grows out from the end of its body furthest from its head. *e.g. The strange animal had a long furry tail.*

tail   430, 442
1 If you **tail** someone or something, you follow them in order to find out where they go or what they do. *e.g. He was tailed by the police car.*
2 A **tail** is a person that follows another person in order to find out where they go or what they do. *e.g. Sergeant, you arrange the tail: this Constable can come with me.*

take   984
1 If you **take** something, especially when someone is offering it to you, you put your hand around it or part of it and hold it. *e.g. Let me take your coat.*
2 If someone **takes** something that belongs to you, they steal it or go away with it without your permission. *e.g. Officer, that man tried to take this lady's purse!*

take a capsule/pill/tablet   476
If you **take a capsule**, **pill** or **tablet**, you swallow one of these objects so as to absorb the chemical it contains. *e.g. She took a pill for her headache.*

take advantage of someone   526, 940
If you **take advantage of someone**, you treat them unfairly or deceive them for your own benefit. *e.g. I took advantage of John's good nature and borrowed two hundred pounds which I know I can't pay back.*

take advantage of someone/something   996
If you **take advantage of someone** or **something**, you make unfair or deceitful use of them or their kindness without caring

about the consequences. *e.g. Basically, the newspapers took advantage of the minister's bad judgement, without any consideration for his family.*

take advantage of something   861
If you **take advantage of something**, you make good use of it while you can. *e.g. Companies took advantage of favourable interest rates, it's as simple as that.*

take a note of   721
When you **take a note of** something, you write it down to help you remember it later, often for another person. *e.g. Take a note of his name, please, Mrs. Hudson.*

take a stand   804
If you **take a stand**, or **make a stand**, you resist attempts to defeat you or to make you change your mind. *e.g. You must be prepared to take a stand on this issue.*

take away   1159
If you **take away** one number or amount from another, you subtract it or deduct it. For example, if you take 3 away from 5, you get 2. *e.g. Now take away the number you first thought of.*

take blood   782
When a doctor or nurse **takes blood**, they draw it from a person's arm in order to test it or store it for emergency use. *e.g. We had to take blood from fifty people that day.*

take it easy   1037, 1400
If you tell someone to **take it easy**, you mean that they should calm down, relax or be patient. *e.g. Take it easy, you won't miss the train.*

taken aback   1092
If someone is **taken aback** by something, or something **takes** them **aback**, they are surprised or shocked by it. *e.g. I was taken aback by this sudden change of heart.*

take no notice   344, 1601
If you **take no notice** of someone or something, you do not allow them to affect what you think or do. *e.g. Take no notice of him. He's always rude to people.*

take notes   720
When you **take notes**, you write down things you want to remember later, especially things that someone has signed or said. *e.g. The secretary will take notes during the discussion.*

take off in an aeroplane/plane   949
If you **take off in an aeroplane** or plane, the aeroplane that you are in leaves the ground and starts flying. *e.g. The pilot must have been crazy to take off in an aeroplane in such bad weather.*

takeoff of an aeroplane/plane   949
The **takeoff of an aeroplane** or a **plane** is the beginning of a flight, when the aircraft leaves the ground. *e.g. The stewardesses brought dinner an hour after takeoff.*

take over   1171
If you **take over** a job, you become responsible for the job after someone else has stopped doing it. *e.g. They want me to take over as editor when Harold Evans leaves.*

take your time   1400
If you tell someone to **take their time** doing something, you instruct them to do it calmly and as slowly as they wish. *e.g. Take your time: precision is what counts, not speed.*

talk   380
1 When you **talk**, you have a conversation with someone. *e.g. They talked about old times.*
2 **Talks** are formal discussions, especially between two countries or two sides in a dispute. *e.g. Talks in London last week produced no hint of a settlement.*

talk   1247
1 If you **talk** about something, you make a presentation about it. *e.g. I'd like to talk to you this afternoon about metaphors in BSL.*
2 A **talk** is a lecture. *e.g. My talk will last about thirty minutes, and then there'll be time for questions.*

talkative   1529
Someone who is **talkative** speaks or signs a lot. *e.g. She is very talkative in class.*

talk on and on   1529
When a person **talks on and on**, they keep speaking or signing for a long time with only brief pauses. *e.g. In the train, Mrs. Lloyd always seems to talk on and on, all the way from Redditch to Birmingham.*

tall   1210, 1217, 1571, 1572
1 Someone or something that is **tall** has a greater height than is normal or average. *e.g. By jove, you're getting tall!*
2 You use **tall** when you refer to people's height. For example, if you are six feet tall, your height is six feet. *e.g. His sister was as tall as he was, both just over five foot six.*

tall (very tall)   1573
Someone or something that is **very tall** has a much greater height than most other people or things. *e.g. He was a very tall, dark man.*

tankard   26
A **tankard** is a large mug with a handle, usually made of metal, which you can drink beer from. *e.g. He was presented with a silver tankard on his retirement*

tap   1128
A **tap** is a device that controls the flow of a liquid or gas from a pipe or container. Taps are often attached to a sink or bath. *e.g. The tap was left running.*

taps   1166
Taps are devices that control the flow of a liquid or gas from a pipe or container. Taps are often attached to a sink or bath. *e.g. What kind of taps would you like in the kitchen?*

taps (turn on taps)   1166
When you **turn on taps**, you open the devices that control the flow of liquid or gas from a pipe, so that it comes out of the pipe. *e.g. I turned on the taps to fill the bath.*

tap (turn off a tap)   1128
When you **turn off a tap**, you shut off the device that controls the flow of liquid or gas from a pipe, so that it stops coming out of the pipe. *e.g. Turn off that tap, there's a water shortage!*

tap (turn on a tap)   1128
When you **turn on a tap**, you open the device that controls the flow of liquid or gas from a pipe, so that it comes out of the pipe. *e.g. I can't even turn on a tap because of my arthritis.*

target   1299
A **target** is a result you are trying to achieve. *e.g. We set a target date four months ahead for completion of the project.*

tart   525, 958
Something that is **tart** has a sharp, unpleasant taste. *e.g. The apples we collected from the garden are very tart.*

Tarzan   138
Tarzan is the name of a strong, well-built and agile man who is the hero of a series of adventure stories which usually take place in the jungle. He was created by the writer Edgar Rice Burroughs and first appeared in a number of stories written by him. *e.g. I went to see a Tarzan film.*

taste   523
1 If you **taste** something, you recognise it when you touch it with your tongue. *e.g. I have never tasted such good fudge before.*
2 The **taste** of something is the special flavour that it has, for example whether it is sweet or salty. *e.g. We put a lot of pepper and spices in the soup to improve the taste.*
3 If a food or drink **tastes** of something, it has a particular flavour, which you notice when you eat or drink it. *e.g. The tea tasted of salt.*

tasty   175, 345, 468
Something that is **tasty** has a fairly

distinctive, pleasant flavour when you eat or drink it. *e.g. That meat was really tasty.*

tatty   740, 812, 825, 1181
Something that is **tatty** is untidy, rather dirty, or looks as if it has not been cared for. *e.g. She wore a tatty old skirt.*

taunt   444, 558, 765, 1016
If you **taunt** someone, you sign or speak offensively to them about their weaknesses or failures in order to upset or annoy them. *e.g. Marchers taunted the police, shouting insults and waving banners.*

taxi   833
1 A **taxi** is a vehicle driven by a person whose job is to take people where they want to go in return for money. Taxis usually have a meter inside which shows how much the journey is costing. *e.g. She said she wanted to drive a taxi.*
2 If you **get a taxi**, you hire such a vehicle. *e.g. Oh, I'll just get a taxi from the station.*

taxi in an aeroplane/plane   951
When **an aeroplane** or **plane taxis**, it is moving slowly along the ground before taking off or after landing. *e.g. The aeroplane taxied to a stop in front of the building.*
2 If you **taxi in an aeroplane** or **plane**, you travel slowly along the ground in it before taking off or after landing. *e.g. We will taxi in the aeroplane to a point where the photographers can get a good view.*

tea   850, 872
1 **Tea** is a drink made by pouring boiling water onto the dried leaves of the tea bush. In Britain, it is usually drunk mixed with milk and often with sugar. *e.g. Would you like tea or coffee?*
2 **Tea** is the chopped, dried leaves that you use to make tea, usually sold in packets or boxes. *e.g. I'll have to go and buy some more tea.*
3 **Tea** is a light meal taken in the afternoon, usually consisting of sandwiches and cakes, often with tea to drink. *e.g. Tea will be ready at four o'clock.*

tea   1501
1 **Tea** is the main meal which you have in the early evening. *e.g. I always come back from work to find tea ready.*
2 **Tea** is a light meal which you eat in the afternoon. *e.g. Come for tea on Tuesday after school, okay?*
3 If you have **tea**, you eat an afternoon or evening meal. *e.g. Is it time to have tea?*

teach   457
If you **teach** or **teach** a subject, you help people to learn about it by explaining it or showing them how to do it, usually as a job at a school, college or university. *e.g. John Bulwer*

used to teach Chirothea in sign language in the seventeenth century.

teacher   457
A **teacher** is a person who helps people to learn about things, usually as a job at a school or similar institution. *e.g. John Dexter, the finest Classics teacher since Tacitus, has been working at this school for many years.*

team   840
1 A **team** is a group of people who play together against another group in a sport or game. *e.g. Keegan deserves the award for assembling such an impressive team.*
2 You can refer to any group of people who work together as a **team**. *e.g. I would particularly like to thank the members of the team for the truly incredible task they have completed today.*

teapot   8, 935
A **teapot** is a container with a lid, a handle, and a spout. You use it for making and serving tea. *e.g. The teapot is on the shelf.*

tear   1510
1 If you **tear** something, or **tear** it into pieces, you pull it violently, causing it to split. *e.g. He picked up the contract and tore it in half.*
2 A **tear** in something is the hole that results, or appears to have resulted, from someone pulling it violently, causing it to split. *e.g. A small tear is not going to upset anyone.*

tear off   1510
If you **tear** something **off** something else, you pull or rip it off by hand. *e.g. He tried to tear off the price tag but was seen by the store detective.*

tears   453, 574
1 **Tears** are the drops of salty liquid that come out of your eyes when you are crying. *e.g. Tears sprang from her eyes.*
2 If someone is in **tears**, they are crying because they are upset or unhappy, or sometimes because they are very happy. *e.g. The next time he saw her, she was in tears.*

tears (burst into tears)   453
If you **burst into tears**, you suddenly begin to cry. *e.g. I burst into tears at the very thought of that awful day.*

tease   444, 765, 1016
If you **tease** someone, you deliberately embarrass them, trick them, or make fun of them, because this amuses you. *e.g. She teased him about his girlfriends.*

teaspoon   842
A **teaspoon** is a small spoon that you use to put sugar into tea or coffee. *e.g. You'll find a teaspoon in the drawer.*

technician   1193
A **technician** is someone whose job involves skilled practical work with scientific equipment, for example in a laboratory. *e.g. The technicians quickly prepared the measuring devices for our experiment.*

technology   1193
1 **Technology** is the activity or study of using scientific knowledge for practical purposes in industry, farming, medicine and business. *e.g. Over recent years, there have been major advances in technology.*
2 A **technology** is a particular area of activity and the equipment it uses which require scientific methods and knowledge. *e.g. Computer technology has become so advanced in recent years.*

teddy bear   141
A **teddy bear** or a **teddy** is a soft toy that looks like a bear. *e.g. Mick has a large collection of teddy bears.*

tedious   1255
Something that is **tedious** is boring and seems to last for a long time. *e.g. This play is very tedious.*

teetotal   395
Someone who is **teetotal** never drinks alcohol. *e..g I can't drink a champagne toast because I'm teetotal.*

teetotaller   395
A **teetotaller** is someone who never drinks alcohol. *e.g. Robert is a member of the Pioneer Association which is made up of teetotallers.*

telephone   944
1 The **telephone** is an electrical system that you use to communicate with someone in another place by dialling a number on a special piece of equipment, typing or speaking into it, and reading or listening to the reply. *e.g. That is a matter for the telephone companies to sort out.*
2 If you **telephone** somebody, you dial their number to have a conversation with them on the telephone, typing or speaking into it, and reading or listening to the reply. *e.g. I have to telephone the dentist.*
3 A **telephone** is the piece of equipment that you use when you communicate with someone by telephone. *e.g. We bought a 1950s Norwegian telephone.*

telephone by Deaf Communicating Terminal/minicom/vistel/text telephone   1019
If you **telephone** or **phone** somebody **by** or **on a Deaf Communicating Terminal, minicom, vistel** or **text telephone**, you dial their number to have a conversation with them on such a piece of equipment,

typing on the keyboard and reading from the small display screen. *e.g. She's Deaf herself, so you'll have to telephone her by minicom: do you know how to do that?*

telephone call   944
If you make a **telephone call** or a **call**, you phone someone. *e.g. I have made two telephone calls but there's no reply. Yes, two calls, no answer.*

television   394
1 A **television**, or a **television set** is a piece of electrical equipment that consists of a box containing a special electronic tube with a glass screen in front of it. You use a television to watch programmes with pictures and sounds, or information broadcasts such as 'Ceefax' and 'Oracle'. *e.g. I watched the news on television.*
2 **Television** is the system of sending pictures, sounds and written information by electrical signals over a distance so that people can receive them on a television set. *e.g. Television pictures of the wedding were transmitted all over the world.*
3 **Television** refers to all the programmes such as plays, films and news, or information broadcasts such as 'No Need To Shout' and 'Earshot', that are broadcast and that you can watch on a television set. *e.g. The boys were watching television.*
4 **Television** is the business or industry concerned with making programmes and information broadcasts, and transmitting them on television. *e.g. Lucy Pickering always thought she'd work in television one day.*

tell   347
If you **tell** someone something, you give them information. *e.g. Tell the nurse your date of birth.*

tell   455, 1383
If you **tell** someone something, you give them a series of pieces of information in signs or spoken words. *e.g. All I did was tell Justine all about him; then she read his letter and asked what I was waiting for.*

tell   1562
If you **tell** someone something of which they are unaware, you let them know that it is the case. *e.g. Tell Mary the phone's ringing.*

tell about an event/story   455, 1383
If you **tell** someone **about an event**, or **tell a story**, you give an account of some real or imagined events by describing them in signs or spoken words. *e.g. Tell a story, do some magic tricks—anything to keep the kids amused.*

tell off   308
If you **tell** someone **off**, you sign or speak to them angrily or seriously because they have

done something wrong. *e.g. I had to tell the kids off when they broke my neighbour's window.*

telltale   625
A **telltale** is someone who reveals information about other people in order to get them into trouble. *e.g. 'You little telltale!' she signed angrily.*

tell tales   625
To **tell tales** is to give away information or to invent false but believable stories, often about something that is meant to be secret, in order to get someone else into trouble. *e.g. We decided we wouldn't invite Clarice to our midnight feast. She was sure to tell tales.*

telly   394
1 A **telly** is the same as a television. *e.g. Dad fell asleep in front of the telly.*
2 **Telly** refers to all the programmes such as plays, films and news and information broadcasts that are transmitted and that you can watch on a television set. *e.g. The kids are in the front room watching telly.*

temper   1185, 1187
1 Your **temper** is the tendency you have to become angry. *e.g. He always had a temper before breakfast.*
2 If you are **in a temper**, you are angry and do not behave calmly. *e.g. The man was in an awful temper and suddenly attacked me.*

temper   1196
1 Your **temper** is the tendency you have to become extremely angry. *e.g. Her temper was wicked when she was under pressure.*
2 If you are **in a temper**, you are extremely angry and cannot control your behaviour. *e.g. My son got into a temper and smashed his bicycle up.*

temperature   388
The **temperature** of something, or the **temperature** in a place, is how hot or cold it is. *e.g. A temperature of ten degrees centigrade is about average for the time of year in this region.*

temper (lose one's temper)   1720
If you **lose your temper**, you become very angry. *e.g. She lost her temper when she missed her train because of the traffic jam.*

temporary   613
Something that is **temporary** lasts or is in a particular situation for only a short time. *e.g. She has a temporary job.*

tempt   845
1 If something **tempts** you, it attracts you and makes you want it, often when it is something which you know you should avoid. *e.g. The prospect of leaving tempts me, to be honest.*

2 If you sign or say that you are **tempted** to do something, you mean that you would like to do it. *e.g. I was tempted to call you last night, but I thought you'd be asleep.*

temptation   845
1 **Temptation** is the state you are in when you feel you want to do something or have something which you know you really ought to avoid. *e.g. He had the strength to resist further temptation.*
2 A **temptation** is something that makes you want to do or have something, although you know it might be wrong or harmful. *e.g. The temptation to go to Sydney was almost overwhelming.*

tend   333
If you **tend** someone or something, you look after them very carefully. *e.g. During the drought, I was asked to tend my neighbours' chrysanthemums.*

tendency   363
A **tendency** is a habit, trend or other piece of behaviour that keeps happening. *e.g. A tendency to tease her classmates is the worst of her characteristics.*

tendency (have a tendency to)   363
If you **have a tendency to** do something in particular, you often behave in that certain way. *e.g. He has a tendency to bowl down the leg side.*

tender   520
1 Meat or other food which is **tender** is soft and easy to cut or chew. *e.g. The steak was so tender you could have eaten it with a spoon.*
2 If an action is **tender**, it is done gently and with care. *e.g. He reached out; just a tender touch, but it woke the baby.*

tennis   59
Tennis is a game played by two or four players on a rectangular court of asphalt, clay, grass, et cetera. They use racquets to hit a ball to-and-fro over a net which is in between them. *e.g. They've gone to play tennis in the park.*

tent   693, 1394
A **tent** is a shelter made of canvas or nylon, which you live in, usually temporarily (for example, when you are camping). It is held up by poles and ropes. *e.g. She pitched her tent in a field.*

terminology   823
The **terminology** of a subject is the set of special signs, words and expressions used in connection with it. *e.g. He used linguistic terminology in his lecture, and the interpreters were not prepared for this.*

terrible   585
A **terrible** experience or situation is very

serious or frightening. *e.g. It was a terrible accident, but we did not panic.*

terrible   904, 911, 914, 918, 992
1 An experience or situation that is **terrible** is very serious and unpleasant. *e.g. It was a terrible accident.*
2 If you feel **terrible**, you feel very ill or feel a very strong and unpleasant emotion. *e.g. I felt a terrible guilt about leaving home.*
3 You describe something as **terrible** when you think it is very bad, unpleasant, or of poor quality. *e.g. This cough medicine tastes terrible.*

terrible   1002
Something that is **terrible** is so unpleasant to experience that you feel disgusted by it. *e.g. There was mould all over the walls of the children's bedroom—it was really terrible.*

terrific   206, 1472, 1710
You describe something as **terrific** when you are very pleased with it or very impressed by it. *e.g. It was a terrific performance.*

terrified   947, 1006, 1143, 1180, 1719
If you are **terrifed** of something or someone, or they **terrify** you, they make you feel extremely frightened. *e.g. My aunt is terrified of the rats that run around in her back yard.*

terrifying   584
If something is **terrifying**, it makes you feel very frightened. *e.g. Watching the hurricane approach the town was a terrifying experience.*

test   690
A **test** is an examination consisting of a set of questions or tasks, which is intended to measure your knowledge or skill. *e.g. He failed the test.*

test   962
1 When you **test** something, you try it, for example by touching it, or using it for a short time, in order to find out what it is, what condition it is in, or how well it works. *e.g. We will test a number of new techniques.*
2 A **test** is a deliberate action or experiment to find out whether something works. *e.g. An underground nuclear test will be carried out.*
3 A **test** is an examination consisting of a set of questions or tasks, which is intended to measure your knowledge or skill. *e.g. He failed the test.*
4 A medical **test** is an examination of a part of your body in order to make sure that it is healthy or find out what is making you ill. *e.g. A blood test is necessary—just routine, of course.*

test tube   484
A **test tube** is a small glass container shaped like a hollow cylinder with a rounded end, that is used in chemical experiments. *e.g. The chemist poured acid into each of the three test tubes.*

text telephone   1019
A **text telephone** is a device enabling visual images to be sent over the telephone network as letters and figures which are typed on a keyboard and read from a small display screen. *e.g. Certain local authorities are making text telephones available to deaf people free of charge.*

thank   1261, 1471
1 When you **thank** someone, you express your gratitude to them for something. *e.g. He thanked her for the books.*
2 When you express your **thanks** to someone, you express your gratitude to them for something. *e.g. He sent a letter of thanks to the staff at Beamish College.*

thankful   1471
When you are **thankful**, you are very happy and relieved that something has happened. *e.g. We were thankful it was all over.*

thank God   894
If you sign or say **thank God** or **thank god**, you mean that you are very relieved about something. *e.g. Thank God it only lasted an hour.*

thank goodness   894
If you sign or say **thank goodness**, you mean that you are very relieved about something. *e.g. He's not here? Oh, thank goodness for that.*

thank heavens   894
If you sign or say **thank heavens**, you mean that you are very relieved about something. *e.g. I sat there thinking 'thank heavens we're not in that situation'.*

thanks   1261, 1471
1 When you express your **thanks** to someone, you express your gratitude to them for something. *e.g. He offered his thanks to Mrs. Perkins for taking over the class in his absence.*
2 You can sign or say **thanks** to express your gratitude to someone for something they have done, signed, said or given to you. *e.g. Thanks, Kyra: I'd have been lost without you.*

thanks a lot   467
You use **thanks a lot** to express anger, scorn or bitterness at what someone signs or does. *e.g. You let him eat my sandwiches? Well, thanks a lot.*

thanks very much   467
You use **thanks very much** or **thank you very much** to express anger, scorn or bitterness at what someone signs, says or does. *e.g. Oh, thanks very much: red wine on the carpet is all I need.*

thank you   1261, 1471
1 You sign or say **thank you** when you wish to express your gratitude to a person or group of

people for something they have done, signed, said or given to you. *eg. Don't just say thank you: give me a kiss!*
2 If you sign, say or give a **thank you** to someone, you express your gratitude to them. *e.g. Finally, I'm sure we'd all like to give a big thank you to Archie for his hard work.*

that   310, 495
You use **that** to refer to an object, animal, place, idea, etc., whose identity has been established or recently mentioned, or to identify one such item in contrast to others. *e.g. That vase came from Salamanca and that one from Prague.*

that is the one   495
You sign or say **that is the one** or **that's the one** to refer emphatically to one particular thing (of a kind that has been mentioned) in contrast to all others of the same kind. *e.g. That's the one I told you about last week.*

that one   495
You sign or say **that one** to identify a particular thing in contrast to all others of the same kind. *e.g. The dress I bought is that one. The others were gifts.*

that's it   1420
If you sign or say **that's it**, you mean you have reached the limit of your patience or tolerance. *e.g. That's it! Everybody stop arguing and let me explain.*

that's the one   495
See **that is the one**.

theatre   143, 968
1 A **theatre** is a building with a stage on which plays and other entertainments are performed. *e.g. We went to the theatre when we were in Washington D.C. to see Bernard Bragg's play 'Tales from a Clubroom'.*
2 You can use **the theatre** to refer to work in the theatre, including acting in, producing, and writing plays. *e.g. She was only really happy when she was working in the theatre.*

their *plural*   13
See **belong to them** *plural*.

their *singular*   11, 63
See **belong to them** *singular*.

their own *plural*   13
1 You use **their own** to emphasise that something is owned by, or relates to, a number of people, things or animals which have already been mentioned or of which the identity is known. *e.g. All of the neighbours brought their own plates, cups and saucers to the street party.*
2 You use **their own** to emphasise that a

number of people, things or animals which have already been mentioned, or of which the identity is known, does something without any help. *e.g. All of the delegates attending the conference are making their own travel arrangements.*

their own *singular*   11, 63
1 You use **their own** to emphasise that something is owned by, or relates to, a single group of people, things or animals which has already been mentioned or of which the identity is known. *e.g. Deaf people have their own social clubs in most cities in Britain.*
2 You use **their own** to emphasise that a single group of people, things or animals which has already been mentioned or of which the identity is known, does something without any help. *e.g. 'Will the Hackney group be there?'—'Yes, they have already arranged their own transport'.*
3 You can use **their own** to emphasise that something is owned by, or relates to, a person or a single group of people that has already been mentioned without their identity being specified. *e.g. I want the culprit to admit their own error, without the rest of you trying to spread out the blame.*

theirs *plural*   13
See **belong to them** *plural.*

theirs *singular*   11, 63
See **belong to them** *singular.*

them   500, 1208
You use **them** to refer to or indicate people, animals or things that are present or whose identity has been established. *e.g. He persuaded them not to strike.*

themselves   557
You use **themselves** to refer to the same people or things that are mentioned as the ones that did something or were affected by another person's action. *e.g. They are trying to educate themselves.*

then   154, 194, 300
You use **then** to indicate that a period or interval of time passes between one thing happening and the next. *e.g. He went to the village school, then to a comprehensive, then to university.*

then   1242
Then means at a particular time in the past. *e.g. I didn't know him then.*

there   161, 977
1 **There** is used when you sign or say that something exists and you want to draw attention to its location. It is used in English with parts of the verb 'to be' such as **am**, **is**, and **are**. *e.g. There*

is a new cushion on one of the settees.
2 Something that is **there** exists in the world and is available and ready for people to use. *e.g. The research information is there.*
3 **There** is used when you are referring to a place which has been mentioned. *e.g. I used to live in India, and some of my family are still there.*

there   495
There is used when you are indicating a place, or referring to a place which has been mentioned. *e.g. The book is there on the table.*

therefore   501
You use **therefore** in formal or technical situations to introduce a conclusion that you are making. *e.g. We conclude, therefore, that the radius is ten per cent larger.*

there is   1124
There is is used when you sign or say that something exists, or when you want to draw attention to a fact. *e.g. Yes, there is a police station near here, just up the road.*

these   500, 1208
You use **these** when you are referring to or indicating several people or things that are present or whose identity has been established. *e.g. These are actually fine quality bone china.*

The States   1051
The States is the United States of America. See **United States of America**.

they   500, 1208
You use **they** to refer to or indicate people or things that are present or whose identity has been established. *e.g. They are rather senior people.*

thick as two short planks   316
If you sign or say that someone is as **thick as two short planks**, you mean that they are very stupid or slow to understand things. *e.g. The administrator must be as thick as two short planks—he keeps sending me the same letter no matter what I tell him.*

thief   1126, 1151
A **thief** is a person who steals something from another person, especially without using violence. *e.g. The thief was arrested.*

thin   1478
A person or animal that is **thin** has very little fat on their body. *e.g. Ernst has always been thin.*

thing   556
1 You use **thing** as a substitute for another sign or word when you do not want to be more precise, when you are referring to something that has already been mentioned, or when you

are going to give more details about it. *e.g. He needed a few things, so we went shopping.*
2 A **thing** is a physical object that is not a plant, animal, or human being. *e.g. He's only interested in things, not people.*
3 Your **things** are your clothes or possessions. *e.g. I like my own things around me.*

think   313
1 When you **think** about ideas or problems, you make a mental effort to consider them. *e.g. Do we need language to think or to communicate?*
2 If you are **thinking** about doing something, you are considering doing it in the future. *e.g. I'm thinking about starting my own business.*
3 If you are **thinking** something at a particular moment, you have words or ideas in your mind without signing them or saying them out loud. *e.g. I lay there thinking how funny it was.*

think   314
1 If you **think** that something is the case, you have the opinion that it is the case. *e.g. I think we should finish work at five o'clock.*
2 If you **think** that something is true, you judge or believe it to be true, but you are not sure. *e.g. I think he is asleep now.*
3 If you **think** of something, you remember it or it comes into your mind when you have been trying to remember it. *e.g. I'm trying to think which other companies I could try for you.*

think   511
1 If you **think** that something is the case, you have the opinion that it is the case. *e.g. I think you're just bluffing.*
2 If you **think** that something is true, you judge or believe it to be true, but you are not sure. *e.g. We've agreed that we think that's a pig.*
3 When you **think** about ideas or problems, you make a mental effort to consider them. *e.g. Do we need language to think or to communicate?*
4 If you **think** of something, you remember it or it comes into your mind, when you have been trying to remember it. *e.g. If I think of his name, I'll tell you.*
5 If you are **thinking** something at a particular moment, you have words or ideas in your mind without signing them or saying them out loud. *e.g. I lay there thinking how funny it was.*

think a lot of   512
If you **think a lot of** someone or something, you admire them very much or think that they are very good, often with the result that you cannot see faults or weaknesses in them. *e.g. You seem to think a lot of her.*

thinker   313
A **thinker** is someone who is famous for their ideas on a particular subject, especially someone who is a philosopher. *e.g. I have always admired great thinkers like Freud and Aristotle who challenged received wisdom.*

thirst 1542
1 **Thirst** is a feeling you have of wanting or needing to drink something. *e.g. All this gardening has given me a real thirst.*
2 **Thirst** is the condition of not having enough to drink. *e.g. She was dying of thirst.*
3 A **thirst** for something is a very strong desire for that thing. *e.g. He couldn't satisfy his thirst for knowledge.*

thirsty 1268
If you are **thirsty**, you feel that you need to drink something. *e.g. Have you any water? I'm thirsty.*

thirsty 1542
1 If you are **thirsty**, you feel that you need to drink something. *e.g. After the match, we were all really thirsty.*
2 If you are **thirsty**, you do not have enough to drink. *e.g. All of the children in the village were hungry and thirsty.*
3 If you are **thirsty** for something, you have a strong desire for that thing. *e.g. He was thirsty for adventure.*

this 310, 495, 497
This is used to refer to or indicate a specific object, animal, place, idea, etc., or to identify one such item in contrast with others. *e.g. I like the information in this newspaper.*

this is the one 495
You sign or say **this is the one** to refer emphatically to one particular thing (of a kind that has been mentioned) in contrast to all others of the same kind. *e.g. I'm telling you, this is the one: the others are all too flat.*

this one 495
You sign or say **this one** to identify a particular thing in contrast to all others of the same kind. *e.g. I didn't like any except this one.*

those 500, 1208
You use **those** when you are referring to or indicating several persons or things which are present or whose identity has been established. *e.g. Talking of cars, what are those doing here?*

thought 313
1 A **thought** is an idea that you have in your mind. *e.g. I had vague thoughts of emigrating.*
2 **Thought** is the activity of thinking. *e.g. She frowned as though deep in thought.*
3 Your **thoughts** are all the ideas in your mind when you are concentrating on something. *e.g. They walked back, each deep in his own private thoughts.*

thousands 1722
You can use **thousands** to mean an extremely large number. *e.g. I've told him thousands of times to be home before ten o'clock.*

threatening 584
Something or someone that is **threatening** seems likely to cause harm. *e.g. He was a very threatening man who was suspected of being cruel to his children.*

throat 365
1 Your **throat** is the back of your mouth and the top part of the tubes inside your neck that go down into your stomach and your lungs. *e.g. Can I have some water? My throat is dry.*
2 Your **throat** is the front part of your neck. *e.g. She has a nasty bruise on her throat.*

throw 312, 1436
If something such as a remark or an experience **throws** you, or someone **throws** you by doing or declaring something, what happens confuses you or surprises you because it is unexpected. *e.g. It will really throw him if you include that in your question!*

throw 1498
1 When you **throw** an object that you are holding to someone, or **throw** someone an object, you move your hand quickly (usually in front of your body) and let go of the object, so that it moves through the air. *e.g. Throw Dad the newspaper.*
2 If you **throw** something into a place or position, you put it there quickly or carelessly, usually letting go of it in front of your body. *e.g. He undressed, throwing his clothes on the floor.*

throw 1703
1 When you **throw** an object that you are holding to someone, or **throw** someone an object, you move your hand quickly (usually from your shoulder) and let go of the object, so that it moves through the air. *e.g. Colleen threw a small ball to Maria.*
2 If you **throw** something into a place or position, you put it there quickly or carelessly, usually letting go of it in front of your shoulder. *e.g. He threw his t-shirt on the chair.*

throw a discus 1738
When you **throw a discus** in an athletics competition, you turn in a circle within a small, marked circular area before releasing the discus at speed into the air. *e.g. He threw the discus seventy metres at the British championships.*

throw a frisbee 1498
When you **throw a frisbee**, you hold it by the rim and move your hand quickly and let go of the frisbee, so that it moves through the air. *e.g. I threw the frisbee to Bunny.*

throw a javelin/spear 19
When you **throw a javelin** or a **spear**, you hold it over your shoulder and move your hand forward quickly and let go of the javelin or spear, so that it moves through the air. *e.g. Steve Backley has thrown the javelin over ninety metres this season.*

throw away 1703
When you **throw away** something that you do not want, you get rid of it, for example by putting it in a dustbin to be removed by refuse collectors. *e.g. You must throw away some of these old shoes which you never wear.*

throw out 1703
If you **throw** something **out**, you get rid of it, for example by putting it in a dustbin to be removed by refuse collectors. *e.g. The broken plates were thrown out.*

throw someone/something over one's shoulder 290
If you **throw someone** or **something over your shoulder**, you grasp them with both of your hands and pull them over your shoulder, causing them to fall in front of you. *e.g. He grabbed Neil Adams by the arm and threw him over his shoulder.*

thump 69
If you **thump** someone or something, you hit them hard with your fist. *e.g. I'll thump you if you don't get out of my way.*

thunder 304
Thunder is the loud noises which occur after flashes of lightning in the sky during violent storms. *e.g. There's going to be thunder tonight.*

thunder and lightning 305
Thunder and lightning refers to the loud noises and very bright flashes of light in the sky that occur during some violent storms. *e.g. Many people believe that thunder and lightning can be interpreted as the anger of the gods.*

thunderstorm 305
A **thunderstorm** is a storm in which there is thunder and lightning. *e.g. The old oak tree came down the night we had the thunderstorm.*

ticket 607, 658
1 A **ticket** is an official piece of paper or card which you are given so that you can prove that you have paid for a journey or for a visit to a theatre or museum. *e.g. A return ticket to Vienna, please.*
2 A **ticket** is a piece of paper or card, often with your name or a number on it, which shows that you are entitled to receive or use something. *e.g. I gave the woman at the dry cleaner's shop my ticket, and she brought my suit.*

tick off 308
If you **tick** someone **off**, you sign or speak angrily to them because they have done

something wrong. *e.g. David had ticked her off for being careless.*

tidy 676, 859

1 Something that is **tidy** is neat and arranged in an orderly way. *e.g. We have a lovely, tidy back yard with a little white shed.*

2 Someone who is **tidy** always keeps their things neat and arranged in an orderly way. *e.g. You only have to look at her desk to see she's not naturally a tidy person.*

tie 605

A **tie** is a long, narrow piece of cloth that is worn round the neck under a shirt collar and tied in a knot at the front so that it hangs in front of the chest. *e.g. I bought him a new tie for his birthday.*

tie 887

1 If you **tie** one thing to another, or if you **tie** something in a particular position, you fasten it to the other thing or fasten it in that position, often using string or ribbon. *e.g. It's one of those labels that you tie onto the handle of a suitcase.*

2 If you **tie** a piece of string or ribbon round something, or **tie** something with the string or ribbon, you put the string or ribbon round it and fasten the ends together in a knot or bow. *e.g. Have you seen a parcel tied with string on this table?*

3 When you **tie** your shoelaces, you fasten the ends together in a bow. *e.g. He was still tying his laces.*

4 If you **tie** a knot or bow in something, or **tie** something in a knot or bow, you fasten the ends of it together and make a knot or bow. *e.g. Will you just tie a knot in your handkerchief and then hurry up!*

tie up 887

1 If you **tie** something **up**, you put string or ribbon round it so that it is firm or secure. *e.g. Jessica came in, carrying some canvasses tied up in brown paper.*

2 When you **tie up** your shoelaces, you fasten them in a bow. *e.g. Tie up your laces. Hurry!*

tiger 1169

A **tiger** is a large, fierce animal that belongs to the cat family and is orange with black stripes. Tigers live in the wild in Asia. *e.g. A tiger terrorised the village.*

tight 1077, 1116

Someone who is **tight** is unwilling to part with or spend their money. *e.g. He's so tight, he won't make any donations.*

tights 147

Tights are a piece of clothing made of a thin, stretchy material. They fit closely round a person's hips, legs, and feet, and are worn by women or performers such as dancers. *e.g. She had a ladder in her only pair of silk tights.*

tilak 321

A **tilak** is a red mark made on the forehead of married Hindu women. The mark is put there by the priest as a sign of blessing and is usually made of kumkum or sandalwood powder. *e.g. Indira explained the significance of the tilak on her forehead.*

time 369

1 **Time** is what we measure in hours, days and years. *e.g. Time passed, and he eventually fell asleep.*

2 You use **time** to refer to a specific point in time which can be stated in hours and minutes and is shown on clocks, watches, et cetera. *e.g. The date and time of his birth are engraved on the handle of the spoon.*

3 **Time** may also refer to the official system of time that is used in a particular place in the world. *e.g. We arrived at six o'clock local time.*

4 You can use **time** to refer to the period of time that someone spends doing something or is available for doing something. *e.g. Do we have time for tea?*

5 If you refer to the **time** at which something happens or is the case, you mean the period when it occurs or is true or correct. *e.g. In my time at school, we had a gymnasium.*

time 410

1 **Time** is what we measure in hours, days and years. *e.g. Time passed, and he eventually fell asleep.*

2 You use **time** to refer to a specific point in time which can be stated in hours and minutes and is shown on clocks, watches, et cetera. *e.g. The date and time of his birth are engraved on the handle of the spoon.*

3 **Time** may also refer to the official system of time that is used in a particular place in the world. *e.g. We arrived at six o'clock local time.*

time 997

1 You use **time** to refer to a specific point in time which can be stated in hours and minutes and is shown on clocks, watches, et cetera. *e.g. Ask the time of the next flight to Vienna.*

2 If you refer to the **time** at which something happens or is the case, you mean the period when it occurs or is true or correct. *e.g. In my time at school, we had a gymnasium.*

3 **Time** is what we measure in hours, days and years. *e.g. Time passed, and he eventually fell asleep.*

4 **Time** may also refer to the official system of time that is used in a particular place in the world. *e.g. We arrived at six o'clock local time.*

time (at the same time) 425

You sign or say **at the same time** to indicate that, according to the measurement given on a clock, two events both take place at one particular moment. *e.g. They started moving at the same time.*

time (from time to time) 299

If you do something **from time to time**, you do it sometimes, but not often. *e.g. From time to time, she stopped and looked round.*

time (once upon a time) 1480, 1481

Once upon a time is used at the beginning of a story, especially a children's story to indicate that the events in it are supposed to have taken place a long time ago. *e.g. Once upon a time there lived a Deaf magician called Glis Guangaen.*

time (over time) 1479

Something that exists or happens or has existed or happened **over time** has developed and continued during that time. *e.g. The number of cigarette smokers in Britain has declined over time.*

times 372

You use **times** in arithmetic to link numbers or amounts that are multiplied together. *e.g. 5 times 50—that's 250.*

time (take one's time) 1003

If you **take your time** doing something, you do it at a moderate speed and do not hurry. *e.g. After the party, I got up at eleven o'clock and took my time tidying up.*

time (through time) 1479

Something that has existed or happened **through time** existed or happened in the past and continues to exist or happen. *e.g. Through time, there have always been some people who would wish to deny deaf children the right to use sign language.*

timid 1632

Someone who is **timid** is shy and shows no courage or self-confidence. *e.g. The new girl is very timid.*

tin 581

Tin is a soft, silvery-white metal. *e.g. Tin was mined in Cornwall and Wales.*

tin 1681, 1683

A **tin** is a metal container with a lid, in which things, such as food, may be kept. It is also used to refer to the food inside a tin or the amount the tin contains. *e.g. A tin of tomatoes, please.*

tiny 612, 618

A **tiny** amount or quantity of something is a very small amount or quantity. *e.g. The proportion of salt in this is actually tiny.*

tiny 637

Something that is **tiny** is very small, and usually of a size that you could hold between your finger and thumb. *e.g. There should be a tiny plug on the back of the machine, just here.*

tiny 1450
Something that is **tiny** is much smaller than is normal or average, and usually of a size that you could fit between your hands if you held them close together. *e.g. For a growing piglet, Oscar was tiny.*

tip 862, 871
If you give someone such as a waiter or a taxi driver a **tip**, you give them some money to thank them for their services. *e.g. The woman left a tip for the waiter.*

tired 230
If you feel **tired**, you want a rest and can't be bothered to do anything. *e.g. Bob was too tired to cook the dinner.*

tired 930
If you feel **tired**, you feel that you want to rest or sleep. *e.g. I feel so tired after that long walk, I could sleep for a day.*

tired 1588
1 If you are **tired**, you feel that you want to rest or sleep. *e.g. I'm sure you must be tired after cycling such a distance.*
2 If you are **tired** of something, you are bored by it. *e.g. Judy was tired of quarrelling with him.*

tissue 1535
A **tissue** is a small, square piece of soft paper that you use as a handkerchief or a dry cloth for wiping things. *e.g. Here's a tissue— wipe that mess off the back seat of the car.*

title 823
1 The **title** of a work of art or literature is the name given to it by the person who wrote it or composed it, or the name by which it is usually known. *e.g. He wrote a book with the title 'The Castle'.*
2 Someone's **title** is a name such as Lord, Lady, Sir or Princess used before their own name in order to show their social rank. *e.g. There were a lot of gentlemen in tweed suits, some with titles and some merely rich.*
3 Someone's **title** is a name such as Mr., Mrs., Doctor or Professor used before their own name in order to show their status or profession. *e.g. Not a lot of academics carry the title of Professor.*
4 Someone's **title** is a name that describes their job or status in an organisation. *e.g. The person in charge usually has a title of some sort: Administration Manager, Sales Chief, that sort of thing.*

toad 820
A **toad** is an animal that looks like a frog with a smooth skin, big eyes, and long back legs, but has a drier skin and lives less in water and more on dry land. *e.g. My sister has a toad for a pet.*

toad hopping 820
If a **toad** is **hopping**, it is leaping from place to place by rapidly straightening its long back legs. *e.g. There was a small toad hopping towards me.*

toad jumping 820
If a **toad** is **jumping**, it is leaping from place to place by rapidly straightening its long back legs. *e.g. The toad was jumping around the meadow.*

toady 941
1 A **toady** is someone who flatters and is pleasant towards people who are important, or have authority, in the hope of being liked by them and of getting some advantage from them. *e.g. Jenkins, you toady, try to act like an adult!*
2 If you **toady** or **toady up** to someone, you flatter or behave with excessive politeness to them in the hope of gaining some advantage. *e.g. She sure knows how to toady up to the boss.*

toast 772, 1202
1 **Toast** is bread which has been cut into slices and made brown and crisp by cooking at a high temperature. *e.g. I like toast for tea.*
2 When you **toast** something, you cook it at a high temperature under a grill so that it becomes brown and crisp. *e.g. You can toast bread from frozen.*

toboggan 1349
A **toboggan** is a vehicle for travelling on snow. It consists of a flat seat with two narrow pieces of a firm material, such as wood or metal, underneath that slide easily over the snow. *e.g. The children were on the toboggan almost at the first sign of heavy snow.*

today 1366, 1625
1 **Today** means the day that is happening at the time when you are signing, speaking or writing. *e.g. I hope you feel better today.*
2 **Today** means the present period of time in the history of the world. *e.g. This is the best translation available today.*

toddler 1211
A **toddler** is a small child who has just learned to walk. *e.g. You were only a toddler when your brother was born.*

toddlers 1216
Toddlers are children who have just learned to walk. *e.g. The toddlers were playing with blocks together.*

together 1101
1 If people do something **together**, they do it with each other. *e.g. We work together as a team in the office.*
2 You use **together** when you are adding two or more things to each other in order to consider the total as a whole. *e.g. The two*

companies together spend more on research than the whole of the rest of the industry.

to hell with 746, 785
Someone who signs or says **to hell with** something is expressing the fact that they are angry or scornful about it or do not want any more to do with it. *e.g. To hell with exams!*

toilet 324, 395, 964, 1186, 1264
1 A **toilet** is a large bowl that is connected by a pipe to the drains which you use when you want to get rid of urine or faeces. *e.g. She heard the toilet flush.*
2 A **toilet** is a small room containing a toilet. *e.g. He opened the door of the toilet.*
3 When you go to the **toilet**, you get rid of urine or faeces from your body in a toilet. *e.g. He wants to go to the toilet.*

toilet 944
If you sign or say that someone goes to the **toilet**, or is at the **toilet**, you are indicating that they are getting rid of urine or faeces from their body in a toilet. This sign is used when you are embarrassed to sign openly about the matter, or you are making a joke of it. *e.g. Well, don't tell anybody, but he had to go to the toilet again.*

toilet (desperate to go to the toilet) 1062
If you are **desperate to go to the toilet**, you very much want to go and get rid of urine or faeces from your body in a toilet. *e.g. Can we stop the bus? Tom's desperate to go to the toilet.*

tolerance 179, 181
Tolerance is the ability or readiness of a person to bear or endure something unpleasant or painful. *e.g. Their tolerance of such bad behaviour surprised him.*

tolerant 1476
If you are **tolerant**, you allow other people to have their own attitudes or beliefs, or to behave in a particular way, even if you do not agree or approve. *e.g. He is a very tolerant person.*

tolerate 179, 181, 1182, 1476
If you can **tolerate** something or someone, you are able to accept them although they are unsatisfactory or unpleasant. *e.g. Why do you tolerate such rudeness?*

toll a bell with a rope 106
When you **toll a bell with a rope**, you ring it slowly and repeatedly by pulling a rope attached to the bell, especially at funerals or as a sign that someone has died. *e.g. The church bell was tolled for him.*

tomato 579
A **tomato** is a soft, small, red fruit that you can eat raw in salads, cooked as a vegetable or

in sauces. *e.g. Please don't touch that huge tomato: I want to show it to Ian, because it's from his greenhouse.*

tomorrow   519
Tomorrow is the day after today. *e.g. They will come tomorrow.*

tonight   810, 811, 1465
Tonight is the evening of today or the night that follows today. *e.g. I think I'll go to bed early tonight.*

too   423
You use **too** when adding another person, thing or aspect that a previous statement applies to or includes. *e.g. We planted cabbages, leeks and potatoes—and carrots, too.*

too bad   1122
When you sign or say **too bad** to someone, seriously or as a joke, you mean you won't give them any sympathy for some problem they have. *e.g. You're hungry? Too bad. You should have eaten your dinner.*

too many   473, 1053
If there are **too many** of something, there are more than is necessary or appropriate. *e.g. Too many cooks spoil the broth.*

too much   473, 1053
If an amount of something is **too much**, it is more than is necessary or appropriate. *e.g. Don't buy too much, though, because it's not cheap.*

toothache   343
If you have **toothache**, your teeth or gums hurt. *e.g. I can't eat ice cream because it gives me awful toothache.*

toothbrush   258
A **toothbrush** is a small brush with a long handle which you use for cleaning your teeth. *e.g. I bought a red toothbrush.*

toothpaste   258
Toothpaste is a thick substance which you put on your toothbrush and use to clean your teeth. *e.g. I prefer the taste of peppermint toothpaste.*

top   1298
1 The **top** of something is its highest point, part or surface. *e.g. He stood at the top of the stairs.*
2 The **top** thing of a series of things is the highest one. *e.g. I have a room on the top floor.*
3 The **top** of an organisation is its highest or most important level. *e.g. The officials at the top make all the decisions.*
4 The **top** of a scale of measurement is the highest point on it. *e.g. The car's top speed is a hundred miles an hour.*

topsy turvy   1161
Something that is **topsy turvy** is in a confused state. *e.g. Kirsteen had left her room topsy turvy, as usual.*

torch   601
A **torch** is a small lamp which you carry in your hand and which gets its power from batteries inside it. *e.g. He took the torch and disappeared into the dark.*

torchlight   601
Torchlight is the light that is produced by one or more small battery-powered lamps (torches) which are carried by hand. *e.g. We looked for the lost coins by torchlight.*

tortoise   600
A **tortoise** is a slow-moving animal that has a hard shell round its back. It can pull its legs and head inside the shell in order to protect itself. *e.g. She was given a tortoise as a pet.*

tortoise walking   600
A **tortoise walking** is an animal with a hard shell on its back, into which it can retract its head and legs (tortoise), moving slowly along by putting one foot in front of the other on the ground. *e.g. There was my tortoise, walking straight towards the flowerbeds.*

torture   558
1 **Torture** is great pain that is deliberately caused to someone in order to punish them or get information from them. *e.g. He lived under the threat of torture and death.*
2 If someone **tortures** another person, they deliberately cause that person great pain in order to punish them or get information from them. *e.g. He saw his relatives being tortured, but they did not give him away.*

Tory   1649
A **Tory** is a member or supporter of the Conservative Party. *e.g. He was a Tory, and always would be.*

toss a coin   617
If you **toss a coin** or **toss**, you decide something by throwing a small piece of metal used as money (a coin) into the air and guessing which side of it will be facing upwards after it falls. *e.g. They decided to toss a coin to see who'd buy the first round of drinks.*

total   1162
1 When you **total** a set of numbers or objects, you add them all together. *e.g. John will total the votes cast for each candidate.*
2 If several numbers **total** a certain figure, that is the figure you get when all the numbers are added together. *e.g. The fine should total £120, according to my calculation.*
3 You can sign or say **in total** to indicate

that the figure you give is the result of a calculation. *e.g. This leaves us, in total, with the grand sum of £26.*
4 A **total** is the number you get when you do a calculation. *e.g. This gives us a total of twenty-two interpreters.*
5 The **total** number of something is the number you get when you add them all together. *e.g. John tells me that the total number is under sixty.*

Total Communication   1685
Total Communication is an educational approach within the field of deaf education in which any one of a number of languages and methods of communication may be used singly or in combination to achieve communication between the deaf child and his or her teachers and parents. These languages and methods include British Sign Language (BSL), Signed English (SE), Sign Supported English (SSE), spoken English, written English, the preferred language of the deaf child's parent or parents if this is not English, and gesture. Audiological equipment is used to maximise whatever hearing the child may have. In Britain, Total Communication has in practice tended to mean the use of Signed Supported English (in which signs that have usually been borrowed from BSL are used in English word order to support spoken English communication), spoken English, written English and the use of the most appropriate audiological equipment available. *e.g. The parents were informed that the school followed a Total Communication approach.*

tot up   1162
If you **tot up** numbers, you add them together. *e.g. Jack will tot up your score.*

touch   1596
1 If you **touch** something, you gently put your fingers or hand on it. *e.g. The metal is so hot I can't touch it.*
2 Your sense of **touch** is the sense that tells you what the surface of something is like, for example when you put your fingers on it. *e.g. The skin was fleshy and slightly waxy to the touch.*
3 The **touch** of something is the feeling when it touches you. *e.g. I will never forget the touch of her hand.*

touch down in an aeroplane/plane   950
If you **touch down in an aeroplane** or **plane**, the aircraft you are travelling in lands. *e.g. We will touch down at about noon local time.*

touchdown of an aeroplane/plane   950
The **touchdown of an aeroplane** or **plane** is the activity or event in which it lands. *e.g. It was a perfect touchdown, the aeroplane's crew agreed.*

tough 68
1 Someone who is **tough** has a strong and independent character and is able to tolerate a lot of pain or hardship. *e.g. He's not a cruel person, just tough.*
2 A **tough** substance is strong, and difficult to break, cut or tear. *e.g. Some plastics are as tough as metal.*
3 **Tough** policies or actions are strict and firm, and show determination. *e.g. He demanded that the government introduce tough anti-discrimination legislation.*

tough 1122
If you sign or say **tough** or **tough luck** to someone, you are showing that you do not have any sympathy for their problems or difficulties and will not do anything to help them. *e.g. 'This machine's stuck again'— 'Tough. You should pay attention when they expain how it works'.*

tour 739, 747
1 A **tour** is a long journey during which you visit several places. *e.g. I made a five-month tour of India and the Far East.*
2 A **tour** is a short trip round a place such as a city or a famous building. *e.g. We went on a tour of Windsor and the castle.*
3 If you **tour** a place, you go on a journey or trip round it. *e.g. This year, we will tour Scotland for our holiday.*

tournament 565
A **tournament** is a sports competition in which players who win a match play further matches, until just one person or team is left as the winner. *e.g. A table tennis tournament will be held next month.*

tow 597
1 If a vehicle **tows** another vehicle or a trailer, it pulls the vehicle or trailer along behind it. *e.g. I'm sorry, I can't tow that in my little car.*
2 If a vehicle is given a **tow**, it is pulled along behind another vehicle. *e.g. If you can't get a tow, you'll have to walk.*

tow a caravan 597
If a vehicle **tows a caravan**, it pulls a vehicle with beds and other equipment inside, in which people live or spend their holidays (a caravan), along behind it. *e.g. A Volvo is an excellent car to tow a caravan with.*

towel 143, 149
A **towel** is a piece of thick, soft cloth that you use to dry your body with, for example after you have had a bath. *e.g. He dried his feet with the towel.*

tower 704
A **tower** is a tall, narrow building, sometimes attached to a larger building such as a castle or church. *e.g. The view from the castle tower was magnificent.*

towering 1573
A **towering** building or tree is very tall and impressive. *e.g. Around the lake were many towering trees.*

town 1125, 1127
A **town** is a place with many streets and buildings where people live and work. Towns are larger than villages and usually have factories, shops, offices, and places of entertainment. *e.g. They moved from London to a small town.*

toy blocks 1688
Toy blocks or **bricks** are small cubes, usually made of wood or plastic, which children use to play with, for example by putting one on top of another. *e.g. Nicola gave her toy bricks to the boy next door.*

toy bricks 1688
Toy bricks are the same as toy blocks. *e.g. We bought her some toy bricks for her birthday.*

track 702
A **track** is a narrow road or path that has an uneven surface made of earth rather than of tarmac or gravel. *e.g. We walked along the track under the trees.*

tractor 503
A **tractor** is a farm vehicle with large rear wheels that is used for ploughing fields, sowing crops and pulling trailers. *e.g. Mr. Carter says I can ride on his tractor.*

tractor driver 503
A **tractor driver** is a person who controls a farm vehicle with large rear wheels used for ploughing fields, sowing crops and pulling trailers (a tractor). *e.g. My mother was a tractor driver during the war.*

trade 975
Someone's **trade** is the kind of work that they do, especially when they have been trained to do it over a period of time. *e.g. His trade was welding.*

trade 1346
Trade is the activity of buying, selling, or exchanging goods or services between, people, firms, or countries. *e.g. Japan is dependent on foreign trade.*

tradition 708, 1207, 1306, 1479
A **tradition** is a custom or belief that has existed for a long time without changing. *e.g. We should respect this tradition which is as old as our tribe.*

traffic 1059
Traffic is all the cars, buses, trucks and other vehicles that are moving along a road at any one time. *e.g. It was a strain getting to school through heavy traffic.*

traffic lights 1702
Traffic lights are the set of red, amber and green lights at a road junction which control the flow of traffic. The red light means 'stop', amber means 'prepare to stop or to go', and green means 'go'. *e.g. Turn right at the traffic lights and the County Hotel is on your left.*

train 17
A **train** is a number of carriages or trucks which are all connected together and which are pulled by an engine along a railway. Trains carry people and goods from one place to another. *e.g. I came by train.*

train 1533
A **train** is an engine with a pointed front plus a number of connected carriages or trucks which travel on a railway, carrying people and goods from one place to another. *e.g. British Rail would like to apologise for the late arrival of this train.*

train 1330, 1732
If you **train** as something, you learn how to do a particular job or task. *e.g. I'd like to train as an accountant, but I can't afford it.*

trainee 442, 1330, 1676, 1732
A **trainee** is someone who is learning how to do a job or task. *e.g. A trainee may spend some time simply observing good practice.*

training 1732
Training for a particular job involves learning the skills that are needed. *e.g. The training course offers Deaf people the opportunity to become computer programmers.*

trampoline 801
A **trampoline** is a piece of equipment on which you can do acrobatic jumps. It consists of a large piece of strong cloth held by springs on a frame. *e.g. In the gym, she liked the trampoline best.*

transfer 1701
1 If you **transfer** something from one place to another, you move it. *e.g. Ten thousand pounds has been transferred into your account.*
2 If you **transfer** to a different place or job, or you are **transferred**, you move to a different place or a different job within the same organisation. *e.g. She's been transferred to another department.*

translate 1319
If you **translate** something that someone has signed, said or written, you sign, say or write it in a different language. *e.g. They want me to

translate videos from BSL into English, so I'm going to need a good dictionary.

translation   1319
1 A **translation** is a piece of signing, writing or speech that has been translated from a different language. *e.g. This is a new translation of the Bible.*
2 **Translation** is the process or activity of reproducing something signed, written or spoken in one language in a different language. *e.g. The hardest part of the job is the translation work.*

translator   1319
A **translator** is a person whose job involves translating signing, writing or speech from one language to another. *e.g. She is employed part-time as a translator.*

transparent   331
If an object or substance is **transparent**, you can see through it. *e.g. The box has a transparent plastic lid.*

transparent   1728
1 If an object or substance is **transparent**, you can see through it. *e.g. The box has a transparent plastic lid.*
2 If something such as a feeling is **transparent** it is easily understood or recognised. *e.g. We wanted our aims to be transparent.*

transport   692
1 If you **transport** goods or people, they are moved from one place to another in a vehicle or vehicles. *e.g. Sculpture is heavy and costly to transport.*
2 **Transport** is the moving of goods or people from one place to another by vehicle. *e.g. The goods were now ready for transport and distribution.*
3 **Transport** is the system of trains, buses and coaches that people can use in order to travel from one place to another. *e.g. Public transport in this country is generally dreadful.*

trap   80
1 If you are **trapped** in a building, or in a particular position, you cannot escape or cannot move because something is in your way or something is holding you down. *e.g. The men were trapped in a tunnel when the roof collapsed.*
2 If you are **trapped**, you are in an unpleasant situation that it is difficult to escape from. *e.g. She felt trapped by the routine of housework.*

travel   739
1 When you **travel**, you go from place to place. *e.g. I travelled around Western Europe for two months.*
2 **Travel** is the activity of visiting various places. *e.g. Travel broadens the mind.*

travel   1229
If you **travel**, you go from one place to another. *e.g. I will have to travel to Colossa by mule.*

treasure   1615
If you **treasure** something, you are very pleased to have it and you regard it as precious. *e.g. The silver locket is very precious and I will treasure it always.*

treasurer   1503, 1508
The **treasurer** of an organisation is in charge of its finances and keeps its accounts. *e.g. The club must appoint a new treasurer.*

tree   1026
A **tree** is a tall plant with a long, wooden trunk, which usually has leaves and branches, and which can live for many years. *e.g. There was a huge tree in the middle of the lawn.*

tremor   1039, 1040
1 A **tremor** is a small earthquake. *e.g. She was frightened by a tremor which shook the foundations.*
2 A **tremor** is a shaking movement which may be caused by such things as heavy vehicles or machinery. *e.g. In our office, you can feel the tremors caused by the traffic outside.*

trial   865, 1367, 1413
A **trial** is a formal legal process in which a judge and jury decide whether someone is guilty after all the evidence about it has been presented. *e.g. He was awaiting trial for murder.*

trial   962
A **trial** is an experiment in which you test something. *e.g. The result of the first trial was very promising.*

tribunal   1367, 1413
A **tribunal** is a special court or committee that is appointed to deal with particular problems. *e.g. An industrial tribunal was hearing cases of unfair dismissal.*

trick   753
If you **trick** somebody, you deceive them, often in order to make them do something. *e.g. She tricked him into marrying her.*

tricycle   93
A **tricycle** is a vehicle similar to a bicycle but with two wheels at the back instead of one. Children often ride small tricycles. *e.g. We gave Liam a tricycle for Christmas.*

trike   93
A **trike** is the same as a tricycle. *e.g. Take that trike out of the hall right now!*

trip   739
A **trip** is a journey that you make from place to place, especially for sightseeing. *e.g. We went for a trip around the Fens.*

trolley   84
1 A **trolley** is a small cart used for carrying heavy things such as shopping or luggage. *e.g. Put the cases on a trolley.*
2 A **trolley** is also a small table on wheels on which things, especially food and drinks, can be taken from one part of a building to another. *e.g. Phyllis wheeled in the tea trolley.*

trouble   1422
1 Your **troubles** are the problems in your life. *e.g. She thought all her troubles were over.*
2 If you are in **trouble**, you have a serious problem. *e.g. If you don't get ready for school, you'll be in trouble.*
3 If there is **trouble**, people are quarrelling or fighting. *e.g. At the demonstration, there was trouble with the police.*
4 If someone is **trouble**, they can lead others into dangerous or unpleasant situations. *e.g. Stay away from him, he's trouble.*

trouble   1604
1 If you have **trouble** doing something, or if it causes you **trouble**, you have difficulties or problems doing it. *e.g. Did you have any trouble finding the house?*
2 If you are in **trouble**, you have a serious problem which will be difficult to solve. *e.g. We are in trouble with the mortgage repayments.*
3 If you are in **trouble**, you are in a situation in which someone in authority is angry with you because of something you have done. *e.g. He got into trouble with the police.*
4 If there is **trouble** between people, there is unpleasant or strongly felt disagreement between them. *e.g. If there is trouble in the Birmingham factory, it may close down.*
5 **Trouble** is also a breakdown or fault in something mechanical. *e.g. Our flight was delayed because of engine trouble.*
6 If you sign or say that one aspect of a situation is **the trouble**, you mean that it is that aspect which is causing problems or making the situation unsatisfactory. *e.g. The trouble is, it's too expensive.*
7 If you have kidney **trouble**, back **trouble**, etc., there is something wrong with your kidneys, back, et cetera. *e.g. He has heart trouble.*

troublesome   1604
Something or someone that is **troublesome** causes annoying problems or difficulties. *e.g. They were troublesome tennants.*

trousers   147, 709
Trousers are a piece of clothing that covers the body from the waist downwards and covers each leg separately. *e.g. Aunty Jean prefers to wear trousers when she goes birdwatching.*

truant   415

A **truant** is a pupil who stays away from school when he or she should be there. *e.g. I found the truant throwing stones in the river.*

truant (play truant)   415

If you **play truant**, you stay away from school when you should be there. *e.g. I used to play truant from school on Wednesday afternoons when I was supposed to be at a games lesson.*

truck   74

1 A **truck** is a large motor vehicle which is open at the back and is used for carrying goods, animals, or people, often on rough roads that are not suitable for cars. *e.g. The farmer drove them out to the orchard in a rusty old truck.*
2 A **truck** is a lorry. *e.g. There as a big truck parked at the side of the road.*

true   1323

1 A story or statement that is **true** is based on facts and on things that really have happened and are not invented. *e.g. The story about the murder is true.*
2 If a dream, wish, or prediction comes **true**, it actually happens. *e.g. My wish had come true.*
3 You use **true** to describe people or things that have all the characteristics of a particular kind of thing. For example, if you describe someone as a **true** Italian, you mean that they have all the characteristics of a typical Italian. *e.g. I suppose it takes time for true democracy to work.*
4 **True** feelings are sincere and genuine. *e.g. We sometimes wish to hide our true feelings.*

truly   1323

1 **Truly** means completely and genuinely. *e.g. He was now truly British.*
2 If you feel something **truly**, you feel it in a sincere and genuine way. *e.g. He knew he had behaved badly and he seemed truly sorry.*

trust   1323

1 If you **trust** someone, you believe that they are honest and sincere and that they will not deliberately do anything that will hurt you in any way. *e.g. Everybody began to like and trust him.*
2 If you **trust** someone to do something, you believe that they are able and willing to do what you want them to do or to act in the way that you want. *e.g. I trust you to find them.*
3 If you **trust** someone with something that you consider to be very valuable or important, you give it or tell it to them. *e.g. She's not a person I can trust with this sort of secret.*
4 If you **trust** in someone or something, you believe deeply in them. *e.g. I slowly found myself able to trust other people again.*
5 If you **trust** a story or someone's account of something, you believe it. *e.g. I'm sure I can trust her story.*

truth   357

1 The **truth** is all the real facts about a situation, event, or person, rather than things that are imagined or invented *e.g. Only two people knew the truth.*
2 If you sign or say that a statement or a story contains **truth**, you mean that it is true, or at least partly true. *e.g. The truth of his statement was not questioned.*

try   373, 374

1 If you **try** to do something, you make an effort in order to be able to do it. *e.g. You can do it if you try!*
2 If you **try** for something, you make an effort to get it or achieve it. *e.g. The school advised Mr. Denby to let his daughter try for university.*
3 A **try** is an attempt to do something. *e.g. For a first try, this is an excellent cake.*

try it on   941

If you **try it on**, you behave in a deceitful, outrageous, or extreme way in order to see how far other people will tolerate your behaviour. *e.g. She is just trying it on to see what you'll let her get away with.*

try out   962

If you **try** something **out**, you test it in order to find out how useful or effective it is. *e.g. Try this out on a piece of spare paper first.*

try to get the attention of   1214

If you **try to get the attention of** somebody, you attempt to get them to notice you in order to be aware of something that you intend to sign, say or show to them. *e.g. Can you try to get the attention of the Chair, because I'd like to add something here.*

tub   1374, 1628

A **tub** is a wide, circular container of any size, into which substances (usually liquids) can be poured. *e.g. All the beer should now be in one tub.*

tube   414, 807

The **tube** is an underground railway. *e.g. She lost her way on the tube and ended up at Charing Cross.*

tug   273

If you **tug** something, you give it a quick pull. *e.g. I tugged at the rope to see if it was tied at the other end.*

tug-of-war   273

A **tug-of-war** is a sport in which two teams test their strength by pulling against each other on opposite ends of a rope. The winners are the team that pull their opponents over a line marked or placed between the two teams. *e.g. My father was a member of a tug-of-war team.*

tumble   566

When something **tumbles**, it moves by rolling and bouncing along. *e.g. Look, Mum!*

It's called a 'Tumbler Jumbler' and it tumbles along all by itself: watch!

tumble dryer   1230

A **tumble dryer** is an electric machine which dries washing by turning it over and over inside a drum and blowing warm air onto it. *e.g. Put the sheets in the tumble dryer.*

tumbler   1671, 1681, 1683

1 A **tumbler** is a drinking glass with straight sides. *e.g. Could you pass me that tumbler, please, and I'll wash it up.*
2 **Tumbler** is used to refer to the amount of liquid which a tumbler contains. *e.g. A tumbler of whisky, added to the punch, will give it a certain depth and bite.*

tunnel   414, 1363

A **tunnel** is a long passage which has been made under the ground, usually through a hill, or under the sea. *e.g. We sped into the tunnel and everything went black.*

turkey   639, 640, 834

1 A **turkey** is a large bird that is kept on a farm for its meat. Turkeys are eaten especially on special occasions, for example on Christmas Day. *e.g. The turkey on the farm made a strange gobbling sound.*
2 **Turkey** is the meat of a turkey. *e.g. We ate roast turkey for Christmas dinner.*

turn   5, 56

When you **turn** or **turn your head**, you move your body or your head so that you are facing in a different direction. *e.g. He turned to smile at his friends.*

turn   503

If something **turns**, or if you **turn** it, it moves quickly in a circle. *e.g. The fan won't turn. It must be broken.*

turn away   5, 56

If you **turn away**, you move your body or your head so that you are facing in a different direction. *e.g. She turned away from him.*

turn (in turn)   156, 157

You use **in turn** to refer to people, things, or actions that are in a sequence one after the other. *e.g. She went along the line of nurses, shaking hands with each in turn.*

turnout   1056

The **turnout** at an event is the number of people who go to it. *e.g. Considering that it was a midweek game, I thought the turnout was not at all bad.*

turn over a page of a calender/notepad   1547

If you **turn over a page of a calender** or a **notepad**, you lift a page and move it to reveal the one underneath or behind it. *e.g. If you turn over a page of your calender, you'll see that the pictures tell a story month by month.*

tutor (a tutor) 457
A **tutor** is a member of staff at a university, college or secondary school who teaches groups of students or gives individual students general help and advice. *e.g. When the students are making their choices, the tutor may well guide them.*

tutor (to tutor) 457
If someone (especially a private teacher) **tutors** a person or a subject, they teach that person or subject. *e.g. I was inexpertly tutored in the subject of deportment and my back still suffers.*

T.V. 394
T.V. is an abbreviation for television. See **television**.

twelve o'clock 738
Twelve o'clock means either noon or midnight. e.g. *They told me to be there at twelve o'clock and to bring a spade.*

twilight 1464
Twilight is the time after sunset when it is getting dark outside. *e.g. Owls begin to hunt at twilight.*

two-faced 675
Someone who is **two-faced** is not sincere or honest in the way that they behave towards other people, and is particularly known for signing or saying one thing and doing another. *e.g. He could be briefly and accurately described as a two-faced liar and opportunist.*

two-handed alphabet 1174
A **two-handed alphabet** is a set of conventional arrangements of handshapes (involving both hands) which form the letters used in writing. Using such a system, you can spell out words on your hands. *e.g. In Britain, we have a two-handed alphabet, but most Deaf communities around the world use one-handed systems.*

two o'clock 749
Two o'clock is the time two hours after noon or midnight. *e.g. Are you crazy? It's two o'clock in the morning!*

two of us 760
You use the **two of us**, or **us two**, to refer to another person and yourself. *e.g. Is there room for the two of us in your car?*

type 1043
1 If you **type** something, you use a typewriter or word processor to write it. *e.g. I type the replies myself.*
2 If you **type** information into a computer or word processor, you put it in by pressing keys on the keyboard. *e.g. The letter was typed into a word processor.*

typewriter 1043
A **typewriter** is a machine that you use to write things in print. It has a series of keys that you press in order to write the letters, numbers, or other characters on the paper. *e.g. She always preferred working on an electric typewriter.*

typist 1043
A **typist** is a person who operates a typewriter. *e.g. Jessica is an excellent typist.*

tyre 503
A **tyre** is a thick ring of rubber which is fitted round each wheel of a vehicle such as a car or bicycle, and which is usually filled with air. *e.g. When he braked, a tyre burst and the car swung off the road.*

U, u

U
U is the twenty-first letter of the British manual and English alphabets. See page 853.

ugly 322, 992
Someone who is **ugly** is considered very unattractive and unpleasant to look at. *e.g. They thought she was ugly and nobody ever asked her for a date.*

ultimate 1298
You use **ultimate** to describe the most important or powerful thing of a particular kind. *e.g. Parliament retains the ultimate authority to dismiss the government.*

umbrella 265
1 An **umbrella** is an object which you carry to protect yourself from the rain. It consists of a long stick with a folding frame covered in cloth or plastic. *e.g. Take your umbrella. It's going to rain.*
2 An **umbrella** is a device like a large sunshade that protects you from the hot sun when you are sitting or lying outdoors. *e.g. Some hotel guests were swimming while others sat under striped umbrellas.*

umpire 641
In games such as cricket and tennis, the **umpire** is the person whose job is to make sure that the game is played fairly and the rules are not broken. *e.g. The umpire got the game underway just before the rain started.*

unable 421
If you are **unable** to do something, you cannot do it, for example because you do not have the necessary skill or knowledge, or because you do not have enough time or money. *e.g. He is unable to write his column for British Deaf News this month due to illness.*

unaware 1570
If you are **unaware** of someone or something, you do not know about them. *e.g. She seemed unaware of the people sitting around her.*

uncertain 1328, 1368
1 If you are **uncertain** about something, you do not know what to do. *e.g. She hesitated, uncertain whether to continue.*
2 If something in the future is **uncertain**, nobody knows what form it will take. *e.g. His future was unclear and uncertain.*

3 If the cause of something is **uncertain**, nobody knows what the cause is. *e.g. The cause of death remains uncertain.*

uncle 393, 815
Your **uncle** is the brother of your mother or father, or the husband of your aunt. *e.g. My uncle is coming to Durham.*

unclean 1020
1 Something that is **unclean** is dirty and may cause disease. *e.g. This food is unclean and unfit for human consumption.*
2 If you sign or say that something or someone is **unclean**, you mean that you consider them to be morally or spiritually bad. *e.g. Jesus, it was said, would cast out all unclean spirits.*

under 1334
1 If something is **under** something else, it is directly below it but some distance away from it. *e.g. The cat was under the car.*
2 If something happens **under** a particular person or government, it happens when that person or government is in charge and is responsible for what is happening. *e.g. He worked under Chairman Mao.*

under   1340
1 If something is **under** a particular amount, number or age, it is less than that amount, number or age. *e.g. Expenditure should be under two million pounds.*
2 If you study or work **under** a person, that person is your teacher or boss. *e.g. He has a large number of executives under him.*

underground   414, 807
The **underground** in a city or town is a railway system in which electric trains travel mainly below the ground in tunnels. *e.g. When we were on the underground, we saw someone steal a bag.*

underground train   414, 807
An **underground train** is a number of carriages pulled along a railway track through a system of tunnels beneath the ground (the underground) by an engine. *e.g. I would hate to drive an underground train for a living.*

underneath   1340, 1341
If one thing is **underneath** another, it is directly below or beneath it. *e.g. He put the box underneath the table.*

underpants   472
Underpants are a piece of clothing worn under other clothes by men and boys. They have two holes to put your legs through and elastic around the waist to keep them up. *e.g. He put on a pair of fresh underpants.*

understand what someone means 167
If you **understand what someone means**, you know what they are referring to *e.g. I understand what you are saying.*

unease   1144
If you have a feeling of **unease**, you feel that something is wrong and you are anxious about it. *e.g. I felt a growing unease as I walked around the deserted house.*

uneasy   1144
If you are **uneasy**, you feel anxious that something may be wrong or that there may be danger. *e.g. He had an uneasy feeling that he was being followed.*

unemployed   668, 1424
1 Someone who is **unemployed** does not have a job. *e.g. The government ought to create more job vacancies for unemployed young people.*
2 People who cannot get a job are often referred to as the **unemployed**. *e.g. They were discussing the problem of the unemployed.*

unemployment   668, 1424
You sign or say that there is **unemployment** in a place when many people cannot get jobs. *e.g. The government is concerned about the level of unemployment in Scotland.*

unemployment benefit   65
In Britain, **unemployment benefit** is money that a person who is out of work receives as of right from the government, subject to certain conditions. It is paid at regular intervals during the person's period of unemployment, for up to a maximum of 52 weeks. *e.g. He receives his unemployment benefit on a Thursday.*

unequal   1639
1 If you sign or say that a political or social system is **unequal**, you mean that it treats people in different ways, for example by giving some people more money or privileges than others. *e.g. You have to acknowledge that a system that allows such things to happen is simply unequal.*
2 Two things that are **unequal** are different in amount or quantity. *e.g. Look, you've given them unequal amounts of work.*

uneven   985
Something that is **uneven** does not have a flat, straight, smooth or regular surface. *e.g. I tripped on the uneven ground.*

unexciting   959
If you describe something as **unexciting**, you mean that it is not interesting, impressive or stimulating. *e.g. It was an unexciting game, with a lot of predictable play.*

unfit   231
If you are **unfit**, you have not been taking regular exercise so that, for example, you get tired quickly when you run. *e.g. I must be unfit to be so out of breath when all I've done is climb these stairs.*

unfold a piece of material 874, 1521
When you **unfold a piece of material**, you hold it at one end and shake it so that it opens to its full extent. *e.g. Please unfold this piece of material so I can see how large it is.*

unfortunate   914, 918
If you sign or say that something that has happened is **unfortunate**, you mean that it is unpleasant or a pity that it happened. *e.g. He had an unfortunate accident.*

uniform   1416, 1417
1 If you describe a number of things as **uniform**, you mean that they all look or are exactly the same. *e.g. The street consisted of uniform tall, white buildings.*
2 If something is **uniform**, it does not vary, but is even and regular throughout. *e.g. We aim to achieve a single, uniform standard nationwide.*

unimpressive   959
You can sign or say that someone or something

is **unimpressive** when they seem to have no good or interesting qualities. *e.g. The town hall was an unimpressive building.*

uninteresting   1255
Someone or something that is **uninteresting** is boring or dull. *e.g. He found her uninteresting, which was a shame, since she was very pretty.*

union   828
1 A **union** is an organisation formed by workers which represents their rights and has the aim of improving such things as the working conditions, pay and benefits of its members. *e.g. She joined the union on her first day at work.*
2 **Union** is used in the name of some clubs and societies. *e.g. The Lesbian and Gay Students' Union has written to complain.*

union   882
Union is the act of joining two or more things so that they become one, or the state of being joined in this way. *e.g. We are working for the union of the two countries.*

union member   828
A **union member** is someone who has joined an organisation which represents their rights (for example, their rights as a worker) and aims to improve conditions for them. *e.g. As a union member, I feel I have someone I can turn to should I have problems at work.*

unit   1447
If you consider something as a **unit**, you consider it as a single, complete thing. *e.g. The family is no longer a self-sufficient unit.*

unite   882
If a group of people or things **unite**, they join together and act as a group. *e.g. Deaf people must unite to combat ignorance about their culture and language.*

United States of America 1051
The **United States of America** is a federal republic in the continent of America consisting of fifty states and the District of Columbia. *e.g. She is going to visit Rochester Institute for the Deaf in the United States of America.*

universal   1044
Something that is **universal** relates to everyone in the world or everyone in a particular group or society; used for example of something that is common to everyone, that is available to everyone or that affects everyone. *e.g. Global warming is a universal concern.*

university   393, 448
A **university** is an institution where students study for academic qualifications (for

example, degrees, diplomas, certificates, etc.) and where scientific and academic research is done. *e.g. She was a student at Edinburgh University.*

unlock with a key   250
If you **unlock** something, such as a door or a container, **with a key**, you open it by placing the key in the lock and turning it. *e.g. He unlocked the door with a key they kept hidden under the mat.*

unlucky   914
Someone who is **unlucky** has very bad luck. *e.g. He was unlucky to be standing there when the wall collapsed.*

unstable   1569
If you are **unstable**, your emotions and behaviour keep changing because your mind is disturbed. *e.g. To be honest, I think he was unstable.*

unsuitable   130
Someone or something that is **unsuitable** has qualities that are not right or appropriate for a particular purpose or occasion. *e.g. The land was unsuitable for farming.*

unsure   982, 1328, 1368
If you are **unsure** of something, you feel uncertain about it or are not confident that it is right. *e.g. This issue is one that many tutors feel unsure about.*

untidy   1370
Something that is **untidy** is messy and disordered and not neat or well arranged. *e.g. The living room was untidy as usual.*

until   1303
You use **until** to sign or say that an activity, situation or event stops at the time or point mentioned. *e.g. We went on duty at six in the evening and worked until two in the morning.*

unwaged   1424
1 People who are **unwaged** do not have a paid job. *e.g. Theatre tickets can be obtained at half price if you are unwaged.*
2 You can refer to people who do not have a paid job as the **unwaged**. *e.g. The unwaged will be charged a reduced fee.*

unwell   231, 318, 931
If you are **unwell**, you are ill. *e.g. I was unwell, so I didn't go to work.*

up   296
Up means towards a higher place or in a higher place. *e.g. Is this lift going up or down?*

up   1201
1 If you are **up**, you are no longer in bed. *e.g.*

They were up early.
2 If a number or an amount goes **up**, it increases. *e.g. The price of tomatoes has gone up again.*

up   1209
1 **Up** means forward towards a higher place. *e.g. We must go up and over the ridge.*
2 If you sign or say that something is on the **up**, you mean that it is improving. *e.g. His health has not been good, but it's on the up now.*
3 If a number or an amount goes **up**, it increases. *e.g. Interest rates are likely to go up again in the near future.*

uphill   1209
If you go **uphill**, you go up a slope. *e.g. She pushed it uphill.*

upland   1209
1 **Upland** places are situated on high hills, plateaus, or mountains. *e.g. These trees can be grown in upland areas.*
2 **Uplands** are areas of land on high hills, plateaus, or mountains. *e.g. Food production in the uplands is high.*

uprising   89
When an **uprising** happens, a group of people start fighting against those in power, for example because they want to bring about a political change in a country. *e.g. He took part in the uprising in Dublin in 1916.*

upside down   1031
1 If you turn a place **upside down**, you create severe disorder or untidiness in it. *e.g. The burglars turned the house upside down.*
2 If a plan or arrangement is up**side down**, it has been spoiled by something that has happened. *e.g. Well, everything's upside down now that Pandeli is away sick.*

upside down   1161
If something is **upside down**, it has been turned round so that the part that is usually lowest is above the part that is usually highest. *e.g. You are holding it upside down.*

upstairs   296
1 If something or somebody is **upstairs** in a building, they are on an upper floor, or on a higher floor than you. *e.g. Upstairs there were three little bedrooms.*
2 The **upstairs** of a building is its upper floor or floors. *e.g. They had to rent out the upstairs to make the mortgage payments.*
3 When you refer to a person **upstairs**, you are referring to someone who lives in a flat or room on an upper floor or on the floor above you. *e.g. The people upstairs are redecorating their flat.*

up to you   1004
If you sign or say to someone that something is **up to you**, you are indicating that you do not

mind whether the person does a particular thing or not and that they should make up their own mind about it. *e.g. It's up to you whether you come to the dance or not.*

upward   1209
1 **Upward** or **upwards** is used to indicate that something rises to a higher level or point on a scale. *e.g. The world urban population is rocketing upward at a rate of 6.5% per year.*
2 If something moves **upward** or **upwards**, it advances towards a higher place. *e.g. We walked upwards towards Scafell.*

urge   560
If you **urge** someone to do something, you try hard to persuade them to do it. *e.g. Roy urged him to take a year off to study drawing.*

urgent   383, 384
Something that is **urgent** needs to be dealt with as soon as possible. *e.g. I got an urgent message.*

us   540
A signer, speaker or writer uses **us** to refer both to himself or herself and to one or more other people as a group. *e.g. There wasn't room for us, so we stayed with Trude.*

USA   1051
USA is an abbreviation for United States of America. See **United States of America**.

use   178, 1582
1 If you **use** something, you do something with it in order to do a job or to achieve something. *e.g. Use a mild detergent to wash this garment.*
2 If you **use** a particular sign, word or expression, you sign, say or write it, because it has the meaning that you want to express. *e.g. It's a phrase I once heard Father Preston use in a sermon.*
3 If you make **use** of something, you do something with it in order to do a job or to achieve something. *e.g. More and more factories are making use of robots to improve productivity.*
4 The **use** of something is the act or fact of using it. *e.g. The pamphlet has been designed for use in schools.*

used to   341
1 If you are **used to** something, you are familiar with it because you have done or seen it often. *e.g. We are used to working together.*
2 If you get **used to** something, you become familiar with it. *e.g. I was beginning to get used to the old iron bed.*

useful   178, 1582
1 If something is **useful**, you can use it in order to do something or to help you in some way. *e.g. She gave us some useful information.*
2 If you are being **useful** you are doing things that help other people. *e.g. Make yourself useful and put the kettle on.*

3 When a possession or a skill comes in **useful**, you are able to use it on a particular occasion. *e.g. This is where your sketch comes in useful.*

useless   222
1 If something is **useless**, you cannot use it. *e.g. Land is useless without water.*
2 If a course of action is **useless**, it does not achieve anything helpful. *e.g. She underwent two useless operations.*
3 If you describe someone or something as **useless**, you mean that they are no good at all. *e.g. I was useless at maths.*

useless   740, 812
If you describe someone or something as **useless**, you mean that they are no good at all. *e.g. The trowel was useless—the blade kept falling out of the handle.*

usherette   601
An **usherette** is a woman who shows people where to sit in a cinema or theatre and who sells refreshments and programmes. *e.g. The usherette showed them to their seats.*

USSR   10
The **USSR** was a federal republic in Eastern Europe and Central and Northern Asia. It was established in 1922 and was the largest country in the world. USSR is an abbreviation for Union of Soviet Socialist Republics. In 1990, the union of republics was dissolved and the individual republics were recognised as independent states. A number of these independent states have formed an association known as the Commonwealth of Independent States (CIS). *e.g. The world will probably never see a republic as large as the USSR again.*

us (two)   760
A person uses **us two** or **us** to refer to him or herself and one other person. *e.g. What do you want us two to do, then?*

usual   204, 207
1 **Usual** is used to describe the thing that happens most often, or that is done or used most often, in a particular situation. *e.g. He sat in his usual chair.*
2 If you do something as **usual**, you do it in the way that you normally do it. *e.g. As usual, he drove far too fast.*
3 You can also use as **usual** to describe something that often happens or is often the case. *e.g. The phone box on the corner is broken as usual—why can't they catch those vandals!*

V, v

V
V is the twenty-second letter of the British manual and English alphabets. See page 854.

vacation   668
1 A **vacation** is a period of the year when universities, colleges, offices and courts are officially closed. *e.g. My son will be home for the vacation but he will have to study.*
2 A **vacation** is a holiday. *e.g. We had a vacation in Canada.*

vaccinate   782
If you **vaccinate** someone, you give them a substance made from the germs that cause a certain disease (usually by injecting it into their body) in order to protect them from that disease by building up their body's defences. *e.g. When were people first vaccinated against measles?*

vaccination   782
Vaccination is the activity of giving people a substance made from the germs that cause a certain disease (usually by injecting it into their body) in order to protect them from that disease by building up their body's defences. *e.g. Vaccination of the entire population is the only solution.*

vacuum   248
1 If you **vacuum** something, you clean it using a vacuum cleaner. *e.g. I'm going to vacuum the car.*
2 A **vacuum** is an electric machine which removes dirt from carpets, furniture, etc., by sucking it into the machine. *e.g. I'll just turn off the vacuum.*

vacuum cleaner   248
A **vacuum cleaner** is an electric machine which removes dirt from carpets, furniture, etc., by sucking it into the machine. *e.g. The vacuum cleaner is in the cupboard.*

vale   1402
A **vale** is a valley. *e.g. The vale was full of lush meadows and blossoms.*

valiant   1200
Valiant means very brave. *e.g. He made a valiant attempt to rescue the struggling swimmer.*

valley   1402
A **valley** is a long, narrow area of land between hills, especially one that has a river flowing through it. *e.g. The sheep grazed in the pastures in the valley.*

valuable   131, 1524
1 **Valuable** help or advice is very useful. *e.g. My mother gave me valuable cooking tips.*
2 When objects such as paintings or jewellery are **valuable**, they are worth a lot of money. *e.g. This antique clock is very valuable.*

value   131, 1524
1 The **value** of something, such as a quality or a method, is its importance or usefulness. *e.g. Everyone realises the value of sincerity.*
2 The **value** of something that you can own, for example a house or a painting, is the amount of money that it is worth. *e.g. What will happen to the value of my property if interest rates fall again?*

3 If you sign or say that something is good **value**, or is **value** for money, you mean that it is worth the money it costs or even a little more. *e.g. The set lunch is good value at five pounds.*
4 If you **value** something, you think that it is important and you appreciate it. *e.g. Which do you value most—wealth or health?*
5 If you **value** something, you decide how much money it is worth. *e.g. Let's suppose we value it at £20,000—will it sell?*

value   199
If you sign or say that something is good **value**, or is **value** for money, you mean that it is worth the money it costs or even a little more. *e.g. The set lunch is good value at five pounds.*

van   74
A **van** is a vehicle bigger than a car but smaller than a lorry that is used for carrying goods. *e.g. A Body Shop van was parked in front of me.*

van   100
A **van** is a vehicle like a large car that is used for carrying people or small quantities of goods. *e.g. My brother borrowed a van to move all the rubbish from the shed.*

vandalise   1031, 1032
Also spelled **vandalize**.
If you **vandalise** something, you deliberately damage it for no good reason. *e.g. All our telephones were vandalised.*

vanish   1534
If something **vanishes**, it moves away quickly

until you can no longer see it. *e.g. I watched the car vanish into the distance.*

vanish   1548
To **vanish** means to disappear suddenly or in a way which cannot be explained. *e.g. On Easter Sunday, Madeleine somehow managed to vanish without trace.*

vanish   1555
1 To **vanish** means to disappear suddenly or in a way which cannot be explained. *e.g. On Easter Sunday, Madeleine somehow managed to vanish without trace.*
2 If something **vanishes**, it ceases to exist. *e.g. A number of protected species vanish each year.*

variation   426, 427, 447
A **variation** is a change in a level, amount or quantity. *e.g. You will see a great variation in the patients' blood pressure: much of this is due to the extent of stress.*

variety   426, 427, 447
1 If something has **variety**, it consists of things which are different from each other. *e.g. Those are the holiday brochures that give you the most variety.*
2 If you have a **variety** of things, you have a number of them of different kinds. *e.g. The college library has a wide variety of books.*

various   426, 427, 447
1 If you refer to **various** things, you mean that there are several different things of the type mentioned. *e.g. There were various questions he wanted to ask.*
2 If a number of things are described as **various**, they are very different from one another. *e.g. His excuses are many and various.*

vase   1455
A **vase** is a jar, usually made of glass or pottery, used for holding cut flowers or as an ornament. *e.g. The vase was made of Waterford crystal.*

vegetable   770
A **vegetable** is a plant such as a cabbage, potato or onion which you can cook and eat. *e.g. Any vegetable is full of vitamins.*

vegetarian   770
Someone who is **vegetarian** or a **vegetarian** does not eat meat or fish. *e.g. She was a strict vegetarian.*

vegetation   1733
Vegetation is plant life in general. *e.g. The Amazon jungle is full of lush vegetation.*

vehicle (small vehicle)   100
See **small vehicle.**

vengeance   48
Vengeance is the act of killing, injuring or

harming someone because they have harmed you. *e.g. I want vengeance for the deaths of my parents and sisters.*

verdict   1329
In a law court, a **verdict** is the decision whether a person is guilty or not guilty. *e.g. The jury in the murder trial gave a verdict of not guilty.*

verger   106
1 A **verger** is a church official who keeps order during services or serves as an usher or sacristan. *e.g. The verger met the congregation at the church gates.*
2 A **verger** is an attendant who carries a rod or staff called a verge as a symbol of a bishop's office. *e.g. The verger came up the aisle preceding the bishop.*

versus   770
1 You use **versus** to say that two ideas or things are opposed, especially when a choice has to be made between them. *e.g. We argued about pipes versus cigarettes.*
2 You use **versus** to say that two people, groups of people, or teams are competing against each other, for example in a sporting event or a case in law. *e.g. The big match tonight is England versus Spain.*

vertigo   323
Vertigo is a feeling of dizziness caused by looking down from a high place. *e.g. Looking down from the top of the Eiffel Tower gave him vertigo.*

very good   213, 220
You sign or say that someone or something is **very good** if you are highly satisfied with what they have done or what you got from them. *e.g. The accommodation at Beamish Hall is very good.*

vibrate   1039, 1040
If something **vibrates**, it shakes with a very slight, quick movement which can often be felt rather than seen. *e.g. I have a bed that vibrates to help me relax.*

vicar   643
A **vicar** is a priest in the Church of England *e.g. The vicar's house is right next to the church.*

video   775
1 **Video** is the recording and showing of television programmes and films using a video recorder, magnetic tapes, and a viewing monitor. *e.g. I know that you use video for teaching these students.*
2 A **video** is a machine which can be used to show video tapes on a viewing monitor and to record television programmes onto magnetic tape. *e.g. Turn off the video: your mother wants to watch television.*

3 A **video** is a film or television programme recorded on magnetic tape for people to watch on a viewing monitor. *e.g. I've seen this video before.*
4 If you **video** something, such as a television programme, you set up a video recorder to record it on magnetic tape as it is being transmitted, in order to watch it later. *e.g. Can you video 'Match of the Day' for me tomorrow, please?*

video cassette   775
A **video cassette** is a plastic container with magnetic tape inside used for recording and playing back sounds and images from real life or television. *e.g. Bring a blank video cassette with you for filming.*

video recorder   775
A **video recorder** or a **video cassette recorder** is a machine which can be used to record television programmes onto magnetic tapes so that people can play them back and watch them later on a viewing monitor. *e.g. John's taped the travel documentary: did you get the video recorder mended?*

video tape   775
Video tape is magnetic tape that is used to record sounds and images from real life or television which you can then play back and watch on a viewing monitor. *e.g. The information can be printed, or put on video tape.*

view   755, 788
1 Your **view** on a particular subject is your opinion about it. *e.g. I've changed my view on this issue.*
2 Your **view** of something is your attitude to it and the way in which you understand it. *e.g. Her view of life is deeply pessimistic.*
3 The **view** from a window or a high place is everything that you can see from it. *e.g. The view was truly breathtaking.*
4 If you have a **view** of something, you can see it. *e.g. I had one last view of the gorge.*

viewer   755, 788
A **viewer** is someone who watches television. *e.g. Many viewers wrote in to complain about this item.*

vinegar   205, 1662
Vinegar is a sharp-tasting liquid, usually made from sour wine, beer or cider, which is used in making things such as chutney or salad dressing, for putting on food such as fish and chips, or for preserving food in. *e.g. Use half a lemon dipped in salt and vinegar.*

violet   1257
Something that is **violet** is of a bluish-purple colour. *e.g. She dyed her dress in blue dye but it came out violet.*

V.I.P.   1298
A **V.I.P.** is someone who is given better

treatment than other people because he or she is famous, influential or important. V.I.P. is an abbreviation for Very Important Person. e.g. *We'll need to get the Chairman here, plus a V.I.P. or two to impress the media.*

virgin 770
A **virgin** is someone who has never had sex. *e.g. Men here still demand that the girls they marry be virgins.*

vision 755
Vision is the ability to see clearly. *e.g. He used to have twenty-twenty vision, but his eyes are older now.*

visit 694, 859, 1607
1 If you **visit** someone or a place, you go to see them and to spend time with them or in that place. *e.g. I went to visit my friends in Edinburgh.*
2 A **visit** is a trip to see and spend time somewhere or with someone in particular. *e.g. My visit to Granma's was like a dream.*

visitor 859
A **visitor** is someone who is visiting a person or place. *e.g. I'm afraid I can't allow your visitor to stay overnight.*

Vistel 1019
Vistel is the particular name of the first text telephone to be marketed in Britain. It is no longer manufactured. *e.g. As soon as I could afford it, I got a Vistel.*

vital 1300
Someone or something that is **vital** is extremely important and necessary in order that something else can take place or succeed. *e.g. A good chairperson is vital to the success of a meeting.*

vodka 770
Vodka is a strong, clear alcoholic drink which is traditionally popular in North Eastern Europe. *e.g. He ordered a vodka with ice.*

voice 365
When someone speaks, their **voice** is the sounds they make which can be heard. *e.g. She had a high-pitched voice.*

volcano 1715
A **volcano** is a mountain which hot melted rock, gas, steam and ash sometimes burst out of, coming from inside the earth. *e.g. He could see the volcano on Manam Island in the distance.*

volcano erupting 1715
When a **volcano** is **erupting**, it throws out lava, ash and steam. *e.g. They stood and watched Mount Etna erupting.*

volleyball 76
Volleyball is a game in which the members of two teams of six hit a large ball with their hands, backwards and forwards over a high net. Points are scored if the ball touches the ground, or if a team fails to keep the ball in play or fails to return it after touching it three times. *e.g. Ernst and Mick are members of the volleyball club.*

volleyball player 76
A **volleyball player** is a person who is a member of a volleyball team. *e.g. Do you need to be tall to be a good volleyball player?*

voluntary 845
1 **Voluntary** work is done by people who are not paid for it, but who do it because they want to. *e.g. A large amount of voluntary work is done by people in the neighbourhood.*
2 A **voluntary** worker is someone who does work, especially socially useful work, without being paid for it, because they want to do it and feel that it needs to be done. *e.g. He was a voluntary assistant in the shelter for homeless people.*

volunteer 845, 1344
1 A **volunteer** is someone who does work, especially socially useful work, for which they are not paid but which they have chosen to do because they feel that the work needs doing. *e.g. Gwen works as a volunteer at Dryburn Hospital.*
2 A **volunteer** is someone who chooses to join the army, navy or air force, especially in wartime, as opposed to one who is forced by law to join. *e.g. He was a volunteer, and a very brave soldier.*
3 If you **volunteer** to do something, you offer to do it without being forced to do it and

without expecting any reward. *e.g. He volunteered to do whatever he could for them.*
4 If you **volunteer** for the army, navy, or air force, you offer to join it, especially in wartime, when you do not have to join by law. *e.g. When World War Two broke out, he volunteered for the Marine Corps.*

vote 413,629
1 A **vote** is a choice made by a particular person or group in a meeting or an election. *e.g. The motion was defeated by 221 votes to 152.*
2 A **vote** is a method of making a decision in which each person involved indicates their own choice, and the choice which most people support is accepted. *e.g. Let's have a vote.*
3 The **vote** is the total number of votes cast or the total number of people who have indicated their choice in an election, or the number or percentage of votes received by a particular group. *e.g. Labour increased its total vote by several million.*
4 If you have the **vote**, you have the legal right to indicate in a political election who you would like to be elected to represent you. *e.g. Women have had the vote for over fifty years.*
5 When you **vote**, you make your choice or state your opinion, especially officially at a meeting or in an election by writing on a piece of paper. *e.g. The students voted to continue the sit-in.*

vote 1344
1 A **vote** is a choice made by a particular person or group in a meeting or an election. *e.g. He gets my vote.*
2 A **vote** is a method of making a decision in which each person involved indicates their own choice, and the choice which most people support is accepted. *e.g. Why do we need a vote?*
3 The **vote** is the total number of votes cast or the total number of people who have indicated their choice in an election, or the number or percentage of votes received by a particular group. *e.g. Scargill got three-quarters of the vote.*

voyeur 1469
A **voyeur** is someone who gets sexual pleasure from secretly watching other people having sex or from watching them undress. *e.g. Stop looking in the window opposite. They'll think you are a voyeur.*

W, w

W
W is the twenty-third letter of the British manual and English alphabets. See page 854.

waddle 1421
To **waddle** means to walk with short, quick steps, swaying slightly from side to side. A person or animal that waddles usually has short legs and a fat body. *e.g. A family of ducks waddled past.*

wad of money 1679
See **money (wad of money)**.

waft 994
If a scent **wafts** or is **wafted** through the air, it

moves gently through the air. *e.g. Her perfume wafted towards me.*

wage   1008, 1558

Your **wage** or **wages** is the amount of money that is regularly paid to you in return for the work you do. *e.g. They stopped work to press for a better wage and improved working conditions.*

waistcoat   1650

A **waistcoat** is a sleeveless piece of clothing with buttons which you wear on the top part of your body. People (usually men) sometimes wear waistcoats under their jackets. *e.g. My grandfather always had a watch in his waistcoat pocket.*

wait   96, 1633

1 If you **wait**, you spend some time, usually doing very little, before something happens. *e.g. He waited patiently for her.*

2 A **wait** is a period of time in which you do very little, before something happens. *e.g. There was a long wait before we were allowed in.*

wait   800

1 If you **wait**, you spend some time standing, without moving much, before something happens. *e.g. I had been prepared to wait, but this was getting ridiculous.*

2 A **wait** is a period of time in which you stand, without moving much, before something happens. *e.g. They told me there might be quite a wait before the next ferry arrived.*

wait   1222, 1435

1 If you **wait**, you spend some time, usually doing very little, before something happens. *e.g. Wait until we sit down.*

2 If you sign or say **just you wait** to someone, you are threatening them or warning them. *e.g. Just you wait! You'll find Steel isn't as gentle as he seems.*

3 If you sign or say **wait** or **just wait** to someone, you are showing how excited, amused, or annoyed you are about something and that you expect it to excite, amuse, or annoy them too. *e.g. Just wait till I tell you what's happened!*

4 If you sign or say that something can **wait**, you mean that it is not important or urgent and so you will deal with it later. *e.g. The dishes can wait.*

wait and see   96

You sign or say **wait and see** to tell someone that they must be patient or that they must not worry about what is going to happen. *e.g. All you can do is wait and see.*

waiter   1011, 1123

A **waiter** is a man who serves people sitting at tables with food and drink, usually as his job. *e.g. The waiter took their order.*

waitress   1011, 1123

A **waitress** is a woman who serves people sitting at tables with food and drink, usually as her job. *e.g. She worked in the restaurant as a waitress.*

wake up   633

1 When you **wake up**, you become conscious again after being asleep. *e.g. When I wake up, the first thing I see is my wife's face.*

2 If you **wake up** or something such as an activity **wakes** you **up**, you become alert and ready to do things after you have been lazy or inactive. *e.g. Those exercises woke me up.*

3 If you **wake up** to something such as a dangerous situation, you become aware of it. *e.g. I've woken up to the fact that CFCs are a danger to this planet.*

Wales   837

1 **Wales** is a country in the west of Great Britain, and a principality, which is part of the United Kingdom. *e.g. Wales has a number of mountainous areas.*

2 The address of the **Wales** Council for the Deaf is: Maritime Offices, Woodland Terrace, Maesycoed, Pontypridd, Mid Glamorgan, CF37 1DZ.

walk   123, 683, 739, 784

1 When you **walk**, you move along, at a fairly slow pace, by putting one foot in front of the other on the ground. *e.g. They walk ten miles to school every day.*

2 A **walk** is a journey which you make by walking. *e.g. He went for a long walk.*

walkabout   739

When a king, queen, or important person goes **walkabout**, or does a **walkabout**, he or she walks through crowds in a public place in order to meet people in an informal way. *e.g. The Pope suddenly decided to go walkabout.*

walk downstairs   806

If you **walk downstairs**, you travel from one floor or level to a lower floor or level, at a fairly slow pace, by putting one foot in front of another on a series of steps. *e.g. Yes, just walk downstairs and it's the fourth door on the left.*

walker   123

A **walker** is a person who walks, especially in the countryside, for pleasure and in order to keep healthy. *e.g. The walkers left the hotel early in the morning.*

walking   123

Walking is the activity or sport of going for long walks. *e.g. Walking holidays have become very popular in recent years.*

walkman   1692

A **Walkman** is a particular radio or cassette player with headphones which people carry around so that they can move from place to place while listening to music, etc., without other people hearing it. *e.g. She bought some batteries for her Walkman.*

walk upstairs   805

If you **walk upstairs**, you travel from one floor or level to a higher floor or level, at a fairly slow pace, by putting one foot in front of another on a series of steps. *e.g. It's hard for me to walk upstairs because of my arthritis.*

walk up steps   1636

If a person or animal **walks up steps**, they travel forwards and away from the ground, at a fairly slow pace, by putting one foot in front of another on a series of flat surfaces at different heights. *e.g. Look at Julie walking up the steps.*

wall   1227

1 A **wall** is one of the vertical sides of a building or room. *e.g. The wall was cracked.*

2 A **wall** is an upright structure made of stone or brick that divides, or marks the boundary of, an area of land. *e.g. We crouched behind the wall and waited.*

wall off   1227

If you **wall off** one area from another, you separate the two areas with a wall. *e.g. We will wall off part of the playground for the infants.*

wallpaper   1347, 1414

1 **Wallpaper** is thick, coloured or patterned paper that is used to decorate the walls of rooms. *e.g. We chose wallpaper with pastel colours.*

2 If someone **wallpapers** a room, they cover the walls with wallpaper. *e.g. We want to wallpaper the bedroom this weekend.*

wally   316

If you call someone a **wally**, you mean that they are stupid or foolish. *e.g. He looked a real wally in that hat.*

walrus   715

A **walrus** is an animal which lives in the sea and looks like a large seal with coarse whiskers and two long teeth pointing down. Walruses are found mainly in the Arctic region. *e.g. A book has been written about the walrus by an Inuit historian.*

want   1281, 1490

1 If you **want** something, you feel a desire to have it or you feel a need for it. *e.g. They really want a holiday.*

2 If you **want** to do something, or **want** something to happen, you have a desire to do it or for it to happen. *e.g. I want to be an actress.*

3 Your **wants** are the things that you want.

e.g. They developed new wants as they grew older: for bicycles, videos and computers.

want (if you want) 1004
If you sign or say **if you want**, you are indicating to someone that they can decide whether or not to do something. *e.g. If you want, we can buy a Chinese take-away.*

war 1120, 1121
1 A **war** is a period of fighting between countries or states. *e.g. They didn't want to lose another war.*
2 If two countries or states **war** with each other, they fight a war with each other. *e.g. India and Pakistan warred in 1965 over Kashmir.*

warden 320
A **warden** is an official who makes sure that certain laws or rules are being obeyed. *e.g. He is a traffic warden.*

ward off 112
If you **ward off** something such as a danger or an illness, you do something to prevent it from affecting you or harming you. *e.g. He placed a cross above his bed to ward off evil spirits.*

warm 1139
1 Something that is **warm** has some heat but not enough to be hot. *e.g. He brought a bowl of warm water.*
2 Clothes and blankets that are **warm** are made of a material such as wool which protects you from the cold. *e.g. I bought him a pair of nice, warm socks.*

warm oneself before a fire 1396
If you **warm yourself before a fire**, you stand near to it so as to absorb some of its heat into your body, especially your hands. *e.g. Pensioners often warm themselves before a fire and forget how much heat is being wasted because the house is not properly insulated.*

warn 308
1 If you **warn** someone about a possible danger or problem, you tell them about it so that they are aware of it. *e.g. I warn you, it will be expensive.*
2 If you **warn** someone not to do something, you advise them not to do it in order to avoid possible danger or punishment. *e.g. I warned him not to lose his temper.*

wary 919, 934
If you are **wary** about something, you are cautious because you are not sure about it, for example because it is a new experience or there may be dangers or problems. *e.g. People are understandably wary of the new government.*

wash 45
1 If you **wash** something, you clean it because

it is dirty, using water and soap or detergent. *e.g. She washes and irons her clothes.*
2 The **wash** is all the clothes, sheets, etc., that are washed together on one occasion, for example once a week. *e.g. I do a weekly wash every Monday.*

wash 1244
1 If you **wash**, you clean part of your body using soap and water. *e.g. You should wash your face—it's dirty.*
2 If you have a **wash**, you clean part of your body using soap and water. *e.g. Children, have a wash quickly, please, and then we'll go.*

washbasin 1374, 1375, 1628
A **washbasin** is a large basin for washing your hands and face. Washbasins are usually fixed to the wall and have taps for hot and cold water. *e.g. The washbasin was cracked.*

wash by hand 45
1 If you **wash** something **by hand** or **handwash** it, you wash it yourself using your hands rather than using a washing machine. *e.g. I'll wash these socks by hand.*
2 If you are advised to **wash** a garment **by hand** or **handwash** it, you should wash it using your hands, as washing it in a washing machine could damage the garment. *e.g. These shirts are not machine-washable. They must be washed by hand.*

washing 45
Washing is a collection of clothes, sheets, etc., which need to be washed or are in the process of being washed or dried. *e.g. My daughter brings her washing home from college every weekend.*

washing machine (front loading) 1230
A **front loading washing machine** is a machine in which you can wash clothes, sheets, etc., which has a door at the front that you open in order to put things into the machine or take them out. *e.g. She bought a front loading washing machine.*

washing machine (top loading) 1622
A **top loading washing machine** is a machine in which you can wash clothes, sheets, etc., which has a lid on the top that you open in order to put things into the machine or take them out. *e.g. They wanted a top loading washing machine because it would be safer with a child around.*

wash one's face with a facecloth/flannel 1244
If you **wash your face with a facecloth** or **a flannel**, you clean your face with a special soft cloth (flannel). *e.g. If you don't wash your face with a flannel, flakes of soap may block your pores.*

wash over 1725
If water from the sea, a lake or river **washes over** its banks or walls, it splashes up and across them. *e.g. The waves grew higher until they washed over the harbour wall.*

waste 1723, 1724
1 If you **waste** time, money, or energy, you use too much of it on something that is not important or necessary. *e.g. You're wasting your time.*
2 If you sign or say that an action or activity is a **waste** of time, money or energy, you mean that it involves using too much time, money or energy, and it is not important or necessary. *e.g. Buying that machine is a waste of money.*
3 **Waste** is the use of too much money or other resources on things that do not need it. *e.g. A committee was set up to avoid future waste of public money.*

wasted 1723, 1724
A **wasted** action is one that is unnecessary. *e.g. My effort to help them was completely wasted: I won't bother next time.*

wasteful 1506
An action that is **wasteful** causes waste, because it uses resources in a careless or inefficient way. *e.g. The wasteful use of scarce resources is a disgrace which shames us all.*

waste of time 1355
If something is a **waste of time**, it takes more time than its importance or value merits. *e.g. Ironing all these shirts has been a waste of time.*

watch 755, 788
1 If you **watch** something, you look at it, usually for a period of time, and pay attention to what is happening. *e.g. A policeman stood watching the shop.*
2 If you **watch** a sports event or something on television, you spend time looking at it, especially when you see it from the beginning to the end. *e.g. When did you last watch a football match?*

watch 829
A **watch** is a small clock which you wear on a strap on your wrist. *e.g. My watch has stopped.*

watch it! 925
You can sign or say **watch it!** in order to warn someone to be careful. *e.g. Watch it! These people are crooks.*

watch out 575
1 If you **watch out**, you are very careful because something unpleasant might happen to you. *e.g. Watch out—or he might stick a knife into you.*
2 If you **watch out** for something or someone, you pay close attention in case it happens or

they appear. *e.g. I told you to watch out for Dad coming back.*

watch over   777
If you **watch over** someone or something, you care for them. *e.g. The women took turns to watch over the children.*

water   943, 1268, 1694
Water is a clear, thin liquid that has no colour, no smell and no taste when it is pure. It falls from clouds as rain and enters rivers and seas. All animals and people need to drink water in order to live. *e.g. We must pay the bill if we want to have water.*

water   981, 994, 1045
1 **Water** is a large amount or area of water, such as a lake. *e.g. As we walked down the hill, the water sparkled in the sun.*
2 **Water** is the surface of an area of water. *e.g. They went snorkelling under the water.*
3 **Water** is a clear, thin liquid that has no colour and no taste when it is pure. It falls from clouds as rain and enters rivers and seas. All animals and people need to drink water in order to live. *e.g. Migrating herds come to drink water early each morning.*

watering can   98
A **watering can** or **watering-can** is a container shaped like a bucket with a long spout on one side and a handle on the other side which you use to water plants. *e.g. The watering can is out by the shed.*

watering can (small watering can)   462
A **small watering can** is a container shaped like a little bucket with a spout on one side and a handle on the other side which you use to water plants. *e.g. We seem to have lost the small watering can—the one I use for the houseplants.*

watermelon   1550
A **watermelon** is a large, round fruit which has a green skin and is pink and juicy inside with a lot of black seeds. *e.g. We ate watermelon for breakfast.*

water off a duck's back   1581
If you sign or say that something that is signed, said or done is **water off a duck's back**, you mean that it has absolutely no effect at all or that nobody takes any notice of it or responds to it. *e.g. My criticisms were water off a duck's back as far as she was concerned.*

water polo   1407
Water polo is a game played in a swimming pool in which two teams of swimmers try to score goals with a ball. *e.g. He is an expert at water polo.*

water polo player   1407
A **water polo player** is someone who plays

water polo. *e.g. You name one famous water polo player, then, if you're so clever.*

waterway   703
A **waterway** is a canal, river or narrow channel of sea which ships or boats can sail along. *e.g. There is a waterway which leads to the harbour.*

water with a small watering can   462
If you **water** plants **with a small watering can**, you pour water from a small watering can into the soil around them to help them grow. *e.g. I'll water them with the small watering can tomorrow, if I can find it; okay?*

water with a watering can   98
If you **water** plants **with a watering can**, you pour water from the watering can over them in order to help them to grow. *e.g. Use the old watering can to water the flowers.*

waves   113, 980, 1045
Waves are raised lines of water on the surface of water, especially the sea, caused by the wind or by tides making the surface of the water rise and fall. *e.g. She stood on the beach watching the waves.*

way   702, 1444
1 If you refer to a **way** of doing something, you are referring to how you can do it. *e.g. This is my favourite way of cooking fish.*
2 The **way** to a particular place is the route that you take in order to get there. *e.g. Do you know the way?*
3 A **way** is also a road; used especially in names. *e.g. Her address is 54, Kingfisher Way.*
4 When you refer to the **way** someone does something, you are referring to the qualities which their action has. *e.g. He hated the way hearing people signed.*

we   540
A signer, speaker or writer uses **we** to refer both to himself or herself and to one or more other people as a group. *e.g. We are members of this club.*

weak   485
1 If something is **weak**, it is likely to break, be destroyed, or fail to work properly. *e.g. These spokes are weak.*
2 If you describe someone as **weak**, you mean that they are easily influenced by other people. *e.g. Nobody could accuse Mandela of being a weak leader.*
3 If an argument or reason is **weak**, it does not convince you that it is right or logical. *e.g. That was a weak answer.*
4 If someone or something is **weak** on a particular subject, they do not have much ability, skill, or information in that subject. *e.g. The book was weak on facts.*

weak   906, 1115, 1117, 1588
1 People who are **weak** do not have very much strength or energy. *e.g. My grandfather was old and weak.*
2 If something is **weak**, it is likely to break, be destroyed, or fail to work properly. *e.g. These spokes are weak.*
3 If you describe someone as **weak**, you mean that they are easily influenced by other people. *e.g. Nobody could accuse Mandela of being a weak leader.*
4 If an argument or reason is **weak**, it does not convince you that it is right or logical. *e.g. That was a weak answer.*
5 If someone or something is **weak** on a particular subject, they do not have much ability, skill, or information in that subject. *e.g. The book was weak on facts.*
6 If you are **weak**, you do not have much importance or influence. *e.g. The union is very weak.*

wealth   1649
Someone who has **wealth** has a large amount of money, property, or valuable possessions. *e.g. A woman of considerable wealth, she married young.*

wealthy   1649
Someone who is **wealthy** has a large amount of money, property or valuable possessions. *e.g. Her parents were wealthy.*

wear   1078, 1083
When you **wear** clothes, you have them on your body or part of your body. *e.g. What are you going to wear to the Garden Party?*

weary   930
If you are **weary**, you are very tired, for example because you have been working hard or because you have lost your enthusiasm for something. *e.g. Weary and dispirited, she opened the door to yet another visitor.*

weather   1073, 1463
The **weather** is the condition of the atmosphere, for example whether it is raining, sunny, hot or windy in an area at a particular time. *e.g. The weather was lovely all week at Bristol.*

wedding   896, 897, 1337
A **wedding** is a marriage ceremony. *e.g. Everybody went to Michelle and Ted's wedding.*

wee   1450
1 Something that is **wee** is not large in physical size, and usually of a size that you could fit between your hands if you held them close together. *e.g. I bought Alison a wee toy for her birthday.*
2 Something that is **wee** does not contain or

occupy a lot of space compared with other things of the same kind. *e.g. Kinlochbervie, which is a wee fishing village, is where my sister lives.*

wee   1574
1 Something or someone that is **wee** is not large in height compared with other things of the same kind, or with other people. *e.g. The other boys in his class can push him around, because he's rather wee.*
2 A **wee** child is a young child. *e.g. Liam was still only a wee bairn when the dictionary was finished.*

week   1048
1 A **week** is a period of seven days, beginning on a Sunday and ending on a Saturday. Some people consider that a week starts on a Monday and ends on a Sunday. *e.g. There was a bad crash last week.*
2 A **week** is the hours that you spend at work during a week. *e.g. Who works a thirty-five hour week anymore?*

week after next   763
The **week after next** refers to the second week from the present, or some time during that week. *e.g. I start my new job the week after next.*

week before   902
The **week before** refers to the week which precedes the one that has been mentioned, or some time during that week. *e.g. I saw him the week before; he'd had his hair cut.*

weekend   1303
A **weekend** is Saturday and Sunday. Sometimes Friday evening is also considered to be part of the weekend. *e.g. I might go skiing this weekend.*

week (every week)   900
Every week is used to describe something that happens or is done each week. *e.g. I'm working at the school for three days every week.*

week (following week)   377, 901
The **following week** refers to the week which comes after the one that has been mentioned, or some time during that week. *e.g. I saw them at the club that Wednesday, but he left her the following week.*

week (in a week's time)   901
You use **in a week's time** to refer to the period which is approximately seven days after today. *e.g. Take my coat to the cleaner's and say I'll be back for it in a week's time.*

week (last week)   381, 902
Last week refers to the week which comes before the present week, or some time during that week *e.g. I spent last week doing part of my interpreting M.A. at Durham.*

week (next week)   377, 901
Next week refers to the week which comes after the present week, or some time during that week *e.g. She will join us next week.*

weekly   900
Weekly is used to describe something that happens, appears, or is done once a week or every week. *e.g. A weekly newspaper is what my children need, not a comic.*

week (one week ago)   381, 902
If you sign or say that something happened **one week ago** or **a week ago**, you mean that it happened approximately seven days before today. *e.g. I left my job one week ago and I have already found another one: it's a miracle!*

weeks (in two weeks' time)   763
You sign or say **in two weeks' time** to refer to the period which is approximately fourteen days after today. *e.g. I won't be here next week, but I'll see you in two weeks' time.*

weeks (two weeks)   748, 763
Two weeks refers to a period of approximately fourteen days. *e.g. Her mother came to stay with her for two weeks.*

weeks (two weeks ago)   750, 764
If you sign or say that something happened **two weeks ago**, you mean that it happened approximately fourteen days before today. *e.g. I went to York two weeks ago.*

weeks (two weeks later)   763
Two weeks later refers to the second week after the one that has been mentioned, or some time during that week. *e.g. Mike bought a new car, but two weeks later it was wrecked.*

weep   453
1 If someone **weeps**, they cry. *e.g. The girl was weeping as she signed goodbye.*
2 If you have a **weep**, you produce tears, usually releasing your feelings when you are unhappy or relieved. *e.g. I think you should have a little weep and then you'll feel much better.*

weigh   1367, 1630
1 If something **weighs** a particular amount, this amount is how heavy it is. *e.g. It's made of steel and weighs ten tons.*
2 If you **weigh** something, you measure how heavy it is using scales. *e.g. The doctor will want to weigh the baby.*
3 If you **weigh** the facts about a situation, you consider them very carefully before you make a decision, especially by comparing the various facts involved. *e.g. We have to weigh the evidence and make a decision.*

weight   1367, 1630
The **weight** of something is its heaviness

which can be measured in units such as kilos, pounds or tons. *e.g. It was twenty five metres long and thirty tons in weight.*

weightlifter   142
A **weightlifter** is a person who does weightlifting. *e.g. The Turkish weightlifter Suleymanoglu should win a gold medal.*

weightlifting   142
1 **Weightlifting** is a sport in which competitors try to lift very heavy weights using certain techniques. The winner is the person who properly lifts the heaviest weight. *e.g. The Russians won the most gold medals in the weightlifting events.*
2 **Weightlifting** is an exercise in which a person lifts weights in order to make their muscles grow bigger or to keep fit. *e.g. The rugby players do weightlifting each morning as part of their general fitness programme.*

weigh up   1367, 1630
1 If you **weigh** things **up**, you consider their importance in relation to each other in order to help you make a decision. *e.g. You have to weigh up in your mind whether to punish him or not.*
2 If you **weigh** someone **up**, you try and find out what they are like and form an opinion of them. *e.g. We chatted for a while, trying to weigh each other up.*

weird   626
Something or someone that is **weird** seems strange and peculiar. *e.g. He is a weird child, always staring at trees and laughing.*

weird   630
If you describe an event or situation as **weird**, you mean it strikes you as unusual or extraordinary in some way. *e.g. That was weird. I didn't expect to see her.*

welcome   1204, 1623
1 If you **welcome** someone, you greet them in a friendly way when they arrive somewhere. *e.g. He moved eagerly towards the door to welcome the Princess Royal.*
2 You sign or say **welcome** to someone when you are greeting them. *e.g. Welcome, welcome: I hope you enjoy your stay in Peking.*
3 If you sign or say that someone is **welcome** in a particular place, you mean that they will be accepted there gladly. *e.g. All members of the public are welcome.*

welfare   661
Welfare is used to describe the activities of an organisation, especially the government, which are concerned with the health, education, living conditions, and financial problems of the people in society. *e.g. Cutbacks in welfare services affect low-income people most.*

welfare officer 661
A **welfare officer** is a person whose job it is to give help and advice to people concerning their rights and responsibilities in society; for example, to people who are very poor or who live in bad conditions. *e.g. His uncle was a welfare officer with the Red Cross.*

well 1382
You sign or say **well** when you are hesitating or about to sign or say something. *e.g. Well, thank you for explaining the problem to me.*

well 1489, 1494
If you are **well**, you are healthy and not ill. *e.g. After my operation last month, I'm feel well.*

well-dressed 230
Someone who is **well-dressed** is wearing smart or elegant clothes. *e.g. She is a well-dressed woman.*

wellingtons 148
Wellingtons or **wellington boots** are long, rubber boots which you wear to keep your feet dry. *e.g. The children were asked to bring their wellingtons to school.*

well (may as well) 198
If you sign or say that you **may as well** or **might as well** do something, you mean that you have nothing better to do, and don't object to doing it. *e.g. I might as well go to the party.*

well-off 1649
Someone who is **well-off** is rich enough to be able to do and buy most of the things that they want. *e.g. She's quite well-off, isn't she?*

Welsh 837
1 Someone or something that is **Welsh** belongs to or relates to Wales or its people. *e.g. There is, in fact, no such thing as Welsh Sign Language, although there are obviously specific Welsh regional signs.*
2 **Welsh** is one of the two official spoken languages of Wales. *e.g. The word for Wales in Welsh is 'Cymru'.*
3 You can refer to people from Wales, or a particular group of people from Wales, as the **Welsh**. *e.g. The Welsh are very proud of the many fine rugby players that have played for their national team.*

west 1048
1 **West** is the direction which you look towards in order to see the sun set. *e.g. The next big town is fifty miles west of here.*
2 The **west** is the part of a place or country which is towards the west. *e.g. He lived in the west of Ireland.*

wet 1549
1 If something is **wet**, it has absorbed or is covered in water, rain, sweat, or another liquid. *e.g. The grass is wet.*
2 If the weather is **wet**, it is raining. *e.g. It was a wet day.*
3 If something such as paint, ink, or cement is **wet**, it is not yet dry or hard. *e.g. Beware of the wet paint on the walls.*

we (two) 760
A person uses **we two** or **we** to refer to him or herself and another person. *e.g. The other four went ahead while we two stayed at the farm.*

what? 306
1 You use **what?** in questions when you are asking for information about something. *e.g. What is your name?*
2 You sign or say **what?** to ask someone to sign or say something again because you did not understand it properly. *e.g. 'Do you want another coffee?' — 'What?' — 'Do you want another coffee?'*
3 You sign or say **what?** to express surprise or disbelief. *e.g. 'Apparently, Chris Waddle's going to play for Gateshead.' — 'What?!'*
4 You can use **what?** if you miss part of what has just been signed or said and you want someone to repeat it for you. *e.g. 'What?' — 'He's just explaining section three: I'll tell you later.'*
5 You can sign or speak about **what** something is, or **what** happens, when you are informing somebody of a fact. *e.g. Now I'll hand you over to Claire who will explain what to do next.*

what do you want? 1274
You use **what do you want?** to ask for information about someone's needs or wishes. *e.g. Come on, what do you want? I haven't got all day!*

what for? 469
You use **what for?** when asking questions about the reasons for something. *e.g. You want to know my address? What for?*

what's the matter? 910
You sign or say **what's the matter?**, or **is anything the matter?**, when you think someone has a problem and you want information about it. *e.g. What's the matter with your leg? You're limping.*

what's the point? 469, 1274
You use **what's the point?** when asking the reasons for a course of action which you do not agree with or are not happy about. *e.g. You want me to take it off again? What's the point?*

what's up? 1274
You use **what's up?** when you think someone has a problem and you want to know what it is. *e.g. What's up with you? Don't look so upset.*

what's wrong? 910
You sign or say **what's wrong?** when you think someone has a problem and you want information about it. *e.g. You look so sad: what's wrong?*

what time? 369, 410
1 You use **what time?** to get information about the precise or approximate hour and minute it is at present, or when something will happen in future. *e.g. What time does the train to Manchester leave?*
2 You use **what time** to specify or refer to the time at which something happens. *e.g. I'm afraid I don't know what time your exam starts.*

wheel 503
A **wheel** is a circular object which turns round on a rod attached to its centre. Wheels are fixed underneath things such as cars, bicycles, and trains so that they can move along. *e.g. The train started, its wheels squealing against the metal tracks.*

wheelbarrow 117
A **wheelbarrow** is a small cart that is used in the garden for carrying things such as plants, soil, or bricks. A wheelbarrow is usually shaped like an open box, with one wheel at the front, two legs at the back, and two handles to lift and push it with. *e.g. She bought a wheelbarrow at the garden centre.*

when? 997
1 You use **when?** to ask questions about the time at which things happen. *e.g. When are you getting married?*
2 You use **when** to refer to the time at which something happens. *e.g. Ask her when the trouble first started.*

where? 1030
1 You use **where?** to ask questions about the place something is in, or is coming from, or is going to. *e.g. Where's Jane? Is she in the car?*
2 You use **where** when you are referring to the place in which something is situated or happens. *e.g. I don't know where the station is.*
3 You use **where** when you are referring to or asking about a situation, a stage in something, or an aspect of something. *e.g. Bryan wouldn't know where to start.*

where from? 1203
1 If you ask **where** someone or something is **from**, you want to know where they live or usually are to be found. *e.g. I'm from London; where are you from?*
2 If you ask **where** someone or something is **from**, you want to know where they were born, made, created or developed. *e.g. Where's this recipe from?*

which? 933
1 You use **which?** to ask questions that have two or more possible answers or alternatives.

e.g. Which is her room?
2 You use **which** to refer to a choice between two or more possible answers or alternatives. *e.g. I don't know which country he played for.*

whichever   938
You use **whichever** to indicate that it does not matter which of several possible alternatives are chosen. *e.g. You can have whichever desk you prefer.*

which of two?   948
1 You use **which of two?** to ask questions when there are two possible answers or alternatives. *e.g. Which is her room? 941 or 942?*
2 You use **which of two?** to refer to a choice between two alternatives. *e.g. I don't know which county he played for, Essex or Derbyshire—anyway, it was one of those two.*

while ago   1250
A **while ago** is a point in time or a period of time that has recently occurred. *e.g. I saw Alice go out a while ago.*

while (in a while)   300
If you sign or say that something will happen **in a while**, you mean that it will happen after a period or interval of time. *e.g. I'll join you at the pub in a while.*

while (once in a while)   299
If something happens **once in a while**, it happens occasionally but not very often. *e.g. Once in a while, she'd give me some lilacs to take home.*

whisk   262
If you **whisk** eggs or cream, you stir air into them very quickly with a special kitchen tool used for this purpose (a whisk) or a similar instrument. *e.g. Whisk all the eggs together.*

whiskers   899
The **whiskers** of an animal are the long, stiff hairs that grow near its mouth. *e.g. The lion licked and groomed its whiskers.*

whiskey   650
Whiskey is a strong alcoholic drink made from grain such as barley or rye, distilled according to Irish or American traditions. *e.g. When we've finished this thing, we'll sit down and drink enough whiskey to forget the bad times.*

whisky   650
Whisky is a strong alcoholic drink made from grain such as barley or rye, distilled according to Scottish tradition. *e.g. A Scotsman never drinks his whisky with ice, remember?*

whisper   1579
1 When you **whisper** something, you say something to someone very quietly, using only your breath and not your throat, so that other people cannot hear what you are saying. *e.g. I whisper the news to my sister.*
2 A **whisper** is a very quiet voice in which you use your breath and not your throat. *e.g. She spoke in a whisper.*

whistle   641
A **whistle** is a small, metal tube which you blow in order to produce a loud sound and attract someone's attention. *e.g. The guard blew his whistle and waved his green flag.*

white   475, 541
1 Something that is **white** is of the lightest colour that there is, the colour of snow or milk. *e.g. A woman dressed in white came up to me.*
2 Someone who is **white** has a pale skin. *e.g. They had never seen a white person before.*

whittle down   1395
To **whittle down** something, or **whittle** something **down**, means to make it smaller or less effective over a period of time. *e.g. We can't whittle down the operation any further or it will disappear completely.*

whizz   158
If you are a **whizz** at something, you are very good or skilled at it. *e.g. She's a whizz at electronics.*

who?   494
1 You use **who?** when you are asking questions about someone's name or identity. *e.g. Who are you?*
2 You use **who** when you are referring to information about a person's name or identity. *e.g. It's not important who I am.*

whole   1104
1 If you refer to the **whole** of something, you mean all of it. *e.g. The whole of Europe will be affected by this war.*
2 A **whole** is a single thing which contains several different parts. *e.g. The earth's weather system is an integrated whole.*
3 If you refer to something **as a whole**, you are referring to it generally and as a single unit. *e.g. Is that just in India, or Asia as a whole?*

why?   306, 368, 469
1 You use **why?** when you are asking questions about the reason for something. *e.g. Why did you do it?*
2 You use **why** when you are referring to the reason for something. *e.g. He wondered why she had come.*

wicked   904, 914, 918, 956
1 Something or someone that is **wicked** is very bad in a way that is deliberately immoral or harmful to other people. *e.g. It was very clear to him that he had done something wicked.*
2 Something or someone that is **wicked** is very dangerous and may cause physical harm. *e.g. Hyenas have a wicked and violent temper.*
3 If you describe something such as a situation as **wicked**, you mean that it is unpleasant or upsetting. *e.g. The prices there are wicked.*

wide   1454
You use **wide** when you refer to how much something measures from one side or edge to the other. *e.g. How wide is the space between the desks?*

widespread   1044
If something is **widespread**, it exists or happens over a large area or to a great extent. *e.g. Pollution is widespread in Britain.*

width   1454
The **width** of something is the distance that it measures from one side or edge to the other. *e.g. The table is two metres in width.*

wife   897
A man's **wife** is the woman he is married to. *e.g. His wife always had to wait for him to get ready.*

wild   1196
If you are **wild**, you are extremely angry. *e.g. When he came home late again, I was wild, and told him so.*

will   21
If you sign or say that you **will** do something, you mean that you intend to do it or are willing to do it. *e.g. I will go to school.*

will do   198, 218
See **do (will do)**.

will not   25
If you sign or say that someone **will not** or **won't** do something, you mean that they cannot do it, refuse to do it, or do not intend to do it. *e.g. Alison will not be at the meeting tonight.*

wimp   485
A **wimp** is someone who lacks confidence and is rather timid and weak. *e.g. Henry is such a wimp. He never speaks up for himself.*

win   255, 1155, 1543
1 If you **win** a fight, a game, or an argument, you defeat the person who you are fighting, playing against, or arguing with. *e.g. Their side will win if we're not careful.*
2 To **win** an election or a competition means to do better than anyone else involved. *e.g. Deborah planned to win a convincing victory at the election.*
3 If you **win** a prize or a medal, you get it because you have been lucky or successful at something. *e.g. Mum might win a microwave oven in a competition.*

4 A **win** is a victory for one participant in a fight, game or argument, and a defeat for the other. *e.g. Another win and we'll be out of sight!*

wind   1073
A **wind** is a current of air that is moving across the earth's surface. *e.g. It was a warm wind.*

wind blowing   1073
If the **wind** is **blowing** or **blows**, currents of air move across the earth's surface. *e.g. By heck, there's a wind blowing up on the moors tonight.*

windfall   1194
A **windfall** is a sum of money that you receive unexpectedly or by luck. *e.g. He had a windfall from the football pools.*

window   441, 575, 581, 1351
A **window** is a space made in a wall or in the side of a vehicle, which usually has glass or a similar material in it so that light can come in and you can see out. *e.g. The kitchen window was broken.*

window cleaner   582
A **window cleaner** is a person who washes the panels of glass in the sides of buildings. *e.g. My daughter wants to be a window cleaner.*

wind someone up   52
1 If you **wind someone up**, you sign or say untrue things in order to trick them. *e.g. Are you winding me up?*
2 If you **wind someone up**, you deliberately sign or say things which annoy them. *e.g. He's always winding his teachers up.*

windy   1073
If it is **windy**, the wind is blowing a lot. *e.g. It was a windy spring day.*

wine   945
1 **Wine** is an alcoholic drink which is made from grapes and is usually described as either red, rosé or white. To make wine, grapes are fermented with water and sugar. *e.g. I like white wine: red wine gives me a hangover.*
2 **Wine** is an alcoholic drink which you can make from any fruit or vegetable by fermenting it with water and sugar. *e.g. John's home-made quince wine tastes excellent.*

wings   1635
The **wings** of a bird or an insect are the two parts of its body that it uses for flying. *e.g. The bird's wings were broken.*

winter   119
1 **Winter** is the season between autumn and spring. In the winter, the weather is usually colder than during the other seasons, and many trees and plants have lost their leaves.

e.g. It was a terrible winter.
2 **Winter** means relating to or characteristic of winter. *e.g. As you can see, the artist has used winter colours such as grey and dark blue to represent the harshness of the season.*

wintry   119
Something that is **wintry** has features that are typical of winter. *e.g. It was a wintry day in early March.*

wipe out   1313
To **wipe out** a place or a group of people means to destroy them completely, especially suddenly or violently. *e.g. The policy of ethnic cleansing has been used to wipe out many of the villagers.*

wire   888
1 **Wire** or **a wire** is a long, thin piece of metal that is used to fasten things or to make things like fences, cages and baskets. *e.g. You can mend it with pliers and a length of wire.*
2 A **wire** is a long, thin piece of metal that carries electricity or electrical signals. *e.g. He touched a wire and was immediately electrocuted.*

wireless   1178
A **wireless** is the same as a radio. *e.g. They always announce the results on the wireless.*

wisdom   166
1 **Wisdom** is a person's ability to use their experience and knowledge in order to make sensible and reasonable decisions or judgements. *e.g. You underestimate your parents' wisdom.*
2 **Wisdom** is the store of knowledge that a society or culture has collected over a long period of time. *e.g. He had access to the wisdom and experience of generations.*

wise   166
1 Someone who is **wise** is able to use their experience and knowledge in order to make sensible and reasonable decisions or judgements. *e.g. He's a wise man.*
2 If you sign or say that a person would be **wise** to do something, you are advising them to do it or suggesting that they should do it, because it is the most sensible and reasonable action or decision in a particular situation. *e.g. You would be wise to accept the offer.*

wish   669
1 If you **wish** that something were the case, you would like it to be the case, even though you know that it is impossible or unlikely. *e.g. I often wish that I were really wealthy.*
2 If you make a **wish**, or **wish** for something, you express your desire for something to yourself in your imagination. In fairy stories, wishes often come true by magic. *e.g. 'What is your wish?' asked the fairy.*

wish   1281, 1490, 1542
1 A **wish** is a longing or desire for something, often something that is difficult to obtain or achieve. *e.g. She told me of her wish to leave the convent.*
2 If you **wish** to do something, you want to do it. *e.g. They wish to marry.*
3 If you **wish** that something were the case, you would like it to be the case, even though you know that it is unlikely or impossible. *e.g. I often wish that John Major were the first Deaf Prime Minister.*

wish (if you wish)   1004
If you sign or say **if you wish**, you are indicating to someone that they can decide whether or not to do something. *e.g. We could go to the Science Museum, if you wish.*

wish something had not happened   1036
If you **wish** that **something had not happened**, you would like it not to have been the case, and the fact that it did happen makes you feel unhappy, dissatisfied or worried. *e.g. I wish I hadn't sent her the letter—it's so embarrassing!*

withdraw   1159
If you **withdraw** money from a bank account or savings account, you take it out of the account in order to spend it or use it. *e.g. You must present your cheque card when you withdraw any money.*

withdraw   1632
1 When troops **withdraw** or are **withdrawn**, they leave the place where they are fighting or where they are based. *e.g. We longed to see the force withdraw.*
2 If you **withdraw** from an activity, you decide that you will no longer take part in it. *e.g. Marsha decided to withdraw from the argument.*
3 If you **withdraw** a remark or statement, you sign or say that you wish to change or deny it. *e.g. I want to withdraw a statement I made earlier on.*
4 If someone is **withdrawn**, they prefer to be alone and do not want to communicate with other people. *e.g. The child was quiet and withdrawn.*

withdrawal   1632
1 The **withdrawal** of something is the act or process of removing it or taking it away. *e.g. They are negotiating the withdrawal of troops.*
2 The **withdrawal** of a remark or statement is the act of signing or saying formally that you wish to change or deny it. *e.g. Please arrange for the withdrawal of their invitations.*
3 Your **withdrawal** from an activity or an organisation is your decision to stop taking part in it. *e.g. There are still people who demand our withdrawal from the Common Market.*

4 Withdrawal is behaviour in which someone prefers to be alone and does not want to communicate with other people. *e.g. She has spells of sulking, withdrawal and vindictiveness.*

withdrawal of money 1558
A **withdrawal of money** is an amount of money that you take from your bank account or savings account. *e.g. It is not the bank's policy to deduct interest if you make a withdrawal of less than £1,000.*

withhold 1632
If you **withhold** something that someone wants, you do not let them have it. *e.g. I decided to withhold the information until later.*

without 1518
1 If you do one thing **without** doing another thing, you do not do the other thing. *e.g. 'No,' she said, without explaining further.*
2 **Without** someone means not in their company or not living or working with them. *e.g. Her husband felt he couldn't face life without her.*

witness 326, 1344
1 A **witness** is a person who sees an event such as an accident and is able to tell other people what happened. *e.g. The witness told reporters what she had seen.*
2 A **witness** is a person who appears in a court of law to tell what he or she knows about a crime or other event. *e.g. Other witnesses were called to the stand.*

witness someone's signature 721
If you **witness someone's signature** on a document, you sign your name on it to confirm that he or she was the person who actually signed it. *e.g. The lawyer asked her to witness their signature.*

wobble 1040
If a person or thing **wobbles**, they make small movements from side to side because they are loose or unsteady. *e.g. You're making the table wobble with your foot.*

wolf 1094
A **wolf** is a wild animal that looks like a large dog and that kills and eats other animals. Wolves live in groups, usually in forests. *e.g. The wolf had left its tracks in the snow.*

Wolverhampton 1094
1 **Wolverhampton** is a town in the West Midlands. *e.g. I have written to the Visual Language Centre at Wolverhampton University for information on their sign language courses.*
2 The address of the Association for the Deaf in **Wolverhampton** is: 38 Rupert Street, Wolverhampton, WV3 9NS.

woman 339
1 A **woman** is an adult female human being. *e.g. We had one woman teaching us and three men, which was most unusual.*
2 You can refer to women in general as **woman**. *e.g. Man's inhumanity to woman is a common theme of lesbian art.*

wonder 313
If you **wonder** about something you do not know or understand, you think about it and try to guess or understand more about it. *e.g. I am beginning to wonder why we invited them.*

wonder 1472
A **wonder** is something or someone that amazes people and makes them feel great admiration. *e.g. These machines are among the wonders of modern technology.*

wonderful 960, 1472, 1710
1 If you describe something as **wonderful**, you mean that it makes you feel very happy and pleased. *e.g. We had a wonderful holiday.*
2 If you describe something as **wonderful**, you mean that it is very impressive or successful. *e.g. The doctor did a wonderful job on Rob's leg.*

won't 25
Won't is the usual spoken form of will not. It appears in writing usually as an informal usage or abbreviation. See **will not.**

wood 195, 1357
Wood is the material which forms the trunks of trees. It can be used to make things such as furniture, or it can be burned to provide heating or to cook food. *e.g. I just love bowls made of wood, especially elm and yew.*

wood 1026
A **wood** is a large area of trees growing near each other. You can refer to a large wood as **the woods.** *e.g. Pooh Bear lived in a wood.*

wooden 195
An object that is **wooden** is made of wood. *e.g. She kept her money in a wooden box.*

woodpecker 639
A **woodpecker** is a bird with a long, sharp beak that makes holes in tree trunks in order to eat the insects which live there. *e.g. He was sure a woodpecker lived in the tree.*

woodwork 134
Woodwork is the activity of making things out of wood, especially when this is done skilfully or artistically. *e.g. He taught woodwork at Northern Counties School.*

wool 1107
1 **Wool** is the hair that grows on sheep and on

some other animals. *e.g. Small bundles of wool had snagged on the fence.*
2 **Wool** is a material made from animals' wool. It is used for making things such as clothes, blankets and carpets. *e.g. She bought a hat made from wool.*

woollen 1107
Woollen clothes or materials are made from wool or from a mixture of wool and artificial fibres. *e.g. You should wear long woollen socks in winter.*

words (eat one's words) 57
If you sign or say that someone has to **eat their words**, you mean that they have to admit, often in humiliating circumstances, that they are wrong about something they have signed or said in the past. *e.g. She said I would never learn sign language. She had to eat her words when I passed my Stage Three C.A.C.D.P. exam.*

words (swallow one's words) 57
If you sign or say that someone has to **swallow their words**, you mean that they have to admit, often in humiliating circumstances, that they are wrong about something they have signed or said in the past. *e.g. I'd been proven wrong and had to swallow my words.*

work 1345, 1354
1 People who **work** have a job which they are paid to do. *e.g. He wanted to work in a bank.*
2 People who have **work**, or who are in **work**, have a job which they are paid to do. *e.g. Many people who have work are nevertheless worried about their future.*
3 When you **work**, you do tasks or duties which are your job or your responsibility, or which you feel need to be done. *e.g. He worked a ten hour day.*
4 **Work** is the tasks which your job involves, or which you do because they need to be done. *e.g. A housewife's work can take ten or twelve hours a day.*

worker 1345
1 A **worker** is a person who is employed by another person or organisation in a particular type of industry or business, and who has no responsibility for managing the industry or business. *e.g. The dispute affected relations between management and workers.*
2 If someone is a good **worker**, a hard **worker**, etc., they work well, hard, et cetera. *e.g. My husband was a hard worker, given the opportunity.*
3 A **worker** is also someone who does a particular kind of job. *e.g. A series of experiments by a Spanish research worker have provided some of the answers.*

work one's guts out 367
If you **work your guts out**, you work as hard

as you can, to the point of being exhausted. *e.g. He made us work our guts out to finish on time.*

world 1418

1 The **world** is the planet we live on. *e.g. There is a growth in world population.*

2 The **world** also refers to all the societies, institutions, and ways of life of people living on this planet. *e.g. The world is now becoming more aware of environmental issues.*

3 **World** is used to describe someone or something that is one of the best or most important of its kind in the world. *e.g. This book is a world classic.*

4 Someone's **world** is the life they lead, the people they have contact with, and the things they experience. *e.g. The world of Deaf people is one which many hearing parents of deaf children are very keen to learn about.*

5 A particular **world** is a particular field of activity and the people involved in it. *e.g. They are well-known names in the sports world.*

6 You can refer to a particular group of living things as the animal **world**, the insect **world**, et cetera. *e.g. Next week's look into the animal world will be at seven o'clock.*

7 A **world** is another planet. *e.g. The film is set on an alien world.*

world-wide 1638

World-wide or **worldwide** is used to describe something that exists or happens throughout the world. *e.g. There was a world-wide economic depression in 1930.*

worm 571, 593

1 A **worm** is a small animal with a long thin body, no bones and no legs, which lives in the soil. *e.g. The garden was dry, but the bird could still feel a worm in the soil.*

2 A **worm** is an insect such as a beetle or moth when it is at a very early stage of its life. These worms often cause damage by eating things. *e.g. All the apples had worms in them.*

3 If animals or people have **worms**, they are ill because they have worms living as parasites in their intestines. These worms enter their body for example when they eat food that is not clean, and often cause disease. *e.g. He wiggled about like a dog with worms.*

worn-out 930, 1555

Someone who is **worn-out** or **worn out** is extremely tired after hard work or a difficult or unpleasant experience. *e.g. You look worn-out after your trip abroad.*

worried 1144

If you are **worried**, you feel uncomfortable or slightly sick because you are anxious about something that might happen. e.g. There was *no news for hours after the accident and I began to feel worried.*

worry 567, 1134

1 If you **worry**, you keep thinking about problems that you have or about unpleasant things that might happen. *e.g. I worry about him all the time.*

2 **Worry** is the state or feeling of anxiety and unhappiness caused by the problems that you have or by thinking about unpleasant things that might happen. *e.g. Worry and stress bring people back to church.*

3 A **worry** is a problem which causes anxiety or unhappiness. *e.g. Money is indeed a worry to her.*

worry 1144

1 If you **worry**, you feel uncomfortable or slightly sick because you are anxious about something that might happen. *e.g. Standing at the top of the roller-coaster, I start to worry.*

2 **Worry** is a feeling of discomfort or slight sickness you get when you are anxious about something that might happen. *e.g. Worry began to gnaw at Judd's vitals: just what lay in the spaceship?*

worse 927

1 Something that is **worse** is further away from being good than it was before. *e.g. Tom's driving is worse than ever.*

2 Something that is **worse** is bad in comparison to something else of a similar kind. *e.g. This one's worse: the paintwork on that one is nicer.*

3 If someone who is ill gets **worse**, they become more ill than before. *e.g. Her mother got worse, so they took her to hospital.*

worsen 926, 927

If a situation **worsens**, or if something **worsens** it, it becomes more difficult, unpleasant, or unacceptable. *e.g. The weather will worsen during the afternoon, and the rain will be heavy by nightfall.*

worship 512

If you **worship** someone or something, you love them or admire them very much, often with the result that you cannot see faults or weaknesses in them. *e.g. Vera worshipped her father, although nobody else could stand him.*

worship 1442

1 If you **worship** a God, you show your respect to the God, by signing or saying your prayers. *e.g. I knelt down and worshipped the Lord.*

2 If you **worship** someone or something, you love or admire them very much. *e.g. The little boy really did worship his brother.*

3 **Worship** is respect for a God, which you show, for example, by saying prayers. *e.g. St. Godric's Church is my place of worship.*

4 **Worship** is love or admiration for someone or something. *e.g. She became an object of worship.*

worship 1461

1 If you **worship** a God, you show your respect to the God, by signing or saying your prayers. *e.g. I knelt down and worshipped the Lord.*

2 If you **worship** someone or something, you love or admire them very much. *e.g. The little boy really did worship his brother.*

3 'Your **worship**' and 'his **worship**' are respectful ways of addressing and referring to a magistrate or a mayor. *e.g. His worship adjourned the court until after lunch.*

4 **Worship** is respect for a god, which you show, for example, by saying prayers. *e.g. St. Godric's Church is my place of worship.*

5 **Worship** is love or admiration for someone or something. *e.g. She became an object of worship.*

worst 923

Something that is the **worst** of its kind is bad in comparison with all others. *e.g. That's the worst BSL interpretation I've ever seen.*

worth 131, 1050, 1524

1 If something is **worth** a particular amount of money, it can be sold for that amount or is considered to have that value in terms of money. *e.g. A two-bedroomed house in this area is worth £50,000 now.*

2 If you refer to a particular amount of money's **worth** of something, you mean the quantity of it that you can buy for that amount of money. *e.g. They stole fifty thousand dollars' worth of equipment.*

3 If you sign or say that something is **worth** doing, **worth** having, or **worth** it, you mean that it is enjoyable or useful, and therefore a good thing to do or have. *e.g. The film's worth seeing.*

would 21

If you sign or say that you **would** do something, you mean that you are willing to do it. *e.g. I would stay if asked.*

would not 25

If you sign or say that you **would not** or **wouldn't** do something, you mean that you refused to do it. *e.g. He would not give up.*

wouldn't 25

Wouldn't is the usual spoken form of would not. It appears in writing usually as an informal usage or abbreviation. See **would not**.

wow 989

You sign or say **wow** when you are very impressed by or pleased with something. *e.g. Have you watched Nigel Mansell driving? Wow, it's hair raising!*

wreck 1031, 1032

1 If you **wreck** something, you break it or destroy it completely. *e.g. I wrecked a good video by not following the instructions properly.*

2 If you **wreck** something, you spoil it completely. *e.g. I'm sorry if I wrecked your weekend.*

3 If you sign or say that someone is a **wreck**, you mean that they are very unhealthy or exhausted. *e.g. If you work like this, you'll end up a wreck.*

wrestler 1736
A **wrestler** is someone who wrestles as a sport. *e.g. All of the children wanted to meet the Deaf wrestler Alan Kilby.*

wrestling 1736
Wrestling is a sport in which two people fight and try to win by throwing and pinning their opponent to the ground. *e.g. She loved to watch wrestling on television, especially when Giant Haystacks was on.*

wring someone's neck 1103
If you sign or say that you could or would **wring someone's neck**, you mean you are very angry with them. *e.g. I'd gladly wring his neck, he's so argumentative.*

wristwatch 829
A **wristwatch** is a small clock which is attached to a strap that you wear round your wrist. *e.g. We gave him a gold wristwatch when he retired.*

write 614, 628
1 When you **write** something on a surface, usually a piece of paper, you use something such as a pen or pencil to produce marks, letters, or numbers on the surface. *e.g. They were learning to read and write.*

2 When you **write** something such as a book, poem, article, essay, or piece of music, you create it and record it on paper or perhaps on a computer. *e.g. I have been asked to write a biography of Dylan Thomas.*

3 If you **write**, you create books, stories, or articles, usually for publication. *e.g. I always felt that I wanted to write.*

4 When you **write** to someone or **write** them a letter or a note, you give them information, ask them something, or express your feelings in a letter or a note. *e.g. She wrote me a letter from Singapore.*

5 If you **write** or **write out** something such as a cheque, receipt, or prescription, you put the necessary information on it and usually sign it. *e.g. The doctor wrote a prescription for me but I couldn't read his handwriting.*

write on a blackboard with chalk 615
When you **write on a blackboard with chalk**, you use a stick of soft, white or coloured rock (chalk) to produce marks, letters, or numbers on a dark-coloured surface made of slate or similar material (blackboard). *e.g. At teacher training college, they show you*

how to write on a blackboard with chalk so that your letters are clear and neat.

write on an upright surface 615
You **write on an upright surface** if you make marks on a board, a flip chart or a wall with a pen or a stick of chalk. *e.g. It would be best if the students could write on an upright surface, and then they wouldn't have to keep bending down.*

writer 628
1 A **writer** is a person who writes books, stories, or articles as a job. *e.g. She wanted to become a writer.*

2 The **writer** of a particular article, report, story, etc., is the person who wrote it. *e.g. On what sources did the original writers base their account?*

write with a ballpoint pen/biro/pen/pencil 614
When you **write with a ballpoint pen**, a **biro**, a **pen** or a **pencil**, you hold and move such an implement so that the ink or lead is transferred from the metal ball or point onto paper or a similar surface. *e.g. My grandfather taught me how to write with a pen, like they used to do in his day.*

written paper 1307
1 A **written paper** is part of an exam in which you have to write your answers (as opposed to signing or speaking them). *e.g. The conversation lasts half an hour and the written paper is three hours.*

2 A **written paper** is an essay produced as an academic text which may be published in a book or journal or used as a discussion document. *e.g. I've cut this from the signed lecture, but it will be included in the written paper.*

written proposal 349, 1307
A **written proposal** is a suggested plan, which is put forward as a document for people to think about and decide upon. *e.g. A written proposal suggesting a change of policy was circulated before the meeting.*

written record 720
If you make a **written record** of something, you record information about it in words on paper, and keep it so that you can refer to it later. *e.g. Do you have a written record of your tutoring work?*

written report 349, 1307
1 A **written report** is an account of something that has happened which is produced as a document. *e.g. When you get back, we need a written report on everything that was discussed at the conference.*

2 A **written report** is an official document which is prepared by a committee or other

group of people who have been working on a particular subject. *e.g. The club committee presented its final written report, recommending rules to prevent discrimination.*

written statement 349, 720, 1307
1 A **written statement** is a specially prepared list of costs and bills for something, showing the total that needs to be paid. *e.g. The lawyer sent them his written statement.*

2 A **written statement** is a document recording someone's formal comments. *e.g. Right sir, we'll just need to take a written statement, then.*

wrong 436
1 Something that is **wrong** is not correct or not suitable. *e.g. I'm afraid I'll make the wrong decision.*

2 If you are **wrong** about something, what you sign, say or think about it is not correct. *e.g. I had to admit the possibility that I might be wrong.*

wrong 910
1 If there is something **wrong**, there is something unsatisfactory about the situation or thing that you are discussing. *e.g. The front door was unlocked: something was wrong.*

2 Something that is **wrong** is not correct or not suitable. *e.g. I'm afraid I'll make the wrong decision.*

3 If something you do is **wrong**, it is bad or immoral. *e.g. I know it was wrong of me to kick the dog, but he was getting on my nerves.*

4 **Wrong** is used to refer to actions that are bad or immoral. *e.g. Parents try to teach their children right from wrong.*

wrong 920
1 If you are **wrong** about something, what you sign, say or think about it is not correct. *e.g. I had to admit the possibility that I might be wrong.*

2 If something you do is **wrong**, it is bad or immoral. *e.g. I never did anything wrong until that fateful day.*

wrong 998
1 If there is something **wrong**, there is something unsatisfactory about the situation or thing that you are discussing. *e.g. The front door was unlocked: something was wrong.*

2 Something that is **wrong** is not correct or not suitable. *e.g. I'm afraid I'll make the wrong decision.*

3 If you are **wrong** about something, what you sign, say or think about it is not correct. *e.g. I had to admit the possibility that I might be wrong.*

4 If something you do is **wrong**, it is bad or immoral. *e.g. I know it was wrong of me to kick the dog, but he was getting on my nerves.*

5 **Wrong** is used to refer to actions that are bad or immoral. *e.g. Parents try to teach their children right from wrong.*

X, x Y, y Z, z

X
X is the twenty-fourth letter of the British manual and English alphabets. See page 854.

Xerox 1545
1 A **Xerox** is a machine that makes photographic copies of pieces of paper which have writing, drawing or printing on them. *e.g. Who's got the key to the Xerox room?*
2 A **Xerox** is a copy of a document made using a Xerox machine. *e.g. Do you have a Xerox of the diagram you sent?*
3 If you **Xerox** a document, you make a copy of it using a Xerox machine. *e.g. That morning, Bernstein had Xeroxed copies of notes from reporters at the scene.*

Xeroxes 1545
Xeroxes are copies of a document made using a Xerox machine. *e.g. I enclose Xeroxes of the letter for your colleagues.*

Xmas 1304
Xmas is the same as Christmas. Xmas is usually used in written English only. See **Christmas**.

Y
Y is the twenty-fifth letter of the British manual and English alphabets. See page 854.

yacht 1459
A **yacht** is a boat with sails, used for racing or for pleasure trips. *e.g. They are building their own yacht.*

yachting 1459
Yachting is the sport or activity of sailing a yacht. *e.g. Yachting holidays are a lot of fun.*

yawn 1255
If you **yawn**, you open your mouth very wide and breathe in more air than usual, often when you are tired or when you are not interested in something. *e.g. I started to yawn after the first five minutes of the film.*

year 416, 417
1 A **year** is a period of 365 or 366 days, beginning on the first of January and ending on the thirty-first of December. *e.g. What will life be like in the year 2000?*
2 A **year** is a period of about twelve months. *e.g. I haven't seen him for a year now.*

year after next 798
The **year after next** is the year that follows the one after this year. For example, if this year is 1993, the year after next is 1995. *e.g. Next year the meeting will be in Bristol, and the year after next it will be in Portsmouth.*

year before 548
If you are discussing the past or the future, the **year before** refers to the period of twelve months preceding the year that has been mentioned. For example, if you refer to the year before the first moon landing (1969), you mean 1968. *e.g. She's been working in Cardiff since April 1975. The year before, she was in Preston.*

year before last 797
The **year before last** is the year that preceded the one before this year. For example, if this year is 1993, the year before last is 1991. *e.g. Last year I went to Rimini, and the year before last I went to Yugoslavia.*

year (every year) 547
You sign or say **every year** to refer to something that happens or happened yearly. *e.g. We go to Rhyl for our holidays every year.*

year (following year) 549
If you are discussing the past or the future, the **following year** refers to the period of twelve months after the year that has been mentioned. For example, if you are discussing the first moon landing (1969), the following year means 1970. *e.g. When you come on the course, you can take four options in the first year, and eight the following year.*

year (last year) 336, 548
Last year is the most recent year before this one. *e.g. Bencie went to Israel last year.*

yearly 547
1 You use **yearly** to describe something that happens or is done once in every year. *e.g. It was a yearly meeting.*
2 You use **yearly** to describe something, such as an amount of money, that relates to a period of one year. *e.g. The workers' yearly income is very small.*

year (next year) 499, 549
Next year is the one immediately after this year. *e.g. We're getting married next year.*

year (one year) 491
One year is a period of twelve months, or 365 or 366 days. *e.g. He'll study in France for one year.*

year (one year after) 549
If you are discussing the past or the future,

one year after refers to the period of twelve months following the year that has been mentioned. For example, if you are discussing the first moon landing (1969), one year after means 1970. *e.g. He will build the foundations in the summer of 1996 and one year after that the house will be finished.*

year (one year later) 549
If you are discussing the past or the future, **one year later** refers to the period of twelve months following the year that has been mentioned. For example, if you are discussing the first moon landing (1969), one year later means 1970. *e.g. In 1912, they got married and a son arrived one year later.*

year (previous year) 548
If you are discussing the past or the future, the **previous year** refers to the period of twelve months preceding the year that has been mentioned. For example, if you are discussing the first moon landing (1969), the previous year means 1968. *e.g. Last year, we went to the ball in Trev's; the previous year, we went to the graduation ball at York*

years 417
You use **years** to emphasise that you are referring to a very long time. *e.g. They've known each other for years, but I wouldn't claim they had ever been friends.*

years (in two years' time) 798
In two years' time means during the year that follows the one after this year. For example, if this year is 1993, in two years' time it will be 1995. *e.g. He plans to retire in two years' time.*

years (two years ago) 797
If you sign or say that something happened **two years ago**, you mean that it is twenty-four months since it happened or that it happened during the year before the one that preceded this year. For example, if this year is 1993, two years ago it was 1991. *e.g. She broke her leg two years ago.*

years (two years later) 798
If you are discussing the past or the future, **two years later** refers to the period of twelve months following the year after the one that has been mentioned. For example, if you are discussing the first moon landing (1969), two years later means 1971. *e.g. John got a job as a bank clerk in 1988 and two years later he was promoted to supervisor.*

yell   1711
1 If you **yell** or **yell** out, you shout loudly, for example because you are excited, angry or in pain. *e.g. I yelled out, but the driver couldn't swerve in time.*
2 If you **yell** something, or if you **yell** it out, you shout it loudly at someone, often when you are angry with them. *e.g. The older boys yelled insults.*
3 A **yell** is a loud and sudden shout given by someone who is shocked, angry, afraid or in pain. *e.g. Ian said he heard a yell inside.*

yellow   417, 624, 1110
1 Something that is **yellow** is the colour of lemons or egg yolks. *e.g. A bright yellow daffodil had shown its joyful face in the garden.*
2 When something **yellows** or is **yellowed**, it becomes yellow in colour, often because it is old. *e.g. A photograph of her, yellowed with age, lay on the dressing table.*

yesterday   337, 338
Yesterday means the day before today. *e.g. It was hot yesterday, but the weather's cooled down now.*

yoghurt   417
Yoghurt is a slightly sour, thick liquid which is made from milk that has had bacteria added to it. You can eat it with fruit or puddings, or with meat or vegetables. *e.g. He lived on a diet of nuts and natural yoghurt.*

you   293
A signer or speaker uses **you** to refer to the person he or she is signing or speaking to. *e.g. What do you think?*

you *plural*   500, 1208
A signer, speaker or writer uses **you** to refer to a group of people he or she is signing, speaking or writing to. *e.g. I want twenty of you to remain in the room.*

your own *plural*   14
1 You use **your own** to emphasise that something belongs or relates to the people you are signing or speaking to. *e.g. If there are cuts in the education service, it will be your own children who will suffer.*
2 You can use **your own** to emphasise that the people you are signing or speaking to do something without any help from other people. *e.g. You must make up your own minds as to what we should do with the money.*
your own *singular*   9
1 You use **your own** to emphasise that something belongs to the person you are

signing or speaking to. *e.g. Your own children are to blame.*
2 You can use **your own** to emphasise that the person you are signing or speaking to does something without any help from other people. *e.g. You are expected to make your own bed.*

your *plural*   14
See **belong to you** *plural*.

yourself   493
1 You use **yourself** to refer to the person you are signing or speaking to when you mention that they do something or are affected by what someone does. *e.g. Did you call yourself an oralist?*
2 You use **yourself** to refer with emphasis to the person you are signing or speaking to. *e.g. You yourself said it was only a routine check.*
3 If you do something **yourself** or by **yourself**, you do it without any help from anyone else. *e.g. You mean you asked him out all by yourself?!*

yourselves   557
1 You use **yourselves** to refer to the people you are signing or speaking to, when you mention that they do something or are affected by what someone does. *e.g. Help yourselves to sandwiches.*
2 You use **yourselves** to refer with emphasis to the people you are signing or speaking to. *e.g. You are now responsible for this job yourselves.*
3 If you and others do something **yourselves** or by **yourselves**, you do it without any help from anyone else. *e.g. You'll just have to do it yourselves.*

your *singular*   9, 63
See **belong to you** *singular*.

yours *plural*   14
See **belong to you** *plural*.

yours *singular*   9, 63
See **belong to you** *singular*.

youth   465
1 Your **youth** is the period of your life after your childhood, but before you are a fully mature adult. *e.g. I used to be pretty rude in my youth.*
2 The **youth** are young people considered as a group. *e.g. There is high unemployment amongst the youth of this country.*

Yugoslav   1269
1 Someone or something that is **Yugoslav** belongs to or relates to Yugoslavia or its people. *e.g. She works at the Yugoslav embassy, as an interpreter.*
2 A **Yugoslav** is a person who comes from, or whose family identity relates to, Yugoslavia. *e.g. Tito was the Yugoslav who was head of state*

in 1945.

Yugoslavia   1269
Yugoslavia is a former federal republic in South East Europe on the Adriatic, which was made up of Bosnia-Herzegovina, Croatia, Macedonia, Montenegro, Serbia and Slovenia. *e.g. Yugoslavia did not take part in the Olympics.*

Yugoslavian   1269
1 Someone or something that is **Yugoslavian** belongs to or relates to Yugoslavia or its people. *e.g. The Yugoslavian mountains are subject to quite frequent landslides.*
2 The address of the **Yugoslavian** Deaf Association is: Savez Organizacija Gluvih i Nagluvih Jugoslavije, Ul. Svetog Save broj 16-18, 11000 Beograd, Yugoslavia.

Z
Z is the twenty-sixth letter of the British manual and English alphabets. See page 854.

zeal   1197
Zeal is great enthusiasm. *e.g. He studied the Torah with impressive zeal.*

zebra crossing   1661
A **zebra crossing** is a place where people can cross the road safely. The road is marked with black and white stripes and vehicles should stop to allow people to cross. *e.g. Cross this busy road at the zebra crossing.*

zero   1704
1 **Zero** is the number 0 which means nought or nothing. *e.g. This scale goes from zero to forty.*
2 **Zero** is also freezing point, 0 degrees centigrade. *e.g. It was fourteen below zero when they woke up.*

zest   1197
1 **Zest** is a feeling of pleasure, enjoyment and interest in what you are doing. *e.g. The children were full of life and zest.*
2 **Zest** is the quality in an activity or in your life which you find exciting and enjoyable. *e.g. She felt that some of the zest had gone out of her life.*

zigzag   1228
1 A **zigzag** is a horizontal line which has a series of angles in it like a continuous series of 'W's. *e.g. This zigzag beside the pedestrian crossing means that no cars can park just here.*
2 To **zigzag** means to move forward by going at an angle first to the right and then to the left. *e.g. You will see the car zigzag as the driver grapples with the steering.*

zoom   1534
1 If you **zoom** somewhere, you go there very quickly. *e.g. We zoom down to the beach whenever we learn that the waves are good for surfing.*
2 If you **zoom** off, you go away from somewhere in a great hurry. *e.g. OK, we'll zoom off now.*